THE DEVELOPMENT OF CHILDREN

The Development of Children

SECOND EDITION

MICHAEL COLE
University of California, San Diego

SHEILA R. COLE

SCIENTIFIC
AMERICAN
BOOKS

Distributed by W. H. Freeman and Company

Cover photograph © 1993 by John Fortunato

Library of Congress Cataloging-in-Publication Data

Cole, Michael, 1938–
The development of children / Michael Cole, Sheila R. Cole.—2nd ed.
p.   cm.
Includes bibliographical references and indexes.
ISBN 0-7167-2238-0
1. Child development.   I. Cole, Sheila.   II. Title.
RJ131.C585   1993
155.4—dc20   92-42001
CIP

Printed in the United States of America

Scientific American Books is a subsidiary of Scientific American, Inc.
Distributed by W. H. Freeman and Company, 41 Madison Avenue,
New York, NY 10010 and 20 Beaumont Street, Oxford OX1 2NQ, England

1 2 3 4 5 6 7 8 9 0 KP 9 9 8 7 6 5 4 3

For our parents and our children,
who have served as the medium of our development, and
for Jonathan Cobb, loyal intellectual midwife whose
experience of these birth pangs has brought a deeper
understanding of development than he ever imagined.

BRIEF CONTENTS

CONTENTS

CHAPTER 3

Prenatal
Development
and Birth   77

CHAPTER 7

Early Experience
and Later Life   243

CHAPTER 8

Language
Acquisition   275

CHAPTER 9

Early Childhood:
Islands of
Competence   315

CHAPTER 10

Social
Development
in Early
Childhood   355

CHAPTER 11

The Contexts of
Early Childhood
Development   395

CHAPTER 16

The Psychological
Achievements of
Adolescence   607

PREFACE

There is a special challenge in the task of writing a textbook to introduce students to the topic of human development. Everyone who picks up this text is already an expert on the topic, in the sense that everyone has had firsthand experience with the process of growing up and vast opportunity to witness and think about the development of other people as well. Our goal in writing this book has been to show our readers how a broad *scientific* framework can enrich their understanding of development, add intellectual excitement to the learning process, and guide the practical applications of work in this dynamic field.

In our view, development is best understood as a life process that emerges from a fusion of biological, social, and psychological factors that interact in the unique medium of human culture. We have thus tried to show not only the role each factor plays but also how they interact in diverse cultural contexts to yield both the striking similarities and important differences in children's development. Because development involves transformations that take place over time, we have adopted a chronological approach in our presentation. We begin with conception and trace the sequence of changes characterizing development from that instant into infancy, childhood, adolescence, and beyond.

Throughout, we have been guided by the belief that it is a mistake to make sharp distinctions between practical, theoretical, and research orientations to questions of development. While some textbook authors focus on one orientation at the expense of others, we believe that truly fundamental knowledge must draw on and illuminate all three orientations.

A PRACTICAL ORIENTATION

The authors of *The Development of Children* have known each other since adolescence. We have shared an interest in children's development from the time we were teenagers working as camp counselors, and we have raised children of our own. We each have a professional interest in child development, as well. Sheila Cole is a journalist who has written articles about children and books for children. Michael Cole is a psychologist who has specialized in the study of children's learning and cognitive development.

Both personally and professionally, our interest in children extends to an active and immediate interest in the design and implementation of practical approaches for fostering their development. So it is natural that our book should focus continually on issues such as the influence of special nutrition programs on the physical and intellectual development of children who have experienced malnutrition early in life; how to reduce aggression among children; controversies surrounding out-of-home care of young children; the importance of extended families in ameliorating the problems facing poor children; the special challenges of learning to read and do arithmetic in school; and the special hazards of teenage pregnancy. We also include many examples drawn from the everyday lives of children that illustrate how a society's beliefs about children influence its children's development by shaping both the laws and the social norms that govern child-rearing practices.

A THEORETICAL ORIENTATION

There is a lot of truth to the saying that nothing is so practical as a good theory. A deep understanding of how children develop requires familiarity not only with the observed phenomena but also with theories that provide coherent interpretations of the facts and suggest the consequences of various courses of action.

A major difficulty for teachers of child development is the number and diversity of theories that contribute significantly to our understanding of basic issues and phenomena. We have adopted two strategies to deal with this problem. First, we frame our presentation in terms of the enduring issues that all theories of development must resolve: how biological and environmental contributions (nature and nurture) are woven together; the extent to which the interaction of these factors results in continuities and discontinuities in the nature of the organism during the dynamic process of development; and the source of individual differences among people. Second, we present competing theories in a constant dialogue with one another and with the practical issues that they were designed to address. Rather than gloss over differences among theories, we have attempted to build an appreciation of the bases for their competing interpretations. Then we have tried to move beyond the differences to show how each theory contributes to an overall understanding of development.

A RESEARCH ORIENTATION

The dialogue between theory and practice leads naturally to disputes about the facts of development and efforts to marshal facts in support of one perspective or another. Research is the process by which scholars gather evidence to settle such disputes and to challenge or support existing theories.

It is essential to understand research methods both as a means of judging the merits of the evidence that psychologists gather and as a means of thinking critically about the conclusions they draw. What is the evidence that sparing the rod spoils the child? How might we determine whether the differences between boys' and girls' games result from social pressures or from deep-seated biological predispositions? What links have been found between watching violent programs on television and subsequent aggressive behavior? And why is it so difficult for psychologists to answer enduring questions about development once and for all? Only through an awareness of the logic, methods, and indeed the shortcomings of psychological research can students come away from a course on development with the ability to evaluate for themselves the relative merits of different scientists' conclusions.

The kind of critical thinking needed to evaluate evidence and to appreciate the process of research

does not develop spontaneously. It requires careful explanation and repeated exposure. Consequently, we have made the detailed discussion of relevant research a constant feature of the book.

A FOCUS ON CULTURE

Our work has taken us to live in many parts of the world: West Africa, Mexico, Russia, Israel, Japan, and Great Britain. Within the United States, we have lived and worked in affluent suburbs and inner-city ghettos. Often our children have accompanied us, providing us with even richer opportunities for getting to know children in a wide variety of circumstances. Such experiences have led us to believe that culture must be a fundamental constituent in any full theory of development. To appreciate this truth fully, it is necessary to overcome as much as possible any ethnocentrism in one's view of children's development.

The task is by no means an easy one. For many, the initial reaction to daily life in an African village, an Asian metropolis, or the slums of a large U.S. city is likely to be "culture shock," a sense of disorientation that stems from the difficulty of understanding why people in other cultures behave the way they do. Very often, culture shock is accompanied by a sense of cultural superiority; the way "we" do it (prepare our food, build our houses, care for our children) seems superior to the way "they" do it. With time and patience, both the disorientation and the sense of superiority diminish.

An appreciation of culture's contribution to development requires more than attention to ways that people far away raise their children. Culture is fundamental to children's experience in *any* society — not something added on to the process of development, but an essential characteristic of human beings. Recognizing how difficult it is to think objectively about the nature of development in unfamiliar cultures, we have tried to keep our readers constantly aware of the diversity of human child-rearing and educational practices and their impact on the lives of children. Only by considering our culture as but one design for living among many can we arrive at a valid understanding of the principles that guide development for all human beings.

A FOCUS ON BIOLOGY

It may seem surprising that authors who espouse a special interest in culture would simultaneously underscore, as we do, the importance of biology to human development; often the two sources of human variability are discussed as opposing each other, as if somehow, by virtue of living within a culture, human beings ceased to be biologically evolving creatures. In our opinion, this is a false opposition. Not only is the ability to create and use culture one of the most striking *biological* facts about our species but there would be no development at all without biological maturation. Advances in the biological sciences have profoundly influenced human development through improved health care and advanced medical procedures. In addition, the biological sciences have increased our understanding of development by shedding light on critical issues such as the intimate links between biological changes in the brain and changes in children's cognitive capacities. The importance of such scientific contributions is made clear throughout this book—not just in the early chapters, where biological influences on development are typically summarized only to be put into the background later.

NEW TO THE SECOND EDITION

In addition to the obvious goal of bringing the text up-to-date in terms of current research, we have made a variety of changes from the first edition that we hope will serve to make the story of development presented in this book clearer and more accessible to students.

- We felt that in seeking to represent cultural variation on a world scale, we had somewhat slighted treatment of cultural variations within the United States. We have established better balance in this respect, although it has proven a difficult job, in part owing to the dearth of new research and in part to the fact that ethnic minority status and social class are so tightly intertwined in contemporary American society.
- We have expanded our discussions of emotional development and personality formation.

- We have placed somewhat greater emphasis on pragmatic aspects of language development, providing clearer links to the discussion of cognitive development in early childhood.
- We have expanded the discussion of modern research on cognition and instruction, introducing a number of promising new developments which have occurred in this area of research.
- We have expanded our treatment of the development of the self in middle childhood.
- We have reorganized the chapters that treat prenatal development, birth, and the first months of postnatal life, consolidating the coverage of these topics in three chapters. Now students can begin to read about the child-in-the-world in Chapter 3.

THE STORY OF DEVELOPMENT AND THE ORGANIZATION OF THIS BOOK

The Development of Children combines traditional chronological and topical approaches to make as clear as possible the idea that development is a process involving *the whole child* in a dynamically changing set of cultural contexts. The book is chronological in its overall structure, describing development from conception to adulthood, as befits our understanding of development as a process that unfolds over time. It also adopts traditional stage boundaries for each of its major sections.

The organization of the text is also topical in two respects. First, within broad, conventionally defined stages, it describes developments as occurring in the biological domain, the social domain, or the psychological domain (including affect and cognition), while at the same time tracing the ways that these developments interweave. Second, it focuses on the way in which stagelike changes emerge from the convergence of events in different developmental domains.

The chronological and topical perspectives correspond to the warp and the woof of development. The pattern that is woven from their combination is the story of development. It is that story we have attempted to tell in this book.

In the first chapter we introduce our main themes: the grounding of scientific concern about children in practical experience; the perennial questions of the field; the nature of developmental psychology as a discipline; and the interplay of research methods, theories, and practice.

Part I is titled "In the Beginning" and describes two types of beginnings: the genetic basis of behavior and mechanisms of inheritance (Chapter 2), and prenatal development and the process of birth (Chapter 3). Part II covers infancy, with Chapters 4, 5, and 6 corresponding to three widely recognized transition points within the first several years after birth — the first 2½ months, the period from 3 to 12 months, and the second year of life. By dividing the period of infancy in this way, we focus on the process of developmental change, highlight the issue of continuity and discontinuity in development, and still retain a picture of the whole developing child. The last chapter of Part II, Chapter 7, examines an enduring issue in the study of development: Is the pattern of development that is established during infancy fixed and unchangeable or can it be significantly influenced by the maturational changes and experiences that occur during childhood and adolescence?

Part III describes the major achievements of early childhood. The four chapters in this section cover the acquisition of language (Chapter 8), cognitive development (Chapter 9), social and personality development (Chapter 10), and the influence of various contexts on children's development in the years from 3 to 6 (Chapter 11).

The first chapter in Part IV describes the biological and cognitive changes that contribute to making middle childhood, the years from 6 to 12, a distinctive stage of development in societies around the world. The next two chapters concentrate on the two contexts of particular importance in most children's lives in these years. Chapter 13 discusses the relationship between schooling and development; Chapter 14 covers the new social relations and changes in self-understanding that emerge during middle childhood, particularly among peers.

Part V covers the transition from childhood to adulthood — a great watershed in development, not only because those formerly considered "children" are now biologically capable of becoming parents but also because this biological change coincides with a fundamental transition in the developing person's responsi-bilities and power. Although this transition is conventionally thought of as a distinct period of development called adolescence, the existence of major cultural and historical variations in the way it is organized have led us to question the sense in which adolescence should be considered a universal, distinctive stage. Chapter 15 highlights biological and social changes; Chapter 16 examines the psychological achievements of this period and critically reexamines the cultural and historical conditions under which adolescence appears as a stage of development.

Chapter 17 completes our narrative by considering both the changes that occur when a child reaches adulthood and the light these changes shed on basic questions of development thoughout life.

A NOTE TO INSTRUCTORS

The Development of Children has been designed to be taught within either a quarter or a semester system. For classes taught on the quarter system in which the curriculum is restricted to childhood, the final section of the book can be left to students to read or not, as they choose, and the remainder can be fit comfortably into a 10-week course. For courses that include adolescence and some treatment of adulthood, sections rather than whole chapters in Part I can be read; Chapter 7 (on the way infant experience shapes later development) and Chapter 8 (on language) could also be skipped or assigned selectively without disrupting the general flow of the presentation.

Those who prefer to organize this course in a topical fashion may also wish to assign segments rather than entire chapters from Part I: These chapters present important foundational issues that can be handled at whatever depth is deemed appropriate. Chapters 4 through 6 can either be read in sequence, or topical issues from each can be abstracted for reading in connection with corresponding chapters from Parts III, IV, and V. The natural sequence of chapters for the remainder of the course then becomes 9, 12, 13, and 16, which emphasize cognitive development, and 10, 14, and 15, which emphasize social and personality development. Parts of Chapter 17 can be read as they correspond to the parallel topical themes being addressed.

PEDAGOGICAL FEATURES AND SUPPLEMENTS

Several pedagogical features have been created to aid students in reading and learning from the text. One particular innovation is the special set of tables we have constructed to help students keep track of the Piagetian stages that serve as a benchmark for so many discussions of children's cognitive development. Also noteworthy are the part introductions, which provide a synthetic framework and, if reread from time to time, help students keep the large picture in mind as they learn about the different periods of development.

The text itself is accompanied by

- An *Instructor's Manual with Test Questions* that has been thoroughly revised for this new edition. It contains teaching suggestions, ideas for student projects, a resource guide to films and books, numerous essay and multiple-choice questions, and a review of each chapter's main points.
- An extensive *Computerized Test Bank* in both IBM/DOS and Macintosh formats.
- *Transparency masters* of key illustrations and tables, to aid in linking lectures and text.
- A *Study Guide,* which, in addition to reviewing the main points of each chapter, provides a variety of practice questions, exercises that help to integrate themes that reappear in various chapters, and information about how to make observations of children and to write research papers. Our experience is that this study guide helps students to read and retain the text material at a higher level than they are likely to achieve by reading the text alone.
- *Readings on the Development of Children,* by Mary Gauvain and Michael Cole, introduces students to well-selected primary source material.

ACKNOWLEDGMENTS

A book of this scope and complexity could not be produced without the help of others. A great many people gave generously of their time and experience to deepen our treatment of different areas of development, particularly the many scholars who consented to review drafts of our manuscript and make suggestions for improvement. The remaining imperfections exist despite their best efforts.

For the first edition, we would like to acknowledge the help of

Kathryn N. Black, Purdue University
Patricia C. Broderick, Villanova University
Urie Bronfenbrenner, Cornell University
Ann L. Brown, University of California at Berkeley
Andrew C. Coyne, Ohio State University
Frank Curcio, Boston University
Judy S. DeLoache, University of Illinois at Urbana-Champaign
Don Devers, North Virginia Community College, Annandale
Shari Ellis, Virginia Commonwealth University
Sylvia Farnham-Diggory, University of Delaware
Mark Feldman, Stanford University
Sam Glucksberg, Princeton University
Mark Grabe, University of North Dakota
Patricia M. Greenfield, University of California, Los Angeles
Harold D. Grotevant, University of Minnesota
William S. Hall, University of Maryland, College Park
Janis E. Jacobs, University of Nebraska, Lincoln
Claire Kopp, University of California, Los Angeles
Alan W. Lanning, College of DuPage
Shitala P. Mishra, University of Arizona
Frank B. Murray, University of Delaware
Nora Newcombe, Temple University
Herbert L. Pick, Jr., University of Minnesota
Ellen F. Potter, University of South Carolina, Columbia
Thomas M. Randall, Rhode Island College
LeRoy P. Richardson, Montgomery County Community College
Barbara Rogoff, University of California at Santa Cruz
Sylvia Scribner, City University of New York
Stephanie Stolarz-Fantino, San Diego State University
Lawrence J. Walker, University of British Columbia
Harriet S. Waters, State University of New York at Stony Brook
Patricia E. Worden, California State University at San Marcos

Joe Campos (University of California at Berkeley), Carol Izard (University of Delaware), and Larry Nucci (University of Illinois, Chicago) each contributed valuable illustrative material from their research for the first edition.

For the second edition we wish to thank

Jeremy M. Anglin, University of Waterloo
Gay L. Bisanz, University of Alberta, Edmonton
Michaelanthony Brown-Cheatham, San Diego State University
Richard Canfield, Cornell University
William E. Cross, Jr., Cornell University
Rosanne K. Dlugosz, Scottsdale Community College
Rebecca Eder, University of California, Davis
Jeffrey W. Elias, Texas Tech University
Beverly Fagot, University of Oregon
Jo Ann M. Farver, University of Southern California
Brenda K. Fleming, Family Service Agency, Phoenix
Mary Gauvain, University of California, Riverside
Herbert P. Ginsburg, Teachers College, Columbia University
Alison Gopnik, University of California, Berkeley
Artin Göncü, University of Illinois at Chicago
Paul Harris, University of Oxford
Jeannette L. Johnson, University of Maryland, College Park
Daniel P. Keating, Ontario Institute for Studies in Education
Gisela Labouvie-Vief, Wayne State University
Jacqueline Lerner, Michigan State University
Elizabeth Levin, Laurentian University
Zella Luria, Tufts University
Sandra Machida, California State University, Chico
Michael Maratsos, University of Minnesota

Patricia H. Miller, University of Florida
Joan Moyer, Arizona State University
Sharon Nelson-LeGall, University of Pittsburgh
Herbert L. Pick, Jr., University of Minnesota
J. Steven J. Reznick, Yale University
Christine M. Roberts, University of Connecticut
Marnie Roosevelt, Santa Monica Community College
Diane N. Ruble, New York University
Felicisima C. Seráfica, Ohio State University
Robert S. Siegler, Carnegie Mellon University
Jerome L. Singer, Yale University
Romy Spitz, University of California, San Diego
Doreen Steg, Drexel University
Michael Tomasello, Emory University
Billy E. Vaughn, California School of Professional Psychology, San Diego
Thomas S. Weisner, University of California, Los Angeles

Paul Baltes (Max Planck Institute for Human Development, Berlin), Joe Campos (University of California at Berkeley), and Robbie Case (Stanford University) merit special thanks for providing us with materials and special advice for the second edition.

We are also grateful to Travis Amos, Jonathan Cobb, Julia De Rosa, Christine Hastings, Moira Lerner, Alison Lew, and Mary Shuford, of W. H. Freeman and Company, who have shepherded us through the ardous process of production.

MICHAEL COLE
SHEILA R. COLE
Solana Beach, California

THE DEVELOPMENT OF CHILDREN

CHAPTER 1

The Study of Human Development

•

> [T]he mature person is one of the most remarkable products
> that any society can bring forth. He or she is a living cathedral,
> the handiwork of many individuals over many years.
>
> — DAVID W. PLATH, *LONG ENGAGEMENTS*

Early one morning in the cold winter of 1800, a naked, dirty boy wandered into a hut at the edge of a French hamlet in the province of Aveyron to beg for food. Some of the people in the area had caught glimpses of the boy in the months before as he dug for roots, climbed trees, and ran at great speed on all fours. They said he was a wild beast. Word spread quickly when the boy appeared in the village, and everyone came to see him.

Among the curious was a government commissioner, who took the boy home and fed him. The child, who appeared to be about 12 years old, seemed ignorant of the civilized comforts that were offered to him. When clothes were put on him, he tore them off. He would not eat meat, preferring raw potatoes, roots, and nuts. He rarely made a sound and seemed indifferent to human voices. In his report, the commissioner concluded that the boy had lived alone since early childhood, "a stranger to social needs and practices. . . . [T]here is . . . something extraordinary in his behavior, which makes him seem close to the state of wild animals" (quoted in Lane, 1976, pp. 8–9).

When the commissioner's report reached Paris it caused a sensation. Newspapers hailed the child as the "Wild Boy of Aveyron." People hoped that by studying the boy's traits and abilities they could resolve questions about the nature and development of human beings, a focus of philosophical and political disputes in Europe for many decades. Put in modern terms, these questions were

- What distinguishes us from other animals?
- What would we be like if we grew up totally isolated from human society?
- To what degree are we products of our upbringing and experience and to what degree is our character an expression of inborn traits?

A CHILD OF NATURE?

Many people hoped that the boy would have a noble character, which would support their claims that children are born good, only to be corrupted by society. But instead of a noble child of nature, examining physicians saw a disheveled creature who was unable to speak and who often moved about on all fours. The physicians diagnosed the boy as mentally deficient and suggested that he had been put out to die by his parents for that reason. They recommended that he be put in an asylum.

One person who disputed the diagnosis of retardation was a young physician, Jean-Marc Itard (1774–1838). Itard argued that the boy appeared to be defective only because his years of isolation from society had not allowed him to develop normal social skills.

(Left) *Victor, the Wild Boy of Aveyron.* (Right) *Jean-Marc Itard, who tried to transform the Wild Boy into a civilized Frenchman.*

Perhaps as many as one in three normal children born in France in the late eighteenth century were abandoned by their parents, usually because the family was too poor to support another child (Kessen, 1965). Itard maintained that what made the Wild Boy unusual was not innate mental deficiency but a remarkable ability to survive in the forests of Aveyron on his own.

Itard took personal charge of the boy, believing that he could teach him to become a full-fledged Frenchman, master of the best of civilized knowledge. France had recently overthrown its monarchy and had embraced the political ideals of liberty, equality, and brotherhood. Itard and other supporters of the republic wanted to demonstrate that it is possible to shape the process of development itself by educating peasant children and improving the conditions of their lives. Itard devised an elaborate set of training procedures to teach the Wild Boy how to categorize objects, to reason, and to talk as a test of his theory that it is the environment of human beings that causes their psychological development (Itard, 1801/1962).

Victor, as Itard named the Wild Boy, made rapid progress at first. He learned to communicate simple needs and to recognize and write several words. He also developed affection for the people who took care of him. But Victor never learned to speak and interact with other people normally. And contrary to Europeans' notions of what a "savage" would be like, he never displayed strong sexual interests.

After 5 years of intense work, Itard abandoned his experiment. Victor had not made enough progress to satisfy Itard's superiors, and Itard himself was unsure about how much more progress the boy could make. Victor was sent to live with a woman who was paid to care for him. He died in 1828, still referred to as the Wild Boy of Aveyron, leaving unsettled the large questions about human nature and the influence of civilized society that had aroused so many people's interest in him. Most physicians and scholars of the time eventually concluded that Victor had indeed been mentally defective from birth. But doubts remain to this day. Victor spent many of his formative years alone. When found, he had already passed the age that appears to be the upper boundary for normal language acquisition. Some modern scholars believe that Itard may have been right in his belief that Victor was normal at birth but was stunted in his development as a result of his social isolation (Lane, 1976). Others believe that Victor suffered from autism, a pathological

mental condition whose symptoms include a deficit in language and an inability to interact normally with others (Frith, 1989). It is also possible that Itard's pioneering methods failed where different approaches might have succeeded. We can only guess.

THE LEGACY OF ITARD

In his work with Victor, Itard created methods for diagnosing mental and linguistic abilities. He combined these diagnostic procedures with a program of instruction that served simultaneously as a test of his scientific, social, and political theories about how society should be organized and as a means to better the life of the individual child he was studying.

The modern science of developmental psychology did not arise until almost a century after Itard's attempts to promote Victor's development. But when the science of developmental psychology did come into being, its practitioners adopted many of Itard's specific techniques as well as his curiosity about the causes of development and his overall faith in science as a means of bettering the human condition.

One legacy of Itard's work was to show that science can provide practical suggestions about raising children based on systematic research into the nature of human development. It also demonstrated that broad philosophical and political debates shape both the questions that scientists ask and the conclusions they draw from their data.

Itard's fusion of science, philosophy, and public policy remains as relevant now in developmental psychology as it was in his time. From one family and community to the next, decisions affecting children's development are influenced by different assumptions about human nature, by different values concerning the goals of development, and by different opinions about the factors that influence development. Whether handicapped children will be enrolled in the same schools as their agemates or in separate facilities will depend on opinions about the conditions under which healthy personality development occurs. The age at which children are taught to read will depend on the importance attached to reading as well as on assumptions about when children are mature enough to profit from reading instruction and about the role of schools in children's education. Attitudes toward divorce are likely to influence beliefs about the effects of divorce on children's development at various ages. Decisions about whether or not to allow very young children to testify in court depend on beliefs about how accurately 4-year-olds can recall past events and about the possible consequences to them of having to relive painful experiences in public.

Modern developmental psychologists engage in research in an effort to provide objective evidence concerning these and many similar questions. The conclusions they reach affect not only the lives of individual children but also the policies of federal, state, and local governments, school boards, and the judicial system.

The Rise of a New Discipline

In Itard's day there was no scientific specialty called developmental psychology. But all during the nineteenth century, interest in children and their development was growing. One stimulus to this trend was the Industrial Revolution, which brought broad social changes to Europe and North America. During the nineteenth century, the industrialization of these continents transformed the basic activities by which people earned their livings. Industrialization also trans-

formed the role of children in society and the settings within which they developed. No longer did the vast majority of children grow up on farms, where they contributed their labor and were cared for by their mothers and fathers until they reached adulthood. Instead, many were employed in factories, alongside and sometimes in place of their parents (Hiner & Hawes, 1985).

Industrialization also fueled urbanization. Huge slums grew up in sprawling industrial cities. When urban children were not at work, they were a liability to their parents, who had little space to accommodate them and little money with which to feed them. They were also a liability to the community, which perceived them as rowdy nuisances. As much for social control as for any academic reasons, public schools were established as places to supervise children's development when neither parents nor employers were supervising them.

Many young children worked long hours in factories and mines, under dangerous and unhealthy conditions. As these conditions became a matter of social concern, philanthropic, medical, and scientific attention began to focus on children. The close links between social concerns, cultural values, and scientific research are evident in some of the earliest studies of children's growth. The Factories Inquiries Committee in England, for instance, conducted a study in 1833 to

Children doing piecework in their home near the turn of the century. The money they earned was usually a vital part of their family's income.

Children provided essential labor in many industries well into the twentieth century. These boys worked in the coal mines of Pennsylvania in 1911.

discover whether children could work 12 hours a day without suffering physical damage. The majority of the committee members decided that 12 hours was an acceptable workday for children. Those who thought a 10-hour workday would be preferable were concerned not about the effects of long work hours on small children's intellectual or emotional well-being but about their morals; these committee members recommended that 2 hours of religious and moral education a day replace 2 of the hours spent working in mine, factory, or shop (Lomax, Kagan, & Rosenkrantz, 1978).

These nineteenth-century pioneers of developmental psychology did more than address concerns arising from changes in society. They used the data they collected in their inquiries to clarify basic questions about human development and how to study it. The early studies of growth and work capacity, for example, implicated environmental factors in development when they revealed that children who worked in textile mills were shorter and weighed less than local nonworking children of corresponding ages. Surveys of intellectual growth, which eventually led to IQ testing, showed wide variations in children's achievements

that seemed to depend on family background and individual experience. Both of these lines of investigation fueled the scientific and social debates that continue to this day.

A crucial event that spurred interest in the scientific study of children was the publication of Charles Darwin's *Origin of Species* in 1859. Wide acceptance of Darwin's thesis that human beings have evolved from earlier species fundamentally changed the way people thought about children. Instead of imperfect adults to be seen and not heard, children came to be viewed as scientifically interesting because they provided evidence about the sources of adults' psychological characteristics. They were also thought to provide evidence that human beings are related to other species (see Figure 1.1). It became fashionable, for example, to compare the behavior of children with the behavior of higher primates to see if they went through a "chimpanzee stage" similar to the one through which human beings were thought to have evolved (Gould, 1977b). As William Kessen (1965) remarks, Darwin initiated "a riot of parallel-drawing between animal and child, between primitive man and child, between early human history and child" (p. 113).

6

(a)

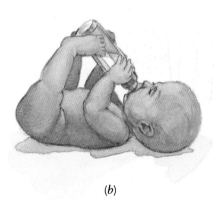

(b)

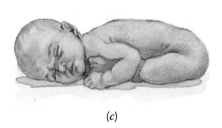

(c)

FIGURE 1.1 *Early evolutionists eagerly scrutinized the motor development of children for evidence that it recapitulated evolutionary stages. Here an infant (a) crawls about on all fours, (b) uses its feet for grasping, and (c) sleeps in an animal-like crouch. (After Hrdlicka, 1931.)*

Late in the nineteenth century, developmental psychologists began to form organizations to promote their work. Important scientific landmarks were the formation in the 1890s of the Child-Study Association by G. Stanley Hall, the first president of the American Psychological Association, and the publication of the first journal devoted to child development, *Pedagogical Seminary*. During the same period, various child welfare organizations were formed to raise money for hospitals and orphanages and to support social reform policies for the benefit of children. Both government agencies and philanthropic foundations began to support specialized magazines such as *Infant Care* and *Parent's Magazine* in the belief that scientific research should reach as wide a public as possible. Today child development issues are widely discussed in the popular media, an indication of broad acceptance of the idea that scientific research on children is a good way "to make this a better world through developing better people" (Young, 1990, p. 17).

A landmark in the institutionalization of concern about children was the creation in 1912 of the U.S. Children's Bureau to monitor the working conditions of children and to disseminate information about effective child-rearing practices. In addition, special institutes and departments devoted to the study of development began to spring up in major universities.

Modern Developmental Psychology

The core concern of developmental psychologists is to understand **development**, the sequence of physical and psychological changes that human beings undergo as they grow older, beginning with conception and continuing throughout life. Interest in development rests on an ancient intuition about personal understanding and self-discovery: If we can discover our roots and the history of changes that brought us to the present moment, we can better understand ourselves. If we then combine insight into our past with information about our present characteristics and circumstances, we are in a better position to anticipate the future and to prepare to meet it on our own terms.

The discipline of developmental psychology translates these personal goals into objective, socially shared procedures for understanding, predicting, and shaping the process of development. It also provides a body of knowledge that can be connected with the insights of scholars who approach the study of development from neighboring disciplines, such as biology, anthropology, linguistics, and sociology.

In the century since psychologists began to concern themselves with the systematic study of human development, they have accumulated a great deal of knowledge about the behavior of human beings at every age level, starting even before birth. They have devised a wide variety of research methods for learning about children, and they have made intensive efforts to explain the developmental processes that underpin the age-related changes they study.

Developmental psychologists are also active in applying their knowledge to promote healthy development. They serve in hospitals, child-care centers, schools, recreational facilities, and clinics. They assess children's developmental status and prescribe measures for assisting children who are in difficulty. They design special environments such as cribs for premature babies, therapeutic methods for children who find it difficult to control their tempers, and more effective techniques for teaching children to read. The many developmental psychologists who believe that development is a lifelong process also take an active interest in the well-being of people of middle age and the elderly (Hetherington, Lerner, & Perlmutter, 1988).

The detailed knowledge and methods that developmental psychologists have accumulated in the course of their research are important, and this book will describe many aspects of them. But as we investigate the facts generated by research and the skills required of developmental psychologists, it is just as important to keep firmly in mind the more general goal of the psychological sciences, which is to increase our understanding of human nature and its development.

THE CENTRAL QUESTIONS OF DEVELOPMENTAL PSYCHOLOGY

Despite great variety in the work they do and the theories that guide their research, developmental psychologists share an interest in three fundamental questions:

1. *Continuity.* To what extent is development characterized by continuous change, and to what extent does it involve discontinuities that result in the emergence of new forms and processes of change?

2. *Sources of development.* Is development guided primarily by the genetic program locked into the body's cells, or is the external environment the driving force that produces change?
3. *Individual differences.* No two human beings are exactly alike. How do people come to have stable characteristics that differentiate them from all other people?

Psychologists are deeply divided on many aspects of these three fundamental issues. Their differing assumptions about continuity, sources of change, and individual differences give rise to competing theoretical systems, each seeking to provide a comprehensive interpretation of developmental processes.

Questions about Continuity

Since the notion of continuity is applied to somewhat different phenomena by different investigators, it gives rise to several areas of inquiry, which we will consider in turn. How similar are human mental capacities and emotions to those of other species? Is individual development a process of gradual accumulation of small quantitative changes, or do we undergo a series of qualitative transformations as we grow older? Lastly, are there periods in a person's life during which specific events must occur if development is to proceed normally?

Are human beings distinctive?

For centuries people have debated the extent to which humans differ from other creatures and the closely related question of whether we are subject to the same natural laws as all other forms of life. This sort of question is about **phylogeny,** the evolutionary history of a species.

The question of continuities and discontinuities between humans and other species is important because the way it is answered shapes our conclusions about the laws governing human development. Insofar as the relation of *Homo sapiens* to other species is continuous, the study of other animals can provide evidence about the processes of human development. To the extent that human beings are distinctive, research findings concerning the development of other species may be misleading when they are applied to humans.

8

Although chimpanzees and human beings share more than 90 percent of their genetic material, the differences between the two species are enormous.

When Charles Darwin (1809–1882) published *The Origin of Species,* the idea of evolution was already a subject of widespread speculation. Darwin's great achievement was to convince most of the Western scientific world, and eventually other people as well, that "the innumerable species, genera and families, with which this world is peopled, are all descended, each within its own class or group, from common parents, and all have been modified in the course of descent" (Darwin, 1859/1958, p. 425).

Darwin was a firm believer in continuity among species. He saw evolution as a slow, steady process of accumulating change. As he put it, the difference between *Homo sapiens* and our near neighbors is "one of degree, not of kind" (Darwin, 1859/1958, p. 107). While modern evolutionary theorists accept Darwin's claim that the origin of new species is a natural process, many of them reject the idea that evolution is gradual and continuous (Eldredge & Gould, 1972). They claim that in relatively isolated environments new species have arisen quite rapidly and have been able to survive momentous environmental changes that have destroyed the species they evolved from. Stephen Gould (1980), a champion of the theory of discontinuous

evolution, likens the process of evolutionary change to the boiling of water:

> Change occurs in large leaps following a slow accumulation of stresses that a system resists until it reaches a breaking point. Heat water and it eventually boils. (pp. 184–185)

To test Darwin's claim that our species evolved gradually and continuously as a part of the natural order, scientists have searched for evidence of evolutionary links—intermediate forms that connect us with other forms of life—and have compared our genetic makeup and behavior with those of other organisms. On the side of continuity between ourselves and other animals, it has been established that we share as much as 98 percent of our genetic material with chimpanzees (Gribbin & Cherfas, 1982). It is also clear, however, that there is something distinctive about the pattern of our species' characteristics. The difficult question is: What is that something?

One characteristic of *Homo sapiens* that is obviously distinctive is the fact that we develop in an environment that has been shaped by countless earlier generations of people in their struggle for survival (Geertz, 1973; White, 1949). This special environment consists of artifacts (such as tools and clothing), knowledge about how to construct and use those artifacts, beliefs about the world, and values (ideas about what is worthwhile), all of which guide adults' interactions with the physical world and with each other and their children. Anthropologists call this accumulation of artifacts, knowledge, beliefs, and values "culture." It is the "man-made" part of the environment that greets us at birth (Herskovitz, 1948) and the "design for living" that we acquire from our community (Kluckhohn & Kelly, 1945).

A key feature of culture is its transmission from generation to generation through language. Thus it is not surprising that since antiquity, language has been proposed as a defining characteristic of our species. In the seventeenth century the philosopher René Descartes stated the traditional view eloquently:

> Language is in effect the sole sure sign of latent thought in the body; all men use it, even those who are dull or deranged, who are missing a tongue, or who lack the voice organs, but no animal can use it, and this is why it is permissible to take language as the true difference between man and beast. (Quoted in Lane, 1976, p. 23)

Even Darwin, who believed so strongly in the continuity of species, agreed that our distinctiveness, insofar as *Homo sapiens* is distinct, is the result of our capacity to communicate through language. In recent years scientists have demonstrated that rudiments of culture and language-like behavior can sometimes be found in chimpanzees and in other primates (Goodall, 1986; Lieberman, 1990; Parker & Gibson, 1990). Still, as we will see in later chapters, human culture and language-using capacities, considered as an ensemble, appear to be qualitatively different from the rudiments exhibited among some other species.

Is individual development continuous?

The second major question about continuity concerns **ontogeny,** the development of the individual organism during its lifetime. As a rule, psychologists who believe development to be primarily a process of continuous, gradual accumulation of small changes emphasize *quantitative* change, such as growth in vocabulary, while those who view development as a process punctuated by abrupt, discontinuous changes emphasize the emergence of qualitatively new patterns in development, such as the change from crawling to walking. These qualitatively new patterns of development are often referred to as **stages.** The contrast between the continuity and discontinuity views is illustrated in Figure 1.2.

In its everyday usage the concept of a developmental stage is sometimes misused to explain behavior. Suzy, we may be told, "behaves wildly *because* she is an adolescent." We would not be satisfied by the explanation that butterflies fly *because* they are in the butterfly, and not the caterpillar, stage. We would want to know what it is about butterflies that enables them to fly and the mechanisms that brought about the transformation from caterpillar to butterfly.

FIGURE 1.2 (a) *The contrasting courses of development of sponges and flowers provide idealized examples of continuous and discontinuous development. According to the continuity view, development is a process of gradual growth (small sponge, bigger sponge, still bigger sponge), whereas according to the discontinuity view it is a series of stagelike transformations (seed, sprout, flowering plant). (b) Human beings appear to exhibit a mixture of the two types of development.*

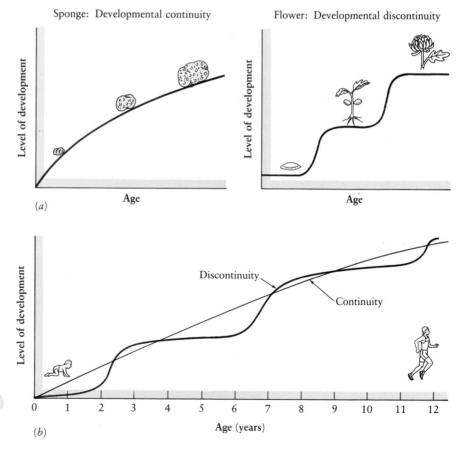

Sponge: Developmental continuity

Flower: Developmental discontinuity

Level of development

Age

(a)

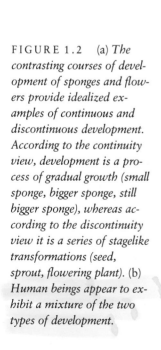

Level of development

Discontinuity

Continuity

0   1   2   3   4   5   6   7   8   9   10   11   12

Age (years)

(b)

The same rule applies to changes as humans grow older. We seek to learn what it is about being an adolescent that gives rise to Suzy's "wild" behavior. Is it the freedom that comes with the right to drive a car? Is it the hormonal changes associated with puberty? Or perhaps Suzy is responding to pressures from her peers. Without a careful specification of the processes that give rise to changes in a person's behavior as she grows older, explanations of behavior that only name the stage the person is presumed to be in add nothing to our understanding.

Sensitive to this problem, psychologists who use the stage concept attempt to specify what they mean by a stage and how the psychological processes that they believe distinguish each stage are related to the behaviors that are characteristic of it. John Flavell (1971) suggests that four criteria are central to the concept of a developmental stage:

1. *Stages of development are distinguished by changes that are qualitative.* Asked to memorize a set of words, adolescents not only remember more than 8-year-olds do, they remember differently, by grouping words according to accepted categories and employing sophisticated strategies of memorization.
2. *The transition from one stage to the next is marked by simultaneous changes in a great many, if not all, aspects of a child's behavior.* About the time of their second birthday, for example, children not only begin to create grammatically complex utterances; they also begin to talk about themselves as distinct individuals, and they start to use objects to represent other objects in their play.
3. *When the change from one stage to the next occurs, it is rapid.* Physical development in childhood, for example, is characterized by relatively slow growth followed by a dramatic spurt at the onset of puberty.
4. *The numerous behavioral and physical changes that mark the appearance of a stage form a coherent pattern.* The new forms of reasoning that arise during middle childhood (approximately ages 6 to 12), for example, are closely linked to new forms of social interaction that appear at the same time.

To the extent that development is punctuated by discontinuous qualitative changes, the way the child experiences the world and the way the world influences the child change as the child progresses from one stage to the next. In short, the process of change itself undergoes changes. Infants are especially sensitive to the sounds of language (Eimas, 1985), for example, but they do not understand what is being said. Once they begin to understand and produce language themselves, the way they learn about the world appears to change fundamentally, and so does the way others interact with them. The discontinuity that accompanies the emergence of the child's active participation in conversation marks the boundary between infancy and early childhood (Flavell, 1985).

Jerome Kagan (1984, p. 91) argues that "each life phase makes special demands, and so each phase is accompanied by a special set of qualities." Kagan believes that discontinuities between succeeding life phases are so marked that some of one's past history is "inhibited or discarded." This strong view of developmental discontinuities implies that early developmental problems do not inevitably lead to later developmental problems; in effect, each new stage presents its own opportunities.

Some psychologists deny that the stage concept is crucial for an understanding of development. Albert Bandura, for example, argues that the mechanisms by which people learn new behaviors are the same at all ages, so there is considerable continuity in the process of developmental change. According to this view, discontinuities in development are relatively rare occurrences that follow abrupt alterations in "social-training and other relevant biological or environmental variables" (Bandura & Walters, 1963, p. 25). Robert Siegler, a psychologist who specializes in studying the development of children's thinking, makes a similar argument: "Children's thinking," he writes, "is continually changing, and most of the changes seem to be gradual rather than sudden" (1991, p. 8).

During most of the twentieth century, stage theories of development have been more numerous and more influential than continuity theories. Yet stage theories are confronted with a variety of facts that appear to violate one or more of the criteria for developmental stages proposed by Flavell.

One acute problem for modern stage theories is that the stage a child appears to be in often varies from one situation to another. For example, 4-year-olds often have difficulty taking another person's point of view, but when they are speaking to a 2-year-old, they simplify their speech appropriately. At 4 years of age children are also likely to overlook the needs of their siblings, yet they frequently become solicitous when the younger child appears to be upset (Hoffman, 1981; Shatz & Gelman, 1973). Such simultaneous occurrences of behaviors thought to appear during different stages seem incompatible with the idea that stages represent general structures of an individual's psychological makeup.

Our own view is that development involves a complex weaving of gradual and abrupt changes, much on the order of Gould's heated water. As Robert Siegler (1991) points out, whether one focuses on gradual or abrupt change depends in part on the time scale one adopts. When we compare a 3-year-old preschooler with a 7-year-old second-grader, the impression of a general, qualitative difference is difficult to avoid. But when we observe a 3-year-old over the course of a year, old and new modes of behavior are so woven together and depend so heavily on the precise task the child is engaged in that change may seem so gradual as to be impossible to perceive.

Are there critical periods of development?

Another question about the continuity of individual development is whether or not there are **critical periods** of development — periods in the growth of an organism during which specific environmental or biological events must occur if development is to proceed normally. The existence of critical periods has been firmly established for some animals (see Figure 1.3) and for some aspects of human physical development, as well. If the newly formed gonads (sex glands) of a human embryo do not produce male hormones about 7 weeks after conception, for example, the development of female genitalia is irreversibly set, even in an embryo with genes for maleness (Austin & Short, 1972a). The strongest evidence for critical periods in human psychological development comes from studies of the development of language (Curtiss, 1977; Goldin-Meadow, 1982; Newport, 1991). Children who for some reason have not had sufficient exposure to language to acquire one before the age of 6 or 7 years may never acquire a language.

FIGURE 1.3   *The ethologist Konrad Lorenz proposed the existence of a critical period in the development of ducklings. These ducklings would not have followed Lorenz had he not been the first moving thing they saw as soon as they were able to walk.*

Questions about the Sources of Development

The second major issue that preoccupies developmental psychologists is the way in which biological factors directed by the genes interact with environmental factors in human development. During much of the twentieth century, this problem has been posed in the form of a choice between "nature" and "nurture." **Nature** refers to the inborn biological capacities of the individual; **nurture** refers to the influences of the social environment on the individual, particularly those of the family and the community. Much of the argument about Victor, the Wild Boy of Aveyron, was essentially about nature and nurture: Was Victor incapable of speech and other behaviors normal for a boy his age because of defective biological endowment (nature) or because of inadequate nurturing? (Early formulations of this issue are discussed in Box 1.1.)

Philosophical Forefathers of Developmental Psychology

When Europeans first became conscious of the peoples of Africa and Asia, in the fifteenth and sixteenth centuries, they debated the source of the obvious physical and behavioral differences between those people and themselves. Were these creatures human? they wondered. Were they also God's children, and if so, why did they look and act so differently? In modern terms, were they different in their basic nature, or were they different because of the conditions of their nurture?

Europeans asked similar questions about one another. Were peasants and princes different because God willed them so? Or were they different because they had been exposed to different experiences after they entered the world? These were not abstract questions, of interest only to philosophers. They were questions of deep political significance. For centuries kings and nobles had claimed that they had a God-given right to rule over others because they were naturally superior by virtue of their birth.

At the beginning of the modern era, two philosophers whose writings were to have great influence on the history of child development, John Locke and Jean-Jacques Rousseau, challenged the view that human differences were determined primarily by birth. Their views of human differences and social inequality were directly connected to their beliefs about children's development.

JOHN LOCKE

The English philosopher John Locke (1632–1704) proposed that the child's mind is a tabula rasa, a blank slate upon which experience writes its story. In *Some Thoughts Concerning Education* (1699/1938), Locke expressed the central intuition that guided his thinking:

The little, and almost insensible Impressions on our tender Infancies, have very important and lasting Consequences: And there 'tis, as in the Fountains of some Rivers, where a gentle Application of the Hand turns the flexible waters into Chanels, that make them take quite contrary Courses, and by this little Direction given them at first in the Source, they receive different Tendencies, and arrive at last, at very remote and distant Places. (pp. 1–2)

Locke did not deny that there are limits to what the "Application of the Hand" can achieve. One cannot make water run uphill. He believed that children are born with different "temperaments and propensities," and he advised that instruction be tailored to fit these differences, a view that remains central to modern theories of education. But Locke clearly asserted that nurture, in the form of adults who "channeled" children's initial impulses, was the key factor in the creation of the main differences between people.

JEAN-JACQUES ROUSSEAU

The French philosopher Jean-Jacques Rousseau (1712–1778) also argued that differences among people were primarily the results of experience, but his view of children and the role of adults in their training differed from Locke's. Rousseau asserted that "natural man" was not born in sin but was corrupted by civilization. In the state of nature all people were equal; inequality appeared with the rise of agriculture, industry, and property. According to this view, the natives of the lands being explored by European seafarers were more virtuous than their "discoverers," who took such pride in their own civilization.

Rousseau claimed for the child at birth what he had claimed for natural man—a nature unspoiled by civilization. In *Emile* (1762/1911), a book that was part novel and part treatise on education, he indicated his opinion of adults' attempts to bring the child "up" to virtue:

> God makes all things good. Man meddles with them and they become evil. He forces one soil to yield the products of another, one tree to bear another's fruit. He confuses and confounds time, place, and natural conditions. He mutilates his dog, his horse, and his slave. He destroys and defaces all things; . . . he will have nothing as nature made it, not even man himself, who must learn his paces like a saddlehorse, and be shaped to his master's taste like the trees in his garden. (p. 5)

In his tale of Emile's education, Rousseau provided a vision of childhood and education in which the role of the caretaker is to protect the child from the pressures of adult society. Emile, who stands for Everychild, is not an incomplete adult who must be perfected through instruction but a whole human being whose capabilities are suited to his age. Emile passes through several natural stages of development. In each, his activities are appropriate to his needs at the time, and they are guided by an adult who uses suitably paced educational practices. As William Kessen (1965) points out, these ideas about stages of development were later taken up by developmental psychologists, and they remain influential to this day.

LOCKE, ROUSSEAU, AND THE MODERN WORLD

Locke's notion of a tabula rasa and Rousseau's vision of natural man have been rightly criticized and sometimes ridiculed in the centuries that have passed since the two philosophers died. Modern research makes it clear that we are not blank slates when we are born; we enter the world with brains that are highly structured. Nor is it plausible that there ever existed a purely "natural" state of humankind, which the modern world corrupts. When Victor, the Wild Boy who really did grow up in a "state of nature," misbehaved outrageously during one of his outings with Itard, people joked, "If only Rousseau could see his noble savage now!"

The common wisdom underlying Locke's and Rousseau's views on the crucial role of experience in the shaping of human behavior remains valid, however. In 1776 the United States of America was founded as a republic based on a profound faith in the "self-evident" truth that "all men are created equal." In an earlier era, when kings and nobles ruled by "divine right," the open expression of such ideas would have been unthinkable. A clear indication of the political significance of the belief that human beings can shape the course of their development by arranging their environments is the fact that when the archbishop of Paris read *Emile*, he sought to have Rousseau arrested. Alerted by friends, Rousseau fled from France.

With the acceptance of the idea that children are born good, or at least not evil, came a deep obligation to confront obvious inequalities in the conditions of developing children's lives. Not only the newly formed United States but France and eventually England as well came to respect the idea that children's welfare—indeed, the welfare of persons of every age—is a concern for which society must accept some responsibility.

Beliefs about the relative contributions of nature and nurture to development can have far-reaching effects on the way society treats children. For example, if it is assumed that girls, by nature, lack interest and ability in mathematics and science, they are not likely to be encouraged to become scientists or mathematicians. If, on the other hand, it is assumed that mathematical and scientific talent is largely a result of nurture, a society may train girls and boys equally in these activities.

Modern psychologists emphasize that we cannot adequately describe development by considering either nature or nurture in isolation because the organism and its environment constitute a single life process (Hinde, 1987). Nonetheless, it is common practice to study living systems by separating definable influences and analyzing them independently. The problem, then, is twofold: (1) to determine the relative contributions of nature and nurture to various kinds of behavior and (2) to discover how nature and nurture interact to produce the developing child.

Disagreements about the relative influence exerted by nature and nurture on development and about how they interact have contributed to the formation of broad, competing theoretical frameworks to explain the developmental process. Four of these frameworks will be discussed repeatedly in this book: the biological-maturation, the environmental-learning, the universal-constructivist, and the cultural-context frameworks (see Figure 1.4). What follows here is only a brief overview. Each of these major theoretical frameworks and specific theoretical approaches within them will be explored in later chapters in conjunction with particular aspects of development.

The biological-maturation framework

The crucial claim of the biological-maturation framework is that the basic sequence of changes that characterize development is **endogenous;** that is, the changes come from inside the organism as a consequence of its biological heritage. The major cause of development is thus **maturation,** genetically determined patterns of change that occur as individuals age from their immature starting point at conception to full adulthood. Psychologists who adopt the biological-maturation framework are likely to believe that psychological development is a progression of stagelike changes that

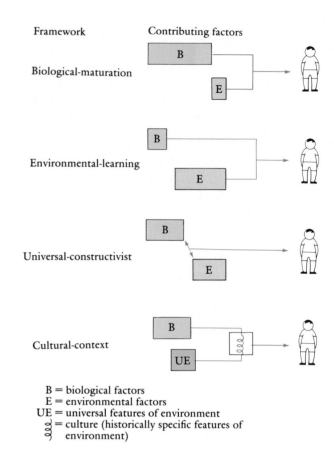

B = biological factors
E = environmental factors
UE = universal features of environment
∮ = culture (historically specific features of
    environment)

FIGURE 1.4 *Four frameworks for interpreting the influence of nature and nurture on individual development. In the first three frameworks, biological and environmental factors directly interact with each other to shape the individual. In the fourth, the cultural-context framework, biological inheritance and universal features of the environment act indirectly through the medium of culture.*

accompany (and are caused by) stagelike changes in the biological structure of the organism.

The secondary role of the environment in shaping the basic course of developmental change according to the biological-maturation view is stated quite forcefully by Arnold Gesell (1880–1961), one of the most influential developmental psychologists of the early twentieth century:

> Environment . . . determines the occasion, the intensity, and the correlation of many aspects of behavior, but it does not engender the basic progressions of behavior development. These are determined by inherent, maturational mechanisms. (1940, p. 13)

Another important maturational theorist was Sigmund Freud (1856–1939), whose theories of personality formation and mental illness have exerted a tremendous influence on modern ideas about human nature. Freud's well-known belief that sex is the primary motive of human behavior places him among the biological-maturation theorists. When he considered the process of individual development, however, Freud, like Gesell, accorded some role to the environment. "The constitutional factor," he wrote, "must await experiences before it can make itself felt" (1905/1953, p. 239). In other words, the basic human drives are biologically determined, but the social environment directs the way these drives will be satisfied, thereby shaping individual personalities.

Biological-maturation theories of human development were out of favor at midcentury, but in recent decades they have enjoyed renewed attention. Again, modern studies of language acquisition are a prominent example, suggesting to some researchers that the environment plays only a "triggering" role in the realization of linguistic potential; the ability to use language appears to mature at a fixed pace and is inherited by all human beings (Piattelli-Palmarini, 1980). In addition, aspects of personality and intelligence have been shown to have a significant inherited component

Arnold Gesell testing a child in the observation room at the Yale Child Study Center.

(Plomin, DeFries, & McClearn, 1990), and several basic intellectual competencies appear to be present in embryonic form at or near birth, suggesting that they initially do not depend on interactions with the postnatal environment (Carey & Gelman, 1991).

The environmental-learning framework

According to the environmental-learning perspective, biological factors provide the basic foundation for development, but the major causes of developmental change are predominantly **exogenous;** that is, they come from the environment, particularly from the adults who reward and punish the child's efforts. The major mechanism of development, according to this framework, is **learning**, the process by which an organism's behavior is modified by experience. John B. Watson (1878–1958), an early behavior theorist, presented an extreme statement of this position:

> Give me a dozen healthy infants, well-formed, and my own specified world to bring them up in and I'll guarantee to take any one at random and train him to become any type of specialist I might select—doctor, lawyer, artist, merchant-chief, and, yes, even beggar-man and thief, regardless of his talents, penchants, tendencies, abilities, vocations, and race of his ancestors. (1930, p. 104)

Modern psychologists who adopt an environmental-learning framework no longer ignore biological differences among children so completely. They do believe, however, that the environment, acting through learning mechanisms, is overwhelmingly important in the shaping of development. In support of their position, they point to evidence that enriching the experience of children who have lived in isolation or who have been brought up in orphanages with little intellectual stimulation dramatically improves their later social and cognitive development (Clarke & Clarke, 1986); that certain styles of parenting appear to promote children's competence (Baumrind, 1980); and that television can influence aggressive behavior (Bandura, 1986).

Their focus on the environment as the major source of development leads many environmental learning theorists to emphasize the gradual and continuous nature of developmental change. This intuition is captured nicely by B. F. Skinner's metaphorical description of how the environment gives rise to new forms:

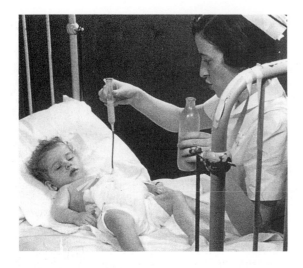

Top: *Because of a birth defect requiring her to be fed through a tube directly into the stomach, Monica was never fed orally or held in arms while being fed during her first two years.* Bottom: *As she grew up, she fed her dolls and, later, bottlefed her infant daughters, who had no such defect, in the same position as she had been fed. For Monica, the cultural mode of holding and feeding babies never felt natural. The persistence of this behavior reflects the enduring importance of children's earliest learning experiences. (Courtesy G. L. Engel et al., 1985)*

Operant conditioning [learning through rewards and punishments] shapes behavior as a sculptor shapes a lump of clay. Although at some point the sculptor seems to have produced an entirely novel object, we can always follow the process back to the original undifferentiated lump, and we can make the successive stages by which we return to this condition as small as we wish. At no point does anything emerge which is very different from what preceded it. The final product seems to have a special unity or integrity of design, but we cannot find a point at which this suddenly appears. (Skinner, 1953, p. 91)

The universal-constructivist framework

Psychologists who adopt the universal-constructivist view maintain that nature and nurture play equal and reciprocal roles as sources of development, so it is inappropriate to attribute more importance to one factor or the other. A leading adherent of this view was the Swiss developmental psychologist Jean Piaget (1896 – 1980), who began his scientific career as a biologist. Piaget paid close attention to processes common to the biological development of all organic life, much like a biological-maturation theorist. "Mental growth is inseparable from physical growth," he argued; "maturation of the nervous and endocrine systems, in particular, continues until the age of sixteen" (Piaget & Inhelder, 1969, p. vii). At the same time, Piaget, like supporters of the environmental-learning framework, believed the environment's role in development goes well beyond triggering the child's innate potential:

The human being is immersed right from birth in a social environment which affects him just as much as his physical environment. Society, even more, in a sense, than the physical environment, changes the very structure of the individual. . . . Every relation between individuals (from two onwards) literally modifies them. . . . (Piaget, 1973, p. 156)

As Piaget conceived it, the universal-constructivist framework attributes to children a greater role as active constructors of their own development than does either the environmental-learning or biological-maturation framework. "Knowledge is not a copy of reality," Piaget once wrote (1964, p. 8). Rather, knowledge comes from modifying and transforming the

Jean Piaget, whose work has had a profound influence on developmental psychology, observing children at play.

world. By actively striving to master their environments, children *construct* higher levels of knowledge from elements contributed by both maturation and environmental circumstances. This constructive process, as Piaget envisioned it, is fundamentally the same in all human groups (which is why we call it a *universal*-constructivist approach).

In addition, Piaget and his followers maintain that the environment does not act in the same way for all children at all ages. Instead, the influences of the environment depend on the child's current stage of development. Development can be speeded up or slowed down by variations in the environment, but the basic sequence of changes is universal.

Contemporary psychologists who follow in the tradition established by Piaget have refined or amended a number of his ideas. Some have focused on his explanations for why children at a given stage of development perform various tasks at seemingly different levels (contrary to the notion of stagelike change) (Fischer & Knight, 1990). Others have attempted to rectify shortcomings in his theories that arise from the fact that he did not study biological contributions to cognitive change (Case, 1991; Dia-

mond, 1991a). Still others have sought to specify more clearly the role of social interaction in the process of construction (Perret-Clermont, Perret, & Bell, 1991). All, however, follow Piaget in adhering to the notion that biology and the environment play reciprocal roles as sources of developmental change.

The cultural-context framework

Psychologists who work within the three theoretical frameworks described thus far assume that development arises from the interaction of factors from two sources, phylogenetic heritage and the ontogenetic environment. Their disagreements focus on the relative weights that should be attributed to the two sources and how they interact to produce development. Psychologists who adopt the cultural-context framework also assume that biological and experiential factors influence each other in development. But they differ with the other frameworks in insisting that the same biological or environmental factor may have quite different consequences for development, depending on the specific cultural-historical context within which it interacts. Emphasizing that the ways people organize

Above and facing page: Cultural-context approaches pay special attention to variations in children's development arising from differences in the human-made parts of the environment.

their activities depend on the experiences of earlier generations passed down through culture, adherents of the cultural-context framework include a third source of development: the history of the child's social group, crystallized in the present in the form of its culture (Baltes, 1987; Bronfenbrenner, 1979; Lerner, 1991; Rogoff, 1990; Valsiner, 1989; Vygotsky, 1978).

The term *culture* as it is used in discussions of development should not be confused with the "culture" popularly attributed to people who have acquired refined manners or an interest in the arts. As we suggested earlier, **culture** consists of human designs for living that are based on the accumulated knowledge of a people encoded in their language and embodied in the physical artifacts, beliefs, values, customs, and activities that have been passed down from one generation to the next.

The way culture influences development can be seen in the development of mathematical understanding. The kinds of mathematical thinking children develop do not depend only on their ability to deal with abstractions and on adults' efforts to teach them mathematical concepts. They also depend on the adults' own mathematical knowledge, which in turn depends on their cultural heritage and the contexts within which mathematical knowledge is relevant. A child growing up among the Oksapmin of New Guinea appears to have the same universal ability to grasp basic

number concepts as a child growing up in Paris or Pittsburgh. The system of counting used in Oksapmin culture — counting by body parts — is unwieldy when children must solve arithmetic problems in school and later when they enter the money economy; but it is no problem at all for a person dealing with the tasks of everyday life in traditional Oksapmin culture (Saxe, 1981). Brazilian market children, who grow up in a country where modern mathematics is a part of the national cultural heritage but who do not attend school, develop remarkable mathematical skills in the context of everyday buying and selling, but they experience difficulties with the same problems if they are presented in a schoollike format (Carraher &

Carraher, 1981). Many U.S. high school students can solve certain physics problems that confounded the Greek philosopher Aristotle in ancient times. In each of these cases, culture has shaped the course of development by arranging particular configurations of interaction between biological and experiential factors.

The cultural-context and universal-constructivist points of view are similar in several respects. Both hold that the developing individual passes through distinctive stagelike changes in the course of development, and both emphasize that development is impossible without the individual's active striving. They differ, however, in three important respects. First, the cultural-context framework assumes that both children and their caretakers are active agents in the process of development. Development is, in this sense, "co-constructed." Second, this framework anticipates wide variability in performance as people move from one kind of activity to another. Third, the cultural-context framework is more open to the notion that the sequence of changes, and even the existence or nonexistence of a particular stage of development, depend on one's cultural-historical circumstances.

The universal-constructivist and cultural-context approaches are sufficiently similar that on occasion it is difficult to classify a theorist as belonging in one camp or the other. For example, Erik Erikson (1902–), a student of Freud whose work figures prominently in later chapters, is sometimes classified as a universal-constructivist theorist because he adheres to the view that nature sets the basic sequence of stages while nurture shapes developmental processes within stages. Erikson draws on evidence from many cultures, however, and he emphasizes that the prior experience of the society into which children are born, embodied in its current culture, plays a major role in development (Erikson, 1963). In these respects his point of view is similar to that of the cultural-context theorists.

Questions about Individual Differences

Every person is in some respects like all other people, like some other people, and like no other person (Kluckhohn, Murray, & Schneider, 1953). All humans are alike because we are all members of the same species; all humans are like some, but not other, people insofar as they share important biological characteristics (males are like each other and different from females) or cultural characteristics (Australian Aborigines are alike in comparison with Inuit Eskimos); and all people are unique. Even identical twins, who have identical genetic constitutions, are not alike in every respect.

When we attempt to understand the nature of development, it is important to take into account two questions about individual differences: (1) What makes individuals different from one another? and (2) To what extent are individual characteristics stable over time?

The question of what makes individuals different from one another is really a question about the sources of development: Are we different from one another because of our nature or because of our nurture? If baby Sam is fussy, is it because he inherited a tendency to be easily upset, or has he been affected by parental anxiety or the fact that his mother was addicted to cocaine during her pregnancy? If baby Georgia has a large appetite, is it because she inherited a tendency to obesity, or is it because her food contains too much sugar? Powerful statistical techniques and ingenious methods of data collection have been used in an effort to tease apart the fundamental sources of individual variation, but disagreements of theory and fact remain (Jensen, 1969; Lewontin, 1982; Scarr, 1992).

Insofar as individual characteristics are stable, they provide a glimpse of what children will be like in the future. If baby Sam is fussy, perhaps he will be an irritable child. If baby Georgia has a large appetite, maybe she will be a big eater as a teenager.

There is an intuitive appeal in the notion that some of our individual psychological characteristics remain constant over extended periods of time, but demonstrating such stability scientifically has proved difficult. The problem is that the indicators that seem appropriate for measuring memory or affability in an infant are not likely to be appropriate for measuring the same traits in an 8-year-old or a teenager. Perhaps for this reason, many studies have failed to support the idea of stable psychological traits (Kopp & McCall, 1982). The refinement of research techniques in recent years, however, has allowed some investigators to find support for stable individual differences in psychological characteristics. There is recent evidence that children who are shy and uncertain at 21 months, for example, are likely to be timid and cautious at 5½ years (Kagan & Snidman, 1991), and that infants who adapt rapidly to novel visual stimuli (an indication that they learn quickly) are likely to score well on tests of mental development 4 or 5 years later (Bornstein, 1989).

The stability of children's psychological characteristics over time depends on stability in their environment in addition to any stable characteristics that might be attributed to their genetic makeup. Studies have found that children who remain in an orphanage that provides only minimal care from infancy through adolescence are lethargic and unintelligent. They are also at risk for intellectual and emotional difficulties as adults. But if the environment of these children is improved — that is, if they are given extra care and stimulating attention by the orphanage staff or if they are adopted into caring families — their condition improves markedly, and many of them become intellectually normal adults (Clarke & Clarke, 1976).

Although adherents of competing approaches and theoretical frameworks have been attempting to explain development all during the twentieth century, the central issues of developmental psychology remain unresolved. Nor is there agreement on a single "correct" framework or theory that should be used in efforts to resolve them. The modern discipline of developmental psychology can usefully be thought of as a social mechanism for organizing scientific inquiry. It allows scholars with conflicting views to compare notes and learn from one another's work despite differing theories about specific phenomena. The resulting discussions about theories and methods encompass every aspect of the field—the observations that are made, the methods for relating facts to theories, and the implications of facts and theories for the way we raise our children.

THE DISCIPLINE OF DEVELOPMENTAL PSYCHOLOGY

Among the sciences that study development, psychology focuses on the individual human being, whereas sociology and anthropology focus on human groups, and the biological sciences encompass our species as a whole, viewing it in relation to other forms of life. This division of scientific labor creates a paradox. On the one hand, psychologists are supposed to seek to understand development in terms of the individual person; on the other, the natural-sciences tradition, which has dominated psychology all during this century, insists that humankind, not the individual human, is the relevant unit of scientific analysis (Danzinger, 1990).

This paradox is eloquently described by the novelist-philosopher Walker Percy:

> There is a secret about the scientific method which every scientist knows and takes as a matter of course, but which the layman does not know. . . . The secret is this: Science cannot utter a single word about an individual molecule, thing, or creature insofar as it is an individual but only insofar as it is like other individuals. (1975, p. 22)

The difference between these two ways of knowing—one based on intimate knowledge of individual characteristics and biography, the other based on characteristics common to many people—is a source of constant tension in psychologists' attempts to understand development. The more psychologists want to know about individuals, the more they need to know about each person's life history and current circumstances. But the more they concentrate on unique histories and patterns of influence, the less they can generalize their findings to other individuals.

This trade-off requires psychologists to vary their research methods, choosing the ones that best accord with their specific goal. If, for example, the goal is to create a beneficial environment for infants born prematurely or to understand the role of symbolic play in toddlers' intellectual development, the appropriate methods are those that treat all children as equivalent with respect to the issue in question. But if the goal is to help Johnny, who suddenly has started to fail in school and misbehave in class, the psychologist may want to know about the circumstances of Johnny's birth, recent changes in his family life, and perhaps even the specific mix of children and activities Johnny is dealing with at school.

The complex web of factors that underpin development and the varied tasks that psychologists are asked to carry out have led them to be self-conscious about the methods they use to arrive at their conclusions. In order to accumulate useful scientific knowledge, they must pay close attention to the adequacy of their descriptions, their techniques for collecting data, and the way they design their research. Only then can the data psychologists collect be related in principled ways to the theories that guide their practical activities on behalf of children.

Criteria of Scientific Description

Every society has its own beliefs about the nature of children and the course of their development. Psychologists, however, are looking for scientific facts that can be universally applied. Like any other scientists, they may begin with common-sense speculation and then attempt to test it in ways that provide clear answers and that allow others to check their reasoning and procedures. Psychologists use four general criteria to judge the conclusions derived from investigations of children's behavior: objectivity, reliability, validity, and replicability.

To be useful in constructing a disciplined account of human development, data should be collected and analyzed with **objectivity;** that is, they should not be biased by the investigators' preconceptions. Total objectivity is impossible to achieve in practice because human beings come to the study of behavior with beliefs that influence their interpretations of what they see. But objectivity remains an important ideal toward which to work.

Data obtained in research should have **reliability** in two senses. First, the descriptions arrived at when the same behavior is observed on two or more occasions should be consistent. Second, independent observers should agree in their descriptions of the behavior. Suppose that one wants to know how upset infants become when a pacifier is taken from them while they are sucking on it (Goldsmith & Campos, 1982). Statements about the degree of an infant's distress are considered reliable in the first sense if the level of distress (manifested as crying or thrashing about) is found to be more or less the same on successive occasions when the baby's sucking is interrupted. The statements are considered reliable in the second sense if independent observers agree on how distressed the baby becomes each time the pacifier is taken away.

Validity means that the data being collected actually reflect the underlying psychological process that the researcher claims they do. Many psychologists believe, for example, that the distress infants display when their sucking is interrupted reflects an enduring predisposition to become irritable (Kagan, 1989). One important test of validity is whether different ways of measuring the same characteristic yield the same outcome. Children who become upset when their pacifier is removed should also become irritable when a rattle is taken away or when they are not fed on time. If different measures do not converge on a single conclusion, doubt is cast on their validity.

Another important test of validity is whether the behavior exhibited at one time can be used to predict future behavior. If the same infants who appear greatly upset when their pacifier is removed also become upset when they are interrupted in future situations (when recess ends in the middle of a game, for example), that is evidence to support the validity of the claim about a predisposition to irritability. If these same infants don't become upset easily in future situations, the original claim — that the behavior is an indicator of an underlying temperamental predisposition to be irritable — is suspect.

In scientific research, **replicability,** the fourth requirement, means that other researchers can use the same procedures as an initial investigator and obtain the same results. In research on the ability to imitate, for example, some researchers report that newborns will imitate exaggerated facial expressions, whereas others have failed to elicit such imitation from newborns (see Chapter 4, pp. 158–159). Only if the same finding is obtained repeatedly by different investigators is it likely to be considered firmly established by the scientific community.

In addition to these four basic criteria, it is important that the group of people studied be a **representative sample** of the people the psychologist wishes to answer questions about. Conclusions drawn from data collected from one group of people may not be applicable to other people with different characteristics. For example, a study of infants from middle-class families in Denver who manifest distress when they are separated from their mothers may yield different results from a study applying the same procedures to infants from working-class homes in Denver or middle-class homes in Tokyo.

Techniques of Data Collection

Over the past hundred years, psychologists have refined a variety of techniques for gathering information about the development of children. Among the most widely used are self-reports, naturalistic observations, experiments, and clinical interviews. No one technique can answer all of our questions about human development, but each has a strategic role in advancing our understanding of it.

Self-reports

Perhaps the most direct way to obtain information about psychological development is through **self-reports,** people's answers to questions about themselves. Psychologists usually conduct interviews to obtain self-reports, but written questionnaires are also commonly used. Topics as diverse as adolescents' developing ideas about friendship and popularity (Savin-Williams & Berndt, 1990) and parents' ideas about child rearing (Sigel, 1985) have been investigated in this manner. In one study (described in Chapter 15), researchers went so far as to provide teenagers with beepers, which sounded at random intervals through-out the day, to signal the teenagers to fill out a questionnaire about what they were doing and feeling at that moment (Csikszentmihalyi & Larson, 1984).

Self-reports can provide intimate accounts of people's life experiences, and they can reveal dynamics of thought and behavior that might otherwise escape notice. A major limitation of this method, however, is that the validity of what people report about themselves is often open to question.

To deal with this problem, investigators often try to make direct observations of the behavior reported on. Research based on this strategy has found only modest agreement between people's reports and their actual behavior (Kochanska, Kuczynski, & Radke-Yarrow, 1989).

Evidence that parents are likely to be selective in what they remember (or at least in what they are willing to report) about themselves and their children comes from a study in which parents were asked to recall their child-rearing practices several years earlier, when their children were 3 years old (Robbins, 1963). The parents' reports could be checked against what they had actually done because they had participated in an earlier study in which their behavior had been observed. Parents' recall, the research found, was distorted to conform to their beliefs about optimum development. Some of the mothers, for example, claimed that their children had never sucked their thumbs, a practice disapproved of by experts at the time of the original observations, even though they were on record as having consulted with their physicians about their children's thumb-sucking. To reduce such distortions in long-term retrospective reports, researchers now often ask parents to focus on specific ongoing behaviors, such as temper tantrums, disobedience, or bed-wetting, and ask for daily reports on these behaviors along with the parents' responses to them (Patterson, 1982; Zahn-Waxler & Radke-Yarrow, 1982).

Naturalistic observations

In the nineteenth century, several scientists began to write **baby biographies,** diaries in which they recorded observations of their children (Kessen, 1965). The most famous of these accounts is Darwin's (1877) daily record of the early development of his eldest son (Figure 1.5). By documenting characteristics shared by human beings and other species, Darwin hoped to

FIGURE 1.5 *The naturalist Charles Darwin became famous for his theory of evolution. His observations of his son, which he recorded in a baby biography, provide one of the first systematic descriptions of infant development.*

support his thesis of human evolution. Darwin's baby biography and others such as W. F. Leopold's (1949) record of his daughter's language development and Piaget's (1952b, 1954) descriptions of his children's mental development have proved to be of enduring scientific value. But at present baby biographies are rarely used outside the area of language development (where they are still a basic source of data) because even scientists usually cannot maintain objectivity when they describe their own children. As Kessen comments, "No one can distort as convincingly as a loving parent" (1965, p. 117). Because of the problems that arise when adults report on their own children's behavior, psychologists prefer to rely on the reports of trained observers who have no personal stake in the children they study. The goal of these **naturalistic observations** is to obtain detailed information about children's actual behavior in the real-world settings they inhabit, including the home, the school, and the community.

Naturalistic observation is one of the major research tools used by developmental psychologists who consider themselves to be *ethologists.* **Ethology** is an interdisciplinary science that studies the biological bases of behavior; ethologically oriented developmental psychologists emphasize the way the behavioral development of children has been conditioned by the evolutionary history of *Homo sapiens* (Hinde, 1987). Ethologists place great emphasis on naturalistic observation because they believe that biologically important behaviors affecting human development are best studied in the settings where they have adaptive significance (Charlesworth, 1976).

F. Francis Strayer (1991) carried out natural observations in this tradition when he studied the way children interact in preschool classrooms. By observing and recording who interacted with whom and the quality of the interactions, Strayer and his colleagues discovered that the spontaneous development of social hierarchies in preschool classes regulates the degree of aggression that little children display toward each other.

OBSERVATION IN MANY CONTEXTS. An important goal of naturalistic observation is to describe the child's **ecology,** a term derived from the Greek word for "house." In the biological sciences, the "house" is the habitat of a population of plants or animals, and the ecology of that population is the pattern of its relationship with its environment. In psychology, *ecology* has come to refer to the range of situations in which people are actors, the roles they play, the predicaments they encounter, and the consequences of those encounters (see Figure 1.6) (Bronfenbrenner & Crouter, 1983; Schoggen, 1989).

Charles Super and Sarah Harkness (1986), who have studied children's development in Kenya as well as the United States, refer to the child's place within the community as a **developmental niche** in order to emphasize the links between children's development and the community within which they are born. They suggest that every developmental niche be analyzed in terms of three components: (1) the physical and social context in which the child lives, (2) the culturally determined childrearing and educational practices of the child's society, and (3) the psychological characteristics of the child's parents.

Thorough ecological descriptions of the variety of real-life experiences of children in their sociocultural contexts, such as those provided by Super and Harkness, provide a sense of the whole child and the many influences that act on the child. We can thereby learn what predicaments loom largest in children's lives and how circumstances might be changed to foster their development.

The most ambitious project launched to study the ecology of human development was conducted by Roger Barker and Herbert Wright (1951, 1955). These researchers spent hundreds of hours observing and describing the natural ecology of schoolchildren in various communities in the United States and abroad. In one such study, they observed a single 7-year-old American boy from the time he awoke on April 26, 1949, until he went to sleep that night. They noted everything the boy did, everywhere he went, and everything that happened along the way. Barker and Wright found that this one child on just one day participated in approximately 1300 distinct activities in a wide variety of settings and involving hundreds of objects and dozens of people. These observations gave some idea of the wide range of skills children possess by the age of 7 and the many social demands made on them.

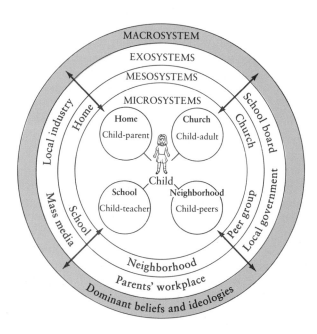

FIGURE 1.6 *The ecological approach sees children in the context of all the various settings they inhabit on a daily basis (microsystems). These settings are related to each other in a variety of ways (mesosystems), which are in turn linked to settings and social institutions where the children are not present but which have an important influence on their development (exosystems). All of these systems are organized in terms of the culture's dominant beliefs and ideologies (the macrosystem).*

Barker and Wright made it a point of pride and principle to write down everything they could notice and get on paper about a child's daily behavior and the contexts in which it occurred. Other investigators who study children across a range of contexts are more selective. They usually decide in advance on a particular type of behavior to observe in different contexts, or they choose a few important contexts within which to make extensive observations of the various behaviors that children exhibit.

In a study of 160 Mayan children between 1 and 14 years of age in a village in Guatemala, for example, Barbara Rogoff (1978, 1981) sampled brief time periods to provide "snapshots" of children's activities. Rogoff drew up a list of the observations she planned to make and worked out a schedule that allowed her or her assistant to observe each child for about 10 minutes several times a day on different days of the week. During these periods she noted whom a child was with and what the child was doing. Rogoff discovered that Mayan children, like U.S. children, spend much of their time apart from adults. When they do spend time with adults, however, their experiences are quite different from those of U.S. children. When Mayan children are with adults, they are expected to help with the grownups' usual jobs. In industrial societies like our own, children cannot (or are not allowed to) help with many adult jobs. Instead, when U.S. children are with adults, they are likely to be instructed by them, even outside school (Schoggen, 1989).

OBSERVATIONS IN A SINGLE CONTEXT. The very breadth of the ecological approach makes it time-consuming and expensive to apply. As a result, developmental psychologists often restrict their observations to a single social setting that is widely encountered and important in children's lives. They observe in minute detail the face-to-face interactions between children or between children and adults and the way participants in these interactions tend to regulate their behavior together.

Lisa Serbin and her colleagues (1973), for instance, examined interactions between teachers and students in 15 preschool classrooms to see whether anything in the teacher's behavior might unwittingly be encouraging aggressiveness in boys and dependence in girls. They found that the teachers did not pay equal attention to the misbehavior of boys and girls. The teachers chastised the boys publicly for a greater proportion of their misdeeds than they did the

DOONESBURY By Garry Trudeau

Cartoonist Gary Trudeau comments on the phenomenon, established in observational research, that teachers respond differently to boys and girls in their classrooms.

girls for theirs. Often this selective treatment seemed to increase aggressiveness among the boys. In a parallel set of observations, the researchers discovered that the teachers rewarded dependent behavior in girls by paying more attention to those girls who were sitting closest to them; they paid equal amounts of attention to all the boys no matter where they were sitting in the classroom. Once such social practices are made explicit, new patterns of interaction can be suggested to the teachers that might foster more effective behavior in schoolchildren of both sexes.

LIMITATIONS OF NATURALISTIC OBSERVATIONS. Observational studies are a keystone of child development research and a crucial source of data about children's social development. As with self-reports, there are limits to what we can learn from them, however. Observers enter the scene with expectations about what they are going to see, and we all tend to observe selectively in accordance with our expectations. An observer cannot write down everything, so information is inevitably lost. In some studies, prearranged note-taking schemes specify what to look for and how to report it. The drawback of such schemes is that they are not flexible enough to take account of unexpected events, so details are often lost in this way, too. If time elapses between an event and note taking, observations may be further distorted because people's selective remembering accentuates the problem of selective observing (D'Andrade, 1974). Recordings of behavior on videotape or film are useful, but they are extremely time-consuming to analyze.

Another difficulty with observational research is that people's behavior changes when they know they are being watched, creating a false impression of their normal behavior (Zegiob, Arnold, & Forehand, 1975). A laboratory study of the interactions between mothers and their children confirmed the problem. Zoe Graves and Joseph Glick (1978) asked mothers to help their 18- to 25-month-old children put together a simple jigsaw puzzle. To determine the influence that being observed had on the mothers' behavior, Graves and Glick told half of them that the video equipment being used to record their interactions was not working. They found that the mothers who believed they were off camera behaved less formally than those who knew they were being taped, but that they were not as helpful to their children.

Perhaps the major problem with naturalistic observation is that it rarely allows researchers to establish the existence of causal relationships between phenomena, a basic aim of science. Collation and comparison of observations can establish whether a **correlation** exists between two factors; that is, whether changes in one factor vary with changes in another. But a correlation doesn't tell us whether one factor causes the other or whether both factors are caused by a third, undetermined factor (see Box 1.2). In their ecological study, for example, Barker and Wright revealed many relationships between the settings in which children find themselves and the characteristics of children's behavior in those settings; similarly, Serbin and her colleagues discovered interesting patterns in the ways teachers treat boys and girls in the classroom. Neither study, however, pinpoints the causes of the patterns it describes.

BOX 1.2
Correlation and Causation

In their attempts to discover factors that cause development, psychologists often begin by determining that different factors are related. Two factors are said to be correlated with each other when changes in one are associated with changes in the other. In later chapters, we will see many examples of correlation: As children grow older, they display increased ability to remember lists of words; that is, age is correlated with memory. The higher the social class of the parents, the greater the achievement of their children in school; that is, school achievement is correlated with social class. These relationships are important hints about causal factors in development, but they fall short of specifying the actual mechanisms involved.

A *correlation coefficient* (symbolized as r) provides a quantitative index of the degree of association between two factors; thus it enables psychologists to distinguish between relationships that occur by chance and those that occur with significant regularity. A correlation coefficient indexing the relationship between factor 1 and factor 2 can vary in both magnitude and direction. When $r = 1.00$, there is a perfect positive correlation between the two factors: As factor 1 changes, factor 2 changes in the same direction and at the same rate. When $r = -1.00$, there is a perfect negative correlation between factor 1 and factor 2. If every increase in age in a population were accompanied by an increase in weight, for example, the correlation between age and weight would be 1.00. If instead people always got smaller as they aged, the correlation would be -1.00. If age and weight were not related at all, the correlation would be .00. Intermediate positive or negative values of a correlation coefficient indicate intermediate levels of association. For example, there is a correlation of approximately .50 between the heights of parents and their offspring, indicating that tall parents tend to have tall offspring (Tanner, 1978).

A correlation may point to a causal relationship between two events, but correlation is not the same as causation; that is, it does not establish that the occurrence of one event depends on the occurrence of the other. The difficulty of distinguishing correlation from

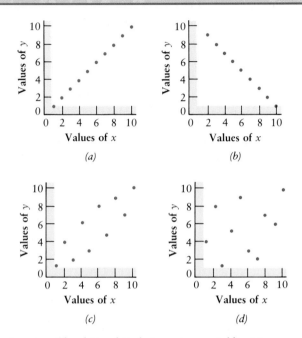

Four possible relationships between two variables: (a)
As values of x *increase, values of* y *increase, producing
a correlation of 1.00.* (b) *As values of* x *increase, values
of* y *decrease, producing a correlation of* −1.00. (c) *As
values of* x *increase, values of* y *often increase, but there
are some exceptions, producing a correlation of .84.*
(d) *As values of* x *increase, values of* y *show a weak but
noticeable tendency to increase, producing a correlation
of .33.*

found between height and scores on tests of mental
ability; that is, taller children tend to score higher on
intelligence tests than their shorter agemates (Tanner,
1978). Since nothing about children's height can plausibly be said to be a cause of their intelligence, or children's intelligence of their height, some other factor
must be the cause of both. One possibility is maturational forces. Taller children may be more mature
overall and thus able to function at a higher level. But
this explanation implies that the correlation between
intelligence test scores and height should disappear in
adulthood, when all individuals are considered mature, yet the correlation remains. Other factors may
be nutritional status and general health; or something
altogether different may cause both greater height
and higher test scores.

The slipperiest cases to deal with are those in
which a scientist has a strong theory about causal
connections among the phenomena under study but
only correlational data to work with. For example,
there is a correlation of .50 between children's current
grades in school and their scores on standard IQ tests
(Minton & Schneider, 1980). It might be tempting to
conclude that intelligence causes cognitive development. That conclusion does not follow from the evidence, however, any more than the conclusion that
age causes changes in weight, although it fits many
people's notion that intelligence causes school
achievement. It could just as plausibly be argued that
students who work hard get their schoolwork done
more often and learn more, thereby boosting their IQ
scores.

The use of correlation coefficients to describe relationships among phenomena is very important in
the study of human development because so many of
the factors of interest to psychologists (social class,
ethnic origin, genetic constitution, and a host of other
factors) cannot be controlled experimentally. Because
correlations often suggest causal relationships but do
not provide crucial evidence of causation, controversies that have no clear resolution often arise, requiring developmental psychologists to exercise caution in
the interpretation of their data.

causation is often a source of scientific controversy. In
the case of the heights of parents and their children,
the problem is not serious. We can be pretty certain
that the height of a child does not cause the height of
the parents. Little confusion is likely to arise about
the relationship between a child's age and weight either. Age by itself cannot cause increases in weight because age is simply another term for the time that
has elapsed since an agreed-upon starting point. Certainly, weight cannot cause an increase in age.

Other cases are less clear-cut. Among schoolchildren, for example, a correlation of about .30 has been

The difficulty in both these cases is that researchers have no means of telling from their observations alone which factors are causal. Did children in Barker and Wright's study act more grown up in church than in a drugstore because church attendance evokes religious feelings or because their parents were there to observe them? In the study by Serbin and her colleagues, did the teachers chastise the boys for their misbehavior more often than they chastised the girls because they had stereotyped the boys as troublemakers who needed discipline to be kept in line or because they simply noticed the boys' misbehavior more often than the girls'? Similar questions can be raised about almost any observational study of behavior. To attempt to resolve such questions, psychologists turn to experimental methods.

Experimental methods

An **experiment** in psychology usually consists of introducing some change in a person's or animal's experience and then measuring the effect of the change on the person's or animal's behavior. Ideally, all the other possible causal influences are held constant while the factor of interest is made to vary to determine if that factor makes a difference. If an experiment is well designed and executed, it should provide a means of confirming a scientific hypothesis about the causes of the behavior observed. A scientific **hypothesis** is an assumption that is precise enough to be tested and can be shown to be incorrect. If there is no way to disprove the hypothesis, it has little scientific value.

An investigation of the development of a fear of high places by Joseph Campos and his colleagues (Bertenthal, Campos, & Barrett, 1984) indicates how the experimental method can help resolve uncertainties about causal factors in development. For many years it was believed that the fear of heights is innate in the human infant. According to this view, the fear of high places becomes apparent when infants begin to locomote, or move about under their own steam, not because either locomotion causes fear or fear causes locomotion, but because both result from general maturational factors and just happen to develop around the same time (Rader, Bausano, & Richards, 1980; Richards & Rader, 1981). Campos and his colleagues disagreed with this hypothesis. They believed that fear of heights is a result of experience, especially the experience that infants acquire when they start to crawl.

Initially Campos and his colleagues studied a group of infants who were between 6 and 8 months old, beginning a week or two after they began to crawl. They discovered that at the first few opportunities the infants were given, all would cross a visual cliff, a transparent platform that gives the illusion of a sharp drop in elevation such as that shown in Figure 1.7. On subsequent trials, however, the infants became increasingly reluctant to cross over the visual cliff, even though they had never experienced any unpleasantness when they had done so. Something seemed to be building up in the infants' minds as they gained experience. But what thing and what experience? To begin to answer these questions, the investigators needed to conduct an experiment.

Campos and his colleagues designed an experiment to test the hypothesis that the onset of the fear of heights results from the experience of moving about (Bertenthal et al., 1984). They located 92 infants who were near the age when they might be expected to start crawling and showing a fear of heights. The infants were randomly assigned to one of two groups. One group was designated as the **experimental group** — the group in an experiment whose environment is changed. Over several days the infants in this group were given more than 40 hours of experience moving about in special baby walkers before they learned to

FIGURE 1.7 *A baby hesitates at the edge of a visual cliff, a transparent platform that makes it appear to the baby that there is a sharp drop just ahead.*

FIGURE 1.8   *Experience in moving around the environment in a walker influences the onset of fear on the visual cliff.*

crawl (see Figure 1.8). The other children, called the **control group** — the group in an experiment that is treated as much as possible like the experimental group except that it does not participate in the experimental manipulation — were provided with no special experience in locomoting. If the hypothesis of Campos and his colleagues was correct, the difference between the experimental and control groups in the amount of experience the infants had in moving around should lead to a difference in their responses to the visual cliff.

Forty hours of careening around a room in a walker may not seem like a lot of experience, but it apparently made a big difference in the way the infants in the experimental group responded when they were placed on the visual cliff. Although responses varied somewhat, in general the infants in the experimental group showed fear on their first exposure to the visual cliff, whereas the infants in the control group, who had no locomoting experience, showed no fear in the initial trials.

This experiment provided strong support for the hypothesis that the development of locomotion plays a large role in the development of the fear of heights. Additional research would be useful to rule out possibilities that this research did not delve into. For example, if children were moved around in little vehicles

that permitted them to explore the environment without locomotion, would they still become fearful when they were placed on the visual cliff? Such uncertainties about research results are almost inevitable. A series of experiments is often necessary to isolate specific causes because the complexities of behavior exceed the researcher's ability to control all the relevant factors in a single experiment (Cole & Means, 1981).

In general, the clear strength of the experimental method is its ability to isolate causal factors in a way no other method of investigation can. Two main factors limit its usefulness as a source of information about development: For ethical reasons, many experiments should not be performed; and the very control of the environment that many experiments require may distort the validity of the results obtained.

ETHICS AND EXPERIMENTATION. The central ethical tenet of all psychological research is: If a research procedure may harm anyone, it should not be carried out. Ethical issues in psychological research are not always so clear-cut as this tenet suggests, however. What is harmful, and how do we assess the risks? Practically any intervention in another person's life may involve some risk, so the judgment can be a difficult one. Furthermore, the factors taken into account often vary from one culture to the next and from one historical era to another. In 1920 John B. Watson, the behavior theorist, and Rosalie Rayner published the results of an experiment to demonstrate that children's fears of animals are not innate but are shaped by the environment. They showed a 9-month-old boy a series of animals (a rat, a white rabbit, a dog, etc.). According to these investigators, the baby played with the animals with no expression of fright. Then they hit a steel bar with a hammer behind the baby as he reached for the rabbit. The boy cried with fear at the loud noise. After several such experiences, the baby cried whenever he saw the rabbit. Watson and Rayner reported that his fear of the white rabbit extended to many white, fuzzy objects he was shown, including a dog, a fur coat, and even a Santa Claus mask. Fear of white rabbits, fur coats, and Santa Claus masks is not inherited, they claimed, it is learned.

Watson and Rayner's research aroused little comment concerning its ethics at the time. In fact, it became a key piece of evidence in favor of environmental theories of development. Since then it has been severely criticized for its failure to conform to important scientific principles of experimentation. The investi-

BOX 1.3
Ethical Standards for Research with Children

The following guidelines are adapted and condensed from the *Ethical Standards for Research with Children* issued by the Society for Research in Child Development.

Children as research subjects present ethical problems for the investigator different from those presented by adult subjects. Not only are children often viewed as more vulnerable to stress, but, having less knowledge and experience, they are less able to evaluate what participation in research may mean. Consent of the parent for the study of the child, moreover, must be obtained in addition to the child's consent. These are some of the major differences between research with children and research with adults.

- No matter how young the children, their rights supersede the rights of the investigator.

- The final responsibility to establish and maintain ethical practices in research remains with the individual investigator.

- The investigator is responsible for the ethical practices of collaborators, assistants, students, and employees, all of whom, however, incur parallel obligations.

- The investigator should inform children of all features of the research that may affect their willingness to participate and should answer children's questions in terms appropriate to their comprehension.

- The investigator should respect children's freedom to choose to participate in research or not, as well as to discontinue participation at any time.

- Informed consent of parents or those who act in loco parentis (e.g., teachers, superintendents of institutions) similarly should be obtained, preferably in writing. Informed consent requires that parents or other responsible adults be told all features of the research that may affect their willingness to allow children to participate.

- The informed consent of any person whose interaction with the child is the subject of the study should also be obtained.

- The investigator may use no research operation that may harm children either physically or psychologically.

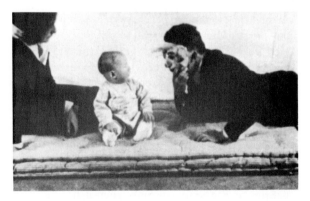

John B. Watson and Rosalie Rayner experimenting with infant fears. (Courtesy of Professor Benjamin Harris.)

gators did not have an appropriate control group; they studied only one child, so they failed to replicate their results; and their reports of the procedures and results were inconsistent (Harris, 1979; Samelson, 1980). What is of interest here, however, is less Watson and Rayner's skill as experimenters than their apparent willingness to override ethical considerations in regard to the baby's welfare in the name of science. Watson's doctrine of learning led him to believe that if fear could be created by events in the environment, it also could be removed. But Watson and Rayner never proved this point in their experiment. They made no attempt to help the child overcome the fears they had induced in him.

- Although we accept the ethical idea of full disclosure of information, a particular study may necessitate concealment or deception. Whenever concealment or deception is thought to be essential to the conduct of the study, investigators should satisfy a committee of their peers that their judgment is correct.

- The investigator should keep in confidence all information obtained about research participants.

- Immediately after the data are collected, the investigator should clarify for the research participant any misconceptions that may have arisen. The investigator also recognizes a duty to report general findings to participants in terms appropriate to their understanding. Where scientific or humane values may justify withholding information, every effort should be made so that withholding the information has no damaging consequences for the participant.

- When, in the course of research, information comes to the investigator's attention that may seriously affect the child's well-being, the investigator has a responsibility to discuss the information with those expert in the field in order that the parents may arrange the necessary assistance for their child.

- When it is learned that research procedures may result in undesirable consequences for the participant, the investigator should employ appropriate measures to correct these consequences, and should consider redesigning the procedure.

- Investigators should be mindful of the social, political, and human implications of their research and should be especially careful in the presentation of their findings. This standard, however, in no way denies investigators the right to pursue any area of research or the right to observe proper standards of scientific reporting.

- When an experimental treatment under investigation is believed to be of benefit to children, control groups should be offered other beneficial alternative treatments, if available, instead of no treatment.

Psychologists' judgments on the ethics of Watson and Rayner's experiment would almost certainly be different today than they were in the 1920s. Psychologists now are less certain of their ability to turn psychological processes on and off than Watson was, and they appreciate more fully that scientific knowledge is by no means certain knowledge. To protect the rights of children, modern researchers are closely monitored by their own institutions and by government agencies. Before they can carry out their research, they must satisfy a committee of their peers that they will not harm the people who participate in their investigations, and that the research promises some benefits to those people in the long run (see Box 1.3).

EXPERIMENTS AND ARTIFICIALITY. When a researcher deliberately constructs a special experimental situation to test a hypothesis, the participants' experiences and resulting behaviors within that artificial situation may be far different from those that occur in everyday life. This artificiality raises doubts about the generality of some experimental results. Indeed, the pervasiveness of the problem has led Urie Bronfenbrenner (1979) to describe many laboratory experiments as studies of "the strange behavior of children in strange situations with strange adults for the briefest possible periods of time" (p. 19).

Often there is no simple solution to the problem of artificiality because the factors being studied in the experiment arise too seldom to be studied systematically in real life. In some cases, however, researchers have partially overcome the problem by introducing experimental variation in naturally occurring situations without significantly disrupting the usual course of events. To investigate how young children add new words to their vocabularies in ordinary circumstances, Elsa Bartlett (1977) and Susan Carey (1978) had a preschool teacher introduce an unusual color, olive, to her charges in the natural course of her classroom routine. To avoid the possibility that some children already knew the name of the color, the teacher referred to it as "chromium." The researchers found that when the new word was introduced casually — "Please pass the chromium crayon"— the children acquired it after very few exposures. Studies of word acquisition in the laboratory, in contrast, typically find that children require extensive instruction by an adult to learn a new word. Thus, by introducing new words to children in a natural way, Bartlett and Carey brought about a basic change in psychologists' understanding of a vitally important aspect of development.

Clinical interview methods

All the research methods discussed thus far, with the exception of diary studies, are designed to apply uniform procedures of data collection to every individual observed. In this respect, clinical interview methods differ fundamentally from the others. The essence of the **clinical method** is the tailoring of questions to the individual subject, with each question depending on the answer to the one that precedes it.

As the term implies, clinical interview methods are often used to investigate the problems of persons who are troubled or unwell. When developmental psychologists use clinical interview methods in this way, they, like medical clinicians, are seeking a set of appropriate remedies. The most famous application of clinical methods in developmental psychology comes from the work of Sigmund Freud, who considered the early family history of the child to be essential to later personality development. From a patient's account, he sought to identify crucial events that produced the difficulty from which the person was suffering. In Freud's use of the clinical method, analysis was coupled with therapy; the analyst's theory was tested by the effectiveness of treatment in resolving the person's difficulty.

Clinical methods are not restricted to pathology, however. Jean Piaget often used clinical interview techniques to explore children's developing understandings of the world. In the example to follow, note that it would have been impossible for Piaget to anticipate this 7½-year-old child's responses. Therefore, he adapted his questions to the flow of the conversation.

Piaget: . . . says that dreams come "from the night." Where do they go?
Child: Everywhere.
Piaget: What do you dream with?
Child: With the mouth.
Piaget: Where is the dream?
Child: In the night.
Piaget: Where does it happen?
Child: Everywhere. In rooms. In houses.
Piaget: Whereabouts?
Child: In the bed.
Piaget: Can you see it?
Child: No, because it is only at night.
Piaget: Would anyone know you are dreaming?
Child: No, because it's near us.
Piaget: Could you touch it?
Child: No, because you are asleep when you dream.
(Adapted from Piaget, 1929, p. 93)

Piaget believed that by interviewing many children of different ages about such familiar phenomena, he could discover basic changes that knowledge undergoes over the course of development.

Alexander Luria (1902–1977), a Russian psychologist, showed that the clinical interview method could also be used to uncover qualitative differences in thinking in different cultural environments. In one study he presented people of varying ages who lived in a pastoral culture in Central Asia with drawings of four objects—a hammer, a saw, a log, and a hatchet—three of which could be grouped into the single category "tools." He then asked which of the objects did not fit with the others (1976, p. 58):

Subject: They all fit here! The saw has to saw the log, the hammer has to hammer it, and the hatchet has to chop it. And if you want to saw the log up really good, you need the hammer. You can't take any of these things away. There isn't any you don't need.

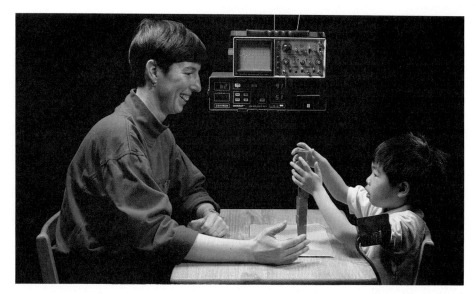

Modern-day psychologists couple measures of children's problem solving behavior with measures of physiological processes in an attempt to understand the complex factors organizing the development of behavior.

Luria: But one fellow told me that the log didn't belong here.

Subject: Why'd he say that? If we say the log isn't like the other things and put it off to one side, we'd be making a mistake. All these things are needed for the log.

Luria: But that other fellow said that the saw, hammer, and hatchet are all alike in some way, while the log isn't.

Subject: So what if they're not alike? They all work together and chop the log. Here everything works right, here everything's just fine.

Here we see a classic use of the clinical interview. The investigator probes the person's understanding by challenging various lines of reasoning and suggesting different (sometimes incorrect) alternatives depending on the person's prior responses. In this case, Luria has encountered someone for whom "similar" seems to mean "enters into the same activity." By contrasting this subject's answers with the answers given by people from other cultural backgrounds, Luria was able to formulate plausible conclusions about the ways in which culture influences the development of intellectual functions.

The strong point of clinical interview methods is that they provide insight into the dynamics of individual behavior. Each adult psychoanalyzed by Freud, each child interviewed by Piaget, and each Central Asian pastoralist interviewed by Luria provided a distinctive pattern of responses that corresponded to their individual experiences. To arrive at general conclusions, however, the clinician must ignore individual differences in order to distill the general pattern, and as the general pattern appears, the individual picture disappears.

Research Designs

If psychological research is to illuminate the process of developmental change, it must be designed to reveal how the supposed factors work over time. There are two basic research designs that psychologists use for this purpose, longitudinal and cross-sectional. Each takes time into account in a distinctive way. The psychologist who uses the **longitudinal design** collects information about a group of children as they age over an extended span of time. The researcher who uses the **cross-sectional** design collects information about children of various ages at one time. These designs can be used in conjunction with each other and with any of the techniques of data collection just discussed. Each design has its own advantages and disadvantages.

Longitudinal designs follow the same persons through the years as they age.

Longitudinal designs

Researchers who choose a longitudinal design select a sample of the population they want to study and gather data from each person in the sample at more than one age. The longitudinal design traces changes in persons over time, and thus is consistent with the basic definition of development as the changes that occur in the physical structure and behavior of the organism during its lifetime. For example, a research team at the Fels Research Institute in Yellow Springs, Ohio, studied personality development in 71 children from their birth until they reached their middle teens (Kagan & Moss, 1962). Observations, tests of personality, and interviews repeated at various times allowed the Fels group to determine the stability of such characteristics as a tendency to become angry or upset when an ongoing activity is disturbed. Without longitudinal measurements, it would be impossible to discover if this particular behavior pattern remains constant or changes as a child grows older. Other influential longitudinal studies have focused on such varied topics as personality (Baumrind, 1971), mental health (Werner & Smith, 1982), temperament and intelligence (Plomin & DeFries, 1985; Rutter, 1985), and language development (Brown, 1973).

Longitudinal designs would seem to be an ideal way to study development because they fit so closely the requirement that development be studied over time. Unfortunately, longitudinal research designs have some practical and methodological drawbacks that have restricted psychologists' reliance on them.

They often require a lengthy commitment on the part of the researcher, and they are expensive to carry out, particularly if they are to be conducted over several years. In addition, some parents may refuse to allow their children to participate in a lengthy study. If such refusals are more frequent in one social, economic, or ethnic group, they may make the sample unrepresentative of the population as a whole. Some of the children who do begin a study may drop out, further changing the sample in ways that weaken the conclusions that can be drawn from the study. To circumvent these problems, some researchers use special procedures called **microgenetic methods.** These procedures are attempts to provoke change in the course of a relatively brief time interval as a means of seeing basic developmental mechanisms in action (Werner, 1948; Siegler & Crowley, 1991; Vygotsky, 1978).

Another difficulty with longitudinal designs is that the people in the sample may become used to the various testing and interviewing procedures; in other words, they may learn how they are expected to respond. As a consequence, it is difficult to know whether a change in a person's responses over time represents the influence of normal causal influences on development or simply practice in taking the tests.

Finally, longitudinal designs confound (mix together) the influence of age-related changes with other sources of change that relate specifically to the subjects' **cohort** — the population of persons born about the same time, who for that reason may share experiences that differ from those of people born earlier or later. For example, a longitudinal study of children's fears from birth onward that began in London in 1932 would coincide in its first years with the Great Depression. At the age of 9 or 10, many of these children would have been sent away from their parents (one or both of whom might later have been killed in World War II) to the countryside in an effort to keep them safe from Hitler's nightly bombings of the city. If the results of such a study indicated that the children's fears centered on hunger in their first years and that later, around the age of 9, they began to fear that they would lose their parents, it would not be possible to determine whether the observed age trends reflected general laws of development, true at any time and any place, or whether they were the result of growing up in a particular time and place, or both (Baltes, Dittman-Kohli, & Dixon, 1984).

Because of these difficulties, some researchers have used a **cohort sequential design,** in which the longitudinal method is replicated with several cohorts, each of which is studied longitudinally. This modification of the longitudinal design allows age-related factors in developmental change to be separated from cohort-related factors.

Cross-sectional designs

The most widely used developmental research design is called the cross-sectional design because groups representing a cross section of ages are studied at a single time. To study the development of memory, for example, one might first test the way samples of 4-year-olds, 10-year-olds, 20-year-olds, and 60-year-olds remember a list of familiar words. By comparing how people in the four age groups go about the task and what the results of their efforts are, one could then form hypotheses about developmental changes in this basic cognitive process. (Figure 1.9 compares longitudinal and cross-sectional research designs.) In fact, a great many cross-sectional studies of memory development have been carried out (Kail, 1990).

The advantages of the cross-sectional design are readily apparent. Because it samples several age levels at one time, this design takes less time and is less expensive than a longitudinal approach to the same question would be, but it can still yield important information. The limited time commitment required of the participants also makes it more likely that a representative sample will be recruited and that few participants will drop out of the study.

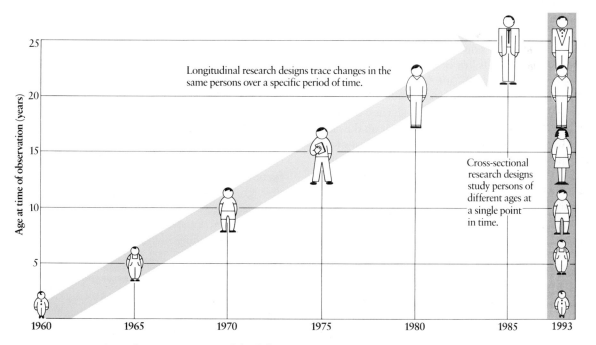

FIGURE 1.9 *A graphic representation of the difference between longitudinal and cross-sectional research designs.*

Despite these attractive features, cross-sectional designs also have drawbacks. Like longitudinal designs, cross-sectional designs can confound age-related changes and characteristics particular to a specific cohort. Only to the extent that people of different ages are equivalent in all relevant ways except for the factor of age will the study be likely to yield accurate information about development.

Consider the possibilities for the hypothetical study of memory development. Suppose that the study was conducted in 1985. Suppose further that the study showed that the 60-year-olds performed significantly more poorly than the 20-year-olds. These results might reflect a universal tendency for memory to decline with age. But the difference might also be caused by differences in childhood nutrition, which has been shown to affect intellectual development (Super, Herrera, & Mora, 1990); nutrition was generally not so good in 1925, when the 60-year-olds were babies as it was in 1965, when the 20-year-olds were babies. Or perhaps memory performance is maintained by the constant practice provided by schooling. In this case, the 60-year-olds may have performed less well because they have been out of school a long time.

A second difficulty with cross-sectional designs is that, by sampling the behavior of different-aged people at one time, they inappropriately slice up development, an ongoing process, into a series of disconnected images. Such a design may be used to contrast the general ways in which 4- and 10-year-olds remember a list of words, for example, but the developmental process by which one form of memory has changed into another is lost because the same children are not being studied over time. Thus when theorists formulate hypotheses about development on the basis of cross-sectional designs, they do a good deal of extrapolation and guesswork about processes of change.

Research Designs and Data-Collection Techniques in Perspective

Each design and each technique for data collection has its uses, but no single design or technique is likely to serve all purposes. *Longitudinal designs* sample behavior of the same individuals over time, but unless they are supplemented by more complex procedures, there is a risk that they will confound age with cohort and that the samples will be biased. *Cross-sectional designs* are more efficient but may artificially break up the process of development. *Self-reports* provide unique insight into the process of development from the perspective of the individual, but they are sometimes of questionable validity. Systematically collected *naturalistic observations* yield essential information about the real-life activities of people, but they are weak when it comes to justifying causal statements about development. *Experiments* can isolate causal factors in specific settings, but the results obtained may not be generalizable beyond the artificial boundaries of the experimental situation. *Clinical interview methods* can reveal the dynamics of individual thought and feelings, but they are difficult to generalize beyond the individual case. In the chapters that follow, the advantages and problems of the various research methods will be discussed time and again as they apply to specific aspects of development.

The Role of Theory

All of the techniques of data collection and both research designs are of practical use to psychologists in their efforts to gather facts about the development of children. However, those facts help us to understand development only if they are embedded in a **theory**, a broad framework or body of principles that can be used to interpret facts. Like heredity and environment, facts and theories go together. Neither comes "first"; they arise and exist together. Nor do facts "speak for themselves"; they speak through theories.

When a newborn infant cries, the physical fact of crying is plain enough. But what does it mean? Is crying a reflex response to gastric pain, or is it an expression of the newborn's distress at being wrenched from the mother's womb? Is the infant asking for help or showing anger? Only an interpretation of crying within a theory gives meaning to the "facts" by providing a framework within which to investigate such questions through research and reason.

Speaking about our understanding of the physical world, Albert Einstein described the central role of theory in extending human knowledge. Observation of the world may be useful, he said:

> But on principle, it is quite wrong to try founding a theory on observable magnitudes alone. In reality the very opposite occurs. It is the theory which decides what we can observe. (Quoted in Sameroff, 1983, p. 243)

Einstein's point applies to psychologists' attempts to understand the human world just as forcefully as it applies to investigations of the physical world. A deeper understanding of human development will not automatically accrue from the continuous accumulation of facts. Rather, it will come through new attempts to make sense of the accumulating evidence on development in the light of some theory.

At the present time in the history of developmental psychology, no overarching theoretical perspective gives unity to the entire body of relevant scientific knowledge. Instead, the field is dominated by a few broad theoretical frameworks, each characterized by its own view of the sources of development (nature and nurture), the dynamics of developmental change (continuity versus discontinuity), and the nature of individual differences. Within each of these broad frameworks, specific theories focus on particular aspects of human development (Piaget, for example, focused on the development of thought, Erikson on the development of personality) and propose specific mechanisms to account for the process of change.

THIS BOOK AND THE FIELD OF DEVELOPMENTAL PSYCHOLOGY

The lack of a comprehensive and widely accepted developmental theory creates difficulties for anyone who seeks an integrated picture of the whole child in the dynamic processes of growth and change. Basic facts are interpreted differently within the various theoretical frameworks. In the face of these difficulties, this book adopts an integrative framework designed to retain the most essential aspects of its subject matter while providing a structured forum within which to evaluate theorists' claims in a systematic way.

This framework starts from the fundamental agreement that unites developmental psychologists: Development is a process that emerges over time; it is directional in the sense that time is directional, moving irreversibly from past to future. Consequently, the text's organization is basically chronological.

In any chronological account of development, two major issues must be resolved. The first is how to segment the flow of time and how much significance to attribute to the various periods that are singled out. The second issue is the problem of keeping track of all the many aspects of development in a systematic way to make clear how they combine and recombine to constitute a whole, living person.

The issue of how to divide the sequence of development into periods is easily settled because adherents of all major theoretical approaches refer to the same seven periods from conception to old age, although they may focus on only a few of them: the prenatal period (the months between conception and birth), infancy, early childhood, middle childhood, adolescence, adulthood, and old age.

Beyond a division of development into at least seven periods, consensus among psychologists breaks down. Some theorists believe that these divisions are little more than verbal conventions, whereas others believe that they represent developmental stages that are both real and of essential importance for understanding the process of developmental change. Stage theorists themselves disagree as to whether significant subperiods should be distinguished. (Table 1.1 indicates how four theorists treat the conventional periods of development.)

At the same time, anthropological and historical studies suggest that the seven developmental periods themselves may not be characteristic of children in all cultures and all historical eras. Many societies recognize no periods that correspond to early childhood and adolescence (Ariès, 1962; Whiting, Burbank, & Ratner, 1986). Modern industrial societies even provide evidence to support the subdivision of almost any of the seven conventional stages into smaller periods (middle childhood, for example, might usefully be thought of as having early, middle, and late substages; adolescence could be divided into early and late substages; and youth could be seen as an early substage of adulthood).

In this book we follow psychological convention and divide the time between conception and adulthood into five broad periods, each of which is accorded a major section of the text; we go on to discuss adulthood and old age, but limitations on space allow us only to illustrate the lifelong nature of development, not to examine the developmental change of the mature individual in detail. Within this chronological framework, our aim is to make clear how the fundamental biological, social, behavioral, and cultural factors of development are woven together in the process of change from one period to the next. We also attempt to show that developmental patterns are not restricted to one or another aspect of the child. Insofar as development is characterized by stagelike changes, the new patterns that emerge at each stage should apply to broad areas of the child's functioning while also reflecting the crucial role of culture and context in

T A B L E 1 . 1
Stages of Development According to Four Theorists

Conventional	Piaget	Freud	Erikson	Vygotsky
Infancy (Birth–2½ years)	Sensorimotor	Oral Anal	Trust vs. mistrust Autonomy vs. shame	Affiliation
Early childhood (2½–6 years)	Preoperations	Phallic	Initiative vs. guilt	Play
Middle childhood (6–12 years)	Concrete operations	Latency	Industry vs. inferiority	Learning
Adolescence (12–19 years)	Formal operations	Genital	Identity vs. role confusion Intimacy vs. isolation	Peer activity
Adulthood (19–65 years)			Generativity vs. stagnation	Work
Old age (65 years–death)			Ego integrity vs. despair	Theorizing

organizing the developmental level manifested at any one time.

The text subdivides infancy, a period when change is particularly rapid, into three subperiods marked by important transition points where distinctively new and significant forms of behavior emerge. Robert Emde and his colleagues (Emde, Gaensbauer, & Harmon, 1976) refer to these transitions as bio-behavioral shifts because the resulting reorganization in the child's functioning emerges from the interaction of biological and behavioral factors. Modifying these researchers' ideas slightly, we refer to such transitions in infancy, and in later development as well, as **bio-social-behavioral shifts.** We add the social dimension because, as Emde and his colleagues themselves note, every bio-behavioral shift involves a change in the relationship between children and their social world. Not only do children experience the social environment in new ways as a result of the changes in their behavior and biological makeup; they are also treated differently by other people.

In addition, we consider the cultural context of children's development to be an essential factor in the bio-social-behavioral shifts and the organization of human behavior as a whole at any age. From the earliest hours of life, cultural conceptions of what children are and what the future holds for them influence the way parents shape their children's experience. For example, parents who believe that girls are destined to be economically and socially dependent on their husbands are likely to treat their newborn daughters very

differently from those whose fondest wish is for their daughter to become an airplane pilot or tennis champion. And as we mentioned earlier, in some cases the timing, the essential character, and even the existence of a developmental period may be strongly influenced by cultural factors (Segall, Dasen, Berry, & Poortinga, 1990).

Our adoption of a bio-social-behavioral framework for the study of development does not imply a commitment to a strict stage theory; rather, it provides a systematic way to keep in mind the intricate play of biological, social, and behavioral forces that combine to produce development. One must approach the notion of stages with caution because stagelike shifts in the functioning of the organism are rarely all-or-nothing phenomena. Behaviors that characterize a new stage of development can almost always be found in embryonic form at an earlier age, and old forms of behavior crop up from time to time after the transition to a new stage. Finally, the existence of important continuities in behavior over time and the significant diversity in a child's behavior at a given age as circumstances vary are fundamental realities that the division of development into periods and subperiods should not be allowed to obscure.

Table 1.2 outlines the bio-social-behavioral shifts that appear to be prominent in the development of the child from conception to adulthood. Not all of the shift points have been equally well established. Nevertheless, they provide a fruitful means of organizing discussions of development because they require us to consider both the sources of change and the evidence concerning developmental continuity and discontinuity in a systematic way.

Throughout the chapters that follow, the large questions of development that captivated Itard and his contemporaries are constantly recurring themes: What makes us human? Can our natures be remolded by experience, or must we be content with the characteristics inscribed in our genes at conception? Can we use our knowledge of development to help us plan our futures and guide the growth of our children? These questions are not likely to be satisfactorily answered until and unless a unified theory of development emerges from the combined efforts of scholars of development working now and in the future. Because the issues are so complex and our knowledge is still so limited, we have tried to design each chapter to set forth basic facts, methods, and theories in a manner that will help the reader to think usefully about the fundamental questions of the field.

TABLE 1.2
Prominent Bio-Social-Behavioral Shifts in Development

Developmental period	Shift point	Prominent changes at point of shift and characteristics of stages
	Conception	Genetic material of parents combines to form unique individual
Prenatal		Formation of basic organs
	Birth	Transition to life outside the womb
Early infancy (birth–2½ months)		Becoming coordinated with the environment
	2½ months	Cortical-subcortical brain connections form; social smiling; new quality of maternal feeling
Middle infancy (2½–9 months)		Increased memory and sensorimotor abilities
	7–9 months	Wariness of novelty; fear of strangers; attachment
Late infancy (9–30 months)		Symbolic thought; distinct sense of self
	End of infancy (24–30 months)	Grammatical language
Early childhood (2½–6 years)		Strikingly uneven levels of performance; sex-role identity; sociodramatic play
	5–7 years	Assigned responsibility for tasks outside of adult supervision; deliberate instruction
Middle childhood (6–12 years)		Peer-group activity; rule-based games; systematic instruction
	11–12 years	Sexual maturation
Adolescence (12–19 years)		Sex-oriented social activity; identity integration; formal reasoning
	19–21 years	Shift toward primary responsibility for self and raising of next generation
Adulthood (19 +)		

SUMMARY

1. Developmental psychology is a scientific discipline that studies the origins of human behavior and the laws of psychological change over the course of a lifetime.
2. The early history of developmental psychology is closely linked to social changes wrought by the Industrial Revolution, which fundamentally changed the nature of family life, education, and work.
3. Many scientific and social questions about development revolve around three fundamental concerns:
   a. Is the process of development gradual and continuous, or is it marked by abrupt, stagelike discontinuities?
   b. How do nature and nurture interact to produce development?
   c. How do people come to have stable characteristics that differentiate them from one another?
4. Concerns about continuity branch into more specific questions:
   a. How alike and how different are we from our near neighbors in the animal kingdom?
   b. Are there qualitatively distinct stages of development?
   c. Are there critical periods in development?
5. Concerns about sources of development have given rise to competing views about the contributions of biology and the environment to the process of development.
   a. According to the biological-maturation framework, the sources of development are primarily endogenous, arising from the organism's biological heritage.
   b. According to the environmental-learning framework, developmental change is caused primarily by exogenous factors.
   c. According to the universal-constructivist framework, development arises from the active adaptation of the organism to the environment. The roles of environmental and biological factors are of equal magnitude.
   d. The cultural-context framework accords importance to both biological and environmental factors in development. In addition, it emphasizes that the interactions out of which development emerges are crucially shaped by the history of the group as embodied in its culture.
6. Developmental psychologists use several data-collection techniques in their efforts to connect abstract theories to the concrete realities of people's everyday experience. These techniques are designed to ensure that the data used to explain development are objective, reliable, valid, and replicable.
7. Prominent among the techniques of data collection used by developmental psychologists are
   a. Self-reports—observations in the form of interviews or responses to a questionnaire.
   b. Naturalistic observation—the systematic description of behavior in naturally occurring settings.
   c. Experimentation—the introduction of a change in a person's experience to test causal hypotheses.
   d. Clinical interview methods—interview techniques for determining the unique circumstances that influence the development of individual people.
8. Research designs that include systematic comparisons among children of different ages enable researchers to establish relationships among developmental phenomena. Two basic research designs are
   a. Longitudinal designs—the same children are studied repeatedly over a period of time.
   b. Cross-sectional designs—different children of different ages are studied at a single time.
9. Theory plays an important role in developmental psychology by providing a broad conceptual framework within which facts can be interpreted.
10. No one method or research design can supply the answers to all the questions that developmental psychologists seek to resolve, just as no one theory can encompass all the questions.
11. The concept of the bio-social-behavioral shift highlights the ways in which biological, social, and behavioral factors interact in a cultural context to produce developmental change. Keeping these factors in mind helps us to maintain a picture of the whole developing child.

KEY TERMS

baby biography
bio-social-behavioral shift
clinical method

cohort
cohort sequential design
control group

correlation
critical period
cross-sectional design

culture	hypothesis	ontogeny
development	learning	phylogeny
developmental niche	longitudinal design	reliability
ecology	maturation	replication
endogenous	microgenetic method	representative sample
ethology	naturalistic observation	self-report
exogenous	nature	stage
experiment	nurture	theory
experimental group	objectivity	validity

SUGGESTED READINGS

ARIÈS, PHILIPPE. *Centuries of Childhood.* New York: Vintage, 1962.

A history of the concept of childhood that reveals many of our unexamined assumptions about children and human nature. This influential book uses paintings, diaries, games, and school curricula dating back to the Middle Ages to show how current conceptions of children and childhood have developed.

CAIRNS, R. B. "The emergence of developmental psychology." In P. H. Mussen (Ed.), *Handbook of Child Psychology,* vol. 1: *History, Theory and Methods.* New York: Wiley, 1983.

The history of developmental psychology as a scientific discipline is traced from the initial pathbreaking publications of the latter half of the nineteenth century. A good source for tracing the changing concerns and theoretical positions that have dominated the field for 100 years.

KESSEN, WILLIAM. *The Child.* New York: Wiley, 1965.

A collection of original writings on children by experts of the past three centuries, supplemented by useful commentary by a leading contemporary developmental psychologist.

LANE, HARLAN. *The Wild Boy of Aveyron.* Cambridge, Mass.: Harvard University Press, 1976.

A fascinating account of the famous wild child and his teacher, Jean-Marc Itard, makes clear the enduring importance of Itard's research for developmental psychology.

LOMAX, ELIZABETH M., KAGAN, JEROME, & ROZENKRANTZ, BARBARA G. *Science and Patterns of Child Care.* New York: W. H. Freeman, 1978.

A historically based discussion of the complex relationships among scientific knowledge about children, child-care practices, and public policy.

MILLER, PATRICIA H. *Theories of Developmental Psychology,* 2nd ed. New York: W. H. Freeman, 1989.

A readable discussion of the major approaches to the study of developmental psychology.

MILLER, SCOTT A. *Developmental Research Methods.* Englewood Cliffs, N.J.: Prentice Hall, 1987.

A thorough survey of the basic research methods used in the study of human development. The author describes the pitfalls of various methods and provides concrete examples to illustrate general principles of research.

SMUTS, HELEN B., & HAGEN, JOHN W. (Eds.), "History and Research in Child Development." In *Monographs of the Society for Research in Child Development* 50 (4–5, Serial No. 211), 1985.

The eight essays in this monograph illustrate ways in which historical research can shed light on contemporary issues in the study of children's development.

PART I

In the Beginning

In Chapter 1 we said that the development of each human being starts with the formation of a single cell at the time of conception. We must acknowledge, however, that this choice of a starting point is only a convention. Each individual human life is but a tiny drop in the vast stream of life that reaches back through thousands of generations and unimaginable millennia of evolutionary time, the beginning of which remains a mystery. As such, it is a product of the evolutionary past of our species. Moreover, the environment each baby will experience is a product of the earth's history and the development of culture and society.

Science views the life process as a constant interplay of forces that create order and pattern on the one hand and forces that create variation and disorder on the other. In the modern scientific view, the interaction of these competing forces is the engine of developmental change.

What are the forces that create order and diversity in human development? In Chapter 2 we will see that the beginning of an explanation can be found in our biological inheritance. Order, the ways in which all human beings are alike, initially arises from the finiteness of our species' pool of genetic possibilities. Variation initially arises through sexual reproduction, which in virtually every instance ensures that each individual will inherit a unique combination of genes from the common pool.

Chapter 2 describes the basic mechanisms of genetic transmission, the processes of gene-environment interaction, and some of the diseases that result from genetic abnormalities. It also discusses the contribution to our development of cultural evolution, a distinctly human mode of inheritance.

Chapter 3, which discusses prenatal development and birth, traces the changes that transform the single cell created at conception into a newborn infant with millions of cells of many kinds, organized into an intricate system of coordinated body parts.

The process of prenatal development illustrates many principles that will recur in later chapters. For example, the changes in form and activity that distinguish the organism at 5 days from the organism at 5 weeks or 5 months after conception are excellent examples of the kinds of qualitative changes that distinguish stages of development from quantitative increases in size. Critical periods in development are exemplified by the great sensitivity of the embryo at certain times to the hormonal secretions that trigger the development of our body's organs and to such external agents as drugs that disturb organ development.

After 9 months of growth and nurturing within the mother's body, chemical changes initiate the birth process. Birth constitutes the first major bio-social-behavioral shift in development. No longer able to obtain life-giving oxygen and nutrients automatically from the mother's body, the baby must use biological capacities developed during the prenatal period in new ways in order to breathe and eat. The behavioral changes that occur at birth are no less remarkable as babies begin to attend to the sights and sounds around them, and to provide some sights and sounds of their own! Without the support of parents who structure their baby's interactions with the environment according to culturally prescribed patterns, the baby would not survive. Parents must feed, clothe, and protect their offspring for many years before they are able to take care of themselves.

Thus begins the lifelong process in which the biological forces that created the new organism at conception interact with the forces of the culturally organized environment that greets the child at birth. Barring unforeseen calamities, in approximately two decades the process will begin again with a new generation.

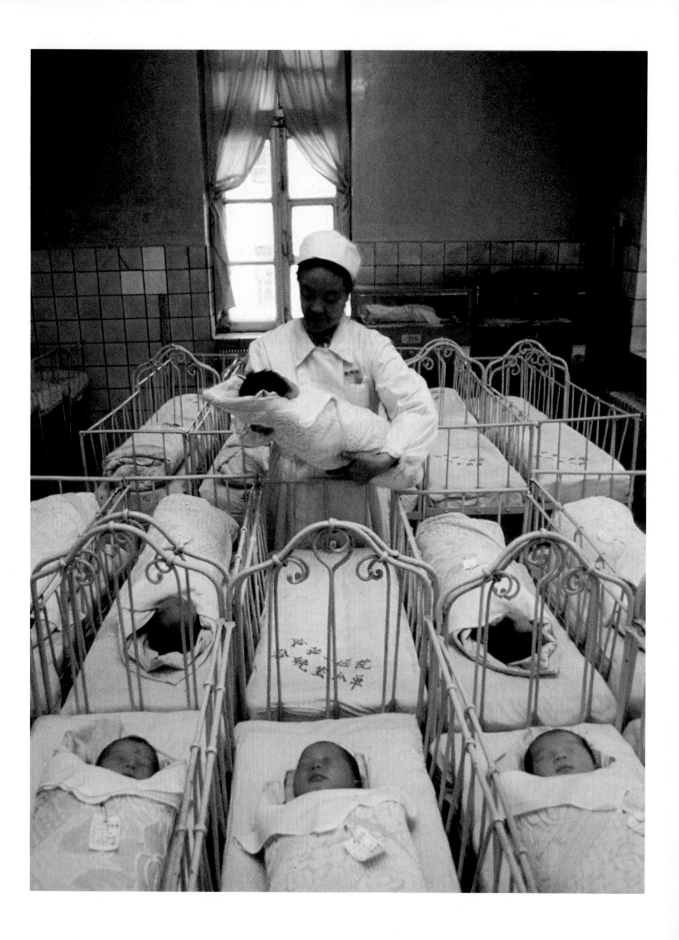

CHAPTER 2

The Human Heritage: Genes and Environment

•

> Every child conceived by a given couple is the result of a
> genetic lottery. He is merely one out of a large crowd of
> possible children, any one of whom might have been conceived
> on the same occasion if another of the millions of sperm cells
> emitted by the father had happened to fertilize the egg cell of
> the mother—an egg cell which is itself one among many. . . .
> If we go to all the trouble it takes to mix our genes with those
> of somebody else, it is in order to make sure that our child will
> be different from ourselves and from all our other children.

— FRANÇOIS JACOB, *THE POSSIBLE AND THE ACTUAL*

A maternity-ward nursery provides an interesting setting for thinking about the origins and development of human beings. In some communities, the babies may look so much alike that it is difficult to tell one from another. In other communities, they may be easily distinguished because some have dark skins and others have light skins. In either case, when these infants are mature adults, 30 years from now, the differences among them will have increased so much that it will be quite easy to tell them apart. Some will be men and some will be women; some will be tall, some short; some will have curly hair, some none at all. They may speak different languages, engage in different types of work, and enjoy different kinds of food. Some will be morose most of the time, whereas others will usually be cheerful; some will be impulsive, others reflective; some will be gifted at mathematics, others at growing rice or selling stocks. Despite this great variation, none will be mistaken for a member of any other species; all will clearly belong to *Homo sapiens*. Such observations raise a fundamental question about the sources of developmental change: What causes us to be so different from each other but at the same time more like each other than like members of any other species?

Both the similarities and the differences between people come ultimately from the interaction between the environments in which they develop and the set of genes they inherit from their parents. The similarities that make us members of a single species arise, on the one hand, because we inherit from other human beings our **genes,** the molecular blueprints for our individual development. On the other hand, human beings are similar to each other because we have evolved in the common environment of the planet Earth.

Because sexual reproduction mixes up the genes we inherit from our two parents, the particular combination of genes each of us inherits is, with rare exceptions, unique. The environment contributes to variations among people by determining which of their characteristics will be most important for adapting successfully to the specific conditions in which they live. For example, children born into families living deep in the forests of the Amazon basin, where people still live by hunting and gathering, must develop physical endurance and become close observers of nature. Conversely, children born into families living in a North American suburb must develop the ability to sit still for long hours in school and acquire the knowledge and skills they will need for economic success as adults. Furthermore, even within a particular family in a particular setting, each child occupies a unique position; thus each child has a unique set of experiences that further shapes the characteristics he or she develops (Plomin, 1990).

We begin this chapter by discussing sexual reproduction, the mechanism for what François Jacob calls the "genetic lottery," and the basic laws of genetic inheritance to which that "lottery" is subject. Next we will discuss the lifelong process of gene-environment interaction, which begins once the specific genetic combination that defines the new organism has been created. The crucial importance of an individual's genetic constitution and the principles of gene-environment interaction will then be illustrated through a discussion of genetic abnormalities. Lastly, we will take a look at the way biology and culture interact in the process of human development.

SEXUAL REPRODUCTION AND GENETIC TRANSMISSION

At his climax during sexual intercourse, a man ejaculates about 350 million sperm into a woman's vagina. For the next several hours, the tiny tadpole-shaped sperm swim through the viscous fluid of the woman's uterus and fallopian tubes. The head of each sperm contains 23 **chromosomes**—threadlike structures consisting of approximately 20,000 genes each. These 23 chromosomes provide half of the genetic information necessary for the development of a new individual. If one of the man's sperm penetrates the woman's ovum (egg), which provides the other half of the genetic information, conception occurs and the cell walls of the ovum and sperm fuse to form a **zygote,** a single cell containing 23 chromosomes from the father and 23 chromosomes from the mother. From this single cell with its 23 pairs of chromosomes will ultimately come all the cells that the child will have at birth.

Mitosis: A Process of Cell Replication

The zygote creates new cells through **mitosis,** the process of cell duplication and division that generates all the individual's cells except sperm and ova. Mitosis begins within a few hours of conception. The 46 chromosomes move to the middle of the zygote, where they produce exact copies of themselves—a process known as replication. These chromosomes separate into two identical sets, which migrate to opposite sides of the cell. The cell then divides in the middle to form two daughter cells, each of which contains 23 pairs of chromosomes identical to those inherited at conception (see Figure 2.1). These two daughter cells go through the same process to create two new cells each, which themselves divide as the process repeats itself again and again. Mitosis is guided by the chromosomes

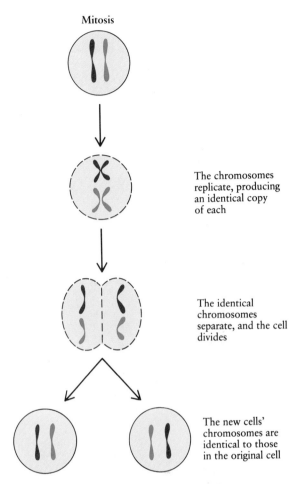

Mitosis

The chromosomes replicate, producing an identical copy of each

The identical chromosomes separate, and the cell divides

The new cells' chromosomes are identical to those in the original cell

FIGURE 2.1   *Mitosis is the process of cell division that generates all the cells of the body except the germ cells. During mitosis each chromosome replicates, creating two that are identical. These then separate in such a way that one is contributed to each new cell. Mitosis ensures that identical genetic information is maintained in the body cells over the life of the organism.*

themselves, complex molecules of deoxyribonucleic acid (DNA) on which the genes are located. The DNA also specifies precisely what kinds of chemical substances will be created by each cell, resulting eventually in the formation of bone cells, blood cells, nerve cells, and so on.

Mitosis continues throughout the life of an individual, creating new **somatic** (body) **cells** and replacing old ones. Each new somatic cell contains copies of the original 46 chromosomes inherited at conception.

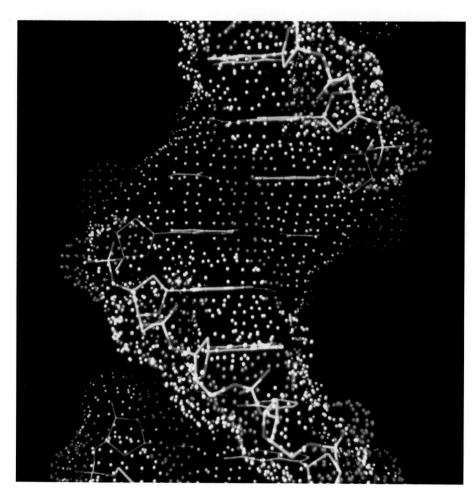

A computer rendering of deoxyribonucleic acid (DNA). Each chromosome is a single DNA molecule consisting of two strands twisted about each other and connected by cross steps to form a laddered spiral called a double helix. A gene is a segment on a strand of the DNA. When a parent DNA molecule replicates to form two identical daughter molecules, the two strands of the double helix separate. Each serves as a template for the synthesis of a complementary strand.

This process ensures the biological continuity of the individual over the course of a lifetime. The genetic material carried by our chromosomes is not altered by the passage of time or by the experiences that shape our minds and bodies under the ordinary conditions of life. There is increasing evidence, however, that direct exposure to radiation and to certain chemicals may alter genes. As we will see later in this chapter, the consequences of such changes can be disastrous.

Meiosis: A Source of Variability

If mitosis governed the production of sperm and ova cells, as well as somatic cells, at conception each individual would receive a full set of 46 chromosomes from each parent for a total of 92, and in each succeeding generation the total number of chromosomes inherited would double. This doubling clearly does not occur. Except in abnormal cases, the number of chromosomes inherited by all members of the human species remains constant at 46.

The zygote contains only 46 chromosomes because the **germ cells,** the cells (sperm and ova) that are specialized for sexual reproduction, are formed not by mitosis but by a different cell-division process called **meiosis.** In the first phase of this process, the 23 pairs of chromosomes in the germ-producing cells produce copies of themselves, just as in mitosis. But then the cell divides not once, as in mitosis, but twice, creating four daughter cells. Each of these daughter cells contains only 23 unpaired chromosomes — half of the parent cell's original set. Meiosis occurs somewhat differently in males and females, as Figure 2.2 explains.

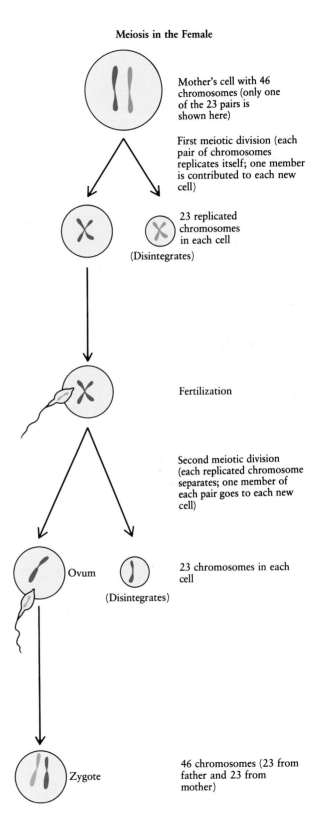

Meiosis in the Male

Father's cell with 46 chromosomes (only one of the 23 pairs is shown here)

First meiotic division (each pair of chromosomes replicates itself: one member is contributed to each new cell)

23 replicated chromosomes in each cell

Second meiotic division (each replicated chromosome separates; one member of each pair goes to each new cell)

23 chromosomes in each sperm

Meiosis in the Female

Mother's cell with 46 chromosomes (only one of the 23 pairs is shown here)

First meiotic division (each pair of chromosomes replicates itself; one member is contributed to each new cell)

23 replicated chromosomes in each cell

(Disintegrates)

Fertilization

Second meiotic division (each replicated chromosome separates; one member of each pair goes to each new cell)

Ovum

(Disintegrates)

23 chromosomes in each cell

Zygote

46 chromosomes (23 from father and 23 from mother)

FIGURE 2.2   (a) *Formation of sperm. As meiosis in the male begins, the chromosome pairs replicate, and one member of each pair is contributed to each new cell. Each new cell then divides and the replicated chromosomes separate. The result is four sperm cells, each of which contains one member (or a copy) of each of the original pairs of chromosomes.*
(b) *Formation of the ovum. Meiosis in the female differs slightly from meiosis in the male. When the first division occurs, the cytoplasm, the matter comprising most of the material of the cell, divides in such a way that the two resulting cells are unequal in size. The smaller of the two cells disintegrates. The large cell, the ovum, does not divide again unless it is fertilized. If fertilization occurs, the replicated chromosomes in the ovum separate into two new cells. Again the cytoplasm divides unequally, and the smaller of the resulting cells disintegrates. The 23 chromosomes of the larger cell fuse with the 23 chromosomes of the sperm to form the zygote with its 46 chromosomes.*

BOX 2.1
Twinning

During the first few mitotic divisions after the zygote is formed, the daughter cells occasionally separate completely and develop into separate individuals. When such a division results in two individuals, they are called **monozygotic twins,** because they are twins that have come from one zygote. Having come from the same fertilized egg, "identical twins" inherit identical genetic information. Thus they potentially have the same physical and psychological makeup, susceptibility to disease, and life expectancy. Monozygotic twins occur about once in every 250 conceptions. It is not understood what leads cells to separate after the first few mitotic divisions; neither the parents' race or their heredity, the mother's age, nor the number of children she has had previously seems to be a factor.

Many twins originate not from a single fertilized ovum but rather from the fertilization by two sperm of two eggs that are released at the same time. The two fertilized eggs develop into **dizygotic twins**—twins that come from two zygotes. Though they shared the same uterus and were born at the same

time, "fraternal twins" are no more alike at birth than are any other children of the same parents. The tendency to have dizygotic twins is influenced by race, heredity, the mother's age, the number of prior pregnancies, and fertility drugs. African American women, mothers who are themselves fraternal twins, women between 35 and 40 years of age, women who have had four or more children, and those who have taken fertility drugs are all more likely to give birth to fraternal twins.

Twins are of special interest to psychologists because a knowledge of their characteristics can help answer questions about the influences of nature and nurture. By comparing resemblances between identical twins (who have the same genes) with resemblances between fraternal twins (whose genes are no more alike than those of any other siblings), researchers can estimate the influence of hereditary factors in the production of different characteristics. For example, Robert Plomin and his colleagues (Plomin & DeFries, 1985) compared identical and fraternal

Monozygotic twins not only look alike naturally, they are often dressed alike and treated similarly by others, which further accentuates their similarity.

These dizygotic twins illustrate the great potential for variety of two individuals conceived by the same parents at the same time.

twins with respect to such temperamental characteristics as emotionality, level of activity, and sociability. They found that identical twins were somewhat similar in their expression of these characteristics: The correlation was .55. For fraternal twins, the correlation was zero; thus fraternal twins resembled each other in the expression of the characteristics no more than would any two children selected at random from the community. These findings indicate that inherited factors probably play a role in the development of temperament.

Because the mother's ovum and the father's sperm contain only 23 chromosomes each, the zygote receives its full complement of 46 chromosomes (23 pairs) when the two germ cells unite at conception. Because half of the zygote's chromosomes come from each parent, each individual conceived is genetically different from both the father and the mother. This biological strategy creates genetic diversity across generations. Genetic diversity is further increased by **crossing over,** a process in which genetic material is exchanged between a pair of chromosomes during the first phase of meiosis. While the pair of chromosomes, each containing genes for the same characteristics, lie side by side, a section of one of the chromosomes may exchange places with the corresponding section of the other chromosome (see Figure 2.3). This exchange alters the genetic composition of each of the two chromosomes; genes originally carried on one chromosome are now carried on the other.

We can now better appreciate the extreme improbability that any two children, even siblings, will be exactly alike, except in the special case of identical twins (see Box 2.1). Although we receive 23 chromosomes from each of our parents, it is a matter of chance which member of any pair of chromosomes ends up in a given germ cell during meiosis. According to the laws of probability, there are 2^{23}, or about 8 million, possible genetic combinations whenever a sperm and ovum unite. It is estimated that when the additional possibilities from crossing over are added, there is only 1 chance in 64 trillion that a particular genetic combination will be repeated (Scheinfeld, 1972).

Sexual Determination: A Case of Variability

Of the 23 pairs of chromosomes found in a human cell, 22 are similar in males and females; the twenty-third pair differs. That pair determines a person's genetic sex, a crucial source of variety in our species. In the chromosomes of normal females, both members of the twenty-third pair are of the same type and are called **X chromosomes.** The normal male has just one X chromosome and a much smaller **Y chromosome.** Since a mother is always XX, each of her eggs contains an X chromosome. Sperm, however, may carry an X or a Y chromosome. If a sperm containing an X chromosome

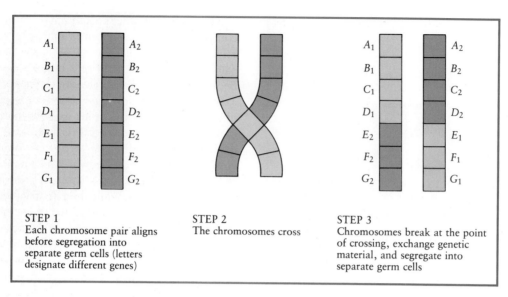

STEP 1
Each chromosome pair aligns before segregation into separate germ cells (letters designate different genes)

STEP 2
The chromosomes cross

STEP 3
Chromosomes break at the point of crossing, exchange genetic material, and segregate into separate germ cells

FIGURE 2.3   *The crossing-over process. (From Shaffer, 1985.)*

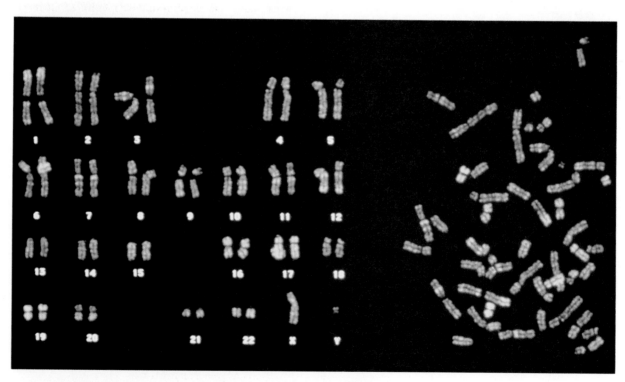

FIGURE 2.4   *Human chromosomes for a male arrayed in matched pairs, an arrangement called a karyotype. Note that the two members (X and Y) of the twenty-third pair for a male differ markedly in size, whereas they would be the same for a female (X and X).*

fertilizes the egg, the resulting child will be XX, a female. If the sperm contains a Y chromosome, the child will be XY, a male (see Figure 2.4). The existence of both X and Y chromosomes in the male might suggest that each conception has a 50–50 chance of resulting in a boy, or a girl. As Table 2.1 indicates, however, many more male than female zygotes are conceived, and slightly more boys than girls are actually born (McMillen, 1979). That fewer male babies are born than are conceived and that the ratio of males to females declines over the life span appear to reflect the greater vulnerability of males to genetic diseases and other problems that lead to death (McKusick, 1975).

A cultural factor that may influence the ratio of males to females at birth is parental preference for one sex or the other. With the recent development of methods for identifying the sex of the fetus, selective abortion has sometimes been used to prevent the birth of female babies. In South Korea, for example, the birth ratio in 1985 was 117 males to 100 females because, according to South Korean obstetricians, some mothers were aborting their female fetuses (Jameson, 1986).

TABLE 2.1
Approximate Sex Ratios for U.S. Whites

Age	Male : Female
Conception	120 : 100
Birth	106 : 100
18 years	100 : 100
50 years	95 : 100
67 years	70 : 100
87 years	50 : 100
100 years	21 : 100

Source: Lerner & Libby, 1976.

THE LAWS OF GENETIC INHERITANCE

When the male and female germ cells come together at conception, the new organism acquires a unique combination of genetic material from its parents and ultimately from its distant ancestors. The mechanisms by which parents transmit their biological characteristics to the next generation were first studied scientifically by Gregor Mendel (1822–1884). On the basis of indirect evidence from experiments in which he cross-bred varieties of garden peas, Mendel proposed that parents transmitted their characteristics unchanged to their offspring via "characters." It was not until later that Mendel's hypothetical "characters" were shown to correspond to actual physical structures—gene-carrying chromosomes in the nucleus of the cell.

In the simplest form of hereditary transmission, a single pair of genes, one from each parent, determines a particular inherited characteristic. Genes that control a particular trait can have alternative forms, called **alleles.** When the corresponding genes inherited from the two parents are of the same allelic form, the person is said to be **homozygous** for the trait. When the alleles are different, the person is said to be **heterozygous** for the trait. The distinction between *homozygous* and *heterozygous* is essential for understanding how different combinations of genes produce different characteristics.

When a child is homozygous for a trait that is controlled by a single pair of alleles, only one outcome is possible: The child will display the characteristic specified by the allele. When a child is heterozygous for such a trait, one of three outcomes is possible:

1. The child will display the characteristic specified by only one of the two alleles. The allele whose characteristics are expressed is referred to as a **dominant allele,** and the allele whose characteristics are not expressed is called a **recessive allele.**
2. The child will show the effects of both alleles and will display a characteristic that is intermediate between the traits of children who are homozygous for one of the alleles and children who are homozygous for the other.
3. The child will display a characteristic that is contributed to by both alleles, but rather than being intermediate, the characteristic will be

distinctively different from that specified by either contributing alleles. This outcome is **codominance.**

The inheritance of blood type illustrates the homozygous outcome and two of the heterozygous outcomes. There are three alleles for blood type—A, B, and O—and four basic blood types—A, B, AB, and O. If children receive two type A, two type B, or two type O alleles, they are homozygous for the trait and will have type A, type B, or type O blood, respectively. But if they inherit either the type A or type B allele from one parent and the type O allele from the other, they will have type A or type B blood, even though their genetic code for blood type is AO or BO. The O allele is recessive, so it does not affect the exhibited blood type. Finally, if children inherit one type A allele and one type B allele, they will exhibit a codominant outcome—type AB blood, which is *qualitatively* different from either type A or type B blood. Figure 2.5 shows some of the outcomes of various combinations of the three alleles for blood type.

There is no intermediate outcome for blood type, but there is one for skin pigmentation and some other characteristics. The skin color of a child of a light-skinned mother and a dark-skinned father, say, may fall between the shades of the parents.

Gregor Mendel, discoverer of the basic principles of genetics.

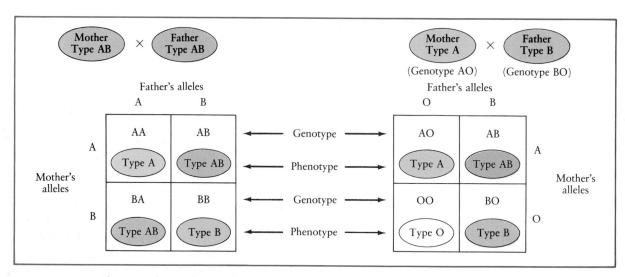

FIGURE 2.5 *Alternative forms of a gene for blood type inherited from parents produce different blood types.*

Genotype and Phenotype

Because an individual's genetic code for blood type may be AO or BO but only the A or B allele is expressed in the blood type itself, knowledge of the person's actual blood type does not permit us to specify the individual's genetic code for blood type. Such differences between the genetic code for a trait and the actual expression of that trait occur for a great many characteristics. As a consequence, geneticists must study organisms on two levels to discover the effects of genes. One level is the **genotype,** the individual's genetic endowment or, in other words, the particular alleles that the individual has inherited. The genotype is constant over the lifetime of the individual. The second level is that of the **phenotype,** the observable characteristics of the individual that develop through interactions between the genotype and the environment.

The study of genotypes focuses on the characteristics of genes and gene combinations, whereas the study of phenotypes focuses on actual organisms as they develop. Discussions about genetic influences on development rely heavily on inferences about genotypes based on observations of phenotypes. Making such inferences is a hazardous and often controversial enterprise because it is usually impossible to isolate genetic from environmental variables. We will discuss some of these controversies, such as those about the degree to which temperament and intelligence are fixed by the genotype, in later chapters.

Determining genetic influences is further complicated by the fact that most human traits are **polygenic;** that is, they are caused not by a single gene but by the interaction of several genes. There is no specific gene for height, for instance; height is believed to be controlled by many genes, each of which has a small effect (Tanner, 1978). What is more, most phenotypical characteristics determined by the interaction of a number of genes are also subject to considerable influence by the environment (Futuyma, 1990).

Genes may interact with each other in a variety of ways. Some genes modify the action of other genes. Human eye color is often said to be controlled by a gene that has two allelic forms, a dominant allele for brown eyes and a recessive allele for blue eyes. If this were actually the case, there would be only two expressions of eye color: blue eyes and brown eyes. Our eyes can be a number of other colors (gray, black, green, or hazel) because **modifier genes** — genes that influence the action or expression of other genes — influence eye color. These modifier genes affect the amount of pigment in the iris, the tone of the pigment (which may be "light," "yellow," or "dark brown"), and the distribution of pigment (over the entire iris, in scattered spots, or in a ring around the outer edge) (Lerner & Libby, 1976).

Other genes are **complementary** to one another — that is, more than one gene is necessary for the expression of a characteristic. Pea flowers are purple, for example, only when both the dominant allele for a gene, designated *C*, and the dominant allele for another gene, designated *P*, are present together. In the absence of either of these alleles, the flowers are always white.

Still other genes may mask the normal expression of a gene; appropriately, they are referred to as **masking genes.** The color of a guinea pig, for example, is affected by two genes. One determines whether melanin, the pigment that determines color, is produced; the other determines how much melanin is deposited. The latter gene has two alleles: one that causes a lot of melanin to be deposited, so that the animal has a black coat; and one that causes a moderate amount of melanin to be deposited, so that the guinea pig has a brown coat. If no melanin is produced, the guinea pig is an albino, and the gene that determines how much melanin is deposited cannot be expressed. In other words, the first gene can mask the second so that it has no effect on the phenotype.

Sex-Linked Genetic Effects

Some inherited human characteristics are determined by genes that are found only on the X or the Y chromosome. Most of these **sex-linked characteristics** are inherited on the X chromosome (we have seen that it is much larger than the Y chromosome). Because females receive two X chromosomes, they get two doses of X-chromosome sex-linked genes, one from each of their parents. Normal males receive only one X chromosome and therefore only one dose of X-chromosome genes, which always comes from their mother. This asymmetry in genetic material leaves men susceptible to a number of genetic defects that ordinarily do not affect females. If a daughter has a harmful recessive gene on one X chromosome, she will usually have a dominant gene on the other X chromosome to override it. Thus the recessive gene is not expressed. A son has no complementary allele to dominate the effects of a harmful recessive gene on his X chromosome, so the harmful gene is expressed.

Red-green color blindness is one sex-linked recessive trait. For a daughter to exhibit this trait, she must be homozygous for it; that is, she must have a father who is red-green color blind and a mother who is either color blind or heterozygous for the trait. By contrast, if a son receives the gene for red-green color blindness on the X chromosome he inherits from his mother, he will be unable to distinguish red from green because there is no corresponding gene on the Y chromosome to counteract the recessive gene.

Harmful sex-linked traits that primarily affect males include hemophilia (a defect that delays the clotting of the blood), certain types of night blindness, atrophy of the optic nerve, hypogammaglobulin (the inability of the body to produce the antibodies necessary to fight bacterial infections), vitamin D resistance (which causes rickets), Duchenne's muscular dystrophy (a progressive wasting away of the muscles that leads to an early death), and some forms of diabetes (Jenkins, 1979), as well as color blindness.

The frequency of sex-linked abnormalities varies greatly depending on the particular trait and the population in which it occurs. For example, one form of genetically caused anemia, a condition in which the blood is deficient in red blood cells, occurs in 60 percent of male Kurdish Jews living in Israel, whereas only 0.5 percent of male European Jews have this condition (Lerner & Libby, 1976). The difference in the incidence of the disease reflects how the allele that causes it differs in frequency in the two gene pools. A **gene pool** is the total genetic information possessed by a sexually reproducing population.

GENES, THE ORGANISM, AND THE ENVIRONMENT

Knowledge about the laws of genetic inheritance is essential if we are to untangle the influences of nature and nurture on development. But this knowledge alone will not allow us to understand genetic contributions to the development of an individual's charac-

teristics because it leaves out an essential ingredient — the **environment**: the totality of things, conditions, and circumstances that surround the organism. Genes do not exist in isolation; they exist only within an environment. And only through the interactions of their genes with their environments do organisms develop.

Studying Gene-Environment Interactions

The relation of genes to their environment is complex and multileveled. Genes are merely chemical codes that specify the sequences of amino acids in the proteins produced by the cells. By so doing, they determine the form and functions of the cells. The cells, in turn, provide the immediate environment of the genes within them. Thus the genes and the cell material are in constant interaction. The system of cells as a whole — the organism — is also in constant interaction with its environment. The outcomes of these organism-level interactions determine the conditions of the individual cells and hence the immediate environment of the genes (Futuyma, 1990).

Variations in the environment at any level can have profound effects on the development of the phenotype. This has been vividly demonstrated in a set of experiments with Himalayan rabbits (Winchester, 1972). The Himalayan rabbit normally has a white body and black ears, nose, feet, and tail. If a patch of the white fur on a rabbit's back is removed and an ice pack is placed over the area, the new fur that grows there will be black (see Figure 2.6). This result shows that the fur-color phenotype depends on the temperature at the specific site where hair grows. The gene for black color is expressed only at low temperatures. But simply specifying the temperature of the rabbit's *general* environment is not sufficient to predict the color of its fur; the temperatures at *specific sites* on the rabbit are the relevant environments for predicting the expression of the gene for black fur. The rabbit's extremities are normally colder than the rest of its body, and this uneven distribution of temperatures causes the typical variations in its coat. This experiment makes it clear that when gene-environment interactions are investigated, the environment must be specified with as much care as the relevant genes.

In conducting research on gene-environment interactions in such organisms as plants, fruit flies, and mice, geneticists use two related approaches. In one

(a)   *(b)*   *(c)*

FIGURE 2.6 *The effect of the environment on the expression of a gene for fur color in the Himalayan rabbit. Under normal conditions (a) only the rabbit's feet, tail, ears, and nose are black. If fur is plucked from a patch on the rabbit's back and an ice pack is placed there (b), creating a cold local environment, the new fur that grows in is black (c). (Adapted from Winchester, 1972.)*

they attempt to keep the environment of various genotypes constant so that any variation in phenotype can be attributed to variations in the genes. In the other they keep the genotype constant while they vary the environment so that variations in the phenotype can be attributed to variations in the environment. The first procedure highlights genetic influences on development; the second highlights the influences of the environment. Either approach by itself would give us only a partial picture of gene-environment interaction.

By charting the changes that occur in the phenotype as the environment of a particular genotype is varied, researchers can discover the **range of reaction** for that genotype. Ideally, this range represents all the possible gene-environment relationships that are compatible with the continued life of the organism, so that it includes all the possible developmental outcomes. In the case of the Himalayan rabbit, the range of reaction for fur color would be bounded at one end by the temperature at which the rabbit would freeze to death and at the other end by the temperature that would be too high to permit it to live. As the temperature approaches the lower boundary, we would expect the rabbit's fur to be predominantly black. As the temperature approaches the higher boundary, even the extremities might remain white. The variations in the phenotypic expression of fur color as the temperature is varied from one extreme to the other is the range of reaction for the Himalayan rabbit's genotype for fur color.

The Range of Reaction for Human Genotypes

Geneticists believe that the principles of gene-environment interactions they have derived from their experiments with plants, insects, and animals also apply to human beings. In actuality, however, we know little about the ranges of reaction for human genotypes. The major problem restricting the study of human genetic expression is that to obtain a range of reaction, researchers must expose organisms with the same genotype to a wide variety of environments, in principle the widest range in which the organism can survive. Obviously, the degree of control over human beings and the risks to their lives that such experiments would require is incompatible with moral precepts and standards of ethical research.

This problem in establishing ranges of reaction for human characteristics has led geneticists and psychologists to resort to **kinship studies**—studies that compare members of the same biological family to see how similar they are in one or more traits (Plomin & DeFries, 1983; Scarr, 1981). If the attribute being studied is controlled largely by heredity, the similarity in that attribute between any two people living in the same environment should increase as the degree to which they share the same genes increases. The ideal cases in kinship studies are those that compare identical (monozygotic) and fraternal (dizygotic) twins of the same sex (see Box 2.1). Identical twins should show the greatest degree of similarity in inherited traits because they have the same genotype. Fraternal twins and siblings, who are estimated to share, on the average, half their genetic material, should differ more than identical twins but less than half sisters and half brothers, who have only one parent in common and therefore share only about 25 percent of their genetic material. Studies that have focused on such varied characteristics as activity level and irritability (Goldsmith & Gottesman, 1981), intelligence test scores (Plomin & DeFries, 1983; Scarr & Weinberg, 1977, 1983), the tendency to respond empathetically to others (Matthews et al., 1981), and susceptibility to mental illness (Gottesman, 1991) have indeed shown that the patterns of similarity decrease with the degree of genetic similarity.

Despite their usefulness, kinship studies are not without problems. Although no two people experience precisely the same environment, the more closely related two people are, the more likely it is that they will be subject to similar environmental influences. This makes it very difficult to isolate genetic influences (Plomin, 1986; Plomin, DeFries, & McClearn, 1990).

An alternative strategy is provided by **adoption studies**. Researchers who use this strategy examine genetically related individuals who have been raised in different environments, usually because they were adopted into different homes. The evidence from adoption studies, like that from the studies of twins, indicates that heredity as well as environment contributes significantly to many human traits.

The most obvious difficulty with adoption studies is that children are by no means assigned at random to the full range of environments available to our species, the condition necessary for establishing a range of reaction. Rather, adoption agencies are likely to make every attempt to place children in secure, loving homes, very often with people whose social and cultural backgrounds match those of the biological parents (Scarr, 1981a). Thus the extent to which adopted children are similar to their biological families cannot be attributed entirely to the similarity of their genes; it may be due to the similarity of their environments.

Feedback in Gene-Environment Interactions

Evidence gathered from kinship and adoption studies indicates that human genotypes interact with their en-

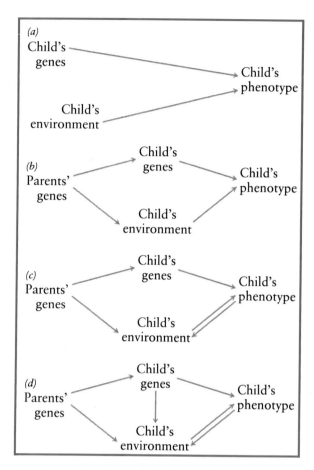

FIGURE 2.7   *The increasingly complex models of gene-environment interactions proposed by Scarr and McCartney.*

vironments in complex ways, leading psychologists to propose the existence of complex feedback mechanisms that mediate between the children's genotypes, phenotypes, and environments. Sandra Scarr and Kathleen McCartney (1983) have proposed a model that encompasses a good deal of the current research on this topic.

The full Scarr-McCartney model is easiest to understand if we work up to it in steps. The simplest model, shown in Figure 2.7a, represents the common wisdom that the whole organism (the phenotype) is created through the interaction between its genes and its environment. For example, there is evidence that some people are genetically predisposed to irritability.

Figure 2.7a represents the idea that the actual expression of irritability in a child will depend on the degree to which the environment interacts with the genetic predisposition for irritability to create irritable behavior.

Figure 2.7b reminds us that the picture is more complicated because the parents' genes not only contribute to their child's genotype but also, through their phenotypic expression, to their child's environment. If, for example, irritability is a highly expressed trait in a baby's mother and father, their presence in the baby's environment may well boost the expression of irritability in the baby. By contrast, if the parents maintain a calm environment in the home despite their own genetic predispositions to irritability, the expression of irritability in the baby may be reduced.

The model in Figure 2.7c comes still closer to real life. It shows that the child's expressed genetic characteristics feed back to influence the environment with which the child is interacting. Given enough provocation, even the most placid parents may become annoyed by an irritable baby and behave in a manner that will increase the baby's irritation. In that case, the infant's genotype is interacting with an environment that is shaped in part by her own phenotypic characteristics.

Finally, Scarr and McCartney add the possibility that the infant's genotype may influence the way the child experiences the environment. An irritable child, for example, may thrash and turn in a way that makes his environment more irritating, as he experiences the sight and feel of his own agitation and the agitation of the physical objects it causes. When this possibility is included, we arrive at the gene-environment interactions of the full model depicted in Figure 2.7d.

The need to consider the full complexity of genotype-environment interactions represented in Figure 2.7d is highlighted by a question posed by Robert Plomin and Denise Daniels (1987): Why are the correlations between biologically unrelated children who are raised in the same family so close to zero if the family is considered a shared environment and environment has been shown to be responsible for 50 percent or more of variations in such traits as sociability, susceptibility to mental illness, and scores on tests of intelligence? Researchers interested in individual differences not only are beginning to estimate the relative contributions of genetic and environmental factors in producing individual differences. They are also seeking to understand the environment in more detail by

studying the ways in which children living in the same family experience different environments (Hoffman, 1991; Scarr, 1992). As the Scarr-McCartney model of gene-environment interactions suggests, a wide variety of factors lead each family member to react in specific ways to each of the others, and these differential reactions create different environments for each of the children living in the home. Birth order, gender, physical appearance, the spacing of children, and temperamental variations, as well as illnesses, accidents, and other idiosyncratic events, all combine to make each person's environment unique.

Picturing Gene-Environment Interactions

The complexities of gene-environment relationships over the course of development have led scientists to try to represent the overall process in a single, easily comprehended picture. Such pictures are necessarily incomplete, but they can be a powerful means of conveying ideas. The biologist C. H. Waddington (1966) likens the developing organism to a ball rolling through a landscape of valleys of differing depths, as in Figure 2.8. The varying depths of the valleys represent

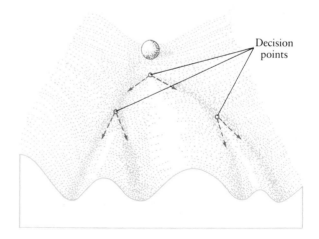

FIGURE 2.8 *Waddington's landscape. The rolling ball represents the developing organism. At each decision point, the organism can go forward along one of two diverging pathways. As development proceeds, it becomes increasingly difficult to move to a different pathway. (Adapted from Waddington, 1957.)*

The kinds of gene-environment interaction that lead a child to perform well with a hoop greatly depend on the cultural context that specifies how it is to be used.

the degrees to which the organism is susceptible or resistant to different environmental influences.

Deep valleys represent characteristics whose development is strongly controlled by the genes. Unless something highly unusual happens, all children will follow the same path in developing these characteristics. They will, for example, develop two arms, two legs, two eyes, a nose, and a distinctive gender. Waddington refers to characteristics that are relatively invulnerable to environmental influence during their development as **canalized characteristics.** Shallow valleys represent traits whose phenotypes are not strongly constrained by the genes. In these cases, the inherited trait is more susceptible to environmental influences, so the range of phenotypes expands. The likelihood that a child will develop an emotional disturbance, for example, is affected by such environmental events as the loss of a parent, a move to a new city, or the support of a sympathetic teacher (Rutter, 1989).

Individual children are pictured as moving through Waddington's landscape and reaching points of transition, labeled "decision points" in Figure 2.8. At these decision points, relatively small differences in environmental influences can affect the direction of the ball (that is, the child), producing large variations in the child's phenotype, although the phenotype will still be constrained by the larger "valley" in which the decision point is located.

To get a concrete idea of how the environment contributes to canalization, consider the fact that in many places in the world, a child's future occupation is greatly influenced by what happens when the child is between 6 and 8 years of age. Will the child become a doctor, a shepherd, a soldier, a shopkeeper, or a homemaker? Environmental factors that influence the direction taken at this decision point include the range of adult occupations in the society in which the child lives, the availability of schools, and the child's access to them. Genetically influenced factors that affect this decision include the child's sex, size, strength, and intellectual ability. If one neglects the fact that both environmental and genetic canalizing forces arise at many levels of the organism-environment system, one may mistakenly think of the child's later life situation as being entirely the outcome of either environmental factors (how can anyone become a physicist in a society that has no universities?) or genetic factors (someone who finds quantitative reasoning difficult is not likely to become a physicist in any society). Either one-sided approach is inadequate.

Waddington's landscape usefully highlights the influences that early developments have on later ones. The farther one has traveled down a particular valley, the harder it is to cross the hill to another path. For example, if illiterate children raised in an isolated area where there are no schools are suddenly offered the opportunity to go to school at the age of 16, most of them are unlikely to do so, and those who do go are unlikely to stay long enough to qualify for work that requires significant schooling.

Four Common Oversimplifications of Gene-Environment Interactions

Because gene-environment interactions are complex, occurring on several levels simultaneously and changing over time, certain errors and oversimplifications are commonly made in efforts to describe them. Richard Lewontin (1982) has summarized the major pitfalls; the following discussion draws on his work.

The assumption that there is a developmental program

An appealing analogy that is often encountered in discussions of development is the comparison of the genetic code to a computer program. Computer programs are physical symbol systems that consist of instructions for processing the data an operator feeds in. It is tempting to think of the genetic code as a program that is specified at conception and determines the output — development — of the organism from then on.

The intricacies of gene-environment interactions indicated by the full Scarr-McCartney model (Figure 2.7d), however, should be sufficient to convince us that the computer-program analogy has only limited application. In the case of a computer, program + data = outcome; but the characteristics of living organisms are not strictly determined by the mechanical unfolding of preset instructions. Instead, they depend to a large extent on the uncertain outcomes of the gene-environment interactions that occur along the way. Computer scientists are beginning to construct self-modifying machines, but at present computer-program analogy should be used with great caution.

The assumption that genes determine the phenotype

As implausible as it may seem in view of the importance of gene-environment interactions, it is still common to encounter the idea that once the genotype is given, the phenotype is fixed. To be sure, some traits do exhibit a one-to-one correspondence between genotype and phenotype for known ranges of reaction. Blood type is one such trait. Phenotypes, however, are generally not fixed by genotypes. Consider alcoholism. Data gathered by behavioral geneticists suggest that there is some genetic influence in alcoholism (Plomin, DeFries, & McClearn, 1990). But no one becomes an alcoholic without consuming large quantities of alcohol. In an environment in which alcoholic beverages are not available or in which it is customary to drink only small amounts of alcohol, any genetic predisposition to alcohol abuse is unlikely to be expressed.

The assumption that genes determine capacity

Another commonly encountered idea is that genes determine capacity. This idea can be illustrated by the hypothetical story of a young woman who wants nothing in the world so much as to be a track star. Through vigorous exercise on the high school track, she develops her stamina so that she will not tire quickly and will have the necessary energy for the final push to the finish line. She practices endlessly at getting quickly off the starting block. She goes to sleep early every night and eats the most healthful foods. But despite all these efforts, she never achieves a running speed that allows her to be a champion. The genes she inherited have given her legs and a torso that do not enable her to run as fast as many of her competitors.

It is true that for a given genotype there is going to be some greatest speed that the organism can achieve over the range of all possible environments. Before we conclude that our hypothetical runner has realized her full genetic capacity for running speed, however, we need to consider the influence of the environment more fully, because hidden in the story is an unexamined assumption about the environment. A high school track is indeed the environment in which many North American runners develop their capacity for speed, but it does not represent the full range of environments in which human beings run. Had our runner grown up and competed in the Himalayas, where the conditions of running are quite different, she might

A cinder track with standardized obstacles provides an excellent standard running surface, but it is only one of the many possible environments within which running abilities may develop, a fact that needs to be kept in mind when investigating the genetic contribution to running speed.

indeed be a champion precisely because her torso and legs are shaped in a way that is suited to running in that environment.

Discussions of the genetic determination of capacity routinely neglect the fact that the effectiveness of the phenotype is always relative to the environment in which it is expressed. An ancestor of a boy growing up in the Peruvian Andes today might have been highly accomplished in performing the mathematical calculations required to conduct business in the Inca empire. The modern boy may possess the same genes pertaining to mathematical ability, but if he does not go to school and instead stays at home to help his parents farm, his presumed mathematical capacity is unlikely to find much expression (Ascher & Ascher, 1981).

The assumption that genes determine tendencies
If genes by themselves do not fix capacities, might they determine tendencies? Perhaps the genetic contribution to excitability is a "tendency to become excited."

This simplification of gene-environment interaction is appealing because it seems to exhibit moderation and a scientific circumspection that is consistent with real-world complexities. But, as in the case of claims about genes and capacity, statements about genes and tendencies are often based on narrow assumptions about the environments in which the tendency is expressed. For example, on the basis of a comparison of a boy named Bob with boys of similar age and family background in some environments in which they all spend time, such as the baseball field and the classroom, one might say that Bob has a tendency to become excitable. And it may be true that in those places Bob is more excitable than his peers by some objective measure. But Bob may still not be generally more excitable than his peers. Is he more excitable when he is reading poetry? When he is talking to his girlfriend? When he is doing homework?

Underlying the proposition that genes determine tendencies is an implicit assumption that the individual's behavior in comparison with that of peers remains consistent across a variety of environments. If this assumption is not valid, if it is made on the basis of only a few environments that are assumed to be typical, the proposition is not really being tested.

MUTATIONS AND GENETIC ABNORMALITIES

Despite its fantastic power to produce diversity among human beings, sexual reproduction is restricted to recombining genes that are already present in the human gene pool. The gene pool can change, however, through **mutation,** an error in the process by which a gene is replicated that results in a change in the molecular structure of the DNA. A mutation can be a qualitative change in a particular gene or a change in the sequence of the genes on the chromosomes. It may also consist of an addition or deletion, as when part of a chromosome is duplicated or lost. Mutations change the overall set of genetic possibilities that sexual reproduction then rearranges.

Mutations sometimes occur in the somatic (body) cells — in cells of the skin, liver, brain, or bones, for example. The somatic cells that carry these mutations pass on the changed genetic instructions to the cells that descend from them by mitosis. These changes affect only the person in whom they occur; they are not passed on to following generations. When a mutation occurs in a parent's sperm or ovum, however, the changed genetic information may be passed on to the next generation.

Geneticists assume that spontaneous mutations have been occurring constantly and randomly since life on earth began, pouring new genes into the gene pool of every species. Indeed, mutation is the driving force behind the evolutionary processes by which new subspecies and species are formed. The fact that mutations are a natural and fundamental part of life does not, however, mean that they usually benefit the individual organisms in which they occur. Each living organism is an intricate whole in which the functioning of every part influences the functioning of every other part. It is little wonder, then, that the introduction of even a small change in the genes can have serious repercussions for the individual.

It is estimated that as many as half of all human conceptions have some sort of genetic or chromosomal abnormality. The majority of these mutations are lethal and result in early spontaneous abortion (Plomin, DeFries, & McClearn, 1990). Still, about 1 out of every 200 babies born has some kind of genetic aberration (Moore, 1982). These mutations tend to be recessive, so an individual who receives one from one parent usually receives a normal gene or chromosome from the other parent to counteract it. Some genetic abnormalities, though, do affect human beings. A few of the more significant conditions attributable to them are listed in Table 2.2.

Developmental psychologists are interested in studying mutations and genetic abnormalities for several reasons:

1. By disturbing the well-integrated mechanisms of development, mutations can help to reveal the intricate ways in which heredity and the environment interact.
2. If the existence of genetic abnormalities can be detected at a very early stage of development, ways may be found to prevent or ameliorate the birth defects that would normally result.
3. When children are born with genetic abnormalities, developmental psychologists are often responsible for finding ways to reduce their impact on the children and their families.

These concerns are reflected in the current research being conducted on sickle-cell anemia, Down's syndrome, certain sex-linked chromosomal abnormalities, and phenylketonuria.

Sickle-Cell Anemia: An Example of Gene-Environment Interaction

In certain environments, some mutations are advantageous to people who are heterozygous for them. The

TABLE 2.2
Common Genetic Diseases and Conditions

Disease or Condition	Description	Mode of Transmission	Incidence	Prognosis	Prenatal/Carrier Detections
Cystic fibrosis	Lack of an enzyme causes mucous obstruction, especially in lungs and digestive tract	Recessive gene	1 in 21,000 live births in U.S.; most common in people of Northern European descent	Few victims survive to adulthood	No (possible in near future)/No
Diabetes melitus (juvenile form)	Deficient metabolism of sugar because body does not produce adequate insulin	Thought to be polygenic	1 in 25 to 40 of all diabetics	Fatal if untreated; controllable by insulin and restricted diet	No/No
Down's syndrome	See text				
Hemophilia (bleeding disease)	Blood does not clot readily	X-linked gene; also occurs by spontaneous mutation	1 in 21,500 live births of males	Possible crippling and death from internal bleeding; transfusions ameliorate effects	No/Yes
Klinefelter's syndrome	See text				
Muscular dystrophy (Duchenne's type)	Weakening and wasting away of muscles	X-linked gene	1 in 200,000 males under age 20	Crippling; often fatal by age 20	Yes/Sometimes
Phenylketonuria (PKU)	See text				
Sickle-cell anemia	See text				
Tay-Sachs disease	Lack of an enzyme causes buildup of waste in brain	Recessive gene	1 in 3600 among Ashkenazi Jews in U.S.	Neurological degeneration leading to death before age 4	Yes/Yes
Thalassemia (Cooley's anemia)	Abnormal red blood cells	Recessive gene	1 in 100 births in populations from subtropical and tropical areas of Europe, Africa, Asia	Listlessness, enlarged liver and spleen, occasionally death; treatable by blood transfusions	Yes/Yes
Turner's syndrome	See text				

Sources: Bergsma, 1979; McKusick, 1986; Nightingale & Meister, 1987.

FIGURE 2.9   *Normal, round red blood cells and sickle-shaped red blood cells from of a person with sickle-cell anemia.*

recessive sickle-cell gene is a case in point. People who inherit this gene from both of their parents, and thus are homozygous for it, suffer from *sickle-cell anemia,* a serious abnormality of the red blood cells. Normal red blood cells are round. In people with sickle-cell anemia, however, these cells take on a curved, sickle shape when the supply of oxygen to the blood is reduced, as it may be at high altitudes or during strenuous exercise (see Figure 2.9). These abnormal blood cells tend to clump together and clog the smaller blood vessels. Because sickle-cell anemia impairs circulation, people who suffer from the disease experience severe pains in the abdomen, back, head, and limbs. The disease causes the heart to enlarge and deprives the brain cells of blood. The deformed blood cells rupture easily, and the rupturing may lead to severe anemia and even to early death. As many as 40,000 African Americans are estimated to suffer from sickle-cell anemia (Lerner & Libby, 1976).

People who are heterozygous for the sickle-cell gene are said to have the *sickle-cell trait.* They usually do not suffer from the symptoms associated with sickle-cell anemia, although about 40 percent of their red blood cells may assume the sickle shape when the supply of oxygen to the blood is reduced, and so may interfere with circulation.

Because many people who suffer from sickle-cell anemia die before they have a chance to reproduce, one would expect that this mutation would eventually die out. This is exactly what is happening in the United States, where the incidence of the trait among African Americans is about 10 percent (Lerner & Libby, 1976). But in West Africa, the area from which the ancestors of most African Americans were brought to this continent, the incidence of the sickle-cell trait is greater than 20 percent (Allison, 1954). For a long time these statistics puzzled scientists. Then investigators noticed that the areas in which the sickle-cell trait was most common also tend to have a high incidence of malaria. This correspondence raised the possibility that there might be some connection between the two.

The link between the sickle-cell gene and malaria was established in 1954 by A. C. Allison of Oxford University, in England. Allison's studies showed that heterozygous carriers of the gene are highly resistant to the malaria parasite. Thus in malaria-infested areas such as the West African coast, people who do not carry the sickle-cell gene are at a disadvantage because they are more likely to suffer from malaria, which can be deadly. Because of the selective advantage the sickle-cell gene affords, its high frequency has been maintained in the population despite the losses caused by the early death of homozygous carriers.

Down's Syndrome: A Chromosomal Error

Down's syndrome was the first human disease to be linked with a specific chromosomal disorder. More than 95 percent of the children born with Down's syndrome have 47 chromosomes, one more than normal. Instead of two copies of chromosome 21, they have three. (For this reason, the disorder is sometimes called *trisomy 21.*) Children with Down's syndrome are mentally and physically retarded and have several distinctive physical characteristics: slanting eyes; a fold on the eyelids; a rather flat facial profile; ears lower than normal; a short neck; a protruding tongue; dental

FIGURE 2.10   *A Down's syndrome child.*

prove the intellectual functioning of some of these children. Thus this genotype apparently has a wide range of reaction.

Down's syndrome occurs in about 1 of every 1000 births in the United States (Hook, 1982). A strong relationship has been found between the incidence of Down's syndrome and the age of the parents, the mother in particular. Up to the age of 30 a woman's risk of giving birth to a live infant with Down's syndrome is less than 1 in 800. The risk increases to 1 in 100 by age 40, to 1 in 32 by age 45, and to 1 in 12 by age 49 (Hook, 1982). The risk is thought to increase because at birth the human female carries all the potential egg cells that she will ever produce. The ova are especially vulnerable to such environmental agents as viruses, radiation, and some chemicals, which can damage the chromosomes or interfere with the process of meiosis. The older a woman is, the more time she has had to be exposed to such harmful agents. This view is supported by the fact that the risk of other chromosomal anomalies, such as Klinefelter's syndrome, also increases with the mother's age.

irregularities; short, broad hands; curved little fingers; a wider space between the toes than normal; and a crease running all the way across the palm (see Figure 2.10). Because of the slanting eyes and the fold on the eyelids of these children, the British neurologist Langdon Down, who first described the syndrome in 1867, called it Mongolism. On the average, children with this disorder are more likely than other children to suffer from heart, ear, and eye problems, and they are more susceptible to leukemia and to respiratory infections. As a result, they are more likely to die young (Bergsma, 1979).

Over 10 percent of the people in institutions for the retarded suffer from Down's syndrome (Plomin, DeFries, & McClearn, 1990); but how effectively Down's syndrome children function as they grow depends not only on the severity of the disorder but also on the environment in which they are raised. Intense intervention by concerned adults can markedly im-

Sex-Linked Chromosomal Abnormalities

Abnormalities of the chromosomes that determine sex are of special interest to developmental psychologists because they provide one means of obtaining information about the genetic basis of sex differences. The most common sex-linked chromosomal abnormality is *Klinefelter's syndrome,* a condition that affects only males. These babies are born with an extra X chromosome (XXY). It is estimated that this abnormality occurs in about one of every 1000 white males born in the United States (McKusick, 1986). XXY males appear to develop normally until adolescence, but then, when they are expected to show signs of maturity, none appears: Their sex organs do not mature, they do not acquire facial hair, their voices do not change, they have low levels of the male hormone testosterone, and they are sterile.

Fragile X syndrome, which accounts for 5 to 10 percent of the nation's cases of mental retardation, is caused by a defect in the X chromosome. The defect is estimated to occur in 1 of every 1250 men (Davies, 1989).

The most common sex-linked abnormality in females is *Turner's syndrome*. About 1 of every 10,000 females is born with only one X chromosome (XO) (McKusick, 1986). At puberty, girls with Turner's syndrome fail to produce the female hormone estrogen. As a result, they do not develop breasts or pubic hair, rarely menstruate, and are sterile. Such girls, as a group, have been found to be about average in verbal ability, although they frequently score below average on tests of spatial ability and have difficulty with such tasks as following a road map and copying a geometric design (Rovet & Netley, 1982).

Phenylketonuria: A Treatable Genetic Disease

The modern history of *phenylketonuria* (PKU), an inherited metabolic disorder that often leads to severe mental retardation if it is not treated, shows dramatically how human beings can change the effects of a genetic defect by changing the environment in which a child develops. It is estimated that 1 in every 15,000 white infants born each year in the United States has PKU and that 1 in 100 people of European descent is a carrier of the recessive mutant gene (Hsia et al., 1956). The incidence of PKU is lower among blacks than among whites (Bergsma, 1979).

PKU was discovered in 1934 in Norway after Dr. Ashborn Folling found that two mentally retarded children who had been brought to him had abnormal amounts of phenylpyruvic acid in their urine. Spurred by this discovery, Dr. Folling tested other retarded children in institutions and found that some of them also had this symptom. We now know that PKU is caused by a defective recessive gene that leads to the absence of an enzyme necessary to metabolize certain proteins. Because PKU children lack this enzyme, they accumulate phenylalanine and phenylpyruvic acid in the bloodstream, and these substances prevent their brain cells from developing normally.

Knowledge of the abnormal biochemistry of the condition led researchers to hypothesize that if the accumulation of phenylalanine and phenylpyruvic acid could be prevented, infants with PKU might develop normally. Physicians have tested this hypothesis by feeding PKU infants a diet low in phenylalanine.

(Phenylalanine is highly concentrated in such basic foods as milk, eggs, bread, and fish.) In many cases the mental retardation that characterizes PKU can be avoided through such intervention. The timing of the intervention is crucial. If phenylalanine intake is not restricted by the time a PKU infant is 1 to 3 months of age, the brain will already have suffered irreversible damage.

In 1961 Dr. Robert Guthrie devised a test to screen newborns for PKU so that preventive measures can be taken before phenylalanine and phenylpyruvic acid have a chance to accumulate. The test is now compulsory in most states. Hospital personnel draw blood from each baby's heel a few days after birth. The blood is then added to a bacterial culture that grows if the phenylalanine level in the baby's blood is high. The test is not infallible, however, so some PKU babies are not identified in time.

Recently a means has been developed to detect PKU prenatally (Nightingale & Meister, 1987). Researchers have also developed a test that can identify people who carry the recessive PKU gene. This test enables carriers of the gene to decide whether they want to risk having a child with the disease. (See Box 2.2 for a general discussion of prenatal detection methods and genetic counseling.)

BIOLOGY AND CULTURE

Today we know that mutations are the source of biological variation among species, but at the time Darwin wrote *The Origin of Species* (1859), the genetic basis of hereditary transmission was unknown. Ignorance of genetics and a limited knowledge of the fossil record helped to fuel a fundamental confusion about precisely how hereditary transmission works. In attempting to account for the differences observed among species and among peoples past and present, many scientists argued that the mechanisms that produce historical change and cultural differences were the same as those that produce biological change. Further examination of this confusion can give us a broader perspective on the relation between our genetic and environmental heritages and on why any attempts to separate the influences of nature and nurture are so problematic.

BOX 2.2
Genetic Counseling

Thanks to recent advances in the field of genetics, many potential genetic problems can be avoided through genetic testing and counseling. The main responsibilities of genetic counselors are to test potential parents to learn whether they are carriers of a genetic disease and to determine the probability that a particular couple will bear a child with such a disease.

Genetic counselors are often called on by couples who have had one child with a genetic defect and who want to know the likelihood that a second child will have the same abnormality. Genetic counselors also advise potential parents who have relatives with a genetic disease, who have physical anomalies they suspect are genetic, who have had several pregnancies that have ended in spontaneous abortion, or who are over the age of 35. Potential parents whose ancestors come from parts of the world where the incidence of a specific genetic disorder is high also use their services. Several inherited disorders in addition to sickle-cell anemia are likely to be found in specific groups of people. For example, the recessive allele for *Tay-Sachs disease*, in which a missing enzyme inevitably leads to death before the age of 4, is carried by 1 in 30 Ashkenazi Jews in the United States. The recessive allele for *thalassemia*, a blood disease, is carried by 1 in 10 Americans of Greek or Italian descent (Omenn, 1978).

Detecting the carriers of the gene for some genetic disorders is relatively simple. The alleles for Tay-Sachs disease and sickle-cell anemia can be detected through blood tests. Female carriers of *Lesch-Nyhan syndrome* (a metabolic disorder affecting male children that leads to the overproduction of uric acid) can be identified through an analysis of their hair follicles. Carriers of chromosomal abnormalities, such as the translocation of chromosome 21, which causes Down's syndrome, can be identified through the analysis of a cell from the body. The carriers of certain chromosomal disorders are sometimes signaled by specific patterns in the prints of their fingers, palms, and soles of their feet.

On the basis of test results and family histories, the genetic counselor tries to determine whether there is a potential problem and what the odds are that a child of the couple will be affected by it. Such predictions can now be made for diseases and traits that are caused by a single recessive or dominant gene or that are sex-linked, and in some cases for those caused by several genes acting together (polygenic defects). They cannot be made for defects caused by spontaneous mutations.

It must be kept in mind that genetic theory generates statistical probabilities that apply to whole populations. Thus a genetic counselor may not be able to say for certain in advance of conception that a particular couple will have a child who will suffer from a genetic abnormality. Once potential parents have been informed of the risks, they must make their own decision.

Acquired Characteristics

In the absence of knowledge of genetics, many prominent biologists in the nineteenth and early twentieth centuries hypothesized that characteristics acquired by individuals during their lifetimes are transmitted biologically to the next generation. This belief raised concerns that parents who engaged in criminal activity, for example, would pass on a tendency to criminality to their children in the same way that they passed on eye or hair color (Gould, 1977b).

The erroneous idea that acquired characteristics can be biologically inherited is referred to as **Lamarckism,** after a French biologist, Jean-Baptiste Lamarck (1744–1829), whose ideas were extremely influential among early evolutionary theorists. Although the in-

After conception, the principal techniques used to determine whether a given fetus suffers from a genetic defect are amniocentesis, sampling of the chorionic villi, and alpha-fetoprotein tests. To perform an **amniocentesis,** the doctor first determines the position of the fetus by means of a **sonogram,** a detailed picture of the fetus formed by high-frequency sound waves that are bounced off the fetus and transformed into a visible image. The doctor then inserts a long, hollow needle into the mother's abdomen and extracts come of the amniotic fluid from the sac surrounding the fetus. The amniotic fluid contains cells and other substances from the fetus that can be analyzed for chemical abnormalities and for the presence of certain genetic disorders. Amniocentesis cannot be performed before the fourth month of pregnancy, and 2 weeks are needed to determine the results.

Another way to detect chromosomal disorders is to sample cells taken from the *villi* (hairlike projections) on the *chorion,* a tissue that forms the placenta. One advantage to such **chorionic villus sampling** is that it can be performed as early as the ninth week of pregnancy and its results are available within a few days; thus an abortion can be performed early, when it is safest, should the woman make that choice. Some controversy still surrounds the procedure with regard to both its safety and the accuracy of the findings (Kolata, 1987).

The **alpha-fetoprotein test** is a blood test that is used mainly to detect the presence of defects in the fe-tus's neural tube, which forms the spinal column and brain. Incomplete closure of the neural tube is the most common birth defect in the United States, occurring in 1 of every 1000 live births. When a fetus has a neural-tube defect, large amounts of alpha-fetoprotein pour out of the open spine or skull into the amniotic fluid. From there it enters the mother's bloodstream, where it can be detected. The results of this blood test are only suggestive, however. Women whose alpha-fetoprotein levels are abnormally high are usually offered sonograms and amniocentesis to verify or disconfirm the problem.

When a genetic disorder is detected by any of these tests, parents usually have only two choices: The woman can carry the pregnancy to term and give birth to a child who is genetically defective in some way, or she can terminate the pregnancy. These are not easy choices, especially since the diagnosis often fails to predict the degree of disability the affected child will suffer or the quality of life that can be expected. The severity of a neural-tube defect, for example, can vary greatly, and many people who suffer from such defects have lived productive lives. In some cases, fetal surgery and other kinds of prenatal and postnatal interventions, such as special diet or blood transfusions, can ameliorate the effects of a defect.

heritance of acquired characteristics has been discredited as a mechanism of *biological* evolution, the idea behind it is not irrelevant to the study of development: *Cultural* evolution does operate in a Lamarckian way. Consider how the habit of making marks on objects has gradually evolved into symbol systems for writing and numerical calculation. Today the millions of children who are learning to read and do arithmetic in schools all over the world are mastering symbol systems that are vastly more complex than those used by any humans as recently as 10,000 years ago. This increased sophistication is not a consequence of biological evolutionary change through the action of genes. Rather, it is the result of *cultural* evolution, in which the successful innovations of earlier generations — knowledge of when to hunt deer or to plant a field, of the alphabet, of the theorems of geometry—are passed on to succeeding generations through language and by example (White, 1959). Evidence of the transmission of innovative forms of behavior from one generation to the next is very meager in nonhuman species (Tomasello, 1990).

Coevolution

For a great many years it was believed that the biological and cultural characteristics of *Homo sapiens* developed in a strict sequence: First the biological capacities we associate with humanity evolved to a critical point, and then an additional biological change allowed *Homo sapiens* to use language and generate culture. Now, however, the situation is believed to have been far more complicated. Contemporary studies of human origins have found evidence that rudimentary forms of culture were already present during early phases of human evolution (see Figure 2.11). *Australopithecus* (one of our primitive ancestors, who lived some 3 million years ago) domesticated fire, built shelters, engaged in organized hunting, and used tools—flints, knives, cooking utensils, and notation systems (Tanner, 1981). Although no one can be certain, many scholars assume that *Australopithecus* also had some form of language (Bates & MacWhinney, 1982; Geertz, 1973).

Such findings indicate that biological evolution of the human line did not end with the appearance of cultural objects. The brain of a modern person is about three times larger than the brain of *Australopithecus*. Most of this increase has occurred in the frontal lobes of the brain, those areas that govern complex, specifically human capacities (Jerrison, 1982; Luria, 1973). Insofar as the capacity to engage in cultural activities and to reason through the use of cultural tools — such as geometry, which permits navigation—confers a selective reproductive advantage, it is probable that the more effective users of culture have been more successful in passing on their genes to succeeding generations. In short, culture *has* influenced biology, and the two forms of evolution, biological and cultural, have interacted with each other in a process called **coevolution** (Futuyma, 1990).

As a consequence of the coevolution of human physical and cultural characteristics, attempts to separate the influences of nature and nurture in the development of contemporary children are even more problematic than our earlier discussion of the range of

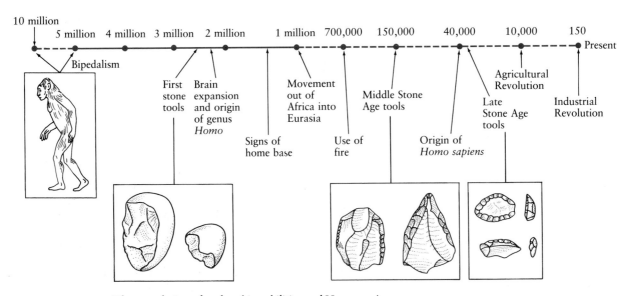

FIGURE 2.11   *The coevolution of tool-making abilities and* Homo sapiens.

reaction suggests. People who have grown up in different parts of the world have lived in environments that make very different physical demands (see Figure 2.12). Furthermore, their cultural histories have differed greatly for tens of thousands of years. These differences in environment and culture have clearly contributed to the physical differences among people, but whether they have also resulted in mental differences is by no means certain. When Japanese children excel at mathematics, for example, what part of their performance should we attribute to genetically transmitted characteristics and what part to the way they are raised in their culture (Gardner, 1983)? Are the extraordinary navigational abilities of Micronesian sailors, who can cross thousands of miles of ocean from one tiny island to another in small canoes without the aid of a compass, the result of genes or cultural tradition (Gladwin, 1970)? There are no general formulas for determining the relative contributions of culture and genes in shaping such human abilities.

The complex interactions between genetic heritage and the environment begin when genes in the zygote start to express themselves and guide the creation of new cells. Each new human being is a variant within the overall range of possibilities that defines *Homo sapiens*. Chapter 3 follows the course of gene-environment interaction from the moment the genetic material of the mother and father come together. In later chapters, as we follow the general patterns of the development of children, we will repeatedly see instances of gene-environment interaction, with culture always playing a mediating role.

FIGURE 2.12   *The physical differences between people who live in different environments reflect evolutionary adaptations to those environments. The ratio of body surface area to body volume is very different for the Eskimo, who lives in a cold climate, than for the Nilotic Negro, who lives in a warm climate. (From Howells, 1960.)*

SUMMARY

1. The particular set of genes each human being inherits comes from the parents. Sexual reproduction rearranges the genetic combination in each new individual. With the exception of identical twins, every person inherits a unique combination of genes, so that great diversity among people is guaranteed.

2. Throughout the life cycle new body cells are created by mitosis, a copying process that replicates the genetic material inherited at birth.

3. The germ cells (sperm and ova) that unite at conception are formed by meiosis, a process of cell division that maintains a constant total of 46 chromosomes in each new individual.

4. The sexes differ genetically in the composition of one pair of chromosomes. In females, the two chromosomes that make up the twenty-third pair are both X chromosomes. Males have one X and one Y chromosome.

5. The genes carried by the twenty-third chromosome pair give rise to sex-linked characteristics. Because females receive two X chromosomes, they get two doses of X-linked genes, one from each parent. Normal males receive only one X chromosome, and therefore only one dose of genes on the X chromosome, which always comes from the mother. Thus men are susceptible to a number of genetic defects that usually do not affect females.

6. It is not possible to determine individuals' genetic constitutions (genotypes) from their visible characteristics (phenotypes) because of dominance and recessiveness and because a genotype can result in a wide variety of phenotypes, depending on the environment in which it develops.

7. The overall relationship between genotype and phenotype can be established only by exposure of the genotype to a variety of environments. By charting the changes that occur in the phenotype as the environment is varied, geneticists can establish a range of reaction. Ideally, such a range specifies all possible phenotypes that are compatible with life for a single genotype.

8. The range of reaction for most human characteristics has not been established because few humans have identical genotypes and because moral precepts and ethical standards make it impossible to carry out investigations that would expose people to all of the environments that are compatible with human life.

9. Mutation is the ultimate source of variability in living organisms. Some mutations are compatible with normal life. Often, however, the changes brought about by mutation result in death or disorders.

10. The presence of culture provides human beings with a mode of adaptation that other species do not have. Cultural evolution occurs when adaptations that arise in one generation are learned and modified by the next.

11. Cultural and biological evolution of human beings have interacted with each other in a process called coevolution, which greatly complicates attempts to separate the influences of nature and nurture in development.

KEY TERMS

adoption study
allele
alpha-fetoprotein test
amniocentesis
canalized characteristics
chorionic villus sampling
chromosome
codominance
coevolution
complementary genes
crossing over
dizygotic twins
dominant allele

environment
gene pool
genes
genotype
germ cells
heterozygous
homozygous
kinship studies
masking gene
meiosis
mitosis
modifier gene
monozygotic twins

mutation
phenotype
polygenic traits
range of reaction
recessive allele
sex-linked characteristics
somatic cells
X chromosome
Y chromosome
zygote

SUGGESTED READINGS

JACOB, FRANÇOIS. *The Possible and the Actual.* New York: Pantheon, 1982.

A brief, provocative inquiry into the sources of human diversity that combines philosophical speculation with a discussion of the mechanisms of human evolution.

JENSEN, ARTHUR. *Bias in Mental Testing.* New York: Free Press, 1980.

A leading proponent of the controversial theory that racial groups differ in their innate intelligence makes his case and answers his critics.

LERNER, MICHAEL I., & LIBBY, WILLIAM J. *Evolution, Heredity, and Society.* New York: W. H. Freeman, 1976.

A general introduction to evolutionary theory that provides a thorough discussion of the many tangled issues that make up the nature-nurture controversy. Chapters deal with such important topics as natural selection, polygenic inheritance, mutation, population genetics, and the political implications of genetic research.

LEWONTIN, RICHARD C. *Human Diversity.* New York: Scientific American Books, 1982.

An excellent introduction to human genetics by a leading population geneticist. The topics covered range from the mechanisms of heredity to the historical migrations of nations and the intermixing of populations.

PERSAUD, T. V. N. *Problems of Birth Defects: From Hippocrates to Thalidomide and After.* Baltimore: University Park Press, 1977.

A compilation of important articles about birth defects that includes fascinating accounts of beliefs about birth defects throughout history.

PLOMIN, ROBERT. *Nature and Nurture: An Introduction to Behavioral Genetics.* Pacific Grove, Calif.: Brooks/Cole, 1990.

A major researcher on the genetic foundations of human behavior provides an introduction to this rapidly growing and important area of research on human development. By working through representative studies in detail, Plomin helps the reader gain a firm grasp of such important concepts as heritability and gene-environment interaction.

CHAPTER 3

Prenatal Development and Birth

•

Every man is some months older than he bethinks him,
for we live, move, have being, and are subject to the actions
of the elements and the malice of disease, in that other world,
the truest Microcosm, the womb of our mother.

—SIR THOMAS BROWNE, *RELIGIO MEDICI* (1642)

Of all our existence, the 9 months we live hidden from view inside our mother's womb are the most eventful for our growth and development. We begin as a zygote, a single cell $^1/_{175}$ of an inch in diameter, about the size of a period on this page, weighing approximately fifteen-millionths of a gram. At birth we consist of some 2 billion cells and weigh, on the average, 3250 grams, or 7 pounds. The changes that occur in our form are no less remarkable than the increase in our size (see Figure 3.1). The first few cells to form from the zygote are all identical, but in a few weeks there will be many different kinds of cells arranged in intricately structured, interdependent organs. A basic task in the study of development is to explain how these prenatal changes in form and size take place.

Many developmental theorists look upon development during the prenatal period as a model for development during all subsequent periods, from birth to death, because many of the principles of developmental change after birth are first seen in action during the prenatal period. For biological-maturational theorists such as Arnold Gesell (1945), all of development can be considered a process of embryogenesis (the technical name given to prenatal development) in which the organism develops in a seemingly preordained manner, without significant shaping by its environment either in the womb or after birth. Even psychologists who accord the environment a larger role in development may believe that the prenatal period provides a model for later development. Jean Piaget, who championed the view that development is a process of constructive interaction between the organism and the environment, claimed that understanding change in the prenatal period is a key to understanding development after birth. "Child psychology," he said, should be regarded as "the embryogenesis of organic as well as mental growth, up to the beginning of . . . the adult level" (Piaget & Inhelder, 1969, p. vii).

Understanding the prenatal period is important for practical as well as theoretical reasons. The developing organism can be adversely affected by the mother's nutritional status, health, drug and alcohol intake, emotions, and surrounding environment. Considerable research has been devoted to understanding how to prevent damage to the growing organism during this critical period.

In order to understand the relation of prenatal development to later development, we first must look at the changes that take place as the organism progresses from zygote to newborn. Then we can look at how the developing organism can be adversely affected by the environment. Finally, we consider the circumstances surrounding the newborn's entrance into the world.

THE PERIODS OF PRENATAL DEVELOPMENT

Through a microscope, the fertilized ovum appears to be made up of small particles inside of larger ones. At the center of the cell, the chromosomes bearing the genes are contained within the nucleus. Surrounding the nucleus is the cell matter, which serves as the raw material for the first few cell divisions. The entire zygote is contained within the **zona pellucida,** a delicate envelope only a few molecules thick that forms its boundary.

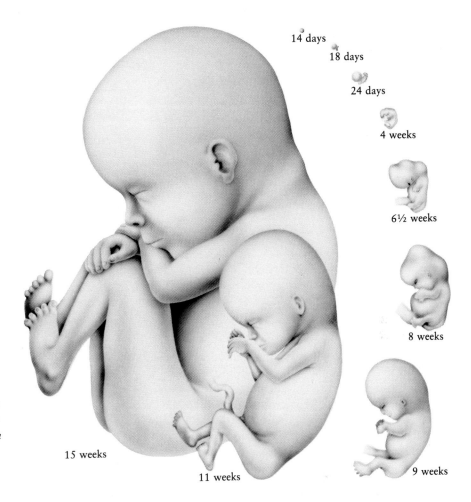

14 days

18 days

24 days

4 weeks

6½ weeks

8 weeks

FIGURE 3.1 *Changes in the size and form of the human body from 14 days to 15 weeks after conception. (Adapted from Arey, 1974.)*

15 weeks

11 weeks

9 weeks

No part of the zygote looks like a bone cell or a blood cell, let alone a newborn baby. Yet within the first few weeks after conception, this single cell will have subdivided many times to form many different kinds of cells. In approximately 266 days it will have been transformed into a wriggling, crying infant. As a first step toward understanding this process, scientists often divide prenatal development into three broad periods, each characterized by distinctive patterns of growth and interaction between the organism and its environment.

1. The **germinal period** begins when the mother's and father's germ cells are joined at conception and lasts until the developing organism becomes attached to the wall of the uterus, about 8 to 10 days later.

2. The **period of the embryo** extends from the time the organism becomes attached to the uterus until the end of the eighth week, when all of the major organs have taken primitive shape.

3. The **period of the fetus** begins the ninth week after conception with the first signs of the hardening of the bones and continues until birth, an average of 30 weeks. During this period the primitive organ systems develop to the point where the baby can exist outside of the mother without medical support.

At any step in these prenatal periods, the process of development may stop. In an estimated 31 percent of cases, for example, the genetic material that comes together when a sperm and egg unite proves to be incompatible with life and the zygote fails to develop at all (Wilcox et al., 1988). If all goes well, however, the creation of a new human being is under way.

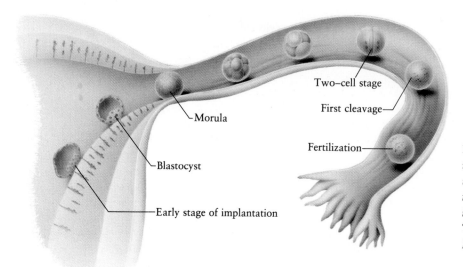

Two–cell stage

First cleavage

Morula

Blastocyst

Fertilization

Early stage of implantation

FIGURE 3.2   *Develop-ment of the human embryo in the mother's reproductive tract from fertilization to implantation. (Adapted from Tuchmann-Duplessis, David, & Haegel, 1971.)*

The Germinal Period

During the first 8 to 10 days after conception, the fertilized ovum moves slowly through the fallopian tube and into the uterus (see Figure 3.2). The timing of this journey is crucial. If the new organism enters the uterus too soon, the uterine environment will not be prepared and the organism will be destroyed. If it arrives too late, the proper conditions for attachment to the wall of the uterus will no longer be present, and the organism will pass out of the mother's body.

The first cells of life

Cleavage, the mitotic division of the zygote into several cells, begins about 24 hours after conception, as the fertilized ovum travels down the fallopian tube. (Mitosis is described in Chapter 2, p. 49.) The single-celled zygote divides to produce two daughter cells, each of which then divides to produce two more daughter cells, and so on (see Figure 3.3). Thanks to this periodic doubling, the developing organism will already consist of hundreds of cells by the time it reaches the uterus.

An important characteristic of cleavage is that the cells existing at any given moment do not divide simultaneously. Instead of proceeding in an orderly fashion from a two-cell stage to a four-cell stage and so on, the cells divide at different rates (Austin & Short, 1972). This difference in the rates of change of different parts of the organism is called **heterochrony** (literally, "variability in time"). Because different parts of the organism

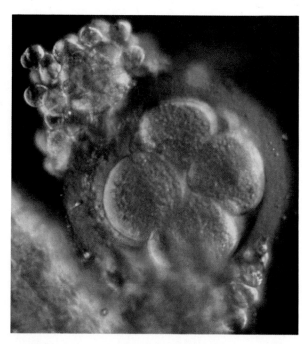

FIGURE 3.3   *A zygote following two cleavages, resulting in four cells of equal size and appearance.*

change at different rates, the organism's behavior will be more or less mature depending on which of the organism's parts are most heavily involved. Thus, the unevenness of development rates gives rise to another prominent feature of development, heterogeneity, or variability, in the *levels* of development of different parts of the organism.

The emergence of new forms

As the first several cleavages occur, a cluster of cells called the **morula** takes shape inside the zona pellucida. For the first 4 or 5 days after conception, the cells in the morula become smaller and smaller with each cleavage until they are all approximately the size of the average body cell. Although the cells in each new "generation" become smaller, they otherwise look identical to their parent cells, and much like a large number of Ping-Pong balls crowded into a balloon.

At this point the cells begin for the first time to interact with the environment outside the zona pellucida to take in nutrients. If they do not, cleavage will cease and the organism will die. The first changes in the organism's internal form emerge simultaneously with these interactions between the organism (morula) and its environment (the fallopian tube).

The first noticeable change in form is the appearance of a fluid-filled cavity within the morula. Simultaneously two distinct kinds of cells can be distinguished for the first time (see Figure 3.4). This transformation of the morula into a **blastocyst** is the earliest instance of a repeating pattern in which development is manifested as a process of differentiation and reintegration. In this case, the identical cells of the morula are differentiated into two kinds of cells that are then reintegrated into the more mature form of the organism called the blastocyst.

The two kinds of cells in the blastocyst play different roles in development, corresponding to two kinds of interactions with the environment. Lumped along one side of the central cavity is a knot of small cells called the **inner cell mass.** This mass will give rise to the organism itself. Around the inner cell mass and the cavity, a double layer of large, flat cells called the **trophoblast** forms a protective barrier between the inner cell mass and the environment. Later the trophoblast will develop into the membranes that will protect the developing organism and transmit nutrients to it. (Appropriately, "trophoblast" is derived from the Greek trophe, "nourishment.") As the cells of the blastocyst differentiate, the zona pellucida surrounding it disintegrates. The trophoblast layer now serves as a kind of pump, filling the inner cavity with energy-giving fluid from the uterus, which enables the cells to continue to divide and the organism to grow.

Although it is easy enough to describe the transformation of the undifferentiated cells of the zygote, first into the two kinds of cells in the blastocyst and eventually into the multitudes of kinds of cells present at birth, the mechanisms by which this occurs remain the central puzzle of development. The leading scientists of the eighteenth century assumed that in some way adult forms — head, arms, legs, brain, liver, and heart — already exist in the very first cell created at conception. According to this view, called **preformationism,** no new forms really develop; they are all there at the beginning.

Critics of the preformationists argued that a fertilized ovum does not look like a baby, so why claim that it "contains" the baby in a form that is simply too small to see? They preferred the idea that each new form emerges through the various kinds of interactions that take place between the preceding form and its environ-

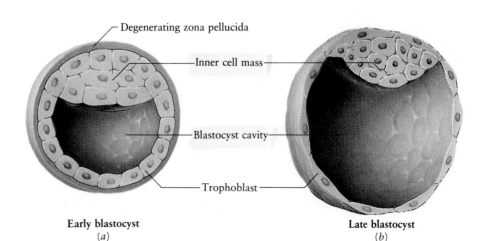

FIGURE 3.4 *Two stages in the development of the blastocyst: (a) the formation of the inner cell mass in the early blastocyst stage, and (b) the differentiation of the trophoblast cells in the late blastocyst stage. By the late blastocyst stage, the zona pellucida has disappeared. (Adapted from Moore, 1982.)*

Degenerating zona pellucida

Inner cell mass

Blastocyst cavity

Trophoblast

Early blastocyst
(a)

Late blastocyst
(b)

ment, a process they called **epigenesis** (from a Greek expression meaning "after being born"). This epigenetic explanation is now generally favored by embryolgists, scientists whose specialty is early organic development (Gottlieb, 1983, 1991a, b). The problem for the epigenetic view of development is to explain how various kinds of interactions account for, say, the emergence of the inner cell mass and the trophoblast from the morula. After all, the cells of the morula are all inside the zona pellucida, which is inside the mother's reproductive tract. How can we say that one cell in the morula has a different kind of contact with the environment than any other cell does?

The answer is to think of "environment" as the immediate surroundings of each individual cell, rather than as the surroundings of the morula as a whole. The cells in the morula do not all have the same surroundings. The cells at the center of the morula are surrounded by other morula cells. Those on the outside have some contact with other morula cells, but on one side they are also in contact with the zona pellucida, which in turn is in contact with the mother's reproductive tract and its fluids.

These differences in location can have significant consequences. When the morula begins to take in nutrients, for example, those nutrients must pass through the cells on the outside to reach the cells on the inside. According to the epigenetic explanation, cell division under such different environmental conditions leads to the creation of different kinds of cells (Austin & Short, 1972) and new forms of organism-environment interaction. This pattern is repeated again and again in the course of an organism's development.

In the nineteenth and early twentieth centuries, the old theory of preformation was considered to have been little more than a mystical substitute for science. Currently, however, it is being remembered more favorably. As Stephen J. Gould (1977a) points out, "the preformationists were . . . right in insisting that complexity cannot arise from formless raw material — that there must be something within the egg to regulate its development" (pp. 205–206). That something, however, is not a minuscule, preformed human being, as the early preformationists thought. Rather, what preexists in the zygote is now understood to be a set of coded instructions contained in the genes.

Implantation

As the blastocyst moves farther into the uterus, the trophoblast cells put out tiny branches that burrow into the spongy wall of the uterus until they come in contact with the mother's blood vessels. Thus begins **implantation,** the process by which the blastocyst becomes attached to the uterus. Implantation marks the transition between the germinal and embryonic periods. Like all of life's transitions (birth being an especially dramatic example), implantation is hazardous for the organism. The danger here arises because the blastocyst, being formed from the genes of both the father and the mother, differs genetically from the mother. If any other bit of alien tissue were introduced into a woman's uterus, it would be attacked by the mother's immune system. But for reasons not well understood, the blastocyst is usually not attacked, despite its genetic uniqueness (Austin & Short, 1972).

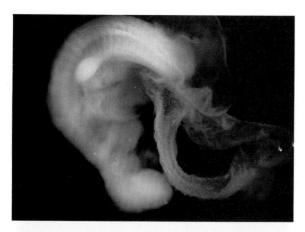

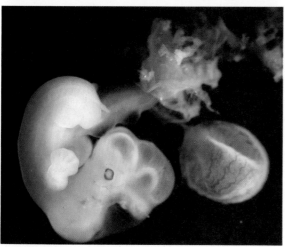

The human embryo at 3 weeks and 5 weeks after conception.

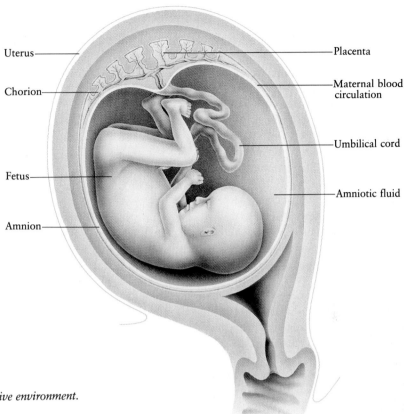

Uterus

Chorion

Fetus

Amnion

Placenta

Maternal blood
circulation

Umbilical cord

Amniotic fluid

FIGURE 3.5   *The fetus in its protective environment.*
(Adapted from Curtis, 1979.)

The Embryonic Period

If the blastocyst is successfully implanted, the developing organism enters the period of the embryo, which lasts for about 6 weeks. During this period, all of the basic organs of the body take shape and the organism begins to respond to direct stimulation. Rapid growth is facilitated by the efficient way the mother now supplies nutrition.

Sources of nutrition and protection

The rapid growth of membranes from the trophoblast ensures that the requisites for the developing organism's survival—nutrients and protection from environmental trauma—are provided early in the embryonic period (see Figure 3.5). The **amnion,** a thin, tough, transparent membrane that holds the amniotic fluid ("bag of waters"), surrounds the embryo. The amniotic fluid protects the organism from hard surfaces

and jolts as the mother moves about, provides liquid support for its weak muscles and soft bones, and gives it a medium in which it can move and change position.

Surrounding the amnion is another membrane, the **chorion,** which becomes the fetal component of the **placenta,** a complex organ made up of tissue from both the mother and the embryo. The placenta and the embryo are linked by the **umbilical cord.** Until birth the placenta acts simultaneously as a barrier that prevents the bloodstreams of the mother and infant from coming into direct contact and as a filter that allows nutrients, oxygen, and waste products to be exchanged. It converts nutrients carried by the mother's blood into food for the embryo. It also enables the embryo's waste products to be absorbed by the mother's bloodstream, from which they are eventually extracted by her kidneys. Thus the mother literally eats, breathes, and urinates for two.

The growth of the embryo

While the trophoblast is forming the placenta and the other membranes that will supply and protect the embryo, the growing number of cells in the inner cell mass begin to differentiate into the various kinds of cells that eventually will become all the organs of the body. The first step in this process is the separation of the inner cell mass into two layers. The **ectoderm,** the outer layer, gives rise to the outer surface of the skin, the nails, part of the teeth, the lens of the eye, the inner ear, and the nervous system (the brain, the spinal cord, and the nerves). The **endoderm,** the inner layer, develops into the digestive system and the lungs. Shortly after these two layers form, a middle layer, the **mesoderm,** appears; eventually it becomes the muscles, the bones, the circulatory system, and the inner layers of the skin (Moore, 1982).

As Table 3.1 makes clear, the embryo develops at a breathtaking pace. The sequence in which the parts of the body form follows two patterns that are maintained until the organism reaches adolescence. In the first, the **cephalocaudal pattern,** development proceeds from the head down. The arm buds, for instance, appear before the leg buds. In the second, the **proximodistal pattern,** development proceeds from the middle of the organism out to the periphery. The spinal cord develops before the arm buds, the upper arm develops before the forearm, and so on. In general, the process of organ formation is the same for all human embryos, but in one major respect — sexual differentiation — it varies. This aspect of development is discussed in Box 3.1.

The emergence of embryonic movement

When the essential organ systems and the nerve cells of the spine have formed, the embryo becomes capable of its first organized responses to the environment. Studies of embryos as they were being removed from the womb during therapeutic abortions indicate that the 8-week-old embryo will turn its head and neck in response to a light touch to the area around the mouth. Its arms will quiver, the upper body will flex, and in many cases its mouth will open (Hooker, 1952). Within the womb, such movements are not detected by the mother because an 8-week-old embryo is still exceedingly small.

TABLE 3.1
Growth and Development of the Embryo

Days 10–13
Cells separate into ectoderm, endoderm, and mesoderm layers. The neural plate, which eventually will become the brain and the spinal cord, forms out of the ectoderm.

Third week
The three major divisions of the brain — the hindbrain, the midbrain, and the forebrain — begin to differentiate by the end of the week. Primitive blood cells and blood vessels are present. The heart comes into being, and by the end of the week it is beating; these movements are a property of the heart muscle and not a response to outside stimulation.

Fourth week
Limb buds are visible. Eyes, ears, and a digestive system begin to take form. The major veins and arteries are completed. Vertebrae are present, and nerves begin to take primitive form.

Fifth week
The umbilical cord takes shape. Bronchial buds, which eventually will become the lungs, take form. Premuscle masses are present in the head, trunk, and limbs. The hand plates are formed.

Sixth week
The head becomes dominant in size. The lower jaw is fused, and the components of the upper jaw are present. The external ear makes its appearance. The three main parts of the brain are distinct.

Seventh week
The face and neck are beginning to take form. Eyelids take shape. The stomach is taking its final shape and position. Muscles are rapidly differentiating throughout the body and are assuming their final shapes and relationships. Neurons are developing at the rate of thousands per minute.

Eighth week
The growth of the gut makes the body evenly round. The head is elevated and the neck is distinct. The external, middle, and inner ear assume their final forms. By the end of this week the fetus is capable of some movement, and responds to stimulation around the mouth.

BOX 3.1
The Development of Sexual Differentiation

Sexual differentiation provides a striking example of the ways in which nature and nurture interact over the course of an organism's development. At each stage of prenatal sexual development we find a new configuration of the parts that were present during the preceding stage and new mechanisms appear that will regulate sexual development in the next stage (Moore, 1982).

The genes that influence sexual determination are located on the X and Y chromosomes inherited at conception. Zygotes with one X and one Y chromosome are genetically male, whereas zygotes with two X chromosomes are genetically female. For the first 6 weeks after conception, however, there is no structural difference between genetically male and genetically female embryos. Both males and females have two ridges of tissue, called gonadal ridges, in the urogenital region. These give no clue to the sex of the embryo.

If the embryo is genetically male (XY), the process of sexual differentiation begins during the seventh week of life, when the gonadal ridges begin to form testes. If the embryo does not have a Y chromosome, no changes are apparent until several weeks later, when ovaries begin to form. Thus the genes inherited at the moment of conception determine whether the sex glands that develop from the gonadal ridges will be male testes or female ovaries. From this point on, though, it is not the presence of the Y chromosome itself but rather the presence or absence of male gonads that determines whether the embryo will develop male or female genital ducts. The male hormones produced by the male gonads, principally testosterone, determine maleness. Femaleness depends not on the secretion of hormones by the ovaries but on the absence of testosterone.

At the end of the seventh week after conception, genetically male and genetically female embryos have the same urogenital membrane and primitive phallus, the future penis or clitoris. If testosterone is present, the membranes are transformed into the male penis and scrotum. In its absence, the female external genitalia are formed. As many researchers have commented, it appears as though nature requires that something be added if the embryo is to become masculine (Halpern, 1986).

The influence of testosterone is not limited to the gonads and the genital tract. During the last 6 months of prenatal development, the presence of testosterone suppresses the natural rhythmic activity of the pituitary gland, located in the brain. If testosterone is absent, the pituitary gland establishes the cyclical pattern of hormone secretion that is characteristic of the female and eventually comes to control her menstrual cycle (Wilson, George, & Griffin, 1981).

Embryologists are still uncertain how the presence of testosterone creates differences in brain activity, but data from animal research suggest that it may shape the development of certain neural pathways in the brain (Toran-Allerand, 1984). These studies show that a dose of testosterone given to a rat at a critical period in the development of its brain will cause it to be responsive to male hormones and insensitive to female hormones from then on, no matter what its genetic sex. If the brain does not receive testosterone at this critical period, it will be responsive to female hormones.

Sensitivity to male rather than female hormones seems to have a striking effect on the organism's later behavior. After William Young and his colleagues (Young, Goy, & Phoenix, 1964) injected pregnant rhesus monkeys with testosterone, the female offspring they bore behaved more like young male monkeys: they threatened other monkeys, failed to withdraw when approached by other monkeys, and engaged in rough-and-tumble play. Their sexual behavior was also masculine in many respects.

During the prenatal period, the development of sexual differences is under strict biological control that is determined directly or indirectly by the genetic code. In later life, however, other factors come into play. Once the baby is born and the parents learn what kind of genitals it has, powerful social, cultural, and psychological factors begin to influence the child's sexual development through a long sequence of interactions between the child and the environments he or she encounters (MacLusky & Naftolin, 1981; Money & Ehrhardt, 1972).

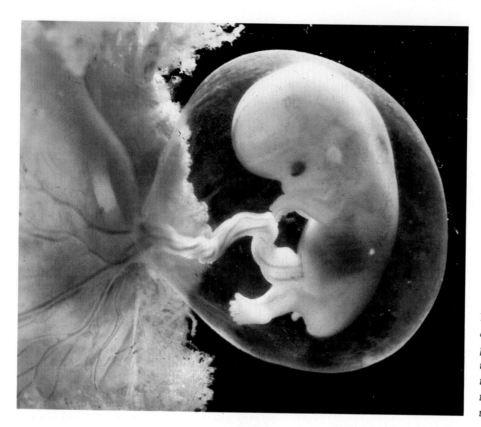

FIGURE 3.6   *The fetus at the beginning of the fetal period (approximately 9 weeks). The way in which the umbilical cord attaches to the placenta is clearly visible.*

The Fetal Period

The fetal period begins once all the basic tissues and organs exist in rudimentary form and the tissue that will become the skeleton begins to harden, or ossify (Arey, 1974). During the fetal period, which lasts from the eighth or ninth week of pregnancy until birth, the fetus becomes 10 times larger and its proportions change dramatically (see Figure 3.6). Each of the organ systems increases in complexity, and the movements become more coordinated. The major events in fetal growth and development are detailed in Table 3.2.

Fetal activity

The increasing complexity of the organism during the fetal period is associated with changes in the level of its activity. The fetus begins to move its arms and head. At 10 weeks the fingers will close fleetingly when the palm is stimulated, and the toes will curl when the sole of the foot is touched. Over the next few weeks body movements become increasingly varied and smooth.

Spontaneous jerks and thrusts of the limbs begin to be accompanied by slower squirming movements of the trunk. Toward the end of the fourth month the fetus is big enough so that the mother can feel its movements.

At 17 or 18 weeks after conception the fetus's activity declines markedly. This decline corresponds with the development of the higher regions of the brain (see Figure 3.7), which eventually makes more complex control of activity possible (Hofer, 1981). As these brain regions mature, they begin to inhibit the primitive activity of the central nervous system characteristic of the less mature fetus. The thrusting and squirming movements of the fetus subside, and it becomes less responsive to stimulation. This period of inhibited activity continues well into the sixth month, at which point the trend toward increasing fetal activity resumes.

As the time of birth draws near, the fetus becomes especially active, moving its limbs, changing its position, even sucking its finger (see photograph on p. 76). In some cases, fetal activity appears to be *endogenous;* that is, it arises directly from the maturation of the organism's tissues. This is the case with the activity of the heart mentioned in Table 3.1. In other cases, it is clearly *exogenous;* that is, the activity arises in response to stimulation from the environment, as when the fetus makes a sudden movement in response to a loud sound.

Functions of fetal activity

Until recently, many embryologists believed that the fetus's activity played no substantial role in its development. The embryologist Viktor Hamburger (1957), for example, claimed that the structure of the nervous system and the behavior patterns it supports "result from self-generating growth and maturation processes that are determined entirely by inherited, intrinsic factors" (p. 56). According to this view, fetal activity has no adaptive value whatsoever for the developing organism; it is simply a by-product of physical growth.

However, evidence discovered in recent decades, some of it supplied by Hamburger himself (Hamburger, 1975), indicates that fetal activity is important to development. Experiments with chick embryos, for example, suggest that their activity is crucial to normal limb development. Under normal circumstances, the spinal cord sends out many more **neurons**—nerve cells—to connect the limbs to the brain than the animal will need when it is fully coordinated. Many of these neurons die off, while the remainder are connected to muscles in an efficient way (Edelman, 1987, refers to this process as "neural darwinism"). If a chick embryo is immobilized by drugs that paralyze its muscles, however, the elimination of excess neurons that ordinarily accompanies neuromuscular development fails to occur. The results are disastrous. In as little as 1 or 2 days, the joints of the chick embryos become fixed into rigid structures, an indication that movement is necessary for articulation between the bones to develop (Bradley & Mistretta, 1975; Provine, 1986).

Many uncertainties remain about the role of the organism's activity during the prenatal period. The data suggest that it plays an important role in some species but not in all, and it has not been possible to gather direct evidence from species similar to *Homo sapiens* because such embryos are difficult or impossible to keep alive when their development is interfered with. It is clear, however, that the human fetus is both active and sensitive to its environment well before birth.

TABLE 3.2
Growth and Development of the Fetus

Tenth week
The head is erect. The intestines have assumed their characteristic position within the body. The spinal cord is a definite internal structure.

Twelfth week
Males and females are externally distinguishable. Blood begins to form in the bone marrow. The eyes take final form.

End of month 4
The fetus looks human. Hair begins to appear. The body has grown larger in relation to the head. The uterus and vagina are recognizable in females. In males, the testes are in position for later descent into the scrotum. Most of the bones are distinct, and the joints appear. The division between the two halves of the brain becomes visible. More reflexes become operational, including swallowing and sucking.

End of month 5
Brown fat, which will help the newborn stay warm, begins to form. New divisions differentiate within the brain. All of the nerve cells that the person will ever have are present. The sheathing of the nerve fibers begins, but it will not be completed until several years after birth.

End of month 6
The lungs begin to make surfactin, a chemical compound that prevents them from collapsing. The fissure between the two sides of the brain is very marked.

End of month 7
The lungs are capable of breathing air, and the central nervous system is sufficiently developed to direct rhythmic breathing movements. Considerable amounts of fat form, smoothing out the wrinkles in the skin. The eyes, which have been closed, open and can respond to light.

End of month 8
The fetus's skin is smooth, and the arms and legs have a chubby appearance. Many folds of the brain are present, although some will not form until after birth.

Month 9
The fetus becomes plumper, adding 50 percent of its weight in the last month. As birth approaches, growth slows. The brain becomes considerably more convoluted. Although the fetus has many reflexes and is active, there is no evidence that the cerebral cortex has any influence on behavior yet.

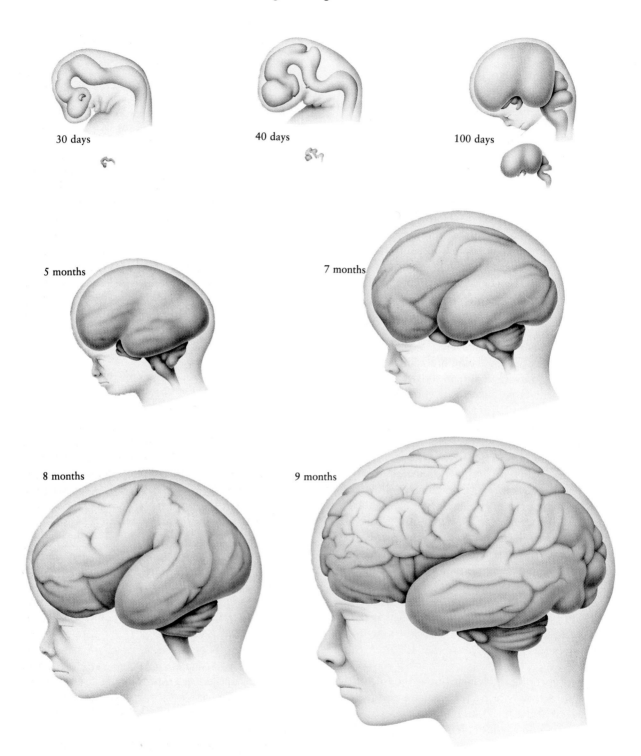

FIGURE 3.7 *The prenatal development of the brain. The primitive parts of the brain are present very early. The cerebral hemispheres, with their characteristic convolutions, do not make their appearance until the middle of pregnancy. (Adapted from Cowan, 1979.)*

THE DEVELOPING ORGANISM IN THE PRENATAL ENVIRONMENT

The marvelous ways in which the mother's body provides a protective and supportive environment for the growth of the human fetus can blind us to the realization that even in the womb the fetus is not independent of the larger world. Modern research makes it clear that the organism is affected not only by its immediate environment but by the world outside the womb as well.

The fetus can be influenced by its uterine environment in a variety of ways. The mother's digestive system and heart are sources of noise, and her movements provide motion stimuli. The fetus comes in contact with the world outside the mother through the wall of her abdomen, and also, less directly, through the placenta and umbilical cord. Nutrients, oxygen, some viruses, and some potentially harmful chemicals all cross the placenta to the fetus. Through these biologically mediated routes a mother's experiences, emotions, illnesses, diet, and social circumstances can affect the child before it is born (Hofer, 1981).

Understanding the effect of the larger environment on the developing fetus is important for several reasons. First, substances and stimulation coming from the environment may have a significant impact on fetal development. Second, the fetus's responses to the environment provide clues about the behavioral capacities that the child will have at birth. Third, when the impact of the environment is detrimental to development, it is important for prospective parents to understand the dangers so that they can take preventive action.

The Fetus's Sensory Capacities

Using modern techniques of measurement and recording, researchers have begun to produce a detailed picture of the development of the human fetus's sensory capacities. This information is essential for determining how the fetus is influenced by its environment.

Motion

The vestibular system of the middle ear, which controls the sense of balance, begins to function in the human fetus about 4 months after conception and is fully mature at birth (Patten, 1968). This early maturity means that the fetus is capable of sensing changes in the mother's posture as it floats inside the fluid-filled amniotic sac.

Vision

Anatomical studies show that the visual system develops only partially during the prenatal period. Little is known for certain about the extent of the fetus's visual experience. Babies born 7 months after conception, however, show changes in brain-wave patterns when a light flashes, an indication that they may be able to respond to light in the womb. Aidan Macfarlane (1977) suggests that toward the end of pregnancy, the fetus may be able to see light that has penetrated the mother's stretched stomach wall. He likens the fetus's visual experience to the glow seen when the palm of the hand covers a flashlight.

Sound

The uterus is a noisy place. Studies in which tiny microphones have been inserted into the uterus adjacent to the fetus's head reveal that the average sound level is approximately 75 decibels, about the level we experience when we ride in a car. This background noise is punctuated by the sound of air passing through the mother's stomach and, every second or so, by the more intense sound of the mother's heartbeat (Birnholz & Benacerraf, 1983).

Because noises from the outside world are muted as they pass through the mother's body and the amniotic fluid, indistinct sounds are unlikely to be discriminated from the normal background noise of the uterus. However, mothers sometimes report an increase in fetal activity when they listen to music or when a door is slammed, and research indicates that they are correct. James Grimwade and his associates (1970) placed a tone generator on the abdomens of 14 pregnant women, along with a sensor to measure the fetus's responsivity when the tone sounded. The mothers wore headphones into which a constant sound was played, to prevent them from hearing or feeling the high-frequency tones played by the generator on their abdomens. The experimenters found that fetal activity increased a few seconds after the tone was turned on, confirming the fact that the fetus perceived the sound directly.

Fetal Learning

The folklore of many societies includes the belief that a pregnant woman's experiences have a significant effect on her child's postnatal development: whatever the mother desires, fears, or admires, the fetus and then the child will come to desire, fear, or admire (Verny & Kelly, 1981). Although such beliefs have met with considerable skepticism during the twentieth century (Carmichael, 1970), there is evidence that at least some events both inside and outside the mother result in fetal learning.

One line of evidence for fetal learning comes from an unusual experiment by Lee Salk (1973). Working in a hospital where mothers and their newborn infants are customarily separated a good deal of the time, Salk arranged for three groups of infants to experience three different experimental conditions. One group was exposed to the sound of a normal heartbeat of 80 pulses per minute, the rate they would have heard while in the womb; another group heard a heart beating 120 times per minute; and a third group heard no special sounds at all. The infants who heard the accelerated heartbeat became so upset that Salk terminated their part in the experiment. The babies who heard the normal heartbeat, however, gained more weight and cried less over the 4 days that the experiment continued than did the group that heard no special sounds. The specific influence of the sound of the normal heartbeat suggests that the infants' experience in the womb had made this sound familiar and therefore reassuring. That newborns found the sound of the mother's heartbeat rewarding was later confirmed by Anthony DeCasper and A. D. Sigafoos (1983).

Salk's experiment suggests that fetuses learn from experiences that originate inside the mother. Evidence of similar learning from stimuli originating outside the mother comes from a study by Anthony DeCasper and Melanie Spence (1986). These researchers asked 12 pregnant women to read aloud a particular passage from *The Cat in the Hat*, a well-known rhyming children's story by Dr. Seuss, twice a day for the last month and a half before their babies were due. By the time the babies were born, the passage had been read to them for a total of about $3^{1}/_{2}$ hours.

Two or three days after the babies were born, DeCasper and Spence tested them with a special pacifier that had been wired to record sucking rates (see Figure 3.8). First the baby was allowed to suck for 2 minutes to establish a baseline sucking rate. After-

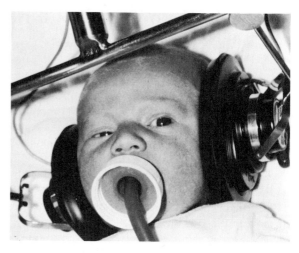

FIGURE 3.8   *This baby is listening to a recording of its mother reading a story. The apparatus permits recordings of changes in sucking to determine if newborns will react to stories read to them while they were in the womb.*

ward, changes in the rate of sucking turned a tape recording of a story on or off. For half of the babies, the story was the one their mothers had read, which presumably they had heard many times from within the womb. For the other half, the story was new. The key finding was that the children modified their rate of sucking when they heard *The Cat in the Hat* but not when they heard the new story. The investigators concluded that the infants had indeed heard the stories being read to them by their mothers and that their learning in the womb influenced the sounds they found rewarding after birth.

The evidence that some kinds of learning occur in the womb is fascinating. Nevertheless, the demonstration that a baby responds more readily to familiar sounds than to unfamiliar ones does not in itself support the claim that prenatal learning has a significant impact on later development.

Maternal Conditions and Prenatal Development

In addition to stimuli that impinge directly on its senses, the fetus is affected by biochemical changes in the mother. Her body chemistry may be altered by factors as diverse as her attitude toward having the baby, her emotional state, the food she eats, and her general health. Many of these changes are transmitted to the fetus through the placenta.

The effects of maternal attitudes and psychological stress

Many physicians who care for pregnant women and newborn infants suspect that a woman's feelings of well-being and her attitude toward her pregnancy affect the well-being of the fetus she is carrying and the child after its birth. A sympathetic mate (see Box 3.2) and other supportive family members, adequate housing, and steady employment—factors that give a woman a basic sense of security—all appear to enhance the prospects for a healthy baby (Pritchard & MacDonald, 1980; Thompson, 1990).

An extensive investigation conducted in Czechoslovakia in the 1960s and 1970s provides the clearest evidence that negative attitudes can adversely affect prenatal development. Henry David (1981) followed up the lives of 220 children whose mothers indicated strong negative attitudes toward having them by twice asking for abortions to end the pregnancy. The refusal of the abortion was an indication that medical authorities believed these women to be capable of carrying through the pregnancy and raising the child.

The children were carefully matched with a control group of children whose mothers either planned for or accepted their pregnancies. The mothers in the two groups were matched for socioeconomic status and age; the children were matched for sex, birth order, number of siblings, and date of birth. The unwanted children weighed less at birth and needed more medical help than the control group, even though their mothers had ready access to medical care and were judged to be in good health themselves. Fewer of the unwanted children were breast-fed, they had more difficulties in school, and they were referred for psychiatric help more often as teenagers.

More recently David and his colleagues (1988) compared wanted and unwanted children in several European countries. They found that children who had not been wanted are at increased risk for a variety of social and psychological dysfunctions into adulthood. They are more likely to be in jail, to abuse drugs or alcohol, and to find their own social relations unsatisfactory.

A moderate amount of stress can be expected to accompany any major life transition, even one that is

welcomed (Holmes & Holmes, 1969). The expectant mother has to adjust her life to accommodate new responsibilities. One who decides to quit working may have to cope with a reduced income. Another may be working so hard that she feels she does not have enough time to take care of herself, let alone her expected child. And if the pregnancy was unplanned, as many are, the stress that normally accompanies pregnancy may be magnified.

Studies have shown that a mother who is under stress or becomes emotionally upset secretes hormones, such as adrenaline and cortisone, that pass through the placenta and have a measurable effect on the fetus's motor activity (Thompson, 1990). When a woman is under extreme stress for a significant amount of time during her pregnancy, she is at increased risk for such complications as miscarriage, long and painful labor, and premature delivery (Blom-

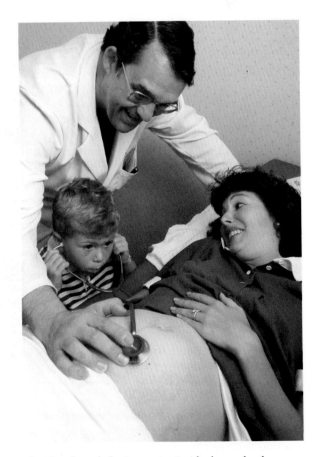

The idea that a baby is growing inside the mother becomes much less abstract when you listen to its heartbeat.

berg, 1980; Sameroff & Chandler, 1975). She is also more likely to give birth to a child who is irritable and hyperactive and who has eating, sleeping, and digestive problems (Friedman & Sigman, 1980; Sontag, 1941, 1944).

In the relatively favored circumstances of middle-class life in industrialized countries, many women may experience little stress during pregnancy; but most of the world's women are poor, live in difficult circumstances, and must worry about how to provide for their child before and after its birth. Even with a sympathetic mate or relatives to ease the burden, stress seems unavoidable under such conditions and is indeed very much a part of a pattern of environmental circumstances that puts many women and their unborn children at risk.

Nutritional influences on prenatal development

Babies in utero are totally dependent on their mothers for the nutrients that keep them alive and allow them to develop. Research indicates that a pregnant woman needs to consume between 2000 and 2800 calories daily in a well-balanced diet that includes all the essential vitamins and minerals (National Academy of Sciences, 1989). The importance of good maternal nutrition to normal prenatal development may seem obvious, but it is often difficult to demonstrate conclusively because maternal malnourishment is closely associated with a host of other factors that can also harm the fetus, such as poor maternal health (Worthington-Roberts & Klerman, 1990).

EXTREME MALNUTRITION. The clearest evidence that insufficient maternal nutrition has a detrimental effect on fetal development comes from studies of sudden periods of famine. During the fall and winter of 1944–1945, for example, famine struck the large cities of western Holland when the Nazi occupation forces embargoed all food shipments because Dutch railway workers had gone on strike to aid the advancing Allied armies. During and after the famine, spontaneous abortions, stillbirths, malformations, and deaths at birth increased markedly. Those babies who were born alive weighed significantly less than normal, as Figure 3.9 indicates (Stein et al., 1975).

A more severe wartime famine occurred in the Soviet Union. In September 1941 Leningrad was encircled by the German army, and no supplies were brought into the city until February 1942. The standard daily ration during this period was 1 pound 2

BOX 3.2
Fathers and Pregnancy

"Pregnancy is a family affair," notes the psychologist Ross Parke (1981, p. 13). Although it is the mother who undergoes the most profound physical and mental changes as the new organism grows inside her body, fathers can play a significant role during pregnancy. In light of research indicating that maternal stress can have negative effects on prenatal development, special attention has been focused on ways the father can help create favorable conditions for the mother and the baby-to-be.

Several factors that commonly cause stress during pregnancy involve the father directly or indirectly. Among them are financial concerns, marital problems, and conception out of wedlock (Blomberg, 1980; Mowbray, Lanir, & Hulce, 1982). A father who denies paternity or refuses to support the mother greatly increases her burden; a father who is mature, flexible, supportive, and loving can greatly reduce her stress.

Harold Rausch and his colleagues (1974) report that many men try to react positively to their pregnant wives' needs for emotional as well as financial support. The researchers observed how expectant couples settled minor disputes, such as deciding what television program to watch. They had seen some of these couples before the women became pregnant, so they were able to identify ways in which the pregnancy affected their interactions. In general, the expectant fathers were more conciliatory than before. Many men showed an increased interest in babies and parenting, taking childbirth and child-care classes with their wives and reading books about pregnancy and child rearing. Some took extra jobs to meet the increased financial obligations that come with having a child.

An important way in which the father can reduce both family tension and the mother's work load is to take a larger role in the care of the couple's other children. Many years ago, the psychologist Alfred Baldwin (1947) observed that when women who already have children become pregnant, they tend to spend less time with their children and behave less warmly toward them. The father's help with older children not only makes life more pleasant for the mother but also sets up a pattern of family interaction that improves the way the older children will react to their new sibling after it is born (Legg, Sherick, & Wadland, 1974).

In some preindustrial cultures, men mark the transition to fatherhood with special rituals called *couvade*, which are intended variously to deflect evil spirits that might harm the mother and baby and to establish paternity (Parke, 1981). As soon as a husband hears that his wife is in labor, he takes to his bed and simulates the agony of giving birth. During the last century it was reported that when a woman of the Erickala-Vandu, a tribe in southern India, went into labor,

> she informs her husband, who immediately takes some of her clothes, puts them on, places on his forehead the mark the women usually place on theirs, retires into a dark room where there is only a dim lamp, and lies down on the bed, covering himself with a long cloth. When the child is born, it is washed and placed on a cot beside the father. (Cain, 1874, quoted in Parke, 1981, p. 15)

Though expectant fathers in modern industrialized societies do not practice such formalized rituals as couvade, an estimated 15 to 20 percent experience what the British psychiatrist W. H. Trethowan and his colleague M. G. Conlon call the *couvade syndrome*: a set of physical symptoms that mimic some of the initial symptoms of pregnancy, including fatigue, backache, headache, loss of appetite, nausea, and vomiting (Trethowan & Conlon, 1965; Liebenberg, 1967). These physical symptoms are often accompanied by such psychological problems as depression, tension, insomnia, and irritability. All the symptoms disappear almost immediately after the mother gives birth.

Data collected by Bittman and Zalk (1978) show how difficult it can be for expectant couples to deal with pregnancy and the new responsibilities of parenthood. As a case in point, they describe Mr. A., a 28-year-old factory worker. Though Mr. A. described his wife's pregnancy of 7 months as "model," he admitted that he himself had been experiencing a great deal of physical discomfort from nausea, vomiting, alternating diarrhea and constipation, head and back pains, and leg cramps. In the course of the interview, he revealed that his wife felt that their apartment was too small for three people but was also concerned about the financial burden of a larger one. Worried about his ability to provide for the baby, Mr. A. was working overtime at a factory job he hated. Now he did not get home until after ten o'clock at night, and then his wife was usually exhausted and often asleep. Although his wife understood that the overtime would help pay for the baby furniture she wanted, she was unhappy about being left alone so long. She complained bitterly, accused Mr. A. of not loving her, and turned away from his embraces. According to Bittman and Zalk, Mr. A. may be an extreme case, especially with regard to the physical symptoms he suffered, but his worries about his ability to provide for his child and the conflicts and stresses he and his wife faced in adjusting to their impending parenthood are not at all unusual.

These expectant parents are attending a class on how to deal with the process of birthing.

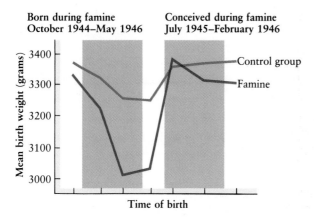

Born during famine
October 1944–May 1946

Conceived during famine
July 1945–February 1946

Control group

Famine

Time of birth

FIGURE 3.9   *Mean birth weights of children born and children conceived in Rotterdam, Holland, during a period of severe famine and in other parts of the country where conditions were less severe. (Adapted from Stein et al., 1975.)*

ounces of bread made with poor-quality rye flour, cellulose, and malt. The number of infants born in the first half of 1942 was much lower than normal, and stillbirths doubled. Very few infants were born in the second half of 1942, all of them to women who had better access to food than the rest of the population did. These babies were, on the average, more than a pound lighter than babies born before the siege, and they were much more likely to be premature. They were also in very poor condition at birth; they had little vitality and were unable to maintain their body temperature adequately (Antonov, 1947).

The sudden famine in Leningrad produced nutritional variations so extreme that normal environmental influences on prenatal development were dwarfed by comparison. Consequently, the specific effects on the developing fetus of maternal malnutrition during particular segments of the prenatal period could be isolated with a high degree of certainty. Severe nutritional deprivation during the first 3 months of pregnancy was most likely to result in abnormalities of the central nervous system, premature birth, and death. Deprivation during the last 3 months of pregnancy was more likely to retard fetal growth and result in low birth weight.

UNDERNOURISHMENT AND ASSOCIATED FACTORS.
Studies of the relation between maternal nutrition, prenatal development, and neonatal health suggest that lesser degrees of malnourishment also increase

risks to the fetus. It is difficult to single out the effects of poor nutrition, however, because malnourished mothers frequently live in impoverished environments where housing, sanitation, education, and medical care are also inadequate (Worthington-Roberts & Klerman, 1990; Rosso, 1990). (Table 3.3 shows just how important prenatal care can be for low-income mothers and their children.) Expectant mothers with low incomes are more likely to suffer from diseases or simply to be in a weakened state than women who live in more materially comfortable circumstances. Their babies are more likely to suffer from a wide variety of birth defects and illnesses and to be born prematurely (Cravioto, De Licardie, & Birch, 1966). Low-income mothers are also more likely to have babies who die at birth or soon after birth, according to a variety of studies conducted in many parts of the world, including the United States (Dott, Fort, & Arthur, 1975a, b; Macfarlane, 1977; Moore et al, 1986).

Not all undernourishment can be attributed to the unavailability of food. Research in both industrial and nonindustrial societies demonstrates that cultural factors also play an important role in determining what foods expectant mothers eat. The Siriono of South America, for example, believe that the characteristics of any animal a woman eats while she is pregnant will be transferred to her unborn child. Pregnant women are therefore not allowed to eat the meat of the owl monkey because their children might develop a tendency to stay awake at night. Jaguar meat is also forbidden for fear that the child will be "quietly born" (stillborn).

In the United States, food choices vary even among people of the same social class. One study of the health of babies born to low-income rural women classified as having either "fair to good" or "poor to very poor" dietary habits found that expectant mothers who ate more nutritious food had markedly healthier babies (Jeans, Smith, & Stearns, 1955).

The possibility of preventing or at least reducing the damaging effects of malnutrition and an impoverished environment has been demonstrated by several studies. In the basic design of this type of research, expectant mothers and their offspring who receive supplemental food and medical attention are compared with those who do not. One of the largest intervention programs, designed to assess the effects of a massive supplemental food program for women, infants, and children — dubbed WIC — was initiated by the U.S. government in 1972 (Kotelchuck et al., 1984).

Low-income women in the program were given vouchers for such staples as milk, eggs, fruit juices, and dried beans. When infants born to these mothers were compared with infants born to mothers not in the program but otherwise matched with respect to age, race, education, and other factors, the program infants were found to have significantly fewer health problems (Worthington-Roberts & Klerman, 1990).

A study that focused on 280 infants in Colombia supports the conclusion that food supplements started in mid-pregnancy and continued for 3½ years enhance the development of children in regions where malnourishment is prevalent (Super, Herrera, & Mora, 1990). When they were assessed at the age of 3, children who received food supplements were found to be somewhat taller and heavier than a group of children who had received no supplementary food. When food supplements were combined with a home-visiting pro-

gram designed to help families stimulate their children's development, the gains were still evident 3 years after the program had ended.

Several studies indicate that maternal nutrition is important to the intellectual development as well as the physical health of the child (Kopp, 1983; Kopp & Parmelee, 1979).

- Many experiments with mammals other than humans point to brain size at birth as a strong predictor of the ease with which the organism learns, retains, and uses new information.
- Although the association is not strong, better-fed mothers have heavier babies with bigger brains.
- Although intellectual deficits are not invariably associated with maternal undernourishment, it is primarily the children of poor mothers who are at risk (Kopp, 1983).
- In a study of children whose mothers had participated in the WIC program in Louisiana, marked differences in the intellectual development of the children were found to depend on *when* their mothers began to receive food supplements (Hicks, Langham, & Takenaka, 1982). The children were evaluated on a variety of intellectual measures when they were 6 or 7 years old and were already enrolled in school. Those children whose mothers had received food supplements during the last 3 months of their pregnancies—the period when the fetal brain undergoes especially rapid development—outperformed the children of mothers who did not receive food supplements until after their children were born.

TABLE 3.3

Birth Complications for Low-Income Women in San Diego, California, Who Did and Did Not Receive Prenatal Medical Care (per 100 births)

Complication	Women Who Received No Prenatal Care	Women Who Received Prenatal Care
Premature rupture of membranes	13	2
Ominous fetal heart rate	10	5
Prematurity	13	2
Low birth weight (less than 2500 grams)	21	6
Low Apgar score (a measure of immediate risk)	8	2
Hospital stay of more than 3 days	24	12
Prenatal death	4	1

Source: Moore et al., 1986.

As important as adequate maternal nutrition is to the growth of the fetus, the long-term effects of prenatal malnutrition are also heavily influenced by the adequacy of the child's diet after birth. The most devastating consequences befall children who were prenatally malnourished in the womb and whose nutrition continues to be inadequate after they are born (Cravioto, De Licardie, & Birch, 1966). Such children are subject to continued health problems as well as deficits in intellectual functioning.

Children who are born malnourished are often apathetic, unresponsive, and irritable (Zeskind & Ramey, 1978, 1981). The negative consequences of this pattern of behavior are seen in a study that found that chronically undernourished toddlers in Santiago, Chile, were less likely to be securely attached to their mothers than children whose weight was within the normal range for their age (Valenzuela, 1990). Such a characteristic makes babies unpleasant to interact with, a situation that can only intensify their problems.

These findings make clear the damage that is done to millions of children throughout the world who are undernourished both before and after birth. Most of these children do not receive food supplements, and even fewer receive high-quality educational help. Quite the opposite. Instead, they experience a cascade of risk factors, of which malnutrition is only one. Associated with malnutrition are a lack of sanitary facilities, a lack of medical care, and a lack of educational opportunities (see Figure 3.10). Together such conditions lead to high rates of infant mortality and shorter life expectancies (Kopp, 1983).

Teratogens: Environmental Sources of Birth Defects

Other threats to the prenatal organism come from **teratogens** — environmental agents that can cause deviations in normal development and can lead to serious abnormalities or death (see Figure 3.11). (The term comes from the Greek *teras*, "monster.") Commonly encountered teratogens include certain drugs and infections, radiation, and pollution.

Drugs

As many as 60 percent of pregnant women take some medications during their pregnancy, primarily over-the-counter analgesics, antinauseants, and sleep medi-

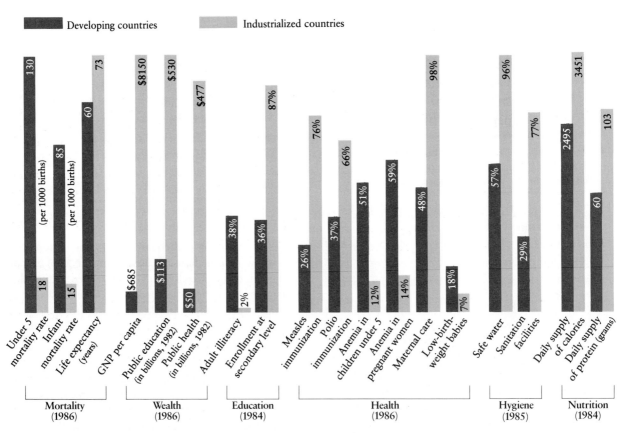

FIGURE 3.10 *In many countries of the world, poor economic conditions create a set of risk factors. For example, poor health conditions and lack of parents' education negatively influence child health and welfare. (Adapted from United Nations Children's Fund [UNICEF], 1987.)*

FIGURE 3.11   *The devastating effects of agent orange,
an environmental pollutant used during the Vietnam War.*

TABLE 3.4

Mean Birth Weight of Babies Born at Various Gestations to Smokers and Nonsmokers (grams)

Maturity (weeks)	Nonsmokers	Cigarettes per Day	
		1–20	Over 20
31	2624	2415	1887
34	2798	2615	2488
37	3007	2848	2816
40	3341	3189	3188
43	3438	3274	3346

Source: Naeye, 1978.

cations (Schnoll, 1986). Some of the drugs they take are not generally thought of as drugs—caffeine, alcohol, the chemical substances in cigarette smoke. Caffeine is not known to be harmful, but tobacco and alcohol have been shown to have a variety of adverse effects on fetal development.

PRESCRIPTION AND NONPRESCRIPTION DRUGS.
From 1956 until 1961, the prescription drug thalidomide was used in Europe as a sedative and to control nausea in the early stages of pregnancy. The women who took the drug were unharmed by it, and many of the children they bore suffered no ill effects. Some children, however, were born without arms and legs; their hands and feet were attached directly to their torsos like flippers. Some had defects of sight and hearing as well. About 8000 deformed children were born before their problems were traced to the drug and it was removed from the market (Persaud, 1977).

Since the disastrous effects of thalidomide were discovered, other prescription drugs have been found to cause abnormalities in the developing organism, including the antibiotics streptomycin and tetracycline, anticoagulants, anticonvulsants, most artificial hormones, Thorazine (used in the treatment of schizo-

phrenia), and Valium (a tranquilizer). In large doses aspirin can also cause abnormalities. Indeed, all drugs are capable of entering the bloodstream of the developing organism, and only a few have been studied well enough to determine whether they are "safe" for expectant mothers. Therefore, pregnant women are advised to check with their physician before taking any nonprescription drug, and physicians are advised to prescribe only the most necessary therapeutic drugs for their pregnant patients.

TOBACCO. Smoking is not known to produce birth defects, but a British study of 150,000 births found the rates of stillbirth and death at birth to be 28 percent higher among the children of mothers who smoked than among those of nonsmokers (Bolton, 1983). Smoking is also associated with lower birth weight (see Table 3.4). This effect appears to be specific to smoking during pregnancy because the children of mothers who smoked during pregnancy were smaller than those born to the same women after they had abstained from smoking (Bolton, 1983).

ALCOHOL. Alcohol is the most commonly abused drug. About 2 percent of all U.S. women of childbearing age suffer from alcoholism (Golbus, 1980). Infants born to mothers who are heavy drinkers during pregnancy — that is, who have five or more drinks a day — have a 30 percent chance of suffering from fetal alcohol syndrome, a set of symptoms that includes an abnormally small head and underdeveloped brain, eye abnormalities, congenital heart disease, joint anomalies, and malformations of the face (see Figure 3.12). The physical growth and mental development of children with this syndrome are likely to be retarded throughout childhood (Hanson, Streissguth, & Smith, 1978). Women who drink heavily during the first trimester of pregnancy and then reduce their consumption of alcohol during the second and third trimesters do not reduce the risk of having children with this affliction (Vorhees & Mollnow, 1987).

The effects of lower levels of alcohol consumption on development are currently in dispute. Some

research indicates that even moderate consumption affects prenatal development adversely. A study of 4-year-olds whose mothers had had three or more drinks a day during pregnancy found the children's intelligence to be significantly below normal. Other studies, however, have found no such difference between the babies of women who abstained from alcohol and those who had one or more drinks a day (Richardson, Day, & Taylor, 1989). Given the potential risks, health professionals advise women to stop drinking before they become pregnant.

COCAINE. Cocaine is an addictive stimulant that, in the concentrated form known as crack, became the drug of choice of many addicts in the late 1980s (Jones & Lopez, 1990). It rapidly produces dependency in the mother, and it has a variety of destructive influences on the fetus, including spontaneous abortion and heart attack. Babies born to cocaine-addicted mothers are irritable, respond excessively to stimulation, and show impaired motor coordination. These effects are still detectable several months after birth.

METHADONE AND HEROIN. Babies of mothers who are addicted to either heroin or methadone are born addicted themselves and must be given drugs shortly after birth if they are not to undergo the often life-threatening ordeal of withdrawal. These babies are more likely to be premature, underweight, and vulnerable to respiratory illnesses. They are twice as likely to die soon after birth as are babies of nonaddicted mothers of the same socioeconomic class (Bolton, 1983; Ostrea & Chavez, 1979).

While these babies are being weaned from the drugs to which they were born addicted, they are irritable and have tremors, their cries are abnormal, their sleep is disturbed, and their motor control is diminished. The effects of the addiction are still apparent in their motor control 4 months later. Even after a year their ability to pay attention is impaired (Jones & Lopez, 1990).

Infections and other conditions

A variety of infection-causing microorganisms can endanger the embryo, the fetus, and the newborn. Most infections spread from the mother to the unborn child across the placental barrier. In a few instances, however, the baby may become infected as it passes through the birth canal. Some of the more common

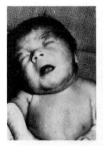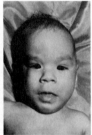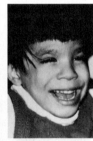
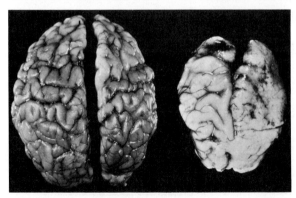

FIGURE 3.12   *Children who suffer from fetal alcohol syndrome do not merely look abnormal; their brains are underdeveloped and many are severely retarded. The IQ scores of the boy pictured here at birth, at 8 months, and at 4½ years were far below normal. The brain of another child who suffered from fetal alcohol syndrome (lower right) lacks the convolutions characteristic of the brain of a normal child (lower left).*

infections and other maternal conditions that may affect the developing human organism are summarized below; Table 3.5 summarizes others.

RUBELLA. In 1941 Dr. N. M. Gregg, an Australian, noticed a sudden increase in the number of infants who were born blind. He interviewed their mothers and found that many of them recalled having had a mild rash, swollen lymph glands, and a low fever—all symptoms of rubella, or German measles—early in their pregnancies. Gregg wrote an article suggesting that there might be some connection between the

---

TABLE 3.5

Some Maternal Diseases and Conditions That May Affect Prenatal Development

SEXUALLY TRANSMITTED DISEASES

Gonorrhea	The gonococcus organism may attack the eyes while the baby is passing through the infected birth canal. Silver nitrate eyedrops are administered immediately after birth to prevent blindness.
Herpes simplex (genital herpes)	Infection usually occurs at birth as the baby comes in contact with herpes lesions on the mother's genitals, although the virus may also cross the placental barrier to infect the fetus. Infection can lead to blindness and serious brain damage. There is no cure for the disease. Mothers with active genital herpes often have a cesarean delivery to avoid infecting their babies.
Syphilis	The effects of syphilis on the fetus can be devastating. An estimated 25% of infected fetuses are born dead. Those who survive may be deaf, mentally retarded, or deformed. Syphilis can be diagnosed by a blood test and can be cured before the fetus is affected, since the syphilis spirochete cannot penetrate the placental membrane before the 21st week of gestation.

OTHER DISEASES AND MATERNAL CONDITIONS

Chicken pox	Chicken pox may lead to spontaneous abortion or premature delivery, but it does not appear to cause malformations.
Cytomegalovirus	The most common source of prenatal infection, cytomegalovirus produces no symptoms in adults, but it may be fatal to the embryo. Infection later in intrauterine life has been related to brain damage, deafness, blindness, and cerebral palsy (a defect of motor coordination caused by brain damage).
Diabetes	Diabetic mothers face a greater risk of having a stillborn child or one who dies shortly after birth. Babies of diabetics are often very large because of the accumulation of fat during the third trimester. Diabetic mothers require special care to prevent these problems.
Hepatitis	Mothers who have hepatitis are likely to pass it on to their infants during birth.
Hypertension	Hypertension (chronic high blood pressure) increases the probability of miscarriage and infant death.
Influenza	The more virulent forms of influenza may lead to spontaneous abortion or may cause abnormalities during the early stages of pregnancy.
Mumps	Mumps is suspected of causing spontaneous abortion in the first trimester of pregnancy.
Toxemia	About 5% of pregnant women in the United States are affected during the third trimester by this disorder of unknown origin. Most common during first pregnancies, the condition mainly affects the mother. Symptoms are water retention, high blood pressure, rapid weight gain, and protein in urine. If untreated, toxemia may cause convulsions, coma, and even death for the mother. Death of the fetus is not uncommon.
Toxoplasmosis	A mild disease in adults with symptoms similar to those of the common cold, toxoplasmosis is caused by a parasite that is present in raw meat and cat feces. It may cause spontaneous abortion or death. Babies who survive may have serious eye or brain damage.

Sources: Moore, 1982; Stevenson, 1977.

rubella epidemic of the summer of 1940 and the subsequent increase in the number of babies who were born blind, alerting the medical community to this danger for the first time (Gregg, 1941). Since then, researchers have found that rubella causes developmental defects in more than 50 percent of all babies born to mothers who suffer from the disease during the first months of pregnancy (Stevenson, 1977). Infection during the first 3 months of pregnancy often results in a syndrome of congenital heart disease, cataracts, deafness, and mental retardation. Infection during the second 3 months may lead to mental and motor retardation and to deafness. A rubella epidemic in the United States during the winter of 1964–1965 resulted in 30,000 stillbirths and 20,000 infants who suffered congenital defects (Lavigne, 1982).

The development of a vaccine for rubella in 1969 has greatly reduced the incidence of the disease, but it has not been eradicated. Women are advised to avoid becoming pregnant for at least 6 months after they receive the vaccine. A few states offer a test for immunity to rubella as part of the blood test given before a marriage license is issued.

ACQUIRED IMMUNE DEFICIENCY SYNDROME (AIDS). The rapid spread of the AIDs virus in the 1980s has made this source of infection a major concern among physicians. Approximately 50 percent of the babies born to mothers who test positive for the AIDs virus acquire this disease. The virus may be transmitted from the mother to her baby either by passing through the placental barrier or through exposure of the baby to the mother's infected blood during delivery (Weber, Redfield, & Lemon, 1986; Whitely & Goldenberg, 1990). There is no known cure for AIDS; it invariably leads to death.

RH INCOMPATIBILITY. Rh is a complex substance on the surface of the red blood cells. One of its components is determined by a dominant gene, and people who have this component are said to be *Rh positive*. Fewer than one in five people inherit the two recessive genes that make them *Rh negative*.

When an Rh-negative woman conceives a child with an Rh-positive man, the child is likely to be Rh positive. During the birth of the baby, some of its blood cells usually pass into the mother's bloodstream while the placenta is separating from the uterine wall. The mother's immune system creates antibodies to

fight this foreign substance, and the antibodies stay in her bloodstream. If the mother again becomes pregnant with an Rh-positive child, the antibodies produced during the birth of her first child will pass into the new baby's bloodstream, where they will attack and destroy its red blood cells. The resultant Rh disease can lead to serious birth defects and even death. Since it takes time for the mother's system to produce Rh antibodies, firstborn children are rarely affected, but the danger increases with each successive child. Fortunately, physicians can prevent Rh disease by giving the Rh-negative mother an injection of anti-Rh serum within 72 hours of the delivery of an Rh-positive child. The serum kills any Rh-positive blood cells in the mother's bloodstream so that she will not develop antibodies to attack them. Children who are born with Rh disease can be treated with periodic blood transfusions (Moore, 1982).

RADIATION. Massive doses of radiation often lead to serious malformations of the developing organism and in many cases cause prenatal death or spontaneous abortion (Moore, 1982). Somewhat lesser doses may spare the life of the organism, but they may have a profound effect on its development. These dangers were made tragically evident following the atomic blasts at Hiroshima and Nagasaki in 1945. Many of the pregnant women who were within 1500 meters of the blasts survived, but they later lost their babies. Of those babies who appeared to be normal at birth, 64 percent were later diagnosed as mentally retarded. The effects of radiation on the fetus's developing central nervous system were found to be greatest during the eighth through the fifteenth week of the prenatal period, a time of rapid proliferation of the cortical neurons (Vorhees & Mollnow, 1987). If the fetus's gonads receive doses of radiation, the germ cells may be affected, so that later generations may suffer genetic damage (Tuchmann-Duplessis, 1975).

The effects of low doses of radiation on human beings have not been firmly established. Because X rays may cause malformations in the embryo, physicians are likely to be cautious about X-raying pregnant women.

POLLUTION. Most of the thousands of chemicals that are used in industrial production and in the preparation of foods and cosmetics have never been tested to see if they are harmful to prenatal development,

The tragic consequences of prenatal mercury poisoning.

although some of these substances reach the embryo or fetus through the placenta (Ames, 1979). Some herbicides and pesticides have been shown to be harmful or even fatal to unborn rats, mice, rabbits, and chicks. Several pollutants in the atmosphere and in the water we drink also appear to be teratogenic. Moreover, some of the effects are cumulative as concentrations of the chemicals build up in the body.

In 1953 it was discovered that the consumption of large quantities of fish from Minimata Bay in Japan was associated with a series of symptoms that have come to be known as Minimata disease. The symptoms include cerebral palsy (a disorder of the central nervous system), deformation of the skull, and sometimes an abnormally small head. The bay was polluted by mercury from waste discharged into the Minimata River from nearby industrial plants. The mercury passed in increasingly concentrated amounts through the food chain from the organisms eaten by fish to humans who ate the fish, including pregnant women

who then passed it on to their unborn babies. "Minimata disease" has since become synonymous with mercury poisoning (Tuchmann-Duplessis, 1975).

The incidence of birth defects is also known to be abnormally high in areas of heavy atmospheric pollution. In the Brazilian industrial city of Cubatão, for instance, the air pollution from petrochemical and steel plants alone exceeds that generated by all the combined industries in the Los Angeles basin of California. During the 1970s, 65 of every 1000 babies born in Cubatão died shortly after birth because their brains had failed to develop, double the rate of this defect in neighboring communities that were not so heavily polluted (Freed, 1983). Fortunately, strong environmental safety efforts have greatly reduced the pollution in Cubatão and the death rate of infants has declined remarkably (Brooke, 1991).

Atmospheric pollution in such U.S. cities as Los Angeles, Elizabeth (New Jersey), Chicago, and Denver is not so high as it used to be in Cubatão, but it is still high enough to cause concern about its effects on prenatal development. And what are the risks to pregnant women and their unborn children who live near chemical dumps? What should a pregnant woman do to minimize these risks? More research is necessary before such questions can be answered.

Principles of teratogenic effects

Although the effects of teratogens on the developing organism vary with the teratogen, several general principles apply to all of them (Hogge, 1990; Moore, 1982):

- *The susceptibility of a developing organism to a teratogenic agent varies with the developmental stage the organism is in at the time of exposure.* Overall, the gravest danger to life is during the first 2 weeks, before the cells of the organism have undergone extensive differentiation and before most women are even aware that they are pregnant (see Figure 3.13). During this critical period, a teratogenic agent may completely destroy the organism. Once the different body systems have begun to form, each is most vulnerable at the time of its initial growth spurt. As Figure 3.13 indicates, the most vulnerable period for the central nervous system is from 15 to 36 days, whereas the upper and lower limbs are most vulnerable from 24 to 49 days after conception.

- *Each teratogenic agent acts in a specific way on specific developing tissue and therefore causes a particular pattern of abnormal development.* Thalidomide, for example, causes deformation of the legs and arms, and mercury compounds cause brain damage that is manifested as cerebral palsy.

- *Not all organisms are affected in the same way by exposure to a given amount of a particular teratogen.* The way a developing organism responds to teratogenic agents depends to some degree on its genotype and the genotype of its mother. Fewer than one-quarter of the pregnant women who used thalidomide during the period when the organism's limbs were forming gave birth to malformed babies.

- *Susceptibility to teratogenic agents depends on the physiological state of the mother.* The mother's age, nutrition, uterine condition, and hormonal balance all affect the action of teratogens on the developing organism. The risk of malformation is highest when the mother is younger than 20 or older than 40. The precise reason is not known. Nutritional deficiency in the mother intensifies the adverse effects of some teratogens. The impact of teratogens also appears to increase if the mother suffers from diabetes, toxemia, a metabolic imbalance, or liver dysfunction, among other disorders.

Industrial pollution is a growing health hazard for children. These children have been playing in an industrial dump site.

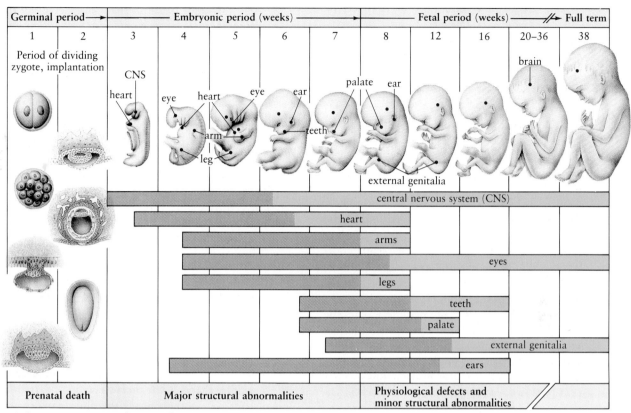

Germinal period→		Embryonic period (weeks) ————————→					Fetal period (weeks) ————→ // → Full term				

* Indicates common site of action of teratogen

FIGURE 3.13   *The critical periods in human prenatal development occur when the organs and other body parts are forming and therefore are most vulnerable to teratogens. Before implantation, teratogens either damage all or most of the cells of the organism, causing its death, or damage only a few cells, allowing the organism to recover without developing defects. The blue portions of the bars represent periods of highest risk of major structural abnormalities; the green portions of the bars represent periods of reduced sensitivity to teratogens. (Adapted from Moore, 1982.)*

- *In general, the greater the concentration of teratogenic agents to which the organism has been exposed, the greater the risk of abnormal development.*

- *Levels of teratogens that can produce defects in the developing organism may affect the mother only mildly or not at all.* Some diseases and drugs that have little or only a temporary effect on the mother can lead to serious abnormalities in the developing organism.

PRENATAL DEVELOPMENT RECONSIDERED

As we noted earlier, many developmental psychologists view the prenatal period as a model for all subsequent development because many of the principles that explain prenatal development also explain development after birth. Before we move on to birth and life outside the uterus, it is worthwhile to review these explanatory principles as they apply to the prenatal period.

- *Sequence is fundamental.* One cell must exist before there can be two. Muscles and bones must be present before nerves can coordinate movement. Gonads must secrete testosterone before further sexual differentiation can occur.
- *Timing is important.* If the ovum moves too rapidly or too slowly down the fallopian tube, pregnancy is terminated. If thalidomide is encountered after the first 3 months, the fetus is unlikely to be affected, but if it is encountered during the first 2 to 3 months of pregnancy, it may have a disastrous effect on the organism. The importance of timing implies the existence of critical periods for the formation of basic organ systems.
- *Development consists of differentiation and integration.* The single cell of the zygote becomes the many, apparently identical, cells of the morula. These cells then differentiate into two distinct kinds of cells, which later are integrated into a new configuration of cells called the blastocyst.
- *Development is characterized by stagelike changes.* Changes in the form of the organism and in the ways it interacts with its environment suggest a series of stagelike transformations. The embryo not only looks altogether different from the blastocyst but also interacts with its environment in a different way.
- *Development proceeds unevenly.* From the earliest steps of cleavage, the various subsystems that make up the organism develop at their own rates. An important special case of such unevenness is physical development that follows a cephalocaudal (from the head down) and proximodistal (from the center to the periphery) sequence.
- *Regressions appear to occur during the course of development.* Although development generally seems to progress through time, there are also periods of apparent regression. Regressions appear to reflect a process of reorganization, such as when fetal activity decreases as higher regions of the brain are beginning to become active.
- *Development is still a mystery.* The process by which the human organism develops from a single cell into a squalling newborn baby continues to mystify investigators. In one sense, the results of development are present at the beginning, coded in the genetic materials of the zygote, which con-

strain the kinds of forms that can emerge out of the interactions between the organism and its environment. In this sense, the preformationist hypothesis is valid. But in another sense, new forms are constantly emerging out of the organism-environment interactions that sustain and propel development. In this sense, the epigenetic hypothesis is confirmed.

BIRTH: THE FIRST BIO-SOCIAL-BEHAVIORAL SHIFT

Among all of life's transitions, birth is the most radical. Before birth, the amniotic fluid provides a wet, warm environment, and the fetus receives continuous oxygen and nourishment through the umbilical cord. By contrast, the environment that greets the newborn as it emerges from the womb is dry and cold. When the umbilical cord is cut and tied, the automatic supply of oxygen and nourishment is abruptly cut off. The lungs inflate to take in oxygen and exhale carbon dioxide for the first time, changing the pressure within the baby's circulatory system and causing the blood flow to reverse direction. Nourishment now comes only intermittently, and the baby must work for it by sucking. The baby no longer has the placenta to provide protection against disease-causing organisms.

The social and behavioral changes that occur at birth are no less pronounced than the biological ones, marking it as the first major bio-social-behavioral shift in human development. The newborn encounters other human beings directly for the first time, and the parents get their first glimpse of their child. From the moment of birth neonates and parents begin to construct a social relationship.

The Stages of Labor

The biological process of birth begins with a series of changes in the mother's body that force the fetus through the birth canal. It ends when the mother expels the placenta after the baby has emerged. Labor normally begins approximately 280 days after the first day of a woman's last menstrual period, or 266 days after conception. It is customarily divided into three overlapping stages (see Figure 3.14).

First stage of labor

Start of second stage

Cervix   Birth canal

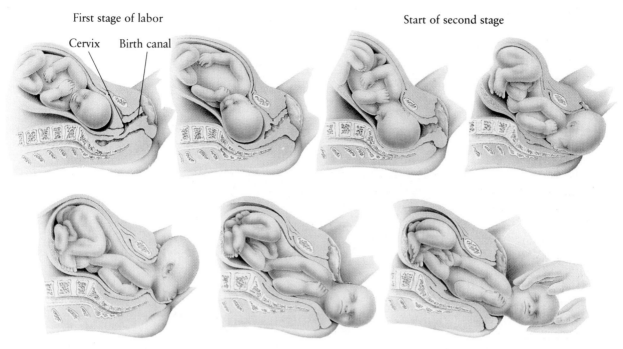

FIGURE 3.14   *During the first stage of labor, which usually lasts several hours, the cervix dilates. During the second stage, the birth canal widens, permitting the baby to emerge. The final stage (not shown) occurs when the placenta is delivered. (Adapted from Clarke-Stewart, 1983.)*

The *first stage of labor* lasts from the first regular, intense contractions of the uterus until the cervix, the opening of the uterus into the vagina, is fully dilated and the connections between the bones of the mother's pelvis become more flexible. The length of this stage varies from woman to woman and from pregnancy to pregnancy: it may last anywhere from less than an hour to several days. The norm for first births is about 14 hours (Niswander, 1981). At the beginning, the muscle contractions come 15 to 20 minutes apart and last anywhere from 15 to 60 seconds. As labor proceeds, the contractions become more frequent and more intense and are longer in duration.

Once the cervix is fully dilated, the baby's head, which is flexible because the bones of the skull have not yet fused, pushes through the cervix into the vagina, beginning the *second stage of labor*. The contractions now usually come no more than a minute apart and last about a minute. The pressure of the baby and the powerful contractions of the uterus typically cause the mother to bear down and push the baby out. Usually the top of the baby's head and the brow are the first to emerge. Occasionally, babies emerge in other

positions, the most common being the *breech position*, with the feet or buttocks emerging first.

The final, *third stage of labor* occurs as the baby is born. The uterus contracts around its diminished contents. The placenta buckles and separates from the uterine wall, pulling the other fetal membranes with it. Contractions quickly expel them, and they are delivered as the *afterbirth*.

Cultural Variations in Childbirth

As a biological process, labor occurs in roughly the same way everywhere. The *experience* of giving birth, however, varies with the traditions of the culture (see Figure 3.15). These traditions provide the mother and the community with a prescribed set of procedures to follow during birthing and a set of expectations about how they are going to feel (Kaye, 1982).

In a few societies, giving birth is treated as an unremarkable process, a routine part of a woman's life. Consider the following description of birth

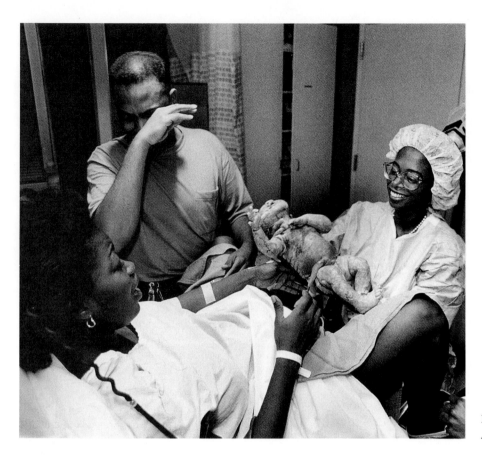

FIGURE 3.15
A new arrival.

among the !Kung, a hunting-and-gathering society in Africa's Kalahari desert:

> Mother's stomach grew very large. The first labor pains came at night and stayed with her until dawn. That morning, everyone went gathering. Mother and I stayed behind. We sat together for a while, then I went and played with the other children. Later, I came back and ate the nuts she had cracked for me. She got up and started to get ready. I said, "Mommy, let's go to the water well, I'm thirsty." She said, "Uhn, uhn, I'm going to gather some mongongo nuts." I told the children that I was going and we left; there were no other adults around. We walked a short way, then she sat down by the base of a large nehn tree, leaned back against it, and little Kumsa was born. (Shostak, 1981, pp. 53–54)

Such unassisted and unheralded birthing is relatively rare. It is far more common to find several peo-ple attending the mother during labor and delivery. Often a special house built outside the village is reserved for childbearing. Special practices, such as having the mother sit or lie in a particular posture as she gives birth or giving her herbal infusions to drink, are used to help her and her baby through the dangerous transition.

In many cultures, the specialists who assist the mother are called "doctors," although there is wide variation in what people believe "medicine" to be. The Onitsha Ibo of Nigeria regard childbirth as an illness. At the end of the third month, a woman places herself in the care of a traditional doctor and begins to take herbal medicines. Certain foods are prohibited and others (such as a soup made of leaves) are recommended (Henderson & Henderson, 1982).

The Ngoni women of East Africa consider themselves to be the childbirth experts, and men are totally excluded from the process. The women even conceal the fact that they are pregnant from their husbands as long as they can. "Men are little children. They are not able to hear those things which belong to pregnancy," the women claim (Read, 1960/1968:20). When a woman learns that her daughter-in-law's labor has begun, she and other female kin move into the woman's hut, banish the husband, and take charge of the preparations. They remove everything that belongs to the husband—clothes, tools, and weapons—and all household articles except old mats and pots to be used during labor. Men are not allowed back into the hut until after the baby is born.

Fifty years ago the Navajo of the southwestern United States treated childbirth as a social event, opening their homes to the whole community when a child was being born. An anthropologist who worked among them at the time reported that "anyone who comes and lends moral support is invited to stay and partake of what food is available" (quoted in Mead & Newton, 1967:171).

Childbirth in the United States

Most babies in the United States today are born in a hospital, a place where people go when they are sick. This emphasis on the medical aspects of childbirth represents a marked shift in cultural practices over the past century. In the nineteenth century, most births took place at home, attended only by a midwife, a woman recognized for her experience in assisting childbirth. By the middle of the twentieth century, 86 percent of all babies were born in hospitals and 95 percent were delivered by a physician (Gordon & Haire, 1981). Underlying this shift from home to hospital were two developments. First, many drugs were developed to relieve the pain of childbirth, and by law they could be administered only by physicians. Second, hospitals came to be better equipped to provide both antiseptic surroundings and specialized help to deal with any complications that might arise during labor and delivery (Cianfrani, 1960).

The lives of thousands of babies and mothers are saved each year by the intervention of doctors using modern drugs and special medical procedures (Figure 3.16). In 1915 approximately 100 of every 1000 babies died in their first year, and almost 7 of 1000 mothers died giving birth. By 1991, infant deaths had been reduced to less than 9 of every 1000 babies born (U.S. D.H.H.S., National Center for Health Statistics, 1992). In 1988, only 8.4 women out of every 100,000 who gave birth in the United States died of causes related to pregnancy, childbirth, or complications after the birth (U.S. Bureau of the Census, 1991). Un-

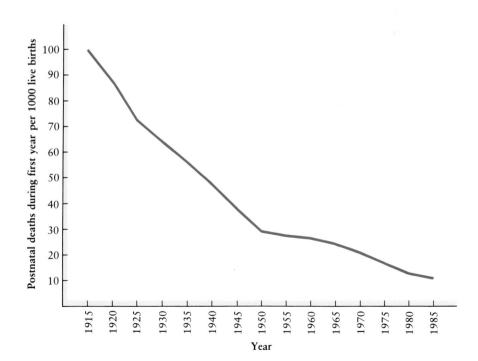

FIGURE 3.16 *During this century the death rate among children under 1 year of age has dropped dramatically in the United States.*

fortunately, the reduction in death rates has not been evenly spread through all segments of the population. While the mortality rate has declined significantly for both African American and white infants, African American infants are still twice as likely to die during the first year of life as white infants. Moreover, African American mothers are more than twice as likely to die in childbirth as white mothers (U.S. Bureau of the Census, 1991).

Despite the reductions in maternal and infant mortality, health-care professionals and parents alike have pointed to problems arising from medical intervention during normal, uncomplicated births (U.S. Congress, Senate Committee on Human Resources, 1978). These concerns center on two questions: (1) What is the safest method for dealing with pain during childbirth? (2) What precautions are necessary to ensure the health of the mother and the baby?

Childbirth pain and its medication

Many drugs have been used to lessen the pain of labor and delivery. They include anesthetics (which dull feeling), analgesics (which reduce the perception of pain), and sedatives (which reduce anxiety). No national data are available on the current use of drugs during childbirth, but a 1974 poll of 18 large teaching hospitals in the United States found that almost 95 percent of the births in those institutions took place under some form of medication (Brackbill, 1979).

Evidence has begun to mount that the drugs administered to the mother to control the pain of labor affect the baby when they pass through the placental barrier and enter the fetus's bloodstream (Abboud et al., 1982). These drugs tend to reduce the mother's oxygen intake; the resultant drop in her blood pressure in turn reduces the supply of oxygen to the fetus and may cause the baby to have difficulty breathing after birth. The baby's immature liver and kidneys are unable to rid the body of these drugs efficiently, so that some of them remain to lodge in the neonate's brain (Wilson, 1977).

Obstetric medications seldom threaten the lives of healthy, full-term babies. But those drugs that have been tested have been found to affect neonatal behavior. The babies of mothers who receive one or another of a variety of drugs during labor and delivery are less attentive and more irritable, have poorer muscle tone, and are weaker than those whose mothers receive no medication (Aleksandrowicz, 1974; Brackbill, 1979; Sepkowski, 1985). The vigor of the newborn infant's sucking response has also been found to be reduced by some obstetric drugs (Brazelton, 1973). As one might imagine, the extent of these effects varies with the drug, the dosage, and the stage of labor at which it is administered (Brackbill, McManus, & Woodward, 1985; Lester, Als, & Brazelton, 1982).

The evidence that obstetric drugs affect the neonate has caused concern that they may have long-term effects on the child's development. Yvonne Brackbill and her colleagues claim, for example, that the heavy use of drugs during birth is implicated in a high incidence of learning disorders among U.S. schoolchildren (Brackbill, McManus, & Woodward, 1985). Most of the existing evidence indicates, however, that low levels of medication do not significantly affect healthy babies. It is only when substantial levels of medication are used in births of babies who are at risk for other reasons that medication may have longer-term effects (Brazelton, Nugent, & Lester, 1987). Because of their concern about the possible adverse effects of drugs on the neonate, many women in the United States and Western Europe are turning to alternative methods of controlling the pain of labor. All of these methods include educational classes that give the expectant mother an idea of what to expect during labor and delivery and teach her relaxation and breathing exercises to help counteract pain. They all recommend that the woman in labor not be left alone. Someone — her husband, a sympathetic friend, or a midwife — should be constantly at her side to provide comfort and emotional support.

Medical interventions during childbirth

In addition to administering drugs to ease the pain of labor, doctors may use medical procedures to safeguard the lives of mother and child. When the baby is significantly overdue or when the mother is confronted with some life-threatening situation, physicians commonly induce labor, either by rupturing the membranes of the placenta or by giving the mother some form of the hormone oxytocin. Another commonly used procedure is the cesarean section, or surgical removal of the baby from the mother's uterus. This procedure is typically used in cases of difficult labor, when the baby is in distress during delivery, or when the baby is not in the headfirst position. The number of cesarean sections performed rose significantly during the 1970s. By 1988, more than 24 percent of all births in the United States were by cesarean section (U.S. Bureau of the Census, 1991).

Although modern medical techniques have made childbirth a great deal safer than it was in the past, some medical personnel claim that they are used more often than they should be (U.S. Congress, Senate Committee on Human Resources, 1978). These critics argue that many of the cesarean operations performed in the United States not only are unnecessary but raise the cost of childbirth, expose the mother to the risk of postoperative infection, and cause mothers to be separated from their infants while they heal from surgery. They may also be detrimental to the babies' well-being (see Box 3.3). Concerns about unnecessary medical intervention also extend to other procedures, such as induced labor and the electronic monitoring of the vital signs of the fetus during labor (Pernoll, Benda, & Babson, 1986).

In part because of such concerns, about 1 percent of U.S. women choose to have their babies at home. Although some of these home births are attended by physicians, most are overseen by certified nurse-midwives, who are specially trained to deal with childbirth. The mortality rate for such births is very low when the mothers have had good prenatal care and are healthy, the births are uncomplicated, and a well-trained medical professional is present (Schramm, Barnes, & Blakwell, 1987). But home births are not recommended for mothers who are at risk for complications of any kind.

BOX 3.3
The Baby's Experience of Birth

What is birth like for the baby? For several hours the fetus is squeezed through the birth canal, where it is subjected to considerable pressure and occasionally is deprived of oxygen. Finally the newborn infant is delivered from the warm, dark shelter of the womb into a cold, bright hospital room. It is difficult to imagine this experience as anything but traumatic.

The psychiatrist Otto Rank (1929), one of Sigmund Freud's first and most valued students, believed that the birth trauma is the cardinal source of neurotic anxiety in the adult, and that he could eliminate this problem by getting his patients to analyze and thereby overcome this "primal trauma." Freud (1937/1953) had reservations about this aspect of his former student's work. "Rank's argument was bold and ingenious," Freud wrote, "but it did not stand the test of critical examination" (p. 316). Although Freud's judgment has generally been sustained (Pratt, 1954), concern continues over the possible long-term effects of the traumatic birth experience.

Modern research on the experience of birth has focused on the biological mechanisms that equip the baby to cope with the stress involved. Hugo Lagercrantz and Theodore Slotkin (1986) have suggested that as the birth process begins, a surge in the fetus's production of adrenaline and other "stress" hormones protects it from the adverse conditions—the pressure on the head and the deprivation of oxygen—it experiences. They go on to suggest that the events that cause the production of stress hormones are of vital importance because these hormones prepare the infant to survive outside the womb.

In support of their hypothesis, Lagercrantz and Slotkin point out that infants delivered by cesarean section often have difficulty breathing. They believe that the procedure deprives babies of the experiences that produce high levels of adrenaline and other hormones in the hours before birth, hormones that facilitate the absorption of liquid from the lungs and the production of surfactin, which allow the lungs to function well. In addition, the hormones appear to produce an increase in the newborn's metabolic rate, which mobilizes readily usable fuel to nourish cells.

Lagercrantz and Slotkin also believe that the stress hormones are instrumental in increasing blood flow to such vital organs as the heart, lungs, and brain and thus increase the chances of survival of a baby who is experiencing breathing difficulties. Furthermore, these researchers speculate that the hormonal surge during the birth process puts the newborn in a state of alertness, which facilitates the attachment between mother and infant during its first hour of life.

THE NEWBORN'S CONDITION

To first-time parents, especially those who imagine that newborn infants look like those pictured on jars of baby food, the real neonate may cause alarm and disappointment. The baby's head is large in proportion to the rest of the body, and the limbs are relatively small and tightly flexed. Unless the baby has been delivered by cesarean section, the head may look misshapen after its tight squeeze through the birth canal. (The head usually regains its symmetry by the end of the first week after birth.) The baby's skin may be covered with vernix caseosa, a white, cheesy substance that protects it against bacterial infections, and it may be spotted with blood.

Medical personnel, accustomed to the way newborns look, are not distracted by the baby's temporarily unattractive appearance. They check the neonate for indications of danger so that immediate action can be taken if something is wrong. They take note of the size of the baby, check its vital signs, and look for evidence of normal capacities.

In the United States, neonates weigh an average of 3200 to 3400 grams (7 to 7½ pounds), although babies weighing anywhere from 5½ to 10 pounds are considered to fall in the normal range. During their first days of life, most babies lose about 7 percent of their initial weight, primarily because of loss of fluid. They usually gain the weight back by the time they are 10 days old.

The average neonate is 20 inches long. To a large extent, the length of the newborn is determined by the size of the mother's uterus. It does not reflect the baby's genetic inheritance, because the genes that control height do not begin to express themselves until shortly after birth (Tanner, 1978).

Assessing the Baby's Viability

A variety of scales and tests are used to assess the neonate's physical state and behavioral condition. The basic procedure in constructing such instruments is first to identify the characteristics that are essential to the newborn's immediate well-being and normal development. Ratings are then collected from a large number of infants to establish norms for comparison. These norms are then used to assess the relative condition of individual babies.

Physical state

In the 1950s Virginia Apgar (1953), an anesthesiologist who worked in the delivery room of a large metropolitan hospital, developed a quick and simple method of diagnosing the physical state of a newborn. The **Apgar Scale** is now widely used throughout the United States to determine if a baby requires emergency care.

The Apgar Scale is used to rate babies 1 minute after birth and again 5 minutes later on five vital signs: heart rate, respiratory effort, muscle tone, reflex responsivity, and color. Table 3.6 shows the criteria for scoring each of the signs. The individual scores are totaled to give a measure of the baby's overall physical condition. A baby with a score of less than 4 is considered to be in poor condition and to require immediate medical attention.

Behavioral condition

During the past half century, many scales have been constructed to assess the more subtle behavioral aspects of the newborn's condition (Brazelton, 1973, 1978; Gesell & Amatruda, 1947; Graham, Matarazzo, & Caldwell, 1956). One of the most widely used is the **Brazelton Neonatal Assessment Scale,** developed by the pediatrician T. Berry Brazelton and his colleagues. A major purpose of this scale is to assess the newborn's neurological condition after the stress of labor and delivery. It is also used to assess the progress of premature infants, to compare the functioning of newborns from different cultures, and to evaluate the effectiveness of interventions designed to alleviate developmental difficulties (Brazelton, Nugent, & Lester, 1987).

Included in the Brazelton scale are tests of infants' reflexes, motor capacities, muscle tone, capacity for responding to objects and people, and capacity to control their own behavior and attention. The only equipment the tests require are a rattle, a bell, a flashlight, a pin, and a cloth. When scoring a newborn on such tests, the examiner must take note of the degree of the infant's alertness and, if necessary, repeat the tests when the baby is wide awake and calm. Here are some typical items on the Brazelton scale:

Orientation to animate objects — visual and auditory:
   The examiner calls the baby's name repeatedly in a high-pitched voice while moving his head up and down and from side to side. Does the baby focus on the examiner? Does she follow the examiner with her eyes smoothly?

TABLE 3.6

The Apgar Scoring System

Vital Sign	Rating		
	0	1	2
Heart rate	Absent	Slow (below 100)	Over 100
Respiratory effort	Absent	Slow, irregular	Good, crying
Muscle tone	Flaccid	Some flexion of extremities	Active motion
Reflex responsivity	No response	Grimace	Vigorous cry
Color	Blue, pale	Body pink, extremities blue	Completely pink

Source: Apgar, 1953.

Pull-to-sit: The examiner puts a forefinger in each of the infant's palms and pulls him to a sitting position. Does the baby try to right his head when he is in a seated position? How well is he able to do so?

Cuddliness: The examiner holds the baby against her chest or up against her shoulder. How does the baby respond? Does she resist being held? Is she passive or does she cuddle up to the examiner?

Defensive movements: The examiner places a cloth over the baby's face and holds it there. Does the baby try to remove the cloth from his face either by turning his head away or by swiping at it?

Self-quieting activity: The examiner notes what the baby does to quiet herself when she is fussy. Does she suck her thumb, look around?

A lively controversy has developed about the usefulness of scales such as Brazelton's (Brazelton, Nugent, & Lester, 1987; Francis, Self, & Horowitz, 1987). Most of these scales are designed with two purposes in mind: (1) to screen for infants at risk and (2) to predict newborns' future development. Research over the past decade shows that they are satisfactory guides for determining when medical intervention is necessary (Francis, Self, & Horowitz, 1987). For predicting later development, however, they appear to be useful only when the newborn is tested repeatedly during the early days and weeks of life so that the

baby's early developmental progress can be estimated reliably (Brazelton, Nugent, & Lester, 1987). Even then, the predictions are not always accurate.

Problems and Complications

Though most babies are born without any serious problems, some are in such poor physical condition that they soon die. Others are at risk for later developmental problems, sometimes fatal ones. Newborns are considered to be at risk if they suffer from any of a variety of problems, including asphyxiation or head injury during delivery (either of which may result in brain damage), acute difficulty breathing after birth, or difficulty digesting food owing to an immature digestive system (Korner, 1987). These are the kinds of problems that are likely to result in low scores on the Apgar Scale. Most of the newborns who are at risk are premature, abnormally underweight, or both (Kopp, 1983; Korner, 1987; Pernoll, Benda, & Babson, 1986).

Prematurity

The time that has passed between conception and birth is known as the baby's gestational age. The normal gestational age is 37 to 43 weeks. Babies born before the thirty-seventh week are considered to be **premature,** or preterm. In the United States, 10 percent of all births are premature (Pernoll, Benda, & Babson, 1986). Disorders related to premature birth

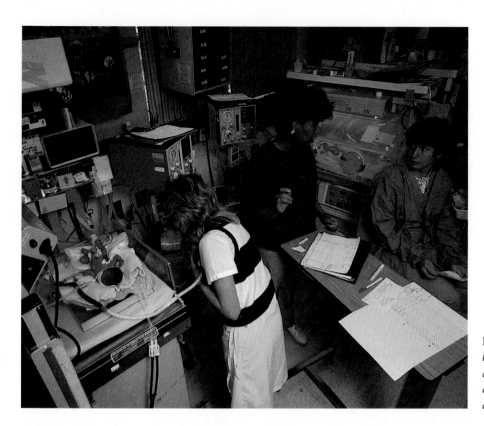

FIGURE 3.17 *Babies born prematurely may require intensive care in an incubator to sustain their early development.*

are the fourth leading cause of infant mortality. With the expert care now available in modern hospitals, mortality rates for premature infants are declining (see Figure 3.17). Eighty percent of those who weigh more than 1020 grams (2¹/₄ pounds) now survive.

The leading cause of death among preterm infants is the functional immaturity of their lungs (Evans & Glass, 1976). The other main obstacle to the survival of preterm infants is immaturity of their digestive and immune systems. Even babies of normal gestational age sometimes have difficulty coordinating sucking, swallowing, and breathing in the first few days after birth. These difficulties are likely to be more serious for preterm infants. Their coordination may be so poor that they cannot be fed directly from breast or bottle, so that special equipment must be used to feed them. Moreover, their immature digestive systems often cannot handle normal baby formulas, so special formulas must be made.

A few of the factors that can lead to prematurity have been identified. Twins are likely to be born about 3 weeks early, triplets and quadruplets even earlier.

Very young women whose reproductive systems are immature and women who have had many pregnancies close together are more likely to have premature babies. So are women who smoke, who are in poor health, or who have intrauterine infections. The chances of giving birth to a premature infant also vary with socioeconomic status (Goldberg & DiVitto, 1983; Pernoll, Benda, & Babson, 1986). Poor women are twice as likely to give birth to small or preterm infants as are women who are more affluent. This disparity can be explained by the fact that poor women are more likely to be undernourished or chronically ill, to have inadequate health care before and during pregnancy, to suffer from infections, and to experience complications during pregnancy.

Many of the causes of prematurity, however, are still not well understood. At least half of all premature births are not associated with any of the identified risk factors. These premature babies are born after otherwise normal pregnancies to healthy women who are in their prime childbearing years and have had good medical care (Goldberg & DiVitto, 1983).

Low birth weight

Premature babies tend to be small, but not all small babies are premature. Babies are considered to have a **low birth weight** if they weigh 2500 grams or less, whether or not they are premature. Newborns whose birth weights are especially low for their gestational age are said to suffer from **fetal growth retardation;** in other words, they have not grown at the normal rate. Multiple births, intrauterine infections, chromosomal abnormalities, maternal smoking or use of narcotics, maternal malnutrition, and abnormalities of the placenta or umbilical cord have all been identified as probable causes of fetal growth retardation (Cunningham, MacDonald, & Gant, 1989).

Developmental consequences

Intensive research has been conducted on the developmental consequences of prematurity and low birth weight (Goldberg & DiVitto, 1983; Kopp & Krakow, 1983). Although premature and low-birth-weight babies are at risk for later developmental problems, they differ in the probable course of development.

Low birth weight increases the risk of developmental difficulty whether the baby is premature or full-term. The smaller the baby, the more likely some sort of congenital abnormality, such as neurological impairment or a permanent impairment of growth potential (Pernoll, Benda, & Babson, 1986). Small babies are also more likely to die in the first year of life than are infants of the same gestational age who are of normal size (Congressional Research Service, 1983).

Many premature babies catch up with full-term babies during infancy, but some do not (Cohen & Parmelee, 1983). Two factors appear to be important in determining what happens to a premature baby in the long run: (1) whether the premature infant also suffers from some form of medical difficulty and (2) what environmental conditions greet the infant after birth. Premature babies who are of normal size for their gestational age are the most likely to catch up with full-term babies. It is those who also are low in birth weight and have medical complications who are most at risk for future developmental difficulties (Goldberg & DiVitto, 1983). Among premature babies who are particularly light for their gestational age, those who have very small heads at birth and whose heads grow slowly during the first 6 weeks of postnatal life are especially likely to suffer long-term developmental problems (Eckerman, Sturm, & Gross, 1985).

Among the factors that determine the effects of prematurity is the way the parents react to their premature baby. Premature babies look tiny and fragile, and they are less responsive and more irritable than full-term infants (Brazelton, Nugent, & Lester, 1987). These characteristics may make it more difficult for parents initially to become attached to them. Furthermore, many premature infants spend their first few weeks in the hospital in heated isolettes that maintain their body temperature and protect them from infection. Although their parents are encouraged to visit their babies often and to establish emotional ties with them, these visits are just that, visits, and then the parents go home and leave the babies alone.

Once the mothers are able to take their premature infants home, however, they tend to spend more time with their babies than do mothers of full-term infants. Although the evidence is somewhat contradictory, it currently appears that for the first year or so of life, premature babies develop more slowly than full-term babies. Keith Crnic and his colleagues (1983), for example, reported that low-birth-weight premature newborns lagged behind a comparison group of full-term babies. In explaining this finding they report that mothers and their premature babies had difficulty maintaining eye contact with each other. The mothers also seemed to have difficulty finding an appropriate level of stimulation for their premature infants, who were either overexcited or bored by their mothers' attempts to engage them. When Crnic and Mark Greenberg studied the same children a year later, however, they found that most of the differences between the two groups had disappeared (Greenberg & Crnic, 1988). Many of the mothers of the premature babies had developed especially positive attitudes toward their roles as parents and toward their babies. The researchers suggest that these positive attitudes helped the mothers to create more favorable contexts for their babies, which in turn helped to compensate for the babies' vulnerability.

The importance of a supportive environment in overcoming the potential risks of prematurity is underscored by research on the social ecology of the families of premature and low-birth-weight infants. Babies who are raised in comfortable socioeconomic circumstances with an intact family and a mother who has had a good education are less likely to suffer negative effects from their condition at birth than are children who are raised without these benefits (Sameroff & Chandler, 1975; Sigman & Parmelee, 1979).

BEGINNING THE PARENT-CHILD RELATIONSHIP

Once the crisis of birth is past, parents can turn their attention to the baby's future. Because human infants are helpless in many basic respects and their very survival depends on the active support and protection of their caretakers, the development of a close relationship between infants and their parents is crucial to infants' well-being. Unfortunately, love between parent and child is neither inevitable nor automatic. The large numbers of infants who are neglected, abused, abandoned, even murdered the world over each year should convince even the most sentimental and optimistic observer of this harsh fact. In 1987, for example, more than 2 million cases of child neglect and abuse were reported to local authorities in the United States (U.S. Bureau of the Census, 1990), and many knowledgeable people believe that the majority of cases are never reported.

Yet most parents love their babies. How, then, is the bond between parent and child formed? When no strong attachment develops, what goes wrong? These are large questions that we will encounter again and again in subsequent chapters because a close parent-child relationship is not formed in an instant; it develops over many years. Here we will examine the factors that come into play immediately after birth and set the stage for the future: the initial reactions of the parents to their baby's appearance, the first hours of contact between parent and infant, and the expectations parents have for their babies.

The Baby's Appearance

In their search for the sources of love between mother and infant, some psychologists have turned to *ethology* — the study of animal behavior and its evolutionary bases. These psychologists believe that examination of the factors that cause nonhuman mothers to protect or reject their young can shed light on the factors that influence human mothers. One important factor that seems to influence animals' responses to their young is their offspring's appearance. Konrad Lorenz (1943), a German ethologist, noted that the newborns of many animal species have physical characteristics that distinguish them from the mature ani-

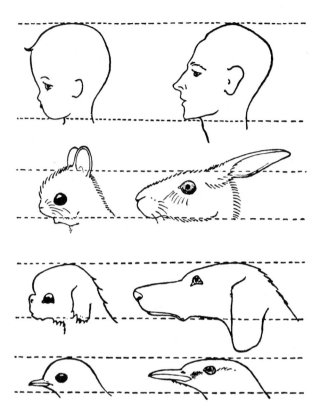

FIGURE 3.18   *The shapes of the heads of infants and adults of four species make clear the distinguishing features of "babyness." (From Lorenz, 1943.)*

mal: a head that is large in relation to the body, a prominent forehead, large eyes that are positioned below the horizontal midline of the face, and round, full cheeks (see Figure 3.18). This combination of features, which Lorenz called **babyness,** seems to appeal to adults and, more significant, to evoke caregiving behaviors in them.

Evidence in support of Lorenz's hypothesis comes from a study by William Fullard and Ann Rieling (1976). These researchers asked people ranging in age from 7 years to young adulthood which of matched pairs of pictures, one depicting an adult and the other depicting an infant, they preferred. Some of the pictures were of human beings; others were of animals. They found that adults, especially women, were most likely to choose the pictures of infants. Children between the ages of 7 and 12 preferred the pictures of adults. Between the ages of 12 and 14, the preference of girls shifted quite markedly from adults to children.

A similar shift was found among boys when they were between 14 and 16. These shifts in preference coincide with the average ages at which girls and boys undergo the physiological changes that make them capable of reproducing.

Patterned responses to the appearance of infants may explain why mothers find it difficult to care for malformed offspring. Mothers of dogs, cats, guinea pigs, and some other species will kill malformed offspring. While human parents usually do not kill their malformed babies, they do interact more frequently and more lovingly with infants they consider attractive than with those they consider homely (Parke & Sawin, 1975; Langlois, 1986). They also attribute greater competence to attractive babies (Stephan & Langlois, 1984). This pattern is particularly noticeable when the baby is a girl. While still in the hospital with their newborn girls, mothers of less attractive babies directed their attention to people other than their babies more often than those whose babies were attractive (Langlois, 1986).

Early Parent-Infant Contact

Further evidence of biological influences on the establishment of the relationship between parents and infants comes from studies of animal species that require early contact between mother and offspring for the formation of an emotional bond between them. If a baby goat is removed from its mother immediately after birth and returned 2 hours later, for instance, the mother will attack it. But if the baby goat is allowed to stay with its mother for as little as 5 minutes after its birth before it is removed for a few hours, the mother will welcome its return (Klopfer, Adams, & Klopfer, 1964).

Marshall Klaus, John Kennell, and their co-workers (1970) claim that there is a similar sensitive period for the bonding of human mothers and their babies. These researchers divided 28 first-time mothers into an experimental and a control group. The mothers in the control group had the amount of contact with their newborn infants that was traditional in many hospitals in the late 1960s: a glimpse of the baby shortly after its birth, brief contact with it between 6 and 12 hours later, and then 20- to 30-minute visits for bottle feedings every 4 hours. In between these periods, the baby remained in the nursery. The

mothers in the experimental group were given their babies to hold for 1 hour within the first 3 hours after delivery. The babies were undressed so that their mothers could touch them. In addition, the mother and child spent 5 hours together each afternoon for the 3 days after delivery. Many of the mothers reported that, although they were already excited by being able to fondle their infants immediately after birth, their excitement rose higher when they succeeded in achieving eye contact with them.

When the mothers and babies in both groups returned to the hospital 1 month later, the mothers in the experimental group were more reluctant to leave their infants with other caretakers. They also seemed more interested in the examination of their infants, were better at soothing them, and seemed to gaze at and fondle their babies more than did the mothers in the control group. Eleven months later the extended-contact mothers still seemed more attentive to their babies and more responsive to their cries than were the mothers in the control group (Kennell et al., 1974).

Drawing an analogy with animal behavior, Klaus and John Kennell (1976) suggest that if a mother and child are allowed to be in close physical contact immediately after birth, "complex interactions between mother and infant help to lock them together" (p. 51). The researchers speculate that hormones generated by the mother's body during the birth process may make her more ready to form an emotional bond with her baby. If these hormones dissipate before the mother has any extended contact with her newborn, presumably she will be less responsive to it (Kennell, Voos, & Klaus, 1979).

These findings received a good deal of attention and prompted doctors and nurses at many hospitals to encourage mothers to have prolonged contact with their newborn babies. They also provoked a lot of criticism. Klaus and Kennell were attacked on methodological grounds because their experimental and control groups were quite small (there were only 14 mothers in each) and composed entirely of unmarried African American women with low incomes, who could not, critics claimed, be considered representative of mothers in general. Furthermore, the mothers in the experimental group were probably aware of the special treatment they received, and some critics suggested that this awareness, rather than the extended contact with their babies, may have been the source of their behavior. In the years since the study was conducted, some follow-up studies have replicated Klaus

BOX 3.4
The Parents' Response to the Baby's Arrival

Aidan Macfarlane, an English pediatrician, recorded the following conversation in a delivery room as Mrs. B., age 27, gave birth to her first child. The concern it reveals about the baby's physical soundness is all but universal, and so is the power of the culture's belief system to shape the parents' initial responses to their newborn child.

Doctor: Come on, junior. Only a lady could cause so much trouble. Come on, little one.

[A baby is delivered]

Mother: A girl.

 D: Well, it's got the right plumbing.

 M: Oh, I'm sorry, darling.

Father: *[laughs]*

 D: What are you sorry about?

 M: He wanted a boy.

 D: Well, you'll have to try again next week, won't you!

 M: *[laughs]*

 D: She looks great. Want to see her? Bloody and messy, but that's not from her.

 M: Oh, she's gorgeous.

 F: Looks like you.

[Mother kisses father]

 M: Is she all right?

 D: Why don't you ask her? She's quite capable of letting you know how she feels about the situation.

 M: She's noisy, isn't she?

 D: Yes, just like the modern generation.

 F: Yes.

 M: Well, Dr. Murphy, I was right. I had a sneaky feeling it was a girl, just because I wanted a boy.

 F: Well, it will suit your mum, won't it?

 M: *[laughs]*

 D: Often tactically best to have a girl first—she can help with the washing up.

[Baby given to mother]

 M: Hello, darling. Meet your dad. You're just like your dad. *[Baby yells.]*

 F: I'm going home!

 M: Oh you've gone quiet. *[laughs]* Oh darling, she's just like you—she's got your little tiny nose.

 F: It'll grow like yours.

 M: She's big, isn't she? What do you reckon?

 D: She's quite gook-looking, despite forcep marks on her head—but don't worry about that. She'll have little bruises around her ears—well they usually have. I don't know if she does.

 M: There's one—there. . . . Oh look, she's got hair. It's a girl—you're supposed to be all little.

 D: What do you think she weighs, Richard? I think about seven and a half.

 M: Oh, she's gorgeous, she's lovely. She's got blue eyes. You hold her. Come on.

 F: No.

 M: Why not? *[laughs]* You're all of a tremble, aren't you?

 D: I dropped the first one I held.

 F: Charming!

 M: Oh look, oh mine. Hello darling. Good lungs, hasn't she? She's got a dimple—where'd she get that from?

 D: That's probably from the forceps. Actually, have you got dimples?

 M: Oh no, neither of us have. Oh, you're lovely. Look . . . she's lovely.

 M: I thought she'd be all mauve and crinkly.

 D: Oh, she's in great nick.

 M: Yes. I was expecting her to be all mauve and shriveled, but she's not, is she?

 D: Not at all. In front of the cameras she's a real lady.

 M: Oh dear. Having your photo taken, darling? Oh.

 D: Ma'am, can I ask you to drop your ankles apart?

 M: She doesn't go much on this.

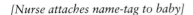

[Nurse attaches name-tag to baby]

F: Like British Rail, labeling her like a parcel.

M: Oh look, darling, look at the size of her feet. She's got no toenails.

D: What do you mean, she hasn't got any toenails?

M: She hasn't got any toenails.

M: They're soft.

D: I don't think you'd like it scratching around inside you.

M: Look—fabulous. Aren't you pleased with her.

F: Yes, of course.

D: I'm not putting her back.

M: You said that if it was a girl it could go back.

D: Back to the manufacturers, yes.

M: Well, it came from him in the first place.

D: It's his spermatozoa that decides the sex.

M: Quite. *[kisses the baby and laughs]*

F: I shall be worried to death when she's eighteen.

M: You'll imagine her going out with all sorts of blokes like you were. *[laughs]* In a sort of odd way I was after his money really.

D: Yes?

M: All two quid. Go, go to dad.

(Macfarlane, 1977:61–67)

Mr. and Mrs. B. are not the only parents who find they must quickly change their plans and make a virtue out of having a daughter instead of a son. In the United States, it is a fairly common occurrence. According to one survey, 80 percent of all Americans want their first child to be a son, and two-thirds of the women polled said that if they were to have only one child, they preferred that child to be a boy (Sanderson, 1982). Despite their initial hopes and expectations, most parents eventually accept the sex of their newborns.

and Kennell's findings, but others have failed to discover any long-lasting, significant differences between the mother-child relationships of experimental and control groups (Chess & Thomas, 1982; de Chateau, 1987; Lamb & Hwang, 1982).

Most researchers today agree that immediate contact is not crucial for the establishment of a long-term, positive emotional relationship between human mothers and normal infants. Parents who do not have immediate contact with their infants for whatever reasons almost always manage eventually to establish emotional ties to them. Most mothers who are anesthetized during delivery or suffer complications and who therefore do not see their babies for several hours or even days after their birth do not reject them; nor do mothers whose babies must be kept in incubators or fathers who are not present for their children's birth. In short, the great majority of mothers and fathers form attachments to their babies under all sorts of circumstances (de Chateau, 1987, and Lamb & Hwang, 1982, review the evidence).

Social Expectations

When a baby is born among the Ngoni of East Africa, the mother-in-law announces its arrival by proclaiming, "A stranger has come!" In a sense, all newborn babies are strangers; they are newcomers no one has seen before. In important ways, however, babies are not total strangers.

While the mother is pregnant, most parents develop specific expectations about what their baby will be like. This is one reason the disappointment and grief parents feel if the baby dies or is deformed can be so devastating. But in normal circumstances, no sooner does a baby emerge from the womb than the parents begin to examine its looks and behaviors for hints of its future. Will she have Grandmother Cameron's high, round forehead? Does his lusty cry mean that he will have his father's quick temper? Naturally, the baby will differ in some respects from the baby the parents' have been imagining. Usually, though, the parents begin to accommodate themselves to the reality of their child at the moment of its birth. According to Aidan Macfarlane (1977), accommodation to the actual sex of the child when the other sex was wanted is one of the adjustments parents most frequently have to make. The initial stages of such an adjustment can be seen in Box 3.4. Many people today find the attitudes displayed in this dialogue offensive, but they are very common. When our own first child was born, the nurse expressed her regret as if to console us for having a daughter.

Whether the baby is a boy or a girl, the parents' beliefs and expectations begin to shape their responses to the baby even before the child displays any truly distinctive features. In one study, for example, first-time mothers and fathers were asked to choose words that described their newborn babies within 24 hours after their birth (Rubin, Provezano, & Luria, 1974). The babies did not differ in birth length or weight or in their scores on the Apgar Scale. Nevertheless, the parents described their daughters as "little," "beautiful," "pretty," or "cute" and as resembling their mothers, whereas they described their sons as "big" and as resembling their fathers. Fathers, the researchers found, were more likely than mothers to sex-type their babies.

There is every reason for their baby's sex to be important to the parents. Children's sex determines what they are named, how they are dressed, how they are treated, and what will be expected of them. Characterizing their baby according to its sex is one important way for parents to gain a sense of the child as a unique individual who belongs to them.

There is a disconcerting side to this process, too. We like to think of ourselves as individuals, and we want to be treated with an awareness of who we are, not of what others expect us to be. It therefore comes as something of a shock to learn that so many important aspects of our future are shaped so early by our parents' expectations. But unless these expectations are held so rigidly that they become destructive, they do not represent a failing on the parents' part.

Parents' responses to their newborns reflect the fact that human infants are not just biological organisms but cultural entities as well. For their parents and for other members of the community, infants have special meanings that are shaped by the culture's ideas about people and about the events that infants are likely to encounter as they grow to adulthood. These meanings in turn shape the ways adults construct the environmental contexts within which children develop. A consistent difference has been found, for example, in the way boys and girls are treated—not just because parents think that infant boys and girls are different to begin with, but more important, because they believe that men and women have different roles to play (Sigel, 1985).

This orientation to the future is expressed in clear symbolic form by the Zincantecos of south-central Mexico (Greenfield, Brazelton, and Childs, 1989). When a son is born he is given a digging stick, an ax, and a strip of palm used in weaving mats, in expectation of his adult role. Newborn girls are given a set of objects associated with the adult female role. Such future orientation is not only present in ritual; it is coded in a Zincantecan saying: "For in the newborn baby is the future of our world."

Organization of the present in terms of the future is a fundamental cultural source of developmental change and a powerful environmental source of developmental continuity. As the anthropologist Leslie White (1949) wrote, only among humans does the world of ideas come "to have a continuity and permanence that the external world of the senses can never have. It is not made up of the present only, but of a past and a future as well" (p. 372).

Just as infants arrive at childbirth with a set of genetically built-in capacities to learn about and to act upon the world, parents arrive at this moment with their own tendencies to respond in certain ways that have developed through their experience as members of their culture. The relationship between child and parents that begins at birth is an essential part of the foundation on which later development builds.

SUMMARY

1. Many developmental theorists look upon the prenatal period as a model for all periods of development from conception to death.

2. Prenatal development is often divided into three broad periods:
   a. The germinal period, when the zygote moves into the uterus and becomes implanted there.
   b. The period of the embryo, which begins with implantation and ends with the first signs of ossification at the end of the eighth week. During this period the basic organs are formed.
   c. The period of the fetus, during which the brain grows extensively and the separate organ systems become integrated.

3. As the organism grows from a single cell to a full-term newborn child, new forms constantly emerge. The preformationist hypothesis holds that all forms are already present in the organism's first cells. According to the epigenetic hypothesis, interactions between the cells and their environment generate the new forms.

4. At implantation, the organism becomes directly dependent on the mother's body for sustenance.

5. The embryo becomes active with the first pulses of a primitive heart, beginning about 1 month after conception.

6. The fetus is subject to environmental influences originating from outside as well as inside the mother. The fetus sometimes experiences outside influences directly through its own sensory mechanisms, but often such influences work indirectly, through their effects on the mother.

7. Babies' reactions to events they first experienced in the womb seem to indicate that fetuses are capable of learning.

8. The mother's reactions to her environment — her feelings and attitudes — are associated with the fetus's well-being. Children born to mothers who do not want them or who are under stress are subject to developmental risk.

9. The nutritional status of the mother is an important factor in fetal development. Extreme malnutrition in the mother has a devastating effect on her ability to produce a normal child. Lesser degrees of malnourishment associated with other forms of environmental deprivation also increase the risks to fetal and postnatal development.

10. Teratogens (environmental agents that can cause deviations in fetal development) take many forms. Drugs, infections, radiation, and pollution all pose threats to the developing organism.

11. Several basic principles apply to the effects of teratogens:
    a. The susceptibility of the organism depends on the stage of its development.
    b. A teratogen's effects are likely to be specific to a particular organ.
    c. Individual organisms vary in their susceptibility to teratogens.
    d. The physiological state of the mother influences the impact of a teratogen.
    e. The greater the concentration of a teratogenic agent, the greater the risk.
    f. Teratogens that adversely affect the developing organism may affect the mother little or not at all.

12. Birth is the first bio-social-behavioral shift in human development.

13. The process of birth begins approximately 266 days after conception, when changes in the mother's body force the fetus through the birth canal.

14. Labor proceeds through three stages. It begins with the first regular, intense contractions of the uterus, and it ends when the baby is born, the umbilical cord is severed, and the afterbirth is delivered. Although the biological process of labor is roughly the same everywhere, there are marked cultural variations in the organization of childbearing.

15. A possible negative outcome of the use of pain-reducing drugs is their impact on the neonate.

16. The infant's physical state at birth is usually assessed by the Apgar Scale, which rates the infant's heart rate, respiratory effort, reflex responsivity, muscle tone, and color. Babies with low Apgar scores require immediate medical attention if they are to survive.

17. Scales have been developed to assess the neonate's behavioral capacities. These scales are satisfactory for identifying neonates who require medical intervention; they appear to be modestly useful, at best, for predicting later patterns of development.

18. Many premature babies who are of normal size for their gestational age can catch up with full-term infants if they are well cared for. Those who have low birth weights and small heads are especially at risk for long-term developmental problems.

19. A newborn's appearance plays a significant role in the parents' responses to it.

20. Some investigators believe that there is a critical period for emotional bonding between mothers and their infants shortly after birth. Attempts to replicate the study on which this claim is based have been only partially successful. Most researchers now believe that contact shortly after birth is not essential to longterm emotional attachment.

21. The parents' expectations patterned by the culture's belief systems influence the child's environment in ways that promote the continuation of cultural traits from one generation to another.

KEY TERMS

amnion

Apgar Scale

babyness

blastocyst

Brazelton Neonatal Assessment Scale

cephalocaudal pattern

chorion

cleavage

ectoderm

endoderm

epigenesis

fetal growth retardation

germinal period

heterochrony

heterogeneity

implantation

inner cell mass

low birth weight

mesoderm

morula

neurons

period of the embryo

period of the fetus

placenta

preformationism

premature

proximodistal pattern

teratogens

trophoblast

umbilical cord

zona pellucida

SUGGESTED READINGS

APGAR, VIRGINIA, & BECK, JOAN. *Is My Baby All Right?: A Guide to Birth Defects.* New York: Trident, 1972.

The originator of the most widely used neonatal assessment method and her coauthor provide an extremely useful summary of the genetic and environmental sources of birth defects.

BRAZELTON, T. BERRY. *Infants and Mothers: Differences in Development* (Rev. ed.). New York: Dell, 1983.

This book by the originator of a widely used neonatal assessment scale provides a solid foundation for thinking about the origins of individuality in early life.

GESELL, ARNOLD. *The Embryology of Behavior.* New York: Harper, 1945.

Although somewhat dated, Gesell's book provides an excellent introduction to the view that all of human development can be thought of as the embryology of behavior.

GOULD, STEPHEN J. "On Heroes and Fools in Science." In Gould, *Ever Since Darwin.* New York: Norton, 1977.

In this lucid essay Gould discusses the history of the preformationist and epigenetic theories of prenatal development and shows how knowledge of modern genetics is blurring the lines between them.

GUTTMACHER, ALAN F. *Pregnancy, Birth, and Family Planning.* Revised and updated by I. H. Kaiser. New York: Signet, 1984.

A prominent expert on conception and family planning provides a detailed account of pregnancy.

KITZINGER, SHEILA. *Giving Birth: The Parents' Emotions at Birth.* New York: Taplinger, 1971.

The core of this book is a set of accounts by parents about their feelings surrounding the birth of their babies. Parents' responses to each other and their initial reactions to their children are also described.

KOPP, CLAIRE B. "Risk Factors in Development." In P. H. Mussen (Ed.), *Handbook of Child Development,* vol. 2: *Infancy and Developmental Psychobiology.* New York: Wiley, 1983.

A thorough summary of the factors that can endanger development from conception through infancy. Major neonatal tests are described and compared, and methods for assessing their predictive power are carefully explained.

MACFARLANE, AIDAN. *The Psychology of Childbirth.* Cambridge, Mass.: Harvard University Press, 1977.

Pregnancy, birth, and the first days of life are described by a British pediatrician in a particularly lucid and sympathetic manner. Special emphasis is placed on the impact of common medical practices on the well-being of the baby and on the nature of early interactions between the parent and infant.

MERKATZ, IRWIN R., & THOMPSON, JOYCE E. (Eds.). *New Perspectives on Prenatal Care.* New York: Elsevier, 1990.

This volume contains 33 articles summarizing the current state of prenatal care in theory and in practice. These accounts show clearly how intervention strategies devised to ameliorate difficulties for mother and child can simultaneously serve as research techniques for understanding the processes of prenatal development.

NILSSON, LENNART. *A Child Is Born: The Drama of Life before Birth*. With text by A. Ingelman-Sundberg and C. Wirsen. New York: Dell, 1981.

A collection of stunning photographs documenting prenatal development.

PURVES, DALE, & LICHTMAN, JEFF W. *Principles of Neural Development*. Sunderland, Mass.: Sinauer Associates, 1985.

This readable undergraduate text on prenatal development highlights the many basic principles that have implications not only for prenatal development but for later development as well.

WALTERS, WILLIAM A. W., & SINGER, PETER. *Test-Tube Babies*. New York: Oxford University Press, 1982.

This book explains the process of in vitro fertilization, which allows a woman to bear children even though her fallopian tubes are so obstructed that natural fertilization is impossible. It also discusses the controversial practice of surrogate motherhood, in which one woman agrees to bear a child for another woman who cannot bear children herself.

PART II

Infancy

All cultures recognize infancy as a distinct period of life. Its starting point is clear; it begins when the umbilical cord is severed and the child starts to breath. The end of infancy is not so easily defined. According to the ancient Romans, an infant is "one who does not speak," and the ability to speak a language is still considered an important indicator that infancy has come to an end. It is not a sufficient marker by itself, however. Modern developmental psychologists look for converging changes in several spheres of children's functioning to establish that one stage has ended and another begun. The acquisition of language is not an isolated event in children's development. It is accompanied by changes in their physical capacities, modes of thought, and social relations. It is this ensemble of changes, rather than changes in any one aspect of children's functioning by itself, that transforms babies from helpless infants into children who, though still dependent upon adults, are on their way to independence.

The chapters in Part II are organized to highlight the important sequences of changes in each sphere and the interactions among them. Chapter 4 begins with a description of infants' earliest capacities for perceiving and acting on the world. It then traces events in infant development from birth to the age of about 2½ months. Although this period is relatively short, it serves as an excellent introduction to the processes of developmental change and the major theoretical frameworks that have been used to explain them. An important requirement of this earliest prenatal period is that the behaviors of infants and their caretakers become sufficiently coordinated for adults to be able to provide infants with enough food and warmth to support their continued growth. This requirement is met through a wide variety of different cultural systems of infant care that call upon infants' basic capacities to learn from experience. If all goes well, the development of crucial brain structures by the end of this period enhances infants' abilities to experience the world and reorders the social and emotional interactions between infants and their caretakers. This ensemble of changes is the first bio-social-behavioral shift.

Between 2½ and 12 months of age, the period covered in Chapter 5, the infant's capacities in all spheres of development progress markedly. Increases in size and strength are accompanied by increases in coordination and mobility: the ability to sit independently appears at about 5 or 6 months, crawling at about 7 or 8 months, and walking at about 1 year. Both memory and problem-solving abilities improve, providing infants with a finer sense of their environment and how to act upon it. Sometime between 7 and 9 months, infants' increased physical ability and intellectual power bring about additional changes in their emotions and social relations. They are likely to become wary of strangers, they become upset when left alone, and they express strong emotional attachments to their caretakers. They also begin to make their first speechlike sounds, heralding the beginning of language acquisition. These changes mark what appears to be a second bio-social-behavioral shift during infancy.

Chapter 6 describes the changes that occur between 12 months and 2½ years, culminating in the bio-social-behavioral shift that signals the end of infancy. Rapid growth in the baby's ability to use language is accompanied by the emergence of pretend play and more sophisticated forms of problem solving. Toward the end of infancy, children begin to show a concern for adult standards and to attempt to meet those standards. As infancy comes to an end, young children stand on their own two feet and announce, "I do it self." Caretakers, for their part, view these changes as a sign that children are no longer "babies." They begin to reason with their children, to explain things to them, and to make demands upon them.

The coverage of infancy ends with Chapter 7, which takes up an enduring question concerning human development: Is the pattern of development that is established during infancy fixed and unchangeable, or can it be significantly altered by the maturational changes and experiences that will occur during later childhood and adolescence? Is there hope that children who have undergone traumatic early experiences can, with proper help, recover to lead normal lives? Will a happy and healthy infancy enable children to develop the capacities they need to cope should they encounter later misfortunes? These scientific questions have practical counterparts: Should society provide special supports for infants and their parents in order to reduce costly problems later on, or should infancy remain purely a family concern? As we shall see, opinions about these matters are sharply divided. Nevertheless, a look at the efforts of psychologists to study them underscores how important it is to consider the whole child in the context of both family and community if we are to gain a scientific understanding of development and make informed decisions about social policies that affect children.

CHAPTER 4

Early Infancy: Initial Capacities and the Process of Change

•

Babies control and bring up their families as much as they are controlled by them; in fact, we may say that the family brings up a baby by being brought up by him. Whatever reaction patterns are given biologically and whatever schedule is predetermined developmentally must be considered to be a series of potentialities for changing patterns of mutual regulation.

— ERIK ERIKSON, *CHILDHOOD AND SOCIETY*

In comparison with guinea pigs and other creatures that at birth are able to negotiate their environments almost as well as their parents, human beings are born in a state of marked immaturity. The capacities of children at birth are not adequate in themselves to ensure their survival. The sucking reflex, for example, is of no help in a newborn's efforts to obtain food unless the mouth is in touch with a source of milk, and newborns are incapable of arranging things so that the sucking reflex can come into play in an adaptive way. They must be physically aided to accomplish even such an elementary function as feeding. The relative helplessness of babies at birth has two obvious consequences. First, human newborns must depend on their parents and other adults for many years for their survival. Second, in order to survive on their own and eventually reproduce, humans must acquire a vast repertoire of knowledge and skills they do not possess at birth.

This chapter describes the earliest capacities of the child at birth and the processes of developmental change that occur in the initial period of infancy. This period begins immediately after birth and ends some 2½ months later when the accumulated changes that have taken place in the central nervous system and the learning the baby has acquired converge to make possible new kinds of behavior and a qualitatively different social relationship between the infant and the caregivers. The convergence of changes in different domains is the kind of qualitative reorganization in developing children that we have designated as a bio-social-behavioral shift.

EARLIEST CAPACITIES

No issue has fired the curiosity of developmental psychologists more strongly than the extent of babies' psychological capacities when they emerge from the womb. How prepared are these newcomers to perceive the sights, smells, and sounds of the world around them? Is the newborn mind a tabula rasa (blank slate) on which the environment writes, as John Locke proposed? (See Box 1.1.) Or do infants come into the world already equipped with highly structured nervous systems, primed to experience an environment for which they have been shaped by their particular genetic endowment?

At the beginning of this century, psychological opinion leaned in Locke's direction. The philosopher-psychologist William James (1890) summarized this view when he described the world the newborn child experiences as a "buzzing, blooming confusion." The new circumstances that greet the infant at birth may well be confusing, but as we will see, the research of recent decades has demonstrated that infants are by no means blank slates. They are born with remarkable capacities to engage the world and to behave in ways that promote their own survival.

Sensory Processes

The sensory systems of an organism are the primary means by which it receives information from the environment. Normal full-term newborns enter the world with all sensory systems functioning, but not all of these systems are at the same level of maturity. The difference in the rates at which the various organ systems develop continues the heterochrony we remarked on with respect to the fetal period (Chapter 3, p. 80), and it will persist throughout the child's development (Werner & Lipsitt, 1981).

The basic method used to determine an infant's sensory capacities is to introduce some change into the environment and observe its effect on the child's physiological processes or behavior (Bornstein, 1988). An investigator might present a tone or a flashing light, for example, and watch for an indication — a turn of the head, a variation in brain waves, a change in the rate at which the baby sucks on a nipple — that the newborn has sensed it. Sometimes the researcher presents two stimuli at once to determine if the baby will attend to one longer than to the other. If so, presumably the baby can tell the stimuli apart, and perhaps even prefers the one it attends to longer.

Another widely used technique is first to repeat or continue a stimulus until the infant stops paying attention to it. This response pattern is called **habituation.** Then some aspect of the stimulus is changed: the frequency of the tone, the language being spoken, or the arrangement of elements within a visual array. If the infant's interest is renewed, the investigator can conclude that the infant did sense the change. To begin paying attention again when some aspect of the stimulus situation has been changed is called **dishabituation.** If the infant continues to ignore the stimulus despite the change, the investigator cannot be certain whether the change in the stimulus was perceived or not.

Hearing

Make a loud noise and infants only minutes old will startle and may even cry. They will also turn their heads toward the source of the noise, an indication that they perceive sound as roughly localized in space (Weiss, Zelazo, & Swain, 1988). Yet newborns' hearing is not so acute for some parts of the sound spectrum as it will be when they are older (Hecox & Deegan, 1985; Werner & Gillenwater, 1990). In the days after birth, the acuity of newborns' hearing improves rapidly as the amniotic fluid left in the ears is absorbed, and it continues to improve for several months.

Infants appear to be able to distinguish the sound of the human voice from other kinds of sounds, and they seem to prefer it. Infants only a few days old will learn to suck on an artificial nipple to turn on recorded speech or vocal music, but they will not suck so readily to hear a rhythmic nonspeech sound or instrumental music (Butterfield & Siperstein, 1972; DeCasper and Fifer, 1980). They are especially interested in speech directed to them and spoken with the high pitch and slow, exaggerated pronunciation known as "baby talk" (Cooper & Aslin, 1990). There is even evidence that some babies have formed a preference for the language spoken around them over a foreign language by the time they are 4 days old (Mehler et al., 1986).

One of the most striking discoveries about the hearing of very young infants is that they are particularly sensitive to the sound categories in human speech (Eimas, 1985), a capacity that appears to be essential for the acquisition of language. These basic language sounds are called **phonemes.**

Phonemes vary from language to language. In Spanish, for example, /r/ and /rr/ are two phonemes; "pero" and "perro" sound different and have different meanings. (Linguists denote phonemes and other language sounds by enclosing them in slashes.) In English, however, there is no such distinction. Similarly, /r/ and /l/ are different phonemes in English but not in Japanese. No wonder learning a new language often seems such a formidable undertaking!

Now consider the even more difficult problem newborn babies confront. Unless they have picked up a sense of the basic rhythms of their native language while in the womb, as a few studies discussed in Chapter 3 suggest (p. 89), babies are born into the world with no experience of language at all. Yet within a year, and with no formal training, they will be making speechlike sounds and may even have begun to produce their first words. What underlies human infants' prodigious ability to acquire language?

Part of the answer is supplied in studies conducted by Peter Eimas and his colleagues (1971) indicating that the ability to perceive basic language sounds is present at birth. These researchers arranged for neonates to suck on a nipple attached to a recording device in a special apparatus (see Figure 4.1). After establishing a baseline rate of sucking for each baby, they presented the speech sound /pa/ to the babies each time they sucked. At first the babies' rate of sucking increased as if they were excited by each presentation

FIGURE 4.1   *Apparatus for presenting artificially manipulated speech sounds to young infants. The infant sucks on a pacifier connected to recording instruments as speech-like sounds are presented from a loudspeaker just above the Raggedy Ann display.*

not. The ability to make phonemic distinctions apparently begins to narrow to just those distinctions that are present in one's native language at about 6 to 8 months of age (see Figure 4.3), the same age at which the baby's first halting articulations of language-like sounds are likely to begin (Eimas, 1985; Kuhl et al., 1992).

Although it is tempting to conclude that human infants are born with perceptual skills that are specially pretuned to the properties of human speech, studies indicate that other species can make similar distinctions (Kuhl & Miller, 1978). The difference is that

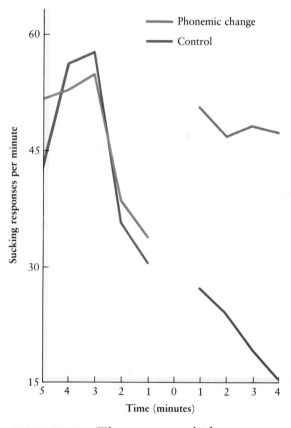

FIGURE 4.2   *When two groups of infants are repeatedly presented a single consonant over a 5-minute period, their rates of sucking decrease to just over 30 sucks per minute. For half of the infants the consonant is changed after the time marked "0" (the curve labeled "phonemic change"). Note that the rate of sucking increases sharply. For the remaining infants who continued to hear the same consonant, the rate of sucking continues to decrease (the curve labeled "control"). (Adapted from Eimas, 1985.)*

of the sound, but after a while they settled back to their baseline rate of sucking. When the infants had become thoroughly habituated to the sound of /pa/, some of them heard a new sound, /ba/, which differed from the original sound only in its initial phoneme — /b/ versus /p/. Others heard a sound that differed an equal amount from the original sound but did not cross the phoneme boundary (see Figure 4.2). The neonates began sucking rapidly again only when the change crossed the phoneme boundary, an indication that they were especially sensitive to the difference.

Other studies have shown that newborns are able to perceive all the categorical sound distinctions used in all the world's various languages. Japanese babies, for example, can perceive the difference between /r/ and /l/ even though adult speakers of Japanese can-humans use this ability as a stepping-stone to the mastery of language, an achievement that is beyond the capacities of other animals.

Vision

The basic anatomical elements of the visual system are present at birth, but they are not fully developed and they are not well coordinated (Aslin, 1987). The lens of the eye is still somewhat immature; it focuses images several millimeters behind the retina, so that the images on the retina are blurred. Also, the movements of the baby's eyes are not coordinated well enough to make the images on the two retinas sufficiently complementary to form a clear composite image. The immaturity of some of the neural pathways that relay information from the retina to the brain further limits the newborn's visual capacities (Atkinson & Braddick, 1982).

COLOR PERCEPTION.   Newborns seem to possess all, or nearly all, of the physiological prerequisites for seeing color, but psychologists disagree about precisely what colors newborns can perceive (Bornstein, 1976; Teller & Bornstein, 1987; Werner & Wooten, 1985). By 2 months of age, however, their color vision appears to be roughly equal to adults' (Bornstein, 1988).

VISUAL ACUITY.   A basic question about infants' vision is how nearsighted they are. To determine newborns' visual acuity, Robert Fantz and his colleagues (Fantz, Ordy, & Udelf, 1962) developed a test based on the fact that when a striped visual field moves in front of the eyes, the eyes start to move in the same direction as the pattern. If the gaps between the stripes are so small that they cannot be perceived, the eyes do not move. By varying the width of the gaps and comparing the results obtained from newborns with those obtained from adults, these researchers were able to estimate that neonates have 20/300 vision — that is, they can see at 20 feet what an adult with normal vision can see at 300 feet. Other researchers estimate the visual acuity, or acuteness, of newborns to be closer to 20/800 (Cornell & McDonnell, 1986). Although these estimates are far apart, both suggest that the newborn is very nearsighted.

Poor visual acuity is probably less troublesome to newborns than to older children and adults. After all,

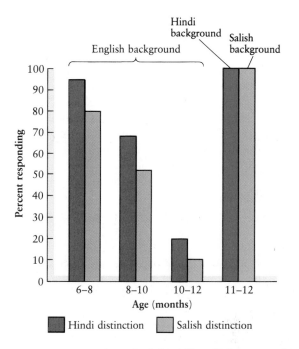

FIGURE 4.3   *A graph of the ability of infants to make phonemic distinctions among contrasting language sounds that are not a part of their native language. The proportion of infants from an English-speaking background who responded to consonants from Hindi and Salish (a North American Indian language) decreases markedly during the first year of life. In contrast, 1-year-old Hindi and Salish infants retain the capacity to perceive the linguistic contrasts native to their respective languages. (Adapted from Eimas, 1985.)*

newborns are unable to move unless someone carries them, and they cannot hold their heads erect without support. Still, their visual system is tuned well enough to allow them to see objects a foot or so away — about the distance of their mother's face when they are nursing. This level of acuity allows them to make eye contact, which is important in establishing the social relationship between mother and child (Stern, 1977). By 7 or 8 months of age, when infants are able to crawl, their visual acuity is close to the adult level (Haith, 1990; Cornell & McDonnell, 1986).

VISUAL SCANNING.   Despite their nearsightedness and their difficulty in focusing, newborns actively scan their surroundings from the earliest days of life (Bronson, 1991; Haith, 1980; Haith, Berman, & Moore,

1977). Marshall Haith and his colleagues developed recording techniques that allowed them to determine precisely where infants were looking and to monitor their eye movements in both light and dark rooms. They discovered that neonates scan with short eye movements even in a completely darkened room. Since no light is entering their eyes, this kind of scanning cannot be caused by the visual environment. It must therefore be endogenous, originating in the neural activity of the central nervous system. Endogenous eye movements seem to be an initial, primitive basis for looking behavior.

Haith's studies also revealed that neonates exhibit an early form of exogenous looking; that is, looking that is stimulated by the external environment. When the lights are turned on after infants have been in the dark, they pause in their scanning when their gaze encounters an object or some change of brightness in the visual field. This very early sensitivity to changes in illumination, which is usually associated with the edges and angles of objects, appears to be an important component of the baby's developing ability to perceive visual forms (Haith, 1980).

PERCEPTION OF PATTERNS.   What do babies see when their eyes encounter an object? Are they able to see objects much as adults do?

Until the early 1960s it was widely believed that neonates perceived only a formless play of light. Robert Fantz (1961, 1963) dealt a severe blow to this assumption by demonstrating that babies less than 2 days old can distinguish among visual forms. The technique he used was very simple. Babies were placed on their backs in a specially designed "looking chamber" (see Figure 4.4) and shown various forms. An observer looked down through the top of the chamber and recorded how long the infants looked at each form. Because the infants spent more time looking at some forms than at others, presumably they could tell the forms apart and preferred the ones they looked at the longest. Fantz found that neonates would rather look at patterned figures, such as faces and concentric circles, than at plain ones (see Figure 4.5).

Fantz's findings set off a search to determine the extent of newborns' capacity to perceive form and the reasons they prefer some forms over others. The resulting research has confirmed that infants visually perceive the world as more than random confusion, but it has also provided evidence that infants do not enter the world prepared to see it in the same way

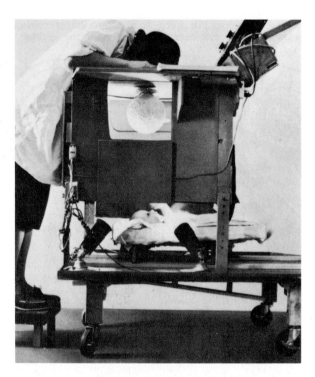

FIGURE 4.4   *The "looking chamber" that Robert Fantz used to test newborns' visual interests. The infant lies in a crib in the chamber, looking up at the stimuli attached to the ceiling. The observer, watching through a peephole, determines how long the infant looks at each stimulus.*

adults do. Gordon Bronson (1991), for example, studied the way 2-week-old and 12-week-old babies scan outline drawings of simple figures, such as a cross or a "v," on a lighted visual field. When adults are shown such figures, they scan the entire boundary. In contrast, Bronson found that babies two weeks of age do not scan the entire figure but instead appear to focus on areas of high contrast, such as lines and angles (see Figure 4.6a). This kind of looking behavior is clearly not random, but it does not provide evidence that children are born with the ability to perceive basic patterns. At 12 weeks of age infants scan more of the figure, but their scanning movements may still be incomplete and still seem to be captured by areas of high contrast (see Figure 4.6b). Bronson also found that some of the older infants scanned the displays very slowly and in the restricted manner of the younger infants, suggesting significant individual differences in rates of perceptual development during the early months of life.

Philip Salapatek (1975) discovered another important limitation to neonates' visual perception. When newborns are presented with a pattern consisting of one contour inside another, they fixate only on the external contour. By 2 or 3 months of age, however, they begin to notice and concentrate more on the internal contour. This finding may seem insignificant by itself, but it is important for interpreting evidence concerning infants' perception of the human face.

PERCEPTION OF FACES.   In Fantz's early studies, one of the complex forms presented to the babies was a schematic human face. The fact that infants looked longer at this form than at any of the others suggested that newborn infants can perceive faces and like to look at them. When Fantz (1961, 1963) presented newborn infants with a schematic face and a form in which facial elements had been scrambled, he found that the infants apparently could distinguish the schematic face from the jumbled face (see Figure 4.7). Such a strong suggestion that newborns have an unlearned preference for a biologically significant form naturally attracted great interest. As you can see in Figure 4.7,

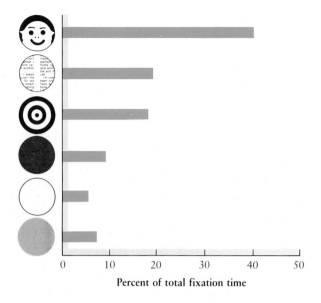

FIGURE 4.5   *Infants tested during the first weeks of life show a preference for patterned stimuli over plain stimuli. The length of each bar indicates the relative amount of time the babies spent looking at the corresponding stimulus. (Adapted from Fantz, 1961.)*

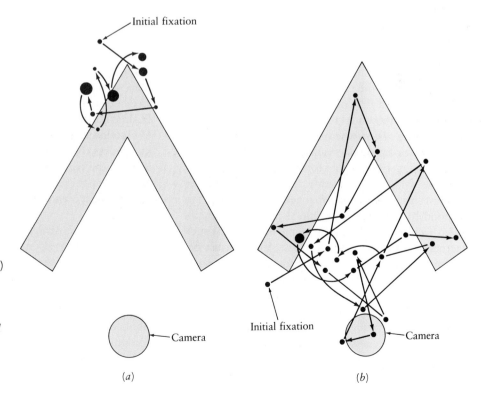

FIGURE 4.6   *Visual scanning of triangles and squares by young infants.* (a) *Note that the 1-month-old concentrates its gaze on a point of high contrast, whereas* (b) *the 12-week-old visually explores the figure more fully. (Adapted from Bronson, 1991.)*

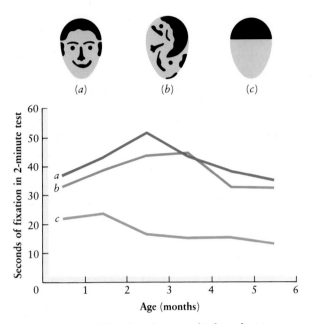

FIGURE 4.7   *Visual preferences of infants for* (a) *a schematic face,* (b) *a scrambled schematic face, and* (c) *a nonfacelike figure, all having equal amounts of light and dark areas. Both facelike forms were preferred over the nonfacelike form, with the "real" face receiving slightly more attention than the scrambled face. (Adapted from Fantz, 1961.)*

however, the preference for the schematic face over the scrambled face is very slight, particularly in comparison with the difference in preference for a complex figure over a plain one shown in Figure 4.7. In the years since Fantz conducted his studies, there has been much debate about whether newborns actually perceive faces or are simply visually attracted to complex figures (Aslin, 1987; Banks & Salapatek, 1983).

The evidence from early follow-ups of Fantz's studies ran against the idea that neonates are primed to respond to "faceness." Lonnie Sherrod (1979) replicated Fantz's research, controlling carefully for such factors as the degree of brightness, the contrast between the forms and their background, and the number of turns and angles within the schematic and scrambled faces. His conclusion, supported by others (Haaf, Smith, & Smitely, 1983), was that the presence of highly contrasting elements or many turns and angles, not "faceness" itself, accounted for Fantz's results. A recent follow-up of this line of research by James Dannemiller and Benjamin Stephens (1988) used

a computer-generated display that allowed the researchers to equate their stimuli in all relevant factors except "faceness." They found that 6-week-olds did not show a preference for one figure over another, but 12-week-olds showed a preference for the face stimulus.

Interesting confirmation of a basic change in infants' perception in the months after birth is provided by studies that demonstrate the importance of movement in young infants' proclivity to look at faces. In Fantz's studies and the later replications we have described, researchers used only stationary schematic representations of faces. Several studies indicate that babies as young as 9 *minutes* old will turn their heads to gaze at a schematic face as it moves in front of them, and will look at it longer than at a scrambled face (Goren, Sarty, & Wu, 1975; Morton & Johnson, 1991). John Morton and Mark Johnson suggest that the very early recognition of faces is a primitive response controlled by innate subcortical mechanisms, whereas the preference for faces among infants older than 2 months arises because the visual cortex has matured and children have begun to learn about faces.

I. W. R. Bushnell (1982) has shown motion to be an important resource for newborns' perception in another way. He presented a group of infants from 1 to 2 months old with stationary compound figures, such as a triangle within a circle. The figure was shown repeatedly, until the infant stopped looking at it for more than a brief moment. When the outside element was then changed (the circle in our example), the infants stared longer at the figure, but when the inside element was changed (the triangle), they did not. Bushnell then arranged his apparatus so that the inside element oscillated back and forth instead of remaining motionless. Now the neonates responded to changes in both the external and internal elements. Bushnell argues that the last experimental condition is analogous to a face with either the eyes or the mouth in motion.

Neonates' visual perceptual abilities are also influenced by degrees of contrast between different parts of an object they are looking at, a factor already mentioned in connection with the evidence of neonates' tendency to concentrate their gaze on lines, angles, and light-dark transitions (Haith, 1980; Haith, Berman, & Moore, 1977). It seems that newborns may recognize their mother's face by the light-dark patterns created by her hairline and the outline of her face.

In real life, people move both their heads and the features of their faces. Under these naturalistic conditions, newborns only 2 days old demonstrate an ability to recognize the face they have seen most often, usually their mother's (Bushnell, Sai, & Mullin, 1989; Field et al., 1984).

TASTE AND SMELL.   Neonates have a well-developed sense of smell (Engen, Lipsitt, & Kaye, 1963; Steiner, 1977, 1979). Trygg Engen and his colleagues demonstrated this sensory capacity in newborns by placing 2-day-old infants on a "stabilometer," an apparatus that measures physical activity. The experimenters held either an odorless cotton swab or a swab soaked in one of various aromatic solutions under the newborns' noses. Babies were judged to react to an odor if their activity increased over the level it had reached in response to the odorless cotton swab. The infants reacted strongly to some odors, such as garlic and vinegar, and less strongly to others, such as licorice and alcohol. Their responses indicated not only that they were sensitive to odors but also that they could tell one odor from another. This early sensitivity to odors has been confirmed in a more naturalistic way by Aidan Macfarlane (1975), who showed that by 5 days of age newborns will turn toward a pad soaked with breast milk, and by 8 to 10 days they will show a preference for the smell of their mother's milk over the milk of another woman.

Newborns' sense of taste, like their sense of smell, is acute. They prefer sweet to sour tastes (Lipsitt, 1977). They will also suck longer, and pause for shorter periods, on a bottle containing sweet substances than on one containing plain water. The characteristic facial expressions they make in response to various tastes look remarkably like those adults make when encountering the same tastes, evidence that these expressions are innate (Rosenstein & Oster, 1988) (see Figure 4.8).

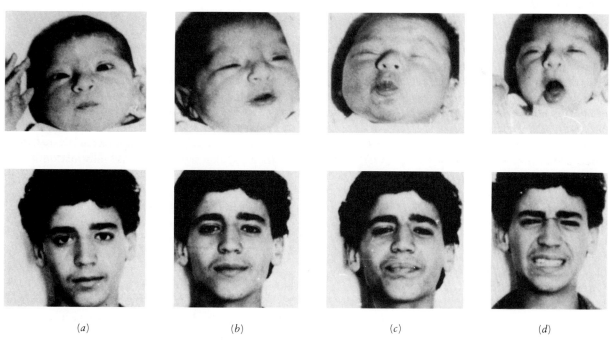

(a)   (b)   (c)   (d)

FIGURE 4.8   *Facial expressions evoked by various tastes are very similar in infants and adults:* (a) *a neutral expression follows the presentation of distilled water;* (b) *a hint of a smile follows the presentation of a sweet stimulus;* (c) *the pucker is in response to a sour stimulus;* (d) *a bitter stimulus evokes a distinctive grimace.*

TOUCH, TEMPERATURE, AND POSITION. The abilities to detect a touch to the skin, changes in temperature, and changes in physical position develop very early in the prenatal period. Although these sensory capacities have not received as much attention as vision and hearing, they are no less important to the baby's survival. Newborns show that they sense they have been touched by making a distinctive movement, such as withdrawing the part touched or turning toward the touch. Some evidence suggests that sensitivity to touch increases in the days after birth (Lipsitt & Levy, 1959). Little is known, however, about whether neonates can distinguish between different tactile stimuli or tell what part of the body is being touched or about how such capacities might develop.

Neonates indicate that they are sensitive to changes in temperature by becoming more active if temperature suddenly drops (Pratt, 1954). They respond to abrupt changes in their physical position, such as being suddenly dropped, with distinctive, reflex-like movements. Such responses indicate that the mechanism for detecting changes in position, which is located in the middle ear, is operating.

Overall, there is extensive evidence that babies come into the world with sensory capacities in good working order and far more structured than they were once thought to be. The question then arises: What capacities do infants have for acting *on* the world? By studying the ability of infants to take in information from the environment and to act on it, researchers can gather the data they need to determine the starting point of postnatal psychological development.

Response Processes

Infants are born with a variety of ways of responding to, and thereby acting on, the world around them. Here we will examine infants' response capacities as displayed in reflexes, emotions, and temperament.

Reflexes

Newborn babies come equipped with a variety of **reflexes** — specific, well-integrated, automatic (involuntary) responses to specific types of stimulation. Some of the reflexes with which infants are born are described in Table 4.1. Virtually all psychologists

agree that reflexes are important building blocks out of which various complex behavioral capacities of later life are constructed. They disagree, however, about the nature of reflexes and how they contribute to the development of more complex capacities.

Some reflexes are clearly part of the baby's elementary survival kit. The eyeblink reflex, for example, has a clear function: it protects the eye from overly bright lights and foreign objects that might damage it. The sucking and swallowing reflexes are essential to feeding. Others, however, such as the grasping reflex (closing fingers around an object that is pressed against the palm) and the Moro reflex (grasping with the arms when suddenly dropped), appear to have no particular function. What, then, is the developmental significance of these reflexes, and how did they evolve in the first place? Some biologically oriented developmental theorists believe that these reflexes serve no purpose now but were functional during early evolutionary stages, when infants needed to cling to their mothers in order to survive (Peiper, 1963). Others, such as John Bowlby (1973), believe that they may still be functional because they promote a close relationship between mother and infant.

Emotions

Emotion — the feeling tone, sometimes referred to as affect, with which individuals respond to their circumstances — is an important aspect of human psychological functioning. Beyond the coloration emotions give to experience, they serve two basic adaptive functions: they motivate and they communicate (Barrett & Campos, 1987). Emotions motivate by energizing us, alerting us to certain information in the environment, and preparing us to respond in particular ways. When something frightens us, for example, our senses become heightened and we become tense, ready to fight or flee. Emotional expressions also communicate to other people how we are responding to situations — an important function for the helpless and inarticulate newborn.

The behaviorist John B. Watson (1930), an early champion of the idea that infants are born ready to feel emotions, claimed that the newborn has three primitive emotions: fear, anger, and love. According to Watson, these emotions are reflected in the way the baby responds to particular events. Fear is aroused by threatening stimuli, and it causes babies to cry and clutch; anger is aroused when babies' ongoing behav-

TABLE 4.1

Reflexes Present at Birth

Reflex	Description	Developmental Course	Significance
Babinski	When the bottom of the baby's foot is stroked, the toes fan out and then curl	Disappears in 8 to 12 months	Presence at birth and normal course of decline are a basic index of normal neurological condition
Breathing	Repetitive, rhythmic inhalation and exhalation	Permanent	Provides oxygen and removes carbon dioxide
Crawling	When the baby is placed on his stomach and pressure is applied to the soles of his feet, his arms and legs move rhythmically	Disappears after 3 to 4 months; possible reappearance at 6 to 7 months as a component of voluntary crawling	Uncertain
Eyeblink	Rapid closing of eyes	Permanent	Protection against aversive stimuli such as bright lights and foreign objects
Grasping	When a finger or some other object is pressed against the baby's palm, her fingers close around it	Disappears in 3 to 4 months; replaced by voluntary grasping	Presence at birth and later disappearance is a basic sign of normal neurological development
Moro	If the baby is allowed to drop unexpectedly while being held, or if there is a loud noise, she will throw her arms outward while arching her back, and then bring her arms together as if grasping something	Disappears in 6 to 7 months (although startle to loud noises is permanent)	Disputed; its presence at birth and later disappearance are a basic sign of normal neurological development; possibly functions as facilitator of mother-infant bonding
Rooting	The baby turns his head and opens his mouth when he is touched on the cheek	Disappears between 3 and 6 months	Component of nursing
Stepping	When the baby is held upright over a flat surface, he makes rhythmic leg movements	Disappears in first 2 months	Disputed; it may be only a kicking motion, or it may be a component of later voluntary walking
Sucking	The baby sucks when something is put into her mouth	Permanent	Fundamental component of nursing

iors are blocked, and they respond by stiffening their bodies and holding their breath; love is aroused by soothing stimulation, which makes babies smile.

In their modern version of Watson's idea, Joseph Campos and his co-workers (1983) believe that the emotions present at birth include pleasure, anger, disgust, surprise, and possibly fear and sadness. They define emotions as states of the central nervous system associated with characteristic configurations of feeling tone and external expression (facial pattern, intonation, and body movements). In their view, emotions are responses to particular relationships between the baby's goals and the events the baby encounters. If babies are given something sour when they are hungry, for example, they will be surprised, and they may also be disgusted and angry. If they are given something exceptionally sweet instead, they will be surprised, but their surprise will be accompanied by pleasure.

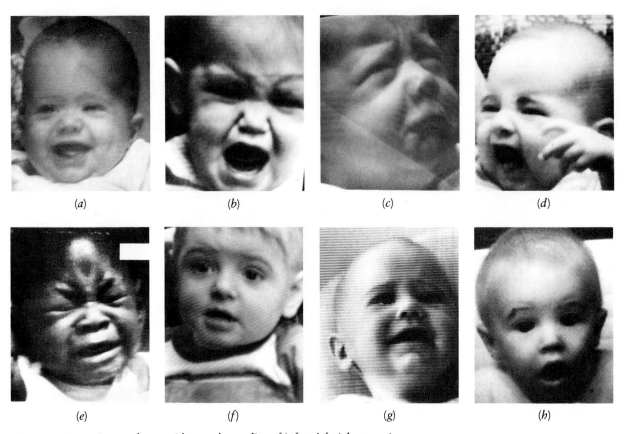

FIGURE 4.9   *Images from a videotaped recording of infants' facial expressions used by Carroll Izard and his colleagues to assess the possible universal relation between emotion and facial expression. What emotion do you think each facial expression represents? The responses most of Izard's adult subjects gave are printed upside down:*

(h) surprise

(a) joy, (b) anger, (c) sadness, (d) disgust, (e) distress/pain, (f) interest, (g) fear,

The evidence that newborns experience emotions depends on the assumption that the crucial defining elements — feelings and goals — can be validly inferred from the infant's facial expressions, noises, and movements (see Figure 4.9). For this reason, some researchers have attempted to establish the existence of emotions in newborns by studying the extent to which newborns' facial expressions in response to various events have the same meaning for everyone. Carroll Izard and his colleagues, for example, videotaped infants' responses to an event such as being inoculated or being reunited with their mothers after a brief separation (Izard, 1977; Izard et al., 1980). They then showed the videotapes, or stills from them, to college students and nurses. These judges agreed fairly consistently on which facial expressions showed interest, joy, surprise, and sadness and to a somewhat lesser extent on which expressions showed anger, disgust, and contempt.

Psychologists who accept the findings of Izard and his co-workers as evidence that infants experience emotions reason that adults agree on the meanings of infants' expressions because the ways in which emotions are expressed facially are universal. Support for this idea comes from the cross-cultural research of Paul Ekman and his associates (Ekman, 1984; Ekman & Friesen, 1972). These researchers asked people in various literate and nonliterate cultures to pose expressions appropriate to such events as the death of a loved one and being reunited with a close friend. Both literate and nonliterate adults configured their faces in the same way to express each emotion. When shown photographs of actors posing the different expressions, the literate and nonliterate adults agreed on the photographs that represented happiness, sadness, anger, and disgust. The nonliterate adults did not distinguish fear from surprise, although they did distinguish them from the other expressions.

Despite the evidence gathered in support of the idea of emotion in the newborn, there is need for caution. Facial expressions, however universal their meanings among adults, may not be reliable indicators of the same emotions among neonates. Newborns may frown simply because they are hungry or cold. Their emotion is a response to immediate physical circumstances. An adult may frown, however, because she has just lost her job and is worried about how she will support herself. Her emotion involves the synthesis of information about her current circumstances and her anticipation of future events. This synthesis requires interaction among the higher brain centers, which are immature at birth. Consequently, the processes that underlie the facial expressions of newborns may differ from those reflected by the same facial expressions in adults. Although Campos, Izard, and others acknowledge that such criticisms have some merit, they maintain that the evidence for the existence of emotions in the neonate is nevertheless convincing.

Temperament

A commonly held intuition about human nature is that people differ from one another and are consistently like themselves in the ways they respond to the world around them and in the quality of their dominant mood. These stable differences are encompassed by the word **temperament** (Allport, 1937; Bates, 1989; Goldsmith, 1987).

A wide variety of characteristics have been read as evidence of infants' temperamental qualities. They include the newborns' activity level, the ease with which they become upset, the intensity of their reactions, their characteristic reaction when something unusual happens, and their sociability (Bates, 1989). Many developmental psychologists believe that these temperamental characteristics are present at birth and are an important source of continuity. These characteristics have proved difficult to pin down scientifically, however (Kohnstamm, Bates, & Rothbart, 1989).

Pioneering studies of temperament and development were conducted by Alexander Thomas, Stella Chess, and their colleagues. Their work has had great influence over the years, both because of the techniques they used to assess temperament and because they followed the children's development into early adulthood. They began their research in the late 1950s with a group of 141 middle- and upper-class children in the United States. Later they broadened their longitudinal study to include 95 working-class Puerto Rican children and several groups of children suffering from diseases, neurological impairments, and mental retardation (Thomas et al., 1963; Thomas & Chess, 1977, 1984). The researchers asked the parents of the children to fill out questionnaires periodically, beginning shortly after the birth of their child. Included were questions about such matters as how the child reacted to the first bath, to wet diapers, and to the first taste of solid food. As the children grew older, the questionnaires were supplemented by interviews with teachers and by tests of the children.

When these researchers analyzed the data they obtained, they found they could identify nine behavioral traits that, taken together, became their definition of temperament (see Table 4.2). After scoring the children on each of these nine traits they found that most of the children could be classified in one of three broad temperamental categories from the time they were infants. Those who were playful, were regular in their biological functions, and adapted readily to new circumstances were labeled *easy* babies. At the opposite extreme were the children who were irregular in their biological functions, were irritable, and often responded intensely and negatively to new situations and tried to withdraw from them. They were classified as *difficult*. The third group of children were low in activity level and their responses were typically mild. They tended to withdraw from new situations, but in a mild way, and required more time than the "easy" babies to adapt to change. These children were categorized as *slow to warm up*.

A critical issue in the study of temperament is the degree to which temperamental characteristics are present at birth and are therefore presumed to be genetically determined. Some researchers *require* that a

TABLE 4.2
Basic Indicators of Temperament According to Chess and Thomas

Trait	Definition
Activity level	The motor component present in a given child's functioning and the proportion of inactive and active periods
Rhythmicity (regularity)	The degree of predictability of biological functions
Approach or withdrawal	The nature of the initial response to a new stimulus, such as food, a toy, or a person
Adaptability	The ease with which initial responses to a situation are modified
Threshold of responsiveness	The intensity level of a stimulus that is needed to evoke a response
Intensity of reaction	The energy level of a response
Quality of mood	The amount of joyful, pleasant, and friendly behaviors in relation to unpleasant and unfriendly behaviors
Distractibility	The effectiveness of extraneous stimuli in disrupting or altering the direction of ongoing behaviors
Attention span and persistence	Two related indicators of the length of time an activity is pursued

Source: Chess & Thomas, 1982.

trait be demonstrably inherited before they will count it as temperament (Buss & Plomin, 1984). Many others do not restrict the definition of temperament to inherited characteristics, although they acknowledge that genetic factors contribute to temperament (Goldsmith & Campos, 1982). It is important to be aware of these differing definitions because they influence the way psychologists conceive of temperament and the extent to which they believe it can be modified through experience.

The strongest evidence for the heritability of temperamental traits comes from twin studies. Arnold Buss and Robert Plomin (1975) found that ratings on emotionality, activity level, and sociability were strongly related in identical twins (who have identical genes) but not in fraternal twins (who inherit different mixes of genes from their parents). H. H. Goldsmith and Irving Gottesman (1981) obtained similar findings in respect to individual differences in activity level.

Daniel Freedman (1974) has documented ethnic differences in excitability among newborn infants, which suggest that excitability has a significant genetic component. He found that during the first days of life Chinese-American babies tend to be more placid and more difficult to perturb than Anglo-American or African-American babies. In one set of observations, Freedman placed a cloth over the babies' noses and observed their reactions. Most African-American and Anglo-American babies quickly turned their heads aside or swiped at the cloth with their hands. In contrast, the Chinese-American babies usually lay quietly with the cloth covering their noses and breathed through their mouths.

The possibility that temperamental traits are stable physiological "biases" in the way individuals respond to their environment could mean that if the right measurements are taken in early infancy, it should be possible to predict the characteristic style with which individuals will behave at later stages of development (Kagan & Snidman, 1981). Some research suggests that this is in fact the case. One study found that the degree of distress displayed by newborn boys when a pacifier they were sucking on was removed from their mouths predicted their attentiveness in nursery school (Bell, Weller, & Waldrop, 1971). Those infants who became the most upset were later the least likely to become absorbed in their nursery school activities. Similar results were reported in a study in which temperament ratings for 88 newborn infants were compared with ratings collected when the children were 5 months old. Cynthia Stifter and Nathan Fox (1990) sampled ratings from physiological measures such as heart rate, behavioral measures such as the degree to which infants became upset when they were interrupted while sucking on a nipple, and parents' judgments about such traits as irritability, resistance to soothing, and cheerfulness. The researchers reported significant temperamental stability over the 5 months between the tests.

Despite these interesting findings, theories of infant temperament remain controversial (Plomin & Dunn, 1986). Researchers disagree about "facts" as much as about theory, because some studies have failed to produce convincing evidence that stable temperamental traits even exist (Goldsmith & Campos, 1982; Lewis & Starr, 1979). One reason for such failures is that the environment is not always stable over the course of development. As Thomas and Chess (1984) suggest, temperament may be like all other psychological phenomena when it comes to stability over time: in any practical consideration of stability, environmental change must also be taken into account. Theoretical disagreements have focused on two issues: (1) the validity of various measures of temperament (the extent to which various tests really tap this hypothetical quality) and (2) the way temperamental characteristics interact with such important psychological processes as emotion and thinking (Kohnstamm, Bates, & Rothbart, 1989).

BECOMING COORDINATED

Neonates, as we have seen, come equipped with reflexes and sensory capacities that give them a tenuous grip on the world around them. But they are still almost totally helpless, depending entirely on the care of their parents and other caregivers for their continued existence.

Parents cannot always be hovering over their baby, anticipating every need before it is expressed. They must find a way to meet their infant's needs within the confines of their own rhythms of life and work. Whether parents work the land and must be up with the sun or work in an office where they are expected to make their appearance at 9 A.M. sharp, they need to sleep at night. If it is the custom to eat a large meal at midday and to take a nap before returning to work, the meal is scheduled for midday. Such circumstances cause parents to attempt to modify their babies' patterns of eating and sleeping so they will fit into the life patterns of the household and the community.

In the United States these attempts to modify an infant's initial pattern of behavior are often referred to as "getting the baby on a schedule." Getting the baby on a schedule is more than a convenience. Through the coordination of activities that results, babies and parents create a system of mutual expectations that serves as the foundation for later developmental change.

Achieving a mutually satisfactory schedule is by no means easy or automatic. Babies come into the world with their own rhythms of activity, and those rhythms frequently do not coincide with their parents'. Every system of mutual accommodation causes some stress and strain. But when, eventually, families and newborns do achieve a common schedule and begin to coordinate their activities more smoothly, the general feeling of well-being that is produced helps to make the baby a welcome addition (Sprunger, Boyce, & Gaines, 1985).

Parents' efforts to achieve a common schedule with their baby focus on the infant's sleeping and eating. Crying is the baby's earliest means of signaling when these efforts fall short.

Sleeping

As with adults, the extent of newborns' arousal varies from complete rest to frantic activity. The patterns of their rest and activity are quite different from those of adults, however, particularly in the first weeks after birth. To find out about newborns' arousal patterns, Peter Wolff (1966) studied babies during their first weeks after birth. On the basis of such observable behaviors as muscle activity and eye movement, Wolff was able to distinguish seven states of arousal. (They are described in Table 4.3.) Additional research has shown that a distinctive pattern of brain activity is associated with each state of arousal (Berg & Berg, 1987; Emde, Gaensbauer, & Harmon, 1976). In this kind of research, a device called an electroencephalograph (EEG) is used to record the tiny electrical currents generated by the brain's cells, which are detected by electrodes placed on the scalp.

EEG recordings of infants' brain waves made shortly after birth distinguish two kinds of sleep that are the precursors of adult sleeping patterns: (1) an active pattern, called *rapid-eye-movement (REM) sleep,* which is characterized by uneven breathing; low-level, rapid brain-wave activity; and a good deal of eye and limb movement; and (2) a quiet pattern, called *non-rapid-eye-movement (NREM) sleep,* in which breathing is regular, brain waves are larger and slower,

TABLE 4.3

States of Arousal in Infants

State	Characteristics
Non-rapid-eye-movement sleep (NREM sleep)	Full rest; low muscle tone and motor activity; eyelids closed and eyes still; regular breathing (about 36 times per minute)
Rapid-eye-movement sleep (REM sleep)	Increased muscle tone and motor activity; facial grimaces and smiles; occasional eye movements; irregular breathing (about 48 times per minute)
Periodic sleep	Intermediate between REM and NREM sleep — bursts of deep, slow breathing alternating with bouts of rapid, shallow breathing
Drowsiness	More active than NREM sleep but less active than REM or periodic sleep; eyes open and close; eyes glazed when open; breathing variable but more rapid than in NREM sleep
Alert inactivity	Slight activity; face relaxed; eyes open and bright; breathing regular and more rapid than in NREM sleep
Active alert	Frequent diffuse motor activity; vocalizations; skin flushed; irregular breathing
Distress	Vigorous diffuse motor activity; facial grimaces; red skin; crying

Source: Wolff, 1966.

and the baby barely moves (see Figure 4.10). During the first 2 to 3 months of life, infants begin their sleep with active, REM, sleep and only gradually fall into quiet, NREM, sleep (Emde, Gaensbauer, & Harmon, 1976). After the first 2 or 3 months, the sequence reverses, and NREM sleep precedes REM sleep. Although this reversal is of little significance to parents, who are most concerned with their child's overall pattern of sleeping and waking, it is an important sign of developmental change because it shows a shift toward the adult pattern.

Neonates spend most of their time asleep, though the amount of sleep they need gradually decreases. This trend is clearly evident in a study in which mothers were asked to keep a record of their babies' sleep time for several weeks after birth (Emde, Gaensbauer, & Harmon, 1976; Thoman & Whitney, 1989). Babies sleep about 16½ hours a day during the first week of life. By the end of 4 weeks, they sleep a little more than 15 hours a day; and by the end of 4 months, they sleep a little less than 14 hours a day.

If babies sleep most of the time, why do parents lose so much sleep? The reason is that though newborns tend to sleep slightly more at night than during the day from the very beginning, they sleep in snatches that last anywhere from a few minutes to a few hours.

Thus they may be awake at any time of the day or night. As babies grow older, their sleeping and waking periods lengthen and coincide more and more with the night/day schedule common among adults (see Figure 4.11).

A marked shift toward the night/day cycle occurs in the first weeks after birth among many babies born in the United States; by the end of the second week, their combined periods of sleep average 8½ hours between 7 P.M. and 7 A.M. (Kleitman, 1963). But their sleep pattern still results in some loss of sleep for their parents because the longest sleep period may be only 3 or 4 hours.

Although babies' adoption of the night/day sleep cycle seems natural to people who live in industrialized countries and urban settings, studies of infants raised in other cultures suggest that it is at least partly a function of culturally patterned social influence on the infant. We see the role of social pressure in rearranging the newborn's sleep (such as putting the baby to bed at certain hours and not picking it up when it wakes during the night) when we contrast U.S. patterns with the development of the sleep/wake behavior of Kipsigis babies in rural Kenya. These infants are almost always with their mothers. During the day they sleep when they can, often while being carried on their

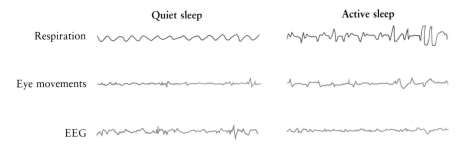

FIGURE 4.10   *The contrast between quiet and active sleep patterns in new-borns is seen in the patterns of respiration, eye movements, and brain activity (EEG). Active sleep is characterized by irregular breathing, frequent eye movements, and continuous low-voltage brain activity. (Adapted from Parmelee et al., 1968.)*

mothers' backs as the mothers go about their daily round of farming, household chores, and social activities. During the night they sleep with their mothers and are permitted to nurse whenever they wake up. Among Kipsigis infants, the longest period of sleep reported at 1 month is only about 3 hours; many shorter periods of sleep are sprinkled throughout the day and night. Eventually Kipsigis infants begin to sleep through the night, but not until many months after American infants have done so. Even as adults the Kipsigis are more flexible than Americans in their sleeping hours (Super & Harkness, 1972).

In the United States, the length of the longest sleep period is often used as an index of the infant's matura-tion. Charles Super and Sara Harkness (1972) suggest that parents' expectations that children will sleep for long periods of time during the early weeks of life may be pushing the limits of what young infants can adapt to. They suggest that the many changes that occur in a newborn's state of arousal in every 24-hour period reflect the immaturity of the infant's brain, which sets a limit on how quickly children can conform to adult routines. This may be the explanation for the failure of some infants in industrialized countries to adopt a night/day pattern of sleeping and waking as quickly and easily as their parents would like them to.

Feeding

Besides attempting to regulate their babies' sleeping patterns, parents also encourage their infants to adjust to a regular pattern of feeding. Pediatricians' recommendations as to when babies should be fed have changed significantly over the years. Today pediatricians often recommend that newborns be fed as often as every 2 to 3 hours. From the early 1930s through the 1950s, mothers were advised to feed their babies only every 4 hours, whether they showed signs of hunger before then or not.

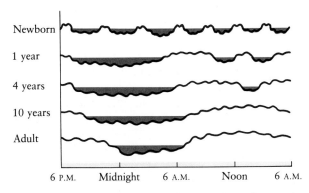

FIGURE 4.11   *The pattern of sleep-wake cycles among babies in the United States changes rapidly during infancy. A long period of sleep comes to replace many brief periods of alternating sleep and wakefulness. (From Kleitman, 1963.)*

Feed him at exactly the same hours every day.
Do not feed him just because he cries.
Let him wait until the right time.
If you make him wait, his stomach will learn to wait.

(Weill, 1930:1)

For a very small infant, 4 hours can be a long time to go without food. In a study in Cambridge, England, mothers were asked to keep records of their babies' behaviors and their own caregiving activities. Included were the time their babies spent in their cradles, the hours at which they were fed, the time the mothers spent bathing their babies and changing their diapers, and the time their babies spent crying. All the mothers were advised to feed their babies on a strict 4-hour schedule, but not all followed the advice. The less experienced mothers tended to stick to the schedule, but the more experienced mothers sometimes fed their babies as soon as 1 hour after a scheduled feeding. Not surprisingly, the reports of the less experienced mothers showed that their babies cried the most (Bernal, 1972).

What happens if babies are fed "on demand"? In one study, the majority of newborn babies allowed to feed on demand preferred a 3-hour schedule (Aldrich & Hewitt, 1947). The interval gradually increased as the babies grew older. At 2½ months, most of the infants were feeding on a 4-hour schedule. By 7 or 8 months, the majority had come to approximate the normal adult schedule and were choosing to feed about four times a day. (Some parents reported the four feedings as "three meals and a snack.") It should be noted, however, that the figures given here are averages; at every age studied, about 40 percent of the babies did not fit the norm.

Crying

One of the most difficult problems parents face in establishing a pattern of care for their babies is interpreting their infants' needs. Parents can ask their newborn babies how they are feeling, but babies cannot answer. Infants do, however, have one important way of signaling that something is wrong—they can cry.

Babies' cries have a powerful effect on those who hear them. Experienced parents and childless adults alike respond to infants' cries with increases in heart rate and blood pressure, both physiological signs of anxiety (Bleichfeld & Moely, 1984; Frodi et al., 1978). New parents react even more strongly to infants' cries than childless adults or experienced parents do (Boukydis & Burgess, 1982). When nursing mothers hear babies' cries, even on recordings, their milk may start to flow (Newton & Newton, 1972).

When newborns cry, it is usually because something is causing them discomfort. The problem for the anxious parent is to figure out what that something is. The cries themselves can sometimes indicate possible causes of distress. Electronic analysis of babies' cries has revealed three distinctive sound patterns: (1) the cries of a baby at birth who has been spanked on the bottom to start breathing; (2) the cries of an infant pricked by a pin; and (3) the cries of a hungry infant (see Figure 4.12). Although there is disagreement about how they do it, adult listeners, even those who are not regularly in contact with newborn babies, can distinguish among these cries (Gustafson & Harris,

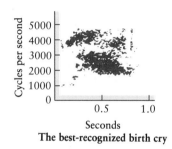
The best-recognized birth cry

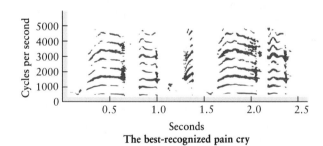
The best-recognized pain cry

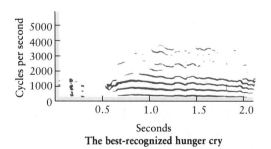
The best-recognized hunger cry

FIGURE 4.12 *Sound spectrograms graphically display the physical differences among the cries that provide adults with information about the causes of babies' distress. (From Wasz-Hökert et al., 1968)*

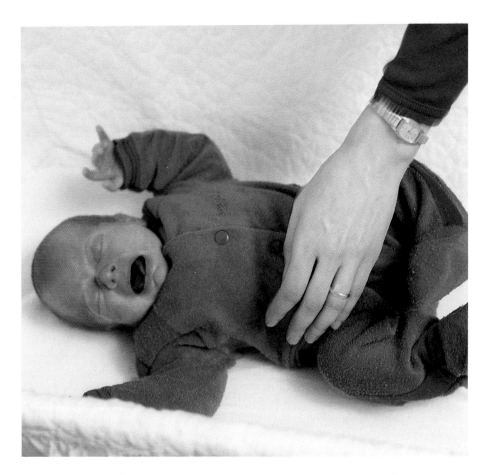

Even without the sound effects, it is clear that this infant's cries are likely to be taken as a peremptory command to anyone listening to do something quickly.

1990; Zeskind et al., 1985). Listeners in a variety of cultures can also distinguish the cries of normal infants from the cries of those at risk for a variety of developmental difficulties (Lester & Zeskind, 1982; Zeskind, 1983; Zeskind et al., 1985). These findings have led Barry Lester (1984) to suggest that an unusual acoustic pattern of crying is a signal that special care is urgently needed.

In spite of their ability to distinguish between types of crying, even experienced parents often cannot tell precisely why their baby is distressed. One reason is that prolonged crying of all kinds eventually slips into the rhythmic pattern of the hunger cry. In many instances, then, only the intensity of the distress is evident. Hunger is, of course, a common reason for a newborn baby to cry. Studies of crying before and after feedings confirm that babies cry less after they are fed (Dunn, 1977; Wolff, 1969). Circumstantial evidence suggests that some crying is the result of gastro-

intestinal pain. Babies will temporarily stop crying after they spit up, are burped, or pass gas, for example.

All these uncertainties make it difficult for parents to know what to do when their baby cries, especially when the cry does not signal acute pain. One natural response is to seek to comfort the infant (see Box 4.1). When parents are under stress or the crying is persistent, however, the uncertainty about how to comfort the child and the negative emotions that crying evokes in adults is sometimes too much to bear, and some parents respond by physically abusing their infants (Frodi, 1985).

Caregivers' efforts to get babies on a schedule and to comfort them when they are distressed continue as the months go by. These parenting activities are so commonplace that it is easy to overlook their significance; but they are crucially important for establishing the background for the more obviously dramatic changes of the first months of life.

BOX 4.1
Comforting the Fussy Baby

All infants occasionally cry and seem to be mildly distressed for no readily identifiable cause, especially during the first 2½ months of life. Generally referred to as fussiness, this distress often peaks in the evenings for reasons not yet understood (Dunn, 1977). Sometimes fussy babies can be soothed by nursing. If they have just been fed and still cry, their mothers often assume that their diapers are wet or that they are cold. And indeed, changing babies' diapers and wrapping them up warmly does tend to quiet them.

To find out just what it is about having their diapers changed that comforts babies, Peter Wolff (1969) arranged for maternity ward nurses to change the diapers of crying babies right after they had been fed, a time when a wet diaper is likely. For half the babies, the nurses changed the diapers as usual. For the other half the nurses went through all the motions of diaper changing but put the wet diapers back on the babies. Most of the babies in both groups stopped crying. This finding suggests that it was the handling and attention the babies received rather than the dry diaper that made the difference.

Mothers and others who care for babies all over the world have long known that babies quiet down when they are being handled or moved. Studies by Annaliese Korner and her associates have confirmed this common knowledge scientifically (Korner & Grobstein, 1966; Korner & Thoman, 1970). These researchers also compared the various ways parents move and hold crying babies—by moving them so that they are lying prone, sitting them up, or picking them up and holding them to the shoulder or to the breast or in an embrace. They found that holding babies to the shoulder is by far the most effective way to make them stop crying. An added benefit when babies are held to the shoulder is that they are more likely to become attentive to their surroundings.

Other methods mothers use to calm crying infants include rocking, patting, cuddling, and swaddling them. Yvonne Brackbill (1971) has found that the important features shared by these techniques are that they provide constant or rhythmic stimulation or that they reduce the amount of stimulation the babies receive from their own movements. Swaddling, or wrapping babies tightly in a blanket so that they cannot move their arms and legs, does both. The blanket provides them with constant touch stimulation and, by restricting their movements, reduces the amount of stimulation they receive from those movements.

Another very effective way to calm crying babies is to give them a pacifier to suck on. Sucking provides the baby with regular and rhythmic stimulation of the mouth, which apparently relaxes both the gut and the major muscles and reduces the baby's random thrashings (Dunn, 1977; Field & Goldson, 1984).

Although it seems natural to ask which technique works the best, there seems to be no single correct answer. Rosemary Gates Campos (1989) reports that sucking on a pacifier appears to be more effective than swaddling at 2 weeks, but that the two techniques are equally effective at 2 months. Brackbill found that of all the techniques that provide continuous stimulation, swaddling was the most effective way to soothe a baby.

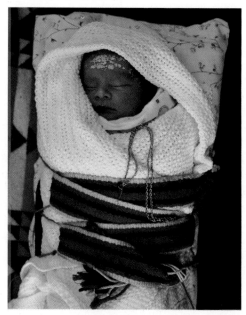

Among the techniques for soothing babies, swaddling, which is used in many cultures, is one of the most effective.

MECHANISMS OF DEVELOPMENTAL CHANGE

Almost immediately after birth, the behavioral repertoire of neonates begins to expand, enabling them to interact ever more effectively with the world around them. In part the changes in behavior that occur during the first months of life are a matter of perfecting capacities that already exist. As infants become able to suck more effectively, for example, they obtain more food, so they can go longer between feedings without distress. The perfecting of existing behaviors does not, however, explain how new behaviors arise. By the age of 2½ months, infants raise their heads to look around, smile in response to the smiles of others, and shake rattles put into their hands. A major goal of developmental psychology is to explain how these new forms of behavior arise.

From Sucking to Nursing

One of the new behaviors that appear in early infancy is nursing. When we compare the way newborn infants feed with the nursing behavior of 6-week-old infants, a striking contrast is evident. Newborns possess several reflexes that are relevant to feeding: rooting (turning the head in the direction of a touch on the cheek), sucking, swallowing, and breathing. These component behaviors are not well integrated, however, so babies' early feeding experiences are likely to be discoordinated affairs. When newborns are first held to the breast, a touch to the cheek will make them turn their heads and open their mouths, but they root around in a disorganized way. When they do find the nipple, they may lose it again almost immediately, or the act of sucking may cause their upper lip to fold back and block their nostrils, eliciting a sharp head-withdrawal reflex (see Figure 4.13). Furthermore, breathing and sucking are not well coordinated at first, so newborns are likely to have to stop sucking to come up for air.

By the time infants are 6 weeks old, a qualitative change is evident in their feeding behavior, a change that is more than just a perfection of the sucking reflex. For one thing, the infants anticipate being fed when they are picked up. More significant, they have worked out the coordination of all the component behaviors of feeding—sucking, swallowing, and breathing—so that they can perform them in a

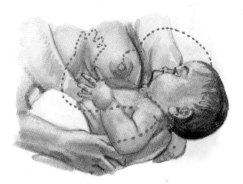

FIGURE 4.13 *In this sequence the infant's nostrils are blocked while he is nursing. The consequent blockage of his breathing elicits a head-withdrawal reflex that interferes with nursing.*

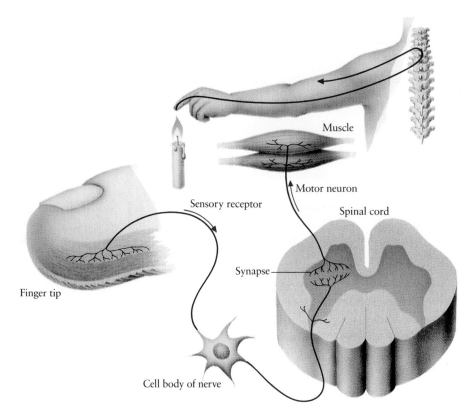

FIGURE 4.14 *How a simple reflex works. The heat of the candle flame sends a sensory message to the spinal cord. The spinal cord sends a message to the arm muscles to pull the hand from the heat. (Adapted from Church, 1974.)*

smooth, integrated sequence (Bruner, 1968). Feeding has become nursing. In fact, babies become so efficient at nursing that they can accomplish in less than 10 minutes what originally took them as long as an hour.

Nursing is clearly not a reflex. It is a new form of behavior that develops through the reorganization of the various reflexes with which infants are born. Although the acquisition of this behavior is commonplace, it raises in clear form the question of how developmental change comes about. Each of the four broad theoretical frameworks — the biological-maturation perspective, the environmental-learning perspective, the universal-constructivist perspective, and the cultural-context perspective — emphasizes different factors in its efforts to explain development (see Chapter 1, pp. 11–20). By examining phenomena spotlighted by each perspective and the way theorists working within these perspectives explain the development of the seemingly simple behavior of nursing, we can gain a sense of how each perspective contributes to our understanding of the development of other behaviors during infancy and beyond.

The Biological-Maturation Perspective

To explain the development of nursing and other new behaviors after birth, biologically oriented developmental theorists invoke precisely the same mechanism that they use to explain all aspects of prenatal development — maturation. New behaviors, they say, arise from old behaviors as a result of distinct maturational changes in the physical structures and physiological processes of the organism. This position was stated most forcefully by Arnold Gesell (1945): "The child comes by his psychic [psychological] constitution through embryological processes" (p. 167). Consequently, the role of the organism's genetic inheritance is considered to be of paramount importance, and the role of the environment in development is considered to be minimal, just as during the prenatal period.

Reflexes and the brain

The emphasis of the biological-maturation perspective on the biological foundations of behavior leads naturally to a focus on the way the development of neonatal behavior depends on the maturation and functioning of the central nervous system. Figure 4.14 shows how a simple nerve reflex works. When a child puts a finger in a candle flame, a *sensory receptor* in the fingertip is excited. This sensory receptor is a neuron, a nerve cell that transmits messages in the form of electrical impulses. *Sensory neurons* are specialized to receive sensory input from the environment and pass it on to cells that are specialized for responding to the environment. The electrical impulse resulting from the heat of the candle travels from the fingertip to the spinal cord, where it comes to a **synapse** — a small gap between interconnecting neurons. The impulse passes across the synapse to a *motor neuron* — a neuron that initiates muscle activity — and then back outward to the muscles in the arm. There it causes the muscles to contract, jerking the hand away from the flame.

For simple reflexes such as this, the circuit that consists of the sensory receptor and the motor neuron reaches only as far as the spinal cord, so regions in the brain play no role in them. The response may occur so quickly that the child does not feel pain or fear until

afterward. Many reflex actions, however, including crying and the various feeding reflexes, may require neural circuitry that is more intricate and involves the more complex structures of the central nervous system. These reflexes, say the biological maturationists, can be expected to change simply because the associated neural structures themselves mature.

In human beings and many other species, the upper end of the spinal cord thickens to form the **brain stem** (see Figure 4.15). Clusters of neurons within the brainstem begin to function during the fetal period. By birth the brainstem is one of the most highly developed areas of the brain. It controls such inborn reflexes as rooting and sucking, as well as such vital functions as breathing and sleeping. The brainstem also contains neural structures that are associated with the emotions.

The nerves of the brainstem do not respond to specific forms of sensory input in a neat, one-to-one manner. Instead, the brainstem contains several distinct neural pathways that mix various sources of sensory input with impulses from other regions of the brain and the body. Stimulation that reaches the

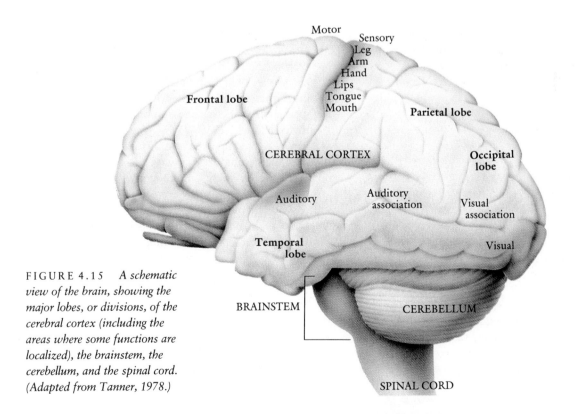

FIGURE 4.15 *A schematic view of the brain, showing the major lobes, or divisions, of the cerebral cortex (including the areas where some functions are localized), the brainstem, the cerebellum, and the spinal cord. (Adapted from Tanner, 1978.)*

brainstem from the environment is modulated and re-organized within these pathways. The fact that inputs from various stimuli follow different pathways allows for activities that are more complex and sustained than those that are characteristic of the simple reflexes that involve only the spinal cord.

In addition to the spinal cord and the brainstem, a third major area of the central nervous system is essential to an understanding of early development — the **cerebral cortex.** In the cerebral cortex, stimulation from the environment travels through fields of interacting neurons so complex that scientists have thus far found it impossible to trace completely the fate of a single stimulus event, such as a touch on the cheek. This complex network of neurons integrates informa-tion from several sensory sources with memories of past experiences, processing old and new information and integrating them in a way that results in the development of new behaviors.

The cerebral cortex is the area of the brain that most clearly distinguishes human beings from other animals. Within the cortex there are regions specialized for the analysis of time, space, and language as well as for motor functions and sensory discriminations. Large areas of the cortical mass, however, are not prewired to respond directly to external stimulation in any discernible way (see Figure 4.16). These "uncommitted" areas provide humans with the capacity to synthesize sensory information in unique ways, making possible such higher psychological functions characteristic of the human adult as voluntary remembering, logical deduction, and written language (Luria, 1973).

Neonates' central nervous systems undergo many changes, continuing processes that began during the fetal period. The number, size, complexity, and even the kinds of cells in the brain increase after birth (Diamond, 1990b; Lecours, 1982) (see Figure 4.17). For example, the hippocampus, which is located in the brainstem and which plays an important role in memory, is estimated to be 40 percent mature at birth, 50 percent mature at 6 weeks, and fully mature at about 1½ years (Kretschmann et al., 1986).

A developmental change in the nervous system that has received much attention is **myelination,** the process by which the neurons become covered by **myelin,** a sheath of fatty cells that insulates the neurons and speeds transmission of nerve impulses along them (Conel, 1939–1963; Yakovlev & Lecours, 1967). Cortical nerve cells, including those that connect the cerebral cortex with the brainstem, are not myelinated at birth. Consequently, the circuitry of the cortex is only tenuously connected to the lower-lying parts of the nervous system that receive stimulation from the environment. At birth these lower-lying areas, which are relatively more mature, can mediate motor reflexes and visual responses without cortical involvement (Woodruf-Pak, Logan, & Thompson, 1990). As the nerve fibers connecting the cortex with regions below the cortex become myelinated, the infant's abilities expand.

Different parts of the cerebral cortex continue to develop at different times throughout infancy and well into childhood and adolescence (Diamond, 1990; Rabinowicz, 1979). Using such criteria as the number and

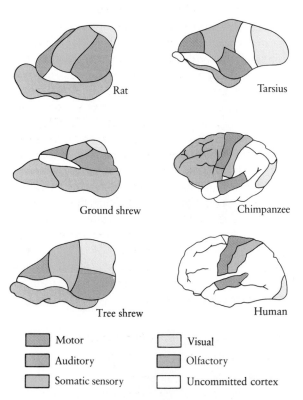

Motor
Auditory
Somatic sensory
Visual
Olfactory
Uncommitted cortex

Rat
Tarsius
Ground shrew
Chimpanzee
Tree shrew
Human

FIGURE 4.16   *In these six mammalian species the proportions of the brain mass that are devoted to different functions vary widely. The areas marked "uncommitted" are not dedicated to any particular sensory or motor functions and are available for integrating information of many kinds. (Adapted from Fishbein, 1976.)*

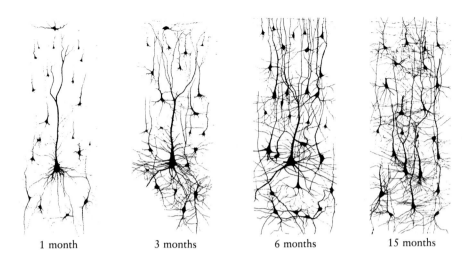

FIGURE 4.17 *These drawings from photomicrographs of infant brain tissue show the marked increases in the size and number of cerebral neurons during the first 15 months of postnatal life. (From Conel, 1939–1963.)*

1 month   3 months   6 months   15 months

size of neurons and the degree of myelination, scientists who study the anatomy of the nervous system estimate that the first area of the cerebral cortex to undergo important developmental change is the **primary motor area,** which is the cortical area responsible for nonreflexive movement (Kolb & Whishaw, 1990). Within the primary motor area, the first cells to become functional are those that control the arms and the trunk. By about 1 month, the neurons in this area are becoming myelinated, so they can now conduct neural impulses more efficiently. The region of the primary motor area that governs leg movements is the last to develop; it is not fully developed until sometime in the second year (Tanner, 1978).

These structural developments in the motor cortex are associated with increases in infants' voluntary movements, that follow a cephalocaudal (from the head down) pattern. At the end of the first month, many infants can raise their heads while lying on their stomachs. At 3 months they show more voluntary movements of the muscles that move the upper trunk, shoulders, arms, and forearms. Voluntary control of leg movements does not come until a few months later.

The **primary sensory areas** of the cortex — those areas that are responsible for the initial analysis of sensory information — also mature in the months after birth. The nerve fibers responsible for touch are the first to become active, followed by those in the primary visual area and then those in the primary auditory area (Huttenlocher, 1990). By 3 months, all of the primary sensory areas are relatively mature (Tanner, 1978).

The prefrontal cortex, which has been implicated in the ability to inhibit movement when movement is inappropriate, and the frontal cortex, which is essential in a wide variety of voluntary behaviors and behaviors that require planning, both begin to function in infancy but continue to mature for an extended time. The prefrontal cortex does not finish maturing for two or more years, and the frontal cortex continues to develop throughout childhood (Diamond, 1990).

According to the biological-maturation perspective, the baby can be expected to engage in more complex and refined interactions with the environment as the brain matures. In this view, the infant's increasing success at nursing, like the gradual lengthening of the intervals between feedings and between periods of sleep, appears to depend at least in part on the maturation of underlying brain structures. Two lines of evidence, one from studies of developmental abnormalities and the other from studies of the relation of reflexes to later behavior, support this view.

Evidence from studies of babies with abnormalities

In rare cases, infants are born without a cerebral cortex. Such babies may have normal reflexes at birth (see Figure 4.18). E. Gamper (1926/1959), for example, observed an infant who was born with an intact brain stem but little or no cerebral cortex. The baby could suck, yawn, stretch, cry, and follow a visual stimulus with his eyes. Robert Emde and Robert Harmon (1972) report REM smiles in such a baby.

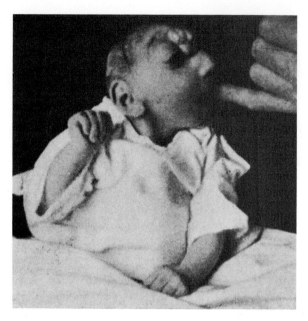

FIGURE 4.18   *Even babies born with little or no cere-bral cortex display basic reflexes such as sucking. (Cour-tesy of the New York Academy of Medicine Library.)*

Babies born without a cerebral cortex seldom live long. Those that do live more than a few days fail to develop the complex, well-coordinated behaviors seen in normal babies. This observation strongly suggests that the cerebral cortex plays an essential role in the development of such coordinated actions as nursing (Emde & Harmon, 1972; Kolb & Whishaw, 1990).

Evidence from studies of reflexes and later behavior

Within the first few months after birth, several of the reflexes infants are born with disappear, never to re-turn. Others disappear for awhile and then reappear as part of a more mature behavior. Still others are trans-formed into more complex behaviors without first disappearing for a time. Many researchers see these changes in the structure of early reflexes as important evidence about the way the maturation of higher brain centers changes behavior (Fox & Bell, 1990; Oppen-heim, 1981).

The **Moro reflex** is a response to a sudden noise or to the sensation of being dropped: infants fling their arms out with their fingers spread and then bring their arms back in toward their bodies with their fingers bent as if to hug something (see Figure 4.19). The Moro reflex usually disappears by the fourth or fifth month, and it is seen again only in the event of injury to the central nervous system. Some researchers con-clude that its disappearance is the result of the matura-tion of higher brain centers (Prechtl, 1977).

The **stepping reflex** is newborns' tendency to make rhythmic leg movements when they are held in an upright position with their feet touching a flat sur-face (see Figure 4.20). It ordinarily disappears at around 2 months of age. At about 1 year of age, babies use similar motions as a component of walking, a vol-untary activity that is acquired with practice.

A lively debate is in progress about the reasons for the disappearance of the stepping reflex and its rela-tion to later walking. According to Philip Zelazo (1983), the disappearance of this reflex is an instance of the suppression of a lower, reflex action as higher, cortical functions begin to mature. After a period of reorganization, he argues, the old reflex reappears in a new form as a component of voluntary walking.

This explanation is rejected by Esther Thelen and her colleagues, who believe that the stepping reflex is really a form of kicking (Thelen, 1986; Thelen, Ulrich, & Jensen, 1989). According to these researchers, early kicking behavior disappears because of changes in the baby's muscle mass and weight, not because of changes in the cortex. They believe that the voluntary walking that appears a year or so after the stepping reflex disappears is not the same movement; it requires not only the maturation of the cortex but also a num-ber of concurrent developments, including increased strength and the ability to balance upright.

A reflex that does not disappear but is instead transformed is **prereaching,** or *visually initiated reach-ing:* newborns reach toward an object that catches their attention and simultaneously make grasping movements (Bushnell, 1985; Trevarthen, 1982; Von Hofsten, 1984). Reaching and grasping are uncoordi-nated just after birth and appear to be independently functioning reflexes. Infants often fail to grasp an ob-ject even after repeated attempts because their hands close too early or too late.

Between 2 and 3 months of age, and coincident with maturational changes in the visual and motor areas of the cerebral cortex, the visually *initiated* reaching reflex is transformed into visually *guided* reaching, a new, voluntary form of behavior in which reaching and grasping are coordinated. A short time thereafter, infants begin to open their hands as soon as

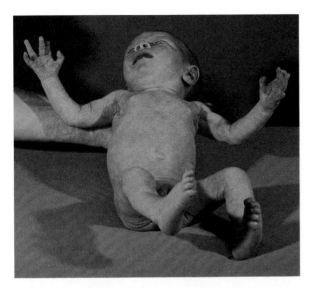

FIGURE 4.19   *Babies exhibit the Moro reflex when they are startled or experience a sudden loss of support.*

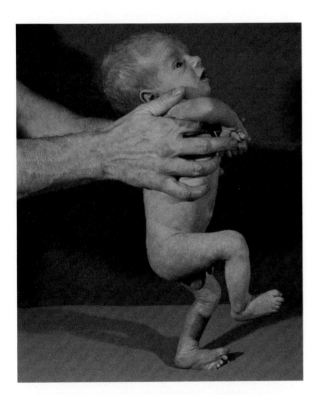

FIGURE 4.20   *Babies held upright with their feet touching the ground move their legs in a fashion that looks like walking. Called the stepping reflex, this form of behavior is currently the subject of debate concerning its origins and subsequent developmental history.*

they begin to reach for an object and begin closing their hands a brief interval before they touch it, clear evidence that they have begun to coordinate reaching and grasping (Von Hoftsten & Rönnquist, 1988).

Although no one has yet pinpointed the cortical areas responsible for such new behaviors as nursing and visually guided reaching, it seems safe to say that the maturation of cortical structures, and probably of the baby's musculature as well, must be accorded a significant role in their development. At the same time, it is not clear that all of the brain connections associated with coordinated reaching and nursing develop before the baby begins to reach and nurse or that they develop in complete independence of environmental influence, as some biological maturationists seem to imply. Rather, some of these brain developments appear to grow out of infants' interactions with their environment (see Box 4.2).

The Environmental-Learning Perspective

Whatever biology may contribute to the changes in the sucking reflex and other reflexes that are present at birth, some form of adaptation to the environment on the part of the infant is clearly necessary for nursing behavior to develop. A mother does not have to continue throughout her child's infancy to be responsible for ensuring that her breast is always presented in precisely the position required to elicit the sucking reflex. Before long infants begin to make the proper adjustments as soon as feeding begins.

Developmental psychologists working within the environmental-learning framework acknowledge that the brain is maturing during early infancy, but they deny that maturation alone can explain how the innate reflexes become coordinated with each other and with appropriate eliciting stimuli in the environment, as is the case when nursing is elicited by the sight of a bottle or the mother's breast. They argue that such coordination requires *learning*, a relatively permanent change in behavior brought about by the experience of events in the environment. Several types of learning are believed to operate throughout development, including habituation (described on p. 129), classical conditioning, and operant conditioning. A fourth type of learning, imitation, is important in later infancy, but the capacity for it may or may not be present shortly after birth. The current controversy surrounding imitation in early infancy is discussed in Box 4.3 (see pp. 158–159).

BOX 4.2
Experience and Development of the Brain

When we attempt to understand the relationship between the brain and psychological development, it seems no more than common sense to expect that increases in the complexity of the brain will precede, or at least accompany, increases in behavioral complexity. An example of such a relationship is the development of social smiling: the cells of the visual cortex and connections between the visual cortex and the brainstem must become functional before children can see others smiling and so be able to smile in return. What this simplified account leaves out, though, is that the development of the brain cells themselves depends on visual experience. The principle that development emerges from the interaction of the organism and the environment applies no less to the development of the brain than to the development of behavior (Gottlieb, 1991a, b; Greenough, 1991).

Early demonstrations of the influence of experience on the brain were provided by studies that Austin Riesen (1950) carried out with normal chimpanzees raised for the first 16 months of their lives in total darkness. When the chimpanzees were then placed in a normally lighted environment, they were unable to learn simple pattern and color discriminations, and their visual acuity was severely impaired. Eye examinations revealed that their retinas had failed to develop normally. Subsequently, anatomical and biochemical analyses have shown that animals deprived of visual experience suffer disturbances of protein synthesis in the visual cortex; as a result, the neurons of the visual cortex have fewer and shorter branches and up to 70 percent fewer synapses than normal (Blakemore & Mitchell, 1973). Significantly, the degree and duration of these effects depend on the age at which the animal is deprived of light. If the deprivation ends early enough, recovery is possible. This finding is consistent with the idea of critical periods.

Additional animal research has shown that the nature of the visual experience plays a role in shaping the neural connections between the eyes and the visual cortex. Certain cells in a cat's brain, for example, normally respond best to horizontal lines, whereas other cells respond best to vertical lines. Both kinds of cells are present in large numbers in kittens that have not yet opened their eyes (Hubel & Wiesel, 1979). When kittens are raised in an environment that allows them to see only horizontal lines for several months, they produce far fewer of the nerve cells that respond to vertical lines than do normal kittens, so their ability to detect vertical lines does not develop normally (Hirsch & Spinelli, 1971).

Evidence that the visual cortex is not the only part of the brain that is affected by experience is provided by the pioneering studies of Mark Rosenzweig and his colleagues (summarized in Rosenzweig, 1984). These researchers raised groups of young male laboratory rats from the same litter in three different environments. The first group were housed individually in standard laboratory cages. Members of the

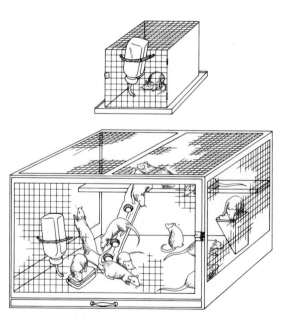

The standard laboratory cage in which laboratory rats are typically housed (top) *provides little opportunity for complex interactions with the environment compared to cages that provide for an enriched environment* (bottom). *Adapted from Rosenzweig, Bennet, & Diamond, 1972.)*

second group were housed together in standard laboratory cages. The third group was provided with enriched conditions. Its members were housed in a large cage that was furnished with a variety of objects they could play with. A new set of playthings, drawn from a pool of 25 objects, was placed in the cage every day. Often the animals in this group were given formal training in a maze or were exposed to a toy-filled open field.

At the end of the experimental period, which lasted anywhere from a few weeks to several months, behavioral tests and examinations of the animals' brains revealed differences that favored the animals raised in enriched conditions:

- Increased rates of learning in standard laboratory tasks, such as learning a maze.
- Increased overall weight of the cerebral cortex.
- Increased amounts of acetylcholinesterase, a brain enzyme that enhances learning.
- Larger neuronal cell bodies and glial (supportive) cells.
- More synaptic connections.

These findings confirm an earlier study that showed that when animals were housed singly in small cages within an enriched environment so that they could do no more than observe what was going on around them, their learning capacity differed in no way from that of the animals that were housed in individual cages away from the enriched environment (Forgays & Forgays, 1952). Active interaction with the environment seems to be the crucial factor in the production of these changes.

Although these results were obtained with nonhuman animal species, they are consistent with what is known about the importance of active involvement with the environment for human development. They show that behavioral changes should not be thought of as secondary consequences of changes that occur in the brain. Behavioral changes induced by environmental stimulation can themselves lead to changes in the brain that then support more complex forms of behavior.

Classical conditioning

Classical conditioning is the process by which an organism learns which events in its environment go with each other. As Carolyn Rovee-Collier (1987), a researcher who has been influential in promoting the study of classical conditioning in infancy, points out, "Because many events in nature occur in an orderly fashion, classical conditioning permits organisms to exploit this orderliness and anticipate events instead of simply reacting to them" (p. 107).

The existence of this very basic learning mechanism was demonstrated at the turn of the century by the Russian physiologist Ivan Pavlov (1849–1936). Pavlov (1927) showed that after several experiences of hearing a tone just before food was placed in its mouth, a dog would begin to salivate in response to the tone, before it received any food. In everyday language, the dog began to expect food when it heard the tone, and its mouth watered at the thought.

In the terminology of environmental learning theories, Pavlov paired a **conditional stimulus** (CS)—a tone—with an **unconditional stimulus** (UCS)—food in the mouth. The food is called an unconditional stimulus because it "unconditionally" causes salivation, salivation being a reflex response to food in the mouth. Salivation, in turn, is called an **unconditional response** (UCR) because it is automatically and invariantly (that is, "unconditionally") elicited by food in the mouth. The tone is called a conditional stimulus because the behavior it elicits depends on ("is conditional on") the way it has been paired with the unconditional stimulus. When the unconditional response (salivation in response to food in the mouth) occurs in response to the CS (the tone), it is called a **conditional response** (CR) because it depends on the pairing of the CS (the tone) and the UCS (the food). The key indicator that learning has occurred is that the CS elicits the CR before the onset of the UCS (see Figure 4.21).

A number of psychologists seized on Pavlov's demonstrations as a possible model for the way infants learn about their environments. One of Pavlov's coworkers demonstrated conditioned feeding responses in a 14-month-old infant (Krasnogorski, 1907/1967). The baby opened his mouth and made sucking motions (CRs) at the sight of a glass of milk (CS). When a bell (a new CS) was sounded on several occasions just before the glass of milk was presented, the baby began to open his mouth and suck at the sound of the bell, an indication that classical conditioning built expecta-

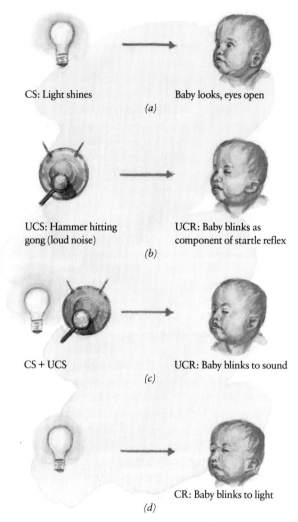

CS: Light shines   Baby looks, eyes open

(a)

UCS: Hammer hitting   UCR: Baby blinks as
gong (loud noise)   component of startle reflex

(b)

CS + UCS   UCR: Baby blinks to sound

(c)

                                         CR: Baby blinks to light

(d)

FIGURE 4.21   *Classical conditioning. In the top panel
(a) the sight of a light (CS) elicits no particular response. In
(b) the loud sound of a gong (UCS) causes the baby to blink
his eyes (UCR). In (c) the sight of the light (CS) is paired
with the loud sound of the gong (UCS), which evokes an
eyeblink (UCR). Finally, (d) the sight of the light (CS) is
sufficient to cause the baby to blink (CR), demonstrating
that learning has occurred.*

tions in the infant based on a process of association.
The crucial point to these observations is that there is
no *biological* connection between the sight of a glass of
milk or the sound of a bell and the mouth-opening and
sucking responses they elicited. Rather, the fact that
the new stimuli elicited these responses shows that
learning has occurred.

Pavlov's ideas soon won a large following in the
United States, and several studies were conducted with
the intention of demonstrating the importance of classical conditioning as a mechanism of infant learning. In
a study mentioned in Chapter 1 (pp. 29–31), John
Watson and Rosalie Rayner purported to show that
infants learn to fear through the process of classical
conditioning. Dorothy Marquis (1931), in one of the
early studies of classical conditioning in newborn infants, showed that sucking motions could be conditioned to the sound of a buzzer if the buzzer sounded
just before the baby was given a bottle.

These early studies were criticized because they
did not entirely rule out other possible causes for the
babies' behavior. The babies in Marquis's study, for
example, may have opened their mouths and made
sucking motions simply because they were excited by
the buzzer and not because they made a specific association between the buzzer and food. These criticisms
took on additional force when several well-controlled
experiments failed to show classical conditioning in
newborn infants (Sameroff & Cavanaugh, 1979).
Thus, as recently as a decade ago, it appeared that
classical conditioning did not occur in infants until 2
or 3 months after birth. Intensive research conducted
during the past 10 years, however, in which stimuli
that are biologically significant to an infant were chosen and great care was taken to make certain that the
infant subjects were alert at the time the experiments
were performed, has demonstrated with virtual certainty that classical conditioning can occur within
hours of birth.

Elliott Blass and his associates, for example, conditioned the sucking response to stroking of the forehead (Blass, Ganchrow, & Steiner, 1984). These researchers assumed that such tactile stimulation occurs
naturally during feeding but that it does not ordinarily
produce sucking. They used a pipette to give infants
only a few hours old a small dose of sugar water (sucrose) immediately after stroking the infants' foreheads. Infants in a control group were also stroked and
given sugar water, but the researchers performed the
two acts independently and at variable intervals to
preclude the possibility that the infants would form an
association between them. The infants in the experimental group began to suck and pucker their faces — a
response pattern the researchers dubbed a "pucker-
suck" — when they were stroked on the forehead. The
infants in the control group did not. One of the most
convincing bits of evidence that classical conditioning
had occurred was the way the infants reacted when the
investigators later stroked their foreheads but did not

give them sugar water. The first or second time this happened, the infants in the experimental group responded by frowning or making an angry face and then crying or whimpering. The researchers also stopped giving sugar water to the infants in the control group, but when their foreheads were stroked, they did not express anger or cry. Rovee-Collier (1987) comments that this finding "suggests that infants in the experimental group had learned the predictive relation between stroking and sucrose delivery and cried because their expectancy was violated" (p. 113).

Lewis Lipsitt (1990) and his colleagues have also succeeded in showing that neonates will form a conditioned reflex to a noxious stimulus—a puff of air to the eye. Infants 10, 20, and 30 days of age learned to shut their eyes in anticipation of an air puff that came 1½ seconds after a tone sounded. The youngest infants did not seem to retain what they had learned, but those 10 and 20 days old showed indications of remembering the experience 10 days later.

Operant conditioning

Classical conditioning is a process by which previously existing behaviors come to be elicited by new stimuli. It explains how infants begin to build up expectations about the connections between events in their environment, but it does little to explain how even the simplest changes take place in infants' behavioral repertoires. The kind of conditioning that gives rise to new and more complex behaviors is called *operant,* or *instrumental,* conditioning, in recognition of the ability the learned response gives the organism to operate more effectively on its environment to bring about desired changes.

The basic idea of **operant conditioning** is that changes in behavior occur as a result of the positive or negative consequences the behavior produces; that is, organisms will tend to repeat behaviors that lead to rewards and will tend to give up behaviors that fail to produce rewards or that lead to punishment (Skinner, 1938; Thorndike, 1911). In the terminology of operant conditioning, a consequence, such as receiving a reward, that increases the likelihood that the behavior that produces it will occur again is called **reinforcement.** According to an operant explanation of the development of nursing, such behaviors as turning the head away from the bottle or burying the nose in the mother's breast will become less probable because they do not lead to a result the infant finds satisfying:

milk. At the same time, well-coordinated breathing, sucking, and swallowing will increase in strength and probability because it is likely to be rewarded with milk.

Until the 1960s, it was generally believed that newborns are capable of simple, reflexive behaviors only, so no one did research on operant conditioning in young infants. Since that time, it has been demonstrated that newborn infants are indeed capable of operant learning, which can be reinforced in them by such varied stimuli as milk, sweet substances, an interesting visual display, a pacifier, and the sound of a heartbeat or the mother's voice (DeCasper & Fifer, 1980; DeCasper & Sigafoos, 1983; Rovee-Collier, 1987; Moon & Fifer, 1990).

An experiment by Einar Siqueland (1968), for example, demonstrated that neonates can learn to turn their heads in order to suck on a pacifier. The key requirement of operant learning is that a behavior has to occur before it can be reinforced. Head turning is ideal in this respect because it is something even the youngest neonates do. While the babies lay in laboratory cribs, Siqueland placed a band around their heads that was connected to a device for recording the degree their heads moved to either side (see Figure 4.22).

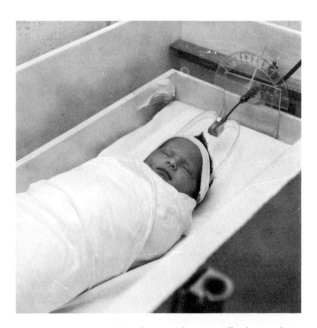

FIGURE 4.22   *A newborn with a specially designed headpiece that records head turning. Head turns of more than 10° were reinforced by the opportunity to suck on a pacifier.*

BOX 4.3

Imitation in the Newborn?

When we consider newborns' limited visual capacities and uncoordinated movements, the notion that neonates can imitate actions they see may seem far-fetched. Yet several studies appear to show that babies are capable of rudimentary forms of imitation from birth (Gardner & Gardner, 1970; Meltzoff & Moore, 1977, 1983a, 1989). These studies have generated intense interest among developmental psychologists because it has long been believed that imitation does not become possible until several months after birth (Abravanel, Levan-Goldschmidt, & Stevenson, 1976; Piaget, 1962). If the capacity for true imitation does exist in newborns, it provides them with an important avenue for learning about the world that they were not previously known to possess.

All that seems necessary to determine whether newborns are capable of imitating is for the researcher to present some behavior to newborns and then observe whether or not they repeat it. Yet a good deal of research has failed to resolve the question of imitation in newborns definitively. Part of the problem is to find behaviors that are within newborns' capacities.

In research conducted by Andrew Meltzoff and Keith Moore (1977, 1983a, 1989), an adult loomed above alert newborn babies and made distinctive facial expressions, such as opening his mouth very wide and sticking out his tongue. Meltzoff and Moore reported that the infants often imitated the facial expression of the adult. Aware that their claims were going to be viewed skeptically, Meltzoff and Moore took special precautions to ensure that their results could not be attributed to procedural errors. As a check of their findings, they photographed the infants and the adult model independently. They then asked judges who had not been present during the experimental sessions to look at the photographs of the infants and guess what sort of face the adult had made. The judges guessed correctly more often than they could have done by chance. The implication is that the infants did indeed imitate the distinctive adult facial expressions they saw.

Yet the results were not so clear-cut as the report of the findings suggests. On the 97 trials when the researcher stuck out his tongue, for example, the babies "most often" stuck out their tongues in return. But

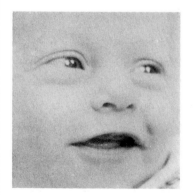  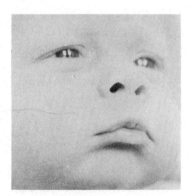

Each pair of photos shows the expression of an infant after observing an adult; the correspondence between the infant's

the "most often" means that they stuck out their tongues 30 times; they opened their mouths 20 times, and they puckered their lips or moved their fingers on the remaining trials. The imitative response won out, but just barely.

The research of Meltzoff and Moore has generated many follow-up studies. Tiffany Field and her colleagues (1982) found support for Meltzoff and Moore's conclusions when they used somewhat different procedures and responses (see the photos below). They arranged for an adult to model three facial expressions—happy, sad, and surprised—for babies who were an average of 36 hours old. The babies showed that they could distinguish among the model's facial expressions by the fact that they habituated to the repeated presentation of a single expression but then began to pay close attention again when the model presented them with a different facial expression. Most important, the babies appeared to imitate these new expressions. An observer who could not see the model and who did not know what expressions were being presented to the babies was able to determine the facial expression of the model from

the facial movements of the babies on a statistically reliable basis. These results are difficult to explain without assuming that the infants somehow matched what they did with what they saw the model doing. Precisely how infants accomplished this matching remains uncertain (Vinter, 1986).

Not everyone who has attempted to replicate Meltzoff and Moore's study has been successful. Some researchers suggest that either there was some peculiarity in their procedures or the behavior they observed is a very special form of imitation (Abravanel & Sigafoos, 1984; Kaitz et al., 1988). One possibility is that imitation in the newborn is a reflex behavior that disappears with time, unless it is specially maintained by operant conditioning.

Even if newborns are capable of imitation, it is uncertain if it should be counted among the important learning mechanisms that are present at birth. It will, however, become an important mechanism of learning when it appears as a prominent part of infants' behavioral repertoire later in the first year of life.

 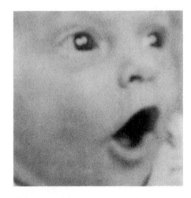 

expression and the adult's expression is taken as evidence that newborns are capable of imitation.

Whenever the designated response occurred, the baby was given a pacifier to suck on.

In the first phase of his study, Siqueland recorded how often the babies naturally turned their heads. Once this baseline rate was established, he set his apparatus to signal when the babies had turned their heads at least 10 degrees to either side. As soon as they did, they were given the pacifier to suck on. After only 25 occasions on which the head turning was reinforced with the pacifier, most of the babies had tripled the rate at which they turned their heads.

To make certain that the increase in babies' head turning was not due to the excitement of being placed in the crib, Siqueland included another group of infants in his experiment who were rewarded with a pacifier for holding their heads *still*. These infants learned to move their heads *less* during the course of the experiment.

Sidney Bijou and Donald Baer (1966), two prominent environmental-learning theorists, summarize the developmental implications of operant conditioning this way:

> Operant conditioning is involved in a vast change in the form and complexity of the infant's responses which may be described as the stringing together of a collection of operants in a chain. An infant may be capable of a variety of arm motions. These may be linked in slightly different order to produce behavior described as a wave or a pat, making patti-cake, beating a drum, grabbing a cookie, fending off, sweeping away, etc. (p. 83)

Support for the argument that behavioral development results largely from learning comes from studies that show that even very young infants are capable of remembering what they have learned from one testing session to the next (Rovee-Collier, 1984, 1987; Vander Linde, Morrongiello, & Rovee-Collier, 1985; Watson, 1984). These studies also suggest that memory for newly learned behaviors improves markedly during the first several months of life, a finding to which we will return at the end of this chapter and again in Chapter 5 (pp. 198–200).

The environmental-learning theorists' emphasis on the power of the environment to shape behavior provides an important counterweight to the biological-maturation theorists' emphasis on the primacy of genetic influences in determining the course of development. But the environmental-learning explanations of developmental change also have some significant shortcomings. In effect, this approach makes no distinction between learning and development; it views development as simply the accumulation of learned modifications in behavior. It acknowledges no qualitative differences that distinguish older and younger children, only quantitative differences in the number and complexity of the behaviors they have acquired. It also has a difficult time dealing with the important issue of individual differences in behavior, including differences associated with sex and temperament. According to this perspective, such differences can be accounted for only by differences in the experiences of individuals; the effects of genetic variation are discounted. Contemporary research on individual differences has made this extreme view difficult to justify (Plomin, 1986).

The Universal-Constructivist Perspective: Piaget

Jean Piaget, the most prominent champion of a universal-constructivist perspective, objected to both the biological-maturation and environmental-learning theories of his day. Although he believed that embryology provides an important model for later development, he criticized biological explanations for their failure to spell out how the environment of human infants interacts with their biological capacities to permit development to occur (Piaget & Inhelder, 1969). At the same time, he was critical of environmental-learning explanations because they assume that the environment is the originator of developmental change and they deny the existence of qualitative, stagelike changes over the course of development.

Piaget's theory of developmental change

The starting point of Piaget's theory of development is his view of the nature of early reflexes. To Piaget, a reflex is a primitive schema, the basic unit of psychological functioning in his theory. The concept of a schema will appear frequently in later chapters because it figures prominently in many modern approaches to development, often with slightly different meanings attached to it. For the present, a **schema** can be thought of as a mental structure that provides an organism with a model for action in similar or analogous circumstances (Piaget & Inhelder, 1969).

During the first month of life, the "reflex schemas" babies are born with provide them with a kind of skeleton for action that is gradually fleshed out by experience. Eventually these initial schemas are strengthened and transformed into new schemas through *adaptation,* a twofold process comprising what Piaget termed *assimilation* and *accommodation.*

During **assimilation,** various experiences are absorbed by the organism and are transformed to fit its existing schemas, strengthening those schemas and making them work more efficiently. Piaget used the process of digestion as a metaphor to help clarify what he meant by assimilation. Reflex schemas, he explained, assimilate experience in much the same way the human body assimilates food. Various kinds of food taken in by the body are assimilated through the process of digestion into such existing physical structures as bone, blood, and brain tissue (Piaget, 1952b).

Sucking is one such primitive schema. It is initially closely tied to a small class of eliciting stimuli, such as a nipple placed in the mouth or a touch on the cheek, but it does not remain strictly bound to particular eliciting conditions for long. At some point babies are likely to find, say, their thumb instead of a nipple touching their face and start sucking on it. Since a thumb is similar to a nipple, the infants can adjust the way the thumb is held so that they can suck on it in pretty much the same way they suck on the nipple. In other words, they assimilate the thumb, a new object, to their existing sucking schema.

Not every object babies encounter can be assimilated to an existing schema. When babies first encounter a blanket, for instance, they may try to suck on it. However, because the qualities of the blanket — the satin binding, perhaps, or the cloth of the blanket itself — are so unlike the qualities of a nipple or a thumb, they are unable to assimilate the blanket as an object to suck on. They will therefore make some **accommodation;** that is, they will modify the way they suck, perhaps by choosing a corner of the blanket and sucking on that, using approximately but not exactly the same schema as they had used to suck on a nipple. In its modified form, the sucking schema can now be applied to old and new environmental experiences. If a baby encounters a toy truck and tries to suck on it, accommodation is unlikely to occur because the toy is so difficult to suck on; in this case, the baby's sucking schema will be unmodified.

Piaget and Barbel Inhelder (1969) expressed the two-sided nature of the process that, in their view, leads to developmental change in the following way:

> [Our] view of assimilation presupposes a reciprocity between S–R [stimulus and response]; that is to say, the input, the stimulus, is filtered through a structure that consists of the action schemes, . . . which in turn are modified and enriched when the subject's behavioral repertoire is accommodated to the demands of reality. The filtering or modification of the input is called *assimilation;* the modification of the internal schemes is called *accommodation.* (p. 6)

One way to summarize Piaget's theory is to view development as a constant tug-of-war between assimilation and accommodation. Piaget referred to this back-and-forth process of seeking a fit between the child's existing schemas and new environmental experiences as **equilibration,** which is basically an attempt to achieve a balance, or equilibrium. At certain times a balance between assimilation and accommodation is achieved, bringing the child to a new level of development. But during childhood the balance does not last for long because the process of biological maturation and the accumulation of experience lead to new imbalances, which cause the tug-of-war between assimilation and accommodation to begin again, pushing development to increasingly higher stages until adulthood is reached.

Piaget was a stage theorist who maintained that development proceeds by a sequence of qualitative transformations in the overall psychological structure of the child. He believed that there are four major developmental stages between birth and adulthood, corresponding to infancy, early childhood, middle childhood, and adolescence.

Table 4.4 provides a summary of the four stages of cognitive development described by Piaget. The sensorimotor stage is discussed below and in Chapters 5 and 6. We examine the preoperational, concrete operational, and formal operational stages in Chapters 9, 12, and 16, respectively.

The sensorimotor period and its substages

Piaget (1952b) referred to infancy as the **sensorimotor stage** because during this period an infant's achievements consist largely of coordinating their sensory perceptions and simple motor behaviors: reaching for an object, for example, or starting to nurse at the mother's breast. This stage lasts from birth to about

TABLE 4.4
Piaget's Stages of Cognitive Development and the Sensorimotor Substages

Age Years	Stage	Description	Characteristics of Sensorimotor Substages
Birth to 2	Sensorimotor	Infants' achievements consist largely of coordinating their sensory perceptions and simple motor behaviors. As they move through the 6 substages of this period, infants come to recognize the existence of a world outside of themselves and begin to interact with it in deliberate ways.	**Substage 1, 0–1½ months** *Reflex schemas exercised:* involuntary rooting, sucking, grasping, looking **Substage 2, 1½–4 months** *Primary circular reactions:* repetition of actions that are pleasurable in themselves
2 to 6	Preoperational	Young children can represent reality to themselves through the use of symbols, including mental images, words, and gestures. Objects and events no longer have to be present to be thought about, but children often fail to distinguish their point of view from that of others, become easily captured by surface appearances, and are often confused about causal relations.	**Substage 3, 4–8 months** *Secondary circular reactions:* dawning awareness of relation of own actions to environment; extended actions that produce interesting change in the environment **Substage 4, 8–12 months** *Coordination of secondary circular reactions:* combining schemas to achieve a desired effect; earliest form of problem solving
6 to 12	Concrete operational	As they enter middle childhood, children become capable of mental operations, internalized actions that fit into a logical system. Operational thinking allows children mentally to combine, separate, order, and transform objects and actions. Such operations are considered concrete because they are carried out in the presence of the objects and events being thought about.	**Substage 5, 12–18 months** *Tertiary circular reactions:* deliberate variation of problem-solving means; experimentation to see what the consequences will be **Substage 6, 18–24 months** *Beginnings of symbolic representation:* images and words come to stand for familiar objects; invention of new means of problem solving through symbolic combinations
12 to 19	Formal operational	In adolescence the developing person acquires the ability to think systematically about all logical relations within a problem. Adolescents display keen interest in abstract ideals and in the process of thinking itself.	

the age of 2 years. Within the sensorimotor period Piaget identified six substages, each of which builds on the accomplishments of the one that precedes it (see Table 4.4). We will discuss the first two substages of the sensorimotor period here because they correspond to the early months of postnatal life. The remaining substages will be described in Chapters 5 and 6.

Substage 1 lasts from birth to approximately 1 to 1½ months. It is the stage during which infants learn to control and coordinate their reflexes. Piaget believed that the reflexes present at birth provide the initial connection between infants and their environments, but at that point they do not, in themselves, add anything new to development because they have undergone very little accommodation and so still reflect the "preestablished boundaries of the hereditary apparatus" (Piaget & Inhelder, 1969:7).

The initial reflexes provide the impetus for their own change, however, because they produce stimulation in addition to responses to stimuli. When infants suck, for example, they experience tactile pressure on the roof of the mouth, which stimulates further sucking, which produces more tactile pressure, and so on. This stimulus-producing aspect of reflexes is the key to the development of the second sensorimotor substage because it results in the earliest extensions of already existing reflexes.

Substage 2 lasts from about 1 month to about 4 months. The first hints of new forms of behavior are found in the way existing reflexes are extended in time (as when infants suck between feedings) or are applied to new objects. Piaget and Inhelder (1969) offered thumb-sucking as an example of the extension of a reflex to accommodate a new object. They noted that babies may suck their thumbs accidentally as early as the first day of life. (We now know they may do so even before birth; see Chapter 3, p. 86.) They believed, however, that the thumb-sucking seen at 2 months of age and beyond is the result of sensorimotor accommodation, which extends the sucking reflex to a new object.

Substage 2 is characterized by what Piaget called **primary circular reactions,** or reactions in which infants repeat a variety of pleasurable motions, such as waving their hands or kicking their feet, for their own sake. These actions are called primary because they are centered on the baby's own body; they are called circular because they lead only back to themselves. (Table 4.4 lists all of Piaget's sensorimotor substages and the behaviors characteristic of each.)

Piaget was a keen observer of his own infants, and evidence in support of many of his ideas about the earliest substages of the sensorimotor period can be seen in the notes he kept about their behavior. The following observations illustrate the kind of behaviors he referred to as primary circular reactions:

> After having learned to suck his thumb, Laurent continues to play with his tongue and to suck, but intermittently. On the other hand, his skill increases. Thus at 1 month, 20 days, I notice he grimaces while placing his tongue between gums and lips and in bulging his lips, as well as making a clapping sound when quickly closing his mouth after these exercises.

> From 2 months, 18 days Laurent plays with his saliva, letting it accumulate within his half-open lips and then abruptly swallowing it. About the same period he makes sucking-like movements, without putting out his tongue. (1952b:65)

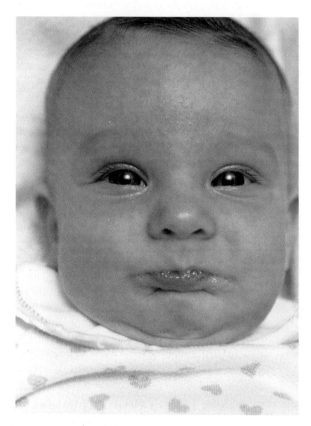

Blowing bubbles is an early instance of a primary circular reaction in which an accidental aspect of sucking is prolonged for the pleasure of continuing the sensation.

Piaget believed that such primary circular reactions are very important because they offer the first evidence of cognitive development. "The basic law of dawning psychological activity," he wrote, "could be said to be the search for the maintenance or repetition of interesting states of consciousness" (1977:202).

Over the first few months of life, these circular reactions undergo *differentiation*—infants learn to use different grasps for different objects and learn not to suck on toy trucks—and *integration*—infants can grasp their mother's arm with one hand while sucking on a bottle in a coordinated way. All the while, infants' experiences are providing more nourishment for their existing schemas and are forcing them to modify those schemas, permitting them to master more of the world.

In contrast to the infants portrayed by biological-maturation and environmental-learning approaches, Piagetian infants are active, problem-solving organisms who virtually from the beginning are busy acting on the environment in the process of adapting to it. All three perspectives discussed thus far designate inborn reflexes as the starting point for development, but they view the significance of these reflexes in different ways. Because Piaget saw reflexes as schemas for action, he downplayed the role of the environment in evoking or reinforcing particular behaviors and instead emphasized the infant's constructive activity in shaping the way the environment will exert its effects.

Piaget's theory and the social environment

Despite Piaget's avowal of the importance of the social environment for development, analysis of the social context for the early development of reflexes is virtually absent from his writings. Yet a close look at the acquisition of new forms of behavior during the first 2½ months of life reveals that changes in a baby's behavior are accompanied by changes in the mother's behavior. These changes in maternal behaviors appear to be just as essential to the infant's development as are the changes that occur in the infant's relations to objects or in its brain functioning.

Nursing clearly demonstrates how the mother's behavior contributes to the infant's development. In the beginning, the mother's nursing behavior may be not much more coordinated than her baby's. She must learn how to hold the baby and adjust herself so that the nipple is placed at exactly the right spot against the baby's mouth to elicit the sucking reflex. She must also learn not to press the baby so tightly to her breast that its breathing is disrupted and the head-withdrawal reflex is brought into play.

When the mother breast-feeds, her reflexes in response to the baby's (reflex) sucking combine with her voluntary efforts to maximize the amount of milk the baby receives. This system of mutually facilitating reflexes in infant and mother, which changes the consequences of reflex sucking, is illustrated in Figure 4.23. The infant's sucking not only transports milk from nipple to mouth but also stimulates the production of more milk, thereby increasing the sucking reflex's adaptive value.

A different type of mutual facilitation arises from the physical movements mothers make while they are feeding their children by either breast or bottle. Kenneth Kaye (1982) and his colleagues found that even during the very first feeding, mothers occasionally jiggle their baby or the bottle. These jiggles come not at random intervals but during the pauses between the infant's bursts of sucking. The jiggles increase the probability of sucking and prolong the feeding session, thereby increasing the amount of milk the neonate receives.

Sucking in response to jiggling is not a reflex in the sense that rooting is a reflex. Rooting is an automatic, involuntary response to being touched on the side of the mouth. There are no known neural connections that make sucking inevitable when a baby is jiggled. Yet it happens, it is to some extent automatic, and it has clear adaptive value. Scholars do not know for sure where such adaptive patterns come from. Kaye calls them "preadapted responses," implying that they may have arisen in the course of human evolution.

Kaye speculates that the mother's jiggle between her infant's bursts of sucking is her way of intuitively "conversing" with her baby by filling in her "turn" during the pauses in the baby's rhythmic sucking. Mothers' reports support Kaye's view. Although they are not aware that they are jiggling their babies in a systematic way, mothers report that they actively try to help their babies nurse. They notice and disapprove of the pauses between bursts of sucking. When mothers are asked about their jiggling behavior, a typical response is that the baby "gets lazy, or dozes off, so I jiggle her to get her back on task."

Kaye's demonstration that mothers contribute to children's behavioral development by actively structuring the children's experiences adds an important ingredient to Piaget's analysis of the mechanisms of

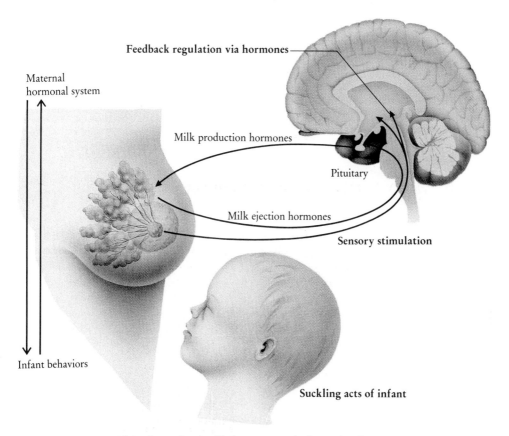

Feedback regulation via hormones

Maternal
hormonal system

Milk production hormones

Pituitary

Milk ejection hormones

Sensory stimulation

Infant behaviors

Suckling acts of infant

FIGURE 4.23   *The reflexes that establish a reciprocal relationship between the infant being fed and the mother. Infant sucking stimulates the release of hormones that increase milk production and help to trigger the ejection of milk from the mammary glands. (From Cairns, 1979.)*

developmental change; *both* the child and the child's environment actively participate in the process of interaction through which development occurs. But in one essential respect, the forms of interactionism advanced by Kaye and Piaget are the same; both investigators assumed that the interactional processes they described are universal features of human behavior and thus apply to children everywhere.

The Cultural-Context Perspective

As we indicated in Chapter 1 (p. 19), the cultural-context perspective shares with Piaget an emphasis on the active strivings of the individual as essential to development as well as his assumption that biology and experience play equal and reciprocal roles in con-

stituting human beings. However, it adds two additional sources of developmental change: (1) the *active* contribution of other people in the child's community and (2) the cultural "designs for living" accumulated over the history of the social group. Such designs for living are present in all human societies, and in this sense they are universal. But their particular shape varies from one society to the next, giving rise to culturally specific modes of interaction. These culture-specific variations encourage development along certain lines while discouraging it along others, thereby producing distinctive patterns of behavior (Laboratory of Comparative Human Cognition, 1983). In the development of sucking into organized feeding we can see how the universal facts of maturation, learning, and maternal support vary culturally in ways that shape infants' behavior in the present and give hints of further changes to come.

FIGURE 4.24 *Although babies are nursed in all cultures, there are wide variations in the way babies' nursing behavior is organized.*

In their discussion of culture and development, Margaret Mead and Frances Macgregor (1951) noted that cultures "differ from each other in the way in which the growth process is interwoven with learning" (p. 26). This principle, they went on to explain, first operates in the various ways adults of different cultures respond to such basic neonatal capacities as the sucking reflex:

> The existence of the sucking reflex at birth . . . will be taken advantage of in some cultures by putting the baby at once to the mother's breast, so that the infant's sucking is used to stimulate the flow of the mother's milk while the infant itself remains hungry, or the infant may be put at the breast of a wet nurse with a well-established flow of milk, in which case the infant's sucking behavior is reinforced but the mother is left without the stimulation that it would have provided. As another alternative, the infant may be starved until the mother has milk, and as still another, the infant may be given a bottle with a different kind of nipple. (p. 26)

These different feeding practices are equivalent in that they are all ways in which parents arrange for infants' innate sucking reflexes to become part of nursing. In this respect, nursing is universal — in every culture, some arrangement is made for the infant's sucking reflex to become a part of nursing (see Figure 4.24).

According to the cultural-context perspective, however, cultural variations in the actual arrangements made with regard to a neonate's initial capacities may have a direct effect on the infant's early experience and an indirect effect on later experiences. To continue with the example provided by Mead and Macgregor, if a baby is bottle-fed until the mother's milk begins to flow, changes in the baby's sucking that are adaptive to bottle-feeding may interfere with subsequent breast-feeding. If the interference is great, breast-feeding may be given up altogether. This outcome will alter both the kind of milk that the infant receives and the forms of social interaction between infant and mother that are a part of feeding. Indirect effects on infants' later development occur when a specific cultural practice, such as bottle-feeding or the use of a wetnurse, is linked to a larger pattern of interaction that will shape the child's future experiences. For example, if a mother who stays at home gives her baby a bottle because she believes that bottled milk is more nutritious than her own, the use of a bottle rather than breast-feeding may have no differential impact on the development of social relations between mother and child. However, if the mother leaves her baby at a day-care center because she is working in an office or factory that makes no provision for on-site childcare, the relationship between mother and baby is less than exclusive. In such a case bottle-feeding is likely to become part of a pattern of social interactions with peers and a succession of caregivers. In either case, the immediate consequences of the specific feeding practice are less important than the larger patterns of life with which they are associated.

An important implication of the cultural-context perspective that is not captured by the example of nursing is that cultures provide people with a framework for interpreting their experiences that even influences their view of their own babies. The way newborn babies are treated depends very much on what a culture defines babies to be. In the United States today, for example, well-educated middle-class adults tend to have a higher opinion of the psychological capacities of young infants than do adults of many other cultures and even of some subcultures within the United States (Super, 1981). When the behavioral consequences of this cultural belief are viewed in isolation from usual childcare contexts, they can be quite striking, as the following description from a study by the pediatrician T. Berry Brazelton and his colleagues illustrates. In this study, 1-week-old infants were placed in infant seats in the laboratory and their mothers were asked to spend several minutes interacting with them. Here's how the scene unfolded:

> Our mothers were faced with the problem of communicating with infants who, if they were not crying or thrashing, were often hanging limply in the infant seat with closed or semi closed eyes or, just as frequently, were "frozen" motionless in some strange and uninterpretable posture — staring at nothing. . . . Perhaps the most interesting response to the challenge of facing an unresponsive infant is this. The mother takes on facial expressions, motions, and postures indicative of emotion, as though the infant were behaving intentionally or as though she and he were communicating. Frequently, in response to a motionless infant, she suddenly acquires an expression of great admiration, moving back and forth in front of him with great enthusiasm; or again in response to an unmoving infant, she takes on an expression of great surprise, moving backward in mock astonishment; or in the most exaggerated manner,

she greets the infant and, furthermore, carries on an animated extended greeting interchange, bobbing and nodding enthusiastically exactly as though her greeting were currently being reciprocated. (Brazelton, Koslowski, & Main, 1974: 67–68)

In sum, most mothers in the United States are unwilling or unable to deal with neonatal behaviors as though they were meaningless or unintentional. Instead, they endow the smallest movements with highly personal meaning and react to them affectively. They insist on joining in and enlarging on even the least possible interactive behaviors, through imitation. And they perform as if highly significant interaction had taken place when there has been no interaction at all.

The Kaluli, who live in the rain forests of Papua New Guinea, have a far different set of beliefs about babies than middle-class Americans do, and they treat their babies quite differently as a result. As Eleanor Ochs and Bambi Schieffelin (1984) report, the Kaluli see their babies as helpless creatures who have "no understanding." Although they may greet their infants by name, they do not talk to them in the way middle-class American adults do. Nor do Kaluli mothers engage in extended eye contact with their babies, because the Kaluli believe that it is impolite to gaze at the person you are talking to. Kaluli mothers hold their infants facing outward so they can see, be seen by, and interact with other members of the social group. Instead of speaking to their infants, Kaluli mothers speak for them. As Ochs and Schieffelin point out, "in taking this role the mother does for the infant what the infant cannot do for itself, that is appear to act in a controlled and competent manner, using language" (p. 290).

Notice that the words Ochs and Schieffelin use to describe the intent of the Kaluli mothers could also be applied to the U.S. mothers, even though the specific actions involved are quite different. In both cultures, beliefs about what babies are, what they can do, and what they will need to do in the future affect the way babies are treated by those around them and thus the way they experience the environment. In short, different cultural patterns lead to different child-rearing practices, which have quite different effects on further development, as we will see in later chapters. It is therefore important to keep cultural factors constantly in mind when we consider the mechanisms of developmental change.

Every culture works out its own best way to transport babies.

INTEGRATING THE SEPARATE THREADS OF DEVELOPMENT

The complexities involved in accounting for the way nursing develops during the first months of life provide some idea of the enormous difficulties facing anyone who seeks to explain human development. Even for this seemingly simple form of behavior, the contributions of biological and environmental factors, including cultural influences and the specific circumstances in which infants find themselves, must all be considered. The difficulties do not end here, however. A child's various behaviors develop not in isolation from one another but rather as parts of an integrated system. Thus psychologists must also study the parts of the system in relation to one another. The requirement that developing organisms must be studied as a whole is expressed with particular clarity by the embryologist C. H. Waddington (1947), whose ideas about nature-nurture interactions were introduced in Chapter 2.

> A new level of organization cannot be accounted for in terms of the properties of its elementary units as they behave in isolation, but is accounted for if we add to these certain other properties which the units only exhibit when in combination with one another. (p. 145)

Nursing, for instance, must be understood as but one element in a system of developing behaviors that includes increasingly longer sleeping and waking periods and the buildup of elementary expectations about the environment.

To meet this requirement that developing behaviors be considered both individually and as parts of a larger whole, the analytical strategy developed by Robert Emde and his associates is especially useful (Emde, Gaensbauer, & Harmon, 1976). As we mentioned in Chapter 1 (pp. 38–39), this strategy involves tracing developments in the biological, behavioral, and social domains *as they relate to one another*. It allows the identification of bio-social-behavioral shifts, those periods when changes in the separate domains converge to create the kind of qualitative reorganization in the overall pattern of behaviors that signals the onset of a new stage of development. We can see the usefulness of this approach by examining the first bio-social-behavioral shift after birth, which occurs when a full-term baby is about 2½ months old.

THE FIRST POSTNATAL BIO-SOCIAL-BEHAVIORAL SHIFT

Emde and his co-workers contend that, although infants learn through active adaptation to their environments and reciprocal interaction with their caregivers during the first 2 months, there is a shift in the "modes and mechanisms" of their behavior during the third month of life (Emde et al., 1976). This shift arises from the convergence of developmental changes that previously have proceeded in relative isolation from one another. Table 4.5 lists in capsule form the changes in the separate domains that converge to create the first postnatal bio-social-behavioral shift.

TABLE 4.5
Elements of the First Postnatal Bio-Social-Behavioral Shift (2½ Months)

BIOLOGICAL DOMAIN

Central nervous system
 Myelination of cortical and subcortical neural pathways
 Myelination of primary neural pathways in some sensory systems
 Increased cortical control of subcortical activity
 Increases in the number and diversity of brain cells
Psychophysiology
 Increases in amount of wakefulness
 Decreases in active (REM) sleep as a proportion of total sleep time
 Shift in pattern of sleep; quiet (NREM) sleep begins to come first

BEHAVIORAL DOMAIN

 Learning is retained better between episodes
 Increases in visual acuity
 More complete visual scanning of objects
 Onset of social smiling
 Decreases in generalized fussiness and crying
 Visually initiated reaching becomes visually guided reaching

SOCIAL DOMAIN

 New quality of coordination and emotional contact between infants and caretakers

---

To appreciate the far-reaching significance of this and subsequent bio-social-behavioral shifts, we must visualize what it means for all of the changes listed in Table 4.5 to occur at about the same time. Emde and his colleagues convey the sense of this meaning by tracing how changes in the infant's smiling are related to other aspects of the developing child.

Smiling during REM sleep.

The Emergence of Social Smiling

During the earliest weeks of life, the corners of a baby's mouth often curl up in a facial expression that looks for all the world like a smile. Most experienced mothers do not pay much attention to these smiles, however, because they are most likely to come when the infant is asleep or very drowsy. Emde and his colleagues studied the nature and origin of infants' smiles by recording their brain waves at times when they were and were not smiling and the nature of social feedback in response to any smiles.

They found that in the days after birth the baby's smiles came primarily during rapid-eye-movement (REM) sleep. They also determined that bursts of brain-wave activity originating in the brainstem accompany infants' early smiles. Emde and Jean Robinson (1979) call these endogenous smiles *REM smiles*. Dur-

ing the second week, smiles also appear when the infant is awake but they are not correlated with any particular events in the environment. Emde and his colleagues found that even when infants were awake their smiles were accompanied by the pattern of brain waves characteristic of drowsiness and REM sleep.

The frequency of the REM smiles decreases rapidly during the next several weeks. In their place there appears an exogenous smile, one that responds to stimulation from the environment. Between the ages of 1 month and 2½ months, infants smile indiscriminately at things or people they see, touch, or hear. Thus this earliest form of exogenous smiling is not really social, even though it is stimulated from the outside.

To become truly social, babies' smiles must be reciprocally related to the smiles of others; that is, the babies must both smile in response to the smiles of others and elicit others' smiles. This is precisely what begins to happen for the first time at the age of 2½ to 3 months as part of the first postnatal bio-social-behavioral shift. This new behavior depends on the changes in the brain and the nervous system that result in marked increases in infants' visual acuity and in their ability to scan objects systematically. The improved visual capacity permits babies to focus their eyes, and thus their smiles, on *people*, so that early exogenous smiling can become truly social smiling.

The changes in infants' behavior that accompany the social smile are not lost on their parents. Quite the opposite, as is indicated by the following observations of mothers on their feelings about their babies before the shift and a description of a mother interacting with her baby after the shift:

BEFORE

> I don't think there is interaction. . . . They are like in a little cage surrounded by glass and you are acting all around them but there is no real interaction. . . . I realized I was doing things for him he couldn't do for himself but I always felt that anyone else could do them and he wouldn't know the difference. (Robson & Moss, 1970:979–980)

AFTER

> His eyes locked on to hers, and together they held motionless. . . . This silent and almost motion-

less instant continued to hang until the mother suddenly shattered it by saying "Hey!" and simultaneously opening her eyes wider, raising her eyebrows further, and throwing her head up and toward the infant. Almost simultaneously the baby's eyes widened. His head tilted up . . . , his smile broadened. . . . Now she said, "Well hello! . . . heello, . . . heeelloooo!," so that her pitch rose and the "hellos" became longer and more stressed on each successive repetition. With each phrase the baby expressed more pleasure, and his body resonated almost like a balloon being pumped up. (Stern, 1977:3)

The Social Smile and Social Feedback

The importance of social feedback to the achievement of bio-social-behavioral shifts is dramatically demonstrated by research conducted by Selma Fraiberg (1974) on the development of congenitally blind infants. Like sighted infants, blind babies exhibit REM smiles. But unlike sighted infants, they may not exhibit the shift to social smiling at 2½ months.

Under normal conditions of growth, the social smile is connected to visual exploration of the world. It depends on increased visual capacity and on visual feedback from people who smile back. Blind infants cannot explore the world visually and hence may not establish the feedback loop they need in order to develop social smiling.

The frequent failure of blind infants to make the expected shift toward social smiling also means that their sighted parents cannot use their baby's facial expressions as a gauge by which to evaluate their own efforts to help their infant. But it does *not* mean that blind infants receive no social feedback or that they cannot acquire social smiling. After all, their brains are maturing like those of sighted children. The problem is that they cannot express their increased capacities in visually related ways. In the absence of this major channel for social feedback, parents must find alternate ways to interact with their blind children.

The intuitive solution that some parents of blind children work out is to establish communication through touch. Fraiberg noticed that many of these parents bounce, nudge, and tickle their children far more than the parents of sighted children. At first all

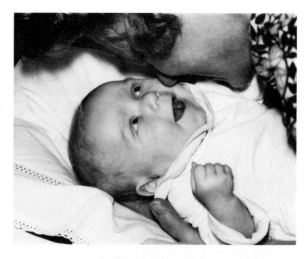

This 2½-month-old blind infant smiled and turned her face toward her mother upon hearing her mother's voice.

this manipulation struck Fraiberg as socially abnormal, but then she noticed that the touching made the children smile and realized that tactile stimulation was a good substitute for the smiling face that elicits the smiles of sighted babies. Through touch the parents had found a way to get the feedback that *they* needed from their infants. Fraiberg used this observation to design a training program to help blind infants and their parents (Fraiberg, 1974). Parents were taught to attend carefully to the way their children used their hands to signal their intentions and reactions and how to organize their baby's environment to encourage interaction. Once the children of these parents were provided with appropriate feedback, they began to develop social smiling.

The success of Fraiberg's training program indicates that social smiling does not arise simply from the fact that an infant's brain has matured to the point where social smiling is possible. For social smiling to emerge, appropriate interaction with others is necessary; when this new behavior does emerge, a new affective quality is able to develop between infants and their parents. As we will see in other periods of a child's life, development results from a complex interaction of biological, social, and behavioral changes that the notion of bio-social-behavioral shifts helps us to keep in mind.

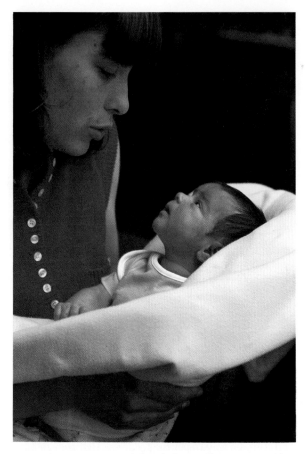

The moment parents and their babies make eye contact is pleasurable for both parties.

SUMMING UP THE FIRST TWO AND A HALF MONTHS

Looking back over the first 2½ months or so of postnatal life, we can see a remarkable set of changes in infants' behaviors. Babies are born with a rudimentary ability to interact with their new environment. They have reflexes that enable them to take in oxygen and nutrients and expel waste products. They are able to perceive objects, including people, although they tend to focus on only a part of the entire stimulus. They are sensitive to the sounds of human language, and they quickly develop a preference for the sound of their mother's voice. Although they sleep most of the time, they are occasionally quite alert.

From the moment of birth, infants interact with and are supported by their parents or other caregivers, who come equipped with the biological and cultural resources necessary to see that their babies receive food and protection. Despite these resources, the first interactions of babies and their caregivers are tentative and somewhat uncoordinated. Within a matter of days, however, a process of mutual adjustment has begun that will provide an essential framework for later development.

The developmental changes that characterize the first 10 to 12 weeks have clear origins in biology and in both the physical and social environments. In the domain of biology, there is rapid maturation of the central nervous system, particularly in the connections between the brainstem and the cerebral cortex. As a consequence of frequent feeding, the baby grows bigger and stronger. As a consequence of practice at feeding, the elementary reflex of sucking becomes efficient feeding, an accomplishment that owes a good deal to the complementary efforts of the baby's caregivers, primarily the mother.

Between the ages of 2½ and 3 months, several lines of development that have been proceeding more or less independently now converge. The consequences are qualitatively different forms of behavior and a new type of social relationship between babies and their caregivers. The story of the development of the seemingly simple behavior of social smiling illustrates the intricate way in which these different lines of development must relate to one another for a transition to a qualitatively new level of development to occur. Maturation of the visual system enables a new level of visual acuity and a new ability to analyze the visual field. As a consequence, smiling, a seemingly unrelated behavior, may be transformed. This transformation will take place, however, only if the infant's caregivers provide proper feedback. Without appropriate feedback, as in the case of some blind children, social smiling does not develop. And if social smiling does not develop, the development of social interactions may be disrupted.

In later chapters we will see versions of this pattern repeated again and again. For a stretch of time the child's overall level of development remains stable while various systems undergo changes in relative isolation. Then there is a brief period during which these separate lines of development converge, resulting in a new level of organization with regard to both the child's behaviors and interactions between child and caregiver. It will not always be possible to identify the specific biological, social, and behavioral factors that contribute to the emergence of higher levels of devel-opment with equal certainty and rigor. But it will always be useful to consider the various domains that enter into the process of developmental change as a means of keeping the whole child in mind.

SUMMARY

1. Infants are born with remarkable sensory and behav-ioral capacities with which to experience and respond to their postnatal circumstances.
   a. Neonates are able to hear sounds in the same range of frequencies that are audible to older children, and they display a special sensitivity to the basic sound categories of human language.
   b. Although infants are nearsighted, they systemati-cally scan their surroundings and are sensitive to the contrast between light and dark. They will track moving facelike forms at birth, and within a few days they seem to be able to distinguish their mother's face from others'.
   c. Neonates can distinguish between tastes and smells. They seem to prefer sweet tastes, and the smells they most enjoy are the ones that seem pleas-ant to older people, too.
   d. The senses of touch, temperature, and position are relatively mature at birth.
2. A variety of reflexes, automatic responses to specific environmental events, are present at birth.
3. It is widely believed that neonates are capable of expe-riencing such elementary emotions as pleasure, anger, disgust, surprise, and perhaps fear and sadness. There is some doubt that these emotions have the same qual-ity as those experienced by older children and adults.
4. Individual variations in temperament—in style of re-sponse and dominant mood—are present at birth. Al-though findings about temperament remain contro-versial, it appears that the temperaments that distinguish individuals are stable for long periods of time, and thus constitute an important source of devel-opmental continuity.
5. The basic behavioral capacities with which infants are born are sufficient for their survival only if they are coordinated with adult caregiving activities.
6. "Getting the baby on a schedule" is more than a conve-nience. By coordinating schedules, babies and their parents create a system of mutual expectations that supports further development.
7. Newborn babies sleep approximately two-thirds of the time, but their periods of sleep are relatively brief and are distributed across all 24 hours of the day. All babies tend to sleep more at night than during the day from the outset, but the time that passes before they begin to sleep through the night depends on the sleep patterns of the adults who care for them, and those patterns vary from culture to culture.
8. Newborn babies tend to eat about every 3 hours if they are given constant access to food. Babies fed only every 4 hours may have trouble adjusting to such a schedule, although most infants adopt a 4-hour sched-ule spontaneously by the time they reach 2½ months of age.
9. Crying is a primitive means of communication that evokes a strong emotional response in adults and alerts them that something may be wrong. The distinctive sound patterns of early cries help cue caregivers as to possible sources of distress. In some cases they indi-cate serious illness.
10. In the beginning, feeding is based on primitive reflex mechanisms that are not well coordinated. Within sev-eral weeks, this form of behavior is reorganized and becomes voluntary; the various constituent reflexes become integrated with one another and the baby be-comes well coordinated with the mother.
11. The four basic perspectives on development can all be applied to the earliest forms of infant development; each emphasizes a different way in which biological and environmental factors contribute to early develop-mental change.
12. According to the *biological-maturation* perspective, postnatal development follows the same principles as prenatal development. New structures are said to arise from endogenous (inherited) capabilities that unfold as the baby matures. Changes in nursing as well as in other behaviors, according to this view, result from such factors as the increased myelination of the neu-rons and the growth of muscles.
13. The maturation of brain structures contributes to the reorganization of early reflexes. Some of these early reflexes disappear completely within a few months of birth. Others may disappear and then reappear later as an element in a new form of activity. Still others re-main and are transformed into voluntary behaviors under the control of the cerebral cortex.

14. *Environmental-learning* theories assign the environment a leading role in the creation of new forms of behavior through the mechanism of learning.

15. Infants' ability to learn from experience increases steadily during the first months of life. *Classical conditioning* permits infants to form expectations about the connections between events in their environment. *Operant conditioning* provides a mechanism for the emergence of new behaviors as a consequence of the positive or negative events they produce. Some studies appear to show that young infants can also learn through *imitation*, but this contention remains in dispute.

16. *Universal-constructivist* theories assign equal weight to biological and environmental factors in development. Reflexes, in this view, are coordinated patterns of action (schemas) that have differentiated from a more primitive state of global activity during the prenatal period.

17. In the view of Jean Piaget, the leading universal-constructivist of the twentieth century, developmental change is constructed through the interplay of *assimilation* (modification of the input to fit existing schemas) and *accommodation* (modification of existing schemas to fit the input). The interplay of accommodation and assimilation continues until a new form of equilibrium between the two processes is reached. New forms of equilibrium constitute qualitatively new forms of behavior; they are new stages of development.

18. According to Piaget, infancy is characterized by sensorimotor ways of knowing. He divides the sensorimotor period into six substages, the first two of which occur during the first 10 to 12 weeks of postnatal life:
    a. Substage 1 is characterized by the exercise of basic reflexes.
    b. Substage 2 is characterized by the beginning of accommodation and the prolongation of pleasant sensations arising from reflex actions.

19. Careful observations of interactions between mothers and infants reveal that some part of the work that Piaget attributed to infants is in fact contributed by the people with whom they interact.

20. *Cultural-context* theories of development emphasize the active roles of the child and of the people around the child, and add historically accumulated "designs for living" as contributors to the process of developmental change.

21. Significant and pervasive cultural variations in parents' interactions with their newborn children influence both short-term and long-term development.

22. At approximately 2½ months of age a bio-social-behavioral shift occurs in the organization of infants' behavior. Changes in brain function owing to maturation are accompanied by increased visual acuity and the ability to perceive the forms of objects and people, increased wakefulness, and social smiling. Caregivers respond with new feelings of connectedness to the infant.

KEY TERMS

accommodation
assimilation
brainstem
cerebral cortex
classical conditioning
conditional response
conditional stimulus
dishabituation
emotion
equilibration
habituation
Moro reflex
myelin
myelination
operant conditioning

phonemes
prereaching
primary circular reactions
primary motor area
primary sensory areas
reflex
reinforcement
schema
sensorimotor stage
stepping reflex
synapse
temperament
unconditional response
unconditional stimulus

SUGGESTED READINGS

BIJOU, SIDNEY W., & BAER, DONALD M.. *Child Development,* vol. 2: *The Universal Stage of Infancy.* New York: Appleton-Century-Crofts, 1966.

An introduction to the topic of developmental change in terms of the basic learning mechanisms of classical and operant conditioning.

EMDE, ROBERT N., GAENSBAUER, THEODORE J., & HARMON, ROBERT J. "Emotional Expression in Infancy: A Behavioral Study." *Psychological Issues,* 1976, *10* (37).

The basic statement of the concept of bio-behavioral developmental shifts, including a discussion of the changes in the social world that are a part of them.

FIELD, TIFFANY. *Infancy.* Cambridge, Mass.: Harvard University Press, 1990.

A readable summary of contemporary research on infants, with a particularly useful survey of research on infants at risk.

KAYE, KENNETH. *The Mental and Social Life of Babies.* Chicago: University of Chicago Press, 1982.

This report of the author's research on early mechanisms of developmental change demonstrates the way in which maternal behaviors help to construct "next steps" in infant development.

MEAD, MARGARET, & MACGREGOR, FRANCES C. *Growth and Culture.* New York: Putnam, 1951.

A study of the cultural organization of infant behaviors in Bali. This richly illustrated book is based on research carried out in collaboration with Arnold Gesell in an early attempt to reconcile maturational and cultural approaches to the explanation of developmental change.

PIAGET, JEAN. *The Origins of Intelligence in Children.* New York: International Universities Press, 1952.

Piaget's account of the earliest stages of development. Piaget's theoretical writings are never easy to read, but his descriptions of children's behavior are fascinating. Because these descriptions are the basic data on which his theory rests, familiarity with them helps readers understand his more abstract statements.

ROSENBLITH, JUDY F., & SIMSKNIGHT, JUDITH E. *In the Beginning: Development during the First Two Years.* Monterey, Calif.: Brooks/Cole, 1985.

An authoritative summary of current theories and research on infant development. An excellent resource for all the chapters in Part II of this book.

STERN, DANIEL. *The First Relationship.* Cambridge, Mass.: Harvard University Press, 1977.

Stern, a psychiatrist, used film and videotape to record parent-child interactions. Through analyses of the moment-by-moment patterns of coordination and discoordination, he demonstrates the importance of close observation for understanding the interpersonal basis of individual development.

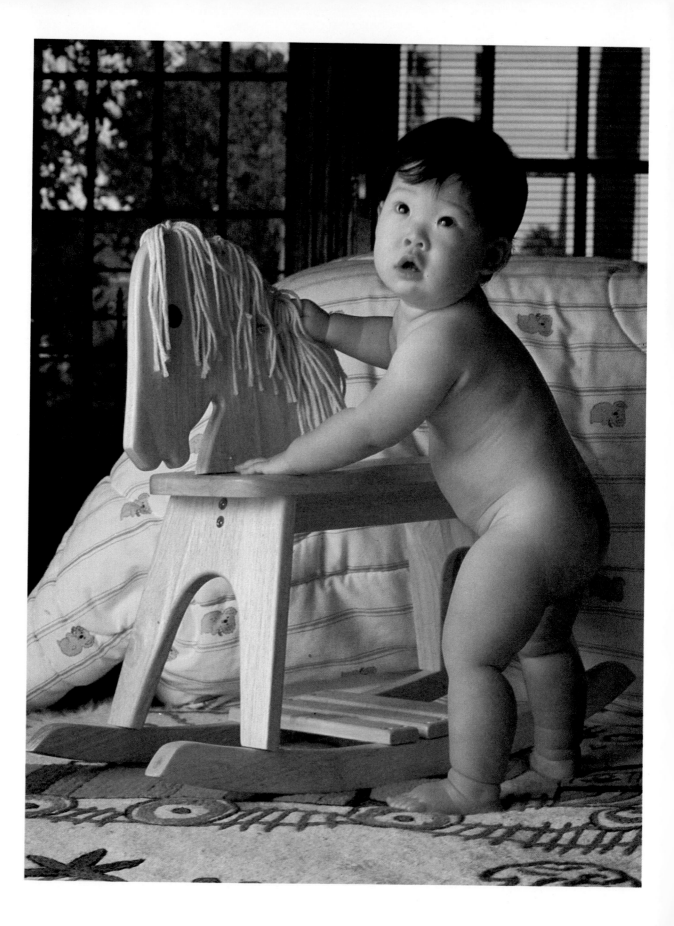

CHAPTER 5

The Achievements of the First Year

•

The question . . . is not where or when mind begins.
Mind in some . . . form is there from the start,
wherever "there" may be.

— JEROME BRUNER, *IN SEARCH OF MIND*

Two neighbors — Jake, who is about to celebrate his first birthday, and his mother, Barbara — have been out for a walk and have stopped by our house. Sheila is in the kitchen preparing dinner. Jake is sitting on his mother's lap at the kitchen table, drinking apple juice from a plastic cup while the two women chat.

Jake finishes his juice, some of which has dribbled onto his shirt, and puts the cup down on the table with a satisfied bang. He squirms around in his mother's lap so that he is facing her. He tries to get her attention by pulling at her face. When Barbara ignores him, Jake wriggles out of her lap to the floor, where he notices the dog.

"Wuff wuff," he says excitedly, pointing at the dog.

"Doggie," Barbara says. "What does the doggie say, Jake?"

"Wuff wuff," Jake repeats, still staring at the dog.

Following his pointing finger, Jake toddles toward the dog. His walk has a drunken, side-to-side quality, and he has a hard time bringing himself to a stop. Barbara grabs hold of Jake's extended hand, redirecting it from the dog's eyes.

"Pat the doggie, Jake."

Jake pats the dog's head.

The dog does not like the attention and escapes into the living room. Jake toddles after her like a pull toy on an invisible string. The dog leads him back into the kitchen, where Jake bumps into Sheila's legs and falls to a sitting position.

"Well, hello, Jake," Sheila says, as she bends over and picks him up. "Did you fall down? Go boom?"

Jake, who has not till then taken his eyes from the dog, turns, looks at Sheila with a smile, and points at the dog. "Wuff wuff," he repeats.

Suddenly Jake's body stiffens. He stares searchingly at Sheila's face for an instant, then turns his head away and holds his arms out to his mother.

Sheila hands Jake to Barbara, who says, "Did you get scared? It's only Sheila."

But Jake eyes Sheila warily and hides in his mother's arms for several minutes.

At almost 1 year of age, Jake behaves far differently than a baby of 2½ months. At that age, Jake's main activities were eating, sleeping, and gazing around the room. He could hold his head up and turn it from side to side, but he could not readily reach out and grasp objects or move around on his own. He took an interest in mobiles and other objects when they were immediately in front of him, but he quickly lost interest in them when they disappeared. Although he seemed most comfortable with his mother, he did not seem particularly unhappy when he was cared for by someone else. His communications were restricted to cries, frowns, and smiles. The contrast between Jake's behavior then and at 1 year gives us a picture of some of the amazing developmental changes that occur in the first year of infancy and present a challenge to the psychologists who seek to explain them.

Several kinds of changes appear to be crucial to the major developments that occur between 2½ months and 1 year. First, babies' mobility and coordination increase. At 3 months, infants are just beginning to be able to roll over. Their parents know that they will remain more or less wherever they are put down. At about 7 to 8 months they begin to crawl, and at about 1 year they begin to walk. They also become much more adept at reaching for objects and grasping them. They prod, bang, squeeze, push, and pull almost anything they can get their hands on, and they often put objects into their mouths to find out about them. Their parents, afraid that they will either harm themselves or destroy property, must be constantly on guard.

As infants near their first birthday, they also exhibit important new cognitive abilities. They learn and remember with markedly greater ease and effectiveness, for example, and they have come to recognize the existence of categories of objects. They can anticipate the course of simple, familiar events, and they act surprised when their expectations are not met. This new level of understanding makes it possible for them to play simple games such as peekaboo.

These changes in infants' motor and cognitive abilities are supported by developments in their biological structure (see Figure 5.1). Jake is visibly larger and stronger than he was at 2½ months. Invisible but essential maturation has also taken place in his cerebral cortex and other brain structures.

Finally, a new form of social and emotional relationship emerges between infants and their caregivers toward the end of the first year. Infants become upset when they are separated from their caregivers, and sometimes they are afraid of strangers, as Jake was when he noticed Sheila. They begin to check their caregivers' faces for indications of how to behave in uncertain situations, and they also begin to comprehend a few words, extending the ways in which they can communicate and maintain contact with their caregivers.

As we shall see, these changes in motor behavior, biological structure, cognitive capacities, and socioemotional relations converge as babies approach their first birthdays, producing a second postnatal biosocial-behavioral shift. The new qualities that emerge from this reorganization of the processes of development bring children to the end of infancy and provide the context for a new stage of development.

BIOLOGICAL CHANGES

The extensive changes in babies' motor behavior and cognitive abilities that occur between the ages of 2½ months and 1 year depend on changes in their body proportions, muscles, bones, and brain structures (Thelen, 1984).

Size and Shape

Most healthy babies triple in weight and grow approximately 10 inches during the first year. As Figure 5.2 shows, the rate of physical growth is greatest in the first months after birth; it then gradually tapers off through the rest of infancy and childhood. Another brief growth spurt comes at the onset of adolescence. The rates at which individual children normally grow vary widely, however, as do the heights and weights they eventually attain (Tanner, 1978). Many factors contribute to these variations, including quantity and quality of food, family income level, exposure to sunlight (a source of vitamin D), and genetic constitution (Johnson, Borden, & MacVean, 1973).

Increases in height and weight are accompanied by changes in body proportions (see Figure 5.3). At birth the head is 70 percent of its adult size and accounts for about 25 percent of the body's total length. At 1 year the head will account for 20 percent of the

FIGURE 5.1   *The differences in size, strength, shape, and motor control between small infants and babies in their second year are evident in the baby being held and the toddler standing nearby.*

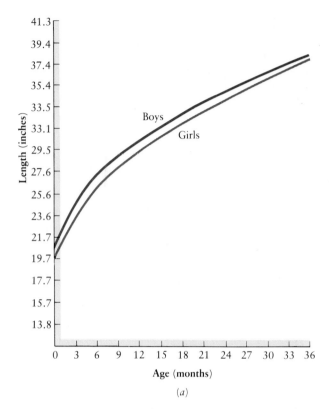

(a)

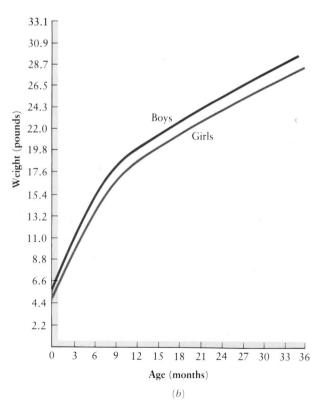

(b)

body's length, and in adulthood the proportion will be 12 percent. Infants' legs at birth are not much longer than their heads. By adulthood the legs account for about half of a person's total height. Changes in body proportions produce a lower center of gravity by about 12 months of age, making it easier for the child to balance on two legs and begin to walk (Thelen, Ulrich, & Jensen, 1989).

Muscle and Bone

As babies grow, the bones and muscles needed to support their increasing bulk and mobility undergo corresponding growth. Most of a newborn's bones are relatively soft, and they harden only gradually as minerals are deposited in them in the months after birth. The bones in the hand and wrist are among the first to ossify (Tanner, 1978). They harden by the end of the first year, making it easier for a baby to grasp objects, pick them up, and play with them.

Although humans are born with all the muscle fibers they will ever have, their muscles change in length and thickness throughout childhood and into late adolescence. In infancy, increases in muscle mass are closely associated with the development of the baby's ability to stand alone and walk.

The Brain

The entire nervous system continues to grow in size and complexity between 3 and 12 months (Bayer & Altman, 1991; Huttenlocher, 1990). Changes are especially notable in the cerebral cortex, which makes crucial contributions to voluntary activity and other higher psychological functions. Sometime between the ages of 7 and 9 months, the frontal lobes and the prefrontal areas of the cortex begin to function more fully as a consequence of the growth and myelination of neurons, and new patterns appear in the electrical

FIGURE 5.2   *Babies' length roughly doubles and their weight increases by 5 or 6 times during the first 3 years of life. (a) Average length by age. (b) Average weight by age. (From the U.S. Department of Health, Education, and Welfare. National Center of Health Statistics, 1976.)*

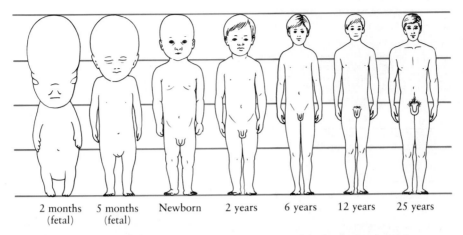

2 months (fetal) 5 months (fetal) Newborn 2 years 6 years 12 years 25 years

FIGURE 5.3   *The proportions of body length accounted for by the head, trunk, and legs at different stages of development change remarkably. The disproportion is greatest during the fetal period, when the head accounts for as much as 50 percent of body length. The head decreases from 25 percent of body length at birth to 12 percent in adulthood. (From Robbins et al., 1928.)*

activity of the cortex as a whole (Diamond, 1990a,b; Fuster, 1990). These changes coincide with similar developments in lower-lying areas of the brain, especially the hippocampus, which plays an important role in memory, and the cerebellum, which is a key center of motor control (Diamond, 1990a,b). Several psychologists believe that these changes in brain structure provide the physical basis for more complex motor behavior and for increases in the ability to learn and solve problems (Case, 1992; Diamond, 1991; Fischer, 1987).

PERCEPTUAL AND MOTOR DEVELOPMENT

One of the most dramatic developments of the first year of life is the enormous increase in infants' ability to explore their environment by looking at it, moving around in it, and manipulating it. Perceiving and acting are intimately connected. Infants, no less than adults, perceive in order to obtain information about how to act and act in order to get more information (Gibson, 1988).

Reaching and Grasping

In Chapter 4 (pp. 152–153) we saw that at the time of the first postnatal bio-social-behavioral shift, at about 2½ months, babies begin to guide their movements visually when they reach for an object. In contrast to the earlier reflex action seen shortly after birth, which is controlled by areas of the brain that lie below the cortex, these voluntary movements are now under cortical control (Von Hofsten, 1984). At first, grasping requires concentration, and babies are likely to glance back and forth between the objects they wish to grasp and their hands. With practice, their eye-hand coordination gradually improves (see Figure 5.4). By the time they are 9 months old, most babies can guide their movements with a single glance, and the movements with which they reach for and grasp objects look as well integrated and automatic as a reflex (Mathew & Cook, 1990).

In the period between 3 and 12 months of age infants also acquire more subtlety in the movements they use to grasp and explore objects manually. As Figure 5.4 indicates, 7-month-olds are still unable to use their thumbs in opposition to their fingers to pick up objects, but by 12 months they are able to move their thumbs and other fingers into position

FIGURE 5.4   (Top) *In the first months after birth, eye-hand coordination takes effort.* (Bottom) *Only after a few months of attention and practice can infants perform such complex actions as eating with a spoon.*

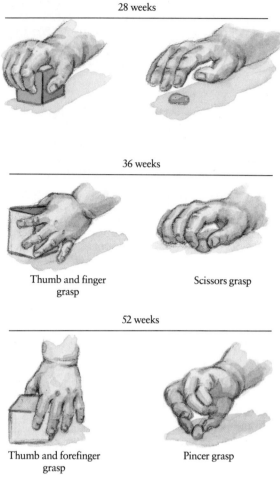

FIGURE 5.5   *Babies find ways to grasp objects from an early age, but good coordination of the thumb and forefinger requires at least a year to achieve. (Adapted from Halverson, 1931.)*

appropriate to the size of the object they are trying to grasp. As their reaching and grasping become better coordinated and more precise, they can perform more complicated action sequences, such as drinking from a cup, eating with a spoon, and picking raisins out of a box (Connolly & Dalgleish, 1989) (Figure 5.5).

Rachel Karniol (1989) found that there is an invariable sequence in the way babies manipulate objects as their fine motor skills increase during the first 9 months of life. They begin by simply rotating an object, then progress to moving it, shaking it, and holding it with one and then two hands, until they can use it as part of a sequence of actions to achieve a goal.

Eleanor Gibson (1988) points out that as babies gain control over their hands, different objects invite them to explore in different ways: "Things can be displaced, banged, shaken, squeezed, and thrown — actions that have informative consequences about an object's properties" (p. 20). Babies seem to sense that different objects invite different kinds of explorations: rattles are to be shaken, pacifiers to be sucked, spoons put in the mouth, and balloons felt (Rochat, 1989).

These recent studies of the development of reaching and grasping leave little doubt that the importance of babies' increasing skills goes beyond the capacity to grab hold of things. Perceptual-motor exploration is an essential means for increasing knowledge about the environment and gaining control over it.

Locomotion

Progress in **locomotion,** the ability to move around on one's own, is central to the pattern of developmental changes that occur toward the end of the first year of postnatal life. As Selma Fraiberg (1959) puts it, "The first time the baby stands unsupported and the first wobbly, independent steps are milestones in personal-

ity development as well as in motor development" (p. 60).

Babies acquire the ability to reach out for and explore objects much earlier than the ability to move around on their own, however. Before any form of locomotion is achieved, they must be able to integrate the movements of many parts of their bodies.

The development of crawling, babies' first effective mode of locomotion, takes several months and progresses through several phases (see Figure 5.6). During the first month of life, when movements appear to be controlled primarily by subcortical reflexes, infants may inadvertently creep across a blanket, propelled by the rhythmic pushing movements of their toes or knees. At about 2 months of age this reflexive pushing disappears, and it will be another 5 or 6 months before babies can really crawl about on their own.

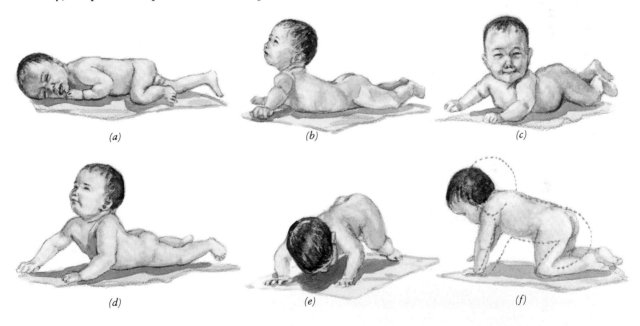

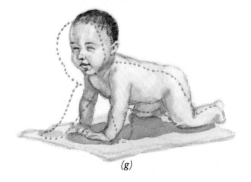

FIGURE 5.6   *Phases in the development of creeping and crawling:*
(a) Newborns creep by making pushing movements with their knees and toes. (b) The head can be held up, but leg movements diminish. (c) Control over movement of head and shoulders has increased. (d) Ability to support the upper body with the arms improves. (e) Babies have difficulty coordinating shoulder and midsection regions; when the midsection is raised, the head lowers. (f) Babies can keep the midsection raised, but they are unable to coordinate arm and leg movements, so they tend to rock back and forth. (g) Coordinated arm and leg movements enable the baby to crawl. (From McGraw, 1975.)

FIGURE 5.7   *Babies who are just beginning to stand up find other people and furniture to be handy aids. Here a Balinese child is holding on to the anthropologist Margaret Mead.*

Although they can hold up their heads from about 2 months of age, young infants still have difficulty moving their arms in a coordinated way. Karniol (1989) places this milestone at the end of the third month. Once they have managed to coordinate their arm movements, babies can pull themselves along, but their legs drag behind uselessly. Slightly later they can get on their hands and knees, but all they can do is rock back and forth because their arms and legs are not yet working together properly. Even as they enter the final phase of crawling at 8 to 9 months of age, their movements may lack precise coordination until, with practice, the various components are knitted into the well-coordinated action of the whole body.

Babies usually do not master walking until several months after they begin to crawl. The transition from crawling to walking requires a reorganization of component skills that is even more complex than the transformation from creeping to crawling (see Figure 5.7).

Table 5.1 shows some of the results of a large-scale study of the ages at which U.S. children achieve various milestones in motor development (Frankenburg & Dodds, 1967). Note the wide variations in the ages at which children are able to perform the various behaviors. Although 50 percent of the babies studied could walk by the time they were just over 1 year old, for example, some 10 percent were still not walking 2 months later.

TABLE 5.1

Ages at Which Infants Reach Selected Milestones in Motor Development (percent)

Motor Milestone	Age (months)			
	25%	50%	75%	90%
Lifts head up	1.3	2.2	2.6	3.2
Rolls over	2.3	2.8	3.8	4.7
Sits without support	4.8	5.5	6.5	7.8
Pulls self to stand	6.0	7.6	9.5	10.0
Walks holding on to furniture	7.3	9.2	10.2	12.7
Walks well	11.3	12.1	13.3	14.3
Walks up steps	14.0	17.0	21.0	22.0
Kicks ball forward	15.0	20.0	22.3	24.0

Source: Frankenburg & Dodds, 1967.

The Role of Practice in Motor Development

Studies of motor development were among psychologists' earliest strategies for discovering the relative roles of nature and nurture in development. During the 1930s and 1940s, when Arnold Gesell's infant scales were in very wide use, it was commonly believed that learning and experience played little or no role in the development of such motor milestones as sitting and walking. One of the studies widely cited to bolster this view was conducted by Wayne and Margaret Dennis (1940) among Hopi families in the southwestern United States. In traditional Hopi families, babies were wrapped up tightly and strapped to a flat cradle board for the first several months of life. They were unwrapped only once or twice a day so that they could be washed and their clothes changed. The wrapping permitted very little movement of the arms and legs and no practice in such complex movements as rolling over. The Dennises compared the motor development of traditionally raised Hopi babies with that of the babies of less traditional parents who did not use cradle boards. The two groups of babies did not differ in the age at which they began to walk unaided, a finding that is consistent with the notion that this basic motor skill does not depend on practice for its development.

In recent decades, however, psychologists have again begun to explore the possibility that experience, as well as maturation, plays a significant role in motor development. Philip Zelazo and his colleagues, for example, provided a group of 2-week-old babies with four 3-minute sessions of walking practice each day for 6 weeks. During these practice sessions, adults supported the infants' stepping activities by holding them erect. Infants trained in this way took their first unaided steps at approximately 10 months of age, 2 months earlier than control groups of babies who were not given equivalent practice (Zelazo, Zelazo, & Kolb, 1972).

Observations of babies from different cultural settings provide further evidence that practice can have an effect on the age at which babies reach universal motor milestones. Charles Super (1976) reports that among the Kipsigis people of rural Kenya, parents begin to teach their babies to sit up, stand, and walk shortly after birth. In teaching their children to sit up, for example, Kipsigis parents seat their babies in shallow holes in the ground that they have dug to support the infants' backs, or they nestle blankets around them to hold them upright. They repeat such procedures daily until the babies can sit up quite well by themselves. Training in walking begins in the eighth week. The babies are held under the arms with their feet touching the ground and are gradually propelled forward. Kipsigis babies reach the developmental milestones of sitting 5 weeks earlier and walking 3 weeks earlier, on the average, than babies in the United States. At the same time they are *not* advanced in skills they have not been taught or have not practiced. They learn to roll over or crawl no faster than American children, and they lag behind American children in their ability to negotiate stairs. Similar results have been reported among West Indian children, whose mothers put them through a culturally prescribed sequence of motor exercises during the early months of infancy (Hopkins & Westen, 1988).

The Ache, a nomadic people living in the rain forest of eastern Paraguay, discourage early motor achievement. Hilliard Kaplan and Heather Dove

The Philippino baby who lives in a house on stilts is being trained at an early age in the essential skill of climbing a ladder.

(1987) report that Ache children under 3 years of age spend 80 to 100 percent of their time in direct physical contact with their mothers and are almost never seen more than 3 feet away from them. A major reason is that Ache hunter-gatherer groups do not create clearings in the forest when they stop to make camp. Rather, they remove just enough ground cover to make room to sit down, leaving roots, trees, and bushes more or less where they found them. For safety's sake, mothers either carry their infants or keep them within arm's reach.

Ache infants perform at North American norms on various tests of social ability, but they are markedly slower to acquire gross motor skills such as walking. They begin walking, on the average, at about 23 months of age, almost a full year later than children in the United States. About the age of 5, however, when Ache children are pushed out of the nest to make way for younger siblings, they begin to spend many hours in complex play activities that serve to increase their motor skills. Within a few years they are skilled at scaling tall trees and at cutting vines and branches while they balance high above the ground in a manner that bespeaks normal, if not exceptional, perceptual-motor skills.

Although special early practice does not appear to have any long-term advantages in the development of basic motor skills, there is some evidence that early practice in culture-specific skills, such as throwing a boomerang, playing tennis, roller-skating, and typing, does make a lasting difference. In one of the classic early studies of the role of experience in motor development, Myrtle McGraw (1935/1975) trained one of a pair of fraternal twins extensively in various activities that required specialized skills, such as riding a tricycle, swimming, and roller-skating. When he had attained proficiency, his twin brother was given training in the same activities. McGraw reported that the second twin caught up rather quickly with the first twin in general skill level. When the twins were adolescents and young adults, however, the first twin was more skilled in these activities and more enthusiastic about them.

As anyone knows who has tried some unfamiliar sport, specialized motor skills are not acquired without extensive practice and in some cases years of instruction as well. In recognition of this fact, specialized training in highly valued skills, such as playing a musical instrument or dancing, is begun quite early in many cultures, producing high levels of proficiency (see Figure 5.8).

FIGURE 5.8   *At the tender age of 7 months, 29 days, young Parks Bonifay is the youngest person to water-ski, according to* The Guinness Book of World Records. *Waterskiing is a skill that requires practice to learn.*

COGNITIVE CHANGES

Just as it was once believed that newborns experienced the world as a confusing jumble of sensations, so it was also believed that understanding basic properties of objects and people built up slowly over the course of infancy and early childhood. Certainly there is impressive evidence that between 3 and 12 months of age children are acquiring a greater ability to think systematically about their surroundings and to remember their experiences.

Today, however, developmental psychologists are divided in their beliefs about the nature of infants' cognitive capacities during the first year of life and about how to account for developmental change. On the one hand, when infants are asked to display their understanding through overt action, they seem to be constructing knowledge slowly over time, much as Piaget claimed. On the other hand, when children's psychological processes are assessed through techniques that require only minimal overt action on their part, such as a change in the interest they show, it appears that a rudimentary understanding of many basic properties of objects is present very early, possibly at birth. The importance of this difference in viewpoints goes well beyond a dispute about observable behavior; it speaks to the basic question of how developmental change comes about.

Piaget's Sensorimotor Substages

As we saw in Chapter 4, Piaget held that development emerges from children's own efforts to master their environments; we come to know the world by acting on it. In his terms, infants actively seek to *assimilate* their environmental experiences into their existing action schemas. To the extent that they are unable to do so they must *accommodate* their existing schemas to the environmental realities they encounter. Development emerges from the interplay between assimilation

and accommodation; sometimes we are able to deal with the world on our own terms—the world adjusts to us—and assimilation dominates. At other times, we must adjust to the world, and accommodation dominates. During those periods when accommodation and assimilation are in equilibrium, the basic structure of the cognitive process does not change. These periods of stability are called "stages" or "substages." Infancy is the sensorimotor stage, in which babies acquire knowledge by perceiving and doing. It has six substages, according to Piaget.

During substages 1 and 2, infants progress from simple reflex activity to the ability to prolong actions they find pleasurable. Even at the end of the second-substage, however, infants appear to have little or no understanding that environment and action are separate. Piaget believed that it is between the ages of 4 or 5 months and 12 months that infants start to form an idea of an external reality as they complete two more substages of sensorimotor development (see Table 5.2).

TABLE 5.2

Sensorimotor Substages and the Development of Object Permanence

Substage	Age Range (months)	Characteristics of Sensorimotor Substage	Developments in Object Permanence
1	0–1½	Reflex schemas exercised: involuntary rooting, sucking, grasping, looking	Infant does not search for objects that have been removed from sight
2	1½–4	Primary circular reactions: repetition of actions that are pleasurable in themselves	Infant orients to place where objects have been removed from sight
3	4–8	Secondary circular reactions: dawning awareness of relation of own actions to environment; extended actions that produce interesting changes in the environment	Infant will reach for a partially hidden object but stops if it disappears
4	8–12	Coordination of secondary circular reactions: combining schemas to achieve a desired effect; earliest form of problem solving	Infant will search for a completely hidden object; keeps searching the original location of the object even if it is moved to another location in full view of the infant
5	12–18	Tertiary circular reactions: deliberate variation of problem-solving means; experimentation to see what the consequences will be	Infant will search for an object after seeing it moved but not if it is moved in secret
6	18–24	Beginnings of symbolic representation: images and words come to stand for familiar objects; invention of new means of problem solving through symbolic combinations	Infant will search for a hidden object, certain that it exists somewhere

[handwritten margin note: A not B error]

Substage 3: Secondary circular reactions (4 to 8 months)

In substage 3, infants are no longer restricted to the maintenance and modification of reflex or body-centered actions. Now they direct their attention to the external world—to objects and outcomes. Accordingly, the characteristic activity observed in infants in substage 3 is the repetition of actions that produce interesting changes in the environment. Piaget termed these new actions **secondary circular reactions** because their focus is on objects external to themselves. When babies kick a bar suspended above their crib and a bell rings, for instance, they will kick the bar repeatedly to make the bell ring again and again. Similarly, when babies make a noise and their mother answers, they will repeat the noise.

The change from primary circular reactions to secondary circular reactions indicated to Piaget that infants are beginning to realize that objects are more than extensions of their own actions. In this substage, however, babies still have only rudimentary notions of objects and space, and their discoveries about the world seem to have an accidental quality.

Substage 4: Coordination of secondary circular reactions (8 to 12 months)

The hallmark of the fourth sensorimotor substage is infants' emerging ability to coordinate several secondary circular reactions in order to achieve a goal. Piaget believed that such coordination is the earliest form of true problem solving because it requires that different schemas be combined to achieve a desired effect.

Piaget tells us that when his son Laurent was 10 months old, Piaget gave him a small tin container, which Laurent dropped and picked up repeatedly (a secondary circular reaction characteristic of behavior in substage 3). Piaget then placed a washbasin a short distance from Laurent and struck it with the tin, producing an interesting sound. From earlier observations, Piaget knew that Laurent would repeatedly bang on the basin to make the interesting sound occur (another typical secondary circular reaction). This time Piaget wanted to see if Laurent would combine the newly acquired "dropping the tin box" schema with the previously acquired "make an interesting sound" schema. Here is his report of Laurent's behavior:

> Now, at once, Laurent takes possession of the tin, holds out his arm and drops it over the basin. I

moved the latter as a check. He nevertheless succeeded, several times in succession, in making the object fall on the basin. Hence this is a fine example of the coordination of two schemas of which the first serves as a "means" whereas the second assigns an end to the action. (Piaget, 1952:255)

According to Piaget, the new way infants relate actions to objects in substage 4 indicates a strengthening of their understanding that objects have an existence independent of themselves. A major means of testing this idea was to create conditions in which the infant responds to objects *when they are not present to the senses.*

Piaget's Test for Object Permanence: Out of Sight, Out of Mind?

As adults, we believe that objects have substance, are external to ourselves, maintain their identity when they change location, and continue to exist when they are out of sight. Piaget referred to this understanding as **object permanence,** and he found it lacking in young infants. Theirs, he claimed, is a world of discontinuous pictures that are constantly being "annihilated and resurrected," in which an object is "a mere image which reenters the void as soon as it vanishes, and emerges from it for no apparent reason" (1954:11). That is, until babies understand that an object exists when they are not perceiving it, out of sight is literally out of mind, according to Piagetian theory.

Evidence consistent with Piaget's view that infants lack object permanence comes from observations of 5- and 6-month-old babies, such as the following:

Observation 1: A baby seated at a table is offered a soft toy. He grasps it. While he is still engrossed in the toy, the experimenter takes it from him and places it on the table behind a screen. The baby may begin to reach for the toy, but as soon as it disappears from sight he stops short, stares for a moment, and then looks away without attempting to move the screen (see Figure 5.9) (Piaget, 1954).

Observation 2: A baby is placed in an infant seat in a bare laboratory room. Her mother, who has been playing with her, disappears for a moment. When the mother reappears, the baby sees three of her, an illusion the experimenter has created through the use of carefully arranged mirrors. The baby displays no consternation as she babbles happily to her multiple mother (Bower, 1982).

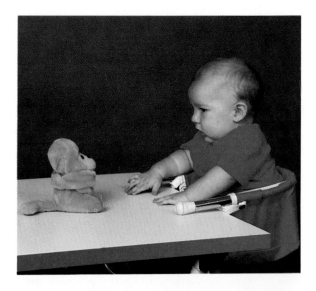

FIGURE 5.9 *Instead of searching behind the screen when his toy disappears, this infant looks dumbfounded. This kind of behavior led Piaget to conclude that objects no longer in view cease to exist for infants less than 8 months of age.*

Observation 3: From the comfort of his mother's lap, a baby follows a toy train with his eyes as it chugs along a track (see Figure 5.10). The baby watches as the train enters a tunnel, at which point instead of continuing to follow the train's progress, his eyes remain fixed on the tunnel's entrance. When the train reappears at the other end of the tunnel, it takes him a few seconds to catch up with it. He displays no surprise when the train emerges from the tunnel in a different color or shape (Bower, 1982).

Piaget maintained that infants respond in this manner because they cannot think of the object when it is absent. Only when they actively search for the absent object can we infer that babies understand that objects continue to exist when they are out of sight.

Stages of Object Permanence

Piaget proposed 6 stages in the development of object permanence, which correspond roughly to the six sub-stages of the sensorimotor period (see Table 5.2). We will discuss the first four of these stages in this chapter and the remaining two in Chapter 6.

Stages 1 and 2 (birth to 4 months)

Piaget observed that during the first 4 months of life babies begin to look toward the source of sounds they hear. He also reported that during this period his own children continued to stare at the place where he was last visible to them (Piaget, 1952b). However, since they *did not actively search* for an object when it disappeared, but instead seemed quickly to turn their attention elsewhere, he denied that these behaviors were evidence that they had a conception of objects.

Stage 3 (4 to 8 months)

Babies 4 or 5 months of age can sit up with some support and can reach out to grasp objects with reasonable accuracy, but their ability to explore is still relatively restricted. Furthermore, their attention to events around them is often fleeting. This is the age of the children in our three observations. Objects that disappear completely seem quickly to be forgotten, and the appearance of the same object in several places

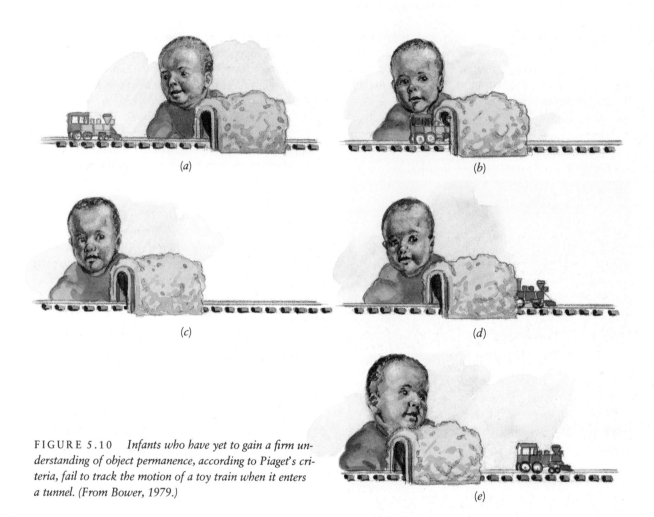

FIGURE 5.10 *Infants who have yet to gain a firm understanding of object permanence, according to Piaget's criteria, fail to track the motion of a toy train when it enters a tunnel. (From Bower, 1979.)*

causes no visible consternation. When objects are only partly hidden, however, the child will reach for them (Piaget, 1954).

Stage 4 (8 to 12 months)

At about 8 months of age, babies begin to show the first evidence, according to Piaget's criteria, that they know objects exist when they are out of sight: they begin to search for them. However, in searching for missing objects, babies in this stage tend to make a characteristic mistake that researchers have called the **A-not-B error**—babies reach for an object in the last place they found it even when they have seen it moved to a new location. Suppose an object is hidden under cover A and the baby is allowed to retrieve it. Then, in full view of the baby, the object is placed under cover B. When allowed to retrieve the object this time, the

baby will regularly look under cover A, where the object was found before, rather than under cover B, where the baby has seen it placed (Piaget, 1954) (see Figure 5.11). The tendency of infants to make this error continues until they are more than a year old, as we will see in Chapter 6.

Explaining the Acquisition of Object Permanence

The sequence of changes in children's developing understanding of object permanence described by Piaget occurs so reliably that tests of object permanence have been standardized for use in assessing the development of children who are at risk because of disease, physical impairment, or extreme environmental deprivation (Decarie, 1969; Uzgiris & Hunt, 1975). Even so, recent experiments have indicated that infants may understand object permanence earlier than Piaget suggested. For example, experiments conducted by Renée Baillargeon, Elizabeth Spelke, and Stanley Wasserman (1985) and by Baillargeon (1987) suggest that under some conditions 3½-month-old infants realize that objects continue to exist when they are hidden. This

evidence of object permanence fully 4½ months earlier than Piaget proposed casts doubt on his explanation of its development.

Baillargeon and her colleagues arranged for babies to watch a screen as it rotated slowly back and forth through a 180-degree arc on a hinge attached to the floor of the viewing surface. In its upright position the screen was like a fence behind which an object might be hidden from view. The screen could rotate toward

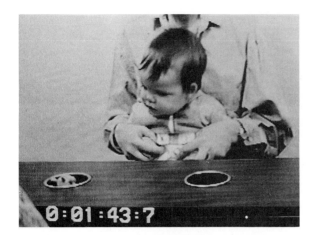
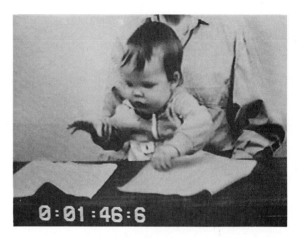
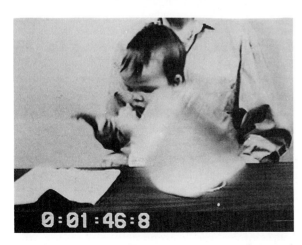
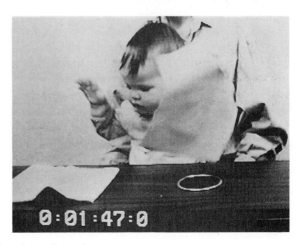

FIGURE 5.11   *In this movie sequence, an object is placed in the circle on the left (position B) and then both circles (positions A and B) are covered with a cloth while the baby watches. In a previous trial, the object had been placed in the right-hand circle (position A), and the baby had correctly retrieved it. This time while remaining oriented toward the hidden object at position B, the baby nonetheless picks up the cloth at position A, where the object was hidden before. (Courtesy of A. Diamond.)*

No elaborate apparatus is necessary to discover babies' growing fascination with the appearance and disappearance of objects in the second half year of life. A simple game of peekaboo is enough to delight children at this age.

the babies until it was lying flat and away from them until it was again lying flat.

When the babies were first shown the rotating screen, they stared at it for almost a full minute, but after several trials they seemed to lose interest in it and looked at it for only about 10 seconds. The experimenters then appeared to place a box behind the screen so that the screen obscured the "box" as it moved into its perpendicular position. (They arranged mirrors to create the illusion of the box.) Next, they did one of two things. For one group of babies, they rotated the screen until it reached the point where it should bump up against the illusory box, then returned it to its starting position. For the second group, they rotated the screen through its full 180-degree arc—a clear demonstration that no box stood in its way (see Figure 5.12).

The researchers reasoned that if the babies thought the box still existed even when it was obscured by the screen, they would stare at the screen longer when the box seemed to have vanished than they would when the screen seemed to bump into the box before returning to its starting point. Baillargeon's data suggest that the babies showed no special interest when the screen seemed to bump into the box (even

though this was a novel event), but they showed great interest when it appeared to pass right through the place where they thought the box was located. Their increased interest when the screen continued to rotate in its original manner is difficult to explain unless it is assumed that the babies expected it to bump into the hidden object.

Their responses to the rotating screen appear to indicate that infants realize hidden objects do not cease to exist simply because they cannot be seen. But if they know this, why do they behave as they do on tests of object permanence of the sort Piaget conducted? Psychologists' attempts to resolve this issue have focused on finding reasons for the A-not-B error.

Adele Diamond (1991) has championed the view that they err because they quickly forget. At 7½ to 8 months of age, the 2-second delay after moving the object from place A to place B is time enough to make the baby look in the wrong place. But by 9 months, they respond correctly after a 5-second delay, and by 12 months the delay must be 10 seconds or more before the baby will make the A-not-B error (Diamond, 1985). A second factor Diamond cites as appearing to affect the babies' performance is that they have trouble stopping themselves from reaching toward a place where they were just rewarded for reaching. Sometimes infants can be observed looking at position B (where they have just seen an object hidden) but reaching toward position A (where they successfully found the object before). If you refer to Figure 5.11, you will see that the baby displays the sort of behavior that Diamond describes. A third factor may be that they have difficulty adjusting their movements in order to reach under and around the obstacles between themselves and the object they are attempting to obtain (Diamond, 1991).

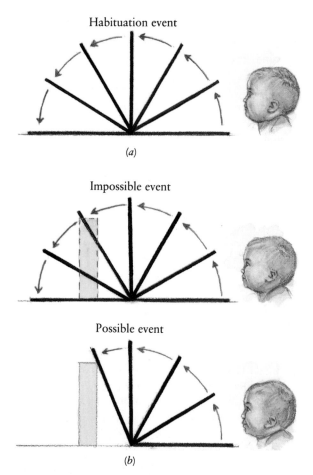

Habituation event

(a)

Impossible event

Possible event

(b)

FIGURE 5.12   *A schematic representation of the* (a) *habituation and* (b) *test events arranged for babies by Renée Baillargeon and her colleagues. In the impossible event, the rotating screen appears to pass through a box that the baby has previously seen behind it. (From Baillargeon, 1987.)*

By themselves, however, none of these explanations can account for the babies' errors. Evidence that insufficient memory for location cannot be the whole story comes from a study by Renée Baillargeon and Marcia Graber (1988). They arranged for 8-month-old infants to observe an object standing on one of two place mats. They then put screens in front of both place mats so that the object was hidden from view. After a 15-second delay the infants showed surprise when they saw a hand reach behind the "wrong" screen and pull out the object, but no surprise when the object was retrieved from behind the screen where they had last seen it. Baillargeon and Graber reasoned that the babies would not react differently to the two displays unless they could remember where they had seen the object. Nor can the difficulty of inhibiting previous actions or of reaching around barriers, alone, explain errors, because 9-month-old infants have been observed to do both in some circumstances (Wellman, Cross, & Bartsch, 1987).

Taken together, the data on the development of object permanence and motor skills between 3 and 12 months suggest the following general picture. By 4 months of age, infants realize that objects do not cease to exist simply because they are out of sight, but they are unable to act on this understanding except to register their surprise when their expectations are not met (Baillargeon, 1987; Spelke, 1991). At this early age, the act of reaching for and grasping an object still takes effort. Infants must monitor their movements carefully by looking back and forth between their hands and the object they are trying to grasp, and they are likely to encounter trouble when they try to reach around and under obstacles. Any such difficulty diverts the infants' attention from the object that has been hidden from sight and hastens their forgetting. By about 9 months, reaching and grasping have become well-integrated responses that no longer require special attention and therefore no longer distract them. In addition, their memory has improved and they are better able to inhibit strong impulses to repeat previously successful actions. These factors combine to enable them to keep their knowledge of the current location of a hidden object in mind long enough to act on it.

This overall picture of the development of behaviors related to object permanence contradicts Piaget's belief that infants under 8 months of age cannot keep in mind the continued existence of objects that they do not see. These recent studies require some

BOX 5.1
Action and Understanding

Piaget's hypothesis that children's own activities are the driving force of their development has led many psychologists to study the developmental consequences of restricted or enhanced movement early in life. A basic intuition guiding such research is the idea that locomotion not only allows babies to learn how to move their bodies in space but also provides them with a new understanding of the objects that fill space. Selma Fraiberg has written:

> Travel changes one's perspective. A chair, for example, is an object of one dimension when viewed by a six-month-old baby propped up on the sofa, or by an eight-month-old baby doing push-ups on a rug. It's even very likely that the child of this age confronted at various times with different perspectives of the same chair would see not one chair, but several chairs, corresponding to each perspective. It's when you start to get around under your own steam that you discover what a chair really is. (Fraiberg, 1959:52)

A classic study demonstrating a close link between locomotor experience and the understanding of spatial relations was carried out by Richard Held and Alan Hein (1963) with kittens who were raised from birth in total darkness. When the kittens were old enough to walk, they were placed two at a time in an apparatus called a "kitten carousel." One kitten, har-nessed to pull the carousel, could use what it saw to control its movements, and its movements determined, to some extent, what it saw. The other kitten was carried in the gondola of the carousel and had no active interactions with the world it saw. The experiences of the passive kitten were controlled largely by the actions of the kitten pulling the carousel. Each pair of kittens was given 3 hours of visual experience in the carousel every day for 42 days. Between these sessions, they were returned to the dark. Thus the only visual experience the kittens had, and hence the only opportunity they had to learn to coordinate vision and movement, was the time they spent in the carousel.

The influence of active versus passive movement on the kittens' responses to their environment became strikingly apparent when Held and Hein lowered them onto the surface of a visual cliff similar to the one shown in Figure 1.7 of Chapter 1 (p. 28). This apparatus had stripes painted on it like the stripes around the sides of the kitten carousel, except that they were painted to look as if one side of the apparatus were far below the other. The kittens that had been active in the carousel shied away from the deep side of the visual cliff and appropriately stretched out their legs to land on it. The passive kittens did not try to avoid the deep side of the cliff, nor did they make appropriate adjustments in the positions of their legs in anticipation of landing on it.

---

modification of his strong emphasis on action as *the* essential motor of cognitive development; in this case knowledge seems to precede the ability to act on it (but see Box 5.1 for additional evidence concerning the role of action in early cognitive development).

Integrating the Various Properties of Objects

Understanding that objects continue to exist even when they are out of sight is by no means all that babies come to know about them. They also come to understand that the various pieces of information they derive from the sight, sound, taste, smell, and feel of an object all go together. This understanding helps them to infer the existence of the whole object from its individual characteristics. They begin to understand, for example, that the voice coming from the other room and the face they see a few moments later are two aspects of the same person, and that the gold color of the stuff on the spoon goes with its awful taste.

During most of this century, developmental psychologists assumed that at birth babies responded to

This finding fits well with the results of the experiment by Joseph Campos and his co-workers described in Chapter 1 (p. 28) that confirmed the importance of movement in human cognitive development (Bertenthal, Campos, & Barrett, 1984). In that study, 5-month-old babies who had not yet begun to crawl did not seem to be afraid of a visual cliff when they first saw it. They began to be afraid of heights only after they had begun to move around on their own or after they had gained experience in locomoting in baby walkers.

Campos and his co-workers have also shown that locomotion enhances the development of infants' memory for the locations of hidden objects. Babies who had extensive experience in moving around in baby walkers before they could move about on their own were more adept at locating hidden objects in standard object permanence tests than were children of the same age who had no such experience (Campos, Benson, & Rudy, 1986).

Finally, unusual support for the close connection between locomotion and development is provided by a study of the development of infants suffering from a neural-tube defect that impedes locomotion (Telzrow, et. al., 1987). Such children were found to be delayed in their development of correct search behaviors by 5 to 6 months. They began to search for hidden objects correctly only after they had begun to move voluntarily. The results of these experiments on how locomo-

tion affects development provide support for the belief that active engagement with the world makes a fundamental contribution to development.

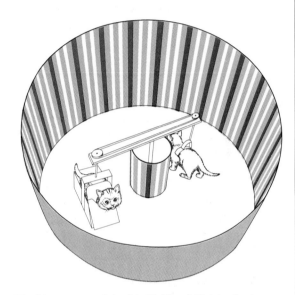

The kitten carousel used in Held and Hein's classic experiment demonstrating the importance of active experience to development. (From Held, 1965.)

the sight, sound, and other sense impressions of objects as if they were completely separate (Harris, 1983; James, 1890). According to this view, infants must learn to integrate mentally the various sensory aspects of an objects as they occur together in the course of everyday experience. Recently, however, several ingenious studies have shown that the ability to integrate at least some combinations of features either does not have to be learned or is learned rapidly and quite early in infancy.

Elizabeth Spelke (1976, 1984) presented pairs of film strips to 4-month-old babies and tested to see if

they knew what sort of sound should accompany each film. In one study she ran two films simultaneously, side by side. One showed percussion instruments being played, and the other showed a game of peekaboo. A loudspeaker located between the two screens would sometimes play sounds appropriate to the percussion instruments, while at other times it played sounds appropriate to the game of peekaboo. The infants looked most often at whatever film corresponded to the loudspeaker's sounds.

Using a similar setup, Arlette Streri and Elizabeth Spelke (1988) arranged for 4-month-old infants to

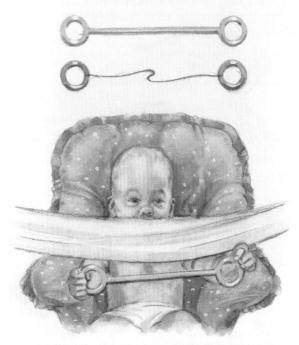

FIGURE 5.13   *Objects and apparatus for experiments on the way that infants use information gained in one sensory modality to recognize it in another. This infant is feeling a rigid object and later will be able to recognize it visually. (From Streri & Spelke, 1988.)*

ties of objects they have experienced by other senses as parts of the same object and do not have to acquire this information through an extended process of associative learning. No techniques have yet been developed to determine if such behavior exists at birth, so the question of how early it develops is still unresolved.

Learning about Kinds of Things

Between 2½ and 12 months, infants show marked improvement in the ability to **categorize,** that is, to perceive objects or events that differ in various ways as equivalent because they share certain common features.

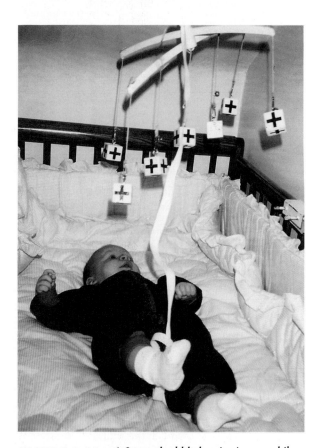

FIGURE 5.14   *A 3-month-old baby viewing a mobile whose +-shaped figures move when the baby kicks. After three 15-minute sessions, each with a different color +, the baby will kick a mobile with yet a fourth color. But if a new form is used in the fourth session (for example, an A), the baby will not kick at first.*

hold two rings, one in each hand, under a cloth that prevented them from seeing the rings or their own bodies (see Figure 5.13). In one case the rings were connected by a rigid bar and moved together. In the other case the rings were connected by a flexible cord so that they moved independently. The infants were handed one pair of connected rings, either rigidly or flexibly connected, until they had largely lost interest and then were shown two *visual* displays of rings, one pair rigidly connected and the other with a flexible connection. The babies looked longer at the visual display *unlike* the pair of rings they had been exploring with their hands. Babies who had been handling the independently moving rings looked longer at a visual display of rigid ones, and babies who had been given the rigidly connected rings to hold looked longer at the flexibly connected ones. These and other data (Meltzoff & Borton, 1979; Spelke, 1990, 1991) strongly suggest that infants perceive the basic proper-

We have already seen that very young infants appreciate differences between such objects as rattles and balloons: they show it by doing different things to them. Carolyn Rovee-Collier and her colleagues have shown that by the time infants are 3 months old, they can also learn to respond to perceptually different objects as equivalent; that is, they are able to form categories (Hayne, Rovee-Collier, & Perris, 1987). Infants were initially shown a mobile with +-shaped trinkets dangling from it and taught that if they kicked their legs the mobile would move (see Figure 5.14). In second and third sessions, the color of the +s was changed (from blue to green to red, say). At the end of the three sessions, infants kicked at a consistently high rate to make the mobile move. Then the infants were shown test mobiles on which the +s were either of yet another color (black, say) or changed in both form and color (a black *B*). Infants responded at high rates to the test mobile with the same form and a novel color, but not to the mobile with a novel form. Apparently, they were categorizing the mobiles on the basis of the specific form of the trinkets.

Between 6 and 9 months of age children develop the ability to make much finer distinctions between categories and to recognize key similarities and differences in objects of greater complexity (Bertenthal, Campos, & Barrett, 1984; Kagan & Hamburg, 1981; Ruff, 1978; Younger & Cohen, 1986). Holly Ruff (1978), for example, compared the amount of time 6- and 9-month-old babies looked at a series of objects that differed in form, size, and color. Each object consisted of a cylinder and a cube that had been glued to a rectangular base. Ruff began with familiarization trials in which she gave the babies the objects depicted in Figure 5.15*a* one at a time. The objects differed in color and size but not in form; that is, each of them had the cylinder and the cube glued to the same side of the rectangular base. The babies were allowed to touch each of the objects for 30 seconds. Then, in two test trials, the babies were shown the two objects depicted in Figure 5.15*b*. In the first test trial, the object was of a different color and size but the same form as the objects with which the babies had become familiar. Since form, not color or size, was the categorizing characteristic of the familiarization objects, the first trial object belonged to the same category. In the second test trial, the cylinder and the cube were glued to opposite sides of the rectangular base. Thus the second trial object was of a new form and therefore belonged to a new category. The 6-month-olds did *not* respond differently to the two test objects; that is, they displayed

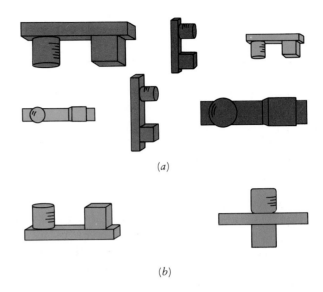

(a)

(b)

FIGURE 5.15   (a) *The familiarization objects in Holly Ruff's experiment differ in size and color—orange, green, and red—but all have the same form.* (b) *The test objects in the experiment are of the same color—blue—and size but differ in form. The differences in color and size between the familiarization objects and the test object on the left did not interest the infants because they had learned that those properties were irrelevant during the first phase of the experiment. (From Ruff, 1978.)*

no knowledge that "rectangle with a cylinder and a square on one side of it" constituted a category. But the 9-month-olds did. They spent more time examining the object that differed from the familiarization objects in form than they did the object that differed in color and size. This behavior indicates that they had formed a perceptual category based on the form of the objects during the familiarization trials.

David Starkey (1981) obtained similar results when he showed 6-, 9-, and 12-month-old infants four yellow plastic pillboxes and four blue clay balls mixed together on a tray. Almost all the 12- and 9-month-olds touched either all the pillboxes or all the clay balls one after the other before turning to the other kind of object. The 6-month-olds, however, touched the two kinds of objects in a completely haphazard manner, indicating that they were not responding to the categorical distinctions between them.

When we combine the results of Ruff's and Starkey's experiments with the findings of Rovee-Collier and her colleagues, it appears that infants can learn to respond to categories through operant conditioning within a few months of birth. Not until 7 or 8 months of age, however, do they begin to respond to categories without special training.

The Growth of Memory

The abilities to make categorical distinctions among objects and to keep in mind the existence of an object that has disappeared from sight indicate that the infant's capacity to structure information from past experience is increasing. The processes underlying such changing memory capacities have been the topic of intensive research.

Using the same general technique as she used to study the formation of categories, Carolyn Rovee-Collier and her colleagues trained infants to make a mobile move by kicking one of their legs, which was attached to the mobile by a ribbon (Sullivan, Rovee-Collier, & Tynes, 1979; Boller et al., 1990). They found that 3-month-olds could remember this experience for 1 week. Brought back to the laboratory, babies started to kick as soon as they were put in the crib and saw the mobile even before the ribbon was tied to their leg. After 2 weeks, however, the babies seemed to have forgotten their training; they took just as long to start the mobile moving as they had taken when they were first trained to do so.

Other studies have shown that if the infants are given a brief visual reminder, they can remember their earlier training even after some time has elapsed. The researchers trained a group of 3-month-old babies to activate a mobile by kicking. They then let a month elapse before putting the baby in the experimental situation again — more than enough time, the researchers thought, for the babies to forget their training. On the day before they tested whether the infants remembered how to make the mobile move, they showed them the mobile but did not allow them to kick. When the babies were tested the next day, they started kicking as soon as they were placed in the crib and the ribbon was tied to their leg (Rovee-Collier et al., 1980). The mere sight of the mobile the day before seemed to remind the babies of what they had learned to do.

FIGURE 5.16 *Not only do young infants imitate live models, but they will also imitate actions they have seen on television (Meltzoff, 1988a). This child observes a televised adult model manipulate blocks and then immediately the child imitates the same actions. Meltzoff also demonstrated that infants who watch a televised model on one day will reproduce the model's behavior 24 hours later. (Courtesy of A. Meltzoff.)*

Recall and Wariness

The work of Rovee-Collier and her colleagues shows that babies begin to remember at a very early age and that their memory continues to improve steadily during the first year of life. On the basis of this evidence, Rovee-Collier (1990) has concluded that the improvement in memory over the course of the first year of life is a continuous process that does not involve any new principles of learning or remembering.

Other investigators argue that sometime after 6 months of age babies begin to display a new form of remembering in which they can call to mind (recall) absent objects and events, even when they have not had an extended opportunity to learn about them (Kagan, Kearsley, & Zellazo, 1978; Mandler, 1988, 1990; Meltzoff, 1990). Recall memory is considered an especially important achievement because it seems to require the generation of a mental representation of the absent stimuli. The demonstration of recall, in children who have not achieved object permanence according to Piaget's criteria would of course be damaging to his account of infant mental development.

One technique used to trace the origins of recall depends on the tendency of young children to imitate the actions of others (Figure 5.16) (Mandler, 1990; Meltzoff, 1990). We discussed early forms of immediate imitation in Chapter 4 (pp. 158–159) and we will discuss the development of imitation more thoroughly in Chapter 6 (pp. 221–222); for now it is sufficient to describe the procedure used to study memory through imitation.

Andrew Meltzoff demonstrated three simple actions to 9-month-old infants seated on their parents' laps (Meltzoff, 1988b). First he took a small board attached in an upright position to a base by a hinge and pushed it until it lay flat on its base; second, he pushed a black button that sounded a beeper; and third, he rattled an orange plastic egg with nuts and bolts in it. After watching these displays, the babies were taken home. The next day they were brought back to the laboratory and allowed to play with a few small toys. Then the board, the buzzer, and the plastic egg were brought out. Although the babies had never themselves done such things, most of them imitated one or more of the actions they had seen Meltzoff do with these objects the day before. McDonough and Mandler (1989) obtained the same findings with 11-month-olds.

Additional evidence for the emergence of recall memory late in the first year comes from the work of Daniel Ashmead and Marion Perlmutter (1979). They describe a 9-month-old girl who was accustomed to playing with ribbons kept in the bottom drawer of a bureau. On one occasion the girl crawled to the bureau and opened the bottom drawer, only to discover that the ribbons were not there. She then opened all of the drawers until she found the ribbons, which had been placed in the top drawer. When she wanted the ribbons the next day, she crawled over to the bureau, immediately opened the top drawer, and removed the ribbons. As Mandler (1988) points out, this kind of behavior implies that the child formed an explicit mental representation of the ribbons' location.

Some researchers believe that the ability to recall earlier events is essential for the changes that occur between 7 and 9 months in the way infants behave when they are confronted with a strange object or person. Sometime during this period, infants become overtly wary and even afraid when something out of the ordinary happens (see Figure 5.17). In a demonstration of this phenomenon, Rudolph Schaffer (1974) repeatedly presented babies between the ages of 4 and 9 months with a strange object until they became habituated to it. He then presented them with a new strange object, a plastic model of an ice cream sundae.

FIGURE 5.17 *The wide-eyed look this child is giving her disguised mother displays the wariness that infants develop sometime between the ages of 7 and 9 months.*

Most 4-month-olds strained toward the sundae immediately, without any hesitation, indicating that they saw nothing strange about it at all. Most 6-month-olds hesitated for a second or two, showing that they noticed the change, and then they reached for the sundae impulsively, often bringing it to their mouths. Nine-month-olds tended to hesitate longer, noting that it was unfamiliar. Some of them even turned away or started to cry. Nathan Fox, Jerome Kagan, and Sally Weiskopf (1979) hypothesize that the 9-month-olds' wariness is caused by their newly acquired ability to compare current events with remembered past events in a systematic way that definitely fits the definition of recall. The babies not only note that the ice cream sundae is unfamiliar but search their memories to determine if it corresponds to any category of things they have seen before, and they become upset because it does not.

Considered as a whole, the data on object permanence, categorization, and the changing bases of remembering support the conclusion that the seemingly separate advances in cognitive development that occur in the latter part of the first year of life are separate neither from each other nor from the development of motor capacities and the biological maturation we described earlier. The new cognitive capacities are intimately linked with changes in the babies' social world, including their emotional relationships with their caregivers and their communicative abilities.

A NEW RELATIONSHIP WITH THE SOCIAL WORLD

The development of infants' understanding of the properties of objects and their increasing ability to remember are reflected in their relationships with other people. Jake's wariness of Sheila at 12 months, described at the start of this chapter, is one of a set of social behaviors that first appear around 7 months of age. When Jake was 10 *weeks* old, Sheila could care for Jake without Jake's showing any overt sign of distress. This does not mean, however, that he did not notice the difference. Keiko Mizukami and her colleagues (1990) have observed that the skin temperature of babies 2 to 4 months old drops—a physiological indicator that they are concerned when their mother

leaves and a stranger appears over their cribs. But at 1 year, Jake not only was surprised when he looked up and saw Sheila where he expected his mother to be; he was distressed, and he showed it by turning away and reaching for his mother.

Many developmental psychologists agree that in the second half of the first year babies' fear of an unfamiliar adult and their distress when their mothers disappear are closely connected to their increasing ability to move around, to categorize, and to remember (Bertenthal, Campos, & Barrett, 1984; Emde, Gaensbauer, & Harmon, 1976; Kagan, 1984).

The Role of Uncertainty in Wariness

When we try to discover why the beginning of locomotion, an increased understanding of the nature of objects, and improved memory should be associated with overt wariness and fear, we have to remember the predicament babies are in. They are constantly encountering new situations and new objects, but they have little experience to guide their responses and little physical strength or coordination to respond with. They cannot eat, dress, or go to the toilet by themselves. What is more, since they have a vocabulary of only a few words at best, they have no reliable system of communication. Therefore, to get through each day reasonably well fed and comfortable, they must depend on adults and older siblings to know what needs to be done and how to do it, as the following vignette illustrates:

Amy, almost four months old, sat in her father's lap in a booth at the coffee shop. He was talking to a friend. Amy was teething on a hard rubber ring he had brought along for her. Her father supported Amy's back with his left arm, keeping his hand free. Twice he used that hand to catch the ring when it fell to her lap or his own lap. When Amy dropped the ring for the third time, he interrupted his conversation, said "Klutz," picked it up and put it on the table. She leaned toward it, awkwardly reached out and touched it, but was not able to grasp it well enough to pick it up. Her father had returned to his conversation, and this time without interrupting it (though he was glancing back and forth between Amy's hand and his friend) he tilted the ring upward toward Amy so that she could get her thumb under it. She grasped the ring and pulled it away from him. Absorbed in chewing on the toy, Amy did not look at him. He went on talking and drinking his coffee, paying no further attention to her until he felt the toy drop into his lap once again. (Kaye, 1982:1–2)

Here we see a few of the ways in which adults who care for babies act for them and with them so that the babies can function effectively despite their relative ineptness. The adult's actions must be finely coordinated with the baby's abilities and needs or the baby will experience some form of difficulty.

The kind of finely tuned adult support that permits children to accomplish with assistance actions that they will later learn to accomplish independently creates what the cultural-context theorist Lev Vygotsky (1978) called a **zone of proximal development.** Vygotsky attributed great significance to such child-adult interactions throughout development. The zone he referred to is the gap between what children can accomplish independently and what they can accomplish when they are interacting with others who are more competent. The term "proximal" (nearby) indicates that the assistance provided goes just slightly beyond the child's current competence, complementing and building on the child's existing abilities instead of directly teaching the child new behaviors. Notice, for example, that Amy's father did not put the teething ring in Amy's hand, nor did he hold it up to her mouth for her to teethe on. Instead, he tilted it upward so that she could grasp it herself, and he did so almost automatically while doing something else. To coordinate behaviors in this way, the adult must know what the child is trying to do and be sensitive to the child's abilities and signals.

The mundane ways in which adults provide a predictable and supportive environment for infants help to explain the onset of wariness during the seventh month of life. There are only certain people that babies can count on to arrange the environment appropriately and in accordance with their expectations. Before babies are 7 months old, their capacity to classify people as "those who can be trusted to help" versus "unpredictable strangers" and to remember the likely implications for themselves is at best quite limited. Once infants can both form such categories and use them to compare their current circumstances with similar past experiences, there is a qualitative change in the way that they respond to strangers. They realize that strangers do not have routines for interacting with them and cannot be depended upon to notice and understand the babies' signals or to do what the babies might need them to do.

A New Form of Emotional Relationship

Recall from Chapter 4 (p. 170) that changes in babies' behavior around 2½ months of age are accompanied by changes in the way caregivers behave toward them. This kind of reciprocity, in which changes in the child go hand in hand with changes in the social world, occurs again in the period between 6 and 9 months.

All of the developments we have discussed thus far play a role in producing a change in the way parents feel about their infants, but according to Joseph Campos and his colleagues, the critical factor in organizing a qualitative change in developmental processes late in the first year of life is locomotion (Campos, Kermoian, & Zumbahlen, 1992). These researchers interviewed parents of 8-month-old infants, some of whom had begun to crawl and some of whom had not. Both the positive and negative feelings about their infants reported by the parents of children who had begun to crawl were more intense than those of the parents whose infants had not yet begun to crawl. The parents of children who were crawling said that they now gave their children tighter hugs, roughhoused with them more, and talked to them more affectionately. They also reported increased feelings of anger at their babies and increased attempts to control them with angry remarks.

Infants' expressions of emotion also seemed to change in conjunction with locomotion. The parents of infants who had begun to crawl reported that the babies' expressions of anger increased in both frequency and intensity when their efforts to achieve a goal were frustrated. They also seemed to become more upset when their parents left their sides. One mother reported:

If I leave [the room] she gets upset unless she's busy and doesn't see it. But as soon as she notices, she starts hollering. I don't think it mattered the first four months. When she started doing more, sitting up, crawling, that's when she'd get upset when I would leave. (Campos et al., 1992:33)

Many developmental psychologists believe that these new forms of emotional expression bespeak a new emotional bond, which they call **attachment**. Eleanor Maccoby (1980) lists four signs of attachment in babies and young children:

1. They seek to be near their primary caretaker. Before the age of 7 to 8 months few babies plan and make organized attempts to achieve contact with the other person; after this age, babies often follow their mothers closely, for example.

2. They show distress if separated from their caretaker. Before attachment begins, infants show little disturbance when their mothers walk out of the room.

3. They are happy when they are reunited with the person they are attached to.

4. They orient their actions to the other person, even when he or she is absent. Babies listen for their mother's voice and watch her while they play.

The special relationship with their mothers that babies begin to display between 7 and 9 months of age undergoes significant changes during the remainder of infancy and beyond. We will take up these later events and describe some of the important research on attachment in Chapter 6.

The Changing Nature of Communication

As babies become mobile and begin to respond warily to novel objects and strange people, the ways in which they communicate with adults also undergo important changes.

We have already seen in Chapter 4 (p. 171) that the advent of social smiling is accompanied by coordinated turn taking; by 3 months of age infants and their caregivers are jointly experiencing pleasure in simple face-to-face interactions (recall Daniel Stern's description of the baby whose "body resonated [with pleasure] almost like a balloon being pumped up" during one such episode [1977:3]). Colin Trevarthen (1980) refers to the coordinated turn taking and emotional sharing between very young infants and their care-

givers as **primary intersubjectivity**. This early form of communication is restricted to direct face-to-face interactions and still depends for most of its support on the adult participant.

Around the age of 7 months babies begin to interact with others in a new and more complex way that Trevarthen calls **secondary intersubjectivity**. The hallmark of secondary intersubjectivity is that the infant and the caregiver can now share understandings and emotions that refer beyond themselves to objects and other people. For example, if a mother and her 5-month-old baby are looking at each other and the mother suddenly looks to one side, the infant will not follow the mother's gaze; but at 7 or 8 months babies look in the direction their mothers are looking and engage in joint visual attention with her (Butterworth & Jarrett, 1991).

This newcomer to the world of upright posture is looking back to see what his mother thinks of his exploits. His enquiring gaze is an example of social referencing.

A striking example of secondary intersubjectivity that also gives evidence of the new emotional relationship between infants and their caregivers as well as the infants' increasingly complex communicative skills is called **social referencing.** Babies use social referencing when they come upon something unfamiliar and look back to their caregivers for some indication of how they should feel and what they are supposed to do. It comes into prominence as a means of communication as soon as babies begin to move about on their own (Campos & Stenberg, 1981). When babies notice that their caregivers are looking at the same thing they are looking at and appear to be concerned, they hesitate and become wary. If their caregiver smiles and looks pleased about the new situation, they relax (Walden & Baxter, 1989).

Smiles and other facial expressions provide only a crude means of communicating, however. As babies become more mobile and more likely to wander out of their caregiver's sight and reach, facial expressions become less available as a source of information. A new means of communication that will allow babies to coordinate their actions with those of caregivers at a distance becomes an urgent necessity.

At 9 months of age, children begin to understand certain words and expressions in highly specific, often ritualized situations. For example, one little girl observed by Elizabeth Bates and her colleagues (1979) touched her head when asked, "Where are your little thoughts?" Another would bring her favorite doll when she was asked to "bring a dolly," but she did not understand the word "doll" to refer to any doll but her own.

The development of the ability to produce language can be traced back to the cooing and gurgling noises babies begin to make at 10 to 12 weeks of age. Soon thereafter, babies with normal hearing not only initiate cooing sounds but begin to respond with gurgles and coos to the voices of others. When they are imitated, they will answer with another coo, thereby engaging in a "conversation" in which turns are taken at vocalizing. They are most likely to vocalize with their mothers and other familiar people.

Babbling begins around 4 months of age in hearing children. It is a form of vocalizing that includes consonant and vowel sounds like those used in speech (de Villiers & de Villiers, 1978). At first babbling amounts to no more than vocal play, as babies discover the wealth of sounds they can make with their tongue,

Even before babies can use words, they are likely to babble in response to adults when they are engaged by them.

teeth, palate, and vocal cords. They practice making these sound combinations endlessly, much as they practice grasping objects or rolling over. They even produce syllables they have never heard before and will not use when they learn to speak. Babbling during the first year of life is the same the world over, whether the baby's family speaks English, French, or Japanese (Oller, 1978; Blake & de Boysson-Bardies, 1992). At about 9 months of age, babies begin to narrow their babbling to the sounds produced in the language they will eventually speak. As babies often babble when they play alone, early babbling does not seem to be an attempt to communicate.

Toward the end of the first year, babies begin to vocalize strings of syllables that have the intonation and stress of actual utterances in the language they will eventually speak. Such vocalizations are called **jargoning.** John Dore (1978) found that before the end of the first year, babies start to repeat particular short utterances in particular situations, as if they had some meaning. When Jake was about 10 months old, for example, if he wanted the bottle of juice from the bag hanging on the back of his stroller, he would turn around in his seat, say, "Dah, dah," and reach toward the bag while looking up at his mother in appeal. She immediately knew what he wanted and gave it to him.

The course of vocalizing done by deaf children provides an instructive contrast to that of hearing children. It used to be thought that deaf children began to babble at the same age as hearing children (Lenneberg, Rebelsky, & Nichols, 1965). Recent work by D. Kimbrough Oller and Rebecca Eilers (1988), however, has shown that the vocalizations of deaf and hearing infants differ markedly in ways that indicate that only deaf children with residual hearing actually babble.

By 1 year of age or so, deaf children rarely vocalize, but a different kind of communication system has revealed itself. At the same time that hearing children begin to babble, deaf children can be seen "babbling" with their hands, making the movements that will become the elements of sign language (Pettito & Maretette, 1991).

These budding linguistic abilities, which we discuss in more detail in Chapters 6 and 8, are part and parcel of the reorganization of babies' perceptual-motor, cognitive, and social capacities that signals the advent of a new bio-social-behavioral shift in the latter half of the first year of life.

A NEW BIO-SOCIAL-BEHAVIORAL SHIFT

Table 5.3 summarizes the set of changes that converge to create a bio-social-behavioral shift in the organization of infants' psychological processes between 7 and 9 months of age. (Brazelton, 1990; Emde, Gaensbauer, & Harmon, 1976). Whereas the crucial biological events at the 2½-month bio-social-behavioral shift centered on changes in the sensory pathways of the brain, the shift that occurs at 7 to 9 months involves changes in the cerebellum and other parts of the brain that control movement and balance, the hippocampus (which is important for memory), and the frontal lobes of the cerebral cortex (which are important for the organization of deliberate action). Also significant are increases in the strength of muscles and bones, which are necessary to support locomotion. Locomotion appears to orchestrate the reorganization of many other functions that have been developing in parallel with it.

> ### TABLE 5.3
> ### Elements of the Bio-Social-Behavioral Shift at 7 to 9 Months
>
> **BIOLOGICAL DOMAIN**
>
> Growth of muscles and hardening of bones
> Myelination of motor neurons to lower trunk, legs, and hands
> Myelination of cerebellum, hippocampus, and frontal lobes
> New forms of EEG activity in cortex
>
> **BEHAVIORAL DOMAIN**
>
> Onset of crawling
> Fear of heights
> Automated reaching and grasping
> Action sequences coordinated to achieve goals
> Object permanence displayed in actions
> Recall memory
> Wariness in response to novelty
> Babbling
>
> **SOCIAL DOMAIN**
>
> Wariness of strangers
> New emotional response to caregiver (attachment)
> Social referencing

New motor skills, for example, lead infants to discover many properties and functions of objects in their immediate environment. They become capable of picking up objects, feeling them, tasting them, moving around them, and attempting to use them for various purposes of their own. As babies learn that some of the objects "out there" move and respond in coordination with them, their interactions with people take on a whole new dimension. Sympathetic adults buffer them against discomfort and danger. These adults can be counted on to understand babies' signals, to complete their actions for them, and to arrange things so that they can act more effectively for themselves.

These experiences would not amount to much, however, if memories of them did not begin to accumulate in infants' minds. Once babies can move away from the immediate presence of watchful adults, they can no longer rely on the adults to help them complete their actions and to rescue them from their mistakes as they did before. It is not enough to recognize that one has seen an object before or to respond with curiosity if it is new. Babies must be able to recall their earlier experiences with objects, including people, in order to behave appropriately.

Both the baby and the caregiver must accommodate themselves to the uncertainties of their increasing separation as babies begin to move about on their own. Caregivers arrange the environment so that the baby is likely to come to no harm, and they keep a watchful eye (or ear) open for anything amiss. Babies anticipate trouble, too. They keep an eye on their caregivers' responses to the things they do. They become openly wary of strange events and people, because they are not sure what unfamiliar adults will do.

As their first birthday approaches, many babies will have progressed from crawling to walking upright, amplifying their powers to move around the world on their own as well as the need to use all of their accumulating cognitive and communicative abilities to coordinate their actions with their caregivers'. Sophisticated as it may be when compared to their behavior at 2½ months, however, the pattern of adaptation that babies achieve by 1 year of age is destined to change. They keep growing, keep exploring, and continue to gain a more reliable understanding of the world in which they find themselves.

SUMMARY

1. Although there is great individual variation, most healthy babies triple in weight during the first year of life. Changes in size are accompanied by changes in overall body proportions that are important for the eventual achievement of balanced walking.

2. Hardening of the bones and increases in muscle mass contribute to the development of crawling, walking, and the coordinated movements of the arms and hands.

3. Development in several areas of the brain is important for the behavioral changes that occur between 3 and 12 months of age:
   a. Primary motor area: general coordination of movements.
   b. Cerebellum: coordination and balance.
   c. Hippocampus: memory.
   d. Frontal lobes: voluntary control and planning.

4. The initial stage of poorly coordinated reaching and grasping, controlled primarily by subcortical brain centers, is followed by a stage of visually guided reaching and grasping, which gives way to swift and accurate voluntary movements after several months of practice.

5. Increasing skill in grasping objects makes possible the discovery of many new properties of objects.

6. Locomotion, which begins during the second half of the first year of life, brings about a fundamental change in infants' relationship with their environments. Motor control of the body begins at the head and neck and proceeds gradually to the trunk and legs. At 7 to 8 months, infants begin to crawl or creep, using a combination of leg and arm movements. Walking is achieved a few months later, around the first birthday.

7. Motor development can be speeded up by extensive practice, but practice has little influence on the eventual level of proficiency at basic motor skills. Extensive early practice may, however, influence the later performance of specialized motor skills such as dancing and swimming.

8. According to Piaget, infants progress through two additional sensorimotor substages before the end of the first year. Between 4 and 8 months they pay increased attention to external objects and prolong actions that produce interesting changes in their environment (substage 3). Between 8 and 12 months of age, they achieve the ability to coordinate separate actions to achieve goals (substage 4).

9. Important changes occur in infants' ability to keep in mind and act upon objects that are out of sight:
   a. For the first 3 months of life, infants appear to forget objects not present to their senses.
   b. At 4 months, many infants seem to understand that objects exist even when they cannot see them, but they are incapable of acting on this knowledge. The object and its location are quickly forgotten.

c. At about 8 months of age, infants begin to search for hidden objects but quickly become confused or forget their location, often remembering their own movements instead.

d. Memory for the locations of objects and the ability to search for hidden objects continue to improve into the second year of life.

10. By 3 to 4 months of age, infants are able to perceive the correspondence between such varied properties of objects as the way they look and the sounds they make. It is not known how early this understanding develops or what aspects of it are present at birth.

11. The ability to perceive a variety of objects as members of a single category appears as early as 3 months of age and continues to develop in tandem with other cognitive capacities.

12. Between the ages of 2½ and 12 months, memory expands steadily. When provided with a specific reminder of training received a month earlier, infants as young as 3 months of age remember how to make a mobile move.

13. About the same time that babies begin to crawl, they show signs of being able to call to mind objects and people that are not present and activities they have not practiced.

14. Changes in social and emotional behavior accompany changes in motor skills and cognition; infants become wary of strangers and upset when they are separated from their primary caregivers.

15. Locomotion is accompanied by a new form of communicative activity. Babies begin to monitor the expression on their caregiver's face to determine the caregiver's reaction to an object or event they are both attending to. Such social referencing helps them to evaluate their environment.

16. Events in the major developmental domains converge between the ages of 7 and 9 months in a bio-social-behavioral shift that ushers in a qualitatively new stage of development.

KEY TERMS

A-not-B error

attachment

babbling

categorization

jargoning

locomotion

object permanence

primary intersubjectivity

secondary circular reactions

secondary intersubjectivity

social referencing

zone of proximal development

SUGGESTED READINGS

FRAIBERG, SELMA H. *The Magic Years: Understanding and Handling Problems of Early Childhood.* New York: Scribner's, 1959.

A richly detailed account of early childhood that incorporates the ideas of Sigmund Freud in a highly readable and sympathetic manner.

HARRIS, PAUL L. "Infant Cognition." In P. H. Mussen (Ed.), *Handbook of Child Psychology,* vol. 2: *Infancy and Developmental Psychobiology.* New York: Wiley, 1983.

A summary of evidence concerning the infant's early intellectual capacities, including an evaluation of competing claims made by theorists of various schools of thought.

LAMB, MICHAEL E., & BORNSTEIN, MICHAEL H. *Development in Infancy: An Introduction,* Third Edition. New York: Random House, 1992.

A thorough, readable introduction to infant behavior and development that covers in greater detail the topics taken up in this chapter.

MCGRAW, MYRTLE B. *Growth: A Study of Johnny and Jimmy.* New York: Arno, 1975.

This classic study of the growth of basic motor skills, which shows its sequential nature and the relative ineffectiveness of special training, makes an important contribution to maturational accounts of development.

PIAGET, JEAN. *The Construction of Reality in the Child.* New York: Basic Books, 1954.

An account of the development of sensorimotor behaviors, with particularly rich descriptions of the stages in the acquisition of object permanence.

STERN, DANIEL N. *The Interpersonal World of the Infant.* New York: Basic Books, 1985.

Stern, an infant psychiatrist, brings together research on infant development with theoretical ideas derived from psychoanalysis as a means of understanding how infants begin to create a sense of themselves and their relationships with those around them.

TANNER, JOHN M. *Fetus into Man: Physical Growth from Conception to Maturity.* Cambridge, Mass.: Harvard University Press, 1978.

A thorough treatment of human growth that includes discussions of the genetic and environmental factors responsible for variability within and among populations.

CHAPTER 6

The End of Infancy

•

The self and its boundaries are at the heart of philosophical
speculation on human nature, and the sense of self and its
counterpart, the sense of other, are universal phenomena that
profoundly influence all our social experiences.

—DANIEL STERN,
THE INTERPERSONAL WORLD OF THE INFANT

Just before Jake's second birthday, his mother, Barbara, and his father and sisters went to Switzerland for a few weeks. Barbara's sister, Retta, said it would be no trouble to look after Jake while they were gone. Before the trip, Barbara arranged to spend a week at her sister's with Jake so that he would have a chance to become familiar with the household.

At first Jake ignored everyone at his aunt's house except his mother and his 4-year-old cousin, Linda. The first afternoon in the sandbox with Linda, he sat and watched with fascination as she conducted a tea party for her teddy bear and bunny rabbit. After a while he placed several small containers in a row on the edge of the sandbox, filled a large container with sand, and then poured its contents into the smaller ones in perfect imitation of his cousin. Then Linda caught his eye. Calling, "Beep-beep! Get out of my way!" she took a toy truck and ran it along the edge of the sandbox, knocking over the teacups and stuffed animals. In an instant Jake was yelling, "Beep-beep!" and knocking over his containers with a toy car. Linda laughed wildly. Jake laughed too and chased her truck around the edge of the sandbox with his car.

From then on Jake followed Linda around the house. If she asked her mother for something to eat or drink, he was right behind her, waiting for his share. Jake did not talk to his aunt directly, and he would not permit her to change his diaper or help him. A lot of the time he refused help from anyone, but if he really couldn't manage, he said, "Mommy do it." Jake knew that Barbara was leaving. "You goin', Mommy?" he asked her several times during that week.

At the airport Jake held Linda's hand and watched bravely as his mother disappeared into the plane. But that afternoon he cried. Linda tried to distract him, but he would not join her in play. Finally she brought him his favorite pillow, which he carried around for the next few days. Then he seemed to adjust to his mother's absence so well that he began to call his aunt "Mommy."

When Jake's family returned 20 days later, there was much excitement at the airport. No one paid any attention when Jake sat on his aunt's lap on the ride back to her house.

That afternoon Jake fell and scraped his knee while he was kicking a ball. He ran crying to his father. His father, who was busy at that moment, suggested that he ask his mother to put a Band-Aid on his scrape. Jake ran into the kitchen where his aunt and his mother were sitting. "Mommy fix it," he said, showing his injured knee to his aunt and ignoring his mother. When Barbara offered to help, Jake refused.

Later, in the swimming pool, Jake was showing his father all the new things he had learned to do. "Show Mommy," his father said, suspecting something. His suspicions were confirmed when Jake turned and tried to get his aunt's attention.

Jake had called his uncle "Daddy" throughout his stay, but as soon as his father was on the scene again, his uncle became "Uncle Len" and his father became "Daddy." No such switch occurred for "Mommy." For the 3 days that Jake's family remained at his aunt and uncle's house, Jake ignored his mother and refused to allow her to do anything for him. When they were preparing to return to their own home, however, Jake looked up at his aunt and said, "Bye, Auntie Retta." Then, turning to his mother, he addressed her directly for the first time since she had returned. "Let's go, Mom," he said, raising his arms up as a signal for her to pick him up.

The changes that have occurred in Jake's behavior since his first birthday reveal the new developments that mark the second year of life. At 12 months, Jake was just beginning to walk; at 24 months, he runs and climbs with ease. He is also far more skilled in manipulating small objects. His vocabulary at 12 months consisted primarily of single words and a few set phrases—"juice," "woof," "Mommy," "All gone"; now Jake's language skills enable him to communicate more effectively and to participate in imaginative play with another child. He is still wary of strange people and places, and he is still so strongly attached to his parents that it was difficult for him to adapt to being left at his aunt's home.

In this chapter we will examine the events that complete the period of infancy and account for the increases in the complexity of children's behavior between the ages of 12 and 30 months. Changes occur in the brain and body; reasoning about the world of objects and people becomes increasingly sophisticated; the child becomes able to imitate sequences of actions, to engage in pretend play, and to communicate; and the form of social relationships between children and their caregivers changes. Each of these facets of development is interesting in its own right. But more significant, each is a single thread in a tapestry, creating a distinctive individual personality with its own distinctive sense of self. About the time that infants celebrate their second birthday or soon thereafter, these biological, cognitive, and social changes converge to create a new bio-social-behavioral shift— the end of infancy—and a new stage of development emerges.

BIOLOGICAL MATURATION

During the second and third years of life, children's bodies continue to grow rapidly, but the rate of their growth is considerably slower than it was in the first year (Eichorn, 1979; Tanner, 1978). Children raised in the United States in recent decades have been found to grow, on the average, from 29 to 38 inches in height and to increase in weight from 20 to 33 pounds during their second and third years, although there is considerable variation from one child to the next. These increases in overall size are accompanied by important changes in the structure of the brain and by increasing neuromuscular control.

Anatomical studies of the brains of children who have died at various ages during infancy have revealed that several changes occur in the brain during the second year (Diamond, 1990a; Fuster, 1990; Rabinowicz, 1979). This evidence has encouraged developmental psychologists to seek links between changes in the brain and the emergence of the new psychological capacities that are characteristic of the last year of infancy.

During the second postnatal year, for example, myelination of the connections between parts of the cerebral cortex and between the brainstem and the cerebral cortex accelerates (see Figure 4.15, p. 150). As a consequence, neurons linking the prefrontal cortex and frontal lobes to the centers in the brainstem where

This child's first steps display the posture and uncertainty characteristic of toddlers.

emotional responses are generated and to cortical centers where visual and auditory input is analyzed function more rapidly and reliably. These changes are important for the development of more complex psychological functions that are governed by the prefrontal portions of the cerebral cortex, including self-awareness, more systematic problem solving, the voluntary control of behavior, and the acquisition of language — characteristics that are widely held to define late infancy (Diamond, 1990a, b; Thatcher, 1991; Luria, 1973).

There is also evidence that toward the end of infancy the length and the degree of branching of the neurons in the cerebral cortex approach adult magnitudes: each neuron now has multiple connections with others. At this time, the various areas of the brain, which have been maturing at very different rates, reach similar levels of development. For the first time, the balance among the various brain systems begins to approximate that of adults (Lecours, 1975; Rabinowicz, 1979). The brain will undergo a few more bursts of growth in later years, but after infancy it will generally develop at a more modest pace. It appears that a great deal of the brain structure that eventually will support adult behavior is present by the end of the second year. This new pattern of growth suggests that later developments are largely refinements of already existing structures.

PERCEPTUAL-MOTOR COORDINATION

Major consequences of these developments in the nervous system are the child's increased control of arm, hand, bladder, bowel, and leg muscles, and increased coordination of perceiving and acting.

Walking

Walking provides an excellent example of a new motor function developing in tandem with increased sensitivity to perceptual input from the environment. In a series of studies, Esther Thelen and her colleagues (Thelen & Ulrich, 1991; Thelen, Ulrich, & Jensen, 1989) traced how a number of separately developing actions converge to enable the child to walk. One crucial element in this process is the ability to coordinate leg movements with shifts of body weight from one foot to the other as each foot steps forward in its turn. They found, for example, that if infants are stood on a treadmill and given the needed support, they can execute the pattern of leg movements needed for walking as early as 7 months of age. But babies this age cannot yet walk on a stationary surface, and without support they are unable to shift their weight and move their arms in a coordinated fashion.

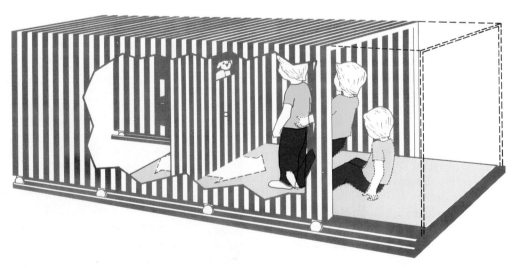

FIGURE 6.1   *The moving-room apparatus. The child inside the room falls backward as she perceives the optical flow produced by the room's movement as indicating a forward sway.*

Walking not only depends on an increase in motor capacities; it also requires babies to be able to evaluate the visual information they receive about the slope of the floor, for example, as they move their bodies through space. They use this information to adjust their posture and to guide their next steps (Bertenthal & Bai, 1989; Butterworth, 1981). Even in adulthood, if visual feedback is somehow distorted, walking becomes difficult, as anyone can testify who has walked through a funhouse with distorting mirrors.

Bennett Bertenthal and Dina Bai (1989) found that it is not until infants begin to locomote on their own that they start making the necessary postural adjustments in response to the visual information they receive from their movement. They tested infants of 5, 7, 9, and 11 months in a special apparatus in which the walls of a small room moved while the infants remained stationary, seated in a specially constructed infant chair that recorded pressure against its back. When the walls of the room moved toward the babies, 9-month-olds pushed firmly back on their infant seats, as if they felt they were falling forward and were seeking to compensate by moving backward. (Eleven-month-olds who were able to stand by themselves actually fell backward [Figure 6.1].) The 7-month-old babies, some of whom were attempting to crawl, showed some traces of postural adjustment, but 5-month-olds showed none at all, indicating that they had not yet acquired the ability to interpret correctly the changes in the visual field in relation to their own motion.

Thelen and Ulrich conclude that no one factor can be seen as *the* cause of walking; rather, walking becomes a smoothly integrated action only when all of its components (upright posture, leg alternation, weight shifting, evaluation of the sensory information one receives as one moves through space) have been developed and the child has had sufficient opportunities to coordinate them within appropriate contexts.

With their first steps babies become "toddlers"; the word describes the characteristic way they spread their legs and toddle from side to side. Most 1-year-olds are unbalanced and fall often, but falling does not stop them. The ground is not far away. Besides, walking is too exciting to give up on, so they simply get up and rush ahead to the next tumble.

Walking brings even more changes to babies' lives than crawling did. As Selma Fraiberg (1959) so eloquently puts it, walking represents

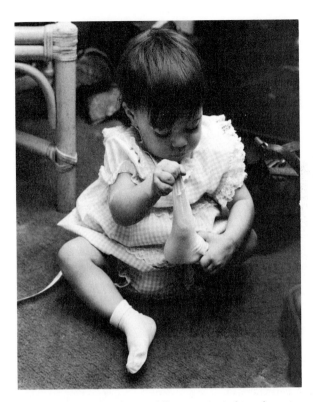

One of the primary ways toddlers express independence is by taking their clothes off and, as their manual dexterity increases during the second year, by putting their clothes on by themselves.

a cutting of the moorings to the mother's body. . . . To the child who takes his first steps and finds himself walking alone, this moment must bring the first sharp sense of uniqueness and separateness of his body and his person, the discovery of the solitary self. (p. 61)

Many months must pass after babies have taken their first steps before they can walk with ease and climb, kick, and jump in a coordinated fashion (see Figure 6.2). Most American children cannot walk up and down stairs until they are at least 17 months old, kick a ball forward until they are 20 months old, or jump until they are almost 24 months old (Frankenburg & Dodds, 1967; Gesell, 1929).

Manual Dexterity

Coordination of fine hand movements increases significantly between 12 and 30 months. Infants 1 year old can only roll a ball or fling it awkwardly; by the time they are 2½, they can throw it. They can also turn the pages of a book without tearing or creasing them, snip with scissors, string beads with a needle and thread, build a tower six blocks high with considerable ease, hold a cup of milk or a spoon of applesauce without spilling it, and dress themselves (as long as there are no buttons or shoelaces) (Gesell, 1929). Each of these accomplishments may seem minor in itself, but each skill requires a good deal of practice to master, and each increases infants' overall competence.

Even an act as elementary as using a spoon, which has been studied in detail by Kevin Connolly and Mary Dalgleish (1989), requires incredibly precise coordination. Figure 6.3 depicts the variety of ways in which infants between 10 and 23 months of age attempt to hold a spoon. After the spoon is dipped into the food, it must be held level so that nothing spills while it is raised to the lips. Then its contents must be emptied into the mouth. At 10 to 12 months babies can do only simple things with a spoon, such as banging it on the table or dipping it repeatedly into the bowl. Slightly older children can coordinate the actions of opening the mouth and bringing the spoon to it, but as often as not the spoon is empty when it arrives. This problem is the next to be solved, as infants learn to get food onto the spoon, carry it to the mouth without spilling it, and put the food in the mouth. Once this elementary sequence of actions is achieved, it is then adjusted until it is smooth and automatic. With all of these coordinated actions to be assembled, no wonder it takes two or more years before a caregiver can leave a child with a spoon and a bowl of cereal and expect much of the cereal to get into the child's mouth!

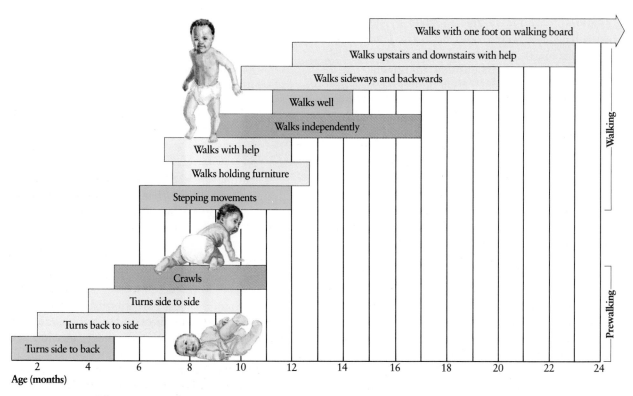

FIGURE 6.2 *The progression from creeping to crawling to walking follows a classic developmental sequence. Each new stage in locomotion allows children to move more rapidly and involves a qualitative change in the pattern of their behavior.*

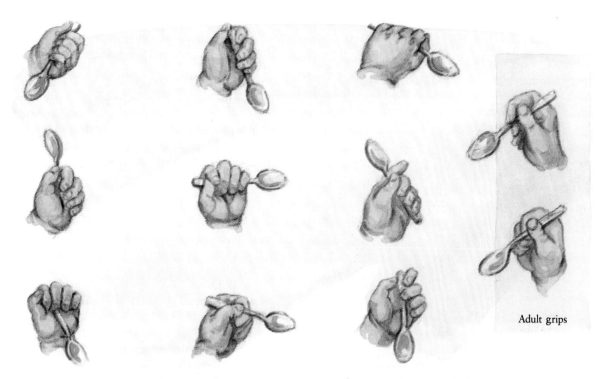

FIGURE 6.3 *Grip patterns. Babies initially grip a spoon in many different ways. As they accumulate experience and greater motor control, they eventually come to adopt an adult grip.*

Control of Elimination

Another important element in the growing ability of children to act on their own is the acquisition of voluntary control over the muscles that govern elimination. In the early months of life, elimination is involuntary. When the baby's bladder or bowels are full, the appropriate sphincter muscles open automatically and empty them. Before a baby can control these muscles voluntarily, the sensory pathways from the bladder and bowels must be mature enough to transmit signals to the cortex of the brain. Children must then learn to associate these signals with the need to eliminate. They must also learn to tighten their sphincters to prevent elimination and to loosen them to permit it. Children are usually not capable of voluntary postponement of elimination until they are at least 15 months of age, but they can be taught to eliminate when they are placed on a potty at 5 to 6 months of age (De Vries & De Vries, 1977). As we will see shortly, several major developmental theorists attribute special importance to the events surrounding toilet training.

In the nineteenth and early twentieth centuries, toilet training was begun as early as possible, not only for convenience in an era before washing machines and disposable diapers but also because it was believed that early training would ensure bowel regularity, which was considered important for good health. The first edition of *Infant Care,* published by the United States Children's Bureau in 1914, advised mothers to begin bowel training by the third month or even earlier (Wolfenstein, 1953).

Because the neural basis for bladder and bowel control is still immature when children are very young, toilet training often takes a while to complete. One study found that toilet training begun before 5 months of age usually requires 10 months to complete; children learn in less than half that time when training is delayed until 20 months of age. Most children are able to remain dry during the day by the time they are 2 years old (Oppel, Harper, & Reder, 1968). But many children do not achieve such control until they are 3 years old, and most children do not learn to stay dry while they are asleep until they are even older.

This little girl has brought along her teddy bear as she practices using a potty.

A NEW MODE OF THOUGHT

As toddlers are perfecting their ability to get around on their own two legs, to eat with utensils, and to control their body functions during the second year of life, they also begin to display a qualitatively new mode of thinking. According to Piaget, this change signals the end of the sensorimotor period. Even psychologists who disagree with much of Piaget's theory agree that developments around the end of the second year enable children to think in a new way (Fischer & Knight, 1990; Kagan, 1982; Vygotsky, 1934/1987).

Completing the Sensorimotor Substages

As we saw in Chapter 4 (pp. 163–164), babies are capable of repeating an action for its own sake during the first months of life, but they seem to be unaware of the relation of the action to the world beyond their own bodies (substages 1 and 2). And, as we saw in Chapter 5 (pp. 187–188), at about 4 months of age, they begin to focus their actions on objects in the external world (substage 3). Then, between 8 and 12 months of age, they develop the ability to combine simple actions to achieve a simple goal (substage 4). Piaget believed that all of the actions of the first four substages are very much tied to the here and now, and that the ability of infants less than 1 year old to think about absent objects is limited.

Substage 5: Tertiary circular reactions (12–18 months)

The fifth substage of the sensorimotor period is characterized by an ability to vary systematically and flexibly the simple instrumental actions of substage 4. Piaget referred to this as the substage of **tertiary circular reactions.** Whereas primary circular reactions are centered on the child's body and secondary circular reactions are focused on objects, tertiary circular reactions are focused on the relationship between the two. Now, in addition to making interesting events last by using already established secondary circular reactions, infants become capable of deliberately varying their action sequences, thereby making their explorations of the world more complex. Piaget referred to tertiary circular reactions as "experiments in order to see" (1952b:272) because children seem to be experimenting in order to find out about the nature of objects. Piaget (1952b) observed this kind of behavior in his son Laurent, then aged 10 months and 11 days. Laurent is lying in his crib:

> He grasps in succession a celluloid swan, a box, etc., stretches out his arm and lets them fall. He distinctly varies the positions of the fall. . . . Sometimes he stretches out his arm vertically, sometimes he holds it obliquely, in front of or behind his eyes, etc. When the object falls in a new position (for example, on his pillow), he lets it fall two or three times more on the same place, as though to study the spatial relations; then he modifies the situation. (p. 269)

This kind of trial-and-error exploration distinguishes tertiary circular reactions from secondary circular reactions, which involve only previously acquired schemas. But infants in substage 5 still do not

TABLE 6.1

Sensorimotor Substages and Stages of Object Permanence

Substage	Age Range (months)	Characteristics of Sensorimotor Substage	Developments in Object Permanence
1	0–1½	Reflex schemas exercised: involuntary rooting, sucking, grasping, looking	Infant does not search for objects that have been removed from sight
2	1½–4	Primary circular reactions: repetition of actions that are pleasurable in themselves	Infant does not search for objects that have been removed from sight
3	4–8	Secondary circular reactions: dawning awareness of relation of own actions to environment; extension of actions that produce interesting changes in the environment	Infant will reach for a partially hidden object but stops if it disappears
4	8–12	Coordination of secondary circular reactions: combining schemas to achieve a desired effect; earliest form of problem solving	Infant will search for a completely hidden object; keeps searching the original location of the object even if it is moved to another location in full view of the infant
5	12–18	Tertiary circular reactions: deliberate variation of problem-solving means; experiments to see what the consequences will be	Infant will search for an object after seeing it moved but not if it is moved in secret
6	18–24	Beginnings of symbolic representation: images and words come to stand for familiar objects; invention of new means of problem solving through symbolic combinations	Infant will search for a hidden object, certain that it exists somewhere

seem able to *imagine* actions and their probable consequences; they are restricted to thinking about manipulating objects in their immediate physical environment.

Substage 6: Representation (18–24 months)

It is not until substage 6, the final stage of the sensorimotor period, that babies indicate that they can carry out actions mentally and think about objects that are not present. **Representation** is the name Piaget gave the new mental capacity characteristic of children who have completed the period of sensorimotor development. It is the basic achievement of this substage and of the sensorimotor stage as a whole. Before substage 6, children can act only on a "present" world. When they can *re*-present the world to themselves—that is, when they can present it to themselves mentally—they can be said to be engaging in true mental actions.

Chief among the new behaviors that Piaget cited as evidence for the appearance of representational thought are the abilities to think about the relations between objects when one is not actually acting on them, to imagine objects that are not present, to imitate events that are not now occurring, to engage in pretend play, and to use language.

The final substages of sensorimotor development, along with the earlier substages described in Chapters 4 and 5, are summarized in the third column of Table 6.1. The fourth column summarizes parallel developments in infants' search behavior in the object-permanence task.

Mastery of Object Permanence

About the time they are 1 year old, babies stop making the A-not-B error; that is, they no longer become confused when an object is first hidden in one location and is then hidden in a second location while they are watching. They now search for the object in its new

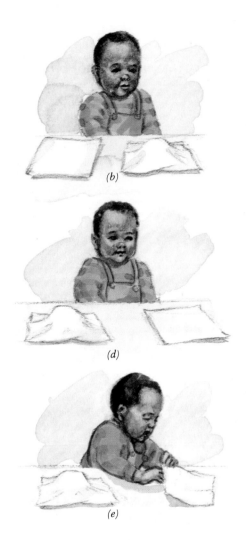

FIGURE 6.4   *Children in stage 5 of the development of object permanence cannot yet maintain a firm idea of the permanence of an object when its location is changed without their knowledge. (a) The infant sees the apple. (b) The apple is hidden beneath the cloth on the right. (c) The position of the hidden apple is changed while the infant's attention is diverted. (d) The infant is confused. (e) The infant searches for the apple under the wrong cloth. (From Bower, 1982.)*

location. This increased ability to keep track of an object's location marks stage 5 of the understanding of object permanence. There is still one substage to go before the baby achieves an understanding of object permanence. If infants in substage 5 do *not* see the object moved, they continue to look where they last saw it, and when they do not find it, they are likely to become confused and stop searching. You can demonstrate this limitation on infants' ability to think about an absent object by pretending to hide an object in your hand while you really hide it behind your back; a stage-5 baby will continue to search for it in your hand, failing to reason that it must be somewhere else nearby. A version of this procedure used in many studies is shown in Figure 6.4.

Piaget (1952b) believed that infants enter stage 6, the final stage of object permanence, between the ages of 18 and 24 months. From that time on, their search for a hidden object is no longer disrupted if the object is moved from one location to another without their knowledge. They appear to be able to reason, "Well, the toy wasn't where I expected, but it must be here somewhere." Then, as they search, they systematically check possible locations until they find the object.

From then on infants are able to anticipate the trajectory of a moving object and the location of its reemergence if it goes behind a barrier. When a ball rolls under a couch, for example, a 2-year-old will go around to the other side of the couch to look for it instead of looking under the couch. Piaget argued that in order to perform successfully in a search for a hidden or moving object, babies must calculate its location mentally. They cannot rely solely on the immediate information given by their senses.

Problem Solving

The ability to reason about the locations of unseen objects is accompanied by increased ability to solve other problems systematically. Piaget's observations of his daughters nicely reveal how these transformations in children's knowledge about objects and events permit them to solve problems systematically instead of by trial and error. Both girls confronted the same problem, Jacqueline at 15 months and Lucienne at 13 months. Each wanted to pull a stick into a playpen from outside through the bars (see Figure 6.5), but the ways they solved the problem differed significantly.

> Jacqueline is seated in her playpen. Outside is a stick 20 centimeters long, the distance of about three spaces between the bars. At first Jacqueline tries to pull the stick into her playpen horizontally, but it will not go through the bars. The second time, she accidentally tilts the stick a little in raising it. She perceives this and reaches through the bars and tilts the stick until it is sufficiently vertical to pass through the bars. But several subsequent attempts make it clear that this is an accidental success; she does not yet understand the principle involved. On the next several tries she grasps the stick by the middle and pulls it horizontally, against the bars. Unable to get it in that way, she then tilts it up. It is not until the seventeenth try that she tilts the stick up before it touches the bars, and not until the twentieth that she does so systematically. (Adapted from Piaget, 1952b: 305)

Jacqueline seemed to have a clear goal in mind because she was certainly persistent. She continued to work at the problem until it was solved. But her efforts were rather hit and miss. When she succeeded, she did not understand why. She grasped the solution only after many trials and many errors. This experience is typical of substage 5 of the sensorimotor period.

Although she was 2 months younger than Jacqueline was when she was presented with this problem, Lucienne's problem solving was more sophisticated, a reminder that age norms associated with Piagetian stages, like other developmental norms, are only approximate.

> Lucienne grasps the stick in the middle and pulls it horizontally. Noticing her failure, she withdraws the stick, tilts it up, and brings it through easily.

When the stick is again placed on the floor, she grasps it by the middle and tilts it up before she pulls it through, or she grasps it by one end and brings it through easily. She does this with longer sticks and on successive days. Unlike her sister Jacqueline, who had to grope her way toward a solution, Lucienne profits from her failure at once. (Adapted from Piaget, 1952b: 336)

In Lucienne's actions we see the essence of substage 6 sensorimotor behavior; she seems to be using information that is not immediately available to her senses to solve the problem. Instead of going through the slow process of trial and error, as her sister did, Lucienne seems to have pictured a series of events in

FIGURE 6.5   *This child in substage 5 of the sensorimotor period carries out deliberate problem solving but still relies on trial and error.*

her mind before she acted. She imagined what would happen if she pulled the stick horizontally. She then inferred that if she turned the stick so that it was vertical and parallel to the bars, it would fit between them. Piaget singled out Lucienne's ability to solve the problem through inference alone as the key evidence for the existence of a new form of thought in substage 6.

Play

During the period from 12 to 30 months, the kinds of behaviors that appear to reflect new mental abilities can be seen in new forms of play (Belsky & Most, 1982; Bretherton & Bates, 1985; Fenson & Ramsay, 1980, 1981; Piaget, 1962; Watson & Fischer, 1977). In a series of observations of babies playing in a room that contained many toys, Jay Belsky and Robert Most (1982) noted a shift that occurred sometime between the ages of 18 and 24 months. From about 12 to 18 months babies use objects in play much as adults would use them in earnest; that is, they put spoons in their mouths and bang with hammers. As they reach the end of infancy, however, babies begin to treat one thing as if it were another. They stir their "coffee" with a twig and comb the doll's hair with a toy rake or, as Jake and his cousin did, act as if the edge of a sandbox were a roadway. This kind of behavior is called **symbolic play**: play in which one object stands for — that is, *represents* — another, as the rake stands for a comb.

Malcolm Watson and Kurt Fischer (1977) traced the increasing complexity of the representational abilities displayed in symbolic play. In observations of 14-, 19-, and 24-month-olds, these researchers were able to distinguish four kinds of pretending that differed with respect to the complexity of the child's actions (see Table 6.2). In the simplest case, which even many of the 14-month-olds demonstrated, the infant was the agent of the action; in the most complicated case (active other agent), a doll manipulated by the infant was the agent of the action. As Figure 6.6 indicates, during their second year children undergo a marked change in ability to pretend. Half or more of the 14-month-olds could pretend to put their heads on a pillow and to put a doll to sleep on a pillow. But the more complicated type of pretending, in which the toddlers had one pretend element operate on another pretend element,

TABLE 6.2	
Four Steps in the Development of Agent Use in Pretending	
Type of Agent Use	Example
Self as agent	The infant puts his head on a pillow to pretend to go to sleep
Passive other agent	The infant puts a doll on a pillow to pretend that it goes to sleep
Passive substitute agent	The infant puts a block on a pillow to pretend that it goes to sleep
Active other agent	The infant has the doll lie down on the pillow and go to sleep, as if the doll were actually carrying out the action itself

Source: Watson & Fischer, 1980.

did not appear until 19 months of age. It was not until they reached the age of 2 years that most of the toddlers could be observed to make such complex symbolic substitutions in their play.

The ability to have one object or concept stand for another, the core accomplishment of symbolic play, continues to develop during the third year of life. Judy De Loache (1987) asked 2½- and 3-year-olds to watch while she hid an attractive toy within a scale model of the room they were in. Then the children were asked to find an analogous toy that had been hidden in the corresponding place in the room itself. The 2½-year-olds could not use the model as a guide and were confused by the task; the 3-year-olds completed it rather easily. De Loache concluded that the younger children could not think of the scale model both as a symbol and as the thing itself.

Why all this scientific attention to something as seemingly frivolous as play? Many developmental psychologists believe that, though play might appear to be quite removed from the serious business of living, it actually serves important functions for the growing organism (Bruner, 1972; Rubin, Fein, & Vandenberg, 1983; Smith, 1988; Vygotsky, 1978). They speculate that early forms of play provide practice in activities that will become important later, just as the seemingly aimless movements of the embryo are a vital part of the process of fetal development. There is widespread agreement that play allows exploration and invention without the possible negative consequences of the "real thing." So, for example, when children begin to play at having tea parties or taking care of a baby, they do so under circumstances in which no one is likely to get burned with hot water or jabbed with a diaper pin. Peter Smith (1982, 1990) describes four major types of play that provide practice for later functions:

1. Locomotor play, such as actions that involve running, jumping, and leaping.

2. Object play, which includes pulling, tugging, and shaking things.

3. Social play, which can be divided into *(a)* play that involves physical contact, such as chasing and wrestling, and *(b)* play that does not, such as building with blocks.

4. Fantasy play, in which the meanings of objects and actions are transformed to fit an imaginary situation.

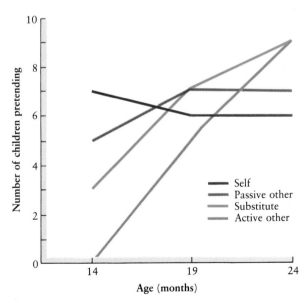

FIGURE 6.6   *The number of infants showing each type of agent use at each age in Watson and Fischer's study. During the second year of life, play with complex substitutions of one object or agent for another becomes common. (From Watson & Fischer, 1980.)*

Smith points out that the first three kinds of play are very common among the young of many species but that clear instances of fantasy play are found exclusively among human beings. This species difference fits with the notion that the use of language and symbolic thought are the distinguishing characteristics of human beings, as well as with Piaget's belief that the advent of symbolic thought is the culminating achievement of cognitive development in the infant.

Lev Vygotsky (1978) emphasized the importance of the social nature of symbolic play for development. He saw the imaginary situations created in play as *zones of proximal development* that operate as mental support systems. (We saw such a support system in Chapter 5, pp. 200–201, where a father supports his infant daughter's attempts to grasp a teething ring before she is able to pick it up on her own.) According to this interpretation, the "as if" nature of social play and the active collusion of other children allow individual children to perform actions that are developmentally more advanced than those they can perform on their own. Thus Jake can "pour tea" in a make-believe game with his cousin in which the demands for precision are far more lenient than they would be if he were to try to pour himself a glass of milk at the breakfast table.

Despite the popularity of the belief that play facilitates general development, studies explicitly designed to demonstrate beneficial effects of play among infants are generally lacking. Peter Smith (1988), who has been active in this field of research, cautions that the belief that play is "good for babies" may be little more than a passing fad. His doubts are supported by cross-cultural work indicating that Central American Mayan infants engage in less play in the first 2 years of life than North American infants but equal them in performance on standardized tests of development (Gaskins, 1990).

Imitation

As we saw in Chapter 4 (Box 4.3, pp. 156–157), some psychologists claim that some form of imitation is present at birth and that by 9 months of age an infant is capable of **deferred imitation;** that is, imitation of an action that occurred many hours earlier. These findings are of special interest because for many years it was believed that deferred imitation does not appear until the second year of life, and that when it does appear, it provides additional evidence that infants are acquiring the ability to represent events to themselves symbolically (Kaye, 1982; Maccoby & Martin, 1983; Piaget, 1962).

The following example, taken from Piaget's work (1962), illustrates both deferred imitation and the importance he attributed to it as evidence that children are beginning to think in a new, more representational way. Jacqueline, now 16 months old, was astonished by the temper tantrum of an 18-month-old boy.

> He screamed as he tried to get out of his playpen and pushed it backwards, stamping his feet. J. stood watching him in amazement, never having witnessed such a scene before. The next day, she herself screamed in her playpen and tried to move it, stamping her foot lightly several times in succession. The imitation of the whole scene was most striking. Had it been immediate, [the imitation] would naturally not have involved representation, but coming as it did after an interval of more than twelve hours, it must have involved some representative or pre-representative element. (p. 63)

A key part of Piaget's argument for the significance of deferred imitation was that it appears during the same period when symbolic play begins. He believed that the two processes are related and that they signal the same underlying change in cognitive capacities, constituting, in effect, two sides of the same developmental coin.

Recall that in Piaget's framework development results from the constant interplay between the *assimilation* of the environment into preexisting patterns of action (called schemas) and the *accommodation* of existing schemas to aspects of the environment. Piaget believed that imitation is closely linked to accommodation because it fits behavior to what is "out there" rather than molding the world to already existing, internal schemas, as play does.

Imitation may well represent a cognitive process in which accommodation plays the leading role. But research by Jean Mandler (1990) and Andrew Meltzoff (1990), designed to demonstrate the origins of recall late in the first year of life (Chapter 5, p. 199), seems to contradict Piaget's claims that deferred imitation emerges only as infants approach their second birthday and is part of a package of simultaneous changes signaling the last substage of sensorimotor develop-

ment. Meltzoff's data indicate rather that deferred imitation makes its first appearance in conjunction with the ability to recall earlier experiences late in the first year of life. However, while the capacity for deferred imitation may exist earlier, it now manifests itself in a far greater range of contexts.

THE GROWTH OF THE ABILITY TO CATEGORIZE

The abilities to engage in symbolic play and to imitate other people's actions provide circumstantial evidence that children become able to engage in the psychological process called mental representation by the middle of the second year. Little is known about the content or form of these mental representations, however, for they cannot be observed directly. The challenge for psychologists is to make good use of the clues provided by children's behaviors to gain insight into the content and structure of these hidden processes.

As we saw in Chapter 5 (p. 197), a rudimentary ability to *recognize* a common characteristic in an array of objects can be observed during the first year of life. During the second year, this rudimentary capacity develops sufficiently for babies to be able to *generate* categories themselves and begin to use them (Gopnik & Meltzoff, 1987; Sugarman, 1983). The growth of this capacity to generate categories was clearly demonstrated by Susan Sugarman (1983). She presented 12- to 30-month-old babies with eight objects that could be classified and subclassified in various ways. Figure 6.7 shows one such set of objects, composed of boats and dolls, which can be grouped by color and form to yield four categories. While sitting on their mother's lap, the toddlers were urged to "fix up" the haphazard array of objects to determine if they would create the same categories as adults. If this suggestion failed to produce results, Sugarman showed them ways to group the objects and then urged them to group the objects themselves. She noted four stages in the progression of categorizing behavior:

1. One-year-olds would pick up one of the toys, look it over, and then touch it to the other toys one at a time. The only indication that they noticed the similarities between individual objects was that they were most likely to touch the toy

they picked up to other toys that had the same shape.

2. The 18-month-olds would create a little work space in front of them and put two or three objects of the same kind in it.

3. The 24-month-old toddlers divided the objects into *two* distinct categories, working on one category at a time. For example, they would select all the boats first and then all the dolls. If Sugarman offered a boat to children of this age who were collecting dolls, they immediately set the boat aside and kept working on the dolls.

4. The 30-month-old children simultaneously coordinated their work on the two major categories and created subcategories as well. They began by making a work space in front of them and then created two categories within it. They filled the categories by picking up whatever toy was nearest at hand and adding it to the appropriate group. If these children were handed a doll right after they had placed a boat in its group, they put it with the other dolls.

Sugarman's results support the findings of David Starkey (1981), reported in Chapter 5, that 1-year-olds show only the most rudimentary awareness of categorical distinctions that are obvious to adults. They are aware of the similarities between objects but express this awareness weakly in their behavior. Eighteen-month-olds create a work space within which they are able to concentrate on the properties of objects that they select in a systematic fashion, but cannot seem to use the work space to represent the existence of more than one category. The behavior of the 24- and 30-month-olds, in contrast, suggests that by the end of infancy, children are able to create multiple categories and subcategories; that is, to represent concepts. This capacity is central to their mastery of language and the more mature forms of thinking that will emerge during early childhood. It also has important implications for understanding other activities, such as pretend play in which they begin to treat certain kinds of objects — teacups, beds, chairs, and so forth — as somehow belonging together.

Sugarman's careful analysis cautions us, however, against overcrediting children with fully developed category representations when play and deferred imitation first appear. When children between the ages of

FIGURE 6.7 *The ability to categorize boats of one color and dolls of another and to subcategorize them according to color and form emerges slowly during late infancy. (From Sugarman, 1983.)*

12 and 24 months begin to operate on objects and to try out possible actions mentally, they may narrow their representations to a single category (such as all the boats) with little understanding that all the other objects also form a category, dolls.

FIRST WORDS

One of the most obvious indicators that children are beginning to think representationally is the appearance of identifiable words that stand for (represent) people, objects, and events. Although many children begin to use a word or two in direct imitation of adults at about 8 or 9 months of age, the first use of words that are not direct imitations usually occurs around the first birthday. Babies of this age respond selectively to their own names and will stop, or at least hesitate, if someone says "No!" (Recall the discussion of the precursors of children's earliest words in Chapter 5, pp. 202–203. We discuss language development further in Chapter 8.)

A large longitudinal study by Robert McCall, Dorothy Eichorn, and Pamela Hogarty (1977) revealed that between the ages of 14 and 18 months, toddlers are able to name a few objects when they are shown them and asked what they are. They can also label pictures of common animals and objects. By 21

This child, who is playing with a peglike doll and a toy train, is engaging in the kind of complicated symbolic play that appears to emerge between the ages of 18 and 24 months.

months of age, toddlers are able to follow relatively complex verbal instructions. When told to "put the block under the doll's chair," for example, they can place the block in the correct location in relation to the chair. They are also able to understand terms that are the opposites of each other. For instance, if you set a large spool and a small spool in front of a child and say "Here is the big one" as you point to the large spool, the child can comply if you then say "Give me the little one."

The use of words that stand for people, objects, and events is sufficient by itself to show that children are beginning to engage in mental representation. But what especially intrigues developmental psychologists is the association between children's use of representational words and the development of the other forms of mental representation—logical search for hidden objects, symbolic play, deferred imitation, and the ability to form categories—discussed in this chapter (Bloom, Lifter, & Broughton, 1985; Bretherton & Bates, 1985; Gopnik & Meltzoff, 1987; McCall, Eichorn, & Hogarty, 1977; Piaget, 1962).

The link between deferred imitation and word acquisition is perhaps the most obvious; a good deal of children's early use of words is closely tied to words they have heard adults speak. "More," for example, was one of the first words used by our daughter Jenny.

Earlier, when she finished drinking a cup of milk or juice, Jenny would bang the empty cup on the tray of her high chair. We would then ask her, "Do you want some more?" Shortly before her first birthday, she began to hold up her cup and say "More" before anyone asked her if that was what she wanted.

Likewise, there is a clear association between language and symbolic play, both of which involve the representation of absent persons, objects, or actions. In symbolic play, arbitrary objects are used to stand for other objects—a banana is treated as a telephone, for example, or a sandbox railing becomes a highway; in language, arbitrary sounds are the substitutes. In the earliest stages, children's fantasy play is restricted to single actions and their utterances are restricted to single words. But at about 18 months of age they begin to combine two actions in play and to use two-word sentences (Bretherton & Bates, 1985; McCune-Nicolich & Bruskin, 1982). So, for example, about the same time that children begin to say "All gone milk," they also begin to pretend that they are pouring water into a cup and helping a baby drink it.

Karen Lifter and Lois Bloom (1989) demonstrated close relationships between the early acquisition of vocabulary and the sophistication with which infants search for hidden objects and play with objects. They found that children's first words appeared at the same time that they first began to search for hidden objects in a systematic way, and that when they demonstrated logical search patterns, they underwent a spurt in the rate of acquiring new words. The same sort of linkages appeared when Lifter and Bloom looked at the sophistication of play; children who had not begun to talk moved toys around but did not combine them to construct new objects. Such combinatory play appeared with children's first words, and more complex constructions appeared in conjunction with a spurt in vocabulary.

Alison Gopnik and Andrew Meltzoff (1987) also found that the ability to classify objects in two groups, sophisticated behaviors in searching for objects, insightful problem solving, and a vocabulary spurt occur at approximately the same age. They report, however, that there is no precise ordering of achievements in the various cognitive tasks and vocabulary developments. Consequently, it is not possible to say that one of these achievements is *the* cause of this ensemble of changes; rather, they all make important contributions to the bio-social-behavioral shift that marks the end of infancy.

THE DEVELOPMENT OF CHILD-CAREGIVER RELATIONS

During the second year of life, children find novelty and excitement everywhere. A walk to the corner drugstore with a 1½-year-old can take forever. Each step presents new and interesting sights to explore: a bottle cap lying by the edge of the sidewalk requires close examination; a pigeon waddling across a neighbor's lawn invites a detour; even the cracks in the sidewalk may prompt sitting down to take a closer look.

Things that attract babies, however, may also cause them to be wary. To toddlers, whizzing cars, strange people, and novel objects are often frightening as well as fascinating. Both interest and fear must be kept in bounds as infants continue to explore and learn about the world. They cannot spend their entire lives tied to their mothers' apron strings, but they cannot survive for long if they wander off on their own too soon. Research with both monkey and human mothers and babies is starting to show us how the balance between exploration and safety is created and maintained in ways that allow continued development. A key element in this balance is the emotional bond that develops between children and their caregivers sometime between the ages of 7 and 9 months, and which we briefly described in Chapter 5 (p. 202). Explaining how this attachment comes about has proved to be a major challenge to developmental psychologists.

Explanations of Attachment

The fact that children everywhere begin at about the same age to become upset when they are separated from their primary caregivers, even though their social experiences may differ in many respects, suggests that attachment is a universal feature of development (Grossmann & Grossmann, 1990). This possibility has led to a lively debate about the evolutionary reasons for attachment, the causes of changes in attachment as children grow older, and the influence of the quality of attachment on children's later development. Three major explanations of the basis of attachment have dominated this debate: Sigmund Freud's suggestion that infants become attached to the people who satisfy their need for food; Erik Erikson's idea that infants

become attached to those they can trust to help them; and John Bowlby's somewhat similar hypothesis that infants become attached to those who provide them with a firm foundation for exploring the world.

Sigmund Freud's drive-reduction explanation

The process of attachment plays an important role in Sigmund Freud's theory of development. Freud held that the early interactions between children and their social environment, particularly the people who care for them, set the pattern for later personality and social development. He believed that human beings, like other organisms, are motivated in large part by **biological drives** — states of arousal, such as hunger or thirst, that urge the organism to obtain the basic prerequisites for its survival. When a drive is aroused, the organism seeks to satisfy the need that gives rise to it. Pleasure is felt as the drive is reduced, the need is satisfied, and the organism returns to a more comfortable biological equilibrium. In this sense, then, pleasure seeking is a basic principle of existence.

Freud (1933/1964) identified the mouth as the primary locus of pleasure during the first year of life, which he dubbed the oral stage of development. During this stage, children become attached to the objects or persons that satisfy their hunger (Freud, 1940/1964). The first person infants become attached to is usually the mother, who is most likely to nourish them; "love has its origin in attachment to the satisfied need for nourishment" (p. 188). Freud believed that attachment to the mother is central to the formation of children's personalities as they progress through later stages of development. In adulthood, the relationship with the mother becomes "the prototype for all . . . love relations for both sexes" (p. 188).

According to Freud (1933/1964), the locus of children's pleasure seeking shifts from the mouth to the anus during the second year after birth. In contrast to oral pleasures, which he characterized as receptive and dependent, anal satisfaction is basically expulsive and reflects a drive for self-control and independence, Freud believed.

Freud's theory of early human attachment has not fared well. One major problem is that research has not substantiated his notion that attachment is caused by the reduction of the hunger drive, as we will soon see. Furthermore, his theory seems to imply that children should begin to act more independently once they enter the anal stage. Thus it fails to explain why children are increasingly likely to become distressed when they are separated from their mothers until well into the second year of life.

Erik Erikson's psychosocial explanation

A more promising explanation of attachment than Freud's, though still within the Freudian tradition, was proposed by Erik Erikson, one of Freud's most influential students. Erikson (1963), whose theory of development will figure in many discussions throughout the remainder of this book, believes that there are eight stages in the human life cycle, each characterized by a distinctive conflict that the individual must resolve. Through the resolution of the conflict at each stage of development, people acquire new skills, such as the ability to act independently of their parents or to do productive work, which open up new opportunities for them. These new opportunities, in turn, increase the demands made on them by society and create new conflicts. Individuals who do not resolve the conflict at each stage satisfactorily will continue to struggle with that conflict later in life.

The conflicts characteristic of the first two stages that Erikson proposes provide an explanation for the increase in children's anxiety when they are separated from their mothers late in the first year of life and its decline during the second year. According to Erikson's scheme, during the first stage of development, which lasts from birth to roughly 1 year of age, babies must develop a favorable balance between trust and mistrust: Will my mother come when I call? Can I trust her to take care of me? In Erikson's view, children become attached to the people who reliably minister to their needs and who foster a sense of trust. Once babies gain faith in their caregivers, usually during the second year, they enter the second stage and their need for autonomy increases; they cease to be distressed during brief separations because they understand that their caregiver will come back.

John Bowlby's evolutionary explanation

In the aftermath of the terrible destruction and loss of life of World War II, many public agencies became deeply concerned about the consequences of an early childhood deprived of normal maternal care. In 1950 the World Health Organization asked John Bowlby, a British psychiatrist, to undertake a study of the mental health problems of children who had been separated from their families and were cared for in institutions (Bowlby, 1969, 1973, 1980).

Bowlby reviewed observations of children in hospitals, nurseries, and orphanages who had either lost their parents or been separated from them for long periods of time. He also looked at reports of clinical interviews with psychologically troubled or delinquent adolescents and adults. He found a similar sequence of behaviors described in these various sources. When children are first separated from their mothers, they become frantic with fear. They cry, throw tantrums, and try to escape their surroundings. Then they go through a stage of despair and depression. If the separation continues and no new stable relationship is formed, these children seem to become indifferent to other people. Bowlby called this state of indifference *disattachment*.

In his attempt to explain the distress of young children when they are separated from their parents, Bowlby adopted a broad evolutionary perspective. His theory incorporated what was then known about mother-infant interactions among large, ground-living apes who defend themselves against predators by banding together with others of their species. Infancy among such primates lasts a long time. Because the growing infants are relatively helpless and vulnerable, they must remain close to their mothers if they are to survive. Counteracting this need for safety through proximity is the infants' urge to explore and play, activities that take them away from their mothers.

Bowlby hypothesized that some mechanism must exist to provide a balance between infants' need for safety and their need for varied learning experiences. He termed this mechanism *attachment* and hypothesized that it works somewhat like a furnace's thermostat. In a thermostat, a switch is thrown to turn on the furnace whenever the temperature falls below a preset minimum. When the heat rises sufficiently, the switch is thrown again to turn the furnace off. As a result, temperature is maintained within comfortable limits.

Bowlby (1969) believes that attachment is a highly evolved system of regulation that normally develops during the first year of life to produce a "dynamic equilibrium between the mother-child pair" (p. 236). Whenever the distance between mother and child becomes too great, one or the other is likely to become upset and act to reduce the distance. Just as babies become upset if their mothers leave them, mothers become upset if their babies wander out of sight. Attachment provides the child with a feeling of security.

The mother becomes a **secure base** from which babies can make exploratory excursions and to which they come back every so often to renew contact before returning to their explorations. At first the mother bears the greater responsibility for maintaining the equilibrium of the attachment system because the infant can do so little. As the child becomes more mobile and spends increasing time away from the mother, the pair enters a transitional state in which they share responsibility for maintaining the equilibrium of the system. Among humans, this transitional phase lasts several years.

Evidence from animal models

Ethical considerations make it difficult, if not impossible, to conduct experiments to determine the source of human attachment. Therefore, scientists have taken to studying our near evolutionary kin, monkeys, whose behavior furnishes researchers with an **animal model** that appears to be somewhat analogous to human behavior.

Throughout the first half of the twentieth century, most American scholars who studied learning believed that animals learn in order to satisfy the needs basic to their and their species' survival—food, drink, freedom from pain, procreation. This drive-reduction theory is similar to Freud's explanation of why babies become attached to their mothers (Miller & Dollard, 1941).

To test the drive-reduction theory of attachment, Harry Harlow and his co-workers (Harlow & Harlow, 1969) carried out an extensive series of studies with rhesus monkeys. In one of these studies, the researchers separated eight baby monkeys from their mothers 12 hours or less after birth and placed them in individual cages with two inanimate surrogate mothers—one made of wire, the other of terry cloth (see Figure 6.8). Four of the infant monkeys received milk from the wire mothers, four from the terry-cloth mothers. The two types of surrogate mothers were equally effective as sources of nutrition, and all eight babies drank the same amount and gained weight at the same rate. Only the feel of the surrogate mothers differed.

Over the 165-day period that they lived with surrogate mothers, the baby monkeys showed a distinct preference for the cloth mothers. Even if they obtained all of their food from a wire mother, the babies would go to it only to feed and would then go back to

FIGURE 6.8 *This baby monkey spent most of its time clinging to the terry-cloth surrogate mother even when its nursing bottle was attached to the wire surrogate mother that can be seen in the background. Harlow concluded that bodily contact and the comfort it gives are important in the formation of the infant's attachment to its mother.*

cling to the terry-cloth mother. From the perspective of drive-reduction theory, it made no sense at all for the four infant monkeys who received their food from a wire mother to prefer to spend their time with a terry-cloth mother that might feel good but satisfied no apparent biological drive, such as hunger or thirst. Harlow concluded, "These results attest the importance—possibly the overwhelming importance—of bodily contact and the immediate comfort it supplies in forming the infant's attachment for its mother" (Harlow, 1959:70).

In later investigations Harlow and his colleagues (Harlow & Harlow, 1969) sought to determine whether attachment to their surrogate mothers had any effect on the infants' explorations, a crucial test of Bowlby's evolutionary theory. Knowing that normal human and monkey babies run to their mothers for comfort when they are confronted with a strange situation, the researchers created such a situation for the monkeys who had received milk from the wire surrogate mothers. They placed a mechanical teddy bear that marched forward while beating a drum in their cages. The terrified babies fled to the terry-cloth mothers, not to the wire ones (see Figure 6.9). Once the babies had overcome their fear by rubbing their bodies against the cloth mother, however, they turned to look at the bear with curiosity. Some even left the protection of the terry-cloth mother to approach the object that had so terrified them only moments before.

The infant monkeys demonstrated their attachment to the terry-cloth mothers after separations of up to a year. The researchers would place the monkey in an apparatus in which pressure on a lever allowed them to look at the terry-cloth mother, the wire mother, or an empty box. The monkeys who had been raised with a wire mother that provided milk and a terry-cloth mother that did not spent more time pressing the lever to get a glimpse of the terry-cloth mother than the lever to see the wire mother. They were no more interested in the wire mother than in the empty box. Even

monkeys who had been raised with only a wire mother showed no signs of attachment when they were given a chance to view it (Harlow & Zimmerman, 1959).

The studies of Harlow and his colleagues undermine the hypothesis that attachment is caused by drive reduction, which implies that infants should become attached to the people who feed them. The idea that receives the most support is that soothing tactile sensations provide the baby with a sense of security that is more important to the formation of attachment than food.

Although soothing tactile sensations appear to be necessary for healthy development, they are not sufficient. As these monkeys grew older, the researchers found that they were either indifferent or abusive to other monkeys. None of them could copulate normally. The researchers concluded that

> the nourishment and contact comfort provided by the nursing cloth covered mother in infancy does not produce a normal adolescent or adult. The surrogate cannot cradle the baby or communicate monkey sounds and gestures. It cannot

FIGURE 6.9   (Above) *This baby monkey clings to its terry-cloth surrogate mother and hides its eyes when it is frightened by the approach of a mechanical teddy bear. (Right) After gaining reassurance, the baby monkey looks at the strange intruder. That the terry-cloth mother, which does not provide nourishment, acts as a secure base rather than the wire mother, which does provide nourishment, contradicts drive-reduction theories of attachment.*

punish for misbehavior or attempt to break the infant's bodily attachment before it becomes a fixation. (Harlow & Harlow, 1962: 142)

The later social behavior of these monkeys supports Bowlby's belief that attachment is a highly evolved system of regulation between the mother and the infant. Such regulation is a two-sided process that requires social *interaction* for healthy emotional development. The infant monkeys clearly turned to the terry-cloth mothers for security, but in the absence of a live mother, all of the adjusting was left to the baby, and a proper regulatory system did not form.

Patterns of Attachment

The maladaptive social behavior of monkeys raised with inanimate surrogate mothers poses a pointed question: What kinds of interactions between mother and child provide the most effective basis for the development of healthy human social relations?

Because no two mother-infant pairs are alike and because the environmental conditions into which human babies are born vary enormously, we should not expect to find "one right pattern" of attachment that meets the basic requirements for social development in all cultures (Hinde, 1982). Many investigators believe, however, that it is possible to identify general patterns of mother-child interaction that are most conducive to development.

Research on the patterns of mother-child interaction has been greatly influenced by the work of Mary Ainsworth. On the basis of observations of mother-infant pairs in Africa and the United States, Ainsworth (1967, 1982) reports that there are consistent, qualitatively distinct patterns in the ways mothers and infants relate to each other during the second and third years of infancy. Most of the mother-infant pairs she observed seemed to have worked out a comfortable, secure relationship by the third year, but some of the relationships were characterized by persistent tension and difficulties in regulating joint activities.

Ainsworth designed a procedure called the **strange situation** as a means of testing the security of the mother-child relationship. The basic purpose of the procedure is to observe how different babies respond to a stranger when they are with their mothers, when they are left alone, and when they are reunited with their mothers. Different patterns of reactions, she

Many small children become strongly attached to a teddy bear, a blanket, or some other object. British psychiatrist D. W. Winnicott (1971) has called such objects "transitional objects." They are the first objects that children perceive to be their very own. They support children in their attempts to understand and deal with the reality that exists beyond their own bodies. The strong attachment this little girl feels for her teddy bear is written all over the bear and the girl's smiling embrace.

reasoned, would reflect different kinds of relationships. The following case study, summarized from research reported by Mary Ainsworth and Barbara Wittig (1969:116–118), illustrates the strange-situation procedure and how a typical 12-month-old middle-class North American child behaves in it.

An observer shows a mother and her baby into an experimental room that has toys scattered on the floor. "Brian had one arm hooked over his mother's shoulder as they came in the room. . . . He looked around soberly, but with interest at the toys and at the observer."

(a)

(b)

The observer leaves the room. "After being put down Brian immediately crept toward the toys and began to explore them [Figure 6.10a]. He was very active. . . . Although his attention fixed on the playthings, he glanced at his mother six times."

After three minutes the stranger enters, greets the mother, and sits down quietly in a chair. Brian "turned to look at the stranger . . . with a pleasant expression on his face. He played with the tube again, vocalized, smiled and turned to glance at his mother. . . . When the stranger and his mother began to converse, he continued to explore actively. . . . When the stranger began her approach by leaning forward to offer him a toy, he smiled, crept forward and reached for it" [Figure 6.10b].

The mother leaves the room, leaving her purse on the chair, while the stranger distracts Brian's attention. "He did not notice his mother leave. . . . He continued to watch the stranger and the toys. . . . Suddenly, he crept to his mother's chair, pulled himself to a standing position, and looked at the stranger. She tried to distract him with a pull toy . . . but he glanced again at his mother's empty chair. He was less active than he had been when alone with his mother and after two minutes his activity ceased. He sat chewing the string of the pull toy and glancing from the stranger to his mother's chair. He made an unhappy noise, then a cry face, then he cried. The stranger tried to distract him by offering him a block; he took it, but threw it away.

When his mother opened the door . . . Brian looked at her immediately and vocalized loudly . . . then crept to her quickly, and pulled himself up, with her help, to hold on to her knee. Then she picked him up, and he immediately put his arms around her neck, his face against her shoulder, and hugged her hard [Figure 6.10c]. . . . He resisted being put down; he tried to cling to her and protested loudly. Once on the floor, he threw himself down, hid his face in the rug, and cried angrily [Figure 6.10d]. His mother knelt beside him and tried to interest him in the toys again. He stopped crying and watched. After a moment she disengaged herself and got up to sit on her chair. He immediately threw himself down and cried again."

Brian's mother gets up and leaves the room again. "As she said 'Bye-bye' and waved, Brian looked up with a little smile, but he shifted into a cry before she had quite closed the door. He sat crying, rocking himself back and forth [Figure 6.10e]."

The stranger, who has earlier left the room, reenters. "Brian lulled slightly when he saw the stranger enter, but he continued to cry. She first tried to distract him, then offered her arms to him. Brian responded by raising his arms; she picked him up and he stopped crying immediately. . . . Occasionally he gave a little sob, but for the most part he did not cry. But when she put him down, he screamed. She picked him up again, and he lulled.

"At the moment that his mother returned Brian was crying listlessly. He did not notice his mother. The stranger half-turned and pointed her out. Brian looked toward her, still crying, and then turned away. But he soon 'did a double take.' He looked back and vocalized a little protest. His mother offered her arms to him. He reached toward her, smiling, and leaned way out of the stranger's arms and his mother took him."

(c)

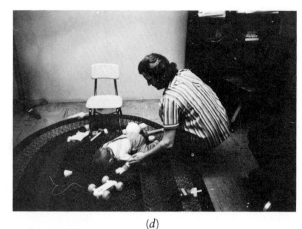

(d)

(e)

To permit systematic companions between children, Ainsworth and her colleagues (Ainsworth, Bell, & Stayton, 1971; Ainsworth et al., 1978) worked out a method of categorizing infants' responses in the "strange situation." It is based on the child's behaviors when the child and mother are alone in the playroom together, when the mother leaves the room, when a strange woman offers comfort, and when the mother returns. The researchers found that the way the child reacts to the return of the mother is the key element, and that the responses fall into three categories:

Anxious/avoidant: During the time the mother and child are left alone together in the playroom, anxious/avoidant infants are more or less indifferent to where their mothers are sitting. They may or may not cry when their mothers leave the room. If they do become distressed, strangers are likely to be as effective at comforting them as their mothers. When the mother returns, these children may turn or look away from her instead of going to her to seek closeness and comfort. About 23 percent of U.S. middle-class children show this pattern of attachment.

Securely attached: As long as the mother is present, the securely attached child plays comfortably with the toys in the playroom and reacts positively to the stranger. These children become visibly and vocally upset when their mothers leave, and they are unlikely to be consoled by a stranger. When the mother reappears and they can climb into her

FIGURE 6.10   *Brian in the "strange situation."*
(a) *Brian explores the toys.* (b) *Brian responds to the stranger.* (c) *Brian hugs his mother when she returns to the room after a brief absence.* (d) *Brian throws himself on the floor when his mother puts him down.* (e) *Brian cries and rocks back and forth when he is left alone again.*

arms, however, they quickly calm down and soon resume playing. This pattern of attachment is shown by about 65 percent of U.S. middle-class children.

Anxious/resistant: Anxious/resistant children have trouble from the start in the strange situation. They stay close to their mothers and appear anxious even when their mothers are near. They become very upset when the mother leaves, but they are not comforted by her return. Instead, they *simultaneously* seek renewed contact with their mother and resist her efforts to comfort them. They may cry angrily to be picked up with their arms outstretched, but they will struggle to climb down once they are in their mother's arms. These children do not readily resume playing after their mother returns. Instead, they keep a wary eye on her. About 12 percent of U.S. middle-class children show this pattern of attachment.

Anxious/avoidant and anxious/resistant children are sometimes labeled *insecurely attached* or simply *anxious.*

Accumulated experience has shown that the basic behaviors described by Ainsworth and her colleagues occur routinely in the strange situation and can be scored with reasonable reliability. Using this method of classifying modes of attachment, psychologists have spent more than two decades seeking to determine the causes of these patterns of behavior (Ainsworth, 1982; Bretherton, 1985; Isabella & Belsky, 1991). Most of this research has focused on the mother-infant relationship, although other attachments that are important in children's lives have also been studied (see Box 6.1).

As often happens when a new scientific technique is introduced, research based on the strange situation has raised many new questions about social and emotional development. Two major questions have dominated the study of patterns of attachment. First, what are the causes of variations in the patterns of attachment? Second, do these variations have important consequences for later development? We will concentrate on the first question here.

The causes of variations in patterns of attachment

Research on what leads to variations in patterns of attachment has focused on several likely factors: the behavior of the mother toward the child, the capacities and temperamental disposition of the child, and the child-rearing patterns of the cultural group to which the mother and child belong.

MATERNAL BEHAVIORS. In an early study of the antecedents of attachment, Mary Ainsworth and Silvia Bell (1969) hypothesized that differences in the responsiveness of mothers to their infants would result in different patterns of attachment. They found

BOX 6.1
Attachment to Fathers and Others

Discussions of infant development tend to focus almost entirely on the role of mothers; other people with whom babies interact have been largely ignored. There are legitimate reasons for this one-sided treatment of babies' social environment.

Perhaps the most legitimate reason for focusing on the mother's role is that the mother spends far more time with her infant than any other adult, not only in advanced industrial societies but in most of the world's societies (Lamb, 1987). Michael Lamb and his colleagues (1987), working in the United States, reported that in two-parent families in which the mothers do not work outside the home, fathers spend only 25 to 30 percent as much time in one-to-one interaction with their infants as mothers do. Even when these fathers are with their children, they assume little or no responsibility for their day-to-day care or rearing.

This state of affairs results not from indifference or lack of ability but from the roles mothers and fathers assume in family life in the United States and in most other cultures. When fathers have been observed feeding their infants, for example, they respond as sensitively as do mothers to their babies' feeding rhythms and engage their babies in social episodes just as often (Parke & Tinsley, 1981). But fathers are far more likely to play with their infants than to care for them. The vast majority of exchanges between fathers and their babies in the U.S. are brief play episodes that come at a specific period of the day (Clarke-Stewart, 1978). Set aside as they are, these periods are likely to be memorable.

Given the differences between fathers and mothers in both the quantity and the quality of their interactions with their infants, psychologists have naturally been interested to learn if and how infants form attachments to their fathers. One early study, by Milton Kotelchuck (1976), suggested that babies become attached to their fathers later than to their mothers. Kotelchuck used a variation of the strange situation to compare the attachment of babies between the ages of 6 months and 2 years to their mothers with their attachment to their fathers. At all the ages he observed, the babies' play was likely to be dis-

Children also form a strong attachment to their fathers, which provides them with an additional secure base for their continued development.

rupted when the mother left the room. Most of the babies did not respond to their fathers' leaving in the same way until they were about 15 months old. The bulk of current evidence, however, indicates that attachment to the two parents occurs at more or less the same time (Lamb, 1979).

Another question that has intrigued researchers is whether or not the attachments infants form to different caregivers are qualitatively the same. In a series of studies, Michael Lamb (1976, 1977a, 1979) observed infants in their homes to determine if they showed a preference for one or the other parent by staying near, approaching, touching, and asking to be held by one parent more than the other. Lamb found that infants displayed no general preference for either parent, but when they became distressed, they were more likely to turn to their mother for comfort.

Several studies have focused on how attachment to one parent affects attachment to the other. If attachment relations depend on infants' history of interactions with particular individuals, as some attachment theorists believe, attachment to one parent ought to be independent of attachment to the other. Yet in a recent analysis of 11 studies comparing at-

tachment to mothers and fathers in the strange situation, Nathan Fox, Nancy Kimmerly, and William Schafer (1991) found that infants who were attached to one parent were also attached to the other.

Fox and his colleagues speculate that one reason for such a linkage is that infants form a "working model" of how to interact with familiar adults in general. Another explanation might be that children's temperaments lead them to interact similarly with their mothers and fathers, so that the emotional bonds are similar in quality.

A recent study by Frits Goossens and Marinus van Ijzendoorn (1990) with a large group of 15-month-old Dutch infants undermines such explanations. These investigators compared the behaviors displayed toward mothers, fathers, and day-care workers in the strange situation. Like Fox and his colleagues, Goossens and van Ijzendoorn found that the attachment behaviors of infants toward mothers and fathers were linked. They found no such linkage, however, between babies' attachment behaviors directed toward their parents and those directed toward day-care workers with whom they spent many hours a day, as one would expect if the children had formed a generalized model of how to interact with adults or if their temperaments caused them to act similarly in all unusual circumstances.

Obviously many questions about the attachments that infants form to the significant adults in their lives remain to be answered. But the fact that such attachments exist and play an important role in children's social development is now well established.

Babies also form attachments with peers and siblings (Stewart & Marvin, 1984; Tronick, Winn, & Morelli, 1985). In some societies, such as that of the !Kung bushmen of the Kalahari Desert, babies are cared for in groups of children of various ages beginning around the age of 1 year, so that their mothers can resume their work (Konner, 1977). Under such circumstances, babies form strong attachments to many older children in the group in addition to adults. In industrialized societies, babies are less upset and more sociable in strange surroundings when an older sibling is present (Dunn, 1984).

The joy of this mother and child at being reunited captures the special emotional feeling of attachment.

These mixed results have caused psychologists to look more carefully at mother-infant interactions in their search for the determinants of positive emotional bonds between infants and caregivers. One finding has been that the mother's responsiveness can have either a positive or a negative effect, depending on the form it takes and how that affects the degree of coordination of mother and infant (Isabella & Belsky, 1991); if responsive mothers are also intrusive and overstimulating, their infants are likely to display evidence of insecure attachment. The key quality that seems to promote secure attachment is a high degree of synchrony between infant and mother.

CHARACTERISTICS OF THE CHILD. Some psychologists have criticized Ainsworth and Bell's initial research for its focus on the caregiver to the exclusion of the role played by the child in the formation of attachment. Joseph Campos and his colleagues (1983) point out that synchrony is a joint accomplishment: just as infants need a responsive mother to develop normally, mothers need responsive infants in order to achieve their full potential as caregivers.

In support of this idea, Michael Lewis and Candice Feiring (1989) observed 174 infant-mother pairs at home when the infants were 3 months old and then tested their reactions in a version of the strange situation 9 months later. They found that infants who spent more time playing with objects than interacting sociably with their mothers were more likely to display symptoms of insecure attachment around their first birthdays.

One infant characteristic that some psychologists think a likely influence on attachment is temperament. Kazuo Miyake, Shing-jen Chen, and Joseph Campos (1985) found that newborns who became extremely distressed when their feeding was interrupted were more likely to be evaluated as insecurely attached at 1 year than newborns who did not become upset. But such findings are rare. Most researchers have found no relationship between temperament and attachment (Bates, Maslin, & Frankel, 1985; Bohlin et al., 1989; Vaughn et al., 1989).

An interesting resolution to the controversy is offered by Jay Belsky and Michael Rovine (1987). After carefully analyzing existing research, these researchers suggest that infant temperament affects the way babies *express* security or insecurity, but that it does not directly affect the actual pattern of attachment. In

that the children of mothers who responded quickly to their cries when they were 3 months old and who were sensitive to their needs during feeding were likely to be evaluated as securely attached at 12 months.

Attempts to replicate Ainsworth and Bell's study have met with mixed success. It has been reliably found, for example, that abusive or neglectful mothers are especially likely to have babies who are rated as anxious/avoidant or anxious/resistant (Schneider-Rosen et al., 1985). When data have been gathered in families where no severe difficulties are present, however, the results have not been so clear-cut. Some studies have found that high ratings of maternal responsiveness predict secure attachment (Grossman et al., 1985), whereas others have detected only weak relationships between ratings of maternal responsiveness and patterns of attachment or no relationship at all (Belsky & Isabella, 1988, review the findings).

addition, Belsky, Margaret Fish, and Russell Isabella (1991) found that the temperaments of many 9-month-old infants are different from the temperaments they displayed at 3 months, undermining both the notion of temperament as a stable personality characteristic and the idea that temperament plays a major role in the formation of attachment.

CULTURAL INFLUENCES.   The pattern of attachment between children and their caregivers may also be influenced by the child-rearing practices of their culture. Children who grow up on Israeli kibbutzim (collective farms), for example, are raised communally from an early age. Although they see their parents daily, the adults who look after them are usually not family members. When such communally raised children were placed in the strange situation with either a parent or a caregiver at the ages of 11 to 14 months, many of them became very upset; half were classified as anxious/resistant, and only 37 percent appeared to be securely attached (Sagi et al., 1985). As we noted earlier, only about 12 percent of the middle-class U.S. children, most of whom were cared for by their parents, were judged to be anxious/resistant (Ainsworth et al., 1978).

A low percentage of securely attached babies has also been observed among German children, though apparently for quite different reasons. One study (Grossmann et al., 1985) found that 49 percent of the 1-year-olds tested were anxious/avoidant and only 33 percent were securely attached. Having made extensive observations of German home life, the researchers were able to reject the possibility that a large proportion of German parents are insensitive or indifferent to their children. Rather, German parents adhere to a cultural value that calls for the maintenance of a relatively large interpersonal distance and a cultural belief that babies should be weaned from bodily contact as soon as they become mobile. The researchers suggest that among German mothers, "the ideal is an independent, nonclinging infant who does not make demands on the parents but rather unquestioningly obeys their commands" (p. 253).

A large proportion of anxious/resistant infants has been found among traditional Japanese families, but no anxious/avoidant infants at all (Miyake, Chen, & Campos, 1985). Kazuo Miyake and his colleagues explain this pattern by pointing out that traditional Japanese mothers rarely leave their children in the care

of anyone else and behave toward them in ways that foster a strong sense of dependence. Consequently, the experience of being left alone with a stranger is unusual and upsetting to these children. This interpretation is supported by a study of nontraditional Japanese families in which the mothers were pursuing careers, which required them to leave their children in the care of others (Durrett, Otaki, & Richards, 1984). Among the children of these mothers, the distribution of the basic patterns of attachment was similar to that seen in the United States.

There is still no agreement about the significance of the differences in the distributions of attachment patterns that have been found in different cultures. Some researchers believe that they indicate basic and important differences in psychological makeup (Grossmann & Grossmann, 1990). Others believe that cultural differences in the meaning attached to the strange situation make it difficult to infer the true nature of the emotional bonds between the mothers and their children, leading to false conclusions when patterns discovered in one culture are used to reason

In resisting her mother's attempt to leave her in someone else's arms, this little girl is showing the distress that babies experience at being separated from their mothers.

about another (Takahashi, 1990). Consequently, while current research clearly demonstrates major cultural differences in the ways in which infants and their caregivers interact in the strange situation, the psychological significance of these differences remains uncertain.

Stability of patterns of attachment

Studies of middle-class children in the United States and Germany have found that the patterns of attachment—anxious/avoidant, securely attached, and anxious/resistant—are likely to remain stable for at least several months (Connell, 1976; Grossmann et al., 1987; Main & Weston, 1981; Waters, 1978). Evidence is accumulating, however, that the stability of a pattern of attachment depends on the stability of the child's life circumstances. If the family is going through a difficult period because of unemployment, poverty, illness, or conflict between the adults, there is a much greater chance that the pattern of attachment displayed by children between the ages of 12 and 18 months will change. Researchers who studied families living below the poverty level found that the pattern of attachment changed for about one-third of the infants (Vaughn et al., 1979). When the level of family stress was high, securely attached infants became less so.

No single factor seems to account for the various patterns of attachment. The complicated interrelationships between the caregivers' behaviors, the innate characteristics of the children, the cultural context, and the children's life circumstances create many developmental paths that lead to many outcomes. This point is made quite forcefully by Robert Hinde (1982), an eminent British ethologist, in his summary of research on human attachment.

> We must accept that individuals differ and society is complex, and that mothers and babies will be programmed not simply to form one sort of relationship but a range of possible relationships according to circumstances. So we must be concerned not with normal mothers and deviant mothers but with a range of styles and a capacity to select appropriately between them.
>
> At one level of approximation, there are general properties of mothering necessary whatever the circumstances. At a more precise level, the optimal mothering behavior will differ according to the sex of the infant, its ordinal position in the family, the mother's social status, caregiving contributions from other family members, the state of physical resources, and so on. *Natural selection must surely have operated to produce conditional maternal strategies, not stereotypy.* (p. 71; italics in original)

Much the same sort of complexity characterizes the long-term consequences of attachment. As we will see when we discuss this hotly debated topic in Chapter 7, there is conflicting evidence about the significance of the various patterns of attachment for later development.

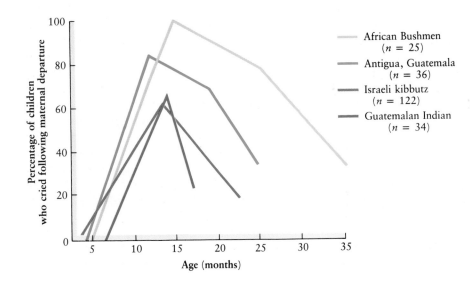

FIGURE 6.11 *The percentage of children of various ages from four cultures who cried after their mother's departure from the room in the "strange situation." (From Kagan, Kearsley, & Zelazo, 1978.)*

The Developmental Course of Attachment

Although there are marked individual and cultural differences in the patterns of behavior that infants display in the various episodes within the strange situation, and interpretations of those differences are a matter of debate among psychologists, infants all over the world appear to display great age-related consistency, no matter what the cultural setting, in their expressions of distress when they are first separated from their mothers. As Figure 6.11 indicates, 5-month-old babies generally do not display distress after the departure of their mothers. The first overt signs of distress appear at about 7 months. After that age the proportion of children who become distressed builds up to about 15 months and then begins to wane. This changing pattern of distress indicates that as time passes the attachment relations established earlier in life become integrated into a new psychological and social system.

A NEW SENSE OF SELF

Thus far in our discussion of the second year of life we have been tracing changes in different realms of children's development one by one. A most striking fact about 2-year-olds is that these separate threads of development come together to provide them with a new and distinctive sense of themselves as people.

The transition that marks the end of infancy is noted by people in many parts of the world. On the South Pacific island of Fiji, parents say that children gain *vakayalo*, sense, around their second birthday; they can be held responsible for their actions because they are supposed to be able to tell right from wrong. The Utku of Hudson Bay say that the 2-year-old has gained *ihuma*, reason. Parents in the United States react to their infants' newly acquired independence and the dwindling of their own control over them by labeling the change as the onset of the "terrible twos."

However it is described, the distinctive pattern of behavior that tells people in many cultures that children have entered a new stage of development seems to comprise several interconnected elements: a growing sensitivity to adults' standards of what is good and bad, a new awareness of their own ability to live up to those standards, and an ability to create plans of their own that they then judge against adult standards (Kagan, 1981). As a result of all of these elements taken

together, children can participate much more adequately in many situations, and their increasing competence provides the basis for the sense of autonomy that Erikson (1963) says characterizes this time of life.

A Sense of Standards

As we have seen repeatedly, infants are sensitive to unusual changes in their environment. Even in the first days of life, babies become habituated to events that occur repeatedly and pay attention to unexpected changes in their surroundings. But around the age of 2 years, children also become sensitive to events that violate the way things are "supposed to be." Children at this age become upset if the plastic eye of their teddy bear is missing or if there is mud on the hem of a new dress. When 14-month-olds are brought to a playroom where some of the toys are damaged, they seem to be unaware of the flaws and play as if nothing were wrong. But 19-month-olds say disdainfully, "Yukky" or "Fix it" (Kagan, 1981:47). Apparently their emerging ability to classify objects extends to an ability to classify events as proper and improper according to adult standards.

Children also express sensitivity to adult standards when they feel they are supposed to imitate an adult. In several studies, Jerome Kagan (1981) had an adult model various activities in a play setting. The adult might make one toy monkey hug another monkey, or build a stack of blocks, or enact a small drama using toy blocks as animals. Many of the acts were too complex for 2-year-olds to imitate. Starting around 18 months of age, the children in Kagan's study seemed to feel that they were expected to do what the adult had done even when they couldn't. As a result, many of them started to fret, stopped playing, and clung to their mothers. Kagan concluded that their distress signaled a new ability to recognize adult standards and an associated sense of responsibility to live up to them.

Further evidence that toddlers develop a sense of standards comes from situations in which adults set goals for children or children set themselves a goal. It is not at all unusual to encounter 2½-year-olds struggling to use all the blocks in the room to build a tower or to fit every available doll into a single toy baby carriage so that all the babies can go on a trip. Merry Bullock and Paul Lütkenhaus (1989) traced the ability of infants to adhere to task standards set by adults. At 17 months the infants had difficulty even beginning to

When things are slightly out of order, the diligent 2-year-old will seek to put them right.

build a tower of blocks, dress a doll, or wash a blackboard. At 20 months, they started out to do the tasks according to adult standards, but got caught up by the materials and ended up playing according to their own whims. It was only at 26 months that they first showed that they could stick to the task until they met adult standards. But it was not until they approached their third birthday that this kind of self-control became the rule rather than the exception. This evidence suggests that until children are able to represent themselves symbolically in relation to a future goal — "I dress the baby" — their problem solving is easily sidetracked.

Accompanying the emergence of children's ability to set a goal for themselves is the appearance of a new kind of smile. As the topmost block is placed on the stack or the last doll is stuffed into the carriage, the child smiles with self-satisfaction. Kagan (1981) refers to this kind of smile as a *mastery smile* (see the photo at the start of this chapter).

Once children can set goals for themselves and realize that there are standards of performance that they must meet, they begin to interact with their parents in a new way; they actively seek their parents' help

in reaching the goals and meeting the standards. When confronted with a task that appeared too difficult, one child is reported to have said, while clinging to his mother, "It's mommy's turn to play" (Kagan, 1981:49). More routinely, children around 20 months of age begin to tell adults what they want them to do. Their success varies, of course, depending on the willingness of adults to let them have their way, which differs from family to family and from culture to culture.

Self-description

When speech first emerges, most one-word utterances name objects in the visual field. Children point at or pick up an object and say its name. These first descriptions include no explicit reference to the self. Between the ages of 18 and 24 months, about the same time that children begin to use two-word utterances, they also begin to describe their own actions. A child completing a jigsaw puzzle exclaims, "Did it!" or "Becky finished." When blocks fall, a child exclaims, "Uh-oh. I fix." In these utterances we see not only children's ability to refer to themselves explicitly but also the ability to represent two aspects of an event in words — their recognition of adult standards and their desire to meet them.

Self-recognition

Consciousness of self is among the major characteristics said to distinguish human beings from other species and 2-year-olds from younger children. This is an interesting idea, but finding a way to demonstrate it convincingly has been a problem.

In 1970 Gordon Gallup reported an ingenious series of mirror experiments with chimpanzees that has since been repeated with children. Gallup showed adolescent wild-born chimpanzees their images in a full-length mirror. At first the chimps acted as if another animal were in the room: they threatened, vocalized, and made conciliatory gestures to the "intruder." After a few days, however, they began to use the mirror to explore themselves; for example, they picked bits of food from their faces, which they could see only in the mirror.

To make certain of the meaning of these reactions, Gallup anesthetized several chimps and painted a bright, odorless dye above one eye and on the ear on the opposite side of the head. When they woke up and

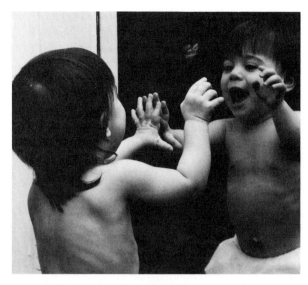

Children's ability to recognize themselves in a mirror attests to the emergence of a new sense of self at the end of infancy.

looked in the mirror, these chimps immediately began to explore the marked spots with their hands. Gallup concluded that they had learned to recognize themselves in the mirror.

This kind of self-recognition is by no means universal among monkey species. Gallup gave a wild-born macaque monkey over 2400 hours of exposure to a mirror over more than 5 months, but it never showed any sign of self-recognition. The problem was not simply dealing with the mirror image; the monkey quickly learned to use the mirror to find food that was out of sight. The monkey simply could not recognize itself.

Gallup's procedure has been used with human infants between the ages of 3 and 24 months. The results fit nicely with the evidence from other studies of the development of self-awareness (Bertenthal & Fischer, 1978; Lewis & Brooks-Gunn, 1979). This research reveals that there are several stages in learning to recognize oneself in a mirror. Before the age of 3 months, children held up to a mirror show little interest in their own images or in the image of anyone else. At about 4 months, if a toy or another person is reflected in the mirror, babies will reach out and touch the mirror image. At this stage, they clearly don't understand that they are seeing a reflection. Babies 10 months old will reach behind them if a toy is slowly lowered behind their back while they are looking in the mirror, but they will not try to rub off a red spot that has been surreptitiously applied to their nose. Not until chil-

dren are 18 months old will they reach for their own nose when they see the red spot. Some try to rub the spot off; others ask, "What's that?" Within a few months, whenever someone points to the child's mirror image and asks, "Who's that?" the child will be able to answer unhesitatingly, "Me."

THE END OF INFANCY

The combined data on the changes in children's autonomy and self-concept between the ages of 18 and 30 months — the decline in the levels of distress they show when separated from their caregivers and their increased ability to engage in symbolic play, to adhere to adult standards and to express themselves in elementary words and phrases — indicate a stagelike transi-

---

TABLE 6.3
The Bio-Social-Behavioral Shift at the End of Infancy

BIOLOGICAL DOMAIN

Myelination of connections among brain areas
Leveling off of brain growth
Maturation of brain areas in roughly equal degrees

BEHAVIORAL DOMAIN

Walking becomes well coordinated
Manual dexterity becomes adequate to pick up small objects
Control over bladder and bowels
Planful problem solving
Symbolic play
Conceptual representations
Elementary vocabulary and beginning of word combinations
Mastery smile

SOCIAL DOMAIN

Decline of distress at separation
Distinctive sense of self
Acceptance of adult standards

tion in the overall pattern of their capacities that we have identified as a bio-social-behavioral shift. The changes that occur in the months surrounding their second birthdays are summarized in Table 6.3. As an ensemble, these changes signal the end of infancy and the advent of a new stage of development.

Table 6.3 provides a timely reminder that the social and cognitive changes that have figured so prominently in this chapter are part and parcel of more mundane behavioral changes, such as coordinated walking and bladder control, and that many of these changes are dependent on the physical development of the body.

The new configuration of characteristics that emerges early in the third year does not, of course, permit children to survive on their own. Far from it. But it does set the stage for a new form of interdependence and a new system of interaction between children and their environments. If all goes well, the individual aspects of development will undergo further modification over time, and this new, distinctive stage of development will give way to the next.

SUMMARY

1. Sometime between their second and third birthdays, children complete the period of development called infancy. Like all major stage transitions, the end of infancy is marked by changes in biological processes, by expanding physical and mental abilities, and by the appearance of a new relationship with the social world.

2. Important connections in the cerebral cortex and between the cortex and the brainstem become myelinated. Neurons in the brain begin to achieve adult length and density, and the rate of overall brain growth slows.

3. Children gain increasing control over several muscle systems, which makes it possible for them to walk upright, run, jump, and execute such movements as eating with a spoon and picking up small objects. They also gain voluntary control over elimination.

4. A new configuration of cognitive abilities is manifested in many domains: problem solving, play, categorization of objects, and communication.

5. Toddlers persist in searching for objects that are hidden and then moved; they no longer give up when they cannot find something in the first place they think to look. Problem solving in general becomes more deliberate; solutions are reached without extensive overt trial and error.

6. Play evolves from a concentration on variation in patterns of movements to the pretend use of objects in imaginary situations. Pretend play itself evolves. Children 1 to 1½ years old can use themselves as agents to carry out a single pretend act at a time. By the time they are 2 years old, children can carry out a sequence of pretend actions in which objects such as dolls are used as the agents.

7. Piaget believed that infants become capable of deferred imitation toward the end of the second year of life as a result of the ability to represent absent objects.

Current evidence indicates that deferred imitation can occur several months earlier.

8. Coincident with the onset of pretend play is the appearance of a new form of categorizing. Presented with a collection of objects to group, toddlers create a separate work space and categorize objects in accordance with adult criteria.

9. Toddlers' vocabularies begin to grow rapidly at the same time that they begin to solve problems insightfully and to search logically for hidden objects.

10. The ability to combine words to make elementary two-word sentences coincides with the ability to combine objects in pretend play.

11. Developmental psychologists interpret infants' distress when they are separated from their mothers as an indicator of feelings of attachment. This distress increases steadily until sometime in the second year and then declines.

12. A variety of theories offer competing explanations for the onset of attachment.

    a. Freud believed that attachment has its roots in the reduction of such biological drives as hunger.

    b. Erikson explains attachment as the establishment of a trusting relationship between parent and child.

    c. Bowlby hypothesizes that attachment serves to reduce fear by establishing a secure base of support from which children can explore their environments.

13. Research with monkeys has disproved the drive-reduction theory and has shown that infant monkeys can become attached to inanimate surrogate mothers that provide soothing tactile sensations.

14. The social incapacity of monkeys raised with inanimate surrogate mothers has focused research on the role of maternal responsiveness in the development of normal social interactions.

15. The "strange situation" has been widely used to assess distinctive patterns of infants' attachment to their primary caregiver. Research has focused on the causes and consequences of three broad patterns of attachment: anxious/avoidant, securely attached, and anxious/resistant.

16. The best predictor of secure attachment is attentive, sensitive caregiving. Abusive, neglectful, and inconsistent caregiving is likely to lead to insecure attachment.

17. Children who are cared for primarily by their mothers also become attached to their fathers and siblings, but these attachments usually develop later.

18. Children's characteristics may contribute to the quality of their attachments. Children who are easily upset when their ongoing activity is interrupted or who dis-play less interest in people than in objects may be more difficult for adults to coordinate with, so that secure attachments are not easily formed.

19. There appear to be marked cultural variations in patterns of response in the strange situation. Traditions both of exclusive mothering and of communal upbringing can result in manifestations of anxiety in the strange situation. The psychological significance of these findings is uncertain.

20. A new sense of self appears around the time of children's second birthday. It is manifested in:
    a. A growing sensitivity to adult standards.
    b. Concern about living up to those standards.
    c. A new ability to set one's own goals and standards.
    d. Self-reference in language.
    e. Immediate recognition of one's image in a mirror.

KEY TERMS

animal model	representation	symbolic play
biological drives	secure base	tertiary circular reactions
deferred imitation	strange situation	

SUGGESTED READINGS

BOWLBY, JOHN. *Attachment and Loss,* vol. 1: *Attachment.* New York: Basic Books, 1969.

Bowlby's ideas have had an enormous and continuing impact on the study of infant development. This first volume in his trilogy provides the rationale and data on which his concept of attachment is based.

BRETHERTON, INGE, & WATERS, EVERETT (Eds.). *Growing Points in Attachment Theory.* Monographs of the Society for Research in Child Development, 1985, *50,* no. 209.

Reports from a wide spectrum of researchers on the current status of research on the growth of attachment.

GELMAN, SUSAN A., & BYRNES, JAMES P. *Perspectives on Language and Thought: Interrelations in Development.* New York: Cambridge University Press, 1991.

Essays by leading researchers that provide in-depth, state-of-the-art theories and findings pertaining to the relationships between the development of thinking and the development of language.

HARLOW, HARRY. *Learning to Love.* San Francisco: Albion, 1971.

A summary of Harlow's research on the role of social interaction in the socioemotional development of monkeys. Although somewhat dated, this work continues to have a great impact on conceptions of emotional development in early childhood.

KAGAN, JEROME. *The Second Year.* Cambridge, Mass.: Harvard University Press, 1982.

A well-rounded description of the interlocking intellectual and social changes associated with the end of infancy. The book is unusual in its inclusion of cross-cultural data and in bringing together modern evidence concerning the biological changes that accompany the distinctive pattern of behaviors that marks the transition to early childhood.

PIAGET, JEAN. *Play, Dreams, and Imitation.* New York: Norton, 1962.

In this account of the end of the sensorimotor stage of development Piaget argues that different domains of infant behavior all point to a single underlying change in thought processes. Many of his observations have become classics in the literature on this age period.

C H A P T E R 7

Early Experience and Later Life

•

Two roads diverged in a yellow wood,
And sorry I could not travel both
And be one traveler, long I stood
And looked down one as far as I could
To where it bent in the undergrowth;
Then took the other, as just as fair,
And having perhaps the better claim,
Because it was grassy and wanted wear;
Though as for that the passing there
Had worn them really about the same,
And both that morning equally lay
In leaves no step had trodden black.
Oh, I kept the first for another day!
Yet knowing how way leads on to way,
I doubted if I should ever come back.
I shall be telling this with a sigh
Somewhere ages and ages hence:
Two roads diverged in a wood, and I—
I took the one less traveled by,
And that has made all the difference.

—ROBERT FROST, ''THE ROAD NOT TAKEN''

One of the most fundamental processes in development
consists in the closing of doors . . . , in the progressive
restriction of possible fates.

—JOSEPH NEEDHAM, *ORDER AND LIFE*

The poet and the scientist agree. Paths taken early in our lives launch us on a course that, once set, may be difficult to change. Insofar as children's fates are shaped by their experiences in the world, it seems reasonable to conclude that their earliest experiences, the paths they first travel down, will be the most significant for their later development. This idea is called **primacy.** We can find the concept in our proverbs— "As the twig is bent, so grows the tree"— and in our heritage from the Greeks. Plato (428–348 B.C.) expressed this view when he wrote:

> And the beginning, as you know, is always the most important part, especially in dealing with anything young and tender. That is the time when the character is being molded and easily takes any impress one may wish to stamp on it. (1945:68)

During the twentieth century, primacy has come to be associated with the idea that children's experiences during infancy determine their future development. This line of thought was greatly influenced by Freud's claim that psychological illness in adulthood can be traced back to unresolved conflicts in the first years of life (Freud, 1940/1964). It is by no means restricted to Freudian theorists, however. In summarizing his research on intellectual development, the psychologist Burton White (1975) argues that *to begin to look at a child's educational development when he is two years of age is already much too late,* particularly in the area of social skills and attitudes" (p. 4, italics added). Similarly, Alan Sroufe and June Fleeson (1986) maintain that the nature of children's first attachments greatly influences the way they form subsequent relationships.

In this chapter we will focus on the questions of whether and to what extent the experiences of infancy exert more influence than later experiences on the course of development. The answers to these questions have an important bearing on such issues as how society and parents can best provide for infants to ensure their optimal development and what can be done to improve the lives of children who suffer deprivation early in life. As we will see, there is no doubt that infants' experiences have a significant effect on their later development. But in many cases there is good reason to doubt extreme claims that the trends begun during the first 2½ years of life are irreversible (Robbins & Rutter, 1991).

A few words of caution are in order about the nature of the research featured in this chapter. In many cases the data that psychologists rely on as evidence about the long-term consequences of infants' experiences arise from the study of children who differ from the norm because of some circumstance that is not under the investigators' control: they have been raised in an orphanage, or in poverty, or by parents who are mentally unstable. In such studies, the basic principle of a true psychological experiment is violated; the subjects are not assigned at random to experimental and control conditions. As a consequence, one has to be cautious in claiming that differences between these and other groups of children in later life are caused by the different circumstances that the children experienced during infancy and early childhood: it is possible that some covarying factor is the real cause of the observed differences.

OPTIMAL CONDITIONS FOR INFANT DEVELOPMENT

The widespread belief that the early experiences of infants are crucial to their later development has produced a continuing effort to identify the conditions that will best foster their early development. Information about these conditions serves as a guide for parents, who want to do all they can to ensure a happy and healthy life for their children, and for policy makers, who must sometimes pass laws concerning children. Ideas about the nature of optimal development depend, of course, on cultural values, but in our society the conditions sought are usually those that will allow as many doors as possible to remain open for the child's future.

It is often suggested that development is best fostered when the mother, or whoever else cares for the baby, is sensitive and responsive to the baby's signals and states. We have encountered this idea in Chapter 6 (pp. 232, 234) in research on the conditions that promote secure attachment. A particularly powerful vision of the sensitive mother is provided by the nineteenth-century Danish philosopher Søren Kierkegaard:

> The loving mother teaches her child to walk alone. She is far enough from him so that she cannot actually support him, but she holds out her arms to him. She imitates his movements, and if he totters, she swiftly bends as if to seize him, so that the child might believe that he is not walking alone. . . . And yet, she does more. Her face beckons like a reward, an encouragement. Thus, the child walks alone with his eyes fixed on his mother's face, not on the difficulties in his way. He supports himself by arms that do not hold him and constantly strives towards the refuge in his mother's embrace, little suspecting that in the very same moment he is emphasizing his need for her, he is proving that he can do without her, because he is walking alone. (Quoted in Sroufe, 1979:462)

Kierkegaard's "loving mother" is so finely tuned to her child's needs that she creates the illusion of physical support where none exists. This illusion provides the child with a sense of individual achievement and self-confidence that encourages maximum effort and courage. These character traits are widely admired

---

TABLE 7.1

Characteristics of Competent 3-Year-Olds

SOCIAL ABILITIES

Getting and holding attention of an adult in socially acceptable ways

Using adults as resources after concluding that they cannot handle the task themselves

Expressing affection and mild hostility

Engaging in role play

GENERAL INTELLECTUAL SKILLS

Understanding and communicating effectively

Engaging in complex problem solving, including finding materials and using them to make a product

Self-control in the absence of external constraints

Ability to plan for and prepare for an activity

Ability to explore novel objects and situations systematically

Source: White & Watts, 1973.

---

in Western European and North American cultures. Consequently, the child-rearing behaviors that foster them are often considered the optimal conditions for development.

Kierkegaard's maternal ideal seems to be embodied in what Burton White and Jean Carew Watts (1973) call *A* mothers. The children of such mothers were judged to be more competent than their peers when they were in kindergarten, on the basis of their performance on a battery of tests and the researchers' observations. (Table 7.1 lists some of the characteristics the researchers evaluated.) The *A* mothers enjoyed being with their toddlers and talked to them on a level they could understand. They placed more importance on their children's happiness and learning than on the appearance of their homes, which were organized to be safe and interesting for toddlers. They allowed their children to take minor risks, but they set reasonable limits for them. They might allow their 1½-year-olds to negotiate stairs while holding on to the banister, for instance, but not to climb up on the edge of the bath-

tub. Their close attention to their children was complemented by their dominant mood: they were busy and happy rather than unoccupied and depressed.

The *A* mothers did not spend all day attending to their toddlers. In fact, they spent less than 10 percent of their time actually caring for them. Some had part-time jobs, and some had several other children. When they were at home, however, they were nearly always available to answer questions, set up a new activity, or give encouragement. The researchers found that neither a lot of money nor a lot of education was necessary to be an *A* mother, although poverty did make a mother's work more difficult. Some of the *A* mothers were on welfare, and some of them had not graduated from high school.

White and Watts's description of effective maternal behaviors tells us about the caretaking environments that foster optimal development in late infancy, as measured by successful early adaptations to a modern, technologically advanced society in which the ability to behave oneself and perform well in school are basic demands. But it does not help answer many important questions that parents and other caregivers must face: What is the "right" kind of responsiveness? How much support is too much, and how much is not enough? Will the same kind of responsiveness that prepares children to succeed in school also prepare them to cope with frustration, inadequate housing, discrimination, or extended periods of unemployment?

As we indicated earlier, answers to questions about what constitutes adequate preparation for later life depend on the historical and cultural circumstances into which a child is born. Japanese mothers, for example, like mothers in the United States, aspire for their children to attain a high level of academic achievement. But in Japanese society, working together with others is valued more than individual achievement, and Japanese mothers stress this value in raising their children. By U.S. standards, Japanese mothers may seem too responsive to their children, thereby encouraging considerable emotional dependence (Miyaki et al., 1986). Japanese mothers' high level of responsiveness, however, does not mean that they provide inappropriate environments for their children's development. Japanese society differs from American society. Therefore both the overall pattern of adult characteristics that Japanese mothers strive to foster in their children and their strategies for achieving this pattern differ.

A quite different situation exists for the people living in the poverty-stricken parts of towns in the northeast of Brazil (Scheper-Hughes, 1992). The environment into which their babies are born is extremely hostile to survival: the drinking water is contaminated, there is little food to eat, there are no sanitary facilities, and there is little medical care. Almost 50 percent of the children born in these communities die before the age of 5 years. For those who survive, success in later life is rarely influenced by academic ability. Little schooling is available; later in life these children can look forward to labor as unskilled farmworkers, which affords no hope of economic advancement or even of a comfortable living.

In many parts of the world large numbers of children do not survive to celebrate their fifth birthday. Often they die of diseases that could be prevented with better sanitary conditions, nutrition, and health care.

In response to these conditions, the mothers of this region studied by Nancy Scheper-Hughes have developed beliefs and behaviors about child rearing that seem harsh and uncaring by the standards of middle-class families in either the United States or Japan. They are fatalistic about their infants' well-being. Children who are developmentally delayed or who have a passive, quiet temperament may be neglected or simply left to die if they are sick, with no attempt being made to give them special care. The favored children are those who are precocious, active, and demanding. Children who survive to the age of 5 or 6 years are expected to begin to contribute to the family's livelihood. The boys are allowed to roam the streets, searching for food and stealing if necessary. The girls are required to pick sugar cane or do housework. But as the report by Scheper-Hughes makes clear, these mothers were simply being practical; they were preparing their children to survive in an environment where weakness almost certainly leads to death.

Spoiling: Responding Too Much?

Even among middle-class families in the United States, beliefs about proper parental behaviors vary. One mother may ignore her toddler's requests for a treat at the store or cries in the middle of the night in the belief that too much responsiveness will foster a false basis for dealing with the world and spoil the child. Another mother may respond to her children's every whim and whimper because she believes that she must buffer them against difficult circumstances until they are strong enough to cope on their own. Which mother is right? *Is* there a right answer to how much parents should cater to the desires and distresses of their infants? Is spoiling a problem?

As we saw in Chapter 4 (pp. 144–145), the meanings of newborns' cries are often ambiguous. Consequently, parents may worry that they will encourage fussiness if they pick up their babies each time they start to cry. Evidence on the short-term effects of being highly responsive to their crying is mixed. A study based on laboratory research shows that the duration of crying episodes decreases if the caregiver ignores the cries but responds quickly to other behaviors, such as smiling (Etzel & Gewirtz, 1967). Observations in home situations, however, suggest

In many parts of the world strenuous labor remains an accepted part of children's lives.

that crying may become more frequent if it is ignored. Silvia Bell and Mary Ainsworth (1972) studied the ways in which 26 mothers responded to their infants' cries. A member of the research team visited each home for 4 hours once every 3 weeks throughout the first year of each baby's life. During the visits the observer recorded how often the baby cried and how the mother responded. Contrary to the common wisdom, the mothers who responded quickly to their infants' cries had babies who cried relatively little. The mothers who ignored their babies' cries for long periods ended up with the babies who cried most often. Bell and Ainsworth suggest that the most important consequence of mothers' quick attention to their infants' cries is that it helps the babies to develop trust in the mother and in their own ability to control what happens to them.

Spoiling does not seem to be a serious risk during infancy. Perhaps there are some parents who cater to their children's every whim, thus giving them an exaggerated sense of their own power that will be maladaptive in the long run. In most cases, however, the everyday demands on parents to earn a living, to maintain a household, and to keep their children from doing things that are potentially dangerous make it almost inevitable that children eventually learn that they cannot always have their own way.

Learned Helplessness: Responding Too Little

Parents' fear that they will create a baby tyrant if they respond to their infant's every demand is balanced by the competing concern that if they never respond on the baby's terms, but only on their own, they will create children who believe that they cannot influence the world around them. Support for the idea that a feeling of helplessness can be learned appeared first in studies of animals. In one such study Bruce Overmier and Martin Seligman (1967) first administered a multitude of shocks to the forepaws of a group of dogs. These dogs received shocks no matter what they did. Then these dogs and a comparison group of dogs that had no experience with unavoidable shock were placed in a large box with a metal grid floor to which shocks could be delivered. If the animal crossed over to the other side of the box quickly enough, it could avoid being shocked altogether. Dogs that were placed in such a box with no history of unavoidable shocks quickly learned to move back and forth across the box to avoid the shock. But the dogs that had previously experienced inescapable shocks did not learn to avoid the shock; they lay down and whined. This is the effect known as **learned helplessness.**

Research on learned helplessness with human adults indicates that when people are put in situations in which events are unaffected by their behavior, they too eventually become passive and lose even the desire to act (Fincham & Cain, 1986; Seligman, 1975).

Studies have shown that infants are capable of learning about their ability to control events, so it seems reasonable to assume that they might also be subject to learned helplessness in the right circumstances. John S. Watson (not to be confused with John B. Watson, the founder of behaviorism mentioned in earlier chapters) set up an apparatus that allowed 8-week-old infants to move a mobile hanging above their cribs by pressing their heads against an air pillow. Because of the direct relationship between pressing down on the pillow and the movement of the mobile, the infants rapidly learned to make the mobile move (Watson, 1972).

Watson reported that once the infants learned to control the mobile, their daily levels of activity increased in comparison with those of a control group whose actions had no effect on the mobile. The babies who were allowed to control the mobile also began to smile delightedly and coo at the sight of it. These observations led Watson to speculate that even very young infants find it pleasurable to control their environment because it gives them a feeling of personal effectiveness. On the basis of similar observations with infants and young children, the psychiatrist Robert White (1959) concluded that human beings have a basic drive to be in control of their environments. He called this drive the *competence motive.*

In another study, Watson (1971) contrasted the behavior of two groups of infants who were provided with mobiles for their cribs at home. One group could set the mobile in motion by pushing down on their pillows; the other group saw the mobile move equally often, but their own actions did not affect its movement. Later both groups were given an opportunity to make a similar mobile move in the laboratory. The infants who had learned to control the mobile at home soon learned to make the laboratory mobile move. The infants who could not control the mobile at home did not learn to control the laboratory mobile. In accord with the idea of learned helplessness, the experience of lack of control over an aspect of the environment in one situation seems to impair later learning in a similar situation.

Neal Finkelstein and Craig Ramey (1977) extended Watson's findings to show that babies who learn a particular behavior to control the environment in one situation may apply what they've learned to establish new behaviors. In the first stage of this study, the researchers placed 8-month-old babies in front of a panel that lit up and made interesting sounds. Half of the babies could produce the interesting outcome by pushing on the panel; the others could push the panel or not, as they pleased, and still see and hear the same things. As expected, the babies whose actions caused the change learned to press the panel, whereas the others did not.

In the second stage of the experiment, both groups could make the sights and sounds occur by engaging in an entirely different kind of behavior, vocalizing. The babies who had learned to push the panel to produce the lights and sounds also learned to activate the panel by vocalizing. But the babies who learned earlier that their behavior was irrelevant to the lights and sounds failed to learn this new way of producing them.

Findings such as Finkelstein and Ramey's suggest that even infants as young as 8 months of age learn more than the direct association between their own actions and specific outcomes, such as the connection between crying and being picked up or between sucking and obtaining nourishment. They also seem to learn something about their ability to control their environment. Although infants cannot tell us directly what they are feeling or thinking, their actions seem to indicate that such experiences shape their sense of personal effectiveness.

An important limitation of the research on spoiling and learned helplessness is that it does not indicate what mix of learning about their ability to control their environment and learning to accept external control provides infants with the optimum foundation for later development. There is no single recipe for the correct amount of responsiveness in every situation. That is why psychologists emphasize that parents' *sensitivity* to their children's needs is a key factor in promoting healthy development.

EFFECTS OF SEPARATION

A variety of situations can separate parents from their children for a time, and during those periods it is impossible for them to fine-tune their children's upbringing. The need to earn a living often separates parents from their young children for many hours several days a week. A family upheaval such as divorce, the death of a parent, or prolonged illness requiring hospitalization also separates children from their parents

Every day large numbers of children are orphaned as a result of war, famine, and disease. This child's father was killed during fighting between Croatians and Serbians following the breakup of Yugoslavia in 1992.

(Wolkind & Rutter, 1985). A major disaster—war, flood, famine—can dislocate a whole population.

Developmental psychologists have long been interested in the consequences of the separation of children from their parents (see Rutter & Hersov, 1985 for a review of the findings). They seek to understand how separation influences development at the time it occurs and how it may affect later development. This knowledge can help them to devise effective therapies for children who have been adversely affected by such separations. In the following discussion, we will consider children who have experienced one or another of a wide range of separations, including those involving day care, hospitalization of themselves or their mothers, and residence in a foster home or orphanage.

Temporary Separation from Parents

Children who spend part of each weekday being cared for by a nonfamily member while their parents work experience a relatively mild form of separation. Many researchers are convinced that high-quality day care has no lasting negative impact on infants' later development. Some, however, claim that no matter what its quality, extensive day care for babies under the age of 1 year has lasting negative effects (see Box 7.1). We will return to the subject of day care in Chapter 11, where we focus on slightly older children.

Another form of separation occurs when young children must spend time in a hospital. Several studies have evaluated the consequences of hospitalization on later emotional development. Michael Rutter (1976), for example, studied 400 10-year-olds to see if early hospitalization had influenced their later psychological adjustment. He found that a single hospital stay that lasted a week or less before the age of 5 produced no emotional or behavioral disturbances that could be detected at the age of 10. Repeated hospitalization, however, was found to be associated with behavior problems and delinquency in later childhood.

As noted earlier, one must always be cautious when one interprets the results of studies in which differences in experience arise naturally rather than as a result of the experimenter's manipulation. Therefore, Rutter is careful to consider other possible explanations for his findings. For example, the later psychological problems may have resulted from the stress of continued ill health rather than from the children's separation from their parents. Another possibility is suggested by subsequent research revealing that children who have been hospitalized repeatedly are more likely than children who have not been hospitalized to come from socially and economically disadvantaged families (Quinton & Rutter, 1976). The negative effect of repeated hospitalization may be less a reflection of disturbed social relations owing to separation than a reflection of chronically difficult home circumstances or ill health.

A more traumatic form of family separation often occurs in time of war. In the early 1940s, the German air force carried out an intensive bombing campaign against the civilian population of London and other English cities. Large numbers of English children were sent to live in the safer countryside with relatives, sponsoring families, or other children in special group living arrangements while their parents remained behind. Dorothy Burlingham and Anna Freud (1942) studied the reactions of a group of such children who ranged in age from a few months to 4 years. They found that many of the children were distressed at being separated from their parents. When these children were examined 20 years later, however, the researchers found no instances of severe mental illness among them; their behavior as young adults fell within normal limits (Maas, 1963).

Extended Separation from Parents

An extreme form of separation is experienced by children who spend their early lives in orphanages because their parents are dead or are unable to care for them. Because many orphanages keep good records of the children they care for, studies of orphanage-raised children provide some of the most systematic data on how multiple caretakers and suboptimal circumstances influence later social and intellectual development.

Children of the crèche

A classic long-range study of orphanage-raised children was carried out by Wayne Dennis (1973) and his colleagues in a crèche (orphanage) in Lebanon. The children were brought to the crèche shortly after birth. Once there, they received little attention; there was only one caretaker for every ten children. These caretakers had themselves been brought up in the crèche until the age of 6, when they were transferred to another institution. According to Dennis, the caretakers showed little regard for the children's individual needs

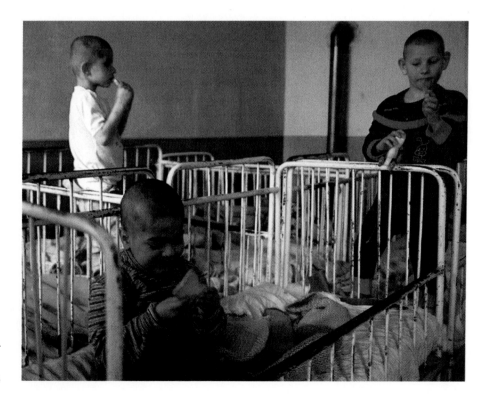

The conditions in orphanages such as this provide insufficient stimulation for normal mental development.

BOX 7.1
Out-of-Home Care in the First Year of Life

Questions about the primacy of infancy reach beyond scientific research into the lives of individuals and the arena of public policy. The increasingly common practice of placing infants in the care of someone other than their parents during the first year of life has sparked a vigorous controversy with obvious political overtones. According to some experts, very early day-care experience puts children at risk for long-term socioemotional difficulties. According to others, little or no risk is associated with early high-quality child care (Belsky, 1990; Clarke-Stewart, 1989; Phillips et al., 1987).

The issue of out-of-home care for infants potentially affects the lives of many people because of two trends in American society: (1) the growing number of single-parent households and (2) the increasing economic need for both parents to work full-time. At the present time, women constitute the fastest-growing segment of the work force, and a majority of mothers who work return to their jobs before their infants are 1 year old. If current trends continue, by the year 2000 the mothers of four out of every five infants under the age of 1 will be in the labor force.

Prominent among those who raise concerns about out-of-home care during the first year of life is Jay Belsky (1986, 1990). He bases his conclusions on evidence that children who have experienced extensive nonmaternal care (more than 20 hours a week) during the first year of life are more likely to exhibit insecure patterns of attachment in the "strange situation," are less compliant in meeting adults' demands, and are more aggressive in their interactions with their peers.

Belsky's concerns are supported by a study conducted by Peter Barglow, Brian Vaughn, and Nancy Molitor (1987). These researchers found that first-born children who had been placed in day-care arrangements before their first birthday were significantly more likely to display insecure forms of attachment when they were 12 to 13 months old than were children who stayed at home with their mothers.

Belsky's conclusions have been criticized on several grounds. Alison Clarke-Stewart (1989) argues that the negative effects of early day care summarized by Belsky are very small in real-life terms. In support of day-care experience during the first year of life, she cites evidence that children enrolled in such care have higher scores on tests of intellectual development. In addition, she suggests that the behaviors labeled "noncompliant" might really reflect increased independence and self-confidence.

Deborah Phillips and her colleagues (1987) agree that Belsky's concerns are misplaced. They maintain that "early entry into day care may be less important than the kind and quality of care children receive while in day care" (p. 20).

A study by Carollee Howes (1990) supports this conclusion. Howes studied how the age at which children enter day care, the quality of the care they receive, and the characteristics of their families influence their social adjustment in preschool and kindergarten. She found that children who entered into low-quality day care before the age of 1 were the ones most likely to have difficulty with their peers in preschool; they were distractible, low in task orientation, and less considerate of others. However, children enrolled in high-quality day care, even during the first year of life, did not seem to be at any risk for such behavior problems. Howes also found that the families who enrolled their babies in low-quality day care early in infancy were under pressures that the other families she studied were not. They were less likely to be involved in supportive social networks and they were more likely to be experiencing a variety of complex problems that had negative effects on their child-rearing efforts.

As Howes's study suggests, when a matter as complex as the effects of day care is at issue, the real-life circumstances of the people involved must be considered. If brief separations with high-quality care are the only disruptions in an otherwise secure family situation, the disruptions appear to have quite different consequences from those experienced by a child whose family is under stress.

In accordance with mounting evidence on the cumulative impact of risk factors, Thomas Gamble and Edward Zigler (1986) conclude that when families are facing a number of life stresses, substitute care during the first year of life increases the likelihood of insecure infant-parent attachments, and that insecure attachments make the infant more vulnerable to stresses they encounter later in life.

The stakes in the debate are very high. On the one hand, everyone is aware that it is in the interests not only of the children in question but also of society as a whole to ensure that children grow up to be emotionally stable and socially competent people. If they do not, society will incur huge costs in later so-

cial services required and economic productivity lost. On the other hand, economic and social pressures are bringing many mothers into the work force and keeping fathers there. The problem is how best to deal with these conflicting realities to maximize children's life chances. Belsky suggests that this goal could best be achieved if parents received support for staying home with their infants during their first year of life. Phillips and her colleagues argue that what is called for is better and more accessible day care.

Many millions of dollars will be spent to deal with the issue of infant and child care in the decades to come, and millions of parents and children will be affected by the policies that are eventually adopted. In fact, virtually everyone will be involved, if only in the role of taxpayer.

With the majority of mothers returning to work within a year of the birth of their children, a growing number of babies are being cared for out of their homes before the age of 1. The effects of such care on their socioemotional development are the subject of intense debate among psychologists.

or temperaments. They rarely talked to the children, did not respond to their infrequent vocalizations, and seldom played with them while bathing, dressing, changing, or feeding them. Instead, they left the babies to lie on their backs in their cribs all day and the toddlers to sit in small playpens with only a ball to play with.

The harmful effects of this low level of stimulation and human contact were evident within a year. Although the children were normal at 2 months, as measured by an infant scale, Dennis found that they had developed intellectually at only half the normal rate when he tested them at the end of the first year.

The later developmental fates of these children depended on their subsequent care. Those who were adopted made a remarkable recovery. The children who were adopted before they were 2 years old were functioning normally when they were tested 2 to 3 years after their adoption, and those who were adopted within the next 4 years were only slightly retarded in their intellectual functioning.

The children who remained institutionalized fared less well. At the age of 6, the girls were sent to one institution and the boys to another. The girls' institution, like the crèche, provided few stimulating experiences and virtually no personal attention. When these girls were tested at 12 to 16 years of age, they were found to be so retarded intellectually that they would be unable to function in modern society. They could barely read, they could not tell time, and they were not able to dial a seven-digit telephone number or to count out change in a store.

The outcome for the boys was quite different. The institution to which they were transferred provided far more intellectual stimulation and more varied experiences than did the crèche. What is more, they had frequent contact with the workers at the institution, who came from the surrounding communities. As a result, the boys showed a substantial recovery from their initial intellectual lag when they were tested at 10 to 14 years of age. Although their performance on standardized tests was below the norm and below the performance of the children who had been adopted, it was within the range that would allow them to function in society.

Children reared in well-staffed orphanages

The grim picture painted by Dennis's research provoked further studies of orphanage-raised children in an effort to determine if the negative consequences he found were the result of particular forms of orphanage care. Barbara Tizard and her colleagues (Tizard & Rees, 1975; Tizard & Hodges, 1978; Hodges & Tizard, 1989a, 1989b) studied 65 English children of working-class backgrounds who were raised in residential nurseries from just after birth until at least the age of 2 years. The nurseries were considered to be of high quality. The children were fed well, the staff was trained, and toys and books were plentiful. The turnover and scheduling of staff members, however, discouraged the formation of close personal relationships between adults and children. Tizard and Hodges estimated that some 24 nurses had cared for each child by the time the children were 2 years old. By the age of 4½, each child had been cared for by as many as 50 nurses. This situation certainly appears to preclude the kind of intimate knowledge and caring that presumably underlies sensitive caregiving.

Tizard and her colleagues evaluated the developmental status of the children when they were 4½ years old and 8 years old, and again when they were 16 years old. They grouped the children into three categories:

1. Children who remained in the institutions.
2. Children who had returned to their families after the age of 2.
3. Children who were adopted between the ages of 2 and 8 years.

For comparison purposes, the researchers also evaluated a group of children with a similar working-class background who had always lived at home.

Leaving institutional care had a positive effect on the children, as Dennis's research might lead us to expect. But how much difference it made depended on what kind of environment they entered and what aspect of psychological functioning one looked at. One of the surprising findings was that the children who were restored to their biological families did not fare as well as the children who were adopted. The adopted children scored higher on standardized tests of intellectual achievement, and they were able to read at a more advanced level. The quality of the adopted children's relationships with their adoptive parents also appeared to be better. Almost all of the children who were adopted formed mutual attachments with their adoptive parents, no matter how old they were when they were adopted. This was not the case for the children who returned to their biological parents. The

Foster care provides an alternative to living in an orphanage. The youngsters pictured here have come to live with the Turner family of Santa Fe, New Mexico.

older they were when they left the nurseries, the less likely it was that mutual attachment developed.

One reason the adoptive homes may have been superior to the biological homes was that many of the families who took back their children were not altogether happy to have them. Many of the mothers expressed misgivings, but they accepted the responsibility because the children were their own. Often the children returned to homes in which there were other children who required their mother's attention or a stepfather who was not interested in them. Most of the adoptive parents, by contrast, were older, childless couples who wanted the children and gave them a good deal of attention. Also, most of the adoptive families were financially better off than the children's biological families had been (Tizard & Hodges, 1978).

One area in which most of the institutionalized children were reported to suffer in comparison with the control group was in their social relations at school. Here both groups of previously institutionalized children were seen to be "overly friendly." They had "an almost insatiable desire for adult attention, and a difficulty in forming good relationships with their peer group" (Tizard & Hodges, 1978:114). Why these children experienced difficulties in social relations at school but not at home is not clear. Perhaps their early experiences in institutions left them with a deficit in their ability to form peer relationships. Alternatively, they may have learned styles of interaction

that were adaptive in the institutions but maladaptive outside them (Rutter & Garmezy, 1983).

When Hodges and Tizard (1989a, b) contacted the children at the age of 16, they found a similar pattern. Children who had returned to their parents showed a high rate of antisocial behavior. Those adopted into new families did not, but even adopted children who developed normal attachment relations to their adoptive parents experienced difficulties dealing with their peers and society at large as teenagers.

The improvements seen in most children who leave institutional care speak against the theory that children can form emotional attachments only during a critical period in early infancy. Although the environment of the English nurseries prevented the children there from forming emotional attachments with their caregivers, most of the children who were adopted into new families formed attachments with their adoptive parents even though the children were well past their second birthday when they left the orphanage. At the same time, the research by Tizard and her colleagues confirms the idea that characteristics of children's environments during *later* periods of their life are influential in determining whether or not the lack of early attachments will prove to be an enduring problem, since the children who returned to indifferent biological parents were less likely to form attachments.

Isolated Children

The most extreme cases of neglect on record are those of children who have been separated not only from their parents but from other human beings as well. During the past 200 years several of these so-called feral children have been discovered, the most famous being the Wild Child, Victor, discussed in Chapter 1. Such children never fail to excite public interest because the idea of a little child fending for itself in nature is so dramatic. But the circumstances of such children's isolation and their condition before they became isolated are usually unknown. As a result, it is rarely possible to draw firm conclusions about the effects of their experiences during their isolation.

There are, however, a few well-documented modern cases of children who have been isolated early in life by sociopathic parents. Because public officials now keep good birth records and other health records, enough is known about the early lives of these children to permit more solidly based conclusions about the developmental impact of their bizarre circumstances (Skuse, 1984b).

Jarmila Koluchová (1972, 1976) studied one of these cases in Czechoslovakia. Identical twin boys were born in 1960 to a mother of normal intelligence who died shortly after their birth. When they were about 1½ years old their father remarried, and his new wife took an active dislike to them. The boys were forced to live in a small, bare closet, without adequate food, exercise, or sunshine. They were not allowed to enter those parts of the house where the other family members lived, and they were rarely visited.

The boys came to the attention of the authorities when they were 6 years old. They were abnormally small and suffered from rickets, a disease caused by a vitamin deficiency that leaves bones soft and bent. They could barely talk, they did not recognize common objects in photographs, and they were terrified of the new sights and sounds around them. The boys were taken to a children's home where they were housed with children younger than themselves in a nonthreatening environment and were well cared for. In these new circumstances, the twins soon began to gain weight, to take an active interest in their surroundings, and to learn to speak. When they were first tested at the age of 8 years, the boys' intelligence measured well below normal. But year by year their performance improved until, at the age of 14, both of them manifested perfectly normal intelligence (see Figure 7.1).

An even more severely neglected child was Genie, who was locked in a room by herself sometime before her second birthday (Curtiss, 1977). For more than 11 years, Genie spent her days chained onto a potty and her nights tied up in a sleeping bag. No one spoke to her. When her father came to tie her in for the night or to bring her food, he growled at her like a beast and scratched her with his fingernails.

Genie was a pitiful creature when she was liberated from these horrible circumstances. Although she was 13 years old, she weighed only 59 pounds and was only 4 feet, 6 inches tall. She rarely made a sound and was not toilet trained. She could not walk normally; instead, she shuffled her feet and swayed from side to side. Remarkably, a battery of psychological tests revealed that Genie had an amazing ability to perceive and think about spatial relationships even though she could barely speak.

Genie did not recover as much as the twin boys did. She learned to control her bowels and to walk normally, but she never developed normal language. She also learned a variety of appropriate social behaviors. When first found, she showed no emotion at all when people left her; eventually, though, she became attached to other people who lived in her hospital rehabilitation unit. She developed ways to make her visitors stay longer and became upset when they finally did leave.

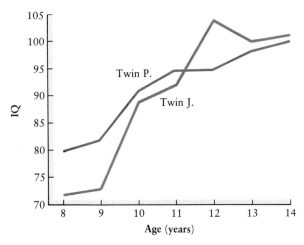

FIGURE 7.1   *Once the twins studied by Koluchová were released from isolation, their intellectual abilities showed gradual recovery until they were normal. (Adapted from Koluchová, 1976.)*

Studies of isolated children leave little doubt that severe isolation can profoundly disrupt normal development, but they also show that extreme early deprivation of caregiving and normal interaction with the environment is not necessarily devastating to later development (Skuse, 1984a). Fortunately, such cases are so rare that we cannot know just how long and how severe a child's isolation has to be before the damage it causes is irreversible. The infrequency of such cases also makes it difficult to assess the impact of isolation on individual aspects of development. Emotional, intellectual, and physical development may all be affected by isolation, but probably not all are affected in the same way (Clarke & Clarke, 1986).

An important question raised, but not answered, by the studies of extreme isolation is, how do the conditions of the isolation environment and the predispositions of isolated children interact to determine the extent of their later recovery? Is it important, for example, that the twins described by Koluchová had each other for company? Was Genie's aptitude for spatial thinking a special intellectual ability that would have shown up whether or not she had been isolated, or did it develop as a consequence of her immobility and her social isolation? The answers to such questions would help us understand the vulnerability to developmental disorders of children raised in less extreme but still adverse circumstances and the factors that enable them to recover despite these circumstances.

VULNERABILITY AND RESILIENCE

Even in times of relative peace and prosperity many adults find life a struggle. In responding to their own pressing needs, they create less than optimal environments for their children. Precisely because these situations are not extreme, they may persist for years and become permanent features of the family environment that shapes the development of the children. They may eventually contribute to delinquent behavior, failure in school, and mental health problems.

Michael Rutter and his colleagues (1975) conducted a large-scale study of the incidence of psychiatric disorders among 150 English families. They found four factors that, taken together, were strongly associated with childhood behavior problems and psychiatric disorders:

1. Family discord.
2. Parental social deviance of either a criminal or a psychiatric nature.
3. Social disadvantage, including low income, inadequate housing, and a large number of children close in age.
4. A poor school environment, including high rates of turnover and absence among staff and pupils and a large proportion of pupils from economically depressed homes.

None of these factors by itself was strongly associated with psychiatric disorders in childhood. But if as few as two of them were present at the same time — for example, if one parent had a personality disorder and the family had a low income — the risk that the child would suffer from a psychiatric disorder increased 400 percent.

The emphasis Rutter and his colleagues placed on the cumulative nature of risk factors is substantiated by a growing body of research. Many studies have demonstrated that a combination of biological, social, and ecological factors, interacting over a considerable period of time, is required to cause serious developmental problems (Garmezy & Rutter, 1988; Kopp & Kaler, 1989; Sameroff, 1989; Werner & Smith, 1982). At the same time, all of these researchers find marked individual differences among children who live in highly stressful circumstances (see Figure 7.2). Some of these children can cope with their difficulties better than others. This observation has led psychologists to search for the sources of such children's resilience in the face of hardship (Garmezy & Rutter, 1988).

Characteristics of the Family

The family is the main support system for the child. We would expect, then, that variations in the kinds of support that families provide for children should be associated with children's ability to withstand threats to their development. This idea is supported by a variety of research (Bronfenbrenner, 1989, reviews the evidence). Many of the ways in which family characteristics influence risk factors and resilience can be seen in the results of an ambitious longitudinal study of a large, multiracial group of children born on the Hawaiian island of Kauai (Werner & Smith, 1982). Statistically, these children were especially likely to

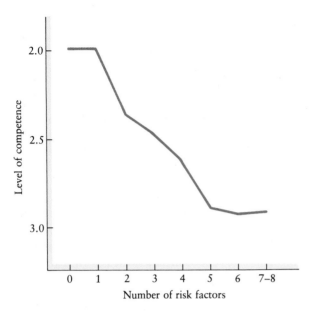

FIGURE 7.2   *The effects of increasing numbers of risk factors on 4-year-old children's social-emotional competence. Note that a single risk factor has no discernible effect, but two or more risk factors markedly lower children's social-emotional competence. (From Sameroff et al., 1987).*

suffer developmental problems because they came from low-income families, their rates of prematurity and stress during the birth process were higher than average, and their mothers had had little formal education. The researchers found that the following circumstances reduced the risk of developmental difficulties:

- The family had no more than four children.
- More than 2 years separated the child studied and the next younger or older sibling.
- Alternate caregivers were available to the mother within the household (father, grandparents, or older siblings).
- The work load of the mother, even when she was employed outside the home, was not excessive.
- The child had a substantial amount of attention by caregivers during infancy.
- A sibling was available as a caregiver or confidant during childhood.
- The family provided structure and rules during the child's adolescence.

- The family was cohesive.
- The child had an informal, multigenerational network of kin and friends during adolescence.
- The cumulative number of chronic stressful life events experienced during childhood and adolescence was not great.

Characteristics of the Community

In general, children in poor communities are more likely to suffer from developmental difficulties than are children in affluent communities (McLoyd, 1990; Rutter, 1989). Other characteristics of the communities in which children live also seem to affect the likelihood that they will develop problems. Those who live in poor inner-city neighborhoods, for example, have a significantly higher risk of developing a psychological disorder than do those who live in relatively poor small towns or rural areas (Lavik, 1977).

One factor found to reduce the impact of negative community characteristics is the strength of the social support networks provided by kin and social service agencies (Pence, 1989). For example, Susan Crockenberg (1987) found that community-based social support services for parents provided by the National Health Service in England significantly increased the amount and quality of teenage mothers' interactions with their infants. These mothers behaved in ways predictive of healthier developmental outcomes according to the criteria we described earlier.

Little is known at present about the factors outside the home that help to buffer children from stressful and depriving life circumstances. One factor that seems to make a difference is the school. Children in disadvantaged and discordant homes are less likely to develop psychological problems if they attend schools that have attentive personnel and good academic records (Rutter, 1987b).

Characteristics of the Child

By itself, no single temperamental trait evident in infancy, such as level of activity or distractibility, has been shown to predict adult psychological adjustment. Young adults who suffer from psychiatric disorders, however, are likely to differ from psychologically healthy adults in their temperamental profiles as infants, according to the findings of a longitudinal study by Alexander Thomas and Stella Chess (1984). These researchers report that infants characterized as "difficult"—those who display irregularity of biological functions, negative responses to new situations and people, and frequent negative moods—are more likely to experience psychological problems as adults.

Whether a difficult temperament is a risk factor, however, depends on one's cultural circumstances. A study by M. W. de Vries (1987) provides dramatic evidence that temperamental characteristics considered difficult in one cultural setting can be crucial to development in another. De Vries administered Chess and Thomas's Infant Temperament Questionnaire to the mothers of 48 4- to 5-month-old Masai (East African) parents. At the time this research was conducted, a severe drought was plaguing Masai country and many people left their native villages in search of food. When de Vries returned several months later to conduct follow-up tests with the 10 most difficult and 10 least difficult infants identified by the earlier questionnaires, he could locate only 13 families, 7 from the "easy" group and 6 from the "difficult" group. To his distress, de Vries found that 5 of the 7 "easy" children had died. Five of the 6 difficult children remained alive.

Additional evidence that characteristics of the child can influence the child's ability to survive difficult circumstances comes from the work of Emmie Werner and Ruth Smith (1982, 1989). On the basis of records provided by health, mental health, and social service agencies and educational institutions, as well as personal interviews and personality tests, they report that the children who were able to cope best with their life circumstances during their first two decades were those described by their mothers as "very active" and "socially responsive" when they were infants. The mothers' reports were verified by independent observers, who noted that these children displayed "pronounced autonomy" and a "positive social orientation." When they were examined during their second year of life, these children scored especially well on a variety of tests, including measures of motor and language development.

Transactional Models of Development

Although the evidence provided by studies of developmental risk shows that several factors increase the probability of long-term developmental damage, it also shows that to consider any one factor in isolation from the others would be a mistake. The various influences on development seem to work in combination. One study found that infants characterized as "difficult" were more likely than those characterized as "easy" to suffer developmental problems when their parents were in conflict and other stresses were acting on the family (Graham, Rutter, & George, 1973). The researchers suggest that temperamentally "difficult" children draw a lot of flak from their families during periods of stress, which makes their already difficult situation worse, whereas "easy" children are able to stay out of the line of fire. Alternatively, "easy" children may simply fail to become upset by experiences, such as family disputes, that severely affect "difficult" children.

Several researchers have developed models that emphasize the interplay among the various factors that influence development (Clarke & Clarke, 1986; Sameroff & Chandler, 1975). These **transactional models** trace the ways in which the characteristics of the child and the characteristics of the child's environment interact across time ("transact") to determine developmental outcomes.

Thomas and Chess (1984) used a transactional model to explain the developmental implications of early temperamental patterns. To show how parents' interpretations can interact with a child's temperamental traits to influence the child's mental health, they describe a girl who

> had severe [neurotic] symptoms starting in her preschool years. She was temperamentally a difficult child, and her father responded with rigid demands for quick, positive adaptation and hostile criticisms and punishment when the girl could not meet his expectations. The mother was intimidated by both her husband and daughter and was vacillating and anxious in her handling of the child. With this extremely negative parent-child interaction, the girl's symptoms grew worse. Psychotherapy was instituted, with only modest improvement. But when she was 9–10 years of age, the girl blossomed forth with musical and dramatic talent, which brought her favorable attention and praise from teachers and other parents. This talent also ranked high in her parents' own hierarchy of desirable attributes. Her father now began to see his daughter's intense and explosive

personality not as a sign of a "rotten kid," his previous label for her, but as evidence of a budding artist. He began to make allowances for her "artistic temperament," and with this the mother was able to relax and relate positively to her daughter. The girl was allowed to adapt at her own pace, and by adolescence all evidence of her neurotic symptoms and functioning had disappeared. (p. 7)

Rutter and his colleagues used a transactional model to explain the later life adjustments of young Londoners who had spent significant parts of their infancy and childhood in child-care facilities (Quinton & Rutter, 1988; Rutter, Quinton, & Hill, 1990). These children had been placed in institutions not because of any behavioral problems but because their parents could not cope with child rearing. Many of them remained in institutions throughout their infancy and early childhood. At 21 to 27 years old, they were compared with another group of the same age from the same part of London.

Focusing first on the "ex-care" women, Rutter and his colleagues found that these young adults had experienced a number of difficulties that were not shared by the women in the comparison group. To begin with, 42 percent had become pregnant before the age of 19 years, and 39 percent of them were no longer living with the biological father of their children. One-third had experienced a relatively serious breakdown in caring for their children. Only 5 percent of the women in the comparison group had become pregnant by the age of 19, all were living with the biological father of their children, and none had experienced a serious breakdown in the care of their children. When the women's current parenting practices were studied, the "ex-care" women were far more likely to receive poor ratings than were the women in the comparison group (see Table 7.2).

At first these findings may appear to be straightforward evidence of the long-term effects of early misfortune. But when they are viewed from the perspective of a transactional model, it becomes clear that the early misfortune set in motion a series of events that tended to perpetuate the difficulty. Institutional care led first to a lack of strong attachments during infancy and childhood and difficulties in forming good relationships with peers. These problems increased the likelihood of teenage pregnancy. The early pregnancy reduced the likelihood of obtaining further education or job training. The ensuing economic pressures created a disadvantaged environment, which in turn created the stresses that were the immediate cause of poor parenting.

Early institutionalization did not necessarily lead to continual misfortune, however. Those women raised in institutions who had supportive husbands were found to be just as effective at parenting as were the women in the comparison group. These positive results led the researchers to conclude that institution-

TABLE 7.2		
Child-Care Behaviors of Mothers Raised in Institutions and of a Comparison Group of Mothers (percent)		
Child-Care Difficulty	**Ex-Care Group** ($n = 40$)	**Comparison Group** ($n = 43$)
Lack of expression of warmth to children	45	19
Insensitivity	65	28
Lack of play with children	33	16
At least two of the above	59	23
Source: Quinton & Rutter, 1985.		

alization during infancy and childhood and the lack of strong personal attachments that goes with it do not necessarily doom women to become poor mothers. If the usual chain of consequences can be broken and favorable transactions can be established, normal behavior is likely to follow.

The profiles of the young men who had spent time in child-care institutions were similar in showing that positive later life experiences decreased their risk of long-term difficulties as well. One particularly interesting gender difference was that men were more likely than women to find a supportive partner in marriage and to raise their children in an intact family, thus blocking the transmission of their own negative early experiences to the next generation (Rutter, Quinton, & Hill, 1990).

RECOVERY FROM DEPRIVATION

The mounting evidence that the long-term consequences of early social or intellectual deprivation depend to a significant degree on later circumstances has spurred a search for principles of successful intervention. A key element in any effort to repair developmental damage is removal from the damaging environment, but such a change alone is not sufficient for recovery. When the Lebanese children were moved from the crèche to other institutions, they did not reach normal levels of development. The girls showed virtually no improvement, and although the boys showed significant recovery, it was by no means complete. Similarly, when Genie was removed from her isolation, she recovered to some degree, but not to a level considered normal for her age.

These findings raise questions about what conditions are necessary to foster recovery from early deprivation. Would the Lebanese girls have recovered as much as the boys if they had been placed in an institution with a more stimulating environment? Might the boys from the crèche have gained totally normal functioning, like the twins described by Koluchová, if they had been treated even better? And what about Genie? Is it possible that some as yet undiscovered environmental conditions might have allowed her to regain normal functioning? Or did her isolation start too early and last too long to permit her ever to recover completely?

Such questions are impossible to answer in full because human babies cannot deliberately be assigned to live in potentially damaging circumstances to satisfy the quest for scientific knowledge. Research with monkeys, however, combined with scattered studies of human subjects, suggests what some of the aids to recovery might be.

Harlow's Monkeys Revisited

In Chapter 6 we examined Harry Harlow's studies of infant monkeys raised in isolation with inanimate surrogate mothers. One of the important findings of that research was the difficulty the infant monkeys had developing normal social relations after they were introduced into cages with their peers. This was the case even with the monkeys who had become attached to surrogate terry-cloth mothers, although the severity of the behavioral disruption varied with the length of the isolation and the age of the monkey when it began (Suomi & Harlow, 1972). Monkeys who were totally isolated for only the first 3 months of life, for example, did not seem to be permanently affected by the experience. When they were moved to a group cage, they were initially overwhelmed by the more complex environment, but within a month they had become accepted members of the social group.

Monkeys who were totally isolated for their first 6 months of life, in contrast, rocked, bit, or scratched themselves compulsively when they were placed in a cage with other monkeys. Monkeys who had been isolated during the *second* 6 months of life (but not the first) became aggressive and fearful when they were put back with other monkeys.

The long-term behavior of these groups of monkeys also differed. Those whose isolation began after 6 months of social interaction in the colony recovered quickly and were able to mate normally when they came of age. But those whose 6-month isolation started at birth recovered only partially. At 3 years of age, when they should have been able to mate, they proved to be incapable of normal sexual behavior.

Isolates may grasp other monkeys of either sex by the head and thrust aimlessly, a semi-erotic exercise without amorous achievement. Another erotic genuflection is that of grasping at another monkey, male or female, at the midline and thrusting across their bodies. This exercise leaves the early totally isolated monkey working at cross-purposes with reality. (Harlow & Novak, 1973:468)

Total isolation for the entire first year of life produced full-fledged social misfits who showed no propensities for social play or social interchange (Harlow & Novak, 1973). When they were placed in a group cage, these monkeys were often the targets of aggression by their peers. As time passed they showed no signs of spontaneous recovery.

Recovery from the Effects of Isolation

After their initial experiments, Harlow and his associates thought that the period from birth to 6 months of age might be critical for social development in these monkeys. If this were the case, recovery would be impossible for monkeys isolated throughout this period, regardless of any subsequent changes in their

This mature female monkey, who was isolated for the first 6 months of life, finds it difficult to react to the baby monkey. But if the baby is sufficiently persistent in its attempts to interact, the older monkey may eventually learn to interact more or less normally with it.

environment. The researchers tried various ways of aiding the adaptation of such monkeys to their new social world. One technique they used was to punish the monkeys for inappropriate behaviors by administering a mildly painful shock. Another approach was to introduce them to the new environment slowly, on the assumption that an abrupt change from total isolation to the busy activity of the group cage induced an "emergence trauma" that blocked recovery. The ineffectiveness of all these efforts seemed to support the idea that there was a critical period for social development. As it turned out, such was not the case at all.

The first hint that there might be an effective therapy for these monkeys came from observations of the maternal behaviors of the females, who had been artificially inseminated (Suomi, Harlow, & McKinney, 1972). Many of them beat their newborns and sat on them, and few of the babies survived. If the baby did live, however, the mother began to recover. As the researchers watched these babies with their mothers, they began to suspect how this change came about. If the baby monkeys could manage to cling to their mother's chest, as newborn infant monkeys normally do, they survived. While clinging, they not only had access to life-sustaining milk but also could usually escape their mothers' attempts to harm them. The longer they held on and the stronger they grew, the more time their mothers spent behaving in ways that were approximately normal, if not loving. By the end of the usual period of nursing, the mothers were no longer abusive and interacted more or less normally with their babies. Even more striking was the caregiving behavior of these mothers when they had a second baby. It was indistinguishable from that of their nondeprived peers. They had recovered normal social functioning.

The recovery of these mothers led Harlow and his colleagues to speculate that it might be possible to reverse the social pathologies of previously isolated monkeys by introducing them into a mother-infant type of relationship with a younger monkey (Harlow & Novak, 1973; Suomi & Harlow, 1972). The researchers introduced normal 2- to 3-month-old monkeys, who were strong enough to survive the abuse they were likely to receive, into a cage with monkeys who had been isolated for 12 months. The playful, love-seeking babies provided just what the older monkeys needed to learn appropriate social behaviors. Over a period of 18 weeks, the former isolates gradually stopped rocking and clasping themselves compulsively. They began to move around more, to explore their environments, and to engage in social play. In the end, all of the former isolates became so well adjusted that even experienced researchers could seldom tell them from monkeys who had been raised normally.

Implications for Human Recovery

Harlow's research with monkeys suggests that placing previously isolated children in an environment in which they can interact with younger children may be therapeutic. This idea seems to be supported by the limited information available about the recovery of human children from extreme social deprivation. When the twins Koluchová (1972, 1976) studied were removed from their isolation, for example, they were at first placed in a special environment in which they lived with younger children. The twins recovered normal functioning despite their years of isolation.

Wyndol Furman, Donald Rahe, and Willard Hartup (1979) conducted a more formal test of the therapeutic potential of interactions with younger children. Through observations in day-care centers, the researchers identified 24 children between the ages of 2½ and 5 years who interacted so little with their peers that they were judged to be "socially isolated." These children were randomly assigned to three groups of eight children each. Each child in the first group participated in one-on-one play sessions with a child 1 to 1½ years old. The children in the second group participated in one-on-one play sessions with a child their own age. The final group served as a control and received no special treatment. Each pair of children had 10 play sessions of 20 minutes each over a 6-week period. During each session, the two children were placed together in a room in which there were blocks, puppets, clothes to dress up in, and other toys that might promote positive social interaction. An observer sitting in the corner of the room took notes but otherwise tried not to interfere with the children.

After the last play session, the social interactions of all the children in the day-care classrooms were rated by observers who did not know which children had participated in the study. Their reports showed that the rate of peer interaction had almost doubled for the socially isolated children who had played with younger children. The children who had played with agemates showed some improvement, but they did not

This baby monkey is "comforting" an older monkey raised in isolation.

differ statistically from the control group. These results show that interactions with younger children can be therapeutic in reducing social isolation, even after a relatively brief period of treatment.

Such evidence of successful therapeutic intervention suggests the intriguing possibility that a given child's failure to recover may actually be due to a psychologist's failure to arrange the proper environment, not to some irreversible damage done to the child. The best environment for a formerly deprived or isolated child is not necessarily one that is common or easy to create. Adults ordinarily have limited time to spend with children, and they may not instinctively provide the special forms of attention and playfulness that will help deprived children to reorganize their patterns of social interaction.

THE PRIMACY OF INFANCY RECONSIDERED

Cases of significant recovery both in young animals and in children who have experienced extreme isolation or lived in deprived environments indicate that practitioners cannot write such a child off; rather, a concerted effort should be made to give that child as therapeutic an environment as possible. When children are left to deal with undesirable life

When single parents marry, conditions for their children's development undergo a significant change. The different emotions of the adults and child in this picture clearly point to their contrasting evaluations of the impending changes in their lives.

circumstances, however, especially circumstances that are abnormal for the society in which they live, it should be expected that negative experiences during infancy will have detectable effects on their later development.

In cases of severe and extended protein malnutrition during infancy, for example, there is disturbing evidence that effects remain at least into adolescence (Hoorweg & Stanfield, 1976; Galler, Ramsey, & Solimano, 1985). Even the children described earlier in this chapter as making remarkable recoveries showed some residual signs of their past deprivation. The children in Dennis's study who were adopted after infancy continued to exhibit somewhat depressed levels of intellectual ability, and Tizard and her colleagues found that the institutionalized children who were adopted continued to display problems in social adjustment.

In attempting to arrive at an overall conclusion about the primacy of infancy, we would do well to return to the proverb "As the twig is bent, so grows the tree." If forces in the environment bend a sapling long enough, the tree may become so bent to the ground that its leaves cannot get the light they must have if the tree is ever to flower and hence to reproduce. But if the forces bending the tree are relieved in time, or if a gardener provides secure stakes to hold the tree upright, the only lasting effect may be a slight bend in the trunk. The tree will go on to flower and reproduce.

In applying this analogy to humans, we must take into account three factors that may modify the role of early experiences in later development. The first is the one we have been focusing on: changes in the environment. Whether these changes are positive (such as entering a supportive school environment or finding community-based social support networks) or negative (such as the outbreak of war or the death of a parent), they may create discontinuities in children's experiences that will set them on a new path of development.

The second factor that may act to modify the long-term effects of experience in infancy is the bio-social-behavioral shift that reorganizes physical and psychological functions into qualitatively new patterns in human babies (but not twigs!) as infancy draws to a close. Such factors as the acquisition of language, new cognitive capacities, and a new relationship with the social world at the end of infancy result in a new way of dealing with the world. A 12-month-old who is easily frustrated when she cannot get her own way may become a placid preschooler once she has learned to speak because she has acquired the ability to coordinate with her surroundings on her own terms. Alternatively, a placid baby who seems to take little interest in objects may suddenly display enormous curiosity and energy once he begins to walk.

The third factor is the change in the way children experience their environments as a result of their increased capacities. The separation anxiety shown by 1-year-olds when their caregivers are not present, for example, may be a realistic response for a helpless, relatively immobile infant because of the loss of crucial support that such separation entails. But 3-year-olds, who have a greater sense of autonomy because they can talk, walk, and run, are less dependent on their caregivers. Consequently, an experience that has a big effect on a 1-year-old may not affect a 3-year-old in the same way.

In recognition of the complicated interplay of the child's developing capacities, the changes these capacities bring about in the way the environment is experienced, and changes in the environment itself, psychologists who study the effects of experience in infancy focus on the *degree* of discontinuity between infancy and later periods, the identification of significant threads of continuity, and the mechanisms by which characteristics evident in early life are transformed or preserved in the transition from infancy to early childhood. Two psychological domains that have been studied intensively with respect to these issues are attachment and cognition.

Attachment

In research on the long-term consequences of the various patterns of attachment, the basic strategy is to assess children's attachment just before their first birthday and then again several years later (Bretherton & Waters, 1985). The evidence concerning later developmental outcomes of particular attachment patterns (see Chapter 6, pp. 229–232) is mixed. Leah Matas, Richard Arend, and Alan Sroufe (1978), for example, found that securely attached infants cooperate with their mothers in a difficult problem-solving task at the age of 2 years more effectively than children who manifest either anxious/avoidant or anxious/resistant attachment patterns. The securely attached babies also achieve higher scores on a scale of infant development (Main, 1973). They are more curious, they play more

effectively with their agemates when they are 3½ years old, and they have better relationships with their teachers (Erikson, Sroufe, & Egeland, 1985; Frankel & Bates, 1990; Sroufe & Fleeson, 1986). In a particularly extensive research project, Alan Sroufe and his colleagues (Elicker, Englund, & Sroufe, 1992; Sroufe, 1988) found that attachment classification during infancy predicted the quality of interactions between 10-year-old children and both their peers and camp counselors. Children who were assessed as securely attached in infancy were more skillful socially, formed more friendships, displayed more self-confidence, and were less dependent than other campers, according to both their counselors' reports and the researchers' observations.

On the other hand, John Bates, Christine Maslin, and Karen Frankel (1985) failed to find a relation between attachment behavior in the "strange situation" at 12 months and behavior problems at 3 years. Even studies that have found a general relationship between insecure attachment and later behavior problems sometimes report significant numbers of exceptions (Erikson, Sroufe, & Egeland, 1985). These inconsistencies in the findings mirror the complexities of predicting development in general.

Researchers who believe that patterns of attachment tend to remain consistent throughout development believe that children's attachment to their primary caregiver serves as the model for all later relationships. This view is similar to Freud's (see Chapter 6, p. 225). Inge Bretherton (1985), drawing on a formulation by John Bowlby (1969), has proposed that infants build up an **internal working model** of the way to behave toward other people and then use it to figure out what to do each time they enter a new situation. As long as the people they interact with behave in ways that allow them to apply their internal working model effectively, children can be expected to continue to use it in all of their relationships.

We saw in Chapter 6 (pp. 231–232) that anxious/resistant children tend to cling to their mothers. Suppose that we observe such children in a preschool setting. According to Sroufe and Fleeson (1986), who believe that children attempt to recapitulate the forms of interaction that are typical in the home — in Bretherton's terms, to apply their internal working models — these children could be expected to try to stay close to the teacher. If the teacher saw such behavior as politeness, cooperation, and eagerness to learn, the children would be likely to find this internal working model effective. Thus the same pattern of interaction would probably continue and might even be reinforced by the teacher. But suppose the teacher interpreted the children's behavior as overly dependent. She might arrange for them to act as helpmates to younger, shyer children, thereby providing them with the experience of a new form of social interaction. As a result, the children's internal working models might change and their subsequent interactions with others might differ from their previous patterns.

Here we see both how internal working models of relationships could produce continuity in social interactions over time and why it might be difficult to predict whether infants' patterns of interaction will be maintained in later life. The degree of continuity would depend on the nature of the initial internal working model and the extent to which it proves to be adaptive in the many contexts children encounter later in life.

Cognitive Development

For many decades researchers believed that individual differences in infants' intellectual development did not predict later achievement, that there was little continuity in cognitive processes from infancy to later life. After reviewing many studies that attempted to correlate scores on infant developmental scales with later test scores, Claire Kopp and Robert McCall (1982) unequivocally concluded that "tests given during the first 18 months of life do not predict childhood IQ to any useful or interesting degree" (p. 35).

Correlations between standardized psychological tests of children's abilities and tests of cognitive abilities in later years improve markedly for children older than 24 months. Still, tests given at 3, 4, and 5 years of age are not sufficiently predictive of children's subsequent behavior to be useful unless their functioning deviates a great deal from the norm (McCall, 1981; Sameroff, 1978).

In recent years psychologists have been somewhat more successful in demonstrating that individual cognitive characteristics measured in infancy do predict later intellectual abilities. The key difference between the earlier (generally unsuccessful) and more recent studies is that the earlier studies did not tap the same psychological processes both times the children were tested; standardized tests of infants' abilities focus

heavily on the sensorimotor sphere, whereas tests of older children's intellectual ability focus on the conceptual sphere.

Several contemporary psychologists argue that it is possible to demonstrate a modest degree of continuity from infancy into childhood when appropriate behaviors are sampled and are measured sensitively (Bornstein & Sigman, 1986; Rose et al., 1991; Sternberg, 1988). One line of support for claims of cognitive continuity between infancy and childhood comes from studies of the rate at which infants process visual information. It has been found, for example, that infants who habituate rapidly to repeated events subsequently display characteristics that psychologists associate with advanced intellectual development in early childhood. These children are, for instance, more likely to explore their environment rapidly, to play in relatively sophisticated ways, and to excel at various problem-solving and concept-formation tasks (Bornstein & Sigman, 1986).

A second technique depends on some infants' proclivity for looking at a novel stimulus. Lee Thompson, Joseph Fagan, and David Fulker (1991) found that children who showed a strong preference for scanning novel pictures were more likely than indifferent scanners to score well on tests of intellectual and language development at 2 and 3 years of age.

Coming to Terms with Limited Predictability

Although recent research into continuity in various psychological spheres indicates that there *are* significant continuities between infancy and later developmental periods, it falls well short of implying that any trait is always continuous and predictable. The correlations between behaviors in infancy and later are generally very modest. Consequently, data showing marked recovery from early traumatic conditions (which suggest that there can be marked changes, or discontinuities, in psychological functioning after infancy) and data showing a moderate correlation in individual behavioral traits over time (which imply continuity of functioning) should not be seen as contradictory. Together they provide evidence that a child's development is both continuous and discontinuous simultaneously.

Many years ago Sigmund Freud (1920/1924) pointed out that whether development seems continuous and predictable or discontinuous and uncertain depends to a certain extent on one's vantage point:

> So long as we trace the development [of a psychological process] from its final stage backwards, the connection appears continuous, and we feel we have gained an insight which is completely satisfactory or even exhaustive. But if we proceed the reverse way, if we start from the premises inferred from the analysis and try to follow these up to the final result, then we no longer get the impression of an inevitable sequence of events which could not be otherwise determined. We notice at once that there might have been another result. . . . (p. 226)

Figure 7.3 is a schematic representation of Freud's insight. If we start at some point in the future, E, and trace a life history back to its beginnings, A, we can build a convincing case for why that precise life history proceeded as it did; the developmental state at time E resulted from events at time D, which resulted from events at time C, and so on. At each decision point, we can sort out the various contributing factors and discern which had the most influence. Only one route leads into the past at each point. But standing at the beginning, A, and looking ahead to the future, we cannot foresee the choices that will be made at points B, C, and D. To borrow Robert Frost's metaphor, the bends in the diverging roads are hidden in the undergrowth.

For parents, the uncertainties of development during infancy are a natural source of anxiety. However, research on primacy shows us that this uncertainty has its good side. A perfectly predictable future

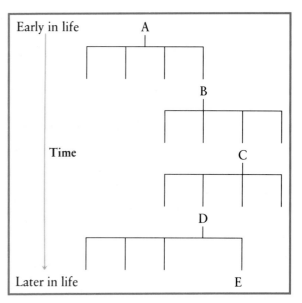

FIGURE 7.3 *It is relatively easy to trace development backward to its origins. But the many decision points with uncertain outcomes that confront organisms during the life span defeat efforts to predict their futures. (Adapted from Emde, Gaensbauer, & Harmon, 1976.)*

holds no possibility of choice. Without the uncertainties that arise from changes in the environment and the changes in the child that accompany development, parents could not dream about influencing the course of their baby's future. It would be immutable. With these uncertainties come the possibility and the challenge of taking advantage of those changes to promote the child's welfare.

SUMMARY

1. There is widespread belief in the primacy of infancy in shaping later behavior.
2. To foster optimal development, the caregiver must be sensitive and responsive to the infant's needs and signals. The kinds of sensitivity and responsiveness that are considered optimal in child rearing, and the way they are expressed, depend on the historical and cultural circumstances into which the child is born.
3. Research does not support the belief that responsive-

ness to an infant's cries will spoil the child and cause unrealistic expectations that will result in antisocial behavior later.
4. Paying too little attention to infants can result in learned helplessness, a state of mind that develops when children believe that nothing they do has any effect on what happens to them. Babies who develop learned helplessness fail to take initiative in their own behalf.

5. Separation from parents is upsetting to babies. However, such separations have long-term negative consequences only when they are of long duration or are repeated.

6. Experts are in dispute about the consequences of short daily separations resulting from out-of-home care during the first year of life.

7. Extended residence in a poorly staffed orphanage retards both mental and social development. Residence in a well-staffed orphanage produces less pronounced developmental difficulties. The degree to which children recover from such experiences depends on their subsequent environments and the age at which they leave the institution.

8. Total isolation leads to severe mental and social retardation. If children are moved to a supportive environment before they are 6 or 7 years old, recovery is sometimes possible. If their circumstances are not changed until adolescence, full recovery appears to be impossible.

9. Living in homes where a high level of discord is combined with social deviance or poverty and in communities where the school environment is poor puts children at risk for later psychiatric disorders.

10. Children's vulnerability to stressful circumstances depends to some extent on:

a. Variations in temperament.

b. Such family factors as the number of siblings, the mother's work load, and the presence of a network of kin and friends.

c. Characteristics of the community, such as whether the neighborhood is in an urban slum or a rural area.

d. The quality of the local school.

11. The processes that lead to various developmental outcomes can be thought of as transactions between child and environment over an extended period of time.

12. Studies of monkeys suggest that recovery from early isolation can be accomplished later than was once thought possible if an adequate therapeutic environment can be arranged. Research has shown that similar principles can be applied to socially isolated children.

13. Three factors limit the degree to which the psychological characteristics of older children and adults can be predicted from their characteristics as infants:

a. Changes in the environment

b. The qualitative reorganization of physical and psychological characteristics

c. Increases in capacities to cope with the environment

KEY TERMS

internal working model

learned helplessness

primacy

transactional models

SUGGESTED READINGS

CHESS, STELLA, & THOMAS, ALEXANDER. *Origins and Evolution of Behavior Disorders: From Infancy to Early Adulthood.* Cambridge, Mass.: Harvard University Press, 1987.

A comprehensive summary of one of the major longitudinal studies of developmental changes in personality. Rich clinical case studies provide excellent illustrations of the transactions between the individual and the environment that regulate continuities and discontinuities in development.

CURTISS, SUSAN. *Genie: A Psycholinguistic Study of a Modern-Day "Wild Child."* New York: Academic Press, 1977.

The amazing case study of a child isolated from normal human contact for many years. It provides thought-provoking evidence about the limits of human plasticity and the role of the environment in development.

NICOL, A. R. *Longitudinal Studies in Child Psychology and Psychiatry: Practical Lessons from Research Experience.* New York: Wiley, 1985.

Evaluation of the long-term effects of experience in infancy generally requires a longitudinal research design. This collection of essays provides insights into the practice and pitfalls of longitudinal research applied to many of the issues raised in this and preceding chapters.

ROBINS, LEE N., & RUTTER, MICHAEL. *Straight and Devious Pathways from Childhood to Adulthood.* New York: Cambridge University Press, 1990.

The essays in this book explore such varied risk factors as illegitimacy, parental absence, or mental illness in a parent to discover how experiences in early life affect later development.

WERNER, EMMIE E., & SMITH, RUTH S. *Vulnerable but Invincible: A Longitudinal Study of Resilient Children and Youth.* New York: McGraw-Hill, 1982.

This important study, which tracks the development of a large sample of children on the Hawaiian island of Kauai, reveals the strengths of longitudinal methods as means of addressing basic developmental issues and their ability to provide realistic data on which social policies affecting children can be based.

PART III

Early Childhood

By the age of 2½ or 3, children are clearly infants no longer. As they enter early childhood—the period between 2½ and 6—they lose their baby fat, their legs grow longer and thinner, and they move around the world with a great deal more confidence than they did only 6 months earlier. Within a short time they can usually ride a tricycle, control their bowels, and put on their own clothes. They can get out of bed quietly on Sunday morning and turn on the TV to amuse themselves while their parents still sleep. They can go over to a friend's house to play and take the role of flower girl or ring bearer at a wedding. Most 3-year-olds can talk an adult's ears off, even if their train of thought is difficult to follow, and they provide an avid audience for an interesting story. They can be bribed with promises of a later treat, but they won't necessarily accept the terms that are offered, and they may try to negotiate for a treat now as well as later. They develop theories about everything, which they constantly test against the realities around them.

Despite their developing independence, 3-year-olds need assistance from adults and older siblings in many areas. They cannot hold a pencil properly, string a loom, or tie their shoes. They do not yet have the ability to concentrate for long without a great deal of support. As a result, they often go off on tangents in their games, drawings, and conversations. One minute a 3-year-old may be mommy in a game of house, the next minute Cinderella, and the next a little girl in a hurry to go to the toilet. Children at this time still understand relatively little about the world in which they live and have little control over it. Thus they are prey to fears of monsters, the dark, dogs, and other apparent threats. They combat their awareness of being small and powerless by wishful, magical thinking that turns a little boy afraid of dogs into a big, brave, gun-toting cowboy who dominates the block.

Despite the long-term interest of developmental psychologists in early childhood, considerable uncertainty remains about how best to characterize this period of life. In some respects, it appears to be a distinctive stage of life with its own special modes of thinking, feeling, and acting. In other respects, it appears to be simply the beginning of a long period of gradual change that extends into adolescence and adulthood. In recent years early childhood has attracted special attention because many achievements once thought to arise no earlier than 7 or 8 years of age have been shown to appear by 3 to 4 years, challenging long-held ideas about childhood development.

Our discussion of early childhood development covers four chapters. Chapter 8 examines the nature of language and its development. Once children begin to acquire language, they can experience the world in an entirely new way. Language is the medium through which their parents instruct them about their roles in the world, acceptable behavior, and their culture's assumptions about how the world works. Simultaneously, language enables children to ask questions, to explain their thoughts and desires, and to make more effective demands on the people around them.

Chapter 9 examines the thinking of preschoolers. Leading theories are compared for their ability to explain how preschool children can behave with logical self-possession at one moment only to become fanciful and dependent the next. The chapter considers whether their apparently illogical behavior is the result of their lack of experience or is governed by its own special logic.

Chapter 10 considers the social development and personality formation of preschoolers: their ideas about themselves, the way they think about rules of proper behavior, and their relations with the people around them. The chapter focuses on the acquisition of sex roles and on children's changing ability to get along with each other, particularly as they learn to balance their own desires with the demands of their social group.

With these general characteristics of early childhood as background, Chapter 11 addresses the influence of various contexts on preschoolers' development: first the family, where children come to learn about who they are and what adults expect of them, then day-care centers, preschools, and the media.

CHAPTER 8

Language Acquisition

•

Both the real conversations of young children and the musings of a poet testify to the fact that learning to "say it right" is a lifelong process. As we have seen, the first blossoming of language around the age of 2 years is a basic component of the bio-social-behavioral shift that separates infancy from early childhood. Language development is by no means complete by age 2½, however. An infant can express only very limited ideas and acquires new vocabulary at a relatively slow rate (Bloom, 1973).

In the period between 2 and 6 years of age, children's mental and social lives are totally transformed by the explosive growth of their ability to comprehend and use language. They are estimated to be learning several words a day during this period, and by the time they are 6 years old their vocabularies have grown to anywhere between 8,000 and 14,000 words (Smith, 1926; Templin, 1957). They can understand verbal instructions ("Go wash your face and don't come back until it's clean"), chatter excitedly about the tiger they saw at the zoo, and insult their sisters and brothers. Although linguistic nuances take additional time to acquire and vocabulary continues to grow, 6-year-old children have become competent language users, an achievement that is essential if they are to perform the new cognitive tasks and social responsibilities that their society will assign them.

In this chapter we begin by reviewing and elaborating on the prelinguistic foundations of linguistic communication and the earliest stages of language formation discussed earlier. Next we trace the course of children's mastery of the four basic subsystems that constitute language: the sound system, the words, the grammar, and the uses to which language is put. With the facts of language development in hand, we turn to competing theories about the processes that underlie this unique and fundamental human capacity. Then we examine what is known about the necessary prerequisites for learning language and how language affects thought.

PRELINGUISTIC COMMUNICATION

The evidence presented in Chapters 3 through 7 leaves little doubt that children are born into the world predisposed to attend to language and to communicate with the people around them. They show a preference for language over other kinds of sounds at birth and are capable of differentiating the basic sound categories characteristic of the world's languages. Within a few days after birth they can distinguish the sounds of their native language from those of a foreign language, and well before they are able to speak intelligibly they have narrowed the categorical distinctions they recognize to the sound categories of the languages they hear around them (p. 130).

The repertoire of sounds newborns can make is initially limited; the only means they have of communicating is to cry. Though variations in cry patterns are not particularly informative, they do provide caregivers with rudimentary information about the causes of distress. At about 2½ months, babies' communication is enhanced by social smiles. Their sound repertoire expands to include cooing, which in turn is supplanted by babbling and jargoning; each change brings the baby closer to producing recognizable words.

At the same time that infants' capacity to distinguish and produce linguistic signals increases, they are also becoming more adept at interacting with the people and objects around them. At birth their weak muscles and blurred vision make it difficult to carry out the most elementary functions, such as nursing and examining an object in a coordinated way. Within a few weeks, with a good deal of support from the parents, these functions become part of a daily routine that gives structure to babies' limited experiences. And within a few months infants are able to engage in playful give-and-take games and to examine objects systematically. *Primary intersubjectivity,* the ability to match their behavior to that of another person and to share experiences in direct face-to-face interaction, emerges at about 3 months of age. It is evident in the rounds of helloing and smiling in which mothers and babies engage, to their mutual delight. At around 9 months, infants acquire the ability to share mental states with another person when the joint focus of attention is a third person, an activity, or an object — an ability called *secondary intersubjectivity*. The close link between secondary intersubjectivity and communication is seen clearly in the form of behavior referred to as social referencing, when babies check their mother's reactions to an uncertain event or an unfamiliar person and respond in accordance with her evaluation. Secondary intersubjectivity is a crucial precursor to language acquisition: when babies and their caregivers talk, they are sharing knowledge about the objects that are the focus of their joint attention (Tomasello, 1992).

Between the ages of 9 and 12 months, babies begin to point at objects (Bruner, 1983; Franco & Butterworth, 1991). Pointing is clearly a communicative act, but a primitive one. When 12-month-olds see a remote-controlled car roll past them, first they point at it and then they look to see how their mothers react to it (social referencing). At 18 months the function of pointing becomes communicative in a more complex way. Now the children are more likely first to look at their mothers to see if they are looking at the car and *then* to point to it. If infants this age are alone in the room when the electric car appears, they do not point until the adult walks back into the room, clearly demonstrating that their pointing is instrumental and meant to communicate.

During the second year of life children's halting first words accumulate, slowly to begin with and then at an increasing rate. At the same time, they acquire greater ability to produce and understand more complex sentences.

In sum, when we look at development from birth to the start of the third year of life, we can see that the capacity for communication has already developed to a remarkable degree before the child has acquired much conventional language at all.

THE PUZZLE OF LANGUAGE DEVELOPMENT

A fundamental issue that we glossed over in our treatment of the precursors and earliest manifestations of language is the strange fact that language, one of the most distinctive characteristics of our species, is still very poorly understood. Linguists, specialists in the study of language, can tell us a great deal about the structure of adult language, the history and meanings of words, and the physical apparatus that transmits utterances from one person to another. But they have not been able to give comprehensive answers to such basic questions as how children acquire language and how either children or adults compose and comprehend it. Developmental psychologists currently play a major part in the effort to understand both the development of language and its role in the development of children. Two questions that have proved difficult to answer are, How do children discover what words mean? (the problem of reference) and How do they learn to arrange words and parts of words in a way that has meaning to others? (the problem of grammar).

The Problem of Reference

Perhaps the most basic intuition that we have about language is that each word refers to something; words name real or fancied objects and relationships in the world. This idea seems so commonsensical that it is difficult to grasp the mystery it conceals, a mystery that no philosopher, linguist, or psychologist has ever adequately explained: How, among all the many things or relations to which any word or phrase may refer, do we ever learn to pick out its intended referent?

In Figure 8.1 we see the difficulty of determining what a word refers to. Look at the picture and try to decide what the father is saying. It's a puzzle, isn't it?

Some people may argue that the example is unfair because the utterance is in a foreign language. A little more reflection reveals that the example may be fair after all; in the beginning, all languages are foreign to newborn children, who must somehow figure out that the sounds they hear are in fact *meant* to refer to something, to indicate an actual object, action, or relation or to express a feeling.

To make the case clearer, suppose you know all of the words that the father says except one: "Look, son, there sits a *ptitsa*." Even this additional information does not tell us which of the objects in the scene is a *ptitsa*. The cat sitting on the wall? The helicopter sitting on the roof? Or the bird sitting in the tree? If you know Russian, you know that the father is pointing at

FIGURE 8.1   *For children just learning to talk, the problem of knowing what words refer to is particularly acute.*

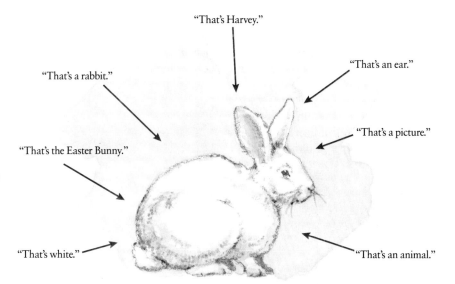

"That's Harvey."

"That's a rabbit."

"That's an ear."

"That's a picture."

"That's the Easter Bunny."

FIGURE 8.2   *An adult can point to the animal in this picture or to many parts of the animal and apply the same declaratory statement: "That's ————."* *How do children know what is being referred to? (From G. A. Miller, 1991.)*

"That's white."

"That's an animal."

the bird. But the language-learning child, even the Russian language-learning child, is not born knowing the meaning of the sound package *ptitsa*. Somehow the child must learn that when the father says *ptitsa* he is talking about the winged creature in the tree and not about any of the other objects.

The problem of how we come to know what words mean is complicated by the fact that a single object or event has many parts and features, which can be referred to in a great many ways. George Miller (1991) illustrates this problem with the example in Figure 8.2. If an adult points to the object in Figure 8.2 and refers to it in the various ways indicated, how is the child to avoid the conclusion that "rabbit," "ear," "white," and "Harvey" are synonyms? Yet somehow, despite all the apparently confusing ways in which objects and actions are referred to, children learn the meanings associated with all of the different kinds of references.

The Problem of Grammar

When we combine words into a comprehensible sentence, the words must be related not only to objects and events but to one another. The rules that govern both the sequence of words in a sentence and the ordering of parts of words (prefixes such as *pre-* begin words; suffixes such as *-ing* end words) are called the **grammar** of a language.

One clear indicator that even children as young as 2½ or 3 years old have some grasp of grammar comes from the errors they make when they string words together. When we hear a child make such statements as "My doggy runned away" or "Mommy, Johnny camed late," we know immediately that the child has confused one grammatical form with another. Such errors are so common that it is easy to overlook their significance. Children cannot have been taught to say such things, nor could they have learned them by simple imitation, because they virtually never hear such incorrect sentences uttered. Where could these sentences come from?

No less puzzling is the appearance in children's language of **recursion,** the embedding of sentences within each other. Recursion is one of the central properties of human language. It provides language with great economy and flexibility of expression. For example, the three sentences "The boy went to the beach," "He saw some fish," and "The boy got sunburned" can easily be combined to create "The boy who went to the beach saw some fish and got a sunburn": three sentences for the price of one. Only human communication exhibits this recursive capacity, and there is no evidence that it is ever consciously taught. How, then, do children develop it?

Here we see the central puzzle of language acquisition. On the one hand, almost all children, even many who are mentally retarded, acquire the ability to speak and communicate with words, so language appears to be a fundamental capacity that is easy for humans to acquire. On the other hand, the complexities and subtleties of language are so great that it is difficult to understand how word meanings or grammatical rules could ever be acquired.

Somehow, in the space of a very few years, children accomplish something denied all other species. What do they do, and how do they manage to do it?

With the early foundations of language and these puzzles in mind, it is now time to turn our attention to language itself, the system of communication fundamental to human life and human development.

FOUR SUBSYSTEMS OF LANGUAGE

Language, according to *Webster's Ninth New Collegiate Dictionary,* is "the words, their pronunciation, and the methods of combining them used and understood by a considerable community." This definition identifies four central aspects of language: sounds, words, methods of combining words, and the communal uses that language serves. We will describe the development of each of these aspects separately, but it is important to keep in mind the *systemic* nature of language: each of its aspects is connected to all of the others, and each aspect is itself a distinctive subsystem of elements. Unless some pathology interferes with normal development, these separate subsystems of language form a unified, organic whole.

Sounds

In the change from babbling to pronouncing words late in the first year, children give up their relative freedom to play with sounds and begin to vocalize the particular sounds and sound sequences that make up the words in their language community (Kuhl et al., 1992). Conformity to a restricted set of sounds brings with it both the ability to create meaningful distinctions between sounds and the freedom to speak rapidly. English-speaking adults talk at an average rate of about 150 words per minute. The words they use contain an average of 5 *phones* (sounds) each. This means that adults can easily produce about 12½ sounds per second, and with extra effort are capable of producing

as many as 25 to 30 sounds per second. According to Philip Lieberman (1984), this feat would be impossible if the set of sounds and sound combinations were not organized, with permissible combinations drastically restricted. These same restrictions help children to discover the system of sounds in the language they hear.

It takes children several years to master the pronunciation of the separate sounds of their native language. Their first efforts may be no more than crude stabs at the right sound pattern, almost as if they were attempting to get the tune right at the same time that they are working on the words. One frequent simplification is to leave out parts of words ("ca" instead of "cat"). Multisyllable words are often turned into a repeating pattern. For example, a child may use the sound pattern "bubba" to say "button," "butter," "bubble," and "baby." A long word, such as "motorcycle," can come out sounding like almost anything: "momo," "motokaka," or even "lomacity" (Preisser, Hodson, & Paden, 1988).

Children's mastery of the sound system of their native language proceeds unevenly. Sometimes a particular sound will prove especially difficult, even after many words that employ that sound are well understood. For example, at the age of 2½ Alexander could not say /l/ sounds at the beginning of words, so he could not pronounce the name of his friend's dog, Lucky. Instead, he consistently pronounced the name "Yucky," much to the amusement of his family. This error didn't concern Alex at all; he knew what other people were talking about when they referred to Lucky, and Lucky didn't seem to notice any problem when Alex called him.

Neil Smith (1971) showed that such substitutions do not arise because children are incapable of pronouncing certain sounds. When he asked one young child to say the word "puddle" it came out as "puzzle," but when he asked for "puzzle" it became "puggle"! Another child would always say "fick" instead of "thick" but he had no difficulty in saying "thick" when he meant to say "sick." Both examples indicate that the basic sounds of a language must be learned as part of the larger system into which they fit, rather than as isolated instances of pronunciation.

Evidently, newborn children can perceive the differences among the basic sounds, or phones, of their language. This does not mean, however, that phonemes, the categories of sound that are meaningful in a language, are "just there" at birth. When, for example, a child learns to employ the English phoneme /l/, more is involved than learning to reproduce a particular sound wave by creating a particular mouth shape. In reality, /l/ is a phoneme (sound category) of English because in our language it contrasts with other phonemes, such as /y/, as part of meaningful words. We hear /l/ and /y/ as different sounds only because they create different meanings: English speakers must learn that "lap" and "yap" or "lard" and "yard" are not simply variations in the pronunciation of a single word. Children's attention to the differences between sounds is not simply a mechanical skill, but develops along with their growing understanding of the meanings of words.

The close connection between phonemes and meanings becomes clear when one is attempting to learn a foreign language. Native speakers of Spanish, for whom the difference between /b/ and /v/ does not correspond to a difference in word meaning, find it difficult to produce or to hear any difference between them. To native English speakers "boat" and "vote" sound quite different; to Spanish speakers, these two words sound the same and thus may be spoken interchangeably. Likewise, the English speaker frequently has difficulty hearing and producing the difference between the French *u* and *ou*, because that difference does not exist in English.

Although it is often convenient to think of words as the basic units of meaning in language, many words contain more than one meaning-bearing part, or **morpheme**. A morpheme may be a whole word or only a part of one. The word "transplanted," for example, is made up of three morphemes. The root of the word is "plant," which means "to fix in place." The morpheme "trans" means "across, over, beyond" and the morpheme "ed" is a marker of past tense. We do not stop to ponder all of these relations when we say a sentence with the word "transplanted" in it. In fact, until the rules are pointed out, we rarely stop to think about the parts of words or the way we mold sounds. Yet every child must learn to decipher and reproduce just such intricate interweavings of sound and meaning.

Words

It takes no effort at all to figure out when children make their first sounds; a shrill cry at birth settles that

Learning to make language sounds properly takes time and practice.

question. It is more difficult to decide when children first use actual words. Adults may be so eager to claim the power of speech for their children that they discover "words" in early cooing and babbling. Genuine words, however, appear only late in the first year, after children have been babbling for some time and after the contours of their sounds have gradually become more speechlike (as we saw in Chapter 5).

It is useful to think of the process of word formation as a peculiar sort of collusion. Neither the adult nor the child really knows what the other is saying. Each tries to gather in a little meaning by supposing that the other's utterance fits a particular sound pattern that corresponds to a particular meaning. This joint effort, or collusion, may eventually result in something common, a word in a language that both can understand. This process may also fail. As the following examples make clear, the process can proceed in a variety of ways, depending on how the parent interprets the relation between the child's sounds and actions.

At 8 months Pablo began to say "dahdee." Although this "first" word sounds like "daddy," Pablo used "dahdee" for commands and requests when daddy was nowhere to be seen, so it must have had some other meaning for him. Adults interpreted "dahdee" to mean either "Take it from me" (when Pablo said it while he offered something to someone) or "Give it to me"; they ignored the fact that Pablo's first word sounded like "daddy." At about the age of 12 months, "dahdee" disappeared from Pablo's

Many first words label familiar objects.

vocabulary (Shopen, 1980). A different fate befell Brenan's first word, "whey." Around 1 year of age, Brenan began to say "whey" at the end of adults' sentences. In this case, the adults had a ready interpretation that allowed them to incorporate the word into the way they spoke to Brenan. "Whey" not only sounded something like "why," it also came at a position in normal conversational turn-taking where "why" would be a possible (if not always appropriate) thing to say. Brenan's parents therefore responded to "whey" as if Brenan had asked a question and rephrased what they had said in order to "answer his question," expanding on their original utterance. Over time, Brenan pronounced and used "whey" more and more like a true "why" until it became a genuine "why" in the English language (Griffin, 1983).

Yet another route to the formation of the first word is taken by Samoans, who believe that once infants begin to walk, they become cheeky and willful. In accordance with this belief, the only word that Samoan parents acknowledge as a child's first word is "tae," which is a Samoan curse word meaning "shit."

They explain this remarkable agreement among their children as confirmation of what every Samoan knows — that all young children are defiant and angry. In fact, young Samoan children may make a number of sounds that *might* be interpreted as words, but Samoan adults choose to hear and acknowledge only "tae" (Ochs, 1982).

Each of these instances differs from the others in significant ways, but all share the characteristics of a single process in which adults collude with each other and their children to create word meanings.

Words as mediators

At some point, usually around 11 to 12 months of age, babies seem to discover that the sound sequences they make can recruit adults' attention and help. What began as a process of making sounds that merely accompanied actions becomes a process of producing sounds that anticipate, guide, and stimulate action. With the emergence of the capacity to use words, children acquire the ability to organize their activity in a new way.

This key feature of language is illustrated in observations that Elizabeth Bates (1976) made of a 13-month-old girl:

> C. is seated in a corridor in front of the kitchen door. She looks toward her mother and calls with an acute sound *ha*. Mother comes over to her, and C. looks toward the kitchen, twisting her shoulders and upper body to do so. Mother carries her to the kitchen, and C. points toward the sink. Mother gives her a glass of water, and C. drinks it eagerly. (p. 55)

In this interaction we see several key features of the process of early word use. First, it is an excellent example of secondary intersubjectivity; initially the linguistic object, "ha," and then its referent, the glass of water, are jointly attended to by mother and child. Second, the episode illustrates clearly that it is the relation of the sound to action, and not just some property of the sound itself, that justifies the conclusion that a word has entered a person's vocabulary. Of course, in this case "ha," the "word" in question, functions in a very small community, the community of mother and child. Nonetheless, the child's use of "ha" displays an important new ability. Instead of seeking to operate *directly* on the object (by, for example, attempting to toddle over to the sink), the child operates *indirectly* through an idiosyncratic sound that evokes the desired behavior from the mother.

In this and the remaining chapters of this book, we will refer to the property of language illustrated in Bates's example as the *mediated* character of linguistic behavior. Until children acquire the ability to use and understand words, they are restricted to *im*mediate, or direct, actions. But with the advent of language, they can also deliberately act *in*directly, in a *mediated* manner. The same principle applies to the way children can be influenced by others; once they start to understand words, children can be influenced by others both directly, via nonverbal actions, and indirectly, through the mediating power of words (see Figure 8.3).

Alexander Luria (1981) beautifully summarized the new intellectual power that human beings obtain when their behavior begins to be mediated by words:

> The enormous advantage is that their world doubles. In the absence of words, humans would have to deal only with those things which they could perceive and manipulate directly. With the help of language, they can deal with things which they have not perceived even indirectly and with things which were part of the experience of earlier generations. Thus, the word adds another dimension to the world of humans. . . . Animals have only one world, the world of objects and situations which can be perceived by the senses. Humans have a double world. (p. 35)

but have memory

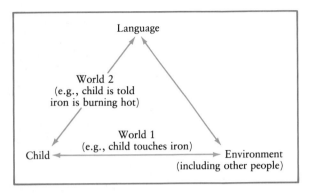

FIGURE 8.3 *Children experience the world in two distinctive ways once they acquire language: directly through their sensory contact with the physical environment (world 1) and indirectly (symbolically) through language (world 2).*

The earliest vocabulary

Evidence concerning children's earliest words comes from diaries kept by interested parents and tape recordings of young children's speech in their homes (Bloom, 1973; Gopnik, 1982; Nelson, 1973). Katherine Nelson (1973), for example, enlisted the aid of 18 families in keeping track of everything their infants said during the months they were acquiring their first words. She found that most early words (65 percent) label things and classes of things at the same time, such as "doggie," "juice," and "ball," or particular things, such as "Mommy," "Daddy," and pet names.

Nelson (1976) points out that the first words acquired are often closely linked to actions that the child can accomplish with the things named. "Hat" and "sock" are common in the initial vocabularies of American children, but "sweater" and "diapers" are

not, perhaps because little children can act more or less effectively on hats and socks, but sweaters and diapers are done to them. In addition, objects that can change and move (such as cars and animals) are likely to be named, whereas large, immobile objects such as trees and houses are "just there" and are not likely to be named. The fact that children tend to use words just at the moment when objects are changing and moving suggests a close link between words and actions in the young child's mind (Greenfield, 1991).

Alison Gopnik and Andrew Meltzoff (1986) found that in addition to labeling things, children use relational words to communicate about changes in the state or location of an object; "gone" may be said when an object disappears and "here" may announce its appearance. One of the most useful relational words in children's early vocabularies is "no," which can fulfill such important communicative functions as rejection, protest, or denial. "No" can also be used to comment on unfulfilled expectations or an object's absence. Given these multiple functions, it is little wonder that "no" is among the earliest and most frequently used words in a child's initial vocabulary (Bloom, 1973).

Gopnik and Meltzoff identify an additional class of early words that children use around the age of 2 to comment on their successes ("There!" "Hooray!") and failures ("Uh-oh"). This verbal evidence appears to fit well with Jerome Kagan's claim that children this age become capable of setting standards for themselves (see Chapter 6, p. 237).

BOX 8.1
Gulliver among the Laputans

The common-sense idea that words can be identified only with things and have fixed, unique meanings is very difficult to overcome. In the following passage from *Gulliver's Travels*, Jonathan Swift highlights the absurdities to which such common sense leads. In the land of Laputa, the people have listened to their literal-minded philosophers too attentively. Swift's hero, Gulliver, tells us:

> Since Words are only names for Things, it would be more convenient for all Men to carry about them such Things as were necessary to express the particular Business they are to discourse on. . . . Many of the most Learned and Wise adhere to the new Scheme of expressing themselves by Things, which hath only this Inconvenience attending it; that if a Man's Business be very great, and of various Kinds, he must be obliged in Proportion to carry a greater Bundle of Things upon his Back, unless he can afford one or two strong Servants to attend him. I have often beheld two of these Sages almost sinking under the Weight of their Packs, like Peddlers among us, who when they meet in the Streets, would lay down their Loads, open their Sacks, and hold Conversation for an Hour together; then put up their Implements, help each other to resume their Burthens, and take their Leave. (Swift, 1726/1970:158)

Early word meanings

To understand how word meanings change during a child's development, it is useful to keep in mind the fact that words do not have unique or fixed meanings. "Table," for example, can refer to an article of furniture or an arrangement of data in rows and columns, among other things. Nonetheless, the illusion that there is one word for each real-world referent remains strong. (See Jonathan Swift's satirical comment in Box 8.1.)

The ambiguity inherent in words can never be completely eradicated. But as children gain familiarity with the way people around them use words, their own uses come to conform more and more closely to the general uses in their cultural group. They achieve this feat by narrowing the set of circumstances in which they use some words while at the same time broadening the application of others (Anglin, 1986).

OVEREXTENSIONS.   Adults are amused when a 2-year-old wanders into a room full of adults and proceeds to call each of the men there "daddy." This form of mislabeling, in which many members of a category are referred to by a single term that adults use to label only one of them, is called **overextension** (Miller, 1991).

Children's early overextensions appear to be strongly influenced by perceptual features of the items named as well as by the way the things named function in children's actions (Anglin, 1977; Clark, 1973). A word such as "kitty" may be extended to cover a wide variety of four-legged animals because of their common shape, or it may cover a variety of soft, furry objects because of their similar texture. (See Table 8.1.)

UNDEREXTENSIONS.   Children also commit the error of **underextension,** using words in a narrower way than adults do (Anglin, 1983). For example, 1½-year-old Emmy used "bottle" only for the plastic bottle she drank from, not other kinds of bottles. Young children may hotly deny that a lizard, a fish, or a mommy is an animal. They may also believe that "cat" applies only to their family's cat, not to cats in the neighborhood or on television.

LEVELS OF ABSTRACTION.   In choosing how to refer to something, children must learn to deal with the fact that several words can be used to refer to the same object. In speaking of someone she sees at the supermarket, a child may point and say:

"Mommy, look at Sally."

"Mommy, look at that girl."

"Mommy, look at her."

"Mommy, look at that person."

Each of these methods of referring is equally accurate, but not equally appropriate in all circumstances. If the girl being talked about is well known to the mother and daughter, it would be inappropriate to refer to her as "that person" or "that girl." It might be appropriate under some circumstances to refer to the girl as "her" instead of "Sally," but to do so would change the meaning of the utterance. Children rapidly learn to distinguish among such nuances if the appropriate words are in their vocabularies.

An interesting characteristic of the early words that children say is that they tend to refer to objects at an intermediate level of abstraction. Only later do children acquire words that are more general or more specific (Nelson, 1979). By the standard of the basic store of words known to adults in the child's culture, these early words classify the world in categories that are neither too big nor too small.

Jeremy Anglin (1977) showed children posters that contained four pictures of objects that could be related at some level of abstraction and asked them for a label that applied to the whole (see Figure 8.4) One poster might have four pictures of roses, which could be labeled by the relatively specific category "roses"; another might have a rose, a daisy, a carnation, and a pansy, which could be labeled at the intermediate category of abstraction as "flowers"; a third might have an elm, a rose, a rubber plant, and a cactus, which could be labeled at a higher level of abstraction as "plants." Anglin found that adults were able to vary the level of generality of their labels appropriately, whereas children between the ages of 2 and 5 who were shown the posters tended to label all the sets at the same intermediate level of generality. They not only called the set containing the daisy, rose, carnation, and pansy "flowers," but also called all four roses "flowers," and were unable to provide a single label for the four plants. Most 4- and 5-year-olds were able both to name specific flowers and to use the general term "plants," but they too tended to use the intermediate term "flowers" far more than the adults did. These same results were obtained with many other category hierarchies, such as "food, fruit, apples" and "animals, dogs, collies."

Children's limitations in labeling specific objects and general categories do not indicate that they fail to understand differences between objects. Even

---

TABLE 8.1

Typical Overextensions in the Speech of Young Children

Child's Word	First Referent	Extensions	Possible Common Property
Bird	Sparrows	Cow, dogs, cats, any moving animal	Movement
Mooi	Moon	Cakes, round marks on window, round shapes in books, tooling on leather book covers, postmarks, letter O	Shape
Fly	Fly	Specks of dirt, dust, all small insects, his own toes, crumbs, small toad	Size
Koko	Cock crowing	Tunes played on a violin, piano, accordion, phonograph, all music, merry-go-round	Sound
Wau-wau	Dogs	All animals, toy dog, soft slippers, picture of old man in furs	Texture

Source: de Villiers & de Villiers, 1979.

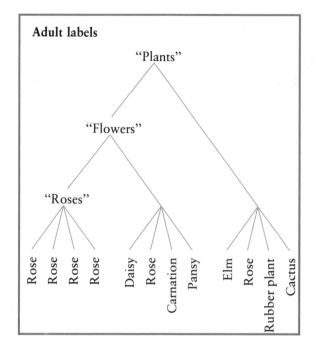
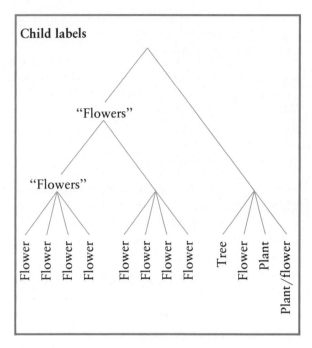

FIGURE 8.4   *Young children fail to differentiate levels of abstractness in the way they label sets of objects, using an intermediate level more frequently than adults do. (Adapted from Anglin, 1977.)*

children who labeled all pictures of dogs and cats as "cat" could still pick out the picture of the proper animal when they were asked to do so (Fremgen & Fay, 1980). Moreover, Jean Mandler and Patricia Bauer (1988) have demonstrated that under some conditions, children less than 2 years of age will show knowledge of superordinate categories (vehicles) as well as basic-level categories (truck, train, airplane), even though they tend to stick to the basic level in the categories they make.

The changing structure of children's vocabularies

Clearly the growth of children's vocabularies involves more than a simple increase in the number of individual words they know and more than a simple improvement in the accuracy with which they apply labels to objects. Vocabulary growth is accompanied by fundamental changes in the ways in which children relate words to one another and in the contexts in which they use words, ultimately creating qualitatively new systems of meaning (Carey, 1985; Luria, 1981; Nelson, 1979).

We can see the changing structure of word meanings by tracing the developmental course of a word such as "dog." The first words and phrases children use are likely to represent the specific circumstances of the first time they associate the sound and its referent, with their feelings playing as important a role as their thoughts. "Dog" may mean something terrible if the child has just been bitten; the same word may mean something wonderful if the dog lies on the rug and allows the child to burrow in its fur.

As children gain experience with dogs, the word "dog" begins to evoke a range of situations in which "dog" is only one element. The structure of the vocabulary at this stage is dominated by the pattern shown in Figure 8.5a. There "dog" is a unifying element in several situations: dog growls, dog barks, dog is petted, dog runs away, dog fights. Each situation is connected to "dog" in a specific way as part of a specific kind of action.

Further experience reveals that dogs are not the only creatures that bite. Cats bite too, and so do babies. At the same time, it becomes clear that cats do not bark (seals do) and they rarely take walks (but mommies do). Some of the things you can say about dogs you can just as easily say about cats (or seals or mommies), but some you cannot. When children are familiar with a large number of concrete situations in which the same word is used, words begin to acquire conceptual meanings that do not depend on any one context, or even on a real-world context. This aspect of language development is depicted in Figure 8.5b.

Once a word's meaning is influenced by the logical categories of the language, the word "dog" evokes more than the single emotion of fear or the single concrete image of Fido begging at the table. It has become part of an abstract system of word meanings independent of any particular situation. "Dog" becomes an instance of the category "domestic animal," or the more general category "animal," or the still more general category "living thing."

These changes in the organization of word meanings can be tracked in many ways. One of the simplest ways to assess the changing structure of children's vocabularies is to ask children of different ages to say the first word that comes to mind in response to each of a set of stimulus words. Early in development, children respond to "dog" with "bites" or "run," depending on the situation that the stimulus word evokes; later they respond to "dog" with "cat" or "animal" (Nelson, 1977). Very similar results are obtained when children are asked, "Tell me all you can about _____s" or "What kind of a thing is a _____?" (Anglin, 1985).

Although new forms of word meaning reshape the child's vocabulary, old forms do not disappear. Adults, no less than children, respond with fear, love, or some other emotion to "dog." And a great deal of adults' use of language depends on a fine-tuned appreciation of the way words relate to each other in particular contexts. What distinguishes the adult's vocabulary from the child's, other than its greater size, is the presence of several alternative forms of meaning for each word, which provide a richer arsenal of linguistic tools for reasoning about dogs, cats, and everything else, and for talking about these things with other people (Anglin, 1985).

Do early words stand for sentences?

The evidence presented so far indicates that children know something about the meanings of individual words very early. But this does not imply that they appreciate the new meanings that can arise from combinations of words or the possible changes of meaning

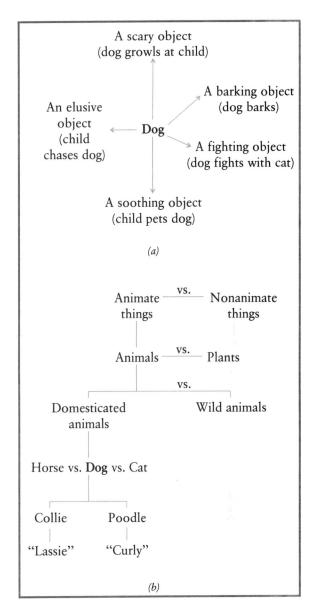

FIGURE 8.5 *(a) For the younger child, word meaning is dominated by the contexts of action in which the words have played a role. (b) As children acquire the formal conceptual categories of their language, the structure of word meanings changes accordingly. (Adapted from Luria, 1981.)*

that can be achieved by changes in word order ("John kissed Mary" versus "Mary kissed John").

Some investigators believe that even when children can utter only single words, these words stand for sentences because they are expressing whole ideas.

This child is making clear the close connection between gestures and words.

These theorists use the term **holophrase** to refer to one-word utterances that may stand for whole sentences. By this account holophrases contain the germ of later, more differentiated language capacities (McNeil, 1970). As children's memory capacity develops and as they become more familiar with language forms, they begin to use increasing numbers of words to articulate the concepts they once packed into one-word utterances.

Patricia Greenfield and Joshua Smith (1976) offer quite a different interpretation of single-word utterances. They believe that a single-word utterance stands not for a whole sentence but only for a particular element of the situation the child wants to talk about. Greenfield and Smith point out that children's single words are almost always accompanied by nonverbal elements, such as gestures and distinctive facial expressions. Thus the single word is not a holophrase but rather one element in a whole complex of communication that also includes nonverbal actions.

It is difficult to decide between competing theories of children's linguistic understanding at the stage of single-word utterances because too little information is available. Certainly, adults respond as if the child's single-word utterances are meaningful. A child says "Shoe," for example, and the father responds by saying, "Oh, you want Daddy to tie your shoelace." But how much of this meaning is the child's, and how much of it is the adult's interpretation of the utterance based on information gleaned from the context in which the child speaks? Until we have more to go on than a single word, it is especially difficult to determine where the child's word leaves off and the adult's interpretation begins. Although this problem of interpretation never completely disappears, it becomes less vexing when the child begins to string words together.

Sentences

As we saw in Chapter 6, a watershed of language development is reached toward the end of infancy, when children begin to produce utterances consisting of two or more words. Although these initial multiword utterances seldom form grammatical sentences, even two-word utterances carry more than twice as much information about the child's meaning as a single word alone. Each of the two words provides hints about what the child is saying, just as the single word provided hints. But now the relationship *between* the two words can also be used. With as few as two words children can indicate possession ("Daddy sock"), nonexistence ("All-gone cookie"), and a variety of other meanings. They can vary the order of the words to create different meanings ("Sock Daddy" and "Daddy sock"). This new potential for creating meaning by varying the arrangement of linguistic elements marks the birth of grammar. Grammatical expression develops over a long period of time.

Two-word utterances

Table 8.2 contains a sample of two-word utterances recorded in one of the first attempts to discover the earliest grammatical rules evident in the speech of infants (Braine, 1963). Several features of the English language stand out in these early "protosentences."

1. *Explicitness.* A child who can say "See boy" instead of being limited to "see" or "boy" in isolation has a better chance of communicating effectively to a listening adult, especially when the context does not make one specific interpretation obvious.
2. *Ordering.* Part of the gain in explicitness comes from the order in which the two words are used.

TABLE 8.2
Sample Two-Word Utterances

See boy	Mail come
See sock	Mama come
Night night office	Bunny do
Night night boat	Want do
More care	Boat off
More sing	Water off

Source: Braine, 1963.

"Boy see" or "Do bunny" does not convey the same meaning in English as "See boy" or "Bunny do." The gains in meaning that result from the order of elements in the utterance are the crucial evidence that something like grammar is beginning to organize the child's talk.

3. *Telegraphic quality.* In these two-word utterances children appear to be coding only the most obvious and essential parts of their ideas, in much the same way adults simplify their language when they send a telegram ("Mom. Cash low. All well. Send money. Love. Johnny"). Such utterances are more informative than single words, but they are often ambiguous.

The shortcomings of two-word utterances are illustrated in an amusing way by a series of incidents in *Higglety, Pigglety, Pop,* Maurice Sendak's tale of an adventurous dog who accepts a job as nanny for Baby, a child caught in the grip of the terrible twos. At first the dog attempts to get the baby to eat, and the baby says, "No eat!" In the second incident, the dog decides to eat the food himself, and the baby again says, "No eat!" Finally the baby and dog find themselves confronted by a lion, and the baby says for the third time, "No eat!"

As adults, we have ready interpretations of what the baby means in each instance. In the first case he appears to mean "I won't eat," in the second case he means "Don't eat my food," and in the third case he means "Don't eat me" (or, if he is feeling generous, "Don't eat us"). The difficulty with these two-word utterances is clear: the same sound pattern ("No eat") has at least three interpretations, and the utterance itself provides no clue to the meaning intended. The ambiguity of many two-word utterances is likely to restrict effective communication to occasions when listeners can reliably interpret the context in which the child is operating. Thus, effective communication about absent or abstract subjects is not yet possible.

Increasing complexity

As children begin to string more and more words together and consistently form complete sentences, they simultaneously increase the number, the complexity, and the variety of words and grammatical devices they use. These changes are illustrated by the following prodigious sentence spoken by an excited 2-year-old: "You can't pick up a big kitty 'cos a big kitty might bite!" (de Villiers & de Villiers, 1978:59).

This sentence is by no means typical of 2-year-olds, but it provides a good opportunity to assess how utterances that are more complex communicate more explicitly. The sentence communicates not only that the little girl doesn't want to pick up a big cat, but that no one should pick up a big cat; it also conveys her understanding that big cats sometimes bite but do not invariably do so. Such complex sentences communicate shades of meaning that help adults to respond sensitively to children's experiences.

As Figure 8.6 indicates, the length of 2-year-olds' utterances grows explosively, along with their vocabularies and grammatical abilities (Brown, 1973; Gopnik & Meltzoff, 1987). Note that the growth in the length of utterances is indicated by the average number of *morphemes* per utterance (or the "mean length of utterance" [MLU]), rather than by the average number of words. The phrase "That big bad boy plays ball," for example, contains six words and seven morphemes, whereas the phrase "Boys aren't playing" contains only three words but six morphemes *(boy, s, are, (not), play, ing).* The procedure of counting morphemes rather than words provides an index of a child's total potential for making meaning in a particular utterance.

GRAMMATICAL MORPHEMES. The complexity of the little girl's long sentence quoted earlier is attributable in large measure to just those little words and word parts that are systematically absent in two-word utterances. The article "a" ("a big kitty") indicates that it is big cats in general, not just this particular big cat, that

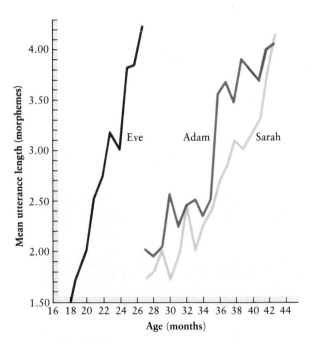

FIGURE 8.6 *This graph shows the rapid increase in the mean length of utterances made by three children during the first four years of life. (From Brown, 1973.)*

is worrisome. The word " 'cos" connects two propositions and indicates the causal relationship between them. The contraction "can't" specifies a particular relationship of negation. These elements are called **grammatical morphemes** because they are units that create meaning by showing the relations between other elements within the sentence. Whether the rate of language acquisition is fast or slow, grammatical morphemes appear in roughly the same sequence in the speech of all children (at least those who acquire English as a first language). As Table 8.3 indicates, the morpheme likely to appear first is *ing*, indicating the present progressive verb case. This verb form allows children to describe their ongoing activity. Morphemes indicating location, possession, and number make their appearance next. Children have many opportunities to use these morphemes in the course of play with toys; blocks are stacked one *on top of* another, dolls go *in* their cribs, and a little girl's lunch belongs *to her*. Morphemes that mark complex relations, such as *am* in "I'm going" (which codes a relation between the subject of the action and the time of the action), are generally slower to emerge.

The appearance of grammatical morphemes is a strong indicator that children are implicitly beginning to distinguish nouns and verbs, because their speech conforms to adult rules that specify which morphemes should be attached to which words in a sentence. Children demonstrate their intuitive grasp of the rules for using grammatical morphemes by the fact that they do not apply a past-tense morpheme to a noun ("girl*ed*"); nor do they place articles before verbs ("*a* walked"). By the time they are 5 or 6 years old, most children will have implicit command of all of the standard parts of speech they will use as adults.

COMPLEX CONSTRUCTIONS.   Between the ages of 2 and 6, children begin to use a great many grammatical devices, the "grammatical rules" that bedevil students in language classes throughout their school days. Some of these grammatical constructions obey rules of such subtlety that, although we follow them intuitively in our speech, we have great difficulty in making explicit the basis of our own judgments.

Small children's two- and three-word utterances may suggest that mastery of grammar requires no more than acquisition of a few ordering rules. But we need more than surface ordering principles to achieve competence in the use of language. Consider, for example, a common grammatical form known as the *tag question* (Dennis, Sugar, & Whitaker, 1982)—words added to the end of a declarative sentence to turn it into a question. "They won the prize, *didn't they?*" and "You will come, *won't you?*" are typical tag questions. It's no easy matter to provide a rule specifying how such questions are formed, is it?

A somewhat more complicated demonstration of the gap between our ability to use language and our ability to understand the principles that underlie our talk is provided by the following sentences:

1. John is easy to please.
2. John is willing to please.

Both sentences seem to follow a single ordering principle. But at some level these sentences, despite their surface similarity, must differ grammatically. We can clarify the difference by adding a single word to the end of each sentence while still preserving the order of elements. Compare the two new sentences:

3. John is willing to please Bill.
4. John is easy to please Bill.

TABLE 8.3
Usual Order of Acquiring Grammatical Morphemes

Morpheme	Meaning	Example
Present progressive	Temporary duration	I walk*ing*
In	Containment	*In* basket
On	Support	*On* floor
Plural	Number	Two ball*s*
Past irregular	Prior occurrence	It *broke*
Possessive inflection	Possession	Adam*'s* ball
To be without contraction	Number; prior occurrence	There it *is*
Articles	Specific/nonspecific	That *a* book
		That *the* dog
Past regular	Prior occurrence	Adam walk*ed*
Third person regular	Number; prior occurrence	He walk*s*
Third person irregular	Number; prior occurrence	He *does*
		She *has*
Uncontractible progressive auxiliary	Temporary duration; number; prior occurrence	This *is going*
Contraction of *to be*	Number; prior occurrence	That*'s* book
Contractible progressive auxiliary	Temporary duration; prior occurrence	I*'m* walking

Source: Brown, 1973.

Sentence 3 is just as acceptable in the English language as sentences 1 and 2, but sentence 4, despite the fact that the surface ordering principles are unchanged, is not grammatically acceptable, and we cannot interpret it.

Such examples suggest that acquiring the grammar of a language involves mastery of highly abstract rules that even adult speakers of a language cannot explain (unless they are linguists!). Yet such rules appear to be acquired by all normal children, regardless of the language they speak. Tag questions, for example, are mastered by the time children are 8 or 9 years old (Dennis, Sugar, & Whitaker, 1982).

Children's difficulties in mastering the subtle grammatical constructions demanded by adult language, even after they know the meanings of the words involved, have been studied by Carol Chomsky (1969). She tells of Lisa, 6½ years old, who was seated at a table on which there was a doll with a blindfold over its eyes.

Adult: Is this doll easy to see or hard to see?

Lisa: Hard to see.

Adult: Will you make her easy to see?

Lisa: If I can get this [blindfold] untied.

Adult: Will you explain why she was hard to see?

Lisa: *[to doll]* Because you had a blindfold over your eyes.

Adult: And what did you do?

Lisa: I took it off.

Before this interchange, Carol Chomsky had made certain that Lisa knew the meaning of "easy." Lisa knew that it is easy to sit in a chair but hard to climb a tree. What, then, was her difficulty in the case of the blindfolded doll? Chomsky argues that children still assume that the person mentioned at the beginning of a sentence is the one who carries out the action (in this case, that it is the doll who does the seeing).

This assumption is often correct, but it is not correct in the case of "easy to see"; children must learn to dig beneath the surface features of the sentence to find the true relationship it codes.

The Uses of Language

In order to communicate effectively, children must master more than the grammatical rules of their language and the meanings of its words. Such knowledge would be of little use if they did not simultaneously master the **pragmatic uses of language**—that is, the ability to select words and word orderings that are appropriate to their actions in particular contexts.

Conversational acts

One way of describing how language is used for pragmatic purposes is to think of utterances as **conversational acts,** actions that achieve goals through language. According to Elizabeth Bates and her colleagues (Bates, Camaioni, & Volterra, 1975), children's earliest conversational acts fall into two categories, proto-imperatives and proto-declaratives. *Proto-imperatives* are ways of engaging another person to achieve a desired object. When our daughter, Jenny, first began holding up her cup and saying "More," she was using a proto-imperative.

Proto-declaratives are ways of referring. Perhaps the earliest form of a proto-declarative is not verbal at all, but the act of pointing. Nonverbal pointing is soon accompanied by words, as when a baby points to a dog and says "Doggie." Another early form of proto-declarative conversation is giving. As infants master this form, they may be seen bringing all of their toys, one after another, to lay at a visitor's feet if each gift is acknowledged by a smile or a comment (Bates, O'Connell, & Shore, 1987).

In the process of acquiring the pragmatic aspects of language, children also come to understand that a single sequence of words may accomplish several alternative goals. A sentence such as "Is the door shut?" has the grammatical form of a request for information (you want to know whether the door is open or shut). But "Is the door shut?" may also be a request for action or a criticism. In these cases, "Is the door shut?" is pragmatically equivalent to "Please shut the door" and "You have forgotten to shut the door again."

As children's vocabularies grow and their command of grammar improves, so does the range of actions they can be induced to perform and the actions they can carry out through language. Marilyn Shatz (1974, 1978) found that children as young as 2 years responded correctly to their mother's indirect commands, such as "Is the door shut?" Instead of responding to the surface grammatical form and answering "Yes" or "No," Shatz's toddlers went to shut the door. A 3-year-old observed by John Dore (1979) used three different ways to accomplish a single goal: "Get off the blocks!" "Why don't you stay away from my blocks?" and "You're standing on my blocks."

In the hope of getting a proper overall picture of language development, a number of scholars have attempted to catalog the full set of language functions that children have to master (Dore, Gearhart, & Newman, 1979). This task has proved to be formidable because there is so much variety in the uses of speech, even by 3-year-olds. The 3- and 4-year-olds these researchers studied have come a long way from mere pointing or the use of idiosyncratic "words" such as "ha." They can solicit information ("What happened?") or action ("Put the toy down!"). They can assert facts and rules ("We have a boat"), utter warnings ("Watch out!"), and clarify earlier statements.

Conversational conventions

As part of the task of learning how to achieve their goals through talking, children must come to appreciate basic rules that apply in any conversation. The master rule of ordinary conversation, according to the philosopher H. P. Grice (1975:45), is the **cooperative principle:** make your contributions to conversation at the required time and for the accepted purpose of the talk exchange. Grice lists four maxims that must be honored if the cooperative principle is to operate effectively:

1. *The maxim of quantity:* Speak neither more nor less than is required.

2. *The maxim of quality:* Speak the truth and avoid falsehood.

3. *The maxim of relevance:* Speak in a relevant and informative way.

4. *The maxim of clarity:* Speak so as to avoid obscurity and ambiguity.

Young children take great delight in their ability to communicate using their rapidly developing linguistic skills.

In conversation among adults everyone understands that these rules are often violated to make deliberately nonconventional statements. The act of encouraging a child, for example, may evoke an exaggerated statement such as "You can do it, Suzie. You're a big girl now, and you know that big girls try hard. They don't give up. I'm sure you can do it." This kind of talk might violate the maxim of quantity (the speaker is saying more than is required) except for the fact that it is acceptable for the special task of providing encouragement.

Some figurative uses of language (such as irony, in which someone says the obvious) depend on deliberate violation of a conversational maxim (see Box 8.2). Learning the circumstances in which the basic speech-act conventions do not apply requires years of additional experience (Winner, 1988).

Children must also acquire knowledge of the social conventions that regulate what is to be said and how to say it. These may vary markedly from one culture to another. In the United States children are expected to say "please" when they request something and "thank you" when they are given something. But in a Colombian mestizo community such verbal formulas are frowned upon in the belief that "please" and "thank you" signal the speaker's inferiority; obedience, not formulaic politeness, is what these adults

expect of their children (Reichel-Dolmatoff & Reichel-Dolmatoff, 1961).

Taking account of the listener

The core meaning of the word "communicate" is "to place in common." Language is said to communicate when speakers and listeners come to share a common interpretation of what is said. Yet a major limitation of the language of young children, as we have seen, is that it leaves so much of the interpretive work to the listener. In this sense, children's language is not fully communicative. Children's increasing knowledge of word meanings and mastery of grammatical rules reduce this problem but by no means eliminate it.

One of the skills that children must master in order to make their language communicative is saying things in such a way that the meaning will be clear from the listener's point of view. An awareness of this necessity is evident at an early age in rudimentary form. The skills required develop slowly, however, in the years from 2½ to 8, and even adults sometimes fail to take their listener's knowledge and perspective into account.

Children as young as 2½ years of age show that they are able to take the listener into account by modifying what they say to include information important

BOX 8.2
Figurative Language

A 2½-year-old runs up to his parents, points at his yellow plastic baseball bat, and says with delight, "Corn, corn!" A 1½-year-old sends a toy car twisting along his mother's arm and exclaims, "Nake" (snake). At first glance these children may appear to be overextending the meanings of their words. But a variety of evidence suggests that not long after children begin to name objects, they begin to use words figuratively as well as literally. They deliberately call objects by the name of something else to which it bears some striking resemblance. Such renamings are in fact deliberate metaphors (Winner et al., 1979). Significantly, the beginnings of metaphorical language coincide with the onset of symbolic play. In both forms of behavior, the 2-year-old child treats objects and events nonliterally.

Figurative use of words provides evidence that language production is a creative process, not a simple imitative one. As Ellen Winner and her colleagues point out, in order to generate a metaphor, children must recognize and express a similarity between two things in some novel way that they have never heard before.

Winner and her co-workers identify two distinct routes for the development of nonliteral, metaphoric speech. Some metaphors are closely tied to action: A 2-year-old rubs a fur teddy bear against a wooden armchair, then holds up the teddy bear and says, "Zucchini." Then he points to the arm of the chair and calls it "grater." A teddy bear does not look at all like a zucchini and most wooden chair arms do not look like vegetable graters; the resemblance that makes these words meaningful depends on the way the objects fit into a typical action sequence. Perceptual metaphors, by contrast, take on meaning from the physical similarities of the objects compared. When a little child exclaims, "Oh, mommy, how balloony your legs look!" or "Can't you see, I'm barefoot all over!" she is using perceptual metaphors (Chukovsky, 1968). Because adults base some of their metaphors on the same kinds of physical similarities that children use to form theirs, adults are often able to figure out what the child means.

Although children between the ages of 2 and 6 years use a good deal of figurative language, they often fail to understand the figurative meaning of adult speech that does not depend on simple actions or on an object's perceptual characteristics. Kornei Chukovsky, a Russian linguist, translator, and children's poet, was especially impressed by the special intelligence revealed by children's misunderstandings of adults' figurative speech. His examples are difficult to improve upon:

> A woman . . . asked her 4-year-old, Natasha: "Tell me, what does it mean to say that a person is trying to drown another in a spoonful of water [a Russian expression]?"
>
> "What did you say? In what kind of a spoon? Say that again."
>
> The mother repeated the adage.
>
> "That's impossible!" Natasha said categorically. "It can never happen!"
>
> Right there and then she demonstrated the physical impossibility of such an act; she grabbed a spoon and quickly placed it on the floor.
>
> "Look, here am I," and she stood on the spoon. "All right, drown me. There isn't enough room for a whole person—all of him will remain on top. . . . Let's not talk about it any more—it's such nonsense!"

> Four-year-old Olia, who came with her mother to visit a Moscow aunt, looked closely at this aunt and her husband as they were all having tea, and soon remarked with obvious disappointment: "Mama! You said that uncle always sits on Aunt Aniuta's neck [a Russian expression for being bossy and controlling] but he has been sitting on a chair all the time that we've been here." (Chukovsky, 1968:12–13)

As children begin to master their native language and approach the age when they will be expected to acquire adult skills, either as apprentices or in school, their freewheeling use of figurative language declines. On the one hand, this narrowing of linguistic adventurism can be considered a good thing: children are learning what is conventional and acceptable in their community. On the other hand, a good deal of the creativity goes out of their speech. It may take some effort for them to regain their sense of delight in discovering new properties of the world through figurative language.

to the listener (Wellman & Lempers, 1977). By the time they are 3½ years old are sufficiently mindful of what other people need to know that they provide extra information to someone who is blindfolded (Maratsos, 1973). They use simpler language when they talk to younger children than when they talk to adults, an indication that in some way they know the younger child's language ability is more primitive than their own (Tomasello & Mannle, 1985).

Marilyn Shatz and Rochel Gelman (1973) found that when 4-year-olds play with 2-year-olds, the older children shorten their sentences, speak more slowly, and simplify both their vocabulary and their grammar to make it easier for the younger children to understand. This ability to modify speech so that younger children can easily understand it does not depend on experience in talking to younger children. Only children are just as likely to simplify their speech as children with little brothers and sisters. Another study demonstrated that small children make the same kinds of simplifications in their speech when they play with a baby doll, but not when they play with a grown-up doll (Sachs & Devin, 1973).

Even four-year-olds adapt their language when speaking to younger children.

EXPLANATIONS OF LANGUAGE ACQUISITION

During much of the twentieth century, two widely divergent theories have organized a great deal of the research on language acquisition. These theories correspond roughly to the polar positions on the sources of human development—nature versus nurture—discussed in Chapter 1. The *learning-theory* approach attributes language to nurture; it accords the leading role in language acquisition to children's environments, especially to the language environment and teaching activities provided by adults. The *nativist* approach attributes language acquisition largely to nature; it assumes that children are born ready to learn language, and that as they mature, their language-using capacity appears as naturally as walking or breathing, without the need for any special training.

In recent decades a variety of *interactionist* approaches to language acquisition have gained prominence. Interactionists hold that both nature and nurture play significant roles in the acquisition of language as in other areas of human development. They also believe that children's language is closely tied to their overall mental development. (Table 8.4 summarizes the basic concepts of the major competing approaches to the development of language.)

Two kinds of interactionist approaches can be distinguished. The first, which is associated with Piaget's universal constructivism, emphasizes the way in which cognitive development sets the stage for language development. The second, which is associated with the cultural-context perspective, emphasizes the way in which linguistic and cognitive developments converge in early childhood to bring about changes in both language and cognition.

The Learning-Theory Explanation

The basic assumption of the learning-theory view is that the development of language is just like the development of other behaviors and conforms to the same laws of learning. According to this point of view, language acquisition depends on imitation and on learning by association through the mechanisms of classical and operant conditioning (Miller & Dollard, 1941; Skinner, 1957; Staats, 1968).

TABLE 8.4
Salient Features of Major Approaches to Language Acquisition

Theory	Major Causal Factor	Mechanism	Major Phenomenon Explained
Learning	Environment	Imitation, conditioning	Word meaning
Nativist	Heredity	Triggering	Syntax
Interactionist (cognitive hypothesis)	Interaction of social and biological factors	Assimilation-accommodation	Correlation of cognitive and linguistic developments
Interactionist (cultural-context approach)	Cultural mediation of social-biological interaction	Coordination in cultural scripts	Language-thought relationships

Perhaps the first statement of this view was provided by the early Christian philosopher St. Augustine (A.D. 354–430). Recalling his childhood, he wrote:

> When they named any thing, and as they spoke turned towards it, I saw and remembered that they called what one would point out by the name they uttered. . . . And thus by constantly hearing words, as they occurred in various sentences, I collected gradually for what they stood; and having broken in my mouth to these signs, I thereby gave utterance to my will. (Augustine, 1961:4)

Classical conditioning

The process of associating objects and words described by St. Augustine is similar to the process that learning theorists refer to as *classical conditioning* (see Chapter 4, p. 155). Table 8.5 shows how the process operates in the acquisition of the word "candy."

A child who hears the word "candy" for the first time cannot know what it means. But if the sound "candy" is reliably paired with a sweet taste, the child begins to associate the sound and the object, thereby learning part of what the sound "candy" means. According to learning theorists, the child grasps the meaning of "candy" as the sum of all the associations that the word evokes after it has been paired with a wide variety of experiences (Mowrer, 1950).

Learning theorists use the classical conditioning model to account for the way children learn to *under-*

stand language, but this mechanism does not account for a child's ability to *produce* language. To explain this aspect of language acquisition, learning theorists point to the mechanism of operant conditioning.

Operant conditioning

The operant explanation begins with the observation, described in Chapter 4 (p. 157), that children emit a rich repertoire of sounds more or less at random during the early phases of babbling. These sounds represent the initial elements of spoken language, which, according to the learning theorists, are gradually shaped through reinforcement and refined through the child's practice. The sound "da," for example, might be shaped into "dog" or "mo" into "more" by a parent's enthusiastic attention to the child's successively closer approximations to the sound of the word.

The process of language acquisition proposed by learning theorists applies to all societies at all times, but the particulars will vary from one language environment to another. An American child growing up in Boston will acquire a different way of pronouncing "Boston" ("Baaston") than a New Yorker ("Bawstin"). A Kpelle child growing up in West Africa will learn to be sensitive to the sound contours of words in order to pronounce the word *kali* with a rising tone on *a* to mean "hoe" and with a falling tone to mean "leopard"; an American child, whose history of reinforcement has rendered rising and falling tones insignificant as meaning-bearing features, may not even hear the difference.

TABLE 8.5

An Example of How Word Meaning Is Acquired Through Classical Conditioning

Stimulus	Response
INITIAL STATE	
Sound of word "candy" ⟶	Orientation (look at candy)
Taste of candy in mouth* ⟶	Salivation Sucking Pleasure
REPEATED PAIRING OF WORD AND OBJECT	
Sound of word "candy" and Taste of candy in mouth ⟶	Salivation Sucking Pleasure
AFTER REPEATED PAIRING	
Sound of word "candy" ⟶	Salivation Pleasure

* After the word "candy" has been paired with the sight of candy and the taste of candy, the word "candy" begins to acquire the meaning "tastes good."

Imitation

It seems obvious that imitation is involved in language acquisition if only because children acquire the languages they hear around them, rather than inventing totally new languages that adults cannot understand. Moreover, modern research has shown that young children often learn to name things by hearing someone else name them and then repeating what they hear (Leonard et al., 1983).

Simple imitation, however, does not appear to explain how children acquire the ability to compose complex grammatical patterns or the tendency to use grammatical forms they have never heard to express new ideas. Children often use a grammatical morpheme correctly the first time they say it and then go through a period of incorrect usage before returning to the correct form. After months of using the correct plural form for "hand," for instance, children may go through a period in which they say "handses" before

returning to "hands." They certainly never heard anyone say "handses," so while they may have learned to say "hands" by imitation, imitation cannot explain the course of the development of this grammatical form.

These and similar complexities have led researchers who believe that imitation is important in language acquisition to a more complicated notion of how imitation is accomplished. With respect to "handses," Gisela Speidel and Keith Nelson (1989) suggest that it is necessary to recognize that imitation can be selectively directed at different stimuli. Initially the child may have attended to and imitated whole words. As the child becomes sensitive to grammatical morphemes, *es* becomes a target of imitation. Eventually, however, the child learns to form some plurals with *s*, others with *es*, and still others in even more irregular ways (mouse/mice, goose/geese, and so on).

Recognizing the need to think more complexly about imitation, Albert Bandura (1977, 1986), a leading learning theorist, proposed that language is acquired through a kind of imitation called **abstract modeling**. This kind of modeling is called abstract because, in Bandura's view, even when children imitate specific utterances, they abstract from them the general linguistic principles that underlie them. Thus a child repeating "Juana walked home" abstracts the grammatical principle of adding *ed* to show past tense, and can then go on to say "Juana fixed the toy" without having to hear those exact words first.

The Nativist Explanation

The nativist view of language acquisition has been dominated by the work of the linguist Noam Chomsky (1975, 1986). According to Chomsky, the fact that children produce a vast array of sentences that they have never before heard makes it implausible that language could be acquired primarily through classical or operant conditioning. The additional fact that children's early original utterances often violate grammatical rules in a systematic way indicates to Chomsky and other nativists that imitation of the kind Bandura described is also insufficient to explain language acquisition, although Chomsky did acknowledge that "children acquire a good deal of their verbal and non-verbal behavior by casual observation and imitation of adults and other children" (1959:49).

Chomsky believes that the capacity to comprehend and generate language is innate, and that the principles by which it develops are not the same as those that underlie other human behaviors. Instead, he argues, the capacity to comprehend and generate language is more like a special human organ with its own structure and function.

Chomsky's strategy for discovering the nature of language and the conditions for its acquisition is to determine the grammatical rules common to many sentences despite variability from one utterance to the next. He refers to the actual sentences that people produce as the **surface structure** of the language. The restricted set of rules from which the surface structure can be derived is called the **deep structure** of the linguistic system.

Unlike researchers who collect their data by observing language behavior in natural settings or in specially constructed experiments, Chomsky uses the intuitions of native speakers about whether a sample sentence is grammatical or not. Of course, native speakers could not actually produce an entire language, which by definition consists of an infinite set of utterances. But native speakers can judge whether any given utterance is a legitimate part of their language because this ability is a basic part of every language user's competence. An English speaker might or might not choose to say "Put the needles in the blue drawer," but any adult English speaker of average intelligence is able to say that "Put the needles in the blue drawer" is grammatical, whereas "Put the needles in the drawer blue" is not.

A key argument of those who believe with Chomsky that language develops through maturation is that children's everyday experience with language provides them with too little feedback to support language acquisition in the absence of some (inborn) linguistic structure that guides their learning (Chomsky, 1980; Pinker, 1989; Wexler, 1990). Attempts to evaluate this argument have focused on documenting children's actual experience with language. In an early and influential study of this kind, Roger Brown and Camille Hanlon (1970) sought to determine if parents show disapproval of their children's ungrammatical utterances and if they correct their children when they make grammatical errors. Would parents react negatively, for example, if a child said, "Why the dog don't eat?" or provide a correct model for the child? Brown and Hanlon found that not only did parents fail to correct their children or to express disapproval, they didn't even seem to notice the errors!

Convergent evidence that the development of language does not depend on learning as a consequence of direct feedback comes from reports that even when parents do attempt explicit instruction to correct erroneous grammar, the effort is likely to fail. The following exchange is reported by David McNeil (1966:106–107):

Child: Nobody don't like me.

Mother: No, say "nobody likes me."

Child: Nobody don't like me.

[This interchange is repeated several times. Then:]

Mother: No, now listen carefully; say "nobody likes me."

Child: Oh! Nobody don't like*s* me.

Extreme resistance to such corrections, even when the child is obviously trying to cooperate, combined with evidence that adults are unlikely to provide explicit feedback about correct and incorrect grammatical forms, undermines the idea that specific teaching is important to language acquisition and bolsters the nativist position that language acquisition depends only minimally on the environment.

In line with the analogy of language as organ, Chomsky proposes that every child is born with a **language acquisition device (LAD),** which is programmed to recognize the universal rules that underlie any particular language that a child might hear. The LAD is like a genetic code for the acquisition of language. Although at birth the child's language acquisition device is still in an embryonic state, as the child matures and interacts with the environment, maturation of the LAD enables the child to acquire more complex language forms that fit the preexisting structure, and the eventual result is the language-using ability of an adult.

In summary, according to the nativist position, the essential structures that make language acquisition possible — the universals of grammar — are determined far more by the evolutionary history of the species than by the experiential history of particular children. Experience does of course determine which of the many possible human languages a child actually acquires. Children without the experience of hearing Chinese spoken will not grow up speaking Chinese, even though they are genetically capable of learning that language. The experience of hearing a particular language, however, does not modify the LAD; it only triggers the innate structures needed to acquire language.

Interactionist Explanations

Surveying alternative explanations of language acquisition in the 1970s, George Miller, a leading researcher on the psychology of language, remarked wryly that psychologists were faced with two unsatisfactory explanations of language development. One of them, the idea that language is acquired by laws of association governed by the environment, was impossible, in his view. The other, nativism, was miraculous. Interactionist approaches to language acquisition may be viewed as attempts to create a bridge between the impossible and the miraculous explanations of language development (Bates, O'Connell, & Shore, 1987; Bloom, 1991; Bruner, 1982; Lock, 1980; Maratsos, 1983). Within this overall position, scholars differ significantly about exactly how such interactions work.

Interactionists believe that children's language development is closely linked to their cognitive achievements, which provide essential resources for language acquisition (Bates, Bretherton, & Snyder, 1988; Meltzoff & Gopnik, 1989; Piaget, 1980). We have already noted (Chapter 6, p. 217) that Piaget associated language acquisition with the emergence of representational thought, which he saw manifested in a variety of ways, including the search for hidden objects, pretend play, and deferred imitation. We now know that some of the achievements that Piaget associated with the end of infancy (such as deferred imitation and some understanding of the continued existence of absent objects) appear in rudimentary form many months earlier than he estimated. As a consequence, some contemporary interactionist theorists direct their research toward identifying more specific links between linguistic and cognitive achievements (Bates, O'Connell, & Shore, 1987; Byrnes & Gelman, 1991; Gopnik & Meltzoff, 1987).

Meltzoff and Gopnik (1989), for example, suggest that the way children use words changes sometime around 18 months in conjunction with a change in the nature of their deferred imitations. Before 18 months, children use "social words" such as "Bye-bye" and "Hereyare" in connection with the events they are actually experiencing (a mother leaving for work, finding a searched-for toy); after 18 months they begin to acquire words for talking about the difference between actual experiences and possible experiences. As we noted earlier, they can now use such expressions as "Uh-oh" to mark the discrepancy between success in accomplishing something they were planning to do and failure.

Explaining the acquisition of grammar has proved particularly difficult for interactionists because grammatical structures appear to be well beyond the ability of infants (or adults, for that matter!) to understand. The solution to this problem suggested by Elizabeth Bates and her colleagues is to treat the mastery of grammatical structures as a by-product of the ability to use language to get things done.

To illustrate how complex grammatical structures may arise from interactions that do not explicitly have the construction of those structures as their goal, Bates and Lynn Snyder (1987) point to the way a complex beehive is formed as a by-product of the process of collecting and storing honey. To make a structure to store the honey, the individual bees deposit the wax that is carried in their heads. As they push their load up against the wax deposited by other bees, they create a honeycomb labyrinth made up of hexagonal cells. It may be tempting to assume that bees have a genetic predisposition to make hexagons to carry out their hive-building functions. But in fact, as Bates and Snyder point out, hexagons are inevitably created whenever circles or spheres are packed together under pressure from all sides. Applying this same logic to linguistic structures, Bates and Snyder propose that grammatical structures result from the packing together of people's various communicative intentions within the narrow confines of language in such a way as to produce usable communicative products.

A *cultural-context* version of the interactionist approach to language acquisition is offered by scholars who emphasize that the social environment is organized to incorporate the child as a member of an already-existing language-using group (Bruner, 1983; Harkness, 1990; Nelson, 1988; Tomasello, 1992). Jerome Bruner (1982) uses the term **format** to refer to a

A great deal of language learning takes place in contexts in which adults play an important role in structuring the activity.

socially patterned activity in which adult and child do things to each other and with each other. Simple formatted activities are games of peekaboo and bedtime routines, which pattern communicative interaction between infants and caretakers even before infants have learned any language and in this way serve as "crucial vehicles in the passage from communication to language."

Bruner (1982) nicely captured the cultural view of language development when he wrote that language acquisition cannot be reduced to

> either the virtuoso cracking of a linguistic code, or the spinoff of ordinary cognitive development, or the gradual takeover of adults' speech by the child through some impossible inductive *tour de force*. It is, rather, a subtle process by which adults artificially arrange the world so that the child can succeed culturally by doing what comes naturally, and with others similarly inclined. (p. 15)

He has suggested that as an ensemble, the formatted events within which children acquire language constitute a **language acquisition support system (LASS)**, which is the environmental complement to the innate, biologically constituted LAD emphasized by nativists.

ESSENTIAL INGREDIENTS OF LANGUAGE ACQUISITION

None of the theories so far advanced provides an overarching explanation of all the processes at work in the development of language. Each approach, however, helps to focus attention on one or more of the many questions that must be answered if we are to understand the overall phenomenon. Three such questions are of special interest: What biological properties must an organism have to be able to acquire human language? What aspects of the environment are crucial to the development of language among human beings, and how do they operate? And finally, how does the acquisition of language influence other aspects of development, particularly the development of thought?

The Biological Prerequisites for Language

The question of biological contributions to language acquisition has been addressed in two fundamentally different ways. The first is to inquire into the possibility that other species are capable of producing and comprehending language; if they are not, then membership in the human species is a biological prerequisite for language development. The second is to investigate children with marked biological deficits to see if and how those deficits affect their acquisition of language.

Is language uniquely human?

For most of human history it has seemed obvious that the basic requirement for acquiring language is that the learner be a human being. Many other species make a variety of communicative sounds and gestures, but none has evolved a communicative system as powerful and flexible as human language (Lieberman, 1991). At this rather crude level, virtually all developmental psychologists agree with Chomsky that the process of language development has a significant inherited component.

One strategy for testing the hypothesis that only human beings can acquire language is to raise a creature of another species in the home along with one's own children. Several researchers have done just that with chimpanzees, hoping that these near phylogenetic neighbors would acquire oral language if they were treated just like human beings (Hayes & Hayes, 1951; Kellogg & Kellogg, 1933; Ladygina-Kots, 1935). These early studies, despite heroic efforts to treat human and chimpanzee infants alike, failed to produce more than the barest rudiments of vocal language (for example, one chimp learned to make a sound corresponding to one word).

In recent decades, the assumption of total discontinuity between *Homo sapiens* and higher primates has been cast into doubt. Several investigators have suggested that earlier studies erred in requiring evidence of oral language, which is likely to be difficult for higher primates because of the structure of their vocal apparatus. In subsequent research it has been claimed that, with intensive training, chimpanzees can be taught to use a manual/visual system of communication, similar in its mode of operation to the sign language used by hearing-impaired people (Gardner & Gardner, 1969; Miles, 1990). These claims are still hotly disputed (Terrace, 1984; Lieberman, 1990), but the research that has resulted from this controversy has revealed that at least some of the elements of human language exist among nonhuman species.

In the wild, chimpanzees and other primates make a variety of communicative sounds and gestures that are important to the social organization of their lives (Cheney & Seyfarth, 1990; Goodall, 1986). Some of these sounds help to coordinate the group when it is foraging for food. Monkey and chimpanzee troops are organized so that if a predator appears, the males, who are on the outside of the group, make a distinctive sound that sends the females and juvenile monkeys, who are in the center, heading for the trees. Some species have distinctive sounds for particular kinds of predators. Infant primates make these same sounds but may confuse the sound for a cheetah with that for a leopard or the sound for a hawk with the sound for an eagle. Additional sounds and gestures signal playfulness, submissiveness, social excitement, and a variety of other states (Cheney & Seyfarth, 1990).

In captivity specially trained chimpanzees and members of other primate species have learned well over 100 "words" that are expressed by hand shapes or plastic chips provided by their human tutors (Miles, 1990; Premack & Premack, 1983). They can also learn to use their signs to make simple requests ("Give stick") not only of their trainer but of other chimpanzees (Savage-Rumbaugh et al., 1986).

In the most successful case yet reported, two chimpanzees who were regularly included in such everyday human activities as taking a bath, looking at a book, going for a car ride, and changing diapers, and with whom the researchers communicated by means of signs and tokens in the course of these activities, acquired the ability to create new sentence-like combinations of words in a manner similar to that of a 2-year-old child (Greenfield & Savage-Rumbaugh, 1990; Savage-Rumbaugh, 1990).

Despite these recent successes, the continuity between human and subhuman language capacities should not be overstated. Current evidence (summarized in Lieberman, 1990, and Parker & Gibson, 1990) indicates that while language-like behavior can be induced in chimpanzees, there is a crucial difference between this behavior and human language. After years of hard work, chimpanzees can learn several dozen signs; but children with no special training learn several thousand. Chimpanzees also learn to construct sequences of signs analogous to an infant's multiword utterances, but the internal complexity of these constructions remains rudimentary; as a consequence, even scholars who emphasize the language-learning abilities of primates are likely to refer to their accomplishments as "protolanguage," emphasizing its underdeveloped status (Greenfield & Savage-Rumbaugh, 1990).

This chimp is signing "I want to hold" (top) *"the cat"* (bottom). *(Courtesy of H. Terrace.)*

Children with severe biological handicaps

In Chapter 2 (pp. 67–68) we briefly described Down's syndrome, a genetic disease that is associated with moderate to severe mental retardation. Although Down's children are able to hold a conversation, their vocabulary is relatively restricted and their talk is grammatically simple. When tested for the ability to produce and comprehend complex linguistic constructions, they fail. Such results suggest that <u>normal</u> <u>language development requires normal cognitive functioning.</u>

This conclusion is challenged, however, by research on children who suffer from a rare metabolic disorder called Williams syndrome. Children afflicted with Williams syndrome are also mentally retarded, yet many of them show nearly normal ability to produce sentences that are grammatical, clearly pronounced, and understandable, and are able to tell stories that are meaningful and display considerable subtlety in their portrayal of human feelings (Bellugi et al., 1990).

Data such as these strongly suggest that at least some aspects of language develop independently of general cognitive functioning. However, coordinated development of the phonetic, grammatical, semantic, and pragmatic aspects of language, all of which are essential to normal linguistic functioning, requires a minimum level of biological integrity below which full language development is impossible.

The Environment of Language Development

Evidence from studies of primates' ability to communicate suggests one absolute biological precondition for full language acquisition: one must be a human being. Evidence from cases such as that of Genie, the girl who grew up in total isolation from normal human interaction and language (described in Chapter 7), suggests the corresponding precondition on the environmental side: one must grow up among humans who behave in a natural human manner. Beyond the specification of these two minimum requirements, however, important questions remain: Which aspects of the environment are necessary to trigger language? How are they arranged? What are the optimal arrangements for ensuring that the language capacity will be fully developed?

Partial deprivation

One way to answer such questions is to find children who are exposed to a great deal of language but are cut off from normal interaction with the speakers. There have been a few reports, for example, of children who are left alone for long periods of time with a television set broadcasting in a language other than the one spoken in the home. Scenes on television portray routine interactions involving normal language, so they might support language acquisition through imitation and the association of sound and action. While children raised in such homes can acquire vocabulary by watching television (Rice & Woodsmall, 1988), children for whom television provides the *only* exposure to language do not seem to acquire the crucial linguistic ability to create and comprehend an infinite number of sentences (Snow et al., 1976). The fact that language does not develop on the basis of television

exposure alone contradicts the idea that mere exposure is all that is required to trigger language development. Children must also test their ideas about language by interacting with other speakers in everyday settings.

The crucial role of active participation in human activity is demonstrated by children who grow up in an environment without language but with normal human interaction. One such situation occurs in the case of deaf children whose hearing parents do not know sign language and discourage its use (Feldman, Goldin-Meadow, & Gleitman, 1978; Goldin-Meadow, 1985; Goldin-Meadow & Mylander, 1990). We know that the biological condition of deafness need not be an impediment to normal language acquisition; deaf children born to deaf parents who communicate in sign language acquire language at least as rapidly and fully as hearing children born into hearing households (Padden & Humphries, 1989). So any delays and difficulties in deaf children's language development cannot be explained by their inability to hear; it must result from differences in the way the environment is organized to permit participation in language-mediated activity.

In the families studied by Susan Goldin-Meadow and her colleagues, the parents did not know sign language and refused to use it because they believed that their deaf children could and should learn to read lips and to vocalize sounds. As a consequence, at an age when other children are hearing (or seeing) language, these children received extremely restricted input in their home surroundings. However, they did participate in everyday, formatted, routine activities coordinated through the language and cultural system of the adults.

Earlier studies had shown that deaf children raised under these circumstances will spontaneously begin to gesture in "home sign," a kind of communication through pantomime (Fant, 1972). Goldin-Meadow and her colleagues wanted to find out if the home-sign systems developed by the deaf children displayed the characteristic features of language acquisition. They discovered that, indeed, the gestures these children developed exhibited certain characteristics of language even though they had no one to show them the signs.

Home sign begins as pointing. The children gesture one sign at a time — at the same age when hearing children develop single-word utterances. Home-sign gestures seem to refer to the same kinds of objects and

FIGURE 8.7   *This little girl is signing the word "sleep."*
(Copyright Ursula Bellugi, The Salk Institute for Biological Studies; reprinted with permission.)

to fulfill the same functions as the early words of hearing children, or of deaf children with signing parents. Remarkably, home-signing children go on to make patterns of two, three, and more signs around their second birthday, at about the same time that hearing children utter multiword sentences.

Analysis of these multipart signs reveals ordering principles much like those seen at the two-word stage in hearing children. In addition, Goldin-Meadow reports that these deaf children were embedding sign sentences within each other ("You/Susan give me/ Abe cookie that is round"). This is the property of recursion, which, as we pointed out at the beginning of this chapter, is characteristic of all human languages and absent from the communicative system of chimpanzees or other creatures even after long training.

Once these children are able to make two- to three-word "utterances" in their home sign and begin to embed sign sentences within each other, their language development appears to come to an end. They fail to acquire grammatical morphemes or to master complex grammatical distinctions. The mere fact of being raised in an environment where the actions of all the other participants are organized by human language and culture is sufficient to allow the child to acquire the basics of linguistic structure. But only access to the additional information provided by the sights (or sounds) of language *as a part of that environment* allows the child to discover its more subtle fea-

tures (Goldin-Meadow, 1982, 1985). Confirmation of this conclusion comes from the case of a hearing child raised by deaf parents (Sachs, Bard, & Johnson, 1981). This child's parents exposed him to neither conventional oral nor conventional manual language input. He heard English only on TV and during a brief time spent in nursery school. The course of development for this child was precisely the same as for the deaf children of hearing parents: he developed the basic features of grammar, but not the more complex ones. Once he was exposed to normal American sign, at the age of 3 years and 9 months, he quickly acquired normal language ability.

Such research narrows the search for the critical environmental ingredients of language development. The beginnings of language may appear during the second year of life even in the absence of direct experience of language, so long as children are included in the everyday life of their family. The kind of language that appears under such linguistically impoverished conditions, however, is by no means fully developed, resembling at best the language behavior of children at the two-word phase. Moreover, some deaf children raised in hearing homes that make no special provisions do not acquire even the rudiments of language, an indication that participation in culturally organized activity, while necessary, is not always sufficient to enable the child to realize that language is part of the environment (Schaller, 1991).

How interaction contributes to language acquisition

The conclusion seems inescapable that if language acquisition is to proceed beyond the rudiments, not only must children hear (or see) language, they also must participate in family or community activity. It is in everyday interactions that hearing children (or deaf children of signing parents) master language as a basic part of the activity, filling in the gaps between nonverbal actions.

Careful examination of the way language is integrated into the joint activity of adults and children goes a long way toward reducing the mystery of how children learn the meanings of words, discussed at the beginning of this chapter (see Figure 8.1, p. 278).

In one series of studies, Michael Tomasello and his colleagues (Tomasello, 1988; Tomasello & Farrar, 1986) videotaped mothers interacting with their 1½- to 2-year-old children in order to identify the precise moment at which the mothers referred to objects in the immediate environment. They found that for the most part the mothers talked about objects that were already a part of the child's ongoing actions and the objects of joint attention, thus greatly reducing the child's problem in figuring out the referents of the mother's words. In a follow-up experimental study, these investigators deliberately taught new words to the children in one of two ways: for half the children the adult labeled an object that was not the focus of the child's attention in an effort to direct the child's attention to it; for the other half, the adult labeled the object after the child had focused on it. The strategy of labeling an object after the child was already attending to it proved more effective than trying to get the child to attend to a new word and a new meaning at the same time.

Other studies of early word learning have shown that young children use verbal labels to help them identify the relevant aspects of the situation being talked about by an adult even before they have had a chance to learn what the label means (Markman, 1987; Waxman & Gelman, 1986). Sandra Waxman and Rochel Gelman introduced children between the ages of 3 and 5 to three "very picky" hand puppets, each of which liked only one kind of thing. All of the children were shown items in three categories (animals, clothing, food) and then asked to help choose the rest of the items that each of the puppets would like. For half of the children the researchers deliberately refrained from naming the things they were talking about; they showed the children that one puppet liked animals, the second clothing, and the third food, without using any labels. For the remaining children, the researchers provided made-up labels instead of the real labels for the categories.

Waxman and Gelman found that if they simply told the children to give each puppet the things the puppet liked without using any labels, the children assigned items to the puppets at random, much as if they didn't realize that each puppet liked only one category of things. But if the researchers used a made-up word to label each category as part of the instructions, the children immediately gave each puppet only the "kind of thing it would like to have." The totally unfamiliar label was just as effective as the words the children did know ("These are the animals, these are the clothes, these are foods"). In short, the children treated the adult's introduction of a label as an invitation to use a category.

The ability of children to home in on words that are closely related to familiar actions is seen in a different way in a study of vocabulary development conducted by Elsa Bartlett (1977) and Susan Carey (1978), which we mentioned in Chapter 1 (p. 32). Bartlett and Carey used the normal routine of a preschool to find out what would happen if a totally new word were introduced into conversation with children. They chose to study the acquisition of color vocabulary. None of the 14 children in the classroom knew the name of the color that adults call olive; some of them called it brown, others called it green, and some didn't refer to the color by name at all. Bartlett and Carey decided to give it an implausible name, chromium, just in case some children had partial knowledge of the real name that they had not revealed.

After the children had been tested to determine that they did not know the name of the color olive, one cup and one tray in the classroom were painted "chromium" (olive). While preparing for snacktime, the teacher found an opportunity to ask each child, "Please bring me the chromium cup; not the red one, the chromium one" or "Bring me the chromium tray; not the blue one, the chromium one."

This procedure worked. All of the children succeeded in picking the correct cup or tray, although they were likely to ask for confirmation ("You mean this one?"). Some of the children could be noticed repeating the unfamiliar word (or some rough approximation of it) to themselves.

One week after this single experience with the new word, the children were given a color-naming test with color chips. Two-thirds of the children showed that they had learned something about this odd term and its referents; when asked for chromium, they chose either the olive chip or a green one. Six weeks later many of the children still showed the influence of this single experience.

A variety of procedures have been used to confirm Bartlett and Carey's observations, including exposure of children to new words in a television program (Rice, 1990). Studies based on Bartlett and Carey's procedure do not support the idea that children acquire language because adults explicitly reward their efforts, nor do they support the idea that children learn by any simple process of imitation. Rather, when children hear an unfamiliar word in a familiar and highly structured situation that constrains the way they are likely to interpret it, they seem to form a quick idea of the word's meaning and the way that new word might fit into their existing repertoire. Mabel Rice (1990) refers to this phenomenon as **fast mapping** and suggests that it provides an essential means for arriving at partial understanding, which is then broadened and solidified through repeated experiences of the word in a variety of contexts.

The conditions that enable fast mapping also illustrate the kinds of adult-guided constructive processes emphasized by cultural context theorists such as Bruner and Vygotsky. As they see it, adults' reinforcement need not come in the form of explicit rewards. Instead, the reinforcement comes from the increased success of communication and the greater freedom children experience once they can use new words as instruments of their own actions.

Is there a role for deliberate instruction?

As we have described it thus far, language acquisition appears to require several elements, each of which is emphasized by one of the major theories:

1. A biologically programmed sensitivity to language present at birth, which develops as the child matures (the nativist view).
2. Imitation of the language behavior of others (the environmental-learning view).
3. Acquisition of basic schemas for actions with objects and people and the ability to represent the world mentally (the universal-constructivist version of an interactionist view).
4. Interaction with caregivers in familiar routines in which language is one of many forms of coordination (the cultural-context version of an interactionist view).

Missing from this list is any role for deliberate instruction with explicit rewards of the kind emphasized in some environmental-learning explanations of language acquisition. Are deliberate efforts to foster language development by teaching about language irrelevant?

Adults in some cultures certainly seem to think that it is important to teach their children how to talk. But the age at which they start such instruction varies widely among cultures. The Kaluli people of New Guinea, for example, believe that children must be explicitly taught language just as they must be taught other culturally valued forms of behavior. The Kaluli make no effort to start teaching language until they

---

TABLE 8.6

Simplifications Used by Middle-Class U.S. Adults Speaking to Small Children

Phonological simplifications
  Higher pitch and exaggerated intonation
  Clear pronunciation
  Slower speech
  Distinct pauses between utterances

Syntactic differences
  Shorter and less varied utterance length
  Almost all sentences well formed
  Many partial or complete repetitions of child's utterances, sometimes with expansion
  Fewer broken sentences
  Grammatically less complex

Semantic differences
  More limited vocabulary
  Many special words and diminutives
  Reference to concrete circumstances of here and now
  Middle level of generality in naming objects

Pragmatic differences
  More directives, imperatives, and questions
  More utterances designed to draw attention to aspects of objects

Source: de Villiers & de Villiers, 1978.

---

believe that the child is ready, a benchmark judged to be the time when the child has begun to use a few words. As soon as those first words are spoken, the parents begin to engage their infants in a form of speech activity called *elema*: the mother provides the utterance she wants to the child to utter followed by the command "*Elema*" ("Say like this"). Eleanor Ochs (1982) described similar practices among Samoans, and Peggy Miller (1982) reported that working-class mothers in Baltimore, Maryland, follow a similar strategy with respect to teaching vocabulary.

Even in societies where adults do not engage in deliberate teaching strategies, many investigators have noted that adults sometimes use a special speech register, dubbed **motherese**: they speak in a special high-

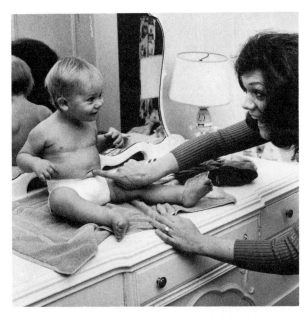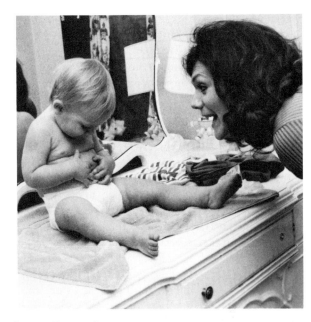

Language is acquired in the context of ongoing activity. This mother is talking and playing with her baby as a routine part of getting him dressed.

pitched voice, emphasize boundaries between idea-bearing clauses, and use a simplified vocabulary when they talk to small children (Fernald, 1991; Snow & Ferguson, 1977).

As Table 8.6 indicates, middle-class parents in the United States simplify virtually every aspect of their language when they speak to their children. Several studies have shown that the complexity of adults' speech to children is graded to the level of complexity of the child's speech (Bohannon & Warren-Leubecker, 1988; Stern et al., 1983).

Catherine Snow (1972) shows how such tailoring processes can work. A child is putting away toys under the mother's direction. Note the sequence of the mother's directions: "Put the red truck in the box now. . . . The red truck. . . . No, the red truck. . . . In the box. . . . The red truck in the box." Snow argues that this kind of graded language environment, in which statements are gradually simplified and their meaning highlighted, provides excellent tutoring because it isolates constituent phrases at the same time that it models the whole correct grammatical structure.

American adults not only simplify what they say as an aid to children's comprehension (and perhaps to aid them in the process of discovering how to use language); they also complicate what children say. This phenomenon was pointed out by Roger Brown and Ursula Bellugi (1964), who called this kind of adult speech "expansion" because it seemed to expand the child's utterance into a grammatically correct adult version. A child who says "Mommy wash," for example, might be responded to with "Yes, Mommy is washing her face"; the declaration "Daddy sleep" might evoke the caution, "Yes, Daddy is sleeping. Don't wake him up."

Despite widespread belief that adult teaching, simplifying, and highlighting behaviors help children to master language, the necessity of such practices has been the subject of a long-standing disagreement among scholars who study language acquisition.

As we noted earlier (p. 298), Brown and Hanlon (1970) found that adults seemed to ignore their young children's grammatical errors. When Courtney Cazden (1965) attempted to "force-feed" children with a heavy diet of feedback in which children's incorrect sentences were expanded and corrected, she found no special effect on language development. Subsequent studies have sometimes found effects of parental expansions or corrections (Farrar, 1992; Nelson, 1976; Hirsh-Pasek, Treiman, & Schneiderman, 1984), but failures to find such effects are at least as numerous

(Gleitman, Newport, & Gleitman, 1984). Consequently, no firm conclusions about the influence of deliberate parental feedback are yet possible.

Perhaps the most important conclusion to come out of several decades of work on the relation between special adult behaviors and children's acquisition of language is that the differences in the everyday, intuitive practices of adults throughout the world make relatively little difference in the rate at which children acquire language: all normally developing children become competent language users. All cultural groups take into account the fact that small children do not understand language and make some provision for seeing that they have the opportunity to acquire it. However, it has not been possible to prove that a particular practice that might be called "teaching the child to speak" has an important impact on language acquisition or that one method of structuring children's language experience is universally essential.

LANGUAGE AND THOUGHT

The research reviewed in this chapter makes it clear that language is complexly related to activity and the surrounding world. Children learn early to use this relationship to influence their interactions with the world. And all the time that their language capacities are growing, they are acquiring more knowledge. How are the development of language and the development of thought processes related?

The Environmental-Learning Perspective

According to learning theorists such as Albert Bandura (1986) and B. F. Skinner (1957), children begin to grasp what different language forms signify by relating what they hear to what they understand to be going on. Eventually a great deal of their thought comes to be based on language. These theorists also believe that there are special advantages to such thinking.

> By manipulating symbols that convey relevant information, one can gain understanding of causal relationships, expand one's knowledge, solve problems, and deduce consequences of actions without actually performing them. The functional

value of thought rests on the close correspondence between the symbolic system [in this case, language] and external events, so that the former can be substituted for the latter. (Bandura, 1986:462)

Language, according to this view, is more than a means of communication with others. Words deepen a child's understanding of certain aspects of objects and of the subtle relations among various events. Associations among words provide a kind of mental map of the world, which shapes the way a child thinks. This view suggests that thinking should change markedly when children begin to acquire language.

The Piagetian Interactionist Perspective

Piaget claimed that a new mode of representation, in which children begin to think in symbols, arises on the basis of sensorimotor schemas accumulated by the end of infancy, as we saw in Chapter 6 (p. 217). Language, he believed, is a verbal reflection of the individual's nonlinguistic understanding (Piaget, 1926, 1983). The acquisition of language provides a means of thinking more rapidly, since a sequence of thoughts can often be carried out more quickly than a sequence of actions. But since language *reflects* thought, language developments cannot *cause* cognitive development. Rather, cognition determines language.

As we saw in Chapters 4 to 6, Piaget believed that cognitive development arises from the child's attempts to assimilate the environment, which are modified through subsequent accommodations. At the end of the sensorimotor period, children have developed a basic understanding that they are a part of a world that exists apart from them, but, as we will see in Chapter 9, they still have difficulty adopting other people's points of view. If language is determined by thought, it follows that early speech, like early thought, must be egocentric and fail to take into account others' points of view. Early in his career, Piaget supported this hypothesis with data collected from preschool children's conversations. What struck him was that while preschoolers appear to be playing and conversing together, their remarks actually focus on what they are doing by themselves, with no real regard for their partner and with no apparent intention of actually communicating. Piaget (1926) called this type of language a **collective monologue.** He believed that collective monologues mirror a profoundly egocentric mode of thought. The following conversation between two American preschoolers illustrates his point:

Jenny: They wiggle sideways when they kiss.
Chris: *(vaguely)* What?
Jenny: My bunny slippers. They are brown and red and sort of yellow and white. And they have eyes and ears and these noses that wiggle sideways when they kiss.
Chris: I have a piece of sugar in a red piece of paper. I'm gonna eat it but maybe it's for a horse.
Jenny: We bought them. My mommy did. We couldn't find the old ones. These are like the old ones. They were not in the trunk.
Chris: Can't eat the piece of sugar, not unless you take the paper off.
Jenny: And we found Mother Lamb. Oh, she was in Poughkeepsie in the trunk in the house in the woods where Mrs. Tiddywinkle lives.
Chris: Do I like sugar? I do, and so do horses.
Jenny: I play with my bunnies. They are real. We play in the woods. They have eyes. We all go in the woods. My teddy bear and the bunnies and the duck, to visit Mrs. Tiddywinkle. We play and play.
Chris: I guess I'll eat my sugar at lunch time. I can get more for the horses. Besides, I don't have no horses now. (Stone & Church, 1957:146–147)

Piaget believed that as children grow older, their ability to adopt others' points of view increases, and collective monologues give way to genuine dialogues.

Piaget's idea that language depends on thought but thought is not influenced by language was tested by Hermione Sinclair-de-Zwart (1967), who taught French-speaking preschoolers the correct meanings of the terms for "more" and "less," then tested their ability to solve problems involving the relationships of more and less. She found that the children who had learned to use the words appropriately in the training situation showed no advantage over untrained children when these relationships were actually needed to solve a problem. This failure of language training to influence problem solving seems to confirm Piaget's theory that language does not affect thought.

The Nativist Perspective

Nativist theorists such as Noam Chomsky explicitly deny that it is possible for language to grow out of sensorimotor schemas, declaring that there are no known similarities between the principles of language and the principles of sensorimotor intelligence (Chomsky, 1980). Rather, as we explained earlier, Chomsky believes that language acquisition is made possible by a specifically human language acquisition device (LAD).

Chomsky (1980) has used the term **mental module** to signal the self-contained nature of the capacity to use language. A mental module is a highly specific mental faculty that is tuned to particular kinds of environmental input. In claiming that language forms a distinctive mental module, Chomsky seems to be declaring that language and thought do not depend on each other. In support of their position, nativists cite evidence that some severely retarded children have relatively advanced linguistic abilities even though their other intellectual abilities are extremely limited (p. 302). However, Chomsky does not go so far as to say that there is no connection between these two domains of mind. When Piaget's colleague Barbel Inhelder challenged Chomsky on this issue, he replied:

> I take it for granted that thinking is a domain that is quite different from language, even though language is used for the expression of thought, and for a good deal of thinking we really need the mediation of language. (Chomsky, 1980:174)

A Cultural-Context Perspective

The most prominent cultural theory of language and thought was developed by the Soviet psychologist Lev Vygotsky (1934/1987, 1978). Pointing out that children's development always occurs in a context organized and watched over by adults, Vygotsky insisted that children's experience of language is social from the outset.

In accord with evidence we presented earlier, Vygotsky (1934/1987) argued that even children's initial words are communicative acts, mediating their interactions with the people around them. More generally, he believed that every new psychological function first appears during children's interactions with others who

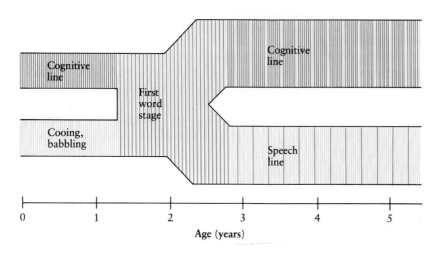

FIGURE 8.8   *The merging and reorganization of cognitive and verbal-communicative lines of development according to Vygotsky. (Adapted from Valsiner, 1989.)*

can support and nurture their efforts. These shared efforts are gradually taken over by the child and transformed into individual abilities. Applied to the area of language, this sequence suggests a progression from social and communicative speech to internal dialogue, or inner speech, in which thought and language are intimately interconnected.

Vygotsky suggests that sometime after children begin to communicate, egocentric speech (speech primarily for oneself) splinters off from social speech and becomes the earliest form of individual, linguistically mediated thought. This type of speech is still a rudimentary form of thought because it is partially external and only some fragments of the child's thought find expression. But even egocentric speech influences the individual's behavior, in Vygotsky's view. This is just the opposite of the way language, cognition, and the social world are related in Piaget's framework, and, as might be expected, Vygotsky's interpretation of collective monologues (or "egocentric speech") also differs from Piaget's.

Vygotsky and his colleagues conducted a series of studies to test Piaget's idea that egocentric speech serves no cognitive or communicative function (Vygotsky, 1934/1987). In one such study, they demonstrated the psychological functionality of egocentric speech: when children were faced with a difficulty in solving a problem, they raised the level of their overt self-regulatory speech. (This finding was replicated by Kohlberg, Yaeger, and Hjertholm [1968].) In a second study they demonstrated that egocentric speech serves a communicative function for others as well as for oneself. In this case preschoolers were placed among deaf-mute children, with whom they had little chance of communicating. Vygotsky reasoned that if egocen-

tric speech was really not intended to communicate, it would not be affected by potential listeners' inability to understand. Instead, the rate of egocentric speech decreased markedly from its level in the presence of hearing children (described in Wertsch, 1985).

A basic innovation in Vygotsky's approach was his assertion that the relationship between language and thought is not constant. Both language and thought develop, and so does the relationship between them. According to Vygotsky, during the first two years of life, language and thought develop along more or less parallel, relatively unrelated lines. Until the end of infancy it is possible to encounter precursors of language that seem unrelated to any intellectual operation (such as babbling) and elements of thought that occur without any language (such as the sensorimotor schemas described by Piaget). Beginning around 2 years of age, however, a fundamental change occurs in the relationship between language and thought. The thought and language that have been developing on more or less independent tracks now begin to intermingle. This intermingling, wrote Vygotsky (1934/1987), fundamentally changes the nature of both thinking and language, providing the growing child with a uniquely human form of behavior in which language becomes intellectual and thinking becomes verbal (see Figure 8.8).

In Vygotsky's framework, language allows thought to be individual and social at the same time. It is the medium through which individual thought is communicated to others while at the same time it allows social reality to be converted into the idiosyncratic thought of the individual. This conversion from the social to the individual is never complete, even in the adult, whose individual thought processes continue to be shaped in part by the conventional meanings present in the lexicon and by the speech habits of the culture.

The relation between language and thought remains one of the most tangled and controversial issues dividing developmental psychologists. There appears to be reasonable agreement that language and thought are separable psychological functions; neither can be reduced to the other. There is also agreement that the two functions intermingle in normal development. The field is still far from agreement, however, on the extent to which development in one domain influences development in the other and on their combined roles in the development of the child as a whole.

THE BASIC PUZZLES OF LANGUAGE ACQUISITION RECONSIDERED

At the beginning of this chapter we introduced two basic questions about the way children acquire language: How do they come to understand what words mean and how do they acquire the ability to arrange words in acceptable sequences to express and understand the complex meanings needed to coordinate with other people?

The information we have presented in this chapter does not definitively answer these questions because neither language nor the way children acquire it is fully understood. But research discussed in this chapter has at least narrowed the scope of the quest.

Consider the problem posed in Figure 8.1, in which the father and son are gazing out of a window and the father tells the boy to look at the *ptitsa* (bird). What this picture leaves out is a history of interaction between parent and child in the course of which they have developed many routines for understanding each other. It also leaves out any indication of what they were in the midst of doing when the father said, "Look, son, there sits a *ptitsa*." Perhaps they had been playing naming games, or perhaps they had been feeding their pet bird. A full account would also need to include what other words the child already knew, because, as we learned from the data on fast mapping (p. 306), children use the words they already know to help them figure out what new words mean.

Knowing these things would certainly reduce the mystery of how the child might come to understand the father, but would not eliminate it entirely. No

chimpanzee would be able to learn in such circumstances. It remains a uniquely human ability.

The puzzle of grammar remains even more mysterious. Perhaps, as nativist theorists claim, linguistic competence is achieved through an innate language acquisition device. But it is still unclear what minimal environmental conditions are needed to permit this device to function properly. Goldin-Meadow's work with deaf children in hearing households tells us that

TABLE 8.7

The Progress of Language Development

Approximate Age	Typical Behavior
Birth	Phoneme perception
	Discrimination of language from nonlanguage sounds
	Crying
3 months	Cooing
6 months	Babbling
	Loss of ability to discriminate between nonnative phonemes
9 months	First words
	Holophrases
12 months	Use of words to attract adults' attention
18 months	Vocabulary spurt
	First 2-word sentences (telegraphic speech)
24 months	Correct responses to indirect requests ("Is the door shut?")
30 months	Creation of indirect requests ("You're standing on my blocks!")
	Modification of speech to take listener into account
	Early awareness of grammatical categories
Early childhood	Rapid increase in grammatical complexity
	Overgeneralization of grammatical rules
Middle childhood	Understanding of passive forms ("The balls were taken by the boys")
	Acquisition of written language
Adolescence	Acquisition of specialized language functions

participation in normal cultural routines can be sufficient for the rudiments of language to appear. And evidence collected in both our own and other societies tells us that children acquire normal linguistic competence without special instruction if they can have access to language (either oral or sign) *and* if they are incorporated in routine, culturally organized activity, which serves as a language acquisition support system. As Jerome Bruner whimsically suggested, language is born from the union of the LAD and the LASS.

Although children 2½ to 3 years of age can properly be considered language-using human beings, we do not want to give the impression that their language development is complete (see Table 8.7). As we have indicated repeatedly, all aspects of language continue to develop all during childhood, and in some cases into adulthood. Moreover, we will see that as children begin to acquire the specialized skills they will need to cope with adult life in their culture, deliberate teaching may begin to play a conspicuous role in language development. Such specialized activities as reciting nursery rhymes, acting in a play, and writing an essay are all forms of language activity that require practice and instruction. We shall return to examine some of the more specialized language developments associated with middle childhood in Chapter 13.

SUMMARY

1. Linguistic communication builds on an extensive foundation of prelinguistic communicative achievements, including babbling, turn taking, and the ability to share a focus of attention on objects and activities with others.
2. Despite intensive investigation, scientists' understanding of language acquisition remains incomplete. No theory is able to explain satisfactorily how children come to understand either the meanings of words or the rules that govern their arrangement (grammar).
3. In the transition from babbling to talking, children begin to conform to the restricted set of sounds of the language their parents speak. The basic sounds of a language (phonemes) are those that distinguish one word from another.
4. Early words for things are associated with actions and with changes in an object's state or location.
5. Early words indicate children's emerging ability to operate on the world indirectly (in a mediated way), as well as directly.
6. Early word meanings often correspond to an intermediate level of abstraction. As a consequence, words may be used too broadly (overextension) or too narrowly (underextension) to conform to adult definitions.
7. As children's vocabularies expand, their understanding of word meanings changes fundamentally; meanings embedded in particular contexts of action are supplemented by meanings dominated by logical categories.
8. Children's first words are often nonconventional; interpretation depends to a great extent on the listener's knowledge of the context in which they are used.
9. Two-word utterances allow children to take advantage of the relationships of words within utterances to convey meaning, marking the birth of grammar. As the length of utterances increases, so does the complexity of the grammatical rules governing the arrangement of words within sentences and of elements (morphemes) within words.
10. The growth of children's vocabularies and their increased ability to use complex grammatical constructions are accompanied by a corresponding growth in their ability to engage in conversational acts that achieve a variety of goals.
11. Central to the successful use of language is the ability to say things in a way that is understandable to one's partner in conversation. Children reveal at an early age their ability to tailor their language to their listeners' needs.
12. Three theories dominate late-twentieth-century explanations of language acquisition.
    a. Learning theories claim that words and patterns of words are learned through imitation and through classical and operant conditioning.
    b. Nativist theories claim that children are born with a language acquisition device (LAD), which is automatically activated by the environment when the child has matured sufficiently.
    c. Interactionist theories emphasize the cognitive preconditions for language acquisition and the role of the social environment in providing a language acquisition support system (LASS).
13. Language is a particularly human communicative ability, but aspects of language-like communication can be found among chimpanzees and other primates.
14. Children acquire the basic elements of language with no special assistance from adults if they are raised in normal speaking or signing homes where communication is appropriate to the hearing ability of the child.

Development of the full range of language abilities, however, requires both participation in human activity and exposure to language as part of that activity.

15. Each of the various theories of language acquisition has its own view of the relationship between language and thought.

    a. According to environmental-learning theorists, language and thought are two aspects of a single process; hence the acquisition of language has a great impact on thinking and vice versa.

    b. According to nativist theorists such as Chomsky, language and thought are independent of each other.

    c. According to Piagetian interactionist theorists, developments in thought are the preconditions for language development.

    d. According to cultural-context theorists such as Vygotsky, language and thought arise independently but fuse in early childhood to create specifically human modes of thinking and communication.

KEY TERMS

abstract modeling
collective monologues *piaget*
conversational acts
cooperative principle
deep structure
fast mapping
format ✔

grammar
grammatical morphemes
holophrase
language acquisition device (LAD)
language acquisition support system (LASS)
mental module

morpheme
motherese
overextension
pragmatic uses of language
recursion
surface structure
underextension

SUGGESTED READINGS

BRUNER, JEROME. *Child's Talk: Learning to Use Language*. New York: Norton, 1983.

For Jerome Bruner, to learn language is to learn to use language. In this slim book Bruner explores the central role of participation in scriptlike interactions between children and adults in the process of language acquisition. He calls the social structuring of children's talk by adults a "language acquisition support system," and considers it a necessary complement to the innate language-learning mechanisms posited by Chomsky.

CHOMSKY, NOAM. *Reflections on Language*. New York: Pantheon, 1985.

This small book by the man who revolutionized the study of language in the latter half of the twentieth century was written for a nonspecialist audience. It provides one of the most accessible summaries of his ideas about language and its relation to human psychological processes.

CHUKOVSKY, KORNEI. *From Two to Five*. Berkeley: University of California Press, 1968.

A renowned Soviet children's writer and translator provides a wealth of wisdom about the creative processes involved in language acquisition. The book is especially rich in concrete examples collected over a lifetime of thinking about children and language.

MILLER, GEORGE A. *Language and Speech*. New York: W. H. Freeman, 1981.

George Miller has probably introduced more fundamentally important concepts of linguistics to American psychology than any other psychologist. This book discusses the origin of language in the human species, the biological bases of language, and all of the major topics covered in this chapter.

MILLER, GEORGE A. *The Science of Words*. New York: Scientific American Library, 1991.

This beautifully illustrated book contains a wealth of information about the nature of words and their relation to human intellectual functioning.

SCHALLER, SUSAN. *A Man without Words*. New York: Summit, 1991.

A fascinating account of a deaf man who discovered language at the age of 27. The book raises many important questions about how language is acquired and how it influences thinking.

CHAPTER 9

Early Childhood: Islands of Competence

•

> In every sentence . . . , in every childish act, is revealed
> complete ignorance of the simplest things. Of course, I cite
> these expressions not to scorn childish absurdities. On the
> contrary, they inspire me with respect because they are
> evidence of the gigantic work that goes on in the child's
> mind which, by the age of 7, results in the conquest of this
> mental chaos.
>
> —KORNEI CHUKOVSKY, *FROM TWO TO FIVE*

A group of 5-year-old children have been listening to "Stone Soup," a folktale retold by Marcia Brown. "Stone Soup" is about three hungry soldiers who trick some selfish peasants into feeding them by pretending to make soup out of stones. "Do stones melt?" asks Rose, one of the children. Master Teacher Vivian Paley reports the conversation that followed this question:

"Do you think they melt, Rose?"
"Yes."
" . . . Does anyone agree with Rose?"
"They will melt if you cook them," said Lisa.
"If you boil them," Eddie added.
No one doubted that the stones in the story had melted and that ours, too, would melt.
"We can cook them and find out," I said. "How will we be able to tell if they've melted?"
"They'll be smaller," said Deana.

The stones are placed in boiling water for an hour and then put on the table for inspection.

Ellen: They're much smaller.
Fred: Much, much. Almost melted.

Rose: I can't eat melted stones.
Teacher: Don't worry, Rose. You won't. But I'm not convinced they've melted. Can we prove it?

Ms. Paley suggests weighing the stones to see if they will lose weight as they boil. The children find that they weigh two pounds at the start. After they have been boiled again, the following conversation ensues:

Eddie: Still two [pounds]. But they are smaller.
Wally: Much smaller.
Teacher: They weigh the same. Two pounds before and two pounds now. That means they didn't lose weight.
Eddie: They only got a little bit smaller.
Wally: The scale can't see the stones. Hey, once in Michigan there were three stones in a fire and they melted away. They were gone. We saw it.
Deana: Maybe the stones in the story are magic.
Wally: But not these.

(Adapted from Paley, 1981:16–18)

We can see that when Ms. Paley entices the children into reconciling the world of the story and the world of their senses, their explanations are a mixture of sound physical theory and magical thinking. The children correctly believe that when things are "cooked down" they grow smaller and that small stones should be lighter than big ones. At the same time they are willing to believe that there really are such things as magical stones that melt, and so they miss the point of "Stone Soup." Their way of thinking appears to wobble back and forth between logic and magic, insight and ignorance, the reasoned and the unreasonable.

A similar patchwork of competence and incompetence can be found in preschoolers' ability to remember. It is quite common for young children to

The experience of being read to during early childhood instills the idea that reading is a pleasurable activity. It also introduces the young child to a good deal of widely held cultural knowledge.

recall the names and descriptions of their favorite dinosaurs, details of trips to an amusement park, or the location of their favorite toy at least as well as their caregivers do (DeLoache, Cassidy, & Brown, 1985; Hamond & Fivush, 1991). But they have difficulty recalling a set of toy objects immediately after they are asked to remember them (Rogoff & Mistry, 1990).

The patchwork-like quality of young children's intellectual performances raises in a new way the basic questions of development. Should the preschool period be considered a distinct stage of development, and if so, how can the unevenness of young children's thinking be accounted for? Are young children simply inconsistent in the way they think? Or do the variations in their thought processes from one task to the next reflect their relative ignorance of some of the topics they are asked to reason about? Or might it be that variations in their abilities result from variable maturation rates of different areas of the brain? In attempting to answer such questions psychologists must also be sensitive to the possibility that preschoolers appear to be illogical or unable to remember things because their still-fragile language skills do not enable them to understand what is expected of them or to communicate their thoughts adequately.

We begin our discussion of these issues by describing Piaget's portrait of early childhood, which has

dominated the study of mental development in the latter half of this century. In recent years Piaget's views on early childhood development have been increasingly questioned, but even specialists who disagree with Piaget often use his observations as the starting point for their work. After describing Piaget's theory and the ways in which he sought his evidence, we will turn to alternative lines of research on preschool thinking that have come to prominence in recent years. At present it appears that preschoolers are more competent than Piaget gave them credit for being, but sharp disagreements remain about both the nature of their abilities and the processes of cognitive change that are evident throughout the period.

PIAGET'S ACCOUNT OF MENTAL DEVELOPMENT IN EARLY CHILDHOOD

In Piaget's theoretical framework, the preschool period is a time of transition between infancy, when thinking is based on action (sensorimotor schemas), and middle childhood, when it is based on internalized (mental) events (Piaget & Inhelder, 1969). With completion of the final sensorimotor substage (described in Chapter 7), children have acquired the rudiments of representational thought. Forever after, they are able to use one thing to stand for another, one of the fundamental capacities on which their newfound ability to use language is based. They no longer rely exclusively on overt trial and error to solve problems; they imitate actions that they have observed in quite different circumstances; they engage in pretend play.

But Piaget believed that preschoolers think about the world in ways that are still decidedly primitive. He was fascinated by their ideas about how the world works. He began by observing the topics that children spontaneously raise in their conversations with each other and with adults: What is a name? What are dreams and where do they come from? Are the clouds alive? What is thinking and how does it work? Does the sun think?

Starting with such questions, Piaget would follow up his inquiry in a way that varied with the child he interviewed, depending on the answers he received. He wanted to make the conversation both as natural and as revealing of the child's thought process as possible (Piaget, 1929/1979). In Chapter 1 (p. 32) we referred to this flexible questioning procedure as a *clinical interview*. Piaget begins a clinical interview with a 5-year-old child identified as Horn by asking, "What is a name?"

> **Horn:** [A name is] what we use. When we want to say something, or call someone.
> **Piaget:** Where is the name of the sun?
> **Horn:** Up in the sky.
> **Piaget:** Where?
> **Horn:** In the sun.
> **Piaget:** Where is your name?
> **Horn:** There [*indicating his throat*].
> (Piaget, 1929/1979:94)

Piaget interpreted Horn's answers as evidence that the child failed to make a distinction between names and the entities to which they refer. When children told him that clouds were alive, he concluded that another failure of distinction — between life and motion — was at fault. He believed that such answers are replaced by more grown-up responses around the age of 7 or 8 because children then become capable of **mental operations,** the mental "actions" of combining, separating, and transforming information in a logical manner. They realize that the sun does not follow

them around to give them light and that dreams do not come from street lamps. They still have many inaccurate theories about the world (as do adults!), but their reasoning loses its make-believe quality.

Piaget's belief that young children are led into error and confusion because they are still unable to engage in true mental operations is captured in the name that he gave to this period of development, the **preoperational stage.** He viewed early childhood as a time when limitations on fully operational thought are gradually overcome. The very name "preoperational" describes 3-, 4-, and 5-year-old children's thinking in terms of what it is *not*: not yet operational. Realizing that this negative definition provides no guide to how they do think, and hence how to teach and help young children, Piaget and his followers have also looked for positive terms to describe the special properties of thinking in early childhood.

Piaget hypothesized that the key feature of thinking during early childhood is the inability of children of this age to focus attention (or "center," as he called it) on more than one salient aspect of whatever they are trying to think about. Only after overcoming this limitation, he believed, do children make the transition to the stage of operational thinking. Two classic examples from Piaget's work have greatly influenced all subsequent work on early childhood development; each is said to illustrate the limitations of centering on a single aspect of a problem.

First, young children appear to become confused about the relationship between a general class of objects and its subclasses. When shown a set of wooden beads, most of which are brown and the remainder white, young children fail to keep simultaneously in mind both the full set ("beads") and the two subsets of differently colored members. When asked, "Which are there more of, brown beads or wooden beads?" they claim that there are more brown beads. According to Piaget, preschoolers make this mistake because they center on only one aspect of the problem at a time — in this case, they appear to concentrate on color. In middle childhood, according to this line of thinking, children can keep in mind more than one feature of the problem. They remember both that there are more brown beads than white beads and that there are more wooden beads than either. Thus the older children are not led into error.

The second example is perhaps Piaget's most famous demonstration of the difference between preoperational and concrete operational thinking.

Children are presented with two identical beakers, each filled with exactly the same amount of water. While the child watches, the water in one of the beakers is poured into a third, narrower and taller beaker, so that the level of the water in the new beaker is higher. From this change in level, 3- and 4-year-olds conclude that the amount of water has somehow increased.

Again Piaget maintained that young children err because they center on only a single dimension of the problem—in this case, the height of the water in the beaker. They are unable to consider the height and width of the beaker simultaneously. Once children are capable of mental operations, they firmly deny that the amount has changed, presumably because their thinking has become decentered and they can consider several aspects of the problem at once. Thus they are able to think through what would happen if the water were poured back into its original beaker at the same time that they keep track of the information about the new beaker. (We will return to research based on these examples in Chapter 12 because it plays a central role in disputes about the nature of mental development in middle childhood.)

Egocentrism

According to Piaget (1983), the inability to center on more than one aspect of a situation at a time is the basis of **egocentrism.** He believed this to be a basic characteristic of preoperational thought from which many of its other characteristics follow. Recall from Chapter 6 that "egocentrism" has a narrower meaning in Piaget's theory than in everyday speech. It does not mean selfish or arrogant. Rather, it means a tendency to consider the world entirely in terms of "ego's" point of view, to "center on oneself." In comparison with infants, who, according to Piaget, are totally centered on their own actions (thus egocentric), preschoolers are far more anchored in external reality. They still, however, have only a hazy sense of how their ideas and desires relate to the world around them, and they tend to assume that everyone else sees things just as they do. He described the difficulties that arise from egocentrism in the following way:

> In order to be objective, one must have become conscious of one's "I." Objective knowledge can only be conceived in relation to subjective

[knowledge], and a mind that was ignorant of itself would inevitably tend to put into things its own pre-notions and prejudices. . . . [O]riginally the child puts the whole content of consciousness on the same plane and draws no distinction between "I" and the external world. (Piaget, 1930:241–242)

The egocentric nature of thought during this period is revealed by the difficulty young children have in imagining what things look like from another person's point of view. The classic example of this form of egocentrism is the three-mountain problem. Piaget and Inhelder (1956) confronted young children with a large diorama containing models of three distinctively marked mountains, each a different size and shape (see Figure 9.1). They first asked the children to walk around the diorama and become familiar with the landscape from all sides. Once the children were familiar with it, they were seated at one side and shown a doll. The doll was placed on the opposite side of the diorama, so that it had a "different view" of the land-

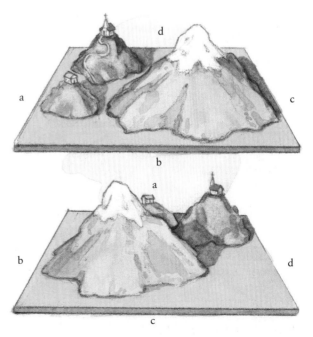

FIGURE 9.1   *Preschool children shown this diorama of three mountains with a distinctive landmark on each mountain were unable to say how the scene might look from perspectives other than the one they had adopted at the moment. (From Piaget & Inhelder, 1956.)*

scape. The children were then shown pictures of the diorama from several perspectives and asked to identify the picture that corresponded to the doll's point of view. Despite the fact that they had traveled around the diorama, the children almost always chose the picture corresponding to their own point of view, not the doll's.

The egocentric quality of children's thought also appears in their speech. Recall from Chapter 8, for example, the tendency of young children to engage in "collective monologues" rather than true dialogues when they play together. This same quality becomes evident when two preschoolers are seated at a table and asked to communicate with each other about identical sets of objects arrayed before them. In experiments of this kind a small screen is placed between the children so that they cannot see each other. (Dickson, 1981, reviews the literature on this type of experiment.) One child is designated the speaker; the other is the listener. The speaker must describe the objects on her side of the screen one at a time, and the listener must choose the corresponding object from her own array. A typical experimental arrangement is shown in Figure 9.2.

Most 4- and 5-year-old children in the role of speaker provide too little information for the listener. If the objects are large and small toys in the shape of dogs, cats, and elephants, for example, the speaker might say only "This one is a dog," or even "Take this one," failing to realize that the listener doesn't have enough information to know exactly which object is being referred to. Young listeners also have difficulty with this task. Even when they are given the chance to ask for more information, 4- and 5-year-olds are unlikely to do so.

A different form of early childhood egocentrism that has attracted a great deal of attention in recent years is evident when children are asked to reason about how other people reason (Astington & Gopnik, 1991). You can demonstrate this kind of egocentrism by telling children the following kind of story, using dolls and toys as props:

> Once there was a little boy who liked candy. One day he put a chocolate bar in a box on the table and went away for a while. While he was gone, his mother came. She took the candy out of the box and put it in the top drawer of the bureau where

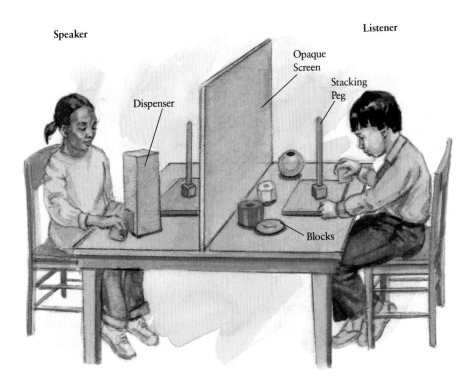

FIGURE 9.2   *The task of keeping in mind what someone else needs to be told in order to communicate with that person effectively often defeats preschoolers. The children shown here must describe the blocks on their side of the screen, being careful to mention their distinguishing features, in order to stack them in the same order. (From Krauss & Glucksberg, 1969.)*

he kept his socks. The little boy came back. He was hungry and went to get his candy.

Then ask the children, "Where do you think the little boy will look?" Three-year-olds act as if the boy who left the room had the same information that they do; they say that the boy will look in the top drawer of the bureau. Five-year-olds are far more likely to say that the little boy will look in the box on the table; they understand that the child who left the room has a false belief about the location of the candy. A variety of evidence indicates that this ability to think about other people's mental states, often referred to as a **theory of mind,** comes into existence during the fourth year of life (Astington & Gopnik, 1991; Frye & Moore, 1991).

The universality of this change in the ability to reason about other people's reasoning at an early age is suggested by the work of Jeremy Avis and Paul Harris (1991). They presented a version of the "hiding the candy bar" task to Baka children between the ages of 3 and 6. The Baka people are preliterate hunter-gatherers who live in southeast Cameroon in West Africa. Avis and Harris found that the Baka children made the transition to understanding that someone might have a false belief at approximately the same age as children who live in the United States and England.

Taken together, the evidence on spatial perspective taking (the three-mountain problem), failure to provide adequate information to others in conversation, and inability to appreciate the possibility that someone may have a false belief all provide support for Piaget's theory of the egocentric nature of young children's thinking.

Confusing Appearance and Reality

A closely associated feature of thought during early childhood, according to Piaget, is a tendency to focus exclusively on what is perceptually most striking about an object; that is, on its surface appearance. He believed that this perceptual tendency makes it difficult for the young child to distinguish between the way things seem to be and the way they are (Flavell, 1985). A common phenomenon that requires a distinction between appearance and reality occurs when a straight stick is partially submerged in water: the stick looks bent, but we know that this appearance is not reality;

FIGURE 9.3   *A straight stick seen through water looks bent. The distinction between a thing as it really is and as it appears under certain circumstances is only partially mastered during early childhood.*

it is an illusion (see Figure 9.3). Young children, however, may believe the stick has actually changed. Likewise, because they have difficulty with the appearance-reality distinction, 2½-year-olds may become frightened when an older child puts on a mask at Halloween, as if the mask had actually changed the child into a witch or a dragon.

Rheta DeVries (1969) took advantage of small children's confusion about the reality behind masks to study the development of the appearance-reality distinction. In separate experimental sessions, each child was introduced to Maynard, an unusually well-behaved black cat. At the start of the experiment, each child was told, "I want to show you my pet. Do you know what it is?" All of the children were able to say that Maynard was a cat. They were encouraged to play with Maynard for a short while, and then DeVries hid Maynard's front half behind a screen while she strapped a realistic mask of a ferocious dog onto his

(a)

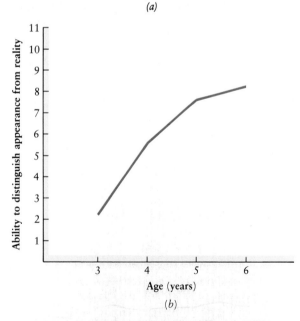

(b)

FIGURE 9.4   (a) *Maynard the cat, without and with a dog mask.* (b) *The growth of the ability to understand that Maynard remains a cat even when his appearance is changed so that he looks like a dog. (Adapted from De Vries, 1969.)*

head (see Figure 9.4a). The children were asked to keep their eyes on the cat's tail while the mask was put on so that they would be certain that she was not switching one animal for another. As she removed the screen, DeVries told each child, "Now this animal is going to look quite different. Look, it has a face like a dog."

DeVries went on to ask a set of questions designed to assess the child's ability to distinguish between the animal's real identity and its appearance: "What kind of animal is it now?" "Is it really a dog?" "Can it bark?" The strength of children's ability to distinguish appearance and reality was measured on an 11-point scale. Children who said that the cat had turned into a dog were given a score of 1, while children who said that the cat only appeared to turn into a dog but could never really become one were rated 11.

By and large, the 3-year-olds focused almost entirely on Maynard's appearance (see Figure 9.4b). They said he had actually become a ferocious dog, and some of them were afraid he would bite them. Most of the 6-year-olds scoffed at this idea, understanding that the cat only looked like a dog. The 4- and 5-year-olds showed considerable confusion. They didn't believe that a cat could become a dog, but they did not always answer DeVries's questions correctly.

Similar confusions between appearance and reality have been reported by John Flavell and his colleagues, who showed young children various objects that appeared to be one thing but were really another: a sponge that appeared to be a rock, a stone that appeared to be an egg, and a small piece of white paper placed behind a transparent piece of pink plastic so that the paper appeared to be pink. The children were shown the objects under a variety of conditions and asked to say what the object looked like and what it "really really" was (Flavell, Flavell, & Green, 1983; Flavell, Green, & Flavell, 1986).

Consistent with Piaget's claims about the difficulties that young children experience in distinguishing reality from appearance, these researchers found that American 3-year-olds are very likely to answer incorrectly. They say (for example) that the white paper under pink plastic really *is* pink or that the fake rock made from a sponge *really really* is a sponge. Four-year-olds seem to be in a transition state; they sometimes answer correctly, sometimes incorrectly. Five-year-olds have a much firmer grip on the appearance-reality distinction in these circumstances and usually answer the experimenters' questions correctly.

Flavell (1990:14–15) offers three lines of evidence to show that young children's difficulties with the appearance-reality distinction are "nontrivial, deep-seated, [and] genuinely intellectual ones."

1. Chinese, Japanese, and British 3-year-olds experience similar difficulties (Flavell et al., 1983; Harris & Gross, 1988).
2. Various attempts to simplify the task do not help young children over their difficulties (Flavell et al., 1987).
3. Attempts to train young children to make the appropriate distinctions have failed (Taylor & Hort, 1990).

Precausal Reasoning

Nothing is more characteristic of preschoolers than their love for asking questions. "Why is the sky blue?" "What makes clouds?" "Where do babies come from?" Adults may not know the answers to such questions themselves or they may prefer not to answer them, but it seems self-evident that children are interested in the causes of things. Despite this interest, Piaget believed that young children are not yet capable of true mental operations, so they do not engage in cause-and-effect reasoning like older children and adults. Instead of reasoning from general premises to particular cases (deduction) or from specific cases to general ones (induction), he claimed, young children think *transductively,* from one particular to another. As a consequence, they are likely to confuse cause and effect. Because transductive reasoning precedes true, causal reasoning, he referred to this aspect of young children's thinking as **precausal** (Piaget, 1930).

Our own daughter gave a splendid demonstration of the transductive reasoning that leads a young child to confuse cause and effect. At the age of 3½, Jenny happened to walk with us through an old graveyard. Listening to us read the inscriptions on the gravestones, she realized that somehow these old moss-covered stones represented people. "Where is she now?" she asked when we finished reading the inscription on one stone.

"She's dead," we told her.

"But where is she?" We tried to explain that after people die they are buried in the ground, in cemeteries.

The idea of death is especially difficult for preschoolers to grasp.

With preschoolers' increased understanding and growing ability to imagine come new fears. A little girl is frightened by a bearded creature in a red suit, whom we know to be Santa Claus.

After that, Jenny steadfastly refused to go into cemeteries with us and would become upset when we were near one. At bedtime every evening, she repeatedly asked us about death, burial, and graveyards. We answered her questions as best we could, yet she kept asking the same questions and she was obviously upset by the topic. The reason for her fear became clear when we were moving to New York City. "Are there any graveyards in New York City?" she asked anxiously. We were exhausted by her insistent questions, and our belief that we should be candid and honest was crumbling.

"No," we lied. "There are no graveyards in New York City." At this response, Jenny visibly relaxed.

"Then people don't die in New York," she said a couple of minutes later. Jenny had reasoned that since graveyards are places where dead people are found, graveyards must be the cause of death. This reasoning led her to the comforting but incorrect conclusion that if you can stay away from graveyards, you are not in danger of dying.

THE STUDY OF YOUNG CHILDREN'S THINKING AFTER PIAGET

The examples we have provided thus far (summarized in Table 9.1) are only a sample of the phenomena that led Piaget to conclude that a distinctive mode of thought is associated with early childhood. But they are sufficient to give the flavor of his approach. Time and again his observations suggest that children's thinking is dominated by a failure to distinguish their own perspective and another's. The inability to reason about two aspects of a thing as part of the same process (an action and its reverse, a set of objects and its subsets) and the child's egocentrism appear to explain the major characteristics of thought during this period of development.

Despite some criticism (Isaacs, 1966; Vygotsky, 1934/1987), the comprehensiveness of Piaget's theory, supported by the vivid and convincing reports of his interviews with young children, won wide acceptance for his characterization of early childhood as the period of preoperational thinking (Flavell, 1985). In recent years, however, a growing tide of studies has produced doubts that Piaget's research methods validly assessed children's mental abilities, and alternative theoretical approaches have been developed to explain the nature of preschoolers' thinking. This new evidence has inspired a broad reexamination of Piaget's theory of early childhood thought processes (Case, 1991; Donaldson, 1978; Gardner, 1991; Siegal, 1991; Wellman & Gelman, 1992).

The Problem of Uneven Levels of Performance

Piaget himself was aware that a child's performance could vary somewhat from one version of a problem to another, even though the problems seemed to require the same logical operations. He referred to such cases as examples of **horizontal decalage** (literally, horizontal misalignment). He believed that subtle differences in the logical requirements of the different versions of a task accounted for these variations in children's performance. He was also aware that the interview technique itself might produce an apparent unevenness in performance by obscuring the thought processes being studied, especially in young children who were still novices in the use of language (Piaget, 1929/1979). His own work convinced him, however, that he had overcome the problems of conversing with young children. Even when interviewing is properly conducted, he believed, preoperational children fail to distinguish their point of view from that of someone else, become easily captured by surface appearances, and are often confused about causal relations.

Nonegocentric reasoning

Recent studies seem to show that young children are not so limited in their ability to appreciate alternative points of view as Piaget thought (Flavell, 1985, and Gelman & Baillargeon, 1983, review the evidence). In one such demonstration, Helen Borke (1975) replicated Piaget and Inhelder's three-mountain experiment and then presented an alternative form of the problem. That is, one version of the task was precisely the same as Piaget and Inhelder's: children were shown a diorama of three mountains, one snow-capped, one with a church on it, and one with a house (see Figure 9.1). In the other version, however, the

TABLE 9.1

Piaget's Stages of Cognitive Development: Preoperational

Age, years	Stage	Description	Characteristics and Examples
Birth to 2	Sensorimotor	Infants' achievements consist largely of co-ordinating their sensory perceptions and simple motor behaviors. As they move through the 6 substages of this period, infants come to recognize the existence of a world outside of themselves and begin to interact with it in deliberate ways.	Centration, the tendency to focus (center) on the most salient aspect of whatever one is trying to think about. A major manifestation of this is egocentrism, the tendency to consider the world entirely in terms of one's own point of view.
2 to 6	Preoperational	Young children can represent reality to themselves through the use of symbols, including mental images, words, and gestures. Objects and events no longer have to be present to be thought about, but children often fail to distinguish their point of view from that of others, become easily captured by surface appearances, and are often confused about causal relations.	* Children engage in collective monologues, rather than dialogues, in each other's company. * Children have difficulty taking a listener's knowledge into account in order to communicate effectively. * Children fail to consider both the height and width of containers in order to compare their volumes. * Children confuse classes, e.g., a set of wooden beads, with subclasses, e.g., the white or brown wooden beads in the set. They cannot reliably say whether there are more wooden beads or more brown beads in the set.
6 to 12	Concrete operational	As they enter middle childhood, children become capable of mental operations, internalized actions that fit into a logical system. Operational thinking allows children mentally to combine, separate, order, and transform objects and actions. Such operations are considered concrete because they are carried out in the presence of the objects and events being thought about.	Confusion of appearance and reality. * Children act as if a Halloween mask actually changes the identity of the person wearing it. * Children may believe that a straight stick partially submerged in water actually does become bent.
12 to 19	Formal operational	In adolescence the developing person acquires the ability to think systematically about all logical relations within a problem. Adolescents display keen interest in abstract ideals and the process of thinking itself.	* Children are likely to answer incorrectly about the color of a sheet of white paper that they see placed under a sheet of transparent colored plastic. Precausal reasoning, characterized by illogical thinking and an indifference to cause-and-effect relations. * A child may think a graveyard is a cause of death because dead people are buried there. A form of moral reasoning that sees morality as being imposed from the outside and that does not take intentions into account.

FIGURE 9.5   *Borke's modification of Piaget's three-mountain perspective-taking task. When a diorama contains familiar objects, preschoolers are more likely to be able to say how it looks from a point of view other than their own.*

landmarks were a small lake with a boat on it, a horse and cow, and a building, placed in approximately the same locations on the diorama as the three mountains (see Figure 9.5).

In Borke's alternative version, Grover, a character from the television program *Sesame Street,* drove around the landscape in a car. From time to time he would stop and take a look at the view. The child's task was to indicate what Grover's view of the scene looked like. Children as young as 3 years old performed well on Borke's farm-scene perspective-taking problem, but their performance on the three-mountain version of the problem was poor, as Piaget and Inhelder's work had suggested. These contrasting levels of performance led Borke to conclude that when easily differentiated objects are used and care is taken to make it easy for young children to express their understanding, they are able to imagine spatial perspectives other than their own. On the basis of similar results from similar experiments, Margaret Donaldson (1978) suggests that 3- to 5-year-old children can display nonegocentric spatial perspective taking, but the motives and intentions of the characters involved in the problem must be clear, so that the task makes what she calls "human sense."

Another piece of evidence contrary to the idea that young children are *generally* unable to take other

people's communicative situations into account has already been provided in Chapter 8 (p. 295): Young children who fail to modify their descriptions of objects for a listener who cannot see the objects are nonetheless likely to modify their language to make it understandable for 2-year-olds who are just beginning to speak.

Distinguishing appearance from reality

In the work of DeVries and Flavell, described earlier (pp. 321–322), children seem to begin to make consistent distinctions between appearance and reality somewhere between the ages of 4 and 6. However, special features of the experimental procedures seem to be at least partly responsible for the difficulties experienced by the youngest children.

In one study designed to explore young children's ability to adhere to the distinction between appearance and reality, 4-year-olds were asked to distinguish between how a character in a story really felt about a situation and how she behaved publicly (Harris et al., 1986). The researchers presented the children with stories such as the following:

> Diana wants to go outside, but she has a tummy ache. She knows that if she tells her mom that she has a tummy ache, her mom will say that she can't go out. She tries to hide the way she feels so that her mom will let her go outside.

When the researchers asked, "How did Diana really feel when she had a tummy ache?" and "How did she try to look on her face when she had a tummy ache?" they found that 4-year-olds were usually able to distinguish between real and displayed feelings. This ability was fragile, however, and the 4-year-olds were generally unable to provide reasonable justifications for their correct judgments.

Perhaps the best evidence that under some circumstances children as young as 3 will exhibit an understanding of the appearance-reality distinction comes from experiments that deliberately focus on children's interpretive problems in conversations with adults. Recall from Chapter 8 (pp. 292–293) that young children first acquire basic conventions of conversation and only later learn to deal with cases in which these conventions are violated. In the experimental studies we have been reviewing in this chapter, the researchers characteristically present the children with a large number of similar problems and question them repeatedly on each problem. Michael Siegal (1991) hypothesized that this sort of inquiry violates the conversational norms that young children know. When a question is repeated, for example, the usual reason is either that the person didn't hear well or that the first answer was incorrect.

Siegal reports that when he and his colleagues replicated the standard procedure, presenting a series of appearance-reality problems and asking the same kinds of questions over and over, 3-year-olds were indeed likely to give answers that seemed to indicate that they were confusing appearance and reality. If they were presented with only a single problem, however, and not queried repeatedly about their responses, three out of four of the children answered correctly.

Children's responses to the following story provide other evidence that they can understand the difference between appearance and reality:

> A grown-up poured milk into a blue glass with a blue lid on top. She asked Sally, a girl your age, what color the milk was truly. Sally said the milk was truly blue. Did she say that because she really and truly thought the milk was blue or was she pretending? (Siegal, 1991:75)

All of the 3-year-olds answered that Sally was only pretending, showing that they could make the appropriate distinction.

Two conclusions can be drawn from the recent research on the appearance-reality distinction. First, many children are able to make such distinctions well before they enter middle childhood at the age of 6 or 7 years. Second, their ability to make such a distinction is fragile and may not appear unless special care is taken to avoid confusing them.

Effective causal reasoning

One of Piaget's best-known examples of precausal reasoning came from his interviews with children about how bicycles work. In the course of the interview, he also asked the children to draw a picture illustrating their explanations (see Figure 9.6). During the interview a bicycle was propped against a chair in front of the child. An interview with Grim, aged 5½, provides the kind of evidence that led Piaget to conclude that the reasoning of young children is precausal (Piaget, 1930:206):

Piaget: How does the bicycle move along?
Grim: With the brakes on top of the bike.
Piaget: What is the brake for?
Grim: To make it go because you push.
Piaget: What do you push with?
Grim: With your feet.

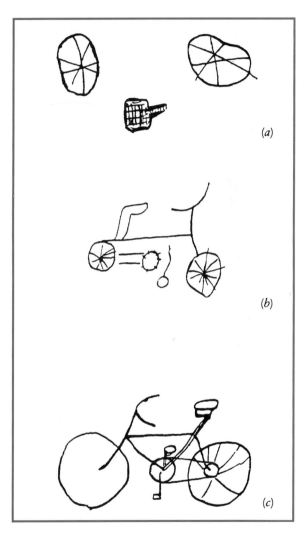

FIGURE 9.6 *These drawings show how children of different ages and mental abilities perceive the way a bicycle works. (a) The child who is 5 years and 3 months old has no clear idea of how the different parts of the bicycle fit together. (b) A retarded 9-year-old has captured part of the mechanism in the illustration but fails to link the pedal to the cogwheel and chain. (c) An 8-year, 3-month-old child can represent all of the essential mechanisms. (After Piaget, 1930.)*

Piaget: What does that do?

Grim: It makes it go.

Piaget: How?

Grim: With the brakes.

In the late 1920s Piaget visited the Malting House School in Cambridge, England, where Susan Isaacs was also conducting research on young children. Isaacs was skeptical about Piaget's ideas on preoperational thought. When she spotted one of her preschoolers riding by on a tricycle, she put her visitor's theory to an impromptu test:

> At that moment, Dan [aged 5 years, 9 months] happened to be sitting on a tricycle in the garden, back-pedaling. I went to him and said, "The tricycle is not moving forward, is it?" "Of course not, when I'm back-pedaling," he said. "Well," I asked, "how does it go forward when it does?" "Oh, well," he replied, "your feet press the pedals, that turns the crank round, and the cranks turn that round" (pointing to the cog-wheel), "and that makes the chain go round, and the chain turns the hub round, and then the wheels go round—and there you are!" (Isaacs, 1966:44)

Isaacs offered this anecdote as evidence against Piaget's theory that young children are incapable of causal reasoning. Before accepting either conclusion, most developmental psychologists would require more information about both boys, their experience with tricycles and bicycles, and the way the interviews were conducted. Is Dan simply an especially advanced preschooler? Is the difference in their performances the result of differences in the way the problems were posed to them? Systematic answers to such questions require experiments that deliberately vary the way in which the problems are presented.

During the 1970s and 1980s, experiments by developmental psychologists provided ample evidence to support the conclusion that when the task is sufficiently simplified, young children's understanding of causation far exceeds the level that Piaget thought typical (Bullock, 1984; Bullock & Gelman, 1979). Merry Bullock and Rochel Gelman, for example, tested the ability of 3-to-5-year-olds to understand the basic principle that causes come before effects, using the apparatus shown in Figure 9.7.

Children observed two sequences of events. In the first, a steel marble was dropped into one of two slots

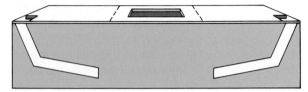

FIGURE 9.7   *The apparatus used by Bullock and Gelman to test preschoolers' understanding that cause precedes effect. A marble was dropped into one of the slots. Two seconds after the marble disappeared, a Snoopy doll popped out of the hole in the middle of the apparatus. At the same moment, a second marble was dropped into the other slot, where it disappeared with no further result. Preschoolers are generally able to indicate which marble caused Snoopy to jump up. (From Bullock & Gelman, 1979.)*

in a box, both of which were visible through the side of the box. Two seconds after the marble disappeared at the bottom of the slot, a Snoopy doll popped out of the hole in the apparatus's middle. At that moment, a second ball was dropped into the other slot. It too disappeared, with no further result. The children were asked which ball had made Snoopy jump up and to give a reason for their answer. Then they were given a ball and asked to drop it into the apparatus on the side where the first ball had made Snoopy jump up.

Even the 3-year-olds were usually correct in selecting the side where the ball had caused Snoopy to jump up. The 5-year-olds had no difficulty with the task at all. However, there was a marked difference between the age groups in their ability to explain what had happened. Many of the 3-year-olds could give no explanation or said something completely irrelevant ("It's got big teeth"). Almost all of the 5-year-olds could provide at least a partial explanation of the principle that causes precede effects. This finding suggests one reason why Piaget underestimated the cognitive competence of young children: His research techniques relied heavily on verbally presented problems and verbal justifications of reasoning, both of which put young children at a disadvantage (see Box 9.1).

The search for alternatives

The various lines of evidence showing that young children's thinking is not as limited as it was once thought to be have been the starting points for several attempts to improve both on Piaget's methods of investigation and on his theory. Each of these approaches is related to one or another of the four basic frameworks for understanding development summarized in Chapter 1 (pp. 14–17).

Psychologists who take the **neo-Piagetian approach** have reaffirmed Piaget's fundamental assumptions about the nature of development but are refining his theory in various ways to account for modern evidence. A second group, those who adopt an **information-processing approach,** have taken a different tack. They conceive of the young child as a limited-capacity information processor whose thinking can best be understood by analogy with the digital computer. Investigators who follow this path generally conceive of developmental change as the result of changes both in children's "hardware," such as myelination of a new brain region, and in children's "software," such as the acquisition of a new strategy for remembering (Siegler, 1991).

Investigators who use the information-processing perspective and the child-as-computer metaphor are not necessarily committed to a particular point of view about the nature of development itself. Some information-processing psychologists adopt a form of environmental-learning theory in which they focus on the ways in which psychological processes are modified as the result of patterns of input from the environment. Psychologists who take this path believe that development is a continuous process in which limitations on memory capacity are gradually overcome; long-term memory capacity gradually increases; behaviors are routinized; and strategies are developed to link input more effectively to output (Klahr & Wallace, 1976; Siegler, 1991). Other psychologists who adopt an information-processing approach believe that gradual changes in one part of the cognitive system — for example, increased short-term memory capacity — lead to discontinuous, stagelike changes in the child's overall functioning. This second group uses the information-processing metaphor to support a Piagetian or neo-Piagetian point of view (Case, 1991).

A third group advocate an approach called **modularity theory,** which is a variant of the biological-maturational view. They believe that Piaget overemphasized both the importance of constructive interaction and the degree to which developmental change occurs in all aspects of children's thinking at the same time. They place much greater weight on inherited, biological factors in explaining developmental change, and they emphasize biological

changes within specific cognitive domains, such as language, number, and space. Finally, a fourth group of psychologists, the **cultural-context theorists,** emphasize the role of culture in structuring the interplay of biological and environmental influences.

Neo-Piagetian Theories of Cognitive Development

There have been three major branches of neo-Piagetian thinking about development in early childhood. Adherents of the first branch retain Piaget's theory in more or less the original form, but seek to refine the way children are observed and the way substages, or levels, are identified in particular problem-solving tasks.

John Flavell and his colleagues, for example, have suggested that it is important to distinguish two levels of difficulty in the process of adopting another's point of view (Flavell, 1986, 1990; Flavell, Green, & Flavell, 1990) (see Figure 9.8). The first level requires only that a child realize that other people may not be able to see what he or she can see; if a card with a cat on one side and a dog on the other is shown to a 3-year-old child and then the card is held vertically between child and experimenter with the dog visible to the child, the child will say that the experimenter cannot see the dog. The same child is unlikely to realize, however, that the way an object appears to people depends on their point of view; if a picture of a cat is laid flat on the table and the child is asked how it looks to the experimenter, the child will tell how it looks from his or her perspective only. Flavell also believes that young children progress through several levels in their ability to understand the distinction between appearance and reality as well as in their ability to predict others' states of mind in false-belief situations. He maintains that when very young children seem to succeed at such tasks, it is because the procedures have distorted and simplified the tasks so drastically that they no longer tap the ability under investigation.

Adherents of a second branch of neo-Piagetian research on early childhood retain Piaget's idea that children construct knowledge through their active engagement with the world but argue that stages in the acquisition of knowledge are narrowly confined to specific spheres of activity, or domains, such as social reasoning, drawing, music, language, and mathematics (Carey & Gelman, 1991; Gelman & Baillargeon, 1983;

BOX 9.1
Young Children as Witnesses

The nature of young children's thought processes becomes an important social issue when they are called upon to give testimony in a court of law. In some cases they may be witnesses to a crime; in others, suspected victims of a crime.

Adults' reluctance to believe the word of a young child has a long history. Psychologists have viewed children as suggestible (Stern, 1910); unable to distinguish fantasy from reality (Piaget, 1926, 1928; Werner, 1948); and prone to fantasize sexual events (Freud, 1905/1953). Judges, lawyers, and prosecutors have also expressed reservations about children's reliability as witnesses (Goodman, 1984; Goodman et al., 1991). Legal rulings on the admissibility of children's testimony reflect these longstanding doubts. In many states, for example, the judge determines whether a child below a certain age (which varies from state to state) is competent to testify (King & Yuille, 1987).

Owing to growing concern over the prevalence of sexual and physical abuse of children in recent years, the legal community has reexamined the reliability of children's testimony. At the same time, psychologists are raising their own doubts about earlier conclusions that young children are unable to testify reliably about past events (Ceci, Toglia, & Ross, 1987).

At the heart of the current discussion of child testimony are two questions: How good are children's memories at various ages and how susceptible are young children to suggestions that change what they remember? Reason for concern is provided by children's behavior both in actual trials and in experimental studies conducted by psychologists.

When young children are asked about events that have personal significance for them, such as whether or not they were given an injection when they went to the doctor's office, they are likely to provide correct answers (Goodman et al., 1990). They have trouble locating events in time, however, and giving specific examples of recurrent events (Nelson, 1986). Adults have a tendency to probe more deeply when a child appears not to remember, but such probes may lead to additional problems. When Katherine Nelson (1978) asked preschoolers about what happens when they eat lunch at school, she found that if she asked for information that children did not have ("Where did the lunch come from?"), they would provide responses that appeared to come from other scripted events, such as a visit to a restaurant or a market, rather than say that they did not know.

These difficulties are seen in a case in which the adults were eventually convicted of sexual abuse, but the child witnesses at first denied that anything unusual had happened. They later recalled events that led to the conviction of their baby-sitter and her husband. But in addition to their accurate testimony they said outrageous, fanciful things—for example, that after assaulting the children, the baby-sitter and her husband ate them for dinner (Goodman, Aman, & Hirschman, 1987).

There are several ways in which the questioning procedures that are standard in criminal proceedings may lead the young child to make false statements. First, the questioning may affect the child's memory of what happened in ways the child is not conscious of. When an interviewer, probing a child's testimony, makes an erroneous suggestion about what happened, the suggestion may become blended with the child's memory of what happened to produce a hybrid "memory." This new, hybrid memory can block the original memory so the child can no longer recall the actual events. It is also possible that the child remembers both what the adult suggested *and* what really happened but can no longer tell which memory is authentic (Ceci & Bruck, in press).

Evidence of young children's vulnerability to suggestion is provided by an experiment in which 3- and 4-year-old children first witnessed a staged incident involving three men and a woman, and were then interviewed by an experienced police officer about the woman's appearance. One session went like this (Dent, 1982: 290–291):

Q: Wearing a poncho and a cap?
A: I think it was a cap.

Q: What sort of a cap was it? Was it like a beret, or was it a peaked cap, or . . . ?

A: No, it had a sort of, it was flared with a little piece coming out. It was flared with a sort of button thing in the middle.

Q: What . . . Was it a peak like that, that sort of thing?

A: Ye—es.

Q: That's the sort of cap I'm thinking you're meaning, with a little peak out there.

A: Yes, that's the top view, yes.

Q: Smashing. Um—what colour?

A: Oh! Oh—I think it was black or brown.

Q: Think it was dark, shall we say?

A: Yes—it was dark colour I think, and I didn't see her hair.

In fact, the woman in the staged scene was wearing neither a poncho nor a hat. The child not only came to "remember" these items, but even added that the woman carried a dark purse to match her hat! As Elizabeth Loftus and Graham Davies (1984) point out, by persistent requests for details, the police officer led the child into error.

Besides pointing up the limitations on their ability to remember and recall information, such episodes may reflect the fact that young children are likely to believe that adults know more than they. When they are being questioned in a legal proceeding, they may incorporate the adult's suggestions in their answers because they want to please the adult, even when they know that the adult's suggestions are wrong. Asked the same questions more than once, they often change their answers because they assume that something was wrong with their first answer (Siegal, 1991).

Children are by no means the only ones whose memories are vulnerable to the suggestions of the people who question them. Adults, too, can be led astray in such situations (Loftus, 1979). Young children are considered to be especially susceptible, however, because of their limited ability to remember, their lack of experience with legal proceedings, and their tendency to try to please adults.

Three-year-old Amanda Conklin looks out at a crowded Van Nuys courtroom as the judge questions her in a case in which her father was accused of murdering her mother.

(a)   *(b)*

FIGURE 9.8   *The two conditions under which the child views the picture of an animal illustrate two levels in perspective-taking ability according to John Flavell and his colleagues. In* (a) *the child knows that the adult does not see what she sees (a cat) and she does not see what the adult sees (a dog is drawn on the other side of the card). This result shows that the child is capable of level 1 perspective taking. However, when a picture is presented as in* (b) *the child confuses the adult view of the picture with her own and assumes that they both see the turtle right-side up. This more difficult (level 2) form of perspective taking does not develop until children are 4 to 5 years old.*

Karmiloff-Smith, 1986). Thus a child may be an expert chess player or a whiz at arithmetic and yet solve typical Piagetian tasks no better than her agemates (Feldman, 1980; Gardner, 1983). The basic intuition of this approach is summarized by Jean Mandler (1983:475): "It may well be that in many areas of thinking there is no generalized competence, only hard-won principles wrested anew from each domain as it is explored." According to this view, there may be little correspondence between the level of development a child displays in one situation and the developmental level he or she displays in another because from the child's point of view, each domain has its own logic and content, both of which have to be mastered.

In another line of neo-Piagetian work, Robbie Case and his colleagues maintain that if researchers can gain a sufficiently precise understanding of the knowledge required by each cognitive domain, they may eventually achieve Piaget's initial goal of defining global stages that apply to all domains (Case, 1985,

1991). According to this view, when researchers make certain that tasks constructed from different domains involve equally demanding content and have the same logical structure, they will find that children perform at the same level of ability in each domain. Under these conditions their performances will reflect the general level of their cognitive development.

To demonstrate the possibility of such synchronous stage transitions in different domains, Case and his colleagues constructed two sets of problems with identical logical structures. The first required children to judge the "juiciness" of a drink made of different mixtures of orange juice and water. Would a mixture of five parts juice and three parts water, for example, taste as juicy as a mixture made of four parts juice and one part water?

The second, logically equivalent problem concerned two boys, each of whom was having a birthday party and each of whom wanted polished stones for his birthday (in the school where the investigators were conducting their research, polished stones were highly prized by the children). The children were shown how many stones each boy wanted and how many he actually received. Then they were asked, "Which child would be happier?" For 89 percent of the young children tested, the estimated level of cognitive development for the two kinds of problems was either the same or only a single problem-solving stage off (Case et al., 1986). The fact that the children reached virtually the same levels of reasoning on the two tasks supports the hypothesis that when enough care is taken to equate the logical structure of two problems with content from different domains, synchronous change across domains of the kind Piaget believed in can be observed.

Information-Processing Approaches

Some psychologists want to replace Piaget's vision with a view of humans as information-processing organisms whose thought processes can best be understood by analogy with the mechanisms of high-speed computers (Klahr & Wallace, 1976; Siegler, 1991).

David Klahr, a leading figure in this movement, expressed his dissatisfaction with Piagetian theorizing about development in colorful terms:

For 40 years now we have had *assimilation* and *accommodation,* the mysterious and shadowy forces of equilibration, the "Batman and Robin" of the developmental processes. What are they? How do they operate? Why is it after all this time, we know no more about them than when they first sprang upon the scene? What we need is a way to get beyond vague verbal statements of the nature of the developmental process. (Klahr, 1982:80)

Figure 9.9 contains a simplified schematic diagram of one influential information-processing approach to human thinking. At the left-hand side is the presumed starting point of any problem-solving process. Some kind of stimulation ("input," in the language of computer programming) is attended to and "read into" the system's sensory register. Then it is stored temporarily in **short-term (working) memory,** where it can be retained for several seconds. The environmental information deposited in short-term memory can be combined there with memory of past experiences (**long-term memory**) or it can be forgotten. Short-term memory is continually monitored by control processes that determine how the information there is to be applied to the problem at hand—for example, whether additional information must be gathered

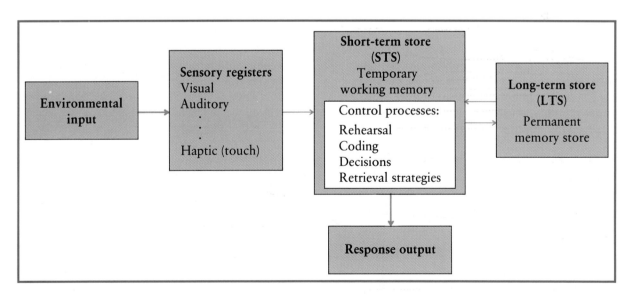

FIGURE 9.9   *The major components of an information-processing model of mental actions. (Adapted from Atkinson & Shiffrin, 1980.)*

from the environment or whether long-term memory must be searched more thoroughly for a better response. Control processes also determine whether a piece of information in short-term memory needs to be retained or can be forgotten.

Despite the differences among them, information-processing psychologists are united by the assumption that human beings, like computers, have limited information-processing capacities. From this perspective, young children's difficulties are caused by insufficient or uneven attention, limited memory, and limited strategies for acquiring and using information (Siegler, 1991). Performance improves in the course of development because these limitations are gradually reduced.

Information-processing limitations show up in many ways. First, a young child's attention is easily captured by loud, flashy stimuli, so young children are easy to distract. When they lose their train of thought in the middle of doing something, their performance naturally suffers.

Second, even when they are not distracted, young children are likely to explore an object in an incomplete and unsystematic way. This limitation was demonstrated some years ago by the Soviet psychologist Vladimir Zinchenko and his colleagues (Zinchenko, Chzhi-tsin, & Tarakanov, 1963), who asked 3- and 6-year-olds to examine various objects and become familiar with them. As Figure 9.10 indicates, the 3-year-olds examined only a few points within the object, whereas the 6-year-olds gave it a thorough examination.

Third, children between the ages of 2½ and 6 have difficulty focusing on the most relevant features of a task if they receive no strong hints from the environment. This limitation was demonstrated by Elaine Vurpillot (1968), who recorded the eye movements of children aged 3 to 10 while they examined pairs of line drawings of houses such as those shown in Figure 9.11. On some trials, children were shown identical houses; on others the houses differed in one or more relatively subtle ways. Children were asked to say whether or not the houses were identical.

Vurpillot found that all of the children responded correctly when the houses were identical, but that the young children were likely to make mistakes when the houses differed, especially if they differed in only one way. Her recordings of eye movements pinpointed the difficulty. The younger children scanned several windows in haphazard order, rather than making a systematic comparison. The older children scanned the windows row by row or column by column until they had checked almost all of them, sometimes scanning back again to check themselves. Young children thus seem to have only limited ability to select relevant details.

The amount of information that young children take in and their ability to store and manipulate it is also limited, according to several studies. For example, Micheline Chi and David Klahr (1975) found that 5-year-olds could perceive no more than three objects flashed simultaneously on a screen, whereas adults could take in six or seven objects at a glance. Many studies have demonstrated age-related increases in the ability to hold several items of information in mind at one time. Thus older children and adults can work through various steps in complex problems without losing track of what they are doing, but young children cannot. Finally, older children and adults have generally accumulated more knowledge than young children, process information more rapidly, and have more effective strategies for dealing with problems. As a consequence, they have more information available in long-term memory storage that can be speedily applied to new problems as they arise, so that they perform more competently (Chi & Koeske, 1983; Siegler, 1991).

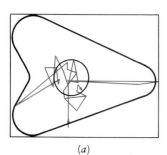

(a)

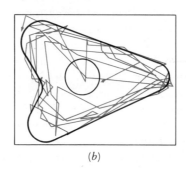

(b)

FIGURE 9.10   *Most 3-year-olds (a) asked to examine a novel figure for 20 seconds are less persistent and thorough than 6-year-olds (b) assigned the same task. (From Zinchenko, Chzhi-tsin, & Tarakanov, 1963.)*

FIGURE 9.11 *Stimuli used by Vurpillot to assess visual search. Preschoolers' failure to scan systematically often leads them to claim that the top pair of houses are identical. (From Vurpillot, 1968.)*

This overview of the limitations on young children's ability to process information suggests that when they are interested in a task, when information is presented slowly, and when they have good background knowledge, their cognitive performance should be enhanced. These are precisely the characteristics of the experiments in which young children demonstrated unexpected competence on Piagetian tasks.

Information-processing psychologists are thus encouraged to believe that their approach, by shifting the focus of study from a search for global stages of development to an assessment of a given task's information-processing demands, may represent a genuine improvement on Piaget's.

Biological Accounts of Mental Development in Early Childhood

So far we have considered efforts to account for the uneven nature of children's problem solving that focus on the content of tasks and the way they are presented: Do the tasks involve familiar content that is presented in a supportive and comfortable way, or are the tasks strange and is the way they are presented confusing? It is entirely possible, of course, that some, if not most, of the limitations on young children's mental abilities and the unevenness of their performance result primarily from variations in the rate of maturation of different parts of the central nervous system.

The growth of the brain

A promising line of evidence suggests that maturational changes in the brains of children between the ages of 2½ and 6 correspond to changes observed in their behavior (Case, 1992; Fischer, 1987; Siegler, 1989). We have already reviewed evidence of similar correspondences in the bio-social-behavioral shifts that occur during infancy in Chapters 5, 6, and 7.

At the start of early childhood, the brain has attained about 50 percent of its adult weight. By the time the child is 6, it will have grown to 90 percent of its full weight (Lecours, 1982; Tanner, 1978). Along with this overall enlargement, myelination occurs within and between several brain areas, and appears to play a particularly important role in cognitive development during early childhood (Figure 4.6 provides an overview of major brain areas). Rapid development of the auditory area is consistent with the speed with which language is acquired in early childhood. More effective connections are established between the temporal, occipital, and parietal areas, which are crucially important for the processing of temporal, visual, and spatial information. The increased connections between these centers allows for more efficient synthesis of information about different aspects of a problem. At the same time, all of these areas become more firmly linked with the speech areas of the brain, a development that fosters the growth of symbolizing and communication abilities. Other areas that undergo rapid myelination during early childhood include the hippocampus, which is important to short-term memory; and the fibers linking the cerebellum to the cerebral cortex, which allow for fine control of voluntary movements, such as those needed to tie a shoelace.

Mental modules

The major theoretical event that brought growth in the brain to the forefront of recent psychological theorizing about mental development was the dissemination of Noam Chomsky's theory of language and its acquisition. As we saw in Chapter 8, children acquire human language without any special tutoring by adults, indicating to Chomsky and his followers the existence of an innate language acquisition device (LAD). Chomsky (1980, 1986) and others have proposed that principles of language acquisition apply to many other cognitive phenomena as well.

Jerry Fodor (1983), for example, has suggested that the mind should be considered as a vast collection of **mental modules**, highly specific mental faculties tuned to particular domains of environmental input. Recognition of faces, the concept of number, perception of music, and elementary perception of causality have all been offered as examples of mental modules (Carey & Gelman, 1991; Leslie & Keeble, 1987). The concept of mental modules shares key assumptions with Chomsky's concept of a language faculty:

1. Psychological operations are presumed to be domain-specific. The mental operations required to perceive a musical tune are different from those required to recognize a face, and the principles of both are different from those that govern talking about perceiving a tune or a face.
2. The psychological principles that organize the operation of each module are assumed to be innately specified; that is, they are coded in the genes and need no special instruction to develop.
3. It is assumed that different modules do not interact directly; each represents a separate mental domain, only loosely connected to the rest.

The concept of modularity has been applied by the Scottish psychologist Alan Leslie and his colleagues in their work on the early development of the concept of causality (Leslie, 1986; Leslie & Keeble,

1987). As we have seen, Piaget's belief that preschoolers are still precausal thinkers has been challenged by Rochel Gelman and her colleagues, who have shown that understanding of causal relations *is* present during early childhood. Leslie's goal was much more ambitious: he sought to show that a primitive sensitivity to physical causality is present as near to birth as could be tested for; that is, he wanted to show that the perception of causality is an innate mental module (point 2 above).

Leslie and his colleagues studied the perception of a cause-effect relationship that results when a rolling billiard ball collides with a stationary billiard ball, which then begins to roll. So strong is this perception that even when adults are shown a series of dots on a page arranged so that one dot draws closer to the other and eventually "bumps into it," they experience the illusion that the first dot "causes" the second to move, even though they know that neither is really moving.

Leslie and his colleagues presented 6-month-old children with a computer display in which one dot appeared to bump into another, causing it to move. In one case the second dot moved immediately, suggesting causation. In the other case there was a delay in the movement of the second dot, suggesting an absence of causation. The researchers compared the pattern of looking when babies were first shown the causal event several times in a row and then shown either a different causal event or the "noncausal" event. The babies stared longer at the noncausal event, indicating that they were sensitive to causality in this restricted context.

Leslie and Stephanie Keeble (1987) suggest that this apparent capacity to perceive causality, even the illusory causality of the computer screen, serves as a template that children use to develop genuine causal understanding even before they have much real-world knowledge. Although this primitive capacity is a very rigid and low-level form of causal understanding, it points babies in the right direction when they attempt to interpret their experiences, and thereby supports the later development of more complex causal knowledge.

A different line of evidence supporting the modularity position comes from children whose overall level of development is exceptionally low but who demonstrate islands of brilliance. Some of these children suffer from **autism,** a poorly understood condition that is defined primarily by an inability to relate to other people. Young autistic children rarely use language to communicate, often fail to make eye contact with others, and do not respond appropriately to other human beings (Frith, 1989).

A remarkable characteristic of some autistic children is their highly developed mental capacity in one specific domain. Some autistic children have been reported to be able to sing an entire opera at the age of 1½, read a text aloud at the age of 2 (without any apparent comprehension), or assemble complicated objects when they are 3 years old (Rimland, 1964).

These extraordinary accomplishments appear to fit the idea of mental modules. Each falls within a domain that has its own distinctive structure (music, language, arithmetic). These are also domains in which there have been child prodigies, children who excel in some specific ability at an astonishingly early age. Prodigious performance in these domains does not seem to require much social support, nor does it affect the normal development of other domains.

Assessing modularity explanations

The evidence that several mental capacities display the properties of modularity proposed by Fodor is too important to ignore. Variability in the rates of development of modular systems almost certainly contributes to the unevenness of behavior during early childhood.

However, this theory has its shortcomings (Fischer & Bidell, 1991; Karmiloff-Smith, 1991). First, we currently have no way of delineating either the full set of mental modules or the boundaries between modules. Second, it is difficult to imagine how the modularity approach would explain many of the uneven performances by young children that we have described. It seems implausible, for example, that there would be a separate module for "taking another's point of view" and others for deductive reasoning, distinguishing between appearance and reality, and so on.

Of course, such possibilities should not be dismissed out of hand. Simon Baron-Cohen, Alan Leslie, and Uta Frith (1986), for example, appear to have discovered a very specific, module-like deficit among autistic children associated with the ability to understand the way other people think and feel. Given the present state of knowledge, however, mental modules do not seem to offer a full-fledged explanation of young children's mental development. Rather, they should be considered one important source of variability that a full theory of early childhood thought should take into account.

Culture and Mental Development in Early Childhood

The cultural-context approach shares Piaget's insistence that children must be seen as active constructors of their own development. But in addition, cultural-context theorists emphasize that parents enter into the process of their children's development by selecting and shaping the environments in which their children grow up. The environments, in their turn, reflect the parents' cultural beliefs, tools, and traditions. This two-sided process, in which both the environment and the child are seen as active agents, is referred to as **social co-construction** (Valsiner, 1988). Earlier we caught glimpses of the process of context-specific social co-construction in the mothers who jiggle their babies to encourage them to nurse (Chapter 4, p. 164), the father who supported his little daughter's attempts to play with a teething ring in a manner that allowed her to achieve a slightly more sophisticated level of play (Chapter 5, pp. 200–201), and the mother who encouraged her toddler son to walk (Chapter 7, p. 245).

The cultural-context view also focuses on specific domains of behavior, a trait it shares with the various neo-Piagetian and modularity theory approaches. Instead of emphasizing domains defined entirely by their logic or content, however, the cultural-contextualists emphasize that contexts are organized in terms of cultural meaning systems. As ordinarily used in modern psychology, **context** is roughly equivalent to "setting." It is not uncommon, for example, to encounter psychologists who speak at one moment of an "educational context" and later of an "educational setting." We often use "context" in this common-sense way in this book. Many scholars point out, however, that context is more properly thought of as a relationship between behavior, the event of which the behavior is a part, and the setting in which they take place (Bateson, 1972; Pepper, 1942).

The intimate relationship between behavior, setting, and meaningful events can be seen in the single physical behavior of waving a hand. This single motion can mean a wide variety of things, depending on its relation to the physical circumstances in which it occurs and the flow of events. A child who waves his hand may be waving good-bye to grandma, petting the cat, patting down Play-Doh to make a pancake, or swatting a fly. Which meaning the action has and its consequent significance for later behavior will depend on the relation of that act to what preceded it, what else is happening at the time, and what follows it. These relationships taken together define the context.

All contexts are cultural in the sense that they are constructed out of the pool of meanings available in the culture of the participants. What the term "cultural" adds to the term "context" is a reminder that people in different cultures engage in different activities, ascribe different meanings to what they see and do, and use different tools. Cultural contexts vary from society to society and perhaps from one generation to the next. Even when particular activities occur in more than one culture (for example, eating), the ways in which the activity is carried out may create very different contexts: In one culture the men may eat by themselves while the women stay out of view in the kitchen, and the children must absent themselves until both the men and the women are through. In another culture children and parents may be expected to eat together, and conversation that includes the children may be considered very important (Ochs et al., 1991). Each of these patterns has consequences for the development of the child.

The mental representation of contexts

A major task of theories of development is to explain how structure in the environment is converted into mental structures during the course of development. As we have seen, Piaget held that in the course of their activity, children construct *schemas,* organized patterns of individual knowledge that represent objects and their interrelationships.

Schemas are also important in cultural-context explanations of development, but they are conceived of somewhat differently. Katherine Nelson (1981, 1986) suggests that as a result of their participation in routine, culturally organized events, children acquire generalized event representations, or **scripts**. Scripts are schemas that specify the people who participate in an event, the social roles they play, the objects that are used during the event, and the sequence of actions that make up the event.

Children's participation in the activity we call "taking a bath" illustrates how script knowledge is acquired and how it functions. "Taking a bath" is done *to* a 2-month-old infant. An adult fills a sink or appropriate basin with warm water, lays out a towel, a clean diaper, and clothing, then slips the infant into the

water, while holding tightly to keep the baby from drowning.

By the age of 2 years, a child has "taken" many baths. Each time, roughly the same sequence is followed, the same objects are used, and the same cast of characters participates. Water is poured into a tub, clothes are taken off, the child gets into the water, soap is applied and rinsed off, the child gets out of the water, dries off, and dresses. There may be variations—a friend may take a bath with the child, or the child may play before or after washing—but the basic sequence is constant. Initially, the role played by the infant is entirely passive. Gradually, as the child becomes familiar with the script used in taking a bath and acquires more competence in various of its parts, he assumes a greater role in the activity.

During the preschool period, adults still play an important role in the scripted activity called "taking a bath." They initiate children's baths and come in to scrub their ears, to wash their hair, or to help them dry off. Not until adulthood will the child be responsible for the entire event, including scouring the tub and worrying about clean towels, hot water, and the money to pay for them.

Nelson points out that, as in the "taking a bath" script, children grow up inside of other people's scripts. As a consequence, human beings rarely, if ever, experience the natural environment "raw." Rather, they experience an environment that has been prepared (cooked up!) according to the recipes prescribed by their culture.

Nelson and her colleagues have studied the growth of scripted knowledge by interviewing children and by recording the conversations of children playing together. When she asked children to tell her about "going to a restaurant," for example, she obtained such reports as:

"Well, you eat and then go somewhere." (Boy aged 3 years, 1 month)

"Okay. Now, first we go to restaurants at nighttime and we, um, we, and we go and wait for a while, and then the waiter comes and gives us the little stuff with the dinners on it, and then we wait for a little bit, a half an hour or a few minutes or something, and, um, then our pizza comes or anything, and um, [interruption]. . . . [The adult says, "So then the food comes . . ."] Then we eat it, and um, then when we're finished eating the salad that we order we get to eat our pizza when it's done, because we get the salad before the pizza's ready. So then when we're finished with all the pizza and all our salad, we just leave." (Girl aged 4 years, 10 months) (Nelson, 1981:103)

Even these simple reports demonstrate that scripts represent generalized knowledge. For one thing, the children are describing *general content:* they are clearly referring to more than a single, unique meal. The 3-year-old uses the generalized form "You eat," rather than a specific reference to a particular time when he ate. The little girl's introduction ("First we go to restaurants at nighttime") indicates that she, too, is speaking of restaurant visits in general.

Besides containing general content, the scripts are organized into a *general structure,* similar to that of adult scripts. Even very young children know that the events involved in "eating at a restaurant" do not take place haphazardly. Instead they report, "First we do this, then we do that." Children evidently abstract the content of a script and its structure from many particular events and then use that knowledge to organize their behavior. But what really differentiates one script from another are the specifics of place, the particular contents, and the amount of detail that make the event a meaningful whole.

The functions of scripts

Scripts are guides to action. They are mental representations that tell children what is likely to happen next in familiar circumstances. Until children have acquired a large repertoire of scripted knowledge, they must use a lot of mental effort to construct scripts as they participate in unfamiliar events. When they lack scripted knowledge, they must pay attention to the details of each new activity. As a consequence, they may be less likely to distinguish between the essential and the superficial features of a context. The little girl interviewed by Nelson, for example, seemed to think that eating pizza is a basic part of the "going to a restaurant" script, whereas paying for the meal was entirely absent. When a little girl grasps even the beginnings of a script ahead of time, she will be free to attend to new aspects of the setting the next time she encounters it. Over time, she will gain a deeper understanding of the events she participates in and the contexts of which they are a part.

A second function of scripts is to allow people within a given social group to coordinate more effectively. This function of scripts becomes possible because script knowledge is knowledge generally held in common. "Without shared scripts," Nelson says, "every social act would need to be negotiated afresh"

Participation in scripted activities such as a birthday party provides a context within which children can develop more complex understandings of their culture's basic concepts and ways of doing things.

(1981:109). In this sense, as Nelson points out, "the acquisition of scripts is central to the acquisition of culture" (p. 110). When children go to the average restaurant in the United States, they learn that first you ask the host or hostess for a table and are assigned a seat. A somewhat different script applies to fast-food restaurants. Discoordination can result if the script is violated (for example, if the child were to enter a restaurant and to sit down at a table where an elderly couple were midway through their meal).

Script knowledge, although generalized, is still tied to particular events (birthday parties, building a block tower, lunchtime, etc.). Somehow children must learn which scripts to use in particular settings on particular occasions. The utility of script-based knowledge also depends on how it is articulated with the knowledge of other participants, for it is only out of behavior coordinated with that of others that a shared, meaningful context can be constructed.

A third function of scripts is to provide a framework within which abstract concepts that apply to many kinds of events can be acquired. When, for example, children acquire scripts for playing with blocks, playing in the sandbox, and playing house, they are accumulating specific examples of play which they can then subsume in a general category (Lucariello & Rifkin, 1986) (see Box 9.2).

Cultural context and the unevenness of development

In the cultural-context view, the fact that children must acquire a large repertoire of scripts and know how to use them in the appropriate contexts provides a natural explanation for the unevenness of development during early childhood. Once children leave the confines of their caregivers' arms and their cribs, they begin to experience a variety of contexts that require them to acquire a variety of new scripts even as they refine their knowledge of scripts with which they are already familiar. The content and structure of the new events in which they participate will depend crucially on the contexts provided by their culture and the roles they are expected to play within those contexts. In familiar contexts, where they know the expected sequence of actions and can properly interpret the requirements of the situation, young children are most likely to behave in a logical way and adhere to adult standards of thought. But when the contexts are unfamiliar, they may apply inappropriate scripts and resort to magical or illogical thinking.

Overall, cultural context influences the unevenness of children's development in four basic ways (Laboratory of Comparative Human Cognition, 1983):

1. *By arranging the occurrence and nonoccurrence of specific contexts.* You cannot learn about something you do not observe and have not heard about. A 4-year-old growing up among the Bushmen of the Kalahari Desert is unlikely to learn about taking baths or pouring water from one glass to another; a child growing up in Seattle is unlikely to be skilled at tracking animals or finding water-bearing roots in a desert.

2. *By determining the frequency of basic contexts.* Children growing up in Bali may be skilled dancers by the age of 4 (Mead & Macgregor, 1951), while Norwegian children are likely to become good skiers and skaters. In each case, adults arrange for children to practice these activities. Likewise, children growing up in a Mexican village famous for its pottery may work with clay day after day, whereas children living in a nearby town known for its weaving may encounter clay only rarely (Price-Williams, Gordon, & Ramirez, 1969; Childs & Greenfield, 1980). Insofar as practice makes perfect, the greater the frequency of practice, the higher the level of performance.

3. *By relating different contexts.* If molding clay is associated with making pottery, it is experienced in the company of a whole host of related contexts: digging from a quarry, firing clay, glazing clay, selling the products. Molding clay as part of a nursery school curriculum will be associated with an entirely different pattern of experience and knowledge.

4. *By regulating the difficulty of the child's role.* As in the script of taking a bath, adults decide how much responsibility the child will bear. Whatever the context, there are likely to be gradations in the contributions that a child must make, beginning with mere presence in the scene and proceeding, as the child grows and gains experience, to a central role with controlling responsibility.

The meaning of an activity such as weaving and the development of the skills needed to do it differ markedly from one culture to another.

Assessing the cultural-context explanation

In the Piagetian view of development, cognitive structures undergo *generalized* transformations as children mature and gain experience. In the cultural-context view, by contrast, children are seen as developing context-specific abilities tied to the content and structure of the events in which they participate. The extent to which new and more sophisticated ways of thinking and acting become general depends crucially on the generality of the content and structure of the contexts in which the new psychological processes emerge (Laboratory of Comparative Human Cognition, 1983). In this view, magical thinking, failure to take another's perspective, and confusion of appearance and reality are not unique to young children; they are also seen in older children and adults (Subbotski, 1991). If adults display these traits more rarely, they do so at least in part because they have much greater direct experience of the world. Adults also have more power than children to shape contexts to suit their own desires and a greater knowledge of the experiences and adaptive solutions of earlier generations.

Piaget too saw that greater experience may influence congitive development. However, he emphasized general transformations in the logic of thought. In contrast, cultural-contextualists hold that qualitative changes in thought will always be as specific as the contexts in which they emerge. Rather than viewing early childhood as a universal stage that follows infancy, cultural-context theorists see a gradual accumulation of restricted changes in many particular domains in the period leading up to middle childhood.

The cultural-context approach also adopts a different view of the mechanism of developmental change. Whereas Piaget saw a "lone child" puzzling out the world unaided, the cultural-context theorist attaches great importance to the ways in which children's interactions with the world of objects and people are co-constructed within adult scripts and activities.

Like the biological modularity view, the cultural-context approach assumes that biological maturation is a basic prerequisite for development. The two approaches contrast markedly, however, in their conceptions of the mechanisms of change and the sources of variability in behavior. Modularity theorists accord a major role to biological maturation and a minimal role to the environment. The development of grammar

BOX 9.2
Sociodramatic Play

Play occupies a conspicuous role in the young child's development. Dorothy and Jerome Singer (1990), researchers who have spent several decades studying the role of imagination in human behavior, refer to early childhood as the "high season of imaginative play."

By the end of infancy a child is able to pretend that a matchbox is a car that can zoom around the sandbox, or that a block is an iron. Such play, however, is largely solitary; even when several children are in a room together, their play is unlikely to be interconnected (Bretherton, 1984).

Pretend play is more social and more complex for preschool-aged children than for infants (Göncü & Kessel, 1988). Instead of solitary pretending, children begin to engage in **sociodramatic play**—make-believe games in which two or more children enact a variety of social roles. These games require shared understanding among the participants, which must be negotiated as part of the game.

Four girls in the doll corner have announced that they will play house and agree upon the roles: mother, sister, baby, and maid.

> **Karen:** I'm hungry. Wa-a-ah!
> **Charlotte:** Lie down, baby.
> **Karen:** I'm a baby that sits up.
> **Charlotte:** First you lie down and sister covers you and then I make your cereal and then you sit up.
> **Karen:** Okay.
> **Karen:** *(to Teddy, who has been observing)* You can be the father.
> **Charlotte:** Are you the father?
> **Teddy:** Yes.
> **Charlotte:** Put on a red tie.
> **Janie:** *(in the "maid's" falsetto voice)* I'll get it for you, honey. Now don't that baby look pretty? This is your daddy, baby.
> (Adapted from Paley, 1984:1)

This transcript illustrates several features of young children's play. The children are enacting social roles and using scripts that they have encountered numerous times in their daily lives, on television, or in stories (Bretherton, 1989). Babies make stereotypic baby noises, maids get things for people, and fathers wear ties. At the same time that they are playing their roles in the pretend world, the children are also outside it, giving stage directions to one another and commenting on the action. The "baby" who sits up has to be talked into lying down, and the boy is told what role he can play. Occasionally, however, the fantasy may become so real and threatening that children stop the game or refuse to join in (Garvey & Berndt, 1977).

Although children draw upon familiar scenes in their sociodramatic play, the scripts and social phenomena that they use are not reproduced in anything resembling precise imitation. As Catherine Garvey (1977) notes, when a boy engaged in sociodramatic play walks into the house and announces, "Okay, I'm all through with work, honey. I brought home a thousand dollars," he has probably never heard that said before. Rather, he has abstracted certain behaviors characteristic of husbands and embellished them with fantasy.

In recent decades developmental psychologists have become intensely interested in sociodramatic play. Many are engaged in a lively controversy about its significance for cognitive and social development (Bretherton, 1989; Fine, 1987; Garvey, 1990). The two main positions in this discussion are derived from the work of Piaget (1962) and Vygotsky (1978).

In Piaget's view, the special quality of play during the preoperational period derives directly from the characteristics of egocentrism. As he phrased it, "For egocentric thought, the supreme law is play" (Piaget, 1928:401). Piaget minimized the significance of play for cognitive development because he assumed that in play, assimilation dominates over accommodation. He predicted that when egocentric thought gives way to logical thought in middle childhood, pretend play should give way to the kind of rule-bound play evident in board games and organized sports.

A number of studies have traced the rise and decline of pretend play during the years of early childhood by observing children and coding the kinds of play they engage in (Rubin, Fein, & Vandenberg, 1983). Though the results are not completely consistent, in general they have confirmed Piaget's belief that sociodramatic play should peak sometime in early childhood and then begin to decline. The disappearance of such play, however, does not mean that children stop pretending. Jerome Singer and Dorothy Singer (1990) believe that once middle childhood is reached, pretend play "goes underground" because other forms of play are considered socially more ac-

Sociodramatic play is a leading activity for children from the age of 2¹/₂ to 6.

ceptable. Douglas Hofstader (1979) believes that pretend play never disappears; throughout their lives people constantly create mental variants on the situations they face:

> [The manufacture of "as-if" worlds] happens so casually, so naturally, that we hardly notice what we are doing. We select from our fantasy a world which is close, in some internal mental sense, to the real world. We compare what is real with what we perceive as almost real. In so doing what we gain is some intangible kind of perspective on reality. (p. 643)

Unlike Piaget, Lev Vygotsky (1978) believed that pretend play provides children with an important mental support system that allows them to think and act in more complex ways. In real life, children depend on adults to help them by providing the rules and by filling in for them in little ways, in what Vygotsky called the zone of proximal development. The freedom to negotiate reality—essential to games of "let's pretend"—provides children with analogous support. As a consequence, wrote Vygotsky, "In play a child is always above his average age, above his daily behavior; in play it is as though he were a head taller than himself" (p. 102).

M. G. Dias and Paul Harris (1988, 1990) provided interesting support for Vygotsky's idea that play creates a zone of proximal development in a study of the way pretending influences young children's ability to reason deductively. Dias and Harris presented 4-to 6-year-old children a series of logical problems in

which they had to reason from two premises to reach a conclusion. Most children do not solve this kind of problem until they are considerably older. In fact, Piaget believed that such reasoning does not emerge until adolescence.

The problems presented by Dias and Harris were of the following kind:

> All fishes live in trees.
> Tot is a fish.
> Does Tot live in the water?

These problems were presented to half of the children in a matter-of-fact tone of voice. With the other half of the children the experimenter started off by saying, "Let's pretend that I am from another planet," and went on to present the problem in the sort of dramatic voice that is ordinarily used in storytelling.

The children's ability to solve these reasoning problems varied greatly from one condition to the other. The children who were instructed in a matter-of-fact tone made many errors; they said that Tot the fish lives in the water. (While it is true that fish live in water, according to the *logic of the problem,* Tot lives in a tree.) These children justified their answers by going outside the boundaries of the problem to draw upon their knowledge of where fish live.

The children who participated in the "let's pretend" version of the problem were much more successful, and the way they justified their answers provided clear evidence that they entered into the hypothetical nature of the tasks. Typical justifications for their correct answers were such statements as "I said Tot lives in a tree because we're pretending that fishes live in trees."

Almost all of the research on pretend play has been carried out in industrially advanced countries where children are likely to attend a preschool (which serves as the setting for a great deal of the existing research). The few analogous studies of pretend play that have been carried out in nonindustrialized societies suggest that in these cultures sociodramatic play sticks much more closely to the models provided by actual adult practices and involves less imaginative transformation of reality (Gaskins & Göncü, 1992). Even in such cultures, however, when children are induced to adopt a "let's pretend" mode of behaving, their logical problem-solving capacities are enhanced (Dias, 1988).

provides the prototype: development of a rudimentary grammar "just happens" when the organism is ripe for it. Variations in the developmental level of children's behavior are assumed to depend on changes in the central nervous system that bring into being the specific biological prerequisites for the behavior in question.

Cultural-context theorists, on the other hand, believe that unless active sociocultural influences operate in tandem with biological ones, development will be stunted, much in the manner of the language of deaf children raised in households where the learning of sign is not permitted (see Chapter 8, p. 303).

Barbara Rogoff (1990), a prominent cultural-context theorist, calls the process by which adults shape young children's development **guided participation.**

> Guided participation involves collaboration and shared understanding in routine problem-solving activities. Interaction with other people assists children in their development by guiding their participation in relevant activities, helping them adapt their understanding to new situations, structuring their problem-solving attempts, and assisting them in assuming responsibility. (p. 191)

Rogoff points out that the kind of guidance she is talking about is rarely explicit or designed specifically to instruct. Rather, it is a process deeply embedded in the casual arrangements and engagements characteristic of everyday activity.

The strength of the cultural-context view is also its greatest weakness. It explains why young children's behavior varies from one context to the next, but it does not provide a comprehensive explanation for the fact that children have general abilities as well as domain-specific ones. Gustav Jahoda (1980) summarized this shortcoming when he wrote that the cultural-context approach

> appears to require extremely exhaustive, and in practice almost endless explorations of quite specific pieces of behavior, with no guarantee of a decisive outcome. This might not be necessary if there were a workable "theory of situations" at our disposal, but . . . there is none. What is lacking . . . are global theoretical constructs relating to cognitive processes of the kind Piaget provides, and which save the researcher from be-

coming submerged in a mass of unmanageable material. (p. 126)

To complicate an already complicated picture, it must be kept in mind that the cultural organization of the child's experience is constantly interacting with the biological properties of the child, which are themselves developing at different rates. Each of these sources of development contributes to *both* generality and specificity in development. When these two sources of development, one from the sociocultural environment and one from biology, are combined, we can appreciate more fully why unevenness is a central feature of early childhood development and why it will remain an important feature of thinking throughout life.

APPLYING THE THEORETICAL PERSPECTIVES

Each of the current theories of early childhood cognition provides a distinctive perspective from which to view development. When proponents of the various approaches attempt to explain the same phenomenon, we have an opportunity to compare the relative strengths and weaknesses of alternative views.

Drawing pictures — an activity with many cognitive components — is a case in point. Children's drawing goes through a regular series of stages (in accord with Piaget's constructivist approach). Children whose linguistic, mental, or social development is severely retarded may nonetheless draw at a high level of competence (in accord with the modularity approach). Stages in drawing can in some cases be tied closely to the ability to hold several aspects of an object in mind at one time (in accord with an information-processing approach). And the development of drawing ability depends on the social organization of the child's activity (in accord with the cultural-context approach).

Constructing the Stages of Drawing

In every culture where children are given an opportunity to draw from an early age, their drawings appear to pass through the same sequence of stages (Gardner, 1980; Golomb, 1974; Kellogg, 1969). In the beginning they scribble. Children are not "making pictures" when they scribble. What seems to matter to them is not the look of the product but the joy of moving their hands and the trail of their movements to which the scribbling bears witness.

Scribbling embodies both of the functions of art in a primitive form. It *expresses* a feeling—the exuberance of motion—and it leaves a trace of the movement, *re-presenting* it for later examination. Scribbling is considered primitive because its expression is uncontrolled and unplanned and because it represents only itself.

Children take a giant step beyond scribbling about the age of 3 when they begin to recognize that their lines can represent things. About this time children begin to draw circles and ellipses that are cleared of the whorls and lines that used to fill their scribble pictures. Most children interpret these circles as "things." The circular line encloses an inside area that seems more solid to them than the field it is on.

As children continue to gain experience with drawing, they are likely to adopt stereotyped ways of depicting objects: a house is a pentagon, a sun is a circle with lines extending from its surface, a flower is a circle surrounded by ellipses, humans and animals appear as tadpole figures (see Figure 9.12). Eventually children begin to combine representations of people and things to make scenes and stories or to depict a variety of experiences.

Between the ages of 7 and 11, children increasingly strive to be realistic in their drawings. At the same time they become more skilled at composition and the techniques of drawing (see Figure 9.13).

Many of the stages observed in the drawings of North American and European children can be found in all societies in which drawing is an expected activity. Such universals in the development of artistic representation are the kind of phenomena that are central to Piaget's theory of cognitive development.

An Information-Processing Account of Drawing

People drew objects for thousands of years before techniques for representing objects in three dimensions became fully developed and exploited (Arnheim, 1954). Yet modern children who grow up with three-dimensional representations all around them acquire the ability to make such drawings at a very early age.

FIGURE 9.12   *Drawing of the human figure develops through a sequence of steps. At first a child draws a big circle that stands for a whole person. The child's global representation of a person soon evolves into a circle or an ellipse with the face in the upper part and two protruding lines underneath. This distinctive form is called a "tadpole figure." Gradually the circle comes to represent only the head, and the body descends between the two vertical lines. Some months later, the child adds a second circle to represent the body, with another pair of lines extending from it as arms. (From Goodnow, 1977.)*

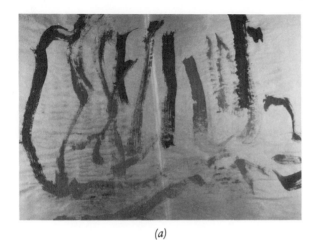

(a)

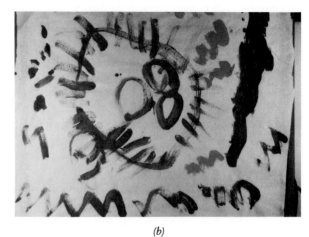

(b)

(c)

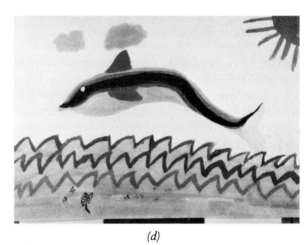

(d)

(e)

FIGURE 9.13   *A sequence of drawings by an American child: (a) at 2½ years, Carrie was drawing lines of different colors; (b) at 3½ years, she began to draw global representations of a person; (c) at 5 years, a body and legs have been added to the creatures she draws, and her main figure is set in a scene; (d) at 7½ years, motion, rhythm, and greater realism are evident in her drawings; (e) at 12 years, she was able to draw a cartoon of a realistic scene. (Courtesy of Carrie Hogan.)*

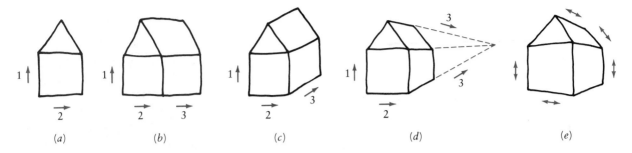

FIGURE 9.14 *The developmental sequence for drawing of an object in three dimensions. Drawing a leaves out the third dimension. Drawings b and c introduce the third dimension in partially correct ways. Drawings d and e represent the full three dimensions according to two conventions. (Adapted from Willats, 1987.)*

Figure 9.14 shows the developmental sequence that children go through in learning to draw a schematic house in three dimensions. The youngest children collapse three dimensions into two. Then the third dimension is partially added, but it is initially collapsed into one of the other two. Finally children acquire ways to represent the third dimension (Willats, 1987). From an information-processing perspective, this sequence follows directly from children's growing acquisition of drawing rules and their ability to remember the need to represent all three spatial coordinates in their drawings.

Drawing as a Mental Module

Although normally the development of children's ability to draw passes through the series of stages we have just described, some important exceptions suggest that drawing ability may be modular in some respects. A compelling example is provided by Nadia, an autistic child in Nottingham, England (Selfe, 1977). At first Nadia seemed to develop normally, but by the age of 3 she had forgotten the few words she had learned, her behavior was lethargic, and she did not engage in pretend play. At the age of 3½, Nadia began to display unusual artistic ability. Without any apparent practice, she began to use perspective and other artistic techniques that are usually acquired only after years of experience in drawing (Figure 9.15). Nadia's dexterity when she was drawing was quite remarkable, yet her hand movements were otherwise uncoordinated. Extensive testing showed that Nadia had an extraordinary ability to form and remember visual images. She would often study a drawing for weeks before producing a version from memory herself. It seemed as if she were building up a mental image so that at some later time her "mind's eye" could guide her hand in recreating the image on paper. Howard Gardner (1980), who has conducted research on the cognitive basis of art, uses terms reminiscent of Chomsky's and of Fodor's idea of mental modules in his discussion of Nadia's case:

> Nadia may have been operating with a high powered mental computational device — one seldom, if ever, exploited by others but perhaps available to at least a sample of the human species. (pp. 186–187)

Lorna Selfe (1983) reports that Nadia's unusual development is not unique. She has found a number of children whose language ability and general mental functioning were quite low but whose ability to create graphic images was exceptionally high. These cases fit nicely with the idea that mental modules, such as language and perception, can develop in relative isolation from one another.

FIGURE 9.15   *Nadia, a preschooler with only minimal exposure to models, displayed an uncanny ability to capture form and movement in her drawings.*

Evidence from less extreme cases also suggests that the ordinary sequence of stages is not necessary to mastery. Gardner (1980) reports that children deprived of the opportunity to draw during early childhood may skip the initial stages of drawing altogether when they finally do get an opportunity to draw. If true, this finding would run counter to the Piagetian position that stages follow each other in an invariant sequence.

A Cultural-Context Account of the Development of Drawing

A cultural-context view of the development of drawing takes for granted both that humans have an innate potential for drawing and that within any particular medium — drawing, writing, music — representations can be constructed at varying levels of complexity. To these axioms it adds its own idea of the processes that transform children's potential for drawing into the actual execution of specific kinds of meaningful representations.

An important indicator of the culturally organized nature of children's drawing is found in the ways adults talk to children about what they are doing. When American adults ask young children, "What are you drawing?" the very form of the question assumes that there is some *thing* to be drawn and that the child is attempting to represent it. When questions of this kind are posed, children often go along by making up stories about what they have drawn after the fact. Initially, these stories are not tied to anything that can be perceived on the paper by adults. After children have gained some experience, however, their explanations may be connected to the discovery that the marks they have made resemble an actual object in the world. But this discovery is made only after the drawing is completed (Golomb, 1974).

The following dialogue between 3-year-olds Roslyn and Don, recorded in a U.S. preschool, illustrates the rudimentary nature of young children's understanding of drawing as well as some of the ways those understandings change (adapted from Gearhart & Newman, 1980:172):

Roslyn: I got brown. *(Holds up her crayon)*
   Don: I got another color. *(Draws short lines back and forth)*

The development of drawing depends on the traditions of the culture into which the child is born. This drawing was done by a 7-year-old Chilean child.

Roslyn: I made a brown circle. *(Illustrates with counterclockwise gesture, holding crayon over the paper)*

Don: I got another color.

Roslyn: I, I, I made a big brown circ-er square. *(Repeats the illustrative gesture)*

Don: *(Makes a counterclockwise form on his paper)* Look what I'm making, Roslyn.

Roslyn: Huh! Ehh! *(Looks)*

Don: I, I went round like this. *(Illustrates with larger counterclockwise movements)*

Roslyn: Well. . . . Now watch what I am making, I'm making mountains. *(Immediately draws a series of short vertical lines)*

Their words and actions clearly indicate that neither child has a fixed, individual drawing in mind. All of their talk refers either to something they have just done ("I *made* a brown circle") or something they are doing ("I'm *making*"). There is little talk about future plans for their pictures. Each child imitates elements introduced by the other, with no overall plan of how that element might fit into the whole.

Even these children's drawings have progressed beyond scribbling, however. As they show each other crayons and figures, swapping comments and ideas, they are talking *as if* the drawings represented something (circles, squares, mountains) even if the correspondence is by no means clear to outsiders.

The way the teacher arranged for a picture to be called "finished" was also important in helping the children to discover what it means to draw a picture. Before writing the child's name on the picture and pinning it up on the board, she asked open-ended questions about what the child had been drawing, again behaving *as if* the child had been drawing a particular thing.

Teacher: Jeff? [Come] tell me about your picture. *(Jeffrey comes and looks at his drawing)*

Jeffrey: Uh, it has two mountains on orange, two orange circles.

Teacher: Two orange circles *(as she writes his name on the drawing)*. (Adapted from Gearhart & Newman, 1980:182)

Learning to draw and paint is an absorbing activity for preschoolers.

In this dialogue the teacher selectively accepts the part of the child's account (two orange circles) that accords with her notion of "thingness." The scribbled "mountains" are ignored. As a consequence, Jeffrey learns something about what sort of marks count as a drawing of a mountain or circles in the eyes of adults and which do not.

The existence of scripted activities for drawing does not contradict the possibility that there is a mental module for drawing or the idea that drawing goes through stages of increasing complexity. Rather, it suggests that the ways in which adults organize instruction provide essential opportunities for modular potential to be triggered and stages constructed. Over the course of a year or two, the teacher's assumptions become second nature to the children. They learn not only the possibility of drawing pictures of "things" but a good many techniques for making those things take shape on the page. Most important, they come to understand and share the teacher's concept of what "drawing a picture" means. This common understanding then becomes the basis for further instruction.

RECONCILING ALTERNATIVE PERSPECTIVES

Scholarly explanations of the phenomena of young children's thought are reminiscent of the parable of the blind men feeling an elephant: The man who feels the trunk believes that the creature is a snake; the man who feels the leg believes that the creature is a tree; and the man who feels the tail is certain that he has hold of a rope. Lacking a coordinated understanding, each man mistakes his part for the whole, which is distinctively different from the parts.

Piaget's young children are incomplete logicians. Having only recently learned to represent the world symbolically, they still have trouble constructing stable cause-effect schemas and they are confused about what is real and what is not. They fail to distinguish their own point of view from the perspectives of others, so they are constantly led into error about what others think and say. It is several years before they can translate conflicting information into useful action- and language-based schemas.

Neo-Piagetian explanations of thinking during early childhood have sought to revise the negative description of young children as egocentric and prelogical. Neo-Piagetians show that young children can reason logically in familiar circumstances as long as their still fragile verbal skills are not overstrained. Still very much at issue among these researchers, however, is whether Piaget's idea of global transformations of mind should be retained or replaced by a piecemeal, domain-specific picture of development.

The information-processing approach to explaining young children's characteristic thought processes focuses on their limited knowledge, attention, and memory capacity and their lack of sophisticated problem-solving strategies. This theoretical framework may be viewed as either a rival to Piaget's theory or as an alternative strategy for research. Some researchers (Case, 1985; Fischer, 1980) use information-processing ideas to support a neo-Piagetian theory. Others (Siegler, 1991) use similar ideas to arrive at a new theory in which cognitive development is seen as a nonstagelike, continuous process of change arising from the accumulation of specific knowledge and strategies.

One major alternative to the Piagetian and various neo-Piagetian approaches, modularity theory, denies that constructive interactions play a prominent role in promoting cognitive development. Viewing the child's mental processes as a collection of separate computational modules, researchers in this tradition attribute the special characteristics of young children's thought primarily to the physical maturation of the brain. In some striking cases these researchers have shown that even infants display rudimentary forms of the cognitive abilities that Piaget denied to young children. From this perspective, the unevenness of behavior during early childhood mirrors unevenness in the rate of physical maturation. As basic brain structures approach maturity, extreme variations among modules decrease, and behavior becomes more consistent and "adult."

Like those who work within a Piagetian or neo-Piagetian framework, cultural-context theorists believe that complex cognitive processes are constructed in social interaction. This approach, however, emphasizes that the process of construction, and hence the mechanism of cognitive development, is shared between children and older members of their communities in scripted activities organized, or at least supervised, by adults.

In our view these competing approaches are most usefully viewed as complementary. Certainly the various phenomena they highlight need to be included in any comprehensive explanation of development during early childhood, even if no single theoretical framework has yet been able to encompass them all. At present a number of promising efforts to provide such a comprehensive explanatory framework are underway (Case, 1991; Fischer, Knight, & Van Parys, 1992; Siegler, 1991).

A child's total psychological development encompasses far more than the restricted abilities described here. Still to be explored are the way young children think about themselves as members of their social worlds, their experiences in nursery school and day care (where they must learn to get along with children their own age under new circumstances), and their induction into the world of books and television. In the remaining chapters of Part III, we will round out our picture of young children as they leave infancy further and further behind and move toward a new bio-social-behavioral shift marking the transition to middle childhood.

SUMMARY

1. Young children's thought processes are characterized by great unevenness; islands of competence exist in a sea of uncertainty and naiveté.
2. Piaget's explanation of thought during early childhood stresses egocentrism and the absence of logical operations. In his view, young children experience difficulty adopting others' perspectives, reasoning about cause and effect, and distinguishing appearance from reality.
3. Piaget's theory has difficulty accounting for the unevenness of children's thought in what he called the preoperational stage. Some developmental psychologists want to refine his theory, while others have suggested alternatives.

4. Neo-Piagetian explanations of young children's thought retain Piaget's theory of stages. Some neo-Piagetians restrict the applicability of stages to specific domains of activity, while others attempt to account for uneven development by citing differences in the requirements of specific tasks.

5. According to the information-processing view, cognitive development is a process of expanding limited attentional, memory, and problem-solving capacities. The unevenness of young children's thought is explained by differences in children's familiarity with specific task settings and in the demands made by the various settings.

6. Biologically oriented theories hold that the brain is organized into mental modules that are domain-specific, innately structured, and relatively isolated from one another. They point to uneven rates of change in brain structures as the major cause of unevenness in young children's thought. The mental capacity of prodigies (children who excel in a single domain at an early age) and of some autistic children support this hypothesis.

7. In the cultural-context view, contexts provide coherence to otherwise isolated actions. Contexts and schemas develop together. Children's interactions with the world are co-constructed within adult scripts and activities.

8. Contexts are represented mentally in the form of scripts—conceptual structures that are guides to action, a means of coordination between people, and a framework in which abstract concepts applicable across contexts are formed.

9. Culture mediates society's influence on mental development by:
   a. Arranging for the occurrence of specific contexts and associated scripts.
   b. Arranging which contexts a child will experience.
   c. Deciding which contexts are associated with particular activities.
   d. Regulating the level of the child's participation.

10. Artistic development demonstrates the complementary nature of the competing explanations. A child learning to draw normally passes through a series of stages. These stages are domain-specific in ways that fit with neo-Piagetian and modularity themes. As one stage follows another, the child's drawings represent more and more aspects of the objects drawn, in line with an information-processing approach. Learning to draw is culturally organized in ways that fit with cultural-context theories.

KEY TERMS

autism
context
cultural-context theory
egocentrism
guided participation
horizontal decalage

information-processing approach
long-term memory
mental modules
mental operations
modularity theory
neo-Piagetian approach
precausal thinking

preoperational stage
scripts
short-term memory
social co-construction
sociodramatic play
theory of mind

SUGGESTED READINGS

FLAVELL, JOHN, MILLER, PATRICIA, & MILLER, SCOTT. *Cognitive Development,* Third Edition. Englewood Cliffs, N.J.: Prentice Hall, 1993.

A leading interpreter of the psychology of Jean Piaget, John Flavell has long been prominent in the study of cognitive development during early childhood. This new edition contains especially useful discussions of the many factors that could account for the unevenness of young children's thought. It also ranges over the full course of cognitive development, and will be a useful reference for later chapters.

GARDNER, HOWARD. *Artful Scribbles.* New York: Basic Books, 1980.

Howard Gardner has written widely on problems of cognitive development, with emphasis on the development of children's aesthetic sensibilities and modes of artistic expression. In this readable account of artistic development, Gardner discusses not only the artistic development of modern children but also the development of art in human history and prehistory. Of special interest is Gardner's account of the artistic achievements of autistic children.

PALEY, VIVIAN G. *The Boy Who Would Be a Helicopter.* Cambridge, Mass.: Harvard University Press, 1990.

This account of life in Paley's classroom focuses on the difficulties a young boy experiences in learning to become a member of the society of preschool children. The book is full of examples of young children's thinking as they express it in their imaginative play and conversations.

PIAGET, JEAN. *The Child's Conception of the World.* New York: Harcourt Brace, 1929.

This early book, much easier to read than Piaget's later theoretical works, contains extensive transcripts of discussions with children about all manner of natural phenomena, among them the nature of thinking, the origin of names, the sources of dreams, and the nature of life. This book helps us understand why Piaget's ideas about young children's thought have had such an enduring effect on developmental psychology.

ROGOFF, BARBARA. *Apprenticeship in Thinking.* New York: Oxford University Press, 1990.

A leading developmental psychologist working within a cultural-context perspective provides myriad examples of the ways adults guide children's participation in the everyday activities of many cultures. She also provides balanced assessments of competing theories of intellectual development.

SIEGLER, ROBERT. *Children's Thinking* (Second Edition). Englewood Cliffs, N.J.: Prentice Hall, 1991.

This is the first general text about the development of children's thinking to be written from the perspective of information-processing theories. Its clear examples help explain how information-processing ideas have contributed to an understanding of cognitive development. Its many excellent discussions of cognitive and language development provide additional information about topics taken up in this chapter.

SINGER, DOROTHY, & SINGER, JEROME. *The House of Make-Believe.* Cambridge, Mass.: Harvard University Press, 1990.

This comprehensive account of imaginative play from infancy to adulthood delves deeply into the central role of imagination in human development.

CHAPTER 10

Social Development in Early Childhood

•

> The incorporation of the individual as a member of a community, or his adaptation to it, seems like an almost unavoidable condition which has to be filled before he can attain the objective of happiness. . . . Individual development seems to us a product of the interplay of two trends, the striving for happiness, generally called "egoistic," and the impulse towards merging with others in the community, which we call "altruistic."
>
> —SIGMUND FREUD,
> *CIVILIZATION AND ITS DISCONTENTS*

———

The process to which Sigmund Freud is referring is called **social development,** a two-sided process in which children simultaneously become integrated into the larger social community and differentiated as distinctive individuals. One side of social development is **socialization,** the process by which children acquire the standards, values, and knowledge of their society. The other side of social development is **personality formation**—the way in which every child comes to have her or his own unique ways of feeling and behaving in a wide variety of circumstances (Child, 1968).

Socialization begins as soon as the child is born and her mother says, for example, "She's never going to be a rugby player" or her father remarks, "I shall be worried to death when she's eighteen" (see Chapter 3, p. 117). Such statements are not idle talk. The beliefs that give rise to them also lead parents to shape the world of the child in ways they deem appropriate on the basis of their cultural experiences. Socialization continues as part of getting the infant on a schedule, clothing girls in dresses and boys in pants, and admonishing children to be polite to their elders, to cover their mouths when they cough, and never to tell a lie.

Both adults and children must play active roles in social development. Adults tell children how they *should* behave, are pleased or displeased by how they *do* behave, and reward, ignore, or punish them accordingly. Adults also select the social contexts within which children have the experiences that allow them to learn about social categories and to become conversant with their culture's fund of knowledge and rules of behavior. But children do not automatically or passively absorb the lessons adults intend. What children learn depends on how they interpret their experiences and what they select from the conflicting messages they receive. If 4-year-old Mark admires his older cousin Eric and wants to be like him, will he select Eric's socially appropriate style of dress to imitate, his socially inappropriate use of slang, or both?

In order to acquire an understanding of the social categories that apply to them, children must somehow figure out what people mean when they say such things as "You are my son" or "Act like a lady." Nor is it sufficient to learn what adults mean by words such as "friend," "boy," "honest," and "Japanese-American"; it is also necessary to learn how to behave in ways that correspond to these concepts. Although we take such matters for granted in our everyday lives, perhaps the most remarkable fact about the process of socialization is that most children come to accept the socially prescribed rules as reasonable and even necessary.

Whereas socialization ensures that children generally subscribe to their society's norms of behavior, the combination of characteristics that emerges from the second side of social development, the child's personality, is unique. No two children, not even identical twins, have precisely the same blend of temperaments, intellectual characteristics, and life experiences. Consequently, no two people ever have precisely the same personality. Even if two children are both nursery school students, friends, nieces, and Japanese-Americans, each will have her own ways of behaving in these roles and her own ways of thinking and feeling.

The origins of personality are no less visible at birth than the presence of socializing influences. As we saw in Chapter 4 (p. 139), neonates display individual differences in characteristic levels of activity, responses to frustration, and readiness to engage in novel experiences. We referred to these patterns of responsivity and associated emotional states as *temperamental traits* and noted that temperament is moderately stable over time; children who draw back from novel experiences in infancy are likely to behave shyly when they first enter a nursery school.

Temperamental traits are the earliest visible manifestations of personality (Buss, 1989; Thomas & Chess, 1989). But when we are speaking of 3- or 5-year-old children, there is more to their personalities than temperament alone. We cannot say that a child is honest or compulsive at birth because there is no temperamental characteristic corresponding to honesty or compulsiveness, or to a host of other characteristics, such as stinginess, compliance, and a desire to please other people. Those characteristics are acquired over the course of a lifetime. As children develop, their initial ways of interacting with their environments (temperament) must be reconciled with their developing cognitive understanding and emotional responses to their experiences. **Personality** is the name we give to the product of this reconciliation process (Lerner, 1988). Personality also includes such cognitive factors as the way children come to conceive of themselves in relation to other people (their **self-concept**).

Viewed in this way, personality development is intimately intertwined with socialization. Crucial to one's sense of self is all of the feedback that one receives from the social environment. This linkage between personality and social development was expressed at the turn of the century by James Mark Baldwin:

The development of the child's personality could not go on at all without the constant modification of his sense of himself by suggestions from others. So he himself, at every stage, is really in part someone else, even in his own thought of himself. (1902:23)

Personality formation and socialization are in constant tension as children discover that their individual desires and ideas often conflict with their culture's norms. A 5-year-old boy who sucks his thumb is likely to be discouraged from doing so by his parents and teased by his peers. A child who is jealous of the attention her baby brother receives must learn that she can't pinch him (or at least can't get caught pinching him!); she must find some socially acceptable way to gain her mother's attention and deal with her socially unacceptable feelings.

By the time children are 6 years old, they will have learned a great deal about the roles they are expected to play and how to behave in accordance with them, how to control aggressive feelings, and how to respect the rights of others. At the same time, they will have developed a relatively explicit sense of themselves, their abilities, and the ways in which they are likely to react in a variety of circumstances. How do these changes take place?

ACQUIRING A SOCIAL AND PERSONAL IDENTITY

Psychologists agree that socialization requires **identification,** a psychological process in which children seek to look, act, feel, and *be* like significant people in their social environment. Experts disagree, however, about the mechanisms by which identification is achieved. Four proposed mechanisms have figured most prominently in discussions of this basic developmental process: differentiation; affiliation; imitation and social learning; and the formation of cognitive schemas.

The development of identification can be studied with respect to almost any social category — becoming a member of a family, a religious group, a neighborhood clique, or a nationality. The overwhelming majority of studies on identification in early

These preschool girls are participating in a beauty contest. This kind of experience gives them an idea of what the adults in their community expect of girls.

childhood, however, focus on the acquisition of sex roles.[1] Consequently, we will devote the lion's share of our attention to this social category before turning to ethnic identity, which is an especially important social category, although only a limited amount of research has been done on it.

Sex-Role Identity

Sex is not a role in the sense that being a big sister, an airplane pilot, or a factory worker is a role. Rather, sex is an attribute that shapes many social roles, determining whether the person is a son or daughter, girlfriend or boyfriend, husband or wife. Sexual identity influences the kind of work children are likely to engage in

as adults, how they are treated by total strangers, and their social status. Because sexual identity is so central to adult experience, the question of how children acquire the understanding that they are a boy or a girl and how they interpret that role is of great interest to developmental psychologists. The central issues in acquiring a sex-role identity are seen in the following conversations:

> "When I grow up," says [4-year-old] Jimmy at the dinner table, "I'm gonna marry Mama."
>
> "Jimmy's nuts," says the sensible voice of 8-year-old Jane. "You can't marry Mama and anyway, what would happen to Daddy?" Exasperating, logical female! Who cares about your good reasons and your dull good sense! There's an answer for that too. "He'll be old," says the dreamer, through a mouthful of string-beans. "And he'll be dead." Then, awed by the enormity of his words, the dreamer adds hastily, "But he might not be dead, and maybe I'll marry Marcia instead." (Fraiberg, 1959:202–203)

The next conversation took place when our daughter, Jenny, was 4 years old. She was lying on her mother's side of her parents' bed, watching her mother comb her hair.

---

[1] Some authors recommend the use of the word "gender" instead of "sex" when this topic is discussed. These authors believe that the term "sex" implies that all sex-typed behavior is ultimately determined by biology. On the other hand, Eleanor Maccoby (1980) argues against the term "gender," which she sees as implying that sex-linked behavior is ultimately determined by the environment. We will continue to use the term "sex," without intending to imply either that sex roles are basically biological or that they are basically environmental.

Jenny: You know, Mommy, when you die I am going to marry Daddy.

Sheila: I don't think so.

Jenny: *(nodding her head gravely)* I am, too.

Sheila: You can't. It's against the laws of God and man.

Jenny: *(close to tears)* But I want to.

Sheila: *(going to comfort her)* You'll have your own husband when you grow up.

Jenny: No, I won't! I want Daddy. I don't like you, Mommy.

These stories are easy to understand. Both of these children have had several years to observe the family life around them. Jimmy knows that he is a boy and Jenny knows that she is a girl. Although neither has a deep understanding of what these labels imply, they know that they want the things that big boys and big girls have. The "big girl" in Jenny's household has a special relationship with Daddy. The "big boy" in Jimmy's household has a special relationship with Mommy. At this early stage of sex-role identification, the best way children can think of to get what they want is literally to take the place of the person they want to be like.

Boys and girls in early childhood tend to choose same-sex parents as models to identify with. Yet the developmental paths that bring the two sexes to their respective identities differ in at least one respect. Although family configurations vary widely both within and among societies, the person who usually looms largest in the lives of both boys and girls during the first two years of life is their mother. She is likely to be the single greatest source of physical comfort, food, and attention for the very young child. As children enter their third year, the behaviors that indicate the strong and obvious attachment of the second year tend to diminish (see Chapter 6, p. 237). During early childhood, the feeling of "wanting to be near" that dominates infancy is supplanted by "wanting to be like." (See Figure 10.1.)

For boys, becoming like their father requires that they become different from the person with whom they have had the closest relationship: their mother. Girls, on the other hand, seek to become like the person with whom they have had the closest relationship. The implications of this sex-linked difference in developmental tasks has sparked intense debate about the process by which children acquire the sex identification they will have as adults.

FIGURE 10.1   *In addition to wanting to be near their parents, young children want to be like them, especially the parent of the same sex.*

Identification through differentiation

By far the best-known account of identity formation is Sigmund Freud's (1921/1949, 1933/1964). Freud believed that early in life, perhaps late in the first year, infants recognize that some objects in the external world are like themselves. He called this primitive recognition **primary identification.** During the third year of life, **secondary identification** occurs. He defined secondary identification as "the endeavor to mold a person's own ego after the fashion of one that has been taken as a model" (Freud, 1921/1949:63). In other words, having noticed that a particular adult, or perhaps an older child, is somehow similar to themselves, children "identify *with*" that person, striving to take on his or her qualities.

By Freud's account, Jimmy is playing out the universal male predicament of boys around the age of 3 or 4, the dilemma of the *phallic stage* (see Box 10.1). This is the period during which children first begin to regard their own genitals as a major source of pleasure.

BOX 10.1
Sigmund Freud

Trained as a neurologist, Sigmund Freud (1856–1939) sought throughout his career to create a theory of human personality that would enable him to cure the patients who came to him with such symptoms as extreme fear, emotional trauma, or an inability to cope with everyday life. Although many of these symptoms appeared similar to neurological disorders, Freud found that he could best understand his patients' problems by tracing their symptoms back to traumatic, unresolved experiences in early childhood.

On the basis of his clinical data, Freud constructed a general theory of development that gave primacy to the manner in which children satisfy their basic drives as the necessary condition for their survival. Survival of the individual child, however, is not sufficient for survival of the species. Influenced by Charles Darwin's theory of evolution, Freud reasoned that whatever their significance for individual adaptation, all biological drives have but a single goal: the survival and propagation of the species. Since reproduction, the necessary condition for the continuation of the species, is accomplished through sexual intercourse, it followed for Freud that, starting from the earliest days of life, all biological drives must ultimately serve the fundamental sex drive, on which the future of the species rests.

Although Freud believed the sexual nature of all gratification remains constant throughout life, the forms of that gratification change. Sexual gratification passes through an orderly series of stages defined in terms of the parts of the body that people use to satisfy their drives. Human beings strive to satisfy the drives that dominate the stage they are in at the moment. Freud held that the way children experience the conflicts they encounter in each of the early stages of development determines their later personality (1920/1955).

The first year of life is the **oral stage,** in which the mouth is the primary source of pleasure. The

Sigmund Freud.

mother's gratification of the baby's need to suck and gain nourishment is critically important.

In the second and third years of life, the **anal stage,** the child is preoccupied with gaining control of the smooth muscles involved in defecation.

Freud believed that during the fourth year children begin to focus their pleasure-seeking on the genital area. During this **phallic stage,** development for boys and girls diverges. Boys become aware that they have a penis. They develop sexual feelings toward their mothers and become jealous of their fathers. Girls become aware that they do not have a penis and begin to resent their mothers for sending them out into the world "ill equipped." Freud believed that resolution of these conflicts produces the most basic form of sexual identification.

Between the ages of 6 and 7 years, the child enters the **latency stage,** which lasts until the beginning of puberty 5 or 6 years later. During the latency stage sexual desires are suppressed and no new areas of bodily excitation emerge. Instead, sexual energy is channeled into the acquisition of technical skills for earning a living that will be needed in adulthood.

The physiological changes of *puberty,* the onset of sexual maturity, cause the repressed sexual urges to reappear in full force, marking the beginning of the **genital stage.** Now sexual urges are no longer directed toward the parents or repressed. This is the onset of adult sexuality, directed toward peers of the opposite sex for the ultimate purpose of reproduction.

Freud believed that from early childhood onward the personality is made up of three mental structures. The **id,** which is present at birth, is the main source of psychological energy. It is unconscious, energetic, and pleasure-seeking (1933/1964). The **ego** is the intermediary between the id and the social world. The ego emerges out of the id as the infant is forced by reality to cope with the fact that simply desiring something will not satisfy its drives. Action is necessary, but a form of action that accomplishes its purpose, that is productive rather than counterproductive. The work of the ego is seen clearly in the distinctive sense of self that children manifest around the age of 2 and it continues to develop throughout childhood and adolescence. The ego's primary task is self-preservation, which it accomplishes through voluntary movement, perception, logical thought, adaptation, and problem solving. It performs its tasks by bringing the instinctual demands of the id under control, and deciding where, when, and how they are to be satisfied.

The **superego,** which begins to form during early childhood, becomes a major force in the personality during middle childhood. It represents the authority of the social group, embodied in the image of the father.

The three structures that make up human personality are rarely if ever in perfect equilibrium. Instead, dominance shifts as the superego and the id battle for control. The constant process of resolving these conflicts is the engine of developmental change, which Freud spoke of as **ego development.** The patterns of individual behavior that arise in this process constitute the personality.

Summarized in this brief fashion, Freud's theory may appear to be fanciful. His theory of infantile sexuality provoked outrage early in this century when he first proposed it and it remains controversial to this day. Freud's psychoanalytic method has been criticized as ineffective and unscientific. It must also be noted that all of Freud's claims about infancy and early childhood are based on his observations of disturbed adults. Freud is certainly vulnerable to criticism on both methodological and theoretical grounds, yet he remains one of the most influential forces in contemporary developmental theorizing.

Robert Emde (1992) points to several of Freud's enduring contributions to developmental psychology. First, Freud was among the most influential champions of the view that understanding of adult personality must rely on a developmental analysis. Thus he made a developmental approach the center of any theory of personality. Second, he emphasized the need to arrive at scientific generalization through intensive study of individual human beings. Third, he was among the first psychologists to point out and study the complex dynamics between unconscious motives and conscious understanding, between fantasy and reality. Finally, he insisted that a human being is a complex, dynamic creature who can be understood only by study of the person as a whole.

Here's how Freud saw the conflict that these new pleasures evoke:

> In a word, his early awakened masculinity seeks to take his father's place with [his mother]; his father has hitherto in any case been an envied model to the boy, owing to the physical strength he perceives in him and the authority with which he finds him clothed. His father now becomes a rival who stands in his way and whom he would like to get rid of. (1940/1964:189)

These feelings cause Jimmy a lot of mental anguish. He is old enough to know that feelings like wanting your father to die are considered bad, and young enough to believe that his parents, who are powerful figures in his life, are always aware of what he is thinking. So he lives in fear of being punished and feels guilty about his bad thoughts.

Freud called this predicament the **Oedipus complex,** referring to the ancient Greek tragedy in which Oedipus, king of Thebes, unknowingly kills his father and marries his mother. Little boys do not, of course, literally repeat this tragedy. Rather, according to Freud, as they leave infancy and enter childhood, boys must mentally reorder their emotional attachments by distancing themselves from their mother and becoming closer to their father. In other words, they must differentiate themselves from their mother and affiliate with their father.

According to Freud, male children achieve this goal at the end of the preschool period, when they enter the next stage of personality development, the *latency stage,* during which their sexual desires are suppressed and they display great interest in learning the skills possessed by adults. The change to latency requires the simultaneous operation of two **defense mechanisms,** Freud's term for the psychological processes by which people protect themselves from unpleasant thoughts. First, boys develop a strong desire to look, act, and feel like their fathers. By literally "playing the role of Daddy" (helping to bring in kindling from the woodpile, pretending to shave), the boy banishes his feelings of hostility and fear. Now he is a powerful figure, too. Second, the boy achieves the needed control over his infantile desire by *repressing* his feelings toward his mother. He stops desiring total possession of her, thus removing the original source of guilty feelings.

Identification through affiliation

Freud believed that female identification is also a defensive adaptation that propels girls into a latency stage, but the process takes place in a different way. According to Freud, the key event in the development of a girl's sex identity is triggered by her discovery that she does not have a penis: the girl is "mortified by the comparison with boys' far superior equipment" (1933/1964:126). She blames her mother for this "deficiency" and transfers her love to her father. Then she competes with her mother for her father's affection.

Now it's the girl's turn to feel guilty. She is afraid that her mother knows what she is thinking and that she will be punished by loss of her mother's love. She overcomes her fear and guilt by repressing her feelings for her father and identifying with her mother. As a result of this sequence, Freud said, a woman's psychological makeup never becomes as independent of its emotional wellsprings as does a man's because the object of her primary identification and the object of her secondary identification are the same person — her mother. This pattern of identity formation in which women affiliate with their mothers, he believed, renders women an "underdeveloped" version of men. He concluded that women show less sense of justice than men, that they are less ready to submit to the great challenges of life, and that their judgments are more often influenced by feelings of affection or hostility (1925/1961:257–258).

Not surprisingly, Freud's argument has been strongly attacked. Even people who support his general line of interpretation point out that his views depended heavily on the historical era in which he lived and were unduly influenced by its rigid sexual mores (Tyson & Tyson, 1990). In particular, Freud has been criticized for claiming that the lack of a penis makes girls feel inferior to boys, for assuming that a girl's sexual identification occurs only as a defense mechanism, and for concluding that women's path to identity renders them inferior to men.

Nancy Chodorow (1974), for example, acknowledges the difference in the two sexes' experience of early social interaction and their differing biological roles, but the conclusion she draws differs from Freud's. Chodorow considers identification a two-way process involving both the parent and the child. She argues that just as daughters identify with mothers, so mothers experience their daughters as like themselves. In contrast, "mothers experience their sons as a male opposite" (pp. 166–167). In defining themselves as masculine, boys reinforce their mothers' reactions to them, aiding in the differentiation process. In defining themselves as feminine, daughters evoke further feelings of similarity in their mothers, fusing the process of attachment with the experience of sex-role identity. Because daughters do not have to go through the alienating experience of differentiating themselves from their mothers, they "emerge from this period with a basis for 'empathy' built into their primary definition of self in a way that boys do not" (p. 167). Put differently, because girls' identity is based upon affiliation with their mothers, girls have a built-in basis for understanding the needs of others.

In many respects Chodorow's formulation is similar to Freud's, but as Carol Gilligan (1982) points out, the difference in its emphasis is important. Freud assumed that because girls experience less differentiation from their mothers, they are less developed than boys of the same age who have gone through separation from the mother and reorientation to the father. Chodorow does not equate differentiation with development. By her account, the two paths to sexual identity result in two complementary developmental endpoints, each with its own strengths and weaknesses. Males achieve identity through separation; as a result, they see themselves as threatened by intimacy. Females, who achieve identity through attachment, see themselves as threatened by separation.

Whereas Chodorow reinterprets Freud's description of sex-role development, other developmental psychologists, including some who are generally supportive of his ideas, believe that Freud's basic description of how sex roles are acquired is incorrect (Emde, 1992). First, they reject Freud's belief that female development is somehow secondary to male development. If either sex could be said to have priority, it would be the female. As we saw in Chapter 3 (p. 85), the sex organs and the brain of all human embryos initially follow a female path of development; these organs become male only if they are modified through the action of male hormones. Second, modern research indicates that children's sexual identities cannot be the *consequence* of resolving the Oedipus complex because aspects of identity formation can be discerned well before the age at which Freud assumed it to be resolved (Stoller, 1980). Third, researchers now consider adults in the child's family, not the child, to be the primary carriers of sexual fantasies. Disturbances in identity formation currently are thought to result from psychological traumas caused by parents who are sexually abusive or seductive and not from children's inability to resolve infantile sexual desires (Cichetti & Carlson, 1989).

However, Freud's ideas continue to exert an influence on popular thinking about the acquisition of sex roles. The challenge facing those who dispute his theories is to provide a better account of the processes at work.

Identification through observation and imitation

Freudian theories of identification assume that the process occurs indirectly: children are caught in hidden conflicts between their fears and their desires, and attempt to resolve these conflicts through identification.

Social-learning theorists have a very different perspective on how children adopt adult roles. They assume that the process of identification is not driven by inner conflict, but is simply a matter of observation and imitation. For example, as a 4-year-old, our son loved to run down the hallway and slide feet first into a pillow. He was not driven by desire for his mother, who disapproved strongly because she feared that his sliding would bother the neighbors downstairs and would certainly wear holes in his pants. Nor was his father's disapproval enough to stop him. Sasha was modeling his behavior on a baseball star who was being given prominence by the media at the time.

Albert Bandura (1969, 1986), Walter Mischel (1966), and other social-learning theorists believe that all behavior, including behaviors such as Sasha's, is shaped directly by the environment. According to this view, children observe that male behavior differs from female behavior. This observation leads the children to develop hypotheses about appropriate male and female behaviors. Further, children learn that boys and girls are rewarded differently by adults for different kinds of behavior, so they choose to engage in sex-appropriate behaviors that will lead to rewards (Perry & Bussey, 1984).

In Bandura's view, the ability to learn from observation depends on several factors:

1. *Availability.* The behavior to be learned must be available in the child's environment either directly or through a medium such as a book or a television program.

2. *Attention.* Children cannot learn from observation unless they pay attention to the model (the mother, the father, or the fictional character) and perceive the significant features of the behavior in question. Children often need to see a complex behavior more than once before they can determine its significant features. A boy who watches Daddy shave, for example, may at first see the application of shaving cream as the salient feature; he may have to watch his father shave several times before he realizes that using a razor is what signifies shaving.

3. *Memory.* Observation will have no lasting effect if children immediately forget what they observe. Bandura believes that when children have a name for modeled events, their observation becomes especially effective and memorable. Significantly, early childhood is the time when children are acquiring both language and knowledge of basic social categories — and their memory capacity is also increasing (see Chapter 9).

4. *Motor reproduction process.* Observation shows the child which behaviors to imitate. If a behavior is too complex, however — doing a backward flip, say — the child will usually not try to perform it.

5. *Motivation.* For modeling, or imitation, and subsequent learning to occur, the observer must perceive some payoff. Children can become motivated, just as they can learn, by observing the experiences of others. When Ben, who wants grownups to think well of him, hears Daddy praise Lisa for taking her glass to the sink when she finishes her apple juice, he may be motivated to take his glass to the sink next time. If Daddy's good opinion means little to him, this observation will probably not motivate him to imitate Lisa.

There is abundant evidence that parents not only provide models for children to imitate but also reward what they consider sex-appropriate behavior and punish cross-sex behavior. Beverly Fagot (1978a, b), who observed children and their parents in their homes, found that many parents rewarded their daughters with smiles, attention, and praise for dressing up, dancing, and playing with dolls, or simply for following them around the house. By contrast, parents rewarded boys more than girls for playing with blocks. The same parents who criticized their girls for manipulating ob-

jects, running, jumping, and climbing discouraged their boys from playing with dolls, asking for help, or volunteering to be helpful. Such findings support social-learning theorists' basic assumption that sex-appropriate behaviors are shaped by the distribution of rewards and punishments.

Despite many attractive features, social-learning theory has a serious problem in defining one of its central concepts — reward. To some degree, a reward, like beauty, is in the eye of the beholder. A 2-year-old boy and a 2-year-old girl may both be pleased when their grandparents give them a doll for good behavior. But two years later, while the girl might find another doll rewarding, the boy might turn away in disgust at "those girl things." Such incidents make it appear that children's conceptions of what is proper behavior for boys and girls shape their ideas of appropriate rewards for boys and girls. Where do these conceptions come from?

Identification through cognition

The belief that a child's own conceptions are central to socialization is the cornerstone of the cognitive-developmental approach to sex-role acquisition proposed by Lawrence Kohlberg (1966). In contrast to the social-learning theorists, Kohlberg argues that "the child's sex-role concepts are the result of the child's active structuring of his own experience; they are not passive products of social training" (p. 85). In contrast to Freud, Kohlberg claimed that the "process of forming a constant sexual identity is not a unique process determined by instinctual wishes and identifications, but a part of the general process of conceptual growth" (p. 98).

In Kohlberg's view, the crucial factor in sex-role identification is children's developing ability to categorize themselves as either "boys" or "girls." This process typically begins during the third year of life, when children are acquiring a distinctive sense of themselves and beginning to form complex concepts. Once formed, children's conceptions of their own sex are difficult to reverse and are maintained regardless of the social environment.

Sandra Bem (1981) has proposed a slightly different version of this cognitive view; she suggests that children acquire a **gender schema,** a network of associations embodying the culture's conception of sex roles, which they then use to guide their own behavior and to structure their perceptions of their environment. In line with the way scripts and schemas structure preschoolers' cognitive development (Chapter 9, pp. 338–339), Bem's view suggests that children learn their society's gender schemas and the attributes and behaviors appropriate to males and females by observing and participating in many events.

In the cognitive view, once children have acquired a concept or schema of themselves as girls or boys, they use that concept to choose actively from the options present in the environment. Whereas the social-learning theorists assume that the thought sequence of male children is "I want rewards, I am rewarded for doing boy things, therefore I want to be a boy," Kohlberg (1966:89) proposed the following sequence: "I am a boy; therefore I want to do boy things; therefore the opportunity to do boy things (and to gain approval for doing them) is rewarding."

Kohlberg acknowledged that children need to feel that they can control their environment and that they are loved by others. But in his view, rewards also come from behaving in a manner that is consistent with one's sexual identity. If the child is to find a sex-typed behavior rewarding, it must be consistent with maintenance of the appropriate identity, which itself is a cognitive judgment by the child.

Sex-role knowledge and sex-role behavior

In their efforts to decide between conflicting theories about how preschoolers form sex-role identities, psychologists have sought to trace the developing relationship between the earliest signs of sex-typed behavior and children's earliest concepts of what adults mean when they use the labels "girl" and "boy." The existing evidence suggests that by the time children are 5 or 6 years old they have a well-articulated concept of what it means to be a boy or girl in their culture, which, as Kohlberg suggested, shapes their behavior. Between the ages of 2½ and 6, however, children are still piecing this conceptual structure together, and the degree to which they use their developing gender schema to guide their behavior varies.

Naturalistic observations of young children in familiar settings, such as the home or a preschool play group, provide a rich source of evidence about young children's sex-stereotyped ideas and behavior. Such research shows that well before children display knowledge of sexual stereotypes, boys' and girls' behavior is likely to differ. Carol Jacklin and Eleanor Maccoby (1978) observed distinctive styles of play

among 2½-year-olds, who were likely to find partners of the same sex more compatible. When boys played together and got into a tug-of-war over a toy, for example, the tug-of-war was likely to become part of the game. But when a girl and boy got into the same kind of tug-of-war, the girl was likely to retreat and simply observe the boy playing. Maccoby is careful not to specify the source of these differences, restricting herself to the conclusion that even at this early age, children "are already developing somewhat distinctive styles of play" (1980:215).

Not only do boys and girls play differently from an early age, they often prefer to play with different things. When children aged 14 to 22 months were observed in their own homes, researchers found that boys were more likely to play with trucks and cars while girls chose dolls and soft toys (Smith & Daglish, 1977). The children spent more time playing with sex-identified toys than with equally available toys that were not sex-typed, suggesting that even at this young age, these children had developed sex-typed preferences. (See Figure 10.2.)

FIGURE 10.2 *Young children often adopt an extreme, stereotyped version of adult sex-role behavior in their dress-up play.*

Around their third birthday, children begin to talk in a manner that indicates they are beginning to develop a conceptual grasp of culturally prominent attributes of sex roles. Judy Dunn (1988), who observed young children in their homes, provided the following example of a conversation between an older brother, a mother, and a 36-month-old girl. The children are arguing over who can play with a toy vacuum cleaner; it belongs to the girl, but the boy has just repaired it. As he plays with it, his sister tries to get it back:

> **Boy:** *(to mother)* I wanted to do it because I fixed it up. And made it work.
> **Mother:** *(to boy)* Well, you'll have to wait your turn.
> **Mother:** *(to girl)* Are you going to let David have a turn?
> **Girl:** I have to do it. *Ladies* do it. (p. 57)

Vivian Paley's classroom, where sociodramatic play is the keystone of children's activity, yields many other examples of young children's developing notions of sex roles:

> **Mollie:** Are you a sister, Margaret?
> **Margaret:** I'm a brother's sister.
> **Mollie:** They call a brother they sometimes call a boy.
> **Margaret:** Brothers are boys, girls are girls.
> **Mollie:** You're a girl, Margaret.
> **Margaret:** So are you, Mollie. L-M-N-O. That spells "girl." (Paley, 1986:35)

Paley (1984) reports a marked change in young children's sex-typed behavior and conceptions of sex roles in the years from 3 to 6.

> Domestic play looks remarkably alike for both sexes at age three. Costumes representing male and female roles are casually exchanged. Everyone cooks and eats pretend food together. Mother, father, and baby are the primary actors, but identities shift and participants seldom keep one another informed. . . . If asked, a boy will likely say he is father, but if he were to say mother, it would cause little concern. (p. x)

At the age of 4, boys become less comfortable playing in the doll corner, although they may sometimes do so, while girls, who sometimes adopt the roles of Wonderwoman or Supergirl, prefer domestic play. In Paley's words, "the doll corner becomes the women's room" (p. xi). By the age of 5, the doll corner becomes a contested battleground, where girls struggle for domestic calm in the face of "boisterous" raids by boys in the guise of superheroes and bad guys. Now all the children seek to adhere to the cultural definition of what it means to be a boy or a girl, and the conflicts between bad guys and princesses are ever present in their play.

The causes of children's developing ideas and preferences concerning their sex-role identities are much debated. Naturalistic studies, which provide the richest source of descriptions of sex-role development, can show us *what* develops but are not so helpful in explaining *how* the changes are brought about. Consequently, experimental studies have been carried out in an effort to pin down when children first become explicitly aware that males and females belong to different social categories, the role of parental behaviors in bringing about this awareness, and how this awareness affects their behavior (Fagot & Leinbach, 1989).

Beverly Fagot, Mary Leinbach, and Richard Hagen (1986) presented children between 21 and 40 months of age with pairs of pictures of boys and girls or men and women and asked them to identify which picture was of a male and which of a female. They found that children less than 26 months of age were likely to fail, whereas those who were 36 months and older generally succeeded. Most important, those of any age who could assign the appropriate sex to the people in the photographs were more likely to play with children of their own sex. In addition, they found that girls who correctly labeled the photographs displayed less aggression than those who did not, suggesting that their increased understanding of sex-role categories was beginning to influence their behavior.

In a follow-up study, Fagot and Leinbach (1991) found evidence of parental behaviors that were shaping their children's conceptions and behaviors. They reported that the mothers of the children who had learned to label pictures correctly according to gender were more likely to initiate play with their children by handing them a toy that fitted the stereotype for their sex. These mothers also expressed more traditional beliefs about sex roles.

Such results don't mean that the children had any deep understanding of the basis for the differentiation between boys and girls or that their behavior was markedly affected when they were left on their own.

Very few of the 2- and 3-year old children who could reliably label boys and girls were able to identify objects usually associated with each sex (such as flowers and butterflies for girls, fire and automobiles for boys). Nor did children who were able to label pictures according to gender category always choose sex-stereotyped toys when they were allowed to play freely on their own (Fagot, Leinbach, & Hagen, 1986). By the time they are 4 years old, however, children know which things are considered "boy things" and which are "girl things." They assign bears, fire, and "rough things" to boys and men, while butterflies and flowers are considered appropriate for women and girls. In addition, their choice of toys becomes more sex-stereotyped, as the evidence from Paley's classroom would lead one to expect (Leinbach & Hort, 1989).

Sex-role constancy

The evidence about what exactly preschoolers understand indicates that while they have some appreciation of adult conceptions, their understanding is limited and frail. A full concept of one's sexual identity goes well beyond a preference for being a bad guy or a princess or the ability to label pictures of boys and girls appropriately. The concept of one's sexual identity also includes knowledge of the anatomical differences between males and females and many characteristics that are a part of each culture's general conceptions of the categories masculine and feminine.

Sandra Bem (1989:662) reports the kind of difficulties that young children can encounter when their knowledge about the basis of sex-role categories is more (or less) sophisticated than their friends'. Her young son, Jeremy, decided one day to wear barrettes to his nursery school. Another boy insisted repeatedly that Jeremy must be a girl because "only girls wear barrettes." Although Jeremy argued that he was a boy because he had testicles and a penis, the other child persisted. Exasperated, Jeremy pulled down his pants to prove his sexual identity. The other boy was not convinced. "Everybody has a penis; only girls wear barrettes," he replied.

Regardless of the theory used to explain it, a good deal of evidence suggests that by the time children are about 6 or 7 years old, they have formed a stable concept of their own identity as male or female. At this point, almost all children strive to imitate behavior that they interpret as appropriate to their sex, as Kohlberg argued (Perry & Bussey, 1984).

There is often very marked sex-role stereotyping in preschoolers' play.

Theories of sex-role identification compared

Developmental psychologists do agree on two points concerning children's discovery of social categories and initial mastery of behavior that is appropriate to their sex: (1) Children conduct some kind of mental "matching" operation that allows them to isolate key features that they share with others; (2) later ideas of sex-appropriate behavior are closely tied to children's ability to categorize, observe, and imitate.

Theorists differ, though, in their view of adults' power to shape the final outcome. For somewhat different reasons, both Freudian and cognitive-developmental theorists believe that the child's sexual identification and subsequent sex-role behavior are unlikely to be affected by any but the most drastic changes in environmental circumstances. In Freud's famous phrase "biology is destiny," males and females are biologically different forms of *Homo sapiens* that no cultural conditioning can change. In the cognitive-developmental view, sexual identity grows out of universal forms of experience and laws of cognitive development; although cultural influence is not absent, it is not primary. The social-learning view implies a far greater role for culture in the shaping of sexual identification and behavior, thus suggesting that changes in the culture can produce significant changes in sex-role behavior. In this view, the essential requirement for changing behavior is changing the models and rewards.

Just how much flexibility exists for redefining *masculine* and *feminine* remains a matter of dispute (Carter, 1987). Although a variety of studies show that individual adults may exert some influence on children's developing concepts of sex roles, such influence is definitely limited. Thomas Weisner and Jane Wilson-Mitchell (1990) studied families that seek to promote sex egalitarianism in their children to see how far they succeeded in modifying the sex-role stereotypes and behaviors of their children. When they compared the sex-typed preferences for friends, toys, and modes of dress of children raised in such families with those of children whose families adhered to existing cultural norms, they found only scattered differences. A similar conclusion is suggested by Vivian Paley (1986). Paley devoted one school year to minimizing the development of sex-stereotyped play patterns among her preschoolers. Although she found that she could bring about changes so long as she remained directly in control of the children's actions, the children "reverted to type" as soon as she relaxed her controls.

Such results do not mean that sex-role acquisition is unaffected by social pressure. Cross-cultural research has shown that many attributes that are sex-typed one way in one society — types of gestures, speech patterns, dress, activities, interests, and occupations — are typed quite differently in another (Rosaldo & Lamphere, 1974). Clearly such behaviors are learned from experience. In various countries and at various times in history, men have worn robes; in the United States, this form of dress is currently associated with femaleness. Such cases reveal that whatever the contribution of biology to the shaping of sex roles, at least part of everyone's conceptions of sex roles and attitudes toward them depends on how sex is bound up with all of the customs and role categories present in one's culture. In fact, the conclusion reached by Weisner and Wilson-Mitchell and by Paley is that the prevailing culture provides so many lessons in how to behave according to its sex-typed scripts that the family and preschool are not sufficiently powerful to make much of a difference.

Ethnic and Racial Identity

In a world populated by many different ethnic groups and races, often interacting with and conflicting with one another, children's developing sense of their ethnic or racial identity is an important social issue. As a consequence, a number of researchers have studied both the developing ability of children to identify their own race or ethnic group and their attitudes toward their own and other groups (Cross, 1991; McAdoo & McAdoo, 1985; Spencer & Markstrom-Adams, 1990).

Perhaps the most famous research on the development of ethnic and racial identity was carried out by Kenneth and Mamie Clark (1939, 1958), who asked American children of African and of European ancestry to choose between pairs of dolls. The children, who were 3 years old and older, were presented with pairs of dolls representing each racial group and asked to choose "which boy [doll] you would like to play with" or "which girl you don't like." The Clarks reported that most of the youngest children could distinguish between the categories of dolls. But more important, the African American children seemed to prefer the white dolls. These findings were used as evidence by the plaintiffs in the case of *Brown* v. *Board of Education of Topeka* (1954) in their argument that racial segregation in the schools leads to a negative sense of self among African American children. On the basis of this and other evidence, the U.S. Supreme Court ruled that racial segregation in the public schools was unconstitutional.

Since that time, both the empirical data about young children's conceptions of their racial and ethnic identity and the interpretation of the data have come under attack (Akbar, 1985; Spencer & Markstrom-Adams, 1990). One concern has been that the Clarks' original study did not produce statistically reliable results. Another concern is that too many psychologists jumped to the conclusion that African American children define themselves entirely in terms of the majority group, thereby denying the importance of their own families and communities in shaping their identities (Cross, 1990).

Studies conducted since the 1950s both confirm the Clarks' original findings (McAdoo, 1985; Spencer, 1988) and extend them to other groups, including Native Americans (Annis & Corenblum, 1987) and Bantu children in South Africa (Gregor & McPherson, 1966).

Perhaps more important, these studies have also cast doubt on the notion that minority-group children acquire a generalized negative ethnic or racial self-concept. Ann Beuf (1977), for example, reports incident after incident in which Native American children who chose white dolls made evident their understanding of the economic and social circumstances that make their lives difficult in contrast to the lives of white people. In one, 5-year-old Dom was given several dolls representing Caucasians and Native Americans (whose skins were represented as brown) to put into a toy classroom.

> Dom: (holding up a white doll) The children's all here and now the teacher's coming in.
> Interviewer: Is that the teacher?
> Dom: Yeah.
> Interviewer: (holding up a brown doll) Can she be the teacher?
> Dom: No way! Her's just an aide. (Beuf, 1977:80)

In Beuf's view, the children's choices were less a reflection of their self-concept than of their desire for the power and wealth of the white people with whom they had come in contact.

Other recent research has shown that in such studies young children's expressed ethnic or racial preferences vary with the circumstances. Focusing on the interview situation itself, one study reports that Native American children show a greater preference for dolls representing their own group when they are tested in their native language (Annis and Corenblum, 1987). Harriet McAdoo (1985) reports that African American preschoolers' professed preference for white dolls has declined since the 1950s. She does not speculate on the reasons for this trend, but the end of racial segregation and several decades of political and cultural activism in the African American community are likely candidates. This conclusion is reinforced by Beuf's (1977) finding that young children of parents who were active in promoting Native American cultural awareness and social rights more often chose dolls representing Native Americans than children whose parents took little interest in Native American affairs.

Additional evidence of the power of the environment to shape children's ethnic preferences comes from an experimental study that rewarded 3-to-5-year-old African American and white children for choosing black rather than white pictures of animals and people (Spencer & Horowitz, 1973). At first all of the children seemed to prefer white stimuli (both animals and people). But this preference changed after training sessions in which they were rewarded either symbolically (by a puppet that praised their choices) or concretely (with marbles that could be traded for cookies) when they chose black stimuli. Their preference for black stimuli was still evident after several weeks.

In sum, the results of studies on ethnic and racial identity indicate that children are aware of these differences by the time they are 4 years old. At the same time, or soon thereafter, they also become aware of their own ethnicity and form judgments about it. Their attitudes toward their own and other people's ethnicity depend both on the attitudes of their adult caregivers and their perceptions of the power and wealth of their own group in relation to others.

Sex and race and ethnicity are by no means the only social categories that young children come to understand and incorporate in their own behavior. Young children are simultaneously learning a vast array of other roles: how to behave as a big sister, a best friend, a visitor in someone else's home, a patient in a dentist's chair, or Mommy's helper at the market. They are also learning something about possible roles they may play in the future: farmer, nurse, daddy, or president.

DEVELOPING THE ABILITY TO REGULATE ONESELF

As children acquire a basic sense of identity, they are also learning which behaviors are considered good and bad. Their parents expect them not only to learn the rules of proper behavior but to follow these rules without constant supervision. In short, children are expected to adopt the standards of conduct appropriate in their culture and to accept them so thoroughly that they "behave themselves."

Because children generally want to please those with whom they identify as well as to be like them, the ways in which the significant people in their lives respond to their behavior give children their first, primitive ideas of what is good and bad. The following discussion with several 5-year-olds clearly shows that adult evaluations are more than an external fact; they are the basis for children's self-evaluations.

Eddie: Sometimes I hate myself.
Teacher: When?
Eddie: When I'm naughty.
Teacher: What do you do that's naughty?
Eddie: You know, naughty words. Like "shit." That one.
Teacher: That makes you hate yourself?
Eddie: Yeah, when my dad washes my mouth with soap.
Teacher: What if he doesn't hear you?
Eddie: Then I get away with it. Then I don't hate myself.
Wally: If I'm bad, like take the food when it's not time to eat yet and my mom makes me leave the kitchen, then I hate myself because I want to stay with her in the kitchen.
Eddie: And here's another reason when I don't like myself. This is a good reason. Sometimes I try to get the cookies on top of the refrigerator.
Teacher: What's the reason you don't like yourself?
Eddie: Because my mom counts to ten fast and I get a spanking and my grandma gets mad at her.
Deana: Here's when I like myself: when I'm coloring and my mommy says, "Stop coloring. We have to go out." And I tell her I'm coloring and she says, "Okay, I'll give you ten more minutes."
Teacher: What if you have to stop what you're doing?
Deana: When she's in a big hurry. That's when she yells at me. Then I don't like myself. (Paley, 1981:54–55)

As Vivian Paley comments, "Bad and good depended on the adult response. . . . An angry parent denoted a naughty child. To the adult, the cause of the punishment was obvious, but the child only saw the stick and judged himself accordingly" (p. 55).

Paley is echoing the opinion of Jean Piaget (1932/1965), who called this pattern of thinking the "morality of constraint" or **heteronomous morality** (*heteronomous* means "subject to externally imposed rules"). According to Piaget, young children's reasoning about moral issues is shaped by three considerations:

1. I should obey the rules set by more powerful people no matter what.

2. I should obey the letter of the rule, not its spirit.

3. What counts is the outcome of my actions. Even if my intentions are good, if the outcome is bad, then I am bad.

Piaget reached these conclusions about the moral reasoning of young children by telling them pairs of stories and then asking them questions. One of his story pairs went as follows (1932/1965:122):

Version A. There was a little boy called Julian. His father had gone out and Julian thought it would be fun to play with his father's ink-pot. First he played with the pen, and then he made a little blot on the table cloth.

Version B. A little boy who was called Augustus once noticed that his father's ink-pot was empty. One day that his father was away he thought of filling the ink-pot so as to help his father, and so he should find it full when he came home. But while he was opening the ink-bottle he made a big blot on the table cloth.

Piaget first asked the child to repeat each of the stories and then asked a series of questions. This kind of task proved too difficult to carry out with preschoolers, so Piaget interviewed somewhat older children who were still young enough, he believed, to retain the kind of moral reasoning characteristic of early childhood. Here is a conversation with a 7-year-old child (1932/1965:126):

Piaget: Are they both equally naughty or not?
Child: No.
Piaget: Which is the most naughty?
Child: The one who made the big blot.
Piaget: Why?
Child: Because it was big.
Piaget: Why did he make a big blot?
Child: To be helpful.
Piaget: And why did the other make a little blot?
Child: Because he was always touching things. He made a little blot.
Piaget: Then which of them is the naughtiest?
Child: The one who made a big blot.

Piaget proposed that children's beliefs grow out of their experience of the restrictions placed on them by powerful elders. It has always been the child's experience that older people announce the rules, compel conformity, and decide what is right and wrong:

> The morality of constraint is that of duty pure and simple and of heteronomy. The child accepts from the adult a certain number of commands to which it must submit whatever the circumstances may be. Right is what conforms with these commands; wrong is what fails to do so; the intention plays a very small part in this conception, and the responsibility is entirely objective. (1932/ 1965:335)

According to Piaget, as children enter middle childhood and begin increasingly to interact with their peers outside of situations directly controlled by adults, the heteronomous morality gives way to a more **autonomous morality,** one that is based on an understanding that rules are arbitrary agreements that can be challenged, and even changed, if the people who are governed by them agree.

Internalization

At the end of infancy, as we saw in Chapter 7, children become sensitive to society's standards of good and bad even when they have not been explicitly instructed about a particular act or have not actually seen how those in authority would respond to it. They begin to anticipate adults' reactions and plan their own actions accordingly. Once children both want to conform to adult wishes and are able to anticipate adults' reactions, they are said to have *internalized* adult standards.

Freud (1940/1964) describes the **internalization** of adult standards and its consequences for the development of self-control this way:

> [About the age of 5] a portion of the external world has, at least partially, been abandoned as an object and has instead, by identification, been taken into the ego and thus become an integral part of the internal world. This new psychical agency continues to carry on the functions which have hitherto been performed by the people [the

abandoned objects] in the external world: it observes the ego, gives it orders, judges it and threatens it with punishments, exactly like the parents whose place it has taken. We call this agency the super-ego and are aware of it in its judicial functions as our conscience. (p. 205)

Once the child has internalized adult standards, a new form of psychological tension begins to emerge—guilt. Children experience guilt when they know what's right but feel unable to conform to it. In the view of Erik Erikson (see Box 10.2), the basic task of early childhood is to resolve the conflict between the need to take initiative and the negative feelings that arise when initiative leads to bad behavior: "Conscience . . . forever divides the child within himself by establishing an inner voice of self-observation, self-guidance, and self-punishment" (1968b:289).

The words that psychologists use to describe the development of conscience reveal the importance of the roles of language and culture in the process of internalization. As in the case of sex-role and ethnic-group identification, culture enters in the form of rules, roles, activities, and beliefs—the *content* of the conscience. But culture also enters into the *process* of developing a conscience, in the internal dialogue between the child and authority figures. The very concept of conscience suggests that the child is imagining what those in authority will say (Vygotsky, 1978).

Self-control

It is possible for children to know the kinds of behaviors that are expected of them, and even to have internalized their culture's standards, yet still fail to behave in a socially acceptable way. In addition to knowing what they should do, children must acquire the capacity to act in accordance with the expectations of their caregivers even when they are *not* being monitored; this kind of compliance is called **self-control** (Kopp, 1987).

At the core of the development of all forms of self-control is the ability to inhibit initial impulses in a situation so that a proper form of action can arise. Eleanor Maccoby (1980) identifies four kinds of inhibition that children must eventually master:

1. *Inhibition of movement.* A number of studies have shown that it is easier for small children to

BOX 10.2
Erik Erikson

Erik Erikson (1902–), a student of Freud's, combined a background in art, teaching, psychoanalysis, and anthropology in his approach to the process of development throughout the individual life span. Erikson is best known for adding an important social dimension to Freud's biological determinism.

Erikson's emphasis on the influence of society has expanded the scope of psychoanalysis, as has his addition of new methods for observing children, his cross-cultural comparisons, and his psychohistories. In his psychohistories he analyzes the psychological development of such well-known figures as Martin Luther and Mahatma Gandhi, basing his conclusions on their writings and on the reports of others (Erikson, 1958, 1969).

Erikson builds on many of Freud's basic ideas about development, including the importance of early childhood in the formation of personality, the existence of the three basic psychological structures (id, ego, and superego), and the existence of unconscious drives. He holds that the main theme of life is the quest for *identity,* which he conceives of as the stable core of personality. Identity in Erikson's terms can be thought of as a relatively stable mental picture of the relation between the self and the social world in the various contexts of socialization. But unlike Freud, he sees identity formation as a lifelong process that goes through many stages. Each stage builds on, reconfigures, and elaborates on the stage from which it emerges. Throughout their lives people ask themselves "Who am I?" and at each stage of life they arrive at a different answer (Erikson, 1963, 1968b).

Whereas Freud's stages of development end in adolescence, Erikson proposes that human development passes through eight stages and continues throughout life. In formulating his stages of *psychosocial* development, he built upon Freud's *psychosexual* stages. Freud's and Erikson's stages of development are outlined in the table on the facing page.

Each stage, Erikson believes, embodies a particular "main task" that the individual must accomplish in order to move on to the next stage of development. Erikson referred to these tasks as "crises" because they are the sources of conflict within the person experiencing them. Each person's sense of identity is formed in the resolution of these crises; these crises are periods of great vulnerability but also of heightened potential. Thus, whether a 2-year-old girl is suc-

Erik Erikson. Copyright © 1988 Jill Krementz.

cessful in acquiring control over her desires and her body will determine whether she feels proud of herself and autonomous or ashamed and doubtful of her ability to control herself. In each stage, maturation opens up both new possibilities and increased social demands. A young girl's pleasure at being able to play the role of flower girl at an aunt's wedding, for example, is matched by the psychosocial demands from those around her to be able to stand still and to follow directions without too much prompting.

Erikson believes that each crisis provides the individual with a "succession of potentialities," new ways of experiencing and interacting with the world. At the same time these potentialities are continuously being shaped by other individuals who are in turn shaped by their culture and social institutions. The "widening circle" of significant individuals who interact with the developing person includes parents, siblings, peers, grandparents, aunts, uncles, teachers, teammates, mentors, colleagues, employers, employees, and grandchildren. The personality undergoes changes appropriate to the person's widening contacts with social institutions and cultural practices.

Each individual's life cycle unfolds in the context of a specific culture. While physical maturation writes the general timetable according to which a particular component of personality matures, culture provides the interpretive tools and the shape of social situations in which the crises and resolutions must be worked out.

Freud's Psychosexual Stages and Erikson's Psychosocial Stages

Approximate Age	Freud (Psychosexual)	Erikson (Psychosocial)
First year	*Oral stage:* The mouth is the focus of pleasurable sensations as the baby sucks and bites.	*Trust vs. mistrust:* Infants learn to trust others to care for their basic needs or to mistrust them.
Second year	*Anal stage:* The anus is the focus of pleasurable sensations as the baby learns to control elimination.	*Autonomy vs. shame and doubt:* Children learn to exercise their will and to control themselves or they become uncertain and doubt that they can do things by themselves.
Third to sixth year	*Phallic stage:* Children develop sexual curiosity and obtain gratification when they masturbate. They have sexual fantasies about the parent of the opposite sex and feel guilt about their fantasies.	*Initiative vs. guilt:* Children learn to initiate their own activities, enjoy their accomplishments, and become purposeful. If they are not allowed to follow their own initiative, they feel guilty for their attempts to become independent.
Seventh year through puberty	*Latency:* Sexual urges are submerged. Children focus on mastery of skills valued by adults.	*Industry vs. inferiority:* Children learn to be competent and effective at activities valued by adults and peers or they feel inferior.
Adolescence	*Genital stage:* Adolescents have adult sexual desires, and they seek to satisfy them.	*Identity vs. role confusion:* Adolescents establish a sense of personal identity as part of their social group or they become confused about who they are and what they want to do in life.
Early adulthood		*Intimacy vs. isolation:* Young adults find an intimate life companion or they risk loneliness and isolation.
Middle age		*Generativity vs. stagnation:* self-absorption Adults must be productive in their work and willing to raise a next generation or they risk stagnation.
Old age		*Integrity vs. despair:* People try to make sense of their prior experience and to assure themselves that their lives have been meaningful or they despair over their unaccomplished goals and ill-spent lives.

start an action than to stop one already in progress (Luria, 1981). A child who does not know when or how to stop is likely, both literally and figuratively, to step on someone else's toes. The same problem applies to verbal commands. In the follow-the-leader game "Simon says," for example, the leader's command is supposed to be obeyed only when it is preceded by the phrase "Simon says." Young children find it very difficult not to respond to the command whether they hear the phrase or not. Even first-graders continue to make errors in this game (Strommen, 1973).

2. *Inhibition of emotions.* During early childhood, children begin to gain control over the intensity of their emotions. Maccoby recounts an incident in which a mother found her 4-year-old with a cut on his hand that ordinarily would have led to tears. When she said to him, "Why, honey,

you've hurt yourself! I didn't hear you crying," the youngster replied, "I didn't know you were home."

3. *Inhibition of conclusions.* Before the age of 6, children presented with a difficult problem tend to respond quickly, failing to note that the task is more difficult than it seemed at first glance. A popular way to assess the ability to inhibit the impulse to jump to conclusions is to ask children to match a familiar figure with its mate in a set of confusing alternatives (Figure 10.3). Young children respond quickly to this task, and they perform poorly. As they grow older, children slow down to reflect on the problem and improve their performance (Figure 10.4) (Messer, 1976).

4. *Inhibition of choice.* An important element of adult self-control is the knowledge that it is often better to pass up short-term gratification for a larger, long-term goal. Given a choice between eating a small candy bar immediately and a large candy bar the next day, kindergartners overwhelmingly take the small candy bar; not until they are about 12 years old do children choose to wait (Mischel, 1968).

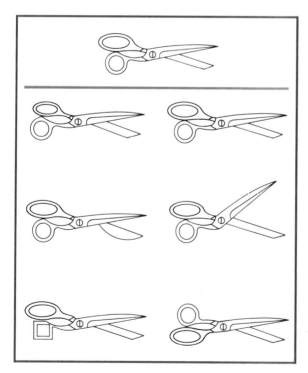

FIGURE 10.3   *An item from the Children's Matching Familiar Figures Test. Which of the six pairs of scissors at the bottom of the figure matches the model at the top? (Courtesy of Jerome Kagan.)*

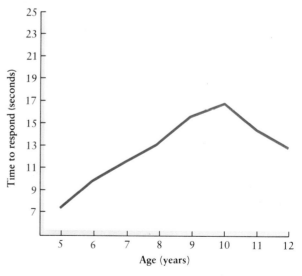

FIGURE 10.4   *Between the ages of 5 and 10, children become increasingly cautious in responding to the task of matching familiar figures. Children older than 10 respond more rapidly because the problems are relatively easy for them. (Adapted from Salkind & Nelson, 1980.)*

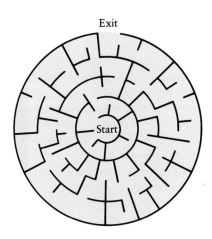

Exit

Start

FIGURE 10.5   *A maze of the kind used by Gardner and Rogoff (1990) to assess children's ability to plan ahead. Trace the route from start to finish to get a feel for how planning is needed to avoid encountering a dead end.*

Claire Kopp (1987) has identified three major phases in the development of children's compliance with adult norms. During the first phase, which occurs between the ages of 1 and 2, children can begin, maintain, modify, and stop actions in response to a direct command from their caregivers. The second phase of self-control begins between the ages of 2 and 3; now the influence of the environment begins to be mediated by the child's internalized knowledge of established rules and expectations. Children who wait until the rest of the family wake up on Sunday morning before turning on the TV set or who accept the rule to "follow the doctor's orders" are displaying self-control.

Kopp believes that children's budding ability to engage in symbolic thinking and to comprehend spoken language, combined with their growing understanding of adult standards, plays a central role in the transition from direct external control to self-control. (These cognitive and linguistic changes are discussed in Chapter 6.) The third phase in the development of compliance with cultural norms occurs between 3 and 6 years of age, when self-control becomes flexible enough to be employed in response to rapidly changing circumstances. The development of self-control also reflects increasing cognitive sophistication, including the ability to plan and to reason more systematically.

The link between the development of the ability to plan ahead and self-control is seen in a study by William Gardner and Barbara Rogoff (1990), who asked young children to solve mazes such as the one shown in Figure 10.5. A glance at this maze quickly indicates that a child who simply begins to trace a path from the nearest opening, without first scanning the maze to see what barriers lie ahead, is certain to fail. Instead of simply jumping in, successful problem-solvers first stop and look over the entire maze. Three-year-olds do not stop to consider what barriers lie ahead and do not solve such a maze. Although they were not always successful at solving the maze, 4-to-6-year-old children planned out their routes in advance about half of the time, indicating the emergence of self-regulation.

AGGRESSION AND PROSOCIAL BEHAVIOR

Up to this point we have focused on the issues of conscience and self-control as more or less individual matters. As we pointed out at the beginning of this chapter, however, individual personality development and socialization are two sides of a single developmental coin. During the preschool years, children begin to spend significant amounts of time interacting with children their own age. In order to be accepted as members of their social group, children must sometimes inhibit their anger when their goals are thwarted; at other times they must subordinate their personal desires for the good of the group. Learning to control aggression and to help others are two of the most basic tasks of young children's social development.

As we saw in Chapter 4 (pp. 136–137), children begin to display the rudiments of both aggression and prosocial behavior shortly after birth. The earliest precursors of aggression are the angry cries and thrashing around of newborns whose rhythmic sucking has been interrupted. The first signs of prosocial behavior are manifested just as early, when newborns react to the cries of other babies by starting to cry themselves (Martin & Clark, 1987). It is widely believed that this "contagious crying" is the precursor of empathy, the sharing of another's feelings, which is the basis for helping and for a variety of other behaviors referred to as prosocial (Eisenberg, 1992; Radke-Yarrow, Zahn-Waxler, & Chapman, 1983).

The Development of Aggression

Aggression is a difficult form of behavior to define. At the core of its meaning is the idea that one person commits an action that hurts another—but not all of the ways a person can hurt another count as aggression. A teething baby who bites the mother's breast while nursing causes pain, as does a toddler who slips and falls on a friend, but these actions aren't usually considered aggressive. To be counted as aggressive, a behavior must be intended to harm someone (Parke & Slaby, 1983). Maccoby (1980) suggests that aggression begins only after children understand that they can be the cause of another's distress and that they can get others to do what they want by causing them distress. This understanding seems to take shape very early, especially within the family situation.

As children mature, two forms of aggression appear (Hartup, 1974). **Instrumental aggression** is directed at obtaining something desirable; for example,

threatening or hitting another child to obtain a toy. **Hostile aggression,** sometimes called "person-oriented" aggression, is more specifically aimed at hurting another person, either for revenge or as a way of establishing dominance, which may gain the aggressor possessions in the long run.

Judy Dunn (1988), who observed young English children and their siblings in their homes, found a rapid increase in children's instrumental aggression toward their siblings during the second year (see Figure 10.6). Perhaps her most interesting finding is that until the age of 18 months, teasing and physical aggression occur with equal frequency. But as children approach their second birthday, they are much more likely to tease their siblings than to hurt them physically. Teasing is a subtle form of aggression requiring the ability to understand specific characteristics of another child. Dunn reports, however, that 16-to-18-month-olds are already capable of leaving a fight in order to go and destroy a sibling's cherished possessions or to push a toy spider at a sibling who is afraid of spiders. (Note that such incidents suggest that children may understand how other people think even earlier than psychologists usually give them credit for—see Chapter 9, pp. 320–321.)

One of the causes of the increased aggressiveness Dunn observed is that as children approach the age of 2 (just when a new and distinctive sense of self seems to emerge, as we saw in Chapter 6, p. 237), they begin to worry about "ownership rights." Taking toys then becomes a serious affair. To trace the early development of aggressive behavior, Wanda Bronson (1975) invited three or four children to a playroom at one time. She gave them toys to play with and she permitted their mothers to be present to give them a sense of security. As the children explored and played, Bronson watched for occasions when two children wanted the same toy.

She noted that often the 2-year-olds struggled over a toy that neither child had shown any interest in before and that neither cared about once the conflict ended. The fact of possession itself, as well as the possibility of "winning out," were new elements in their interactions. Reports from several cultures suggest that similar changes occur in all societies (Kagan, 1981; Ochs & Schieffelin, 1984; Raum, 1940/1967).

Between the ages of 3 and 6, the expression of aggression undergoes several related changes. First, physical tussles over possessions decrease, while the amount of verbal aggression, such as threats, teasing, or insults, continues to increase. Second, "person-

Teeth are a favorite weapon when preschoolers engage in person-oriented aggression.

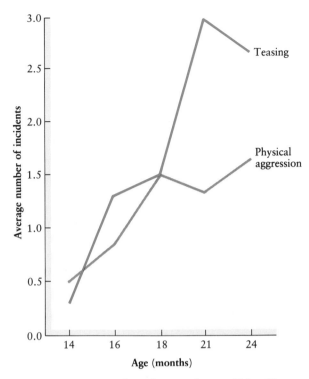

FIGURE 10.6   *Early in the second year of life, siblings are as likely to hurt each other physically as to tease each other; but as they approach their second birthday, teasing becomes much more frequent than physical aggression. (Adapted from Dunn, 1988.)*

What Causes Aggression?

More people have died in war during this century than in all earlier centuries combined. Every day our newspapers carry stories of people killing each other in search of money, to avenge a perceived wrong, or for no apparent reason at all. Among all the questions that can be asked about human social relations, none is more fraught with concern and uncertainty than the causes of aggression and the means of controlling it.

Explanations for the development of aggressive behavior focus on three major factors: the presence of aggression among the evolutionary precursors of our species, the ways societies reward aggressive behaviors, and the tendency of children to imitate the behavior of older role models.

The evolutionary argument

Noting that no group in the animal kingdom is free from aggression, many students of animal behavior have proposed that aggression is an important mechanism of evolution (Lorenz, 1966). According to Darwin (1859/1958), a species gradually comes to assume the characteristics of its most successful individuals. Darwin defined as "most successful" those individuals who manage to pass on their inborn characteristics to

oriented" or "hostile" aggression, in which one child attempts to hurt another even though no possessions are at stake, makes its appearance (Hartup, 1974).

Many studies show boys to be more aggressive than girls in a wide variety of circumstances, although the causes of the difference are uncertain. This difference seems to emerge during the second and third years of life (Legault & Strayer, 1990; Fagot & Leinbach, 1989). As we see in Figure 10.7, which plots the frequency of overtly aggressive acts in a preschool setting, girls' aggression drops markedly as they approach their second birthday, while boys become slightly more likely to behave aggressively at this time. According to Beverly Fagot and Mary Leinbach (1989), these patterns are related to children's growing understanding of male and female sex roles, suggesting that the expression of aggression is coming under increasing cognitive control.

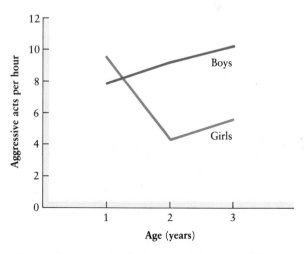

FIGURE 10.7   *As children in a nursery school approach their second birthday, acts of aggression decline significantly among girls but increase slightly among boys. (After Legault & Strayer, 1990.)*

the next generation. Because each individual is, in some sense, competing with every other individual for the resources necessary for survival and reproduction, evolution would seem to favor competitive and selfish behaviors. Such animal behaviors as territorial defense, which ensures a mating pair access to food, have been interpreted as survival-oriented competition (Wilson, 1975). According to this interpretation of evolution, aggression is natural and necessary; its appearance automatically accompanies biological maturation of the young.

Rewarding aggression

A second explanation, generally associated with the social-learning view, is that people learn to behave aggressively because they are often rewarded when they do so (Patterson, DeBaryshe, & Ramsey, 1989). G. R. Patterson and his colleagues (1967) spent many hours watching the aggressive behavior of nursery school children. Whenever they observed an incident of aggression, they noted who the aggressor was, who the victim was, and what the consequences were. They found that aggressive actions occurred several times an hour and that well over three-quarters of the aggressive acts they observed were followed by positive consequences for the aggressor: the victim either gave in or retreated. These victories increased the probability that the aggressor would repeat the attack.

These researchers also found that parents of aggressive children often reinforce aggressive behaviors (Snyder & Patterson, 1986). In some cases, they provide positive reinforcement by paying more attention, laughing, or signaling approval when their children are aggressive. In other cases, children are successful at getting their parents to stop coercing them by becoming even more coercive themselves. Patterson and his colleagues (1989) remark that in coercive households aggressive behavior is functional because it makes it possible for the child to survive in punishing social circumstances.

Modeling

Social-learning theorists believe that in the act of punishing their children, parents may inadvertently teach them how to behave aggressively. One line of evidence for this mechanism comes from a famous series of experiments conducted by Albert Bandura and his co-workers (Bandura, Ross, & Ross, 1963; Bandura,

1965, 1973). They arranged for several groups of preschool children to watch as an adult yelled at a large, inflatable "Bobo" doll, hit it on the head with a mallet, threw it across the room, punched it, and otherwise abused it (see Figure 10.8). In some cases the children watched a normally dressed adult attacking the doll; in others, they saw a filmed version of the same events; in still another case, the model was costumed as a cartoon cat.

After the children watched the episodes of aggressive behavior, the experimenters arranged for them to engage in other activities for a while. Then they brought the children to a playroom containing a Bobo doll and invited them to play, in order to see if they would imitate the adult they had observed. As Bandura's social-learning theory had led them to expect, the aggressive behavior of children who had observed adult aggression was substantially higher than that of children in a control group who had watched nonaggressive interactions. Not only did the children who had been exposed to an aggressive model imitate specific forms of aggression, they also made up forms of their own, such as pretending to shoot the doll, or spanking it. It made little difference whether the adult models were live or filmed, but the children were somewhat less likely to imitate the aggression of the cartoon character. The conclusion seems inescapable: once children are old enough to understand that they can get their way by harming others, they learn from adults both specific types of aggression and the general idea that acting aggressively may be acceptable (Figure 10.9).

A second line of evidence that children learn to behave aggressively by observing adults comes from cross-cultural research. Douglas Fry (1988) compared the levels of aggression of young children from two Zapotec Indian towns in central Mexico. On the basis of anthropological reports, Fry chose one town that was notable for the degree to which violence was controlled and a second town that was notable for the fact that people often fought with each other at public gatherings, husbands beat their wives, and adults punished children by beating them with sticks.

Fry and his wife established residences in both towns so that they could get to know the people and to establish enough rapport to be able to make their observations unobtrusively. They then collected several hours of observations of 12 children from each town as they played in their houses and around the neighborhood. When the researchers compared the aggres-

FIGURE 10.8   *In the top row of photos, an adult behaves aggressively toward a Bobo doll. In the two lower rows, youngsters imitate her aggressive behavior.*

sive acts of the children in the two towns they found that those from the town with a reputation for violent behavior performed twice as many as the children from the other town.

Because these data were collected in naturally occurring interactions, it is not possible to say that observational learning was the only factor causing the differences in the levels of aggression displayed by the children. Fry reports, for example, that adults in the more violence-prone town sometimes directly encouraged their sons and daughters to be aggressive and did not always break up fights between their children. However, the differences he observed could not plausibly be explained in terms of differing biological dispositions, so the result fit most comfortably within an environmental-learning or cultural-context approach. At the same time, it should not be overlooked that even in the town that discouraged aggression the children sometimes acted aggressively, a fact that is difficult to explain purely in terms of learning mechanisms.

Taken as a whole, the evidence concerning causes of aggression cautions us not to pit environmental and biological explanations of behavior against each other in a simplistic way. Such either/or thinking is not sufficient to explain a complex form of behavior like aggression, which grows out of the interactions between deep-seated biological characteristics and culturally organized environmental influences. Nor can we understand aggression without looking at the various mechanisms that counteract it, since aggression is just one among several factors that regulate social behavior.

Controlling Human Aggression

The same theories that attempt to explain aggression also point to mechanisms that are likely to be effective in controlling it. Two such mechanisms that have been

FIGURE 10.9   *Among the Dani of New Guinea, boys are socialized to be aggressive and warlike from an early age through organized practice sessions and many opportunities to observe admired older males in battle. (a) Father teaching his young son how to use a bow and arrow. (b) Boys observing men from their village fight against men from another village. (c) Boys practicing spear throwing.*

extensively studied are the evolution of hierarchical systems of control and the use of reward and punishment.

Evolutionary theories

While aggression is widespread among animal species, so are mechanisms that limit aggression. Changes in the aggressive behavior in litters of puppies, for example, follow a maturational timetable (James, 1951). At about 3 weeks, puppies begin to engage in rough-and-tumble play, mouthing and nipping one another. A week later the play has become rougher; the puppies growl and snarl when they bite, and the victim may yelp in pain. A few weeks later, if littermates are left together, there is little doubt that serious attacks occur. Often the larger puppies concentrate their attacks on the runts of the litter, and among some breeds, it is necessary to remove the smallest animals to keep them from being killed. Once injurious attacks become really serious, a hierarchical social structure emerges, with some animals dominant and others subordinate. After such a **dominance hierarchy** is formed, the dominant puppy needs only to threaten to succeed in getting its way; it has no need to attack. At this point, the frequency of fighting diminishes (Cairns, 1979). Throughout the animal kingdom one finds such hierarchies, which regulate interactions among members of the same species (see Figure 10.10).

The developmental history of aggression and its control among puppies is similar in some interesting ways to development in human children. F. F. Strayer and his colleagues (Strayer, 1980, 1991) observed a close connection between aggression and the formation of dominance hierarchies among 3- and 4-year-olds in a nursery school. They identified a specific pattern of hostile interactions among children: when one child would aggress, the other child would almost always submit by crying, running away, flinching, or seeking help from an adult. These dominance en-

counters formed an orderly pattern of social relationships within the group. One child who dominated another also dominated all children below that child in the dominance hierarchy of the group.

As dominance hierarchies in the nursery school take shape, they influence who fights with whom, and under what circumstances. Once children know their position in such a hierarchy, they challenge only those whom it is safe for them to challenge. They leave others alone, thereby reducing the amount of aggression within the group.

The existence of some similarities across species in these patterns of aggression and its control should not blind us to some important differences. The young of other species often must rely entirely on the dominance hierarchy, whereas human offspring are watched over by their parents and older siblings, who set limits to small children's initial expressions of ag-

FIGURE 10.10   *Many species of animals have innate mechanisms for signaling defeat to allow the establishment of a social dominance hierarchy without bloodshed. (From Eibl-Eibesfeldt, 1970.)*

gression to keep them from harming others. These older members of the group also invoke rules about proper behavior which the children begin to internalize, thus helping to pave the way for self-control.

Frustration and the catharsis myth

One of the most popular and persistent beliefs about aggression is that providing people with harmless ways to be aggressive will reduce their aggressive and hostile tendencies. This belief is based on the assumption that unless aggressive urges are "vented" in a safe way, they build up until they explode violently. Psychologists refer to this process of "blowing off steam" as **catharsis,** a general term for the release of fear, tension, or other intense negative emotions. According to this theory, the way to control aggression is to arrange for "venting" before trouble erupts (Quanty, 1976).

Despite its popularity in folk belief and clinical practice, there is little convincing evidence to support catharsis as a means of controlling aggression. In a rare experimental study of the efficacy of catharsis, Shahbaz Mallick and Boyd McCandless (1966) asked two groups of third-grade boys to build a house of blocks within a limited amount of time in order to win a cash prize. The activities of one group were interfered with by a boy who was a confederate of the experimenters. These children were angered because they lost the opportunity to win the prize. The other group was allowed to work uninterrupted. Some of the boys were then given the opportunity to shoot a play gun at animated targets of people and animals, or at a bull's-eye target. Others were asked to solve arithmetic problems. Next, the boys were asked to administer uncomfortable shocks to the boy who had interrupted their building task (actually, no shocks were delivered to the boy). The number of "shocks" they gave was used as the measure of aggression.

The experimenters found that frustration *did* appear to increase the children's aggression. The boys who had been interrupted administered more "shocks" than the other children. Contrary to the catharsis hypothesis, however, the opportunity to blow off steam did not reduce the boys' aggressive behavior; the boys who shot at targets delivered just as many "shocks" as the children who had solved arithmetic problems.

The ineffectiveness of catharsis contrasts sharply with a noncathartic treatment included as part of the experiment. Some of the boys were told that the child

who had interrupted their building was "sleepy and upset." This sympathetic reinterpretation was sufficient to dissipate their anger. This finding underlines both the role of interpretation in human aggression and the specifically human possibilities of controlling aggression.

Punishment

Another common belief about aggressive behavior is that it can be eliminated if it is punished whenever it occurs. This approach suppresses aggressive behavior under some circumstances, but often it does not. Several studies have found that attempts to control children's behavior by means of physical punishment, or by threats to apply raw power, actually increase the children's aggressiveness (Bandura & Walters, 1959; Sears, Maccoby, & Levin, 1957).

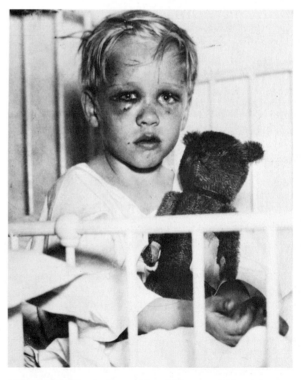

When a family adopts coercive child-rearing behaviors, the levels of violence may escalate to create serious patterns of abuse. Evidence suggests that such patterns may perpetuate themselves in the next generation when young parents who were abused as children abuse their own children (Crowell, Evans, & L'Donnell, 1987).

Patterson and his colleagues have observed how this effect is produced under natural conditions. They observed two groups of boys aged 3 to 13½ along with parents in their homes. The boys in the first group had been referred to the researchers by schools and clinics because of their excessively aggressive behavior. The second group of boys had not been referred for help. The investigators found that punitive child-rearing tactics were more frequent in the homes of the referred boys and that these tactics often increased the level of aggression in the family as a whole (Patterson, 1976, 1979, 1982). Patterson's findings indicate that such learning typically occurs in the following way:

> A younger brother hits his older sister in order to obtain a toy. His sister hits him back. He shouts at her, and while pulling on the toy, hits her again. She resists. Their mother comes running to see what is the matter. She shouts at them to stop, but they do not listen. Exasperated, she lashes out and slaps her son, and roughly shoves her daughter. The boy withdraws, breaking the cycle for the moment. If matters stopped here, this would be a simple case of punishment. But now the mother's behavior has been modified. Since the mother's slap successfully stopped the children's fighting, she is more likely to be aggressive at a later time. Since she models successful aggression, her children may also learn to interact in that way.

Patterson points out that in interactions of this kind, which he calls "coercive," children may inadvertently influence their parents to use physical punishment and make themselves still more aggressive as a result. Coercive situations such as this teach children both how to be aggressive and how to be the victim.

If punishment is used as a means of socialization, it is most likely to suppress aggressive behavior when the child identifies strongly with the person who does the punishing (Eron, Walder, & Lefkowitz, 1971) and when it is employed consistently. Used inconsistently, punishment is likely to provoke children to further aggression (Block, Block, & Morrison, 1981; Parke & Slaby, 1983).

Rewarding nonaggressive behaviors

Since young children sometimes become aggressive in order to gain attention, one strategy for reducing aggression is to ignore it and to pay attention to children only when they are engaged in cooperative behavior.

When teachers are trained to use this selective-attention technique, aggression in their classroom declines significantly (Brown & Elliot, 1965).

A successful technique is for adults to step in between the children involved in an altercation and to pay attention to the victim, while ignoring the aggressor (Allen, Turner, & Everett, 1970). The adult may comfort the injured child, give the child something interesting to do, or suggest nonaggressive ways in which the victim might handle future attacks. Children are taught to say, for example, "No hitting," or "I'm playing with this now."

In such selective-attention procedures the aggressor is not rewarded either by the adult's attention or by the victim's submission. The victim is taught how to deal with such attacks without becoming an aggressor, thus keeping the aggression from escalating. In addition, other children who may have observed the scene are shown that it is appropriate to be sympathetic to the victim of aggression, and that nonviolent assertion in the face of aggression can be effective.

Cognitive training

Another way to control aggression is to use reason. Though it is sometimes difficult to hold a rational discussion with a 4-year-old who has just grabbed a toy away from a playmate, such discussions have been found to reduce aggression even at this early age.

Shoshana Zahavi and Steven Asher (1978) arranged for the teacher in a preschool program to take the most aggressive boys aside, one by one, and engage them in a 10-minute conversation aimed at teaching them that (1) aggression hurts another person and makes that person unhappy; (2) aggression does not solve problems, it only causes resentment in the other child; and (3) children can often resolve conflicts by sharing, taking turns, and playing together. The teacher taught each concept by asking the child leading questions and encouraging the desired response. After these conversations, the boys' aggressive behavior decreased dramatically and their positive behavior increased.

An important component of this technique was that the children were made aware of the feelings of those they aggressed against. All of the successful techniques for teaching self-control of aggression go beyond the mere suppression of aggressive impulses. Instead, children are encouraged to stop their direct attacks and to consider another way to behave.

The Development of Prosocial Behavior

When Charles Darwin published *The Origin of Species,* the public's understanding of evolution was dominated by such famous phrases as Herbert Spencer's "survival of the fittest" and Tennyson's "Nature, red in tooth and claw." Even Darwin said that Spencer's expression was "more accurate" than his own "natural selection" (1859/1958: chap. 3). Yet we recognize now that it presents an inaccurate, one-sided picture of evolution, for it takes no account of behaviors that offer no direct reward to the benefactor but do benefit the group. Such **prosocial behaviors** — altruism, cooperation, helping, empathy — are common. When a preschooler offers her teddy bear to a friend who is crying because she scraped her knee or another brings candy to share with friends, they are engaging in prosocial behavior. Why do such behaviors occur and how do they develop?

Evolutionary explanations

Prosocial behavior, like aggression, is not an exclusively human trait. Many animals, among them social insects, hunting dogs, and chimpanzees, exhibit behaviors that at least appear to reflect altruism. The challenge to theories of biological evolution is to show how these behaviors have evolved and how they apply to human beings.

Edward O. Wilson, a biologist, has posed the problem and its solution as follows:

> . . . how can altruism, which by definition reduces personal fitness, possibly evolve by natural selection? The answer is kinship: if the genes causing the altruism are shared by two organisms because of common descent, and if the altruistic act by one organism increases the joint contribution of these genes to the next generation, the propensity to altruism will spread through the gene pool. This occurs even though the altruist makes less of a solitary contribution to the gene pool as the price of its altruistic act. (1975:3–4)

Wilson reasoned that if natural selection "looked for" altruism among lower animals, there must also be a direct genetic basis for altruism among human beings.

Wilson's argument set off a controversy that is still in progress. Among the lower animals studied by Wilson, altruism seemed explicable because it was re-stricted to *kin,* those with very similar genes. But among human beings, altruism extends well beyond kin to include total strangers. While the argument can be made that altruism to strangers may increase a person's chance for survival because it may eventually be reciprocated (a modern version of the notion of casting bread upon the waters), to many investigators, such a connection to human behavior seems too remote to be useful (Kitcher, 1985).

When we consider this aspect of social development, it is important to keep in mind that both antisocial and prosocial behaviors develop within a single integrated social system. Empathetic impulses develop in the context of social interactions just as aggressive ones do; both are essential parts of a child's personality and both are subject to the process of socialization.

Empathy

The emotional state that corresponds to prosocial behavior in the way that anger corresponds to aggression is **empathy,** the sharing of another's emotions and feelings. Empathy is widely believed to provide the emotional foundations of prosocial behavior (Eisenberg, 1992; Hoffman, 1975). According to Martin Hoffman (1975), a child can feel empathy for another person at any age. As children develop, however, their ability to empathize broadens and they become better able to interpret and respond appropriately to the distress of others.

Hoffman has proposed four stages in the development of empathy. The first stage occurs during the first year of life, even before a baby appears to be aware of the existence of others. As we noted earlier, babies as young as 2 days cry at the sound of another infant's cries (Martin & Clark, 1987). Nancy Eisenberg (1992) calls this phenomenon "emotional contagion." These early "sympathy cries" are akin to innate reflexes, since babies obviously can have no understanding of the feelings of others. Yet they respond as if they were having those feelings themselves.

As children gradually become aware of themselves as distinct individuals during the second year of life, their responses to others' distress change. Now when babies are confronted by someone who is distressed, they are capable of understanding that it is the other person who is upset, not they. This realization allows children to turn their attention from concern for their own comfort to comforting others. Since they have difficulty keeping other people's points of view in

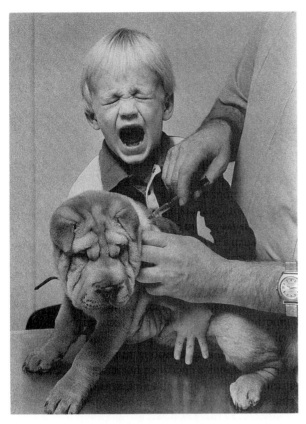

This child's empathy for his pet is so strong one might think that it is he, not the dog, that is being innoculated.

mind, however, some of their attempts to comfort or help may be inappropriate, such as giving a security blanket to a daddy who looks upset.

The third stage in the development of empathy, corresponding roughly to the preschool period, is brought on by the child's increasing command of language and other symbols. Language allows children to empathize with a range of feelings that require more subtlety to express, as well as with people who are not present. Information gained indirectly through stories, pictures, or television permits children to empathize with people whom they have never met.

The fourth stage in the development of empathy occurs sometime between the ages of 6 and 9. Children now appreciate not only that others have feelings of their own but that these feelings occur within a larger set of experiences. Children at this stage begin to be concerned about the general conditions of others, their poverty, oppression, illness, or vulnerability, not just their momentary emotions. Since children in this age range are aware that there are classes of individuals, they are capable of empathizing with groups of people, and thus can take a budding interest in political and social issues.

It might be noted that Hoffman's theory of empathy is linked to Piaget's theory of cognitive development. Each new stage of empathy corresponds to a new stage of cognitive ability that allows children to understand themselves better in relation to others.

Perhaps because it is linked so closely to what children *understand,* Hoffman's explanation of the development of empathy tends to leave out how they *feel.* It is tacitly assumed that the more children understand, the more intensely they adopt the feelings of the person in distress. The catch, as Dunn (1988) points out, is that children may understand perfectly well why another child is in distress and feel glad as a result.

Evidence on the development of prosocial behaviors

Several studies document the development of such prosocial behaviors as sharing, helping, caregiving, and showing compassion as early as the second year of life (see Figure 10.11). For example, Carolyn Zahn-Waxler and Marion Radke-Yarrow (1982) studied the development of prosocial action over a 9-month period among three groups of children, who were 10, 15, and 20 months of age at the start of the observations. Their findings were based on mothers' reports of occasions when their children expressed sympathy for others.

Consistent with Hoffman's theorizing, when confronted with someone else's distress, the youngest children responded by crying themselves. As the children grew older, crying decreased and was replaced by worried attention. At the age of 1, most of the children were observed to comfort a person who was crying or who was in pain by patting her, hugging her, or presenting her with an object. In the period between 12 and 18 months of age, most children had progressed from diffuse emotional responses to active caregiving and comforting behavior in response to another's distress. The comforting behavior of 1½- and 2-year-olds was sometimes quite elaborate. Children this age did such things as try to put a Band-Aid on someone's cut or cover their resting mother with a blanket. They also began to express their concern verbally and to give suggestions about how to deal with the problem.

FIGURE 10.11   *One twin brother shows his sympathy for the other as he tries to comfort him.*

Dunn (1988) reports that the tendency of young children to comfort a sibling in distress increased between 15 and 36 months, as we would expect on the basis of the results reported by Zahn-Waxler and Radke-Yarrow. But she found that such comforting occurred only when the child did not cause the sibling's distress in the first place. Moreover, children of all ages were sometimes observed to respond to their sibling's distress by laughing or seeking to make matters worse.

Other evidence about the development of prosocial behavior comes from observations of young children as they follow their parents through their daily rounds of activities, often trying or offering to help. Harriet Rheingold (1982) invited parents and their 18-, 24-, and 30-month-old children into a laboratory setting that simulated a home. The setting included several undone chores—a table to be set, scraps to be swept up, dusting to be done, a bed to be made, and laundry to be folded. The parents and other adults were instructed to do these chores without asking the children for help. Yet in a 25-minute session, all the 2-year-olds helped their mothers, and 18 of the 20 helped an unfamiliar woman. While they were helping,

the children said things that indicated that they knew the goals of the tasks and were aware of themselves as working with others to accomplish these goals. They worked spontaneously and eagerly, and went well beyond imitation in their helpfulness.

Nancy Eisenberg-Berg and Cynthia Neal (1979) obtained analogous results when they observed 3-to-5-year-olds in nursery schools helping, sharing with, and comforting their playmates. Such prosocial behaviors were by no means numerous, however. They occurred only about once every 4 hours during the time the children spent together.

Promoting prosocial behavior

Adults are of course eager to encourage children's prosocial behavior. Research has identified many strategies that adults use in this endeavor, most notably rewarding children for prosocial activity.

Offers of explicit rewards such as a piece of candy or a gold star, however, may well encourage children to behave prosocially *only* if they are rewarded. This unwanted consequence of explicit rewards was demonstrated by Mark Lepper and his colleagues (Lepper & Greene, 1978). These researchers knew that 3-to-5-year-old children enjoy drawing with colored felt pens. They promised one such group of children a special certificate if they would draw a picture for a visiting adult, while others were allowed simply to draw on their own. They found that during free-play periods a week or two later, the children who had made their drawings "under contract" and had been rewarded for their efforts spent only half as much time drawing with pens as the children who had not been rewarded for drawing.

As a consequence of such findings, developmental psychologists suggest less direct means of promoting prosocial behavior. Two methods that recent research has shown to be effective are **explicit modeling,** in which adults behave in ways they desire the child to imitate, and **induction,** in which adults give explanations that appeal to children's pride, their desire to be grownups, and their concern for others (Eisenberg, 1992).

Most studies of explicit modeling contrast the behavior of two groups of children. In the "nonmodeling" group, no special arrangements are made for teachers to model prosocial behaviors such as helping and sharing. In the "modeling" group, teachers are told to stage periodic training sessions in which they demonstrate sharing and helping behaviors: they share candies among the children with explicit fairness, read books about helping a child who is feeling sad or who is being teased, and so on. Such techniques have been found to increase prosocial behavior among children (Fukushima & Kato, 1976; Yarrow, Scott, & Waxler, 1973). Marion Yarrow and her colleagues also found that when the training was carried out in a nurturant, loving way, children showed the effects of the training as long as 2 weeks later—evidence that the effects of modeling can last for some time.

Studies of the efficacy of induction strategies, in which adults attempt to reason with children, have usually been carried out with older children. A study of early prosocial behaviors in the home found that younger children, too, performed more prosocial acts when their mothers attempted to induce prosocial behavior (Zahn-Waxler, Radke-Yarrow, & King, 1979). Reason by itself, however, was not the crucial factor; the most effective mothers combined reason with loving concern.

It is worth remembering that in real life, outside of research settings, the strategies to increase prosocial behavior do not occur in isolation from efforts to decrease aggressive behavior. Rather, a great variety of techniques are likely to be brought into play, interacting with and reinforcing one another to create overall patterns of socialization. (This patterning of socialization is discussed further in Chapter 11.)

THE EMERGENCE OF NEW EMOTIONS

Throughout our discussion of development in early childhood, we have written about cognitive and social development as somewhat separate topics. They are not separate in everyday life, of course. Thinking about the world and interacting with other people are intimately connected in virtually all of children's waking moments. Children's developing cognitive capacities influence and are influenced by their social relations just as their social relations depend on how they interpret and evaluate other people's actions. Moreover, whether one focuses on the cognitive or the social aspect of children's experiences, a third aspect—how children *feel* about their experience—

must also be taken into account. Consequently, our discussion would be incomplete if we did not consider how emotion, the "feeling tone" that accompanies children's actions, develops during this period.

According to Kurt Fischer and his colleagues (Fischer, Shaver, & Carnochan, 1989), every emotion emerges from a stepwise process: we first perceive and then evaluate the events we encounter. Upon first perceiving a situation, the individual rapidly appraises it to decide if it has positive or negative implications. Once this good/bad or positive/negative decision is made, a second look-see and appraisal evokes the emotional reaction.

We know that children come into the world capable of experiencing a small set of emotions—pleasure, anger, disgust, and surprise (Chapter 4, pp. 136–137). By 6 to 9 months of age their reactions to strange adults and to heights indicate that fear can be added to this set (Chapter 5, p. 200). Psychologists refer to these as *primary* emotions because they appear so early in life and the facial expressions that accompany them are universally recognizable.

At the end of infancy, as children develop a distinct sense of themselves and a sensitivity to cultural standards, they begin to show the first signs of *secondary* emotions, each of which relates to one of the small set of primary emotions. (Figure 10.12 shows the relations of the secondary emotions to the primary ones.) The cardinal feature of these new emotions is their dependence on the development of a more refined concept of oneself in relation to others.

Michael Lewis and his colleagues (1989) refer to the secondary emotions as *self-referential* to emphasize the special sense of "in relation to others" that evokes these emotions. We feel embarrassed, for example, when we are the objects of unwelcome attention. We feel guilty when we have failed to live up to the cultural standards of behavior we have internalized. We feel envy when someone receives praise, attention, or an object that we would like for ourselves. We feel proud when we have excelled in respect to our culture's standards and others praise our accomplishments.

To test out the idea that a distinct sense of self is important to the development of secondary emotions, Lewis and his co-workers assessed children's self-concepts and understanding of secondary emotions in two situations, and then sought to determine if success on the self-image test was necessary for the development of embarrassment. The test of self-image was the same one we discussed in Chapter 6—do children

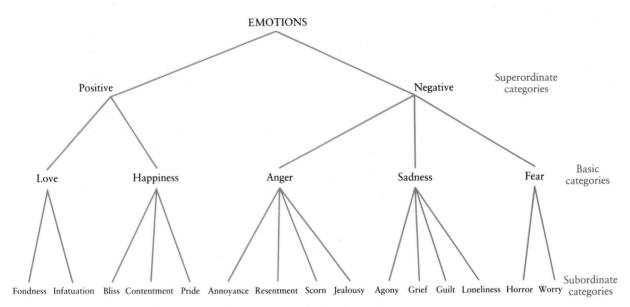

FIGURE 10.12   *A simplified version of the emotion hierarchy, showing how some of the secondary (subordinate) emotions relate to the primary (basic) ones. (Only a few of the secondary emotions are included here.) (From Fischer, Shaver, & Carnochan, 1989.)*

recognize themselves in a mirror and reach up to rub a red spot off their nose? To test for secondary emotions the researchers assessed the children's reactions when asked to dance for an adult. They obtained the result they expected on the basis of the assumption that self-recognition and self-referential emotions develop together. The children who did not recognize themselves in a mirror were not embarrassed when they were asked to dance, while those who did recognize themselves were likely to become embarrassed.

The intimate link between children's ability to experience secondary emotions and their cognitive understanding of social events is brought out in a different way in another study. Linda Michalson and Michael Lewis (1985) presented the pictures shown in Figure 10.13 to children between the ages of 2 and 5. Each picture was accompanied by a story about a little girl called Felicia. In Figure 10.13*a*, for example, Felicia is having a birthday party, and the children were asked to say how Felicia feels. At 2 years of age the children could say that Felicia was happy about the birthday party. But they could not say that Felicia was

afraid when she was lost in the supermarket (Figure 10.13*f*) or sad when her dog ran away (Figure 10.13*c*). As children grow older and approach the age when they will be attending elementary school, they become much better at "reading" situations for the emotional reactions they are likely to evoke.

When we take into account the fact that the organization of the contexts in which children grow up varies from culture to culture, it is also clear that the development of emotion includes a cultural component. For young children in the United States, being asked to dance for a grownup may elicit embarrassment. Such a performance is unusual and the attention it evokes is unwelcome. But in Bali, where very young girls are taught to dance and such performances are routine, the request is more likely to elicit pride than embarrassment.

Although secondary emotions first emerge at the start of early childhood, their variety and the situations that elicit them change markedly as children grow older (Harris, 1989). A 4-year-old may be embarrassed when she is asked to recite a poem for a family

FIGURE 10.13 *As children's understanding of social events increases, so does their ability to predict Felicia's feelings in these scenes:* (a) *Felicia has a birthday party;* (b) *Felicia's mother has pink hair;* (c) *her dog runs away;* (d) *her food tastes awful;* (e) *her sister knocks over Felicia's tower of blocks;* (f) *Felicia gets lost in the supermarket.*

gathering; it is not until many years later that she will experience embarrassment if someone tells her that her slip was showing when she rose to address a room full of people. As children grow older and gain both more social experience and more cognitive sophistica-

tion, the pattern set in early childhood continues to become more refined. Consequently, we can expect the development of secondary emotions to be a lifelong process that will vary in its particulars with the cultural milieu (Lewis & Saarni, 1985; Lutz, 1987).

TAKING ONE'S PLACE IN THE SOCIAL GROUP AS A DISTINCT INDIVIDUAL

The kindergartners in Vivian Paley's classroom are discussing the fate of Tico, a wingless bird who is cared for by his black-winged friends. Their discussion reveals considerable sophistication about the dilemma described by Freud at the beginning of this chapter: How can a person achieve happiness as an individual and at the same time win acceptance as a member of the group?

In the story, the wishingbird visits Tico one night and grants him a wish. Tico wishes for golden wings. When his friends see his golden wings in the morning, they are angry. They abandon him because he wants to be better than they. Tico is upset by his rejection and wants to gain readmission to the group. He discovers that he can exchange his golden feathers for black ones by performing good deeds. When at last he has replaced all the golden feathers with black ones, he is granted readmission by the flock, who comment, "Now you are just like us" (Leoni, 1964).

Teacher: I don't think it's fair that Tico has to give up his golden wings.

Lisa: It is fair. See, he was nicer when he didn't have any wings. They didn't like him when he had gold.

Wally: He thinks he's better if he has golden wings.

Eddie: He is better.

Jill: But he's not supposed to be better. The wishingbird was wrong to give him those wings.

Deana: She has to give him his wish. He's the one who shouldn't have asked for golden wings.

Wally: He could put black wings on top of the golden wings and try to trick them.

Deana: They'd sneak up and see the gold. He should just give every bird one golden feather and keep one for himself.

Teacher: Why can't he decide for himself what kind of wings he wants?

Wally: He has to decide to have black wings. (Paley, 1981:25–26)

This conversation shows that the children understand that by wishing for golden wings, Tico has wished himself a vision of perfection. Each child has done the same thing countless times: "I'm the beautiful princess"; "I'm Superman. I'll save the world." For the blissful, magic moments when the world of play holds sway, perfection is attainable, even by a lowly bird or a preschool child. Wally and his friends also appreciate the dilemmas of perfection. In their eyes, Tico not only thinks he is better, he *is* better—but he is not supposed to be. Try as they may to conceive of a way for Tico to retain his prized possessions, the children realize that conformity is unavoidable. Wally's summary is difficult to improve upon: Tico has to choose to conform.

The children discussing the fate of Tico and his community of birds reveal more than an appreciation of the heavy hand of society as it is experienced by every child growing up. They are also able to see that individuals have a responsibility for regulating social relations. Since wishingbirds grant wishes, it is not the wishingbird's fault that Tico wished himself better than the others. Tico should have known better. He should have been able to control *himself* and make a reasonable wish.

This story returns us to the theme with which this chapter began—that social development and personality development are two aspects of a single process. When children engage in acts of sharing and comforting, they reveal their ability to know another person's mental state. At the same time, they are displaying their own ways of thinking and feeling—in other words, their personalities. Lawrence Blum (1987) captures the interconnectedness of one's relation to the social group and one's identification as an individual when he writes:

> To be concerned for a friend, or for a community with which one closely identifies and is a member, is not to reach out to someone or something which is "wholly other" than oneself, but to that which shares a part of one's own self and is implicated in one's sense of one's own identity. (p. 318)

As they approach their sixth birthday, children have by no means completed the socialization process. They have attained only a rudimentary understanding of their social worlds, and their ability to think about themselves is correspondingly general and undifferentiated (Eder, 1989). They demonstrate great sensitivity to the social world, however, and a readiness to engage it with all the intelligence and energy that their developing cognitive and physical abilities permit.

Before we turn in Part IV to the wide range of new roles and rules that children encounter in middle childhood and the corresponding changes that take place in their sense of themselves, we need to round out the discussion of early childhood by investigating the range of contexts and social influences that make up the world of the young child. As we shall see in Chapter 11, even young children are exposed to a great variety of social influences and cultural prescriptions. It is in the course of dealing with the variety of concrete circumstances that structure their everyday experiences that children create the synthesis of cognition and emotion called personality and acquire their social identities.

SUMMARY

1. Social development is the two-sided process in which children become integrated into their community while differentiating themselves as distinct individuals.

2. One side of social development is socialization, the process by which children acquire the standards, values, and knowledge of their society.

3. The other side of social development is personality formation, the process by which children come to have distinctive and consistent ways of feeling and behaving in a wide variety of contexts.

4. Identification, the process of molding one's behavior to that of a person one admires, contributes to children's distinctive sense of themselves at the same time that it places each of them in salient social categories, such as male and female.

5. Competing theories of identification emphasize four mechanisms:
   a. Identification as a process of differentiating oneself.
   b. Identification as a process of empathy and attachment.
   c. Identification resulting from observation and imitation of powerful others, and from the rewards gained by appropriate behaviors.
   d. Identification resulting from the cognitive capacity to recognize oneself as a member of a social category.

6. Early ability to identify oneself as a boy or girl does not depend on anatomical knowledge of sex differences. Not until the end of the preschool period do boys and girls fully understand that sex is a permanent characteristic.

7. Sex-role categories serve as an important basis for acquiring other roles that contribute to the child's personality.

8. Children acquire a sense of ethnic identity around the age of 4. Their attitudes toward their race or ethnicity depend heavily on how their social group is perceived in the society as a whole.

9. The social standards displayed by adult models with whom children identify become the basis for children's initial judgments of good and bad behavior.

10. Internalization of social roles and standards of behavior provides children with a framework for gaining control of their own impulses.

11. Self-control requires persistence and inhibition of action. Children develop four kinds of inhibition:
    a. Inhibition of motion.
    b. Inhibition of emotion.
    c. Inhibition of conclusions.
    d. Inhibition of choice.

12. Children display the rudiments of both aggression and altruism shortly after birth.

13. Aggression in the sense of an act that is intended to hurt others does not appear until the second year of life.

14. Aggression is observed among animals of many species. From an evolutionary perspective, aggression is seen as a natural consequence of competition for resources.

15. Instrumental aggression is directed at obtaining desirable resources. Hostile aggression may also gain resources, but it is more directly aimed at causing pain to another person.

16. Aggressive behavior may increase among children either because they are directly rewarded for it or because children imitate the aggressive behavior of others.

17. The development of aggression is accompanied by the development of social dominance hierarchies that control aggression.

18. Among humans, additional effective means for controlling aggression are rewards for nonaggressive behaviors and cognitive training that induces children to consider the negative consequences of aggressive behaviors.

19. Prosocial behavior, no less than aggression, is a characteristic of our species. Empathy—the ability to feel what another person is feeling—may be the basis for the development of prosocial behavior.

20. The development of the ability to hurt other people is paralleled by and interacts with the ability to help others. Helping, sharing, and other prosocial behaviors can be observed as early as the first 3 years of life.

21. Increased cognitive ability in combination with increased social knowledge leads to the emergence of secondary emotions, such as embarrassment and envy.

22. In acquiring a distinctive way of interacting with other people, both prosocially and antisocially, children acquire a sense of themselves and their own personalities.

KEY TERMS

aggression

anal stage

autonomous morality

catharsis

defense mechanisms

dominance hierarchy

ego

ego development

empathy

explicit modeling

gender schema

genital stage

heteronomous morality

hostile aggression

id

identification

induction

instrumental aggression

internalization

latency stage

Oedipus complex

oral stage

personality

personality formation

phallic stage

primary identification

prosocial behaviors

secondary identification

self-concept

self-control

social development

socialization

superego

SUGGESTED READINGS

DUNN, JUDY. *The Beginnings of Social Understanding.* Cambridge, Mass.: Harvard University Press, 1988.

By studying children as they interact with their brothers and sisters in everyday family settings, Judy Dunn has discovered a great deal about early social development. This book is especially helpful in illuminating the intimate relationship between intellectual and social development.

EISENBERG, NANCY (Ed.). *The Caring Child.* Cambridge, Mass.: Harvard University Press, 1992.

An excellent and readable summary of current theory and research on the development of prosocial behavior. Separate chapters are devoted to such important topics as the early origins of prosocial behavior, motives for prosocial behavior, individual differences, cultural variations, and the biological bases of prosocial behavior.

ERIKSON, ERIK. *Childhood and Society.* New York: Norton, 1963.

This early and classic statement of Erikson's theory of development includes extended case studies of development in a variety of cultural circumstances. The case studies make clear Erikson's indebtedness to Freud but demonstrate that he accords culture a larger role in development than Freud did.

FREUD, SIGMUND. *An Outline of Psychoanalysis.* In J. Strachey (Ed. and Trans.), *The Standard Edition of the Complete Psychological Works of Sigmund Freud* (Vol. 17). London: Hogarth, 1964; New York: Norton, 1970.

This series of lectures provides an excellent introduction to Freud's theory of personality development, particularly his view of sexuality as a fundamental source of development.

McDONALD, KEVIN B. *Social and Personality Development: An Evolutionary Synthesis.* New York: Plenum, 1988.

The subtitle indicates the special emphasis of this book, which seeks to link social development to its biological foundations without neglecting the way in which the social world constructs the self and others. Particularly noteworthy is a chapter on socialization at a national level, which takes up examples as distant from each other in time as the societies of ancient Greece and twentieth-century Europe and America.

PALEY, VIVIAN. *Boys and Girls.* Chicago: University of Chicago Press, 1984.

The preschool classroom is the setting for this book about the development of sex-role identity during early childhood. To an unusual degree, the children are allowed to speak for themselves. Paley is a teacher who believes that an understanding of preschool development requires adults to listen with great care and sympathy to what children are trying to say.

PERRY, DAVID G., & BUSSEY, KAY. *Social Development.* Englewood Cliffs, N.J.: Prentice Hall, 1984.

A thorough introduction to the topic of social development from the perspective of social-learning theory.

CHAPTER 11

The Contexts of Early Childhood Development

•

A new level of organization is in fact nothing more
than a new relevant context.

—C. H. WADDINGTON,
ORGANIZERS AND GENES

Thus far we have treated the settings that children inhabit during early childhood primarily as background to our discussions of their cognitive, physical, and social development. In this chapter we alter our focus to highlight the ways in which the contexts within which children live and the activities they engage in contribute to their development.

As we shift our attention to the contexts of early childhood, it is helpful to refer once again to Figure 1.6 (p. 24), which represents the environments of development as a "nested arrangement of concentric structures, each contained within the next" (Bronfenbrenner, 1979:22). The innermost circles in this diagram are the specific events and contexts of children's direct experience: eating dinner, playing on the jungle gym, having a drawing lesson, and so forth. These events take place in a variety of community settings, such as the home, the church, the local park, and the nursery school. On a somewhat more global level are settings and social institutions such as the parents' workplaces, government offices, and the mass media, which influence children either directly, as in the case of television, or indirectly, through their impact on parents and other family members.

Each level of context in Urie Bronfenbrenner's model is reciprocally related to its neighbors. Children are influenced by parents; they also influence their parents. The parents' behavior at home is influenced by the experiences they have at work and in their communities, while the society, of which the community is a part, both shapes and is shaped by its members.

The context that most directly influences young children's development is the family. Parents influence their children's development in two complementary

ways. First, they shape their children's personalities by the ways they respond to particular behaviors, the values they promote, and the patterns of behavior they model. But that is only part of the story. As the anthropologist Beatrice Whiting (1980) has observed, parents also influence their children's development by selecting many of the other contexts to which children are exposed, including the settings outside of the home they visit, the television programs they watch, and the other children they play with.

Even before children utter their first defiant no in response to a parent's command or request, they are shaping their parents' behavior: each child's distinctive emotional responsivity, appearance, verbal ability, and many other characteristics all play their roles in the socialization process (Goodnow, 1990; Lamb & Rosenblum, 1974).

We begin by comparing family configurations and personality development in two markedly different societies. Every cultural-ecological setting gives rise to a distinctive family configuration, which in turn shapes children's social and cognitive development. This cross-national comparison is followed by an examination of the major varieties of family configuration and child-rearing patterns in the United States. Next, we examine the influence of books and television—two communications media that link the family to the larger context of the society. Finally, we discuss the socializing effects of two social institutions designed specifically to serve young children and their families in modern industrialized societies: day care, which substitutes for parental care at home; and nursery schools, which go beyond "minding" children to fostering their cognitive and social development.

THE FAMILY AS A CONTEXT FOR DEVELOPMENT

During most of the twentieth century, the conventional image of a family in the United States has been a household with a husband, a wife, and two or three children (see Box 11.1). This kind of family is referred to by anthropologists as the *nuclear family* (Murdock, 1949). Although such picture-book families can be found in many communities in the United States, they are by no means representative of the full range of family configurations currently existing here. In many households children are raised by a single parent (usually the mother) or by several adults in an *extended family*. When we consider variations in family configuration on a world scale, the nuclear family that is the American ideal is in a minority. *Polygyny,* in which one man is married simultaneously to more than one woman, is the dominant pattern (Stephens, 1963).

A Cross-Cultural Study of Family Organization and Socialization

In the 1950s, Beatrice and John Whiting (1975) organized teams of anthropologists to observe child rearing in six locales, including towns in New England and India and villages in Kenya and Mexico. The families studied lived in societies that differed in social complexity, economic development, cultural belief systems, and domestic living arrangements.

A comparison of two groups studied by these teams, the Gusii of Nyansongo, Kenya, and Americans in a small New England town, reveals the extent to which cultural variations in family organization can affect individual development. It shows how differences in life circumstances produce variations in basic economic activities and family life, which influence the way parents treat their children and affect the children's development.

At the time of the Whitings' work, the Gusii, who at one time were herders, were an agricultural people living in the fertile highlands of western Kenya. Women, who were the main farm laborers, usually lived in their own house with their children, apart from their husbands. Men, no longer active as cattle herders, sometimes took wage-earning jobs but also spent a lot of time in local politics. The community had no specialized occupations, few specialized buildings, and almost no differences in social rank or wealth among its inhabitants.

Because of their farmwork, Gusii mothers were often separated from their infants, who were left to play in the care of older siblings and elderly family members. Beginning at the age of 3 or 4, children were

A major way in which parents influence their children's development is by selecting the contexts they spend time in. However, parents cannot directly control how successfully their children perform nor the enthusiasm with which they enter new forms of activity.

BOX 11.1
Siblings and Socialization

Most theories of socialization concentrate on relations between one child and two parents when they address such questions as the development of sex-role identity, aggression, and prosocial behavior. But actual families—and actual socialization—are more complex. Single-child families are a distinct minority the world over. In North America, most families include at least two children.

A number of recent studies show that although parents are of primary importance in children's socialization, siblings also play significant roles (Dunn, 1988). The roles of siblings are most obvious in agricultural societies, where much of the child care is performed by older siblings or by the mother's younger sisters. It is through these child caretakers, who are sometimes no more than 5 years older than their charges, that many of the behaviors and beliefs of the social group are passed on (Zukow, 1989). In industrialized societies, where families tend to have fewer children and those children attend school from the age of 5, boys and girls have less responsibility for their younger siblings. Nevertheless, siblings still influence one another's socialization in important ways (Dunn, 1988).

Judy Dunn and Carol Kendrick (1979) studied the influence of siblings by observing 40 lower-middle-class English families in their homes from late in the mother's second pregnancy through the infancy of the second child. They visited the family again when the first child was 6 years old. Their observations, supplemented by reports from the mothers, reveal that siblings are prominent persons in each other's lives.

One of the most obvious indications that the newcomer makes a difference is the fact that in fully 78 percent of the occasions when one of the parents interacted with the new baby, the older sibling joined in. Sometimes the older siblings were friendly and cooperative; at other times they were openly disruptive. Many instances were also observed in which the older sibling responded to signs that the baby was upset or was engaged in a forbidden act.

New babies are not only charges to be taken care of, they are people to play with (Abramovitch, Corter, & Lando, 1979). A lot of the play is imitative. During the first year, it is the firstborn who imitates the new baby; then the tables are turned and it is the little sibling who becomes the imitator (Abramovitch, Pepler, & Corter, 1982). Younger siblings take an increasingly active role in their relationships with their older siblings as they approach the age of 4. Their interventions in the interactions between their mothers and their older siblings become more effective (Dunn & Shatz, 1989). They also become more interesting as conversation partners for their older siblings (Brown & Dunn, 1991). Even so, the older sibling continues to dominate the relationship and is most likely to initiate play as well as altruistic and aggressive interactions (Abramovitch et al., 1986).

Sibling relationships are often ambivalent; it is not possible to characterize them as either consistently friendly or consistently hostile. The obvious explanation is that children compete for their parents' love and attention. Despite features common to all sibling relationships, there are marked differences in the ways pairs of siblings interact. One pair may be friendly and protective of each other, while another pair may dislike each other intensely and fight frequently. The temperaments of the individuals involved in the relationship and the match between the temperaments seem to influence the way siblings get along (Stocker, Dunn, & Plomin, 1989). Children who have difficult temperaments, who are hostile, active, or intense, are more likely than children who have "easy" temperaments to have conflictual relationships with their siblings (Munn & Dunn, 1988).

One might expect that the sexual composition of the sibling pair would affect the nature of the relationship, but the findings here are weak and inconsistent. Some studies show that same-sex sibling pairs get along better than mixed-sex pairs (Dunn & Kendrick, 1979) and some show the opposite (Abramovitch et al., 1986).

What does reliably affect the nature of the sibling relationship is the emotional climate of the family of which they are a part (Brody & Stoneman, 1987). Siblings fight more when their parents are not getting along well together, when they divorce, and when a stepfather enters the family, especially if one or both of the siblings are boys (Hetherington, 1988). At the same time there is evidence that siblings provide im-portant support for each other in such situations by confiding in each other and offering comfort (Jenkins, Smith, & Graham, 1989).

Mothers who treat their children differently con-tribute to their children's antagonism toward each other, according to the findings of several studies (Boer, 1990; Brody & Stoneman, 1987; Stocker, Dunn, & Plomin, 1987). One study of 200 pairs of siblings conducted in the Netherlands found that parental favoritism is related to increased hostility be-tween the siblings, with both children acting nega-tively toward each other (Boer, 1990).

Faced with conflicts between their children, par-ents frequently intervene to try to settle their disputes. But several studies have found that the more often parents intervene in their children's disputes, the more disputes there are. What is not clear is what is cause and what is effect. Parental intervention may increase fighting between siblings because the children quarrel in order to get their parents' attention and because parental intervention deprives them of the opportu-nity to learn how to resolve their conflicts. But it may also be that parents intervene in their children's quar-rels when they become intense; in this case, the proper conclusion would be that children who have intense quarrels also have frequent ones regardless of what their parents do (Dunn & McGuire, 1991).

The birth of a second child is often upsetting for firstborns, especially if they are less than 4 years old. Since the firstborn had no competition until the sec-ond child arrived on the scene, this is understandable. In many families the added demands on the mother's attention reduce the amount of time she interacts with her firstborn child. The firstborn may respond to the mother's inattentiveness by being demanding and showing more negative behavior, by becoming more independent, by taking a larger role in initiating con-versations and play, or by becoming more detached from the mother (Dunn, 1984; Dunn & Kendrick, 1979).

Siblings play an important role in each other's lives.

In many rural traditional communities children of both sexes are responsible for the care of their infant siblings. This kind of socialization-for-nurturance appears to have a long-term impact on children's personality development.

expected to start helping their mothers with simple household tasks. By the age of 7, their economic contributions to the family were indispensable.

New England's "Orchard Town" represents the opposite extreme in terms of family organization and social complexity. Most of the adult men of Orchard Town were wage or salary earners who lived with their wives and children in single-family dwellings, each with its own yard. A few of the mothers had part-time jobs, but most of them spent their time caring for their children, their husbands, and their property. The town has many specialized buildings (see Figure 11.1) and a wide variety of specialized occupations — doctor, fire fighter, auto mechanic, teacher, librarian, merchant, and many more.

Children in Orchard Town were observed to spend more time in the company of adults than did the children of Nyansongo. At home, Orchard Town children played in the house or in the yard within earshot of their mother. At school they were constantly supervised by their teachers. In contrast to the Gusii, Orchard Town children were rarely asked to do chores. Instead, they often sought their parents' help in activities of their own choosing.

When the Whitings inquired into the children's behavior patterns, they found that most children in the two societies behaved in both prosocial and aggressive ways. The overall patterns of children's behavior differed, however. Gusii children were more likely to engage in "nurturant-responsible" behaviors — offering help and support, and making responsible suggestions to others. Orchard Town children were less prone to display those particular prosocial behaviors and were often observed seeking help and attention or trying to dominate other children, in what the Whitings called a "dependent-dominant" pattern of behavior.

The Whitings' data, summarized in Table 11.1, do not allow us to conclude simply that Gusii children are prosocial while U.S. children are self-centered. Gusii children also reprimanded and assaulted others, behavior that the Whitings characterized as "authoritarian-aggressive." The Orchard Town children, by contrast, were characterized as "sociable and intimate." They were more often observed engaged in sociable horseplay, touching others, and joining groups in an amiable way. To explain the social behavior of children in the two societies, both the nurturant-responsible versus dependent-dominant and the sociable-intimate versus authoritarian-aggressive dimensions of their behavior need to be related to conditions of family life in the two societies.

The Whitings believed that children of preindustrial societies, such as the Gusii, were more nurturant

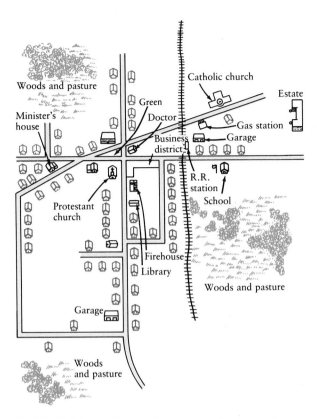

FIGURE 11.1 *A map of the village of Orchard Town in the United States. Husbands and wives live with their children in their own houses. (From Whiting & Whiting, 1975.)*

children were born, and helped to care for them. These conditions, made possible and even necessary by the economic demands and cultural traditions of modern New England, helped create the intimacy within U.S. families.

The authoritarian-aggressive aspect of Gusii children's behavior was also shaped by their household arrangements, which in turn reflected their society's strategy for dealing with their physical environment. Gusii marriages were polygynous (each man typically had more than one wife) and exogenous (one could not marry a member of one's own clan). In addition, the Gusii lived in extended families headed by a grandfather. Property was owned by the family as a group. Children belonged to their father's clan, so that a man lived in the village where he grew up, surrounded by his parents, brothers, and other kinsmen, whereas young girls left their home communities when they married. As Figure 11.2 indicates, each wife had her own house. Her husband may have slept in the same house with her, but not in the same bed, and the preferred pattern was for him to sleep and eat in a separate house. By

and responsible because the nature of their parents' work made it necessary for them to help at an early age. As early as 3 to 5 years of age, Gusii children did economically vital work. Children of industrialized societies, such as those in Orchard Town, were less nurturant and responsible because their chores were less clearly related to their families' economic welfare and may even have seemed arbitrary. Orchard Town children also spent their days in school, where instead of helping others, they competed with them for good grades and were encouraged to think of themselves as individuals rather than as members of a group.

The same set of factors helps to explain why the Orchard Town children were more sociable-intimate than the children of Nyansongo. Orchard Town children lived in nuclear households. Fathers ate at the same table with their wives and children, slept with their wives, were likely to have been present when the

TABLE 11.1

Patterns of Social Behavior Distinguishing Gusii and U.S. Children

Specific Kinds of Behavior	Category of Behavior	Cultural Group
Offers help Offers support Makes responsible suggestions	Nurturant–responsible	Gusii
Seeks help Seeks dominance Seeks attention	Dependent–dominant	U.S.
Acts sociably Engages in horseplay Touches	Sociable–intimate	U.S.
Reprimands Assaults Insults	Authoritarian–aggressive	Gusii

Source: Whiting & Whiting, 1975.

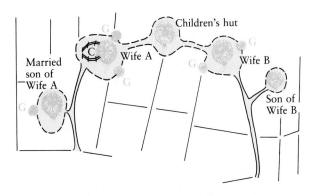

Married
son of
Wife A

Children's hut

Wife A

Wife B

Son of
Wife B

FIGURE 11.2   *A plan of a typical residential compound in the village of Nyansongo, Kenya. Each wife lives in her own house. Older children also live in separate houses. Husbands may live in the same house as their wives but do not share their beds with them. (From Whiting & Whiting, 1975.)*

American standards, there was little intimacy between husbands and wives or between fathers and children.

From a middle-class North American point of view, these arrangements may appear strange, even unpleasant. Most Americans believe it is immoral for a man to have more than one wife, and they are unlikely to approve when children behave in a way they consider authoritarian and aggressive. But to the Gusii, these arrangements and behaviors are both proper and desirable. The behavior of Gusii children fits Gusii expectations and the Gusii way of life. Here we see the power of culture to shape the socialization of new members.

Family Configurations and Socialization Practices in North America

Research on family socialization practices conducted in the United States has shown that while child-rearing practices vary widely, the dimensions along which they vary are fairly restricted. Precisely how many dimensions there are and how they are defined differ somewhat from one researcher to another (Maccoby & Martin, 1983). When Earl Schaefer (1959) carried out statistical analysis of his observations of parent-child interactions, he found that parental behavior varied

along two dimensions. The first corresponds to the degree to which parents try to control the way their children behave — are they strictly controlling or do they allow a good deal of autonomy? The second dimension is the amount of affection that parents display toward their children — are they warm and loving or cool and indifferent? Eleanor Maccoby and John Martin (1983) have also proposed a two-dimensional scheme that seeks to incorporate the basic properties of parental styles encountered in a number of studies (see Table 11.2).

Recent studies of family socialization not only have sought to identify patterns, such as those seen in Table 11.2, but also have looked for answers to several related questions. How do parenting styles affect children's development? What mix of control, autonomy, and expression of affection is most supportive of healthy development? How are family socialization patterns influenced by social class and ethnicity? We begin our examination of these questions with research on the middle-class nuclear family. We then examine the socialization practices of other family types frequently encountered in North America at the end of the twentieth century.

TABLE 11.2
A Two-Dimensional Classification of Parenting Patterns

	Accepting, Responsive, Child-Centered	Rejecting, Unresponsive, Parent-Centered
Demanding, Controlling	Authoritative-reciprocal High in bi-directional communication	Authoritarian Power assertive
Undemanding, Low in Control Attempts	Indulgent	Neglecting, ignoring, indifferent, uninvolved

Source: Maccoby & Martin, 1983.

Parenting styles in the middle-class North American nuclear family

In one of the best-known research programs on the developmental consequences of parenting styles, Diana Baumrind (1967, 1971, 1972, 1980) arranged for trained observers to record children's behavior during routine activities in a nursery school. The children's behavior could then be correlated with the teaching styles of their parents, as measured by observations and interviews. The observers rated the children's behavior on a 72-item scale. These ratings were then correlated to obtain seven clusters of scores, representing seven dimensions of preschool behavior (such as hostile vs. friendly, resistive vs. cooperative, domineering vs. tractable) (Table 11.3).

The researchers also interviewed each child's parents, both separately and together, about their child-rearing beliefs and practices. Then they visited the children's homes twice to observe family interactions from just before dinner until after the child went to bed (Table 11.4).

When the interviews and observations were scored and analyzed, Baumrind and her colleagues found that parenting behaviors in 77 percent of their families fitted into one of three patterns:

- Parents who follow an **authoritarian parenting pattern** try to shape, control, and evaluate the behavior and attitudes of their children according to a set traditional standard. They stress the importance of obedience to authority and discourage verbal give and take between themselves and their children. They favor punitive measures to curb their children's "willfulness" whenever their children's behavior conflicts with what they believe to be correct.
- Parents who demonstrate an **authoritative parenting pattern** take it for granted that they have more knowledge and skill, control more resources, and have more physical power than their children, but they believe that the rights of parents and children are reciprocal. Authoritative parents are less likely than authoritarian parents to use physical punishment and less likely to stress obedience to authority as a virtue in itself. Instead, these parents attempt to control their children by explaining their rules or decisions and by reasoning with them. They are willing to consider their child's point of view, even if they do not always accept it. Authoritative parents set high standards for their chil-

dren's behavior and encourage them to be individualistic and independent.
- Parents who exhibit a **permissive parenting pattern** exercise less explicit control over their children's behavior than either authoritarian or authoritative parents, either because they believe children must learn how to behave through their own experience or because they do not take the trouble to provide discipline. They give their children a lot of leeway to determine their own schedules and activities, and often consult them about family policies. They do not demand the same levels of achievement and mature behavior that authoritative or authoritarian parents do.

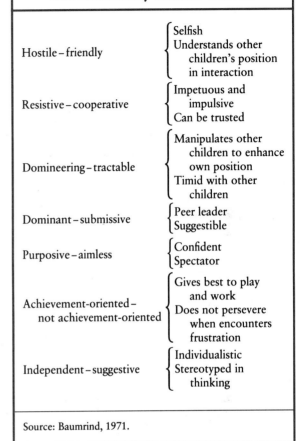

TABLE 11.3

Sample Items from the Baumrind Rating Scale for Preschool Behavior Grouped into Statistically Related Clusters

Cluster	Items
Hostile – friendly	Selfish Understands other children's position in interaction
Resistive – cooperative	Impetuous and impulsive Can be trusted
Domineering – tractable	Manipulates other children to enhance own position Timid with other children
Dominant – submissive	Peer leader Suggestible
Purposive – aimless	Confident Spectator
Achievement-oriented – not achievement-oriented	Gives best to play and work Does not persevere when encounters frustration
Independent – suggestive	Individualistic Stereotyped in thinking

Source: Baumrind, 1971.

TABLE 11.4

Sample Items in Baumrind's Scale of Parental Behaviors Observed in Home Interactions

Set regular tasks

Demand child put toys away

Provide intellectually stimulating environment

Set standards of excellence

Many restrictions on TV watching

Fixed bedtime hour

Mother has independent life

Encourage contact with other adults

Demand mature table behavior

Clear ideals for child

Stable, firm views

Cannot be coerced by child

Use negative sanctions when defied

Force confrontation when child disobeys

Parents' needs take precedence

Regard themselves as competent people

Encourage independent action

Solicit child's opinions

Give reasons with directives

Encourage verbal give and take

Inhibit annoyance or impatience when child dawdles or is annoying

Become inaccessible when displeased

Lack empathetic understanding

Source: Baumrind, 1971.

Baumrind found that, on the average, each style of parenting was associated with a different pattern of children's behavior in the preschool:

- Children of *authoritarian* parents tended to lack social competence in dealing with other children. They frequently withdrew from social contact and rarely took initiative. In situations of moral conflict, they tended to look to outside authority to decide what was right. These children were often characterized as lacking spontaneity and in-

tellectual curiosity (Baumrind, 1971; Hoffman, 1970).

- Children of *authoritative* parents appeared more self-reliant, self-controlled, and willing to explore, as well as more content than those raised by permissive or authoritarian parents. Baumrind believes that this difference is a result of the fact that, while authoritative parents set high standards for their children, they explain to them why they are being rewarded and punished. These explanations improve children's understanding and acceptance of the social rules.

- Children of *permissive* parents tended to be relatively immature; they had difficulty controlling their impulses, accepting responsibility for social actions, and acting independently.

Baumrind also reported differences in the way girls and boys responded to the major parenting patterns. The sons of authoritarian parents, for example, seemed to show more pronounced difficulties with social relations than the daughters did. They were also more likely than other boys to show anger and defiance toward people in authority. The daughters of authoritative parents were more likely to be independent than their brothers, while the boys were more likely to be socially responsible than the girls.

Research conducted in the two decades after Baumrind's initial publications has generally supported her overall conclusions and extended them to older children (Dornbusch et al., 1987; Steinberg, Elmen, & Mounts, 1989). Sanford Dornbusch and his colleagues found, for example, that authoritative parenting is associated with better school performance and better social adjustment among high school students, just as it is among preschoolers.

Despite the consistency of these findings, it is important to remember that the basic strategy for relating parental behaviors to child behaviors used in this line of research relies on correlational data. Consequently, there can be no certainty that differences in parenting styles *caused* the differences in children's behavior (we discussed this problem in Chapter 1, pp. 26–27). Michael Lamb (1982), among others, has pointed out that, in fact, preexisting differences among children may influence their parents' choice of child-rearing strategies. A particularly active and easily frustrated child, for example, might elicit authoritarian responses; the parents might respond differently to an easygoing or timid child.

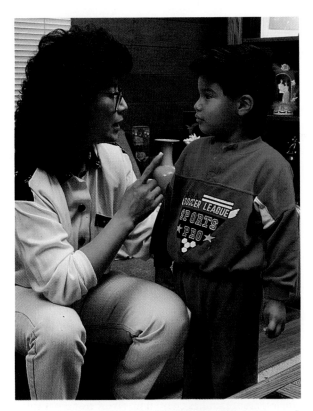

The use of verbal discipline coupled with explanation is characteristic of the authoritative pattern of parenting.

In support of this view, recent research on the personalities of biologically unrelated children in the same household has shown these children to be quite different from one another, even though they were being raised by the same parents (Plomin & Bergeman, 1991). Such findings imply either that patterns of caregiving do not have much effect on a child's behavior or that parents' patterns of caregiving vary from one child to the next. Either conclusion undermines the idea that parental styles of socialization are the causes of variations in children's development.

Baumrind is well aware of these difficulties. She agrees that children's temperaments influence parenting styles, but she is convinced that the evidence shows clearly that parenting styles have a significant impact on children's personalities (Baumrind, 1980, 1991). Researchers are currently using a variety of strategies to isolate the causal effects of parenting styles on patterns of child development (Crockenberg & Litman, 1991; Hoffman, 1991; Scarr, 1992; Sigel, 1985).

A second limitation of Baumrind's research program is that her families were not representative of North American families as a whole: they were, in general, suburban, white, largely middle-class, two-parent families. If we are to get a broad understanding of the family as a context of development, we have to consider how various family configurations, in combination with economic circumstances, race, and ethnic heritage, influence socialization within the family.

Patterns of socialization in single-parent families

In 1989, the last year for which statistics are available, approximately 27 percent of U.S. children were living in single-family households, almost always with the mother (U.S. Bureau of the Census, 1991). Among African American families the percentage is 57 percent. What are the consequences of growing up in a single-parent family? Does it matter whether the mother has never been married or has been divorced?

YOUNG MOTHERS AND THEIR CHILDREN.   Many single women who are raising children are teenagers. As Figure 11.3 indicates, the number of births among unmarried teenagers has grown rapidly over the past three decades. This situation is of great concern because research has shown that children of unmarried teenage mothers are at a developmental disadvantage. Preschool children of single teenage mothers have been found to be more aggressive, less self-controlled, and less cognitively advanced, for example, than the

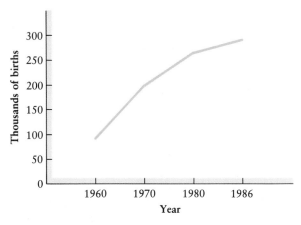

FIGURE 11.3   *The number of children born to unmarried teenage mothers, 1960–1986.*

children of older, married mothers (Furstenberg, Brooks-Gunn, & Chase-Lansdale, 1989).

Frank Furstenberg and his colleagues (1989) believe that three factors contribute to the negative developmental effect of being raised by a young unmarried mother:

1. Young mothers tend to be less equipped emotionally to be competent parents.

2. Young mothers are often less prepared to bring up children and less interested in doing so. As a consequence, they tend to vocalize less with their babies than older mothers do. A lack of verbal communication in turn seems to lead to lowered cognitive ability in preschool and elementary school.

3. Young mothers, especially those without husbands, are likely to have very limited financial resources. As a consequence, they are likely to be poorly educated, to live in disadvantaged neighborhoods, to obtain poor health services for themselves and their children, and to be socially isolated.

It has proved difficult to specify how much each of these factors contributes to the developmental problems of children raised by young unmarried mothers because the factors are closely intertwined.

We will return to examine the question of unwed single mothers in connection with a discussion of how poverty and racial prejudice shape family configurations and socialization practices (pp. 000–000 below).

THE CONSEQUENCES OF DIVORCE.   Studies conducted in the 1970s and 1980s seemed to indicate with virtual certainty that divorce has a negative effect on children's academic achievement and social development. Judith Wallerstein (1983, 1984, 1987) found that when parents first separated, their young children tended to worry about being abandoned by both of them. They felt responsible for the separation, had sleep disturbances, were likely to become irritable, tearful, and aggressive, and did not play as much as other children. Children who were 7 or 8 years old when their parents separated were likely to become depressed. They tended to be preoccupied with their father's departure, to long for his return, and to fear their mother's remarriage. The children interviewed by Wallerstein desperately wanted their parents to rec-

oncile and felt a conflict of loyalty between their mother and father.

In general, a divorce is likely to be followed by lowered academic performance and various problems of social development (Hetherington, Stanley-Hagan, & Anderson, 1989; Hetherington & Clingempeel, 1992). Some researchers have suggested that children in one-parent households do poorly in school because they tend to lack self-control and therefore become disruptive in the classroom (Guidubaldi et al., 1983). Mavis Hetherington (1989) agrees, and attributes this lack of self-control to a breakdown in the mother's control over her children in the wake of divorce. She and her colleagues observed that in the 2 years immediately after a mother's marriage broke up, she exercised less control over her children than she did before, made fewer demands on them, and did not communicate as often as she once did (Hetherington, Cox, & Cox, 1982).

Divorce leads to several other changes in children's life experiences that might be expected to harm their development. Many of the problems associated with divorce are of the same kind as those faced by unmarried single women. First, the average income of single-parent families created by divorce or separation falls by 37 percent within 4 months of the breakup, according to a recent study by the U.S. Bureau of the Census (1991). Only 44 percent of children living with their mothers receive child support from their absent fathers. As a consequence, many children whose parents' marriages have broken up find themselves living in poverty. (In 1990 the Census Bureau defined a family of four as poor if its annual income fell below $13,359.)

Second, a mother raising children alone is trying to accomplish by herself what is usually a demanding job for two adults. Divorce, separation, and widowhood force many mothers to enter the work force at the same time that they and their children are adapting to a new family configuration. Eighty percent of divorced mothers are in the labor force; most of them work full-time (U.S. Department of Labor, 1988). Because of the many demands on their mothers' time, children of divorce not only receive less guidance and assistance but tend to lose out on important kinds of social and intellectual stimulation (Medrich et al., 1982).

Third, the divorced mother is often socially isolated and lonely (Hetherington, Cox, & Cox, 1982). She has no one to support her when the children ques-

When parents feel overwhelmed, they are more likely to be coercive in their interactions with their children.

tion her authority, nor does anyone act as a buffer between her and the children when she is not functioning well as a parent.

Although it makes intuitive sense that the losses associated with the breakup of a family are the *causes* of these children's difficulties, a number of studies that collected data about children *before* their parents divorced have cast doubt on the belief that the divorce itself is the major cause of the problems that have been observed. Noting that divorce is a consequence of disharmony in the family, several researchers have suggested that it is conflict between the child's parents, and not divorce itself, that poses the greatest risk for children (Wolkind & Rutter, 1985; Block, Block, & Gjerde, 1986).

This conclusion is confirmed by two longitudinal surveys of children conducted in Great Britain and the United States (Cherlin et al., 1991). The two studies began with a large sample of children living in intact families. All the parents were interviewed about their children's behavior when the children were 7 years old and again when they were 11 years old.

Children whose parents divorced or separated between the two interviews were compared with children whose families remained intact. Both studies found, in line with earlier research, that children whose parents had divorced between the two inter-

views had more behavior problems than children whose families had remained intact. However, when the researchers looked back at the reports on those same children when they were 7 years old and the family was still intact, they found that the children were already exhibiting many behavior problems, including tantrums, bad dreams, resistance to going to school, disobedience at home, and fighting with other children. These are the kinds of behaviors that tend to accompany parental conflict.

There is great diversity in the ways children respond to conflict between their parents and to their subsequent divorce, but some general patterns have emerged. The effects of marital disharmony and of divorce seem to be greater in boys than in girls (Hetherington et al., 1989). Boys who live with single mothers show a higher rate of behavior disorders and problems in their relations with others than girls who live with single mothers or children who live with both their parents.

Temperamentally difficult children are also at special risk when their parents are in conflict or get divorced (Rutter, 1981; Hetherington, 1989). They are more likely to become targets of their parents' anger and criticism than are children who are more easygoing, and they have a harder time coping with these negative parental behaviors.

Children's age at the time of the marital conflict and divorce is another factor that plays a role in the way they adapt to their changing family situation. One study found that children who were young when their parents divorced initially blamed themselves for their parents' separation and were afraid of being abandoned. But when they were interviewed 10 years after the divorce, they could barely remember either the conflict between their parents or their own responses to it (Wallerstein, 1987). Adolescents are in a better position to assess the problems that cause parents to divorce and to cope with the attendant stresses. They are also better able than young children to take advantage of the support of friends and others outside of their families, and in fact many adolescents do respond to their parents' marital problems by disengaging from their families (Hetherington, 1989). Whether the result is good or bad depends on the kind of people and activities the adolescent turns to instead.

By 2 or 3 years after the divorce, most children and parents have adapted to the new situation, but this equilibrium does not last long. In many families today, the custodial parent remarries within 3 to 5 years after the divorce, so that the children have to cope with yet another major change in their family life. Several studies have found that the early stages of remarriage are stressful for everyone, parents included (Furstenberg & Cherlin, 1991). Children's long-term adjustments to the new family configurations seem to be determined by several factors, including their sex, their age when the parent remarries, and the duration of the marriage itself (Chase-Lansdale & Hetherington, 1990).

The impact of poverty on child rearing

We have already noted that poverty is a major factor affecting children in single-parent families. Poverty touches all aspects of family life: the quality of housing and health care, access to education and recreational facilities, and even one's safety as one walks along the street (Wilson, 1987).

Cross-cultural studies have found that in many parts of the world, poor families who are living close to the subsistence level are likely to adopt controlling parenting styles akin to the authoritarian pattern described by Baumrind. According to the anthropologist Robert LeVine (1974), parents who know what it means to eke out a living "see obedience as the means by which their children will be able to make their way in the world and establish themselves economically in young adulthood when the basis must be laid for the economic security of their nascent families" (p. 63).

Chronic poverty such as that experienced by Irish tinkers creates multiple risk factors for children's development.

FIGURE 11.4 *An analytic model of how poverty and economic loss affect African American children. In this model, poverty increases psychological distress and weakens the marital bond. These factors also have an adverse effect on parents' social relations with their children, which may lead to socioemotional problems in the children. Special characteristics of the parents, social support systems, and the child modify the way these effects play themselves out in individual cases. (After McLoyd, 1990.)*

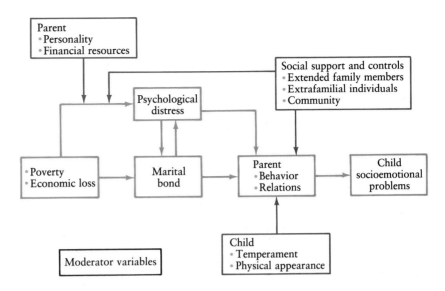

An emphasis on obedience, among other features of authoritarian parenting, is also frequently encountered in poor families in the United States. Echoing LeVine's conclusions concerning the child-rearing patterns of people living at a subsistence level in other countries, some researchers have suggested that poor minority mothers place a high value on unquestioning obedience and discourage curiosity because the dangerous circumstances of daily life make mistaken judgment on the part of their children too risky (Silverstein & Krate, 1975).

One important way in which poverty influences adult socialization practices is by raising the level of stress. Adults who are under stress are less nurturant, more likely to resort to physical punishment, and less consistent when they interact with their children (see Figure 11.4 and the discussion of child abuse in Box 11.2). This relationship between stress and authoritarian parenting was observed by Forgatch and Wieder (summarized in Patterson, 1982), who studied interactions between mothers and children at home over the course of several days. The researchers obtained daily reports from the mothers about such stressful events in their lives as unexpectedly large bills, illness in the family, and quarrels with their husbands. A mother's irritability usually increased when things outside her relationship with her children were going badly, and she was more likely to hit or scold her children and more likely to refuse their requests.

The kinds of stress documented by Forgatch and Wieder are by no means restricted to families living in poverty. But as Robert Halpern (1990) points out, poverty makes these universal sources of stress more serious because it increases the likelihood that a variety of stresses are chronically present simultaneously. At the same time, poverty decreases the likelihood that the family will have the resources to deal with multiple stresses.

Although multiple stresses and scant resources offer one explanation for obedience-oriented parenting styles, they are not the only factors. Melvin Kohn and his colleagues (1977) have found that the kinds of work the parents engage in are directly related to their emphasis on obedience. Middle-class occupations place a premium on the ability to work without close supervision. The content of such work is often complex and the flow of work is nonroutinized; therefore workers must be self-directed. Working-class occupations, by contrast, demand obedience and punctuality. The flow of work is often so routinized that a robot can — and increasingly does — carry out the job just as efficiently as a human being (assembly-line jobs are a classic example). The high incidence of authoritarian parenting styles among the economically disadvantaged is perfectly understandable in light of the facts that poverty creates stressful circumstances in the family context and that working-class occupations require obedience in the face of routine work. At the same

BOX 11.2
Child Abuse and Neglect

In a report to Congress and the Department of Health and Human Services, a federal advisory panel has declared that abuse and neglect of children by their parents constitute a national emergency in the United States (Cimons, 1990). According to the report, more than 2 million children "are starved and abandoned, burned and severely beaten, raped and sodomized, berated and belittled annually in the United States" (Advisory Board on Child Abuse and Neglect, 1990).

A sharp increase in public awareness and the mobilization of scientists, physicians, policy makers, and social workers to address the problem in the past decade might lead one to believe that child abuse is a new problem. Infanticide was routinely practiced in ancient Greece, Rome, Arabia, and China. In more recent times, children have been routinely beaten in schools and forced to work long hours at backbreaking tasks under the worst possible conditions (Zigler & Hall, 1989). While it is possible that the maltreatment of children has increased, it is just as likely that the current concern results from changing social attitudes toward parents' responsibilities and children's rights.

A major problem in all discussions of child abuse is that we have no reliable data on its prevalence. One reason for the lack of data is the absence of an agreed-upon definition of child abuse. In our multicultural society there is little consensus on acceptable and unacceptable child-rearing practices. As a consequence, definitions of abuse vary from the very narrow, which include only intentional physical abuse so severe as to be life-threatening, to the very broad, which include anything that interferes with a child's "optimal" development.

Another reason is that, no matter how broadly or narrowly child abuse is defined, many cases of neglect and brutality and of sexual abuse go undetected and unreported. Many experts consider the officially reported cases of abuse and neglect to be just the tip of the iceberg. The only certainty is that large numbers of children are harmed by their parents.

Researchers trying to understand child abuse have been concerned with several basic questions: Who are the abused children? Who are the abusers? Under what circumstances is abuse most likely to occur? What are the developmental consequences of abuse? And what can be done to prevent abuse and to help abused children?

WHO IS ABUSED?

While any child may be neglected or abused, some children seem to be at greater risk than others. Age is one factor: several studies have found that children under 3 are slightly more likely to be abused than children who are older (Zigler & Hall, 1989). Poor health is a second factor. Premature and low-birth-weight infants are often irritable, unresponsive, and active, and thus difficult to care for. Premature infants make up nearly 25 percent of the population of battered infants, though they account for only 8 percent of all infants born (Klein & Stern, 1971; Parke & Collmer, 1975). Personality is a third factor: among babies and toddlers, it is the emotionally unresponsive, irritable, or hyperactive child who faces the greatest risks (Egeland & Sroufe, 1981; Sherrod et al., 1984). But passive, lethargic children are not immune; they are the ones who are most likely to be neglected (Belsky, 1980). Among older children, defiance in the face of discipline can lead some parents to escalate discipline until it becomes abusive. Socioeconomic class is a fourth factor: children living in poverty are more likely than middle-class children to be abused. The sex of the child seems to be irrelevant to all forms of maltreatment but one: sexual abuse is committed four times more often against girls than against boys (U.S. Department of Health and Human Services, 1988).

It is important to remember, however, that most children who fall into these at-risk categories are *not* abused and that many healthy, even-tempered children are. Consequently, it is still necessary to determine why some adults are abusive and neglectful and others are not.

WHO DOES THE ABUSING?

A popular assumption is that people who abuse or neglect their children must be mentally ill. While a small percentage of those who abuse children are mentally ill (10 percent, according to one estimate), most are not (Kempe & Kempe, 1978).

Another widespread belief is that parents who abuse their children were abused as children themselves (Kempe et al., 1962). Once again, the facts are not so simple. People who were abused as children *are* more likely to abuse their own children, but only about 30 percent of those who have a history of being abused as children mistreat their own children (Kaufman & Zigler, 1989). A history of abuse also fails to explain child abuse by parents who were not abused as children.

The perpetrator of sexual abuse is often a stepfather or the mother's live-in boyfriend; less often it is the child's natural father, an uncle, or an older brother (Alter-Reid et al., 1986).

THE LIKELIHOOD OF CHILD ABUSE

There is a good deal of evidence that children are much more likely to be maltreated when families are under stress. The stress factors can be of many kinds and compound one another: chronic poverty, recent job loss, marital discord, and social isolation have all been linked to increases in the incidence of child abuse. The likelihood of abuse is also higher when the mother is very young, is poorly educated, or receives little financial support from the father (Belsky & Vondra, 1987; Pianta, Egeland, & Erickson, 1989).

Many scholars who have studied the physical abuse of children in the United States believe that it is a mistake to blame either the parents or the child for child abuse. They see child abuse as a social disease that accompanies the society's acceptance of violence in general and corporal punishment in particular (N. Fesbach, 1980). Two kinds of evidence support this position: (1) Most child abuse occurs when parents set out to discipline their children by punishing them physically and then end up hurting them (Zigler & Hall, 1989); (2) Cultures in which the physical punishment of children is frowned upon have very low rates of child abuse (Belsky, 1980; Gil, 1970).

In the case of sexual abuse, children who reside in homes where marriages and separations are frequent and new partners are often being introduced, are vulnerable. But sexual abuse occurs in relatively stable middle-class households (Gomes-Schwartz, Horowitz, & Cardarelli, 1990).

EFFECTS OF BEING ABUSED

Recent studies that compare the intellectual, social, and emotional consequences of child abuse attest to its negative effects (Belsky & Vondra, 1987, and Cicchetti & Carlson, 1989, review the research). In infancy, maltreated infants are often sad, fearful, and frequently angry. They rarely initiate social contact, and their attachment behavior in the strange situation is likely to be classified as insecure or avoidant. As toddlers, they find it difficult to get along with other children and are likely to be fearful at the approach of a stranger. As they become older, abused children are generally more aggressive and cognitively less advanced than other children. In short, there is little doubt that the effects of abuse extend well beyond any physical damage that the parents inflict.

Like children who have been abused in other ways, children who have been sexually abused tend to be depressed, to be angry, to have poor social skills, to have difficulties with self-control, and to behave in a fearful manner. In addition, they often show a precocious interest in sex and behave seductively (Haugaard & Reppucci, 1988).

WHAT CAN BE DONE?

Suggestions on how to intervene in the lives of vulnerable families to reduce child abuse have targeted virtually all known risk factors (Belsky & Vondra, 1987; Olds & Henderson, 1989). Some analysts have focused on changing the macrosystem, proposing a guaranteed minimum income as a way to reduce poverty or arguing for a reduction of violence in the media, but most programs intervene at more local levels. One strategy is to create social networks of support for hard-pressed parents: special hotlines for parents to call if they feel themselves getting too upset and special organizations, such as Parents Anonymous. Another strategy is to use the medical establishment to provide special training programs before or soon after the birth of a child. A third strategy is to provide teenagers with formal training for parenthood, including extensive firsthand experience with children.

The long history of child abuse cautions us not to expect results from piecemeal efforts and expressions of community concern. A systematic campaign that attacked several risk factors simultaneously would appear to offer the best hope of eliminating the problem in the long run.

time, the links between adult work and family socialization make the long-term situation facing poor children even more difficult. Halpern pinpoints the issue when he remarks that "patterns of care and nurturance designed to prepare low-income children for the immediate contexts of their lives may not always be consonant with those that mainstream psychology offers as optimal" (1990:7).

Coping with economic disadvantage: The extended family and social networks

According to a number of scholars concerned with the socialization of poor minority children, the extended family acts as a problem-solving and stress-reducing social institution that provides important resources to many young children (Halpern, 1990; Wilson, 1989). An extended family is one in which not only parents and their children but other kin — grandparents, cousins, nephews, or more distant family relations — share a household. In some cases it includes children from other people's families who are sent for a period of time to trusted friends or business partners or godparents (Harrison et al., 1990).

It is uncertain just how widespread the phenomenon of extended families has become in recent decades. Melvin Wilson (1986) estimates that perhaps 10 percent of African American children live in extended families, and there are indications that the figure may be much higher when the mothers are young and single (Sandven & Resnick, 1990). Extended families are also common among Hispanic, Asian Pacific, and Native American households in the United States (Harrison et al., 1990).

Scholars identify two major sources for the formation of an extended family: cultural traditions and economic hardship. Extended family arrangements of various kinds were the norm among the African peoples brought to the Americas and sold into slavery. Strong family affiliations persisted during slavery, despite attempts to destroy them (Genovese, 1976). Richard Griswold del Castillo (1984) offers a similar explanation of the high incidence of extended families among Hispanic Americans. He traces the contemporary Hispanic American family back to the period before the Spanish conquest. Extended kin relations were a central feature of the cultures of these people's ancestors.

Many scholars see the extended family as a natural strategy for dealing with the combined handicaps of low income and low social standing (Harrison et al., 1990; McLoyd, 1990). Extended families appear to play an especially important role in providing support for children born out of wedlock (McLoyd, 1990; Wilson, 1989). They provide income, child care, and help in maintaining the household as well as such less tangible assistance as emotional support and counseling. Grandmothers in particular provide sustained care that tends to be more responsive and less punitive than that of their teenaged daughters (Stevens, 1984). In addition, the presence of other adults in the house makes it possible for the children's mothers to obtain additional education, which in turn improves the family's economic circumstances.

The evidence that extended family relations help to buffer children against the harmful effects of poverty is part of a broader range of studies that emphasize the importance of social networks in shaping parental behaviors toward their children (Bronfenbrenner, 1986; Salzinger, 1990). When poor families are isolated from their communities, and especially when single young women attempt to raise their children without a social support system, children are especially at risk. By contrast, young mothers who are incorporated into a social network that allows them to interact regularly with friends and neighbors, to attend church, and to participate in other community activities raise their children in a more nurturant and sensitive way (Crockenberg, 1987; McLoyd, 1990).

MEDIA LINKING COMMUNITY AND HOME

Parents are by no means the only ones in the home to shape children's behavior. Children are affected by their brothers and sisters, and sometimes by their grandparents, aunts, uncles, and cousins, as well as by people from the surrounding community who come into the home as visitors, to perform services, or to bring news of the world outside. In modern societies like our own, the outside world also enters the home through letters, magazines, newspapers, television, radio, and books. The sheer magnitude of children's exposure to modern communications media makes it important to understand the impact of these media on child development.

Both the content of what children encounter through communications media (fairy tales, adventure stories, advertisements, or news programs) and the form in which the information is presented (brief images flashed on a screen or stories read aloud) are widely claimed to exert lasting effects on the development of children's interests, cognitive skills, and social behavior (Greenfield, 1984). Here we will discuss what is known about the developmental effects of watching television and of being read to.

One of the most effective ways of giving children both a love of books and basic reading skills is to read to them.

Television: What Is Real? What Is Pretend?

Although estimates vary, they indicate that a TV set is on for 6 or more hours each day in the average American home and that young children are to be found in front of it for 2 or more of those hours (Comstock & Paik, 1991). According to Dorothy and Jerome Singer (1990), "No other extraparental influence has penetrated the lives of children as television has."

The evidence that young children and even infants learn from watching TV is irrefutable. In Chapter 5 (p. 196) we saw how Andrew Meltzoff (1988) demonstrated that infants only 14 months old will imitate actions they have seen on a TV screen. Meltzoff arranged for infants to watch an adult on television taking apart and reassembling a dumbbell-shaped object. When presented with this unfamiliar object the next day, many of the infants proceeded to take it apart and put it back together again. Infants also imitate the language they hear on TV. Dafna Lemish and Mabel Rice (1986) report that one 2-year-old they observed at home approached her father, pointed at the bottle of beer in his hand, and declared, "Diet Pepsi, one less calorie." Young children identify with superheroes and mythical creatures in their fantasy play, imitate their clothing, and eat the cereals they endorse — clear evidence that what children learn from television influences their everyday behavior.

A special concern about the influence of television viewing on young children arises from the fact that they easily confuse make-believe and reality. Research such as that summarized in Chapter 9 (pp. 321 – 322) has shown that young children have a hard time distinguishing reality and appearance. Television is thought to compound the difficulty because most programs are presented in a realistic format and show believable people engaging in behavior and events that could be happening. A fictitious story about a cowboy who goes to Dallas and rides in a rodeo may even be acted out by real cowboys at a real rodeo in Dallas.

An early study of children's responses to televised commercials found that two out of three children 3 to 4 years old believed that characters in the ads could see into their homes, and almost half said that they could talk to the televised character (Atkin, Hocking, & Gantz, 1979). A more recent study by John Flavell and his colleagues (1990) also found that 3-year-olds were likely to interpret the images on the television screen as real, physically present objects. But 4-year-olds seemed to understand that what they were seeing were pictures, not the people and objects themselves. These researchers believe that the younger children erred because they had not yet come to appreciate the ways in which one thing can represent another.

Even after children realize that the objects on the screen are pictures, not the real objects, they are still unclear about whether the events depicted are real or fictitious. Aimee Dorr (1983) reports that children under the age of 7 years often have difficulty understanding that on television, when a bad guy is shot, the actor isn't really dead, or when a husband beats his wife, the actress isn't really hurt. Even 7- and 8-year-olds will claim that actors and actresses who play married couples must be friends and that actors wear bulletproof vests in case the bullets are real.

Susceptibility to confusion about the reality of television is not restricted to children. From time to time, for example, one reads of an irate adult assaulting an evil character in a soap opera. But the problem is more acute for young children because they have little independent knowledge of the world against which to compare the "reality" of what they see on television. Some physical features of the medium and the way it is used may also cause confusion for them.

The problem of television form

Television, like film, allows extraordinary flexibility in the way realistic visual images can be made and sequenced. Human beings' attention is attracted by movement and change. Television plays on this characteristic by using quick cuts from one scene or one camera angle to another, jolting expectations to maintain attention. The popular children's program *Sesame Street,* for example, uses a new cut on the average of every 30 seconds (Lesser, 1974).

Many techniques of television production help to focus adult viewers' attention and highlight the central message: close-up shots pick out essential details, camera placement gives hints about point of view, flashbacks fill in earlier parts of the story. These thought-shaping techniques are a great resource for conveying meaning, but they have their negative side as well, particularly for young children.

Young children do not understand special television techniques (Singer & Singer, 1980; Smith, Anderson, & Fischer, 1985). They become confused by quick scene changes without transitions; they need both long shots and close-ups to understand the action; and they fail to infer the location of one aspect of the action from a view of another (see Figure 11.5).

In an evaluation of a number of standard shows watched by preschoolers, Andrew Collins (1975) found that children had difficulty keeping track of the programs' content. When they were tested for memory of what they had seen happen, they might recall as little as 30 percent of the central events (Friedlander, Whetstone, & Scott, 1974). Their comprehension is better when the programming has been designed to be educational (Blosser & Roberts, 1985), although young children still misunderstand a great deal of what

FIGURE 11.5   *An item from the space construction test, which assesses children's ability to re-create an entire setting on the basis of partial glimpses that correspond to the various camera angles used in making films and television programs. Children are asked to put the four cards together to make a meaningful scene. (From Greenfield, 1984.)*

Those inseparable friends, Calvin and Hobbes, parody exaggerated concerns about the evils of television.

they watch. Comprehension improves markedly during middle childhood, but even 9- and 10-year-olds have difficulty understanding fast-paced programs that do not clearly show the continuity of action from one sequence to the next (Wright et al., 1984).

To the extent that television techniques communicate successfully, they raise a different concern. Television provides a prefabricated, alternative world that requires little mental effort to comprehend once a viewer has sufficient background knowledge and mastery of its forms. Furthermore, its fast pace makes it impossible to stop and ponder what is being presented. Do these characteristics affect children's responses to the world off the air? Evidence that they do has been reported by Gavriel Salomon (1984). He found that children socialized to learn from television had lower than normal expectations about the amount of mental work required to learn from written texts. As such a finding suggests, children who watch a great deal of television read less and fare relatively poorly when they get to school (Comstock & Paik, 1991).

The problem of television content

To the extent that children accept the ideas and behavior presented on television as appropriate models for their own behavior, there is good reason to be concerned about the *content* of what they view.

One major concern about television is the widespread presence of *stereotyping*: people who belong to an identifiable category (Latinos, women, scientists) are portrayed as if they all had the same personality characteristics, lived in the same kinds of surroundings, and engaged in the same occupations. In one of

the earliest studies of ethnic stereotyping, Dallas Smythe (1954) found that African Americans (who made up only 2 percent of TV characters at the time) were portrayed only as servants, entertainers, or buffoons. By the 1980s, the proportion of African American characters appearing in TV had increased markedly, but stereotyping had not disappeared, it had only changed; with a few exceptions, African Americans now appeared primarily as criminals or victims of crime. The same was (and still is) true of portrayals of other minority groups in the United States, as well as characters depicted as foreigners; Italians are stereotyped as gangsters and Latin Americans as lazy or as drug-smuggling criminals (Gerbner et al., 1986).

Stereotyping in television is by no means restricted to the category of ethnicity. Summarizing the available data, Robert Liebert and Joyce Spravkin (1988) report that women occupy only between 25 and 30 percent of the roles in entertainment television. When they do appear as characters, they are mainly assigned supporting roles as wives, girlfriends, or other family members. If they are employed, they are likely to be nurses or secretaries. The elderly fare no better. When a comment is made about an elderly person on Saturday-morning programming for children, it is almost always negative (Bishop & Krause, 1984).

Research indicates that the way various social groups are presented on TV influences young children's everyday behavior in the direction suggested by the TV portrayals. Children who watch episodes of *Sesame Street* in which children of various ethnic groups are portrayed in positive ways are increasingly willing to play with children of those groups (Gorn, Goldberg, & Kanango, 1976). Young children who

Parents often use television as a baby-sitter. Research shows, however, that children get more out of television viewing when their parents are there to discuss the programs with them.

watch televised episodes in which children play with sex-stereotyped toys adopt similar biases. If the televised episodes portray children playing with dolls representing their own sex, sex-stereotyped toy selection increases; if the televised children play with toys associated with the opposite sex, cross-sex toy selections increase (Comstock & Paik, 1991).

Research on the effects of depictions of violence shows conclusively that television offers models for behavior in real life. Fully 80 percent of the television programs that young Americans watch include at least one violent event, and many contain more. Evidence has accumulated in recent decades that violence on television increases violent behavior among many viewers, not just among those "predisposed" to be violent (Comstock & Paik, 1991; Liebert & Spravkin, 1988; Potts, Huston, & Wright, 1986). Lynette Friedrich and Aletha Stein pinpointed violence in programming as the key to aggressive behavior among the young children in their 1973 study. Preschoolers who watched *Batman* and *Superman* became more aggressive in their play, whereas those who watched episodes of *Mister Rogers' Neighborhood,* a children's program noted for its positive values, did not.

Family influences

The evidence that television affects children's behavior is complemented by equally strong evidence that the family can temper those influences. When Jerome and Dorothy Singer (1980) studied patterns of family viewing in a working-class community in the eastern United States, they found that the homes of highly aggressive preschoolers who watched a lot of television had relatively few books or records. These children were often permitted to stay up late to watch any program they wanted to. Their parents rarely took them out of the house, except to the market or to the movies. The families of less aggressive children, in contrast, tended to keep tighter control on the way their children spent their time. They restricted their children's television viewing to educational and children's programs. Their children were more likely than those in the more aggressive group to go to bed early and to be taken to parks, museums, and cultural events.

When parents watch television with their children and talk about what they see, the children absorb more of the content (Ball & Bogatz, 1979). The parents can provide connections that the children miss and remind them of related events in their own lives, helping them to make sense of what is happening on the screen.

The message of these findings is that if parents are concerned about the negative effects of television on their children's behavior, they should restrict the amount of time the children spend watching television and increase the amount of time they join their children in front of the television set. Some informative guides have been written to help parents and children get the most out of watching television (see Figure 11.6) (Dorr, Graves, & Phelps, 1980; Singer, Singer, & Zuckerman, 1980).

EDITING: THE BIONIC PUZZLE

Here are three pictures showing how a bionic jump is done. How does the bionic jump look on TV? You can find out by cutting out the three small pictures at the bottom of the page and pasting them onto the big TV screen.

MATCHING CAMERA EFFECTS

Here are four different pictures taken with a TV camera. Draw a line from each TV set to the TV camera that is taking that picture.

FIGURE 11.6   *Sample exercises to help people interpret the conventions of editing used in television production. (From Singer, Singer, & Zuckerman, 1981.)*

Books

While parents worry that extensive television viewing may impede their children's development, many share an equally pervasive belief that reading will enhance it. Their positive opinion of reading comes in part from a belief that reading to children stimulates their mental development and in part from general approval of the content of the stories written for children.

In some ways being read to is much like watching television. In both cases, children must extract meaning from words and pictures that represent familiar elements of the everyday world. They encounter problems with both media when their limited experience of the world makes it difficult for them to arrive at a plausible interpretation of what they are seeing and hearing. The evidence on the effects of reading to children is not so extensive as that on television viewing, but the limited data available provide an instructive contrast between the two media.

This little boy has acquired part of the idea of what it means to read just by watching those around him, but there are many crucial elements still to be learned.

The form of early literacy experiences

In the United States, young children of every social class are exposed to print in some form almost every day, even if only for a few minutes (Anderson & Stokes, 1984; McLane and McNamee, 1990). Sometimes the children are just "hanging around" while their parents read a letter or discuss their big sister's homework. But young children are also likely to be seen talking about the messages on cereal boxes, asking for help with a television schedule or instructions for a game, and carrying notes from nursery school. These experiences teach them that the marks on paper somehow convey information, a form of knowledge about reading and writing that is currently referred to as "emergent literacy" (Teale & Sulzby, 1986) (see Figure 11.7).

Evidence indicates that young children who are often read to at home learn to read relatively easily once they start school (McLane & McNamee, 1990; Wells, 1981). Anat Ninio and Jerome Bruner's (1978) study of parents reading to their 1-to-2-year-old children suggests how such experiences might help children's later reading. For example, Richard, who is seated on his mother's lap, is engaged by his mother in a stylized, cyclical form of dialogue focused on the picture in a book. With few exceptions, each cycle in their conversation goes something like this:

Mother: *(pointing to a picture)* Look at this!
　Child: *(touches picture or gives some other indication of attention)*
Mother: What is it?
　Child: A doggy.
Mother: Right! *(turns pages and initiates a new round)*

Once children begin to attend school, the vast majority of their instructional experience will occur in a similar format:

Teacher: Who knows the capital city of France?
Student: Paris.
Teacher: That's right! *(then the teacher initiates a new round)*

When children are young, adults may fill in the labels for objects and accept any sort of contribution from the child as an adequate turn. As the child's knowledge increases, adults supply less help in keeping

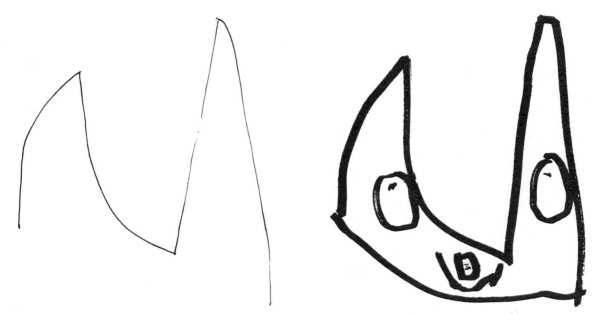

FIGURE 11.7   Left: *"An* M . . . *What does that spell? It spells* M *for Molly."* Right: *"And it could be a rabbit. See, it's got big ears."* Here 3½-year-old Molly uses the letter M in two different ways as she begins to get the idea of writing. For Molly, the letter and the drawing are only fragilely differentiated.

the game going. Instead they raise the stakes by choosing more complex texts and pictures, or by asking more complicated questions about old favorites (De-Loache, 1984). This kind of tailored support that keeps changing to fit children's growing competence creates the "zone of proximal development" discussed in earlier chapters.

Parents who introduce their children to books in the way Ninio and Bruner described also talk to their children about book contents at odd times of the day when no books are present (Heath, 1982; Crago & Crago, 1983). These parents make it clear to their children that the pictures and texts in books are relevant to the world at large, thus helping them to acquire more powerful cognitive schemas.

Shirley Brice-Heath (1982, 1984) has found that when parents seldom read picture and storybooks to their children, the whole structure and purpose of reading are likely to differ from the pattern described by Ninio and Bruner. In some families she observed, being read to was an occasion more for learning to sit still than for making sense of pictures and words. Children who learn that kind of lesson well may have trouble learning to read once they begin school, even if they sit very quietly and behave themselves in class.

The content of early reading

Perhaps the most crucial difference between young children's television viewing and their being read to is seen in the degree to which adults control the content their children are exposed to. Because few young children can read, most are exposed only to those books that adults deem appropriate for them and are willing to read to them. By contrast, once small children can toddle over to the television set and push the correct buttons, they are likely to hear and see programs that were not designed for them, including adult programs with relatively high levels of sex and violence.

From time to time books that have traditionally been read to children have come under fire for the harm they allegedly do to a child's view of the world. Most fairy tales and myths were created in the centuries before childhood was considered a special period of life and before any literature had been specifically devised for children (Sale, 1978). Adults have occa-

BOX 11.3
The Sense of Nonsense Verse

Kornei Chukovsky, a Soviet author of poems for children, was sometimes accused of damaging children by his use of fantasy. The following letter is typical of such criticism.

> Shame on you, Comrade Chukovsky, for filling the heads of our children with all kinds of nonsense, such as that trees grow shoes. I have read with indignation in one of your books such fantastic lines as:

> Frogs fly in the sky,
> Fish sit in fishermen's laps,
> Mice catch cats
> And lock them up in
> Mousetraps.

> Why do you distort realistic facts? Children need socially useful information and not fantastic stories about white bears who cry cock-a-doodle-doo. That is not what we expect from our children's authors. We want them to clarify for the child the world that surrounds him, instead of confusing his brain with all kinds of nonsense.

In defense of his nonsense verse, Chukovsky had this to say of the man who sent the critical letter:

> Had he had other resources than "common sense," he would have realized that the nonsense that seemed to him so harmful not only does not interfere with the child's orientation to the world that surrounds him, but, on the contrary, strengthens in his mind a sense of the real; and that it is precisely in order to further the education of children in reality that such nonsense verse should be offered to them. For the child is so constituted that in the first years of his existence we can plant realism in his mind not only directly, by acquainting him with the realities in his surroundings, but also by means of fantasy. (1968:89–90)

sionally argued (echoing arguments about television) that fairy tales should not be read to children because they are brutal, cruel, and frightening, and are not realistic portrayals of the world. Such stories are condemned as not sensible or "educational." Others, such as the psychoanalyst Bruno Bettelheim, have insisted that children need fairy tales. "Like all great art, fairy tales both delight and instruct; their special genius is that they do so in terms which speak directly to children" (Bettelheim, 1977:56). Bettelheim believed that the very unreality of such stories allows children to use them to find solutions to their own inner conflicts; it is certainly less threatening to think about Cinderella's evil stepmother than to think consciously about real negative feelings toward one's own mother or father (see Box 11.3).

Another frequent complaint is that too many children's books ignore or misrepresent certain ethnic and racial groups, women, and working-class and poor people. As in the case of television, these concerns have frequently been supported by surveys of the contents of children's books (Council on Interracial Books for Children, 1976; Tanyzer & Karl, 1972; White, 1976).

Whether in the form of a television situation comedy, an evening news bulletin, or a story about a beautiful princess, the larger world of adult relationships enters the homes of children through a great variety of media. Evidence supports the conclusion that the influence of a particular *form* of mediated experience is neither good nor bad in any fixed objective sense. How one assesses the value of, say, reading fairy tales or Bible stories or watching adult programming on television depends upon the values one wishes to perpetuate in the home and the community and one's idea of the future life for which the child is being prepared.

THE YOUNG CHILD IN THE COMMUNITY

As long as parents remain at home with their young children, they can retain relatively direct control over outside influences, even the influence of television. But when the parents leave their children in the care of others for several hours a day, the nature of that control—not to mention the nature of their children's experiences—changes in a decisive way. In the United States and other industrialized countries, one of the most important tasks many parents face is to select the day care or nursery school that will provide the upbringing of their children during those hours.

Varieties of Day Care

In 1989 more than 60 percent of U.S. mothers with children below the age of 6 years were working and their children were in some form of day care (U.S. Bureau of Labor Statistics, 1991). The most popular arrangement is *family day care,* in which children go to the home of someone who is not a family member. The

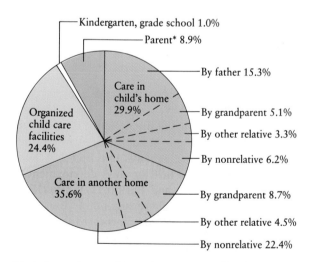

*Includes mothers working at home or away from home.

FIGURE 11.8 *Primary child care arrangements used by working mothers for children under 5 years of age in 1987. (From U.S. Bureau of the Census, Current Population Reports, Series P-70, No. 20 [1988].)*

least-used arrangement—although it has attracted the most public attention—is the *day-care center.* In between is *home care,* in which children are cared for in their own home by either a relative or a baby-sitter (U.S. Bureau of the Census, 1991). Choices among the various kinds of care are usually based on availability, cost, the parents' judgments about the quality of care offered, and the age and number of children in need of care (Belsky, Steinberg, & Walker, 1982) (see Figure 11.8).

Home care

Because child care in the home is so private, relatively little is known about it. One study comparing various types of care confirmed what common sense might lead one to expect (Clarke-Stewart, 1982). Children cared for at home experience the least change from normal routine: they eat food provided by their parents and take naps in their own beds. They also come in contact with relatively few children their own age.

Family day care

Family day care exposes children not only to caretakers from outside the family circle but also to new settings and often to children of other families. The children in a family day-care setting may range widely in age, forming a more diverse social group than is likely to exist at home. The routine of activities in family day care, however, is usually very similar to the routine at home (Clarke-Stewart, 1992).

State, county, or local government agencies grant licenses to family day-care homes that meet basic health and safety requirements and maintain acceptable adult-child ratios. Most family day-care homes, however, are unlicensed. Observers have found that unlicensed providers are less likely than licensed ones to give comfort, verbal stimulation, and guidance to the children in their care (Goelman, 1988).

Day-care centers

Licensed day-care centers generally offer a wider variety of formal learning experiences than family or home day care, and are likely to employ at least one trained caretaker. Waiting lists for places in day-care centers tend to be long, however, since the demand far exceeds the available openings.

These children at a day-care center in Czechoslovakia are obtaining the kind of experience in getting along in groups that is one of the major features of the day-care experience.

Because licensed day-care centers often receive public financing, they have been more accessible to researchers, who have studied both their characteristics and the way these characteristics affect children's development. Here are some of their findings:

- Day-care centers with populations of more than 60 children place more emphasis on rules than smaller centers do, are relatively inflexible in their scheduling, and offer children fewer opportunities to initiate or control their own activities. Teachers in large centers tend to show less sensitivity to the needs of individual children, perhaps because there are so many children for them to supervise (Clarke-Stewart & Fein, 1983).
- The most important factor for 3-to-5-year-old children is the size of the day-care group (Travers & Ruopp, 1978). Groups of fewer than 15 to 18 children allow for more individual contact and more verbal interaction between children and adults, and for more active involvement in group activities (McCartney et al., 1985; Ruopp et al., 1979; Howes & Rubenstein, 1985).

The programs offered by day-care centers vary in style and philosophy. Some offer an academic curriculum, emphasize discipline, and have a schoollike atmosphere. Others emphasize social development and allow children to exercise more initiative in their activities. In accord with the class differences in modes of parenting discussed earlier in this chapter, most lower-class parents have been found to prefer the more schoollike day-care centers, while middle-class parents are likely to choose the less structured centers (Joffe, 1977).

Developmental Effects of Day Care

Psychologists disagree sharply about the developmental impact of day care on young children, just as they do about its impact on infants (see Box 7.1). Such notable figures in the field of child development as Selma Fraiberg (1977) and Burton L. White (1975) claim that prolonged daily separation of young children from their mothers is detrimental to their development. Others conclude that as long as day care is of high quality, it is not bad for young children and can even make positive contributions to their later intellectual and social development (Clarke-Stewart & Fein, 1983; McCartney, 1984; Scarr, Phillips, & McCartney, 1990). (Table 11.5 lists the features that contribute to high quality in day care.)

TABLE 11.5
Federal Interagency Day-care Requirements

1. A planned daily program of activities that are developmentally appropriate and that are designed to promote children's intellectual, social, emotional, and physical development.
2. Caregivers with specialized training in childcare who have also had an orientation to health and safety procedures for the particular setting.
3. Adequate and nutritious meals.
4. A health record for each child.
5. Opportunities for parents to observe the setting and to discuss the child's needs before enrollment and during the time the child attends the center.
6. Small group sizes and low student-to-staff ratios.

Source: Clarke-Stewart, 1992.

Shortcomings of the evidence

These disagreements are difficult to resolve because intensive research on day care is still in its infancy, and the studies completed so far have been subject to some important limitations. First, a great deal of the early research on the effects of day care was conducted in university-affiliated day-care centers of high quality. The experience of children in these centers is probably not representative. This problem is being redressed by comparative studies of high- and low-quality day care (McCartney, 1984; McCartney et al., 1985), but caution must be exercised when one attempts to generalize about programs that differ both in the backgrounds of the families involved and in the quality of care offered (Howes & Olenick, 1986).

Second, most research has looked only at the immediate effects of day care, leaving open the question of possible long-term effects. Finally, the families of children in day care are not a random sample of all families with young children. The lack of clear data comparing families that do and don't use day care raises the possibility that differences between children found at the end of the program were there at the beginning, and resulted not from day care but from other aspects of the family situation (Belsky & Stein-

berg, 1978; Howes & Olenick, 1986). Despite these limitations, suggestive findings have emerged.

Intellectual effects

The intellectual development of middle-class children in adequately staffed and equipped day-care centers is at least as good as that of children raised at home by their parents (Clarke-Stewart, 1982; Clarke-Stewart & Fein, 1983; Kagan, Kearsley, & Zelazo, 1978) (see Figure 11.9). In some cases it may actually be accelerated (Clarke-Stewart, 1984).

Experience in day-care enrichment programs seems in some cases to lessen or prevent the decline in intellectual performance that sometimes occurs after the age of 2 when children of low-income families remain at home with poorly educated parents. Enrichment programs may even lead to marked gains in language and cognitive development among these children (Burchinal, Lee, & Ramey, 1989; McCartney, 1984; McCartney et al., 1985; Wasik et al., 1990).

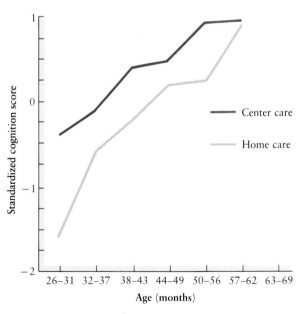

FIGURE 11.9 *Performance on tests of intellectual development by children cared for in day-care centers and by those cared for at home. The tests were specially constructed to assess children's ability to use language, form concepts, and remember information. (From Clarke-Stewart, 1984.)*

Impact on social development

Children who attend day-care centers in the United States tend to be more self-sufficient and more independent of parents and teachers, more helpful and cooperative with peers and mothers, more verbally expressive, more knowledgeable about the social world, and more comfortable in new situations. Some of them also tend to be less polite, less agreeable, less compliant with adults, and more aggressive than children who do not attend day-care centers (Clarke-Stewart & Fein, 1983; Haskins, 1985; Howes & Olenick, 1986). These effects may vary with the quality of day care and the involvement of the child's parents. Many parents whose children are in low-quality day care have very stressful lives and consequently are less involved in their children's activities than those whose children attend high-quality day-care centers (Howes & Olenick, 1986).

It isn't necessary to look far for an explanation of day care's effects on a preschooler's social development. At home the wishes and needs of small children are often anticipated, their social incompetence is overlooked, and their failures at communication are filled in. Care supplied outside of the home requires children to get along with adults who do not know their special likes and dislikes and who must fit several children into a common schedule. In addition, children who receive day care must learn to interact successfully with a variety of other children, often when few adults are present.

These children usually have more opportunities to turn to peers for companionship, affection, amusement, and a sense of identity and belonging. Experience with groups their own age helps children to learn about their strengths and weaknesses by comparing themselves with others. The flowering of language at the end of the second year and the beginning of the third adds an important dimension to children's social interactions that influences their experiences in day care. By the time children are 2½ they are able to manage interactions with one another that contain, in fledgling form, all the basic features of social interactions among older children or adults — sustained attention, turn-taking, and mutual responsiveness (Rubin, 1980).

Day-care arrangements of various kinds also provide children with their first experiences at forming friendships with other children of the same age who are not kin. Carollee Howes (1987) found that friendship formation among preschoolers grows out of mutual social attraction in which the partners reciprocate and complement each other's behaviors, creating a "climate of agreement." Friendships provide children with experience at cooperating and communicating with others. According to Howes, preschoolers who have formed a stable friendship are able to carry out more complex actions together than nonfriends can manage, an indication that this important form of social relation has positive effects on children's cognitive abilities as well as on their social behavior.

Children's experiences with each other in day-care centers and nursery schools usually occur around a shared activity, such as playing fantasy games or building with blocks. Observations conducted by William Corsaro (1981) at a state university child-study center indicate that most voluntary interactions among groups of 3- and 4-year-olds are extremely fragile. Such group interactions usually last less than 10 minutes and often end abruptly when a playmate leaves the play area without warning. The fragility of such groups requires that children learn how to gain access to another group — or face the prospect of playing alone.

An attempt to enter a preexisting group may be rebuffed, especially if the group is made up of good friends. Corsaro (1981) observed the outcome of 128 bids to gain access to a group's ongoing activities.

It requires a good sense of the game and good timing to gain entry to someone else's ongoing activity. Most children spend some time hovering on the periphery watching before they try.

An important aspect of the preschool experience is the opportunity to make friends with children one's own age.

More than 50 percent met with initial resistance. Typical of the reasons children gave for refusing admission to a newcomer are "We don't like you today" and "We only want boys here."

The key to success in entering a group seems to lie in understanding what is going on in the group, what its structure is, and who is doing what, and then using that knowledge to act as if one were already a member of the group. Good communication skills are also an asset (Hazen & Black, 1990). Children who ask socially inappropriate questions about what is going on, criticize what group members are doing, or tell the others how they feel are likely to be rejected when they try to join a group (Putallaz & Gottman, 1981).

Fearing rejection, most young children hover around the periphery of the group before making their first attempt to gain access to it (Corsaro, 1981). As their experience increases, they are less likely to be found playing by themselves or hovering on the periphery of a group (Schindler, Moely, & Frank, 1987).

As they approach middle childhood, popular children (those with whom other children most often choose to play) do not require as much time as those who are unpopular to gain entry to a group composed of popular children. However, it is more difficult for them to enter a group composed of unpopular children. The situation is just the opposite for children

who are not well liked by other children. They have a more difficult time gaining admittance to an activity in which popular children are involved, but an easier time when the group is composed of other unpopular children.

No matter how socially skilled a girl is, she can expect to have particular difficulty gaining entry to a group composed of boys. A little girl who asks to join two boys who are playing on the swings is likely to be told "No! We don't want girls here." At the start of early childhood, boys have a somewhat easier time joining a group of girls, but as they grow older they encounter more resistance from the girls.

Such exclusive behavior may be cruel, but according to Corsaro, it functions to preserve existing groups. By excluding others, the members of a group give themselves a special identity. They become "we," as opposed to outsiders, who are "they." Their rejections protect their ongoing interactions from the disruption of a newcomer, especially one who plays differently.

It is these kinds of experiences—gaining access to group activities, learning to become desirable companions, and dealing with rejection—that are the most likely social benefits of day care. On the negative side, some of the behavior children learn in day care may conflict with their parents' standards of appropriate behavior at home and elsewhere.

BOX 11.4
Cultural Variations in Preschool Education

When we compare the lives of young children in a traditional agricultural society and a modern industrialized society (as the Whitings did in their study of children in Kenya and New England), we are not surprised to discover that they occupy vastly different developmental niches in the two societies. But when we look at two industrialized societies with apparently similar institutions for socializing children, we may not expect cultural variations to be so prominent. Yet when Joseph Tobin, David Wu, and Dana Davidson (1989) compared preschools in Japan and the United States, they found that even though the nursery schools were physically similar, the differences in the adults' socialization practices were very marked.

On the day that Tobin and his colleagues were videotaping the 4-year-old group at Komatsudani Hoikuen, a Buddhist preschool in Kyoto, Hiroki was acting up. He greeted the visitors by exposing his penis and waving it at them. He initiated fights, disrupted other children's games, and made obscene comments.

American preschool teachers who observed the videotape disapproved of Hiroki's behavior, his teacher's handling of it, and many aspects of life in the Japanese classroom in general. They were shocked to see 30 preschoolers and only one teacher in the classroom. How could this be in a country as affluent as Japan? they asked. They could not understand why the teacher ignored Hiroki instead of isolating him or giving him "time out" as punishment.

The Japanese viewed the matter very differently. First, though Japanese teachers acknowledged that it would be very pleasant for *them* to have a smaller classroom, they believed it would be bad for the children. Children, they said, "need to have the experience of being in a large group in order to learn to relate to lots of children in lots of kinds of situations" (p. 37). When they were asked what they thought would be the ideal class size, the Japanese preschool teachers generally said 15 or more students per teacher; the American preschool teachers preferred classes of four to eight students. When the Japanese teachers observed a tape of an American preschool with 18 children and two teachers, they worried for the children. "A class that size seems kind of sad and underpopulated," one remarked. Another added, "I wonder how you teach a child to become a member of a group in a class that small."

Members of the two cultures also had very different interpretations of the probable reasons for Hiroki's outrageous behavior. One American teacher speculated that Hiroki misbehaved because he was intellectually gifted and easily became bored. The Japanese educators rejected this notion out of hand. To them, "smart" and "intelligent" are almost synonymous with "well behaved" and "praiseworthy," neither of which applied to Hiroki. Hiroki, they believed, had a "dependency disorder." Because his mother was absent from the home, he had not learned how to be properly dependent, so he did not know how to be sensitive and obedient. Isolating

Nursery School

Day care originated in response to the needs of adults who wanted their children supervised while they worked or went to school. By contrast, the purpose of *nursery schools* (sometimes termed *preschools*) is primarily educational. Nursery schools came into being early in the twentieth century out of educators' and physicians' concern that the complexities of urban life

were overwhelming children and stunting their development. The nursery school was conceived as "a protected environment scaled to [children's] developmental level and designed to promote experiences of mastery within a child-sized manageable world" (Prescott & Jones, 1971: 54). The basic intuition justifying nursery schools as environments for development is contained in the botanical metaphor of the child as a budding flower. At the age of 5 many children "gradu-

Hiroki, they reasoned, would not help. Rather, he needed to learn to get along in his group. To this end his teacher encouraged the other children in the class to take responsibility for helping Hiroki to correct his behavior. Tobin and his colleagues point out that

> Japanese teachers and Japanese society place [great value] on equality and the notion that children's success and failure and their potential to become successful versus failed adults has more to do with effort and character and thus with what can be learned and taught in school than with raw inborn ability. (p. 24)

The Japanese preschool teachers who watched a videotape of an American preschool classroom disapproved of the individualism they observed, believing that "a child's humanity is realized most fully not so much in his ability to be independent from the group as his ability to cooperate and feel part of the group" (p. 39). But the very qualities the Japanese deplored in the Americans—independence, self-reliance—were the ones the Americans most wished to promote.

At the American preschool, disputes between children were negotiated daily, with the children "playing the roles of plaintiff, defendant, and attorney, and teachers playing the role of judge" (p. 166). This means of resolving classroom disputes struck some of the Japanese as cumbersome and heavy-handed. They believed that children should be left, as much as possible, to devise their own techniques for resolving conflicts. "I was surprised by the way the American teacher got right in the middle of the children's disputes," one Japanese teacher wrote after viewing a fight between two American boys. A Japanese school administrator added:

> For my tastes there is something about the American approach [where children are taken aside when they misbehave and confronted and talked to by their teachers] that is a bit too heavy, too adultlike, too severe and controlled for young children. (p. 53)

This comparison of American and Japanese preschools reveals a fundamental fact about the influence of culture on children's development. The difference in the sizes of the classes was not a result of necessity. The Japanese have the resources to limit their classes to 15 children if they chose to do so. The pattern of preschool education in each society is shaped by what the adults imagine the future will be for their charges, both in later grades and in later life. The American preschool educators imagine that it is desirable for the children in their classrooms to become self-sufficient and independent adults; the Japanese educators want their young charges to become sensitive adults who have a strong sense of interdependence with their group. Much as parents treat their newborn boys and girls differently, not because they are so very different but because they *will be* different as adults, the American and Japanese teachers are helping the children in their classrooms to develop the characteristics they imagine they will need as adults in their society.

ate" from nursery school to kindergarten, a "garden for children" (from the German *kinder* [children] and *garten* [garden]). According to this same intuition, 3- and 4-year-old children are not ready for the rigors of this garden where rain falls, wind blows, and birds forage for seeds. Like the seedlings at a local garden store (a nursery!), they are most likely to develop healthily if they are specially protected until they are ready for transplanting.

A typical nursery school's layout and schedule reveal prevalent ideas of how best to foster development from the age of 2½ to 6 (see Box 11.4). There are likely to be several kinds of play areas: a sandbox, a water-play table, a doll corner, a block area, a large area with a rug where children can gather to listen to stories or sing songs, a cluster of low tables used for arts and crafts projects and for snacks, and an outdoor area with jungle gyms, slides, and swings. Each area provides an environment for developing a different aspect of children's overall potential: their ability to understand physical transformations in play materials; to control their own bodies; to create in language, song, clay, and paint; to adopt various social roles; and to get along with other children.

During the 2½ to 3 hours that children may spend in a nursery school, they are guided from one activity area to another. The developmental spirit of nursery schools is reflected in their lack of pressure on children to perform correctly on preassigned tasks and in their emphasis on exploration.

Preschools and the "War on Poverty"

In the 1960s a variety of scientific and social factors combined to create great interest in preschools' potential to increase the educational chances of the poor. On the scientific side was a growing belief that environmental influence during the first few years of life is crucial to all later abilities, especially intellectual ones (see Chapter 7). This belief coincided with broader historical pressures to improve the status of ethnic and racial minorities and with widespread political concern that social barriers between the rich and the poor and between whites and blacks were creating a dangerous situation in the United States. In 1963, for example, Michael Harrington warned that the United States was creating

> an enormous concentration of young people who, if they do not receive immediate help, may well be the source of a kind of hereditary poverty new to American society. If this analysis is correct, then the vicious circle of poverty is, if anything, becoming more intense, more crippling, and problematic. (1963:188)

This combination of social, political, and scientific factors led the U.S. Congress to declare a "war on poverty" in 1964. One of the key programs in this "war" was Project Head Start. Its purpose was to intervene in the cycle of poverty at a crucial time in children's lives by providing them with important learning experiences that they might otherwise miss. Federal support allowed Head Start programs to offer these experiences at no charge to low-income families.

This strategy of social reform through early childhood education rested on three crucial assumptions:

1. The environmental conditions of poverty-level homes are insufficient to prepare children to succeed in school.
2. Schooling is the social mechanism that permits children to succeed in our society.
3. Poor children could succeed in school, and thereby overcome their poverty, if they were given extra assistance in the preschool years.

When President Lyndon Johnson initiated Head Start, he declared that because of this project, "thirty million man-years—the combined life span of these youngsters—will be spent productively and rewardingly, rather than wasted in tax-supported institutions or welfare-supported lethargy."

Originally conceived as a summer program, Head Start soon began operating year round, serving approximately 200,000 preschool children at a time (Consortium for Longitudinal Studies, 1983). Three decades later, Head Start programs continue to play an important role in the lives of many U.S. children (Darlington, 1991).

What difference does Head Start make?

Because nursery schools have gained considerable social acceptance since the 1960s, it might be assumed that the preschool experience had proved to have positive benefits for children. The data are not so clear-cut.

Planners of Project Head Start and other preschool programs were sensitive to the need for scientific demonstrations of the usefulness of nursery schools (Zigler & Valentine, 1979). The logical requirements for proving the effectiveness of preschools were simple enough: select a large sample of children; give half of them (the experimental group), chosen at random, the experimental nursery school experience; and let the other half of the sample (the control group) stay home. But the demand for nursery school was so great that everyone who could be given access to a program received it. No parents wanted their children to be part of a control group, so the logic of experimental design was bypassed. As a consequence, there has been a great deal of controversy over the developmental consequences of Head Start programs.

The first reports were promising. Children who attended the summer program showed marked gains in standardized test scores. Hundreds of thousands of parents were involved in their children's school lives for the first time, whether as members of Head Start

These children attending a Head Start program are learning skills and acquiring attitudes that are intended to help them succeed in school in later years.

planning boards, as participants in special training programs for parents, or as classroom helpers. A great many children received improved nutrition and health care through Head Start (Condry, 1983).

Doubts about the effectiveness of the program were soon heard, however. In 1969 it was reported that the effects of Head Start slowly disappeared during the first 3 years of elementary school (Grotberg, 1969). A widely publicized evaluation by the Westinghouse Learning Corporation (1969) concluded that although "full-year Head Start appears to be a more effective compensatory education program than summer Head Start, its benefits cannot be described as satisfactory" (p. 11).

People who had never favored Head Start programs felt their doubts had been confirmed by the Westinghouse report. But supporters were by no means persuaded. They pointed out that the Westinghouse study lacked any proper control groups, substituting a variety of doubtful statistics instead.

In 1989 Ron Haskins, a psychologist and staff member of the Ways and Means Committee of the House of Representatives, reviewed all of the major studies of Head Start programs for which data concerning later developmental impact were available. The evidence included model experimental nursery

school programs and ordinary Head Start programs mounted without support from researchers. By 1989 it was possible to assess follow-up evaluations of children as they reached their early 20s and broader developmental indicators such as crime rates and earned income.

This broad evaluation revealed a mixed picture. On the positive side, Haskins found that the children who had attended regular Head Start programs and special, model programs showed clear evidence of meaningful gains in intellectual performance and socioemotional development. Preschool attendance also reduced the likelihood that children would be assigned to remedial special-education classes while they were in school. Only the model programs, however, yielded positive outcomes on such indicators of life success as delinquency, teenage pregnancy, and employment. An important finding was that unless the preschool experience—whether in Head Start or a model program—is followed up by a special program later in the child's educational career, the impact of the early "head start" grows smaller and smaller, and often fades out altogether.

Overall, the evidence indicates that nursery school experience for the children of low-income families *can* make a difference in their later school achievement, and perhaps in their later life success, but this positive outcome is by no means guaranteed. High-quality programs that are maintained longer than the initial "head start" are necessary to realize the hopes placed in preschool education by Head Start's founders.

The future of compensatory preschool programs

Compensatory preschool programs face an uncertain future in the United States. In addition to uncertainty about the permanence of gains from programs that last only a year, two major philosophical objections have been raised to the propagation of compensatory preschool programs. First, there is the question of how public money should be spent. Congressional committees that oversee the uses of tax dollars have questioned whether even successful programs are successful enough to justify their costs. In his summary of the relationship between the costs and benefits of Head Start programs, Haskins (1989) concludes that the savings to taxpayers from Head Start programs (measured in the dollars that would otherwise have to be spent for special services and for law enforcement and the criminal justice system) are relatively small. This conclusion leads naturally to a search for more effective ways to use the funds. Second, some critics argue that educational programs cannot compensate for the damage caused by poor housing, inadequate nutrition, discrimination, and parental unemployment. They say that President Johnson and the planners and implementers of Project Head Start were misleading the public. Giving the children of the poor a "head start" would not reduce their poverty.

Despite uncertainty about the long-term effects and cost-efficiency of the Head Start program, there are reasons to believe that the program may continue to play a role in the government's efforts in support of children. As Ron Haskins (1989) noted, the Head Start program has become a national symbol of the desire to help poor children advance through self-improvement. Head Start children receive much-needed food, health care, and dental care. They also obtain intellectual stimulation that increases the chances that they will begin their formal schooling with a firmer foundation and greater hopes of long-term success.

ON THE THRESHOLD

This chapter has by no means surveyed all of the contexts that significantly influence early childhood development: young children also learn from trips to the beach, attendance at houses of worship, and visits to the doctor's office. Each new context brings with it new social challenges as young children gradually piece together a deeper understanding of their world and their place in it.

Adding the influence of contexts to early childhood development helps make sense of the variable picture each young child presents to the world. In familiar contexts, where children know the appropriate scripts and their own roles in them, they may display mature reasoning and surprising competence. But often they find themselves novices in new settings, where they do not know the appropriate scripts, where they are expected to work out social relationships with strangers, and where they are set new tasks that require them to master new concepts. In these circumstances, their powers of self-expression and self-control are put under great strain, and their thought processes may be inadequate to the heavy demands placed upon them.

The problem of being a novice is by no means unique to young children; people face it throughout their lives. But the difficulties are particularly acute at the beginning of early childhood because young children know so little about how their culture works. Consequently, children of this age need almost constant supervision. When they play together, they need some powerful organizing activity, such as pretend play, to support their fragile ability to coordinate with one another.

By the end of early childhood, children's vocabularies and command of grammatical forms have grown immensely. They have greater knowledge about a wide variety of contexts and a more sophisticated sense of themselves; and they are vastly more competent to think about the world, to control themselves, and to deal with other children. In these and many other ways they indicate a readiness to venture into new settings, to take on new social roles, and to accept the additional responsibilities that await them as they enter middle childhood.

SUMMARY

1. The factors that influence children's lives can be usefully thought of as a nested set of contexts.
2. The various levels of context have reciprocal influences on one another.
3. The family influences children's development in two ways: by shaping their behavior within the family context and by selecting other contexts for them to inhabit.
4. Cross-cultural comparisons of family life and personality configurations reveal that children develop to fit the overall demands of economic activity and community life in their society.
5. Family socialization patterns vary within societies, depending on such factors as the family configuration and the values, beliefs, education, income, and personalities of the family members.
6. Patterns of socialization can be grouped for purposes of comparison. Child-rearing practices in the United States in most cases follow one of three patterns:
   a. Authoritarian families use set standards and emphasize conformity.
   b. Authoritative families emphasize control through reasoning and discussion.
   c. Permissive families avoid overt control and believe that children should make their own decisions.
7. Among white middle-class two-parent families, authoritative child-rearing practices are associated with children who are more self-reliant, self-controlled, and willing to explore than those raised by permissive or authoritarian parents.
8. A significant number of U.S. children grow up in single-parent families headed by a young unwed mother. These children tend to be more aggressive, less self-controlled, and less cognitively advanced than the children of older married couples.
9. Children whose parents have divorced often display a variety of negative reactions, including sleep disturbances, irritability, and aggressiveness. The severity and duration of the dislocation resulting from divorce depend on a variety of factors, including the family income and the configuration of the new family that results if the custodial parent remarries.
10. Poverty affects family life in many ways, increasing the stress on parents at the same time that it reduces their resources for dealing with it. Stress, in turn, is associated with authoritarian parenting styles.
11. Extended family arrangements provide one means of coping with poverty. The presence of several adults reduces the stress on the parent or parents and provides resources for dealing with the causes of stress.
12. Influences from the community enter the family context through such media as newspapers, television, radio, and books. Each medium of communication is assumed to influence children's development in specific ways.
13. A major factor in television's influence on children is the great amount of time they spend watching it.
14. Television's potential for realism makes it difficult for children to distinguish reality from fiction in television content, and their understanding of the content is confused by such cinematic techniques as rapid cuts and zoom shots.
15. Television content influences people's underlying beliefs about the world. Insofar as reality is distorted by television, children who watch television acquire false beliefs about the world.
16. A variety of evidence indicates that violence depicted on television increases aggressiveness in children.
17. Parents can influence television's impact on their children by controlling what their children watch and by watching with them and talking about what is happening on the screen.
18. Reading to young children furnishes them with an early model of activities that will be important in school. Parents have far greater control over the pace and the content of the reading material that the child encounters than over what the child sees on television.
19. Once children begin to spend time outside of the home, their experience changes in fundamental ways.
20. Day-care centers vary widely in social setting, philosophy, and physical facilities. The size of the group is of special importance to the quality of day care: the smaller the group, the higher the quality.
21. Day care in the United States has more clear-cut effects on children's social behavior than on their cognitive behavior. Major effects include
   a. Increased self-sufficiency and decreased compliance with adults' wishes.
   b. Increased ability to engage in peer-led group activity.
22. Nursery schools developed during the twentieth century as a means of promoting the development of children who had to cope with the complexities of urban life.
23. Since the early 1960s, nursery school education has been promoted as a means of combating school failure among people living in poverty.

KEY TERMS

authoritarian parenting pattern   authoritative parenting pattern   permissive parenting pattern

SUGGESTED READINGS

CLARKE-STEWART, ALISON. *Daycare*, 2nd ed. Cambridge, Mass.: Harvard University Press, 1992.

Alison Clarke-Stewart, who has extensive experience in day-care research, provides both a concise discussion of the critical scientific issues surrounding day care and practical advice about evaluating day-care facilities.

CONSORTIUM FOR LONGITUDINAL STUDIES. *As the Twig Is Bent: The Lasting Effects of Preschool Programs*. Hillsdale, N.J.: Erlbaum, 1983.

The history and background of modern preschool programs is presented through case studies and pooled analyses of programs. An excellent entry point into research that attempts to apply developmental theories as a means of promoting development.

GREENFIELD, PATRICIA M. *Mind and Media*. Cambridge, Mass.: Harvard University Press, 1984.

Too many discussions of the effects of television on children's development neglect other forms of media that children begin to encounter, such as radio, books, and computers. Greenfield compares the various media in interesting ways and examines their implications for development.

MACCOBY, ELEANOR E., & MARTIN, JOHN. "Socialization in the Context of the Family: Parent-Child Interaction." In P. H. Mussen (Ed.), *Handbook of Child Psychology*, Vol. 4: E. M. Hetherington (Ed.), *Socialization, Personality, and Social Behavior*. New York: Wiley, 1983.

An authoritative summary of research on the special quality of families as contexts for development.

MONTESSORI, MARIA. *The Montessori Method*. New York: Shocken, 1964.

Maria Montessori, the first Italian woman physician, was a pioneer in the study of intellectual development and early childhood education. This comprehensive summary of her ideas includes both statements of her general theory and detailed descriptions of her program for a "scientific pedagogy." In one form or another, many of Montessori's ideas remain influential in early childhood education today.

WHITING, BEATRICE, & EDWARDS, CAROLYN. *Children of Six Cultures*. Cambridge, Mass.: Harvard University Press, 1988.

This volume summarizes evidence from many parts of the world to provide a convincing account of the ways ecological and cultural factors shape adults' economic activities, which in turn shape their socialization practices, and eventually the personalities of their children.

PART IV

Middle Childhood

In societies around the world, adults behave as if children between the ages of 5 and 7 enter a new stage of development that lasts until about age 12 (Harkness & Super, 1985; Rogoff et al., 1975). Among the Ngoni of Malawi in central Africa, for example, adults believe that the loss of milk teeth and the acquisition of second teeth (which begins around the age of 6) signal that children are ready for a different kind of life. When this physical change occurs, adults expect children to begin to act more independently. Children of both sexes are held accountable for being discourteous. They are supposed to stop playing childish games and start learning skills that will be essential when they grow up. The boys leave the protection and control of women and move into dormitories, where they must adapt to a system of male dominance and male life. Margaret Read describes the associated stresses for Ngoni boys:

> There was no doubt that this abrupt transition, like the sudden weaning [several years earlier], was a shock for many boys between six-and-a-half and seven-and-a-half. From having been impudent, well fed, self-confident, and spoiled youngsters among the women many of them quickly became skinny, scruffy, subdued, and had a hunted expression. (1960/1968:49)

In his book on the history of the idea of childhood, Philippe Ariès tells us that a change in children's status around age 7 has a long history, reaching back even before the advent of industrialization and compulsory schooling:

> In the Middle Ages, at the beginning of modern times, and for a long time after that in the lower classes, children were mixed with adults as soon as they were considered capable of doing without their mothers or nannies, not long after a tardy weaning (in other words, at about the age of seven). They immediately went straight into the great community of men, sharing in the work and play of their companions, old and young alike. (1962:411)

Even the brief descriptions provided by Read and Ariès indicate one universal feature of the period developmentalists call middle childhood: children are no longer restricted to the home or to settings where they are carefully watched by adults. They are now responsible for behaving themselves in a variety of new contexts. Those new contexts are of three principal types: *solitary* contexts, where children are expected to play or carry out chores on their own; *instructional* contexts, which are designed to impart culturally valued knowledge and are controlled by one or a few adults; and *peer* contexts, where children spend time with others in the absence of adult supervision. There are important differences within and among societies in the particular mix of contexts that children begin to inhabit in middle childhood as well as in the nature of the activities that go on there.

We can appreciate cultural variation most clearly by comparing societies that expect children to work with those that emphasize instruction and education during the middle years of childhood. Among some indigenous peoples in the highlands of Guatemala, boys go out to herd cattle, a solitary activity that takes them well beyond the range of watchful adults, while girls spend more time at home helping their mothers and the older women of the village (Rogoff, 1978). In the United States, boys and girls alike spend long hours in school, with their peers, receiving formal education.

At first glance, time spent with peers when no adults are present may appear less important to development than time spent in educational contexts. After all, a good deal of peer interaction is taken up with games, gossip, or simply "hanging out." But this informal interaction with peers provides children with important opportunities for exploring social relationships and moral feelings and for the development of personal identities.

These changes in the social contexts of development would be impossible to adjust to if children did not also acquire the cognitive capacities needed to support their newly granted autonomy. Evidence gleaned from experiments and clinical interviews makes clear that a defining characteristic of middle childhood is a greatly increased ability to think more deeply and logically, to follow through on a problem once it is undertaken, and to keep track of more than one aspect of a situation at a time.

This section is divided into three chapters: Chapter 12 describes the nature of children's biological and cognitive capacities between the ages of 5 and 12. Chapter 13 examines the influence of schooling on development, with particular attention to the organization of school activities and to the intellectual capacities that schooling both demands and fosters. Chapter 14 focuses on the developmental significance of the new social relations that emerge during middle childhood, particularly among peers.

CHAPTER 12

Cognitive and Biological Attainments of Middle Childhood

•

Walking was my project before reading. The text I read was the town; the book I made up was a map. . . . I pushed at my map's edges. Alone at night I added newly memorized streets and blocks to old streets and blocks, and imagined connecting them on foot. . . . I felt that my life depended on keeping it all straight — remembering where on earth I lived, that is, in relation to where I walked. It was dead reckoning. On darkened evenings I came home exultant, secretive, often from some exotic leafy curb a mile beyond what I had known at lunch, where I had peered up at the street sign, hugging the cold pole, and fixed the intersection in my mind. What joy, what relief, eased me as I pushed open the heavy front door! — joy and relief because, from the very trackless waste, I had located home, family, and the dinner table once again.

An infant watches her hands and feels them move. Gradually she fixes her own boundaries at the complex incurved rim of skin. Later she touches one palm to another and tries for a game to distinguish each hand's sensations of feeling and being felt. What is a house but a bigger skin, and a neighborhood map but the world's skin ever expanding?

— ANNIE DILLARD, *AN AMERICAN CHILDHOOD*

One of the best ways to gain a sense of middle childhood is to observe what goes on in children's everyday lives. Roger Barker and Herbert Wright (1951) arranged for observers to follow one child living in "Midwest," a small community in the United States, through every minute of the waking day. The resulting portrait of 7-year-old Raymond Birch reveals the new independence, the greater responsibility, and the new variety of contexts that characterize middle childhood. The following account was adapted from Barker and Wright's *One Boy's Day:*

Raymond gets up, dresses himself (although his clothes have been laid out for him by his mother), and takes care of his own grooming. He eats breakfast with his mother and father. Then he helps his father to clear the dishes. He negotiates with his mother about the need to wear a jacket to school and grudgingly accepts her judgment that a jacket is in order. He decides on his own not to take his bike to school because it might rain.

After spending a few minutes casting a fishing rod with his father in the backyard (he is the only one who caught fish on their last outing), he accompanies his mother to the courthouse where she works. At the courthouse he greets adults politely, and holds the door open for a man who is going out at the same time he is. He plays by himself outside while his mother works. When it is time for him to go to school, he walks the few blocks by himself, crossing the street cautiously. On the playground, he and the other children are unsupervised. A few minutes before 9 A.M. he enters his classroom, which the second-graders share with the first grade. While waiting for school to begin, he draws on the board, looks at a book with a friend, and chats quietly with other children. When the teacher comes into the room promptly at 9 A.M., he turns in his seat (all the seats are arranged in rows, facing front). While the teacher readies the first-graders to go to music, Raymond, who has become worried that he left his coat on the playground, asks permission to search for it. He has forgotten that he has hung it in the cloakroom. When he discovers this, he comes back and makes May baskets out of paper strips with the rest of the second-graders. He goes to music, listens to other children's stories, and goes outside for recess.

In the afternoon he does poorly on the spelling test. When another boy asks, "What did you get on your spelling?" he blushes and looks down at his desk. In a swift hoarse whisper he tells the boy that his grades are his own business. He seems embarrassed when he speaks. Close to dismissal time, the class searches for the money another boy has reported lost. When it turns out to have been in his desk the entire time, Raymond smiles companionably at him and leans back to pat his hand. Then the boy pats Raymond's hand. They pat harder and harder, grinning broadly, until the teacher intervenes with a directive for the entire class.

While his mother is preparing dinner after work, Raymond pushes the lawn mower for a minute. He then joins his 11-year-old neighbor Stewart Evarts, and Clifford, Stewart's 3½-year-old nephew, in the vacant lot across the street. Playing with their trucks in a pit that was once the basement of a house, Raymond discovers a dilapidated wooden crate about 5 feet long buried in the weeds. He drags the crate out, and the boys devise several ways to play with it, despite its unwieldy size. They lift it out of the pit and send it crashing back in, get in the crate and pretend it is a cage and that they are monkeys, and hang on with their hands and feet as it rocks and tumbles over and over. At the same time, the older boys are careful that Clifford is not harmed by their games.

From such observations carried out with many children, Barker and Wright (1955) concluded that of the more than 200 activity settings in which Midwest's children might have participated on an average weekday — such as the street, the classroom, the playground, and the grocery store — they actually partici-

pated in about a dozen settings, each associated with its own special set of skills, expectations, values, and attitudes.

Adults were present in many of these places. But generally, the amount of time that children such as Raymond Birch spend unsupervised by adults increases markedly during the course of middle childhood (see Figure 12.1). In about one-third of the settings where children Raymond Birch's age spend their time — the streets between home and school and the empty lot across from Raymond's home, for example — they have no adult supervision. Similar increases in unsupervised time have been reported in urban centers as well as the rural Midwest, and in quite different societies in several parts of the world (Ellis, Rogoff, & Cromer, 1981; Whiting & Whiting, 1975).

The new independence and responsibility that adults around the world confer on children between 5 and 7 suggest how much more adults expect of them than of younger children. These expectations stem both from cultural traditions and from adults' observations of how well their children cope with new demands (Goodnow, 1984; Sigel, 1985) (see Figure 12.2).

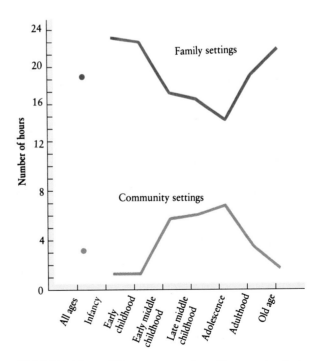

FIGURE 12.1   *The average number of hours a day that people of various ages in "Midwest" spent in family and community settings. (From Wright, 1956.)*

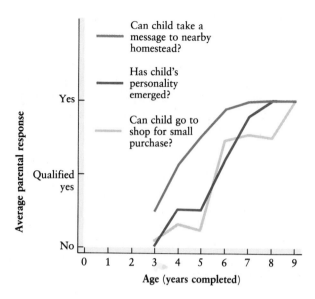

FIGURE 12.2 *The ages at which Kipsigis mothers in Korwet, Kenya, believe their children undergo basic developmental changes. Note that there is a sharp discontinuity in this culture's estimates of personality development and the ability to carry out an errand involving money. But according to this culture there is continuity in the development of memory. (From Harkness & Super, 1983.)*

The Ifaluk of Micronesia believe that at the age of 6 years children acquire "social intelligence," which includes both the requisite knowledge and the ability to work, adhere to social norms, and demonstrate compassion for others—all valued adult behaviors (Lutz, 1987). Raymond Birch's parents have similar ideas, except that they consider his work to be the job of getting an education. They would not have allowed him to play around the courthouse unattended if they had not expected him to behave appropriately. If he were to become so fascinated with a playground game that he lost his jacket, he would be held responsible for his mistake because he was supposed to know better. His teacher and his parents expected him to have learned his spelling words, and he knew enough to be embarrassed when he did not do well on his test.

Children entering middle childhood can meet these higher standards because their physical and cognitive capacities have increased. They are strong and agile enough to catch a runaway goat or to carry their little sister on her hip. They know enough not to let the baby crawl into the fire. They can wait for the

school bus without wandering off. They can, sometimes under duress, sit still for several hours at a time while adults attempt to instruct them, and they can carry out their chores in an acceptable manner. In short, they can perform tasks independently, can formulate goals, and can resist the temptation to abandon them.

In this chapter we will investigate the changes in children's biological and cognitive functioning that justify adults' new demands. Are these changes the same all over the world, or do they vary from one society to the next? Are they signs of a distinctive new stage of development, or can they be accounted for on the basis of continuous buildup of capacities already present in early childhood?

BIOLOGICAL DEVELOPMENTS

One reason for what appears to be a universal change in children's status is their physical maturation (Gesell & Ilg, 1943). In many cultures the first loss of a baby tooth, which occurs about age 6, is seen both as an index of a child's age and as a sign of new capacities that permit a new status (Rogoff et al., 1975) (see Figure 12.3). While the loss of baby teeth is clearly a sign of physical maturation, there is no reason to believe that the arrival of new teeth is the cause of changes in children's behavior or in their parents' expectations. Other biological changes—increases in physical size and strength and brain developments that support better coordination and more complex thinking—are more likely sources of new capacities that lead adults to accord children a new social status.

Physical Growth

Children's size and strength increase significantly during middle childhood, although more slowly than in earlier years. Average 6-year-olds in the United States are about 3½ feet tall and weigh about 50 pounds. At the start of adolescence, 6 or 7 years later, their average height will have increased to almost 5 feet and their weight to approximately 100 pounds (see Figure 5.2, p. 180). Strength increases even more dramatically than size. Most boys double their muscular strength

FIGURE 12.3   *The loss of one's front teeth is a widely accepted sign that middle childhood is beginning.*

during this period and girls become significantly stronger as well (Tanner, 1978).

As in other periods of development, children's growth depends upon both nutritional and genetic factors. Margaret Janes (1975) investigated nutritional factors by comparing the sizes of Nigerian boys of well-off families with those of less advantaged boys. During middle childhood, the less advantaged children were, on the average, almost 4 inches shorter than their well-off counterparts.

When groups of equally well-nourished children are compared, the genetic contribution to size can be clearly seen. Phyllis Eveleth and J. M. Tanner (1976) compared the sizes of European, Asian, and African American children from the ages of 1 to 18. The Asian boys and girls, even those who received better than average care, were found to be distinctively shorter than children in the other two groups — a clear demonstration that genetic constitution interacts with the cultural environment to determine children's size.

Brain Developments

Physical growth and an increase in strength are only two of the factors that account for children's increased competence during middle childhood. Children in this period also become more agile and finely coordinated, so that they are able to ride bikes, weave on looms, and write legibly with a pencil.

Some researchers have suggested that these new skills are made possible by a change in the working relationship between the two halves of the brain (Brown & Jaffe, 1975; Lenneberg, 1967). This hypothesis is based on the idea that at birth the two halves of the brain are not specialized. As children grow older, however, various psychological functions become controlled by one hemisphere, a process known as **lateralization** (see Figure 12.4). According to this line of reasoning, the onset of middle childhood is accompanied by an increase in lateralization, which supports

Left hemisphere   Right hemisphere

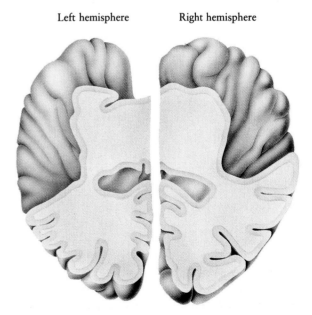

FIGURE 12.4   *The two hemispheres of the brain are not symmetrical, either anatomically or in function. Perception of language-related sounds, letters, words, and verbal memory are generally controlled by the left hemisphere. Perception of music, of other nonspeech sounds, and of visual patterns as well as visual memory are generally controlled by the right hemisphere. (From Kolb & Whishaw, 1985.)*

Middle childhood is a time when a combination of physical changes and extended practice enables children to acquire complex, culturally valued skills.

more subtle and coordinated action and more complex thought.

Evidence in favor of this idea comes from research showing that lateralization of such complex behaviors as writing, throwing, and kicking a ball increases during middle childhood (Coren, Porac, & Duncan, 1981). Researchers have also noted that in many cultures it is not until about age 6 that children are punished for violating social norms that require them to use their right hand for such functions as eating and shaking hands (Rogoff et al., 1975).

Recent research, however, has cast doubt on the idea that lateralization is responsible for developments seen between the ages of 5 and 7. First, it has been shown that even during the first few months of life, the two halves of the brain produce different electrical patterns, an indication that they are already functioning differently (Kinsbourne & Hiscock, 1983). Moreover, in infants, as in older children and adults, the right ear is dominant in the perception of speech sounds (Best, Hoffman, & Glanville, 1982), and infants display a preference for one hand over the other

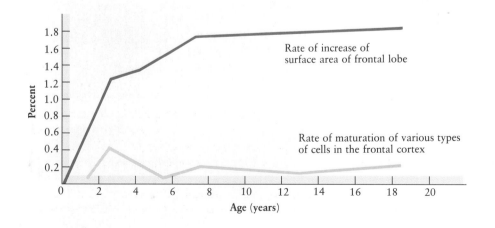

FIGURE 12.5   *The rate of increase in the area of the frontal lobes and in the maturation of nerve cells during development. (From Luria, 1973.)*

when they reach for something (Michel, 1981). Thus, if lateralization does play a role in the advent of middle childhood, it is only part of the story.

Other biological changes associated with middle childhood include an increase in brain size and changes in the pattern of electrical activity in the brain. The rate of growth in the surface area of the brain's frontal lobes rises sharply until the age of 2. Another sharp increase occurs between ages 5 and 7, after which the rate of growth remains level, as Figure 12.5 indicates (Luria, 1973).

The years between 6 and 8 also witness the near completion of the myelination of the cortex, which induces a change in the interconnections between parts of the brain (Lecours, 1982). (Recall from Chapter 4 that myelination provides each cortical neuron with an insulating sheath of tissue to speed transmission of nerve impulses along the neurons.)

Myelination between 6 and 8 years of age is also accompanied by a fundamental shift in the pattern of waking brain-wave activity (Corbin & Bickford, 1955). As Figure 12.6 indicates, until the age of 5, EEGs (electroencephalograms) recorded when children are awake display more theta activity (characteristic of adult sleep states) than alpha activity (charac-

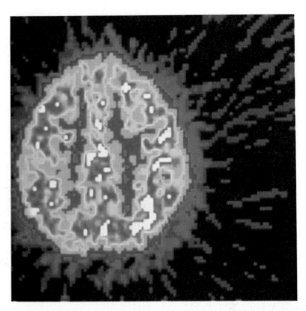

FIGURE 12.7 *An example of a positron emission tomographic (PET) scan used to assess the activity of different parts of the brain while a child is engaged in various forms of problem solving. This modern technique is based upon the ability to detect the extent to which parts of the brain take up and use glucose. Orange and white on the scan indicate areas where more glucose is being taken up and used. By comparing the changing patterns of activity in different brain centers as children grow older it is possible to specify with greater precision the relation between brain changes and problem-solving activities.*

teristic of engaged attention). Between 5 and 7 years the amounts of theta and alpha activity are about equal, but thereafter alpha activity (engaged attention) predominates.

Several researchers who have attempted to explain the relationship between the brain and cognitive development (Case, 1992; Luria, 1973; Thatcher, 1991) argue that the pattern of brain changes between the ages of 5 and 7 permits the frontal lobes to coordinate the activities of other brain centers in a qualitatively more complex way, enabling people to control their attention, to form explicit plans, and to engage in self-reflection, all behaviors that appear to undergo important developments in middle childhood (see Figure 12.7). This view is supported by the fact that when the frontal lobe is damaged in humans and in other animals, their behavior deteriorates in specific ways: they

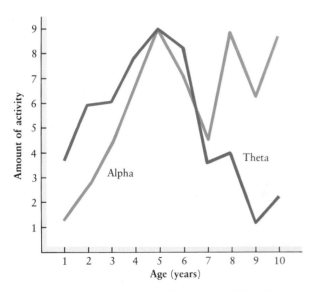

FIGURE 12.6 *Changes in the amount of theta (sleep-like) and alpha (alert) EEG activity during development. Note that alpha waves come to predominate over theta waves around the age of 7. (From Corbin & Bickford, 1955.)*

are unable to maintain goals; their actions become fragmentary and uncontrolled; they respond to irrelevant stimuli and are easily thrown off track by interruptions and pauses. These deficits are so similar to those attributed to young children (see Chapter 9) that it seems plausible to suppose that the increasing role of the frontal lobes in overall brain organization may account for the behavioral changes of middle childhood.

Yet we must be cautious about inferring direct causal links between particular changes in the brain and specific changes in behavior. Much of the evidence we have cited is correlational: as children grow older, we observe changes in their brains and changes in their behavior, but the direction of causation is uncertain. Do children perform in more sophisticated ways because of changes in their brains, or have their brains become larger and more complicated because they are put in more challenging situations? (This possibility is discussed in Box 5.1, pp. 194–195.)

Many studies designed to establish causal relationships between biological and behavioral changes have in fact failed to do so. When Robert McCall and his colleagues (1983) tested the hypothesis that a spurt in head growth precedes a spurt in cognitive development, for example, they found no such relation between the physical and psychological changes. Psychologists currently investigating such relationships, mindful of past failures, are seeking more precise measures of both brain change and behavioral change to overcome the shortcomings of earlier research (see Fischer, 1987).

A NEW QUALITY OF MIND?

During the middle decades of this century there was a broad consensus among developmental psychologists that children's thought processes undergo a qualitative change between early and middle childhood. Currently, however, the evidence surveyed in Chapter 9 and other evidence about the cognitive abilities of young children are raising considerable doubt that any such qualitative change occurs. Some psychologists have argued that middle childhood is merely a collection of gradual advances in the cognitive developments that first appeared at the end of infancy (Biddel & Fischer, 1992; Flavell, 1985; Siegler, 1991).

New Forms of Remembering

As long as children remain in the company of their parents or other caretakers, their behavior can be guided step by step. Once they begin to spend time on their own, however, they must be able to follow directions without being constantly reminded. According to a variety of evidence, when children reach middle childhood, they are increasingly able to carry out tasks on their own after an adult has issued a set of instructions (Luria, 1961; Miller, Shelton, & Flavell, 1970). In parts of Africa, Asia, and Central America (as in the United States of 100 years ago) a variety of chores are commonly assigned to children of this age — gathering wood or kindling, bringing food to parents working in the fields, guarding crops from pigs or birds, bringing a horse in from the field, running errands, making small purchases, shelling and husking corn (Hareven & Adams, 1982; Tietjen, 1989). All these tasks require the execution of a series of actions and are often performed without supervision (Nerlove et al., 1974).

Oleg Tikhomirov (1978), investigating changes in the ability to follow instructions, asked children to squeeze a rubber bulb according to different preliminary directives; for example, "Squeeze when the green light flashes" or "Squeeze twice each time a light flashes." Tikhomirov reported that when young children were asked to squeeze whenever a green light flashed but not when they saw a red light, they quickly became confused and pressed every time a light flashed, regardless of its color. They could cope with the task only if the experimenter repeated the instructions before each flash of light. Eight-year-olds, however, quickly mastered the task on the basis of preliminary instructions alone.

Perhaps the most obvious interpretation of the difficulties young children have in following directions is that they simply forget what has been asked of them. This conclusion is bolstered by a vast experimental literature that shows marked increases in memory between early childhood and middle childhood (Kail, 1990). In light of this evidence, psychologists often link improvements in memory to other increases in cognitive competence during middle childhood (Case, 1991; Siegler, 1991).

Four factors appear to combine to create the changes in memory between early and middle childhood: (1) an increase in memory capacity; (2) the development of strategies for remembering; (3) an increase

Adults around the world assign children chores in middle childhood that call upon their increased physical strength as well as their ability to control themselves so that they can complete the assigned tasks.

in knowledge about the things one is trying to remember; and (4) the development of knowledge about one's own memory processes (Siegler, 1991).

Memory capacity

In Chapter 9 we noted that as children grow, the number of randomly chosen numbers or letters that they can keep in mind at one time increases steadily (p. 334). This number is called a *digit span*. Most 4- and 5-year-olds can recall four digits presented one after another; most 9- and 10-year-olds can remember about six. Several investigators propose that this increase reflects an underlying maturation of the child's capacity to hold information in short-term (or "working") memory (Pascual-Leone, 1988; White & Pillemer, 1979; Figure 9.9, p. 333, shows a general model of memory). According to this view, 5-to-7-year-olds' new ability to keep track of a task while they carry it out can be explained by increases in their ability to hold information in working memory long enough to execute actions involving several steps.

Not all developmental psychologists agree with this explanation. Robbie Case (1985, 1991), for example, believes that the absolute size of children's memory storage capacity does not increase with age. What does increase, he contends, is children's efficiency at using their mental capacities. In order to remember several numbers presented at random, for example,

children must somehow represent each number to themselves, perhaps by silently repeating "Ten, six, eight, two." Case and his colleagues have shown that young children take longer than older children simply to repeat a number such as 10 or 2, indicating that they must use much of their information-processing capacities on this part of the task alone. Older children name individual numbers quite quickly, so that more of their information-processing resources are left for the task of actually retaining the numbers in memory (Case, Kurland, & Goldberg, 1982).

Cross-cultural research enriches these conclusions. When Chuansheng Chen and Harold Stevenson (1988) compared the digit spans of U.S. and Chinese children aged 4 to 6 years, they found that the Chinese children were able to recall more digits at each of the ages tested. This finding might suggest that their capacity for short-term memory was larger. In line with the work of Case and his colleagues, however, Chen and Stevenson pointed to the fact that the Chinese words for the digits are shorter than the American words, so the task was easier for the Chinese children, just as it had been easier for the older American children. This conclusion was strongly supported by a study in which Stevenson and his colleagues (1985) used lists of objects whose names were equal in length in English and Chinese. When these words were presented for remembering, Chinese and American children were found to have equal memory capacities.

The ability of older children to repeat digits more quickly appears to be just one instance of a more general tendency for older children and adults to carry out cognitive operations of many kinds faster than younger children. In a series of studies, Robert Kail (1986, 1991) has shown that the time it takes to retrieve information from memory or to match two letters presented in different spatial locations decreases from early childhood well into adulthood. As a consequence of this increase in mental processing speed, older children and adults can be expected to execute more cognitive operations than younger children, and therefore to demonstrate increased intellectual effectiveness.

Memory strategies

A second factor that might lead to better memory is the increased ability of older children to employ memory strategies (Kail, 1990). A **strategy** is a deliberately selected action performed for the purpose of attaining a particular goal (Paris, Newman, and Jacobs, 1985). When we say that children use *memory strategies,* we mean that they are able to engage in deliberate actions to achieve the goal of remembering something.

Elementary strategies can be observed in children even before their second birthday if just the right procedures are used. For example, Judy DeLoache, Deborah Cassidy, and Ann Brown (1985) told 1½-to-2-year-old children to remember the location of an attractive stuffed animal that they hid while the children watched. The children were then induced to play with several attractive toys. After 4 minutes had elapsed, a bell rang and the children were urged to retrieve the stuffed animal. During the time they were playing with the toys, the children often interrupted themselves to look at, point at, peek at, or talk about the hidden stuffed animal. They did not engage in such behaviors when the stuffed animal was not hidden, indicating that their behaviors were specific to cases in which forgetting was a potential problem. DeLoache and her colleagues point out that such behaviors are similar to well-known strategies observed in older children, such as rehearsing.

Such young children often fail to use special strategies to help them to remember, however. In many cases that appear to be relatively simple, children do not create strategies for remembering until they are 7 or 8 years old (Ritter, 1978).

Two memory strategies whose development has been intensively studied are rehearsal and organization. **Rehearsal** is repetition of material that one is trying to memorize, such as a list of words, a song, or a phone number. In order to study the development of rehearsal strategies in children, John Flavell and his colleagues (Keeney, Canizzo, & Flavell, 1967) presented 5- and 10-year-olds with seven pictures of objects to be remembered. The children were asked to wear a "space helmet" with a visor that was pulled down over their eyes during the 15-second interval between the presentation of the pictures and the test for recall. The visor prevented the children from seeing the pictures and allowed the experimenter to watch their lips to see if they repeated to themselves what they had seen. Few of the 5-year-olds rehearsed, but almost all of the 10-year-olds did. Within each age group, children who rehearsed the pictures recalled more than children who did not. When those who had not rehearsed were later taught to do so, they did as well on the memory task as those who had rehearsed on their own. More recent research shows that under some conditions, young children use some of the same memory strategies as children in middle childhood, but less frequently. Jill Weissberg and Scott Paris (1986), for example, observed rehearsal in 43 percent of the 3-to-4-year-olds they tested and in 79 percent of the 6-to-7-year-olds.

There are also marked changes in the use of **memory organization,** another strategy associated with the advent of middle childhood. Children who use this strategy mentally group the materials to be remembered in meaningful clusters of closely associated items, so that they have only to remember one part of a cluster to gain access to the rest. Research has demonstrated that 7- and 8-year-olds are more likely than younger children to impose their own ordering principles on what they have to remember by grouping the items in easy-to-remember categories (Kail, 1990). The kinds of groupings that children impose on lists of things to be remembered also change. Younger children often use sound features, such as rhyme *(cat–sat)*, or situational associations *(cereal–milk)* to group words they are trying to remember. In middle childhood, children are more likely to link words according to the categories to which they belong, such as *animals:* cat–dog–horse; *plants:* tree–flower–grass; or *geometric figures:* triangle–square–circle (Hasher & Clifton, 1974). The consequence of these changes is an enhanced ability to store and retrieve information deliberately and systematically.

Knowledge base

In general, children in middle childhood are likely to know more about any given topic than younger children do simply by virtue of having accumulated more experience in the world (Cole & Means, 1981; Lange, 1978). At least some of the increases in memory, then, may result from neither increased biological capacity nor more powerful strategies, but from an accumulation of experience that provides older children with a richer **knowledge base,** or store of information upon which to draw in a new situation.

Two studies conducted by Michelene Chi dramatically demonstrate how a child's knowledge base influences memory performance. In one experiment Chi (1978) compared memory for the arrangement of chess pieces among 10-year-old chess buffs with the memory abilities of college-age chess amateurs. The 10-year-olds recalled the chess arrangements better than the college students, though when the two groups were compared on their ability to recall a random series of numbers, the college students' performances were far superior.

A second study (Chi & Koeske, 1983) focused on a 4½-year-old boy's ability to recall the names of dinosaur species. Chi and Randi Koeske first elicited the names of all the dinosaurs the child knew (46 in all for this unusually well-versed child!) by questioning him on various occasions. They selected the 20 dinosaurs

Skill at cards requires the ability to remember the cards that have been previously dealt and the relative values of different hands, as well as the ability to use strategies to defeat your opponent.

he mentioned most frequently and the 20 he mentioned least frequently in order to study how the child's comparative knowledge influenced his memory of each group.

The child's knowledge about these 40 dinosaurs was probed in a game in which the experimenter and the child took turns generating clues from which the other had to guess the dinosaur in question ("Lives in forest, eats plants, moves on four legs, is very big—what is it?"). The dinosaurs the child most frequently mentioned were those that were most familiar to him, and they were also closely associated with each other in his mind.

Chi and Koeske subsequently read the two lists of dinosaurs to the child three times each and asked him to remember them after each presentation of a list. He recalled twice as many items from the list of dinosaurs he knew more about (an average of 9.7) as from the list with which he was less familiar (an average of 5.0). The researchers concluded that the more one knows about a topic, the easier it is to recall items that pertain to it. Since a great deal of a person's knowledge base is stored as concepts, and the richness and elaborateness of these concepts are likely to increase as one's knowledge grows, the experiences children have accumulated by the time they reach middle childhood are likely to account for at least a part of the increase in their ability to remember.

Metamemory

Most 7- and 8-year-olds not only have more elaborate knowledge about the world than preschoolers but also are likely to possess more knowledge about memory itself (a concept referred to as **metamemory**). Even 5-year-olds have some understanding of the process of remembering. In one study, for example, they knew that it is easier to remember a short list of words than a long one, to relearn something you once knew than to learn it from scratch, and to remember something that happened yesterday than something that happened last month (Kreutzer, Leonard, & Flavell, 1975).

Most 8-year-olds have a much better understanding of the limitations of their own memories than most 5-year-olds, however. When shown a set of ten pictures and asked if they could remember them all, most of the 5-year-olds but only a few of the 8-year-olds claimed that they could. The 5-year-olds also failed to evaluate correctly how much progress they had made in remembering. Given unlimited time to master the set of pictures, the 5-year-olds announced that they were ready right away, even though they succeeded in remembering only a few of the items. The 8-year-olds, by contrast, knew enough to study the materials and to test themselves on their ability to remember (Flavell, Friedrichs, & Hoyt, 1970).

The combined picture

These data on the development of memory capacity and the use of remembering strategies, the increase in the knowledge base, and metamemory all confirm that memory improves between early childhood and the age of 7 or 8. Considered one at a time, they also undermine the hypothesis that a *qualitatively* new form of remembering arises in middle childhood. When familiar materials are presented to preschoolers in a simple format that they can understand easily, very young children are seen to use many of the strategies common in middle childhood, and their level of performance can be impressive.

But such similarities between the memory abilities of young children and 7- or 8-year-olds should not be overstated. Memory experiments conducted for research purposes are designed to pare away all but one focal process. But in a great many everyday circumstances the four aspects of remembering we have highlighted do *not* occur one at a time; two or more of them are likely to be simultaneously relevant. Children's ability to remember a list of words, for example, is affected by how rapidly they can store the words in short-term memory, how practiced they are at using such strategies as rehearsal and organization, and how well they can evaluate which parts of the list need the most attention. Because young children are less proficient in each of these processes, their performance outside of experiments is likely to suffer quite substantially. When deliberate remembering is viewed as a kind of cognitive activity that recruits and deploys a variety of specific mental resources, older children's common propensity to remember well in a wide variety of circumstances calling for deliberate remembering contrasts sharply with a younger child's fleeting and fragile competence in highly restricted contexts.

Concrete Operations: New Forms of Reasoning?

Without denying that changes in memory contribute to the new behaviors observed in middle childhood, Piaget believed that the key to these new behaviors lies in the crystallization of a new form of thought he referred to as **concrete operations** (Piaget, 1983; Piaget & Inhelder, 1969; Piaget, 1952b). An *operation,* in Piaget's terminology, is an internalized (mental) action that fits into a logical system (see Chapter 9, p. 318). When children begin to engage in concrete operational thinking, they become capable of combining, separating, ordering, and transforming objects in their minds. These mental operations, summarized in Table 12.1, are termed *concrete* because, during middle childhood, children still cannot manipulate objects mentally unless the objects are physically present.

Young children can physically manipulate objects, but in Piaget's view they cannot do so mentally. This puts them at the mercy of momentary appearances. Most 8-year-olds, by contrast, can manipulate blocks or clay or glasses full of water mentally, imagining not only what would happen if the physical materials were

TABLE 12.1

Piaget's Stages of Cognitive Development: Concrete Operational

Age, years	Stage	Description	Characteristics and Examples
Birth to 2	Sensorimotor	Infants' achievements consist largely of coordinating their sensory perceptions and simple motor behaviors. As they move through the 6 substages of this period, infants come to recognize the existence of a world outside of themselves and begin to interact with it in deliberate ways.	Features of thinking governed by concrete operations include * Decentration: Children can notice and consider more than one attribute of an object at a time and form categories according to multiple criteria. * Conservation: Children understand that certain properties of an object will remain the same even when other, superficial ones are altered. They know that when a tall, thin glass is emptied into a short, fat one, the amount of liquid remains the same.
2 to 6	Preoperational	Young children can represent reality to themselves through the use of symbols, including mental images, words, and gestures. Objects and events no longer have to be present to be thought about, but children often fail to distinguish their point of view from that of others, become easily captured by surface appearances, and are often confused about causal relations.	* Logical necessity: Children have acquired the conviction that it is logically necessary for certain qualities to be conserved despite changes in appearance. * Identity: Children realize that if nothing has been added or subtracted, the amount must remain the same. * Compensation: Children can mentally compare changes in two aspects of a problem and see how one compensates for the other. * Reversibility: Children realize that certain operations can negate or reverse the effects of others.
6 to 12	Concrete operational	As they enter middle childhood, children become capable of mental operations, internalized actions that fit into a logical system. Operational thinking allows children mentally to combine, separate, order, and transform objects and actions. Such operations are considered concrete because they are carried out in the presence of the objects and events being thought about.	Declining egocentrism * Children can communicate more effectively about objects a listener cannot see. * Children can think about how others perceive them (social perspective taking). * Children understand that a person can feel one way and act another.
12 to 19	Formal operational	In adolescence the developing person acquires the ability to think systematically about all logical relations within a problem. Adolescents display keen interest in abstract ideals and the process of thinking itself.	Changes in social relations owing to concrete operational thinking * Children can regulate their interactions with each other through rules and begin to play rule-based games. * Children take intentions into account in making judgments of "good" and "bad" behavior (autonomous moral reasoning) and believe the punishment must fit the crime.

transformed in some way but how such transformations could be undone.

In the transition from early to middle childhood, newly acquired logical underpinnings of thought transform all aspects of psychological functioning, according to Piaget. The world becomes more predictable because children come to understand that certain physical aspects of objects, such as size, quantity, and number, remain the same even when certain aspects of their appearances have changed. Children's thinking also becomes more flexible. They can think about alternatives when they try to solve problems, or mentally retrace their steps if they want to, as Raymond Birch did when he thought he had left his coat on the playground and asked permission to search for it.

Piaget believed that the advent of concrete operational thinking also changes children's social behavior: they gain an understanding of how to play games according to rules, and, as we shall see in Chapter 14, they can better understand social and moral rules. Children also become less susceptible to being caught in their own point of view and more skilled at interpreting other people's intentions. With these new insights the scope and complexity of their social relations increase.

Piaget invented a number of problem-solving tasks to enable him to diagnose the presence or absence of concrete operational thinking. Those involving conservation of quantities and logical classification demonstrate with special clarity his distinction between preoperational and concrete operational thinking (Inhelder & Piaget, 1964; Piaget & Inhelder, 1973).

Conservation

Conservation was Piaget's term for the understanding that some properties of an object or substance remain the same even when its appearance is altered in some superficial way. In the most famous version of the conservation task, touched on briefly in Chapter 9, children are presented with two identical glass beakers containing the same amounts of liquid (see Figure 12.8). The experimenter begins by asking, "Are the amounts of liquid in the two glasses the same?" If the child does not think so, the amounts are adjusted until the child agrees that the two glasses contain exactly the same amounts. Then the experimenter pours the contents of one of the beakers into a third beaker that is taller and thinner. Naturally, the liquid rises higher in the new beaker. Now the experimenter asks the child,

"Does the new beaker contain more liquid than the old beaker, does it contain the same amount, or does it contain less?"

Piaget claimed that young children are incapable of conservation because they lack concrete operations. In Piagetian interviews, 3- and 4-year-old children say that the amount of liquid has changed; the taller beaker has more. When asked why, they explain, "There's more because it's higher" or "There's more because it's bigger" or even "There's more because you poured it." They appear to focus their attention on a single aspect of the new beaker—its height. (Focusing on a single attribute of an object is the phenomenon of "centering," introduced in Chapter 9, p. 318.) Even when the experimenter points out that no liquid was added or subtracted, and even after a demonstration that the amount has not changed when the liquid is poured back into the original beaker, 3- and 4-year-olds still claim that there is more liquid in the taller beaker. When Piaget made these observations, he found that sometime around the age of 5 or 6 children's understanding of conservation goes through a transitional stage. At this point they seem to realize that it is necessary to consider both the height and the circumference of the beakers, but they have difficulty keeping both in mind simultaneously so that they can properly compare them.

According to Piaget, children begin to master the principle of conservation fully around the age of 8, when they understand not only that the new beaker is both taller and thinner but that a change in one dimension of the beaker is offset by a change in the other. Children who have acquired the concept of conservation of liquid recognize that it is *logically necessary* for the amount of liquid to remain the same despite the change in appearance. When asked the reasons for their judgment, they make such statements as "The liquid *can't* change just because you poured it." When pressed further, they offer several arguments showing that they understand the logical relationships involved:

- "They were equal to start with and nothing was added, so they are the same." This mental operation is called **identity;** the child realizes that a change limited to outward appearance does not change the amounts involved.
- "The liquid is higher, but the glass is thinner." This mental operation is called **compensation;** changes in one aspect of a problem are mentally

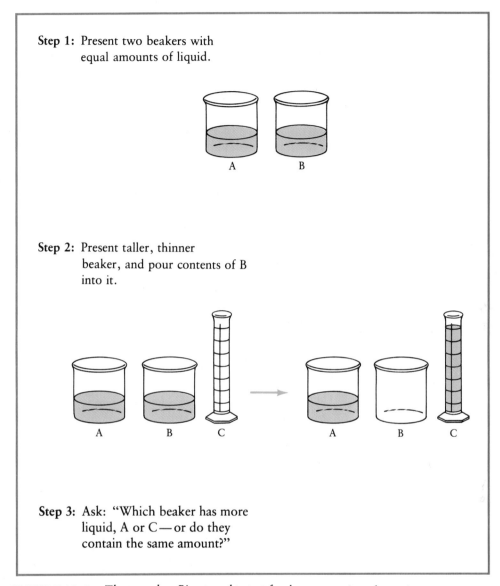

Step 1: Present two beakers with equal amounts of liquid.

Step 2: Present taller, thinner beaker, and pour contents of B into it.

Step 3: Ask: "Which beaker has more liquid, A or C — or do they contain the same amount?"

FIGURE 12.8   *The procedure Piaget used to test for the conservation of quantity.*

compared with and compensated for by changes in another.

• "If you pour it back you will see that it is the same." This mental operation is called **negation or reversibility;** the child realizes that one operation will negate, or reverse, the effects of another.

Children's developing understanding of number is another of the changes associated with concrete operations. Piaget called the ability to recognize one-to-

one correspondence between two rows of objects, despite a difference in the sizes of the objects or in their spatial positions, "conservation of number" (Piaget, 1952a).

The basic procedure for testing children's ability to conserve numbers is to present them with two rows of objects such as those shown in Figure 12.9a. Both the number of objects and the lengths of the two lines are equal, and children are asked to affirm that they are. Then one of the rows is spread out, as in Figure

Children's ability to reason more effectively as they grow older complicates the kinds of questions they begin to ask and the kinds of mischief they can get into.
(From Love Is Hell © 1985 by Matt Groening. All Rights Reserved. Reprinted by permission of Pantheon Books, a division of Random House, NY.)

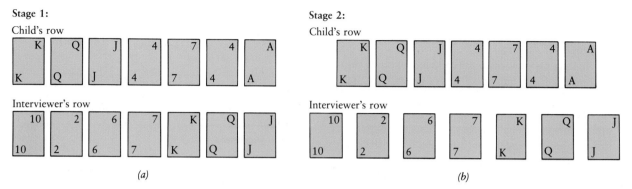

FIGURE 12.9 *The procedure used by Herbert Ginsburg to test for the conservation of number. (a) In stage 1, the child's and the interviewer's seven cards are arrayed at equal intervals. (b) In stage 2, the interviewer spreads out his cards and asks the child if she and the interviewer still have the same number of cards. (From Ginsburg, 1977.)*

12.9*b*, and children are asked if the numbers of objects in the two rows are still equal. Usually younger children fail to realize that number is conserved despite changes in location, whereas older children realize that the number remains the same.

The following interview with 6-year-old Deborah reveals the typical pattern of confusion experienced by children who have not fully mastered concrete operations. In this case, one attribute that Deborah perceives—length—overpowers her ability to use logic.

The interviewer *(I)* placed seven playing cards in a line on the table in front of Deborah *(D)*:

> **I:** How many cards?
> **D:** Seven.
> **I:** Make another line of cards that's the same number.

Deborah counted out seven cards—"One, two, three, four, five, six, seven"—and placed them directly above the interviewer's cards. The interviewer pointed to the bottom row, saying it was his, and to the top row, identifying it as Deborah's.

> **I:** Now does your line have just as many as my line? Is it just as many cards?
> **D:** Yes.
> **I:** All right, now watch what I do with my line.

The interviewer spread out his row of cards as Deborah watched. This is the "conservation" problem. The question is whether Deborah will *conserve* the initial equivalence despite the change in the appearance of the array.

> **I:** See. Now do we both have as many cards? Does this line have as many cards as this line?
> **D:** *(shakes her head no)*
> **I:** Which line has more?
> **D:** *(points to the interviewer's line)*
> **I:** Why does this line have more?
> **D:** Because it is out here. *(indicating that the interviewer's line is longer than hers)*
> **I:** O.K. I see . . . but how many cards are in my line?
> **D:** Seven.
> **I:** How many cards are in your line?
> **D:** Seven.
> **I:** How come this one has more if they both have seven?
> **D:** Because you spread them out. (Adapted from Ginsburg, 1977:26–27.)

In the first part of this interview, Deborah shows that she grasps the principle of one-to-one correspondence, which she uses to create a row of cards equal in number to the row created by the experimenter. When the length of the rows is made unequal because the experimenter spreads out his cards, however, the child fails to conserve the property of number of items in the row and instead makes her judgment on the basis of the length of the row.

In Piaget's view, once the child is capable of thinking operationally, individual bits of knowledge are no longer isolated or merely juxtaposed in the mind, as they were earlier. The capacity to perform concrete operations permits children to unify their experience into a coherent logical structure, which in turn enables them to think more systematically and effectively. In particular, the ability to perform the crucial operation of reversing something in their minds allows children to coordinate their representations of present and future states of objects and people. They can think ahead to see how actions may change the objects and then bring their thoughts back to the scene before them. If Deborah were able to apply concrete operations to the number conservation task, she would be able to say to herself, in effect, "There must be the same number of cards, because if the experimenter moved the cards in his row back to where they were at the beginning, nothing would have changed."

Alternative interpretations

It is difficult to overestimate the influence that Piaget's conservation experiments and his interpretations of the results have exerted on psychologists' interpretations of cognitive development. Dozens of books and hundreds of research papers have been written in attempts to extend, modify, or criticize Piaget's methods and conclusions.

By and large, when other investigators have replicated Piaget's methods, they have also replicated his results. But that has not prevented controversy over the conclusions he drew or attempts to create alternative problem-solving tasks to support conflicting interpretations of cognitive development in middle childhood.

Perhaps the most important criticism and source of alternative approaches focuses on the idea that Piaget's procedures actually create the phenomenon they were designed to explain. In its most general form, this criticism boils down to a claim that young children misinterpret what is being asked of them. The responses of 6-year-old Deborah, reported on page 454, can show how such misunderstandings might occur. Deborah understands the idea that numbers stand in a one-to-one correspondence with objects. She knows how many objects are in each row of playing cards. But

FIGURE 12.10   *A possible reason for wrong answers in conservation tasks. (From Siegal, 1991.)*

she still says that the more spread-out row of cards "has more."

Two alternative interpretations of children's failures in conservation tasks have received the bulk of experimental attention (Parsonson & Naughton, 1988; Siegal, 1991). First, perhaps children do not interpret such words as "same" and "more" in the way adults intend. Deborah, for example, may believe that cards that are spread out are "more" in the sense that they extend over a greater area.

The major way to test the idea that children interpret the experimenter's words incorrectly has been to present children with conservation tasks over and over again until they make the correct response and give a logical explanation as a way of making sure that they knew what was expected of them. The specific training procedures used have varied from one study to the next, but the experiments that produced the most convincing results demonstrated not only that non-conserving children could be trained to conserve and give logical answers, but that they spontaneously demonstrated conservation on problems different from the one they had been trained on. If they were trained to conserve number when an array of buttons was spread out, for example, they also conserved when balls of clay were deformed to make them long and thin or when glasses of water were poured into beakers of different shapes. When they are given some training and a small number of objects is used, children as young as 3 or 4 years can recognize one-to-one correspondence and conserve numbers (Gelman & Baillargeon, 1983).

The fact that children ordinarily too young to display understanding of conservation should "change developmental stages" as a result of a simple training procedure speaks against the idea that any deep misunderstanding is involved and shifts suspicion to children's misunderstanding of the words the adults use.

Another popular interpretation of children's failure in Piagetian tasks is that they are confused when adults repeat questions. (In the case of Deborah, the experimenter asks if the two arrays contain the same number twice: once before spreading out one array and again right after spreading it out.) If young children are at all uncertain about the right answer, they may change their answers when the experimenter repeats the question. In effect, they interpret the repeated question as an indication that their judgment of "same" was wrong (see Figure 12.10). In several experiments, Michael Siegal (1991) found evidence that children were falling prey to this kind of misunderstanding, again suggesting that it was the experimental procedures, not the logical concepts, that were causing them to err.

At present such controversies have yet to be resolved. The situation is not unlike the one we encountered in the case of developmental changes in remembering. Younger children show some understanding of conservation in simplified situations when the sources of confusion have been pared away. But children as old as 6 or 7 can still become confused if a conservation task involves a relatively large number of objects or a variety of other complications (Cowan, 1987). Piaget's argument that young children are *unable* to conserve numbers appears to be an exaggeration, but the increasing ability of older children to zero in on the required aspects of the task and to interpret what adults are asking of them remains to be explained.

Logical classification

Another important way in which children grasp relationships and unify their experiences into logical wholes is by classifying events or objects according to a variety of attributes. As we saw in Chapter 6 (p. 223), even in the third year of life children are able to separate a collection of objects into two categories (such as blue objects and red objects), even when other attributes differ (some of the blue objects are toy boats, say, and others are wooden dolls). The ability to classify increases during early childhood, but it remains fragile and breaks down quickly as soon as the situation is made more complex (Gelman & Baillargeon, 1983).

During middle childhood the ability to create categories increases in ways that support Piaget's ideas about children's emerging capacity to engage in mental operations. When children begin to collect stamps or

Systematic cataloguing of a rock collection requires the ability to classify according to multiple criteria.

baseball cards, for example, they often organize their collections according to multiple criteria. Stamps come from different countries, and are issued in different denominations and in different years. There are stamps depicting insects, animals, sports heroes, and space exploration. Children who organize their stamps according to type of animal and country of origin (so that, for example, within "France," all the tigers are together, all the rabbits are together, and so on) are creating a multiple classification for their collections. Similarly, the child who groups baseball cards according to league, team, and position creates a multiple classification.

When psychologists seek to demonstrate the changes that take place between early and middle childhood in children's ability to group objects into categories, they often ask children to classify objects such as those depicted in Figure 12.11. Unlike the very simple materials presented to 1- and 2-year-olds (Chapter 6, p. 223), the three kinds of objects (cars, boats, and airplanes) in Figure 12.11, all in three colors — red, blue, and yellow — permit multiple possibilities for grouping.

Younger children are unlikely to create a consistent classification of the objects (Frith & Frith, 1978). Instead, they usually create a number of small groups, each according to its own principle (a red and a blue airplane in one group, three yellow objects in a second group, a row of alternating boats and cars in a third group, etc.). Children over the age of 8 quickly figure out the underlying principle of cross-classification and create classification matrices like the one shown in Figure 12.11. They also are able to combine classes of objects, such as cat, dog, rabbit, into more general categories, such as animals.

The change in classifying abilities between early and middle childhood becomes apparent when children are asked to think simultaneously about the relationship between a category and its members, as in Figure 12.12 (Inhelder & Piaget, 1964). To make the task concrete, the animals in Figure 12.12 are usually presented to the child as toy figurines. Suppose that children are presented with ten figurines — five dachshunds, three poodles, and two cats. The children are asked a series of preliminary questions to make certain that they can identify each of the figurines and that they understand the words being used. Once the investigator is satisfied that the children are able to discuss the objects in question, they are asked the key question designed to reveal their comprehension of the relationship between a category and its parts: Are there more dogs or more dachshunds?

Children who are about 8 years old may find it peculiar to be asked such a question but they quickly

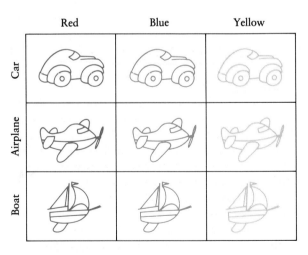

FIGURE 12.11   *Typical stimuli used to determine whether children are capable of systematically categorizing objects according to two or more dimensions simultaneously. Initially the objects are arrayed randomly. The child is then asked to place them in the two-dimensional matrix.*

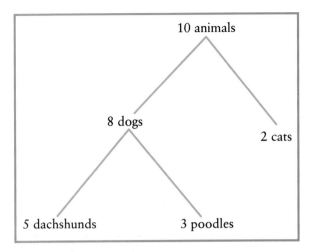

FIGURE 12.12 *A class inclusion problem. Before middle childhood, children find it difficult to keep in mind the fact that there are more dogs than dachshunds and more animals than dogs, even when concrete objects embodying these objects are there for them to see.*

figure out how to respond appropriately; younger children are likely to say that there are more dachshunds than dogs, and that there are more dogs than animals. This confusion about the relationship of parts to wholes makes it difficult for young children to reason systematically about objects or to communicate effectively with other people.

Considering Two Things at a Time

The ease with which 7- and 8-year-olds solve conservation and classification problems in comparison with the difficulties that younger children experience with the same problems demonstrates the power of what Piaget calls concrete operational thinking, the process in which elements of a problem are mentally combined, ordered, and reordered in a systematic way that corresponds to the actual relationships between the objects being thought about.

The common element underlying the many manifestations of concrete operational thinking is the two-sided, reversible nature of mental operations. In effect, children begin to think simultaneously about two aspects of a thing at a time. This common element influences children in a variety of ways.

Perceiving two things at a time

Clearly children would not be able to think logically about two aspects of a problem at a time if they had not perceived both aspects in the first place. It has been suggested that as children reach middle childhood, their reasoning improves not only because they use mental operations but also because they perceive more of the elements of a problem (Elkind, 1978; O'Bryan & Boersma, 1971). Younger children often fail to notice more than a single aspect of the problem, focusing on only one of its salient features (height, in the case of the conservation-of-liquid problem illustrated in Figure 12.8).

David Elkind (1978) showed children the pictures depicted in Figure 12.13, each of which is either ambiguous or made up of several elements. Children over 8 were generally able to see the alternative possibilities in the drawings right away, but the 6-year-olds rarely gave more than one interpretation of each drawing unless the alternatives were pointed out to them. Among 4- and 5-year-olds the tendency to latch on to a single interpretation was so strong that they did not perceive the alternative possibilities even when they were pointed out.

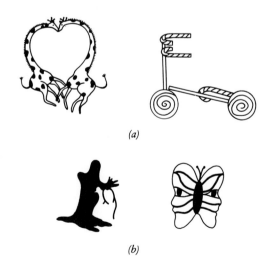

(a)

(b)

FIGURE 12.13 (a) *Parts and wholes: these figures depict objects constructed from other objects — a heart made of giraffes, a scooter made of candy canes and lollipops.* (b) *Ambiguous figures: a tree/swan and a butterfly/face. Until middle childhood the double significance of these kinds of figures is unlikely to be perceived. (From Elkind, 1978.)*

Research by Kenneth O'Bryan and Frederic Boersma (1971) suggests a relationship between young children's tendency to fasten onto only one attribute of a problem and their difficulty in the conservation task discussed on page 450. Using a camera that records eye movements, O'Bryan and Boersma found that children who did not understand the principle of conservation failed to look systematically at the various parts of the display. Their gaze seemed to be captured by—or centered on—a single attribute, which they used to guide their answer about the amount of liquid.

Declining egocentrism

Young children's bias toward interpreting events only from their own point of view never completely disappears. John Flavell, who has conducted a great deal of research on children's developing thought, comments:

> I believe we are "at risk" (almost in a medical sense) for egocentric thinking all of our lives, just as we are for certain logical errors. The reason lies in our psychological designs in relation to the jobs to be done. We experience our own points of view more or less directly, whereas we must always attain the other person's in more indirect manners. Our own points of view are more cognitively "available" to us than another person's. (1985:125)

Despite continuing slips and difficulties, however, children's reasoning becomes less egocentric in a broad range of situations during middle childhood. No longer is it necessary to create a friendly farm scene with a puppet driving around in a car to help children imagine how things look from the other side of the diorama in the three-mountain problem (see Chapter 9, p. 326). Now that children can keep two perspectives in mind more easily, they can also communicate more effectively, consider the views of others, and anticipate how other people will behave.

The growth of effective communication

A series of studies begun by Robert Krauss and Sam Glucksberg (1969), later replicated with many variations (summarized in Shatz, 1983), show that the decline in egocentrism during middle childhood can increase the effectiveness of communication. In these

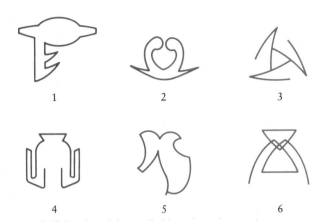

FIGURE 12.14   *Six novel figures used by Krauss and Glucksberg to study the development of communication skills. (From Krauss & Glucksberg, 1969.)*

studies (described in Chapter 9, p. 320) children sit facing each other across a table but are prevented from seeing each other by a barrier between them. They have duplicate sets of figures on the table before them. One child is asked to describe one figure at a time so that the other child can pick it out.

In many of Krauss and Glucksberg's experiments, children are shown novel figures that are difficult to describe with simple labels (see Figure 12.14). Children under the age of 7 typically respond to this task by choosing labels that are peculiar to their own experience ("It looks like my mommy's hat"). In middle childhood, children realize that they must choose features and labels that will mean something to their listener. They may say, "It looks like a flying saucer with a saw hanging off it." (The reader might check to see if this description is adequate!) Between the ages of 6 and 10, children double the number of features they mention to identify the target item for listeners (Rubin, 1973), indicating their growing ability to attend to more features of the blocks and to take their listeners into account.

Social perspective-taking

Tests of spatial perspective-taking (such as the three-mountain problem) and tests of communication require children to think about how objects will be perceived by others. Children must also develop ability in **social perspective-taking:** they must learn to think about how their actions and ideas will be perceived by others.

Children's understanding of others' social perspectives has been studied by Robert Selman (1976a, 1980). Selman asked children to listen to a brief story and then to answer questions posed in a clinical interview format. Here is one of the stories Selman used:

Holly is an 8-year-old girl who likes to climb trees. She is the best tree climber in the neighborhood. One day while climbing down from a tall tree she falls off the bottom branch but does not hurt herself. Her father sees her fall. He is upset and asks her to promise not to climb trees any more. Holly promises.

Later that day, Holly and her friends meet Sean. Sean's kitten is caught up in a tree and cannot get down. Something has to be done right away or the kitten may fall. Holly is the only one who climbs trees well enough to reach the kitten and get it down, but she remembers her promise to her father. (1980:36)

Once the story is read, children are asked to make judgments about the feelings and possible actions of the various characters. The comments of two children, one a preschooler, the other in middle childhood, indicate the differences in their understandings of other people's points of view.

A PRESCHOOLER'S UNDERSTANDING

Q: What do you think Holly will do, save the kitten or keep her promise?
A: She will save the kitten because she doesn't want the kitten to die.
Q: How will her father feel when he finds out?
A: Happy, he likes kittens.

A 9-YEAR-OLD'S UNDERSTANDING

Q: What punishment does Holly think is fair if she climbs the tree?
A: None.
Q: Why not?
A: She knows that her father will understand why she climbed the tree so she knows that he won't want to punish her at all. (Selman, 1976a:303, 305)

The preschooler clearly fails to consider that Holly and her father may not have the same point of view. The 9-year-old is aware that each person in the story has a distinct point of view. Moreover, the 9-

year-old's answers coordinate the points of view of Holly and her father in a plausible way. Note, however, that the older child still does not systematically take both persons' points of view into account. When children achieve the ability to be systematic about such questions, sometime in adolescence, they will find it difficult to say for certain how Holly's father will react. They will begin to realize that while the father may understand Holly's motive, he may not accept it.

The increase in children's social perspective-taking skills depends in part on their growing ability to consider both a person's external behavior and his or her psychological state. This developmental change is evident in a study by Dorothy Flapan (1968), who showed 6-to-12-year-old children an edited version of the film *Our Vines Have Tender Grapes*.

In a key episode of this film, a father punishes his daughter because she refuses to share her roller skates with a neighbor boy. But the father feels uncomfortable about the harshness of his punishment. Later, he seeks to make it up to his daughter by taking her to the circus.

After the children had viewed the film, Flapan asked them to explain what happened in a scene that takes place after the father has punished his daughter but before he tries to make up for his harshness. Contrast the account of a 6-year-old with that of a 12-year-old.

THE 6-YEAR-OLD'S ACCOUNT

At the beginning, her daddy was sitting in the chair in the living room looking at the paper, and the little girl got out of her bed and said, "Pa, will you kiss me good night?" And the daddy said, "Go to bed," and the little girl went to bed crying. And he tore up the paper and he threw it down on the floor. Then he went into the kitchen and was getting ready to go out to the barn. And the lady said, "Where are you going?" And he said, "Out to the barn." And the lady said, "At this time of the night?" And the man said, "Yes."

THE 12-YEAR-OLD'S ACCOUNT

The father was reading the newspaper, but he was thinking about something else. He couldn't really read it. And the little girl was looking down and asked her father if he didn't want to kiss her good night. The father wanted to say good night, but then he thought she did something bad, so he said,

"No. Go back to bed." And the girl was crying and did go back to bed. And the father tried to read the newspaper again, but he couldn't read it, so he threw it away. He wanted to go up to her and say it wasn't so bad. But he decided he better not. So he went to the kitchen and said to his wife he was going out. And the mother said, "I think you just want to be by yourself." And he said, "Yes." And the mother said, "There is a circus coming to town tonight." I think he is going to go to the circus with the girl now. (Flapan, 1968:31–32)

A striking difference in quality is evident in the two accounts. The 6-year-old makes virtually no reference to psychological states, while the 12-year-old provides a plausible interpretation of the father's internal conflict and explains the film's actions in psychological terms.

Cultural Variations in Cognitive Change

So far we have seen that adults around the world expect 7-to-12-year-old children to be capable of performing complex tasks independently. We have also seen that these children have become capable of more sophisticated forms of problem solving, in which they weigh two or more aspects of a problem or points of view simultaneously. We have remained cautious about concluding that such achievements signal a qualitatively new level of cognitive development, however,

because even younger children demonstrate similar abilities in some circumstances. In addition, researchers have raised questions about the universality of the presumed cognitive changes we have described. Do cognitive changes observed in Switzerland, Japan, or the United States occur in all of the world's cultures?

When psychologists use their standard procedures to test the performances of children in nonindustrial societies, where literacy and schooling either are absent or have been introduced only in recent decades, they often find cultural differences. It appears that many children in some cultures do not display the cognitive changes characteristic of the transition to middle childhood in industrialized societies (Segall et al., 1990; Jahoda, 1980).

The possibility that the development of problem solving and memory varies with the culture raises a new set of questions. Are the cultural conditions of industrialized countries necessary for the development of the cognitive abilities said to characterize middle childhood? Or do cultural circumstances merely influence the *rate* at which children proceed through universal stages? Does the evidence from nonindustrial cultures require a reevaluation of the whole idea of a universal stage of middle childhood (Laboratory of Comparative Human Cognition, 1983)?

Figure 12.15 summarizes the kinds of developmental growth patterns that might be found in different cultures. The figure refers specifically to concrete operations, but equivalent curves could be drawn for

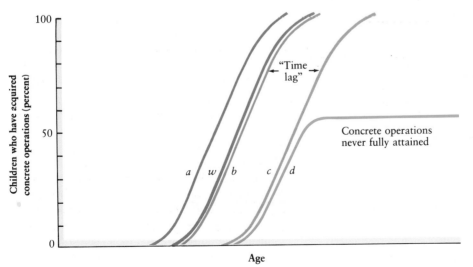

FIGURE 12.15 *Hypothetical curves representing the percentage of children who have acquired the concept of concrete operations at various ages. Curve w is assumed to be the developmental curve for a sample of children with a Western technological background. Curves* a, b, c, *and* d *are possible developmental curves derived from cross-cultural studies; their interpretation is discussed in the text. (From Dasen & Heron, 1981.)*

metamemory, egocentrism, or any other cognitive process. The curve labeled *w* (for "Western, technologically sophisticated cultures") represents the performance typical of children such as those Piaget worked with in Geneva. As these children grow older, more and more of them show that they understand the concepts being tested, until the curve levels off at 100 percent.

Curves *a*, *b*, *c*, and *d* represent possible patterns that might be observed in other cultures. Curves *a*, *b*, and *c* differ from curve *w* only in the rate of change: curve *a* represents earlier acquisition of the cognitive process; *b* represents development at essentially the same rate as the Western norm; *c* represents delayed development by Western standards. Curve *d* differs from the other curves not only in the rate of cognitive development but in the final level of performance, which remains significantly below 100 percent. Were researchers to discover a society in which the acquisition of concrete operations resembled curve *d*, it would counter the hypothesis that concrete operations are universal, because people whose development follows curve *d* never reach this stage of understanding at all.

Curves *a*, *b*, and *c* were the results that Piaget anticipated when he reviewed the meager data available in the mid-1960s, when research to test his theory in other cultures was just gaining momentum. Piaget (1966) assumed that the common phylogenetic heritage of our species would ensure that people everywhere would eventually attain the level of concrete operations.

A great deal of research has been conducted in other cultures to test these speculations as they apply not only to concrete operations but to other cognitive abilities as well (Laboratory of Comparative Human Cognition, 1983; Segall et al., 1990). Two of the most frequently studied cognitive abilities are conservation and free-recall memory, each of which raises important questions about universal stagelike changes in children's development, the role of culture in development, and standard psychological methods of assessment.

Studies of concrete operations

Studies of cultural variations in cognitive development using Piaget's conservation tasks have often found that children in traditional, nonindustrial societies follow pattern *c*, lagging 1 or more years behind Western

children in attaining the stage of concrete operations (Dasen, 1972, 1977; Dasen & Heron, 1981). But in several cultures investigators have encountered 12- and 13-year-old children and even adults who demonstrate no understanding of conservation in the Piagetian tasks (Dasen, 1977a, b, 1982).

Patricia Greenfield (1966) conducted a series of conservation studies among Wolof children in the West African nation of Senegal. Following the classical procedure, Greenfield first presented children with two beakers containing equal amounts of liquid, then poured the contents of one beaker into a taller, thinner beaker. Although the likelihood that children would display an understanding of conservation increased with age, only 50 percent of those 10 to 13 years old showed that they understood that the amount of liquid was not changed when it was poured from one beaker to another.

Similar results were obtained in studies of adults in cultures as varied as those found in central Australia, New Guinea, the Amazon jungle of Brazil, and rural Sardinia (Dasen, 1977a, b). Reviewing the evidence available in the early 1970s, Pierre Dasen wrote, "It can no longer be assumed that adults of all societies reach the concrete operational stage" (1972:31).

This conclusion was immediately challenged because of its wide-reaching implications. If adults lacked concrete operations, they would be severely handicapped in everyday life. Like preschool-aged children, they would not be able to think through the implications of their actions and would believe that objects changed simply because of their spatial distribution. They would be unable to understand another person's social perspective or to engage in causal reasoning. Dasen's conclusion would also justify the belief, popular in the nineteenth and early twentieth centuries, that "primitives think like children" (Hallpike, 1979).

Such implications led Gustav Jahoda (1980), a leading cross-cultural psychologist, to reject outright the possibility that in some cultures children did not eventually achieve the ability to think operationally. As Jahoda points out, it is difficult to see how a society could survive if its members were indifferent to causal relations, incapable of thinking through the implications of their actions, or unable to adopt other people's points of view. He concluded that "no society could function at the preoperational stage, and to suggest that a majority of any people are at that level is nonsense almost by definition" (1980:116).

Words alone do not suffice to settle such questions, however. To prove Dasen incorrect, one would have to produce evidence that the methods of observation used in these studies, which seemed straightforward enough, were misrepresenting their subjects' mental capacities.

One plausible explanation of the findings is that the people being tested failed to understand what was expected of them, either because they were unfamiliar with the test situation or because the experimenters did not make their intentions clear in an unfamiliar culture and language. (This is the same line of reasoning used to challenge Piaget's views on the thought processes of preschool-aged children—see Chapter 9.) Dasen and his colleagues tackled this problem by training subjects to solve conservation tasks (Dasen, Ngini, & Lavallée, 1979). They reasoned that if subjects were truly able to engage in concrete operational thinking but did not display their ability because they were unfamiliar with the tests, training on similar tasks should be sufficient to change their performance.

In a series of studies, the researchers demonstrated that by the end of middle childhood, relatively brief training in procedures similar to the standard conservation task was sufficient to change the pattern of performance on the conservation task itself. One such result is shown in Figure 12.16, which compares rural Australian Aborigine children with children in the city of Canberra. Without training, half of the Aborigine children appear not to acquire the concept of conservation of quantity at all (curve *d* in Figure 12.15). But when they are trained, their test results show that they do understand the basic concept of conservation of quantity. Even with training, the Aborigine children exhibit curve *c* in Figure 12.15: in acquisition of the concept of conservation they lag behind the Canberra children by approximately 3 years, suggesting that their culture does not provide the kind of experiences that in other cultures accelerates the acquisition of this concept.

This modified interpretation of cultural differences in the development of concrete operations is challenged by African psychologists who suggest that specialized training may be unnecessary and that no lags will appear if the researchers are of the same culture as the children they are testing and know the local language well. Psychologists native to the culture are able to follow the flexible questioning procedures that are the hallmark of Piaget's clinical interviews, procedures that seem to be even more effective than training in bringing out children's best performance.

Raphael Nyiti (1982), for example, compared the conservation performances of 10- and 11-year-old children of two cultural groups, both living on Cape Breton, Nova Scotia. Some of the children were of English-speaking European backgrounds and some

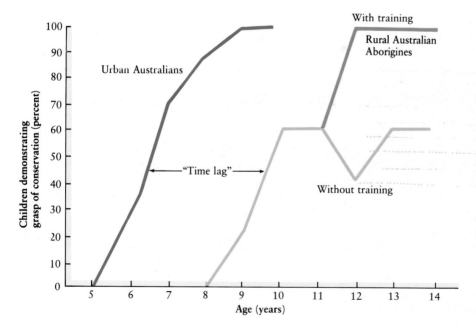

FIGURE 12.16 *Curves representing the actual percentages of Australian children who demonstrated a grasp of the concept of conservation. Australian Aborigines lagged behind urban Australian children with European backgrounds. Without training, 50 percent of the Aborigine children as old as 14 years failed to demonstrate an understanding of the concept of conservation. (From Dasen, Ngini, & Lavalleé, 1979.)*

The kinds of work that children are assigned afford different kinds of learning opportunities. Young street vendors acquire a variety of arithmetical skills that sometimes surpass those of children the same age who attend school.

were of the Micmac Indian tribe. The Micmac children all spoke Micmac at home, but they had spoken English in school since the first grade. The children of European backgrounds were all interviewed in English by an English speaker of European background. The Micmac children were interviewed in English once and in Micmac once.

The results of Nyiti's experiment clearly suggest that inadequate communication between researchers and children can be the source of apparent developmental lags in children of some cultures. When all children were interviewed in their native languages, no difference at all was found in the performances of the two cultural groups. But when the Micmac children were interviewed in English, only half as many of them as of the other children seemed to understand the concept of conservation. Nyiti (1976) obtained similar results in a study of children in his native Tanzania, as did other researchers in the West African country of Sierra Leone (Kamara & Easley, 1977).

Children of some nonindustrial societies appear to make a cognitive transition *earlier* than the industrialized norm (curve *a* in Figure 12.15). This result is obtained when the tasks used to assess cognitive development tap a nonindustrialized society's special experiences directly, as occurred in Jahoda's 1983 study of the development of the concept of profit (which has been shown to develop through several Piagetian-like stages). Jahoda arranged for 107 fourth-to-sixth-graders in the Central African country of Zimbabwe and 48 Scottish children of the same ages to act as shopkeepers in several mock business transactions. This task was assumed to be closer to the experience of the Zimbabwean children, all of whom had helped their parents with marketing and for whom trading was part of life.

Some of the hypothetical problems required the children to sell such goods as cloth and rice from a "store"; others required them to buy goods from a supplier. The main question was whether the children would know that they needed to sell the goods for more than they had paid for them, thereby demonstrating their understanding of the concept of profit. Jahoda hypothesized that the Scottish children would lag behind the children of Zimbabwe because they had had less experience buying and selling at a profit. This was exactly what he found: fully 84 percent of the Zimbabwean children displayed full or partial understanding of the concept, compared to only 45 percent of the Scottish children.

Taken as a whole, recent evidence appears to demonstrate that when Piaget's clinical procedures are properly applied, concrete operations are a universal cognitive achievement of middle childhood, just as Piaget (1966) assumed they were. However, there are quite dramatic cultural variations in children's familiarity with content and testing procedures, and these variations clearly influence children's performances (Greenfield, 1976; Jahoda, 1980; Laboratory of Comparative Human Cognition, 1983).

Studies of memory

Cross-cultural studies of memory call the universality of cognitive developments into question in a somewhat different way (Rogoff, 1982). Like the investigators of conservation, researchers who study memory find that children's familiarity with materials and procedures influences their performance. But unlike similar conservation research, when memory tests do make use of materials with which children are familiar, the results still show cultural differences in the kind of remembering that takes place.

For example, Michael Cole and his colleagues (1971; Cole & Scribner, 1974) studied the development of memory among tribal people in rural Liberia. To overcome the barriers of language and culture, these researchers observed everyday cognitive activities before conducting their experiments and worked closely with the college-educated local people who acted as the experimenters. Even with these precautions, they found striking cultural differences in the way tribal people went about remembering and solving the problems presented by their experimental tasks.

The nature of these cultural differences can be seen in studies of the development of *free-recall memory*. In a free-recall task people are shown a large number of objects, one at a time, and then asked to remember them. This kind of memory is called "free" recall because people are free to recall the items in any order they wish.

Below is a list of objects used in several of Cole's studies. The list shows that the objects appear to fall into four distinct categories. To make certain that American categories were not simply being imposed on Liberian reality, the researchers made preliminary investigations to ensure that Liberian subjects were

familiar with the items used and that they readily separated these items into the four groups indicated in the list (Cole et al., 1971).

plate	cutlass
calabash	hoe
pot	knife
pan	file
cup	hammer
potato	trousers
onion	singlet
banana	headtie
orange	shirt
coconut	hat

The researchers found that unlike children in industrial societies, Liberian children showed no regular increase in memory performance during middle childhood — unless they had attended school for several years. The nonschooled people improved their performance on these tasks very little after the age of 9 or 10. These subjects remembered approximately ten items on the first trial, and managed to recall only two more items after 15 practice trials. The Liberian children who were attending school, by contrast, learned the materials rapidly, much the way schoolchildren of the same age did in the United States.

Important clues to the causes of these differences were revealed by detailed analyses of the order in which the words were recalled. Schoolchildren in Liberia and the United States not only learned the list rapidly but used the categorical similarities of items in the list to aid their recall. After the first trial they clustered their responses, recalling first, say, the items of clothing, then the items of food, and so on. The nonschooled Liberian subjects did very little such clustering, indicating that they were not using the categorical structure of the list to help them remember.

To track down the source of this difference, the researchers varied aspects of the task. They found that if, instead of a list of objects presented in random order, the same objects were presented in a meaningful way as part of a story, their nonschooled Liberian subjects recalled them easily, clustering the objects according to the roles they played in the story.

Similar results on tests of children's memorization skills have been obtained in research among Mayan people of rural Guatemala. When Mayan children were presented with a free-recall task, their performances lagged considerably behind those of agemates in the United States (Kagan et al., 1979). Their performances changed dramatically, however, when Barbara Rogoff and Kathryn Waddell (1982) gave them a memory task that was meaningful in local terms.

Rogoff and Waddell constructed a diorama of a Mayan village located near a mountain and a lake, similar to the locale in which the children lived. Each child watched as a local experimenter selected 20 miniature objects from a set of 80 and placed them in the diorama. The objects included cars, animals, people, and furniture — just the kinds of things that would be found in a real town. Then the 20 objects were returned to the group of 60 others remaining on the table. After a few minutes, the children were asked to reconstruct the full scene they had been shown. Under these conditions, the memory performance of the Mayan children was slightly superior to that of their United States counterparts.

The implication of these memory studies differs from that of the cross-cultural studies of concrete operational thinking. The basic mental operations studied by Piaget and his followers are presumed to reflect the logic underlying everyday actions in any culture. The ability to remember is also a universal intellectual requirement, but specific forms of remembering are not universal. Those forms of memory most often studied by psychologists are usually associated with formal schooling.

Schooling presents children with specialized information-processing tasks — committing large amounts of information to memory in a short time, learning to manipulate abstract symbols in one's head and on paper, using logic to conduct experiments, and many more tasks that have few if any analogies in societies without formal schooling. The free-recall task that Cole and his colleagues initially used to assess memory among Liberian tribal people has no precise analogy in traditional Liberian cultures, so it is not surprising that the corresponding way of remembering would not be acquired.

The same conclusion applies to the vast majority of tasks psychologists use to assess other mental transformations that occur in middle childhood. Such tasks embody forms of activity that are specific to certain kinds of settings, especially schools and the modern technological workplace — settings that only some cultures provide. Performance on these tasks can be expected to be closely related to children's experience in school, but the relation of these tasks to other contexts of development is still poorly understood (Rogoff & Lave, 1984).

Is middle childhood a universal stage of development?

The evidence presented thus far provides a mixed picture with respect to the idea that middle childhood is a distinctive stage of development. The changes in adults' behavior that propel children into new activity contexts and the increase in children's biological capacities (including greater physical strength, dexterity, and perhaps a more complex brain structure) seem to occur in every culture during the years from 5 to 7. However, because the contexts into which children are put and the skills they are expected to acquire there vary markedly from one culture to the next, it is more difficult to determine whether the cognitive changes that Piaget and others have associated with middle childhood are universal.

These complexities require us to withhold judgment on the competing views about the distinctiveness of middle childhood. First, it is necessary to examine the special context of schooling, which is such an important part of growing up in industrialized countries. What are the cognitive demands specific to schooling? Is it possible that mastery of school-based tasks is essential to the production of basic changes in the way children think? Second, it is necessary to look into the kinds of activities that go on in peer groups, where children in middle childhood begin to spend so much of their time. Piaget, among others, argued that experiences in peer groups are crucial to the cognitive changes he associated with middle childhood. What is the evidence to support such a claim? Once we have a more well-rounded picture of children's experiences in these different contexts, we can return to examine the central issue of the distinctiveness of middle childhood and the forms of thought that are said to characterize it.

SUMMARY

1. The onset of middle childhood is recognized in cultures around the world. When children begin to lose their baby teeth, adults begin to assign them tasks that take them away from adult supervision and to hold them responsible for their own actions. This reorientation in adult behavior implies an increase in children's physical capacities, in their ability to follow instructions, and in their ability to keep track of what they are doing.

2. Around the start of middle childhood, the cerebral cortex reaches approximately adult size. This new level of growth is accompanied by myelination of pathways between brain areas and by changes in the basic pattern of electrical activity in the brain.

3. Increased lateralization of complex behaviors during middle childhood may play a role in the improvement of children's motor coordination.

4. It is widely speculated that changes in brain capacity produce distinctive cognitive changes during middle childhood, but there is little direct evidence to confirm these speculations.

5. Changes in memory associated with middle childhood in Western industrialized countries are manifested in children's increased capacity to hold several items of information in mind at one time, increased speed of storing and retrieving information, use of memory strategies, ability to think about remembering, and development of a relevant knowledge base.

6. There is evidence both for continuity and for discontinuous change in the quality of remembering between early and middle childhood. Many of the memorizing behaviors characteristic of middle childhood can be seen during early childhood in simplified and carefully supported contexts, but the range of circumstances in which children deliberately remember, rehearse, and reorganize to-be-remembered material expands during middle childhood.

7. Piaget believed that around the age of 7 children begin to think in terms of concrete operations, which permit them to combine, separate, reorder, and transform objects mentally. The advent of concrete operations is said to be manifested in:

   a. An understanding that the appearance of objects may change while their quantity or some other feature remains the same.

   b. The ability to classify objects according to multiple criteria, which enables children to think more systematically about the relation of one object to another.

   c. The ability to perceive alternative images in specially constructed pictures made up of many unrelated elements.

   d. The ability to communicate effectively about objects not visible to another person.

   e. The ability to adopt other people's social perspectives and to understand their intentions.

8. Cross-cultural research often identifies cultures in which children in middle childhood fail to display the changes in mental abilities that are characteristic of children in industrialized societies.

9. Cross-cultural differences on Piagetian conservation problems disappear when the subjects are provided special training or when the studies are conducted by experimenters who are versed in the language and familiar with the culture of the people studied.

10. Sizable variations in memory performance differentiate nonschooled people from those who attend school. These differences are most evident when the materials to be remembered are items selected at random or related to one another in ways that do not fit the patterns of the subjects' everyday activities. When the test materials are organized in ways meaningful to the subjects, however, no cross-cultural differences in performance can be detected.

11. Cross-cultural evidence on cognitive development indicates that culture-specific contexts are important contributors to development during middle childhood. Study of schooling and peer groups is required to resolve questions about development in middle childhood.

KEY TERMS

compensation	knowledge base	rehearsal
concrete operations	lateralization	reversibility
conservation	memory organization	social perspective-taking
identity	metamemory	strategy
	negation	

SUGGESTED READINGS

COLLINS, W. ANDREW (Ed.). *Development during Middle Childhood*. Washington, D.C.: National Academy Press, 1984.

This volume, summarizing the status of basic research on children from 6 to 12 years of age, was produced for the National Research Council. Individual essays focus on biological, behavioral, and social factors in development, as well as the important contexts of middle childhood — the family, the school, and the peer group.

KAIL, ROBERT. *The Development of Memory in Children* (3rd ed.). New York: W. H. Freeman, 1990.

A clear description of such important issues in the development of memory as the use of strategies, the growth of the ability to think about and monitor one's own memory, and the role of increasing knowledge of the ability to remember.

LABORATORY OF COMPARATIVE HUMAN COGNITION. "Culture and Cognitive Development." In P. Mussen (Ed.), *Handbook of Child Development*, Vol. 1: *History, Theory, and Methods*. New York: Wiley, 1983.

A thorough review of research on cognitive development in different cultures, focusing on middle childhood. In addition to information on cultural variability in cognitive development, the work explores the methodological problems of assessing memory and problem solving when children do not share a common cultural heritage with the experimenter and test constructor.

PIAGET, JEAN. *The Child's Conception of Number*. New York: Humanities Press, 1952.

The classic discussion of the logic of the conservation experiments as crucial evidence of the transformation from preoperational to concrete operational thinking. In addition, the book provides rich detail on Piaget's use of the clinical method as a means of studying cognitive development.

ROGOFF, BARBARA, & LAVE, JEAN (Eds.). *Everyday Cognition: Its Development in Social Context*. Cambridge, Mass.: Harvard University Press, 1984.

Essays by psychologists and other social scientists examining the impact of context on the process of cognitive development. The book also suggests ways to modify methods of studying children to take the role of context into account for the purpose of psychological assessments.

CHAPTER 13

Schooling and Development in Middle Childhood

•

I spent that first day picking holes in paper, then went home in a smoldering temper.

"What's the matter, Love? Didn't he like it at school, then?"

"They never gave me the present."

"Present? What present?"

"They said they'd give me a present."

"Well, now, I'm sure they didn't."

"They did! They said: 'You're Laurie Lee, aren't you? Well you just sit there for the present.' I sat there all day but I never got it. I ain't going back there again."

—LAURIE LEE, *CIDER WITH ROSIE*

In many parts of the modern world going to school is a legal obligation from the age of about 6 to 16. For 9 or more months of the year, 5 or 6 days a week, children spend 5 to 7 hours listening to teachers, answering questions, reading from books, writing essays, solving arithmetic problems in workbooks, taking tests, and generally "being educated." Before they take their places as adult workers, most young Americans will have spent more than 15,000 hours in classrooms. In some countries the amount of time children spend in school is even greater (Stevenson & Stigler, 1992). It would be very surprising indeed if the activities that children engage in at school did not play a central role in defining the characteristics of their middle childhood and in shaping their later lives.

To determine the influence of schooling on children's development, we need to address a series of questions:

- What is the nature of school as a context for children's development, and under what historical conditions do schools arise?
- How does learning in school differ from learning in other contexts?
- How does schooling influence cognitive development?
- What special abilities does schooling require and what factors account for success in school?

Answers to these questions have far-reaching significance in modern societies. Children who fail to thrive in school or who drop out may be confined as adults to less interesting and less secure work as well as to substantially lower incomes than children who meet society's expectations by completing high school (Sexton, 1961). Despite the emphasis society places on education, many millions of young people in the United States do not thrive in school. In the opinion of policy makers, resulting low levels of literacy and mathematics skills jeopardize the country's ability to compete effectively in the international arena (Educational Testing Service, 1988; U.S. Department of Education, 1983). These concerns have made the study of learning and development in school contexts one of the most active areas of research in developmental psychology.

THE CONTEXTS IN WHICH SKILLS ARE TAUGHT

In Chapter 10 we examined socialization in the family, concentrating on the ways in which young children are raised to acquire the basic knowledge, skills, and beliefs essential in their community. Socialization is a universal human process; as far as anyone knows, it has always been a part of human experience everywhere. In addition, as we discussed in Chapter 11, sometime around the sixth or seventh year of life, all societies begin to involve children in new tasks that are designed to provide them with the skills necessary for adult life. What is not universal is the specific content of the preparation and the way it is socially organized. Although formal schooling is an enduring fact of life in industrialized countries, it is only one of several ways in which societies have arranged for children to acquire adult skills and knowledge.

Education is a form of socialization in which adults engage in *deliberate teaching* of the young to ensure the acquisition of specialized knowledge and skills. It is not known if education existed among the hunter-gatherer peoples who roamed the earth hundreds of thousands of years ago, but deliberate teaching is not a conspicuous part of socialization in contemporary hunter-gatherer cultures (LeVine, 1974). Among the !Kung Bushmen of Africa's Kalahari Desert, for example, basic training in the skills expected of adults is embedded in everyday activity:

> There is . . . very little explicit teaching. . . . What the child knows, he learns from direct interaction with the adult community, whether it is learning to tell the age of the spoor left by a poisoned kudu buck, to straighten the shaft of an arrow, to build a fire, or to dig a spring hare out of its burrow. . . . It is all implicit. (Bruner, 1966:59)

In cultures such as the !Kung, inclusion of children in grownups' activities is the basic means by which adults ensure that children acquire culturally valued skills and knowledge.

In fact, the sharp divide between "grownups' activities" and "children's activities" that is characteristic of industrialized societies is far less sharply defined in much of the world (Whiting & Edwards, 1988). Children who have reached middle childhood in most societies are assigned tasks that are essential to their families—shopkeeping, weeding gardens, herding, cooking, hauling water, minding smaller children (the situation among the Gusii, discussed in Chapter 11). In such societies adults ensure that young children acquire valued adult skills by arranging for them to be with older children to whom tasks have been assigned.

When societies achieve a certain degree of complexity and specialization in the roles people play, the tools they use, and the ways they secure food and housing, preparation for some occupations is likely to take the form of an **apprenticeship**: a novice spends an extended period of time working for an adult master and learning the trade on the job (Coy, 1989; Greenfield & Lave, 1982; Lave, 1991). The settings in which apprentices learn are not organized primarily for the purpose of teaching. Rather, instruction and productive labor are combined; from the beginning, apprentices contribute to the work process.

Several of apprenticeship's distinctive features follow directly from the fact that the apprentice participates in adult work. Jean Lave (1977) found that apprentice tailors in Monrovia, Liberia, often have a hand in producing complicated items of clothing, with the level of their contribution scaled to the level of their expertise. The novice begins by cleaning the shop, running errands, and learning how to use a needle, thread, tape measure, and other tools. The master then oversees the child's practice in the tailor's craft in easy stages: sewing buttonholes, cutting cloth for inexpensive items such as hats and shorts, and finally the more difficult jobs of making gowns and suits. This regime gives apprentices a good overview of the entire process they need to learn while at the same time providing safeguards against costly mistakes.

Researchers have found that novice apprentices receive relatively little explicit instruction in their craft (Rogoff, 1990). Instead, they are given ample opportunity to observe skilled workers and to practice specific tasks. Manning Nash (1967) reported that in Guatemala novices learn to weave on a foot loom by sitting next to a skilled weaver for several weeks and observing him carefully. No explanations are offered. In other cases, as among Lave's tailors in Liberia, the master turns over responsibility for more and more complex aspects of the work until the apprentices are ready to go out on their own as masters themselves.

In many societies the apprentice's relationship with the master is part of a larger web of family relationships. Sometimes the master is a relative who trains the novice in exchange for training that the novice's parents give one of the master's children. Often the apprentice lives with the master and does farming or household chores to help pay for his upkeep. In this way the tasks of socialization, community building, and education are woven together (Goody, 1989).

Apprenticeship arrangements in which children learn by observing adults and participating in their work remains an important form of education despite the spread of formal education.

Although on-the-job training is still important in the industrialized world, formal education has surpassed it as the primary form of socialization. Schooling differs both from informal instruction in family settings and from apprenticeship training in four main ways (Greenfield & Lave, 1982; Scribner & Cole, 1973).

First, the *motives* for learning are different. When students begin school, they must work for years to perfect their skills before they can put their knowledge to any practical use. Apprentice tailors, by contrast, are present for the entire process of making a garment. Unlike students, they do not go through a long period of training without any notion of how the skills they are learning fit into the overall logic of an adult activity.

Second, the *social relations* of child and teacher differ from those of apprentice and master. Schoolteachers are assigned a carefully prescribed role in their pupils' upbringing that separates education from kinship obligations and real-life economic contributions. The teacher is likely to be a stranger who has been hired as an "educational expert." In the United States it is not uncommon to find a white, middle-class adult from the suburbs teaching in an inner-city classroom with predominantly ethnic minority pupils. The social background and values of teachers may thus differ substantially from those of their pupils' families, so

that effective teaching becomes difficult (Moll & Greenberg, 1990).

Third, the *social organization* of schooling differs from that of apprenticeship. Apprentices are most likely to learn in a workshop among people of diverse ages and levels of skill, so they have more than one person to turn to for assistance. At school, children usually find themselves in large rooms in the company of other children of about the same age and only one adult. They are expected to work individually, rather than cooperatively, or risk being labeled "cheaters."

Fourth, the *medium* of formal schooling is distinctive. Apprenticeship instruction is usually conducted in spoken language in the context of production. Speech is also important to formal schooling, but it is speech of a special kind that requires children to acquire skills and knowledge through the manipulation of *written* symbols.

It has sometimes been suggested that apprenticeship and schooling create fundamentally different kinds of learning environments that promote different kinds of cognitive skills. Sylvia Scribner and Michael Cole (1973) suggested, for example, that formal schooling is more likely to promote *general* strategies for learning, remembering, and problem solving, and that apprenticeship learning results in more *context-specific* skills. Recent studies indicate that the generality of the effects of a form of instruction depends upon how it is taken up into subsequent forms of activity (Cole, 1990; Lave & Wenger, 1991). As a consequence, there is a growing movement to include more aspects of apprenticeship in school curricula as a means to increase the effectiveness of school-based teaching (Collins, Brown, & Newman, 1989; Gardner, 1991).

To convey a deeper understanding of the distinctive nature of formal schooling as a context for development we will first examine more closely the historical development of literacy, numeracy, and schooling, as well as the special language of schooling. Such historical background also throws some revealing light on why many children experience difficulty in school.

THE NATURE OF SCHOOL LEARNING

Evidence indicates that formal schooling is historically recent and by no means universal. Formal systems of education are closely associated with the rise of large population centers and the use of systems of writing and record keeping (Harris, 1986; Goody, 1987).

The Historical Development of Literacy and Schooling

The remains of some of the earliest permanent settlements of human beings are found in the Middle East. In such early, predominantly agricultural villages, archaeologists discovered the first precursors of modern literacy: small clay tokens, such as those depicted in Figure 13.1. A settled, nonnomadic life permitted people to accumulate surplus goods to trade for things they could not grow or make themselves, and the tokens were very likely used to keep track of personal possessions and business transactions (Pfeiffer, 1977).

In a primitive way, these tokens served the fundamental purposes of writing systems. They were artificial signs that represented natural objects and regulated people's interactions with the physical world and with one another (Schmandt-Besserat, 1978). Because the tokens stood for actual objects, they enabled people to keep track of their goods over time without

FIGURE 13.1   *These tokens, found in the Middle East and dating from 10,000 B.C., are believed to be the earliest precursors of literacy. The shapes of the tokens and the marks on them stand for the identity and quantity of different objects. (From Schmandt-Besserat, 1978.)*

having to count them over and over again; because the tokens were small and sturdy, they could be carried from place to place as a kind of "promissory note" for purposes of trade.

The system of tokens remained unchanged for several thousand years until about 4000 B.C., when people discovered a means of smelting copper and tin to form bronze. Bronze revolutionized their economic and social lives. With implements of bronze, the earth could be tilled more deeply, extensive irrigation canals could be built, and armies could fight more effectively. For the first time, one sector of a population could grow enough food to support a large number of others besides themselves. This fact made possible a substantial division of labor and the development of city-states.

With the development of early cities, token-based record-keeping systems rapidly expanded, allowing kings to monitor the wealth of their lands, the sizes of their armies, and the collection of taxes. As the number of tokens increased, the system became cumbersome, and people began to draw pictures of tokens on clay tablets instead of using the tokens themselves (see Figure 13.2). This practice gave rise to *cuneiform writing* (cuneiform means, literally, "wedge-shaped," in reference to the shape of the symbols etched in clay) (Larsen, 1986; Schmandt-Besserat, 1978).

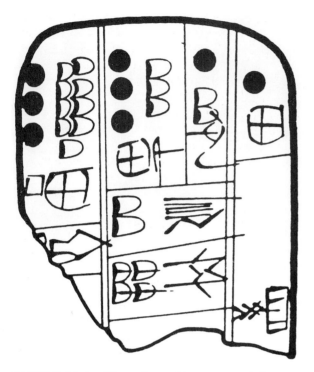

FIGURE 13.2   *The earliest writings were symbols etched on clay tablets. This tablet records information about a herd of sheep. It is thought to be the annual account of a shepherd, who records that of the 33 sheep in the herd, 12 gave birth to lambs, 2 were taken away for some reason, and 4 died. (From Strauss, 1988.)*

This transformation in the medium of recording made possible a crucial change in the way people related inscribed symbols to objects. The tokens stood for objects, and the earliest cuneiform writing retained pictures of the tokens as part of its notation system. But the newly complex political and economic conditions of cities required a writing system that could represent *relationships* among objects (such as "owed" or "paid") as well as the objects themselves. At this juncture a revolutionary discovery was made: pictures representing objects could be supplemented by symbols representing the sounds of language (Larsen, 1986).

Written symbols for words and numbers are direct extensions of the mediating capacity of spoken language. Since, as we noted in Chapter 8, language is a representation of reality, the written form of a language must be considered a representation of a representation of reality. The essential advantage shared by all written notation systems is that they extend the power of language in time and space (Goody, 1977, 1987). Sounds disappear as soon as they are spoken, and even the loudest speakers can project their voices over only a short distance. Words that are written down, by contrast, can be carried great distances with no change in their physical characteristics. Writing freezes words in time; what is once written down can be returned to and thought about time and again in its original form. In this respect, written notations are a form of memory.

The system of cuneiform writing that arose in connection with the earliest large cities could be mastered only after long and systematic study. But so important was this new system of written communication that societies began to devote resources to support selected young men with the explicit purpose of making them *scribes,* people who could write. The places where young men were brought together for this purpose were the earliest schools.

Activities in these early schools were in some ways specific to the societies in which they arose, and in other ways startlingly modern. Two dozen or more students sat in rows facing a teacher, who lectured to them and drilled them in "the basics" while they scratched out their lessons on writing tablets. In addition to learning the rudiments of writing, reading, and arithmetic, these early students learned the record-keeping procedures they would use as civil servants after they graduated.

Literacy and Schooling in Modern Times

Evidence from the Middle East and elsewhere indicates that once literacy and numeracy became central to the functioning of society, schooling arose as a means of ensuring that children would master the new technologies for representing, preserving, and communicating information (Goody, 1987).

For centuries the tradition of literacy and schooling in the Western world was confined largely to the children of the elite. Not until the nineteenth century, in response to the Industrial Revolution, did nations begin to institute mandatory schooling and strive for mass literacy.

The spread of schooling in the past two centuries has created a distinctive set of social problems with important implications for children's development.

Two hundred years ago, when mass literacy programs were in their infancy, there were two kinds of education. "Higher education," intended for a small elite, included some mastery of classical literature and the rudiments of geometry and algebra. A tutor was hired to see that the children of the wealthy gained a degree of learning equal to their status in life. These children received individual attention and as much explanation as the tutor could provide.

The "mass education" provided to the great majority of children was quite different. It enabled them to recite from a religious text such as the Bible or the Koran, to write simple messages, and to calculate simple sums, but the instruction provided the masses was not intended to give them a general education as we understand that term today. When teachers were confronted by 20, 40, or more students instead of one or two, instruction was based largely on drill and practice combined with oral imitation of the teacher (Resnick & Resnick, 1977). Today many societies expect all of their children to attain a level of education that was once reserved for small elites, but the children are still expected to do so in large classes in which they receive little or no individual instruction.

In two respects, the task facing children in the modern classroom is far more difficult than the task faced by their ancient predecessors in the Middle East.

First, since the advent of literacy some 6000 years ago, human knowledge has been accumulating far more rapidly than it did in all the prior history of *Homo sapiens*. While civilizations have waxed and waned, scientific and technological knowledge has continued to accumulate, adding progressively to the lessons that children have been asked to master as part of "the basics." Second, the mode of representing knowledge has undergone fundamental changes that have made reading and writing a more complex undertaking.

Development of the Alphabet

Methods of representing language have developed in different ways in different parts of the world. Some societies developed a symbol to correspond to each distinct concept, as occurred in China, while in other societies the system of representation focused on units of sound, as occurred in Greece (Harris, 1986). Each representational strategy has certain costs and benefits to its users (Hatano, 1987). Here we will concentrate on the alphabet, a system descended from cuneiform writing.

The first written symbols that stood for units of sound corresponded to syllables. Thus a word such as

Mastery of written symbol systems is the focus of most early eduction.

"lackadaisical" would be written with five symbols corresponding to *lack-a-dai-si-cal*. This kind of writing continued in use for about 2000 years. The process of creating a system for representing language sounds reached what many people consider its height around the seventh century B.C., when the Greeks began to use a new system of writing that represents each significant sound variant (phoneme) with a single symbol (Harris, 1986; Logan, 1986).

A phoneme-based writing system might seem very inconvenient. The two-syllable word "zygote," for example, is written with a total of six symbols instead of two. But in fact the system, which in English came to be called the alphabet (after the first two characters representing two phonemes in the Greek language, alpha and beta), enabled spoken language to be represented by only two dozen or so basic symbols and a few punctuation marks. By contrast, there are more than 8000 basic syllables in English. Representing each syllable with its own symbol would make mastery of written English a formidable task indeed!

The economy of using phonemes, however, is offset by the fact that phonemes are abstractions; they cannot be pronounced in isolation, but only in combinations that we perceive as syllables. As a consequence, it is difficult for teachers to communicate clearly about the basic correspondences that children must acquire in order to read.

DEVELOPMENT AND ACADEMIC SKILLS

From the earliest schools of the ancient Middle East to neighborhood schools throughout the modern world instruction has focused on the mastery of two basic symbol systems, written language and mathematics. Each challenges children in a special way.

Learning to Read

There is a broad agreement among psychologists that reading is a complex cognitive skill that requires the coordination of a number of interrelated sources of information (Crowder & Wagner, 1992; National Academy of Education, 1985). A good deal is known

about how skilled readers translate marks on a page into meaningful messages (Hall, 1989). But despite intensive research efforts throughout this century, and especially over the past two decades, the process of *learning* to read is still not well understood (see Adams, 1990, and Foorman & Siegel, 1986, for a juxtaposition of conflicting views). The problem is an important one because at present a great many children of normal intelligence fail to acquire reading skills deemed adequate for productive participation in a modern society (Miller, 1988).

The components of reading

Current theories of reading recognize two major component processes: **decoding,** the process by which letters of the alphabet are associated with corresponding phonemes of the spoken language, and **comprehension,** the process by which meaning is assigned to the text. There is also broad agreement that the full act of reading entails both fluent decoding and the ability to read for meaning. Controversy centers on the details of how these two processes combine and how they should be taught.

All widely used methods of instruction focus on the communicative functions of print and the importance of understanding the author's message, but strategies for achieving this goal differ. Some reading researchers believe that children should learn to decode *before* they are asked to derive meaning from the written word. Others believe that reading for meaning should be a part of the instruction from the beginning.

The process of learning to decode the symbols of the writing system into the sounds of spoken language is more complex than it may at first appear (recognizing the symbol *a* as the sound /a/, for instance). Although even very small children can say their ABC's, rote recitation is not the same as knowing how an alphabet represents sounds. When children recite the alphabet, they are pronouncing the *names of letters;* they are *not* making sounds that they recognize as representing parts of words.

A special problem that affects children who are learning to read and write in English is that there is no one-to-one relationship between letters of the alphabet and the phonemes that make up English words. Instead, the 26 letters of the English alphabet represent 52 different basic phonemes (Henderson, 1982). So, for example, a child acquiring literacy in English must grasp the fact that while *t* remains *t*, it is not

Learning letter-sound correspondences so that written symbols can be decoded to find the corresponding sounds is one of the essential tasks confronting beginning readers.

pronounced the same way in the words "tea" and "both," while such seemingly different letters as *g* and *f* can be used to produce a single sound, as in "muff" and "rough."[1] Similar lessons must be mastered for the entire alphabet.

A second difficulty in teaching children to decode an alphabetic writing system stems from the fact that teachers cannot demonstrate isolated phonemes, the linguistic units represented by alphabetic characters. At best they can try to illustrate individual sounds by pronouncing whole words or syllables and suggesting how the separate sounds are blended. Suppose, for example, that you ask a child to say the word "caterpillar." After each attempt, ask for a slower pronunciation. The result will be something like this:

    caterpillar
    caaaterrpiiilarr
    caaaaaat eerrrr piiiiiiil laaarrrrrrr

The word takes longer and longer to say, but most significant, it breaks down into parts corresponding to

syllables. It does not and cannot isolate the sounds so that *c* is pronounced separately from *a*, which is pronounced separately from *t*, and so on.

Faced with this problem, the teacher may start out with a short word such as "cat" and attempt to illustrate the sounds corresponding to the pattern of letters. Even if children have learned the names of the three letters, "cee," "ay," and "tee," this learning may not help much. No matter how quickly the children pronounce these names in sequence, the result will not be the sound blend that transforms *c-a-t* into "cat."

Top-down versus bottom-up processing

The other point on which experts agree is that reading requires the coordination of two kinds of information: "lower-order" information, about the actual letters and words in the text, and "higher-order" information, about the topics being referred to. This notion of reading as a synthesis of qualitatively different kinds of information is a relatively recent development. Early in the twentieth century, the process that resulted in reading comprehension was believed to progress from the "bottom up": the instructor began either by teaching children to recognize a basic set of words or by first sounding out the letters that compose the words, thereby giving access to individual word meanings;

---

[1] A famous example of the alphabet's complex relation to spoken English is attributed to the British writer George Bernard Shaw (1963). Shaw suggested that the word "fish" should be written "ghoti": *gh* as in "cough," *o* as in "women," *ti* as in "nation."

these individual words were then put together into phrases, then into sentences, then into paragraphs, and so on. A good deal of research in recent years has demonstrated that such bottom-up processes are only half of the story (Crowder & Wagner, 1992; National Academy of Education, 1985). When we read for meaning, information supplied by words and phrases must simultaneously be integrated with the knowledge we already have. Interpretation based on prior knowledge is often referred to as "top-down" processing because it begins with general knowledge that becomes increasingly focused as the reader combines it with the bottom-up information obtained from letters and words.

The kind of top-down information needed for meaningful reading can be seen in the following two passages. Although the words in each are of roughly equivalent difficulty (that is, the "bottom" components are similar), note how much more difficult it is to understand the second passage:

PASSAGE 1

When Mary arrived at the restaurant, the woman at the door greeted her and checked for her name. A few minutes later, Mary was escorted to her chair and was shown the day's menu. The attendant was helpful but brusque, almost to the point of being rude. However, her meal was excellent, especially the main course. Later she paid the woman at the door and left.

PASSAGE 2

The procedure is really quite simple. First you arrange items into different groups. Of course, one pile may be sufficient depending on how much there is to do. If you have to go somewhere else due to lack of facilities that is the next step, otherwise you are pretty well set. It is important not to overdo things. That is, it is better to do too few things at once than too many. In the short run this may not seem important but complications can easily arise. A mistake can be expensive as well. . . . After the procedure is completed, one arranges the materials into different groups again. Then they can be put into their appropriate places. Eventually they will be used once more and the whole cycle will then have to be repeated. (Bransford, 1979:135)

The first passage is easy to comprehend because we realize right away that it is about a restaurant. We have well-worked-out scripts for restaurants (see Chapter 9) that allow us to anticipate what will happen, thereby providing top-down constraints on our reading of the passage. The second passage is harder to comprehend because it fails to provide a top-down indication of what it is about. You can verify this difference by trying to remember, without looking back, what the second passage says. As soon as you are told that the passage is about washing clothes, however, the separate sentences fall into place as you read, and the passage is easily interpreted. If readers cannot imagine what a passage is about, even if they can decode all of the words, the interpretation that is crucial to true reading does not occur.

When children are just learning to read, all three aspects of the process—low-level text information, high-level general information, plus the act of combining the two to produce an interpretation—can be sources of serious difficulty. If children do not know how to assign letters to sounds, they may struggle over the interpretation of specific words letter by letter ("c-c-che-check"). As the child struggles with the letter-sound correspondences, the knowledge that the passage is about a restaurant experience may be momentarily forgotten, and the child may substitute "cheek" for "check." After only a few such misreadings a child becomes confused and discouraged, and further reading becomes even more difficult.

Controversy continues over the best way to ensure that children learn all the necessary aspects of reading. Where should reading instruction begin? Should word recognition and decoding come first, or should reading for meaning be a part of each lesson from the beginning?

Jean Chall, who advocates the code-emphasis-first approach, proposes a stage theory of reading acquisition (Chall, 1983; Chall, Jacobs, & Baldwin, 1990):

Stage 0. Prereading: birth to age 6   Children arrive at school with at least some notion of what it means to read. For several years they have been "reading" in the broad sense of interpreting events on the basis of partial signs. They know that when they see the car in the driveway, their mother is home from work, and that a stormy look on their father's face means they should stay out of his way until his mood brightens. They can also "read" in the somewhat more conventional sense of identi-fying the logo of their favorite fast-food restau-rant, and they have acquired some knowledge about words, such as that some words have the same beginning or ending sounds (alliteration, rhyme); that some words can be broken into parts; that words can be put together in various combi-nations. They may also know that books are sources of good stories. But with few exceptions, children entering school for the first time cannot read in the sense of scanning alphabetic print and interpreting what it says.

Stage 1. Decoding: grades 1–2, ages 6–7 The basic task of stage 1 is to learn the arbitrary set of letters in the alphabet and their correspondence to the sounds of spoken language. Some researchers be-lieve that children best learn to decode when they are drilled on the correspondences of sounds and letters in all of the basic patterns in the language (a "phonics" approach); others believe that children can naturally figure out these patterns if they learn to recognize enough words (a "whole word" ap-proach). The evidence favoring one or the other approach is hotly disputed (Crowder & Wagner, 1992).

Stage 2. Confirmation, fluency, ungluing from print: grades 2–3, ages 7–8 During this stage, new readers are supposed to confirm and solidify the gains of the previous stage. They move from rela-tively halting and uncertain application of their decoding skills to rapid, fluent, automatic decod-ing. Chall argues that once they no longer read letter by letter or word by word, children can begin to think about the topic while they are read-ing about it, a process that she refers to as "unglu-ing." Their reading, however, is restricted to texts that they know well.

Stage 3. Reading for learning something new: grades 4–8, ages 9–14 Chall believes that a basic shift in the reading process occurs in the late elemen-tary school years. Children in the primary grades *learn to read*, whereas in secondary school they *read to learn:*

During Stages 1 and 2 what is learned concerns more the relating of print to speech while Stage 3 involves more the relating of print to ideas. Very

little new information about the world is learned from reading before Stage 3; more is learned from listening and watching. It is with the beginning of Stage 3 that reading begins to compete with these other means of knowing. (1983:20–21)

Stage 4. Multiple viewpoints: grades 9–12, ages 15–18 This stage involves the kind of reading ex-pected in high school. Various theories and facts are juxtaposed, and the reader must reconcile the different viewpoints in order to interpret a text's meaning.

Stage 5. Construction and reconstruction: postsecond-ary level At this stage readers are doing more than learning what the writer has to say. They are engaged in their own process of knowledge con-struction in which written texts become aids in solving problems. At this stage readers know when to skim, when to reread, and when to take notes. As Chall phrases it, this highest level of reading entails "a struggle to balance one's com-prehension of the ideas read, one's analysis of them, and one's own ideas about them" (1983:24).

Many teachers adhere to some version of Chall's approach. In the early grades they emphasize "word-attack skills" and use a variety of workbook assign-ments to foster the ability to decode automatically (see Figure 13.3). The texts used in this approach are spe-cially designed to give intensive practice in phonetic analysis and as a consequence do not make for very interesting reading. Aesop's tale of the tortoise and the hare, for example, has been presented like this:

Rabbit said, "I can run. I can run fast. You can't run fast."
Turtle said, "Look, Rabbit. See the park. You and I will run. We'll run to the park."
Rabbit said, "I want to stop. I'll stop here. I can run, but Turtle can't. I can get to the park fast."
Turtle said, "I can't run fast. But I will not stop. Rabbit can't see me. I'll get to the park." (Quoted in Green, 1984:176)

Some psychologists and reading teachers believe that in their zeal to ensure that all children "break the code," those who follow Chall's approach are leaving

Color the part brown if the word ends like 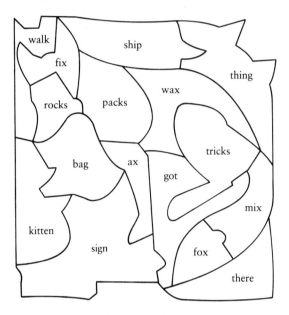. What is the surprise?

FIGURE 13.3   *A great deal of reading instruction in the elementary school grades is carried out in workbook exercises, such as this one for building decoding skills.*

out the basic purpose of reading—to be able to interpret the world in a new and exciting way. In effect, critics charge, curricula that require children to be efficient decoders before they learn about meaning give them the wrong idea about reading. The narrow focus on decoding, it is argued, may even cause some children to fail: because they get stuck on the fine points of decoding for so long and are given such uninteresting materials to read, they stop trying to read for meaning altogether (Coles, 1990).

Alternatives to the code-emphasis-first approach are based on the idea that reading is a special case of comprehending the world through symbols, an ability that children acquire when they learn language in the first place. Advocates of a "comprehension first" approach argue that reading for comprehension should not be put off until the children are fluent decoders. Since children arrive at school already able to "read the world," the main requirement of a good reading curriculum is many rich opportunities to experience written language as a useful tool for exploring and problem solving. Emphasis on correct and automatic decoding is replaced by a belief that children should be allowed

to invent their own spellings for words they do not know and to read any texts they perceive as instrumental to their goals. At first their spelling and text interpretation may not be strictly correct according to conventional standards, but that is not a matter for concern. What matters is that the children perceive reading and writing as good ways to achieve important goals; gradual mastery of conventional forms will follow.

Kenneth and Yetta Goodman refer to such a comprehension-based alternative as a *whole-language* curriculum, because reading is not taught in isolated lessons. Instead, literacy is made a part of the ongoing intellectual life of the classroom; when children begin to experience reading and writing as useful, they will naturally incorporate it into their repertoire of cognitive skills (K. Goodman et al., 1987; Y. Goodman & K. Goodman, 1990).

Once children catch on to reading, it can become a source of pleasure. This boy's comic book promises him not only the adventures of Tarzan, but knowledge of the world of zoology as well.

Evidence indicates that it is not appropriate to take an either/or approach to teaching children how to read. On the basis of their review of methods for teaching reading, Steven Stahl and Patricia Miller (1989) argue that teachers should use a strategy that integrates the use of interesting and motivating literature with specialized training in decoding. The proper mix of methods may vary from one child to the next, so no rigid guide can be provided. The main task is to maintain children's interest in learning to read for the pleasure it can bring them and at the same time to provide assistance to ensure that children achieve high levels of word recognition and decoding skills.

Reciprocal teaching

Reciprocal teaching, a method devised by Annemarie Palincsar and Ann Brown (1984), is one way in which instruction can be organized to permit integration of decoding skills and comprehension. Palincsar and Brown began with the observation that some students who are trained in the code-emphasis-first approach manage to develop reasonably good decoding skills but have great difficulty comprehending what they have just read (Walczyk, 1990).

In the reciprocal teaching procedure, a teacher and a small group of students read silently through a segment of text and then take turns leading a discussion of its meaning. The discussion leader (adult or child) begins by *asking a question* about the main idea and then *summarizes* the content in his or her own words. If members of the group disagree with the summary, the group rereads the passage and discusses its contents to *clarify* what it says. Finally, the leader asks for *predictions* about what will come next.

Note that each of the key elements in reciprocal teaching—*asking questions about content, summarizing, clarifying,* and *predicting*—presupposes that the purpose of the activity is to figure out what the text means. And because these strategies are talked about (and argued over), the children are able to see and hear the teacher and other children model the behaviors necessary for comprehension. As Brown and her colleagues (1992) point out, reciprocal teaching is an application of Vygotsky's notion of a "zone of proximal development" that allows the children to participate in the act of reading for meaning even before they have acquired the full set of abilities that independent reading requires.

A number of studies (summarized in Brown & Campione, 1990) have found reciprocal teaching to produce rapid and durable increases in children's reading skills. Figure 13.4 shows the findings of a recent study of a group of junior high school students who had problems reading for meaning. Here reciprocal teaching is compared with procedures in which the

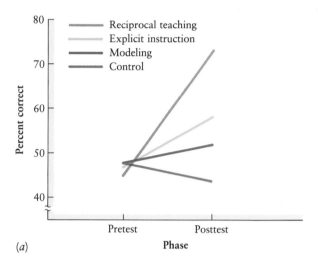

(a)

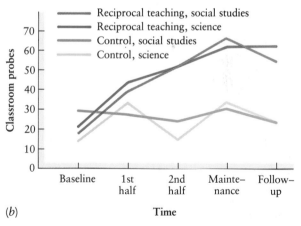

(b)

FIGURE 13.4   (a) *The effectiveness of reciprocal teaching is compared with explicit instruction, modeling, and a control group that received no practice. All forms of instruction led to improved reading, but reciprocal teaching was by far the most effective procedure.* (b) *Reciprocal teaching instruction generalizes to social studies and science classrooms. When compared to students who received no special reading instruction, students given practice in reciprocal reading showed large and sustained improvements in their social studies and science courses. (From Brown et al., 1992.)*

teacher modeled comprehension strategies aloud or taught procedural rules but did not arrange for students to take turns. Reciprocal teaching not only proved to be more effective than the other two procedures when the students were tested in their reading classes (Figure 13.4*a*), but it also produced marked improvement in their reading in social studies and science (Figure 13.4*b*).

The work of Brown and her colleagues does not imply that decoding is irrelevant to mature reading; rather, it emphasizes the importance of integrating decoding with the process of comprehension. Most important, it provides examples of relatively simple procedures that make a large difference in learning outcomes.

Learning Arithmetic

The teaching of formal mathematics, like the teaching of reading, has been the subject of intense investigation during most of this century. Rochel Gelman and her colleagues (Gelman, Meck, & Merkin, 1986) write that learning mathematics requires the acquisition and coordination of three kinds of knowledge:

1. *Conceptual knowledge,* or the ability to understand the principles that underpin the problem.
2. *Procedural knowledge,* or the ability to carry out a sequence of actions to solve a problem.
3. *Utilization knowledge,* or the ability to know when to apply particular procedures.

As we indicated in Chapters 9 (p. 324) and 12 (p. 444), most children arrive at school with some of each kind of knowledge, and cross-cultural research reveals that even societies with no tradition of schooling and literacy use methods of counting and solving arithmetic problems (see Box 13.1). Young children know, for example, that numbers and objects can be put into one-to-one correspondence with each other and that the last number used in counting an array stands for the total (conceptual knowledge). They have an intuitive grasp of how to add and subtract very small quantities (procedural knowledge). They also know that if Suzie has two candies and her mother gives her one more, they need to add, not subtract, to arrive at the total (utilization knowledge) (Klein & Starkey, 1987). These rudimentary kinds of knowledge provide an es-

sential starting point for learning more advanced mathematics in school, but each must be constantly expanded to keep up with the increasingly complex forms of mathematics that schooling introduces.

Jeffrey Bisanz and Jo-Anne Lefevre (1990) provide a demonstration of the development of children's *conceptual* knowledge in their study of children's understanding that adding a number to a given quantity and then subtracting it leaves the total unchanged. They presented problems of the form "$a + b - b$" (for example $10 + 8 - 8$) to subjects ranging in age from 6 years to adulthood. They found that between 6 and 9 years of age, calculating became progressively speedier, but the children did not seem to grasp the principle. They would dutifully add the second number to the first and then subtract the third number from the sum. The larger the second and third numbers, the longer it took them to get an answer (it required more time to figure out the answer to $10 + 28 - 28 = ?$, for example, than to solve $10 + 8 - 8 = ?$). Most 11-year-olds and virtually all adults ignored the particular value of the second and third numbers; they responded very rapidly, no matter how large the second and third numbers were, indicating that they had mastered the principle involved.

Investigators have also documented the development of children's *procedural* knowledge in the course of mathematics instruction (Hughes, 1986; Siegler, 1991). For example, Robert Siegler and his colleagues have studied the development of strategies that are essential to mastery of addition, subtraction, and other mathematical operations (Siegler & Shrager, 1984; Siegler, 1991). To add two numbers, such as 4 and 4, first- and second-graders may count on their fingers starting with one (1-2-3-4 . . . 5-6-7-8). Eventually they may hit on the strategy of holding up fingers corresponding to the first of the pair and counting up (4 . . . 5-6-7-8). If asked to add 2 + 9, first-graders may start with 2 and then use their fingers to add nine more; a year or so later children are more likely to convert "2 + 9" into "9 + 2," a strategy that both simplifies the task and shows their understanding of the principle that order is not important in addition. And, of course, if they think they know the sum "by heart," children will recall the answer (or what they believe to be the answer) directly. As children grow older and more knowledgeable, direct recall comes to dominate addition of small numbers, and a variety of paper-and-pencil procedures replace fingers as strategic tools under most circumstances.

BOX 13.1
The Human Body as a Calculator

Early in their developing understanding of numbers, youngsters hit upon the use of their bodies as aids in keeping track of quantity. Throughout the ages and in many cultures children have used their fingers when they began to count (Conant, 1896); in some societies much more elaborate counting systems based on the body have been devised. The Oksapmin of New Guinea, for example, use a system involving 29 body parts (Saxe, 1981). Other societies have used such conventional counters as kola nuts and cowry shells (Gay & Cole, 1967; Zaslavsky, 1973). Such systems can be more powerful than one might imagine. West Africans who exchanged cowry shells for goods supplied by Portuguese merchants in the seventeenth century could calculate sums running into the tens of thousands using cowry shells as counters.

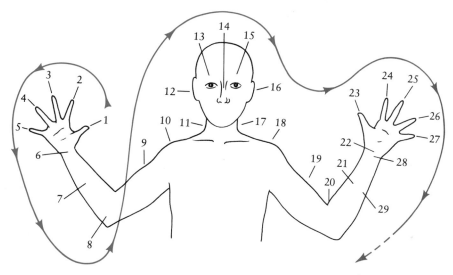

The Oksapmin of New Guinea do their arithmetic by using a basic set of 29 numbers corresponding to a conventionalized sequence of body parts. (From Saxe, 1981.)

Utilization knowledge (knowledge of which procedures to use in order to solve a given problem) increases as children grow older and receive more instruction, but it also depends a great deal on the particular way a problem is presented. This was made clear by Terezinha Carraher, David Carraher, and Analúcia Schliemann (1985) in a study of mathematical problem solving among child street vendors in Recife, Brazil. Carraher and her colleagues first posed arithmetic problems to the children on street corners or at the market as part of the process of buying the goods the children were selling. A typical exchange with a 12-year-old child went like this:

Interviewer: How much is one coconut?
     Child: 35.
Interviewer: I'd like ten. How much is that?
     Child: *(Pause)* Three will be 105; with three more, that will be 210. *(Pause)* I need four more. That is . . . *(pause)* . . . I think it is 350.

After the interviewers posed a number of such questions, they gave the children a paper and pencil and asked them to solve identical problems. In the follow-up interview they presented two different kinds of problems. In some cases the problems were

Counting on their fingers is a universal strategy for beginning arithmetic students.

presented strictly as mathematical operations (How much is 10 times 35?) and in others the mathematical operations were presented as word problems. During the informal first interview, the children were correct 98 percent of the time. In the second interview they were correct on the word problems 74 percent of the time, but could solve only 37 percent of those that required mathematical computation but had no real-world connections.

Analysis of the interviews revealed that in the formal interview the children failed to use the successful computational strategies they had applied in their selling activity. One 9-year-old quickly responded to an offer to buy 12 lemons at 5 cruzeiros each by counting "10, 20, 30, 40, 50, 60" while separating out two lemons at a time. But when she was asked to solve the problem "12 × 5," she "brought down" first the 2, then the 5, and then the 1 and came up with an answer of 152. She failed to employ a strategy she knew to be effective and was unable to replace it with a correct, school-based form of computation. Such results indicate that the way problems are posed influences the extent to which children utilize their existing knowledge.

Recommendations for effective teaching of mathematics vacillate between two poles, analogous to the dichotomy between code emphasis and meaning emphasis in reading instruction. At one end are psychologists who believe that instruction is best carried out through intensive drill and practice on small parts of the overall process; at the other end are psychologists who believe that learning should begin with understanding and then proceed to practice (Resnick & Ford, 1981).

The drill-and-practice approach is exemplified by the work of E. L. Thorndike (1922), an early pioneer in educational research. Thorndike believed that learning arithmetic was a matter of building strength in a large number of specific habits orchestrated within a single system. Once automated, the individual parts could fit into a total problem-solving organization, "as a soldier fighting together with others," to produce the correct answer (Thorndike, 1922:139).

Although Thorndike's emphasis on drill to create automatic knowledge became a standard part of educational practice, it met with strenuous objections from psychologists and educators who believed that drill would promote only a low level of competence in arithmetic. The alternative approach, learning with understanding, was championed by William Brownell (1928), who believed that it is important to make problems meaningful to children so that their drill and practice will enable them to calculate automatically without sacrificing understanding. Proper understanding, Brownell claimed, would enable students to go beyond the narrow confines of the practice problems and apply their knowledge in novel situations. In terms of the theory advanced by Gelman and her colleagues (p. 482 above), Brownell's approach can be understood as advocating teaching methods that enable children to use their conceptual knowledge to support their procedural and utilization knowledge.

Research has supported Brownell's view. For example, T. R. McConnell (1934/1958) compared a strict drill method with meaningful instruction. The drill method simply repeated arithmetic "facts" (5 + 7 = 12, 4 + 5 = 9, etc.). The meaningful instruction presented the same facts in conjunction with pictures and objects that allowed students to verify their answers against real-world knowledge. McConnell found that straight drill was an efficient way to acquire rapid and automatic responses to the training materials, but when the students were tested on novel combinations, the meaningful approach led to significantly better results.

It is now agreed that both drill in computation and practice in generalizing computations to a variety of meaningful new problems are necessary. There is no single agreed-upon procedure for mixing these two aspects of instruction, but a variety of effective instructional procedures have been worked out for specific content domains (Dienes, 1966; Rasmussen, Hightower, & Rasmussen, 1964; Resnick & Ford, 1981).

The Special Language of Schooling

As we have seen, schooling is a distinctive form of socialization in which children are expected to learn how to gain information about the world by manipulating symbols — while sitting at their desks. Instead of learning by doing, children must learn by reading, writing, and calculating. In most cases, the real world to which their learning applies is outside the classroom. At times, such as when students are asked, "What is 5 + 5?" there is no allusion to the real world at all.

Instructional discourse

In addition to reading, writing, and calculating, schoolchildren must also learn a way of using language that is peculiar to the classroom. Classroom conversation, or **instructional discourse,** differs in both structure and content from the ways adults and children speak in their everyday lives outside of school. The central goals of instructional discourse are to give children information stipulated by the curriculum and feedback about their efforts to learn it while providing teachers with information about their progress (Mehan, 1979; Shuy & Griffin, 1978; Sinclair & Coulthard, 1975).

Learning the proper ways to behave in the classroom is an important part of children's school experience.

One of the distinctive characteristics of instructional discourse is the **initiation-reply-evaluation sequence,** demonstrated in Table 13.1. In this pattern, the teacher initiates an exchange, usually by asking a question; a student replies; and then the teacher provides an evaluation.

The initiation-reply-evaluation sequence includes a form of question-asking that is rarely encountered in everyday conversation, the "known-answer question" (Searle, 1969). When the teacher asks Beth, "What does this word say?" that teacher already knows the answer; he or she is really seeking information about Beth's ability to read, so the question is really a way to evaluate Beth's progress. Learning to respond easily to known-answer questions, in addition to learning the academic content of the curriculum, is an important early lesson of schooling (Mehan, 1979).

The initiation-reply-evaluation sequence can be quite flexible. When Ramona hesitates (Table 13.1), the teacher immediately calls on Kim, who provides the answer. This arrangement allows Ramona to learn from Kim's answer and the teacher's response to it at the same time that it allows the teacher to assess Ramona's need for more instruction.

Another special facet of school-based language is the emphasis placed on the linguistic form of students' replies, as we see in the lesson on the use of prepositions shown in Table 13.2. This interchange has several interesting aspects. First, note that the teacher gradually builds an understanding of the linguistic form that she considers appropriate by using the turn-taking rules of classroom discourse. Second, note that for the purposes of this lesson, the truth of what the children say is less important than the way they say it. Cindy gave the full answer the teacher was looking for but, as Richard noticed, Cindy had used a crayon of a different color! She was correct in school terms, although she clearly violated norms of everyday language use.

In everyday conversations one usually has ample opportunity to check one's expectations against reality. But in the closed world of the classroom, the real-world objects and events that are the content of the conversation are not available to help children interpret what is being said. Consequently, children must learn to focus on language itself as the vehicle of information in order to master the specialized knowledge taught in school. (Box 13.2 discusses the special problems that arise when children come to school speaking only a foreign language.)

Learning notation systems

The writing of numbers in mathematical notation systems is another distinctive feature of school language. One of the first tasks children face when they encounter mathematics at school is to learn to write the first ten digits. Since it is only a cultural convention that the symbol 9 should stand for the spoken word "nine," the first stage of this process is memorization.

Once children learn the first ten digits, they must learn the conventions for writing larger quantities and the concept of place value that underpins our notation system. The required correspondences are not intuitively obvious. Some first-graders, for example, have

---

TABLE 13.1
Initiation-Reply-Evaluation Sequence

Initiation	Reply	Evaluation
T [Teacher]: . . . what does this word say? Beth.	*Beth:* One.	*T:* Very good.
T: What does this word say? Jenny.	*Jenny:* One.	*T:* Okay.
T: Now look up here. What does this word say? Ramona.	*Ramona:* Umm.	
T: Kim.	*Kim:* First.	*T:* Okay.

Source: Mehan, 1979.

TABLE 13.2

Lesson on Use of Prepositions

Initiation	Reply
T [Teacher]: Make a red flower under the tree. *(pause)* Okay, let's look at the red flower. Can you tell me where the red flower is?	*Children:* Right here, right here.
T: Dora?	*Dora:* Under the tree.
T: Tell me in a sentence.	*Dora:* It's under the tree.
T: What's under the tree, Dora?	*Children:* The flower.
T: Tell me, the flower . . .	*Dora:* The flower is under the tree.
T: Where is the red flower, Richard?	*Richard:* Under the tree.
T: Can you tell me in a sentence?	*Richard:* The flower is under the tree.
T: Cindy, where is the red flower?	*Cindy:* The red flower is under the tree.
Richard: [*noticing that Cindy actually drew the "red" flower with a yellow crayon*] Hey, that's not red.	

Source: Mehan, 1979.

---

written "23" as "203" (Ginsburg, 1977). This representation, although erroneous, follows the conventions of our way of speaking ("twenty-three" or 20-3) and our system for representing spoken language in print. Unfortunately, from the child's point of view, conventions for representing place value in arithmetic do not follow the conventions of the writing system. While numbers such as 203 ("two hundred and three") are, so to speak, pronounced from left to right, they are actually constructed right to left from the decimal point, which is ordinarily written only when some fraction of a whole number is to be indicated. So, for example, "Two hundred and three and forty-five hundredths" is written 203.45.

It takes most children several years to master these complexities, a fact that influences their ability to carry out such basic operations as addition and subtraction. Common mistakes are to add numbers in the order in which they are said — from left to right — and line up numbers from the left. Misunderstandings of this kind produce such errors as

$$\begin{array}{r} 123 \\ +1 \\ \hline 223 \end{array}$$

Children who produce such answers are behaving as they are expected to do in school in one important respect: they are applying previously acquired knowledge to solve new problems. As long as they don't become discouraged, they eventually catch on to the logic underlying the written number system their teachers present to them.

THE COGNITIVE CONSEQUENCES OF SCHOOLING

It seems reasonable to assume that many thousands of hours spent sitting in classrooms learning about the world through reading and writing should have considerable impact on cognitive development during middle childhood and beyond. After all, schooling expands children's knowledge base, provides massive experience in deliberate remembering, and trains children in systematic problem solving, all of which, as we saw in Chapter 12, are areas of cognitive functioning that appear to undergo fundamental changes in middle childhood.

BOX 13.2
School Success and Bilingualism

Over 2.5 million children in the United States come to school unable to understand or speak the English language. In a landmark decision in 1974, the U.S. Supreme Court declared that these children are denied equality of treatment even if they are given the same facilities, textbooks, and teachers because they are "effectively foreclosed from meaningful education" (*Lau v. Nichols,* p. 26). Since that time local school districts have spent well over $1 billion on programs intended to remedy this situation.

Although educators agree that the major goals of their programs are to increase these children's proficiency in the English language and promote their scholastic achievement, opinion continues to be sharply divided on how this goal should be achieved (McGroarty, 1992; Moll, 1992). On one side of the debate are those who believe that children should be immersed in the English language so that they can quickly achieve the competence necessary to participate in all aspects of the curriculum. Educators who favor this view believe that time spent communicating in the child's native language only postpones the day when the child will be fluent in English. On the other side are those who believe that a firm grounding in basic literacy and numeracy skills in the child's home language will serve as a foundation for later academic achievement in courses taught in English.

Research on this issue is clouded by the difficulty of conducting experiments in which ideal versions of the two strategies can be pitted against each other. Researchers have had to take advantage of the fact that some schools have adopted an "English-only" approach while others have provided instruction in children's native language for 2 or 3 years before moving them to English-based instruction. The difficulty with this kind of comparison is that it is virtually impossible to ensure that only the variable being studied—the use of English-only versus home-language-first instruction—differs in the programs being compared. Additional factors, such as the cultural and socioeconomic backgrounds of the children, the training and enthusiasm of the teachers, and the resources available for teaching, may vary in uncontrolled ways that undermine the logic of experimental comparisons.

Stephen Krashen and Douglas Biber (1988) summarize the evidence on the effectiveness of California's extensive bilingual education effort by declaring that "the fastest route to second language learning is through the first language" (p. 19). Acknowledging that bilingual education is not always successful, however, Krashen and Biber identify three characteristics of successful programs:

1. High-quality teaching of subject matter in the first language without translation.
2. A firm foundation of literacy in the first language.
3. After items 1 and 2 are accomplished, special teaching of English as a second language and supplementary subject matter instruction in English.

Another important factor not named by Krashen and Biber is that the process of acquiring the second language be given enough time. A study among Navaho children compared the English-language skills of children who were taught only in English (including special instruction in English as a second language) with the progress made by children in a bilingual program in which they were first taught to read in Navaho and later transferred to English classes. Initially the children in the bilingual program fared poorly, but after three or four years the bilingual group was outperforming those who had experienced instruction in English from the beginning (Rosier, 1977).

The need to allow time for children to learn enough English to take full advantage of school instruction is also highlighted in studies by Lily Wong-Filmore (1985). She found that although minority-language children generally become reasonably fluent in spoken English in two or three years after starting school in the United States, much more time is needed to become proficient in using the language they encounter in school. Wong-Filmore reported that as many as four to five years were required to master the language skills needed for academic success.

A major obstacle that educators face in attempting to apply the lessons from this line of research is that there are far too few bilingual teachers who are qualified to teach the many languages represented by the school-aged population of the United States. In California, for example, nearly 1.5 million children for whom English was a second language were attending school in 1990. Almost 60 percent of them were judged to have limited proficiency in English, a

Number of Limited- and Fluent-English-Proficient Students in California Public Schools, 1990, by Language

Language	Limited-English-Proficient Students	Fluent-English-Proficient Students	Total
Spanish	655,097	408,280	1,063,377
Vietnamese	34,934	27,681	62,615
Filipino	16,338	35,135	51,473
Cantonese	21,154	23,113	44,267
Korean	13,389	20,178	33,567
Cambodian	19,234	5,243	24,477
Hmong	18,091	3,824	21,915
Mandarin	7,201	13,257	20,458
Lao	12,177	4,275	16,452
Armenian	9,046	3,021	12,067
Japanese	5,505	6,541	12,046
Farsi	4,875	7,041	11,916
Other Chinese	3,293	4,220	7,513
Portuguese	2,830	4,601	7,431
Arabic	2,771	3,248	6,019
Punjabi	2,093	2,161	4,254
Hindi	1,754	1,892	3,646
Mien	2,834	508	3,342
Samoan	1,490	1,842	3,332
Ilocano	1,041	1,468	2,509
Hebrew	904	1,399	2,303
Russian	1,510	669	2,179
Thai	852	985	1,837
Tongan	956	610	1,566
Taiwanese	560	899	1,459
Other Filipino	584	853	1,437
Rumanian	820	504	1,324
German	307	956	1,263
Gujarati	501	705	1,206
Urdu	396	413	809
French	265	539	804
Assyrian	415	384	799
Italian	153	443	596
Pashto	375	128	503
Polish	247	201	448
Indonesian	295	152	447
Greek	103	310	413
All other languages	17,141	33,956	50,967
State totals	861,531	621,505	1,483,036
Percent	58.0%	42.0%	100.0%

Source: Adapted from California State Department of Education, 1990.

situation that would seem to call for bilingual instruction if the current research is valid. But the schools had to contend with more than 50 languages! Except in districts that have a large concentration of children with the same linguistic background, the creation of high-quality bilingual programs is all but impossible. The great challenge facing these schools is how to cope with the linguistic variety in their classrooms in a manner that works for children who enter the system with limited English-language skills.

If the cognitive performances of children who have attended school are compared with those who have not, it is possible to begin to specify the special contributions of schooling to cognitive development. One way to make such comparisons is to take advantage of bureaucratic rules concerning how old a child must be to attend school. Another is to conduct research in societies where schooling is not universal.

The School Cutoff Strategy

In many countries school boards set the birth date that a child must have passed in order to begin attending school. To enter grade 1 in September, children in Edmonton, Alberta, Canada, must have passed their sixth birthday by March 1 (Morrison, 1988). Six-year-olds born after that date must attend kindergarten instead and their formal education is delayed for a year. If the intellectual performances of children who were born in January or February are compared with those born in March or April at the beginning and end of the following school year, it is possible to assess the impact of schooling with age held virtually constant. This procedure is known as the *school cutoff strategy*.

A number of studies that have used this strategy indicate that schooling brings about a marked increase in the sophistication of some cognitive processes but not others. Lisa Smith (1989) compared the ability of first-graders and kindergartners to recall pictures of nine common objects. The first-graders were, on average, only a month older than the kindergartners, and at the start of the school year the performances of the two groups were virtually identical. At the end of the school year, the first-graders almost doubled the number of pictures they could remember, and they were seen to engage in active rehearsal strategies. The kindergartners did not improve at all, and for the most part did not engage in active rehearsal. Clearly, one year of schooling had brought about a marked change in performance.

Frederick Morrison (1989) found that children who attended first grade improved in their ability to analyze the sound components of words, a cognitive skill that seems to be promoted by reading instruction. Sorel Cahan and Nora Cohen (1989) obtained very similar results with respect to the ability of Israeli children to solve a variety of cognitive tasks that are often included in IQ tests.

There is an interesting exception to these findings. Jeffrey Bisanz (1989) tested children's responses to a standard Piagetian test of number conservation (see Chapter 9, p. 319) and also asked them to add small numbers. He found that performance in the conservation task improved largely as a consequence of *age* but that mental arithmetic improved almost exclusively as a consequence of *schooling*. Bisanz's findings both confirm the importance of schooling in promoting a variety of relatively specific cognitive abilities and support Piaget's belief that the ability to conserve quantity develops without any special instruction at some time between the ages of 5 and 7.

Cross-cultural Research on the Effects of Schooling

The school cutoff strategy provides an excellent way to assess the cognitive consequences of small amounts of schooling but it is applicable for only one year. Studies in societies where schooling is available to only a part of the population provide the other major route for assessing the contribution of formal education to cognitive development in middle childhood. Four cognitive domains have figured heavily in this research: concrete operations, lexical organization (the organization of word meanings), memory, and metacognitive skills (the ability to reflect upon one's own thought processes).

Concrete operations

As we saw in Chapter 12, studies of concrete operational thinking are more or less evenly split between those that find an advantage for children who have attended school and those that do not (Rogoff, 1981). When schoolchildren do well on the standard Piagetian tests, their success appears to have less to do with concrete operational thinking than with a greater familiarity with the circumstances of test taking. Such specialized knowledge includes familiarity with the forms in which questions are asked, a greater ease in speaking to unfamiliar adults, and an ability to speak the language when the testing is not conducted in the child's native language. Overall, this evidence, supplemented by Bisanz's findings, suggests that the development of concrete operational thinking increases with age and is relatively unaffected by schooling, in accord with Piaget's theory.

Lexical organization

We have seen that unlike children who are assigned to tend sheep, to care for younger siblings, or to weave rugs to be sold in the market, children who attend school spend vastly more time learning through talking and listening than through doing. Moreover, the talk encountered in school differs in content and form from the talk familiar to children who do not attend school. Not only does talk in school require the mastery of abstract concepts, it requires that mastery to be used away from the real-world contexts to which they apply. A biology lesson about the way sunlight influences plant growth, for example, may be taught in a windowless room with no plants in it. As a consequence, children must learn to create meaning from subtle differences in the ways words are combined. This feature of schooling has led some psychologists to suggest that the underlying organization of children's *lexicons*—the total store of words in their vocabulary—is changed by schooling (Luria, 1976; Olson, 1978).

The impact of schooling on lexical organization was demonstrated by Donald Sharp and his co-workers in a study of Mayan Indians on the Yucatan peninsula of Mexico (Sharp, Cole, & Lave, 1979). When adolescents who had attended high school one or more years were asked which words they associated with the word "duck," they responded with other words in the same taxonomic category, such as "fowl," "goose," "chicken," and "turkey." When adolescents in the same area who had not attended school were presented with the same word, their responses were dominated by words that describe what ducks do ("swim," "fly") or what one does with ducks ("eat").

The results of this study and findings from other parts of the world (such as Cole et al., 1971) suggest that schooling sensitizes children to the abstract, categorical meanings of words, in addition to building up their general knowledge. Not that word meaning fails to develop in children who have not attended school. The nonliterate Mayan farmers studied by Sharp and his colleagues knew perfectly well that ducks are a kind of fowl. Although they did not refer to this fact in the artificial circumstances of the free-association task, they readily displayed awareness of it when they talked about kinds of animals on their farms.

Memory

In Chapter 12 we saw that during middle childhood children in some cultures do not show the same increase in memory skills that U.S. children do on the standard tests that psychologists generally use. Research comparing schooled and nonschooled children in other societies, like the comparative data on first-graders and kindergartners presented earlier in this chapter, has shown that schooling is the crucial experience underlying these cultural differences. When children in other cultures have had an opportunity to go to school, their memory performance on these standard tests is more similar to that of their American counterparts in the same grade than it is to that of their age-mates in the same village (Cole et al., 1971).

These Liberian boys are learning to read passages from the Koran by an early morning fire.

A study by Daniel Wagner (1974) suggests the kind of memory-enhancing information-processing skills that children acquire as a consequence of schooling. Wagner conducted his study among educated and uneducated Mayans in Yucatan. He asked 248 people varying in age from 6 years to adulthood to recall the positions of picture cards laid out in a linear array (see Figure 13.5). The items pictured on the cards were taken from a popular game called *lotería,* so Wagner could be certain that all the pictures were familiar. On each trial, each of seven cards was displayed for two seconds and then turned face down. As soon as all seven cards had been presented, a duplicate of a picture on one of the cards was shown and people had to point to the position where they thought its twin was located. By selecting different duplicate pictures, Wagner in effect manipulated the length of time between the first presentation of a picture and the moment it was to be recalled.

Earlier research in the United States had demonstrated a marked increase in the ability of children to remember the locations of cards once they reach middle childhood (Hagen, Meacham, & Mesibov, 1970). The older children's increased ability was attributed to their rehearsal of each card's location as it was presented. Two of Wagner's key findings, which he replicated several years later in Morocco (Wagner, 1978), suggest that it is schooling that leads to improved memory for the locations of objects by promoting the development of rehearsal strategies. First, performance improved only among children who were attending school (see Figure 13.6). Second, the pattern of improvement among the educated children as they grew older was the pattern to be expected if they were using rehearsal strategies.

As with lexical organization, the evidence from studies of schooling's impact on memory should not be interpreted to mean that memory simply fails to develop among children who have not attended school. The difference between educated and uneducated children's performance in cross-cultural memory experiments is most noticeable after several years of schooling and when the materials to be learned are not related to each other according to any everyday script. When the materials to be remembered are part of a meaningful setting, as in Rogoff and Waddell's study of memory for objects placed in a diorama of the subjects' town (see Chapter 12, p. 465), the effects of schooling on memory performance disappear (see also Mandler et al., 1980). It appears that schooling helps children to develop specialized strategies for remembering, enhancing their ability to commit arbitrary material to memory for purposes of later testing. There is no evidence to support the conclusion that schooling increases an individual's memory capacity in general.

Metacognitive skills

Schooling appears to influence the ability to reflect on and talk about one's own thought processes (Luria, 1976; Rogoff, 1981; Tulviste, 1991). When children have been asked to explain how they arrived at the

FIGURE 13.5 *Cards used to test short-term memory. Seven cards are selected and then turned face down. The person being tested is then shown a duplicate of one of the cards (here a rooster) and asked to select the card that corresponds to it from the seven that are face down. (From Wagner, 1978.)*

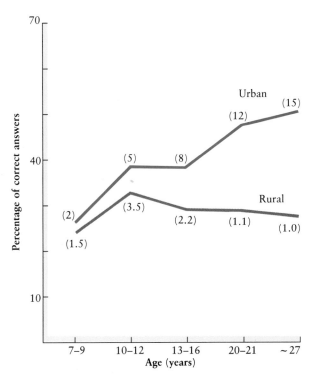

FIGURE 13.6 *Short-term memory performance as a function of age and number of years of education. In the absence of further education, performance does not improve with age. Thus schooling appears to be a key factor in one's ability to do well on this task. (Numbers in parentheses represent the average number of years of education for the designated group.) (From Wagner, 1974.)*

answer to a problem or what they did to make themselves remember something, those who have not attended school are likely to say something like "I did what my sense told me" or to offer no explanation at all. Schoolchildren, on the other hand, seem better able to describe the mental activities and logic that underpin their cognitive activities. This ability is called **metacognition.**

Attendance at school also seems to affect children's ability to think about their own language-using skills (referred to as *metalinguistic awareness*). Sylvia Scribner and Michael Cole (1981), for example, asked educated and uneducated Vai people in Liberia to judge the grammatical correctness of several phrases spoken in Vai. Some of the sentences were grammati-

cal, some not. Education had no effect on the ability to *identify* the ungrammatical phrases; but those who were educated could generally *explain* just what it was about a phrase that made it ungrammatical, whereas uneducated people could not.

The evidence in overview

Overall, the picture that emerges from recent decades of intense research on schooling provides only minimal support for the idea that schooling changes the cognitive processes associated with middle childhood in any deep and general way. In those cases where schooling has been found to affect cognitive performance, the effect appears to be restricted to rather specific information-processing strategies or to a specific context that is relevant primarily, if not exclusively, to school itself (Cole, 1990).

This conclusion in no way detracts from the importance of schooling in modern life. Schooling need not produce a generalized increase in the level of cognitive ability to be of great significance for children's development. And indeed, the central goal of schooling is not to transform mental machinery but to make people more effective problem solvers and rememberers when they have pencils, books, and computer at hand. In many societies reading, writing, and calculating have real importance outside of school, and the impact of schooling may be more appropriately sought in people's use of these skills than in any general mental transformations that schooling may produce.

Perhaps the most important aspect of schooling for the majority of people is that it is a gateway to economic power and social status (see Table 13.3). Most work in modern industrial societies requires the level of literacy that a high school education usually provides, and most highly paid jobs require a college-level education and perhaps specialization beyond that. The associations between years of schooling, income, and job status are strong (Jencks, 1972); on the average, the more years of schooling people complete, the higher their incomes are and the more likely they are to obtain white-collar and professional jobs.

Developmental psychologists and educators interested in enhancing children's development have therefore investigated the factors that account for success in school because it is such an important contributor to their later well-being in literate societies. They have

	TABLE 13.3 **School Enrollment in Selected Countries**				
Country	Percentage in Primary School		Percentage Who Enter Grade 1 and Complete Primary School (Both Sexes)	Percentage in Secondary School	
	Male	Female		Male	Female
Afghanistan	16	8	54	11	5
Senegal	50	34	86	17	8
Sierra Leone	46	32	48	23	10
Nicaragua	72	74	27	38	47
Indonesia	97	93	68	42	31
Philippines	97	98	71	61	66
Hungary	100	100	93	74	73
France	97	97	95	83	95
Japan	98	99	100	93	95

Source: United Nations Children's Fund, 1987.

paid particular attention to the possibility that some children come equipped with a special "aptitude for schooling" that others lack. Considerable research has also been conducted on the roles of the home, the community, and the school itself in a child's academic success.

APTITUDE FOR SCHOOLING

In *The Mill on the Floss,* the nineteenth-century novelist who called herself George Eliot provides a particularly vivid account of the difficulties facing a poor student:

> "You feel no interest in what you are doing sir," [Tom's teacher] Mr. Stelling would say, and the reproach was painfully true. Tom had never found any difficulty in discerning a pointer from a setter, when once he had been told the distinction, and his perceptive powers were not at all deficient. I fancy they were quite as strong as those of the Rev. Mr. Stelling, for Tom could predict with accuracy what number of horses were cantering behind him, he could throw a stone right into the center of a given ripple, he could guess to a fraction how many lengths of his stick it would take to reach across the playground, and could draw almost perfect squares on his slate without any measurement. But Mr. Stelling took no note of these things; he only observed that Tom's faculties failed him before the abstractions hideously symbolized to him in the pages of the Eton Grammar and that he was in a state bordering on idiocy with regard to the demonstration that two given triangles must be equal, though he could discern with great promptitude and certainty the fact that they were equal. (pp. 150–151)

Mr. Stelling's judgment that Tom's difficulties were attributable either to "natural idiocy" or to deliberate efforts to avoid learning proved to be mistaken. A few years later, when his family lost its middle-class standing, Tom demonstrated both his ability to learn and his diligence as a businessman.

Children who struggle in school but later are successful are by no means restricted to fiction, yet in the real world of today people must have basic reading and arithmetic skills if they are to function well in their society, and thousands of youngsters leave school without having acquired them. It is estimated that as many as 25 percent of adults in the United States read so poorly that they cannot cope adequately with the demands of everyday life (Kozol, 1985).

Why is it that some children experience exceptional difficulty in school while others do not? And what can be done to promote the kind of learning that takes place in school? All during this century, this inquiry has been influenced by the idea that people vary in an aptitude called "intelligence," and that these variations explain the differences in their school performance.

The concept of intelligence is very widely accepted. All languages have terms that describe individual differences in the way people solve problems and the kinds of problems they are good at solving (Nerlove et al., 1974; Segall et al., 1990). But the precise meanings of these terms vary among cultures, and it has proved difficult — some people say impossible — to define intelligence so that it can be measured as precisely as weight or height. Nonetheless, almost all children growing up today in the United States can expect to take an intelligence test at some time before they complete their education. Such tests are used to decide the education they will receive and the kind of work they will do, which in turn will influence the kind of lives they will lead as adults. It is thus important to understand the nature of intelligence as a factor in children's development as well as the nature of intelligence testing.

The Origins of Intelligence Testing

Interest in measuring intelligence became widespread at the turn of the century, when mass education was becoming the norm in Europe and the United States. Though most children seemed to be able to profit from the instruction they were given, some seemed virtually unable to learn in school. Concerned educational officials sought to determine the causes and cures for these difficulties.

In 1904 the French minister of public instruction named a commission to ensure the benefits of instruction for what he termed "defective" children. The commission asked Alfred Binet, a professor of psychology at the Sorbonne, and Theophile Simon, a physician, to create a means of examining children to identify those who needed special instruction. Binet and Simon set out to construct a psychological examination to diagnose mental subnormality that would have all the precision and validity of a medical examination. They were especially concerned about children incorrectly diagnosed as subnormal because, as they put it, "to be a member of a special class can never be a mark of distinction" (Binet & Simon, 1916:10).

The diagnostic strategy adopted by Binet and Simon was to present children with a series of problems whose solution was considered indicative of intelligence in the culture of their time. The problems were tailored to differentiate between children at each age, so that children who were far behind could be identified and given special instruction. Binet and Simon surmised, for example, that one aspect of intelligence is the ability to follow directions while keeping several task components in mind at once. To test for this ability, they presented children aged 4 to 6 with the following task:

> Do you see this key? You are to put it on the chair over there (pointing to the chair); afterwards shut the door; afterwards you will see near the door a box which is on a chair. You will take that box and bring it to me. (1916:206)

At 4 years of age, few children could carry out all parts of this task without help. At 5 years, about half of the children responded adequately, and at 6 years, almost all children passed. This age-linked pattern of achievement provided Binet and Simon with the test characteristics they needed. A 4-year-old who passed the test was considered precocious while a 6-year-old who failed was considered retarded with respect to this ability.

Other tasks required children to identify the missing parts of a picture, to name colors, to copy geometric figures, to remember strings of random digits, to count backward from 20, to make change for 20 francs, and so on. After extensive pretesting, Binet and Simon tested slightly more than 200 children ranging in age from 3 to 12 years, giving a different set of questions to each age group. As they had hoped, almost precisely 50 percent of these children scored at the expected age level. Of the remainder, 43 percent were within one year of expectation and only 7 percent deviated above or below the norm by as much as two years.

Binet and Simon concluded that they had succeeded in constructing a scale of intelligence. They called the basic index of intelligence for this scale **mental age (MA)**. A child who performed as well on the test as an average 7-year-old did was said to have an MA of 7; a child who did as well as an average 9-year-old was said to have an MA of 9, and so on. The MA provided Binet and Simon with a convenient way to characterize mental subnormality. A "dull" 7-year-old child was one who performed like a normal child one or more years younger.

To verify that their scale reflected more than a lucky selection of test items, Simon and Binet tested their conclusions against teachers' judgments. Their success in picking out the children judged most and least able by teachers confirmed their hopes.

Binet and Simon offered two explanations for school failure: a child might lack either the "natural intelligence" (the "nature") needed to succeed in school or the cultural background (the "nurture") presupposed by the school.

> A very intelligent child may be deprived of instruction by circumstances foreign to his intelligence. He may have lived far from school; he may have had a long illness . . . or maybe some parents have preferred to keep their children at home, to have them rinse bottles, serve the customers of a shop, care for a sick relative or herd the sheep. In such cases . . . it suffices to pass lightly the results of tests which are of a notably scholastic character, and to attach the greatest importance to those which express the natural intelligence. (1916:253–254)

This approach may appear intuitively plausible, but in fact it contains a crucial ambiguity: nowhere do Binet and Simon offer a definition of "natural intelligence" that would allow them to separate tests of natural intelligence from tests of a "scholastic character." Instead of defining natural intelligence in a way that distinguishes it from cultural experience (which they refer to as a problem of "fearful complexity"), they contented themselves with pointing out that whatever natural intelligence is, it is not equivalent to success in school. In their view, not only is there more to intelligence than schooling, there is also more to schooling—and to life—than intelligence:

> Our examination of intelligence can not take account of all these qualities, attention, will, regularity, continuity, docility, and courage which play so important a part in school work, and also in after-life; for life is not so much a conflict of intelligences as a combat of characters. (1916:256)

The Legacy of Binet and Simon

Educators immediately adopted Binet and Simon's tests, and their use spread rapidly. By 1916 more than 20,000 translated test booklets had been distributed by a single American institution devoted to education of the retarded. This was only the beginning. The tests were later translated and used in such far-flung countries as Australia, China, the Soviet Union, and South Africa.

Many refinements of the original tests have been made in the past 90 years. In the United States, Lewis Terman at Stanford University modified the original scales to create the Stanford-Binet Intelligence Scale in an attempt to determine the origins of mental giftedness (Terman, 1925), and David Wechsler devised tests for use with both adults and children (Wechsler, 1939) (see Figure 13.7). Updated versions of these tests are still widely used today.

From mental age to IQ

William Stern (1912), a German developmental psychologist, introduced an important refinement in the way tests were thought about and applied. He suggested that intelligence be considered the ratio of children's mental age to their actual, or chronological, age (CA). Thus was born the unit of measurement that we use today, the "intelligence quotient" (**IQ**): IQ = (MA/CA) × 100. The stratagem of multiplying the relative magnitude of MA/CA by 100 is simply a convenience. Calculation of IQ in this fashion ensures that when children are performing precisely as expected for their age, the resulting score will be 100, so that 100 is an "average IQ" by definition (see Figure 13.8). A 9-year-old child with a mental age of 10, for example, is assigned an IQ of 111 (^{10}/9 × 100 = 111), while a 10-year-old child with a mental age of 10 is assigned an IQ of 100.

Stern's IQ score was quickly adopted as the basic unit for comparison of mental performances. It pro-

Information (30 items)

How many wings does a bird have?
What is steam made of?

Picture Completion (26 items)

What is the missing part of the picture?

Similarities (17 items)

In what way are a lion and a tiger alike?
In what way are an hour and a week alike?

Picture Arrangement (12 items made up of 3 to 5 picture cards each)

(The person is asked to arrange the cards so that the story of the woman weighing herself makes sense.)

Comprehension (17 items)

What should you do if you see someone forget his book when he leaves a restaurant?
What is the advantage of keeping money in a bank?

FIGURE 13.7 *Simulated items from the Wechsler Intelligence Scale for Children. (Copyright © 1948, 1974, 1991 by the Psychological Corporation. Reproduced by permission. All rights reserved.)*

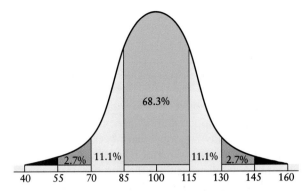

FIGURE 13.8 *An idealized bell-shaped curve of the distribution of IQ scores. A bell-shaped curve is a distribution of scores on a graph in which the most frequent value, the mode, is in the center and the less frequent values are distributed symmetrically on either side. By definition, the modal IQ score is 100.*

vided psychologists and educators with a convenient index that could be used to specify the correlation between intelligence test scores and grades in school. (Correlation is discussed in Chapter 1, pp. 26–27.)

In recent decades the method of calculating IQ has been refined to take into account the fact that mental development is more rapid early in life than later. Raw IQ scores do not take into account the fact that the difference in mental functioning between 4- and 5-year-olds, for example, is greater than the difference between 14- and 15-year-olds. To overcome this difficulty, psychologists now use a score referred to as a **deviation IQ** (Wechsler, 1974). Calculation of IQ scores as deviations takes advantage of the statistical fact, illustrated in Figure 13.8, that the raw IQ scores calculated for a large sample form an approximately normal distribution. When psychologists base the IQ scores assigned to children on the differences between their raw scores and the standardized mean of 100, they have a statistical standard that is the same for all children.

Despite various revisions, the logic of the procedures devised by Binet and Simon is still the basis of standardized intelligence tests. The key tasks in the creation of an IQ test are:

1. To select a set of items that produces a range of performances among children at the same age level.

2. To arrange the items in the order of difficulty, so that as children grow older, they are more likely to answer each succeeding item correctly.
3. To make certain that performance on the test corresponds to performance in school.

Only part of Binet and Simon's legacy is to be found in the adoption and refinement of their testing methods. Equally important have been the questions they left unresolved, three of which have dominated research on intelligence since the start of their pioneering efforts. The first question focuses on the nature of intelligence itself: How is intelligence to be defined? Is it a general characteristic of a person's entire mental life, or is it a bundle of relatively specific abilities? Second is the nature-nurture question: What causes variations in intelligence test scores? Third, why do variations in IQ scores predict variations in school performance?

The nature of intelligence: General or specific?

Although Binet and Simon were skeptical about the possibility of defining intelligence, the nature of their assignment forced them to attempt to specify the quality of mind they were trying to test for. They offered the following characterization:

> It seems to us that in intelligence there is a fundamental faculty, the alteration or lack of which is of the utmost importance for practical life. This faculty is judgment, otherwise called good sense, practical sense, initiative, the faculty of adapting oneself to circumstances. To judge well, to comprehend well, to reason well, these are the essential activities of intelligence. (1916:43)

This definition served to guide Binet and Simon's choice of items for their test, but it did not by any means settle the question of the essential properties of intelligence.

In 1921, when educators were embracing intelligence tests with enthusiasm, the editors of the *Journal of Educational Psychology* asked a number of experts to give their views on the nature of intelligence. The contributors mentioned these characteristics, among others:

- The power to think one's way to the truth or facts of a situation.

- The ability to think abstractly.
- The ability to learn and adjust oneself to the environment.
- The ability to adapt to new situations in life.
- The capacity to inhibit instinctive judgment.

As John Carroll (1982) comments, these definitions vary so substantially that one wonders whether the experts in 1921 were talking about the same thing. But in one respect, these respondents agreed with Binet and Simon's early definition. In their view, intelligence, whatever it is, is a *general* characteristic. This view has been supported over the years by some statistical evidence that the separate tasks on the test are highly correlated with one another; people who score high on one task tend to score high on the others (Jensen, 1980; Spearman, 1927).

One participant in the 1921 symposium on intelligence, V. A. C. Henmon, disagreed with his colleagues. He believed that intelligence tests measure only "the special intelligence upon which the schools place a premium" (1921:197). The idea that intelligence tests measure only school-specific aptitudes has been championed in recent years by a number of scholars (Ceci, 1990).

Several characteristics seem to distinguish the intellectual tasks demanded by schools from tasks encountered in many other settings, as we have seen (see also Neisser, 1976; Scribner & Cole, 1973; Wagner & Sternberg, 1985):

- School tasks are formulated by other people.
- School tasks are of little or no intrinsic interest to the learner.
- All the needed information is present at the start of a school task.
- School tasks are separate from everyday experience.
- School tasks are usually well defined, with a single correct answer.
- Often only one method for finding the solution to a school task is considered correct.
- School tasks are usually presented in written symbols (words, numbers).

These characteristics of school tasks have led several modern investigators to agree with Henmon that there is a special form of intelligence that is specific to such tasks. Ulric Neisser (1976) speaks of "academic" versus "everyday" intelligence. Robert Sternberg

(1985) distinguishes academic and practical intelligence, both of which he considers to differ from a third kind of intelligence, which he calls wisdom.

The search for separate intelligence factors by no means stops at two or three types. The psychologist Louis Thurstone (1938) proposed the existence of seven "primary mental abilities": verbal comprehension, word fluency, number, space, memory, perceptual speed, and reasoning. J. P. Guilford (1967) went further. He proposed 120 separate mental abilities, all of which could be tapped by appropriate test items.

More recently Howard Gardner (1983) has proposed a theory of multiple intelligences, each of which follows a separate developmental path (see Table 13.4). Musical intelligence often appears at an early age; logical mathematical intelligence seems to peak in late adolescence and early adulthood; the kind of spatial intelligence on which artists rely may reach its peak much later.

There is at present no firm agreement on the best way to characterize intelligence. Part of the problem is that different statistical techniques for assessing the correlations between subtests of IQ tests yield different answers (Gould, 1981). But researchers' personal intuitions about what intelligence is also play a role in their theorizing on this topic. Should great musical ability be called a form of intelligence, or is it better thought of as a "talent"? Conversely, couldn't the ability to solve IQ test problems be considered a talent, or is it really useful to identify it as intelligence? There are no obvious right answers to these questions.

Population differences and the nature-nurture controversy

Disagreements over general intelligence versus specific intelligences are accompanied by disagreements about why people's test performance varies. As mobilization for World War I was beginning, Robert Yerkes proposed that all recruits be given an intelligence test to determine their fitness to serve in various military capacities as well as to generate data about the intelligence of the U.S. population as a whole. Approximately 1.75 million men were administered tests in groups—written tests for those who could read English, a picture-completion test for those who could not (see Figure 13.9). Men who failed were given an individually administered version of the Binet and Simon scales (Yerkes, 1921). Never before had IQ tests been administered to such large groups of people at

TABLE 13.4	
Howard Gardner's Idea of Multiple Intelligences	
Kind of Intelligence	**Characteristics**
Linguistic	Special sensitivity to language, which allows one to choose precisely the right word or turn of phrase and to grasp new meanings easily
Musical	Sensitivity to pitch and tone, which allows one to detect and produce musical structure
Logical-mathematical	Ability to engage in abstract reasoning and manipulate symbols
Spatial	Ability to perceive relations among objects, to transform mentally what one sees, and to recreate visual images from memory
Bodily-kinesthetic	Ability to represent ideas in movement; characteristic of great dancers and mimes
Personal	Ability to gain access to one's own feelings and to understand the motivations of others
Social	Ability to understand the motives, feelings, and behaviors of other people.

Source: Gardner, 1983.

one time, or to people for whom the language of testing differed from their native languages.

Both because of the chaotic conditions of testing and because of the results, Yerkes' research began a controversy that has continued to the present time (Gould, 1981). Two results appeared to be particularly problematic. First, the average mental age of native-born white Americans was assessed at 13 years. Since, by the standards of the time, a mental age of 8 to 12 years was considered subnormal for an adult, it appeared that a substantial part of the white population consisted of "morons."

FIGURE 13.9 *Items from the picture-completion test used by Robert Yerkes and his colleagues to test recruits during World War I. Each picture is incomplete in some way; the task is to identify what is missing. (From Yerkes, 1921.)*

Second, there was a substantial difference between the scores obtained by European immigrants and African Americans. Overall, the average for recruits of European origin was a mental age of 13.7 years, although the recruits whose families came from southern and eastern Europe scored lower than northern Europeans, with an average mental age of about 11 years. African Americans scored lowest of all, with an average tested mental age of slightly more than 10 years.

Several of the pioneer mental testers interpreted such differences as the results of innate, immutable differences in natural intelligence ("nature"). Terman's book on mental giftedness, for example, bore the title *Genetic Studies of Genius*. Cyril Burt (1883–1971) was another early test developer who exercised great influence on the field, although some of his data have subsequently been shown to be fraudulent (Hearnshaw, 1979). Burt believed both that intelligence is an innate quality and that each person has one general "intelligence," rather than a set of specific intelligences:

By intelligence the psychologist understands inborn, all-round intellectual ability. It is inherited, or at least innate, not due to teaching or training; it is intellectual, not emotional or moral, and remains uninfluenced by industry or zeal; it is general, not specific, i.e., it is not limited to any particular kind of work, but enters into all we do or say or think. Of all our mental qualities, it is the most far-reaching. (Quoted in Carroll, 1982:90)

In short, according to this **innatist hypothesis of intelligence,** some people are born generally smarter than others and no amount of training or variation in the environment can alter this fact. Many psychologists of the 1920s rushed to embrace this conclusion. In an address titled "Is America Safe for Democracy?" William McDougall, then head of Harvard University's psychology department, stated, "The results of the Army tests indicate that about 75 percent of the population has not sufficient innate capacity for intellectual development to enable it to complete the usual high school course" (quoted in Chase, 1977:226). The generally lower test scores of members of ethnic minority groups and the poor (who often, but not always, are the same people) were widely interpreted to mean that such groups were innately and irrevocably inferior.

During the 1930s and 1940s scholarly opinion was seriously divided on this issue (Cronbach, 1975). The general-intelligence, innatist position championed by Terman, Burt, and others was balanced by an **environmentalist hypothesis of intelligence** as both specific and heavily dependent upon experience (Klineberg, 1980). It was demonstrated, for example, that after people had moved from rural areas to the city, their intelligence test scores rose (Klineberg, 1935), and that when orphans were removed from very restricted early environments, their intelligence test scores improved markedly (see Chapter 7).

The scientific and social debates about the differences in tested intelligence between ethnic groups and social classes erupted again when Arthur Jensen (1969) published an article with the title "How Much Can

We Boost IQ and Scholastic Achievement?" Jensen was disenchanted with the federally sponsored Head Start program (see Chapter 11). He suggested that it was a mistake to expect scholastic improvements from Head Start because poor and minority children were genetically less capable of the mental processes demanded by school. His provocative thesis fueled a heated controversy. Jensen's critics charged that he used biased tests, misused statistical techniques, and misrepresented the data; Jensen has disputed the charges (Block & Dworkin, 1981; Gould, 1981; Jensen, 1980).

IQ performance and the logic of testing

At the present time no responsible scholar believes that the variation in intelligence test scores from person to person can be attributed entirely to either environmental or genetic factors, or that school success is caused entirely by inherited intelligence (Ceci, 1990; Sternberg & Powell, 1983). Rather, it is accepted that all behavior, including performance on IQ tests and in school, is an aspect of one's *phenotype* (that is, one's observable characteristics), which arises from interactions between one's *genotype* (the set of genes one inherits) and the environment.

As we pointed out in Chapter 2, the study of gene-environment interactions in human beings is especially difficult for several reasons. First, for ethical reasons, it is impossible to study the full range of reaction. To do so would be to expose some newborn children to hostile environments for the express purpose of satisfying scientific curiosity. Second, almost all human characteristics are *polygenic*—that is, they are shaped by several genes acting in combination in a given set of environmental conditions. Thus, even when it has been possible to estimate the genetic contribution to a trait, little can be said about precisely which genes are interacting with the environment in what way. Third, the fact that parents contribute both to their children's genetic material and to the environment in which their children grow up complicates the process of separating the various influences on the phenotype. Finally, children actively shape their own environments, further complicating an already complicated situation (see Figure 2.7 for a reminder of these complexities).

Attempts to understand how genetic and environmental factors combine to create the phenotypic behavior called "intelligence" face another, even greater difficulty. As we noted earlier, psychologists disagree profoundly about what, precisely, they are measuring when they administer an intelligence test. All they can say with any degree of confidence is that these tests predict later school performance to a moderate degree. (The typical correlation between test performance and school performance is .50 [Snow & Yalow, 1982].) We can understand this problem better if we compare the gene-environment interactions that might determine intelligence with those that determine height.

To determine how environmental variation influences height, we might study sets of monozygotic (identical) and heterozygotic (fraternal) twins. Suppose that the twins to be studied were all born in Minnesota. Suppose further that some of the twins were separated, with the second member of each pair sent to live among the !Kung Bushmen of the Kalahari Desert. Although these environments do not represent the most extreme variations compatible with human life, they are sufficiently different in climate, diet, daily activities, and other relevant factors to represent a plausible test of the relative importance of genetic and environmental contributions to height.

If, within this environmental range, genetic factors dominate the expression of the phenotype (measured height), then we would expect two facts to emerge:

• The heights of identical twins should be roughly as similar to each other when the twins are raised far apart as when they are raised in the same family.

• The similarity between the heights of identical twins should be greater than the similarity between the heights of fraternal twins. In fact, the similarity of the heights of identical twins raised in very different environments might be greater than that of fraternal twins raised in the same environment.

Whether the children are in Minnesota or in the Kalahari Desert, we can be pretty confident about our measure of height. Whether we use a yardstick or a metric scale, we have a standardized measure to determine the heights of the twins, regardless of the context in which they are measured. At first glance IQ tests may appear to be standard measures logically similar to a yardstick. But this appearance is an illusion.

Precisely because intelligence tests take their meaning from their correlation with schoolwork, they are inherently bound to the schooled society in which they are developed. As we have seen, central to all schooling are graphic systems of representation. But these modes of representation are generally absent in nonliterate societies. To be administered to a !Kung child, every existing intelligence test would thus require some modification, if only translation from English to !Kung. If, for example, a !Kung child were asked how many fingers are on two hands, the modification seems minimal, but caution is still necessary. The number system used by the !Kung is not the same as that used by Minnesotans, and it plays a different role in their lives. What in !Kung society is the relative importance of knowing the number of fingers on a hand versus, say, knowing how to tie knots with those fingers?

When it comes to the tests that require interpretation of pictures or copying from written figures, even more serious difficulties arise. The !Kung have no tradition of either drawing or writing. Research with young children in the United States (Klapper & Birch, 1969) and nonliterate peoples in several parts of the world (Deregowski, 1980) shows that people do not automatically interpret two-dimensional pictures of objects as they would the objects themselves. So the tests that use pictures and require copying are inappropriate, as are any tests that depend upon the ability to read. We thus cannot assume that an IQ test is like a yardstick, yielding equivalent measures across cultural environments.

Various attempts to create "culture-free" tests have been made (Cattell, 1949; Davis, 1948), but no generally satisfactory solution has yet been found: all tests of intelligence draw on a background of learning that is culture-specific (see Figure 13.10). (More recent attempts to deal with the difficulties of comparing intelligence across racial and cultural lines are described in Irvine & Berry, 1987, and Cole, 1985.)

The fact that intelligence cannot be tested independently of the culture that gives rise to the test greatly limits the conclusions that can be drawn from IQ testing in different social and cultural groups. A good deal of research uses comparisons of identical and fraternal twins to distinguish genetic from environmental contributions to intelligence, but these studies suffer an important limitation. According to the logic of twin studies, the environmental variations for separated twins ought to be great enough to allow such

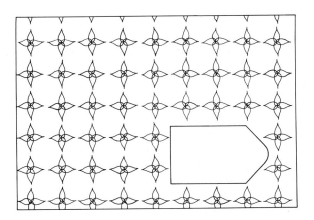

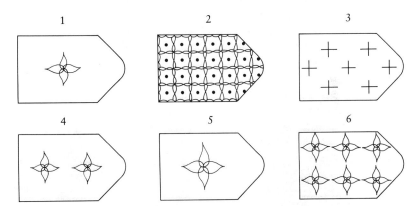

FIGURE 13.10 *Items from a "culture-free" intelligence test. Note that though these test items do not require elaborate verbal formulation, they assume that the test taker is familiar with two-dimensional representations of figures, a convention that does not exist in many cultures. (From J. C. Raven, Coloured Progressive Matrices [London: H. K. Lewis & Co. Ltd., 1962]. Reprinted with permission of J. C. Raven Limited.)*

influences to be visible. But if the environmental variation is too great, as in the case of a child transported from Minnesota to the Kalahari Desert, both twins' intelligence cannot be validly measured by the same test.

Despite these difficulties, a large literature has grown up around studies of twins' IQ test performance, along with studies of children of interracial marriages and of children adopted across racial and ethnic lines (Mackenzie, 1984; Scarr, 1981). Controversy continues to attend this work, but the following conclusions appear most defensible:

1. Some part of individual differences in performance on IQ tests is attributable to inheritance. The degree of heritability is in dispute: some investigators claim that it is very high (Jensen, 1980); some claim that it is very low or indeterminate (Lewontin, Rose, & Kamin, 1984). One influential recent summary estimates that perhaps 50 percent of the variation in test performance *within population groups* is controlled by genetic factors (Plomin, 1990).

2. There are significant differences between the average IQ scores of African Americans and white Americans. Whites score approximately 15 points higher than African Americans; other ethnic groups in the United States, such as Native Americans and Hispanics, score at some intermediate level (Jensen, 1980).

3. There is *no evidence* that the average difference in scores between ethnic groups in the United States is the result of inherited differences in intelligence, however defined. Nonetheless, great uncertainty remains about precisely what environmental factors are involved in producing the group differences.

At first glance, the first two facts may appear to conflict with the third: if inheritance is responsible for a large part of the differences between individuals in tested intelligence, and if there are large differences between groups in tested intelligence, why wouldn't it be reasonable to conclude that the source of the differences between groups is the same as the source of the differences between individuals?

There are two answers to this question, one logical and the other empirical. The logical answer was provided by Richard Lewontin (1976). It can be illustrated simply by an example from plant genetics (see Figure 13.11). Suppose that a farmer has two fields, one fertile and the other depleted of nutrients. He randomly takes corn seed from a bag containing several genetic varieties and plants them in the two fields. He cares for them equally. When the plants have reached maturity he will discover that *within* each field some plants have grown taller than others. Since all the plants within each field experienced roughly the same environment, their variation can be attributed to genetic factors. But the farmer will also discover variation *between* the fields; the plants grown in the fertile field will be taller than the plants grown in the nutrient-poor field. The explanation for this average difference in the heights of the plants lies in their environments, even though the degrees of heritability in the two fields may be equal.

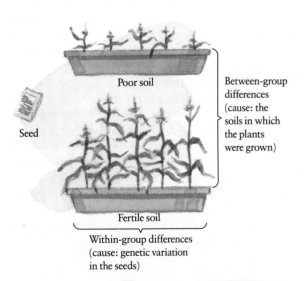

Poor soil

Between-group differences (cause: the soils in which the plants were grown)

Seed

Fertile soil

Within-group differences (cause: genetic variation in the seeds)

FIGURE 13.11   *The reason that differences within groups do not explain differences between groups. Here the difference in the heights of the plants within each box reflect genetic variations in the seeds planted in it. The difference between the average heights of the plants in the two boxes is best explained by the quality of the soil, an environmental factor. The same principle holds for IQ test scores of human groups. (Adapted from Gleitman, 1963.)*

This same argument applies to variations in test performance between ethnic and racial groups. Even though the heritability of intelligence *within* ethnic or racial groups may be the same, the average difference in performance *between* groups may still be caused not by their genetic endowment but by differences in the environments within which the children have been raised.

Lewontin's example illustrates another important point about heritability that applies equally to IQ. Heritability is a *population statistic*. It applies to groups, not to individuals. If the heritability statistic for a field of corn or a set of IQ scores is .50, it does *not* mean that 50 percent of the height of each corn plant or each IQ score is determined by genetic factors. Instead, it means that 50 percent of the *variation* in a field of corn or a group of IQ scores can be traced to genetic differences. The other 50 percent of the variation must be explained in another way.

Research evidence also speaks strongly against the idea that ethnic, racial, and class differences in tested IQ can be explained by inheritance. In a particularly important study, Sandra Scarr and Richard Weinberg (1976, 1983) evaluated the impact on children of African American working-class parents of being adopted by white middle-class families. Had the African American children remained at home, they would be expected to achieve an average IQ score of 85. Raised in white middle-class families, these children had an average IQ score of 97, almost precisely the national average, despite the fact that they had been adopted more than a year after birth. Children adopted closer to birth had even higher scores. This kind of evidence points squarely to children's environment as a major factor in the abilities tapped by standardized intelligence tests, abilities that are important to success in school.

THE SCHOOL AND THE COMMUNITY

In seeking to identify the environmental factors that contribute to IQ scores as well as school success, researchers have focused on factors operating in the family, in children's peer groups, and in the schools. (Box 13.3 takes an even broader cross-national look at factors that contribute to academic achievement.)

Family Influences

Research described in Chapters 7 and 11 suggests some of the home characteristics that are likely to be influential in school achievement (Baumrind, 1967; White & Watts, 1973). Parents who encourage exploration, who take care to explain what they are doing and to listen to their children, and who tailor the difficulty of the environment to their children's abilities and interests tend to raise children who are more successful academically. Such results are not restricted to the United States; similar patterns of parental influence are found in Japan as well (Stevenson, Lee, & Stigler, 1986).

The family's contribution to academic achievement is strikingly evident among the refugees from Vietnam, Cambodia, and Laos who fled to the United States during the 1970s and 1980s. These refugees have been conspicuously successful in both economic and educational pursuits (Caplan, Whitmore, & Choy, 1989). Although they had lost from 1 to 3 years of formal education in refugee camps and most were unable to speak English when they entered school in the United States, eight out of ten students surveyed had a B average or better within 3 to 6 years. Almost half received A's in mathematics. These achievements are all the more noteworthy because they were attained in schools in low-income, inner-city areas traditionally associated with fewer resources and less motivated, more disruptive student bodies.

In trying to account for the spectacular success of these immigrants, Nathan Caplan, John Whitmore, and Marcella Choy (1989) found the parents' involvement with the child to be crucial. Almost half of the parents surveyed said they read to their children, many in their native language. Apparently the parents' knowledge of English has less effect on the children's school performance than the emotional associations of being read to and the cultural wisdom they shared as they read the stories. The parents demonstrated their commitment to education not only by owning books and reading to their children but also by the number of hours of homework they required the children to do. Parents reported that an average of almost three hours of every weekday evening was spent doing homework, twice the average for native-born American children.

Homework was also found to be a family affair. Caplan and his colleagues report that parents and older siblings took an active part in homework assignments.

An interesting indicator of the effectiveness of this kind of involvement was the finding that the more children a family had, the higher were the grade point averages. This result is just the opposite of the usual pattern in American households, where a large family is associated with poor school performance. Homework time was so much a family affair, in fact, that Caplan and his colleagues were unable to assess how much time each child spent on specific parts of the curriculum because they helped each other while they were doing their own work. The researchers comment that "a great amount of learning goes on in these homes in terms of course content and study habits, and it becomes understandable that children socialized in these settings would feel at home in school" (1989:106).

Evidence that some patterns of family interaction promote success in school does not mean that the socialization practices of the home and the school have to be closely matched before the schools can teach children effectively. Studies carried out among Hawaiian children have shown that teachers can successfully build upon some features of family socialization practices while ignoring or reversing others (Jordan, 1981; Weisner, Gallimore, & Jordan, 1988). These investigators found, for example, that they could build upon the strong value Hawaiians place on cooperation and harmony by encouraging small groups of children to cooperate in carrying out school assignments. At the same time, they found that it was possible to ignore the fact that children speak a creole dialect at home because this language variation did not interfere with their learning to read. By contrast, they advocated reversing the children's tendency to avoid looking directly at adults because eye contact is important in classroom discussion. This kind of culture-sensitive approach to the organization of classroom learning requires knowledgeable and flexible teaching, but when it is carried out by skilled teachers, it makes instruction more effective.

Peer Influences

The possibility that peers will have a negative impact on a child's school performance is a common source of concern (Bishop, 1989). Evidence indicates, however, that when peer interactions are properly organized,

BOX 13.3
Schooling in Three Cultures

Typical classrooms and curricula appear very similar whether they are found in crowded cities such as New York and Tokyo or small rural towns in West Africa and Australia. Yet, many studies of classroom life and academic performance in different societies reveal that despite surface similarities, both the process and the products of schooling vary markedly from one culture to the next.

In the classrooms of rural Liberia, for example, children are taught basic reading, writing, and arithmetic through rote instruction (Cole et al., 1971). A favorite method used by Liberian teachers is to have the entire class recite lessons in unison, with little attention devoted to the meaning of the recitation. John Gay and Michael Cole (1967) report that when one of the children they studied was asked questions about arithmetic, he launched into a singsong patter ("La lala lala, la lala lala, la la la lala"). When asked what he was doing, he answered that he was adding numbers, but so far he had learned only the tune, not the words. Not surprisingly, the academic achievement of the typical Liberian child is low by U.S. standards.

But the achievement of American schoolchildren is itself low in comparison with that of children in other industrialized societies (McKnight et al., 1987). This finding has spurred attempts to identify the factors responsible for variations in children's achievement from one society to the next. A series of studies initiated by Harold Stevenson has provided a good deal of insight into the ways in which cultural differences in the conduct of elementary school education lead to variations in children's performance (Stevenson, Lee, & Stigler, 1986; Stevenson & Stigler, 1992; Stigler & Perry, 1990). These studies focused on classrooms in three countries: the United States, Japan, and Taiwan.

The accompanying diagrams provide a capsule look at schoolchildren's mathematical performance in the three societies on three tests of mathematical achievement: computational skill, word problems, and conceptual knowledge of mathematics. With the single exception of the test of conceptual understanding in the first grade, American children performed far below the level of both Asian groups. As might be expected, this evidence of marked national differences

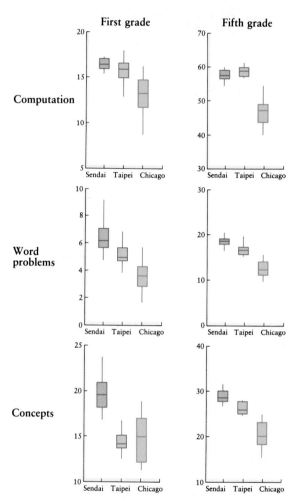

Distribution and mean number of correct answers on three mathematics-related tests in schools in Sendai (Japan), Taipei (Taiwan), and Chicago. (From Stigler & Perry, 1990.)

in the development of mathematical thinking has spurred a debate about their causes. Richard Lynn (1982) argued, on the basis of comparative performance on IQ tests, that Japanese children enjoy a genetic superiority in intelligence. However, careful evaluations of this hypothesis have shown it to be false. Large comparative studies demonstrating differences in mathematics performance showed no corresponding differences in intelligence scores (Stevenson et al., 1985).

Acknowledging that other factors, such as encouragement of school work at home and different forms of socialization, may contribute to the cultural differences observed, Stevenson and his colleagues have focused on the process of instruction in the classroom, arguing that a lot can be learned from study of these settings, whatever other factors may be at work. They found that the two factors in which American and Asian schooling differed the most were the amount of time spent in the teaching and learning of mathematics and the social organization of classroom interactions.

The Asian children in both the first and fifth grades attend school more days each year than the American children (240 days versus 180). At the fifth-grade level, Japanese children go to school 44 hours a week, Chinese students 37 hours a week, and American children 30 hours a week. On each school-day the two Asian groups spent as much time on mathematics as they did on reading and writing, but the American groups spent almost three times as much on language arts. As James Stigler and Michelle Perry (1990:336) note, the disparity in the sheer number of hours spent on mathematics lessons is large enough to "go a long way toward explaining the differences in mathematics achievement."

But the differences are not restricted simply to gross amounts of time spent on mathematics; the Asian classrooms were organized quite differently from the American classrooms. By and large, classrooms in the two Asian countries are centrally organized and the teacher instructs the whole class at once. The American classrooms are generally more decentralized; often the teacher devotes attention to one group at a time while the other children work independently at their seats. Two important differences in the quality of teacher-student interactions are correlated with these differences in classroom organization. First, American children spend a good deal of time being instructed by no one. This might not make much of a difference if the children were absorbed by their workbooks and truly working independently. But here another difference in students' behavior comes into play: to a significant degree American chil-

dren do not use their independent study time well; they are out of their seats or engaged in inappropriate behavior such as gossiping with friends or causing mischief almost half of the time. Asian children spend far more time attending to schoolwork than their American counterparts do.

There are also differences in the content of the lessons. First, the Japanese teachers devote twice as much instruction time to helping children reflect on and analyze mathematics problems as do the Chinese and American teachers. Second, both the Chinese and Japanese teachers are more likely than their American counterparts to use concrete manipulable objects and to provide a meaningful context for the mathematics problems they teach. Third, the Asian teachers stress the connections between problems encountered at different points in the lesson, or even between problems in one lesson and another, giving greater coherence to their teaching.

An attractive conclusion is that if American educators want children to match the performance of their Asian counterparts, all they need to do is lengthen the school year and copy Japanese or Taiwanese classroom teaching methods. Proposals to extend the school year are on the agendas of many state legislatures and local school boards. It is not at all obvious, however, that a shift to teacher-led whole-group lessons will improve the quality of instruction or children's performance. In fact, a sizable body of evidence indicates that a curriculum organized around small-group activities is an especially effective mode of instruction in American classrooms (Cole & Griffin, 1987).

Stigler and Perry (1990) sound a similar caution: their research suggests that instruction can be organized so that children learn mathematics at a higher level than they are currently doing in American schools, but it does not indicate how to draw on American cultural traditions to achieve this result. Quoting the sociologist Merry White (1987), they remind us that cross-cultural research does not provide a blueprint for improving the education of children. Rather, it provides a mirror that sharpens awareness of our own cultural practices and provides some hints about how they might be changed to make teaching and learning more effective.

they can have a positive effect on children's school-based learning (Azmitia & Perlmutter, 1989).

On the negative side, William Labov and Clarence Robbins (1969) studied the way children's participation in peer groups may interfere with their success in school. Their reserach, carried out in central Harlem, focused on groups of boys in grades 4 to 10. Although these groups were not "gangs" in the sense that they did not fight other groups as a unit, fighting was common and intergroup conflict was an important source of group cohesion.

The major values of group members were incompatible with those of the school, according to Labov and Robbins:

> Sources of prestige within the group are physical size, toughness, courage and skill in fighting; skill with language in ritual insults, verbal routines with girls, singing, jokes, and story-telling; knowledge of nationalist lore; skill and boldness in stealing. . . . Success in school is irrelevant to prestige within the group, and reading is rarely if ever used outside of school. (1969:55)

By comparing the reading scores of group members and nonmembers at different grade levels, Labov and Robbins could assess the influence of participation in certain peer groups on academic achievement. They found that as boys who were not group members progressed through the grades, their reading scores rose steadily, whereas group members improved hardly at all.

On the other hand, Margarita Azmitia and Marion Perlmutter (1989) found that peers can have positive effects as well. They reviewed a wide range of studies that assessed the effects of asking school-aged children to work collaboratively on academic tasks with their peers. Working with peers improved children's problem solving, they found, so long as the children got along well enough to collaborate in a mutually facilitating manner. It is particularly important that the children be able to reach agreement about the best way to tackle the problem and to agree when they have achieved a good result. But this outcome is by no means guaranteed. Consequently, current research is focusing on means to enhance the collaborative aspects of peer interaction so that the potential of peers for academic achievement can be maximized (Forman, 1989).

School Atmosphere

Research in recent years demonstrates convincingly that the quality of experience within the school can make a decisive difference in students' academic success. Michael Rutter and his colleagues (1979), for example, carried out a large-scale study of secondary schools in central London, where housing conditions are poor, unemployment and crime rates are high, levels of education among adults are low, and handicapping psychiatric disorders are common. These are just the conditions that one might expect would lead to poor educational achievement, and in many cases they do. What makes this research important is its demonstration that the school can make a difference. The most successful school in the researchers' sample was more than four times more successful in educating pupils than the least successful school.

Rutter and his colleagues discovered that contrary to expectations the successful schools were not more modern, their teachers were not better trained or better paid, and their students did not have higher IQs or more favorable conditions at home. The differences were traced to educational conditions within the schools. Four conditions were found to be most important:

Academic emphasis Schools that clearly demonstrated their expectation that students were in school to master academic subjects produced higher levels of achievement. These expectations were communicated in a variety of ways, such as assignment of homework and regular displays of excellent work on classroom bulletin boards. Figure 13.12 shows the relationship between the amount of homework assigned and the average examination score pupils achieved. (See also Box 13.4.)

Teachers' behaviors When teachers must stop to discipline individual children, everyone tends to lose the thread of the lesson. Successful classrooms were those where teachers could coordinate the entire class at one time; often these teachers expected their students to work silently, on their own.

Distribution of rewards and punishments The most successful classrooms were those where punishment was less frequent than praise.

BOX 13.4
Teachers' Expectations and School Success

We have all spent more than a dozen years in class-rooms and we all know from personal experience that teachers' attitudes toward students vary. Teachers expect some students to do better than others in mastering academic material. Modern research has shown that these attitudes and expectations influence students' performance in a variety of ways.

Perhaps the most famous, and certainly the most controversial, research on the effect of teachers' expectations was initiated in the 1960s by Robert Rosenthal and his colleagues (Rosenthal, 1987; Rosenthal & Rubin, 1978). These researchers found that a teacher's expectations about a child's academic ability may become a self-fulfilling prophecy, even when the expectations are groundless.

To demonstrate the power of teachers' expectations, Rosenthal and Lenore Jacobsen (1968) gave children in all six elementary grades a test that, they told the teachers, would identify children who were likely to "bloom" intellectually during the coming year. After the testing, teachers were given the names of those children who, the researchers said, would show a spurt in intellectual development during the school year. In fact, the names of the presumed "bloomers" were chosen at random (with a few exceptions, to be described in due course).

At the end of the school year the children were tested again. This time the researchers found that at the first- and second-grade levels there was in fact a difference between the "bloomers" and "non-bloomers": the children who had been randomly identified as likely candidates for rapid intellectual growth really did grow. They gained an average of 15 points on their IQ scores over their scores at the beginning of the school year, while their classmates' IQ scores remained unchanged. In this study, the IQs of children in grades 3 through 6 did not change, but in a follow-up study Rosenthal and his colleagues found that older schoolchildren's performance on IQ tests could also be influenced by the teachers' expectations (Rosenthal, Baratz, & Hall, 1974).

Since the children identified as those likely to bloom intellectually were chosen at random, Rosenthal and his colleagues concluded that teachers' expectations influence their own behavior and thus their students', so that their teaching is more effective with children who they believe are academically able.

A particularly provocative finding in Rosenthal and Jacobsen's (1968) study concerned race, ethnic, and class differences in academic performance. Teachers often have lower expectations for the academic performance of minority-group and poor children than they do for their white, middle-class counterparts (Minuchin & Shapiro, 1983). To test the possibility that these lowered expectations actually lower minority and poor children's academic performance, Rosenthal and Jacobsen included a group of poor Mexican-American children among those they identified as likely to bloom during the coming year. These children made particularly large gains in IQ test performance. In fact, the children whom the teachers identified as most "Mexican-looking" made the largest gains, perhaps because they were the ones from whom the teachers would ordinarily have expected the least.

Such results immediately attracted the attention of researchers and the public at large. More than 500 studies have been conducted on the role of teachers' expectations in students' academic performance (Wineberg, 1987). Many school districts even have special training programs to ensure that their teachers are sensitive to the ways in which their expectations may negatively affect some children.

Despite general acceptance that teachers' expectations are a significant factor in children's academic performance, some psychologists and educators remain skeptical (Wineberg, 1987). One basis for doubt is that many studies fail to find any such effects. Why do they not find the effects that other studies do?

In an attempt to answer this question, researchers observed teachers and children interacting in classrooms. They found that not all teachers

(continued)

BOX 13.4
Teachers' Expectations and School Success *(continued)*

behave the same way toward the children for whom they have low expectations. Some teachers ignore those from whom they expect little academically and focus on the children they consider more capable. But other teachers seem to compensate by giving extra help and encouragement to the children for whom they have low expectations, and still others are even-handed in apportioning attention (Good, Sikes, & Brophy, 1973). This research also makes it clear that children are not passive recipients of teachers' expectations. Children influence those expectations by their own classroom behavior (Brophy, 1983).

Research by Carol Dweck and her colleagues has shown one way in which the interplay between teachers' expectations and children's behavior may shape academic development. Dweck's research has focused on teachers' differing expectations for boys and girls. In general, girls are better behaved than boys during the elementary school years. Consequently, teachers expect boys to challenge classroom decorum and girls to support it. Dweck and her colleagues found that these differences in children's behavior and teachers'

expectations led teachers to respond differently to boys and girls (Dweck & Bush, 1976; Dweck et al., 1978; Dweck & Goetz, 1978). Overall, teachers criticize boys more than girls. Often this criticism focuses on boys' lack of decorum, their failure to do their work neatly, or their inattentiveness. Their criticism of girls, by contrast, is likely to focus on their ability and intellectual performance. At the same time, when teachers offer praise, its focus is likely to be girls' cooperative social behavior and boys' intellectual accomplishments.

These differences in teachers' expectations for boys and girls and in the kind of feedback they give them have been found to be related to the kinds of expectations that children form about their own behavior (Dweck & Elliott, 1983). When girls are told that they have failed, they usually believe that the teacher has correctly assessed their intellectual capacity, so they tend to stop trying. Boys interpret such criticism differently: they blame their poor performance on someone else or on their situation and retain faith in their own ability to do better next time.

Evidence that teachers may discourage children for whom expectations are low has prompted a variety of programs to encourage broad participation in academic work. This young girl is participating in a program to encourage excellence in mathematics.

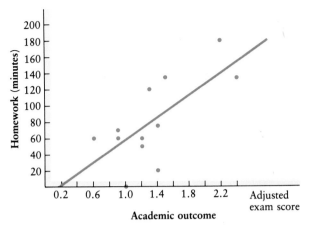

FIGURE 13.12   *As the amount of homework assigned each week increases (a measure of the academic emphasis of the school), students' grades improve. (From Rutter et al., 1979.)*

Student conditions   Schools in which students were free to use the buildings during breaks and at lunchtime, had access to a telephone, and were expected to keep the classrooms clean and pleasant produced better student achievement than schools that were run entirely by adults.

The most intriguing finding was that in the successful schools, each individual factor seemed to feed the others, creating an overall environment, or "school atmosphere," conducive to success. This positive school atmosphere cannot be legislated; it must be created by the staff and the students together. Each successful school arrived at its own conducive atmosphere in its own way, taking a distinctive mix of approaches.

Out of School

Although literate societies have come to equate success with schooling, it should not be forgotten that there is more to life than school. On weekday afternoons and evenings, on weekends and holidays, 6-to-12-year-old children are likely to be found among their friends, engaged in activities of their own choosing. Participation in these peer groups provides a kind of preparation for adult life that is quite different from that organized by adults in classrooms and in the home. A full understanding of the nature of middle childhood requires investigation of this context as well, to which we turn in Chapter 14.

SUMMARY

1. School is a specialized child-rearing environment that is specific to certain societies and historical eras. Formal education in schools differs from traditional training, such as apprenticeship, in the motives for learning as well as in the social relations, the social organization, and the medium of instruction.
2. Schooling arose as a means of training large numbers of scribes to keep the records on which complex societies depend.
3. The use of a written notation system is essential to formal education. The technology of writing has undergone a long evolution. The early notation systems that represented objects gave way to systems of symbols representing language. The evolution of the written notation system called an alphabet decreased the number of symbols that people needed to learn but increased the abstractness of the resulting system for representing sounds.
4. Reading an alphabetic language is a complex cognitive skill in which information the reader obtains by decoding the correspondences between letters and sounds must be coordinated with higher-order information about the content of the text.
5. Researchers are divided in their ideas about how reading should be taught.
   a. Those who favor the code-emphasis-first approach believe that reading is acquired in several stages. The transition around third or fourth grade from decoding individual words to reading for the purpose of learning something new is particularly difficult for many children.
   b. Those who favor a meaning-emphasis-first approach believe that from the outset decoding should be learned in the context of reading for meaning.
6. Reading instruction has undergone changes in response to demands for higher levels of proficiency. Current curricula seek to balance an emphasis on de-

coding with an emphasis on reading for meaning. Special teaching methods, such as reciprocal teaching, have been devised to enable students to integrate their decoding skills with reading for meaning.

7. Children arrive at school with rudimentary knowledge about practical arithmetic, including the idea of one-to-one correspondence between number words and objects and the ability to count.

8. Learning mathematics in school requires students to acquire and coordinate three kinds of knowledge:
   a. Conceptual knowledge, or the understanding of mathematical principles.
   b. Procedural knowledge, or the ability to carry out sequences of actions to solve a problem.
   c. Utilization knowledge, or the knowledge of when to apply particular procedures.

9. Theories of how best to teach mathematics vary between two extremes, one emphasizing the need for drill and practice, the other emphasizing the centrality of conceptual understanding. Most current teaching techniques attempt to balance drill with explanation.

10. Classroom instruction is characterized by a special kind of talk.
    a. With respect to spoken language, children must learn to acquire knowledge through verbal exchanges in which teachers ask questions, students reply, and teachers evaluate.
    b. With respect to written language, children must learn to use notation systems that differ systematically from their spoken equivalents.

11. The great emphasis placed on the use of correct linguistic forms in classroom discourse reinforces the hypothetical, "as if" nature of classroom problem solving.

12. Research comparing the cognitive performances of schooled and unschooled children reveals that in several domains—including the organization of the lexicon, memory, and metacognitive skills—formal schooling appears to enhance the development of certain cognitive skills during middle childhood. Positive cognitive consequences of schooling, however, turn out to be restricted to materials and procedures that closely match classroom practices. There is no evidence that schooling enhances cognitive development in general.

13. Tests of aptitude for schooling first appeared when public education became a mass phenomenon. The earliest tests were designed to identify children who needed special support to succeed in school.

14. The key innovation in Binet and Simon's test of school aptitude was to sort test items according to the age at which typical children could cope with them, thus producing a scale of "mental age."

15. The aptitude measure called IQ represents a child's mental age (as determined by the age at which average children pass each test item) divided by chronological age ($IQ = [MA/CA] \times 100$). By definition this ratio yields an average IQ of 100.

16. IQ test scores have been found to correlate significantly with later school success.

17. An important unresolved question about intelligence tests is the degree to which the aptitudes they tap are general across all domains of human activity, or are closely related to specialized activities, such as those involved in schooling and music.

18. Persistent class, racial, and ethnic differences in IQ test performance have inspired fierce debates about the possibility that some races, ethnic groups, and classes are genetically inferior.

19. Modern research comparing the IQs of identical and fraternal twins indicates that IQ has a genetic component that accounts for perhaps 50 percent of the variation in test performance within groups.

20. African American children adopted by white middle-class families develop normal IQs, an indication that average differences in IQ scores are the result of environmental factors.

21. Peer-group values antithetical to school values can exert a powerful negative effect on students' achievement. Peer groups can also be used to enhance classroom learning.

22. Schools with a strong academic emphasis, teachers skilled in classroom management, an emphasis on praise over punishment, and a welcoming attitude toward students have positive effects on students' achievement in school.

KEY TERMS

apprenticeship

comprehension

decoding

deviation IQ

education

environmentalist hypothesis of intelligence

innatist hypothesis of intelligence

initiation-reply-evaluation sequence

instructional discourse

IQ

mental age (MA)

metacognition

reciprocal teaching

SUGGESTED READINGS

FARNHAM-DIGGORY, SYLVIA. *Schooling.* Cambridge, Mass.: Harvard University Press, 1990.

The topics covered in *Schooling* provide a useful supplement to the materials covered in this chapter. After exploring the historical background of the theory and practice of schooling in the United States, Sylvia Farnham-Diggory summarizes various scientific approaches to the study of school-based learning and prospects for change in schooling guided by modern research.

GARDNER, HOWARD. *The Unschooled Mind: How Children Think and How Schools Should Teach.* New York: Basic Books, 1991.

Howard Gardner brings together knowledge about cognitive development from birth to middle childhood as the foundation for a variety of suggestions about how to reform schooling to make it more in tune with children's talent for learning. The early portions of his book provide an excellent review of topics that we covered in earlier chapters. Later chapters show how his theory of multiple intelligences can be applied to the organization of school-based instruction.

GINSBURG, HERBERT. *Children's Arithmetic: The Learning Process.* New York: Van Nostrand, 1977.

This book analyzes the development of mathematical reasoning, focusing primarily on children's struggles with arithmetic tasks in school. It is particularly rich in its detailed descriptions of individual children's reasoning as their intuitive ways of thinking about numbers confront the written notation system of mathematics.

GOULD, STEPHEN J. *The Mismeasure of Man.* New York: Norton, 1981.

Professor of biology, geology, and the history of science, Stephen J. Gould here surveys the historical origins of the idea that intelligence is a single entity, located in the brain, that can legitimately be used to rank people along a single dimension of ability.

HOLT, JOHN. *How Children Fail.* New York: Dell, 1964.

A firsthand account of the dynamics that make failure in school an integral part of middle childhood for a large percentage of the world's children.

SAXE, GEOFFREY B. *Culture and Cognitive Development: Studies in Mathematical Understanding.* Hillsdale, N.J.: Erlbaum, 1991.

Geoffrey Saxe conducted an extensive series of studies on the development of mathematical thinking among children who sell candy on the streets of Recife, Brazil. Here he provides an exceptionally well-rounded comparison of the thought processes the schools promote and those used in everyday mathematical practices.

STERNBERG, ROBERT J. *Handbook of Intelligence.* New York: Cambridge University Press, 1982.

An authoritative compendium of essays on the history and theory of intelligence testing.

STEVENSON, HAROLD, & STIGLER, JAMES. *The Learning Gap: Why Our Schools Are Failing and What We Can Learn from Japanese and Chinese Education.* New York: Summit, 1992.

The educational and economic achievements of the Japanese and of the Chinese in Taiwan have won widespread admiration. This book describes the cultural values, social policies, and classroom practices that underlie recent educational successes in these two Asian countries and contrasts them with practices in the United States.

CHAPTER 14

The Social Relations of Middle Childhood

•

We went home and when somebody said, "Where were you?"
we said, "Out," and when somebody said, "What were you
doing until this hour of the night," we said, as always, "Nothing."
But about this doing nothing: we swung on the swings. We
went for walks. We lay on our backs in the backyards and
chewed grass . . . and when we were done, he [my best
friend] walked me home to my house, and when we got there
I walked him back to his house, and then he —.
We watched things: we watched people build houses, we
watched men fix cars, we watched each other patch bicycle
tires with rubber bands . . . [we watched] our fathers playing
cards, our mothers making jam, our sisters skipping rope, curl-
ing their hair. . . .
We sat in boxes; we sat under porches; we sat on roofs; we sat
on limbs of trees.
We stood on boards over excavations; we stood on tops of
piles of leaves; we stood under rain dripping from the eaves;
we stood up to our ears in snow.
We looked at things like knives . . . and grasshoppers and
clouds and dogs and people.
We skipped and hopped and jumped. Not going anywhere —
just skipping and hopping and jumping and galloping.
We sang and whittled and hummed and screamed.
What I mean, Jack, we did a lot of nothing.

— ROBERT PAUL SMITH, *WHERE DID YOU GO? OUT.*
WHAT DID YOU DO? NOTHING.

Between the ages of 6 and 12, U.S. children typically spend over 40 percent of their waking hours in the company of **peers,** children of their own age and status, often "doing nothing." This figure is more than double the amount of time they spent with peers when they were preschoolers. The increase in time spent among peers is accompanied by a complementary decrease in the time spent with parents (Baldwin, 1955; Barker & Wright, 1955; Hill & Stafford, 1980).

Comparisons of the same children's behavior in different settings suggest two obvious differences between contexts where adults supervise and contexts dominated by peers. First, the content of the activity is different. When adults preside over children's activities, some form of instruction or work is likely to take place; when several children get together with no adults present, they will probably play a game or "just hang out."

Second, the forms of social control are different. When children are under the watchful eyes of adults, either at home or in school, it is the adults who keep peace and maintain the social order. If Sarah takes more than her share of ice cream, or if Tom and Jimmy refuse to let Sam on the swings, the adult is there to invoke society's rules ("Share and share alike"; "Everyone gets a turn") and to settle disputes. But when children are on their own in peer groups, they must establish the distribution of authority and responsibility themselves. Sometimes might makes right, and an especially strong child dominates the group. By and large, however, authority is established through negotiation, compromise, and discussion (Youniss, 1980). Power within the group may also shift with the children's activities. A leader in making mischief may not be the leader in organizing an afternoon trip to the movies (Sherif & Sherif, 1956).

The increased time that children spend among their peers is both a cause and an effect of their development during middle childhood. Adults begin to allow their children to spend extensive time with friends because they recognize the children's greater ability to think and act for themselves. At the same time, the new experiences with peers challenge children to master new cognitive and social skills (Hartup, 1992; Schneider et al., 1989; Selman & Schultz, 1990).

Learning to get along without fighting is a difficult task, especially when a smaller child is threatened and one's honor is at stake.

These boys are playing in the ocean without any supervision from their parents, a situation which would not have been allowed just a few years earlier.

Children's sense of themselves and their relations with others also changes in middle childhood. So long as they spend their time primarily among family members, their place in the social world is determined for them. They are accepted as "Mrs. Smith's little girl, Suzie," or "Juan López's brother Tony." When children spend more time among their peers, the sense of self they acquired in their families no longer suffices and they must learn to reconcile their old identities with the new ones they begin to form in the new contexts they inhabit (Damon & Hart, 1988). The responsible older sibling who watches the baby, the classroom comedian, the star volleyball player, and the kid who spends a lot of time reading adventure stories may well be one and the same person.

Middle childhood also brings changes in the quality of children's relations with their parents (Maccoby, 1984). Parents can no longer easily pick them up and physically remove them from danger or from sibling squabbles. Instead they must rely on their children's greater understanding of the consequences of their actions and on their desire to conform to adult standards. As a result, parents' socialization techniques become more indirect: they rely more on discussion and explanation than on physical force to influence their children's behavior.

Unfortunately, psychological research methods cannot always do justice to the greatly increased diversity of experience during middle childhood. Scientists' study of preschoolers is impeded by the children's imprecise grasp of language; it is difficult to distinguish fact from fancy in what they say. On the other hand, young children, whether at home or in a day-care center, are restricted to relatively few environments, where adults can keep an eye on them and record what they do; and the presence of an adult does not affect their spontaneity. Most 8- and 9-year-olds, in contrast, are perfectly capable conversationalists, but their behavior with their peers is likely to change radically when an adult observer appears on the scene.

Scientific knowledge about middle childhood is therefore fragmentary in several respects. We have extensive information about children's behavior in school, but systematic knowledge about their life in other contexts is often skimpy. A great many studies have been conducted on how children respond to questions about hypothetical moral dilemmas, their explicit conceptions of friendship, and the way they attempt to solve a variety of intellectual puzzles adults pose for them. But we have little systematic information about their actual moral behavior, their qualities as friends, or their ability to recognize and solve problems in everyday life. In this chapter we will discuss the evidence on the social aspects of middle childhood and then return at the end to the questions of whether middle childhood represents a distinctive stage of development.

GAMES AND GROUP REGULATION

The appearance of peer groups among children 6 to 12 years old raises a central question about middle childhood: How do children learn to regulate their social relations by themselves? The precise psychological mechanisms are still uncertain, but it appears that one important arena for this development is game playing (Piaget, 1967; Sutton-Smith, 1979).

Games and Rules

Like preschoolers, children who have entered middle childhood engage in fantasy role play, with each child taking a part in an imaginary situation: cops chase robbers; tree houses become havens for shipwrecked families; and forts hide runaway children (Singer & Singer, 1990). But now a new form of play comes into prominence — the playing of games based upon rules.

The rules and the styles of interaction that these games promote vary from culture to culture. In West Africa children divide into teams and challenge each other to remember the names of leaves gathered in the forest. Children in the United States are more likely to play Twenty Questions or Trivial Pursuit. In many cultures we find variations on games in which a ball is kicked, hit, or thrown as part of a team sport, or games that resemble tag or hopscotch (Rubin, Fein, & Vandenberg, 1983; Schwartzman, 1980). But even in cultures in which children are more likely to begin to work than to attend school, middle childhood is the time when games with explicit rules make their appearance.

Although fantasy play is based on *roles* and games are based on *rules,* rules are not totally absent from fantasy play in early childhood, nor are roles totally absent from rule-based play. Rules are a part of young children's social pretend play in two ways. First, when young children perform their roles, they typically fol-low implicit social rules. The pretend teacher tells the pretend children to sit quietly; the children do not tell the teacher what to do.

Second, young children use rules to negotiate the roles they adopt and to maintain the make-believe context: "Only girls are allowed to be Superwoman"; "Go away, Darth Vader, we're having a birthday party and spacemen are not allowed at birthday parties" (Paley, 1984).

The balance between rules and roles is reversed in the games that become prominent during middle childhood. About the age of 7 or 8, rules become the essence of many games, especially among boys. In such games, the rules determine what roles are to be played and what one can and cannot do in playing those roles. Rules also enter differently into the content of the games of middle childhood. Preschool fantasy play can change from moment to moment, allowing children constantly to merge their whims with their play. But in the games characteristic of older children, participants must agree ahead of time about the rules that will govern their activity. Anyone who changes the rules without common consent is "cheating."

Rule-based games seem to require the kind of mental abilities that form the basis for adults' assignment of new tasks and responsibilities to 6- and 7-year-olds (see Chapter 12). Children must be able to keep in mind the overall set of task conditions specified ahead of time as they pursue the goals of the moment. At the same time, they need to engage in social perspective-taking, understanding the relation between the thoughts of the other players and their own actions if they are going to be successful ("If I move my checker into this opening, she'll double-jump me").

Rule-based games also differ in purpose from fantasy play. In fantasy play, the play's the thing. Satisfaction comes from exercising the imagination in the company of others. In rule-based play, the object is to win through competition governed by rules (see Box 14.1). The following description of an attempt to involve a preschooler in a rule-based game captures beautifully this difference in orientation:

> The experimenter is playing hide-and-seek with a 3-year-old child. When the child has hidden, the experimenter does not "find" it immediately, but deliberately waits near the child for a minute or two pretending not to be able to find it. Then the tot cannot restrain itself from breaking the rule,

BOX 14.1
Socialization for Adulthood: Little League Baseball

Little League Baseball is the best-known and most successful sports program for boys in the United States (although girls are now making inroads on this institution). Every spring and summer, well over half a million boys between the ages of 9 and 12 spend two or three afternoons a week learning "the American pastime." In addition to providing instruction in the skills of baseball, the Little League coaches try to teach their players to work hard, to cooperate and compete with one another, to adhere to ideals of good sportsmanship, and to be good members of their communities.

For three seasons in the early 1980s the sociologist Gary Alan Fine (1987) was a frequent visitor to several Little League teams in various leagues. He not only attended practices and games but from time to time got together with the team members in other community settings. Although he rarely participated directly as a coach or an umpire, he won acceptance as a friendly outsider, "one of the boys," and his detailed field notes are a rich source of information about American boys growing up under the tutelage of older males in their community. Fine notes:

> If we hope to understand how adult sex roles are shaped, we must observe the blossoming of those roles in childhood peer groups. . . . Most nonfamilial guardians of boys are women; yet in sports, boys are taught to be men, and these men (at least in Little League) see themselves as having specific didactic roles. (1987:1)

Fine discovered that participation in Little League provides many opportunities for socialization in basic community values.

Play and work. Playing baseball in Little League is a mixture of play and work. Once a boy becomes a member of a team, it is not enough for him simply to turn up at gametime. He is expected to attend practices and to concentrate on building his skills even if he is bored or tired. During games he is expected to pay attention and provide encouragement to his teammates even if he is not in the game.

Effort. In an obvious sense, the object of playing baseball is to win. But Little League coaches make clear that it is at least as important to try hard as to win. Typical of coaches' comments is this one:

> Your goal for the year is to be a winner. That doesn't mean winning every game. Sometimes you will be up against teams that are better than you. It does mean to give everything you've got. If you give everything you've got, you're a winner in my book. (p. 62)

Sportsmanship. Although a coach may consider his players to be winners if they try hard, there is no avoiding the fact that losing is as much a part of the game as winning. When a boy strikes out or makes an error, he may feel a powerful urge to throw his bat or to cry. But the knowledge that he is performing in public provides an extra incentive at least to appear to take mistakes and losing gracefully.

When a player does lose his self-control—and it is not uncommon for a boy to become overtly upset or hostile—it is up to his coach and teammates to help him regain his equanimity. Of course, in the heat of the game, the coach himself may engage in unsportsmanlike conduct, yelling at the boys, suggesting underhanded ways for them to gain the advantage, or cursing other adults. Observation of several such scenes moved Fine to comment that "successful socialization is learning when to express the moral verities proclaimed by adults, discerning which ones they 'really' mean, and knowing what moral rhetoric to adopt when caught redhanded" (p. 60).

Teamwork. Perhaps no aspect of participation in Little League is so overtly linked to adult life as teamwork. One of the coaches whom Fine interviewed said that "teamwork is very important. That's one of the things that life is all about, is working with a team. Little League is that opportunity" (p. 71).

Supporters of Little League believe that this form of organized sports activity is good for the children who participate. The former major-league star Bob Feller sums up the view of many when he says:

> Little Leagues not only foster friendships, develop coordination and good health habits in boys, but they break down social barriers to make a more closely knit community. . . . No one

pays attention to how much money a boy's father has, or his social standing. . . . Where else is there a more practical training for democracy? (p. 196)

Little League also has its critics. Noting that some coaches are so determined to win that they forget the lofty ideals of the organization, some observers argue that Little League is too competitive. Others suggest that the presence of umpires and fixed schedules rob children of the opportunity to engage in sports spontaneously and also exposes them to physical danger and to the tender mercies of untrained coaches.

Fine surveyed existing research on the impact of Little League on children's development and conducted an interview study of his own. By and large, the data he was able to gather appeared to be more supportive of Little League than critical of it. Parents generally think that Little League is beneficial for their children, and fathers report that they spend more time with their sons engaged in mutually satis-

fying activity. Other research shows that participation in Little League is correlated with popularity, positive self-esteem, higher ratings of leadership ability by teachers, and reduced delinquency. In every case, however, the direction of causation is open to dispute, because Little League is a voluntary activity; boys don't have to play in Little League, they must want to. As a consequence, a positive correlation between some desirable attribute (such as popularity or positive self-esteem) may be logically explained either as a result of the fact that popular or more self-confident children join Little League or as a result of participation in Little League.

Surveying the results of his own and others' research on the merits and demerits of participation in Little League, Gary Alan Fine hands down a verdict of "not proven." On balance, his own personal opinion is positive: "Basically Little League is fun for those preadolescents who participate, and while we should never stop trying to curtail its flaws, we should be satisfied that it brings a little joy into the lives of our children" (p. 221).

Games with rules are prominent in the lives of children during middle childhood.

and almost immediately begins to shout: "Uncle, here I am!" A 6-year-old plays hide-and-seek quite differently. For it, the main thing is to stick to the rules. The experimenter conceived the idea of telling both children (the 3-year-old and the 6-year-old) to hide together. He again pretended that he could not find them. Soon the children's excited voices were heard, and then a muffled noise. The little one was trying to give itself up while the 6-year-old was preventing it from doing so. Exclamations were heard: "Quiet, keep still!" Finally the older child tried to stop the little one's mouth—matters came to very vigorous measures to make the younger child observe the rule. (Leontiev, 1981:381)

The shift from fantasy play to rule-based games greatly expands both the number of children who can play together and the likely duration of their joint activity. In a typical preschool setting, only two or three children play together at a time, and their play episodes are likely to last less than 10 minutes (Corsaro, 1981). When larger groups gather, it is almost certainly because the teacher has taken the trouble to coordinate their activity, which is unlikely to be fantasy play. School-age children, by contrast, often play for hours in groups numbering up to 20 or so (Hartup,

1984). The increased duration and complexity of children's play provide evidence that at least under some conditions, children who have entered middle childhood are capable of regulating their own behavior according to agreed-upon social rules.

Games and Life

The link between young children's pretend play and their social surroundings is fairly obvious because they use adult roles and familiar scripts as the basis of their fantasy. It is less obvious how a game of hopscotch or checkers relates to adult life. Nonetheless, the idea that rule-based games are preparation for life has widespread appeal (see Box 14.1).

Piaget (1965) believed that the appearance of rule-based games in middle childhood has a double significance for children's development. First, he saw the ability to engage in rule-based games as a manifestation of concrete operations in the social sphere, corresponding to decreasing egocentrism, the appearance of conservation, and other cognitive abilities discussed in Chapter 12. Second, he believed that such games create structured circumstances within which children obtain practice in balancing their own desires against the rules of their society. Commenting on the decrease in pretend play in middle childhood and the advent of rule-based games, Piaget wrote that

> The more the child adapts himself to the natural and social world, the less he indulges in symbolic distortions and transpositions, because instead of assimilating the external world to the ego he progressively subordinates the ego to reality. (1962:145)

In other words, the replacement of pretend play by rule-based play brings about a shift from the dominance of assimilation toward more accommodation.

Rule-based games are a model of society for children in two closely related respects, Piaget argued. First,

> games with rules are social institutions in that they remain the same as they are transmitted from one generation to the next and they are independent of the will of the individuals who participate in them. (Piaget & Inhelder, 1969:119)

Like other social institutions—a school lesson, for example—games provide an already existing structure of rules about how to behave in specific social circumstances.

Second, like all social institutions, rule-based games can exist only if people agree to their existence. In order to play a game such as checkers or hide-and-seek, children must learn to subordinate their desires and behavior to a socially agreed-upon system. Piaget linked this ability to work within a framework of rules to children's acquisition of respect for rules and a new level of moral understanding:

> All morality consists in a system of rules, and the essence of all morality is to be sought for in the respect which the individual acquires for these rules. . . . The rules of the game of marbles are handed down, just like so-called moral realities, from one generation to another, and are preserved solely by the respect that is felt for them by individuals. (1965:13–14)

In Piaget's view, it is through the give and take of negotiating plans, settling disagreements, making and enforcing rules, and keeping and breaking promises that children come to develop an understanding that social rules provide a structure that makes possible cooperation with others (Piaget, 1965).

On the basis of his observations of the way children play games, Piaget proposed a developmental progression in children's understanding of social rules. The game on which he based most of his discussion is marbles. He maintained that very young children play marbles with little regard for the rules and with no notion of competition. They pile marbles up or roll them around as suits their fancy. At this stage, marbles is not a true game at all.

In middle childhood they try to win according to preexisting rules. At first they tend to believe that the rules of the game have been handed down by such authority figures as older children, adults, or even God; therefore, the rules are sacred and cannot be changed. Piaget asked one 5½-year-old if it would be all right to allow little children to shoot their marbles from a position closer to the marbles they were trying to hit.

"No," answered Leh, "that wouldn't be fair."—"Why not?"—"Because God would make the little boy's shot not reach the marbles and the big boy's shot would reach them." (1965:58)

Piaget suggested to Ben, aged 10, that he might invent a new version of marbles. Ben agreed reluctantly that it would be possible to think up new rules, and suggested one. Piaget asked if such a new rule would be acceptable:

Piaget: Then people could play that way?
Ben: Oh, no, because it would be cheating.
Piaget: But all your pals would like to, wouldn't they?
Ben: Yes, they all would.
Piaget: Then why would it be cheating?
Ben: Because I invented it: it isn't a rule! It's a wrong rule because it's outside of the rules. A fair rule is one that is in the game. (1965:63)

Most children begin to treat the rules of games with less awe sometime between the ages of 9 and 11, according to Piaget. They realize that game rules are social conventions resulting from mutual consent. The rules must be respected if you want to play together, "but it is permissible to alter the rules as long as general opinion is on your side" (1965:28).

Although he focused his attention on the game of marbles, which in Geneva was played almost exclusively by boys, Piaget wanted to show that the developmental progression he had encountered was universal. However, he reported that he could not find any collective games played by girls that used as many rules and had as many fine-grained codifications as marbles. After observing many girls playing hopscotch, he remarked that girls seemed more interested in inventing new configurations of hopscotch squares than in elaborating the rules.

Piaget's observation that boys and girls not only play different games but play games differently has generated a good deal of subsequent research. When José Linaza (1984) observed English and Spanish boys and girls playing marbles, he found that though the boys might play marbles more often and more skillfully than girls, there were no marked sex differences in the children's understanding of the rules of the game. Janet Lever (1978), however, confirmed Piaget's finding that rules enter into the play of boys and girls differently (see Box 14.2). Overall, the research suggests that, despite some observed sex differences, middle childhood is a time when play based on explicit rules begins to assume prominence in the interactions of both sexes.

BOX 14.2
Boys' Games, Girls' Games

Piaget's observation that during middle childhood boys are more likely than girls to engage in competitive games based on explicit rules was corroborated many years later by Janet Lever (1978). Lever observed children in the United States on playgrounds, interviewed them, and had them keep diaries of their after-school play. She then rated the children's play according to its complexity. She defined as complex those games that require each player to take a different role (such as baseball); that require a relatively large number of participants; that require players to compete for an explicit goal, such as scoring a goal in soccer or checkmating an opponent; that have a number of specified rules that are known by all the players before the game begins and whose violations are penalized; and that require teams.

According to Lever's data (see the accompanying table), both boys and girls engage in a wide variety of play activities, including complex games. But on the average, girls play less complex games with fewer participants than boys do. Boys are almost twice as likely as girls to engage in competitive games, even when they are not playing team sports. Girls tend to play cooperatively. When their games allow competition, as jump-rope and jacks do, it is indirect: each player acts independently, competing by turn against the others' scores, rather than in face-to-face confrontations, as boys do.

Not only are boys' games different from girls'; their play groups tend to be larger. Team sports, which they are more likely to engage in than girls, require from 10 to 25 participants to be played properly. Lever rarely observed girls playing in groups as large as 10; they favored such games as hopscotch and tag, which can be played with as few as two people and seldom include more than six. Some girls talked more than they played.

Lever conjectures that such differences provide girls and boys with markedly different sets of social-

Percent of Time Girls and Boys Were Observed Playing Games of Various Degrees of Complexity

	Girls	Boys
Complexity score 0 Roller skating, bike riding, listening to records	42%	27%
Complexity score 1 Singing, playing catch, bowling, racing electric cars	7	12
Complexity score 2 Indoor fantasy, jump-rope, tag, simple card games	31	15
Complexity score 3 Board games, checkers	8	15
Complexity score 4 Capture the flag	2	1
Complexity score 5 Team sports	10	30

Source: Lever, 1978.

ization experiences and social skills. Boys' games, she contends, provide them with the opportunity to deal with diversity, to coordinate with a large number of people, to cope with impersonal rule systems, and to work for collective as well as personal goals. In particular, participation in team sports furnishes boys with the opportunity to be rewarded for improving their skills, to gain experience in leadership positions, and to deal with competition in a depersonalized fashion, as well as to maintain self-control. Most girls' play activities tend instead to recreate primary human relationships and to concentrate on intimacy.

REASONING AND ACTION IN DIFFERENT RULE DOMAINS

In the transition to middle childhood, children must come to understand several domains of rules, each with its own nature and content. The various types of social rules can be distinguished by their importance, their presumed source, their apparent permanence, and their generality (Turiel, Killen, & Helwig, 1987) (see Table 14.1). At the most general level are **moral rules,** social regulations based on principles of justice and the welfare of others. One important category of moral rules applies to moral *transgressions,* such as the prohibition against killing another human. A second category of moral rules applies to issues of *fairness,* such as the assumption that resources ought to be distributed equitably among people. Moral rules are often believed to derive from a divine source and therefore are obligations that cannot be transgressed. Such rules are found in some form in all societies (Rawls, 1971).

At the next level of generality are social norms, or **social conventions** — rules that are particular to a given society — such as prescriptions about the kinds of behavior that are appropriate for males and females or the kind of clothes people should wear in public, as well as rules about who has authority over other people, how authority is exercised, and how it is acknowledged (Turiel, 1983). **Group norms,** a more restricted kind of social convention, apply to small groups such as peer groups. They include special modes of greeting (such as secret handshakes) and styles of dress. Social conventions coordinate the behavior of individuals within a social system, but vary from society to society and from group to group.

At the most specific level are **personal rules** governing particular events, such as "Do homework before watching TV" and "Brush teeth before going to bed every night." Personal rules are often created by individuals to regulate their own behavior.

Larry Nucci (1981) has demonstrated that at least from middle childhood on, North American children can distinguish among all three kinds of rules. Nucci presented cartoon strips depicting violations of moral, conventional, and personal rules to children and adolescents (see Figure 14.1). Asked to judge the seriousness of each incident, subjects of all ages ranked moral violations the most serious; then came violations of social convention and finally violations of personal rules.

TABLE 14.1

Sample Event Types and Infractions in the Domains of Moral Rules, Social Conventions, and Personal Rules

Sample Event Types	Sample Infractions
MORAL RULES	
Physical harm	Hitting, pushing, killing
Psychological harm	Hurting feelings, ridiculing
Fairness and rights	Stealing, breaking a promise
Prosocial behaviors	Never donating to charity, refusing help to someone in distress
SOCIAL CONVENTIONS	
School rules	Chewing gum in class, talking back to the teacher
Forms of address	Calling a physician "Mr." when he is working
Attire and appearance	Wearing pajamas to school
Sex roles	Boy wears barette to keep hair out of eyes while playing football
Etiquette	Swearing, making loud noises while eating
PERSONAL RULES	
Hygiene	Not brushing teeth, forgetting to change sheets
Social	Neglecting to call parents, forgetting best friend's birthday
Financial	Overdrawing account at bank

Source: After Turiel, Killen, & Helwig, 1987.

(a)

Kathy is playing with her doll.	Meg comes over and takes Kathy's doll away from her.	Kathy is upset. Meg is not supposed to take things away from other children.

(b)

Karen is watching her very favorite TV program, "The Mickey Mouse Club."	Her big sister tells her, "Karen, you're not allowed to stay inside on sunny days. Mom says you have to go outside and play."	"Those are the rules."

(c)

Larry is eating lunch in the school cafeteria. He is eating with his fingers.	Laura tells Larry, "You shouldn't eat meat with your fingers."	"You should use a knife and fork when you're eating in the cafeteria."

FIGURE 14.1 *Cartoon strips used to evaluate the relative importance that children attach to infractions of* (a) *moral rules,* (b) *personal rules, and* (c) *social conventions. (Courtesy of L. Nucci.)*

Although children seem to understand the distinction between rule types from an early age, their understanding of each type continues to develop throughout childhood. A major research goal is to determine the extent to which development within one rule domain is related to development within others, and to grasp how children's understanding of rules relates to their behavior in everyday life.

Thou Shalt Not: Reasoning about Moral Transgressions

As we described briefly in Chapter 10 (p. 370), preschoolers believe that rules are always imposed by adults and that an act is bad if it breaks the rules that adults formulate. Piaget referred to this kind of moral reasoning, in which morality is imposed from the outside, as "the morality of constraint." Earlier we saw how Piaget came to the conclusion that as children begin to understand that the rules of games can be changed if everyone agrees, their reasoning about moral questions should also change because moral development depends upon respect for social rules. In particular, he believed that when they enter middle childhood and begin to play rule-based games, children should begin to base their judgments of "good" and "bad" behavior on autonomous moral reasoning that takes the intentions of the rulebreaker into account.

Lawrence Kohlberg modified Piaget's ideas about moral thinking to provide a more complete theory of how moral reasoning develops in relation to children's changing cognitive abilities and social experiences (Gilligan, 1977; Hoffman, 1983; Kagan & Lamb, 1987; Kohlberg, 1969, 1976, 1984; Kurtines & Gewirtz, 1991; Lickona, 1976; Rest, 1983). Kohlberg proposed that reasoning about moral issues generally progresses through five stages. He also believed in the existence of a sixth, ideal stage based on what he called "universal moral principles," but he encountered this stage so rarely that he abandoned efforts to score it.

Kohlberg's stages are grouped according to three levels of moral judgment, corresponding to Piaget's three major stages of cognitive development from age 3 to adulthood. At the *preconventional* level (corresponding to the stage of preoperational thinking), moral judgments are based on the direct physical consequences of the action in question and on the child's own desires. At the *conventional* level (corresponding to the stage of concrete operations), moral judgments depend on what other people think; acts that violate social standards are bad. At the *postconventional* level (corresponding to the stage of formal operations, which typically emerges after middle childhood), moral judgments are based on abstract moral principles. Table 14.2 summarizes Kohlberg's stages.

According to Kohlberg (1984), one must be able both to reason logically and to take the perspectives of others before one can attain a higher level of moral development. A person who cannot reason in a logical and systematic way is limited to stages 3 and 4 in this sequence. Similarly, people who have difficulty interpreting the thoughts and feelings of others will be restricted to lower levels of moral development (Kohlberg, 1976).

Since children in middle childhood rarely go beyond stage 3, we will describe only the first three stages in Kohlberg's moral development theory here. The remaining three stages will be discussed in Chapter 16.

Kohlberg's approach to assessing moral reasoning was to create a series of story dilemmas, each of which embodies a traditional question of moral philosophy: the value of human life and property, people's obligations to each other, the meaning of laws and rules. The story dilemmas pose these abstract issues in a concrete, dramatic way to engage the subjects' interest.

In the manner of Piaget's clinical interview technique, Kohlberg would read the story, ask the child's opinion, and then probe the reasoning behind that opinion with a set of questions tailored to the individual child's answer. Kohlberg's most famous story is the "Heinz dilemma":

> In Europe, a woman was near death from cancer. One drug might save her, a form of radium that a druggist in the same town had recently discovered. The druggist was charging $2,000, ten times what the drug cost him to make. The sick woman's husband, Heinz, went to everyone he knew to borrow the money, but he could get together only about half of what it cost. He told the druggist that his wife was dying and asked him to sell it cheaper or let him pay later. But the druggist said no. The husband got desperate and broke into the man's store to steal the drug for his wife. Should the husband have done that? Why? (Kohlberg, 1969:379)

TABLE 14.2
Kohlberg's Six Moral Stages

Level and Stage	What Is Right	Reasons for Doing Right	Social Perspective
LEVEL I—PRECONVENTIONAL			
Stage 1—Heteronomous morality	Adherence to rules backed by punishment; obedience for its own sake; avoidance of physical damage to persons and property.	Avoidance of punishment; superior power of authorities.	Egocentric point of view: Doesn't consider the interests of others or recognize that they differ from one's own; doesn't relate two points of view. Actions are considered in physical terms rather than in terms of psychological interests of others. Confusion of authority's perspective with one's own.
Stage 2—Individualism, instrumental purpose, exchange	Following rules only when it is to one's immediate interest; acting to meet one's own interests and needs and letting others do the same. Right is also what's fair, what's an equal exchange, a deal, an agreement.	To serve one's own needs or interests in a world where other people have their own interests.	Concrete individualistic perspective: Aware that all people have their own interests to pursue and these interests conflict, so that right is relative (in the concrete individualistic sense).
LEVEL II—CONVENTIONAL			
Stage 3—Mutual interpersonal expectations, relationships, and interpersonal conformity	Living up to what is expected by people close to you or what people generally expect of people in your role as son, brother, friend, etc. "Being good" is important and means having good motives, showing concern about others. It also means keeping mutual relationships by such means as trust, loyalty, respect, and gratitude.	The need to be a good person in your own eyes and those of others. Your caring for others. Belief in the Golden Rule. Desire to maintain rules and authority that support stereotypical good behavior.	Perspective of the individual in relationships with other individuals: Aware of shared feelings, agreements, and expectations that take primacy over individual interests. Relate points of view through the concrete Golden Rule, putting oneself in the other guy's shoes.
Stage 4—Social system and conscience	Fulfilling the actual duties to which you have agreed. Laws are to be upheld except in extreme cases when they conflict with other fixed social duties. Right is also contributing to society, group, or institution.	To keep the institution going as a whole, to avoid the breakdown in the system "if everyone did it," or the imperative of conscience to meet one's defined obligations (easily confused with stage 3 belief in rules and authority).	Differentiates societal point of view from interpersonal agreement of motives: Takes the point of view of the system that defines roles and rules. Considers individual relations in terms of place in the system.

TABLE 14.2 *(continued)*

Level and Stage	What Is Right	Reasons for Doing Right	Social Perspective
LEVEL III — POSTCONVENTIONAL, OR PRINCIPLED			
Stage 5 — Social contract or utility and individual rights	Being aware that people hold a variety of values and opinions, that most values and rules are relative to your group. These relative rules should usually be upheld, however, in the interest of impartiality and because they are the social contract. Such nonrelative values and rights as *life,* and *liberty,* however, must be upheld in any society, regardless of majority opinion.	A sense of obligation to law because of one's social contract to make and abide by laws for the welfare of all and for the protection of all people's rights. A feeling of contractual commitment, freely entered upon, to family, friendship, trust, and work obligations. Concern that laws and duties be based on rational calculation of overall utility, "the greatest good for the greatest number."	Prior-to-society perspective: Perspective of a rational individual aware of values and rights prior to social attachments and contracts. Integrates perspectives by formal mechanisms of agreement, contract, objective impartiality, and due process. Considers moral and legal points of view; recognizes that they sometimes conflict and finds it difficult to integrate them.
Stage 6 — Universal ethical principles	Following self-chosen ethical principles. Particular laws or social agreements are usually valid because they rest on such principles. When laws violate these principles, one acts in accordance with the principle. Principles are universal principles of justice: the equality of human rights and respect for the dignity of human beings as individual persons.	The rational belief in the validity of universal moral principles, and a sense of personal commitment to them.	Perspective of a moral point of view from which social arrangements derive. Perspective is that of any rational individual recognizing the nature of morality or the fact that persons are ends in themselves and must be treated as such.

Source: Adapted from Kohlberg, 1976.

Stage 1 coincides with the end of the preschool period and the beginning of middle childhood. Children at stage 1 adopt an egocentric point of view; they do not recognize the interests of others as distinct from their own. Their judgments about the rightness and wrongness of an action are based on its objective outcome, which in this case is how authorities respond to it. Stage 1 children might assert that Heinz must not steal the medicine because he will be put in jail. Or they might reason that he might as well take the medicine because it is not worth much money, so no one will get very upset. In either case, the stage 1 child focuses on the likely consequences of the man's actions.

At stage 2, which ordinarily appears around 7 to 8 years, children continue to adopt a concrete self-interested (egocentric) perspective but can recognize that other people have other perspectives. Justice is seen as an exchange system: you give as much as you receive. Kohlberg referred to the moral reasoning of children at this stage as "instrumental morality," because they believe it is perfectly acceptable to use others for their own interests. Children at this stage might respond to the Heinz dilemma by saying that Heinz should steal the drug because someday he might have cancer and would want someone to steal it for him.

Children at stage 3 make their judgments on the basis of a social-relational perspective. They see shared feelings and agreements, especially with people close to them, as more important than individual self-interest. One child quoted by Kohlberg said, "If I was Heinz, I would have stolen the drug for my wife. You can't put a price on love, no amount of gifts make love. You can't put a price on life either" (1984:629).

Stage 3 is often equated with the kind of moral reasoning associated with the Golden Rule. In Jewish tradition, this precept is attributed to Rabbi Hillel, who lived in the decades just before the birth of Christ. Rabbi Hillel phrased this injunction as "Do not unto others what you would not have them do unto you." This same idea was expressed in positive form in the Sermon on the Mount, when Jesus exhorted his followers to "do unto others as you would have them do unto you" (Matt. 7:12).

Though stage 3 is undoubtedly a more humane way of thinking about morality than either stage 1 or 2, stage 2 is the key transition associated with the new ability to get along without adult supervision that appears during middle childhood. No longer do children depend upon a strong external source to define right and wrong; instead, reciprocal relations between group members regulate behavior. Adults may not find the resulting behaviors desirable ("I won't tell your mom you went to see that R-rated move if you won't tell mine"), but at least this form of thinking allows children to regulate their actions with each other.

Thou Shalt: Reasoning about Rules of Fairness

William Damon's approach to the study of moral development differs somewhat from Kohlberg's. Instead of examining situations that might lead to the breaking of rules, Damon (1975, 1977, 1980) investigated children's conceptions of **positive justice:** how to divide resources or distribute rewards.

TABLE 14.3
Levels of Reasoning about Positive Justice

LEVEL 0-A (AGE 4 AND UNDER)

Positive-justice choices derive from wish that an act occur. Reasons simply assert the wishes rather than attempting to justify them ("I should get it because I want to have it").

LEVEL 0-B (AGES 4 TO 5)

Choices still reflect desires but are now justified on the basis of external, observable realities such as size, sex, or other physical characteristics of persons (e.g., we should get the most because we are girls). Such justifications, however, are invoked in a fluctuating, after-the-fact manner, and are self-serving in the end.

LEVEL 1-A (AGES 5 TO 7)

Positive-justice choices derive from notions of strict equality in actions (i.e., that everyone should get the same). Equality is seen as preventing complaining, fighting, "fussing," or other types of conflict.

LEVEL 1-B (AGES 6 TO 9)

Positive-justice choices derive from a notion of reciprocity in actions: that persons should be paid back in kind for doing good or bad things. Notions of merit and deserving emerge.

LEVEL 2-A (AGES 8 TO 10)

A moral relativity develops out of the understanding that different persons can have different yet equally valid justifications for their claims to justice. The claims of persons with special needs (e.g., the poor) are weighed heavily. Choices are attempts to reconcile competing claims.

LEVEL 2-B (AGES 10 AND UP)

Considerations of equality and reciprocity are coordinated so that choices take account of more than one person's claims and the demands of the specific situation. Choices are firm and clear-cut, yet justifications reflect the recognition that all persons should be given their due (though, in many situations, this does not mean equal treatment).

Source: Damon, 1980.

In order to study age-related changes in forms of reasoning, Damon, too, adopted the popular technique of telling a story and then posing a series of questions. One of his stories went like this:

> A classroom of children spent a day drawing pictures. Some children made a lot of drawings; some made fewer. Some children drew well; others did not draw as well. Some children were well-behaved and worked hard; others fooled around. Some children were poor, some were boys, some were girls, and so on. The class then sold the drawings at a school bazaar. How should the proceeds from the sale of the drawings be fairly distributed? (Adapted from Damon, 1975)

Damon probed the answers that children 4 to 12 years old gave to such questions, challenged them, and followed them up to determine the reasoning behind them. He found that children's conceptions of positive justice, like the moral judgments studied by Kohlberg, develop through a sequence of levels as children grow older (see Table 14.3).

Before the age of 4, children do not give objective reasons for their choices; they simply state their wants. Most 4- and 5-year-olds still focus primarily on gratifying themselves, but now they begin to justify their decisions with appeals to such arbitrary characteristics as size and sex—"The biggest should get the most"; "We should all get some because we're girls."

Between the ages of 5 and 7, children begin to believe that all participants have a claim to the rewards. They usually assert that the way to resolve conflict is to give everyone an equal share. Their arguments recognize no mitigating circumstances; the only fair treatment is equal treatment.

From approximately the age of 8 onward, children seem to believe that some individuals within the group may have a legitimate claim to more than an equal share of the group's rewards if they contributed more to the group's work or if they are handicapped in some way, as by poverty or by a physical disability. However, it is still difficult for 8-year-olds to balance all of the competing considerations to produce a fair outcome. Changes after the age of 8 reflect children's increased sophistication at logically weighing all of the relevant factors. Damon (1983), whose initial studies were in the United States, reports that this same progression has been found in a number of other countries, including Israel, Puerto Rico, and parts of Europe.

The ability of children to take particular circumstances into consideration when they make decisions about fairness was tackled in a somewhat different way by Theresa Thorkildsen (1989). Thorkildsen noted that adults' judgments about fairness often depend on the context of the actions being judged (Figure 14.2). Helping someone to fill out an application for a job, for example, is likely to be considered fair, but helping the same person to fill out the correct answers on a driver's test is likely to be considered cheating.

Thorkildsen sought to determine if children's judgments of fairness depend on context in the same way. To make sure that the contexts of different kinds of fairness judgments would be familiar and meaningful to the children, she asked them questions about events that they encountered regularly in school.

In the case of a classroom lesson, Thorkildsen told the children, who ranged in age from 6 to 11, about a classroom where everyone is trying hard to learn how to read, but some children finish the assignments more quickly than others. She then asked the children if it is fair for those who already read well to help those who are slower in each of three situations:

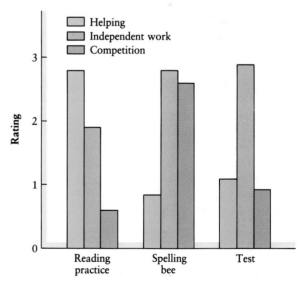

FIGURE 14.2 *Fairness ratings assigned by children 6 to 11 years old to three kinds of rules as applied to three school activities: reading practice, a spelling bee, and a test. A rating of zero indicates unfair; a rating of 3 indicates fair.*

TABLE 14.4

Excerpts from Damon's Transcripts Comparing 6- and 10-year-olds'
Reasoning about and Practice of Positive Justice

Three 6-year-olds: Jay, Juan, and Susan	Three 10-year-olds: Craig, Norman, and Bonnie
Experimenter: So what Jay said is he put them out, three for him and three for Juan, two for Susan and two for Jennifer *[not present]*. And Susan said that's OK too. That's the way she did it.	*E:* . . . What do you think is the best way to give it out?
Jay: *[to Juan]* You should think that's fair too. You have three, and I have three, and they have two.	*Craig:* Would Dennis *[the younger child]* get some?
Juan: I don't think that's fair.	*E:* If you think so.
Jay: Why?	*Norman:* He has to be here too.
Juan: We shouldn't give the boys more than the girls. We should break them in half and give the girls two, the boys two, and then . . .	*E:* Well, you all decide among you.

Experimenter: So what Jay said is he put them out, three for him and three for Juan, two for Susan and two for Jennifer *[not present]*. And Susan said that's OK too. That's the way she did it.

Jay: *[to Juan]* You should think that's fair too. You have three, and I have three, and they have two.

Juan: I don't think that's fair.

Jay: Why?

Juan: We shouldn't give the boys more than the girls. We should break them in half and give the girls two, the boys two, and then . . .

Jay: No. No. No. I said ours were the prettiest, that's why we get more.

Juan: Wait a second. Whose is this?

Jay: Yours.

Juan: No, it isn't.

Jay: See, we made the prettiest. I say we made the prettiest. Do you think that's a nice one? And you made the nice ones, and we made the prettiest. I think that's fair because we made the prettiest. . . .

E: What do you think, Susan? Didn't you at one point say you thought we should split them in half?

Susan: That's what I said. Now I say . . . *[Susan gives them out—three, three, two, two, as Jay wishes.]*

E: What? This way?

Jay: Yeah. Because she thinks that we made the prettiest.

Juan: She got some in her lunch box. Do you have candy? . . .

E: Susan says it's OK. How about Jennifer?

Jay: I think she would say it's OK.

Juan: If she didn't leave, I think it wouldn't be OK. . . .

Jay: Think that would be fair! She would have three, and we would all have three.

E: We don't have eleven, we have ten.

Jay: But she only made one, and it's not pretty.

Juan: It's good. She's only in kindergarten. She would think it's fair, I think. Yeah, she would.

E: What are you guys going to do?

Jay: If you think it's fair, and Susan thinks it's fair, and I think it's fair, she *[Jennifer]* might think it's fair.

E: Well, let's see what Juan thinks. What do you suggest, Juan? What's the best way? What's the best thing to do with the candy bars?

Juan: I think that's *[three, three, two, two]* the best way, if she's only in kindergarten.

Jay: She had two, and we have three.

E: . . . What do you think is the best way to give it out?

Craig: Would Dennis *[the younger child]* get some?

E: If you think so.

Norman: He has to be here too.

E: Well, you all decide among you.

Bonnie: I was thinking, we could give out one a bracelet, because Dennis did one and we all did three. Or give two and a half to everybody. That way everybody gets the same thing.

Craig: Maybe he *[Dennis]* should get one and we get three.

Norman: No. It ain't fair.

Bonnie: Also, Dennis is younger and he left earlier.

E: Well, what do you think? Is that the best way?

Norman: No.

E: Why not, Norman?

Norman: Because if he were here too, and he's a child too, so he should get even.

Bonnie: Yeah, well, lookit. His was bigger so it would have taken longer. And he used more black, but that made it shorter. But he left earlier, he's younger and, you know, didn't do it neat.

Norman: I know. That's beside the point. That means we don't expect much from him. . . .

Craig: Or give three to her *[Bonnie]*, three for Norman, and three for me, and one for Dennis.

E: And why do you think that is the best way, Craig?

Craig: *[No reply.]*

Norman: You're not putting his *[Dennis's]* mind into your little mind. . . .

Craig: Yes, I am.

Norman: Well, you're not reasoning about him. If we did that he would say *[mimics child's whining voice]* "Come, come, you guys got this and I only got this" and he'd start bawling his brains out.

Bonnie: Well, his isn't that neat or anything.

Norman: I know, but he is younger.

Bonnie: Well, wouldn't you say, supposing that you had a younger dog and an older dog, right? You could teach them both the same tricks. And if you had a box of dog bones, you'd give them a bone for every trick. Supposing the little one or even the big one just wanted the dog bones and he wouldn't do any tricks. You wouldn't give him one for that.

Norman: I know, but he did something. It's not like he didn't do anything. Least he did one. You're getting on the point like he didn't do anything.

TABLE 14.4 (continued)

Three 6-year-olds: Jay, Juan, and Susan	Three 10-year-olds: Craig, Norman, and Bonnie
Juan: You made the most. *Jay:* You see I had four bracelets. *Juan:* I had the second most. Give these two candy bars to her. *Jay:* You see, what I was thinking was, Juan and I get three 'cause we, ours are pretty and I made the most. Susan already has one in her lunch box. *Juan:* And Jennifer's only in kindergarten. *Jay:* She does't get more, 'cause she just made one and it's not pretty. *E:* Do you agree, Susan? *Susan:* OK.	*Bonnie:* No, I know he did something. He did the best he could. *Norman:* Yeah, so he should get as much as we do.

Source: Damon, 1977.

1. Is it fair for the teacher to ask the fast readers to help the slow readers during a reading lesson?

2. Is it fair for the good readers to help the slow readers by whispering answers during a spelling bee?

3. Is it fair for the good readers to help the slow readers during a test?

Children's judgments depended on the activity being described, as Figure 14.2 indicates. They thought it was fair to have a reading lesson in which children were told to work independently or to help each other, but it would be unfair to make the lesson competitive. If the activity was a spelling bee, they thought it was unfair to help, but both independent work and competition were considered to be fair. If the activity was a test, independent work was seen as the only fair alternative; neither helping nor competition was seen as appropriate.

These findings indicate that children take the particular circumstances into account when they judge fairness. Moreover, the 6-year-olds seemed to take the social context of an action into account as well as the 11-year-olds did.

Thus far the studies of moral reasoning we have discussed have been restricted to hypothetical situations. This restriction naturally raises the question of how children's abstract reasoning about moral issues is related to their actions in a real-life situation. How, for example, would children actually divide up the rewards if some had done more of the work than others? Would their actions fit their words?

To answer this question, Damon arranged for 144 children to be divided into groups of four. Each group was asked to make bracelets, for which the group would be rewarded. After the children had been at work for a while, he brought the work period to a close and gave each group 10 candy bars to divide among themselves as payment for their work. In order to ensure that the relevant issues of positive justice arose as a problem for the children, Damon arranged the composition and working conditions of each group so that there would be several different claims: one of the children would have made more bracelets than the others, for example, and another might be substantially younger. As Table 14.4 indicates, the children's reasoning about fairness varies markedly with their age. The 6-year-olds insist that fairness means equal outcomes, whereas the older children are better able to adjust the outcome to fit the profile of abilities and contributions in the group.

Damon compared the hypothetical reasoning of children with their actual behavior in this real situation. In half of the cases, the children's behavior matched their reasoning. About 10 percent of the children actually exhibited more advanced reasoning in the face of a real task, while almost 40 percent scored lower in reality than in their reasoning. When these children were faced with real candy bars, they were likely to give in to temptation and claim more than they would consider their due if they followed the reasoning they displayed in the hypothetical situation.

Reasoning about Social Conventions

Elliot Turiel and his colleagues (Nucci & Turiel, 1978; Turiel, 1983) have shown that by the time North American children are 5 or 6 years old they evaluate the consequences of moral infractions, such as hurting someone, differently from violations of social conventions, such as dressing according to the school dress code. These findings led Turiel to conclude that moral reasoning and reasoning about social conventions are independent domains. In a series of studies, he and his colleagues have provided evidence that each domain—that of moral rules and that of social conventions—is judged according to its own criteria and undergoes its own sequence of developmental transformations (Tisak & Turiel, 1988; Turiel, 1983; Turiel, Killen, & Helwig, 1987).

Turiel's method, like that of other researchers who have probed children's reasoning about social rules, was to tell brief stories and then interview the children to investigate their reasoning about the stories. One story he told was about a young boy who wants to become a nurse and care for infants when he grows up, but his father doesn't want him to.

The following interview, based on the nurse story, illustrates the earliest stage of reasoning about social conventions. The child seems to believe that conventions reflect the natural order of things. To violate the convention would be to behave unnaturally.

> Joan (6 years, 5 months): (Should he become a nurse?) *Well, no, because he could easily be a doctor and he could take care of babies in the hospital.* (Why shouldn't he be a nurse?) *Well, because a nurse is a lady and the boys, the other men would just laugh at them.* (Why shouldn't a man be a nurse?) *Well, because it would sort of be silly because ladies wear those kind of dresses and those kind of shoes and hats. . . .* (Do you think his father was right?) *Yes, because, well, a nurse, she typewrites and stuff and all that.* (The man should not do that?) *No, because he would look silly in a dress.* (Turiel, 1978:62–63)

At the second level of reasoning about social conventions, evident around the age of 8 or 9, children realize that just because most doctors are men and most nurses are women, the empirical association of activities, roles, and modes of dress does not mean that other combinations are impossible. At this level, children reject the need for social conventions; they see no necessity for such rules to coordinate human activities. They are even sophisticated enough to realize that traditional social conventions may mislead people:

> Emily (8 years, 11 months): (Why do you think his parents see that job as for women only?) *Being a nurse—because not many men are nurses so they get used to the routine. I know a lot of ladies who are doctors, but I don't know a man who is a nurse, but it is okay if they want to.* (Turiel, 1978:64)

At level 3, children display a dawning awareness that social conventions, arbitrary though they are, have a legitimate role in the regulation of social life. Eventually, sometime in early adulthood, they come to view social conventions as a positive force because they facilitate the coordination of social interactions, which is essential to the functioning of any social group.

At present a serious source of uncertainty about developmental sequences in reasoning about social rules is the generally low level of correspondence between the levels children reach when they are asked to reason about different sorts of rules. They often think at one level about moral rules, at another about fairness, and at still another about social conventions (Turiel & Davidson, 1986; Shweder, Mahapatra, & Miller, 1987). Though it is clear that children's thinking about various aspects of social life becomes more complicated as they grow older, the existing data raise considerable doubt as to whether a unitary process governs the kinds of games children play, the kinds of rules they invoke, and the way they reason about morality.

In addition, it is not clear whether children around the world think about moral rules and social conventions in the same way children in North America do. Using culturally appropriate versions of Turiel's stories, some researchers have replicated his basic findings in a wide variety of societies (Nucci, Turiel, & Encarnación–Gawrych, 1983; Song, Smetana, & Kim, 1987). When anthropologists have studied children's moral reasoning in naturally occurring situations, however, or have used somewhat different techniques to elicit judgments, they have found that people in at least some cultures are more likely to consider breaches of social convention to be moral issues than North Americans do (Shweder, Mahapatra, & Miller, 1987). The issue of cultural variations in the development of reasoning about moral rules and social conventions is discussed at some length in Chapter 16.

RELATIONS WITH OTHER CHILDREN

Once children begin to spend significant amounts of time among their peers, they must learn to create a special place for themselves within the social group. Their greater appreciation of social rules and their increased ability to consider other people's points of view are essential resources for this new task. But no matter how sophisticated or sensitive they may be about social relations, there is no guarantee that they will be accepted by their peers. In seeking friends, all children must come to terms with the possibility that they may not be liked, learn to compete for social status, and deal with the conflicts that inevitably arise.

Friendship

Friendship is generally considered to be a relationship characterized by affection, reciprocity, and commitment between people who consider themselves more or less equals (Hartup, 1992). Willard Hartup identifies four developmental functions of friendships:

1. They are contexts in which such basic social skills as communication, cooperation, and ability to enter an already formed group are acquired and elaborated.

2. They are sources of information about oneself, others, and the world.

3. They provide emotional and cognitive resources for having fun and dealing with the stress of everyday life.

4. They provide models of intimate relationships that will become important in later life.

Age-related changes in friendship

Among 3- and 4-year olds, "friend" is often synonymous with "playmate," as in "I won't be your friend anymore if you won't give me the hammer." By the end of middle childhood, however, friendship and children's ideas about it have become quite complicated. An account written by an 11-year-old girl in the United States makes this clear:

> What a wrong day! Lindsey is getting me more and more irritated every day. I think we're both beginning a bad relationship. She bothers me a lot. We kind of made a commitment to tell each other everything. But no, she had just recently started to tell me things, about her and Alan, and that she hated me during the summer. I wonder if she still does hate me, maybe. . . . I always have to listen to how she feels but she won't listen to how I feel. I hate her as of the present moment, but I will never take off the bead ring I have that she gave me. I love her a lot and never want to part as a friend, but there are times I just can't stand when she does things like this. (Rubin, 1980:74)

Age-related changes in the nature of friendship are also apparent in the responses children give when they are interviewed about their conceptions of friendship and their ideas of how to make friends with someone (Goodnow & Burns, 1985; Hartup, 1992; Youniss, 1980; Youniss & Volpe, 1978). James Youniss and his colleagues found that 6- and 7-year-olds in the United States speak of friends as playmates with whom they share activities and things. In answer to the question "What is a best friend?" they say, "When they play together" or "Play with them and give them stuff."

By the time they are 9 and 10 years old, children say that friends are people you have spent enough time with to know well, people who have common interests, similar abilities, and compatible personalities. Asked how one makes friends, 9- and 10-year-olds say such things as "They'll play around on the playground and talk to each other" or "They might find out they like the same things." They believe that a friend is "someone who really cares about you and doesn't want to betray you . . . a person who would want to help out when he needs his help." The older children Youniss interviewed believed that friendship transcends momentary interactions and is an ongoing relationship whose continued existence depends on mutual responsibility, support, caring, and commitment.

Table 14.5 summarizes Australian children's conceptions of friendship, which are quite similar to those found among children in North America.

Factors that influence the formation of friendships

Before you can become friends with someone, the two of you have to spend some time together, so it is no surprise that one of the major determinants of friendship between children is proximity (Epstein, 1989). But proximity cannot be the full story, because most children are in the company of other children several hours every day and become friends with only a few of them.

Children tend to pick friends who are similar to them in a variety of ways (Epstein, 1989). Friendships are most common among children who are of the same age, the same race, and the same sex. Friends are also likely to feel the same way about school (a child who likes school and gets good grades is likely to have a friend who also likes school and gets good grades) and to share preferences in such aspects of popular culture as sports and music.

Occasionally, though, children of different sexes, ages, and races become friends. Such cross-category friendships may arise when family friends get together, when there is a large project such as a school play to be put on, or when the children are simply "playing on the block" (Ellis, Rogoff, & Cromer, 1981).

John Gottman (1983) provides an extensive and detailed description of the process of becoming friends. Gottman arranged for pairs of children of the same age to meet and play together in one of the children's homes for three sessions within the space of a month. The children, who were strangers to each other at the start of the study, ranged from 3 to 9 years in age. In order to find out if the children became friends during the experiment, Gottman asked the mothers to fill out a questionnaire that probed the strength and quality of the children's relationship.

To determine *how* children make friends, Gottman tape-recorded each play session and analyzed the tapes, comparing children who became friends with those who did not. Five aspects of the children's social interaction appeared to distinguish pairs who became friendly from those who did not:

1. *Common-ground activity* Children who became friends found quickly something they

---

TABLE 14.5

The Main Qualities Mentioned by Australian Children in Definitions of a Good Friend (Percent of All Qualities Mentioned)

	Grades 1 & 2	Grades 3 & 4	Grades 5 & 6
A caring attitude			
Likes, cares for, comforts you	22%	25%	21%
Does not hit/fight	5	3	5
Protects, looks after you	5	3	5
Is available, is "there"	3	2	3
Understanding and sharing			
Makes you feel special	19	19	26
Understands you	2	3	10
You understand them	2	5	9
Shares fun with you	25	24	11
Shares activities, interests, things with you	6	7	6

Source: Goodnow & Burns, 1985.

Being with friends is one of life's special pleasures.

could do together. In addition, they explored their similarities and differences.

2. *Communication clarity* Children who became friends were less likely to engage in what Piaget referred to as "collective monologues" (see Chapter 8, p. 309). They listened to each other, requested clarification when they did not understand, and spoke in ways that were relevant to the task at hand.

3. *Exchanging information* Children who became friends both asked for and provided information relevant to their partners.

4. *Resolving conflict* Children who became friends gave good reasons when they disagreed and were able to bring conflicts to a quick resolution.

5. *Reciprocity* Children who became friends were likely to respond to their partner's positive behaviors with an appropriate positive contribution of their own.

Although children all over the world must learn how to sustain intimate and mutually supportive relationships with their peers, in a great many societies the children who become friends are not strangers who happen to have been placed in the same class at school or who happen to be in the same carpool. Instead, friendships are formed with children who are part of the same family or kinship group (Weisner, 1984). These circumstances alter the task of making friends. Summarizing cultural variations in childhood friendships, the anthropologist Tom Weisner wrote that in many parts of the world the conditions for forming friendships

do not require the child to personally initiate interaction, then display such personal skills as mutuality and verbal appropriateness. Rather, the child first must understand how the culture has already classified him or her into a preexisting set of alliances and feuds; second, the child must incorporate the acquaintance into his or her immediate sibling group. In addition, children ages 6–12 will very early have to consider what work, tasks, and chores must be done along with this child as a friend. Friendship will require much more than play, games, and childhood intimacy. (1984:348)

Detailed data on the psychological processes involved in friendships in such societies are generally lacking. But Weisner's point should be kept in mind as we explore friendships among children in industrially advanced countries.

What do friends do together?

In early childhood the focus of friendship is pretend play. Young children's descriptions of their actual friendships and of their beliefs about friendship in general reveal that they clearly place a premium on other children's potentials as playmates (Berndt, 1986). A good playmate is someone with whom the child can achieve a high level of coordination, leading to more fun, more solidarity, and more humor.

Belonging and social acceptance are the major themes of friendship in middle childhood. At this point in their lives children recognize that their age-mates have different statuses and that play groups are hierarchically organized. Children's awakened sensitivity to their relative status among their peers leads them to be particularly concerned about the possibility that they will be rejected or have their feelings hurt (Parker & Gottman, 1989).

As a result, according to Jeffrey Parker and John Gottman, gossip becomes "the mortar as well as much of the brick of friendship conversation during middle childhood" (1989:114). It is through gossip that children now carry out the basic social reciprocities and information exchanges that are central to friendship. When a clear cultural norm is at issue (such as the norms that regulate sharing, aggression, and lying), gossip reaffirms the norm, as can be seen in a conversation between Erica and Mikaila as they gossip about Katie's bossiness:

> M: She's mean. She beat me up once *[laughs]*. I could hardly breathe, she hit me in the stomach so hard.
> E: She acts like . . .
> M: She's the boss.
> E: "Now do this." *[mimicking Katie]*
> M: "And I'll . . ."
> E: "And Erica, you do this. And you substitute for people who aren't here, Erica."
> M: "And you do this, Mikaila. And you shouldn't do that, you shouldn't, you have to talk like this. You understand? Here. I'm the teacher here."
> E: I know. She always acts like she's the boss. (Parker & Gottman, 1989:114)

When a topic comes up that is not covered by a clear cultural norm, gossip allows children to find out what their friends think so that they can tailor their behavior accordingly.

Of course, childhood friends do more than just gossip; they also disagree and make up, compete with each other, go to school together, hang out after school, play games together, and engage in all those forms of "doing nothing" that Robert Paul Smith describes in the epigraph to this chapter.

Boys and girls as friends

Children in all cultures are sexually segregated for a good part of the time during middle childhood. In nonindustrialized societies, sexual segregation may stem from the kinds of chores that children are assigned by adults. The girls help their mothers around the village by fetching water, doing the wash, sweeping, and helping to prepare food, while the boys watch the herds, hunt, and fish (Harkness & Super, 1985; Weisner, 1984; Whiting & Edwards, 1988). In industrialized societies, children's tendency to gather in same-sex groups appears to depend more on their preferences for different kinds of activities and styles of interaction. Studies that ask children to nominate a "best friend" have found that at 6 years of age roughly 68 percent choose a child of the same sex; and by the age of 12 this figure has grown to about 90 percent (Daniels-Beirness, 1989).

Sex segregation is by no means total during middle childhood (Hartup, 1992; Whiting, 1986). In industrialized societies boys and girls often meet ritually in schoolyards and parks and on neighborhood streets. Some of these meetings have the qualities of a foray into enemy territory. Others, such as chase-and-kiss games and teasing, have sexual overtones. But there are also occasions when the two sexes naturally merge in joint activities.

Similar patterns of partial segregation of the sexes emerge from observations in various parts of the world. On the basis of their observations in a Kipsigis village in Kenya, Sara Harkness and Charles Super (1985) report that companions were often kin from nearby homesteads who were likely to vary in age and sex. Pamela Reynolds (1989), who observed children in a South African shantytown, estimated that boys and girls played together about 25 percent of the time. It seems that boys and girls are most likely to play together when the supply of potential companions is limited, as it may be in both a rural village and a U.S. suburban neighborhood.

Boys' and girls' experiences with peers often differ considerably, as we have already seen in the kinds of

These children playing during recess illustrate the kind of sex segregation that appears during middle childhood.

games they play. Observational studies of children on playgrounds repeatedly find that girls congregate in groups of two or three, whereas boys move around in "swarms" (Daniels-Beirness, 1989). Girls tend to have fewer friends than boys and to make friends less rapidly (Eder & Hallinan, 1978). They seem to be more sensitive to the boundaries that differentiate close friends from acquaintances, and they are more likely to discourage interactions with those who are not close friends. Girls' friendships are often more intimate than boys'; they are characterized by the sharing of feelings, exchanges of presents and compliments, and lengthy discussions about likes and dislikes, embarrassments and triumphs (Waldrop & Halverson, 1975). Boys are more likely to have larger groups of friends and more friends of different ages. They are also more likely than girls to play physical, boisterous, competitive games with their friends and to interact with one another in places where they are free from direct adult supervision.

A clear pattern of differential sex-role socialization emerges from the existing data. Boys appear to be socialized to compete with one another in activities bound by rule systems, while girls are socialized for cooperation and interpersonal sensitivity in circumstances in which rules are only implicit. In the United States this pattern may change as more women enter the workplace to compete with men. Girls may come to be socialized more for competition than they have been in the past, but if such a change is occurring, it is not yet visible in the social relations among peers during middle childhood.

Friendship and social competence

Psychological research on the development of friendship demonstrates that peer interaction provides an important context for the development of social skills. Collectively, skills that result in successful social functioning with peers are referred to as **social competence** (Howes, 1987). According to Jacqueline Goodnow and Ailsa Burns (1985:134), the most important elements of social competence are these:

1. Making successful overtures.

2. Learning what is expected at various stages of friendship.

3. Working out which people are unlikely candidates for friendship.
4. Deepening relationships with those seen as likely to be rewarding friends.
5. Keeping things going in a manner pleasing to both parties.
6. Making sure that each party puts a similar effort into the relationship, without keeping too close a tally.
7. Avoiding the risk of placing too much trust in someone likely to prove fickle.
8. Fighting off challenges from those who want to "steal" one's friends.
9. Avoiding getting stuck with friends one no longer finds appealing.
10. Avoiding a reputation for disloyalty and self-seeking.
11. Avoiding being stranded without friends.
12. Achieving resilience in the face of being dumped.

These skills at negotiating social interactions with peers depend in turn on children's growing ability to understand how others think and feel (Selman, 1976a, 1980). Recall from the discussion of perspective-taking in Chapter 12 (the story of Holly the tree-climber and her father, p. 459) that 8-to-10-year-olds are able to coordinate the perspectives of two characters in a story, while most 5-to-6-year-olds are not. In one set of studies designed to test his theory that the social skills needed for forming friendships depend on the ability to take other people's perspectives, Robert Selman (1980) compared children's social perspective-taking skills (as revealed by their interpretations of stories) with their understanding of friendship (as revealed by structured clinical interviews). He found that children who responded at a high level to perspective-taking problems were also likely to have more sophisticated ideas about friendship. Table 14.6 summarizes Selman's view of the way perspective-taking is related to stages of friendship.

Table 14.6 reveals an interesting parallel between changes in children's understanding of friendship and their ability to see different perspectives. Children's reasoning in each domain develops from uncoordinated, individualistic understanding to understanding that coordinates two perspectives, and then to a stage in which individual perspectives are viewed in the context of a more complex system. This sequence fits closely with Piaget's theory that young children's egocentricity restricts them to their own point of view,

whereas older children can keep two aspects of a problem in mind at the same time (see Chapter 9, p. 318, and Chapter 12, pp. 456–457).

To see if there was any connection between children's conceptions of friendship and their actual behavior as friends, Selman undertook research on interpersonal relations at a clinic for emotionally disturbed children. A notable characteristic of such children is that they have difficulty getting along with others and often behave immaturely. Selman (1981) found a very complex range of relationships between children's understanding of friendship displayed in interviews and their actual relationships. As expected, the children who displayed lower levels of understanding in clinical interviews had difficulties forming and maintaining friendships because they failed to take the other's point of view or understand the reasons for the other's behavior. However, children who reasoned at significantly higher levels than the other children in their school classes also ended up at the clinic because of interpersonal difficulties with their peers. In some cases, these children were disliked for being bossy or hard to understand.

Overall it appears that higher levels of reasoning about interpersonal relationships, including friendships, provide children with **social repair mechanisms,** strategies that allow friends to remain friends even when serious differences temporarily drive them apart. Examples of social repair mechanisms include disengaging before a disagreement escalates into a fight, staying nearby after a fight, and minimizing the importance of a conflict once it is over.

Social repair mechanisms take on importance in middle childhood because of children's changed social circumstances. In middle childhood, there is often no caretaker present, so children must settle conflicts on their own.

In this confluence of changed social circumstances and increased social competence we see that neither the social nor the cognitive characteristics of middle childhood could emerge without the other. They are two facets of a single developmental process.

Peer Relations and Social Status

Most people care deeply about how their peers feel about them, but not all members of a group are equally well liked. Whenever a group exists for a while, a social

TABLE 14.6

How Selman Relates Developmental Levels of Perspective-Taking to Developmental Levels of Friendship

Developmental Level in Coordination of Perspectives	Stage of Understanding Reflected in Close Friendships
LEVEL 0 (APPROXIMATELY AGES 3 TO 7)	**STAGE 0**
Egocentric or undifferentiated perspective. Children do not distinguish their own perspective from that of others. They do not yet recognize that others may interpret the same social experience or course of action differently from the way they do.	*Momentary playmates.* A close friend is someone who lives close by and with whom one is playing.
LEVEL 1 (APPROXIMATELY AGES 4 TO 9)	**STAGE 1**
Subjective or differentiated perspectives. The child understands that others' perspectives may differ from her own.	*One-way assistance.* A friend does what one wants. A close friend is someone who shares the same dislikes and likes.
LEVEL 2 (APPROXIMATELY AGES 6 TO 12)	**STAGE 2**
Self-reflective or reciprocal perspective. The child is now able to view his own thoughts and feelings from another's perspective.	*Fair-weather cooperation.* With their new awareness of the reciprocal nature of personal perspectives, children become concerned with coordinating their thoughts and actions, rather than adjusting them to a fixed standard, as they did before. Relationships depend on adjustment and cooperation and fall apart over arguments.
LEVEL 3 (APPROXIMATELY AGES 9 TO 15)	**STAGE 3**
Third-person or mutual perspective. The child at this level can step outside of an interaction and take the perspective of a third party.	*Intimate and mutually shared relationships.* Friendships are seen as the basic means of developing mutual intimacy and mutual support. At this stage friendship transcends momentary interactions, including conflicts. The primary limitation of this stage is possessiveness and jealousy.
LEVEL 4 (APPROXIMATELY AGES 12 TO ADULTHOOD)	**STAGE 4**
Societal or in-depth perspective. Children at this level are able to take the generalized perspective of society, the law, or morality.	*Autonomous, interdependent friendships.* This stage is characterized by an awareness of the interdependence of friends for support and a sense of identity and at the same time an acceptance of the other's need to establish relations with other people.

Source: Adapted from Selman, 1981.

structure emerges in which it is possible to identify a few members whom almost all the others name as people they would like to be with or sit near, a few who are more or less ignored, a few who are actively rejected, and several who occupy an intermediate position in the hierarchy. Developmental psychologists study children's social status both as a means to understand the development of personality and because there is evidence that children's social status is related to later developmental outcomes (Dodge & Feldman, 1990; Kupersmidt, Coie, & Dodge, 1990; Parker & Asher, 1987).

Researchers who study the relative social status of group members usually begin by constructing a sociogram of group relations. A **sociogram** is a graphic representation of how each child feels about every other child in the group (Asher & Dodge, 1986) (see Figure 14.3). In constructing a sociogram, the investigators may ask members of a group to name the children they would like to sit near, to play with, or to work with, or simply to name their friends in the group. This is referred to as a *nomination* procedure. Alternatively, they may use a *ranking* procedure, asking children to rank each other according to a criterion such as popularity or desirability as a friend. The picture of social

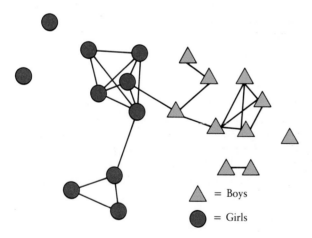

FIGURE 14.3   *A sociogram of the relationships among a group of fifth-grade boys and girls. Note that the one boy who has a relationship with a girl is only marginally related to the two groups of boys. The girl in this relationship, by contrast, is part of a group of girls. Two girls and one boy are social isolates, while a pair of boys have chosen each other in isolation from the group. (Adapted from Gronlund, 1959.)*

△ = Boys
● = Girls

relations given by the sociogram and other *sociometric data* (measures of social relations) is then used to investigate the relation between children's individual characteristics and their group standing. The children nominated most often or ranked highest are assumed to be the most popular in the group; those who are not named by anyone are assumed to be either neglected or rejected.

One of the most pervasive findings of such research is that the degree of popularity within a group is related to a person's physical attractiveness (Langlois, 1986). In one such study, boys were categorized in five subgroups on the basis of their popularity as indicated by a sociogram of their standing among their peers. Then adult raters who did not know the boys were asked to judge their attractiveness from photographs. In general, the lower the boys' ratings on attractiveness, the lower the popularity standing of their subgroup (Dodge, 1983). Brian Vaughn and Judith Langlois (1983) obtained similar results and found also that attractiveness and popularity are more highly correlated among girls than among boys.

There is more to popularity than good looks, however. To assess factors associated with various kinds of social status in middle childhood, researchers have developed the technique of bringing children together in play groups to observe how differential social status arises and is maintained (Coie & Kupersmidt, 1983; Dodge, 1983). Kenneth Dodge, for example, brought together unacquainted fourth-grade boys in play groups that met once a week for eight weeks. He videotaped the boys' interactions for later analysis, and at the end of the eight weeks asked them to name the two boys they liked most and the two they disliked most. To assess the role of attractiveness, ten college students rated photographs of the boys.

At first, of course, no one in these groups could be considered to be more popular than anyone else because the boys did not know one another. But by the end of the eight sessions it was possible to identify popular, neglected, and rejected boys on the basis of peer nominations. The videotapes enabled Dodge to observe the emergence of group structures and the behaviors that led to popularity, neglect, or rejection.

Attractiveness played a role in the boys' preferences. Popular boys were judged to be more attractive than neglected boys, who in turn were judged to be more attractive than rejected boys. The children's behavior was also important. Boys who became popular were helpful, reminded others of the rules, provided suggestions in ambiguous and difficult situations, and were almost never aggressive. The rejected boys were more talkative, active, and aggressive than the other members of the group, and they often wandered off on their own. Boys who were neglected by the others interacted with their peers the least but rarely offended anyone.

Additional findings about how children come to have high or low social standing was reported by John Coie and Janis Kupersmidt (1983). Like Dodge, they created artificial play groups. They began, however, by going to the children's classrooms to collect sociometric data on the children who would later be interacting with one another, so that later they could determine if their eventual findings coincided with the children's social status elsewhere. Coie and Kupersmidt also arranged for half of the play groups to be made up of boys from the same classrooms, so they knew each other. Sociometric data were collected after every play session, as each child was being driven home by one of the participating experimenters. During these informal interviews, the child was asked how things went, whom he had gotten along with, whom he liked, and so on.

Coie and Kupersmidt, like Dodge, found that rejected boys were active and disruptive while popular boys were helpful and group-oriented. They also found that there were *no noticeable differences in social status among the boys during the first few sessions.* Thus the children did not automatically transfer their judgments about each other from school to the play group. By the end of the third session, however, the boys had become clearly differentiated by social status. Moreover, the statuses that emerged in the play group coincided with the children's social status in their classrooms at school.

One of the important social skills that appears to differentiate popular and unpopular children is the ability to enter an already existing group, according to Martha Putallaz (1983). In the first phase of her study she invited 22 boys who were about to enter first grade to play one at a time with two unfamiliar children who were her confederates. The two confederates were already playing a game when the child being studied arrived on the scene. Putallaz introduced the children and told them that later on she would be asking them to tell her how they liked the game. Then she left them alone and observed the new boy's attempts to join the ongoing game. The two confederates were instructed to engage in several preplanned social interactions that

were designed to cause problems for the newcomer. For example, the two confederates pretended to have an argument.

Putallaz videotaped the social interactions in these episodes and then used the tapes to predict each boy's popularity in his first-grade classroom four months later, using a sociometric rating technique like the one described on page 542. She found that the boys later rated as most popular by their classmates were those who had been able to fit into the experimental group by making constructive contributions to the ongoing conversation, to adopt the group's frame of reference, and to understand the rules of the social interaction.

Kenneth Dodge and his colleagues (1986) extended these findings with slightly older children who were known to be unusually aggressive and socially rejected. These children and a group of average children viewed videotaped interactions in which two child actors who were playing a board game were joined by a third child actor who behaved differently on each of several tapes: competently, aggressively, in a self-centered manner, and so on. After each taped interaction the children participating in the study were asked a series of questions designed to assess their ability to think about different aspects of the videotaped interactions they had just seen. The aggressive children were less likely to pick up important social cues from the tape. They were less likely to identify the child who became annoyed, for example, and they had more difficulty suggesting appropriate social responses to the behaviors they observed.

These children were also asked to participate in a scene like the one they observed on the videotape. The aggressive children had more difficulty entering the ongoing game, just as they had more trouble interpreting the videotaped interactions. Dodge and his colleagues concluded that deficient social understanding contributes to both the children's aggressive behavior and their low social status. Here we see two attempts to enter an ongoing game, one successful, the other not.

SUCCESSFUL ATTEMPT

Mark enters, pauses for a moment, and moves forward to the proximity of the two peer hosts, who are playing a board game.
  Mark: Can I play?
  Host 1: Okay.

Host 2: Okay.
Host 1: Get yourself a seat.
Mark seats himself.
Host 2: What grade you in?
 Mark: Fourth. What grade are you in?
Host 2: Third.
Host 1: Third. I'm eight.
 Mark: I'm nine.
Host 2: I'm eight.
Host 1: This — if I were — today was my birthday and if I was, if I was nine, I'd be as old as you. (p. 52)

UNSUCCESSFUL ATTEMPT

David enters, hovers, motionless, while looking down at the table. Hosts are seated. Host 1 motions to Host 2 to spin the dial for the game they are playing.
Host 2: Line.
Host 1: I get to go again.
Host 2: I know.
Host 2 looks at David, who is still standing. After a long pause, Host 2 speaks.
Host 2: What are you staring at?
 David: Just watching . . . [inaudible mumble].
Host 2 giggles under his breath. The hosts continue playing the game. (Dodge, et al., 1986, p. 53)

Martha Putallaz and Aviva Wasserman (1990) showed that there is more to children's success in such situations than their social skills, just as there is more to popularity than attractiveness. The researchers observed first-, third-, and fifth-graders on the school playground as they attempted to join a group already at play. So far as the researchers could tell, low-status and high-status children (as determined by a sociometric questionnaire) differed only slightly in the skill with which they sought entry. Low-status children, however, were more than twice as likely to be ignored as high-status children. In the familiar setting of a school playground, apparently, children may be rejected because the group has already formed a negative opinion of them before they utter a word or make a move.

Evidence in favor of such a two-sided view of social rejection is reviewed by Shelley Hymel, Esther Wagner, and Lynda Butler (1990). They found that children's reputations ("He is always hitting"; "She never gives anyone else a turn") can become self-perpetuating. In a number of cases they discuss, a peer

group's expectations cause the members to interpret a child's behavior as aggressive or unfriendly even when, by objective standards, it is not. It is not difficult to imagine how such biased interpretations make the task of winning acceptance more difficult and how they might evoke the very behaviors that led the child to be rejected in the first place.

Parental influences on children's status among peers

Peer-group interactions are never entirely free of adult influence. Even when no adult is actually present, behavioral patterns that children have acquired at home and social norms accepted by the adult community are likely to influence children's behavior.

In Chapter 10 we reviewed evidence that parents may unwittingly encourage their children to behave aggressively by engaging in coercive, power-assertive modes of socialization. Since aggressive behavior in children is thought to lead to rejection by their peers, a number of researchers have investigated coercive family interaction patterns as a possible source of low social status in middle childhood (Dishion, 1990; Hart, Ladd, & Burleson, 1990; Putallaz & Heflin, 1990).

In one such study, Thomas Dishion (1990) collected information on social status by interviewing the teachers and classmates of over 200 boys between the ages of 9 and 10. He obtained evidence about family socialization patterns and the children's behavior from interviews with the parents and the boys themselves and through observations in the boys' homes.

Dishion found that boys who were judged to fall within the rejected category on the basis of sociometric analysis were exposed to more coercive family experiences than were children judged as average. These boys were more aggressive with their peers and also behaved badly in the classroom. Although boys from lower-income homes were more likely to fall within the rejected category, Dishion's data showed that socioeconomic class was *not* a direct cause of lower peer status or aggressive behavior. In accord with findings discussed in Chapter 11 (pp. 408–409), he found that poverty affected social status and behavior *indirectly* by increasing the general level of stress within the family. When parents coped well enough with the pressures of poverty to treat their children in a noncoercive way, the children were less likely to have low social status among their peers. This pattern, in which the children of coercive mothers tended to be less accepted by their peers, was confirmed by Craig Hart, Gary Ladd, and Brant Burleson (1990).

Complementary data were collected by Martha Putallaz (1987), who observed pairs of mothers and their first-graders as they played a specially constructed word game. Both children in each pair were of the same social status (either high or low, as determined by a sociometric analysis carried out on data obtained at their school). In a second phase of the study the children were left alone to play for 15 minutes while the experimenter kept the mothers busy elsewhere.

Putallaz then analyzed the mother-child interactions in the first phase of the study and the interactions between children in the second phase to determine how they might be related. She obtained two main results. First, mothers of high-status children were more likely to interact in a positive and agreeable manner with their children and to be more concerned with feelings—both their own and their children's—whereas the mothers of low-status children exhibited more negative and controlling behavior. Second, low-status children behaved more disagreeably than high-status children.

The results of these studies linking children's social status to parenting styles appear to confirm the findings of research focused on younger children (Chapter 10, p. 383; MacDonald & Parke, 1984): the modes of interaction that children acquire in the home tend to serve as models for their behavior with their peers, affecting the children's social status for better or for worse.

Competition and cooperation within groups

Children's social behavior may be influenced by the socialization patterns of a cultural group as well as by those of their parents. The particular aspect of social interaction that has been the focus of this research is the extent to which a culture values cooperation relative to competition among members of a group.

Millard Madsen and his colleagues (Kagan & Madsen, 1971; Madsen & Shapira, 1970; Shapira & Madsen, 1969) studied the way members of small peer groups chose to cooperate or compete in solving a problem. The purpose of the studies was to contrast problem-solving strategies of children whose cultures emphasize cooperation with the strategies of those whose cultures emphasize competition.

One of the early studies in this series contrasted two groups of Israeli children (Shapira & Madsen, 1969). One group was composed of children in agricultural communes, or kibbutzim; the other group was made up of children in a middle-class urban neighborhood. Middle-class urban Israelis, like their U.S. counterparts, encourage their children to achieve as individuals. Kibbutzim, by contrast, prepare children from an early age to cooperate and work as a group. Kibbutz adults deliberately reward cooperation and punish failure to cooperate (Spiro, 1965). Competition is so discouraged that children may feel ashamed to be at the top of their class (Rabin, 1965).

Six-to-ten-year-old children of both communities were brought together four at a time to play a game with the apparatus depicted in Figure 14.4. At the start of each round of the game, four children were seated at the corners of the board. In the center of the board was a pen connected to each corner by a string. Each child could pull the string to move the pen. The board itself was covered with a clean piece of paper, on which the pen left a mark as it moved.

The game called for the children to move the pen to specific places on the game board marked by four small circles. To bring the pen to one of these circles,

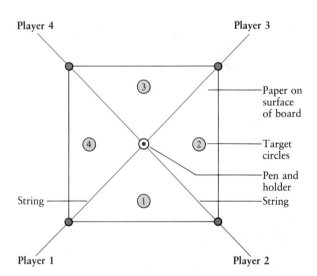

FIGURE 14.4 *Diagram of apparatus used to assess children's predispositions to compete or cooperate. The pen at the center of the board must be moved to the target circles, an act that requires changes in the lengths of the strings manipulated by all four players. (From Shapira & Madsen, 1969.)*

the children had to cooperate in pulling the strings; otherwise the pen would remain in the center or move erratically.

Each group of children was asked to play the game six times. For the first three trials Madsen and Ariella Shapira told them that the object of the game was to draw a line over the four circles in one minute. If they succeeded, each of them would get a prize. If they covered the four circles twice, they would get two prizes, and so on. But if they covered fewer than four circles, no one would receive a prize. Under these circumstances, children from both kinds of communities responded similarly, in a generally cooperative manner (see Figure 14.5).

After the first three trials, the experimenters changed the way rewards were given. Now, whenever

the pen crossed the circle to the right of a child, that child received a reward. Under these new conditions, a cultural difference quickly became apparent. The urban children changed tactics, and each started pulling the pen toward him- or herself. They persisted in competing even on the fifth trial, by which time they had ample opportunity to see that they were getting nowhere. In some cases the children would agree to cooperate, but the cooperation would break down as soon as one child pulled a little too hard on the string. As a result, their rate of success was greatly reduced.

The children from kibbutzim responded quite differently to the new condition. They quickly set up cooperative rules, saying such things as "Okay, gang, let's go in turns." They also directed one another during the game with such suggestions as "We'll start here, then here. . . ." The kibbutz children were concerned that no one be rewarded more than the others, and they set up rules to see that they all shared equally in the prizes.

Madsen's studies, which have been repeated in other countries under varying conditions (Kagan & Madsen, 1971; Madsen & Shapira, 1970), show that the pattern of socialization that a culture fosters significantly influences the way peers work together. Cultures that emphasize group cohesion over individualism produce children with a greater readiness to cooperate for the mutual benefit of the group.

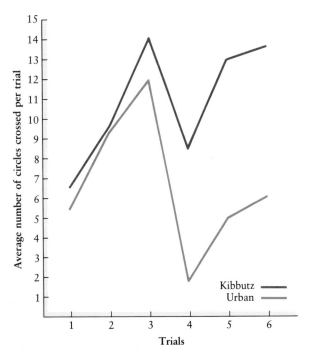

FIGURE 14.5   *The average number of successful attempts to cross a target circle by urban Israeli children and by Israeli children raised in a kibbutz. On the first three trials, children were rewarded for cooperating. On the second three trials, rewards were distributed for individual achievement. Children raised on a kibbutz continued to cooperate and succeed, but urban children began to compete, lowering their success rate. (From Shapira & Madsen, 1969.)*

Competition and conflict between groups

Except in small, widely separated communities, peer groups are unlikely to be isolated. In a single urban neighborhood there may be several groups, some based on common interest, others on membership in a church or athletic team, or simply residence on the same block. In some locales, children may become involved in street gangs in middle childhood, a social phenomenon that has aroused growing concern in recent decades.

When we turn from the study of interaction *within* a single peer group to interaction *between* two groups, many of the issues repeat themselves in a new form. Just as individual children must learn to get along with each other without strict adult control, so groups of children must find a way to regulate their interactions with other groups.

A classic series of studies by Muzafer and Carolyn

Sherif (1953) provides the best evidence to date about the conditions that foster different kinds of interaction between peer groups. In the most famous of these studies, 11-year-old boys—all strangers to one another—were brought to one of two summer camps in Robbers Cave State Park in Oklahoma. The boys all came from stable middle-class homes. They were all in the upper half of their class in academic standing, and all were judged to be physically healthy and well adjusted.

The boys in the two encampments went canoeing, swam, played ball, and engaged in other typical camp activities. To ensure that the boys at each encampment formed a cohesive group, the adults arranged for them to encounter problems that the boys could solve only by cooperating. They provided ingredients for dinner, for example, but left it to the boys themselves to prepare and apportion the food. During the first week of the experiment the two groups lived in ignorance of each other.

At the end of the week, friendships had formed and leaders had emerged within each group. Each had adopted a name: they were the Rattlers and the Eagles. They had made their own group flags, constructed their own hideouts, and claimed particular swimming holes as their own.

When it was clear that both the Rattlers and the Eagles had formed a stable pattern of group interactions, the adults let it be known that there was another group in the area. The boys expressed a keen desire to compete, and each group immediately issued a challenge to the other.

The adults arranged for a tournament, with prizes going to the winners. At the end of the first day of competition, the Eagles lost a tug-of-war. Stung by their defeat, they burned a Rattlers flag that had been left behind. When the Rattlers returned the next morning and discovered the burned flag, they immediately seized the Eagles' flag. Scuffling and name-calling ensued.

Over the next five days hostilities escalated. The Rattlers staged a raid on the Eagles' camp, causing the Eagles a good deal of inconvenience and frustration. The Eagles retaliated with a destructive raid of their own. At the end of this period the two groups disliked each other intensely.

Once the intergroup hostility had reached a high level, the experimenters took steps to reverse it. First they tried bringing the boys together in a series of pleasant social gatherings—joint meals, attendance at a movie, shooting firecrackers—but these attempts all failed miserably. The boys used these occasions to escalate hostilities by throwing food and calling names.

Next the experimenters introduced a series of *superordinate* problems that affected the welfare of both groups equally, requiring them to combine efforts to reach a solution. The most successful application of this technique occurred during an overnight camping trip. The adults arranged for the truck that was to bring food to get stuck in a position where it could not be pushed. The boys came up with the idea of using their tug-of-war rope to pull the truck out of its predicament. Now, instead of pulling against each other, the boys were pulling together for a burning common reason—hunger. The Sherifs describe the outcome:

> It took considerable effort to pull the truck. Several tries were necessary. During these efforts, a rhythmic chant of "Heave, heave" arose to accent the times of greatest effort. This rhythmic chant of "Heave, heave" had been used earlier by the Eagles during the tug-of-war contests in the period of intergroup competition and friction. Now it was being used in a cooperative activity involving both groups. When, after some strenuous efforts, the truck moved and started there was jubilation over the common success. (1956:322–323)

After this joint achievement, there seemed no point in preparing separate meals. The two groups cooperated without much discussion and with no outbreaks of name-calling or throwing of food. The experimenters arranged for the truck to get stuck again. This time the boys immediately knew what to do, and the two groups mixed freely as they organized the rope pull.

At the end of the series of joint-activity problems, the boys' opinions of each other had changed significantly. Mutual respect had largely replaced hostility, and several of the boys had formed friendships in the opposite group.

The Sherifs' experiment carries an important lesson. Cooperation and competition are not fixed biological characteristics of individuals or of groups. They are forms of interaction that can be found at some time in all social groups and in all individuals; they can be, and are, heavily influenced by social organization.

Developmental consequences of peer interaction

Several lines of research suggest that peer interaction in middle childhood is important to the development of social-cognitive skills and to later social well-being (Doise, Mugny, & Perret-Clermont, 1975; Piaget, 1965; Sullivan, 1953). Evidence that peer interaction promotes social competence is provided by Marida Hollos (Hollos, 1975; Hollos & Cowan, 1973), who studied children growing up in three distinctive social settings in Norway and Hungary: towns, villages, and isolated farms. Hollos sought to determine if differences in the children's experiences with peers led to distinctive patterns and rates of cognitive development.

Many Norwegian children live on remote farms that are difficult to reach, especially during the winter, so they experience relatively little peer interaction. Except on holidays, young farm children rarely interact with children other than their brothers and sisters. At the age of 7, when they begin school, they are bused to a neighboring community three times a week and bused home again as soon as school is over, so they have no free time to play with the other children. At home they spend most of their time playing alone or watching their mothers work. Communication in their families is generally simple and direct, perhaps because the family members spend so much time in one another's company that they have little new to talk about.

Young children living in villages and towns, by contrast, spend most of their free time playing with other children. They bicycle together all over, explore the waterfront, visit one another's homes, ski together in winter, and play out on the streets at all times of the year. They also interact with adults in shops, on the street, and in their friends' homes. Village children encounter fewer people than the town children do, but the peer interactions they experience are similar. Hollos found the same general patterns in Hungary.

To assess the impact of these different peer experiences on development, Hollos presented 7-, 8-, and 9-year-old children in these settings with a battery of tests drawn from two Piagetian categories. The first set consisted of classification and conservation tasks, designed to test the development of logical operations. The second set was designed to measure social perspective-taking and communication skills.

One perspective-taking task presented the child with a seven-picture cartoon sequence suggesting an obvious story that the child was asked to recount.

Then three of the pictures were removed. The remaining four pictures suggested a different story. A second experimenter then entered the room and the child was asked to pretend to take the first experimenter's place and tell the story that the experimenter would tell. The key question was whether the child would simply repeat the first story or adjust to the new circumstances.

Hollos (1975) obtained similar results with both the Norwegian and the Hungarian children. As Figure 14.6 indicates, the scores of the three groups of Hungarian children were about equal on the test of logical operations. All groups improved with age. On the social perspective-taking tasks, however, the farm children, who spent little time interacting with others, did less well than the village and town children. In a study conducted in Iceland, other researchers also found that urban children's performance on social perspective-taking tests was superior to that of rural children (Edelstein, Keller, & Wahlen, 1984). Further evidence that peer interaction helps children develop the ability to take other people's perspectives comes from a study conducted in Canada, which found that elementary school children who played with their peers on the playground less often than their agemates also scored lower on social perspective-taking tests (Le Mare & Rubin, 1987).

A quite different kind of hypothesis about the consequences of peer relationships comes from the work of the psychiatrist Harry Stack Sullivan (1892–1949), who considered the experience of friendship during middle childhood to be an essential precursor to adult intimacy, with which it shares some important features:

> If you will look very closely at one of your children when he finally finds a chum . . . you will discover something very different in the relationship—namely, that your child begins to develop a new sensitivity to what matters to another person. And this is not in the sense of "what should I do to get what I want," but instead "what should I do to contribute to the happiness or to support the prestige and feeling of worthwhileness of my chum." So far as I have been ever able to discover, nothing remotely like this appears before the age of, say, 8½, and sometimes it appears decidedly later. (1953:245–246)

Sullivan believed that the tendency of children to pick out one or a few other children with whom they

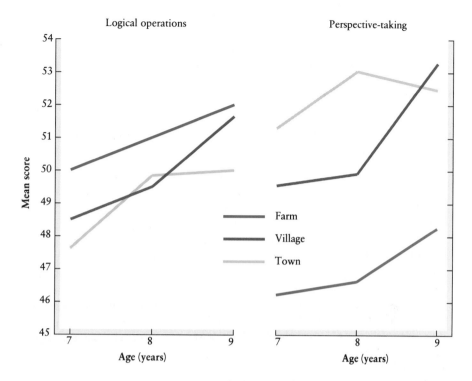

FIGURE 14.6 *The cognitive development of Hungarian children from isolated farms, villages, and towns. The graph on the left depicts their performance on tests of logical operations. The graph on the right depicts their performance on perspective-taking tasks. (From Hollos, 1975.)*

feel this kind of special affinity is the childhood precursor of the need for interpersonal intimacy that will be called love when it is encountered again in adolescence. He further claimed that the failure to form such friendships in childhood creates a social deficit that is difficult to remedy later. As evidence, he cites several of his psychiatric patients who had failed to form friendships as children and who now were extremely uncomfortable in their business and social dealings with others. Figure 14.7 shows one person's interpretation of the consequences of failure to participate in a peer group.

Since Sullivan's time there has been considerable interest in the link between problematic relations with peers during childhood and later maladjustment. A number of studies using both follow-back and follow-forward designs have been conducted to investigate this relationship. Researchers who use **follow-back designs** begin by selecting a sample of adults who are known to be deviant in some way (poor mental health, criminality, failure to complete school) and a second sample of adults who are free of that problem. The researchers then examine available childhood school and clinic records to determine which aspects of childhood functioning seem to be associated with the

adult's problems. Researchers who use **follow-forward designs** (a form of longitudinal design) begin by selecting groups of children who differ in their social acceptance or their behavior (shy, aggressive, etc.) and then compare their subsequent adjustment.

A review of a number of studies by Jeffrey Parker and Steven Asher (1987) found that childhood aggression is the most consistent predictor of later problems for boys. Follow-back studies show that most adolescent males who are charged with delinquent behavior were aggressive as children. Follow-forward studies show that boys who are more troublesome and antisocial than their peers when they are children are more likely to become delinquent during adolescence. Aggression during childhood is also linked to early withdrawal from school, especially among boys (Cairns, Cairns, & Neckerman, 1989).

Being rejected is not so closely linked with criminality as aggression is (Kupersmidt, Coie, & Dodge, 1990), but it is a frequent precursor of dropping out of school. Rejected children are three to five times more likely to drop out of school than children who are accepted by their peers.

Despite some weaknesses, the existing data support the belief that peer interactions and childhood

DEAR DR

I read the report in the Oct. 30 issue of
_____ about your study of only children. I am
an only child, now 57 years old and I want to tell you
some things about my life. Not only was I an only
child but I grew up in the country where there were no
nearby children to play with. My mother did not want
children around. She used to say 'I don't want my kid
to bother anybody and I don't want nobody's kids
bothering me.'

. . . From the first year of school I was teased and
made fun of. For example, in about third or fourth
grade I dreaded to get on the school bus to go to
school because the other children on the bus called
me 'Mommy's baby.' In about the second grade I
heard the boys use a vulgar word. I asked what it
meant and they made fun of me. So I learned a lesson
— don't ask questions. This can lead to a lot of confusion to hear talk one doesn't understand and not be
able to learn what it means . . .

I never went out with a girl while I was in school —
in fact I hardly talked to them. In our school the boys
and girls did not play together. Boys were sent to one
part of the playground and girls to another. So, I
didn't learn anything about girls. When we got into
high school and the boys and girls started dating I
could only listen to their stories about their experiences.

I could tell you a lot more but the important thing is
I have never married or had any children. I have not
been very successful in an occupation or vocation. I
believe my troubles are not all due to being an only
child, but I do believe you are right in recommending
playmates for preschool children and I will add playmates for the school agers and not have them strictly
supervised by adults. I believe I confirm the experiments with monkeys in being overly timid sometimes
and overly aggressive sometimes. Parents of only children should make special efforts to provide playmates
for [their children].

Sincerely yours,

FIGURE 14.7   *A letter from a friendless man giving his
account of the importance of childhood friendships for development. (From Hartup, 1978.)*

friendships play an important part in development
during middle childhood. It would be a mistake, however, to attribute all social development during this
period to peer interactions. Children's relationships
with their parents continue to play an important role.

CHANGING RELATIONS WITH PARENTS

When Alfred Baldwin (1946) studied American parent-
child relationships and compared parents of 3-year-
old children with parents of 9-year-olds, he found that
parents were less warm to their 9-year-old children,
more severe, and more critical of them. Two related
factors combine to account for this change in parental
standards and behavior as children enter middle childhood. First, parents in every culture have their own
ideas of the ages when their children should be able to
do certain things (Goodnow et al., 1984; Hess et al.,
1980; Warton & Goodnow, 1991). Second, the strategies parents adopt to correct their children's misbehavior change as the level of their children's competence
increases.

Japanese, American, Australian, and Australian-
Lebanese mothers were asked the approximate age
when they expected children to be capable of each of
38 kinds of behavior: before the age of 4 years, between 4 and 6 years, or after 6 years of age. Table 14.7
shows the ages at which they expect their children to
behave competently in various spheres. As the table
indicates (note that low scores indicate *late* expectations of competence), Japanese mothers expected
their children to display emotional maturity, compliance, and ritual forms of politeness at an earlier age
than mothers in the other three groups. The American
and Australian mothers expected their children to develop social skills and the ability to assert themselves
verbally relatively early. The Lebanese mothers were
distinctive in their willingness to leave the children to
attain the needed competencies in their own good
time; their developmental timetables were usually later
than those of the other groups. Despite cultural variations in the precise age at which the various competencies were expected to be achieved, all parents expect
their children to master these basic competencies
sometime during middle childhood (Rogoff et al.,
1980).

TABLE 14.7

Mean Ages at Which Mothers in Four Cultural Groups Expect Their Children to Attain Various Competencies

(1 = 6 years or older; 2 = 4–5 years; 3 = younger than 4 years)

Item	Japan	U.S.A.	Australia A*	B†
Emotional maturity				
Does not cry easily	2.49	2.08	1.66	1.95
Can get over anger by self	2.67	1.69	1.93	1.38
Stands disappointment without crying	2.34	1.97	1.83	1.65
Does not use baby talk	2.07	1.91	2.66	2.76
Compliance				
Comes or answers when called	2.66	2.21	1.79	1.13
Stops misbehaving when told	2.57	2.33	2.28	1.57
Gives up reading/TV to help mother	1.33	1.54	1.59	1.51
Politeness				
Greets family courteously	2.90	2.22	2.69	2.38
Uses polite forms (please) to adults	2.08	2.37	2.76	2.73
Independence				
Stays home alone for an hour or so	1.78	1.04	1.10	1.05
Takes care of own clothes	2.17	1.87	1.55	1.35
Makes phone calls without help	1.41	1.21	1.14	1.21
Sits at table and eats without help	2.95	2.76	2.79	2.59
Does regular household tasks	2.03	1.97	2.07	1.32
Can entertain self alone	2.74	2.78	2.72	1.78
Plays outside without supervision	1.98	2.19	2.38	1.40
Social skills				
Waits for turn in games	2.31	2.12	1.97	1.89
Shares toys with other children	2.62	2.72	2.72	1.73
Sympathetic to feelings of children	1.86	2.13	1.79	1.22
Resolves disagreement without fighting	1.41	1.70	1.45	1.11
Gets own way by persuading friends	1.40	1.94	1.97	1.30
Takes initiative in playing with others	1.59	2.48	2.24	1.73
Verbal assertiveness				
Answers a question clearly	2.10	1.98	2.14	1.46
States own preference when asked	1.72	2.25	2.00	1.30
Asks for explanation when in doubt	1.71	2.30	2.21	1.38
Can explain why s/he thinks so	1.48	2.09	1.76	1.32
Stands up for own rights with others	1.62	2.27	2.10	1.24
Miscellaneous				
Uses scissors without supervision	2.00	1.54	1.52	1.11
Keeps feet off furniture	2.74	2.30	2.31	2.05
Disagrees without biting or throwing	2.43	2.34	2.38	1.92
Answers phone properly	1.52	1.49	2.10	1.98
Resolves quarrels without adult help	1.52	1.73	1.52	1.46

* Born in Australia.
† Born in Lebanon.
Source: Goodnow et al., 1984.

BOX 14.3

Maternal Employment and Child Welfare

All parents must rely on their children's good sense and self-control when they are not around to supervise, and such reliance becomes an urgent necessity when employed mothers are unavailable to their children during the greater part of each day. In the United States nearly 60 percent of all mothers of school-aged children are employed (see the accompanying table). The National Research Council formed a panel of scholars to review the research on how these children are affected by their mothers' employment.

Contrary to popular belief, this report concludes that available research "has not demonstrated that mothers' employment *per se* has consistent direct effects, either positive or negative, on children's development" (Hayes & Kamerman, 1983:221). More recent research has confirmed this conclusion (Hoffman, 1989).

The effects of a mother's employment on her children depend on how her work interacts with other factors, including the family's income, race, family structure (are the parents married, divorced, single?), the parents' attitudes toward their role as parents, their work and housework, as well as where the family lives (rural area, suburb, city, near relatives, etc.). It also depends on what happens to the children when their parents are at work. Although the data permit no sweeping generalizations, some specific findings are of interest.

As might be expected, school-aged children with employed mothers spend less time in their parents' presence than children whose mothers are not employed. One survey found that mothers who were not employed outside the home spent roughly 13 hours each week in such primary child-care activities as feeding their children, taking them places, talking to them, and helping them with their homework, whereas mothers who worked 40 or more hours a week spent about 5 hours a week in such activities (Robinson, 1989). What might not be expected is that although they spend less time with their parents, the amount of time that they spend actively doing things with their parents does not vary significantly from the average recorded for children whose mothers are not employed (Hayes & Kamerman, 1983; Easterbrooks & Goldberg, 1985; Hoffman, 1984). One can only speculate about how children are affected by the amount of time they spend with their parents, and whether it matters if the time is spent actively doing something together or just being in each other's company.

Mothers who work outside of the home are more likely to emphasize independence in training their children than mothers who are not employed. In line with this orientation, children of employed mothers have been found to spend somewhat more time on household chores than do their peers whose mothers do not work (Medrich et al., 1982). This emphasis on independence begins early. When both parents are wage earners, securely attached 18-month-olds show comparatively less dependency behavior than toddlers whose mothers are not employed (Weinraub, Jaeger, & Hoffman, 1988).

Socioeconomic status influences the way maternal employment affects children's development. Many children of single, impoverished, poorly educated mothers appear to benefit when their mothers hold a job. An increase in family income is one factor, but also important is the improvement in the mothers' social circumstances, morale, and self-confidence

To learn how parental expectations concerning children's competencies affect the way they react when their children misbehave, Theodore Dix and his colleagues (Dix, Ruble, & Zambarano, 1989) interviewed over 100 mothers of children ranging in age from 4 to 12 years. Each mother was read two descriptions of children the same age as her own who either stole quarters from a neighbor's house or ate the family's dessert at a picnic. Some of the descriptions were unclear as to whether the child understood that the behavior was wrong; other descriptions made it obvious that the child understood. In the first case, mothers said that they would try to explain to the children how the behavior hurt other people, but that they were not likely to punish them. In the second case, mothers were more likely to say that the child should be punished although they also thought that they should explain why the behavior was wrong. In

(Bronfenbrenner, 1986). This finding is confirmed by a study that found that third- and fifth-grade children who were cared for after school by their single, nonemployed mothers had higher ratings for antisocial behaviors, anxiety, and peer conflicts and lower scores on a picture vocabulary test than their peers who were under other types of adult-supervised after-school care (Vandell & Ramana, 1991).

Children are also affected by the number of hours their mothers work. Being employed more than 40 hours a week increases a mother's anxiety and affects the sensitivity of her mothering. It is also likely to have a negative effect on her child's achievement and adjustment (Gottfried, Gottfried, & Bathhurst, 1988; Owen & Cox, 1988).

Overall, it appears that maternal employment has a positive influence on girls. Daughters of employed mothers are reported to be more "indepen-dent, outgoing, higher achievers, to admire their mothers more, to have more respect for women's competence, and to show better social and personal adjustment" (Hoffman, 1984:116).

Boys fare less well when their mothers hold jobs. The evidence suggests that in poor families these boys are less well adjusted than the sons of mothers who do not work outside of the home, and in middle-class families they do not perform so well in school (Hoffman, 1980, 1989).

Since the general social trend in industrialized countries is toward full- and part-time maternal employment, considerable attention has been devoted to the evidence suggesting that in some conditions boys are at risk if the mother works outside the home (Hoffman, 1984); but precisely what those conditions are is is not yet clear.

Percentage of Women in U.S. Labor Force with Children in Five Age Categories, 1990

	Children 18 and under	Children 14–17	Children 6–13	Children 3–5	Children under 3
All women	66.6%	76.4%	73.6%	64.4%	54.5%
White	66.9	77.2	73.9	64.4	54.8
Black	66.1	73.8	74.3	66.8	53.3
Hispanic	51.5	64.3	61.9	50.5	38.5

Source: U.S. Department of Labor, Bureau of Labor Statistics, *Current Population Survey*, March 1991.

accord with the findings on parental timetables described above, mothers believed that older children ought to be aware when they are misbehaving and consequently favored more severe responses to their transgressions.

Related to this change in parents' expectations is a change in the issues that arise between parents and children, according to Eleanor Maccoby (1980). Parents of young children are concerned with establishing daily routines and controlling temper tantrums and fights, as well as teaching children to care for, dress, feed, and groom themselves. Some of the issues of early childhood, such as fights among siblings, are still of concern during the years from 6 to 12. In addition, a whole new set of problems crops up when children start to take responsibility for chores at home, attend school, work, and spend increasing amounts of time away from adult supervision (see Box 14.3).

In economically developed countries, parents start to focus on their children's achievement during middle childhood, even though it may have no immediate economic consequences for the family. School is the arena in which children's achievement is most prominently judged. Parents worry about how involved they should become in their child's schoolwork, what they should do if a child has academic problems, and how to deal with behavior problems. Other concerns that emerge during middle childhood are whether to require children to do chores and what standards of performance should be expected of them, whether children should be paid for work they do around the house, and the extent to which parents should monitor their children's social life (Maccoby, 1984; Warton & Goodnow, 1991).

In less developed countries, where a family's survival often depends on putting children to work as early as possible, parents worry about their children's ability to take care of younger kin in the absence of adult supervision and to carry out important economic tasks such as the care of livestock or the hoeing of weeds (Weisner, 1984).

As children grow older and spend increasing amounts of time out of adults' sight, parents reason with their children more, appeal to their self-esteem ("You wouldn't do anything that stupid") or to their sense of humor, and seek to arouse their guilt. They remind children that they are responsible for themselves. When school-aged children break rules, they are not so likely to be punished as they were when they were younger (Clifford, 1959), and when they are punished, their parents are more likely to deprive them of privileges and confine them to the house or their room rather than to spank them (Newson & Newson, 1976).

As the parents' behavior changes, so does the children's. Children openly express anger toward their parents less often than they did when they were younger (Goodenough, 1931/1975). They are less likely to use such coercive behaviors as whining, yelling, hitting, and ignoring others' overtures (Patterson, 1982). Now they argue with their parents, sometimes (to their parents' consternation) at great length, even going so far as to point out their parents' inconsistencies. When conflict breaks out, however, or when they become angry, children do not recover so quickly as they did when they were younger. Parents report that children at this stage are often sulky, depressed, or passively noncooperative, or that they avoid them after an angry conflict (Clifford, 1959).

In sum, parents increasingly share control with the children themselves. Maccoby (1984) terms this sharing of responsibility **coregulation.** Coregulation is built on parent-child cooperation. It requires parents to work out methods of monitoring, guiding, and supporting their children when adults are not present, using the time they are together to reinforce their children's understandings of right and wrong, what is safe and unsafe, and when they need to come to adults for help. For coregulation to succeed, children must be willing to inform their parents of their whereabouts, their activities, and their problems.

These changes in child-parent interaction are consistent with Freud's characterization of middle childhood as a time when the superego becomes dominant, causing children to be preoccupied with mastering adult standards. It is a time when the superego "observes the ego, gives it orders, judges it and threatens it with punishments, exactly like the parents whose place it has taken" (Freud, 1940/1964:205) (see Chapter 10, p. 371). As a result, children want to conform to their parents' expectations and feel distressed when they fail to meet them. They blame this distress partly on their parents and partly on themselves, which causes both interpersonal and psychological conflict.

Despite differences in emphasis and terminology, researchers who focus on socialization in middle childhood generally agree that children's social relations undergo a significant rearrangement during this period. These changes in social relations can be viewed both as a cause and an effect of changes taking place in the children's sense of themselves.

A NEW SENSE OF SELF

Research on changes in children's self-concept during middle childhood has focused on how they define themselves, the emergence of sensitivity to their relative standing among peers, and their resulting efforts to maintain their self-esteem.

Concepts of the Self

Researchers have used interviews, story dilemmas, and questionnaires to probe developmental changes in the way children think about themselves. Although results depend slightly on the procedure used, in general preschool children think of themselves primarily in terms of the activities they engage in and to some extent of their physical characteristics. When Ann Keller, LeRoy Ford, and John Meacham (1978) asked 3-to-5-year-old children to complete such sentences as "I am a boy/girl who . . . ," the children described themselves in terms of what they did: "I am a girl who walks to school" or "I am a boy who plays baseball." After the age of 7, children increasingly distinguish among the mental, physical, social, and psychological aspects of themselves, and their view of the relationship between self and activity becomes more complex (Broughton, 1978; Damon & Hart, 1988; Secord & Peevers, 1974).

Table 14.8, based on an extensive study of changes in children's self-concept by William Damon and Daniel Hart (1988), displays both the variety of children's answers when they are asked to describe themselves and the increasing complexity of their self-conception as they grow older. Damon and Hart report that children at all of the ages they studied refer to their appearance, their activities, their relations to others, and their psychological characteristics when they describe themselves; but both the weight they give to the various characteristics and the complexity of their self-concept change with age. Children 6 to 7 years old sometimes describe themselves in terms of particular categories that apply to them ("I'm 6 years old") and sometimes in terms of others ("I'm older than she is"). Between 8 and 11 years of age, these two ways of thinking about oneself are supplemented by self-conceptions that include the interpersonal implications of the characteristics they pick out. Instead of

---

TABLE 14.8

A Developmental Model of Self-concept

Level	Physical	Activity-based	Social	Psychological
1. Categorical identification (4–7 years)	I have blue eyes. I'm 6 years old.	I play baseball. I play and read a lot.	I'm Catholic. I'm Sarah's friend.	I get funny ideas sometimes. I'm happy.
2. Comparative assessments (8–11 years)	I'm bigger than most kids. I have really light skin because I'm Scandinavian.	I'm not very good at school. I'm good at math, but I'm not so good at art.	I like it when my mom and dad watch me play baseball. I do well in school because my parents respect me for it.	I'm not as smart as most kids. I get upset more easily than other kids.
3. Interpersonal implications (12–15 years)	I am a four-eyed person. Everyone makes fun of me. I have blonde hair, which is good because boys like blondes.	I play sports, which is important because all the kids like athletes. I treat people well so I'll have friends when I need them.	I am an honest person, so people trust me. I'm very shy, so I don't have many friends.	I understand people, so they come to me with their problems. I'm the kind of person who loves being with my friends; they make me feel good about being me.

Source: After Damon & Hart, 1988.

The way one looks is often central to self-definition.

at face value. They deny that what people say may not be what they think. Selman calls this conception of the self physicalistic because the self is equated with specific body parts. Children at this level, Selman reports, will say that their mouth tells their hand what to do or that their ideas come from their tongue (Selman, 1980).

About the age of 6, the children in Selman's study believed that psychological and outward appearance are different but claimed that they must be consistent with each other. Then, about the age of 8, they realized that there can be a discrepancy between inner experience and outer appearance; the self can fool itself. Thus Mike might really want another puppy (the psychological experience), even though he says he doesn't (outer appearance). At this point children have developed the idea that each person has a private, subjective self that behavior does not always reveal.

Social Comparison

As children enter middle childhood they begin to define themselves by comparison with other children. When children are asked, "What kind of person are you?" a preschooler might answer, "I ride a bike," but a third-grader is more likely to respond, "I ride a bike better than Sammy" (Secord & Peevers, 1974). In short, during middle childhood the self starts to be defined in relation to one's peers.

There is no mystery as to why social comparison begins to play a significant role in children's sense of themselves during middle childhood. The increased time they spend with their peers and their greater ability to understand others' points of view lead children to engage in a new kind of questioning about themselves. If the setting is the playground, they must decide "Am I good at sports?" "Am I a good friend?" "Do the other kids like me?" If the setting is the classroom, the comparison is likely to be along academic lines ("Am I good at math?"). Such questions have no absolute answer because there are no absolute criteria of success. Rather, success is defined by one's relation to the social group. As a consequence, the children's developing self-concepts must take into account their relative standing, a process called **social comparison.** From specific comparisons in a wide variety of settings, children begin to formulate a new overall sense of themselves.

saying "I'm smarter than other kids," for example, children now are likely to say, "I'm smarter than other kids, so they don't like to hang out with me."

Robert Selman (1980) posed story dilemmas such as this one to obtain evidence about children's changing self-concept:

> Eight-year-old Tom is trying to decide what to buy his friend Mike for a birthday party. By chance, he meets Mike on the street and learns that Mike is extremely upset because his dog, Pepper, has been lost for two weeks. In fact, Mike is so upset that he tells Tom, "I miss Pepper so much that I never want to look at another dog again." Tom goes off, only to pass a store with a sale on puppies: only two are left, and these will soon be gone. (1980:94)

After telling this story, Selman asked children if Tom should buy a puppy for Mike and followed up the question with probes about the child's ideas concerning the self and others: "Is there an inside and an outside to a person?"; "Can you ever fool yourself into thinking that you feel one way when you really feel another?"

Before middle childhood, children take Mike's statement that he never wants to look at another dog

Of course, most preschoolers are not complete strangers to social comparison. When cookies are being distributed at snacktime in a day-care center, preschoolers make certain they get as many as their peers. Kindergartners are likely to know whether other children in their class can run faster than they can. And certainly jealousy among siblings reflects awareness of comparative levels of attention from parents. But around the age of 8 or 9 years, children's sensitivity to themselves in relation to others their own age increases significantly (Ruble & Frey, 1991).

To study the beginnings of one common form of social comparison, the extent of athletic ability, Diane Ruble and her colleagues (1980) arranged for 5-, 7-, and 9-year-old children to play a modified game of basketball, the objective of which was to throw the ball into a basketball hoop concealed behind a curtain. Because the children could not see for themselves if they were successful, they had to depend on what the experimenter told them. The unusual procedure was explained as a test of their ability to remember the location of the hoop when it was no longer visible. To make this story plausible, the children were given a brief practice session with the hoop visible.

Once the experimenters were satisfied that the children knew what was expected of them, each child was given four chances to throw the ball through the hoop. All the children were told that they were successful on the second and fourth throws. This part of the procedure set the stage for the social comparison manipulation to follow.

Each of three groups of children at each age level was provided with different information about how they performed in relation to a hypothetical group of other children their own age. To make the comparison clear, the experimenter pasted paper symbols on a large scorecard to mark the child's performance. Each child saw two balls and two X's pasted on the board to mark his or her two "hits" and two "misses." Children in the relative-success group also saw the hypothetical scores of eight other children, only one of whom scored even one hit. Children in the relative-failure group saw scores of eight children, all of whom scored three or more hits. Children in a control group saw only their own scores. The children were asked both how good they were at this game and how pleased they were with their performance.

If the children assessed their own performance by comparing their scores with others', one would expect that those who experienced relative failure would assess themselves as failures and those who experienced relative success would assess themselves highly. This is exactly what Ruble and her associates observed among the 9-year-olds. Nine-year-old children in the relative-success group had the highest self-assessment, followed by those in the control group; those in the failure group gave themselves the lowest assessment. But these findings did not hold true for the 5- and 7-year-olds. These children did not seem to assess their own performance in relation to those of others. They were equally pleased with their performance whether they had experienced relative failure, relative success, or no social comparison at all.

In real life, children have a great deal of experience evaluating their relative abilities in all sorts of endeavors, from piano recitals to spelling bees and playground games, and the process of social comparison can be quite complex. The following example is taken from an interview with an aspiring ballet dancer. Gwen, who is 12½ years old, is in a special class from which members of a leading national ballet company are chosen. Gwen knows that she is constantly being graded, much as she might be in school.

> Partly because she is so much younger, Gwen is smaller and doesn't have as much strength and stamina as the other girls in her class. They also have more experience on toe than she does and she takes fewer classes than they do. "Mostly it doesn't really bother me that much," she says. "But sometimes I think I'm doing really badly and I start comparing myself to them. Then I say, 'Hey, look, I'm not as old.' But I like having people a little bit older than me because that way I can look up to them and see what they're doing and then try to work up to that, instead of having kids my own age. Because when I was with the kids my own age I was always better than they were," she states matter-of-factly. Then, catching herself, she adds, "I feel badly saying that, but it's true." (Cole, 1980a:159)

Evidence suggests that deliberate and pervasive social comparison becomes important around 8 years of age, after children have accumulated experience both in activities dominated by their agemates and in the explicit comparative evaluations that are so prominent a feature of schooling (Ruble & Frey, 1991).

FIGURE 14.8   *A sample item to elicit information about children's self-esteem. Children were asked which picture corresponded most closely to themselves by marking the appropriate circle. The small circle means that the picture applies a little, the large circle that it applies a lot. (From Harter & Pike, 1984.)*

Self-esteem

As we mentioned in Chapter 10 (p. 371), Erik Erikson (1963) thought of middle childhood as the time when children have to resolve the crisis of industry versus inferiority. We discussed the "industry" side of this formulation at length in Chapters 12 and 13, which described the new assignments adults give children who work or go to school. Here we focus on the "inferiority" side of the crisis by considering the challenges to self-esteem that arise from children's efforts to demonstrate that they are capable and worthy of others' love and admiration.

Self-esteem is considered to be a critical index of mental health (Jahoda, 1958). High self-esteem during childhood has been linked to satisfaction (Crandall, 1973) and happiness (Bachman, 1970) in later life, while low self-esteem has been linked to depression, anxiety, and maladjustment both in school and in social relations (Damon, 1983).

To study self-evaluations, Susan Harter and Robin Pike (1984) presented 4-, 5-, 6-, and 7-year-old children with pairs of pictures like those in Figure 14.8 and asked them to say whether each picture was a lot or a little like them. Each picture was selected to tap the children's judgments in one of four domains

thought to be important to self-esteem: cognitive competence, physical competence, peer acceptance, and maternal acceptance. Older children were presented comparable items, but the specific content was changed to be age-appropriate (for example, an item such as "Knows the alphabet," used to assess cognitive competence in the 4- and 5-year-olds, corresponded to the item "Can read alone" for the 6- and 7-year-olds). Children's responses to these self-evaluation tasks revealed that they evaluated their own worth in terms of two broad categories—competence and acceptance. In effect, they lumped cognitive and physical competence together in a single category of competence and combined peer and maternal acceptance in the category of acceptance. Nevertheless, the scale seemed to tap children's feelings of self-worth in a realistic way. Harter and Pike found, for example, that children who had been held back a grade rated themselves low in competence while newcomers to the school rated themselves low in acceptance.

In work with somewhat older children (8 to 12 years old), Harter (1982) presented the self-esteem questions in the written format shown in Figure 14.9. She found that these children were able to make more differentiated self-evaluations; for example, they distinguished between cognitive, social, and physical

Really true for me	Sort of true for me	Some kids often forget what they learn	but	Other kids can remember things easily	Sort of true for me	Really true for me
☐	☐				☐	☐

FIGURE 14.9   *A sample item from Harter's scale of self-esteem. Choices to the left of center indicate degrees of poor self-esteem; choices to the right indicate degrees of positive self-esteem. (From Harter, 1982.)*

competence (Harter, 1987). Older children were also able to provide evaluations of their overall self-worth, whereas the younger children evaluated themselves only in specific domains. (Table 14.9 shows the content of sample items in each domain of self-esteem included in Harter's scale for 8-to-12-year-olds.

Harter and others also report that there is an age-related change in the extent to which children's self-evaluations fit the views of others (Harter, 1982; Stipek, 1981). Younger children, like those who are older, are able to rate their peers' "smartness" at school in a way that agrees with teachers' evaluations. The way they rate themselves, however, does not correlate with either their teachers' or their peers' ratings. Around the age of 8, children's evaluations of themselves are validated by both their peers and their teachers. This pattern of results fits nicely with those reported by Ruble on social comparison (discussed on p. 557) and supports the conclusion that an overall sense of oneself in relation to others arises around the age of 8.

Self-esteem has also been linked to patterns of child rearing (Bishop & Ingersoll, 1989; Coopersmith, 1967; Loeb, Horst, & Horton, 1980). In an extensive study of 10-to-12-year-old boys, Stanley Coopersmith found that parents of boys with high self-esteem (as determined by their answers to a questionnaire and their teachers' ratings) employed a style of parenting strikingly similar to the "authoritative" pattern described by Diana Baumrind in her study of parenting (see Chapter 10). Recall that authoritative parents were distinguished by their mixture of firm control, promotion of high standards of behavior, encouragement of independence, and willingness to reason with their children. Coopersmith's data, taken from a significantly older group of children, suggest that three parental characteristics combine to produce high self-esteem in late middle childhood:

Acceptance of their children The mothers of sons with high self-esteem had closer, more affectionate relationships with their children than mothers of children with low self-esteem. The children seemed to appreciate this approval and to view their mother as favoring and supportive. They also tended to interpret their mother's interest as an indication of their personal importance, as a consequence of which they came to regard themselves favorably. "This is success in its most personal expression—the concern, attention, and time of significant others" (Coopersmith, 1967:179).

Clearly defined limits When parents impose strict limits on their children's activities, they make it clear when deviations are likely to evoke action; enforcement of limits gives the child a sense that norms are real and significant, and contributes to the child's self-definition.

Respect for individuality Within the limits set by the parents' sense of standards and social norms, the children are allowed a good deal of individual self-expression. Parents show respect for their children by reasoning with them and taking their points of view into account.

Taken together, these data suggest that the key to high self-esteem is the feeling, transmitted in large part by the family, that one has some ability to control one's own future by controlling both oneself and one's environment (Harter, 1983). This feeling of control is not without bounds. Children who have a positive self-image know their boundaries, but this awareness does not detract from their feeling of effectiveness.

TABLE 14.9

Harter Self-esteem Scale for 8-to-12-Year-Olds

Area of Self-evaluation	Content of Sample Items
Cognitive competence	Good at schoolwork, can figure out answers, remember easily, remember what is read
Social competence	Have a lot of friends, popular, do things with kids, easy to like
Physical competence	Do well at sports, good at games, chosen first for games
General self-worth	Sure of myself, do things fine, I am a good person, I want to stay the same

Source: Harter, 1982.

Rather, it sets clear limits within which the person feels considerable assurance and freedom.

A strong and positive sense of who they are within the family context cannot completely shield children against buffeting by their peers, but it does provide a secure foundation for the trials they undergo when they are on their own.

MIDDLE CHILDHOOD RECONSIDERED

With the evidence from this and the preceding two chapters before us, it is appropriate to return to the question of whether the transition from early to middle childhood constitutes a bio-social-behavioral shift. Is middle childhood a stage of development characterized by a common set of features in every culture?

Table 14.10 summarizes the changes that appear to distinguish middle childhood from early childhood. We have placed the social domain at the top because surveys of the world's cultures make it clear that adults everywhere assign 6- and 7-year-olds to a new social category and require them to behave themselves in new (and often stressful) contexts. Whether individual children are fully prepared or not, they must adapt to their new duties and roles or face the displeasure of their parents and the scorn of their peers.

Another universal characteristic of middle childhood is the rise of the peer group as a major context for development. For the first time children must define their status within a group of relative equals without the intervention of adults. In many cultures, perhaps all, interactions with peers become coordinated, with games governed by rules serving as surrogates for adult control. The experience of negotiating these interactions and comparing themselves with peers contributes to children's mastery of the social conventions and moral rules that regulate their communities. Peer interactions also provide crucial contexts within which children arrive at a new, more complex, and global sense of themselves.

The new cognitive capacities that develop at this time are less accessible to observation than changes in the social domain, but no less important in creating a qualitatively distinct stage of development. As we saw in Chapter 12, thought processes in middle childhood become more logical, deliberate, and consistent. Children become more capable of thinking through ac-

---

TABLE 14.10
The Bio-Social-Behavioral Shift That Initiates Middle Childhood

SOCIAL DOMAIN

Peer-group participation
Rule-based games without direct adult supervision
Deliberate instruction
Golden Rule morality
Coregulation of behavior between parent and child
Social comparison

BEHAVIORAL DOMAIN

Increased memory capacity; strategic remembering
Concrete operations
Logical classification
Decreased egocentrism and improved perspective-taking

BIOLOGICAL DOMAIN

Loss of baby teeth and gain of permanent teeth
Growth spurt in frontal lobes and in overall brain size
Predominance of alpha activity over theta in EEG

---

tions and their consequences; they are able to engage in concentrated acts of deliberate learning in the absence of tangible rewards; they keep in mind the points of view of other people in a wider variety of contexts; and they learn to inhibit actions that would lead them into difficulty with their parents and their peers. In effect, the children learn to "behave them*selves*."

Least visible are the biological changes that underpin children's apparent new mental capacities and modes of social interaction. The fact that children are bigger, stronger, and better coordinated is obvious enough. But only recently has modern anatomical and neurophysiological research provided evidence of such subtle changes as the proliferation of brain circuitry, changing relations between different kinds of brain-wave activity, and the greatly expanded influence of the brain's frontal lobes in guiding behavior.

If we were to consider each element in the transition to middle childhood separately, it would be difficult to sustain the argument that it is initiated by a bio-social-behavioral shift and represents a qualitatively stagelike change from earlier periods. After all, preschoolers are often found in neighborhood groups with older children when no adults are present. They have been shown to exhibit logical thinking and the use of memory strategies in some contexts, and their play contains elements of rules as well as social roles.

But the changes we have documented do not occur separately; they occur as a loosely coordinated ensemble. Although the details vary from one culture and one child to the next, the overall pattern is consistent and thus suggests a distinctive stage of life.

The existence of a universal pattern of changes associated with middle childhood in no way contradicts the fact that there are significant variations among cultures in the particular ways they conceive of and organize 6-to-12-year-old children's lives. Societies in which formal schooling is a central arena for children's development are especially likely to encourage uniformity in the age at which children begin to enter into the mode of life typical of middle childhood. Rural agrarian societies in which the change in children's activities is less extreme are less precise in the specific age at which a child is accorded the responsibilities and rights of middle childhood. But a few months' variation in the occurrence of various elements in the bio-social-behavioral shift does not substantially change their significance in the overall process of development.

SUMMARY

1. Middle childhood, the years from 6 to 12, is a time when children begin to spend significant amounts of time beyond direct adult control in the company of children roughly their own age.
2. During middle childhood the nature of children's play changes from role-based fantasy to games that require adherence to rules.
3. Social rules are of three types: moral rules, social conventions, and personal rules. Especially important for the functioning of peer groups are basic moral rules and social conventions.
4. The distinction between moral rules and social conventions is understood during early childhood. Within each domain of rules, children's thinking goes through a sequence of developmental stages.
5. Moral reasoning changes during middle childhood from a belief that moral authority resides naturally in a more powerful other (heteronomous morality) to a "market mentality" based on mutual support and, in some cases, to a belief in reciprocal responsibility (the Golden Rule).
6. Ideas about the fair distribution of resources change from reliance on arbitrary criteria to a recognition of the rights of all to share in the group's resources. Further development consists of children's increasingly sophisticated ability to appreciate the legitimacy of distributing resources unequally under certain conditions.
7. When children first reason about social conventions, they treat conventions as more or less equivalent to natural laws. With increased sophistication they begin to separate empirical associations ("Most nurses are women") from necessity ("A nurse has to be a woman"). Finally, children come to appreciate the usefulness of social conventions in the regulation of social interaction.
8. Children's conceptions of friendship develop from an emphasis on participating in joint activities to an emphasis on sharing interests, building mutual understanding, and creating trust.
9. The development of conceptions of friendship is closely associated with an increased ability to adopt other people's points of view and to repair misunderstandings when they arise.
10. Middle childhood is a period of relative segregation of the sexes. Boys tend to have more friends than girls, but girls' friendships tend to be more intimate than boys'.
11. Social differentiation in peer groups creates preference patterns as to who likes to spend time with whom. Physical attractiveness is a major factor in popularity, but relevant social skills—such as making constructive contributions to group activity, adopting the group's frame of reference, and understanding social rules—also play important roles in it.
12. Cultures vary markedly in the value they place on cooperation versus competition in peer interactions.
13. When conflicts arise between peer groups, the most likely way to reduce the tension is to involve both groups in solving a common problem.
14. Participation in peer groups is important to later development because it fosters the ability to communicate, to understand others' points of view, and to get along with others.
15. As children begin to participate in peer groups, their relationship with their parents undergoes significant changes.
    a. Parents become more demanding of their children,

with respect to both their domestic duties and their achievement in school.

    b. Parents shift from direct to indirect methods of control—to reasoning, humor, appeals to self-esteem, and the arousal of guilt.

16. Increased time spent among peers poses challenges to children's sense of themselves. Their basic conceptions of the self change from a fusion of the physical and the mental toward a recognition that people can feel one way and behave another.

17. Special challenges to the sense of self arise from the process of social comparison, which occurs when children compete in games and in school.

18. A strong sense of self-esteem is important to mental health. Family practices that emphasize acceptance of children, clearly defined limits, and respect for individuality are most likely to give rise to a firm sense of self-worth.

19. Social development is an essential part of the biosocial-behavioral shift that occurs in the years between 5 and 7. Understood as a unique configuration of biological, social, and behavioral characteristics, middle childhood appears to be a universal stage of human development.

KEY TERMS

coregulation

follow-back designs

follow-forward designs

group norms

moral rules

peers

personal rules

positive justice

social comparison

social competence

social conventions

social repair mechanisms

sociogram

sociometric data

SUGGESTED READINGS

COLES, ROBERT. *The Moral Life of Children.* Boston: Atlantic Monthly Press, 1986.

    The child psychiatrist Robert Coles provides many examples of children's moral thinking about important issues: school segregation, social inequality, and the threat of nuclear annihilation.

DAMON, WILLIAM. *Social and Personality Development.* New York: Norton, 1983.

    An excellent summary of many topics treated in this chapter: changing senses of the self, friendship, the roles of parents and peers in social and personality development, and the importance of cultural context.

GOLDING, WILLIAM. *The Lord of the Flies.* New York: Putnam, 1954.

    A terrifying fantasy of what might happen if a group of boys were marooned on an island with no supervision.

RUBIN, ZICK. *Children's Friendships.* Cambridge, Mass.: Harvard University Press, 1980.

    Beginning with an examination of the question "Do friends matter?" this book describes the evolution of children's friendships in a nontechnical and readable fashion, with special emphasis on middle childhood.

SOYINKA, WOLE. *Ake, the Years of Childhood.* New York: Random House, 1981.

    In this fascinating autobiographical account of growing up in an African village, a Nobel Prize–winning playwright, poet, and novelist gives us a glimpse into a culture that provides its children with their own distinctive ways of making sense of the world.

YOUNISS, JAMES. *Parents and Peers in Social Development.* Chicago: University of Chicago Press, 1980.

    Drawing on the theories of Jean Piaget and Harry Stack Sullivan, James Youniss examines the nature of social development as it is revealed in hundreds of interviews with children about the nature of their interactions with other people.

PART V

Adolescence and Beyond

The cascade of biochemical events that begins around the end of the first decade of life alters the body's size, shape, and functioning. The most revolutionary of these alterations is the development of an entirely new potential, the ability to engage in biological reproduction. This biological fact has profound interpersonal implications for the simple reason that reproduction cannot be accomplished by one human being alone. As their reproductive organs reach maturity, boys and girls begin to engage in new forms of social behavior because they begin to find the opposite sex attractive.

There is more to human reproduction than sex, however. The process of *biological* reproduction, by itself, is not sufficient for the continuation of our species. Central to human reproduction is the fact that biological reproduction must be complemented by an extended period of *cultural* reproduction, in which the "designs for living" evolved by the group are handed down to the next generation. In addition to mastering the basic skills necessary for economic survival, young people must achieve new and more mature relations with agemates of both sexes, learn the appropriate masculine or feminine social roles associated with adult status, develop emotional independence from parents and other adults, acquire their culture's values and ethical system, and learn to behave in a socially responsible manner (Havighurst, 1967).

In the United States and other industrialized societies, a gap of 7 to 9 years typically separates the biological changes that mark the onset of sexual maturity from the social changes that confer adult status (such as the right to marry without parental consent and to run for elective office). This lengthy period is necessary because it takes young people many years to acquire the knowledge and skills that will ensure them economic independence and enable them to reproduce their culture. It is in developed societies that a well-formed concept of adolescence as an intermediate stage of development between middle childhood and adulthood is most likely to be found.

Some societies recognize little or no gap between the beginning of sexual maturity and the beginning of adulthood (Whiting, Burbank, & Ratner, 1986). These are usually societies in which biological maturity occurs late by our standards and in which the level of technology is relatively low. By the time biological reproduction becomes possible, about the age of 15 in many nonindustrial societies, young people already know how to farm, weave cloth, prepare food, and care for children. In such societies, there may be no commonly acknowledged stage of development equivalent to adolescence.

The wide variation from one society to another in the time that elapses between the achievement of sexual maturity and the attainment of adult status raises the possibility that adolescence is not a universal stage of development. Some historians of childhood argue that adolescence exists as a distinct stage of development only in societies where prolonged education is necessary for people to become fully competent members of the community (Aries, 1962; Demos & Demos, 1969; Modell & Goodman, 1990). Other scholars argue that there is a period in every society during which children strive to attain adult status and that this striving produces similar experiences wherever it occurs (Bloch & Niederhoffer, 1958; Schlegel & Barry, 1991). They believe, therefore, that adolescence should be considered a universal developmental stage.

We will return to the question of the universality of adolescence as a distinctive stage at the end of Chapter 16. First, however, in Chapter 15, we examine the advent of biological maturity and its intimate links with changes in social life, including changes in the nature of interactions with peers, of friendships, and of relationships with one's family, as well as with entry into the work force. Chapter 16 concentrates on what have traditionally been thought of as the psychological characteristics of adolescence: the new modes of thought that are needed to perform the economic tasks and fulfill the social responsibilities of adulthood, the changed sense of personal identity that is occasioned by a transformed physique and altered social relationships, and the new beliefs about morality and the social order that accompany preparation for adulthood.

Chapter 17 sketches the course of development in later life. Whether or not one considers adolescence a universal stage of life, there is no doubt that eventually children enter adulthood. According to some schools of thought, once a person reaches adulthood, development stops. People are no longer in the process of "growing up." They *are* grownups.

Those who see culture as an essential factor in development, however, are likely to believe that development continues across the entire life span. From this perspective, adulthood, no less than infancy or middle childhood, is a time when changing biological, social, and behavioral characteristics transform the individual.

CHAPTER 15

Biological and Social Foundations of Adolescence

•

How is it that, in the human body, reproduction is the only function to be performed by an organ of which an individual carries only one half so that he has to spend an enormous amount of time and energy to find another half?

— FRANÇOIS JACOB, *THE POSSIBLE AND THE ACTUAL*

One of the most poignant accounts of what it feels like to enter adolescence appears in the diary of Anne Frank, a Jewish girl who lived in Holland during the German occupation of World War II. Unable to leave her hiding place and go outside for fear of being captured, Anne turned her diary into the friend she longed for. The entries quoted here were written shortly before Anne and her family were discovered and sent to their deaths in a concentration camp.

WEDNESDAY, 5 JANUARY 1944

Yesterday I read an article about blushing by Sis Heyster. This article might have been addressed to me personally. Although I don't blush very easily, the other things in it certainly all fit me. She writes roughly something like this — that a girl in the years of puberty becomes quiet within and begins to think about the wonders that are happening to her body.

I experience that, too, and that is why I get the feeling lately of being embarrassed about Margot, Mummy, and Daddy. Funnily enough, Margot, who is much more shy than I am, isn't at all embarrassed.

I think what is happening to me is so wonderful, and not only what can be seen on my body, but all that is taking place inside. I never discuss myself or any of these things with anybody; that is why I have to talk to myself about them.

Each time I have a period — and that has only been three times — I have the feeling that in spite of all the pain, unpleasantness, and nastiness, I have a sweet secret, and that is why, although it is

nothing but a nuisance to me in a way, I always long for the time that I shall feel that secret within me again. (1975:116–117)

THURSDAY, 6 JANUARY 1944

My longing to talk to someone became so intense that somehow or other I took it into my head to choose Peter.

Sometimes if I've been upstairs into Peter's room during the day, it always struck me as very snug, but because Peter is so retiring and would never turn anyone out who became a nuisance, I never dared stay long, because I was afraid he might think me a bore. I tried to think of an excuse to stay in his room and get him talking, without it being too noticeable, and my chance came yesterday. Peter has a mania for crossword puzzles at the moment and hardly does anything else. I helped him with them and we sat opposite each other at his little table, he on the chair and me on the divan.

It gave me a queer feeling each time I looked into his deep blue eyes, and he sat there with that mysterious laugh playing round his lips. I was able to read his inward thoughts. I could see on his face that look of helplessness and uncertainty as to how to behave, and at the same time, a trace of his sense of manhood. I noticed his shy manner and it made me feel very gentle; I couldn't refrain from meeting those dark eyes again and again, and with my whole heart I almost beseeched him: oh, tell me, what is going on inside you, oh can't you look beyond this ridiculous chatter?

But the evening passed and nothing happened, except that I told him about blushing—naturally not what I have written, but just that he would become more sure of himself as he grew older. (pp. 118–119)

These diary entries, written less than 24 hours apart when Anne was 14½ years old, vividly reveal the intimate connection between the physical changes of puberty and the social characteristics of adolescence. They touch on many aspects of the bio-social-behavioral shift that marks the end of middle childhood. First, the biological changes of puberty transform the size and shape of young people's bodies and evoke new, initially strange feelings. These changes are accompanied by changes in social life: after many years of relatively little interest in the opposite sex, boys and girls begin to find each other attractive, and their mutual attraction brings about changes in their interactions with peers and with close friends. Simultaneously, their relationships with their parents change, as if in recognition of the fact that independence, work, and the responsibility of caring for others must replace reliance on their parents' support. Lastly, the combination of biological and social developments is accompanied by changes in the way young people think about themselves and the world.

In attempting to gain a comprehensive picture of psychological development during adolescence, developmental psychologists face several difficulties. On the one hand, adolescents are able to talk more reflectively about their feelings and thought processes than are younger children. On the other hand, many of the topics that preoccupy them are socially awkward to talk about, and more of the things they do cannot be observed directly, so the actual facts of adolescents' behavior are difficult to document. Despite these difficulties, the nature of adolescence has long excited the interest of scholars, who have sought to understand its special characteristics both as a transition from middle childhood to adulthood and as a stage of development in its own right.

Societies' conceptions of adolescence are of vital importance to young people because they determine the demands made of them and the rights they are accorded. If they live in a society that considers puberty to be the onset of adulthood, they will be expected to maintain themselves economically, to care for others, and to be legally responsible for their ac-

tions. Conversely, if 15- and 16-year-olds are still considered children, they will be cared for by others and will remain free of many of the responsibilities adults must face. But they will also be expected to bend to adult demands as the price for their dependence.

TRADITIONAL CONCEPTIONS OF ADOLESCENCE

Present-day conceptions of adolescence in Western cultures are still heavily influenced by the eighteenth- and nineteenth-century European scholars who wrote about adolescence as a distinct period of life. The first great theorist of adolescence was Jean-Jacques Rousseau (see Chapter 1, pp. 12–13). In *Emile* (1762/1911), his treatise on human nature and education, Rousseau suggested three characteristics of adolescence.

1. Adolescence is a period of heightened instability and emotional conflict that is brought on by biological maturation. As Rousseau phrased it:

   As the roaring of the waves precedes the tempest so the murmur of rising passions announces this tumultuous change, a suppressed excitement warns us of the approaching danger. A change of temper, frequent outbreaks of anger, a perpetual stirring of the mind, make the child almost ungovernable. He becomes deaf to the voice he used to obey; he is a lion in a fever; he distrusts his keeper and refuses to be controlled. (p. 172)

2. In important respects, adolescence recapitulates—repeats in concise form—the earlier stages of life through which the child has passed. Rousseau expressed this idea in this way: "We are born, so to speak, twice over; born into existence, and born into life; born a human being and born a man" (p. 172).

3. The biological and social changes that figure prominently in adolescence are accompanied by a fundamental change in psychological processes. The transition to adolescence, Rousseau believed, brought with it self-conscious thought and the ability to reason logically.

When developmental psychologists began to turn their attention to the phenomenon of adolescence, at the end of the nineteenth century, Rousseau's ideas were picked up and modified by, among others, G. Stanley Hall, the first president of the American Psychological Association and a major figure in the shaping of developmental psychology (Cairns, 1983; Kessen, 1965). Hall's goal was to construct a theory of individual development based on Darwin's ideas about the evolution of the species. Hall proclaimed that

> adolescence is a new birth, for the higher and more completely human traits are now born. The qualities of body and soul that now emerge are far newer. The child comes from and harks back to a remoter past; the adolescent is neo-atavistic, and in him the later acquisitions of the race become prepotent. Development is less gradual and more saltatory, suggestive of some ancient period of storm and stress when old moorings were broken and a higher level attained. (1904:xiii)

This key passage contains two controversial ideas, both of which can be traced back to Rousseau. One is that adolescence is characterized by a heightened state of emotionality, stress, stratospheric highs and abyssal lows, and love of excitement. The other is that adolescence is a period of rebirth after childhood, although Hall, unlike Rousseau, believed that adolescence recapitulates earlier stages in the life of the *species,* not of the individual child. In the flush of late nineteenth-century enthusiasm for Darwinism, **recapitulationism**—the idea that each creature's individual development repeats the entire evolutionary history of the species—was so popular that it inspired a tongue-twisting aphorism: "Ontogeny recapitulates phylogeny" (see Box 15.1).

According to Hall, middle childhood corresponds to an ancient period of historical development when human reason, morality, feelings of love toward others, and religion were presumably underdeveloped by modern standards. As he put it, the end of childhood

> was once, and for a very protracted and relatively stationary period, the age of maturity in the remote, perhaps pigmoid, stage of human evolution, when in a warm climate the young of our species once shifted for themselves independently of further parental aid. (1904:ix – x)

BOX 15.1
Recapitulation and Development

In their attempts to understand the laws governing the evolution of life, nineteenth-century scholars revived an idea that can be traced back to antiquity: that the development of an individual organism recapitulates the entire evolutionary history of the species. In the decades before the publication of Darwin's *Origin of Species* (1859), this debate focused not on human beings but on lower species whose origins could be traced through fossils (Gould, 1977b).

Louis Agassiz, a geologist who believed that "ontogeny recapitulates phylogeny," offered the development of the tail of the fish *Pleuronectes* as a prime example. As the left half of the illustration in this box indicates, the tail of an individual *Pleuronectes* undergoes a predictable sequence of changes as the fish matures. First the tail is symmetrical and pointed, then the top half extends well beyond the lower half, and finally symmetry is reestablished when a new and more complex structure connects the tail to the fish's spinal cord.

This progression also describes the evolution of *Pleuronectes* as a species, as the right half of the illustration indicates. These drawings depict the adult tails of three kinds of fish that represent three stages in the evolution of *Pleuronectes,* as revealed by the fossil record. Clearly the sequence of changes in the lifetime of individual *Pleuronectes* on the left parallels the evolutionary history of the species on the right.

Once Darwin made the claim that the evolutionary laws that apply to lower species apply to human beings as well, the idea that human children recapitulate earlier stages of human evolution during their development became enormously popular (Gould, 1977b; Kessen, 1965). The heyday of speculation about parallels between human origins and individual development coincided with the flowering of developmental psychology. Consequently, many early developmental psychologists believed in some form of the recapitulationist theory and applied it in their work.

In the early twentieth century, the doctrine of recapitulationism came under heavy attack within the scientific community. It was not that scholars suddenly decided that ontogeny and phylogeny were totally unrelated. As biological knowledge expanded at

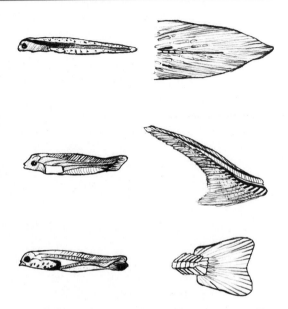

Parallels between individual development and evolutionary change provided key evidence for the hypothesis that ontogeny recapitulates phylogeny. On the left are changes in the tail of a single Pleuronectes *as it develops. On the right is fossil evidence of three stages in the evolution of the species* Pleuronectes. *(From Gould, 1977b.)*

the turn of the century, however, it became clear that the evidence on which recapitulationists had drawn was selective; many cases did not fit the law of recapitulation. Even more damaging, the mechanism of heredity that recapitulationists relied on to explain human development from birth to adulthood required them to assume that acquired characteristics were inherited, an assumption that was totally rejected in biology once the genetic basis of evolution became established. (The idea that acquired characteristics can be inherited is discussed in Chapter 2, p. 70.)

Despite its demise as a scientific theory, the idea of recapitulationism has had a major influence on professionals who have concerned themselves with child development throughout the twentieth century. As recently as 1968, Dr. Benjamin Spock, whose book on child rearing influenced generations of parents and their children, wrote:

> Each child as he develops is retracing the whole history of mankind, physically and spiritually, step by step. A baby starts off in the womb as a single tiny cell, just the way the first living thing appeared in the ocean. Weeks later, as he lies in the amniotic fluid in the womb, he has gills like a fish. Towards the end of the first year of life, when he learns to clamber to his feet, he's celebrating that period millions of years ago when man's ancestors got up off all fours. . . . The child in the years after six gives up part of his dependence on his parents. He makes it his business to find out how to fit into the world outside the family. . . . He is probably reliving that stage of human history when our wild ancestors found it was better not to roam the forest in independent family groups but to form larger communities. (p. 229)

One of the areas where recapitulationist ideas have continued to be important is education, where they are still used to organize the early classroom experience of many children. It was to help children "traverse the path of human development" that Maria Montessori (1912/1964), whose methods of preschool education are still in wide use, recommended that young children be shown how to grow plants and tend animals. She believed that by discovering how to intensify "the production of the soil," young children, like their remote ancestors, would "obtain the reward of civilization" (p. 160). John Dewey (1916), perhaps the most influential of all American educational theorists, adopted recapitulationist ideas in advocating that children participate actively in farming, building houses, and the like as a way to break through the abstract, formal nature of much school instruction. He insisted that the goal of allowing children to learn about and thus vicariously experience earlier epochs in human history was to help them to understand human life today.

Hall saw adolescence as a time for the development of the highest human capacities and as the period during which human progress could be promoted.

Modern texts on adolescence tend to treat Hall as a figure of purely historical interest. His insistence that the young recapitulate the entire history of the human species has been discredited (Gould, 1977b; Medicus, 1992), and his portrait of adolescence as a period of emotional excess is considered to be exaggerated (Feldman & Elliot, 1990). But Hall's ideas, like Rousseau's, live on in our culture's stereotype of modern adolescence, and they appear in modified form in the ideas of several influential twentieth-century psychologists, including Freud, Gesell, Piaget, and Erikson.

MODERN THEORIES OF ADOLESCENCE

The challenge to modern theorists of adolescence is to understand the biological, social, behavioral, and cultural factors involved in the transition from childhood to adulthood and how they are woven together. Each of the four theoretical perspectives we have been examining offers insights into this question, but there is as yet no widely accepted, unified theory of adolescence, and a great many researchers do not identify themselves with any of the established theoretical perspectives (Feldman & Elliott, 1990).

The Biological-Maturation Perspective

Biological-maturation theories of adolescence, like similar theories of development during earlier periods, emphasize that development is primarily the unfolding of inherited biological potentials. Two early modern adherents of this view whose ideas we have been tracking are Arnold Gesell and Sigmund Freud.

Arnold Gesell

Gesell admitted that the environment may exert a more powerful influence during adolescence than it did during infancy, but he still maintained that environmental conditions do not alter the *basic* pattern of development during adolescence in any fundamental way:

> Neither he [the adolescent] nor his parents in their zeal can transcend the basic laws of development. He continues to grow essentially in the same manner in which he grew as he advanced from the toddling stage of two years through the paradoxical stage of two and a half, and the consolidating stage of three. (Gesell & Ilg, 1943:256)

Gesell agreed with Hall that the child recapitulates the history of the species during the course of development. He asserted that the "higher human traits," such as abstract thinking, imagination, and self-control, make their appearance late in the development of the individual because they were acquired late in the history of the species. Although Gesell may be criticized for overemphasizing the effects of maturational changes on adolescents' behavior, his insistence that biological factors determine the basic pattern of psychological functioning in adolescence currently enjoys considerable support.

Sigmund Freud

As we saw in Chapter 1 (p. 15), Freud's ideas are often best thought of as reflecting a maturational position with respect to the sources of development, although he also attributed importance to social factors in developmental change. Here we must treat him as a biological theorist because he viewed adolescence as a distinctive stage of development during which human beings can at last fulfill the biological imperative to reproduce themselves and hence the species. This evolutionary assumption underlay Freud's emphasis on sex as the master motive for all human behavior, even behavior in the earliest stages of life. He called adolescence the *genital stage* because this is the period during which sexual intercourse becomes a major motive of behavior.

In Freud's theory, the emotional storminess that accompanies the adolescent stage is the culmination of the psychological struggle between the three parts of the personality: the id, the ego, and the superego (see Chapter 10, pp. 360–361). As Freud saw it, the upsurge in sexual excitation that accompanies puberty reawakens primitive instincts, increases the power of the id, and upsets the psychological balance achieved during middle childhood. This imbalance produces psychological conflict and erratic behavior. The main developmental task of adolescence is therefore to reestablish the balance of psychological forces by reintegrating them in a new and more mature way that is compatible with the individual's new sexual capacities.

Freud, like Hall, was greatly influenced by the doctrine of recapitulationism (Gould, 1977b; Sulloway, 1979). He argued, for example, that when sexual maturation reawakens the oedipal urges that were repressed at the start of middle childhood, the young person must rework this "old" conflict under the new conditions.

Freud's theory of adolescence is rooted in biology because of its assumption that the imperative to reproduce is the engine of individual development, but it does not ignore the social world. The superego is, after all, the internal representation of society, and the ego mediates between the social world embodied in the superego on the one hand and the demands of the id on the other. Consequently, personality development during adolescence, as in earlier periods, involves social as well as biological factors.

Ethological approaches

In recent years there has been a growing interest in applying theories and methods developed in the field of ethology, the study of animal behavior within an evolutionary framework, to the study of adolescence (MacDonald, 1988). As we saw in our discussion of social development in early childhood (Chapter 10, p. 381), there are striking similarities between the development of dominance relations in nonhuman species and in human children, and some psychologists hypothesize a common biological mechanism behind these similarities (Strayer, 1991). Research by Ritch Savin-Williams (1987) on the development of social hierarchies and aggressive behavior among teenagers confirms the continued importance of such social control mechanisms during adolescence.

An interesting finding to emerge from a number of ethological studies of nonhuman primates is the presence of a transition period for males between the juvenile and adult stages of life. In some respects it resembles human adolescence (Montemayor, 1990). Nonhuman primate females enter adulthood as soon as they become sexually mature, but males go through a conflictual period in which they must aggressively fight for access to females. One investigator, impressed

by the stress and danger of this transitional period, characterizes the adolescence of the nonhuman male primate as "the most dangerous and traumatic stage in his life" (Dolhinow, 1972:383). In some human cultures, as we shall see, similar sex differences in the transition from childhood to adulthood can be observed.

The Environmental-Learning Perspective

Beginning with the ascendance of behaviorist explanations of human behavior in the 1920s, biologically oriented accounts of development were criticized for underestimating the degree to which the social environment shapes children's behaviors and for overestimating the degree of discontinuity that distinguishes adolescence from middle childhood. For example, Albert Bandura and Richard Walters (1959) argued that the aggressiveness that is often associated with adolescent boys is a product of societal reinforcement, not innate predispositions. They found that aggressive boys were encouraged by their parents to be aggressive outside the home — to "stick up for their rights" and use their fists. The fathers of aggressive boys even seemed to get vicarious enjoyment from their sons' aggressive behavior. By being aggressive, then, the boys could have the satisfaction of pleasing their fathers.

Arguing that the same principles of learning that apply to human development at younger ages continue to apply during the teenage years, Bandura (1964) has been skeptical about claims that adolescence is a distinctive stage of development. He has been particularly critical of the idea that adolescence is inevitably a period of stress, tension, and rebellion, citing evidence that the rate of emotional difficulties is no higher among adolescents than among adults.

Investigators who give the most weight to environmental factors in development have sought out societies in which teenagers do not display the presumed universal characteristics of adolescence. They then point to those cultural variations as supporting the idea that the social environment shapes adolescents' behavior. One of the most famous of such studies was undertaken by the anthropologist Margaret Mead (1901–1978), who went to the Pacific islands of Samoa in 1926. Mead posed the question to be answered by her research in a characteristically straightforward manner:

Is adolescence a period of mental and emotional stress for the growing girl as inevitably as teething is a period of misery for the small baby? Can we think of adolescence as a time in the life history of every girl child which carries with it symptoms of conflict and stress as surely as it implies a change in the girl's body?

Her conclusion was equally straightforward:

Following the Samoan girls through every aspect of their lives we have tried to answer this question and we found throughout that we had to answer it in the negative. The adolescent girl in Samoa differed from her sister who had not reached puberty in one chief respect, that in the older girl certain bodily changes were present which were absent in the younger girl. There were no other great differences to set off the group passing through adolescence from the group which would become adolescent in two years or the group which had become adolescent two years earlier. (1928/1973:109)

Mead attributed the tranquility of Samoan adolescence to the general casualness of Samoan society, particularly its relaxed attitude toward sexual relationships among adolescents, in contrast to the wide variety of conflicting attitudes and choices that confront young people in the United States and in western European societies.

Although later investigators have claimed that there was a much higher level of conflict and stress among Samoan girls than Mead recognized (Freeman, 1983; Raum, 1940/1967), Mead's work has exerted enormous influence on modern ideas about adolescence. She forced psychologists to pay serious attention at last to the cultural and social factors that contribute to the characteristics of adolescence proposed by Hall, Freud, and other biologically oriented psychologists.

A second, environmental-learning approach to the study of adolescence is to identify naturally occurring socioenvironmental variations within cultural groups or to create environmental variations experimentally and to look for ways in which those variations might affect behavior. The first of these paths has been followed by Diana Baumrind (1989), whose work on the influence of parenting behaviors on young children's social, academic, and personality development was discussed in Chapter 11 (pp. 403–404).

When Baumrind returned to her sample of families after the children entered adolescence, she found that the children of "authoritative" parents (those who imparted clear standards, demanded high performance, and were responsive to their children) were as "outstandingly competent" as adolescents as they had been earlier. The children of "directive," or "authoritarian," families achieved less in school, engaged in more antisocial behavior, and precipitated more family conflict. By this account, parenting styles are important environmental factors in the regulation of behavior during adolescence.

In a persuasive experiment, Nancy Guerra and Ronald Slaby (1990), following the lead of Kenneth Dodge (see Chapter 14, p. 543), designed a 12-session program to teach inmates of a state juvenile correction facility how to recognize important social cues, seek additional information when problems arose, generate alternative solutions to problems, and make good choices among the alternatives they came up with. Even this relatively short training program produced marked reductions in aggression, impulsivity, and inflexibility in the adolescents' everyday interactions outside the training environment. A major virtue of such approaches is that they provide procedures for modifying behaviors that are unacceptable to society at large (McCord, 1990).

The Universal-Constructivist Perspective

Two of the most influential theorists of adolescence, Erik Erikson and Jean Piaget, sought to reconcile the biological and environmental-learning explanations of adolescence by showing how the distinctive qualities of this period of development arise from the interaction of biological and social factors found in all societies, irrespective of their cultural organization. Although Erikson and Piaget approached the problem in different ways, their theories of adolescent psychology are similar in many respects (Kegan, 1982; Kohlberg, 1984).

Jean Piaget

At the core of Piaget's theory of adolescence is the idea that as young people begin to take on adult roles they must simultaneously begin to plan ahead and to think more systematically about the world. As we will see in

Chapter 16, Barbel Inhelder and Jean Piaget (1958) believed that the systematic nature of adolescent thinking indicates an advance from the *concrete* operational to the *formal* operational level. They argued that this new mode of thinking changes all aspects of psychological functioning, including adolescents' understanding of themselves, their relations with peers, their ability to work, and their attitudes toward social ideals.

Erik Erikson

As we mentioned in Chapter 1, Erik Erikson's theory of development is difficult to classify. Although he is a student of Freud, Erikson is as concerned as Mead was to show that the development of human personality is not totally controlled by biological instincts; in this respect he is similar to the environmental-learning and cultural-context theorists. Yet he accepts Freud's emphasis on the role of biological factors in shaping the characteristics of adolescence, and he also maintains that adolescence is a universal, qualitatively distinct period of development.

Erikson believes that the task for young people about to enter adulthood is to incorporate their new sexual drives and the social demands placed upon them into a fully integrated and healthy personality. The result of this integration is what Erikson calls *identity,* which he defines as a "sense of personal sameness and historical continuity" (1968a:17). Our identity tells us how we fit in with the people around us and with our selves of the past and future. Identity is not a single trait or belief. Rather, it is a pattern of beliefs about the self that adolescents construct to reconcile the many ways in which they are like other people with the ways in which they differ from them.

The formation of identity becomes crucial during adolescence, in Erikson's view, because this is the time when the child's beliefs, abilities, and desires must be reconciled with adult norms; that is, individual identity and social identity must be made compatible. For this reason, Erikson characterizes the central crisis of adolescence as one of "identity versus identity confusion" (1968a:94). Identity confusion leads to social deviance and conflict.

Erikson's approach to adolescence is also notable in that he does not view adolescence as the end point of development; like cultural-context theorists, he views development as a lifelong process. (It may be helpful to refer back to Table 1.1, p. 38, for a summary of the developmental stages posited by leading theorists, and Box 10.2, p. 373, for a summary of Erikson's stages.)

Both Piaget and Erikson have inspired a wide range of research that uses their ideas as guides, as we shall see in Chapter 16.

The Cultural-Context Perspective

The theories of adolescence discussed so far have differed from one another in several respects: whether or not they consider development to end with adolescence, the emphasis they place on biological versus social factors as determinants of the psychological characteristics of the period, and the distinctiveness they attribute to the psychological characteristics of adolescence. The biological-maturation and Piagetian views are alike in their assumption that adolescence is a universal period of development that encompasses some part of the teenage years. Environmental-learning theorists also accept the universality of adolescence but deny its stagelike qualities. Psychologists who take the cultural-context perspective, in contrast, contend that adolescence is a developmental stage in some cultural circumstances but not in others (Whiting, Burbank, & Ratner, 1986). Its recognition as a distinct stage depends largely on whether or not the process of enculturation required to ensure reproduction of the culture extends beyond the age at which biological reproduction becomes possible.

Among traditional !Kung San of the Kalahari Desert, for example, there is no delay between puberty and marriage. During middle childhood, !Kung San children become sufficiently competent at carrying out hunting and gathering activities to sustain themselves. When they become ready for biological reproduction, they are also ready to engage in the tasks of cultural reproduction; they can sustain a family economically and can bring their children up to deal with the world as they know it (Lee & Devore, 1976; Shostak, 1981). When 13- or 14-year-olds in the United States have children, by contrast, both the parents and the children face great hardships because the parents cannot sustain either themselves or their children (Furstenberg, Brooks-Gunn, & Chase-Lansdale, 1989).

According to the cultural-context view, the kinds of activities that one must master to carry out the full process of human reproduction shape the psychological characteristics that one develops at the end of childhood. The intellectual skills of a teenage girl in Detroit, say, who spends her days studying mathematics, the natural sciences, and literature, are likely to differ from those of a girl in a nonliterate society who spends her days helping her mother-in-law with farming, cooking, and child-rearing chores. She is also likely to have a distinctly different sense of herself and different relationships with her peers, parents, and other kin.

As we have found for each of the earlier periods of development, data supporting one theoretical perspective do not necessarily discredit rival perspectives. In some cases, when the facts to be accounted for are similar and have been generated in similar ways, theoretical disputes can be settled by further observation. But often the aspects of development addressed in rival theories differ too much to permit direct comparisons or choices among them.

With these words of caution, we will now turn to the major phenomena of the adolescent period that the alternative theories attempt to explain. We will start with a description of puberty, the biological changes that initiate the capacity for sexual reproduction. We will then turn to the reorganization of social life that the potential for biological reproduction requires as an essential part of the transition to adulthood.

PUBERTY

During the second decade of life, the series of biological developments known as **puberty** transforms individuals from a state of physical immaturity to one in which they are biologically mature and capable of sexual reproduction. Puberty begins with a signal from the hypothalamus, located at the base of the brain, that activates the pituitary gland, a pea-sized organ appended to the hypothalamus. The pituitary then increases its production of growth hormones, which in turn stimulate the growth rate of all body tissue. The pituitary also releases hormones that trigger a great increase in the manufacture of the two gonadotrophic ("gonad-seeking") hormones. The gonads, or primary sex organs, are the ovaries in females and the testes in males. In females these hormones stimulate the ovaries to manufacture the hormones estrogen and progesterone, which trigger the numerous physical events, in-

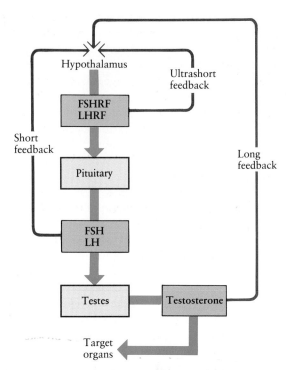

FIGURE 15.1   *Puberty in males is initiated by complex interactions among the hypothalamus, the pituitary gland, and the testes. When the hypothalamus releases gonadotropin-releasing factors (FSHRF, LHRF), it causes the pituitary to discharge the gonadotropins FSH and LH into the blood. These hormones stimulate the testes, promoting the production of testosterone, which in turn stimulates changes in other body organs and provides feedback to the hypothalamus. (From Katchadourian, 1977.)*

cluding the release of mature ova from the ovaries, that eventually allow for reproduction. In males, gonadotrophic hormones stimulate the testes and adrenal glands to manufacture the hormone testosterone, which brings about the manufacture of sperm (Katchadourian, 1977) (see Figure 15.1).

The Growth Spurt

One of the first visible signs of puberty is a spurt in the rate of physical growth. Boys and girls grow more quickly now than at any other time since they were babies. A boy may grow as much as 9 inches taller and a girl as much as 6 to 7 inches taller during the 2 to 3 years of the growth spurt. Although adolescents continue to grow throughout puberty, they reach 98 percent of their ultimate adult height by the end of the growth spurt (Tanner, 1978).

Some parts of the body spurt ahead of others during adolescence. As a rule, leg length reaches its peak first, followed 6 to 9 months later by trunk length. Shoulder and chest breadths are the last to reach their peak. As J. M. Tanner has quipped, "A boy stops growing out of his trousers (at least in length) a year before he stops growing out of his jackets" (1978:69).

Even the head, which has grown little since the age of 2, participates in the growth spurt. The skull bones thicken, lengthening and widening the head. The brain, which attains 90 percent of its adult weight by the age of 5, grows little during this period (Tanner, 1978).

Changes in physical size are accompanied by changes in overall shape. During puberty males and females acquire the distinctive physical features that characterize the two sexes. Girls develop breasts and their hips expand. Boys acquire wide shoulders and a muscular neck. Boys also lose fat during adolescence, which makes them appear more muscular and angular than girls. Girls continue to have a higher ratio of fat to muscle, so that they have a rounder, softer look.

Most boys not only *appear* to be stronger than girls after puberty, they *are* stronger (see Figure 15.2). Before puberty, boys and girls of similar size differ little in strength. But by the end of this period, boys can exercise for longer periods and can exert more force per ounce of muscle than girls of the same size. Boys develop relatively larger hearts and lungs, which give them higher blood pressure when their heart muscles contract, a lower resting heart rate, and a greater capacity for carrying oxygen in the blood, which neutralizes the chemicals that lead to fatigue during physical exercise (Katchadourian, 1977).

The physiological differences between males and females may help to explain why males have traditionally been the warriors, hunters, and heavy laborers throughout human history. They also help to explain why most superior male athletes can outperform superior female athletes. In some important respects, however, females exhibit greater physical prowess than males: they are, on the average, healthier, longer lived, and better able to tolerate long-term stress (Tavris & Offir, 1977).

Sexual Development

During puberty all the **primary sex organs,** those organs involved in reproduction, enlarge and become functionally mature. In males the testes begin to produce sperm cells and the prostate begins to produce semen, which come together in the vas deferens. Males

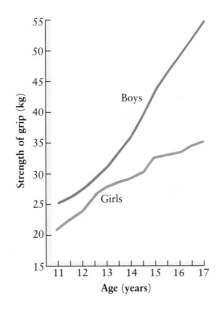
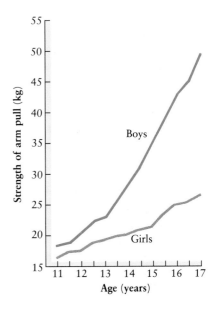

FIGURE 15.2 *After the onset of puberty the difference in strength between males and females increases steadily. (Adapted from Katchadourian, 1977.)*

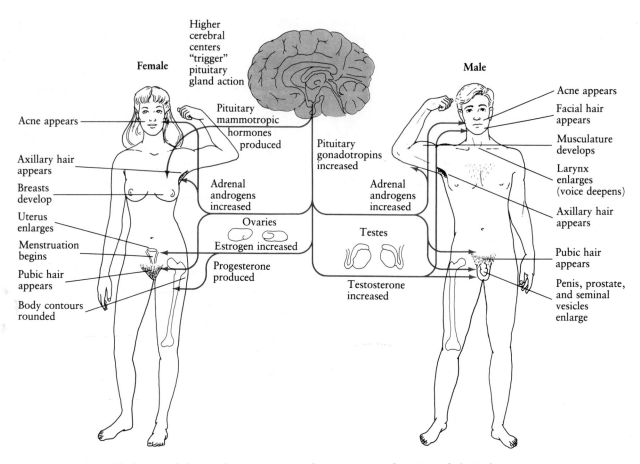

FIGURE 15.3   *The hormonal changes that accompany puberty cause a wide variety of physical changes in both females and males. (Adapted from CIBA Pharmaceutical Company, 1965.)*

gain the capacity to ejaculate the semen, which contains the sperm. In females the ovaries begin to release mature ova into the fallopian tubes. When conception does not take place, menstruation does. **Secondary sex characteristics,** the anatomical and physiological signs that outwardly distinguish males from females, appear as the primary sex organs are maturing (see Figure 15.3). The first signs that boys are entering puberty are an enlargement of the testes, a thickening and reddening of the skin of the scrotum, and the appearance of pubic hair. These changes usually occur about a year before boys begin their growth spurt. About the time the growth spurt begins, the penis begins to grow; it continues to do so for about 2 years. About a year after the penis begins to grow, boys become able to ejaculate semen. The first ejaculation often occurs spontaneously during sleep and is called a *nocturnal emission.*

At first the sperm in the semen are less numerous and less fertile than in adult males (Katchadourian, 1977).

Underarm and facial hair usually appear about 2 years after a boy's pubic hair begins to grow, but in some individuals underarm and facial hair may appear first. Most men do not develop a hairy chest until late adolescence or early adulthood. A boy's voice usually does not deepen until late in puberty, and then does so gradually as the larynx expands and the vocal cords lengthen. During this process, cracks in a boy's voice announce to the world the changes that are taking place in his body.

The first visible sign that a girl is beginning to mature sexually is often the appearance of a small rise around the nipples called the *breast bud.* Pubic hair usually appears a little later, just before the growth spurt begins, but sometimes it appears first. About the same time that girls' outward appearance is beginning to change, their ovaries enlarge and the cells that eventually will evolve into ova begin to ripen. The uterus begins to grow and the vaginal lining thickens.

Girls' secondary sex characteristics develop throughout puberty. The breasts continue to grow with the development of the mammary glands, which allow for lactation, and the accumulation of adipose (fatty) tissue, which gives them their adult shape.

Menarche—the first menstrual period—occurs relatively late in puberty, about 18 months after the growth spurt has reached its peak velocity. Early menstrual periods tend to be irregular, and they often occur without *ovulation*—the release of a mature egg. Ovulation typically begins about 12 to 18 months after menarche (Boxer, Tobin-Richards, & Petersen, 1983).

The Timing of Puberty

A glance around a seventh-grade classroom is sufficient to remind even the most casual observer of the wide variations in the age at which puberty begins. Some of the 12- and 13-year-old boys may look much as they did at the age of 9 or 10, whereas others may have the gangly look that often characterizes the growth spurt. Among the girls, who on the average

begin to mature sexually somewhat earlier, some may look like mature women with fully developed breasts and rounded hips, some may still have the stature and shape of little girls, and some may be somewhere in between. Figure 15.4 shows typical differences in the maturity of an adolescent girl and boy.

The timing of the changes of puberty depends, as do all events in development, on complex interactions between genetic and environmental factors. The importance of genetic factors is demonstrated by comparisons of identical and fraternal twins. The average difference in the age at which menarche occurs in identical twin sisters is only 2 months, whereas the average difference for fraternal twin sisters is 8 months (Marshall & Tanner, 1974).

Environmental factors, such as nutrition, stress, physical exercise, family size, and socioeconomic background, also influence the age of menarche. Girls in the higher socioeconomic classes have been found to go through menarche as much as 11 months earlier than girls in poor families (Marshall & Tanner, 1974). Researchers believe that better nutrition, especially higher protein intake, is primarily responsible for this difference, but since such factors as health care and stress are closely intertwined with socioeconomic class, the specific factors have not been completely isolated (Frisch, 1978; Tanner, 1978).

FIGURE 15.4 *Differences in the timing of puberty can result in startling differences in size between adolescents who are close in age.*

Historical changes in the age at which menarche is reached are even more striking than class differences. In industrialized countries and in some developing countries as well, the age when menstruation begins has been declining among all social groups (see Figure 15.5). In the 1840s the average age of menarche among European women was between 14 and 15 years, whereas today it is between 12 and 13 (Bullough, 1981). A similar trend is apparent in the United States, where menarche occurs about a year and a half earlier than it did in 1905.

The onset of puberty among males also seems to be occurring earlier, but the evidence for this change is less direct. Fifty years ago the average American male gained his maximum height at the age of 26; now this marker of the end of puberty occurs, on average, at the age of 18 (Marshall & Tanner, 1974).

Studies of the physical changes associated with puberty indicate that it ordinarily lasts about 4 years (Tanner, 1978). The duration of puberty, however, is as variable as the age at which it begins. One boy may go through all the events of puberty in the time it takes another's genitals to develop.

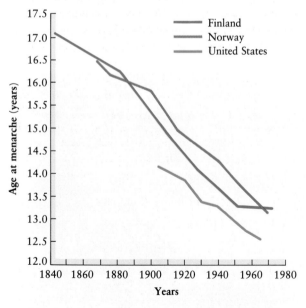

FIGURE 15.5   *The age of menarche has been declining in many countries during the past 150 years. (Adapted from Katchadourian, 1977.)*

The Developmental Impact of Puberty

The changes associated with puberty are of special significance both to the young people themselves and to the community of which they are a part, but the way these changes are perceived and portrayed varies with cultural circumstances and personal characteristics.

Rites of passage

In many societies the transition into adolescence is recognized by ritual. These ceremonies are often public events that express the contributions to society the young person is expected to make in his or her adult life (Schlegel & Barry, 1991). When Margaret Mead visited the Arapesh of New Guinea several decades ago, a girl's first menstruation was accompanied by ceremonial rites that symbolized her emergence as a woman ready to become a productive member of the community. Here Mead describes the preparations for the ceremony, which takes place in the girl's husband's home:

> Her woven arm and leg bands, her earrings, her old lime gourd and lime spatula are taken from her. Her woven belt is taken off. If these are fairly new they are given away; if they are old they are cut off and destroyed. There is no feeling that they themselves are contaminated, but only the desire to cut the girl's connection with her past.
>
> The girl is attended by older women who are her own relatives or relatives of her husband. They rub her all over with stinging nettles. They tell her to roll one of the large nettle-leaves into a tube and thrust it into her vulva: this will ensure her breasts growing large and strong. The girl eats no food, nor does she drink water. On the third day, she comes out of the hut and stands against a tree while her mother's brother makes the decorative cuts on her shoulders and buttocks. . . . Each day the women rub the girl with nettles. It is well if she fasts for five or six days, but the women watch her anxiously, and if she becomes too weak they put an end to it. Fasting will make her strong, but too much of it might make her die, and the emergence ceremony is hastened. (Mead, 1935:92–93)

Among the Mano in Liberia and in several other West African tribes, boys undergo a ceremonial

Every society has evolved customs that mark the end of childhood and the transition to adult status. Here an Apache girl is inducted into her new status role.

"death" at puberty and are then spirited away by older men to an isolated grove deep in the forest. There they are taught the secret lore of the men, as well as farming and other skills they will need to earn a living. When they emerge from "behind the fence," in some cases several years later, they have a new name and a new identity (Harley, 1941).

Psychological responses to pubertal events

Modern societies have nothing that corresponds to a full initiation ceremony marking the passage out of childhood. The events of puberty are rarely talked about publicly by the individuals who are experiencing them or by their community. Until fairly recently, when people recalled menarche or their first ejaculations it was often in negative or comic terms. The onset of menstruation is typically traumatic in such accounts (Brooks-Gun & Reiter, 1990). Yet menarche is a sign that one is becoming an adult female. This paradox has led modern researchers to wonder how young people going through puberty view the changes their bodies are undergoing, and how they adapt to them. By and large, this research has focused on white middle-class girls and their responses to their first menstrual period.

When girls who had recently started to menstruate were asked how they felt about their first menstruation, about 20 percent reported feeling positive, about 20 percent said they felt negative, and another 20 percent were indefinite. The remaining 40 percent reported being both "excited and pleased" and "scared and upset," but for the most part their feelings were not very intense (Ruble & Brooks-Gunn, 1982). Those who menstruate earlier than their peers and who are unprepared for menstruation report more negative experiences at menarche than other girls.

In a series of studies (summarized in Brooks-Gunn & Reiter, 1990) Jeanne Brooks-Gunn and her colleagues have found that girls' attitudes and beliefs about menstruation are only in part a result of their direct experience of menstruation. A girl's physical symptoms during menstruation are often correlated with the expectations she had before menarche (Brooks-Gunn, 1987). Girls who reported unpleasant symptoms were more likely to have been unprepared for menarche, to have matured early, and to have been told about menstruation by someone they perceived negatively.

Very little is known about the meaning of pubertal changes to boys. Two-thirds of the mid-adolescent boys interviewed in one study reported being a little frightened by their first ejaculations, but on the whole, positive responses were stronger than negative ones (Gaddis & Brooks-Gunn, 1985).

Both boys and girls are initially secretive about the onset of nocturnal emissions and menarche. Girls report telling far fewer friends that they have begun menstruating than they thought they would ahead of time. About one-fourth of all girls questioned report telling only their mothers. This reticence does not last, however. By the time they have been menstruating for 6 months, most have talked to their friends about it (Brooks-Gunn et al., 1986). Boys are far more likely to continue to be reticent about the onset of puberty and thus receive far less social support from their parents and peers than girls do.

Consequences of Early and Late Maturation

Several studies have sought to determine whether relatively early or late sexual maturation influences young people's peer relations, personality, and social adjustment. This research has produced a mixed picture (Brooks-Gunn & Petersen, 1983; Lerner & Foch, 1987; Simmons & Blyth, 1987).

One of the earliest of these studies, conducted by Mary Cover Jones and Nancy Bayley (1950), reported different consequences for early- and late-maturing boys in the United States. Using data from an ongoing longitudinal study of growth and development, these researchers identified 16 adolescent boys who were maturing late and 16 who were maturing early, according to X-ray analyses of their bone growth. They then asked adults and peers who knew the boys to rate them on a variety of social and personality scales to see if the boys' state of physical maturation affected other people's perceptions of them.

Both adults and peers rated the early-maturing boys as more psychologically and socially mature. These boys did not appear to need to strive for status, and they were the group from which school leaders emerged. The boys who were slower to mature physically were rated as less mature both psychologically and socially. Both adults and peers thought that they often sought attention to compensate for their late development and that some of them tended to withdraw from social interaction. Other studies have confirmed some parts of this picture. In general, early-maturing boys seem to have a more favorable attitude toward their bodies, largely because their greater size and strength make them more capable athletes, and athletic prowess in turn brings them social recognition (Brooks-Gunn & Petersen, 1983; Simmons & Blyth, 1987).

Apparently, however, not all the effects of early maturation are positive. On the basis of data from a longitudinal study that used a personality test to measure maturity instead of ratings by other people, Harvey Peskin (1967) found that early-maturing boys become significantly more somber, temporarily more anxious, less exploratory, less intellectually curious, and less active after the onset of puberty than do late-maturing boys. He argued that early-maturing boys are actually handicapped by the early end to childhood because they are less prepared for the hormonal and social changes taking place. Thus the experience of puberty is more intense and less manageable than it is for those who mature more slowly. In Peskin's view, the social advantages of maturing early also exact a price: later these boys tend to cling too rigidly to the patterns that brought them their early success.

Peskin's conclusions are supported by more recent research that associates early sexual maturation with lower self-control and less emotional stability, as measured by psychological tests (Sussman et al., 1985). Adolescent boys who reach puberty at a relatively early age are also more likely to smoke, drink, use drugs, and get in trouble with the law (Duncan et al., 1985).

The picture for girls is also mixed, but the overall effect of early maturation appears to be more negative (Brooks-Gunn & Petersen, 1983; Simmons & Blyth, 1987; Stattin & Magnusson, 1990). In some cases, early maturation brings greater social prestige based on sexual attractiveness. Girls who had reached puberty by the sixth or seventh grade considered themselves more popular with boys and more likely to be dating than girls who had not yet reached puberty (Simmons et al., 1987). A longitudinal Swedish study of adolescent girls found that early-maturing girls were also more likely to have a stable boyfriend and sexual experience by mid-adolescence and, perhaps as a consequence, were also more likely to have unwanted pregnancies than their later-maturing peers (Stattin & Magnusson, 1990).

Although the attention of older boys, drawn by their fuller figures, can be gratifying for early-maturing girls, there is a down side to their precocious biological development. They are larger than other children their age, especially boys, who generally enter puberty later. This may be one reason why early-maturing girls are more likely than their peers to say that they are dissatisfied with their height and weight (Simmons & Blyth, 1987; Stattin & Magnusson, 1990). Early-maturing children of both sexes tend to weigh more and to be slightly shorter than late-maturing children when they finish puberty, and this difference persists throughout life (Malina, 1975). This is an advantage for early-maturing boys, because robust males are considered attractive, but it is a disadvantage for early-maturing girls, who are less likely to fit Western industrialized society's current preference for a thin, long-legged, prepubertal body shape in women.

Recent research in the United States has found that early-maturing girls tend to have somewhat lower emotional stability and self-control, perhaps as a consequence of the increased uncertainties and social pressures they experience (Petersen & Crockett, 1985). In Sweden it was found that they are also more likely to get into trouble with adults because of a decline in their academic performance, truancy, drug and alcohol use, shoplifting, and running away (Stattin & Magnusson, 1990).

A relatively late passage through puberty may be a negative experience for girls at first, but the overall consequences are generally positive. Late-maturing sixth-grade girls in the United States report dissatisfaction with their appearance and their lack of popularity, but in a few years they may actually be more satisfied with their appearance and more popular than their early-maturing peers (Simmons & Blyth, 1987).

Unfortunately, evidence concerning the impact of the timing of puberty on *later* life is both skimpy and inconclusive. Mary Cover Jones (1965), who followed groups of early-maturing and late-maturing boys into their early thirties, concluded that early maturation has positive psychological benefits that continue into manhood. She found the early maturers to be poised, cooperative, and responsible; they held good positions at work and were leaders in their social organizations. The late developers were more likely to be impulsive, touchy, and nonconforming; they were not so successful, and some felt rejected and inferior. When John Clausen (1975) tested the same men at the age of 38, however, he could find only two differences between the groups: the early maturers took more pride in being objective and in being seen as conventional than those who matured late did. More recently Hakan Stattin and David Magnusson (1990) found that the early-maturing Swedish girls they studied were likely to have children earlier and to complete fewer years of school than other girls their age.

THE REORGANIZATION OF SOCIAL LIFE

The marked changes in young people's biological capacities are associated with equally marked changes in the way they interact with their families and their peers.

The Effects of Puberty on Family Relations

Studies conducted in the United States (summarized in Hill, 1988) indicate that the onset of puberty contributes to a reorganization in family relationships for both boys and girls. By and large, pubertal maturation is associated with increased emotional distance between young people and their parents and increased autonomy. Within this overall trend, however, the pattern of change differs somewhat for boys and girls.

For the first few months after a girl's menarche, both her parents are likely to increase their attempts to control her, and disagreements between the girl and her mother may increase. After a year or so has passed, the parents' attempts at control and the disagreements diminish markedly. The particular age when menarche begins does not seem to make a great deal of difference; it is pubertal status, not age, that seems to count. A similar pattern of mother-child dynamics is found among boys, but in their case age does make a difference: early maturation is especially likely to increase conflict with their mothers.

A striking finding is that adolescents' relations with their mothers change more noticeably than their relations with their fathers. Perhaps mothers have lower status than fathers in their children's eyes, so adolescents assert their independence in interactions with their mothers in the belief that their mothers are less likely to challenge them. Or perhaps they have formed closer emotional relationships with their mothers and so the process of achieving autonomy with respect to their mothers is psychologically more difficult.

A New Relationship with Peers

The social patterns established during middle childhood undergo marked reorganization during adolescence. Now young people are no longer satisfied to socialize almost exclusively with people of their own sex, and they begin to gather in groups that are increasingly heterosexual. Same-sex friendships change too, reaching new heights of complexity and intensity.

Friendship

Not counting classroom time, teenagers in the United States spend an average of 22 hours a week with their peers. They report spending more time with their friends than they do with their families or by themselves, and the amount of time they spend this way increases over the course of adolescence (Csikszentmihalyi & Larson, 1984). It should come as no surprise, then, that teenagers typically say they enjoy the time they spend with their friends more than anything else they do (Youniss & Smollar, 1985). They feel their friends understand them and allow them to be themselves.

Because adolescents in the United States are more mobile than younger children and attend larger schools, they have more opportunities to meet peers of other social classes and ethnic backgrounds. Nevertheless, their close friends tend to be even more similar to them than they were in elementary school (Epstein, 1989).

Several large-scale studies conducted in the United States reveal a changing basis of friendships as children enter adolescence (Bigelow & La Gaipa, 1975; Douvan & Adelson, 1966; Selman, 1980; Youniss, 1980). Table 15.1 summarizes these changing expectations. Between the ages of 6 and 12 (grades 1 to 4), participation in common activities, including organized play, is a major reason given for considering a peer a friend. This criterion does not disappear in adolescence but is supplemented by other factors. In grade 7 (12 to 13 years of age), for example, common interests, similarity of attitudes and values, loyalty, and intimacy become important to friendship.

Teenagers choose friends who share their interests, values, beliefs, and attitudes because such friends are more likely to be supportive and understanding (Youniss & Smollar, 1985). High school friends tend to have similar feelings about drug use, drinking, and delinquency (McCord, 1990). They also tend to be similar in their behavior, their views of school, their academic achievement, their dating, and other leisure-time activities.

It is not difficult to understand why intimacy and loyalty become major criteria of friendships in adolescence, especially among girls. It is in the context of intimate, self-disclosing conversations with close friends that teenagers define themselves and explore their identities. According to Jeffrey Parker and John Gottman (1989), who observed and recorded teenage conversations, there is a difference between the self-disclosures of friends in middle childhood and those during adolescence.

> At younger ages, a self-disclosure prompts a statement of solidarity ("Oh, I know! Me too!"), but little else. In adolescence, self-disclosures occasion psychological attributions and lengthy discussions about the nature of the problem and possible avenues to its resolution. (1989:120–121)

In the later stages of group development during adolescence, relationships become increasingly heterosexual.

TABLE 15.1

Incidence of Various Types of Friendship, by Grade Level (Percent)

Type	Grade Level*							
	1	2	3	4	5	6	7	8
Help (friend as giver)	5	12†	14	7	14	25	33	35
Common activities	3	7	32	52	24	40	60	60
Propinquity	7	5	9	12	12	20	38	32
Stimulation value	2	3	12	23	30	51	52	61
Organized play	2	0	15	26	9	10	17	20
Demographic similarity	0	3	7	35	15	15	10	23
Evaluation	2	5	13	13	17	33	21	30
Acceptance	3	0	5	9	9	18	18	38
Admiration	0	0	5	23	17	24	32	41
Incremental prior interaction	2	7	4	10	10	17	32	34
Loyalty and commitment	0	0	2	5	10	20	40	34
Genuineness	0	3	0	2	5	12	10	32
Help (friend as receiver)	2	5	3	5	2	12	13	25
Intimacy potential	0	0	0	0	0	0	8	20
Common interests	0	0	5	7	0	5	30	18
Similarity of attitudes and values	0	0	0	0	2	3	10	8

* At each grade level, the number of subjects (*n*) = 60.

† An underlined score indicates the grade level at which the incidence of the type of friendship first becomes significant.

Source: Bigelow & La Gaipa, 1975.

As evidence, Parker and Gottman offer the following excerpt from a conversation between two teenagers:

> **A:** You missed two weeks of school.
> **B:** I know. That's what Dad said. He said, "I guess London didn't help your grades," and I said . . .
> **A:** No, and then you came back and were depressed and that didn't help school too much either. I mean, not wanting to be there doesn't help things at all.
> **B:** I've got to get my grades up.
> **A:** You're only allowed one B this quarter.
> **B:** Yep.
> **A:** You work your tail off in English.
> **B:** Yeah, I'll get an A in English now.
> **A:** OK. [That bad grade] was your fault.
> **B:** [giggle]
> **A:** Because you were a stubborn little twit. [jokingly] (Parker & Gottman, 1989:121)

Because of the biological changes of puberty and growing involvement with the opposite sex, one of the most important aspects of the self that teenagers explore in their intimate conversations with their friends is their sexuality and how they feel about it:

> **A:** [joking] I think you should take Randy to court for statutory rape.
> **B:** I don't. I'm to the point of wondering what "that kind of girl" is. . . . I don't know about the whole scene.
> **A:** The thing is . . .
> **B:** It depends on the reasoning. And how long you've been going out with somebody.
> **A:** Yeah. I'm satisfied with my morals. (Parker & Gottman, 1989:119)

Obviously no one would want to have such a conversation with a friend who was not loyal or who might gossip. Nor would one want to share such confidences with a person who was not understanding and supportive, even of feelings and beliefs she does not share.

During the late teen years, girls' friendships seem to lose the feverish, jealous qualities that characterize them during the middle phase of adolescence. Elizabeth Douvan and Joseph Adelson, two leading researchers on adolescence, suggest that "needing friendship less, they are less haunted by fears of being abandoned and betrayed" (1966:192). By the time they are in their late teens, most girls show an increased capacity to tolerate friends who differ from them. This trend is consistent with the sequence of Selman's developmental stages of friendship (see Chapter 14, p. 541). According to Selman's (1981) evidence, there is a shift during adolescence from stage 3 (in which friendships are seen as a means of developing mutual intimacy and support) to stage 4 (which is characterized by a new acceptance of a friend's need to establish relations with other people).

The friendships of boys between the ages of 14 and 16 years are likely to be less close than those of girls, according to Douvan and Adelson (1966). These researchers suggest that this difference arises because boys are more concerned with their relations to authority than girls are. To assert and maintain their independence from control by parents and other adults, boys need the alliance of a *group* of friends. Duane Buhrmester and Wyndol Furman (1987) suggest that these sex differences in friendship are a matter more of style than of substance. They have found that boys form friendships "in which sensitivity to needs and validation of worth are achieved through actions and deeds, rather than through interpersonal disclosure of personal thoughts and feelings" (pp. 111–112). Their view is supported by findings that boys are generally less articulate than girls about the nature and meaning of friendship per se and tend to focus their descriptions of friendship on the qualities that are important in doing things together. Like girls of 11 to 13, the 14-to-16-year-old boys studied by Douvan and Adelson (1966) said that they wanted their friends to be amiable, cooperative, and able to control their impulses and to share a common interest with them. Like girls in their late teens, they said they expected their friends to help them in times of trouble. What differed between the sexes was the kind of trouble they expected and therefore the kind of friendly support they sought. Girls wanted their friends to be people they could confide in about their relations with

Calling a boy is likely to be a group project at first.

boys, whereas boys wanted their friends to support them when they got into trouble with authority.

Adolescent friendships for both boys and girls play a developmental role similar in certain respects to the role of attachment in infancy. During infancy babies engage in "social referencing"—continually looking to their mothers to see how they evaluate what is going on—and they use their mothers as a "secure base" to which they can retreat when they feel threatened as they explore their environment (see Chapters 5 and 6). During adolescence, friends help each other to confront and make sense of uncertain and often anxiety-provoking situations. The first time a boy calls up a girl for a date, his best friend may well be standing at his elbow. And no sooner has the girl hung up than she is likely to call her best friend. The two pairs of friends will decide together if the call was a success or a failure and lay plans for the next move. For both the infant and the adolescent, successful interaction with the world "out there" modifies the attachment bond; eventually the baby will leave the mother and the adolescent will begin to depend less on the best friend.

Popularity

In the world of the American high school, some friends are more desirable than others because they have more status. James S. Coleman (1962) conducted a classic study of the factors that determine individual status and membership in high-prestige groups among U.S. high school students. He based his conclusions on an analysis of questionnaires distributed to thousands of students at ten high schools in small towns, small cities, large cities, and suburbs.

In every school he studied, Coleman found that students could identify a "leading crowd" against which they evaluated themselves. The responses he obtained to the question "What does it take to get into the leading crowd in this school?" reveal some of the values of American adolescent society a generation ago and the characteristics that were considered important to be a success within it:

GIRLS SAID

- Money, clothes, flashy appearance, date older boys, fairly good grades.
- Be a sex fiend, dress real sharp, have own car and money, smoke and drink, go steady with a popular boy.
- Have pleasant personality, good manners, dress nicely, be clean, don't swear, be loads of fun.
- Hang out at ____'s, don't be too smart, flirt with boys, be cooperative on dates. (Coleman, 1962:37)

BOYS SAID

- Money, cars, the right connections, and a good personality.
- Be a good athlete, have a good personality, be in

everything you can, don't drink or smoke, don't go with bad girls.
- Prove you rebel [against] the police officers, dress sharply, go out with sharp freshman girls, ignore senior girls.
- Good in athletics, "wheel" type, not too intelligent. (Adapted from Coleman, 1962:40–41)

When Coleman tabulated the responses to his questionnaires, he found that both boys and girls said a good personality was the most important characteristic of people in the leading group. For boys, the next most important characteristics were having a good reputation, being a good athlete, being good-looking, wearing good clothes, and getting good grades. For girls, the most important characteristics after a good personality were good looks, good clothing, and a good reputation.

The leading crowd seemed to have great influence in adolescents' lives. When Coleman asked for responses to the statement "If I could trade, I would be someone different from myself," he found that one out of five boys and girls expressed a desire to change themselves so that they would be accepted by the leading crowd. The importance of membership in the leading crowd was also reflected in the answers to Coleman's questions about popularity (see Figure 15.6).

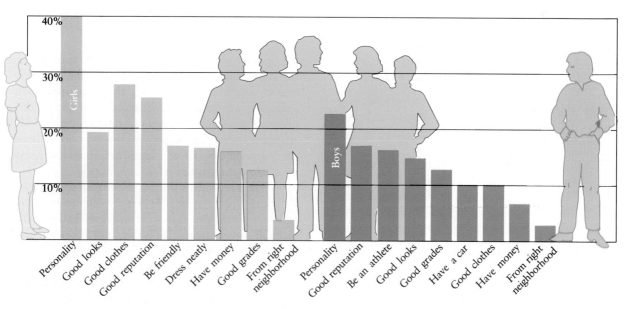

FIGURE 15.6   *The average ranks given by boys and girls to major criteria of popularity. (Adapted from Coleman, 1962.)*

Subsequent research has confirmed Coleman's general point that there is a leading crowd to whom others are oriented, but the ranking of characteristics that make someone popular has varied according to such factors as grade level, ethnicity, and socioeconomic status (Butcher, 1986; Sebald, 1981; Williams & White, 1983).

In another classic study, carried out in the late 1940s and followed up in the 1970s, August Hollingshead (1975) added a socioeconomic dimension to the picture of adolescent social relations. Hollingshead found that adolescents at every grade level tended to form friendships and cliques with others of the same socioeconomic background. Only rarely did adolescents date or have friends whose socioeconomic backgrounds diverged widely from their own, and when they did, they were usually censured by their parents and other adults in the community. When a lower-class girl dated a boy of the highest class, for example, not only did his parents object but the townspeople predicted trouble. They made such remarks as "She's flying too high"; "After high school she is going to take a fall"; and "Ten years from now she will be taking in laundry like her sister on Beacon Street" (p. 158).

In some groups academic achievement leads to a *decrease* in popularity (Ishiyama & Chabassol, 1985). In some working-class African American communities, for example, academically able young people mask their abilities to avoid being labeled a "brain" and being ostracized (Fordham & Ogbu, 1986).

The transition to sexual relationships

Often it is the popular boys and girls, those who are members of the leading crowd in high school, who lead their peers in making the transition from participation in same-sex peer groups to participation in heterosexual groups. Dexter Dunphy (1963), an Australian sociologist, traced the way adolescent peer groups helped to organize the development of heterosexual relationships among Australian adolescents in the late 1950s. Dunphy observed and interviewed 303 young people between the ages of 13 and 21 over a 2-year period in largely middle-class areas of Sydney. He supplemented his notes and records with data from questionnaires and diaries kept by his subjects.

CLIQUES AND CROWDS. Dunphy distinguished between two kinds of adolescent peer groups, which he labeled "cliques" and "crowds." Cliques are small groups whose six to seven members "hang around" together. Dunphy noted that cliques are about the size of a two-child family with the grandparents present. "Their similarity in size to a family," Dunphy wrote, "facilitates the transference of the individual's allegiance to them and allows them to provide an alternative center of security" (p. 233).

Cliques differ from families in an important respect: they are voluntary groups that adolescents are free to leave, whereas membership in a family is not normally a matter of choice for them. The element of choice in peer-group membership reflects the increased control adolescents have in choosing the settings in which they find themselves, the people they associate with, and the things they do.

Cliques exist as a part of a larger social unit, the crowd. Whereas cliques are organized on the basis of interactions among their members, crowds are typically organized around important attitudes or activities that give them a separate identity in the eyes of adolescents (Brown, 1990). Crowd labels—"jocks," "brains," "nerds," "druggies"—indicate the ways in which crowds are identified.

The crowds Dunphy studied ranged in size from 15 to 30 members, with an average of about 20. Like cliques, crowds are, by and large, voluntary groups. Much of what goes on in the crowd, again as in cliques, is under the control of its members. But unlike the cliques, which at least initially were composed of young people of the same sex, the crowds were often heterosexual groups in which the fact of heterosexuality was the issue.

As the adolescents Dunphy studied grew older, the relationship between their participation in cliques and crowds changed in a way that supported their transition to heterosexual intimacy. Dunphy diagrammed the stages of this transition as in Figure 15.7. At stage 1 there are as yet no crowds, only isolated same-sex cliques. These cliques are, in effect, carryovers from the days of middle childhood.

Stage 2 represents the first movement toward heterosexual peer relations. At first the cliques come together to form crowds at such places as skating rinks, football games, swimming pools, and ice cream parlors, where boys and girls get together under conditions in which anonymity precludes the danger of intimacy, which they fear.

In stage 3 the members of the crowd with the highest status initiate heterosexual contacts across

Early adolescence

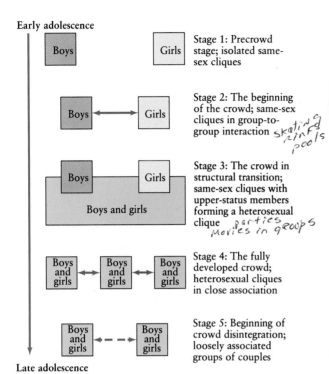

Stage 1: Precrowd stage; isolated same-sex cliques

Stage 2: The beginning of the crowd; same-sex cliques in group-to-group interaction *skating rinks pools*

Stage 3: The crowd in structural transition; same-sex cliques with upper-status members forming a heterosexual clique *parties Movies in groups*

Stage 4: The fully developed crowd; heterosexual cliques in close association

Stage 5: Beginning of crowd disintegration; loosely associated groups of couples

Late adolescence

FIGURE 15.7 *The stages of group development during adolescence. At the start of this period, peer-group interactions are largely segregated by sex; at the end, there is far more heterosexual peer-group interaction. (Adapted from Dunphy, 1963.)*

cliques while still maintaining membership in their same-sex cliques. At this stage boys and girls start going to parties and the movies together in groups, but they continue to spend a great deal of time with same-sex peers.

During stages 2 and 3, social events that require more intimate interaction, such as dances and parties, become prominent. Here again the size of the crowd is important. There is safety in numbers! The presence of others makes it less likely that anyone will step over the bounds of propriety.

Eventually cross-clique pairing begins to transform the peer-group structures. In stage 4, same-sex cliques are transformed into heterosexual cliques, whose members are often paired. These arrangements allow a greater degree of intimacy, should the pair want it, but also provide a group of co-conspirators with whom each member can talk about what is going on.

Stage 5 sees the slow disintegration of the crowd and the formation of loosely associated groups of couples who are going steady or are engaged to be married. It coincides with the transition to marriage and the reorganization of social life that is associated with adulthood and parenting.

The crowds Dunphy observed were themselves connected in a loose hierarchy of prestige that depended on the relative ages of their members. The most prestigious crowds were those with the oldest members. The crowds emerged as part of a loosely structured cultural system in which the oldest, most mature, and most knowledgeable members of the social group modeled the next developmental steps for the members of the crowd below them in the status/age hierarchy.

PEER-GROUP LEADERS. The leaders of cliques and crowds not only were the most popular and most emulated group members but also were likely to be the most sexually active. According to Dunphy, the leaders of adolescent groups facilitated the transition of other members to heterosexual relations because they simultaneously participated in both the clique and the crowd. Their dual membership gave them wider and more frequent contact with those outside the clique than their followers had. Clique leaders were better informed than their followers about what was going on in the generally older and more sexually active crowd. Other members of the cliques came to rely on them for information about people in other cliques and crowds and their activities. Taken together, the intimate friendship, the clique, and the crowd constituted a sequence of social mechanisms that orchestrated the adolescents' transition from same-sex to heterosexual pairings. They provided an interlocking set of social relations that sequentially linked the individual to the social (friendship), the friends to the same-sex friendship group (clique), the same-sex group to the heterosexual group (crowd), and finally the individual back to his or her intimate friend, this time a person of the opposite sex. In its institutionalized form this relationship is called first "going steady" and eventually "marriage."

The young people whom Dunphy identified as leaders by virtue of their positions in these interlocking social relationships literally led their followers by being the first of their set to be admitted to the crowd of the next higher age bracket. They were the ones

whose behavior was expected to be heterosexual earlier than that of their peers.

The social arrangements that are a part of the transition from small same-sex friendship groups to large heterosexual groups and eventually back to exclusive relationships are strikingly analogous to the zone of proximal development that was introduced in Chapter 5 (p. 201) as a useful characterization of the way adults support young children's cognitive development. In the case of adolescents' social development, this zone is created by the hierarchy of group arrangements and the group leaders who have, so to speak, one foot in the future. It allows young people to learn something about what the future has in store for them before they are responsible for behaving in a more advanced way themselves.

As plausible as this description of adolescent social mechanisms may be, it should be kept in mind that the pattern described by Dunphy may well vary from one society or one historical era to another because of variations in such factors as geographic mobility, education, social institutions, and the timing of marriage. Dunphy's research was carried out more than 30 years ago, and the social ecology of the young people he studied was certainly unique in some respects to their particular society. Nevertheless, his findings continue to enjoy wide acceptance among researchers who study adolescence (Brown, 1990).

Sexual Activity

It should be clear by now that a great deal of the social behavior associated with sex roles must be learned from observation and practice. Less obvious, perhaps, is the fact that the physical act of uniting with another person sexually also requires a good deal of learning. Moreover, because boys and girls have different biological roles and social histories, the processes by which they learn to engage in sexual intercourse—often referred to as "coitus," from a Latin word meaning "to come together"—differ in important respects.

One line of evidence about the role of social experience in sexual intercourse comes from Harry Harlow's studies of monkeys raised in isolation. As we saw in Chapter 7 (p. 262), monkeys deprived of the opportunity to interact with their mothers and peers during the first 6 months of life were incapable of engaging in intercourse (Harlow & Novak, 1973).

A second line of evidence for the role of social learning in sexual activity comes from the wide range of behaviors that lead up to and accompany sexual intercourse. Social learning appears to play some role even in the choice of the sex of the partner. In heterosexual activity, the changing incidence of petting—erotic caressing that does not include the union of male and female genitals—also reveals the role of social experience in sexual behavior. According to Dr.

Alfred Kinsey and his associates, whose famous surveys of sexual behavior were published at mid-century (Kinsey, Pomeroy, & Martin, 1948; Kinsey et al., 1953), the practice of petting increased substantially among Americans born after 1900, and it has continued to increase in the decades since the Kinsey surveys (Scanzoni & Scanzoni, 1976).

Sex as scripted activity

Petting is often viewed as part of a larger sequence of actions that make up sexual behavior in Western culture. John Gagnon and William Simon (1973) use the concept of scripts to describe this sequence, which in recent years proceeds from lip kissing to tongue kissing to touching breasts through clothing to touching breasts under the clothing to touching the genitals through clothing to touching genitals, and finally to genital contact. Oral sex, which has become fairly common, may or may not precede coitus (Katchadourian, 1990). This sequence is more common among white American adolescents than among African American teenagers, who are likely to move toward intercourse earlier and with fewer intervening steps (Smith & Udry, 1985).

In Chapter 9 we saw that the concept of scripts is important for understanding the mental development of preschool children. Scripts allow very small children, who clearly do not understand fully what is expected of them, to participate with adults in such activities as eating in a restaurant, attending a birthday party, and drawing a picture. A similar use of scripts is evident among adolescent boys and girls who are engaging in sexual activity for the first time. Their peer-group experiences, their observations of adults, and their general cultural knowledge provide them with a rough idea of the scripts they are supposed to follow and the roles they are supposed to play. In the United States, for example, the male is traditionally active and controls the interaction while the female responds. (Box 15.2 provides a glimpse of a very different way of organizing the transition to heterosexual behavior.)

A script also gives sexual meaning to individual acts that may have no such meaning in other contexts. Hand-holding, kissing, and unzipping one's pants are not inherently sexual acts; each occurs often in nonsexual contexts. It is only within the context of the larger script of dating or of coitus that these acts take on sexual meanings and give rise to sexual excitement.

Sexual expectations

Evidence from a wide variety of sources indicates that males and females come to sexual activity with different expectations as a result of their different histories (Gagnon & Simon, 1973; Sorenson, 1973). To begin with, biological differences between the two sexes set the stage for males and females to have divergent experiences with the erotic potential of their bodies.

Sexual arousal is more obvious in males than in females because of its expression in clearly visible penile erection. Among newborns erections are reflexive. Just when and how this reflexive response becomes sexual is still a mystery (Katchadourian & Lunde, 1975). Erections continue to occur during childhood, so it is easy for a boy to discover that stimulating his penis gives him pleasure. At puberty the frequency of erections and the sensitivity of the genitals increase dramatically. Within 2 years after puberty, most males experience orgasm, usually through masturbation (Gagnon & Simon, 1973). According to Kinsey and his co-workers (1948), 82 percent of the men they surveyed reported they had masturbated to orgasm by the age of 15 years. Sexual arousal is more ambiguous in females. The clitoris, the center of female sexual pleasure, is small and hidden within the vulva, so girls are less likely to discover its erotic possibilities. In fact, Kinsey and his colleagues (1953) found that only 20 percent of the women they surveyed reported having masturbated to orgasm by the time they were 15.

According to Gagnon and Simon (1973), differences in the masturbatory behavior of boys and girls have a number of consequences for later sexual behavior. First, masturbating to orgasm reinforces males' commitment to sexual behavior early in adolescence. Second, experience with masturbation tends to focus the male's feelings of sexual desire on the penis, whereas most females, lacking such experiences, do not localize their erotic responses in their genitals until much later, and then primarily as a result of sexual contacts with males.

Differences in the socialization of males and females give rise to differences in the fantasies that accompany masturbation. Male gender training in U.S. culture emphasizes aggressive, competitive, and achievement-oriented behaviors. Correspondingly, males report having masturbatory fantasies that involve sexual aggression, unattainable excesses (such as a harem at one's command), and sexual dominance. Their fantasies are rich in specific sexual behaviors and

The Traditional Kikuyu Script for Adolescent Sex

Among the Kikuyu people of central Kenya at the turn of the century, boys and girls underwent an initiation ceremony, or rite of passage, just before the start of puberty, after which the boys were considered to be junior warriors and the girls were considered to be maidens (Worthman & Whiting, 1987). For the next several years, approved sexual relations between the young men and women followed a script that differed in many ways from those typically followed by teenagers in the United States.

In addition to helping their mothers with household chores and gardening, Kikuyu maidens were expected to strengthen the social cohesion of the group by entertaining the bachelor friends of their older brothers. The entertainment included not only dancing and feasting but a kind of lovemaking called *ngweko*. Jomo Kenyatta (1938), the first president of Kenya after it won its independence in 1962, described *ngweko* in his autobiography:

> The girls visit their boy-friends at a special hut, *thingira*, used as a rendezvous by the young men and women. . . .
>
> Girls may visit the *thingira* at any time, day or night. After eating, while engaged in conversation with the boys, one of the boys turns the talk dramatically to the subject of *ngweko*. If there are more boys than girls, the girls are asked to select whom they want as their companion. The selection is done in the most liberal way. . . . In such a case it is not necessary for girls to select

their most intimate friends, as this would be considered selfish and unsociable. . . .

> After the partners have been arranged, one of the boys gets up, saying "*ndathie kwenogora*" (I am going to stretch myself). His girl partner follows him to the bed. The boy removes all his clothing. The girl removes her upper garment . . . and retains her skirt, *motheru*, and her soft leather apron, *mwengo*, which she pulls back between her legs and tucks in together with her leather skirt, *motheru*. The two V-shaped tails of her *motheru* are pulled forward between her legs from behind and fastened to the waist, thus keeping the *mwengo* in position and forming an effective protection of her private parts. In this position, the lovers lie together facing each other, with their legs interwoven to prevent any movement of their hips. They begin to fondle each other, rubbing their breasts together, whilst at the same time engaged in love-making conversation until they gradually fall asleep. (pp. 157–158)

Sexual intercourse was explicitly not allowed as a part of this premarital sexual activity. In fact, both the boys and the girls were taught that if either of them directly touched the genitals of the other, they would become polluted and have to undergo a costly purification rite. Boys who did not adhere to this restriction were ostracized by their peers. Not until marriage was sexual intercourse sanctioned.

---

are seemingly devoid of affiliative emotions (Gagnon & Simon, 1973). Female gender training, in contrast, emphasizes affiliation and pleasing others—parents when they are young and males as they grow older (Chodorow, 1974). Although fewer females than males report masturbating during adolescence, those who have done so report having fantasies that are limited to the sexual acts they have already performed and are set in a context that emphasizes love, marriage, and, in some cases, mild forms of masochism (Gagnon & Simon, 1973).

These differences between male and female experience have led Gagnon and Simon to suggest that when males and females come together in later adoles-

cence, the males are committed to sexuality but are relatively untrained in the rhetoric of romantic love, whereas the females are committed to romantic love but are relatively untrained in sexuality. "Dating and courtship may well be considered processes in which persons train members of the opposite sex in the meaning and content of their respective commitments" (1973:74).

Initial responses to sexual intercourse

Boys and girls differ in the ways they approach and respond to sexual intercourse, according to a survey of

TABLE 15.2
Feelings about First Intercourse (Percent)

	Sorry	Ambivalent	Glad	No Feelings
Boys	1%	34%	60%	5%
Girls	11	61	23	4

From Coles & Stokes, 1985.

more than 1000 American adolescents conducted by Robert Coles and Geoffrey Stokes (1985). In all but a very few cases, girls and boys reported having their first intercourse with someone they knew, usually a boyfriend or girlfriend. The boys' choices of partners, however, were more casual than the girls'. Thirty-two percent of them described their first partner as a friend, but for 75 percent of the girls the partner was definitely a *boyfriend*.

In general, boys responded more positively to the first experience of intercourse. Very few said they were sorry, but the girls were more likely to say that they experienced pain and to express ambivalence (Table 15.2).

Changing sexual habits

Conventional social wisdom has it that a "sexual revolution" in the 1960s markedly changed the sexual habits of young Americans. In this view, the advent of the Pill combined with the social unrest surrounding the civil rights and anti–Vietnam War movements created a new climate of social permissiveness. Liberated by these new conditions, teenagers presumably began their sexual careers earlier, expressed their sexuality more openly, and were less concerned about exclusive sexual relationships.

Evidence to support these beliefs comes from a variety of sources, most notably questionnaire studies of sexual activity and attitudes. In 1953 Kinsey and his colleagues reported that 3 percent of 14-year-old girls and 20 percent of college-age young women had experienced sexual intercourse. Harold Christensen and Christina Gregg (1970) obtained similar figures for college-age women in 1958. By 1968, however, the percentage of college-age women reporting sexual intercourse had leaped to 34 percent. The most recent evidence (National Centers for Disease Control, 1992) indicates that the trend toward increasing sexual activity among teenagers has continued. As Table 15.3 indicates, the percentage of never-married females between the ages of 15 and 19 who had experienced sexual intercourse was quite a bit higher in 1990 than that reported by Kinsey in the 1950s. The most rapid increase has been among white females.

TABLE 15.3
Percentage of Never-Married Girls Who Are Sexually Active, United States, 1971–1990

Race and Age	1990	1982	1979	1976	1971	Percent Change, 1971–1990
All races	48.0%	42.2%	46.0%	39.2%	27.6%	+73.9%
15	31.9	17.8	22.5	18.6	14.4	+121.5
16	42.9	28.1	37.8	28.9	20.9	+105.2
17	52.7	41.0	48.5	42.9	26.1	+101.9
18	66.6	52.7	56.9	51.4	39.7	+67.8
19	n.a.	61.7	69.0	59.5	46.4	—
White	47.0	40.3	42.3	33.6	23.2	+102.6
Black	60.0	52.9	64.8	64.3	52.4	+14.5

Source: Zelnick & Kantner, 1980; U.S. Department of Health and Human Services, National Center for Health Statistics, 1992.

It is also important to realize, however, that changes in the sexual habits of Americans are not restricted to recent decades. The most dramatic increase in premarital sexual intercourse in this century occurred around the time of World War I, when the number of women who were not virgins when they married doubled (Reiss, 1972).

Although the greater availability of contraceptive devices probably played some role in the more recent increases in teenage sexual activity, contraception is unlikely to have been the decisive factor. During the 1970s and 1980s, when there was a clear trend toward increased sexual activity, many teenagers made no attempt to prevent conception when they first had sexual intercourse (Zelnik & Shah, 1983). The average delay between the initiation of sexual activity and the first use of prescription methods of birth control, which are the most effective, was reported to be about 1 year. A more recent survey of high school students found that the use of condoms and other forms of birth control has increased, influenced at least in part by increased awareness of the danger of AIDS and other sexually transmitted diseases. Still, more than half of those high school students who are sexually active do not protect themselves against these threats (National Centers for Disease Control, 1992).

It appears that we cannot attribute the changes in sexual habits to a hypothesized sexual revolution or to any other single factor. The evidence suggests that the pattern of increasing sexual activity among unmarried people, teenagers in particular, is part of a long-term trend that reflects many interlocking factors. Ira Reiss provides an excellent overview of this trend:

> In the 50 years from World War I to the late 1960's the predominant change was not in the proportion of women non-virginal but rather in the attitudes of women and men toward premarital sexuality. During that half century, guilt feelings were reduced, the public discussion of sex increased radically, probably the number of partners increased, and the closeness to marriage required for coitus to be acceptable decreased. For males, other changes were occurring. Males were becoming more discriminate; they were beginning to feel that sex with someone they felt affection for, person-centered sex, was much to be preferred to body-centered coitus. (1972:169)

Teenage pregnancy

According to a survey of 37 countries, the United States leads nearly all other developed nations in the incidence of pregnancy among girls between the ages of 15 and 19 (National Research Council, 1987). Though the survey found that U.S. teenagers were no

The high incidence of teenage pregnancy and child bearing has led to the organization of special programs to ensure that young mothers can complete their education.

more sexually active than those in the other countries surveyed, they were far more likely to become pregnant. The rate of pregnancy among U.S. teenagers is nearly double that of British and French teenage girls and six times that of Dutch girls. Of the girls between the ages of 15 and 19 who become pregnant, an estimated 40 percent choose to terminate their pregnancy by abortion; among girls under the age of 15, over 50 percent of all pregnancies end in abortion (National Research Council, 1987). Of the girls who go on to give birth, an increasing number are unmarried. Unlike unwed mothers of earlier decades, these mothers are more likely to keep and raise their babies than to give them up for adoption (National Research Council, 1987).

Race, social class, education, and the strength of religious beliefs all affect a teenager's decision about whether or not to have and keep her child. Black teenagers are more likely than white teenagers to become single mothers. White teenagers are more likely to choose to have an abortion or to get married before the baby is born. The more education a pregnant teenager's mother has (which is an indirect measure of her social class) and the better the teenager is doing in school, the more likely she is to decide to abort the pregnancy. Teenagers with strong religious convictions are likely to have and keep their babies, no matter what their race or social class (Eisen et al., 1983).

Several studies have found that teenage motherhood usually imposes lasting hardships on both the mother and the child (National Research Council, 1987, summarizes this research). Teenage mothers are, on the average, more likely to drop out of high school, to be poor, and to be dependent on welfare. Of the women under the age of 30 who receive benefits under Aid to Families with Dependent Children, 71 percent had their first child as teenagers (National Research Council, 1987). Rates of mortality and illness are also higher among the babies of teenage mothers than among babies born to older women.

Parents versus Peers

As we indicated earlier, puberty is associated with changes in young people's relationships with their parents, both emotionally and physically; as young people become more distant from their parents, they are more likely to turn to their peers for advice on a variety of questions about how to conduct themselves (Brown, 1990).

While psychologists agree that young people's increased reliance on interactions with their peers and their greater sense of personal autonomy accompany changes in their relationships with their parents, they disagree about the basic nature of these changes. The disagreement focuses on two questions:

1. What is the major source of change? Is it primarily the result of factors operating within the family, or does the peer group play the major role?
2. Are changes in parent-child relations best thought of as a process of "breaking away" from the family or as one of renegotiating an ongoing relationship?

The relative influence of parents and peers

Traditional ideas about the rebelliousness of youth have given rise to the idea that people who have grown or are growing up in industrialized countries during the late twentieth century are part of a distinctive "youth culture" that is separated from the culture of their parents by a "generation gap" (Eisenstadt, 1963). In *The Adolescent Society* (1962) James Coleman made perhaps the strongest case for a distinctive youth subculture:

> [The adolescent] is "cut off" from the rest of society, forced inward toward his own age group, made to carry out his whole social life with others his own age. With his fellows, he comes to constitute a small society, one that has most of its important interactions within itself, and maintains only a few threads of connection with the outside adult society. In our modern world of mass communication and rapid diffusion of ideas and knowledge, it is hard to realize that separate subcultures can exist right under the very noses of adults—subcultures with languages all their own, with special symbols, and, most importantly, with value systems that may differ from adults'. (p. 3)

Evidence for the existence of a separate youth culture can be found on any American Main Street on a Saturday night. One is likely to find traffic lanes full of cars that have been carefully (and often expensively) modified to fit prevailing styles. The young people riding in those cars or strolling in suburban shopping malls are no less painstakingly decked out in styles that systematically deviate from adult tastes. The jargon that these teenagers speak and the music blasting from their cars or hand-held radios are equally distinctive. The specific manifestations vary from one country or region to the next, but the conspicuous display of behaviors and styles that seem (to older generations) to have been chosen because they are incomprehensible to adults or offend people in authority may be encountered in many parts of the world.

Despite the plausibility of claims for a discontinuous, self-contained youth culture, research by psychologists and sociologists reveals considerable continuity between the culture of adolescents and that of their parents as well as agreement between the generations about most important issues (Brown, 1990; Collins, 1990; Youniss & Smollar, 1985). Writing a decade after the publication of Coleman's book, the psychologists Denise Kandel and Gerald Lesser (1972) summarized their extensive study of high school students in the United States and Denmark with an outright rejection of Coleman's ideas:

> We find no evidence, in the two societies we studied, for the alienation of the young . . . or for the segregation and isolation of adolescents from the adult world proposed by Coleman. . . . Most adolescents have a close relationship with their parents. (p. 7)

When Kandel and Lesser analyzed data from questionnaires filled out by more than a thousand teenagers and their mothers, they found that most teenagers respect their parents. Dialogue rather than outright conflict or rejection was the major method of resolving disagreements. When asked how they felt about their parents, approximately 60 percent of the adolescents said that they were "extremely" or "quite" close, and only 11 percent denied that they felt close at all. Almost 60 percent also said that they wanted to be like their parents in many or most ways.

Several years later, Kandel (1986) asserted that psychologists had been asking the wrong question about the influence of parents and peer groups during adolescence. Instead of pitting the general influence of peers against the general influence of parents, researchers should be asking "What are the areas of influence for friends and what are the areas of influence for parents?" (p. 213).

Other researchers have reached the same conclusions. Ian Chand, Donald Crider, and Fern Willits (1975), for example, reported that adolescents and their parents tend to agree on issues related to religion and marriage, although they disagree about issues related to drugs and sex. Similarly, Robert Kelley (1972) found that parents and adolescents are in basic agreement about moral issues, but not about dress styles, hair length, and hours of sleep.

Studies reveal that adolescents' interactions with their fathers differ from their interactions with their mothers. Among the differences are the kinds of topics they are likely to discuss (Gjerde, 1986; Kandel & Lesser, 1972; Smetana, 1989; Youniss & Smollar, 1985). James Youniss and Jacqueline Smollar describe a "family division of labor" in which fathers are authority figures who are responsible for providing their adolescent children with long-range goals. They are brought into personal matters only when special advice is needed. By contrast, adolescents talk to their mothers about personal topics both to obtain practical advice and to validate their feelings and impressions.

Despite the great importance of peer groups in the lives of adolescents, most continue to maintain close relationships with their parents.

Adolescents are conspicuous for their unusual styles of dress and behavior, which change from one generation to the next. The only constant in these styles is their deviation from adult norms.

These conversations may be argumentative. The adolescents interviewed by Kandel and Lesser reported that they disagreed with their mothers about the value of academic success, dating, involvement in athletics, financial independence, and popularity. On a great many issues, however, mothers and teenagers agreed: it is important to plan for the future, to have a good reputation, and to respect one's parents. Overall, the relationships of adolescents with their mothers were found to be considerably more intimate than those with their fathers.

Young people not only consult their parents frequently but also continue to spend time with them. From telephone interviews with 64 youngsters ranging in age from 12 to 15 Raymond Montemayor (1982) found that adolescents spend a good deal of time with their parents as well as their peers, but their activities in the two contexts are so different that Montemayor called them "contrasting social worlds." Time spent with parents is devoted largely to eating, shopping, and household chores, whereas relaxation and play are the leading activities with peers. That adolescents consider the time spent with parents to be important is evidenced by the fact that when they get into disagreements with one parent, they are not driven to spend more time with their peers. Instead, they spend more time with the other parent.

Peer pressure to conform

No less widespread than the idea of a generation gap is the belief that adolescents are especially susceptible to peer pressure (Coleman, 1980). Adults worry that peer pressure may lead adolescents into antisocial behavior (Glynn, 1981; Huba & Bentler, 1980). The evidence suggests that young people are indeed especially sensitive to peer pressure during early adolescence, but their willingness to go along with the group depends greatly on the particular issue and peers in question (Lansbaum & Willis, 1971; Savin-Williams & Berndt, 1990).

Thomas Berndt (1979) addressed the question of special susceptibility to peer pressure at various ages by posing such problems as:

> You are with a couple of friends on Halloween. They're going to soap windows, but you're not sure whether you should or not. Your friends all say you should, because there is no way you could get caught. What would you *really* do? (p. 610)

Overall, Berndt found that adolescents were more likely than younger children to report that they would be willing to follow their peers; he also found that the tendency to conform with peers decreases in later adolescence. This pattern of increased susceptibility to peer pressure during early adolescence followed by a later decline appears to be well established (Brown, Clasen, & Eicher, 1986; Constranzo, 1970) (see Figure 15.8).

Evidence that the effectiveness of peer pressure varies according to the kind of activity involved comes from a variety of questionnaire studies (Berndt, 1979; Brittain, 1963; Brown, Clasen, & Eicher, 1986; Brown, Lohr, & McClenahan, 1986). To a certain extent, these studies confirm adults' concern that adolescents are susceptible to antisocial peer pressure. B. Bradford Brown, Donna Clasen, and Sue Ann Eicher (1986), for example, found that the more pressure adolescents feel to engage in misconduct, the more likely they are to do so. On the whole, however, adolescents report that they are more likely to give in to peer pressure that is prosocial than to pressure to misbehave.

Brown and his co-workers (1986) found that peer pressure to smoke, drink alcoholic beverages, and engage in sexual intercourse increases with age. It should be noted, however, that adults consider many of these same behaviors acceptable for themselves. This fact has led Richard and Shirley Jessor (1977) to argue that age-related increases in drinking should be viewed as attempts to model adult behavior rather than as social deviance. This argument may also apply to some of the other behaviors considered to be antisocial during adolescence, such as sexual intercourse and smoking.

The content and severity of adolescent-parent conflict

The studies of adolescents' relations with parents and peers reviewed so far suggest that in the United States the cultural stereotype of intergenerational conflict is exaggerated. Unfortunately, this conclusion depends heavily on self-reports and questionnaires, and the data secured by these techniques may not be representative of everyday interactions between adolescents and their parents.

A study by Mihaly Csikszentmihalyi and Reed Larson (1984) provides a partial solution to the imperfections of typical questionnaire studies and fills a gap in our knowledge. These researchers asked adolescents to carry an electronic beeper with them for a week, from the time they got up in the morning until they went to sleep at night. At a randomly chosen moment every 2 hours or so the subjects were "beeped," at which point they filled out a standard report about what they were doing and experiencing (see Figure 15.9). This technique provided detailed

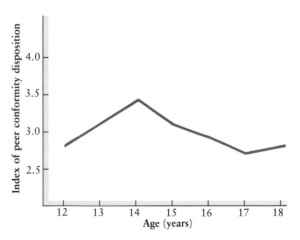

FIGURE 15.8   *Susceptibility to peer pressure increases during early adolescence and then begins to decline. (Adapted from Berndt, 1979.)*

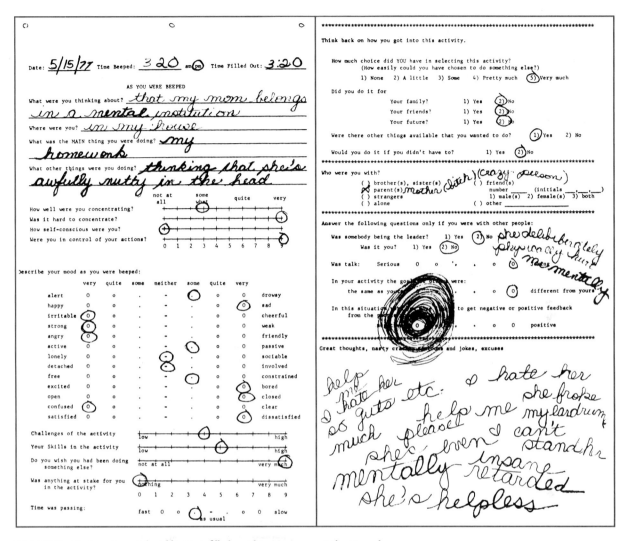

FIGURE 15.9   *A sample self-report filled out by a teenager at the time she was "beeped." (From Csikszentmihalyi & Larson, 1984.)*

information about the kinds of activities adolescents engage in at home as well as their moods and their thoughts. The following sample of the responses to the question "As you were beeped, what were you thinking about?" gives some sense of the conflicts that occurred between the subjects and their parents:

- Why my mother manipulates the conversation to get me to hate her.
- How much of a bastard my father is to my sister.
- How ugly my mom's taste is.

- How incompetent my mom is.
- My bitchy mom.
- How pig-headed my mom and dad are.
- About my mom getting ice cream all over her.
- How f____ing stupid my mom is for making a big f____ing fuss.

Notice that issues that are highlighted in the survey studies of Brown and his colleagues and of Kandel and Lesser, such as the importance of grades and the undesirability of drinking, are missing from this sample of complaints. Csikszentmihalyi and Larson report that the conflicts between adolescents and their parents often seem to center on seemingly unimportant matters of taste. But the appearance of triviality is deceiving:

> Asking a boy who has spent many days practicing a song on the guitar Why are you playing that trash? might not mean much to the father, but it can be a great blow to the son. The so-called "growth pains" of adolescence are no less real just because their causes appear to be without much substance to adults. In fact, this is exactly what the conflict is all about: What is to be taken seriously? (1984:140)

Adults naturally try to structure adolescents' realities to correspond to their notions of how the world works. And adolescents, who are at the threshold of adulthood themselves, can see the shortcomings of their parents' realities. In large and small ways, they resist having their realities defined for them on their parents' terms and seek to assert their own preferences. At the same time, adolescents realize they are dependent on their parents. When Robert Sorenson (1973) asked his national sample of adolescents between the ages of 13 and 19 to respond yes or no to the statement "I am not a child anymore, but I'm not an adult yet," 73 percent agreed with it. Approximately 50 percent agreed with the statement "If I had to go out into the world on my own right now, I think I would have a pretty hard time of it."

Here we see the real dilemma of adolescence and the major source of conflict between adolescents and their parents. Teenagers are caught between two worlds, one of dependence, the other of responsibility. Quite naturally, they would like to have the best of both worlds. But their parents, who pay the bills and pick up the clothing tossed on the floor, demand that independence be matched by responsibility. Once we realize that conflicts over "little things" are also disagreements about the major issues of growing up — the power to decide for oneself and to take responsibility for oneself — the issue of adolescent-parent conflict is brought into proper focus.

Overall, the data on the role of parents and peers in shaping adolescents' behavior speak against the existence of a broad generation gap. Some adolescents really do "break away" and establish relationships outside the family that remove them from their parents physically and emotionally. The more common pattern, however, is a process of individuation whereby adolescents and their parents negotiate a new form of interdependence that grants the adolescent a more equal role and more nearly equal responsibilities (Collins, 1990; Youniss, 1983). Neither the peer group nor the family can be assigned the primary role in this process. Instead, the two social contexts play complementary roles in reorganizing adolescents' social life.

Work

A vital factor in the rearrangement of adult-child relations is the young person's ability to make the transition to adult work responsibilities. Until young people can participate in adult work — work that sustains them and the family of which they are a part — they will not gain adult status.

In many countries, including the United States, access to adult jobs and adult status comes only after a long period of preparation during which young people learn to work and acquire skills that are required by particular jobs (Coy, 1989; Taggart, 1980). American children's first work experience often consists of doing household chores, such as setting the table, washing dishes, and caring for pets, usually without pay. About the age of 12 years, many children begin to work at odd jobs around the neighborhood — babysitting, delivering newspapers, mowing lawns. In most households, the money they earn from these jobs is theirs to spend with a minimum of adult supervision (Cole, 1980a). By the age of 15, many adolescents have progressed from working in casual jobs to regular part-time employment (Taggart, 1980). Some drop out of high school and plunge directly into the full-time labor market. The most conservative estimate is that 10.7 percent of students leave school before graduating, but the dropout rate in inner-city neighborhoods has been estimated to run as high as 50 percent (U.S. Bureau of the Census, 1991).

Because many teenagers work in jobs that the U.S. Department of Labor does not monitor and because some are paid "off the books" by employers who want to avoid paying the minimum wage and social security taxes, no accurate count of student workers is possible. Surveys indicate that more than 75 percent of all

Part-time jobs do not usually provide young people with on-the-job training that will prove useful in adulthood, but they do provide young people with some practical knowledge about work in addition to giving them spending money and a sense of accomplishment.

high school seniors and juniors and as many as 60 percent of all tenth-graders are employed at some time during the school year (Bachman, Johnston, & O'Malley, 1987).

The employment rate is higher for white students than for minority groups. Among 15- and 16-year-olds, the employment rate for African Americans is half that for whites (U.S. Department of Labor, 1985). White teenagers are more likely than minority teenagers to live near suburban shopping malls and other locations where part-time jobs can be found, and they are more likely to be successful in competing for jobs when they are available (Fine, Mortimer, & Roberts, 1990).

The number of hours a week that teenagers work varies with their social class and sex. When teenagers from minority and less advantaged homes find jobs, they tend to work longer hours than middle-class youths. Boys work longer hours than girls. Among boys, sophomores typically work 15 hours a week, while seniors work 21 hours. By comparison, sopho-

more girls work 11 and senior girls 18 hours a week (Fine, Mortimer, & Roberts, 1990). Many teenagers work even longer hours during school vacations.

It was once widely believed that extensive work experience during adolescence is all to the good. Government policy advisers contended that work is a good complement to school. Holding a job, so the argument went, teaches adolescents responsibility, develops positive attitudes toward work, provides on-the-job training, brings youngsters into contact with adults from whom they could learn, and keeps them out of trouble (Carnegie Commission on Policy Studies in Higher Education, 1980; National Commission on Youth, 1980; National Panel on High School and Adolescent Education, 1976; President's Science Advisory Committee, 1974).

Research during the past decade has been less positive, finding that working during adolescence confers disadvantages as well as advantages. These more recent studies support the idea that working provides a way for young people to acquire certain kinds of practical knowledge that eases their transition into adulthood. Their work experience teaches them how to find and hold a job, how to manage money, and how the business world functions (Greenberger & Steinberg, 1986). In addition, working requires adolescents to learn to budget their time and to assess their goals: Do they have the time to see their favorite television program and also get their homework done? Which is more important, working a few more hours a week or getting good grades?

When they handle work situations well, youngsters often feel the pride and self-confidence that come with a sense of accomplishment. Not surprisingly, even when they dislike their jobs, most adolescents enjoy the sense of power and independence they get from earning their own money. Dating and other social activities can be expensive. For most boys and for some girls, earning their own money is an essential prerequisite for participation in the social scene.

Contrary to the beliefs of many advocates of adolescent work experience, however, part-time jobs do not typically provide students with on-the-job training that will prove useful in adulthood, nor do they usually bring adolescents into contact with many adults. The vast majority of U.S. adolescents who are employed work in jobs that pay the minimum wage, offer no job protection, and provide few opportunities for advancement (Cole, 1980a). Few adults can afford to work in such jobs. As a result, adolescents frequently work with other adolescents in segregated sections of the labor market. They work primarily in food service, retail sales, clerical, and manual laboring jobs—all jobs that offer little formal instruction in work-related skills (Greenberger & Steinberg, 1986).

To complicate matters, part-time employment does not, as its advocates assume, keep teenagers out of trouble. Ellen Greenberger, Laurence Steinberg, and Mary Ruggiero (1982) found that holding a job is associated with higher rates of alcohol and marijuana use. Many adolescent part-time workers also admitted taking goods from their employers, which they usually either gave away or sold at a discount.

 Given the close correlation between years of schooling and the ability to find work as an adult, the data with perhaps the most serious negative implications for the future are those showing that adolescents who work part-time are generally less involved in school than their nonworking classmates (D'Amico, 1984; Steinberg & Dornbusch, 1991). The employed adolescents surveyed by Greenberger and Steinberg (1981) reported being absent more and enjoying school less than their classmates who did not work. This distaste for school typically increases in tandem with the number of hours a youngster works, perhaps because holding a job gives youngsters a chance to compare school (where some report they are not permitted to do the things they feel they do best) with other environments. More than 27 percent of the teenagers in Greenberger and Steinberg's study reported a decline in their grades after they began working, whereas only 16 percent reported an improvement.

It is not the mere fact of working that seems to cause the grades of teenagers to fall but rather the number of hours they work. Long work hours during the school year are associated with lower investment in school and a drop in grade point average (Steinberg & Dornbusch, 1991). But the evidence with respect to grades is mixed. Michael Finch and Jeylan Mortimer (1985) found that working long hours depresses high school students' grades when they are sophomores and juniors but not when they are seniors. Those sophomores and juniors who work more than 20 hours a week during the school year are more likely to drop out of school than are their classmates who do not work so much (D'Amico, 1984). Less intensive commitment to work during those years, however, is asso-

ciated with an increase in the probability of completing high school.

Even as late as the high school years, many U.S. adolescents know little about the occupations available in their geographic region, the content of people's work, or their earnings (De Fleur & Menke, 1975). Adolescents' information about the labor force increases slowly as they begin to work themselves and as their network of working friends grows. Only gradually do they develop some sense of what work they want to do as adults.

Each subsequent job that an adolescent holds tends to be more substantial and more responsible and to provide greater exposure to the options in the labor market. In the period after high school, many adolescents gradually enter jobs in which they stay long enough to learn a skill, either formally or informally. Others seek career training in professional schools, colleges, public programs, or the military. By the time they are in their mid-twenties, most young people have acquired vocational competency and are beginning to work in an adult career (Office of Educational Research and Improvement, 1991; Taggart, 1980).

THE BIO-SOCIAL FRAME AND ADOLESCENT DEVELOPMENT

The basic bio-social dilemma of adolescence is clear. In all societies where the assumption of adult rights and responsibilities is delayed well beyond puberty, young people must cope with bodies that allow mature sexual activity but social circumstances that keep them in a state of dependence and immaturity. These circumstances complicate a developmental transition that could be expected to be difficult in any event because biological maturity fundamentally changes the power relations between children and their parents. In a phrase, the child becomes "too big to be spanked." Parents continue to exert considerable influence over their children, but this influence must be renegotiated.

In modern industrialized societies such as our own, the transition to adulthood is further complicated by two interrelated facts. First, the earlier onset of puberty and the increasingly longer years of education required for economic productivity have combined to lengthen adolescence. Second, the ways in which schooling and work are organized separate adolescents and adults, increasing the influence of peers and dividing generations.

Taken together, the biological and social reorganizations that define modern adolescence provide the essential conditions for the psychological changes that characterize this developmental period. We have touched only briefly on how cultural context influences the social perception of adolescence as a distinctive period of development. In Chapter 16 we will first examine the special qualities of mind that develop as

young people struggle to understand their new circumstances and to master the complex systems of technical knowledge that will structure their adult work lives. Then we will consider all three domains of developmental change—the biological, the social, and the psychological—simultaneously as an interacting system of influences in a cultural context. This approach leads to a deeper understanding of the universal and the culture-specific aspects of adolescence. It also leaves us better able to evaluate the success of competing theories in accounting for the transition to adulthood.

SUMMARY

1. Since the time of Rousseau, three key issues have preoccupied those who theorize about adolescence:
   a. The degree to which rapid biological changes increase behavioral instability.
   b. The possibility that development in adolescence recapitulates earlier stages in achieving an integration appropriate to adulthood.
   c. The relation of biological and social changes to cognitive changes.
2. Common to all theories of adolescence is recognition of the child's need to integrate new biological capacities with new forms of social relations. Theories vary in this regard as they do in respect to earlier periods:
   a. Biological theories emphasize the universal physical changes in children's bodies as the central causes of adolescent behavior.
   b. Environmental-learning theories emphasize the continuity of adolescence with earlier periods and the power of society to shape its psychological characteristics.
   c. Universal-constructivist theories emphasize the discontinuity of adolescence from earlier periods and the complementary roles of biological and social factors in provoking the emergence of a new level of psychological organization.
   d. Cultural-context theories do not assume that adolescence is a universal stage of development. Instead, they hold that it will appear only under conditions that create a delay between biological maturity and adulthood.
3. Puberty, the sum of the biological changes that lead to sexual maturity, is accompanied by a growth spurt

during which boys and girls attain approximately 98 percent of their adult size. During puberty the bodies of males and females take on their distinctive shapes.
4. Menarche, or the first menstrual period, usually occurs late in a girl's puberty, after her growth spurt has reached its peak. Among males, the ability to ejaculate semen signals the maturation of the primary sex organs.
5. The age at which biological maturation occurs influences a child's social standing with peers and adults.
6. The dominant mode of peer relations at the start of adolescence is same-sex friendship focused on shared activities. As adolescence proceeds, same-sex friendship is increasingly characterized by an emphasis on trust, loyalty, and mutual understanding.
7. Social standing within one's peer group depends upon social factors, such as membership in the leading crowd, and personal factors, such as girls' physical attractiveness and boys' athletic ability.
8. The transition to two-person heterosexual relations goes through a number of stages. It begins with membership in small same-sex cliques and participation with the other members in social events that draw heterosexual crowds. Within these crowds, heterosexual cliques are formed as couples begin the process of pairing off preparatory to going steady, becoming engaged, and marrying.
9. Achieving an intimate, mutually satisfactory heterosexual relationship requires learning as well as biological maturation.
10. The transition to heterosexual relations proceeds in opposite directions for males and females in our culture because of differences in their histories. Males

begin with the highly developed goal of sexual satisfaction and only gradually learn to include a deeper social and emotional commitment in their heterosexual relations. Females begin with the highly developed goal of social and emotional affiliation and only gradually acquire the goal of sexual satisfaction.

11. Biological maturation and the increasing time spent with peers alter parent-child relations. Parental authority, which decreases in relation to the influence of peers, must now be exercised even more through persuasion than was true in middle childhood.

12. Contrary to the hypothesis of a separate youth culture, most adolescents share their parents' values. Dialogue, rather than outright conflict or rejection, is the major method of resolving disagreements between adolescents and their parents.

13. Conflicts with parents during adolescence seem to center on matters of taste, though often they are actually about larger issues of control.

14. Most U.S. adolescents have considerably more intimate relationships with their mothers than with their fathers.

15. Sensitivity to peer pressure seems to peak around the age of 15. Most adolescents report that they are more likely to go along with peer pressure that is prosocial than with pressure to misbehave. The more pressure adolescents feel to engage in antisocial behavior, however, the more likely they are to do so.

16. Evidence concerning the developmental impact of work experience in the United States is mixed. Moderate amounts of work enhance feelings of independence and efficacy, but too much work reduces achievement in school.

17. The bio-social-behavioral shift to adulthood is complicated by the fact that sexual maturity does not necessarily coincide with adult status. The resulting conflict between biological and social forces gives this transition its unique psychological characteristics.

KEY TERMS

menarche
primary sex organs
puberty
recapitulationism
secondary sex characteristics

SUGGESTED READINGS

FELDMAN, S. SHIRLEY, & ELLIOTT, GLEN R. (Eds). *At the Threshold: The Developing Adolescent.* Cambridge, Mass.: Harvard University Press, 1990.

A broad summary of research on adolescence written by outstanding scholars in the field. Individual chapters are rich sources of ideas about specific topics and the volume as a whole provides definitive coverage of most of the topics discussed in this chapter.

FRANK, ANNE. *Diary of a Young Girl.* New York: Pocket Books, 1975.

The classic autobiographical description of the experience of early adolescence. The very normality of this account, written under fearful circumstances, attests to the universality of many of the psychological changes evoked by coming of age.

KATCHADOURIAN, HERANT. *The Biology of Adolescence.* New York: W. H. Freeman, 1977.

A wide-ranging and readable account of the biological changes associated with adolescence. The author does an especially good job of presenting information about the biology of development in a way that connects with students' everyday knowledge.

KETT, JOSEPH F. *Rites of Passage: Adolescence in America, 1790 to the Present.* New York: Basic Books, 1977.

This historical account is full of information about the quality of adolescence since the founding of the United States. In addition to providing glimpses of lives that vary considerably from our own, the book provides insights into universal and historically determined characteristics of adolescence as a stage of development.

MEAD, MARGARET. *Coming of Age in Samoa: A Psychological Study of Primitive Youth* (1928). New York: American Museum of Natural History, 1973.

The book that is the high-water mark of the idea that the stresses of adolescence in our society are created by cultural practices that inhibit sexual activity and restrict adolescents' autonomy. Not only an important document in the anthropological study of child development, this book continues to exert an influence on our basic conceptions of human nature.

SAVIN-WILLIAMS, RITCH C. *Adolescence: An Ethological Perspective.* New York: Springer-Verlag, 1987.

An expert on social and personality development during adolescence who has championed an ethological approach to development, Ritch Savin-Williams devotes this book to a naturalistic study of adolescents at a summer camp. By collecting his data in settings where young people "act themselves," Savin-Williams provides an exceptionally rich description of the way psychological processes are manifested in social interactions.

YOUNISS, JAMES, & SMOLLAR, JACQUELINE. *Adolescent Relations with Mothers, Fathers, and Friends.* Chicago: University of Chicago Press, 1985.

This book uses extensive interviews to provide a picture of the social reorganization that is fundamental to adolescence.

CHAPTER 16

The Psychological Achievements of Adolescence

•

Now I look into myself and see the I of me, the weak and
aimless thing which makes me. I is not strong and needs be, I
needs to know direction, but has none. My I is not sure, there
are too many wrongs and mixed truths within to know. I
changes and does not know. I knows little reality and many
dreams. What I am now is what will be used to build the later
self. What I am is not what I want to be, although I am not
sure what this is which I do not want.
But then what is I? My I is an answer to every all of every
people. It is this which I have to give to the waiting world and
from here comes all that is different.
I is to create.

—JOHN D., AGE 17, QUOTED IN PETER BLOS,
ON ADOLESCENCE

Theorists of development have agreed at least since Rousseau that the transition from middle childhood to adulthood requires the development of a new quality of mind. The basic logic behind this consensus is similar to the logic we have invoked to explain earlier bio-social-behavioral shifts: changes in children's capacity for biological reproduction are necessarily accompanied by changes in social relations that propel them into a new social status, with new rights and responsibilities; these changed circumstances, in turn, require more complex forms of thinking.

One manifestation of this new mode of thinking is the disdain adolescents express for adults' opinions and behavior. They become critical of received wisdom and even more critical of the discrepancies between adults' ideals and behavior. At the same time, the adolescent

> seeks out among [adults] models to imitate; heroes to worship. He also seeks out heroes of history and of biography. . . . Literature, art, religion take on new meanings and may create new confusions in his thinking. He has a strangely novel interest in abstract ideas. He pursues them in order to find himself. (Gesell & Ilg, 1943:256)

In the end, neither slavish adherence to nor rejection of existing cultural expectations will suffice; rather, young people must reconcile their own desires and ways of doing things with their community's requirement that they become economically productive and law-abiding citizens. Viewed in this way, adolescent thinking is, on the one hand, the adolescent's most important psychological *means* to come to grips with the tasks of adult life and, on the other hand, a *result* of his or her struggle to reconcile competing social demands. This process of reconciliation requires a level of systematic thought that strains or exceeds the capacity of younger children.

We begin this chapter by examining the experimental evidence for and against the idea that the thought processes of young people become more systematic and logical as they begin the transition to adulthood. This evidence raises a number of questions: Under what circumstances do adolescents engage in systematic, logical thinking? Is the quality of thinking exhibited in scientific experiments also revealed in the way young people think about such pressing issues as the laws that govern their society, their rights and obligations as citizens, and their own personal sense of identity? Is the new quality of mind that is observed among young people in modern industrialized societies universal or does it result from the extended schooling they receive? And finally, when the entire pattern of biological, social, and cognitive changes is examined in different cultural contexts, does it support the idea of adolescence as a universal stage of development?

RESEARCH ON ADOLESCENT THOUGHT

In 1980, Daniel Keating suggested five basic characteristics that distinguish adolescent thinking from thought during middle childhood:

Thinking about possibilities Unlike younger children, who are more at ease reasoning about what they can directly observe, adolescents are likely to think about alternative possibilities that are not immediately present to their senses.

Thinking ahead Adolescence is a time when young people start thinking about what they will do when they grow up. Adolescents by no means always plan ahead, but they do so more often and more systematically than younger children. Contemplating the upcoming summer holiday, an adolescent might think, "Well, I could go to Montana and work on a ranch. Or I could stay home and make up that D in algebra, which isn't going to look too good when I apply to college." A younger child would be more likely to focus only on having a good time and forget other responsibilities.

Thinking through hypotheses Adolescents are more likely than younger children to engage in thinking that requires them to generate and test hypotheses and to think about situations that are contrary to fact. In thinking about going to a beach party with a boy she does not know well, a teenage girl may reason, "What if they get drunk and rowdy? What will I do? I guess if things get out of hand, I can always ask someone to take me home. But then they'll think I'm a drag." A younger child would make a decision without contemplating the wide range of possible scenarios.

Thinking about thought During adolescence, thinking about one's own thought processes—the

"metacognitive thinking" we described in Chapter 12—becomes increasingly complex. Adolescents also acquire the ability to engage in **second-order thinking**; that is, they can develop rules about rules, holding two disparate rule systems in mind as they mull them over. At the same time, they can think more systematically and deeply than younger children about other people's points of view, a development seen in the changing nature of adolescent friendships (see Chapter 15, p. 585).

Thinking beyond conventional limits Adolescents use their newly sophisticated cognitive ability to rethink the fundamental issues of social relations, morality, politics, and religion—issues that are debated by the adults in their community and that have perplexed human beings since the dawn of history. Now acutely aware of the disparities between the ideals of their community and the behavior of individual adults around them, adolescents are highly motivated to figure out how to "do it right." Arnold Gesell and Frances Ilg, as we just saw, link this aspect of adolescent thought to youth's idealism and search for heroes.

One can certainly find many adolescents in the United States who display the characteristics that Keating describes. In addition, evidence from standardized tests shows that American adolescents can routinely solve problems that younger children cannot. When adolescents are asked to solve such analogies as "*under* is to *beneath* as *pain* is to *[pleasure, doctor, feeling, hurt]*," they err very seldom, whereas 9- and 10-year-olds have considerable difficulty (Sternberg & Nigro, 1980). Recent research, however, has raised basic questions about the distinctiveness and the universality of cognitive development during adolescence. Reviewing the field again in 1990, Keating noted that the view that adolescent thinking could be characterized by a small set of general characteristics had given way to the belief that adolescents' thought processes depend heavily on the content of the problems they think about and the context in which they encounter that content.

The importance of content and context for understanding adolescent thought processes is nowhere more clear than in current research on the formal operations posited by Piaget.

Formal Operations

It was Piaget's contention that changes in the way adolescents think about themselves, their personal relationships, and the nature of their society have a common source: the development of a new kind of thought process, based on a new logical structure that

Piaget called **formal operations** (see Table 16.1). As you will recall, an *operation* in Piaget's terminology is a mental action that fits into a logical system. Inhelder and Piaget distinguished formal operations, which they believed emerge by age 12, from concrete operations, which are characteristic of middle childhood, in this way:

TABLE 16.1

Piaget's Stages of Cognitive Development: Formal Operational

Age, years	Stage	Description	Characteristics and Examples
Birth to 2	Sensorimotor	Infants' achievements consist largely of coordinating their sensory perceptions and simple motor behaviors. As they move through the 6 substages of this period, infants come to recognize the existence of a world outside of themselves and begin to interact with it in deliberate ways.	Formal operational reasoning, in which each partial link in a chain of reasoning is related to the problem as a whole * Young people solve the combination-of-chemicals problem by systematically testing all possible combinations. * In forming a personal identity, young people take into account how they judge others, how others judge them, how they judge the judgment processes of others, and how all this corresponds to social categories available in the culture.
2 to 6	Preoperational	Young children can represent reality to themselves through the use of symbols, including mental images, words, and gestures. Objects and events no longer have to be present to be thought about, but children often fail to distinguish their point of view from that of others, become easily captured by surface appearances, and are often confused about causal relations.	
6 to 12	Concrete operational	As they enter middle childhood, children become capable of mental operations, internalized actions that fit into a logical system. Operational thinking allows children mentally to combine, separate, order, and transform objects and actions. Such operations are considered concrete because they are carried out in the presence of the objects and events being thought about.	Application of the newly mastered logical and mathematical principles to a wide variety of life's problems * Young people think about politics and law in terms of abstract principles and are capable of seeing the beneficial, rather than just the punitive, side of laws. * Young people are interested in universal ethical principles and critical of adults' hypocrisies.
12 to 19	Formal operational	In adolescence the developing person acquires the ability to think systematically about all logical relations within a problem. Adolescents display keen interest in abstract ideals and in the process of thinking itself.	

Although concrete operations consist of organized systems (classifications, serial ordering, correspondences, etc.), [children in the concrete operational stage] proceed from one partial link to the next in step-by-step fashion, without relating each partial link to all the others. Formal operations differ in that all of the possible combinations are considered in each case. Consequently, each partial link is grouped in relation to the whole; in other words, reasoning moves continually as a function of a "structured whole." (Inhelder & Piaget, 1958:16)

Formal operational thinking is the kind of thinking needed by anyone who has to solve problems systematically. This new ability is needed by the owner of a gasoline station who, in order to make a profit, has to take into account the price he pays for gasoline, the kinds of customers that pass by his station, the kinds of services he needs to offer, the hours he needs to stay open, and the cost of labor, rent, and utilities. A lawyer, too, must take into account a wide variety of alternative developments in order to present her client's case adequately and counter the arguments of the attorney on the opposing side.

Classic studies in formal operations

Inhelder and Piaget asked children to combine chemicals or to reason about weights suspended from a bal-ance beam, problems that required them to hold one variable of a complex system constant while systematically searching mentally through all the other variables. To clarify the contrast between childhood and adolescent thought, the investigators chose children aged 6 through 14.

The combination-of-chemicals problem illustrates both the ability to combine variables and the idea of a "structured, psychological whole" that Inhelder and Piaget believed to be the key characteristics of formal operational thinking. At the start of the task, four large bottles, one indicator bottle, and two beakers are arrayed on a table in front of the child, as in Figure 16.1. Each bottle contains a clear liquid. The liquids are chosen so that when liquid from bottles 1 and 3 are combined in a beaker and then a drop of the chemical from the indicator bottle (*g*) is added, the liquid turns yellow. If the chemical in bottle 2 is added to a beaker containing liquid from both 1 and 3, the solution remains yellow, but if 4 is then added, the liquid turns clear again.

The experimenter begins with two beakers already full of liquid. One contains liquid from bottles 1 and 3, the other liquid from bottle 2. He puts a drop from bottle *g* in each beaker, demonstrating that it produces a yellow color in one case but not in the other. Now the child is invited to try out various combinations in an attempt to determine which combination of chemicals will transform the color of the liquid.

These young women are engaged in a task that requires them to combine variables in the manner Piaget associated with formal operations.

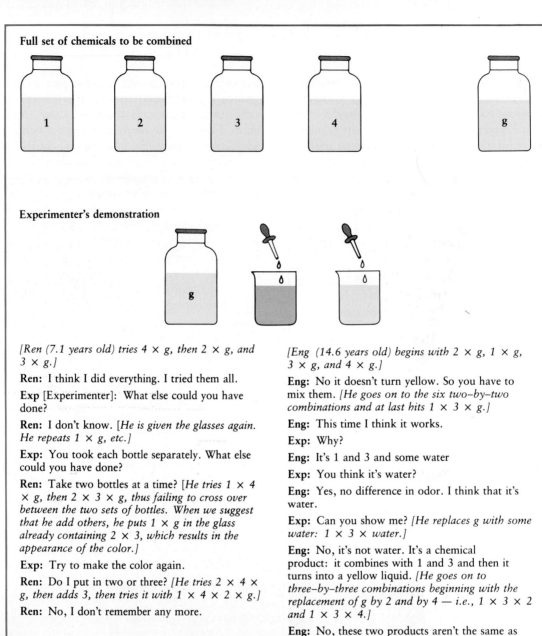

Full set of chemicals to be combined

1 2 3 4 g

Experimenter's demonstration

g

[Ren (7.1 years old) tries 4 × g, then 2 × g, and 3 × g.]

Ren: I think I did everything. I tried them all.

Exp [Experimenter]: What else could you have done?

Ren: I don't know. *[He is given the glasses again. He repeats 1 × g, etc.]*

Exp: You took each bottle separately. What else could you have done?

Ren: Take two bottles at a time? *[He tries 1 × 4 × g, then 2 × 3 × g, thus failing to cross over between the two sets of bottles. When we suggest that he add others, he puts 1 × g in the glass already containing 2 × 3, which results in the appearance of the color.]*

Exp: Try to make the color again.

Ren: Do I put in two or three? *[He tries 2 × 4 × g, then adds 3, then tries it with 1 × 4 × 2 × g.]*

Ren: No, I don't remember any more.

[Eng (14.6 years old) begins with 2 × g, 1 × g, 3 × g, and 4 × g.]

Eng: No it doesn't turn yellow. So you have to mix them. *[He goes on to the six two–by–two combinations and at last hits 1 × 3 × g.]*

Eng: This time I think it works.

Exp: Why?

Eng: It's 1 and 3 and some water

Exp: You think it's water?

Eng: Yes, no difference in odor. I think that it's water.

Exp: Can you show me? *[He replaces g with some water: 1 × 3 × water.]*

Eng: No, it's not water. It's a chemical product: it combines with 1 and 3 and then it turns into a yellow liquid. *[He goes on to three–by–three combinations beginning with the replacement of g by 2 and by 4 — i.e., 1 × 3 × 2 and 1 × 3 × 4.]*

Eng: No, these two products aren't the same as the drops: they can't produce color with 1 and 3 *[Then he tries 1 × 3 × g × 4.]*

Eng: It turns white again: 4 is the opposite of g because 4 makes the color go away while g makes it appear.

FIGURE 16.1   *A 7-year-old and an adolescent tackle the combination-of-chemicals task. Note that the 7-year-old starts by testing only one chemical at a time. When it is suggested that he try working with two chemicals at a time, he becomes confused. The 14-year-old also starts with one chemical at a time but quickly realizes that he must create more complicated combinations, which he does in a systematic way until he arrives at the solution to the problem. (From Inhelder & Piaget, 1958.)*

Interviews with two of Inhelder and Piaget's subjects are shown at the bottom of Figure 16.1: one with a 7-year-old boy who does not have the kind of overall conceptual grasp of the problem that indicates the presence of a **structured whole** (a system of relationships that can be logically described and thought about) and one with a 14-year-old boy who does. The first child is unsystematic in his sampling of possible combinations, even with hints from the experimenter. The second, an adolescent, sets about his task systematically. He starts with the simplest possibility (one of the chemicals, when combined with *g*, turns yellow), then proceeds to the next level of complexity—the possibility that two, and later three, chemicals must first be combined. When he combines pairs, he discovers that when *g* is added to a mixture of 1 and 3, the yellow color appears, but because he is methodical in exploring all the logical possibilities, he also discovers that 4 counteracts *g*, thereby arriving at a systematic understanding of the miniature chemical system that Inhelder and Piaget have arranged for him. The adolescent is exhibiting formal operational thinking par excellence.

In a second problem, which highlights somewhat different features of formal operations, Inhelder and Piaget asked children to make judgments about the conditions under which a balance beam would be in equilibrium (see Figure 16.2). The youngest children failed to understand the problem at all. The 8-year-olds concentrated on the weight on each side of the

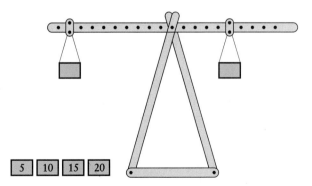

FIGURE 16.2   *The balance beam used by Inhelder and Piaget. On each trial of the experiment, weights of varying magnitude are hung at varying distances from the fulcrum. It is the child's task to determine if the beam will be in balance, and if not, to predict which side will be the heavier. (From Inhelder & Piaget, 1958.)*

fulcrum: if these weights were equal, they predicted that the beam would balance, disregarding the distance of the weights from the fulcrum. Only the adolescents consistently considered both weight and distance in solving the problem (Inhelder & Piaget, 1958; Siegler, 1976).

The correct solution to the balance-beam problem exemplifies the key properties of formal operational thinking because this problem requires that the values of both variables—weight and distance from the fulcrum—be systematically varied and combined. Equally important is the fact that to arrive at a general rule for solving the problem, adolescents must develop an understanding of logical and mathematical principles. They can then use those principles to solve an infinite variety of weight and distance problems.

Although Inhelder and Piaget selected these problems from specific scientific domains, they claimed that the quality of reasoning needed to solve them was quite general. Formal operations, they declared, are "like a center from which radiate the various more visible modifications of thinking which take place in adolescence" (1958:335).

Are formal operations universal?

A casual reading of Inhelder and Piaget's 1958 monograph on adolescent thought processes or of a standard text on adolescence can easily lead one to conclude that formal operational thinking is universal. These writings suggest both that formal operational thinking suffuses all domains of adolescent thought and that the social conditions that give rise to formal operational thinking—the demands of the adult roles and responsibilities the young person is preparing to shoulder—are just as universal a part of adolescence as puberty. One would thus expect to see formal operations organizing adolescent and adult thought in all societies and in all cultural contexts. The actual evidence tells a far more complicated story.

In studies of well-educated American teenagers, as few as 30 to 40 percent have solved such problems as the combination of chemicals and the balance beam, which, according to Piaget, exemplify universal characteristics of formal thinking (Capon & Kuhn, 1979; Keating, 1980; Linn, 1983; Neimark, 1975; Siegler & Liebert, 1975). Such widespread failure raises serious doubts as to whether this kind of thought process is universally acquired. A good deal of research has been carried out to determine whether formal operational thinking is or is not a universal achievement of adolescence, and what kinds of factors promote or block its development and expression.

STUDIES AMONG U.S. SUBJECTS.   Robert Siegler and Robert Liebert (1975) designed a combination-of-variables problem in which children ranging in age from 10 to 13 were asked to find the combination of open and closed positions on four switches needed to make a model train go along a track. This arrangement made the problem logically similar to Inhelder and Piaget's combination-of-chemicals problem.

Some children were introduced to the problem as Inhelder and Piaget would have presented it. The experimenters tutored others, using one of two supplementary procedures. In the first supplementary procedure, they showed the children a systematic way to check through the various combinations of open and closed switches. In the second procedure, after showing the children the checking method they coached them on two problems that were logically equivalent to the one they would be asked to solve. Siegler and Liebert then compared the performances of the three groups of children.

The tutoring helped. With no training or tutoring, none of the 10-year-olds and only 20 percent of the 13-year-olds searched systematically through all the alternatives as formal operational thinkers are supposed to do. With training in checking but no tutoring in similar problems, the 13-year-olds showed only modest improvement and the 10-year-olds showed none at all. All the children who received both training and tutoring in analogous problems solved the problem correctly. (Similar findings are reported by Stone & Day, 1980.)

These results suggest that children on the threshold of adolescence are capable of the kind of systematic, logical manipulation of variables that is the hallmark of formal operations if they are given proper instruction and if the benefits of the systematic manipulation are made clear. But such coached performance cannot be considered evidence of the spontaneous development of a new mode of thought in early adolescence.

Difficulties with formal operational thinking do not disappear in later adolescence, nor do they show up only in laboratory problems. Noel Capon and Deanna Kuhn (1979) approached adult shoppers at a supermarket and asked them to judge which of two sizes of garlic powder was a better buy: a 67-gram bottle at 77 cents or a 35-gram bottle at 41 cents. The shoppers were provided with paper and pencil to help them reach a solution.

Only 20 percent of the shoppers followed the formal operational procedure of determining the ratio of amount to price; most shoppers relied instead on the conventional belief that the bigger bottle must be a better buy. These results led Capon and Kuhn to conclude that "there does in fact exist significant variability in the level of logical reasoning among an adult population" (p. 421).

SEX DIFFERENCES IN FORMAL OPERATIONS.   A good deal of research in recent decades has sought to determine whether there are sex differences in children's performance on formal operational tasks — that is, whether males have greater talent in these areas and are superior in their ability to engage in formal operational thought. The reasons for this interest are social as well as scientific. If formal operations are a universal capacity, both sexes can acquire this kind of reasoning. Yet the belief is pervasive that men have greater talent in such areas as mathematics, science, and engineering, fields that appear to require formal operational thinking. This stereotype is bolstered by (and bolsters) the fact that more men than women currently work in these fields.

Anita Meehan (1984) surveyed 150 studies in which both males and females were asked to solve the same formal operational problems. In many of the studies she surveyed, no differences were found between the performances of males and females, but when sex differences were found, they generally favored males.

Several attempts have been made to discover why males sometimes perform better than females on experimental tasks that require formal operations. J. Peskin (1980) found that female high school students who reported little interest in science performed better on "female-oriented" formal operational tasks whose content captured their interest. Female students interested in science, by contrast, performed no better on the special "female-oriented" problems than on the standard Piagetian tasks. Since in contemporary American schools fewer girls than boys are interested in science, these findings suggest that sex differences such as those Meehan documented may be caused by boys' greater interest in the content of the standard Piagetian tasks that require formal operations, as well as by their greater familiarity with the procedures.

Many tasks that call for formal operational reasoning require the exercise of spatial ability. Since boys, on average, outperform girls on tasks in which spatial ability plays a large role (Hyde, 1981), perhaps the difference between them on some formal operational tasks is simply the result of sex-linked differences in spatial ability (Linn & Sweeney, 1981). No clear link between spatial ability and formal reasoning performance, however, has been established (Linn & Pulos, 1983).

Current evidence favors the idea that the capacity to solve formal operational problems develops equally in males and females, but one's success in using this ability to solve particular problems depends on one's experience. This conclusion, as we will see, is supported by evidence from the other line of research on the universality of formal operations, which compares the performances of children of different cultures.

CULTURAL VARIATIONS IN FORMAL OPERATIONS. In our review of research on cultural variability in the development of concrete operations (Chapter 12) we found that children of different cultures vary considerably in the age at which they use concrete operational reasoning to solve conservation problems. We also saw, however, that this variability appears to result from relatively superficial difficulties in understanding the tasks because of the ways they are presented. Concrete operational ability does appear to be universal. Evidence across cultures on the development of formal operations offers a far sterner challenge to the idea that this stage is universal. People in small, technologically unsophisticated societies rarely demonstrate formal operations when they are tested with Piagetian methods (Jahoda, 1980; Laboratory of Comparative Human Cognition, 1983; Rogoff, 1981; Segall et al., 1990).

In the course of his career Piaget shifted position on the universality of formal operational thinking. According to his general framework, the acquisition of formal operations should be universal, reflecting universal properties of biological growth and social interaction. Nonetheless, he did say that "in extremely

disadvantageous conditions, [formal operational thought] will never really take shape" (Piaget, 1972:7). This is the position that Inhelder and Piaget (1958) adopted:

> The age of about 11 to 12 years, which in our society we found to mark the beginning of formal thinking, must be extremely relative, since the logic of the so-called primitive societies appears to be without such structures. (p. 337)

In such statements we see Piaget explicitly rejecting formal operations as a universal cognitive ability and claiming differences in cultural development as the reason.

An alternative possibility, which Piaget also entertained,

> is to envisage a difference in speed of development without any modification of the order of succession of the stages. These different speeds would be due to the quality and frequency of intellectual stimulation received from adults or obtained from the possibilities available to children for spontaneous activity in their environment. (1972:7)

The conclusion that Piaget preferred toward the end of his life was that all normal people attain the level of formal operations. "However," he wrote,

> they reach this stage in different areas according to their aptitudes and their professional specializations (advanced studies or different types of apprenticeship for the various trades): the way in which these formal structures are used, however, is not necessarily the same in all cases. (1972:10)

In other words, a lawyer might think in a formal manner about law cases but not when sorting the laundry, or a baseball manager might employ formal operational thinking to choose his batting lineup but fail to do so in the combination-of-chemicals task.

Later we will consider in more detail the importance of formal operations for adolescent cognitive development. First, however, we will consider evidence from other research traditions about the universality of the psychological processes required to solve complex logical problems.

Alternative Approaches to Adolescent Thought

Investigators who question Piaget's account of adolescent cognition have sought alternative explanations. Those who work in the information-processing tradition have explained adolescents' improved performance on logical reasoning tasks in much the same way they attempt to explain advances in thought processes at earlier ages. Cumulative changes in memory capacity, the acquisition of more powerful strategies, and metacognitive understanding are the major mechanisms they focus on. Researchers from a variety of traditions have suggested that adolescents discover a new relation between thought and language that is the key to their cognitive development during this period. Those who emphasize the importance of cultural context have pursued the path that Piaget himself suggested, concentrating on the way specialized practice in particular domains of experience gives rise to the kind of systematic thought that appears to underlie the new quality of adolescent cognition.

Information-processing theories

In recent years psychologists who work within the information-processing tradition have provided provocative alternatives to Piaget's analysis. These scholars reject Piaget's idea that children develop a qualitatively different mode of thought during adolescence. They maintain that characteristics of adolescent thought are best accounted for by an increasing capacity to process information. According to this view, adolescents develop more efficient strategies for solving problems and become better able to retain information in their memory while they relate the components of a task to one another (Siegler, 1983).

Adopting an information-processing perspective, Siegler (1976) analyzed the various ways in which Inhelder and Piaget's balance-beam problem (Figure 16.2) can be posed. The impression one gets from Inhelder and Piaget's account is that this problem is a single logical puzzle that older children come to master by applying more powerful logic. Siegler demonstrated, however, that what seems like a single logical problem is really several tasks, each of which makes its own cognitive demands.

In one such demonstration Siegler contrasted 5-to-17-year-olds' performance on balance-beam problems in which the weights were equal but distributed at different distances from the fulcrum with children's performance on problems in which both the weights and their distances from the fulcrum were unequal (see Figure 16.3). He found that the adolescents were much more likely than the children to respond correctly to the problem in which the weights were equal but the distances were unequal. The youngest children took only weight into account and hence incorrectly concluded that the beam was balanced. When both weight and distance were varied and the larger weight was closer to the fulcrum, however, the 5-year-olds performed better (89 percent correct) than the 17-year-olds (51 percent correct). But the *reason* for their correct answers was itself incorrect: Since they continued to concentrate only on weight, they correctly predicted that the side with the greater weight would go down. The 17-year-olds considered both weight and distance, but since they had not arrived at the rule for solving this problem, they simply

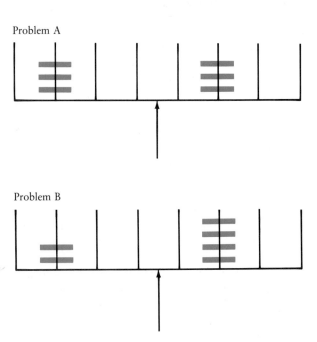

Problem A

Problem B

FIGURE 16.3   *The balance beams used by Siegler and his colleagues to demonstrate the development of different problem-solving strategies. In problem A the weights are equal but distance is varied; in problem B both weight and distance from the fulcrum are varied. Surprisingly, 5-year-olds, who use faulty reasoning, outperform adolescents on problem B (see text). (From Siegler, 1976.)*

muddled through, performing better than chance, but not very well.

These results challenge the notion that adolescents achieve a new general mode of thought. Only a quarter of the 17-year-olds demonstrated the ability to solve the balance-beam problem in all its forms, whereas if the acquisition of formal operational thinking were universal, the whole group would have been expected to find the solution. Such evidence suggests that the increased problem-solving skills of adolescents, rather than demonstrating a global, qualitative change in modes of thinking, are better described as the gradual acquisition of more powerful rules that can be applied to particular problem-solving situations with increasing reliability.

A changing relation of thought to language

Scholars associated with several theoretical traditions believe that an increased ability to use abstract verbal concepts is central to such characteristics of adolescent thought as the ability to conceptualize alternative worlds and plan future ways of life (Vygotsky, 1934/1987; Werner & Kaplan, 1952). This new level of ability is evident both in the way adolescents make sense of unfamiliar words and in the way they make inferences from relations between familiar words.

Heinz Werner and Bernard Kaplan (1952) devised a clever way to show how children figure out the meanings of unfamiliar words. They made up a series of sentences, each of which contained a nonsense word whose meaning the child had to figure out from the context. For example:

1. You can't fill anything with a contavish.
2. The more you take out of a contavish, the larger it gets.
3. Before the house is finished, the walls must have contavishes.
4. You can't feel or touch a contavish.
5. A bottle has only one contavish.
6. John fell into a contavish in the road.

These sentences were presented one at a time. Each time a definition for "contavish" was decided on, the next sentence was presented, until the whole set was included. The children in the sample ranged from 9 to 12 years old. The 9- and 10-year-olds were more likely to try to figure out each sentence as a separate entity, ignoring the fact that the same word was present and must make sense in all the sentences. So, for example, a 9-year-old might respond to sentence 3 by saying that before the house is finished the walls must have paint and to sentence 4 by saying that you can't feel or touch air. Such children were unlikely to come up with a common definition for "contavish" that could be used in all of the sentences.

By contrast, 11- and 12-year-old children often had difficulty coming up with a good definition of "contavish" in the first sentence or two (as did we when we first encountered this research), but they were able to compare the possible meanings in each sentence and eventually find a meaning that fitted all of the cases ("hole").

The complementary ability to build analogies such as "day is to night as ____ is to dark" also seems to develop during adolescence (Levinson & Carpenter, 1974; Lunzer, 1965). This kind of problem is encountered on many IQ tests and on the Miller Analogies Test, which is widely used in the United States as one of the criteria for evaluating candidates for admission to graduate school.

Philip Levinson and Robert Carpenter (1974) presented children 9 through 15 years old with two kinds of analogies in order to distinguish between abstract and concrete modes of thinking about words. The first kind of analogy, which they referred to as "real" or "true" analogies, were of the form "Bird is to air as fish is to ____ ." The concepts they embodied were expressed more concretely in the second kind of analogy, which the researchers referred to as quasi-analogies: "A bird uses air; a fish uses ____ ."

The 9-year-olds found the quasi-analogies significantly easier to grasp than the true analogies. The 15-year-olds found quasi-analogies and true analogies equally easy to solve. Thus the ability to coordinate isolated word meanings into a single logically consistent system seems to be a key achievement of adolescent thought.

The experiments on the development of verbal concepts suggest that new structures of word meaning begin to take shape during adolescence (Sternberg & Powell, 1983; Vygotsky, 1934/1987). These studies do not contradict the idea that a new form of logic contributes to adolescent thinking, but they demonstrate that changes in the structure and use of language, as well as in the logic of problem solving, are important aspects of adolescent cognitive development.

The cultural-context perspective

The cultural-context approach to adolescent thought begins with an observation similar to Inhelder and Piaget's: qualitatively new modes of thought become prominent as teenagers prepare to adopt adult roles. Both approaches start by analyzing the structure of adult activity. Whereas Piaget sought a single new logic underlying all adult thought, the cultural-context theorists emphasize variation in the contexts of adult activity and the consequent heterogeneity of adult thought processes. Thus these theorists believe that it is necessary to analyze the structure of activity and the scripts encountered in various kinds of settings that adults frequent. (See Box 16.1.)

To the extent that different contexts require different degrees of systematic thought, the cultural-context perspective leads one to expect variability in the kind of thinking exercised in different contexts; in particular, in the likelihood that someone would use formal operational thought. In this respect, the cultural-context position is similar to the approach Piaget (1972) adopted when he proposed that systematic, theoretically precise thinking is most likely to appear where it is most demanded. This perspective differs from Piaget's, however, in its assumption that all cultures have contexts that require some formal operational thinking; thus adolescents in all cultures can be expected to use formal operational thought in some contexts. What is universal from this perspective is the acquisition of the ability to think systematically about systems. What is variable is the contexts in which such ability will be used. This approach emphasizes that Inhelder and Piaget's experiments are based on the kinds of activity that scientists are assumed to engage in and that schoolchildren are exposed to when they are taught principles of science. According to the cultural-context perspective, it is inappropriate to use these specialized scientific procedures as the standard for assessing formal operations in general. Instead, formal operational thinking, like all other forms of thinking, should be regarded as dependent on the specific properties of an activity and the context in which it is occurring. Without denying that formal operational procedures can come to play a role in people's thinking in different cultures, psychologists who favor a cultural-context approach start by analyzing actual activities, finding occasions when formal operational thinking is required and therefore when it is likely to be manifested.

A common occasion that requires formal operational thought is the event called "planning a holiday meal." The following example was provided by Peg Griffin, a sociolinguist, who obtained it from a 40-year-old college-educated woman who declared on the basis of reading Piaget that she "did not have formal operations."

On the holiday in question it is customary to eat one of several main dishes: turkey, goose, or ham. The choice of the main course depends on several variables: What is available? How expensive is each of the alternatives? Is anyone coming who is on a low-cholesterol diet? Is anyone a vegetarian? Do the guests like to try new dishes, or are they meat-and-potatoes people? If turkey is on sale and a lot of people are expected, turkey can be very tempting. Goose, on the other hand, is more unusual, but the fattiness may bother guests who worry about cholesterol.

These calculations do not stop with the main course. If the hostess serves turkey, she has to serve cranberry sauce; with ham, Cumberland sauce is essential. What about starches? Stuffing? Rice? Potatoes? Sweet potatoes? What about the soup? Clam chowder goes with turkey, but will it go with goose, or would a clear broth be better?

Social factors also have to be taken into account. First, who is coming to dinner? Are all the guests old friends who expect a turkey, or are some "important personages" also invited? Social factors also include such elements as how to present and serve the food and how to keep everyone happy (who will sit next to chatty Aunt Betty or deaf Uncle Norm)?

The ability of this woman to engage in such thinking while she stands at the meat counter on the eve of a holiday illustrates several essential features of formal operational thinking. First, she is able to sort through several variables, holding one constant while she works on the others ("Hmmm, ham, candied sweet potatoes, cranberries . . . uh-oh, no cranberries, gotta start over again. . . . Besides, John keeps begging for goose, but will one goose be enough for 12 people? Two would make dinner too expensive. Well, let's see . . ."). Second, this kind of thinking clearly is a form of planning. Third, the plan results in a "structured whole" organized by concepts significant to the shopper; one of them is the concept "holiday meal." Finally, the shopper is able to reflect on and describe her thought processes.

This example differs from Inhelder and Piaget's characterization of formal operations in that the

John decided to bake a cake. But he ran out of some ingredients. So:
He used margarine instead of butter for the shortening
He used honey instead of sugar for the sweetening and
He used brown whole wheat flour instead of regular white flour.

The cake turned out great because it was so moist.

John thought that the reason the cake was so great was the honey. He thought that the type of shortening (butter or margarine) or the type of flour really didn't matter.

 = Great cake

What should he do to prove this point?

He can bake the cake again but use sugar instead of honey, and still use margarine and brown whole wheat flour.

He can bake the cake again but this time use sugar, butter, and regular white flour.

He can bake the cake again still using honey, but this time using butter and regular white flour.

FIGURE 16.4   *A combination-of-variables task involving an everyday situation. Children were asked to choose one of the three hypothetical problem-solving strategies. When the outcome of the hypothetical event was positive, as in this case, neither children nor adults used rigorously logical testing procedures. (From Tschirgi, 1980.)*

shopper fails to consider literally *all* of the possible combinations of relevant factors. Instead, like the people in the market deciding which size of garlic powder is a better buy, she pursues each of the variables in her problem only long enough to come up with a usable solution. Nevertheless, the process by which she plans the meal clearly involves the kind of systematic variation of alternatives indicative of formal operations.

Several recent experimental studies suggest that it is quite common for people to reason differently in everyday situations than they do in formal experiments designed as logical puzzles (Lave, 1988; Linn, 1983; Tschirgi, 1980). Marcia Linn, Tina de Benedic-

tus, and Kevin Delucchi (1982) compared reasoning performance in Piagetian-style problems with reasoning about the truthfulness of advertising. The researchers were questioning Piaget's hypothesis that once individuals can engage in formal reasoning, it becomes a general characteristic of their thinking. They found virtually no correlation between the quality of reasoning used in the Piagetian problems and that used in the advertising problems. Apparently, then, the participants did not use one single characteristic mode of thinking. In any case, the level of formal reasoning was so low in both kinds of problems that it cast doubt on the universality of this mode of thought among adults in the first place.

BOX 16.1

Formal Operations in a Nonliterate Culture

In a great many of the situations that seem to call for the use of formal operations in our everyday lives, most of us use written notes as a means of keeping track of our thoughts. Even scientists, who are likely candidates for having achieved the stage of formal operations, routinely resort to paper and pencil or a computer when they have to sort through a large number of variables to solve a problem. Only rarely, as in a chess game or a psychological test, does the thinking have to go on entirely inside a person's head.

Attempts to determine the universality of a new mode of thinking associated with the transition to adulthood are undermined by the fact that many cultures do not have writing systems or the formal scientific procedures that tests of formal operations typically model. Consequently, the standardized procedures are completely alien to many cultures. Fortunately, however, research by anthropologists familiar with psychological theories has begun to provide evidence on complex problem solving in a variety of settings (Hutchins, 1980; Rogoff & Lave, 1984).

An interesting instance of complex problem solving in a nonscientific culture is seen in the navigational practices of South Sea islanders (Goodenough, 1953; Gladwin, 1970). Until such devices as magnetic compasses became readily available after World War II, natives of Polynesia and Micronesia, groups of islands northeast of New Guinea, sailed their small outrigger canoes over hundreds of miles of ocean to get from one tiny island to another without the help of conventional instruments. Even very experienced sailors from other parts of the world would not presume to sail such distances without a compass for fear of sailing off into the vast Pacific and probable death.

The technique the islanders have developed for finding their way over the sea requires an external record-keeping system, a hypothetical reference point, and constant estimates of speed—all combined in a single problem-solving process that lasts as long as the voyage itself. It depends heavily on 14 distinctive "star paths"; that is, a set of stars that always rise from the same point on the eastern horizon and set at the same place in the west, appearing to move in an unvarying arc across the sky. Instruction in how to navigate with this system begins in adolescence and continues for several years. A practiced navigator is able to construct the entire "star compass" mentally from a glimpse of two or three stars on the horizon (see diagram). As Edwin Hutchins phrases it, "The star compass is an abstraction which can be oriented as a whole by determining the orientation of any part" (1983:195).

The star compass is only one part of the navigator's mental model of the voyage. An essential additional element is a "reference island" whose bearing on the star compass is known for any island from which a boat might set out. The term "reference island" is placed in quotation marks because in many cases the island is purely hypothetical, a reference point needed only to make calculations of relative distance from the destination.

In the actual process of sailing, navigators mentally combine the information about the star paths,

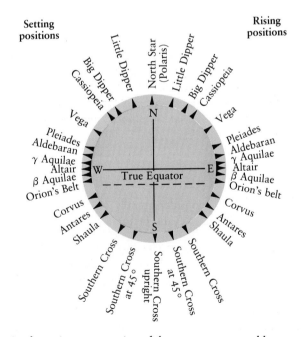

A schematic representation of the star compass used by navigators in the Caroline Islands to guide their outrigger canoes from one island to another. (From Goodenough, 1953.)

Navigators from one Caroline Island conduct a lesson in how to use the star compass.

the location of the reference island, and their rate of speed in order to discover their current position and distance from their destination. So skillful are they at making these calculations that they can tack away from their destination to catch the wind and still keep track of their location and find their way.

Some of the earlier researchers who investigated this kind of navigation believed that the navigators could not talk logically about the system they were using (Gladwin, 1970). Their explanations seemed to be inconsistent with the anthropologists' analysis of their navigational system. If they were indeed incapable of describing their own thought processes, the claim that their problem solving demonstrated formal operations would be considerably weakened.

Hutchins (1983) showed, however, that the navigators' explanations were perfectly logical for the system they were using. The apparent illogicality arose from a basic cultural difference in the way people think about compasses and relative motion. It seemed obvious to Gladwin that the canoe moved across the water while the islands remained still. The navigators, however, had developed their system by imagining that the boat stood still while the reference island moved. When Hutchins took their accounts completely seriously, he was able to show that the anthro-pologists had simply failed to work out the full system.

Although Micronesian navigators demonstrated that they can engage in formal operational thought at sea, they showed no such ability when they were presented with a standard Piagetian combination-of-variables task (Gladwin, 1970). Gladwin presented adolescents and adults with stacks of poker chips and asked them to find all the possible combinations of colors. Even expert navigators responded to this task at a very low level within Piaget's framework; most paired only a few colors, falling far short of the formal operational ideal. Only a few young men who had attended high school managed to display some aspects of systematic combinatorial activity. These young men, however, had not been trained in the sailors' system of navigation!

These results suggest that formal operational thinking may occur far more widely than the evidence from typical experiments suggests, and that this type of thinking may indeed be universal in human groups. At the same time, the data make it clear that formal operations do not uniformly replace earlier modes of thought. Their use remains highly restricted to contexts in which they are appropriate and in which the individual has had the greatest experience.

Judith Tschirgi (1980) found that even when two problems were analogous, the kind of reasoning used to solve each one depended on whether the outcome of the situation was one the subject viewed as positive (and hence wanted to maintain) or negative (and hence wanted to change). An example is seen in Figure 16.4. The boy has baked a cake with margarine, honey, and whole wheat flour, and the cake is a great success because it is so moist. The boy hypothesizes that the cause of the success is the honey. The question is: What should he change when he bakes another cake to check his hypothesis? In the negative case, the cake is too runny and the boy again hypothesizes that honey is the crucial factor. The question remains: What must be done to test this hypothesis?

The logic of these problems is the same. In each case, the best way to test the hypothesis is to hold the kind of shortening and flour constant while varying

Even such everyday adult tasks as shopping may require the kind of systematic thinking that Piaget referred to as formal operations.

the kind of sweetener. But in this experiment, only when the cake was a failure did participants agree that the boy should substitute sugar for honey. When the cake was a success, they kept honey constant and changed other factors. College students were as likely to follow this pattern as second-graders, an indication that this illogical pattern may be a general characteristic of human reasoning. As Tschirgi comments, when people are confronted with an everyday problem, their expectations about the outcome, rather than their underlying cognitive competencies, control the way they reason (see also Linn, 1983).

The shortcuts taken by Griffin's shopper and the errors of the participants in Tschirgi's study do not conform to Piaget's idealized scientific solution, but even studies of the way experts solve problems suggest that such unscientific habits are typical (Chi, Glaser, & Rees, 1982). In fact, the systematic reasoning of the shopper displays more aspects of formal operations than skilled adults often display when they solve highly demanding intellectual problems. Expert chess players, for example, do not usually run through all possible combinations of moves, preferring instead to match the overall board pattern to a successful pattern they recall from past experience (Chase & Simon, 1973). Similarly, scientists follow their intuitions and take shortcuts that clearly violate the canons of scientific reasoning (Latour, 1987).

These data fit with Piaget's final speculation (1972) that formal operations are acquired in a context-specific manner, casting doubt on his and Inhelder's earlier description of formal operational thinking as a totally systematic pattern that comes into routine use during adolescence.

The evidence from both the information-processing and cultural-context approaches has blurred the concept, central to traditional Piagetian theory, of a discontinuity between middle childhood and adolescence (Flavell, 1982, 1985). According to these approaches, the improvements in cognitive ability during this transition may appear either continuous or discontinuous, depending on the depth of the young person's knowledge about a particular context or problem. Consequently, to resolve the question of whether thinking undergoes a stagelike change in adolescence, we must assess the extent to which adolescent thinking is systematic in a variety of contexts. Only if a qualitatively new mode of thinking appears across a broad range of contexts is it legitimate to conclude that a stagelike change has taken place.

ADOLESCENT THINKING ABOUT THE SOCIAL ORDER

The experimental tasks discussed thus far have been confined to the world of objects (chemicals, balance beams, groceries) and the relationships between them. In this section we examine the characteristics of adolescents' thought processes when they are asked to reason about issues of much greater personal concern: why their society is organized as it is; what might be done to improve it; how to be a moral person in a world where immoral behavior is so prevalent.

Thinking about Politics

Although children as young as 9 think seriously about the nature of society (Furth, 1980), they still have little understanding of political issues, according to Joseph Adelson and his colleagues. On the basis of interviews with hundreds of children and adolescents in the United States, Germany, and England, Adelson wrote:

> Unable to imagine social reality in the abstract, he [the child] enters adolescence with only the weakest sense of social institutions, of their structure and functions, or of that invisible network of norms and principles which link these institutions to each other. Furthermore, the failure to achieve abstractness does not permit him to understand, except in a most rough and ready way, those concepts essential to political thought — such ideas as authority, rights, liberty, equity, interests, representation, and so on. (1972:109)

Adelson and his colleagues investigated how young people's reasoning about politics changes during the course of adolescence. To overcome national differences in knowledge about political figures and the fact that adolescents may have little specific knowledge about their political system, they asked teenagers to imagine that a thousand people move to a Pacific island where they have to set up a new society. The researchers then posed a series of questions about how the new society should be organized. Some questions required the young people to choose among different forms of government and to decide on the laws governing personal freedom and the rights of minorities. Others posed such hypothetical problems as whether a

dissenting religious group should be allowed to refuse vaccinations.

These researchers found a major change in adolescents' reasoning about politics sometime around the age of 14 (Adelson & O'Neil, 1966; Adelson, Green, & O'Neil, 1969). This change was so little affected by such factors as gender, social class, and nationality that Adelson declared: "A twelve-year-old German youngster's ideas of politics are closer to those of a twelve-year-old American than to those of his fifteen-year-old brother" (1972:108). The change was particularly evident in three areas: the way adolescents reason about laws, the level of social control they think appropriate, and the frequency of their appeal to overarching political ideals when they express their views.

Laws

Whereas 12-to-13-year-olds respond to questions about society in terms of concrete people and events, 15-to-16-year-olds respond in terms of abstract principles, as in these answers to the question "What is the purpose of laws?" (Adelson, 1972:108):

12-TO-13-YEAR-OLDS

> They do it, like in school, so that people don't get hurt. If we had no laws, people could go around killing people. So people don't steal or kill.

15-TO-16-YEAR-OLDS

> To ensure safety and enforce the government. To limit what people can do. They are basically guidelines for people.

In their responses to questions about whether the law should allow the government to take private property for public use, the older adolescents demonstrated that they could reason hypothetically, taking many aspects of the problem into account. Adelson presented them with the case of a government that wanted to build a highway through land that an owner refused to sell. An older adolescent answers:

> If it's a strategic point like the only way through a mountain maybe without tunneling, then I'm not too sure what I'd do. If it's a nice level stretch of plain that if you didn't have it you'd have to build a curve in the road, I think that the government might go ahead and put a curve in the road. (1972:114)

Social control

The way 12-to-13-year-olds think about social control becomes evident when they are asked about crime, punishment, and retribution. In response after response, the youngest adolescents suggest that severe punishment is the best way to deal with lawbreakers, leading Adelson to conclude that "the young adolescent's authoritarianism is omnipresent" (1972:119). One such boy who was asked how to teach people not to commit crimes in the future answered:

> Jail is usually the best thing, but there are others. . . . In the nineteenth century they used to torture people for doing things. Now I think the best place to teach people is in solitary confinement. (1972:116)

As adolescents grow older, ideas of reform and rehabilitation begin to enter into their answers. Older adolescents also conceive of the beneficial side of laws, whereas younger ones think of laws only as a way of keeping people from behaving badly. When a law seems not to be working, older adolescents suggest that perhaps the law should be changed, while younger adolescents tend to say that the level of punishment should be increased.

The younger adolescents in Adelson's study seem to find it difficult to conceive of social and political regulation as ongoing processes, assuming instead that "what is, has been; what is, will be." What "has been" for them is a world in which they were told what to do, so they project this regime into the future. The older adolescents, perhaps because they have experienced the need to be responsible for their own good behavior, seem capable of reasoning about a world in which they must provide their own rules and regulations voluntarily.

Adelson points out that this mid-adolescent shift in reasoning about politics corresponds to changes that Inhelder and Piaget found in their studies of scientific problem solving. He suggests that the thinking of the younger adolescents, with its emphasis on one right answer that is right in all cases, doesn't require formal operational thinking, whereas conceptions of modifiable, flexible, well-balanced political systems do. Younger adolescents are only beginning to engage in real formal operational thinking and are not yet capable of some of the more difficult operations; older adolescents are more likely to explore all possibilities.

Political idealism

In this century many adolescents have been attracted to political and religious ideologies. Young people were prominent in the civil rights movement in the United States in the 1960s and in China in the late 1980s.

According to many students of adolescence, young people are both pushed and pulled toward ideologies (Coles, 1967; Erikson, 1963; Inhelder & Piaget, 1958). They are pushed by their desire to become independent of their parents and to show that they can govern their own affairs; they are pulled by a seemingly coherent system that offers an alternative to the imperfections of the adult world.

With the search for inconsistencies between long-held beliefs—one aspect of adolescents' ability to think logically—comes an increased interest in ideal systems of thought. Jerome Kagan (1972) suggests that this tendency arises when adolescents use the following sort of syllogism:

Parents are omnipotent and omniscient.

My parent has lost a job, or failed to understand me, or behaved irrationally (or any other liability the teenager cares to select).

If my parents were omniscient, they would not be tainted with failure and vulnerability.

Having concluded that their parents are not perfect, they confront a new psychological problem. Up until now, parents have been their role models. The adolescent has identified with them and been attached to them since early infancy. What is to replace them? Identification with a person or system that is ideal is one possible answer.

Since no ideal person or political system has yet appeared on earth, adolescents' newly adopted ideologies are frequently utopian or religious. This proclivity was especially visible in the civil rights and commune movements of the 1960s, both of which drew heavily for support on adolescents who saw in them a consistent alternative to the imperfect society in which they lived (Berger, 1981; Coles, 1967).

Although adolescents have traditionally been viewed as idealistic and can think about ideal systems, most teenagers have not worked out any systematic alternatives to the existing political order for themselves. With rare exceptions, when asked directly to

Their increased understanding makes teenagers critical of society and eager to suggest better ways of doing things.

imagine an ideal society, teenage respondents came up with such platitudes as these:

> A society that everyone gets along and knows each other's problems and try to sit down and figure out each other's problem and get along like that.

> I think right now that the only society I would have would be the exact same one as we have now, although it does have its faults, I think we do have a good government now.

> Well, I would set up a society of helping out people like when there would be crime, like I said before, I would put these criminals in there for life because when they get out they would want to do it again and all that. (Adelson, 1975:74–75)

Many young people become increasingly cynical about political processes (Torney-Purta, 1990). They can see the problems and inconsistencies in political life but they are unable to work out practical solutions. Table 16.2 shows adolescents' pessimistic responses to the question "Would it ever be possible to eliminate . . . (crime, poverty, racial prejudice)?" In general, the older adolescents are pretty certain that political solutions to the world's ills are unlikely. At

TABLE 16.2
Percentage of Pessimistic Responses, by Age, to the Question "Would It Ever Be Possible to Eliminate . . . ?"

Age	Crime	Poverty	Racial Prejudice
12	48%	9%	45%
14	66	40	80
16	72	54	85
18	75	53	76

Source: Adelson, 1975.

the same time, since they are in the process of defining themselves in contrast to their parents' generation, they are still attracted to the promises of someone who declares that, given the right beliefs and behavior, a more rational organization of life on earth *is* possible.

Thinking about Moral Issues

When adolescents think about their own and others' behavior, they become preoccupied by such questions as: What is right? What is wrong? What principles should I base my behavior on and use to judge the behavior of others? Evidence suggests that the processes people use to think about such questions, like those they use to think about science problems or politics, change during adolescence.

The single largest body of research on the development of moral reasoning during adolescence has focused on Lawrence Kohlberg's elaboration of Piaget's ideas (Modgil & Modgil, 1986; Power, Higgins, & Kohlberg, 1989). Kohlberg, it may be recalled (Chapter

14, p. 527), posited three levels of moral reasoning, each consisting of two stages. (Table 16.3 summarizes these levels and stages; a more detailed description of them appears in Table 14.2, pp. 528–529.) According to Kohlberg, moral reasoning at the start of middle childhood is at the *preconventional* level; in other words, children's reasoning is not based on social conventions or laws. Stages 1 and 2 fall within this level. Toward the end of middle childhood, children attain the level of *conventional* moral reasoning, so named because they are said to begin taking social conventions into account. Kohlberg called stage 3 reasoning "good-child morality" because being moral now means to live up to the expectations of one's family, teachers, and other significant people in one's life.

TABLE 16.3	
Kohlberg's Stages of Moral Reasoning	
Level and Stage	**What Is Right**
Preconventional Stage 1. Heteronomous morality (reasoning based on obedience and punishment)	To avoid breaking rules backed by punishment; obedience for its own sake.
Stage 2. Instrumental reasoning	Following rules only when it is to someone's immediate interest; acting to meet one's own interests and needs and letting others do the same.
Conventional Stage 3. Good-child morality	Living up to what is expected by people close to you or what people generally expect of you in your role as son, brother, friend, etc.
Stage 4. Law-and-order morality	Fulfilling the actual duties to which you have agreed. Laws are to be upheld except in extreme cases, when they conflict with other fixed social duties.
Postconventional Stage 5. Social-contract reasoning	Being aware that people hold a variety of values and opinions, that most values and rules are relative to the group that holds them.
Stage 6. Universal ethical principles	Following self-chosen ethical principles. Particular laws or social agreements are usually valid because they rest on such principles.

Source: Kohlberg, 1976.

Moral reasoning at stage 4 is like that at stage 3 except its focus shifts from relations between individuals to relations between the individual and the group. People who reason at stage 4 believe that the point of view of society is primary and accept its existing laws and customs. Moral behavior from this point of view is behavior that maintains the social order. For this reason, stage 4 is sometimes referred to as the law-and-order stage (Brown & Herrnstein, 1975:289). Stage 4 reasoning begins to appear during adolescence, but stage 3 is still the dominant mode of reasoning about moral questions (Colby et al., 1983).

Kohlberg believed that moral thinking in stages 3 and 4 depends on partial attainment of the ability to engage in formal operational reasoning, in particular the ability to consider simultaneously all *existing* factors relevant to moral choices (Kohlberg, 1984). People who are reasoning at stages 3 and 4, however, are still reasoning concretely because they do not yet consider all *possible* relations, nor do they form abstract hypotheses about what is moral.

With the transition from stage 4 to stage 5 in Kohlberg's scheme comes another basic shift in the level of moral judgment. Reasoning at stage 5 requires people to go beyond social conventions to more abstract principles of right and wrong. This perspective, which he called *postconventional,* involves a social-contract orientation to moral problems. People still accept and value the social system, but instead of insisting on maintaining it as it is, they are open to democratic processes of change and to continual exploration of possibilities for improving upon the existing social contract. Recognizing that laws are sometimes in conflict with moral principles, they become creators as well as maintainers of laws. Kohlberg found that stage 5 moral reasoning does not appear until early adulthood, and then only rarely.

People reach stage 6 when they make moral judgments in accordance with universal ethical principles that transcend the rules of individual societies. The idea that human life is of supreme value and cannot be taken under any circumstances is such a universal moral principle. A person who reasons at this level believes that certain precepts are sacrosanct no matter what the personal consequences. The civil disobedience practiced by Mahatma Gandhi in India and Martin Luther King, Jr., in the United States exemplifies behavior based on Kohlberg's stage 6 reasoning.

As we noted in Chapter 14, stage 6 reasoning is rarely encountered. But under extraordinary circumstances, otherwise ordinary people will put their own lives at risk because of moral beliefs guided by stage 6 reasoning. Such was the case during World War II, when many European Gentiles rescued Jews scheduled for extermination. According to Samuel and Pearl Oliner (1988), most of them were motivated by ethical principles that they believed apply to all of humanity, the hallmark of stage 6 moral reasoning.

Despite its comprehensiveness and its ability to inspire research, Kohlberg's theory of moral development has had a somewhat stormy history (Kurtines & Gewirtz, 1991, and Shweder, 1982, are representative discussions; Kohlberg, 1984, contains an extensive reply to his critics). Several studies have confirmed that children progress through Kohlberg's stages of moral reasoning in the predicted order (Walker, 1986), but others have failed to do so. Instead of steadily progressing upward, subjects sometimes regress in their development or seem to skip a stage (Kuhn, 1976; Gilligan & Murphy, 1979; Kohlberg & Kramer, 1969; Kurtines & Grief, 1974).

Another controversial assumption of Kohlberg's theory is that his levels of moral reasoning correspond to the levels of cognitive development described by Piaget. The expected correspondences (summarized in Table 16.4) have been found by some researchers (Colby et al., 1983; Walker, 1986) but not others (Haan, Weiss, & Johnson, 1982). Some investigators have taken these failures as evidence that Kohlberg's stage theory was incorrectly formulated (e.g., Hoffman, 1980), but others argue that the problem lies in the way the data have been interpreted (Walker, 1988).

One problem of interpretation arises from the procedures used to score the answers to Kohlberg's questions (Kurtines & Gewirtz, 1984). Recall from Chapter 14 that Kohlberg presented dilemmas in the form of stories and asked children to reason about them in a give-and-take interview session. Some investigators report having trouble sorting interview answers reliably into the correct categories (Kurtines & Grief, 1974). Unreliable scoring makes it difficult to evaluate the accuracy with which the theory predicts reality. In response to this criticism, Ann Colby and Kohlberg (1984) created a standardized scoring scheme that they claim is both easy to use and reliable. Using the revised procedures, Lawrence Walker (1986) found improved correspondence between the theory and the data.

Kohlberg's theory is also criticized for failing to address the question of how hypothetical reasoning

---

TABLE 16.4
Parallel Stages of Cognitive and Moral Development

Cognitive Stage	Moral Stage
Preoperations The "symbolic function" appears but thinking is marked by centration and irreversibility.	**Stage 1. Heteronomy** The physical consequences of an action and the dictates of authorities define right and wrong.
Concrete operations The objective characteristics of an object are separated from action related to it; classification, seriation, and conservation skills develop.	**Stage 2. Exchange** Right is defined as serving one's own interests and desires, and cooperative interaction is based on terms of simple exchange.
Beginning formal operations The ability to use propositional logic develops.	**Stage 3. Expectations** Emphasis is on good-person stereotypes and concern for approval.
Early basic formal operations The hypothetico-deductive approach emerges, involving the ability to develop possible relations among variables and to organize experimental analyses.	**Stage 4. Social system and conscience** Focus is on maintaining the social order by obeying the law and doing one's duty.
Consolidated basic formal operations Operations are now completely exhaustive and systematic.	**Stage 5. Prior rights and social contract** Right is defined by standards that have been agreed upon by the whole society.

Source: Walker, 1980.

---

about moral dilemmas is related to actual moral behavior (Gilligan & Belenky, 1980; Kohlberg, Hickey, & Scharf, 1972). It is commonly observed that perfectly respectable, law-abiding citizens who are likely to score at stage 3 or 4 on Kohlberg's scale sometimes fail to help strangers in need, or riot at football games, causing great pain and loss to others. Clearly the ability to reason about morality does not inevitably lead to moral behavior.

One well-known study did support a positive relationship between moral reasoning and action. It was conducted at the University of California in the mid-1960s and enlisted the participation of students who were involved in the free-speech movement there (Haan, Smith, & Block, 1968). Some of their activities, such as engaging in sit-ins to attest to their beliefs, put these students at risk of arrest for civil disobedience. Hypothetical moral dilemmas were described both to

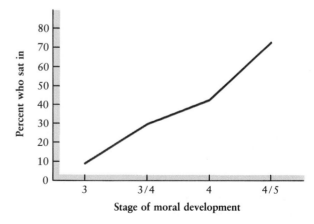

FIGURE 16.5   *The percentage of students who participated in the Berkeley sit-ins increases as the level of their assessed moral reasoning increases, illustrating a link between moral reasoning and moral action.*

students who actually engaged in sit-ins and to other students who did not. As Figure 16.5 indicates, students who risked arrest by sitting in scored at higher moral stages than those who did not, providing support for Kohlberg's claim that levels of moral reasoning are related to levels of moral action.

Sex differences in moral reasoning

Piaget attributed the new, autonomous form of moral reasoning that appears in middle childhood to the ways children in that age group play games with their peers (see Chapter 14). He also claimed to find clear sex differences in children's play: girls seemed to be more interested in elaborating social relations, whereas boys seemed to be more interested in rules and infractions. Insofar as some people consider the kinds of games played by boys to be more advanced cognitively (as Piaget did), this line of reasoning leads naturally to the inference that there are sex differences in moral development as well. Both this line of reasoning and the evidence gathered to test it are hotly disputed (Baumrind, 1986; Walker, 1986, 1991; Walker, de Vries, & Trevethan, 1987).

In some of the first tests of moral reasoning in adolescents, boys appeared to score higher than girls (Haan, Langer, & Kohlberg, 1976; Holstein, 1976). The data in Figure 16.6, taken from Constance Holstein's (1976) study of moral reasoning, display a pattern of results that sparked a great deal of controversy. Adolescent boys were most frequently found to be in stage 4, whereas adolescent girls most frequently scored at stage 3. In studies of adults, men's answers

almost always displayed reasoning at a level higher than stage 3, whereas women's responses were hardly ever at the level of stage 5.

Data such as Holstein's spurred Carol Gilligan (1977, 1982) to question whether Kohlberg's description had left out a dimension of morality of particular concern to women. She argued that women's responses to moral dilemmas are lower on Kohlberg's scale than are those of men because women's moral thinking is oriented toward interpersonal relationships and coupled with an ethic of caring and responsibility for other people. This difference in what she referred to as "moral orientation" inclines women to suggest altruism and self-sacrifice rather than to invoke rights and rules as the solutions to interpersonal problems and moral dilemmas.

In effect, Gilligan was arguing that men and women really use different moral criteria. According to the criteria that Gilligan found to be of importance to women, stage 3, which emphasizes mutual caring, should be ranked more highly than Kohlberg's stage 4.

Gilligan illustrated this difference in moral orientation by contrasting men's and women's responses to questions about morality:

A 25-YEAR-OLD MAN'S RESPONSE TO THE QUESTION "WHAT DOES THE WORD 'MORALITY' MEAN TO YOU?"

Nobody in the world knows the answer. I think it is recognizing the right of the individual, the rights of other individuals, not interfering with those rights. Act as fairly as you would have them treat you. I think it is basically to preserve the human

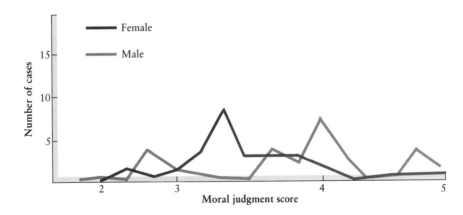

FIGURE 16.6 *The distribution of moral judgment scores for a sample of male and female 16-year-olds. Note that in this study the most frequent score for females is near level 3, whereas the most frequent score for males is in the range of level 4. (From Holstein, 1976.)*

being's right to existence. I think that is the most important. Secondly, the human being's right to do as he pleases, again without interfering with somebody else's rights.

A 25-YEAR-OLD WOMAN'S RESPONSE TO THE QUESTION ''IS THERE REALLY SOME CORRECT SOLUTION TO MORAL PROBLEMS OR IS EVERYBODY'S OPINION EQUALLY CORRECT?''

No, I don't think that everyone's opinion is equally right. I think that in some situations there may be opinions that are equally valid, and one could conscientiously adopt one of several courses of action. But there are other situations in which I think there are right and wrong answers, that sort of inhere in the nature of existence, of all individuals here who need to live with each other to live. We need to depend upon each other, and hopefully it is not only a physical need but a need of fulfillment in ourselves, that a person's life is enriched by cooperating with other people and striving to live in harmony with everybody else, and to that end, there are right and wrong, there are things which promote that end and that move away from it. (1982:19–20)

In Gilligan's view, these answers capture the difference between male moral reasoning, which she sees as focused on individual rights, and female moral reasoning, which she believes is based on a sense of responsibility for other people.

A well-developed sense of empathy is an important element in the moral development of adolescents.

At present there is no consensus with respect to male/female differences in moral development, and no simple resolution to the disputes about them is in sight. Contrary to expectations based on either Piaget's analysis of game playing or Gilligan's hypothesis, sex differences in moral reasoning show up relatively rarely, and when they do appear, they are small (Nunner-Winkler, 1984; Rest, 1979; Snarey, 1985; Walker, 1986, 1988, 1991). In a review of 80 studies of moral reasoning involving 152 groups of subjects, Walker and de Vries (1985) found only 22 that showed significant sex differences, and in nine of them females scored higher on Kohlberg's scale than males. Beyond the test data there remains the unanswered question of whether these and other hypothesized differences in reasoning about morality manifest themselves in actual moral behavior.

Cultural variation in moral reasoning

Standard studies of cross-cultural variability in moral reasoning, like those of formal operational reasoning, reveal far greater differences between cultural groups than between the two sexes (Snarey, 1985). Although there are some exceptions (Shweder, Mahopatra, & Miller, 1987), most studies show that people who live in relatively small, face-to-face communities in technologically unsophisticated societies rarely reason beyond stage 3 on Kohlberg's scale and often justify their decisions at the level of stage 1 or 2 (Edwards, 1982; Harkness, Edwards, & Super, 1981; Kohlberg, 1969; Tietjen & Walker, 1985) (contrast the scores in Figure 16.7 with those in Figure 16.6).

Kohlberg explained cross-cultural data such as those in Figure 16.7 by suggesting that cultural differences in social stimulation produce differences in the ability to engage in formal operational reasoning, which in turn explain differences in moral reasoning:

. . . an absence of cognitive stimulation necessary for developing formal logical reasoning may be important in explaining ceilings on moral level. In a Turkish village, for example, full formal operational reasoning appeared to be extremely rare (if the Piagetian technique for intellectual assessment can be considered usable in that setting). Accordingly, one would not expect that principled (Stage 5 or 6) moral reasoning, which requires formal thinking as a base, could develop in that cultural context. (1984:198)

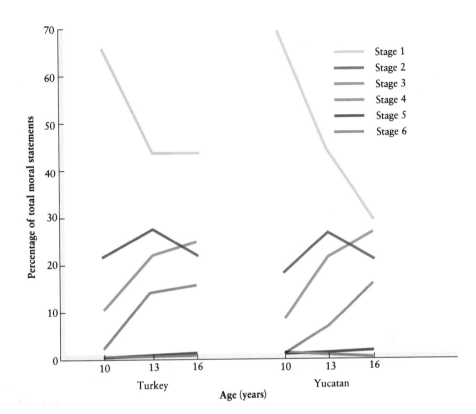

FIGURE 16.7 *Age trends in the moral judgments of boys in small isolated villages in two nations. Note the continuing high incidence of level-1 responses even by 16-year-olds. (From Kohlberg, 1969.)*

Critics have pointed out the unfortunate implications of Kohlberg's willingness to accept the validity of Piagetian techniques and to apply his own moral standards to different cultures. The anthropologist Richard Shweder (1982), for example, claims that culture-specific value judgments built directly into Kohlberg's stage sequence itself make it no more than a justification for the special cultural perspective of Anglo males, inheritors of the political ideology of liberal democracy. Are we to believe, such critics ask, that people who grow up in a traditional Third World village are less moral than the residents of a city in an industrially advanced country (Simpson, 1974)? Isn't it more reasonable to assume that because Turkish villagers live in face-to-face contact with the people who govern their fate, they are bound to give the greatest moral value to the Golden Rule, a morality of caring and responsibility?

The historian Howard Kaminsky (1984) expresses the same doubts:

Is a Stage 6 refusal to support a friend who is wrong superior to a Stage 3 loyalty to that friend? A medieval nobleman would say no, and history suggests to us that if we repudiate the nobleman's sense of right, we are also repudiating the civilization created in resonance with his mentality, as well as those elements of the aristocratic ideal that have formed the modern sense of individuality. . . . [P]ersonal loyalty has obvious virtues that are lost when friendship or affection is made conditional on abstract rightness. (p. 410)

Kohlberg denied claims that bias in his scales fosters the conclusion that some societies, the United States among them, are more moral than others. He echoed the classical position of modern anthropology, that cultures should be thought of as unique configurations of beliefs and institutions that help the social group adapt to both local conditions and universal aspects of life on earth (Boas, 1911; Geertz, 1984). In accord with this relativist view, Kohlberg wrote that "we do not understand how a 'moral ranking' of cultures could either be done or be scientifically useful" (1984:311). In this view, a culture in which stage 3 was the height of moral reasoning would be considered "morally equivalent" to a culture dominated by stage 5 or 6 reasoning, even though the specific reasoning practices could be scored as less "developed" according to Kohlberg's universal criteria.

Kohlberg's position on cultural levels of moral development would be logically consistent, whatever else one thought of it, were it not for the nagging problem that he had already proposed that people of other cultures are at a lower level of cognitive development — not a relative matter. As a result of this crucial link between formal operational thinking and moral judgment, Kohlberg's view is vulnerable to his critics' claims that higher scores on his scale of moral development really do imply "moral superiority" at both individual and cultural levels (e.g., Liebert, 1984; Simpson, 1974).

Despite many uncertainties arising from disagreements about how data about "moral development" should be gathered and interpreted, evidence collected around the world indicates that by the time most people become adults, they are capable of reasoning at a level that corresponds at least to the Golden Rule. That their actions fall short of this basic moral tenet reflects the wry wisdom contained in the old admonition "Do as I say, not as I do."

INTEGRATION OF THE SELF

One of the most widely held ideas about adolescence is that this is the period when the individual forges the basis for a stable adult personality. Teenagers' ability to take several factors into account when they think through a problem, their broader knowledge of society's norms and moral codes, and their increasing awareness that adulthood is approaching all contribute to the establishment of an integrated, adult sense of self.

Changing Attributes of the Self

In Chapter 14 we saw that at about the age of 6, when American children enter school, they begin to think of themselves in comparative terms: Instead of saying (for example), "I am a girl who likes to skate," they begin to

provide such self-descriptions as "I am a better skater than most of my class." A little later they begin explicitly to include the interpersonal consequences of their attributes: "I am a good skater so lots of kids like to skate with me" (see Table 14.9, p. 559).

During adolescence a fourth kind of self-description makes its appearance, in which personal identity is expressed in terms of general beliefs, values, and life plans, as in the following dialogue:

Interviewer: What kind of person are you?
Adolescent: I am someone who believes that everybody is created equal.
Interviewer: Why is that important?
Adolescent: Because I want to work for equal rights for everybody.
Interviewer: What do you mean?
Adolescent: I am going to be a lawyer and take cases and see that everyone gets rights, even if he's very poor or the wrong color or something. (Damon & Hart, 1988:69)

As children enter adolescence, their self-descriptions also shift from relatively concrete attributes (for instance, "I'm a good listener" or "I am easy-going") to more inclusive, higher-order concepts ("I am tolerant"). As Susan Harter (1990:355) points out, "To consider oneself 'sensitive,' one must potentially combine such attributes as being understanding, friendly, and caring."

Another feature that distinguishes the self-concepts of adolescents from those of younger children is the greater variety of attributes they include. In middle childhood, children describe themselves in terms of either their cognitive, physical, and social competence or a global notion of self-worth (Harter, 1982). Adolescents describe themselves in terms of scholastic competence, athletic competence, job competence, physical appearance, social acceptance, close friendship, romantic appeal, and conduct — categories that overlap but are not identical to those that are prominent in middle childhood (Harter, 1990). Moreover, adolescents tailor their descriptions of themselves to the particular context they are being asked about. If they are asked what they are like when they are with their friends or in a class at school, their answers will differ from those they give when they are asked to describe what they are like when they are having dinner at home.

The appearance of "multiple selves" in adolescents' descriptions of themselves makes it necessary for them to deal with the fact that they are, in some sense, different people in different contexts. It is at this point that the question "Who is the real me?" comes to the fore.

Susan Harter (1986) reports that the appearance of several selves, each depending on whom one is with and what role one is fulfilling, is especially troublesome to 14- and 15-year-old Americans. When asked about the contradiction between being nice to some people but not to others, a 13-year-old responded, "I guess I just think about one thing about myself at a time and don't think about the other until the next day" (p. 45). An older adolescent, by contrast, asked about problems in a romantic relationship, replied in a way that indicates her sensitivity to variations in herself as the situation changes: "I hate the fact that I get so nervous! I wish I wasn't so inhibited. The real me is talkative: I want to be natural, but I can't" (p. 45). Harter and her colleague Ann Monsour (1992) report that as young people move through adolescence, they become increasingly better at resolving and normalizing the contradictory selves that they see themselves to be in different contexts.

Adolescent Self-esteem

When adolescents begin routinely to notice the disparities between the way they behave and the way they ought to behave if they are to be true to their "real selves," they begin to be preoccupied with themselves. Once they start dwelling on their own characteristics, they are confronted with the question "How much do I like myself?" This question of self-esteem, first discussed in Chapter 14 (p. 558), takes on a new form at this point because adolescents' self-concepts are more differentiated than children's and because adolescents are more thoughtful about them.

To a considerable degree, attributes associated with high self-esteem in adolescents are the same ones that are attributed to popular peers. Attractiveness heads the list, especially for girls, followed by peer acceptance. All other characteristics trail behind.

This heavy emphasis on female attractiveness has an unfortunate impact on the self-esteem of girls, because many of them do not believe that they are attractive. Studies in a wide range of countries have found that, on average, girls have a lower sense of self-esteem than boys (Offer et al., 1988; Simmons & Blyth, 1987).

The girl on the left is displaying the increased concern with personal appearance that is an important feature of adolescence.

A number of studies show a marked decline in children's self-esteem in early adolescence followed by a steady increase as they enter their 20s (McCarthy & Hodge, 1982). Researchers believe that this early decline in self-esteem is due in part to the transition from elementary school to junior high school, which confronts children with increased academic demands at the same time that it puts them at the bottom of the social ladder (Simmons & Blyth, 1987). The steady increase thereafter is less well understood; it may reflect the increasing freedom young people have to choose their friends, contexts, and activities, so that they can live up to their own standards, or it may indicate that they are bringing their hoped-for ideal selves more into line with reality.

As adolescence comes to an end, young people face the task of reconciling the multiple, often conflicting self-images that have developed over the years. This so-called identity crisis and the resolution of their sexual identity are two of the most fundamental issues they must deal with during the transition from child to adult.

Resolving the Identity Crisis

Recall from Chapter 15 that Erikson sees the fundamental task of adolescence to be **identity formation.** The adolescent must either achieve a secure sense of personal identity or confront a variety of psychological problems in later life (Erikson, 1968a; Kroger, 1989). Like Freud, Erikson believes that success in dealing with the developmental challenges of adolescence requires a reworking of previously resolved developmental crises. He explains the idea of a **developmental crisis** this way:

> At a given age, a human being, by dint of his physical, intellectual and emotional growth, becomes ready and eager to face a new life task, that is, a set of choices and tests which are in some traditional way prescribed and prepared for him by his society's structure. A new life task presents a *crisis* whose outcome can be a successful graduation, or alternatively, an impairment of the life cycle which will aggravate future crises. Each crisis prepares the next, as one step leads to another; and each crisis also lays one more cornerstone for the adult personality. (1958:254; italics in original)

According to Erikson, adolescents must rework four earlier developmental crises:

Establishing trust, the problem that infants encounter as part of the attachment process, reappears in adolescence as the search for people to have faith in, people to whom one can prove one's own trustworthiness. This search goes on at several levels simultaneously, in both personal and social spheres. First, one seeks trustworthy and admirable friends. At the beginning of adolescence these are friends of the same sex who can be trusted to share your anxieties without making fun of you. Later, the focus shifts to partners of the opposite sex who will find you attractive and love you.

In the larger social world, the need to establish trust takes the form of a search for political causes and leaders worth supporting. To succeed at this level, adolescents must think systematically about human nature and society in order to select an *ideology* in which to place their trust. The difficulties of this search are often expressed in mistrust of adult social institutions and cynical indifference to them.

Establishing autonomy was expressed at the end of infancy as the 2-year-old's demand to "do it myself!" Now autonomy means choosing one's own path in life instead of going along with decisions imposed by one's parents.

Taking initiative, which was expressed as pretend play during early childhood, now means setting goals for what one might become rather than settling for the limited reality that adults have arranged. The imaginary situations of preschool play find their counterparts in new dreams of greatness that the adolescent can seek to realize.

Industry takes on a new meaning toward the end of adolescence, quite different from its meaning during middle childhood. No longer will the tasks be set by the teacher; the relative independence of adulthood carries with it the duty to take responsibility for setting one's own goals and for the quality of one's work.

A special feature of the process of identity formation during adolescence is that for the first time physical maturation, cognitive skills, and social expecta-

Adolescence is a time when young people must confront adult stereotypes and come to their own decisions about who they are and what kind of identity they want to achieve.

tions come together in a way that makes it possible for young people to "sort through and synthesize their childhood identifications in order to construct a viable pathway toward adulthood" (Marcia, 1980:160).

As we noted earlier, Erikson saw this process of identity formation as involving the integration of more than the individual personality. In order to forge a secure sense of self, adolescents must resolve their identities in both the individual and the social spheres or, as Erikson put it, establish "the identity of these two identities" (1968a:22). Some idea of the intellectual complexity of this task can be gleaned from Erikson's attempt to specify the thought processes required to achieve identity formation:

> . . . in psychological terms, identity formation employs a process of simultaneous reflection and observation, a process taking place on all levels of mental functioning, by which the individual judges himself in the light of what he perceives to be the way in which others judge him in comparison to themselves and to a typology significant to them; while he judges their way of judging him in the light of how he perceives himself in comparison to them and to types that have become relevant to him. (1968a:22–23)

Although Erikson's description of the kind of thinking required to achieve a sense of an integrated identity may seem unnecessarily convoluted, this passage is worth careful study because it corresponds to Piaget's descriptions of formal operational thinking, suggesting a link between Piaget's theory of cognitive development and Erikson's theory of personality development.

Erikson's core idea is that adolescents engage in an identity-forming process that depends on:

• How they judge others.
• How others judge them.
• How they judge the judgment processes of others.
• Their ability to keep in mind social categories ("typologies") available in the culture when they form judgments about other people.

Note that it is not enough to take only one or two of these elements into account — say, the fact that you base judgments of others on social categories of importance to you: "Sam is a jerk for allowing himself to be caught drinking beer behind the gym." Rather, you must simultaneously consider both your own and other people's judgments, plus the perspective of society (embodied in the linguistic categories used to formulate the judgments), if your judgment of Sam is to be complete with respect to your own identity. Sam may have been caught drinking behind the gym, but if you too drink beer, or if you also cut class, does that make you a jerk too? Or is getting caught the only way to be a jerk? And wouldn't Sam think you were a jerk for attending a dumb civics class just because you're the teacher's pet? And what would your teacher think if he knew whom you had been with at 11:30 last night and what you were doing?

Viewed in this way, Erikson's ideas about the mental processes involved in resolving the identity crisis of adolescence fit not only with Piaget's ideas of formal operational thinking but also with the findings of a variety of studies on the development of self-understanding during adolescence. As we noted earlier, adolescents begin to describe the self primarily in abstract, general terms, to be more self-reflective, and to show concern for integrating their past selves with an imagined future self (Damon & Hart, 1988; Secord & Peevers, 1973; Selman, 1980).

Erikson's characterization of the developmental tasks of adolescence also makes it clear that the process of identity formation is likely to be difficult for families and friends as well as for adolescents them-

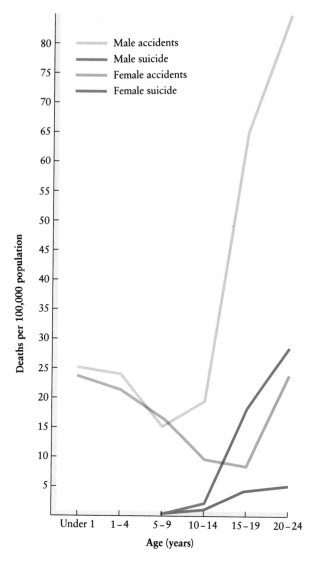

FIGURE 16.8   *Adolescence is a time when young people are at increasing risk of death by accident or suicide. Especially striking is the precipitous increase in male mortality by accident or suicide. Researchers contend that many suicides are reported as accidents because of the social stigma attached to suicide. Experts estimate that there are at least 50 suicide attempts for every successful suicide (U.S. Select Panel for the Promotion of Child Health, 1981). More girls than boys attempt suicide, but fewer are successful.*

selves. (While this process is painful for many adolescents, it seems to be especially so for those who assume a homosexual identity. See Box 16.2.) Young people who are in the midst of working out a coherent notion of themselves sometimes take out their mixed feelings on themselves and others, and the result can be antisocial, sometimes self-destructive, behavior (see Figure 16.8). As Erikson summarized it, a frequent result of identity confusion is that

> youth after youth, bewildered by the incapacity to assume a role forced on him by the inexorable standardization of American adolescence, runs

away in one form or another, dropping out of school, leaving jobs, staying out all night, or withdrawing into bizarre and inaccessible moods. (Erikson, 1968a:132)

Here we have the Eriksonian version of Hall's and Freud's visions of an emotionally stormy adolescence (see Chapter 15, pp. 570, 572), clothed in modern terminology.

It has proved difficult to create explicit, objective methods for testing Erikson's ideas about identity. Many threads enter into the process of establishing an identity, and each person must create a unique synthesis of all those disparate parts (Marcia, 1987; Waterman, 1985).

One of Erikson's favorite means of testing his ideas was the detailed biographical case study, such as his famous biographies of Martin Luther and Mahatma Gandhi (Erikson, 1958, 1969). These studies produced fascinating interpretations of these great men's psychological states. But to apply such a method to the everyday problems of contemporary teenagers who are experiencing identity confusion is time-consuming, expensive, and difficult.

The great popularity of Erikson's ideas has created a demand for simpler psychodiagnostic techniques that will achieve the same end, a portrait of an identity in the process of consolidation (Constantinople, 1969; Grotevant, 1986; Marcia, 1966; Waterman, 1985). James Marcia, for example, interviewed 86 male college students about their choice of occupation and their beliefs about religion and politics. Harold Grotevant, William Thorbecke, and Margaret Meyer (1982) extended Marcia's interview questions to include the interpersonal domains of friendship, dating, and sex roles. Their questions were designed to elicit information on the degree to which individuals have adopted and fully committed themselves to a point of view.

On the basis of the students' answers, Marcia (1966) identified four patterns of coping with the task of identity formation:

Identity achievement Adolescents who display this pattern have gone through a period of decision making about their choice of occupation, for example, or their political or religious commitment. They are now actively pursuing their own goals. When people in this group were asked about their political beliefs, for instance, they responded with such answers as "I've thought it over, and I've decided to be a _____. Their program is the most sensible one for the country to be following."

Foreclosure Young people who display this pattern are also committed to occupational and ideological positions, but they show no signs of having gone through an identity crisis. In a sense they never really undergo a personality reorganization. Instead, they just take over patterns of identity from their parents. They respond to questions about their political beliefs with such answers as

"I really never gave politics much thought. Our family always votes _____, so that's how I vote."

Moratorium This pattern is displayed by adolescents who are currently experiencing an identity crisis. They are likely to answer a question about their political beliefs by saying, "I'm not sure. Both parties have their good points, but neither one seems to offer a better chance for my economic future."

Identity diffusion Adolescents who manifest this pattern have tried out several identities without being able to settle on one. They are likely to take a cynical attitude toward the issues confronting them, so they may answer questions about political commitment by declaring, "I stopped thinking about politics ages ago. There are no parties worth following."

If Erikson's ideas about identity formation are successfully captured by Marcia's categories, and if both are accurate reflections of reality, research should show a consistent shift away from identity diffusion toward identity achievement as adolescents grow older. This expectation is confirmed by a large number of studies summarized by Alan Waterman (1985). The proportion of identity achievers increases steadily from the years before high school to the late college years, while the proportion manifesting identity diffusion decreases (Table 16.5 shows the relevant data in the realm of occupational choice). In agreement with Erikson's belief that identity formation is a process rather than a trait, researchers find a general shift toward identity achievement well into adulthood as individuals readjust their understandings of themselves to accord with their experiences (Waterman & Waterman, 1971). In addition, Waterman (1985) reports that the level of identity achievement varies with the domain in question; it is considerably lower for political ideology than for vocational choice.

A number of studies have explored the influence of experiences within the family on identity achievement. Harold Grotevant and Catherine Cooper (1985), for example, looked at the way family interactions in a specially constructed "family interaction task" correlated with scores on identity achievement. In this task a mother, father, and their adolescent are asked to make plans for a two-week vacation together.

BOX 16.2
Homosexuality

Although the dominant form of sexual behavior centers on the union of male and female, a sizable number of people exhibit a homosexual preference—that is, a preference for members of their own sex as sexual partners—at various times in their lives. Because of the social stigma attached to homosexuality in many societies and the resulting reticence about such matters, there is no way to know for sure how many people have engaged in homosexual practices. Still, that homosexual activity is common is borne out by survey data collected almost 40 years ago by Alfred Kinsey and his colleagues (1948, 1953). These researchers found that about a third of men and 13 percent of women reported having reached orgasm with a partner of the same sex at least once in their lives. Such behavior is by no means limited to our culture. It has been documented by anthropologists in most of the world's cultures (Ford & Beach, 1951).

While homosexual activity is widespread, only a small number of the people who engage in it consider themselves to be homosexuals. Both in the Kinsey surveys and in more recent investigations of adolescent sexual behavior, the young people who indicated that they had engaged in homosexual activity far outnumbered those who described themselves as homosexuals (Cole & Stokes, 1985).

In other cultures, adolescent homosexual behavior is only rarely viewed as an expression of a lifelong sexual identity (Gonsiorek & Weinrich, 1991; Herdt, 1989; Savin-Williams, 1990). Instead it is viewed as either necessary because of the separation between the sexes, as a way for young men to learn about sex, as part of the ritual of becoming a man, or as a playful acting out of the sex drive by young men who have excess energy.

Because of such disparities between sexual behavior and sexual identity, several contemporary researchers distinguish between homosexual orientation, homosexual behavior or practices, and homosexual identity. Homosexual *orientation* consists of a preponderance of sexual or erotic feelings, thoughts, fantasies, and behaviors involving members of the same sex. Homosexual *behavior* is sexual behavior between members of the same sex. Homosexual *identity* "represents a consistent, enduring self-recognition of the meanings that sexual orientation and sexual behavior have for oneself" (Savin-Williams, 1990). Some researchers maintain that a public declaration of one's homosexuality is a necessary part of assuming a homosexual identity; others disagree (Savin-Williams, 1990; Troiden, 1988).

In the United States, arrival at a heterosexual identity fits approved American social categories. Homosexuality is stigmatized in our society. How, then, do young men and women come to commit themselves to a homosexual identity?

Leading researchers seem to agree that for many people the development of a homosexual identity goes through several stages, such as those described by Richard Troiden (1988).

Stage 1: Sensitization; feeling different. In retrospective reports one often encounters people who say that during middle childhood they had social experiences that made them feel different from other children and that served later to make homosexuality personally relevant to them, although they assumed at the time that they were heterosexual (Bell, Weinberg, & Hammersmith, 1981). Typical comments from girls: "I was very shy and unaggressive" (p. 148); "I felt different: unfeminine, ungraceful, not very pretty, kind of a mess" (p. 156). Typical comments from boys: "I couldn't stand sports, so naturally that made me different. A ball thrown at me was like a bomb" (p. 74); "I just didn't feel like I was like other boys. I was very fond of pretty things like ribbons and flowers and music" (p. 86).

Stage 2: Self-recognition; identity confusion. When such children enter puberty, they realize that they are attracted to members of the same sex and begin to label such feelings as homosexual. This recognition is the source of considerable inner turmoil and identity confusion; they can no longer take their heterosexual identities as given, and they know that homosexuals are stigmatized.

"You are not sure who you are. You are confused about what sort of person you are and where your life is going. You ask yourself the questions 'Who am I,' 'Am I a homosexual,' 'Am I really a heterosexual?'" (Cass, 1984: 156)

By middle or late adolescence such young people begin to believe that they are probably homosexual because they are uninterested in the heterosexual activities of their peers. Many homosexual adults recall adolescence as a time when they were loners and social outcasts. This upsetting psychological and social situation provokes denial and attempts to rationalize their different sexual orientation in socially approved ways.

Stage 3: Identity assumption. Some young people who have had homosexual experiences and who recognize that they prefer sexual relations with members of their own sex do not act on their preference. Many others, however, move from private acknowledgment of their homosexual preference to admitting it openly, at least to other homosexuals. Although homosexual identity is assumed during the early stages of this process, it often is not fully accepted. Vivienne Cass (1984) describes people at this stage of identity formation:

"You feel sure you're a homosexual and you put up with, or tolerate this. You see yourself as homosexual for now, but you are not sure of how you will be in the future. You usually take care to put across a heterosexual image. You sometimes mix socially with homosexuals, or would like to do this. You feel a need to meet others like yourself." (p. 156)

People who have achieved this level of homosexual identity deal with it in a variety of ways. Some try to avoid homosexual contacts and attempt to pass as heterosexual because they are afraid of the stigma attached to homosexuality. Others adopt the broader society's stereotypes of homosexuals and behave in extreme ways that fit those stereotypes. Still others begin to align themselves with the homosexual community.

Stage 4: Commitment; identity integration. This final level is reached by those who adopt homosexuality as a way of life. Identity integration is indicated by a fusion of one's sexuality and emotional commitments, by expressions of satisfaction with one's lifestyle, and by public disclosure of one's homosexual identity.

Troiden notes that commitment to a homosexual identity may vary from weak to strong, depending on such factors as the individual's success in forging satisfying personal relationships, being accepted by his or her family, and functioning well at work or in a career. By middle age, the inner and outer person may have become so well integrated that homosexuality ceases to be an important issue in the individual's life.

TABLE 16.5
Percentage of Students Manifesting Four Identity Statuses in Domain of Vocational Choice, by Age Group

Age Group	Identity Achievement	Moratorium	Foreclosure	Identity Diffusion
Pre–high school years	5.2%	11.7%	36.6%	46.4%
High school underclass years	9.0	14.6	37.1	39.3
High school upperclass years	21.3	13.5	36.0	29.2
College underclass years	22.8	28.3	25.7	23.2
College upperclass years	39.7	15.5	31.3	13.5

Source: Waterman, 1985.

They have twenty minutes to arrive at a day-by-day plan that covers both the location and the activity for each day. The discussions were scored by the way the family members express their individuality (for example, through stating their own point of view or through disagreeing with another family member) and their connectedness (as displayed by their responsiveness and sensitivity to others' points of view).

Grotevant and Cooper interviewed the adolescents in these families to find out how thoroughly they had explored a variety of options for their futures. They hypothesized that identity exploration would be related to individuality (the adolescent had to learn how to develop a distinctive point of view) and to connectedness (the family had to provide a secure base from which the adolescent could explore). In their study of white middle-class families, these researchers found that adolescents' interactions with their parents *were* associated with identity exploration, but in different ways for sons and daughters. For sons, greater identity exploration was associated with their fathers' willingness to allow disagreement, to compromise, and to modify their own suggestions in light of what the boys said — to engage in genuine give and take. For daughters, a higher degree of identity exploration was associated with family communication in which the girls expressed their disagreements with their parents and were assertive in making suggestions. Despite the

different patterns, it appears safe to say that a family system that offers support and security while encouraging the adolescent to create a distinct identity appears to be most effective in promoting identity achievement.

When adolescents are struggling to achieve a stable identity, they often prefer to spend time by themselves.

The Psychosexual Resolution

In the years of middle childhood, when most young people strongly prefer to spend time with members of their own sex, children's sense of self depends heavily on how other children of the same sex respond to them. As a result of the changes brought on by puberty, the childhood sense of self must change from one based on opposition to the opposite sex to one based on the interdependence of males and females.

As we noted in Chapter 15 (p. 573), Freudian psychologists view adolescence as a period when children reexperience the conflicts of earlier stages in new guises (Blos, 1962, 1972). Unless these problems are worked through and resolved, the adult personality will be distorted.

Central among the early developmental problems that must be reworked, according to Freud, is the child's primitive desire to possess the parent of the opposite sex. The way young children resolve this conflict, which Freud called the *Oedipus conflict,* is to repress illicit desire by identifying with the same-sex parent. Freud maintained that this infantile resolution is essential to proper sex-role identification (see Chapter 10, p. 362).

These early oedipal feelings are encountered again in adolescence, but repression and identification with members of the same sex are no longer the adaptive responses that they were at the end of infancy. Puberty reawakens sexual desire at a time when adolescents are fully capable both of carrying out the forbidden acts and of understanding the incest taboo that denies them the parent as a sexual partner.

The combination of awakened desire and social constraint leads the adolescent to seek people outside the family to love. The basis for this search was laid during the peer-group experience of middle childhood, but the adolescent's reorientation is nonetheless fraught with difficulties. To begin with, the young person has had little experience of friendship with opposite-sex peers and virtually no experience interacting with peers as sexual partners; new modes of social behavior will have to be learned. Second, a shift in the object of affection from a parent to a peer requires emotional disengagement from the family, which has been the bedrock of emotional security since birth. Recognizing the difficulty of this task, Freud referred to the adolescent's reorientation of affection as "one of the most painful psychical achievements of the pubertal period" (Freud, 1905/1953a:227).

Painful or not, the adolescent's reorientation from family to peers is viewed as essential by Freudian scholars. If, for example, a girl refuses to give up her dependence on her parents' love and authority, she may lack the capacity to love her husband. She may also, Freud (1905/1953) claimed, become a sexually cold wife because she is fixated at a level of development where love is asexual. Similarly, a young man who fails to reorient his affections may find himself attracted only by older women, and may later involve his mother too intimately in his marriage, angering and alienating his wife. Successful adjustment in adolescence, therefore, requires the reawakening of old conflicts and the subsequent attainment of a new equilibrium within socially acceptable constraints.

Freud believed that these demands and the stress they induce make the adolescent personality especially susceptible to disorders that may have lasting effects. Freud's daughter, Anna, an influential psychoanalyst herself, concentrated on the period of adolescence because of her concern about its special dangers. As she conceived it, to regain psychological balance the ego must avoid overassociation with either the superego or the id. If the ego "allies itself too closely with the superego" (to use her terminology), the adult will be inflexible in personal relations, a slave to social rules. Such a person will experience difficulty in forming attachments to the opposite sex. At the other extreme, if the ego sides too much with the id, "no trace will be left of the previous character of the individual and the entrance into adult life will be marked by a riot of uninhibited gratification of instinct" (A. Freud, 1946:163).

Sexual Variations in Identity Formation

Investigations of possible sex differences in identity formation have raised problems typical of all attempts to understand adolescent modes of thinking. Freud (1905/1953b) claimed that the psychosexual dynamics of development are different for the two sexes. In contrasting the adolescent resolution of males and females, the psychoanalyst Peter Blos has claimed that a boy's

> energies are directed outward toward control of and dominance over the physical world. The girl, in contrast, turns—either in fact or fantasy—with deep-felt emotionality, mixed of romantic

tenderness, possessiveness, and envy, to the boy. While the boy sets out to master the physical world, the girl endeavors to deal with relationships. (1972:61)

Erikson also believes that there are significant sex differences in the process of forming an identity. He agrees with Freud that "anatomy is destiny." According to this view, a woman's biological makeup determines her social role as an adult, a role that assigns her the greater responsibility for child rearing and homemaking. At times Erikson has softened his stance by noting that "nothing in our interpretation . . . is meant to claim that either sex is doomed to one . . . mode or another; rather . . . these modes 'come more naturally' " (1968a:273). Within the limits set by the norms of the social group, adolescent girls, like adolescent boys, try out various roles and modes of life.

The endurance of war in the modern world creates conditions for identity formation among youthful males who are the majority of the fighters. These adolescents are learning how to look and act like soldiers.

Recent research provides mixed evidence on Erikson's claims about sex differences. Waterman (1985) summarized several studies in which interviews of the kind designed by Marcia (1966) were used. He found only "weak and inconsistent evidence" that boys and girls follow different paths to identity achievement in the domains of vocational choice, religious belief, political ideology, and sex roles. Thorbecke and Grotevant (1982), however, found in similar interviews that adolescent girls score higher levels of identity achievement than boys in the domain of friendship, and Sally Archer (1985) found that girls score higher in the domain of choices about combining career and family. Archer's interviews also reveal American girls' ambivalence and confusion as they confront the dilemmas that are inherent in the cultural expectations and standard social roles that await them (see Table 16.6).

Minority-Group Status and Identity Formation

In a recent review of research on identity formation among minority-group children in the United States, Margaret Spencer and Carol Markstrom-Adams (1990) remark that identity formation is especially complicated for these young people. The factors that influence this process—skin color; behavioral, linguistic, and physical differences; and long-standing social stereotypes—vary from one group to the next. Spencer and Markstrom-Adams note, for example, that skin color is more of an issue among African Americans and Native Americans than among Hispanics. Young people in all such groups, however, must contend with negative social stereotypes and the generally low income that accompanies minority-group status.

Research on identity formation among minority-group children has focused primarily on two areas: progression through Marcia's stages of identity formation and ethnic identity of the kind we examined in our discussion of socialization during early childhood (Chapter 10, pp. 368–369). Researchers have found that minority-group adolescents (African American, Hispanic American, Asian American, Native American) are more likely than other adolescents to fall within the category of foreclosure, an indication that they have not fully explored possible identities (Abraham, 1986; Markstrom, 1987). Spencer and

TABLE 16.6
Views of Adolescent Girls and Boys on Family and Career Priorities

Views of Girls	Views of Boys
I might be a mother and not a wife. Having a husband is just like your father. You can't go out, can't do anything. You have to cook, clean, take care of the children and still work.	If I was into sports, my wife and kids would have to travel and stay in a little room—but there's nothing that couldn't be worked out.
If I have a career and a husband who doesn't want me to work, I'll do what I want.	If I am a musician, on tour, my wife's going to get worried. I wouldn't try to bring it home. We'd talk and just give it some time. Sometimes it shouldn't interfere.
I intend to have a career. Being a wife is okay; it's not so much of a strain. Kids are a strain. Maybe I can talk him into adopting a 5-year-old; or stop my career. If I am into my career, especially at my peak, it would really hurt.	I would enjoy something like marriage and family. I'd love to have my own kid at the right time. I look forward to it. You have a wife to be with and share time with. Helping each other out. But you're tied down. Can't go out with the guys.

Source: Archer, 1985.

Markstrom-Adams (1990) suggest that in some cases the early cessation of identity exploration is the result of racial prejudice; young people are actively discouraged from involvement with people outside of their reference group. In the case of Japanese Americans, it has been suggested that parents' strong expectations for their children's success in school and for what their future roles will be cut off their exploration of their identities (Nagata, 1989).

William Cross (1991) writes that it is not at all unusual for African American adolescents to experience an identity crisis in which they question how they feel about their ethnic identity. Often such a crisis results from an encounter in which they experience rejection or humiliation because of their race. The specifics of such encounters are quite varied (Fordham & Ogbu, 1986). A teacher may accuse a student of cheating when she does outstanding work, on the assumption that African Americans or Puerto Ricans or Samoans are incapable of such work; or a boy may be told he may no longer socialize with a girl he has been friends with for years because he has the wrong skin color, ethnic background, or religion.

One reaction to such encounters is to distance oneself from one's own group and try to win acceptance by the majority group. More common is the opposite reaction: the young person rejects everything associated with the majority group and strongly identifies with his or her group (Cross, 1991). Signithia Fordham and John Ogbu (1986) describe several cases in which African American adolescents attempt to purge themselves of patterns of dress, speech, mannerisms, and attitudes associated with white American society and adopt an oppositional or separate identity. These researchers believe that the process of oppositional identity formation provides one of the major explanations for the school failure of African American children. Although research is sketchy, evidence suggests that similar identity processes are at work in the development of adolescents of many minority groups (Gibbs & Huang, 1989).

A word of caution is needed in regard to these findings. The economic inequalities that go with minority-group status make it very difficult to isolate minority-group status as *the* crucial variable in the development of children's personal and social identities, just as in the case of their IQs (Chapter 13, pp. 503–504). By and large, comparisons that are supposed to be about differences in ethnicity or race are also about socioeconomic class, especially poverty. As a

consequence, we cannot be certain why foreclosure is more frequent among minority-group adolescents or why some of them appear to identify less with their own ethnic or racial group than with that of the dominant group in American society.

Cross-cultural Variations in Identity Formation

In comparison with the relatively shaky evidence concerning sex and minority-group differences, differences in identity formation between broadly different cultural groups seem a virtual certainty (Fogelson, 1982; Geertz, 1984; Hallowell, 1955; Rosaldo, 1984). First, there is ample evidence that self-concepts vary from one historical era to the next and from one culture to another (Baumeister, 1987; Markus & Kitayama, 1991; Shweder & Bourne, 1984). In a review of cultural variations in concepts of the self, Hazel Markus and Shinobu Kitayama (1991:226) note that cultures that adhere to an **independent construal of self**, described by such labels as "individualistic," "egocentric," "separate," "autonomous," "idiocentric," and "self-contained," are quite distinct from cultures that adhere to an **interdependent construal of**

self, described by such labels as "relational," "collectivist," "connected," "contextual," "holistic," and "sociocentric."

According to Markus and Kitayama, people whose cultures encourage an independent sense of self are oriented to being unique, to promoting their individual goals, and to expressing their own thoughts and opinions. People whose cultures emphasize an interdependent sense of self, by contrast, seek to fit into the group, to promote the goals of others (that is, of the group), and to develop the ability to "read" the minds of others (see Table 16.7).

A study by Steven Cousins (1989) reveals several contrasts between these two modes of self-construal. Cousins chose American and Japanese high school students as representatives of cultures that adhere to independent and interdependent self-construals. Each student was asked to describe him- or herself in one of two circumstances. The first, context-free case presented the student with the simple question "Who am I?" 20 times. The second, context-specific case asked the student to describe him- or herself in several specific situations (me at home, me at school, me with friends, etc.).

When asked to say 20 things about themselves in the context-free circumstance, the American students

2 modes of self-construal

TABLE 16.7

Key Differences between an Independent and an Interdependent Construal of Self

Feature Compared	Independent	Interdependent
Definition	Separate from social context	Connected with social context
Structure	Bounded, unitary, stable	Flexible, variable
Important features	Internal, private (abilities, thoughts, feelings)	External, public (statuses, roles, relationships)
Tasks	Be unique Express self Realize internal attributes Promote own goals Be direct; "say what's on your mind"	Belong, fit-in Occupy one's proper place Engage in appropriate action Promote others' goals Be indirect; "read other's mind"
Role of others	*Self-evaluation:* others important for social comparison, reflected appraisal	*Self-definition:* relationships with others in specific contexts define the self
Basis of self-esteem[a]	Ability to express self, validate internal attributes	Ability to adjust, restrain self, maintain harmony with social context

[a] Esteeming the self may be primarily a Western phenomenon, and the concept of self-esteem should perhaps be replaced by self-satisfaction, or by a term that reflects the realization that one is fulfilling the culturally mandated task.
Source: Markus & Kitayama, 1991.

most often mentioned psychological traits or general attributes ("I am friendly," "I am a good athlete"). The Japanese students most often referred to kinds of behavior they engaged in ("I play tennis after school").

When the students were asked to answer the question "Who am I?" in particular contexts, the pattern of answers changed. This time it was the Japanese students who offered generalizations about themselves. Asked to say who they are in their families, for example, they might answer "I am good natured," whereas the American students qualified their answers. Cousins remarks that the American students' answers, such as "I am *usually* open with my brother," implied that just because they behave a certain way in one setting doesn't mean that they are always like that (see Figure 16.9).

As Markus and Kitayama point out, this difference in orientation to the self creates different sets of problems for forging a unified sense of identity. For one thing, the American emphasis on the autonomous self presupposes that identity formation is an individual, personal process. In societies where the self is seen in relation to others, by contrast, "others are included *within* the boundaries of the self because others and specific contexts are specific features of the self" (pp. 245–246). Moreover, adolescents in collectivist societies do not have to make many of the decisions and choices that American adolescents must face in order to resolve their identity. It makes little sense to assert that healthy identity formation requires adolescents to make a "commitment to a sexual orientation, an ideological stance, and a vocational choice" (Marcia, 1980:160) in societies in which marriages are arranged by the family, one's vocation is whatever one's father or mother does, and strict subordination to one's elders is a moral imperative.

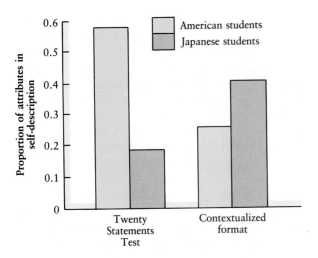

FIGURE 16.9   *Mean proportion of psychological attributes endorsed by American and Japanese students who were asked to give statements about themselves in two self-description tasks. One, the Twenty-Statements Test, was decontextualized; the other had a contextualized format that asked for self-descriptions in particular settings. (From Cousins, 1989.)*

Unfortunately, virtually no research has been done on the development of identity in nonindustrial societies of the kind that has been conducted in technologically sophisticated societies. We have to turn to the reports of anthropologists who have concerned themselves with identity formation in small hunter-gatherer or agricultural societies, such as those found in parts of West Africa, the Arctic regions, and New Guinea (Condon, 1987; Harley, 1941; Raum, 1967; Schlegel & Barry, 1991). The most distinctive fact about identity formation in such groups is that, as in the collectivist societies discussed by Markus and Kitayama, it involves little of the cognitive deliberation and personal choice that play such large roles in psychologists' accounts of identity formation. There are so few distinct adult roles in such societies that a young person has few decisions to make. The transition to adult identity in such societies, however, is often forged in ritual initiation ceremonies that are obligatory and painful. These circumstances must certainly influence identity formation, but existing psychological research does not permit us to draw conclusions about the processes involved.

THE TRANSITION TO ADULTHOOD

As we commented in the introduction to our discussion of adolescence, no developmental transition after birth is so well marked as the end of middle childhood. Profound changes in the size and shape of children's bodies are unmistakable signs that they are "ripening." Certainty about the end of middle childhood, however, is not the same as certainty that a distinctive stage intervenes between middle childhood and adulthood. Is adolescence really a stage in the same way that infancy or middle childhood is, or is it more like an uneven transition between stages, as Piaget sometimes conceived early childhood to be?

We have seen that in at least two key respects, the period between middle childhood and adulthood does not fit the pattern of earlier stages. First, since in many societies the onset of puberty coincides closely with marriage and the adoption of an adult role, it is by no means certain that adolescence—considered as the stage *before* adulthood—is universal. Second, in societies such as our own, where adult status is delayed for years after puberty, the kinds of factors that usually make up a bio-social-behavioral shift do not seem to converge in the relatively well-coordinated manner of earlier stages. Consequently, we have to take seriously the possibility that adolescence is not a stage of development but instead reflects a slow transition between childhood and adulthood in which aspects of the two stages commingle (Fox, 1977).

Is Adolescence a Distinctive Stage of Development?

A first step toward resolving uncertainties about adolescence as a distinctive stage is to note that we have been using two terms, "the transition from middle childhood to adulthood" and "adolescence," as if they were more or less synonymous. In fact, as psychologists ordinarily use them, "transition" and "stage" are not synonyms. A stage is a more or less stable, patterned, and enduring system of interactions between the organism and the environment; a transition is a period of flux, when the "ensemble of the whole" that makes up one stage has disintegrated and a new stage is not firmly in place. The transition from middle childhood to adulthood is universal, but what part of the phenomenon called the adolescent *stage* should also be considered universal?

Herbert Bloch and Arthur Niederhoffer (1958) suggest one of the universal features shared by both a transition to adulthood and adolescence: a struggle for adult status. In all societies, the old eventually give way to the young. It is not easy for people in power to give it up, so it is natural that to some degree the granting of adult status, and with it adult power, involves a struggle. Freud's focus on the difficulties of making the transition from latency to mature sexuality highlights a second universal feature, one that also involves tension but that is necessary for the continuation of human society. It is not easy for children, who have long identified strongly with members of their own sex, to become attached to a member of the opposite sex. Whether these necessary changes require an entire stage devoted to a struggle for their realization, however, remains to be demonstrated.

Often the argument for the universality of adolescence as a stage of development is based on historical evidence:

> The young are in character prone to desire and ready to carry any desire they may have formed into action. Of bodily desires it is the sexual to which they are most disposed to give way, and in regard to sexual desire they exercise no self-restraint. They are changeful too, and fickle in their desires, which are as transitory as they are vehement. . . . They are passionate, irascible, and apt to be carried away by their impulses. . . . They regard themselves as omniscient and are positive in their assertions; this is, in fact, the reason for their carrying everything too far. . . . Finally, they are fond of laughter and consequently facetious, facetiousness being disciplined insolence. (Quoted in Kiell, 1964:18–19)

This description has a certain timeless quality. It could describe a high school clique in almost any modern town or Romeo and his friends in medieval Verona. In fact, it is a description of Greek youth in the fourth century B.C., written by the philosopher Aristotle. When such historical evidence is set beside similar accounts from a tribal village in Africa and a Winnebago Indian village in Nebraska, it seems self-evident that the experience of adolescence is universal. These data, however, by no means clearly establish the universality of adolescence as a unified stage.

First, the evidence available from ancient societies has a noticeable shortcoming: women are invisible. In Aristotle's description and all the others from ancient societies (Kiell, 1964), the people being talked about were clearly males. Moreover, they were urban males of the moneyed classes who did indeed undergo a period of extended training, often including formal schooling, which created a delay between puberty and full adult status. Generally speaking, women and most members of the lower classes underwent no such specialized training, nor is there evidence that they were ever included in the category of adolescents.

Second, the evidence from other cultures may support the idea that the transition to adult status is universally fraught with anxiety and uncertainty, but it provides equally strong evidence that adolescence, as the term is used in modern industrialized societies, exists only under particular cultural circumstances (Whiting, Burbank, & Ratner, 1986). When researchers make the assumption that adolescence exists in societies that have no concept for it and no set of social practices corresponding to it, they do violence to the facts.

The Inuit of the Canadian Arctic at the turn of the century, for example, used special terms to refer to boys and girls when they entered puberty, but these terms did not coincide with the usual notion of adolescence (Condon, 1987). Young women were considered adult at menarche, a change in status marked by the fact that they were likely to be married by this time and ready to start bearing children. Young men were considered fully grown as soon as they were able to build a snow house and hunt large game unassisted. They might be able to do both shortly after the onset of puberty, but boys usually achieved adult status somewhat later because they had first to prove that they could support themselves and their families. In view of the life circumstances of these people, it is not surprising that they developed no special concept corresponding to adolescence that applied to boys and girls alike; such a concept did not correspond to their reality.

Adolescence in Modern Societies

Granted that a social category corresponding to adolescence may arise only in certain cultural circumstances, we are still left with the problem of understanding the developmental dynamics of young people who fit this category in modern industrialized societies. If we want to claim that adolescence is a stage of development in modern societies, does it adhere to the same rules of organization and transition as earlier stages, or is it unique in important respects?

When the roots of adolescence in the United States and other modern industrialized societies are traced, it appears to be closely associated with apprenticeship training or formal schooling; or with a period of waiting until the designated adult role becomes available, either through a marriage proposal or an inheritance (Ariès, 1962; Fox, 1977; Gillis, 1974; Kett, 1977). Although scattered instances of the concept of adolescence can be found in ancient civilizations, it was only during the nineteenth century, when formal schooling was introduced for the mass of boys and girls, that adolescence became a generally recognized and pervasive category defining children of a certain age regardless of sex and social class.

The crucial factors introduced by formal schooling are a long delay in achieving economic self-sufficiency and prolongation of socialization in contexts that are institutionally separated from the real processes of production and adult life. In the United States, for example, young people are expected to attend school for 12 or more years and to abstain from starting a family during their junior and senior high school years. In these circumstances, there can be no doubt that adolescence as a stage of development is a social reality.

In fact, adolescence has been elaborated in such detail in the United States and other industrially advanced societies that psychologists who specialize in this developmental stage often distinguish three substages: early adolescence (11–14 years), middle adolescence (15–18 years), and late adolescence (18–21 years). As Larry Steinberg (1989) notes, these divisions correspond to the way modern societies group children in schools: early adolescence corresponds roughly to middle or junior high school, middle adolescence to high school, and late adolescence to college.

This correspondence between age and the context of development presents analysts of adolescence with a problem: they can determine that younger adolescents are more susceptible to peer pressure than older adolescents (Figure 15.8, p. 598) and reason differently about political processes (p. 623), but it is difficult to determine why. The differences may arise from some factor closely associated with age (greater social experience, more advanced reasoning skills) or from the differences in experience afforded by the various ways children's school life is organized.

A peculiar fact about adolescence in societies such as ours is that not all aspects of the bio-social-behavioral shift that initiates it coincide as they do in earlier stages. To be sure, biological maturation simultaneously gives rise to new desires and emotions and to new forms of social relationship. Intimate friendships with peers of the same sex are supplemented by, and in some cases supplanted by, intimate love relationships with members of the opposite sex. As these relationships develop, family ties loosen, as if in anticipation of the new family configuration to come. Although theorists dispute the details (they argue, for example, about how much conflict and discontent the process engenders), they agree about the overall pattern of change during adolescence, because the observed connections between the biological and social domains seem to form a logical pattern.

Yet an important element in the "social" part of the bio-social-behavioral shift that defines the transition to adulthood for Piaget and other stage theorists (see Table 16.8) is the partial failure of part of the social system to change at the expected time. With some exceptions, such as participation in adult work, modern young people are offered carefully arranged substitutes for real adult roles. Instead of the responsibility for conducting real chemistry experiments, students are given exercises that model the ideal practice of chemists. Instead of responsibility for running their own school, students are given a student government with elected officers, laws, and legislatures but no power. Instead of responsibility for informing the community of important events, students are allowed to run student newspapers whose topics are carefully circumscribed by rule and custom. If modern adolescence is to be considered a separate stage of development, we must admit that it combines biological, social, and behavioral factors in a way we have not seen in any of the stages that precede it.

The unevenness of adolescent thinking grows directly out of the artificiality of some of the changes in the social sphere. When adolescents throw themselves into an activity as if it were a lifetime commitment or in those rare instances when they are allowed or required to take on an adult role (in a work situation, say, or when a mother falls ill), they may display the formal

---

TABLE 16.8
The Bio-Social-Behavioral Transition to Adulthood

BIOLOGICAL DOMAIN

Capacity for biological reproduction
Development of secondary sexual characteristics
Attainment of adult size

BEHAVIORAL DOMAIN

Achievement of formal operations in some areas
(systematic thinking)
Formation of identity

SOCIAL DOMAIN

Sexual relations
Shift toward primary responsibility for oneself
Beginning of responsibility for next generation

---

operational cognitive ability that is supposed to appear at this time. In many other situations, however, both their social roles and their thought processes can be expected to remain distinctly "adolescent."

In summary, the historical and cross-cultural evidence, in combination with what we know about the transition from childhood to adulthood in our own society, suggests the following formulation: The tran-

sition to adulthood universally engenders conflict as young people come to terms with sexual maturity and the need to adopt adult roles. As a recognized stage of development during which the young person becomes prepared for adult roles, however, adolescence is not universal. Consequently, the way one experiences the transition to adulthood depends on one's cultural circumstances.

Looking Ahead

The modern trend toward extending and intensifying adolescence springs from the same forces that created the concept of adolescence in the first place. It is a virtual certainty that in the decades to come, young people will be expected to achieve higher levels of learning than ever before (U.S. Department of Education, 1983). This increased achievement will be sought in part through intensification of education in the lower grades, longer school hours, and more days of schooling per year. But to gain access to higher-paying and more secure jobs, young people will also be expected to spend more years in school, which will further delay their independent working lives and prolong their economic dependence. These economic factors suggest that we will either see adolescence extended further or, as the psychologist Kenneth Keniston (1970) has suggested, invent a new stage of development between adolescence and adulthood, during which young people will achieve some forms of autonomy that adolescents are denied but will still stop short of taking on the full responsibilities of adults.

SUMMARY

1. The thinking of adolescents often manifests five characteristics not usually observed in the thinking of younger children:
   a. Thinking about possibilities.
   b. Thinking through hypotheses.
   c. Thinking ahead.
   d. Thinking about thought.
   e. Thinking beyond conventional limits.
2. Piagetian theory attributes these characteristics to the emergence of formal operations, in which all possible

logical aspects of a problem are thought about as a structured whole. The core of Piaget's evidence comes from observations of adolescents working on problems modeled on scientific experiments.
3. Contrary to classical Piagetian theory, not everyone proves capable of solving Piagetian formal operational tasks, even in adulthood. In some societies, virtually no adults can solve these problems. Non-Piagetian versions of formal operational thinking occur in some contexts in all societies, however.

4. Difficulties with Piaget's explanations of adolescent thought processes have inspired attempts at alternative explanations.

   a. Information-processing approaches hypothesize that increased memory capacity, increased efficiency in the use of strategies and rules, and the ability to form abstract verbal concepts, rather than changes in the logic of thought, account for adolescents' new thought processes.

   b. Theorists of several persuasions have suggested that developments in the domain of language are crucial to the emergence of new cognitive ability during adolescence.

   c. Cultural-context theorists propose that involvement in new activities creates the conditions for a new level of systematic thought. Systematic thought is assumed to occur in all societies but is always bound to the demands of particular contexts.

5. The more powerful thought processes manifest themselves in new ways of thinking about the social world, including moral problems and politics.

6. Though some psychologists assume that increased intellectual capacity results in a higher level of moral and political behavior, the evidence linking reasoning ability with actual behavior shows that many other factors are involved.

7. Variability in the way sex and culture affect adolescents' and adults' reasoning about moral standards has led some theorists to propose that there are a variety of moral orientations, rather than a single sequence of moral development.

8. Personality development during adolescence requires that new sexual capacities and new social relations be integrated with the personality characteristics accumulated since birth.

9. Adolescents describe themselves in more varied, generalized, and abstract ways than they did during middle childhood, an indication of the need to reconcile their "multiple selves."

10. Self-esteem declines at the onset of adolescence, especially for girls in the United States, reflecting the difficulties of adjusting to social and biological changes. It then rises throughout the remainder of adolescence.

11. According to Freud, the reintegration of personality begins when new sexual desires upset the balance of id, ego, and superego; the resolution of this imbalance requires the individual to find an appropriate person to love, bringing to a close the oedipal conflict of infancy.

12. According to Erikson, adolescence is the time when the person recapitulates and resolves all earlier developmental crises in order to form an adult identity.

13. According to both Freudian and Eriksonian theories, failure to resolve past crises during adolescence leads to a neurotic adult personality.

14. Both Freudian and Eriksonian theories hypothesize sex differences in adolescent personality formation, but the evidence they offer about the course of female development is weak.

15. There is ample evidence that self-concepts vary with sociocultural circumstances, but evidence on cultural variations in the process of adolescent personality formation is generally lacking.

16. Historical variations in the cultural organization of young people's lives after middle childhood suggest that adolescence is not a universal stage of development.

17. In modern industrial societies, where adolescence is an institutionalized stage of development, the discoordination of biological, social, and psychological changes creates a developmental configuration unlike those of earlier stages of development.

KEY TERMS

developmental crisis
formal operations
identity formation
independent construal of self

interdependent construal of self
second-order thinking
structured whole

SUGGESTED READINGS

ERIKSON, ERIK H. *Identity: Youth in Crisis*. New York: Norton, 1968.

This is the classic monograph by perhaps the most influential theorist of adolescent psychology in the twentieth century.

GILLIGAN, CAROL. *In a Different Voice: Psychological Theory and Women's Development*. Cambridge, Mass.: Harvard University Press, 1982.

A major statement on sex differences in psychological development. Gilligan argues that women's orientation to the social world, and hence to themselves, differs from men's. These distinctive orientations in turn lead each sex to develop a distinctive basis for moral reasoning.

INHELDER, BARBEL, & PIAGET, JEAN. *The Growth of Logical Thinking from Childhood to Adolescence*. New York: Basic Books, 1958.

This is the classic monograph on formal operational thinking. To obtain an overall grasp of the Piagetian view of adolescent thought patterns, it is helpful to read the final chapter before plunging into the details of particular studies.

KOHLBERG, LAWRENCE. *The Psychology of Moral Development: The Nature and Validity of Moral Stages*. New York: Harper & Row, 1984.

This volume brings together many of Kohlberg's seminal papers on moral development. His theoretical papers give the overall approach and his empirical papers provide the basic evidence for and against the theory.

KROGER, JANE. *Identity in Adolescence*. London: Routledge, 1989.

Each of the major theories of identity formation and the data on which they are based receive careful attention in this clearly written book. An especially attractive feature of Kroger's presentation is her biographical accounts of the major theorists, which place their work in a cultural-historical context.

TROIDEN, RICHARD R. *Gay and Lesbian Identity: A Sociological Analysis*. Dix Hills, N.Y.: General Hall, 1988.

Although this book is labeled "a sociological analysis," it does an admirable job of integrating information about the interplay of psychological and social processes involved in identity formation for the homosexual population.

CHAPTER 17

Development
and Later Life

•

We leave childhood without knowing what youth is, we marry
without knowing what it is to be married, and even when we
enter old age, we don't know what it is we're heading for:
the old are innocent children of their old age. In that
sense, man's world is a planet of inexperience.

— MILAN KUNDERA, *THE ART OF THE NOVEL*

We shall not cease from exploration
And the end of all our exploring
Will be to arrive where we started
And know the place for the first time.

— T. S. ELIOT, *"LITTLE GIDDING"*

People who have completed the transition from childhood to adulthood are expected to support themselves economically and to take on new roles, including those of wife or husband and parent. The process of "growing up" has come to an end and the individual is recognized as an adult — "one who has grown up." If adulthood is thought of in this way, it follows that once adulthood is reached, development is over. People continue to change, of course, but instead of growing *up* they grow *old.*

Is this view correct? Should the trajectory of human development be viewed as a rapid rise to full physical maturity, followed by a longer period of equilibrium or decline? Or might it be, as Milan Kundera and T. S. Eliot suggest, that development is really a lifetime process, during which we are constantly children in the world of inexperience who return again and again to our starting point, only to know it for the first time?

In our discussions of earlier periods of life, the conviction that we were dealing with developmental change was supported by the fact that many of the changes we observed could in some respect be considered "advances" because they involved a change from less (smaller, weaker, less self-sufficient) to more (larger, stronger, more independent). Generally speak-ing, change during adulthood does not clearly "progress" in an upward direction.

In our view, questions about developmental change during adulthood help to illuminate the nature of development in infancy and childhood because they force one to confront basic questions about human development in general. In addressing these questions we will apply the same analytic strategy we used to investigate earlier periods of life. To begin with, we will examine the historical and cultural conditions that lead societies to divide life after adolescence into periods. As we shall see, the identification of adulthood as a stage of life is itself a cultural phenomenon, and the boundaries of that stage vary according to sociohistorical circumstances. Next we will discuss briefly the major theories of psychological change after adolescence; some of these theories claim that development effectively comes to a close, while others posit a sequence of developmental transformations up to the time of death. With this information as background, we will briefly review evidence concerning biological, social, and behavioral changes and their interactions in adulthood and old age. In light of our earlier analyses, we will pay special attention to the applicability of the idea of bio-social-behavioral shifts to the pattern of later life changes.

THE DISCOVERY OF ADULTHOOD

People in all cultures at all times have known perfectly well that some individuals are grownups and others are children. They have not always agreed, however, as to whether the period or periods after childhood have qualitatively distinct psychological characteristics. Nor have they agreed on the ages at which they expect significant transitions to occur.

The age period most recently conceived of as a separate life stage is **adulthood,** a period bounded on one side by adolescence and on the other by old age (Hareven, 1978). In adulthood the individual has reached full maturity and responsibility before the law. It was not until the middle of the twentieth century that psychological change during adulthood began to command the attention that had been devoted to infancy and childhood.

The first stirrings of social awareness that adulthood might be considered a distinct period of life can be traced back to nineteenth-century Europe and the United States. At that time, public attention focused on the two social categories that would come to provide the boundaries of adulthood: adolescence, which evoked concerns about the need for extended education and the consequences of failure to integrate young people properly into society; and old age, which evoked concerns about maintaining people who could no longer care for themselves.

Adolescence was institutionalized as a distinct developmental stage several decades before old age was. Extended schooling and the passage of child labor laws at the beginning of this century created a separate status for adolescents that the elderly did not enjoy. To be sure, it had long been recognized that old age was a time of reduced physical capacities that might cause the elderly to be dependent. Caring for old people had always been a significant family issue, and in the late nineteenth century care of the elderly began to be seen as a social problem as well. Both urbanization and the predominance of wage labor reduced the economic importance of elderly family members and separated a growing number of elderly people from their families. Because relatively few people survived into old age, however, the problem, though acknowledged, did not seem to threaten the social order in the way adolescence did.

Explicit recognition of a stage of life called old age resulted from improvements in health conditions and modern medicine, which combined to create a dra-

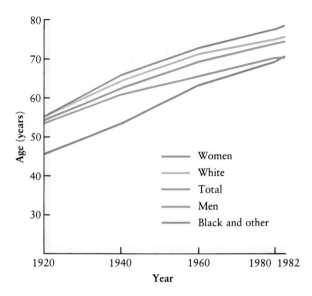

FIGURE 17.1 *Life expectancy at birth has increased 60 percent in the United States since 1920. (From* Vital Statistics of the United States, *annual of the U.S. National Center for Health Statistics.)*

matic increase in the proportion of elderly people in society (Uhlenberg, 1980). When the United States was being formed, at the end of the eighteenth century, only 20 percent of the population lived to the age of 70 years; now more than 80 percent do. In 1900 the average life expectancy in the United States was 47 years; today it is approximately 75 years, a 60 percent increase in life expectancy in less than a century (see Figure 17.1).

This increase in life expectancy, combined with the reduction in economic contributions made by the elderly, placed a great burden of support and care on younger adults. At the same time, growth in the number of elderly people led to an increase in their political power and made their needs a part of the national consciousness.

The Great Depression of the 1930s brought these issues to a head. In a time of massive unemployment, many adults had no way to maintain themselves as they grew older. This loss of income and the population's greatly increased longevity crystallized public perception of the elderly as the source of a severe social problem. In response, Congress enacted legislation to provide financial assistance in the form of social security payments to working people when they reached age 65, the age at which most people retired.

When the mandated age arrives, it is time to retire, regardless of how alert and active one feels. Here a retiring college professor is congratulated by her students.

Once old age was legally recognized as a distinct period of life, people naturally developed a more finely honed awareness of adulthood, the life stage bounded by old age on the one side and by adolescence on the other. In recent decades research has greatly increased our knowledge of the special psychological characteristics of both adulthood and old age as periods of human development.

THEORETICAL APPROACHES TO ADULTHOOD AND OLD AGE

The major conceptual division between theorists who believe that the term "development" should be restricted to the period from conception to adulthood and theorists who believe development to be a lifelong process is the role they assign to cultural-historical factors in the process of developmental change (Figure 1.4, p. 14). From a purely biological point of view, the endpoint of development is death; and from the standpoint of biology, it stands to reason that once humans are capable of biological reproduction, further change is on a downward course. When culture is assigned a central role in development, however, developmental change is seen as a lifelong process in which adults and the elderly play important parts: they are responsible for ensuring that the process of *cultural*

reproduction accompanies the process of biological reproduction as one generation follows the next.

Since psychologists are sharply divided over the relative roles of biology and culture in the process of development, it is only natural that they should be sharply divided on the question of whether development continues into adulthood and old age.

According to G. Stanley Hall (1922), whose influential book on adolescence we discussed in Chapter 15, the period from puberty to death should be divided into only two parts: adolescence and senescence. Adolescence, he believed, lasted a long time, into the thirties and forties, and senescence began where adolescence ended. As he wrote, "All that we have thought characteristic of middle life consists of only the phenomena which are connected with the turn of the tide" (1921:294).

Sigmund Freud also believed that once young people reach the genital stage and complete the process of sexual reproduction, they have fulfilled their fundamental biological role — to ensure the continuation of the species. To be sure, adults must care for their offspring until they are mature enough to repeat the cycle, but Freud attributed no particular developmental significance, for the parents, to the activities of parenting.

In Piagetian theory, formal operations are the logical endpoint of development because they provide a comprehensive logical apparatus that allows a person to maintain a state of cognitive equilibrium. Piaget did recognize that pure logic is an insufficient basis for mature action, pointing out that some of the less attractive aspects of teenage behavior result from adolescents' infatuation with the newly discovered power of logic, which leads them to act "as though the world should submit itself to idealistic schemes rather than systems of reality" (1967:64). Experience brings about a more realistic balance between the adolescent's newfound powers of systematic thinking and the messiness of life. "Just as experience reconciles formal thought with the reality of things," Piaget wrote, "so does effective and enduring work, undertaken in concrete and well-defined situations, cure dreams" (1967:68–69).

For Piaget, however, this coming to terms with reality did not imply *developmental* change; in his view, there was no stage of thought beyond formal operations. At best, he believed, changes after adolescence represent a process of consolidation and an increase in judgment about how to employ one's (fundamentally unchanged) cognitive resources.

In recent years researchers have attempted to extend Piagetian theory by demonstrating a new set of cognitive abilities that grow out of (or in parallel with) formal operations (Alexander & Langer, 1990; Commons, Richards, & Armon, 1984). Kurt Fischer, Sheryl Kenny, and Sandra Pipp (1990) argue, for example, that the development of formal operations, the ability to reason about an abstract system, is followed by the ability to relate one abstract system to another and eventually to think about entire systems of abstract relations. These further cognitive developments, according to Fischer and his colleagues, take place well into people's twenties and thirties.

Toward the end of his life Lawrence Kohlberg came to believe that beyond the ability to make judgments about specific moral dilemmas lies a qualitatively different seventh stage that centers on the question "Why be moral?" People who come to believe that it is necessary to be moral because it is through morality that one becomes most fully human have, according to Kohlberg and Robert Ryncarz (1990), solved for themselves the fundamental question of the meaning of human life. The Greek philosopher Socrates and the Reverend Martin Luther King, Jr., stand as exemplars of people who achieve this highest level.

Erik Erikson, who accords a major role in adult development to the accumulation of cultural knowledge and experience, divides life after adolescence into three stages, each with its own developmental crisis (Erikson, 1980; Erikson, Erikson, & Kivnik, 1986):

1. **Early adulthood**—the years between the ages of 20 and 35—is a period when adults commit themselves to a love relationship or else develop a sense of isolation.

2. **Middle adulthood**—roughly ages 35 to 65—is a time when adults must commit themselves to productive work, including the raising of the next generation, or become stagnant and self-centered.

3. **Old age**—65 years and beyond—is a time when people attempt to make sense of life and to incorporate the choices they have made in the past into a meaningful and satisfying pattern. Failure at this stage leads to despair; success results in that elusive quality known as wisdom.

Especially in his treatment of later life development, Erikson's ideas are similar to those of psychologists who adopt a cultural-context approach. Followers of L. S. Vygotsky distinguish two broad developmental periods after adolescence. They see the years from 18 to 30 as a time when psychological processes are organized to achieve competence at productive work, and the years from 30 to 60 as "the period of real creativity, when the individual enriches and perhaps reorders" the nature of social life in the community (Markova, 1979:26).

Many contributions to the study of adult development in recent decades have come from psychologists and scholars of other disciplines who speak of "life-span" and "life-course" development. Like the cultural-context theorists, these psychologists seek to provide detailed accounts of the way biological, behavioral, and social changes interact with cultural-historical circumstances to shape the human experience (Baltes, Featherman, & Lerner, 1990; Binstock & George, 1990; Birren & Schaie, 1990). Although the life-span and life-course approaches are similar in many respects, they differ somewhat in emphasis. In the **life-span approach,** for example, psychological phenomena such as affective relationships, the sense of self, and memory are traced from infancy through old age to determine how they are transformed as a result of biological, cognitive, and social changes (Perlmutter, 1986; Takahashi, 1990; Waterman & Archer, 1990). The **life-course approach** is more concerned with how the timing of major life events, such as the onset of schooling, the time at which someone leaves home, the beginning of childbearing, and retirement from the labor force, influence an individual's life and overall psychological well-being. Life-course psychologists might ask, for example, what difference it makes to one's self-esteem if an economic depression coincides with the birth of one's first child (Elder, Liker, & Cross, 1984; Hareven & Adams, 1982).

Paul Baltes, a major life-span theorist, believes that during adulthood some people develop a qualitatively distinct form of thinking that he calls wisdom. Baltes defines **wisdom** as "exceptional insight and judgment involving complex and uncertain matters of the human condition" (Baltes, Smith, & Staudinger, 1991:136). He likens wisdom to expertise, pointing out that experts are people who have deep experience in the domain or domains of their expertise. The domain of wisdom is daily life in society.

It is possible in principle for someone to gain this kind of deep insight at an early age, but few people are likely to do so because human social life is so complex that the necessary expertise normally requires many years to acquire. By and large, therefore, the people we refer to as wise are likely to be relatively old. They are also likely to be people who have the time to look back over a long span of experience, to theorize productively about life itself, and to pass on to the next generation the results of their theoretical activity.

Gisela Labouvie-Vief, another influential life-span theorist, believes that to achieve wisdom people must integrate two distinct aspects of the personality: thinking and emotion (Labouvie-Vief et al., 1989; Labouvie-Vief, 1990). She points out that children are encouraged to stop and think, to control their emotions, and to "behave themselves." Such self-control requires them to keep their immediate impulses in check, to subordinate emotion and momentary desire to cognition.

Labouvie-Vief goes on to note that adolescents are able to exert considerable cognitive control over their feelings and actions. But this control comes at a cost: the emotional aspects of life experience are not well connected with life's cognitive aspects. The new developmental task in adulthood, write Labouvie-Vief and her colleagues (1989), is to find a way to reconnect the cognitive and the emotional aspects of experience in order to achieve a more meaningful and organic sense of self.

EMPIRICAL RESEARCH ON CHANGE IN LATER LIFE

Knowledge about biological, social, and psychological aspects of adulthood and old age has burgeoned in the past few decades even amidst the continuing controversy over whether adult change should be considered "development" or simple "aging." We will first review the results of this research and then return to consider their implications for human development as a whole.

Biological and Cognitive Change

Developmental psychologists once saw adulthood as a featureless plateau; now many have come to see it as a complex landscape with its own special qualities. The scientific challenge is to find a way to describe this newly perceived complexity. The task is difficult because change does not seem to follow as predictable a course during adulthood as in the earlier years. As Bernice Neugarten and Gunhild Hagistad (1976) point out,

> Ours seems to be a society that has become accustomed to 70-year-old students, 30-year-old college presidents, 22-year-old mayors, 35-year-old grandmothers, 50-year-old retirees, 65-year-old fathers of preschoolers, 60-year-olds and 30-year-olds wearing the same clothing styles and 85-year-old parents caring for 65-year-old offspring. (p. 52)

Despite these difficulties, some major trends are discernible in the ways adults function as they age.

Biological changes

As we charted biological growth from conception through adolescence, at every step we encountered *increases*—growth in the size of the body, increased myelination of the brain, improved visual acuity, greater strength. By about the age of 20 years, this general pattern of increase levels off and biological capacities gradually begin to decline (see Figure 17.2) (Fries & Crapo, 1981; Katchadourian, 1987).

It may be many years before the decreases in biological functioning make themselves felt because our various organs have greater capacity than they need. Athletes and people who engage in heavy labor, however, begin to "feel their age" in their early thirties. Muscles no longer have the elasticity and recuperative power they once did; aging of the brain has begun to slow reaction time; and eyesight begins to dim as a result of decreased transparency of the lens and a loss of elasticity in the muscles that focus the lens of the eye. The inability to adjust the shape of the lens is likely to become noticeable sometime around the age of 40 and may become acute around the age of 60. Similar declines are experienced in respect to hearing and other senses (Corso, 1990).

By the age of 50, the decline in biological functioning becomes evident in most people. It is rare for athletes to continue to compete with younger men or women when they enter their fifth decade. Workers engaged in heavy labor or assembly-line jobs find that they can no longer keep up with younger workers.

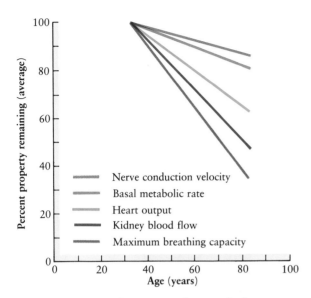

FIGURE 17.2 *The capacity of various body organs declines in a linear fashion after the age of 35. (From Shock, 1960.)*

Perhaps the most dramatic biological discontinuity in adult functioning before the age of 65 or 70 occurs in women, who usually stop ovulating and menstruating sometime between the ages of 45 and 55, a process called **menopause.** At one time menopause was considered a major turning point in a woman's life because it signaled a change in hormonal output and meant that she could no longer bear children. Research has shown, however, that women who are going through menopause or have already done so are less concerned about it than younger women who have yet to experience it (Neugarten et al., 1963).

The evidence suggests that women's response to menopause is strongly influenced by their culture and their immediate physical and social environments as well as by physiological factors (Voda, Dinnerstein, & O'Donnell, 1982). A study of Belgian women of various socioeconomic classes found that women of higher classes who held jobs outside the home had fewer complaints about menopause and tended to be more satisfied with life than lower-class women and full-time homemakers (Severne, 1982). Women in largely nonwestern cultures have more positive attitudes toward menopause than women in technologically advanced cultures and have fewer or no symptoms. Rural Mayan Indian women, for example, perceive menopause as an opportunity to participate in

a greater range of activities than they could earlier, when they were usually either pregnant or worried about becoming so (Beyene, 1991).

Some researchers have speculated that men also undergo a rapid decrease in hormonal output, a form of "male menopause." However, men continue to produce testosterone and sperm throughout their lives, although in progressively smaller quantities (Katchadourian, 1987).

For both sexes, the body's functioning begins to deteriorate markedly sometime after age 65, although there are wide individual variations in the age at which a precipitous decline in biological functioning sets in. As in other periods of life, people's physical condition depends on their unique biological makeup, the healthiness of the environment, and their way of life.

Declining physical capacities do not preclude the elderly from participating in athletic events, but they can no longer compete on an equal basis with younger adults, so special categories of competition are created for them.

In some cases, deterioration may reflect an accumulation of small defects, as when the buildup of residue inside veins and arteries triggers a heart attack or stroke. But even in the absence of any detectable disease, the body's cells eventually stop dividing, and the individual dies (Hayflick, 1980).

In general, scientists agree on a picture of biological functioning that in many respects matches G. Stanley Hall's image of adulthood as a plateau of peak capacity followed by a gradual decline. Uncertainty focuses on how long the period of "level ground" lasts for various capacities and how sharp a "downward turn" occurs at the end of life.

Cognitive changes

During the greater part of this century it was believed that cognitive capacity advanced and declined on the same schedule as biological capacity: rapid development from birth to adolescence; relatively little change during adulthood; and then a decline in old age that ended with senility, or "mindlessness."

Though current experts acknowledge that some cognitive capacities eventually decline, there is considerable uncertainty about which capacities change and in what ways. Cognitive change is inherently more difficult to assess than biological change. For one thing, each cognitive function follows its own course of change, and for another, the estimates of cognitive change are often influenced by the methods used to measure it.

TWO KINDS OF COGNITIVE CHANGE. The ability to perform certain intellectual tasks appears to decline during adulthood, while for other tasks it appears to remain about the same or even to improve. Starting with the curve at the bottom of Figure 17.3, we see that scores on tasks that require the subject to construct novel analogies from common words, such as "Sonata is to composer as portrait is to ?" (answer: painter), or to complete a series such as 32 11 33 15 34 19 35 — — — (answer: 23 36 27), or to memorize a list of unrelated words all decrease markedly after the age of 30. The ability to recall information from the distant past, however, improves slightly into middle age and by the age of 60 shows only a slight decline. The ability to interpret a spoken or written communication actually increases markedly up to the age of 60 before it too begins to decline.

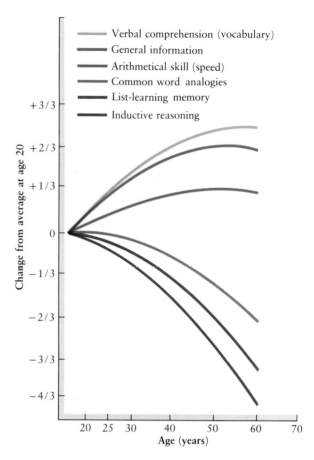

FIGURE 17.3   *Changes in the performance of various cognitive skills after the age of 20. Performance that depends on the manipulation of novel information declines with age; highly practiced mental operations such as arithmetic calculation improve slightly; performance that depends on accumulation of culturally transmitted knowledge continues to improve up to old age. (Adapted from Horn & Donaldson, 1980.)*

John Horn and Gary Donaldson (1980) explain this divergence as a reflection of two fundamentally different kinds of intelligence. The kinds of performance that improve over the course of adulthood, they argue, are those that make use of **crystallized intelligence** — intelligence that is built up over a lifetime on the basis of experience. The kinds of performance that begin to decline during adulthood they see as depending on **fluid intelligence** — intelligence that requires the manipulation of new information to solve a problem.

In Horn and Donaldson's view, fluid intelligence is largely an inherited biological predisposition that parallels other biological capacities in its growth and decline. Crystallized intelligence, by contrast, consists of culturally organized, accumulated experience; thus it continues to increase until the biological foundations that support all behavior have markedly deteriorated.

Baltes and his colleagues offer a similar "dual process" explanation of cognitive change during adulthood (Baltes, Smith, & Staudinger, 1991). They distinguish between **mental mechanics,** which depend on inherited, universal features of human thinking, and **pragmatic features,** which depend on a rich base of knowledge and the cultural context in which cognitive demands arise. In Baltes's view, a person's overall intellectual functioning always reflects a mixture of these two sources of performance. The major characteristic of cognitive change during adulthood is people's use of their growing pragmatic abilities to compensate for the brain's declining efficiency.

PROBLEMS OF MEASUREMENT. Firm conclusions about cognitive change in adulthood are complicated by several problems of measurement. So many real-life tasks seem to demand mixtures of the two kinds of abilities distinguished by Horn and Donaldson and by Baltes that it is difficult to predict how actual performance will change over time. To obtain a driver's license, for example, one has to pass a written test of one's knowledge of the law. Often such tests require the application of fluid intelligence to decide between two plausible alternatives or to figure out what the examiner is getting at with a particular question. This aspect of the test may put older people at a disadvantage. But these same older people have long experience with such laws and a great deal of general knowledge to help them pick the correct answers when they are uncertain. Consequently, they may do better than younger people with more fluid intelligence but less background knowledge.

Another difficulty of measurement can be seen in criticisms of studies such as Horn and Donaldson's, whose cross-sectional designs compare people of different ages at a single point in time (Schaie, 1990; Schaie & Hertzog, 1985). Recall from Chapter 1 (pp. 35–36) that cross-sectional designs are especially vulnerable to confounding by social and cultural factors, such as changes in the average level of education, eco-

nomic conditions, and exposure to information through the mass media. A study conducted in 1985, for example, might compare the cognitive performances of 20-, 30-, 40-, 50-, 60-, and 70-year-olds and find few differences among subjects under 50 and a marked decline thereafter. Is age the cause of the decline? Or might it be that the poor performance of the 60-year-olds resulted from the fact that they grew up during the Great Depression of the 1930s, when they and their mothers were ill fed, and that the 70-year-olds' performances suffered from the fact that their education was cut short when they quit school during the Depression to pick up what odd jobs they could and save the cost of the school clothes their parents could no longer afford?

A useful though still not trouble-free method of overcoming these weaknesses is to conduct a longitudinal study, testing the same people several times over several years. When longitudinal studies of adult cognitive change are compared with cross-sectional ones, or when cross-sectional designs are supplemented by follow-up observations, much of the apparent decline of cognitive functions disappears (Kliegl & Baltes, 1987; Labouvie-Vief, 1982; Schaie, 1990).

A large-scale study by Warner Schaie and his colleagues combined aspects of cross-sectional and longitudinal designs (Schaie & Hertzog, 1985; Schaie & Labouvie-Vief, 1974). The study began in 1956, when a large group of adults ranging in age from 22 to 70 were tested on the Thurstone test of primary mental abilities. In 1963 all of these people who could be found and persuaded to participate were retested. The same procedure was repeated again in 1970, 1977, and 1984. Each of these studies was a cross-sectional study; but by tracking the performances of all subjects who participated in all five cross-sectional studies, Schaie and his colleagues also obtained longitudinal data spanning 28 years.

Figure 17.4 summarizes the data obtained from the first three cross-sectional and longitudinal comparisons on the subtest that assesses "verbal meaning" (the ability to understand ideas expressed in words). When the cross-sectional data for the 1956, 1963, and 1970 samples are plotted, performance is found to rise slightly between 25 and 45 years of age and then to undergo a steady decline. When the data from repeated testing of the same subjects are considered, however (Figure 17.4b), little or no decline in functioning is evident except among the oldest subjects. Such results strongly suggest that at least part of the decline

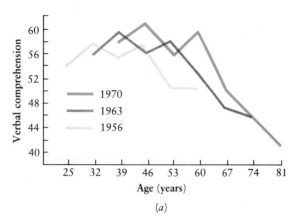

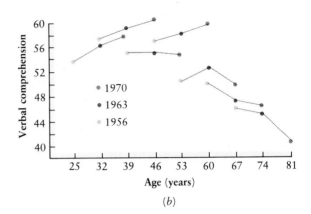

FIGURE 17.4   (a) *Performance on a test of verbal comprehension given to three groups of people varying in age from 25 to 81 years in 1956, 1963, and 1970. Note that in this cross-sectional approach, the generally downward slope of the curves begins as early as age 40. (b) Scores attained on initial tests and retests by groups tested in 1956, again in 1963, and again in 1970. The performance of these longitudinally tested groups begins to deteriorate only after the age of 65. (From Schaie & Labouvie-Vief, 1974.)*

in function found by cross-sectional studies reflects differences in life experiences and exaggerates the decline of memory with advancing age.

There are other reasons for caution in drawing conclusions about cognitive changes during adulthood. When we consider the fact that everyday intellectual activity is rarely carried out under tightly controlled laboratory conditions, we have good reason to question the practical significance of the data reported so far. For one thing, the content of laboratory tasks is often trivial by everyday standards; remembering a list of nonsense words, creating verbal analogies outside of any recognizable context, or mentally rotating geometric figures is scarcely the kind of challenge that would motivate a worldly adult to think hard. When elderly subjects are asked to memorize interesting material relevant to their lives and allowed to use the memory strategies they have developed over their lifetimes, excellent performance has been reported (Kliegl & Baltes, 1987). Consequently, laboratory studies may systematically underestimate the abilities of older people simply by virtue of the testing materials themselves.

Marion Perlmutter and her colleagues, who studied restaurant workers from 21 to 67 years of age, have shown that real-world competence may increase despite declines in physical ability and selected cognitive processes (Perlmutter, Kaplan, & Nyquist, 1990).

After first assessing the kinds of cognitive, physical, and social skills considered necessary for competent performance in actual restaurants, these researchers administered a series of standardized tests to measure manual dexterity, strength of grip, short-term memory, and the ability to attend to and act upon social cues. By and large, performance on these standardized tests declined with age. On-the-job performance, however, improved with age. The older workers were better able to balance the conflicting demands of the work, take into account what was important for customers, and adjust the level of their effort so that during times of peak demand their performance was at its peak.

Such findings have sparked a lively debate among psychologists about the nature of cognitive changes during adulthood and old age (Horn & Donaldson, 1980; Labouvie-Vief, 1982). As no resolution to this question is in sight, perhaps the best that can be concluded is that the stereotype of a steady and inevitable intellectual decline during adulthood is overdrawn, except near the very end of a long life. While certain aspects of intellectual functioning may decline — for example, the flexibility to deal rapidly with novel problems — this loss is compensated for in most everyday tasks by skills, knowledge, and a lifetime of experience (Baltes, 1987).

Social Factors and Psychological Change

The changes observed in the biological and cognitive spheres appear to accumulate gradually and continuously, with no hint of stagelike discontinuities or bio-social-behavioral shifts. At the same time, they appear to require qualitatively new patterns of thinking that permit accumulating cultural knowledge to compensate for declining "fluid" or "mechanical" abilities. Before we try to draw general conclusions about psychological change in later life, however, we should examine the possibility of stagelike changes and dis-continuities in the social rather than the biological or cognitive domain.

One useful method for tracing social events that might be expected to create discontinuities in development over the entire life course has been proposed by Robert Atchley (1975), who focused on the influence of age-related changes in family life, occupational status, and economic power. At the top of Figure 17.5 is a time line, marked in ten-year intervals, against which Atchley evaluates the parallel influences of various age-graded aspects of life. A second time line depicts the normative life stages of people in modern

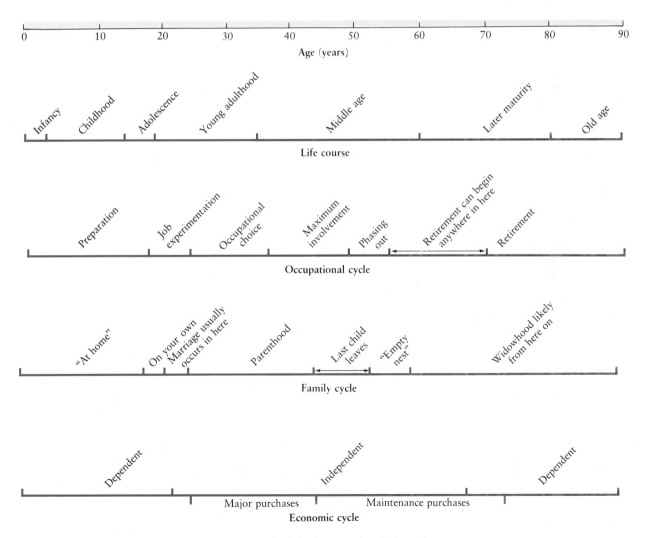

FIGURE 17.5   *Relationships between age, standard developmental periods, and major socially determined life events. These relationships vary widely according to sex, social class, culture, and historical era. (From Atchley, 1975.)*

industrialized societies, as contemporary life-span theorists describe them (e.g., Baltes & Brim, 1979; Baltes, Featherman, & Lerner, 1988; Erikson, 1968b). The next three lines chart important landmarks in an individual's changing social life.

On the occupational time line Atchley depicts birth to mid-adolescence as a time of preparation for an occupational role. The individual's work life, once it begins, goes through its own stages: experimentation, settling on a choice of jobs, a period of heavy involvement in work, and then, around the age of 50, a gradual phasing out followed by retirement and absence from the workplace.

The family cycle roughly parallels the work cycle. The individual starts out life "at home," in the family setting. Then, after a period "on one's own," family life once again becomes important, this time as a parent. In late middle age, when the individual's children are grown and begin to leave the house, the family in the home shrinks (the "empty nest" situation) and finally, through the loss of the spouse, disappears, unless the individual is absorbed into the home of one of the children or remarries.

The economic cycle plays a large role in an individual's dependence on others; until an occupational choice has been made and the power to earn a living is secure, the person is dependent on others for a livelihood. According to Atchley's scheme, a long period of relative economic independence is then followed by decreased earning power and, often, in old age, dependence once again.

As some theorists see it, all the social factors combined produce a typical "developmental contour," a social life cycle characterized by heavy involvement in many domains during youth and middle age and decreased activity later (Barker & Barker, 1968; Frenkel-Brunswik, 1963; Smelser, 1980) (see Figure 17.6; see also Figure 12.1, p. 439). From their late twenties until sometime in their fifties, most people in Western industrialized societies are simultaneously building a family, making major purchases such as a house, and becoming involved in the most responsible and time-consuming aspects of their chosen occupation. This pattern does not go unnoticed in American popular culture, where it has been humorously noted that the convergence of social involvements in middle age results in a kind of "midlife bulge" not unlike the expanding waistlines of people in their forties.

In a general way, the contour of social involvements parallels the buildup and decline of biological

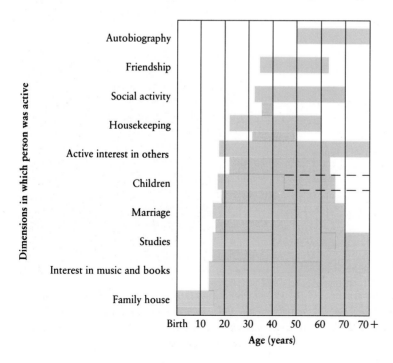

FIGURE 17.6 *Growth and decline of involvement in representative activities over the life course. The bars indicate the kinds of activity engaged in by Elizabeth Textor Goethe, mother of the eighteenth-century German poet Johann Wolfgang von Goethe. The shaded background represents a summation of the activities she engaged in simultaneously. (From Frenkel-Brunswik, 1963.)*

and cognitive capacities. In one respect, however, social changes during adulthood differ sharply from biological and cognitive changes at this time; unlike cognitive and biological changes, changes in the social sphere are marked by clear—sometimes very dramatic—*discontinuities*. There are two major reasons. First, a change in social category is often associated with a change in the contexts one encounters and the roles one plays. Second, a change in social categories causes one to be treated differently by others even in familiar contexts; because the way others treat us so largely determines the way we experience ourselves, our sense of self is likely to change quite suddenly when we experience a change in social category.

Consider the transition from the period of job preparation (which in technologically advanced societies is often synonymous with formal schooling) to being employed in a permanent full-time job. A young person entering an office, a factory, or some other workplace is immediately confronted with the need to learn a new set of skills and to get along with a group of more experienced strangers. In place of a group of classmates of similar age and perhaps similar background and adults who set the rules "for your own good," there are co-workers and supervisors of many ages and backgrounds and employers who set rules "for the good of the company." Similarly, the act of getting married and setting up housekeeping with another person requires a reorientation of authority relationships and responsibility. The appearance of children introduces an even more dramatic discontinuity into one's social identity and responsibilities (see Box 17.1).

Changes in social category are related to psychological change in complicated ways. It can be quite a shock to the sense of identity of a young adult who has just earned a teaching credential when he first walks into a classroom and is addressed as Mr. Smith by the somewhat anxiously deferential children there. It may be even more disconcerting, and an even more powerful stimulus to psychological change, for new teachers to realize that, no longer students themselves, they must now exert authority over their students, who may prefer talking with friends to learning the day's spelling words. Similarly, young adults may experience a discontinuous drop in self-esteem when marriage causes a sudden decrease in the amount of attention and open admiration they receive from members of the opposite sex.

The transitions marked by marriage, the birth of a first child, and the death of a spouse all bring about a marked change in adults' social and economic circumstances, creating a discontinuity in experience.

BOX 17.1
Suddenly I'm the Adult?

(This essay by Richard Cohen originally appeared in Psychology Today, *May 1987.)*

Several years ago, my family gathered on Cape Cod for a weekend. My parents were there, my sister and her daughter, too, two cousins, and, of course, my wife, my son and me. We ate at one of those restaurants where the menu is scrawled on a blackboard held by a chummy waiter and had a wonderful time. With dinner concluded, the waiter set the check down in the middle of the table. That's when it happened. My father did not reach for the check.

In fact, my father did nothing. Conversation continued. Finally, it dawned on me. Me! I was supposed to pick up the check. After all these years, after hundreds of restaurant meals with my parents, after a lifetime of thinking of my father as the one with the bucks, it had all changed. I reached for the check and whipped out my American Express card. My view of myself was suddenly altered. With a stroke of a pen, I was suddenly an adult.

Some people mark off their life in years, others in events. I am one of the latter, and I think of some events as rites of passage. I did not become a young man at a particular year, like 13, but when a kid strolled into the store where I worked and called me "mister," I turned around to see whom he was calling. He repeated it several times—"Mister, mister"—looking straight at me. The realization hit like a punch: Me! He was talking to me. I was suddenly a mister.

There have been other milestones. The cops of my youth always seemed to be big, even huge, and of course they were older than I was. Then one day they were neither. In fact, some of them were kids—short kids at that. Another milestone.

The day comes when suddenly you realize that all the football players in the game you're watching are younger than you. Instead of being big men, they are merely big kids. With that milestone goes the fantasy that someday, maybe, you too could be a player—maybe not a football player but certainly a baseball player. I had a good eye as a kid—not much power, but a keen eye—and I always thought I could play the game. One day I realized that I couldn't. Without having ever reached the hill, I was over it.

For some people, the most momentous milestone is the death of a parent. This happened recently to a friend of mine. With the burial of his father came the realization that he had moved up a notch. Of course, he had known all along that this would happen, but until the funeral, the knowledge seemed theoretical at best. As long as one of your parents is alive, you stay in some way a kid. At the very least, there remains at least one person whose love is unconditional.

For women, a milestone is reached when they can no longer have children. The loss of a life, the in-

At the other end of the adult spectrum, the chairperson of the board who retires and is no longer in a position to exert authority may find it difficult not only to keep herself occupied but also to adjust to a long-forgotten feeling of powerlessness. The social category of "retired person" has much in common with that of "child to be seen and not heard." Likewise, a man whose wife of many years dies may experience a dislocation of his identity when he finds himself once again the object of attention from female acquaintances now that he again fits the social category of "bachelor."

These socially engendered changes in life experience ensure that the aging individual is confronted with qualitatively new experiences which demand the kind of active social and psychological adaptation that was a part of development early in life.

Variation in the Social Structuring of the Life Course

Although family, occupational, and economic timetables must be considered along with chronological age in any study of adult development, the ones depicted in Figure 17.5 are far from universal, as Atchley himself points out. To begin with, Atchley's version of important life events inadequately represents the conditions of women. Until the twentieth century there were few occupational choices for women; the nor-

ability to create one—they are variations on the same theme. For a childless woman who could control everything in life but the clock, this milestone is a cruel one indeed.

I count other, less serious milestones—like being audited by the Internal Revenue Service. As the auditor caught mistake after mistake, I sat there pretending that really knowing about taxes was for adults. I, of course, was still a kid. The auditor was buying none of it. I was a taxpayer, an adult. She all but said, Go to jail.

There have been others. I remember the day when I had a ferocious argument with my son and realized that I could no longer bully him. He was too big and the days when I could just pick him up and take him to his room/isolation cell were over. I needed to persuade, reason. He was suddenly, rapidly, older. The conclusion was inescapable: So was I.

One day you go to your friends' weddings. One day you celebrate the birth of their kids. One day you see one of their kids driving, and one day those kids have kids of their own. One day you meet at parties and then at weddings and then at funerals. It all happens in one day. Take my word for it.

I never thought I would fall asleep in front of the television set as my father did, and as my friends' fathers did, too. I remember my parents and their friends talking about insomnia and they sounded like members of a different species. Not able to sleep?

How ridiculous. Once it was all I did. Once it was what I did best.

I never thought that I would eat a food that did not agree with me. Now I meet them all the time. I thought I would never go to the beach and not swim. I spent all of August at the beach and never once went into the ocean. I never thought I would appreciate opera, but now the pathos, the schmaltz and, especially, the combination of voice and music appeal to me. The deaths of Mimi and Tosca move me, and they die in my home as often as I can manage it.

I never thought I would prefer to stay home instead of going to a party, but now I find myself passing parties up. I used to think that people who watched birds were weird, but this summer I found myself watching them, and maybe I'll get a book on the subject. I yearn for a religious conviction I never thought I'd want, exult in my heritage anyway, feel close to ancestors long gone and echo my father in arguments with my son. I still lose.

One day I made a good toast. One day I handled a headwaiter. One day I bought a house. One day—what a day!—I became a father, and not too long after that I picked up the check for my own. I thought then and there it was a rite of passage for me. Not until I got older did I realize that it was one for him, too. Another milestone.

mative female career was that of mother and housewife. A young woman had no "time on her own" between living "at home" and marriage, and no period of economic independence. When women's life paths did deviate from this norm, it was seldom in the direction taken by men. The youngest daughter, for example, was often expected to forgo marriage and a family of her own altogether in order to remain at home and help her parents (Hareven & Adams, 1982). And since the average life expectancy was much shorter than it is today, many women died before their youngest child was grown.

In the United States these conditions have been mitigated somewhat by improvements in health care, changes in occupational roles, and social security legis-lation. But the social circumstances of elderly women are still difficult—and different in many ways from those of men.

Atchley's normative picture is also oriented toward the highly educated middle class, and so misrepresents the life course of working-class and poor people of both sexes (Espenshade & Braun, 1983). People who are born into families with few financial resources are likely to drop out of school early, and their jobs are likely to require physically demanding labor. These workers, whose health care is likely to be rudimentary and housing inadequate, are not likely to be capable of sustaining "maximum involvement" at work into their fifties and sixties. By their mid-fifties, they may be relegated to sweeping up or running errands, the kinds of jobs that used to be assigned to 10- or 12-year-olds just entering the work force. Thus their life trajectory is not at all the one Atchley describes.

Finally, Atchley is providing a picture of people living in a modern industrialized society (see Figure 17.7). When we turn to nonindustrial societies, we find enormous variation in the culturally accepted stages of adult development (Falk, Falk, & Tomashevich, 1981; Fry, 1988; Holmes, 1983) and in the social significance assigned to various age periods. At the same time, nonindustrialized societies generally seem to have no social institutions comparable to what we call retirement (Jacobs, 1975). Old people are likely to continue to play active roles in these societies.

The continued importance of old people in such societies grows out of their importance in the process of cultural reproduction. Most such societies lack writing systems to preserve the experiences of the group, so the elders are repositories of vital information. Old people in general, and old men in particular, often wield power in many spheres. As repositories of the culture's knowledge, the old rise rather than decline in status. Among the Ashanti of West Africa, for example,

the grandparents . . . on both sides are the most honored of one's kinsfolk. Their position and status are of very great importance in the social system. In Ashanti it is the grandparents who are the prototypes of persons and institutions commanding reverence and submission to the norms of tradition. (Fortes, 1950:276)

The situation of the elderly in nonindustrialized societies should not, however, be overly romanticized. In agricultural societies the elderly are generally expected to contribute to the economic well-being of the household until they die. In many subsistence-level hunter-gatherer societies the old and feeble suffer a loss of prestige, and if the group is put under extreme pressure, they may be killed or left to die (Falk et al., 1981).

Thus the patterns of individual lives vary in accordance with sex, social class, culture, and historical period. In a longitudinal study of the impact of some of these factors on people living in Oakland, California, the life-course psychologist Glen Elder (1974) showed that the effects of the Depression and World War II depended on a person's age and economic status at the start of the Depression and the severity of its impact on the family's income. The people who were teenagers during the Depression experienced the fewest difficulties. Although they were required to help their families by finding odd jobs and doing housework, these responsibilities gave them a sense of usefulness and spurred them to greater efforts. Although the young men faced the terrors of war, those who survived returned to a booming economy and a period of unexcelled material well-being. The young women entered the work force in record numbers during the war, and when it ended they and the returning men started the baby boom.

The Depression was a much more difficult time for younger children, who experienced family disruption all during their childhoods — first because their fathers were out of work and their families faced the loss of their homes and a life of desperation, then because their fathers went to war while their mothers went to work.

When Elder (1982) studied the same families after the participants had entered old age, he found that the effects of these early experiences often lingered. Women from middle-class households that had experienced only mild economic difficulties reported that

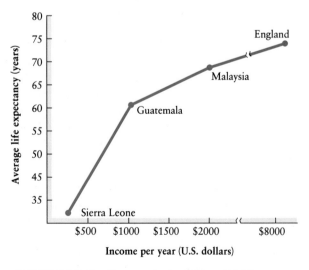

FIGURE 17.7 *In many parts of the world, life expectancy is still relatively short. As a nation's income increases, so does the average life expectancy. (From United Nations Children's Fund, 1988.)*

they found the transition to retirement and lowered income less difficult because they had learned to cope with such circumstances as young mothers. Women who had decided not to have children because of their experience of severe deprivation in the 1930s, however, found themselves in very difficult circumstances in the 1970s when their husbands had died and they had no adult children to help them deal with the problems of old age.

Such complexities in actual lives argue for caution in drawing conclusions from simplified schemas of the life course. While Atchley's overall approach has merit, it must be continually modified to take actual historical and cultural contexts into account.

The Influence of Social Factors on Cognition and Biology

In assessing the nature of the changes experienced in later life, we must keep in mind a principle that was central to our understanding of early development: Biology not only shapes experience but is shaped by it (see Chapter 4, p. 154). This principle alerts us to the strong possibility that variations in experience produced by socially mandated life changes such as retirement can affect development in the biological and cognitive spheres.

A variety of evidence indicates that the disengagement that accompanies retirement, the loss of a spouse, or placement in an old-age home—all events that change one's social world—contribute substantially to biological and cognitive decline (Schooler & Schaie, 1987). Even when elderly people are in a comfortable institution where they receive high-quality health care and food, the mere fact of being in the institution seems to hasten their death (Lawton, 1977).

Precisely which features of that environment exert such negative effects? Part of the answer seems to be that when elderly people are confronted with new and unfamiliar social contexts over which they have little control, they may lose the courage to engage in the kind of active adaptation necessary to allow them to develop (Rodin, 1986). Echoing the problem of learned helplessness seen under certain circumstances during infancy (Chapter 7, pp. 248–249), such people respond by simply giving up on life, and their development comes to an abrupt halt.

The transition to life in an institution that cares for the elderly and disabled can be a source of severe stress, even if there is adequate provision of basic necessities.

Even if elderly people do not simply give up hope when they enter a nursing home, they may develop dependent behaviors because it is the best way to get attention from the staff. Several studies by Margaret Baltes and her colleagues (summarized in M. Baltes & Wahl, 1991) have shown that displays of independence reduce the amount of social interaction the elderly receive; the paradoxical result is that dependency is a way to overcome social isolation.

But just as learned helplessness can be overcome by rearrangement of the newborn's environment, the negative impact of social changes in adulthood can be mitigated by deliberate intervention to change the social environment (Langer & Rodin, 1976; Rodin & Langer, 1977; Middleton, Buchanan, & Suurmond, 1991). Ellen Langer and her colleagues (1979) intervened in a nursing home in an attempt to reverse the intellectual decline typically found among its residents. The researchers focused on memory function as the variable they would attempt to improve. First they gave a memory pretest to all residents who participated in the study. Then they visited the home four or five times over a 6-week period and posed simple, readily understandable questions to the residents, explaining that they were interested in learning more about life in such institutions. They asked about what was going on in the home that day, what residents had eaten for breakfast or for dinner the night before, and so on. They also asked about the residents' former lives — their families, jobs, and earlier life experiences.

They carried out these interviews in two ways, creating two groups of subjects. With one group the researcher talked about his or her own life experiences in addition to asking about the residents' experiences, a procedure that Langer and her colleagues called "reciprocal self-disclosure." On the basis of prior research, the investigators believed that if they reciprocated the residents' trust by talking honestly about their own lives, they would build interest and motivation, enhancing the residents' willingness to engage in mental work. The researchers asked the second group the same questions and showed the same level of interest in their answers but did not talk about themselves.

Despite its apparent simplicity, this manipulation had a significant impact. On the basis of nurses' estimates of the residents' level of awareness, sociability, health, and other measures of well-being, as well as on the basis of formal memory testing, the residents who engaged in reciprocal discussions outscored those who were engaged in a less interactive way. Such results provide evidence that environmental arrangements that increase people's social connectivity promote healthy development when they are appropriately applied.

As Ronald Abeles and Matilda Riley (1987) point out, these and similar results demonstrate that aging is

As simple an act as taking the time to chat with elderly people living in a home for the aged has been shown to increase their mental alertness and improve their overall health.

not determined solely by biology; rather, like development at the start of life, it reflects complex interactions of social, behavioral, and biological processes. We would add the reminder that these interactions are themselves shaped by and help to shape the cultural contexts in which they occur.

DECLINE OR CONTINUING DEVELOPMENT?

It is now time to return to the question with which we started: Does development continue throughout life or do the principles of psychological change themselves undergo a change after the transition to adulthood?

Although the data are not unequivocal, the growth of biological capacities to the age of approximately 30 years and their subsequent slow decline appear to follow the course of change described metaphorically by many psychologists over the years: From birth through puberty and a few years more, the tide of life rises, sometimes with a rush, sometimes with a smooth, imperceptible advance. At some vaguely definable time, the high-water mark is reached, and the tide slowly retreats.

A similar story appears adequate to describe those intellectual capacities referred to as "fluid" and believed to depend heavily on biological factors. This pattern of rise and decline can also be seen in the social domain: Infants begin life confined entirely to contexts where they can be watched over and protected; the range of contexts where the growing person can act as an independent agent expands steadily into middle age; then the contexts for independent action shrink until life ends as it began, with the elderly person dependent on others and capable of acting only within a restricted range of contexts.

At the same time, aspects of intellectual and social change suggest both the qualitative rearrangement of psychological processes and discontinuities in the process of change. Qualitatively new forms of thinking arise from the fact that "crystallized," "pragmatic" abilities increase while "fluid," "mechanical" abilities decrease, requiring people to reorganize their thinking to maintain their effectiveness as they grow older. This changing balance among mental resources interacts with the social discontinuities in one's life, such as retirement or the loss of a spouse, which bring about

In many traditional, nonliterate societies, the elders retain high status because of the store of knowledge they have accumulated over a lifetime.

dramatic changes in the contexts of one's everyday activities.

When we take into consideration the complex psychological trade-offs that changes in the biological, cognitive, and social domains require, the picture of adulthood as a period of stability followed by a gradual decline often fails to correspond to a particular individual's actual experience of psychological change. Instead of a subjective feeling of gradual decline, what emerges from studies of adult development is an intricate, shifting mosaic in which gradual change and predictable experiences are mixed with sudden, unexpected events—new insights, conceptual reintegrations, and triumphs as well as disappointments, loss of power, and decline. Even as one's physical powers decrease, the accumulated experiences of a lifetime, the "crystallized" and "pragmatic" aspects of cognition, provide adults with resources for dealing with life that are well beyond the reach of the young.

This perception of later life as a form of development comes through very clearly in interviews with middle-aged and elderly people:

There is a difference between wanting to feel young and wanting to *be* young. Of course, it would be pleasant to maintain the vigor and appearance of youth; but I would not trade those things for the authority or autonomy I feel—no, nor the ease of interpersonal relationships nor the self-confidence that comes from experience.

You feel you have lived long enough to have learned a few things that nobody can learn earlier. That's the reward . . . and also the excitement. I now see things in books, in people, in music that I couldn't see when I was younger. . . . It's a form of ripening that I attribute largely to my present age.

It's as if there are two mirrors before me, each held at a partial angle. I see part of myself in my mother who is growing old, and part of her in me. In the other mirror, I see part of myself in my daughter. I have had some dramatic insights, just from looking in those mirrors. . . . It is a set of revelations that I suppose can only come when you are in the middle of three generations. (Neugarten, 1968:97–98)

As the novelist Milan Kundera reminded us in the passage at the beginning of this chapter, the old, no less than the young, are innocent of the experiences yet to come. Except for the unavoidable fact of death, little can be known for certain about the new experiences that await us each day. Consequently, as long as one actively engages the environment, one has the possibility of gaining new insights even into the most familiar of life's experiences, feeling the pleasure of knowing one's life in a fresh way each time. In this sense, development shares features common at all ages; it is always a process of becoming.

SUMMARY

1. The study of adulthood poses a major problem for students of development: Does development continue after the transition to adulthood, or does it cease and some other process of change begin?
2. Adulthood is the last major period of the life span to attract detailed scholarly study. Analysis of adulthood followed legislation that institutionalized its upper boundary at age 65, the point at which retirement is usual and old-age benefits normally begin.
3. Concern with old age and adulthood was spurred by changes in public health and medicine that resulted in a major shift in society's age profile. During the past century, average life expectancy has increased by 60 percent.
4. Major theoretical approaches to the study of child development have offered three basic theories of adult development:
   a. The biological maturation approach: Development ceases and a period of gradual decline ensues.
   b. The universal constructivist view: Development ceases but there is no marked decline until shortly before death.
   c. The cultural-context view: Development continues throughout life, but the particular mix of biological, social, and behavioral factors that become reintegrated at successive stages varies as a function both of age and of cultural and historical circumstances.
5. Physiological indicators of organ capacity decline steadily from approximately the age of 30.
6. Menopause represents a biological discontinuity in a woman's ability to bear children; men experience no comparable biological discontinuity.
7. A period of rapid deterioration in biological capacity begins sometime after the age of 65 and proceeds until death.
8. It is widely believed that different cognitive abilities follow different paths of change during adulthood and old age. Performance improves in tasks that require crystallized intelligence and declines in tasks that depend on fluid intelligence.
9. Efforts to document cognitive change are complicated by problems of measurement. Longitudinal designs often fail to confirm the decline in performance suggested by cross-sectional designs. An elderly person's performance depends heavily on the conditions of testing and the test materials used, an indication that poor performance does not always reflect low ability.
10. Socially determined changes in the spheres of family and work introduce major discontinuities into the process of development during adulthood and old age. These changes bring qualitatively new experiences that require the kind of active adaptation associated with earlier development.
11. As the particular pattern of individual life events varies in accordance with sex, social class, culture, and historical era, it is difficult to specify a single pattern for adult development. Generalization is further impeded by the unpredictability of many life events that influence the course of development.
12. Causal relations among biological, behavioral, and social factors in adulthood, as in early life, are multidirectional: biology not only influences behavioral and social factors but is influenced by them.
13. At the level of individual psychological experience, development appears to be a lifelong process of encountering the new and unexpected and acquiring greater insight into human experience through a process of active adaptation.

KEY TERMS

adulthood
crystallized intelligence
early adulthood
fluid intelligence
life-course approach
life-span approach

menopause
mental mechanics
middle adulthood
old age
pragmatic features
wisdom

SUGGESTED READINGS

ALEXANDER, C. N., & LANGER, ELLEN J. (Eds.). *Higher Stages of Human Development*. New York: Oxford University Press, 1990.

The dozen essays in this volume provide up-to-date discussions of a great many of the topics covered in this chapter. They can serve as a good summary of current issues in the study of psychological change during adulthood and old age.

ERIKSON, ERIK H. (Ed.). *Adulthood*. New York: Norton, 1978.

A seminal series of essays by leading students of adult development in many scientific disciplines. Erikson himself uses Ingmar Bergman's classic film *Wild Strawberries* as an exemplary case study of development during adulthood and old age.

ERIKSON, ERIK H., ERIKSON, JOAN M., & KIVNICK, HELEN Q. *Vital Involvement in Old Age*. New York: Norton, 1986.

The leading proponent of development as a lifelong process, his wife and co-worker, and another co-worker summarize a lifetime of reflections about development through interviews with the surviving participants in a longitudinal study begun 60 years earlier.

FRIES, JAMES F., & CRAPO, LAWRENCE M. *Vitality and Aging*. New York: W. H. Freeman, 1981.

A readable and comprehensive survey of the aging process.

HAREVEN, TAMARA K. *Family Time and Industrial Time*. Cambridge: Cambridge University Press, 1982.

A detailed account of the links between family life and work in a New England mill town after the turn of the century, showing the intimate links between the social organization of people's lives and their experience of lifelong development.

SCHAIE, K. WARNER, & WILLS, S. L. *Adult Development and Aging* (3rd ed.). New York: Harper & Row, 1991.

This textbook, written by two leaders in the study of adulthood and aging, provides a comprehensive overview of psychological change in later life. The text is an especially good source for clear and accessible discussions of the complex methodological issues involved in the use of cross-sectional and longitudinal designs in the study of human development.

SKINNER, B. F., & VAUGHAN, BARBARA E. *Enjoy Old Age*. New York: Norton, 1988.

This informal, engaging, and well-informed view of how to cope with aging combines personal experience with insights gained from a half-century of research about the behavior of organisms.

GLOSSARY

ABSTRACT MODELING A kind of modeling in which children abstract general linguistic principles from specific utterances. According to Bandura, this is one of the main ways in which children acquire language.

ACCOMMODATION In Piaget's theory, the process by which children modify their existing schemas in order to incorporate or adapt to new experiences.

ADOPTION STUDY Studies in which genetically related individuals who are raised in different family environments are compared to determine the extent to which heredity or environment controls a given trait.

ADULTHOOD From the Latin word meaning "one who has grown up." A period bounded on one side by adolescence and on the other by old age. In adulthood, the individual has reached full maturity and responsibility before the law.

AGGRESSION An act in which someone intentionally hurts another.

ALLELE An alternate form of a gene coded for a particular trait.

ALPHA-FETOPROTEIN TEST A blood test used mainly to detect prenatal defects of the neural tube.

AMNIOCENTESIS A medical procedure in which a long, hollow needle is inserted through the mother's abdomen into the amniotic sac surrounding the fetus and amniotic fluid is withdrawn for later analysis. It is one of the principal techniques for discovering whether a fetus suffers from certain genetic defects.

AMNION The amnion is the thin, tough, transparent membrane that holds the amniotic fluid surrounding the prenatal organism. It arises out of the trophoblast and is sometimes called the amniotic sac.

ANAL STAGE In Freudian theory, the period during the second year of life when the child is preoccupied with gaining control of the smooth muscles involved in defecation.

ANIMAL MODEL Research conducted on animals that are close evolutionarily to humans and whose patterns of behavior therefore serve as models for drawing inferences about human development.

A NOT B ERROR A characteristic of stage 4 of Piaget's six stages of object permanence; babies will look for a hidden object where they first found it even after they have seen it moved to a new location.

APGAR SCALE A quick, simple test used to diagnose the physical state of newborn infants.

APPRENTICESHIP A special process of training in which a novice spends an extended period of time working for a master in a particular trade or craft while learning on the job.

ASSIMILATION In Piaget's theory, the process by which children incorporate new experiences into their existing schemas.

ATTACHMENT An enduring emotional bond that infants form with specific people, usually beginning with their mothers, sometime between the ages of 6 and 9 months. Children are said to be attached to someone when they seek to be near that person, are distressed when they are separated from the person, are happy when they are reunited with the person, and orient their actions to the person even in the person's absence.

AUTHORITARIAN PARENTING PATTERN Authoritarian parents try to shape and evaluate the behavior and attitudes of their children according to a set standard. They stress the importance of obedience to authority and favor punitive measures to bring about their children's compliance.

AUTHORITATIVE PARENTING PATTERN Authoritative parents try to control their children by explaining their rules or decisions, and by reasoning with their children. They are willing to listen to their children's point of view, even if they do not always accept it. They set high standards for their children's behavior and encourage them to be individualistic and independent.

AUTISM A poorly understood condition in which children are unable to interact with others normally, their language development is retarded, and their behavior is often ritualistic and compulsive.

AUTONOMOUS MORALITY Morality based on the belief that rules are arbitrary agreements that can be changed if those governed by them agree.

BABBLING A form of vocalizing that includes consonant and vowel sounds like those used in speech. Babies begin to babble at approximately 4 months of age.

BABY BIOGRAPHY A parent's detailed record of an infant's behavior over a period of time.

BABYNESS The combination of physical features that ethologists believe attracts adults to the young of the species. Babyness includes a large head relative to body size; a large and protruding forehead in relation to the rest of the face; eyes that are positioned below the horizontal midline of the face; and round, protruding cheeks.

BIOLOGICAL DRIVES Aroused states, such as hunger and thirst, that urge the organism to obtain the basic requirements for survival.

BIO-SOCIAL-BEHAVIORAL SHIFT The process of change arising from the convergence and reorganization of biological, social, and behavioral elements of development in which distinctively new and significant forms of behavior emerge.

BLASTOCYST The hollow sphere of cells that results from the differentiation of the cells in the morula into trophoblast cells on the outside and the inner cell mass on the inside.

BRAIN STEM A central nervous system structure located at the upper end of the spinal cord. It becomes active during the fetal period. At birth, it is one of most highly developed areas of the brain and controls such vital functions as breathing, sleeping, the inborn reflexes, emotions, and states of alertness.

BRAZELTON NEONATAL ASSESSMENT SCALE A scale used to assess the newborn's neurological condition. Included in it are tests of infants' reflexes, motor capacities, muscle tone, capacity for responding to objects and people, and capacity for controlling their own behavior and attention.

CANALIZED CHARACTERISTICS Characteristics that are relatively invulnerable to environmental influence during their development.

CATEGORIZE To perceive objects or events that differ in various ways as equivalent.

CATHARSIS The reduction of an urge, or an emotional release.

CEPHALOCAUDAL PATTERN The sequence of body development from head to foot.

CEREBRAL CORTEX The uppermost part of the central nervous system. Within the cortex there are specialized regions for the analysis of time, space, and language; as well as for motor functions and sensory discriminations. Large areas of this part of the brain are not prewired to respond directly to external stimulation in any discernible way.

CHORION One of the membranes that develops out of the trophoblast. It forms the placenta.

CHORIONIC VILLUS SAMPLING A medical procedure in which cells are taken from the villi (hairlike projections) on the chorion. This procedure can reveal the presence of chromosomal defects.

CHROMOSOME A threadlike structure made up of genes; in humans there are 46 chromosomes in the nucleus of each cell.

CLASSICAL CONDITIONING The process by which an organism learns which events in its environment go with others. It is the establishment of a connection between a response (such as salivation) and a previously neutral stimulus (such as a tone), resulting from the neutral stimulus being paired with an unconditional stimulus (such as food).

CLEAVAGE The initial mitotic divisions of the zygote into several cells as it travels down the fallopian tube into the uterus.

CLINICAL METHOD A method of observation in which questions are tailored to the individual, with each question depending on the answer to the one that precedes it.

CODOMINANCE A trait that is determined by two alleles but is qualitatively different from the trait produced by either of the contributing alleles alone.

COEVOLUTION The combined process that emerges from the interaction of biological and cultural evolution.

COHORT A group of persons the same age who are therefore likely to share some common experiences that are different from those of younger or older groups.

COHORT SEQUENTIAL DESIGN An experimental design in which the longitudinal method is replicated with several cohorts, each of which is studied longitudinally. This design allows age-related factors in developmental change to be separated from cohort-related factors.

COLLECTIVE MONOLOGUES The speech that occurs when children are playing near each other and each of them is talking, but their remarks focus on what they are doing by themselves, with no real regard for their partner and with no apparent intention of actually communicating.

COMPENSATION A mental operation that allows the child to consider how changes in one aspect of a problem are related to (and potentially compensated for by) changes in another.

COMPLEMENTARY GENES Genes that can only produce their phenotypical effect if they work in combination with other genes.

COMPREHENSION In reading the process by which meaning is assigned to the text.

CONCRETE OPERATIONS In Piaget's theory, internalized mental actions that fit into a logical system. Such thinking allows the child to combine, separate, order, and transform objects in their minds, and is termed concrete because it is restricted to objects and events actually present in the child's environment.

CONDITIONAL RESPONSE In classical conditioning, a response that occurs following a previously neutral stimulus as a result of pairing the neutral stimulus with an unconditional stimulus.

CONDITIONAL STIMULUS In classical conditioning, a stimulus that evokes no particular response by itself but which can come to elicit a response after training. For example, a tone can become the conditional stimulus for salivation if it is repeatedly sounded before food is presented.

CONSERVATION Piaget's term for the understanding that the properties of an object or a substance remain the same even though its appearance may have been altered in some superficial way.

CONTEXT In cultural-context theory, it is the interrelationship of a particular behavior, the event in which the behavior is a part, and the setting in which the behavior and event take place.

CONTROL GROUP The persons in an experiment who are treated as much as possible like the persons in the experimental group except that they do not undergo the experimental manipulation.

CONVERSATIONAL ACTS The term used to describe how language is used for pragmatic purposes to achieve goals.

COOPERATIVE PRINCIPLE The master rule of ordinary conversation which is to make your contributions to conversation at the required time and for the accepted purpose of the talk exchange.

COREGULATION The sharing between parent and child of responsibility for the child's behavior.

CORRELATION Two factors are said to be correlated with one another when changes in one are associated with changes in the other.

CRITICAL PERIODS Periods in the growth of the organism during which specific biological or environmental events must occur for development to proceed normally.

CROSSING OVER The process during the first phase of meiosis in which genetic material is exchanged between chromosomes containing genes for the same characteristic.

CROSS-SECTIONAL DESIGN A research design in which children of different ages are studied at a single time.

CRYSTALLIZED INTELLIGENCE Intelligence that is built up over a lifetime on the basis of experience.

CULTURAL-CONTEXT THEORY A theory that emphasizes the role of culture in structuring the interplay of biological, social, physical, and environmental influences in development.

CULTURE The pattern of human designs for living that is based on the accumulated knowledge of a people as encoded in their language and embodied in the physical artifacts, beliefs, values, customs, and activities that have been passed down from one generation to the next.

DECODING In reading, the process by which letters of the alphabet are associated with corresponding phonemes of the spoken language.

DEEP STRUCTURE The restricted set of rules of a language from which the actual sentences that people produce can be derived.

DEFENSE MECHANISM Freud's term for psychological processes, such as repression, that people use to protect themselves from unpleasant thoughts and feelings.

DEFERRED IMITATION In Piagetian terms, the imitation of actions that have occurred at an earlier time.

DEVELOPMENT The sequence of physical and psychological changes that human beings undergo as they grow older, beginning with conception and continuing throughout life.

DEVELOPMENTAL CRISIS In Erikson's theory, a set of choices and tests that an individual faces as he or she becomes ready to face a new life task. The outcome of a crisis can be either successful transition to the next stage or failure and an impairment of the life cycle.

DEVELOPMENTAL NICHE The term used by Super and Harkness to refer to the child's place within the community. They suggest that every developmental niche be analyzed in terms of the physical and social context in which the child lives, the culturally determined child rearing and educational practices of the child's society, and the psychological characteristics of the child's parents.

DEVIATION IQ A method of calculating IQ that takes account of the fact mental development is more rapid early in life than later. In this method IQ scores are assigned to children based on the difference between their raw scores and the standardized mean of 100.

DISHABITUATION   To begin paying attention again when some aspect of the stimulus situation has been changed.

DIZYGOTIC TWINS   Twins that result from the fertilization by two sperm of two eggs that are released at the same time; also called "fraternal" twins.

DOMINANCE HIERARCHY   A hierarchical social structure in which some individuals are dominant and others subordinate to them; associated with the control of conflict.

DOMINANT ALLELE   The allele that is expressed when there are two different alleles for the same trait.

EARLY ADULTHOOD   In Erikson's theory, the years between 20 and 35 when adults commit themselves to a love relationship or else develop a sense of isolation.

ECOLOGY   In developmental psychology, the range of situations in which people are actors; the roles they play; and the predicaments they encounter.

ECTODERM   One of the layers of cells that develops out of the inner cell mass of the blastocyst. The ectoderm eventually develops into the outer surface of the skin, the nails, part of the teeth, the lens of the eye, the inner ear, and the central nervous system.

EDUCATION   A specialized form of socialization in which adults engage in deliberate teaching of the young to ensure the acquisition of specialized knowledge and skills required in adult life.

EGO   In Freud's theory, the mental structure that emerges out of the id. Its major task is self-preservation, which it accomplishes through voluntary movement, perception, logical thought, adaptation, and problem solving, and by gaining control over the instinctual demands of the id.

EGOCENTRISM   The interpretation of the world from one's own (ego's) point of view without taking into consideration alternative perspectives.

EMOTION   The feeling tone, or affect, with which people respond to their circumstances.

EMPATHY   The sharing of another's emotional experience.

ENDODERM   The inner layer of cells that develops from the inner cell mass of the blastocyst. The endoderm eventually develops into the digestive system and the lungs.

ENDOGENOUS CAUSES   Causes of development arising from inside the organism as a consequence of its biological heritage.

ENVIRONMENT   The totality of things, conditions, and circumstances that surround the organism.

ENVIRONMENTALIST HYPOTHESIS OF IQ   The position that intelligence is both specific and heavily dependent on experience.

EPIGENESIS   The hypothesis that new forms emerge through the interactions that take place between the preceding form and its environment.

EQUILIBRATION   The term Piaget used for the back-and-forth process of seeking a balance between existing psychological structures and new environmental circumstances. When children achieve a balance between accommodation and assimilation, they enter a new stage of development.

ETHOLOGY   An interdisciplinary science that studies the biological bases of behavior and its evolutionary context.

EXOGENOUS CAUSES   Causes of development arising from the environment, particularly from the adults who reward and punish the child's efforts.

EXPERIMENTAL GROUP   The persons whose environment is changed as part of an experiment.

EXPERIMENTS   Research procedures in which the investigator introduces some change in the person's experience and then measures the effect of that change on the person's behavior.

EXPLICIT MODELING   A method of increasing prosocial behavior in which adults behave in the ways they desire children to imitate.

FAST MAPPING   The way in which children quickly form an idea of the meaning of an unfamiliar word they hear in a familiar and highly structured situation.

FETAL GROWTH RETARDATION   The term used to describe the conditions of babies who are especially small for their gestational age at birth.

FLUID INTELLIGENCE   Problem-solving ability that enables a person to manipulate new information.

FOLLOW-BACK DESIGNS   Such designs begin by selecting a sample of adults who are known to be deviant in some way and a second sample of adults who are free from such problems. The researchers then examine available records to determine which aspects of childhood functioning seem to be associated with the adults' problem.

FOLLOW-FORWARD DESIGNS Researchers using such designs begin by selecting groups of children who differ on a particular dimension such as their aggressiveness and then compare their subsequent adjustment.

FORMAL OPERATIONS The ability to think in a systematic manner about all the logical relations in a problem. Piaget hypothesized that formal operational thinking emerges at about the age of 12. It is the final stage in his theory of development.

FORMAT The term Bruner uses to refer to activities like games of peekaboo and bedtime routines in which the communicative interaction between children and their caregivers are socially patterned.

GENDER SCHEMA According to Sandra Bem and others, a network of associations embodying the culture's conception of sex roles, which children use to structure their perceptions of the various scenes they inhabit and guide their behavior.

GENE POOL The total genetic information possessed by a sexually reproducing population.

GENES The molecules that transmit the hereditary blueprints for the development of the individual from one generation to the next.

GENITAL STAGE In Freudian theory, the period of mature sexuality that begins with adolescence, in which sexual urges are no longer directed toward the parents but are transferred to peers of the opposite sex.

GENOTYPE The total complement of genes that an individual inherits.

GERM CELLS Sperm and ova; the cells specialized for sexual reproduction that have only half the number of chromosomes normal for a species (23 in humans).

GERMINAL PERIOD The period from conception to implantation, which occurs about 8 to 10 days after conception.

GRAMMAR The rules of a language that govern both the sequence of words in a sentence and the ordering of parts of words.

GRAMMATICAL MORPHEMES Words and parts of words that create meaning by elaborating relations among elements in a sentence.

GROUP NORMS Rules that apply only to particular groups, such as peer groups or professional groups.

GUIDED PARTICIPATION The collaboration between adults and children built upon shared understanding in routine problem-solving situations by means of which adults shape young children's development.

HABITUATION The gradual decrease of attention paid to a repeated stimulus.

HETEROCHRONY The variability in the rates of change of different parts of the organism over time.

HETEROGENEITY The variability in the levels of development of different parts of the organism at a given time.

HETERONOMOUS MORALITY The morality of constraint, according to Piaget. Such morality is characterized by unquestioning obedience to rules and to more powerful individuals; by attention to the letter of the law, rather than its spirit; and by a conception of responsibility in which outcomes are crucial and motives irrelevant.

HETEROZYGOUS Having inherited two genes of different allelic forms for the same attribute.

HOLOPHRASE A term for babies' single-word utterances; the term indicates a belief that these single words stand for entire phrases or sentences.

HOMOZYGOUS Having inherited two genes of the same allelic form for a single attribute.

HORIZONTAL DECALAGE Piaget's term for a child's uneven performance at a given stage of development when the same logical problem is presented in different forms.

HOSTILE AGGRESSION An act aimed at hurting another, either for revenge or to establish dominance.

HYPOTHESIS An experimental hypothesis is an assumption that is precise enough to be tested and can be shown to be incorrect.

ID In Freudian theory, the first mental structure. It is the part of ourselves responsible for our innate desires and is the main source of mental energy. It is unconscious, energetic, and pleasure-seeking.

IDENTIFICATION A process that provides individuals with a sense of who they are and who they want to be. In Freudian terms, identification is the strong desire to look, act, and feel like another person of the same sex.

IDENTITY According to Erikson, an individual's sense of personal sameness and historical continuity. It is a pattern of beliefs about the self that reconciles the many ways in which one is like other people with the ways in which one differs from others. According to Piaget, identity refers to the ability of children to realize that objects and quantities remain invariant when surface appearances change.

IDENTITY FORMATION According to Erikson, the development crisis faced by adolescents. To forge a secure identity, adolescents must bring about a resolution of the identity crisis in both the individual and the social spheres. They must establish the "identity of these two identities."

IMPLANTATION The process by which the blastocyst becomes attached to the uterus.

INDEPENDENT CONSTRUAL OF SELF A sense of self that is described by such labels as "individualistic," "egocentric," "separate," "autonomous," "idiocentric," and "self contained."

INDUCTION A method of increasing children's prosocial behavior through the use of explanations that appeal to their pride, concern for others, and their desire to be grown-up.

INFORMATION-PROCESSING APPROACH A strategy of explaining cognitive development using the analogy of a modern computer. Research in this tradition is greatly concerned with a detailed analysis of each intellectual task and each step in solving a problem.

INNATIST HYPOTHESIS OF IQ The position that some people are born generally smarter than others and no amount of training or normal variation in the environment can alter this fact.

INITIATION-REPLY-EVALUATION SEQUENCE A pattern within instructional discourse that begins when the teacher initiates an exchange, a student replies, and the teacher provides an evaluation of the student's reply.

INNER CELL MASS The knot of cells inside the blastocyst that eventually becomes the embryo.

INSTRUCTIONAL DISCOURSE A specialized use of language within the context of the classroom that is designed to give students information about the content of the curriculum and feedback about their efforts, while providing teachers with information about student progress.

INSTRUMENTAL AGGRESSION Aggression committed in order to obtain a goal.

INTERDEPENDENT CONSTRUAL OF SELF A sense of self that is described by such labels as "relational," "collectivist," "connected," "contextual," "holistic," and "sociocentric."

INTERNAL WORKING MODEL A mental model that infants build up as a result of their experience with their caregivers that they then use to guide their behavior in their subsequent relationships.

INTERNALIZATION The process by which children come to accept standards without being explicitly instructed or needing to wait for those in authority to respond.

IQ A score on a test of intelligence; a child's mental age (as determined by the age at which average children pass the test items) divided by chronological age, multiplied by 100 ($IQ = MA/CA \times 100$). By definition, this ratio yields an average IQ of 100.

JARGONING Vocalizations of strings of syllables that have the intonation and stress of actual utterances in the language that the baby will eventually speak.

KINSHIP STUDIES Studies in which members of the same biological family are compared to see how similar they are in one or more attributes.

KNOWLEDGE BASE The store of information upon which the child can draw in a new situation in order to remember, reason, and solve problems.

LANGUAGE ACQUISITION DEVICE (LAD) According to Chomsky, the LAD is an innate language-processing capacity that is programmed to recognize the universal grammar common to all languages. The LAD is realized in the particulars of the language the child hears.

LANGUAGE ACQUISITION SUPPORT SYSTEM (LASS) According to Bruner, the LASS is the set of parental behaviors that structure children's language environment to support the development of language.

LATENCY In Freudian theory, the stage of development that lasts from about the age of 6 years until the beginning of puberty. During latency, sexual desires are suppressed and sexual energy is channeled into acquiring the technical skills that will be needed during adulthood.

LATERALIZATION The process by which one side of the brain takes the lead in organizing a particular mental process or behavior.

LEARNED HELPLESSNESS People's perception that their behavior does not matter because of their inability to affect events; as a consequence, they lose the desire to act and become passive.

LEARNING The process by which an organism's behavior is modified by experience.

LIFE-COURSE APPROACH An approach to development from birth to death that focuses on how the timing of major life events (onset of schooling, retirement, etc.) influence an individual's psychological development.

LIFE-SPAN APPROACH A framework for studying development that assumes it to be a lifelong process arising from the interaction of biological, social, and historical influences on the individual. Such an approach traces various psychological phenomena from infancy to old age to determine how they are transformed as a result of biological, cognitive, and social changes.

LOCOMOTION The ability to move around on one's own.

LONGITUDINAL DESIGN A research design in which data are gathered from the same group of people at several ages, making it possible to trace change over time.

LONG-TERM MEMORY Memory from past experience.

LOW BIRTH WEIGHT A baby's weight of 2500 grams or less at birth.

MASKING GENE A gene that masks the normal expression of another gene.

MATURATION The genetically determined patterns of change that occur as individuals age from conception through adulthood.

MEIOSIS The reduction division process that produces sperm and ova, each of which contain only half of the parent cell's original complement of chromosomes (23 in humans).

MEMORY ORGANIZATION A strategy for remembering in which the materials to be remembered are grouped in meaningful clusters of closely associated items. This strategy does not come into use until middle childhood.

MENARCHE A girl's first menstrual period.

MENOPAUSE The cessation of ovulation and menstruation in women, signaling the end of the period of biological reproduction.

MENTAL AGE The basic index of intelligence for an age-graded scale such as that developed by Binet and Simon. A child who does as well on such a test as an average 9-year-old is said to have a mental age of 9.

MENTAL MECHANICS Baltes's term for intelligence that depends on the inherited, universal features of human thinking.

MENTAL MODULES Highly specific mental faculties tuned to particular kinds of environmental input. Mental modules are said to be specific to particular domains such as music and language and are only loosely connected to one another. The psychological principles that organize the operation of each domain are generally claimed to be innate.

MENTAL OPERATION In Piaget's terms the mental "actions" of combining, separating, and transforming information in a logical manner. Children become capable of mental operations at around the age of 7 or 8.

MESODERM The middle layer of cells that develops from the inner cell mass of the blastocyst. It eventually becomes the muscles, the bones, the circulatory system, and the inner layers of the skin.

METACOGNITION The ability to describe one's own mental activities and the logic underpinning one's attempts to solve problems.

METAMEMORY Knowledge about one's own memory processes.

MICROGENETIC METHODS Experimental procedures that provoke change in the course of a relatively brief time interval as means of seeing basic developmental mechanisms in action.

MIDDLE ADULTHOOD In Erikson's theory, the years between 35 and 65 when adults must engage in productive work and raise the next generation or else become stagnant and self-centered.

MITOSIS The process of cell duplication and division that generates all of an individual's cells except sperm and ova.

MODIFIER GENE A gene that influences the action or expression of other genes.

MODULARITY THEORY A theory that emphasizes biological changes within specific cognitive domains such as language, number, and space in developmental change.

MONOZYGOTIC TWINS Babies that come from the same zygote and therefore have identical genotypes; also called "identical" twins.

MORAL RULES Obligatory social regulations based on principles of justice and welfare.

MORO REFLEX In response to an abrupt noise or to the sensation of being dropped, very young babies fling their arms out with their fingers spread and then bring their arms back toward their bodies with their fingers bent as if to hug something.

MORPHEMES The parts of a word that carry meaning. A word may contain more than one morpheme; for example, actor ("act" + "or") or unmanageable ("un" + "manage" + "able").

MORULA The mass of cells that results from the cleavage of the zygote as it moves through the fallopian tube.

MOTHERESE The term for the special speech register that adults use in speaking to small children. When they are using motherese, adults speak in a special, high pitched voice, emphasize the boundaries between idea-bearing clauses, and use a simplified vocabulary.

MUTATION An error in the process by which a gene is replicated that results in a change in the molecular structure of the genetic material itself.

MYELIN The sheath of fatty cells that covers the neurons, stabilizing them and speeding the transmission of impulses.

MYELINATION The process by which myelin covers nerve cells.

NATURALISTIC OBSERVATIONS A research method for obtaining detailed evidence about the actual behavior of people in the real world settings they inhabit, including home, school, and community.

NATURE With respect to the "nature-nurture" issue, the inborn, genetically coded biological capacities and limitations of individuals.

NEGATION The mental operation that allows the child to think back and imagine undoing or reversing—negating—an action.

NEO-PIAGETIAN APPROACH A theoretical approach that accepts Piaget's basic framework but seeks to refine the way in which children are observed and the way substages, or levels, are identified in particular problem-solving tasks.

NEURON A nerve cell.

NURTURE With respect to the "nature-nurture" issue, the influence of the environment exerted on the individual by the social group, particularly the family and the community.

OBJECTIVITY A requirement that the information on which scientific knowledge is based not be distorted by the investigator's preconceptions.

OBJECT PERMANENCE The understanding that objects have substance, are external to oneself, and continue to exist when out of sight. Piaget maintained that we cannot infer that babies understand object permanence until they begin to search actively for an object they no longer see.

OEDIPUS COMPLEX In Freudian terms, the fear, guilt, and conflict evoked by a little boy's desire to get rid of his father and take his place in his mother's affections.

OLD AGE A time late in life (usually 65 years or older) of reduced physical capacities and (in many societies) reduced social responsibilities, often producing a state of dependence. In Erikson's theory, a stage of life leading either to integration and wisdom, or to despair.

ONTOGENY The course of development during an individual's lifetime.

OPERANT CONDITIONING Sometimes called instrumental conditioning, this is the modification of behavior as a result of the positive or negative consequences that the behavior produces. In this view, organisms tend to repeat behaviors that are rewarded and to give up behaviors that fail to produce rewards or that lead to punishment.

ORAL STAGE In Freudian theory, the first stage of development, in which the mouth is the primary source of pleasure.

OVEREXTENSION A term used for the error of applying verbal labels too broadly. Young children commonly overextend the meaning of words when they are learning to talk; for example, using "cat" to mean all four-legged animals.

PEER An individual of comparable age and status to other individuals; the term is often used to refer to children of about the same age as one another.

PERIOD OF THE EMBRYO The period from when the organism becomes attached to the uterus until the end of the eighth week when all of the major organs have taken primitive shape.

PERIOD OF THE FETUS The period from about 9 weeks after conception until birth. During this period, the primitive organs grow in size and complexity until the baby can exist outside the mother without medical support.

PERMISSIVE PARENTING PATTERN Permissive parents exercise less explicit control over their children's behavior than do other parents. They give their children a lot of leeway to determine their own schedules and activities and often consult them about family policies. They make relatively few demands on their children for achievement or mature behavior.

PERSONALITY The pattern of characteristic behaviors that results from each person's unique mix of genetic endowment and personal experience. It also includes the way one conceives of oneself and one's characteristic style of dealing with others, as well as the idiosyncrasies that make one distinctive.

PERSONALITY FORMATION The way in which every child comes to have her or his own unique ways of feeling and behaving in a wide variety of circumstances.

PERSONAL RULES Rules created by individuals to regulate their own behavior.

PHALLIC STAGE In Freud's theory the period around the fourth year when children begin to focus their pleasure seeking on the genital area. It is during this period that children develop sexual feelings toward their opposite-sex parent and jealousy of their same-sex parent.

PHENOTYPE The organism's observable characteristics that result from the interaction of the genotype with the environment.

PHONEMES The sound categories that signal differences among meaningful units in a language. Phonemes differ from language to language.

PHYLOGENY The evolutionary history of a species.

PLACENTA A complex organ made up of tissue from both the mother and the fetus that serves as both a barrier and a filter. As a barrier, it keeps the bloodstreams of the mother and the fetus separate. As a filter, it converts nutrients carried in the mother's bloodstream into nourishment for the fetus, and it enables the fetus's waste products to be absorbed by the mother's bloodstream.

POLYGENIC TRAITS A genetic trait that is determined by the interaction of several genes. Most human traits are polygenic.

POSITIVE JUSTICE Damon's term for the process of reaching a decision about how to divide resources or distribute rewards fairly.

PRAGMATIC FEATURES Intellectual functioning that depends on a rich base of knowledge and the cultural context in which the cognitive demands arise, in Baltes's terms.

PRAGMATIC USES OF LANGUAGE The ability to select words and word orders that convey what the speaker intends to communicate.

PRECAUSAL THINKING According to Piaget, a form of thinking observed in young children in which they do not engage in cause-and-effect reasoning, but instead reason from one particular to another.

PREFORMATIONISM The hypothesis that the adult form is present in some way in the cells out of which it develops.

PREMATURE Born before the thirty-seventh week of gestation.

PREOPERATIONAL STAGE In Piagetian theory, the period between 2½ and 6 years, during which the child's thought does not have the clear-cut properties of the sensorimotor stage that precedes it or the stage of concrete operations that follows. During this period children often fail to distinguish their point of view from that of others, become easily captured by surface appearances, and are often confused about causal relations.

PREREACHING A reflexlike movement in which newborns reach toward an object that catches their attention and simultaneously, but independently, make grasping movements.

PRIMACY The idea that the earliest experiences of children determine their later development.

PRIMARY CIRCULAR REACTION Behavior characteristic of the second substage of Piaget's sensorimotor period, which lasts from about 1 to 4 months, in which the baby repeats simple actions for their own sake. These actions are called primary because they are centered on the baby's own body; they are called circular because they lead back only to themselves.

PRIMARY IDENTIFICATION Freud's term for infants' recognition that some objects in the external world are like themselves.

PRIMARY INTERSUBJECTIVITY The term used to describe the coordinated turn taking and emotional sharing between very young infants and their caregivers. It is restricted to direct face-to-face interactions.

PRIMARY MOTOR AREA The area of the cerebral cortex that controls nonreflexive, voluntary movement.

PRIMARY SENSORY AREA Those areas of the brain that are responsible for the initial analysis of sensory information.

PRIMARY SEXUAL ORGANS Those organs, like the ovaries in females and the testes in males, that are involved in reproduction.

PROSOCIAL BEHAVIORS Behaviors that benefit the group with no direct reward for the benefactor. Prosocial behaviors include empathy, sharing, helping, and cooperation.

PROXIMODISTAL PATTERN The sequence of body development from the middle outward.

PUBERTY A revolutionary series of biological developments that transforms individuals from a state of physical immaturity to one in which they are biologically mature and capable of reproduction.

RANGE OF REACTION/NORM OF REACTION All the possible phenotypes for a single genotype that are compatible with life.

RECAPITULATE To repeat in concise form. The idea that human children recapitulate earlier stages of human evolution during their development was popular in the period when the study of child development began. The idea that older children recapitulate earlier stages in their own development remains central to Freud and Erikson's theories of adolescence.

RECESSIVE ALLELE The allele that is not expressed when there are two different alleles for the same trait.

RECIPROCAL TEACHING A method of teaching reading in which instruction is organized to permit integration of decoding skills and comprehension. In this procedure a teacher and a small group of students read silently through a segment of text and then take turns leading a discussion of its meaning.

RECURSION A term for the embedding of sentences within each other.

REFLEXES Specific, well-integrated responses; behaviors that are automatically elicited by specific aspects of the environment.

REHEARSAL A strategy for remembering that involves repetition of material.

REINFORCEMENT In operant conditioning, reinforcement refers to the consequences of a behavior that increases the likelihood that the behavior produced will be repeated.

RELIABILITY A requirement of scientific knowledge that the phenomenon under study can be observed repeatedly and that different observers agree on what they observe.

REPLICATION A study is replicated when the same procedures are used on another occasion and the same results are obtained.

REPRESENTATION The capacity to go beyond actions in a present world to "present" the world to oneself mentally.

REPRESENTATIVE SAMPLE A sample of individuals included in a study who are representative of the people about whom the psychologist wishes to answer questions.

REVERSIBILITY Piaget's term for mental operations in which children can think through an action and then reverse it.

RULE-BASED GAMES Games in which the rules are agreed upon ahead of time and in which the objective of the game is to win by competing within the confines of the rules.

SCHEMA A mental structure that provides an organism with a model for action in similar or analogous circumstances.

SCRIPTS Generalized event representations developed by individuals as a result of their repeated participation in routine activities. Scripts specify the appropriate people who participate in an event, the social roles they play, the objects that are used, and the sequence of actions that occur. Scripts serve as guides to action for the participants and help the participants coordinate themselves with one another.

SECONDARY CIRCULAR REACTIONS The diligent repetition of an action by a baby in order to produce an interesting change in its environment. This is a characteristic behavior of the third substage of Piaget's sensorimotor period, which occurs approximately between the ages of 4 and 8 months.

SECONDARY IDENTIFICATION Freud's term for the endeavor to mold one's own ego to be like one that has been taken as a model.

SECONDARY INTERSUBJECTIVITY The sharing between infants and their caregivers of understandings and emotions that refer beyond themselves to objects and other people.

SECONDARY SEXUAL CHARACTERISTICS The anatomical and physiological signs that outwardly distinguish males from females. These characteristics make their appearance as the primary sexual organs are maturing.

SECOND-ORDER THINKING The ability to develop rules about rules and to hold competing thoughts in mind while mulling over both thoughts.

SECURE BASE Bowlby's term for the source of security provided by the persons to whom a child is attached. The secure base helps to regulate the baby's explorations of the world.

SELF-CONCEPT The way individuals conceive of themselves in relation to other people.

SELF-CONTROL The capacity to act in accordance with the expectations of those in authority even when one is not being monitored.

SELF-REPORT A method of gathering data through diaries, interviews, or questionnaires, in which people report on their own psychological states and behaviors.

SENSORIMOTOR STAGE The first of Piaget's four developmental stages, during which the behaviors that develop involve coordination between the infant's sensory experiences and simple motor behaviors. Piaget distinguished six substages in this period, which lasts for the first 2 years of life.

SEX-LINKED CHARACTERISTIC An attribute determined by genes that are found on the X chromosome.

SHORT-TERM MEMORY Working memory that retains new information for a period of several seconds; as opposed to long-term memory, in which information is held in storage.

SOCIAL CO-CONSTRUCTION The two-sided process in which both the environment and the child are active in constructing the child's development.

SOCIAL COMPARISON A process in which children come to define themselves by comparing themselves with their peers. Social comparison comes to prominence in middle childhood.

SOCIAL COMPETENCE Skills that result in successful social functioning with peers.

SOCIAL CONVENTIONS Rules that are specific to a given society, such as prescriptions about the kind of behavior that is appropriate to males or females, or about who has authority over people and how it is exercised.

SOCIAL DEVELOPMENT A double-sided process in which children simultaneously become integrated into the larger social community and differentiated as distinctive individuals.

SOCIALIZATION The process by which children acquire the standards, values, and knowledge of their society.

SOCIAL PERSPECTIVE-TAKING The ability to think about how one's actions and ideas will be perceived by others.

SOCIAL REFERENCING The communicating behavior in which babies keep a watchful eye on their caregiver's expression to see how they should interpret unusual events.

SOCIAL REPAIR MECHANISMS Strategies that allow friends to remain friends even when serious differences temporarily drive them apart.

SOCIODRAMATIC PLAY Make-believe games in which two or more children enact a variety of social roles.

SOCIOGRAM The graphic representation of how each child feels about every other child in a group. A sociogram is derived from children's answers to questions about which children in a particular group they would like to be with or sit near, or about which children they like the most.

SOCIOMETRIC DATA Measures of social relations.

SOMATIC CELLS All the cells in the body except for the germ cells (ova and sperm).

STAGE A distinctive period of development that is qualitatively different from the periods that come before and after.

STEPPING REFLEX The rhythmic leg movements newborn infants make when they are held in an upright position with their feet touching a flat surface.

STRANGE SITUATION A procedure designed by Mary Ainsworth to assess children's responses to a stranger when they are with their parent (usually the mother), when they are left alone, and when they are reunited with their parent.

STRATEGY A deliberate action performed for the purpose of attaining a particular goal.

STRUCTURED WHOLE A system of relationships that can be logically described and thought about.

SUPEREGO Freud's term for the part of the psyche that represents the authority of the social group.

SURFACE STRUCTURE Chomsky's term for the actual sentences that people construct when using in a language.

SYMBOLIC PLAY Play in which one object stands for another. Children begin to participate in symbolic play during their second year.

SYNAPSE The small space between interconnecting neurons across which nerve impulses must flow.

TEMPERAMENT The basic style with which an individual responds to the environment, as well as his or her dominant mood.

TERATOGENS Environmental agents that can cause deviations in normal development and lead to serious abnormalities or death.

TERTIARY CIRCULAR REACTIONS Piaget's term for the behaviors characteristic of substage 5 of the sensorimotor period in which infants become capable of performing varied action sequences, thereby making their explorations of the world more complex. Piaget referred to tertiary circular reactions "as experiments in order to see." They are typical of babies from about 8 to 18 months of age.

THEORY A broad framework or body of principles used to interpret a set of facts.

THEORY OF MIND The ability to think about other people's mental states is often referred to by psychologists as a theory of mind.

TRANSACTIONAL MODELS Models of development that trace the ways in which the characteristics of the child and the characteristics of the child's environment interact across time to determine developmental outcomes.

TROPHOBLAST The outer cells of the blastocyst that eventually develop into the membranes that support and protect the embryo.

UMBILICAL CORD A soft tube containing blood vessels that connects the embryo to the placenta.

UNCONDITIONAL RESPONSE In classical conditioning, a response that occurs unconditionally whenever a particular stimulus is present. Salivation, for example, is the unconditional response to food in the mouth.

UNCONDITIONAL STIMULUS In classical conditioning, a stimulus that always elicits a particular response without prior training. For example, food placed in the mouth is an unconditional stimulus for the salivary response.

UNDEREXTENSION A term for applying verbal labels too narrowly. Young children learning language commonly underextend the meaning of some words, using "cat" to apply only to black kittens, for example.

VALIDITY The scientific requirement that a description of behavior correctly reflects the underlying psychological process that the investigator claims it does.

WISDOM According to Baltes, it is exceptional insight and judgment involving complex and uncertain matters of the human condition.

X CHROMOSOME The larger of the two chromosomes that determine the sex of the individual. Normal females have two X chromosomes, while normal males have only one.

Y CHROMOSOME The smaller of the two chromosomes that determine the sex of the individual. Normal males have one Y chromosome inherited from their fathers and one X inherited from their mothers. Normal females do not have a Y chromosome.

ZONA PELLUCIDA The thin, delicate envelope that surrounds the zygote and later the morula.

ZONE OF PROXIMAL DEVELOPMENT The kind of support provided by adults and more competent others that permits children to accomplish with assistance actions that they will later learn to accomplish independently.

ZYGOTE The single cell formed at conception by the union of the 23 chromosomes of the sperm and the 23 chromosomes of the ovum.

REFERENCES

ABBOUD, T. K., KHOO, S. S., MILLER, F., DOAN, T., & HENRIKSEN, E. H. (1982). Maternal, fetal, and neonatal responses after epidural anesthesia with Bupevacaine, 2-Chloraprocaine, or Zedocaine. *Anesthesia and Analgesia, 61,* 638–643.

ABELES, R. P., & RILEY, M. W. (1987). Longevity, social structure and cognitive aging. In C. Schooler & K. W. Schaie (Eds.), *Cognitive functioning and social structure over the life course.* Norwood, NJ: Ablex.

ABRAHAM, K. G. (1986). Ego-identity differences among Anglo-American and Mexican-American adolescents. *Journal of Adolescence, 9,* 151–166.

ABRAMOVITCH, R., CORTER, C., & LANDO, B. (1979). Sibling interaction in the home. *Child Development, 50,* 997–1003.

ABRAMOVITCH, R., CORTER, C., PEPLER, D., & STANHOPE, L. (1986). Sibling and peer interaction: A final followup and comparison. *Child Development, 57,* 217–229.

ABRAMOVITCH, R., PEPLER, D., & CORTER, C. (1982). Patterns of sibling interaction among pre-school-aged children. In M. Lamb & B. Sutton-Smith (Eds.), *Sibling relationships: Their nature and significance across the lifespan.* Hillsdale, NJ: Erlbaum.

ABRAVANAL, M. (1991). Neonatal imitation. *Developmental Review, 11,* 60–97.

ABRAVANEL, E., LEVAN-GOLDSCHMIDT, E., & STEVENSON, M. B. (1976). Action imitation: The early phase of infancy. *Child Development, 47,* 1032–1044.

ABRAVANEL, E., & SIGAFOOS, A. D. (1984). Exploring the presence of imitation during early infancy. *Child Development, 55,* 381–392.

ADAMS, M. J. (1990). *Learning to read: Thinking and learning about print.* Cambridge, MA: MIT Press.

ADELSON, J. (1972). The political imagination of the young adolescent. In J. Kagan & R. Coles (Eds.), *Twelve to sixteen: Early adolescence.* New York: W. W. Norton.

ADELSON, J. (1975). The development of ideology in adolescence. In S. E. Dragastin & G. H. Elder, Jr. (Eds.), *Adolescence in the life cycle.* Washington, DC: Hemisphere.

ADELSON, J., GREEN, B., & O'NEIL, R. P. (1969). Growth of the idea of law in adolescence. *Developmental Psychology, 1,* 327–332.

ADELSON, J., & O'NEIL, R. P. (1966). Growth of political ideas in adolescence: The sense of community. *Journal of Personality and Social Psychology, 4,* 295–306.

ADVISORY BOARD ON CHILD ABUSE AND NEGLECT (1990). *Child abuse and neglect: Critical first steps in response to a national emergency.* Washington, DC: Department of Health and Human Services, Office of Human Development Services.

AINSWORTH, M. D. S. (1967). *Infancy in Uganda: Infant care and the growth of love.* Baltimore: Johns Hopkins Press.

AINSWORTH, M. D. S. (1982). Attachment: Retrospect and prospect. In C. M. Parkes & J. Stevenson-Hinde (Eds.), *The place of attachment in human behavior.* New York: Basic Books.

AINSWORTH, M. D. S., & BELL, S. M. (1969). Some contemporary patterns of mother-infant interaction in the feeding situation. In A. Ambrose (Ed.), *Stimulation in Early Infancy.* New York: Academic Press.

AINSWORTH, M. D. S., BELL, S. M., & STAYTON, D. J. (1971). Individual differences in strange-situation behavior of one-year-olds. In H. R. Schaffer (Ed.), *The origins of human social relations.* New York: Academic Press.

AINSWORTH, M. D. S., BLEHAR, M. C., WATERS, E., & WALL, S. (1978). *Patterns of attachment: A psychological study of the strange situation.* Hillsdale, NJ: Erlbaum.

AINSWORTH, M. D. S., & WITTIG, B. A. (1969). Attachment and exploratory behavior of one-year-olds in a strange situation. In B. M. Foss (Ed.), *Determinants of infant behavior* (Vol. 4). London: Methuen.

AKBAR, N. (1985). Our destiny: Authors of a scientific revolution. In H. P. McAdoo & J. L. McAdoo (Eds.), *Black children: Social, educational, and parental environments.* Beverly Hills: Sage.

ALDRICH, C. A., & HEWITT, E. S. (1947). A self-regulating feeding program for infants. *Journal of the American Medical Association, 35,* 341.

ALEKSANDROWICZ, M. K. (1974). The effect of pain relieving drugs administered during labor and delivery on the behavior of the new born: A review. *Merrill-Palmer Quarterly, 20,* 121–141.

ALEXANDER, C. & LANGER, E. (Eds.). (1990). *Higher stages of human development: Perspectives on adult growth.* New York: Oxford University Press.

ALLEN, K. E., TURNER, K. D., & EVERETT, P. M. (1970). A behavior modification classroom for headstart children with problem behavior. *Exceptional Children, 37,* 119–127.

ALLISON, A. C. (1954). Protection afforded by sickle-cell trait against subtertian malarial infection. *British Medical Journal, 1,* 290–294.

ALLPORT, G. (1937). *Personality: A psychological interpretation.* New York: Holt, Rinehart and Winston.

ALTER-REID, K., GIBBS, M. S., LACHEN-MEYER, J. R., SIGAL, J., & MASOTH, N. A. (1986). Sexual abuse of children: A review of empirical findings. *Clinical Psychology Review, 6,* 249–266.

AMES, B. N. (1979). Identifying environmental chemicals causing mutations and cancer. *Science, 204,* 587–593.

ANDERSON, A., & STOKES, S. (1984). Social and institutional influences on the development and practice of literacy. In H. Goelman, A. Oberg, & F. Smith (Eds.), *Awakening to literacy.* Exeter, NH: Heinemann.

ANGLIN, J. M. (1977). *Word, object, and conceptual development.* New York: W. W. Norton.

ANGLIN, J. M. (1983). Extensional aspects of the preschool child's word concepts. In T. Seiler & W. Wannenmacher (Eds.), *Concept development in the development of word meanings.* New York: Springer-Verlag.

ANGLIN, J. M. (1985). The child's expressible knowledge of word concepts: What preschoolers can say about the meanings of some nouns and verbs. In K. E. Nelson (Ed.), *Children's language* (Vol. 5). Hillsdale, NJ: Erlbaum.

ANGLIN, J. M. (1986). Semantic and conceptual knowledge underlying the child's words. In S. S. Kuczaj & M. D. Barrett (Eds.), *The development of word meaning.* New York: Springer-Verlag.

ANNIS, R. C., & CORENBLUM, B. (1987). Effect of test language and experimenter race on Canadian Indian children's racial and self-identity. *Journal of Social Psychology, 126,* 761–773.

ANTONOV, A. N. (1947). Children born during the siege of Leningrad in 1942. *Journal of Pediatrics, 30,* 250.

APGAR, V., & BECK, J. (1972). *Is my baby all right?: A guide to birth defects.* New York: Trident.

ARCHER, S. L. (1985). Identity and the choice of social roles. In A. S. Waterman (Ed.), *Identity in adolescence: Processes and contents (New directions for child development,* No. 30). San Francisco: Jossey-Bass.

AREY, L. B. (1974). *Developmental anatomy: A textbook and laboratory manual of embryology* (7th ed.). Philadelphia: Saunders.

ARIES, P. (1962). *Centuries of childhood: A social history of family life.* New York: Vintage Books.

ARNHEIM, R. (1954). *Art and visual perception.* Berkeley: University of California Press.

ASCHER, M., & ASCHER, S. R. (1981). *Code of the quipu.* Ann Arbor, MI: University of Michigan Press.

ASHER, S. R., & DODGE, K. A. (1986). Identifying children who are rejected by their peers. *Developmental Psychology, 22,* 444–449.

ASHMEAD, D. H., & PERLMUTTER, M. (1979). Infant memory in everyday life. Paper presented at the meeting of the American Psychological Association, New York.

ASLIN, R. N. (1987). Visual and auditory development in infancy. In J. D. Osofsky (Ed.), *Handbook of Infant Development* (2nd ed.). New York: Wiley.

ASTINGTON, J. W., & GOPNIK, A. (1991). Theoretical explanations of children's understanding of the mind. *British Journal of Developmental Psychology, 9,* 7–31.

ATCHLEY, R. C. (1975). The life course, age grading, and age-linked demands for decision making. In N. Datan & L. H. Ginsberg (Eds.), *Life-span developmental psychology: Normative life crises.* New York: Academic Press.

ATKIN, C. K., HOCKING, J., & GANTZ, W. (1979). How young children perceive television commercials. Paper presented at the Eastern Communication Association Convention, Philadelphia.

ATKINSON, J., & BRADDICK, O. (1982). Sensory and perceptual capacities in the neonate. In P. Stratton (Ed.), *Psychology of the human newborn.* Chichester, England: Wiley.

ATKINSON, R. C., & SHIFFRIN, R. M. (1980). The control of short-term memory. In R. L. Atkinson & R. C. Atkinson (Eds.), *Mind and behavior: Readings from Scientific American.* New York: W. H. Freeman.

ST. AUGUSTINE (1961). *Confessions*. Baltimore: Penguin Books.

AUSTIN, C. R., & SHORT, R. V. (Eds.). (1972). *Reproduction in mammals: Embryonic and fetal development*. Cambridge: Cambridge University Press.

AVIS, J., & HARRIS, P. L. (1991). Belief–desire reasoning among Baka children: Evidence for a universal conception of mind. *Child Development, 62*, 460–467.

AZMITIA, M., & PERLMUTTER, M. (1989). Social influences on children's cognition: State of the art and future directions. *Advances in Child Development and Behavior, 22*, 89–144.

BACHMAN, J. G. (1970). *The impact of family background and intelligence on tenth grade boys: Vol. 2. Youth in transition*. Ann Arbor, MI: Survey Research Center, Institute for Social Research.

BACHMAN, J. G., JOHNSTON, L. D., & O'MALLEY, P. M. (1987). *Monitoring the future: Questionnaire responses from the nation's high school seniors, 1986*. Ann Arbor, MI: Survey Research Center, Institute for Social Research.

BAILLARGEON, R. (1987). Object permanence in 3½- and 4½-month old infants. *Developmental Psychology, 23*, 655–664.

BAILLARGEON, R., & GRABER, M. (1988). Evidence of location memory in 8-month old infants in a nonsearch AB task. *Developmental Psychology, 24*, 502–511.

BAILLARGEON, R., SPELKE, E., & WASSERMAN, S. (1985). Object permanence in five-month-old infants. *Cognition, 20*, 191–208.

BALDWIN, A. L. (1946). Differences: Parent behavior toward three- and nine-year-old children. *Journal of Personality, 15*, 143–165.

BALDWIN, A. L. (1947). Changes in parent behavior during pregnancy: An experiment in longitudinal analysis. *Child Development, 18*, 29–39.

BALDWIN, A. L. (1955). *Behavior and development in childhood*. New York: Dryden Press.

BALDWIN, J. M. (1902). *Social and ethical interpretations in mental development* (3rd ed.). New York: Macmillan.

BALL, S., & BOGATZ, G. A. (1972). Summative research of Sesame Street: Implications for the study of preschool children. In A. D. Pick (Ed.), *Minnesota symposia on child psychology* (Vol. 6). Minneapolis: University of Minnesota Press.

BALTES, M. M., & WAHL, H. W. (1991). The behavior system of dependency in the elderly: Interaction with the social environment. In M. Ory, R. P. Abeles, & T. D. Lipman (Eds.), *Aging, health, & behavior*. Beverly Hills: Sage.

BALTES, P. B. (1987). Theoretical propositions of life-span developmental psychology: On the dynamics between growth and decline. *Developmental Psychology, 23*, 611–626.

BALTES, P. B., & BRIM, O. G., JR. (Eds.). (1979). *Life-span development and behavior* (Vol. 2). New York: Academic Press.

BALTES, P. B., DITTMANN-KOHLI, F., & DIXON, R. A. (1984). New perspectives on the development of intelligence in adulthood: Toward a dual-process conception and a model of selective optimization with compensation. In P. B. Baltes & O. G. Brim, Jr. (Eds.), *Life-span development and behavior* (Vol. 6). New York: Academic Press.

BALTES, P. B., FEATHERMAN, D. L., & LERNER, R. M. (Eds.). (1990). *Life-span development and behavior* (Vol. 10). Hillsdale, NJ: Erlbaum.

BALTES, P. B., SMITH, J., & STAUDINGER, U. (1992). Wisdom and successful aging. *Nebraska Symposium on Motivation, 39*, 123–167.

BANDURA, A. (1964). The stormy decade: Fact or fiction. *Psychology in the School, 1*, 224–231.

BANDURA, A. (1965). Influence of models' reinforcement contingencies on the acquisition of imitative responses. *Journal of Personality and Social Psychology, 1*, 587–595.

BANDURA, A. (1969). Social-learning theory of identificatory processes. In D. A. Goslin (Ed.), *Handbook of socialization theory and research*. Chicago: Rand McNally.

BANDURA, A. (1973). *Aggression: A social learning analysis*. Englewood Cliffs, NJ: Prentice-Hall.

BANDURA, A. (1977). *Social learning theory*. Englewood Cliffs, NJ: Prentice-Hall.

BANDURA, A. (1986). *Social foundations of thought and action: A social cognitive theory*. Englewood Cliffs, NJ: Prentice-Hall.

BANDURA, A., ROSS, D., & ROSS, S. A. (1963). Imitation of film-mediated aggressive models. *Journal of Abnormal and Social Psychology, 66*, 3–11.

BANDURA, A., & WALTERS, R. H. (1959). *Adolescent aggression*. New York: Ronald Press.

BANDURA, A., & WALTERS, R. H. (1963). *Social learning and personality development.* New York: Holt, Rinehart and Winston.

BANKS, M. S., & SALAPATEK, P. (1983). Infant visual perception. In P. H. Mussen (Ed.), *Handbook of child psychology: Vol. 2. Infancy and developmental psychobiology.* New York: Wiley.

BARGLOW, P., VAUGHN, B. E., & MOLITOR, N. (1987). Effects of maternal absence due to employment on the quality of infant-mother attachment in a low-risk sample. *Child Development, 58,* 945–953.

BARKER, R. G., & BARKER, L. S. (1968). The psychological ecology of old people in Midwest, Kansas, and Yoredale, Yorkshire. In B. L. Neugarten (Ed.), *Middle age and aging.* Chicago: University of Chicago Press.

BARKER, R. G., & WRIGHT, H. F. (1951). *One boy's day: A specimen record of behavior.* New York: Harper Brothers.

BARKER, R. G., & WRIGHT, H. F. (1955). *Midwest and its children.* New York: Harper & Row.

BARON-COHEN, S., LESLIE, A. M., & FRITH, U. (1986). Mechanical behavioral and intentional understanding of picture stories in autistic children. *British Journal of Developmental Psychology, 4,* 113–125.

BARRETT, K. C., & CAMPOS, J. J. (1987). Perspectives on emotional development: II. A functionalist approach to emotions. In J. D. Osofsky (Ed.), *Handbook of Infant Development* (2nd ed.). New York: Wiley.

BARTLETT, E. (1977). The acquisition of the meaning of color terms. In P. T. Smith & R. N. Campbell (Eds.), *Proceedings of the Sterling Conference on the Psychology of Language.* New York: Plenum Press.

BATES, E. (1976). *Language and context: The acquisition of pragmatics.* New York: Academic Press.

BATES, E., BENIGNI, L., BRETHERTON, I., CAMAIONI, L., & VOLTERRA, V. (1979). *The emergence of symbols: Cognition and communication in infancy.* New York: Academic Press.

BATES, E., BRETHERON, I., & SNYDER, L. (1988). *From first words to grammar.* Cambridge: Cambridge University Press.

BATES, E., CAMAIONI, L., & VOLTERRA, V. (1975). The acquisition of performatives prior to speech. *Merrill Palmer Quarterly, 21,* 205–226.

BATES, E., & MACWHINNEY, B. (1982). A functionalist approach to grammatical development. In L. Gleitman & E. Wanner (Eds.), *Language acquisition: The state of the art.* Cambridge: Cambridge University Press.

BATES, E., O'CONNELL, B., & SHORE, C. (1987). Language and communication. In J. D. Osofsky (Ed.), *Handbook of infant development* (2nd ed.). New York: Wiley.

BATES, E., & SNYDER, L. (1987). The cognitive hypothesis in language development. In I. Uzgiris & J. McV. Hunt (Eds.), *Infant performance and experience: New findings with the ordinal scales.* Champaign, IL: University of Illinois Press.

BATES, J. E. (1989). Concepts and measures of temperament. In G. A. Kohnstamm, J. E. Bates, & M. K. Rothbart (Eds.), *Temperament In Childhood.* New York: Wiley.

BATES, J. E., MASLIN, C. A., & FRANKEL, K. A. (1985). Attachment, security, and temperament as predictors of behavior: Problem ratings at three years. *Monographs of the Society for Research in Child Development, 50,* (Serial No. 209).

BATESON, G. (1972). *Steps to an ecology of mind.* New York: Ballantine Books.

BAUMEISTER, R. F. (1987). How the self became a problem: A psychological review of historical research. *Journal of Personality and Social Psychology, 52,* 163–176.

BAUMRIND, D. (1967). Child care practices anteceding three patterns of preschool behavior. *Genetic Psychology Monographs, 75,* 43–88.

BAUMRIND, D. (1971). Current patterns of parental authority. *Developmental Psychology Monographs, 4* (1, Part 2).

BAUMRIND, D. (1972). An exploratory study of socialization effects on Black children: Some Black-White comparisons. *Child Development, 43,* 261–267.

BAUMRIND, D. (1980). New directions in socialization research. *American Psychologist, 35,* 639–652.

BAUMRIND, D. (1986). Sex differences in the development of moral reasoning: A response to Walker's (1984) conclusion that there are none. *Child Development, 57,* 511–521.

BAUMRIND, D. (1989). Rearing competent children. In W. Damon (Ed.), *Child development today and tomorrow.* San Francisco: Jossey-Bass.

BAUMRIND, D. (1991). To nurture nature. *Behavioral and Brain Sciences, 14,* 386.

BAYER, S. A., & ALTMAN, J. (1991). *Neocortical development.* New York: Raven.

BELL, A. P., WEINBERG, M. S., & HAMMERSMITH, S. K. (1981). *Sexual preference: Its development in men and women.* Bloomington, IN: Indiana University Press.

BELL, R. Q., WELLER, G., & WALDROP, M. F. (1971). Newborn and preschooler: Organization of behavior and relations between periods. *Monographs of the Society for Research in Child Development,* 36 (1–2, Serial No. 142).

BELL, S. M., & AINSWORTH, M. (1972). Infant crying and maternal responsiveness. *Child Development,* 43, 1171–1190.

BELLUGI, U., BIHRLE, A., JERNIGAN, T., TRAUNER, D., & DOHERTY, S. (1990). Neuropsychological, neurological, and neuroanatomical profile of Williams Syndrome. *American Journal of Medical Genetics Supplement,* 6, 115–125.

BELSKY, J. (1980). Child maltreatment: An ecological integration. *American Psychologist,* 35, 320–335.

BELSKY, J. (1986). Infant day care: A cause for concern. *Zero to Three,* 6(5), 1–9.

BELSKY, J. (1990). Developmental risks associated with infant day care. In S. Chehrazi (Ed.), *Psychosocial issues in day care.* Washington, DC: American Psychiatric Press.

BELSKY, J., FISH, M., & ISABELLA, R. (1991). Continuity and discontinuity in infant negative and positive emotionality: Family antecedents and attachment consequences. *Developmental Psychology,* 27, 421–431.

BELSKY, J., & ISABELLA, R. (1988). Maternal, infant, and social-contextual determinants of attachment security. In J. Belsky & T. Nezworski (Eds.), *Clinical implications of attachment.* Hillsdale, NJ: Erlbaum.

BELSKY, J., & MOST, R. K. (1982). Infant exploration and play. In J. Belsky (Ed.), *In the beginning.* New York: Columbia University Press.

BELSKY, J., & ROVINE, M. (1987). Temperament and attachment security in the strange situation: An empirical rapprochement. *Child Development,* 58, 787–795.

BELSKY, J., & STEINBERG, L. D. (1978). The effects of day care: A critical review. *Child Development,* 49, 929–949.

BELSKY, J., STEINBERG, L. D., & WALKER, A. (1982). The ecology of day care. In M. E. Lamb (Ed.), *Nontraditional families: Parenting and child development.* Hillsdale, NJ: Erlbaum.

BELSKY, J. & VONDRA, J. (1987). Child maltreatment: Prevalence, consequences, causes, and interventions. In D. Crowell, I. Evans, & C. O'Donell (Eds.), *Childhood Aggression and Violence: Sources of Influence, Prevention and Control.* New York: Plenum Press.

BEM, S. L. (1981). Gender schema theory: A cognitive account of sex-typing. *Psychological Review,* 88, 354–364.

BEM, S. L. (1989). Genital knowledge and gender constancy in preschool children. *Child Development,* 60, 649–662.

BERG, W. K., & BERG, K. M. (1987). Psychophysiological development in infancy: State, startle, and attention. In J. D. Osofsky (Ed.), *Handbook of infant development* (2nd ed.). New York: Wiley.

BERGER, B. M. (1981). *The survival of a counterculture: Ideological work and everyday life among rural communards.* Berkeley: University of California Press.

BERGSMA, D. (Ed.). (1979). *Birth defects compendium* (2nd ed.). New York: Alan R. Liss.

BERNAL, J. F. (1972). Crying during the first few days, and maternal responses. *Developmental Medicine and Child Neurology,* 14, 362–372.

BERNDT, T. J. (1979). Developmental changes in conformity to peers and parents, *Developmental Psychology,* 15, 608–616.

BERNDT, T. J. (1986). Children's comments about their friendships. In M. Perlmutter (Ed.), *Minnesota symposia on child psychology.* Vol. 18: *Cognitive perspectives on children's social and behavioral development.* Hillsdale, NJ: Erlbaum.

BERTENTHAL, B. I., & BAI, D. L. (1989). Infants' sensitivity to optical flow for controlling posture. *Developmental Psychology,* 25, 936–945.

BERTENTHAL, B. I. & CAMPOS, J. J. (1990). A systems approach to the organizing effects of self-produced locomotion during infancy. In C. Rovee-Collier & L. P. Lipsitt (Eds.), *Advances in infancy research,* (Vol. 6). Norwood, NJ: Ablex Publishing Corp.

BERTENTHAL, B. I., CAMPOS, J. J., & BARRETT, K. C. (1984). Self-produced locomotions: An organizer of emotional, cognitive, and social development in infancy. In R. Emde & R. Harmon (Eds.), *Continuities and discontinuities in development.* New York: Plenum Press.

BERTENTHAL, B. I., & FISCHER, K. W. (1978). Development of self-recognition in the infant. *Developmental Psychology,* 14, 44–50.

BEST, C. T., HOFFMAN, H., & GLANVILLE, B. B. (1982). Development of infant ear asymmetries for speech and music. *Perception and Psychophysics, 31,* 75–85.

BETTELHEIM, B. (1977). *The uses of enchantment: The meaning and importance of fairytales.* New York: Vintage Books.

BEUF, A. H. (1977). *Red children in white America.* Philadelphia: University of Pennsylvania Press.

BEYENE, Y. (1991). Menopause: A biocultural event. In A. J. Dan & L. L. Len (Eds.), *Menstrual health in women's lives.* Champaign, IL: University of Illinois Press.

BIDDEL, T. R., & FISCHER, K. W. (1992). Beyond the stage debate: Action, structure, and variability in Piagetian theory and research. In C. Berg & R. S. Sternberg (Eds.), *Intellectual development.* New York: Cambridge University Press.

BIGELOW, B. J., & LAGAIPA, J. J. (1975). Children's written descriptions of friendship: A multidimensional analysis. *Developmental Psychology, 41,* 857–858.

BIJOU, S. W., & BAER, D. M. (1966). *Child development:* Vol. 2. *The universal stage of infancy.* New York: Appleton-Century-Crofts.

BINET, A., & SIMON, T. (1916). *The development of intelligence in children.* Vineland, NJ: Publications of the Training School at Vineland. (Reprinted by Williams Publishing Co., Nashville, TN, 1980.)

BINSTOCK, J. E., & GEORGE, L. K. (Eds.). (1990). *Handbook of aging and the social sciences.* San Diego: Academic Press.

BIRNHOLZ, J. C., & BENACERRAF, B. R. (1983). The development of human fetal hearing. *Science, 222,* 516–518.

BIRREN, J. E., & SCHAIE, K. W. (Eds.). (1990). *Handbook of the psychology of aging.* San Diego: Academic Press.

BISANZ, J. (1989). Development of arithmetic computation and number conservation skills. Paper presented at the annual meeting of the American Educational Research Association, San Francisco.

BISANZ, J., & LEFEVRE, J. (1990). Mathematical cognition: Strategic processing as interactions among sources of knowledge. In D. P. Bjorkland (Ed.), *Children's strategies: Contemporary views of cognitive development.* Hillsdale, NJ: Erlbaum.

BISHOP, J. H. (1989). Why the apathy in American high schools? *Educational Researcher, 18,* 6–10.

BISHOP, J. M., & KRAUSE, J. M. (1984). Depictions of aging and old age on Saturday morning television. *The Gerentologist, 24,* 91–94.

BISHOP, S. M., & INGERSOLL, G. M. (1989). Effects of marital conflict and family structure on the self-concepts of pre- and early adolescents. *Journal of Youth and Adolescence, 18,* 25–38.

BITTMAN, S. J., & ZALK, S. R. (1978). *Expectant fathers.* New York: Hawthorn Books.

BLAKE, J., & DE BOYSSON-BARDIES, B. (1992). Patterns in babbling: A cross-linguistic study. *Journal of Child Language, 19,* 51–74.

BLAKEMORE, C., & MITCHELL, D. E. (1973). Environmental modification of the visual cortex and the neural basis of learning and memory. *Nature, 241,* 467–468.

BLASS, E. M., GANCHROW, J. R, & STEINER, J. E. (1984). Classical conditioning in newborn humans 2–48 hours of age. *Infant Behavior and Development, 7,* 223–235.

BLEICHFELD, B., & MOELY, B. (1984). Psychophysiological response to an infant cry: Comparison of groups of women in different phases of the maternal cycle. *Developmental Psychology, 20,* 1082–1091.

BLOCH, H. A., & NIEDERHOFFER, A. (1958). *The gang: A study in adolescent behavior.* New York: Philosophical Library.

BLOCK, J. H., BLOCK, J., & GJERDE, P. (1986). The personality of children prior to divorce: A prospective study. *Child Development, 57,* 827–840.

BLOCK, J. H., BLOCK, J., & MORRISON, A. (1981). Parental agreement–disagreement on child-rearing orientations and gender-related personality correlates in children. *Child Development, 52,* 965–974.

BLOCK, N. J., & DWORKIN, G. (Eds.). (1976). *The I.Q. controversy.* New York: Pantheon.

BLOMBERG, S. (1980). Influences of maternal distress during pregnancy on complications in labor and delivery. *Acta Psychiatria Scandinavia, 62,* 399–404.

BLOOM, K., LIFTER, K., & BROUGHTON, J. (1981). What children say and what they know. In R. Stark (Ed.), *Language behavior in infancy and early childhood.* New York: Elsevier.

BLOOM, L. (1973). *One word at a time: The use of single word utterances before syntax.* The Hauge: Mouton.

BLOOM, L. (1991). *Language development from two to three.* New York: Cambridge University Press.

BLOS, P. (1962). *On adolescence.* New York: Free Press.

BLOS, P. (1972). The child analyst looks at the young adolescent. In J. Kagan & R. Coles (Eds.), *Twelve to sixteen: Early adolescence.* New York: W. W. Norton.

BLOSSER, B. J., & ROBERTS, D. F. (1985). Age differences in children's perceptions of message intent: Responses to TV news, commercials, educational spots, and public service announcements. *Communication Research, 12,* 455–484.

BLUM, L. (1987). Particularity and responsiveness. In J. Kagan, (Ed.), *The emergence of morality in young children.* Chicago: University of Chicago Press.

BOAS, F. (1911). *The mind of primitive man.* New York: Macmillan.

BOER, F. (1990). *Sibling relationships in middle childhood.* Leiden: DSWO University of Leiden Press.

BOHANNON, J. N., III, & WARREN-LEUBECKER, A. (1988). Recent developments in child-directed speech: We've come a long way baby-talk. *Language Sciences, 10,* 89–110.

BOHLIN, G., HAGEKULL, B., GERMER, M., ANDERSSON, K., & LINDBERG, L. (1989). Avoidant and resistant reunion behaviors as predicted by maternal interactive behavior and infant temperament. *Infant Behavior and Development, 12,* 105–118.

BOLLER, K., ROVEE-COLLIER, C., BOROVSKY, D., O'CONNOR, J., & SHYI, G. (1990). Developmental changes in the time-dependent nature of memory retrieval. *Developmental Psychology, 26,* 770–779.

BOLTON, P. J. (1983). Drugs of abuse. In D. F. Hawkins (Ed.), *Drugs and pregnancy: Human teratogenesis and related problems.* Edinburgh: Churchill Livingston.

BORKE, H. (1975). Piaget's mountains revisited: Changes in the egocentric landscape. *Developmental Psychology, 11,* 240–443.

BORNSTEIN, M. H. (1976). Infants are trichomats. *Journal of Experimental Child Psychology, 21,* 425–445.

BORNSTEIN, M. H. (1988). Perceptual development across the life cycle. In M. H. Bornstein & M. E. Lamb (Eds.), *Developmental Psychology: An Advanced Textbook.* Hillsdale, NJ: Erlbaum.

BORNSTEIN, M. H. (1989). Stability in early mental development: From attention and information processing in infancy to language and cognition in childhood. In M. H. Bornstein & N. A. Krasnegor (Eds.), *Stability and continuity in mental development: Behavioral and biological perspectives.* Hillsdale, NJ: Erlbaum.

BORNSTEIN, M. H., & SIGMAN, M. D. (1986). Continuity in mental development from infancy. *Child Development, 57,* 251–274.

BOUKYDIS, C. F. Z., & BURGES, R. L. (1982). Adult physiological response to infant cries: Effects of temperament of infant, parental status, and gender. *Child Development, 53,* 1291–1298.

BOWER, T. G. R. (1982). *Development in human infancy.* New York: W. H. Freeman.

BOWLBY, J. (1969). *Attachment and loss:* Vol. 1. *Attachment.* New York: Basic Books.

BOWLBY, J. (1973). *Attachment and loss:* Vol. 2. *Separation.* New York: Basic Books.

BOWLBY, J. (1980). *Attachment and loss:* Vol 3. *Loss, sadness, and depression.* New York: Basic Books.

BOXER, A. M., TOBIN-RICHARDS, M., & PETERSEN, A. C. (1983). Puberty: Physical change and its significance in early adolescence. *Theory into Practice, 22,* 85–90.

BRACKBILL, Y. (1971). Cumulative effects of continuous stimulation on arousal level in infants. *Child Development, 42,* 17–26.

BRACKBILL, Y. (1979). Obstetrical medication and infant behavior. In J. D. Osofsky (Ed.), *Handbook of infant development.* New York: Wiley.

BRACKBILL, Y., MCMANUS, K., & WOODWARD, L. (1985). *Medication in maternity: Infant exposure and maternal information.* Ann Arbor, MI: University of Michigan Press.

BRADLEY, R. M., & MISTRETTA, C. M. (1975). Fetal sensory receptions. *Physiological Review, 55,* 352–382.

BRAINE, M. D. S. (1963). The ontogeny of English phrase structure: The first phase. *Language, 39,* 3–13.

BRANSFORD, J. D. (1979). *Human cognition: Learning, understanding, and remembering.* Belmont, CA: Wadsworth.

BRAZELTON, T. B. (1973). *Neonatal behavior assessment scale.* London: Spastics International Medical Publications.

BRAZELTON, T. B. (1990). Saving the bathwater. *Child Development, 61,* 1661–1671.

BRAZELTON, T. B., KOSLOWSKI, B., & MAIN, M. (1974). The origin of reciprocity: The early mother-infant interaction. In M. Lewis & L. Rosenblum (Eds.), *The effect of the infant on its caretaker.* New York: Wiley.

BRAZELTON, T. B., NUGENT, K. J., & LESTER, B. M. (1987). Neonatal behavioral assessment scale. In J. D. Osofsky (Ed.), *Handbook of Infant Development* (2nd ed.). New York: Wiley.

BRETHERTON, I. (1984). Representing the social world in symbolic play: Reality and fantasy. In I. Bretherton (Ed.), *Symbolic play: The development of social understanding.* New York: Academic Press.

BRETHERTON, I. (1985). Attachment theory: Retrospect and prospect. *Monographs of the Society for Research in Child Development, 50* (1-2, Serial No. 209).

BRETHERTON, I. (1989). Pretense: The form and function of make-believe play. *Developmental Review, 9*(4), 383–401.

BRETHERTON, I., & BATES, E. (1985). The development of representation from 10 to 28 months: Differential stability of language and symbolic play. In R. N. Emde & R. J. Harmon (Eds.), *Continuities and discontinuities in development.* New York: Plenum Press.

BRETHERTON, I., & WATERS, E. (Eds.). (1985). Growing points in attachment theory. *Monographs of the Society for Research in Child Development, 50,*(1-2, Serial No. 209).

BRITTAIN, C. V. (1963). Adolescent choices and parent-peer cross pressures. *American Sociological Review, 28,* 385–391.

BRODY, G. H., & STONEMAN, Z. (1987). Sibling conflict: Contributions of the siblings themselves, the parent-sibling relationship, and the broader family system. *Journal of Children in Contemporary Society, 19,* 39–53.

BRONFENBRENNER, U. (1979). *The ecology of human development.* Cambridge, MA: Harvard University Press.

BRONFENBRENNER, U. (1986). Ecology of the family as a context for human development: Research perspectives. *Developmental Psychology, 22,* 723–742.

BRONFENBRENNER, U. (1989). Ecological systems theory. In R. Vasta (Ed.), *Annals of child development* (Vol. 6). Greenwich, CT: JAI Press.

BRONFENBRENNER, U., & CROUTER, A. C. (1983). The evolution of environmental models in developmental research. In P. H. Mussen (Ed.), *Handbook of child psychology: History, theory, and methods* (Vol. 1). New York: Wiley.

BRONSON, G. (1991). Infant differences in rate of visual encoding. *Child Development, 62,* 44–54.

BRONSON, W. C. (1975). Development of behavior with age-mates during the second year of life. In M. Lewis & L. A. Rosenblum (Eds.), *The origins of behavior: Friendship and peer relations.* New York: Wiley.

BROOKE, J. (1991, June 15). Cubato journal: Signs of life in Brazil's industrial valley of death. *New York Times,* Pt. 1, p. 2.

BROOKS-GUNN, J. (1987). Pubertal processes and girls' psychological adaptation. In R. Lerner & T. T. Foch (Eds.), *Biological-psychosocial interactions in early adolescence: A lifespan perspective.* Hillsdale, NJ: Erlbaum.

BROOKS-GUNN, J., & PETERSEN, A. (Eds.). (1983). *Girls at puberty: Biological and psychosocial perspectives.* New York: Plenum Press.

BROOKS-GUNN, J., & REITER, E. O. (1990). Pubertal Processes. In S. S. Feldman & G. R. Elliott (Eds.), *At the threshold: The developing adolescent.* Cambridge, MA: Harvard University Press.

BROPHY, J. E. (1983). Research on the self-fulfilling prophecy and teacher expectations. *Journal of Educational Psychology, 75,* 631–661.

BROUGHTON, J. (1978). Development of concepts of self, mind, reality, and knowledge. In W. Damon (Ed.), *Social cognition (New directions for child development,* No. 1). San Francisco: Jossey-Bass.

BROWN, A. L., & CAMPIONE, J. C. (1990). Interactive learning environments and the teaching of science and mathematics. In M. Gardner, J. G. Greeno, F. Reif, A. H. Schoenfeld, A. DiSessa, & E. Stage (Eds.), *Toward a scientific practice of education.* Hillsdale, NJ: Erlbaum.

BROWN, A. L., CAMPIONE, J. C., REEVE, R. A., FERRARA, R. A., & PALINCSAR, A. S. (1992). Interactive learning and individual understanding: The case of reading and mathematics. In L. T. Landsmann (Ed.), *Culture, schooling, and psychological development.* Hillsdale, NJ: Erlbaum.

BROWN, B. B. (1990). Peer groups and peer cultures. In S. S. Feldman & G. R. Elliott (Eds.), *At the threshold: The developing adolescent.* Cambridge, MA: Harvard University Press.

BROWN, B. B., CLASEN, D. R., & EICHER, S. A. (1986). Perception of peer pressure, peer conformity dispositions, and self reported behavior among adolescents. *Developmental Psychology, 22,* 521–530.

BROWN, B. B., LOHR, M. J. L., & MCCLENAHAN, E. L. (1986). Early adolescents' perceptions of peer pressure. *Journal of Early Adolescence, 6,* 139–154.

BROWN, J. R., & DUNN, J. (1991). 'You can cry, mum': The social and developmental implications of talk about internal states. *British Journal of Developmental Psychology, 9*, 237–256.

BROWN, J. W., & JAFFE, J. (1975). Hypothesis on cerebral dominance. *Neuropsychologia, 13*, 107–110.

BROWN, P., & ELLIOT, R. (1965). Control of aggression in a nursery school class. *Journal of Experimental Child Psychology, 2*, 103–107.

BROWN, R. (1973). *A first language: The early stages.* Cambridge, MA: Harvard University Press.

BROWN, R., & BELLUGI, U. (1964). Three processes in the child's acquisition of syntax. *Harvard Educational Review, 34*, 133–151.

BROWN, R., & HANLON, C. (1970). Derivational complexity and the order of acquisition of child speech. In J. R. Hayes (Ed.), *Cognition and the development of language.* New York: Wiley.

BROWN, R., & HERRNSTEIN, R. J. (1975). *Psychology.* Boston: Little, Brown.

BROWN v. BOARD OF EDUCATION OF TOPEKA, KANSAS (1954). 347 U.S. 483; 7455 Ct. 686.

BROWNE, SIR THOMAS (1642/1964). *Religio Medici.* London: Oxford University Press.

BROWNELL, W. A. (1928). *The development of children's number ideas in the primary grades.* Chicago: University of Chicago Press.

BRUNER, J. S. (1966). On cognitive growth. In J. S. Bruner, R. R. Olver, & P. M. Greenfield (Eds.), *Studies in cognitive growth.* New York: Wiley.

BRUNER, J. S. (1968). *Process of cognitive growth: Infancy.* Worcester, MA: Clark University Press.

BRUNER, J. S. (1972). The nature and uses of immaturity. *American Psychologist, 27*, 687–708.

BRUNER, J. S. (1982). Formats of language acquisition. *American Journal of Semiotics, 1*, 1–16.

BRUNER, J. S. (1983a). *Child's talk.* New York: W. W. Norton.

BRUNER, J. S. (1983b). *In search of mind: Essays in autobiography.* New York: Harper & Row.

BUHRMESTER, D., & FURMAN, W. (1987). The development of companionship and intimacy. *Child development, 58*, 1101–1113.

BULLOCK, M. (1984). Preschool children's understandings of causal connections. *British Journal of Developmental Psychology, 2*, 139–142.

BULLOCK, M., & GELMAN, R. (1979). Preschool children's assumptions about cause and effect: Temporal ordering. *Child Development, 50*, 89–96.

BULLOCK, M., & LÜTKENHAUS, P. (1989). The development of volitional behavior in the toddler years. *Child Development, 59*, 664–674.

BULLOUGH, V. (1981). Age of menarche: A misunderstanding. *Science, 213*, 365–366.

BURCHINAL, M., LEE, M., & RAMEY, C. (1989). Type of day-care and preschool intellectual development in disadvantaged children. *Child Development, 60*, 128–138.

BURLINGHAM, D., & FREUD, A. (1942). *Young children in wartime.* London: Allen and Unwin.

BUSHNELL, I. W. R. (1982). Discrimination of faces by young infants. *Journal of Experimental Child Psychology, 33*, 298–308.

BUSHNELL, I. W. R. (1985). The decline of visually guided reaching. *Infant Behavior and Development, 8*, 139–155.

BUSHNELL, I. W. R., SAI, F., & MULLIN, J. T. (1989). Neonatal recognition of the mother's face. *British Journal of Developmental Psychology, 7*, 3–15.

BUSS, A. H. (1989). Temperament as personality traits. In G. A. Kohnstamm, J. E. Bates, & M. K. Rothbart (Eds.), *Temperament in childhood.* New York: Wiley.

BUSS, A. H., & PLOMIN, R. (1975). *A temperament theory of personality development.* New York: Wiley.

BUSS, A. H. & PLOMIN, R. (1984). *Temperament: Early developing personality traits.* Hillsdale, NJ: Erlbaum.

BUTCHER, J. (1986). Longitudinal analysis of adolescent girls' aspirations at school and perceptions of popularity. *Adolescence, 21*, 133–143.

BUTTERFIELD, E. L., & SIPERSTEIN, G. N. (1972). Influence of contingent auditory stimulation upon nonnutritional sucking. In J. Bosma (Ed.), *Oral sensation and perception: The mouth of the infant.* Springfield, IL: Charles Thomas.

BUTTERWORTH, G. E. (1981). The origins of auditory-visual perception and visual proprioception in human infancy. In R. D. Walk & H. L. Pick (Eds.), *Intersensory perception and sensory integration.* New York: Plenum Press.

BUTTERWORTH, G. E. (1991). The ontogeny and phylogeny of joint visual attention. In A. Whitten (Ed.), *Natural theories of mind.* Oxford: Blackwell.

BUTTERWORTH, G., & JARRET, N. (1991). What minds have in common in space: Spatial mechanisms serving joint visual attention in infancy. *British Journal of Developmental Psychology, 9,* 55–72.

BYRNES, J. P., & GELMAN, S. A. (Eds.). (1991). *Perspectives on Language and Cognition: Interrelations in Development.* Cambridge: Cambridge University Press.

CAHAN, S., & COHEN, N. (1989). Age versus schooling effects on intelligence development. *Child Development, 60,* 1239–1249.

CAIRNS, R. B. (1979). *Social development: The origins of interchanges.* New York: W. H. Freeman.

CAIRNS, R. B. (1983). The emergence of developmental psychology. In P. H. Mussen (Ed.), *Handbook of child psychology:* Vol. 1. *History, theory and methods.* New York: Wiley.

CAIRNS, R. B., CAIRNS, B. D., & NECKERMAN, H. J. (1989). Early school dropout: Configurations and determinants. *Child Development, 60,* 1437–1452.

CALIFORNIA STATE DEPARTMENT OF EDUCATION (1990). *Language census report for California public schools — 1990.* Sacramento: California Department of Education, Educational Demographics Unit.

CAMPOS, J. J., BARRET, K. C., LAMB, M. E., GOLDSMITH, H. H., & STENBERG, C. (1983). Socioemotional development. In P. H. Mussen (Ed.), *Handbook of child psychology:* Vol 2. *Infancy and developmental psychobiology.* New York: Wiley.

CAMPOS, J. J., BENSON, J., & RUDY, L. (1986). The role of self-produced locomotion in spatial behavior. Posterpaper presented at the meeting of the International Conference for Infant Studies. Beverly Hills, CA.

CAMPOS, J. J., & BERTENTHAL, B. (1987). Locomotion and psychological development in infancy. In K. Jaffe (Ed.), *Childhood powered mobility: Developmental, technical, and clinical perspectives.* Washington, DC: Rehabilitation Engineering Society of North America.

CAMPOS, J. J., KERMOIAN, R., & ZUMBAHLEN, M. R. (1992). Socioemotional transformations in the family system following infant crawling onset. In N. Eisenberg & R. A. Fabes (Eds.), *Emotion and its regulation in early development (New directions for child development, 55).* San Francisco: Jossey-Bass.

CAMPOS, J. J., & STENBERG, C. R. (1981). Perception, appraisal, and emotion: The onset of social referencing. In M. E. Lamb & L. R. Sherrod (Eds.), *Infants' social cognition: Empirical and social considerations.* Hillsdale, NJ: Erlbaum.

CAMPOS, R. G. (1989). Soothing pain-elicited distress in infants with swaddling and pacifiers. *Child Development, 60,* 781–792.

CAPLAN, N., WHITMORE, J. K., & CHOY, M. H. (1989). *The boat people and achievement in America: A study of family life, hard work, and cultural values.* Ann Arbor: University of Michigan Press.

CAPON, N., & KUHN, D. (1979). Logical reasoning in the supermarket: Adult females' use of proportional reasoning strategy in an everyday context. *Developmental Psychology, 15,* 450–452.

CAREY, S. (1978). The child as word learner. In M. Halle, J. Bresnan, & G. A. Miller (Eds.), *Linguistic theory and psychological reality.* Cambridge, MA: MIT Press.

CAREY, S. (1985). *Conceptual change in childhood.* Cambridge, MA: MIT Press.

CAREY, S., & GELMAN, R. (Eds.). (1991). *The epigenesis of mind: Essays on biology and cognition.* Hillsdale, NJ: Erlbaum.

CARMICHAEL, L. (1970). Onset and early development of behavior. In P. H. Mussen (Ed.), *Carmichael's manual of child psychology:* Vol. I, Part I. *Infancy and early experience.* New York: Wiley.

CARNEGIE COMMISSION ON POLICY STUDIES IN HIGHER EDUCATION. (1980). *Giving youth a better chance.* San Francisco: Jossey-Bass.

CARRAHER, T. N., & CARRAHER, D. W. (1981). Do Piagetian stages describe the reasoning of unschooled adults? *Quarterly Newsletter of the Laboratory of Comparative Human Cognition, 3,* 61–68.

CARRAHER, T. N., CARRAHER, D. W., & SCHLIEMANN, A. D. (1985). Mathematics in the streets and in schools. *British Journal of Developmental Psychology, 3,* 21–29.

CARROLL, J. B. (1982). The measurement of intelligence. In R. J. Sternberg (Ed.), *The handbook of human intelligence.* Cambridge: Cambridge University Press.

CARTER, D. B. (1987). *Current theories and conceptions of sex roles and sex typing: Theory and research.* New York: Praeger.

CASE, R. (1985). *Intellectual development: A systematic reinterpretation.* New York: Academic Press.

CASE, R. (1991). *The mind's staircase.* Hillsdale, NJ: Erlbaum.

CASE, R. (1992). The role of the frontal lobes in the regulation of cognitive development. *Brain and Cognition, 20*(1), 51–73.

CASE, R., KURLAND, D. M., & GOLDBERG, J. (1982). Operational efficiency and growth of short-term memory span. *Journal of Experimental Child Psychology, 33,* 386–404.

CASE, R., MARINI, Z., MCKEOUGH, A., DENNIS, S., & GOLDBERG, J. (1986). Horizontal structure in middle childhood: Cross domain parallels in the course of cognitive growth. In I. Levin (Ed.), *Stage and structure: Reopening the debate.* Norwood, NJ: Ablex Publishing Corp.

CASS, V. C. (1984). Homosexual identity formation: Testing a theoretical model. *Journal of Sex Research, 20,* 143–167.

CATTELL, R. B. (1949). *The culture free intelligence test.* Champaign, IL: Institute for Personality and Ability Testing.

CAZDEN, C. (1965). *Environmental assistance to the child's acquisition of grammar.* Unpublished doctoral dissertation, Harvard University.

CECI, S. J., & BRUCK, M. (in press). The suggestibility of the child witness: An historical review and synthesis. *Psychological Bulletin.*

CECI, S. J., TOGLIA, M. P., & ROSS, D. F. (Eds.). (1987). *Children's eyewitness memory.* New York: Springer-Verlag.

CHALL, J. (1983). *Stages of reading development.* New York: McGraw-Hill.

CHALL, J., JACOBS, V. A., & BALDWIN, L. E. (1990). *The reading crisis: Why poor children fall behind.* Cambridge, MA: Harvard University Press.

CHAND, I. P., CRIDER, D. M., & WILLITS, F. K. (1975). Parent–youth disagreement as perceived by youth: A longitudinal study. *Youth and Society, 6,* 365–375.

CHARLESWORTH, W. R. (1976). Intelligence as adaptation: An ethological approach. In L. Resnick (Ed.), *The nature of intelligence.* Hillsdale, NJ: Erlbaum.

CHASE, A. (1977). *The legacy of Malthus.* New York: Knopf.

CHASE, W. G., & SIMON, H. A. (1973). Perception in chess. *Cognitive Psychology, 4,* 55–81.

CHASE-LANSDALE, P. L & HETHERINGTON, E. M. (1990). The impact of divorce on life-span development: Short and long-term effects. In P. B. Baltes, D. L. Featherman, & R. M. Lerner (Eds.), *Life-span development and behavior,* (Vol. 10). Hillsdale, NJ: Erlbaum.

CHEN, C., & STEVENSON, H. W. (1988). Cross-linguistic differences in digit span of preschool children. *Journal of Experimental Child Psychology, 46,* 150–158.

CHERLIN, A. J., FURSTENBERG, F. F., JR., CHASE-LANSDALE, P. L., KIERNAN, K. E., ROBINS, P. K., MORRISON, D. R., & TEITLER, J. O. (1991) Longitudinal studies of the effects of divorce on children in Great Britain and the United States. *Science, 252*(5011), 1386–1389.

CHESS, S., & THOMAS, A. (1982). Infant bonding: Mystique and reality. *American Journal of Orthopsychiatry, 52,* 213–221.

CHEYNEY, D. L., & SEYFARTH, R. M. (1990). *How monkeys see the world.* Cambridge: Cambridge University Press.

CHI, M. T. H. (1978). Knowledge structures and memory development. In R. S. Siegler (Ed.), *Children's thinking: What develops?* Hillsdale, NJ: Erlbaum.

CHI, M. T. H., GLASER, R., & REES, E. (1982). Expertise in problem solving. In R. J. Sternberg (Ed.), *Advances in the psychology of human intelligence* (Vol. 1). Hillsdale, NJ: Erlbaum.

CHI, M. T. H., & KLAHR, D. (1975). Span and rate of apprehension in children and adults. *Journal of Experimental Child Psychology, 19,* 434–439.

CHI, M. T. H., & KOESKE, R. D. (1983). Network representation of a child's dinosaur knowledge. *Developmental Psychology, 19,* 29–39.

CHILD, I. (1968). Personality in culture. In E. F. Borgatta & W. W. Lambert (Eds.), *Handbook of personality theory and research.* Chicago: Rand McNally.

CHILDS, C. P., & GREENFIELD, P. M. (1980). Informal modes of learning and teaching: The case of Zinacanteco learning. In N. Warren (Ed.), *Studies in cross-cultural psychology* (Vol. 2). New York: Academic Press.

CHODOROW, N. (1974). Family structure and feminine personality. In M. Z. Rosaldo & L. Lamphere (Eds.), *Women, culture and society.* Stanford, CA: Stanford University Press.

CHOMSKY, C. (1969). *Acquisition of syntax in children from 5 to 10.* Cambridge, MA: MIT Press.

CHOMSKY, N. (1959). Review of *Verbal Behavior* by B. F. Skinner. *Language, 35,* 26–58.

CHOMSKY, N. (1965). *Aspects of a theory of syntax.* Cambridge, MA: MIT Press.

CHOMSKY, N. (1975). *Reflections on language.* New York: Pantheon Books.

CHOMSKY, N. (1980). Initial states and steady states. In M. Piatelli-Palmerini (Ed.), *Language and learning: The debate between Jean Piaget and Noam Chomsky.* Cambridge, MA: Harvard University Press.

CHOMSKY, N. (1986). *Knowledge of language: Its nature, origins, and use.* New York: Praeger.

CHRISTENSEN, H. T., & GREGG, C. F. (1970). Changing sex norms in America and Scandinavia. *Journal of Marriage and the Family, 32,* 616–627.

CHUKOVSKY, K. (1968). *From two to five.* Berkeley: University of California Press.

CIANFRANI, T. (1960). *A short history of obstetrics and gynecology.* Springfield, IL: Charles Thomas.

CICCHETTI, D., & CARLSON, V. (Eds.). (1989). *Child Maltreatment: Theory and research on the causes and consequences of child abuse and neglect.* Cambridge: Cambridge University Press.

CIMONS, M. (1990, June 12). Panel Calls Child Abuse A National Emergency. *Los Angeles Times,* Section A, p. 12.

CLARK, E. V. (1973). What's in a word? On the child's acquisition of semantics in his first language. In T. E. Moore (Ed.), *Cognitive development and the acquisition of language.* New York: Academic Press.

CLARK, K. & CLARK, M. (1939). The development of consciousness of self and the emergence of racial identity in Negro pre-school schoolchildren. *Journal of Social Psychology, 10,* 591–599.

CLARKE, A. M., & CLARKE, A. D. B. (Eds.). (1976). *Early experience: Myth and evidence.* London: Open Books.

CLARKE, A. M., & CLARKE, A. D. B. (1986). Thirty years of child psychology: A selective review. *Journal of Child Psychology and Psychiatry, 27,* 719–759.

CLARKE-STEWART, A. (1978). And daddy makes three: The father's impact on mother and young child. *Child Development, 49,* 466–479.

CLARKE-STEWART, A. (1982). *Daycare.* Cambridge, MA: Harvard University Press.

CLARKE-STEWART, A. (1984). Day-care: A new context for research and development. In M. Perlmutter (Ed.), *Parent-child interaction and parent-child relations in child development: The Minnesota Symposia on Child Psychology* (Vol. 17). Hillsdale, NJ: Erlbaum.

CLARKE-STEWART, A. (1989). Infant day care: Maligned or malignant? *American Psychologist, 44,* 266–273.

CLARKE-STEWART, A. (1992). *Daycare* (2nd ed.). Cambridge, MA: Harvard University Press.

CLARKE-STEWART, A., & FEIN, G. G. (1983). Early childhood programs. In P. H. Mussen (Ed.), *Handbook of child psychology: Vol. 2. Infancy and developmental psychobiology.* New York: Wiley.

CLAUSEN, J. A. (1975). The social meaning of differential physical and sexual maturation. In S. E. Dragastin & G. E. Elder, Jr. (Eds.), *Adolescence in the life cycle.* Washington, DC: Hemisphere Press.

CLIFFORD, E. (1959). Discipline in the home: A controlled observational study of parental practices. *Journal of Genetic Psychology, 95,* 45–82.

COHEN, R. (May, 1987). Suddenly I'm an adult? *Psychology Today, 21,* 70–71.

COIE, J. D., & KUPERSMIDT, J. B. (1983). A behavioral analysis of emerging social status in boys' groups. *Child Development, 54,* 1400–1416.

COLBY, A., & KOHLBERG, L. (1984). Invariant sequence and internal consistency in moral judgement stages. In W. M. Kurtines & J. L. Gewirtz, (Eds.), *Morality, moral behavior, and moral development.* New York: Wiley.

COLBY, A., KOHLBERG, L., GIBBS, J., & LIEBERMAN, M. (1983). A longitudinal study of moral development. *Monographs of the Society for Research in Child Development, 48,* (1–2, Serial No. 200).

COLE, M. (1985). Mind as a cultural achievement: Implications for IQ testing. In E. Eisner (Ed.), *Learning and teaching the ways of knowing.* Chicago: National Society for the Study of Education.

COLE, M. (1990). Cognitive development and formal schooling. In L. C. Moll (Ed.), *Vygotsky and education: Instructional implications and applications of sociohistorical psychology.* Cambridge: Cambridge University Press.

COLE, M., GAY, J., GLICK, J. A., & SHARP, D. W. (1971). *The cultural context of learning and thinking.* New York: Basic Books.

COLE, M., & GRIFFIN, P. (1987). *Contextual factors in education.* Madison: Wisconsin Center for Education Research.

COLE, M., & MEANS, B. (1981). *Comparative studies of how people think.* Cambridge, MA: Harvard University Press.

COLE, M., & SCRIBNER, S. (1974). *Culture and thought*. New York: Wiley.

COLE, S. (1980). *Working kids on working*. New York: Lothrop, Lee and Shepard.

COLEMAN, J. C. (1980). *The nature of adolescence*. London: Methuen.

COLEMAN, J. S. (1962). *The adolescent society*. Glencoe, IL: Free Press.

COLES, G. S. (1990). Literacy and mental illness. *Readings, 5*, 20–24.

COLES, R. (1967). *Children of crisis: A study of crisis and fear*. Boston: Atlantic-Little, Brown.

COLES, R. (1986). *The moral life of children*. Boston: Atlantic Monthly Press.

COLES, R., & STOKES, G. (1985). *Sex and the American teenager*. New York: Harper & Row.

COLLINS, A. (1975). The developing child as viewer. *Journal of Communication, 25*, 35–43.

COLLINS, A., BROWN, J. S., & NEWMAN, S. E. (1989). Cognitive apprenticeship: Teaching the crafts of reading, writing, and mathematics. In L. B. Resnick (Ed.), *Knowing, learning and instruction: Essays in honor of Robert Glaser*. Hillsdale, NJ: Erlbaum.

COLLINS, W. A. (Ed.). (1984). *Development during middle childhood*. Washington, DC: National Academy Press.

COLLINS, W. A. (1990). Parent-child relationships in the transition to adolescence: Continuity and change in interaction, affects, and cognition. In R. Montemayor, G. Adams, & T. Gullota (Eds.), *Advances in adolescent development* (Vol. 2). Beverly Hills: Sage.

COMMONS, M., RICHARDS, F., & ARMON, C. (Eds.). (1984). *Beyond formal operations: Late adolescent and adult cognitive development*. New York: Praeger.

COMSTOCK, G., & PAIK, H. (1991). *Television and the American child*. New York: Academic Press.

CONANT, L. L. (1896). *The number concept*. New York: Macmillan.

CONDON, R. G. (1987). *Inuit youth*. New Brunswick, NJ: Rutgers University Press.

CONDRY, S. (1983). History and background of preschool intervention programs and the Consortium for Longitudinal Studies. In the Consortium for Longitudinal Studies (Ed.), *As the twig is bent . . . lasting effects of preschool programs*. Hillsdale, NJ: Erlbaum.

CONEL, J. L. (1939–1967). *The postnatal development of the human cerebral cortex* (8 vols.). Cambridge, MA: Harvard University Press.

CONGRESSIONAL RESEARCH SERVICE. (1983, June). *Infant mortality*. Washington, DC: U.S. Government Printing Office.

CONNELL, D. B. (1977). *Individual differences in attachment: An investigation into stability, implications, and relationships to the structure of early language development*. Unpublished doctoral dissertation, Syracuse University.

CONNOLLY, K., & DALGLEISH, M. (1989). The emergence of a tool using skill in infancy. *Developmental Psychology, 25*, 539–549.

CONSORTIUM FOR LONGITUDINAL STUDIES (1983). *As the twig is bent*. Hillsdale, NJ: Erlbaum.

CONSTANTINOPLE, A. (1969). An Eriksonian measure of personality development in college students. *Developmental Psychology, 1*, 357–372.

CONSTANZO, P. (1970). Conformity development as a function of self-blame. *Journal of Personality and Social Psychology, 14*, 366–374.

COOPER, R. P., & ASLIN, R. N. (1990). Preference for infant-directed speech in the first month after birth. *Child Development, 61*, 1584–1595.

COOPERSMITH, S. (1967). *The antecedents of self esteem*. New York: W. H. Freeman.

CORBIN, P. F., & BICKFORD, R. G. (1955). Studies of the electroencephalogram of normal children. *Electroencephalography and Clinical Neurology, 7*, 15–28.

COREN, S., PORAC, C. E., & DUNCAN, P. (1981). Lateral preference behaviors in preschool children and young adults. *Child Development, 52*, 443.

CORNELL, E. H., & MCDONNELL, P. M. (1986). Infants' acuity at twenty feet. *Investigative Ophthalmology and Visual Science, 27*, 1417–1420.

CORSARO, W. A. (1981). Friendship in the nursery school: Social organization in a peer environment. In S. R. Asher & J. M. Gottman (Eds.), *The development of children's friendships*. Cambridge: Cambridge University Press.

CORSO, J. F. (1990). Sensory-perceptual processes and aging. In K. W. Schaie & C. Eisdorfer (Eds.), *Annual Review of Gerentology, 7*. New York: Springer-Verlag.

COUNCIL ON INTERRACIAL BOOKS FOR CHILDREN. (1976). *Human (and anti-human) values in children's books*. New York: Racism and Sexism Resource Center for Educators.

COUSINS, S. D. (1989). Culture and selfhood in Japan and the United States. *Journal of Personality and Social Research, 56,* 124–131.

COWAN, R. (1987). Assessing children's understanding of one-to-one correspondence. *British Journal of Developmental Psychology, 5,* 140–153.

COY, M. (1989). *Apprenticeship: From theory to method and back again.* Albany, NY: SUNY Press.

CRAGO, M., & CRAGO, H. (1983). *Prelude to literacy.* Carbondale: Southern Illinois University Press.

CRANDALL, R. (1973). The measurement of self-esteem and related concepts. In J. P. Robinson & P. R. Shaver (Eds.), *Measures of social psychological attitudes* (rev. ed.). Ann Arbor, MI: Institute for Social Research.

CRAVIOTO, J., DE LICARDIE, E. R., & BIRCH, H. G. (1966). Nutrition, growth and neurointegrative development: An experimental and ecological study. *Pediatrics, 38,* 319–372.

CRNIC, K. A., RAGOZIN, A. S., GREENBERG, M. T., ROBINSON, N. M., & BASHAM, R. R. (1983). Social interaction and developmental compliance of preterm and fullterm infants during first year of life. *Child Development, 54,* 1199–1210.

CROCKENBERG, S. (1987). Support for adolescent mothers during the postnatal period. In C. Boukydis (Ed.), *Research on support for parents and infants in the postnatal period.* Norwood, NJ: Ablex Publishing Corp.

CROCKENBERG, S., & LITMAN, C. (1991). Effects of maternal employment on maternal and two-year-old child behavior. *Child Development, 62,* 930–953.

CRONBACH, L. J. (1975). Beyond the two disciplines of scientific psychology. *American Psychologist, 30,* 116–127.

CROSS, W. (1991). *Shades of black.* Ithaca, NY: Cornell University Press.

CROWDER, R. G., & WAGNER, R. K. (1992). *The psychology of reading* (2nd ed.). New York: Oxford University Press.

CSIKSZENTMIHALYI, M., & LARSON, R. (1984). *Being adolescent: Conflict and growth in the teenage years.* New York: Basic Books.

CUNNINGHAM, F. G., MACDONALD, P. C., & GANT, N. F. (1989). *William's Obstetrics* (18th edition). Norwalk, CT: Appleton & Lange.

CURTIS, H. (1979). *Biology.* New York: Worth.

CURTISS, S. (1977). *Genie: A psychological study of a modern-day wild child.* New York: Academic Press.

D'AMICO, R. (1984). Does employment during high school impair academic progress? *Sociology of Education, 57,* 152–164.

DAMON, W. (1975). Early conceptions of positive justice as related to the development of logical operations. *Child Development, 46,* 301–312.

DAMON, W. (1977). *The social world of the child.* San Francisco: Jossey-Bass.

DAMON, W. (1980). Patterns of change in children's social reasoning: A two-year longitudinal study. *Child Development, 5l,* 1010–1017.

DAMON, W. (1983). *Social and personality development: Infancy through adolescence.* New York: W. W. Norton.

DAMON, W., & HART, D. (1988). *Self-understanding in childhood and adolescence.* Cambridge: Cambridge University Press.

D'ANDRADE, R. G. (1974). Memory and assessment of behavior. In H. M. Blalock, Jr. (Ed.), *Measurement in the social sciences.* Chicago: Aldine.

DANIELS-BEIRNESS, T. (1989). Measuring peer status in boys and girls: A problem of apples and oranges. In B. H. Schneider, G. Attili, J. Nadel, & R. P. Weissberg, (Eds.), (1989). *Social competence in developmental perspective.* Boston: Kluwer Academic Publishers.

DANNEMILLER, J. L. & STEPHENS, B. K. (1988). A critical test of infant pattern preference models. *Child Development, 59,* 210–216.

DANZINGER, K. (1990). *Constructing the subject.* Cambridge: Cambridge University Press.

DARLINGTON, R. B. (1991). The long-term effects of model preschool programs. In L Okagaki & R. J. Sternberg (Eds.), *Directors of development: Influences on the development of children's thinking.* Hillsdale, NJ: Erlbaum.

DARWIN, C. (1859/1958). *The origin of species.* New York: Penguin.

DASEN, P. R. (1972). Cross-cultural Piagetian research: A summary. *Journal of Cross-Cultural Psychology, 3,* 29–39.

DASEN, P. R. (1977a). Are cognitive processes universal? A contribution to cross-cultural Piagetian psychology. In N. Warren (Ed.), *Studies in cross-cultural psychology* (Vol. 1). London: Academic Press.

DASEN, P. R. (1977b). *Piagetian psychology: Cross cultural contributions.* New York: Gardner.

DASEN, P. R. (1982). Cross-cultural data on operational development: Asymptotic development curves. In T. G. Bever (Ed.), *Regressions in Development*. Hillsdale, NJ: Erlbaum.

DASEN, P. R., & HERON, A. (1981). Cross-cultural tests of Piaget's theory. In H. Triandis & A. Heron (Eds.), *Handbook of cross-cultural psychology*: Vol. 4. *Developmental psychology*. Boston: Allyn and Bacon.

DASEN, P. R., NGINI, L., & LAVALLEE, M. (1979). Cross-cultural training studies of concrete operations. In L. H. Eckenberger, W. J. Lonner, & Y. H. Poortinga (Eds.), *Cross-cultural contributions to psychology*. Amsterdam: Swets & Zeilinger.

DAVID, H. P. (1981). Unwantedness: Longitudinal studies of Prague children born to women twice denied abortions for the same pregnancy and matched controls. In P. Ahmed (Ed.), *Pregnancy, childbirth, and parenthood*. New York: Elsevier.

DAVID, H. P., DYTRYCH, Z., MATEJCEK, Z., & SCHULLER, V. (1988). *Born unwanted: Developmental effects of denied abortion*. Prague: Avicenum, Czechoslovak Medical Press.

DAVIES, K. E. (1989). *The fragile X syndrome*. Oxford: Oxford University Press.

DAVIS, A. (1948). *Social class differences in learning*. Cambridge, MA: Harvard University Press.

DECARIE, T. G. (1969). A study of the mental and emotional development of the thalidomide child. In B. M. Foss (Ed.), *Determinants of infant behavior* (Vol. 4). London: Methuen.

DE CASPER, A. J., & FIFER, W. P. (1980). Of human bonding: Newborns prefer their mother's voices. *Science, 208*, 1174–1176.

DE CASPER, A. J., & SIGAFOOS, A. D. (1983). The intrauterine heartbeat: A potent reinforcer for newborns. *Infant Behavior and Development, 6*, 19–25.

DE CASPER, A. J. & SPENCE, M. J. (1986). Prenatal maternal speech influences newborn's perception of speech sounds. *Infant Behavior and Development, 9*, 133–150.

DE CHATEAU, P. (1987). Parent-infant socialization in several Western European countries. In J. D. Osofsky (Ed.), *The handbook of infant development* (2nd ed.). New York: Wiley.

DE FLEUR, L., & MENKE, B. (1975). Learning about the labor force: Occupational knowledge among high school males. *Sociology of Education, 48*, 324–345.

DELOACHE, J. (1984). What's this? Maternal questions in joint picture book reading with toddlers. *Quarterly Newsletter of the Laboratory of Comparative Human Cognition, 6*, 87–95.

DELOACHE, J. S. (1987). Rapid change in the symbolic functioning of very young children. *Science, 238*, 1556–1557.

DELOACHE, J. S., CASSIDY, D. J., & BROWN, A. L. (1985). Precursors of mnemonic strategies in young children. *Child Development, 56*, 125–137.

DEMOS, J., & DEMOS, V. (1969). Adolescence in historical perspective. *Journal of Marriage and the Family, 31*, 632–638.

DENNIS, M., SUGAR, J., & WHITAKER, H. A. (1982). The acquisition of tag questions. *Child Development, 53*, 1254–1257.

DENNIS, W. (1973). *Children of the creche*. New York: Appleton-Century-Crofts.

DENNIS, W., & DENNIS, M. (1940). The effect of cradling practices upon the onset of walking in Hopi children. *Journal of Genetic Psychology, 56*, 77–86.

DENT, H. R. (1982). The effects of interviewing strategies on the results of interviews with child witnesses. In A. Trankell (Ed.), *Reconstructing the past*. Deventer, the Netherlands: Kluwer.

DEREGOWSKI, J. B. (1980). *Illusions, patterns, and pictures: A cross-cultural perspective*. London: Academic Press.

DE VILLIERS, J. G., & DE VILLIERS, P. A. (1978). *Language acquisition*. Cambridge, MA: Harvard University Press.

DE VILLIERS, J. G., & DE VILLIERS, P. A. (1979). *Early language*. Cambridge, MA: Harvard University Press.

DEVRIES, M. (1987). Cry babies, culture, and catastrophe: Infant temperament among the Masai. In N. Scheper-Hughes (Ed.), *Child survival: Anthropological approaches to the treatment and maltreatment of children*. Boston: Reidel.

DE VRIES, M. W., & DE VRIES, M. R. (1977). The cultural relativity of toilet training readiness: A perspective from East Africa. *Pediatrics, 60*(2), 170–177.

DEVRIES, R. (1969). Constancy of genetic identity in the years three to six. *Monographs of the Society for Research in Child Development, 34*, (Serial No. 127).

DEWEY, J. (1911). Culture epoch theory. In P. Monroe (Ed.), *A cyclopedia of education* (Vol. 2). New York: Macmillan.

DIAMOND, A. (1985). Development of the ability to use recall to guide action, as indicated by infants' performance on AB. *Child Development, 56,* 868–883.

DIAMOND, A. (1990a). Introduction. *Annals of the New York Academy of Sciences, 608,* xiiii–vi.

DIAMOND, A. (Ed.). (1990b). The development and neural basis of higher cognitive functions. *Annals of the New York Academy of Sciences, 608,* 267–317.

DIAMOND, A. (1991). Frontal lobe involvement in cognitive changes during the first year of life. In K. Gibson, M. Konner, & A. Patterson (Eds.), *Brain and behavioral development.* Hillsdale, NJ: Erlbaum.

DIAS, M. G., & HARRIS, P. L. (1988). The effect of make-believe play on deductive reasoning. *British Journal of Developmental Psychology, 6*(3), 207–221.

DICKSON, P. (Ed.). (1981). *Children's oral communication skills.* New York: Academic Press.

DIENES, Z. P. (1966). *Mathematics in the primary school.* London: Macmillan.

DILLARD, A. (1987). *An American childhood.* New York: Harper & Row.

DISHION, T. J. (1990). The family ecology of boys' peer relations in middle childhood. *Child Development, 61,* 874–892.

DIX, T., RUBLE, D. N., & ZAMBARANO, R. J. (1989). Mothers' implicit theories of discipline: Child effects, parent effects, and the attribution process. *Child Development, 60,* 1373–1391.

DODGE, K. A. (1983). Behavioral antecedents of peer social status. *Child Development, 54,* 1386–1399.

DODGE, K. A., & FELDMAN, E. (1990). Issues in social cognition and sociometric status. In S. R. Asher & J. D. Coie (Eds.), *Peer rejection in childhood.* Cambridge: Cambridge University Press.

DODGE, K. A., PETTIT, G. S., McCLASKEY, C. L., & BROWN, M. M. (1986). Social competence in children. *Monographs of the Society for Research in Child Development, 51,* (2, Serial No. 213).

DOISE, W., MUGNY, G., & PERRET-CLERMONT, A. N. (1975). Social understanding and the development of cognitive operations. *European Journal of Social Psychology, 5,* 367–383.

DOLHINOW, P. (Ed.). (1972). *Primate patterns.* New York: Holt, Rinehart and Winston.

DONALDSON, M. (1978). *Children's minds.* New York: W. W. Norton.

DORE, J. (1978). Conditions for acquisition of speech acts. In I. Markova (Ed.), *The social concept of language.* New York: Wiley.

DORE, J. (1979). Conversational acts and the acquisition of language. In E. Ochs & B. B. Schieffelin (Eds.), *Developmental Pragmatics.* New York: Academic Press.

DORE, J., GEARHART, M., & NEWMAN, D. (1979). The structure of nursery school conversation. In K. E. Nelson (Ed.), *Children's language* (Vol. 1). Hillsdale, NJ: Erlbaum.

DORNBUSCH, S. M., RITTER, P. L., LEIDERMAN, P. H., ROBERTS, D. F., & FRALEIGH, M. J. (1987). The relation of parenting style to adolescent school performance. *Child Development, 58,* 1244–1257.

DORR, A. (1983). No shortcuts to judging reality. In P. E. Bryant & S. Anderson (Eds.), *Watching and understanding TV: Research on children's attention and comprehension.* New York: Academic Press.

DORR, A., GRAVES, S. B., & PHELPS, E. (1980). Television literacy for young children. *Journal of Communication, 30,* 71–83.

DOTT, A., FORT, B., & ARTHUR, T. (1975a). The effects of maternal demographic factors on infant mortality rates: Summary of the findings of the Louisiana Infant Mortality Study: Part 1. *American Journal of Obstetrics and Gynecology, 123,* 847–853.

DOTT, A., FORT, B., & ARTHUR, T. (1975b). The effects of availability and utilization of prenatal care and hospital services of infant mortality rates: Summary of the findings of the Louisiana Infant Mortality Study: Part 2. *American Journal of Obstetrics and Gynecology, 123,* 854–860.

DOUVAN, E., & ADELSON, J. (1966). *The adolescent experience.* New York: Wiley.

DUNCAN, P. D., RITTER, P. L., DORNBUSCH, S. M., GROSS; R. T. & CARLSMITH, J. M. (1985). The effects of pubertal timing on body image, school behavior, and deviance. *Journal of Youth and Adolescence, 14,* 227–235.

DUNN, J. (1977). *Distress and comfort.* Cambridge, MA: Harvard University Press.

DUNN, J. (1984). *Sisters and brothers.* Cambridge, MA: Harvard University Press.

DUNN, J. (1988). *The beginnings of social understanding.* Cambridge, MA: Harvard University Press.

DUNN, J., & KENDRICK, C. (1979). Young siblings in the context of family relationships. In M. Lewis & L. A. Rosenblum (Eds.), *The child and its family.* New York: Plenum Press.

DUNN, J., & MCGUIRE, S. (1992). Sibling and peer relationships in childhood. *Journal of Child Psychology and Psychiatry and Allied Disciplines, 33*(1), 67–105.

DUNN, J., & SHATZ, M. (1989). Becoming a conversationalist despite (or because of) having a sibling. *Child Development, 60,* 399–410.

DUNPHY, D. C. (1963). The social structure of urban adolescent peer groups. *Sociometry, 26,* 230–246.

DURRETT, M. E., OTAKI, M., & RICHARDS, P. (1984). Attachment and mothers' perception of support from the father. *Journal of the International Society for the Study of Behavioral Development, 7,* 167–176.

DWECK, C. S., & BUSH, E. S. (1976). Sex differences in learned helplessness: I. Differential debilitation with peer and adult evaluators. *Developmental Psychology, 12,* 147–156.

DWECK, C. S., DAVIDSON, W., NELSON, S., & ENNA, B. (1978). Sex differences in learned helplessness: II. The contingencies of evaluative feedback in the classroom. III. An experimental analysis, *Developmental Psychology, 14,* 268–276.

DWECK, C. S., & ELLIOTT, E. S. (1983). Achievement motivation. In P. H. Mussen (Ed.), *Handbook of child psychology:* Vol. 4. *Personality and social development.* New York: Wiley.

DWECK, C. S., & GOETZ, T. E. (1978). Attributions and learned helplessness. In J. H. Harvey, W. Ickles, & R. F. Kidd (Eds.), *New directions in attribution research* (Vol. 2). Hillsdale, NJ: Erlbaum.

EASTERBROOKS, M. A., & GOLDBERG, W. A. (1985). Effects of early maternal employment on toddlers, mothers, and fathers. *Developmental Psychology, 21,* 774–783.

ECKERMAN, C. D., STURM, L. A., & GROSS, S. J. (1985). Different developmental courses for very-low-birth-weight infants differing in early head growth. *Developmental Psychology, 21,* 813–827.

EDELMAN, G. M. (1987). *Neural Darwinism.* New York: Basic Books.

EDELSTEIN, W., KELLER, M., & WAHLEN, K. (1984). Structure and content in social cognition: Conceptual and empirical analysis. *Child Development, 55,* 1514–1526.

EDER, D., & HALLINAN, M. T. (1978). Sex differences in children's friendships. *American Sociological Review, 43,* 237–250.

EDER, R. A. (1989). The emergent personologist: The structure and content of 3¹/₂-, 5¹/₂-, and 7¹/₂-year-olds' concepts of themselves and other persons. *Child Development, 60,* 1218–1228.

EDUCATIONAL TESTING SERVICE. National Assessment of Educational Progress (1988). *The mathematics report card: Are we measuring up?* Princeton, NJ: Educational Testing Service.

EDWARDS, C. P. (1982). Moral development in comparative cultural perspective. In D. Wagner & H. Stevenson (Eds.), *Cultural perspectives on child development.* New York: W. H. Freeman.

EGELAND, B., & SROUFE, L. A. (1981). Attachment and early maltreatment. *Child Development, 52,* 44–52.

EIBL-EIBESFELDT, I. (1970). *Ethology: The biology of behavior.* New York: Holt, Rinehart and Winston.

EICHORN, D. H. (1979). Physical development: Current foci of research. In J. Osofsky (Ed.), *The handbook of infant development.* New York: Wiley.

EIMAS, P. D. (1985). The perception of speech in early infancy. *Scientific American, 204,* 66–72.

EIMAS, P. D., SIQUELAND, E., JUSCZYK, P., & VIGORITO, J. (1971). Speech perception in infants. *Science, 171,* 303–306.

EISEN, M., ZELLMAN, G. I., LEIBOWITZ, A., CHOW, W., K., & EVANS, J. R. (1983). Factors discriminating pregnancy resolution decisions of unmarried adolescents. *Genetic Psychology Monographs, 108,* 69–95.

EISENBERG, N. (1992). *The caring child.* Cambridge, MA: Harvard University Press.

EISENBERG-BERG, N., & NEAL, C. (1979). Children's moral reasoning about their own spontaneous prosocial behavior. *Developmental Psychology, 15,* 228–229.

EISENSTADT, S. N., (1963). Archetypal patterns of youth. In E. H. Erikson (Ed.), *The challenge of youth.* Garden City, NY: Doubleday.

EKMAN, P. (1984). Expression and the nature of emotion. In P. Ekman & K. Scherer (Eds.), *Approaches to emotion.* Hillsdale, NJ: Erlbaum.

EKMAN, P. & FRIESEN, W. V. (1986). A new pan-cultural expression of emotion. *Motivation and Emotion, 10,* 159–168.

ELDER, G. H. (1974). *Children of the great depression.* Chicago: University of Chicago Press.

ELDER, G. H., JR. (1982). Historical experiences in the later years. In T. K. Hareven & K. J. Adams (Eds.), *Aging and life course transitions: An interdisciplinary perspective.* New York: Guilford Press.

ELDER, G. H., JR., LIKER, J. K., & CROSS, C. E. (1984). Parent-child behavior in the great depression: Life course and intergenerational influences. In P. B. Baltes & O. G. Brim, Jr. (Eds.), *Life-span developmental psychology: Historical and generational effects.* New York: Academic Press.

ELICKER, J., ENGLUND, M., & SROUFE, L. A. (1992). Predicting peer competence and peer relationships in childhood from early parent-child relationships. In R. Parke & G. Ladd (Eds.), *Family-peer relationships: Models of linkage.* Hillsdale, NJ: Erlbaum.

ELDREDGE, N., & GOULD, S. J. (1972). Punctuated equilibria: An alternative to phyletic gradualism. In T. J. M. Schopf (Ed.), *Models in paleobiology.* New York: W. H. Freeman.

ELIOT, G. (1860/1965). *The mill on the floss.* New York: New American Library.

ELIOT, T. S. (1971). Little Gidding. In *The complete poems and plays: 1909 to 1950.* Orlando, FL: Harcourt Brace Jovanovich.

ELIOT, T. S. (1971). East Coker. In *The complete poems and plays: 1909 to 1950.* Orlando, FL: Harcourt Brace Jovanovich.

ELKIND, D. (1978). *The child's reality: Three developmental themes.* Hillsdale, NJ: Erlbaum.

ELLIS, S., ROGOFF, B., & CROMER, C. (1981). Age segregation in children's interactions. *Developmental Psychology, 17,* 399–407.

EMDE, R. N. (1992). Individual meaning and increasing complexity: Contributions of Sigmund Freud and René Spitz to developmental psychology. *Developmental Psychology, 28,* 347–359.

EMDE, R. N., GAENSBAUER, T. J., & HARMON, R. J. (1976). Emotional expression in infancy: A behavioral study. *Psychological Issues Monograph Series, 10,* (1, Serial No. 37).

EMDE, R. N., & HARMON, R. J. (1972). Endogenous and exogenous smiling systems in early infancy. *Journal of the American Academy of Child Psychiatry, 11,* 77–100.

EMDE, R. N., & ROBINSON, J. (1979). The first two months: Recent research in developmental psycho-

biology and the changing view of the newborn. In J. Noshpitz & J. Call (Eds.), *Basic handbook of child psychiatry.* New York: Basic Books.

ENGEN, T., LIPSITT, L. P., & KAYE, H. (1963). Olfactory responses and adaptation in the human neonate. *Journal of Comparative and Physiological Psychology, 56,* 73–77.

EPSTEIN, J. L. (1989). The selection of friends: Changes across the grades and in different school environments. In T. J. Berndt & G. W. Ladd (Eds.), *Peer relations in child development.* New York: Wiley.

ERIKSON, E. H. (1958). *Young man Luther.* New York: W. W. Norton.

ERIKSON, E. H. (1963). *Childhood and society* (2nd ed.). New York: W. W. Norton.

ERIKSON, E. H. (1968a). *Identity: Youth and crisis.* New York: W. W. Norton.

ERICKSON, E. H. (1968b). Life cycle. In D. L. Sills (Ed.), *International encyclopedia of the social sciences* (Vol. 9). New York: Crowell, Collier.

ERIKSON, E. H. (1969). *Gandhi's truth.* New York: W. W. Norton.

ERIKSON, E. H. (1978). *Adulthood.* New York: W. W. Norton.

ERIKSON, E. H. (1980). *Identity and the life cycle.* New York: W. W. Norton.

ERIKSON, E. H., ERIKSON, J. M., & KIVNICK, H. Q. (1986). *Involvement in old age.* New York: W. W. Norton.

ERIKSON, M. F., SROUFE, L. A., & EGELAND, B. (1985). The relationship between the quality of attachment and behavior problems in preschool in a high-risk sample. *Monographs of the Society for Research in Child Development, 50,* (1–2, Serial No. 209).

ERON, L., WALDER, L., & LEFKOWITZ, M. (1971). *Learning of aggression in children.* Boston: Little, Brown.

ESPENSHADE, T. J., & BRAUN, R. E. (1983). Economic aspects of an aging population and the material well-being of older persons. In M. W. Riley, B. B. Hess, & K. Bond (Eds.), *Aging in society: Selected reviews of recent research.* Hillsdale, NJ: Erlbaum.

ETZEL, B. C., & GEWIRTZ, J. L. (1967). Experimental modification of caregiver maintained high-rate operant crying in a 6-week - and a 20-week-old infant (Infant tyranno-tearus): Extinction of crying with reinforcement of eye contact and smiling. *Journal of Experimental Child Psychology, 5,* 303–317.

EVANS, H. E., & GLASS, L. (1976). *Perinatal medicine*. Hagerstown, MD: Harper & Row.

EVELETH, P. B., & TANNER, J. M. (1976). *Worldwide variation in human growth*. Cambridge: Cambridge University Press.

FAGOT, B. I. (1978a). The influence of sex of child on parental reactions to toddler children. *Child Development, 49,* 459–465.

FAGOT, B. I. (1978b). Reinforcing contingencies for sex role behaviors: Effect of experience with children. *Child Development, 49,* 30–36.

FAGOT, B. I. & LEINBACH, M. D. (1989). The young child's gender schema: Environmental input, internal organization. *Child Development, 60,* 663–672.

FAGOT, B. I., LEINBACH, M. D., & HAGEN, R. (1986). Gender labeling and adoption of sex-typed behaviors. *Developmental Psychology, 22,* 440–443.

FAGOT, B. I., & LEINBACH, M. D. (1993). Gender-role development in young children: From discrimination to labelling. *Developmental Review 13.*

FALK, G., FALK, U., & TOMASCHEVICH, G. V. (1981). *Aging in America and other cultures*. Saratoga, CA: Century Twenty-One Publishing.

FANT, L. (1972). *Ameslan*. Silver Springs, MD: National Association for the Deaf.

FANTZ, R. L. (1961). The origins of form perception. *Scientific American, 204,* 66–72.

FANTZ, R. L. (1963). Pattern vision in newborn infants. *Science, 140,* 296–297.

FANTZ, R. L., ORDY, J. M., & UDELF, M. S. (1962). Maturation of pattern vision in infants during the first six months. *Journal of Comparative Physiological Psychology, 55,* 907–917.

FARNHAM-DIGGORY, S. (1990). *Schooling*. Cambridge, MA: Harvard University Press.

FARRAR, M. J. (1992). Negative evidence and grammatical morpheme acquisition. *Developmental Psychology, 28,* 90–98.

FELDMAN, D. (1980). *Beyond universals in cognitive development*. Norwood, NJ: Ablex Publishing Corp.

FELDMAN, H., GOLDIN-MEADOW, S., & GLEITMAN, L. (1978). Beyond Herodotus: The creation of language by linguistically deprived, deaf children. In A. Lock (Ed.), *Action, symbol, and gesture: The emergence of language.* New York: Academic Press.

FELDMAN, S. S., & ELLIOTT, G. R. (Eds.). (1990). *At the threshold: The developing adolescent*. Cambridge, MA: Harvard University Press.

FENSON, L., & RAMSAY, D. S. (1980). Decentration and integration of child's play in the second year. *Child Development, 51,* 171–178.

FENSON, L., & RAMSAY, D. S. (1981). Effects of modelling action sequences on the play of twelve, fifteen, and nineteen month old children. *Child Development, 52,* 1028–1036.

FERNALD, A. (1991). Prosody in speech to children: Prelinguistic and linguistic functions. In R. Vasta (Ed.), *Annals of child development* (Vol. 8). London: Jessica Kingsley Publishers.

FESBACH, N. D. (1980). Corporal punishment in the schools: Some paradoxes, some facts, some possible directions. In G. Gerbner, C. J. Ross, & E. Zigler (Eds.), *Child abuse: An agenda for action*. New York: Oxford University Press.

FIELD, T. (1990). *Infancy*. Cambridge, MA: Harvard University Press.

FIELD, T. M., COHEN, D., GARCIA, R., & GREENBERG, R. (1984). Infant response to facelike patterns under fixed trial and infant-control procedures. *Child Development, 54,* 172–177.

FIELD, T. M., & GOLDSON, E. (1984). Pacifying effects of nonnutritive sucking on term and preterm neonates during heelstick procedures. *Pediatrics, 74,* 1012–1015.

FIELD, T. M., WOODSON, R., GREENBERG, R., & COHEN, D. (1982). Discrimination and imitation of facial expressions by neonates. *Science, 218,* 179–182.

FINCH, M. D. & MORTIMER, J. T. (1985). Adolescent work hours and the process of achievement. In A. C. Kerckhoff (Ed.), *Research in sociology of education and socialization* (Vol. 5). Greenwich, CT: JAI Press.

FINCHAM, F. D., & CAIN, K. M. (1986). Learned helplessness in humans: A developmental analysis. *Developmental Review, 6,* 301–333.

FINE, G. A. (1987). *With the boys: Little League baseball and preadolescent culture*. Chicago: University of Chicago Press.

FINE, G. A., MORTIMER, J. T., & ROBERTS, D. F. (1990). Leisure, work, and the mass media. In S. S. Feldman & G. R. Elliott (Eds.), *At the threshold: The developing adolescent*. Cambridge, MA: Harvard University Press.

FINKELSTEIN, N. W., & RAMEY, C. T. (1977). Learning to control the environment in infancy. *Child Development, 48,* 806–819.

FISCHER, K. W. (1980). A theory of cognitive development: The control and construction of hierarchies of skills. *Psychological Review, 87,* 477–531.

FISCHER, K. W. (1987). Commentary—Relations between brain and cognitive development. *Child Development, 58,* 623–632.

FISCHER, K. W. & BIDELL, T. R. (1991). Constraining nativist inferences about cognitive capacities. In S. Carey & R. Gelman (Eds.), *The epigenesis of mind: Essays on biology and knowledge.* Hillsdale, NJ: Erlbaum.

FISCHER, K. W., KENNY, S. L., & PIPP, S. L. (1990). How cognitive processes and environmental conditions organize discontinuities in the development of abstractions. In C. Alexander & E. Langer (Eds.), *Higher stages of human development: Perspectives on adult growth.* New York: Oxford University Press.

FISCHER, K. W., & KNIGHT, C. C. (1990). Cognitive development in real children: Levels and variations. In B. Presseisen (Ed.), *Styles of learning and thinking: Interactions in the classroom.* Washington, DC: National Education Association.

FISCHER, K. W., KNIGHT, C. C., & VAN PARYS, M. (1991). Analyzing diversity in developmental pathways: Methods and concepts. In W. Edelstein & R. Case (Eds.), *Constructivist approaches to development: Contributions to human development.* Basel, Switzerland: S. Karger.

FISCHER, K. W., SHAVER, P. R., & CARNOCHAN, P. (1989). A skill approach to emotional development: From basic-to-subordinate-category emotions. In W. Damon (Ed.), *Child development today and tomorrow.* San Francisco: Jossey-Bass.

FLAPAN, D. (1968). *Children's understanding of social interaction.* New York: Teachers College Press.

FLAVELL, J. H. (1971). Stage-related properties of cognitive development. *Cognitive Psychology, 2,* 421–453.

FLAVELL, J. H. (1982). Structures, stages and sequences in cognitive development. In W. A. Collins (Ed.), *The concept of development: Minnesota Symposia on Child Psychology* (Vol. 15). Hillsdale, NJ: Erlbaum.

FLAVELL, J. H. (1985). *Cognitive development* (2nd ed.). Englewood Cliffs, NJ: Prentice-Hall.

FLAVELL, J. H. (1986). The development of children's knowledge about the appearance-reality distinction. *American Psychologist, 41,* 418–425.

FLAVELL, J. H. (1990, June 2). Perspectives on perspective-taking. Paper presented at the 20th Annual Symposium of the Jean Piaget Society, Philadelphia.

FLAVELL, J. H., FLAVELL, E. R., & GREEN, F. L. (1983). Development of the appearance-reality distinction. *Cognitive Psychology, 15,* 95–120.

FLAVELL, J. H., FLAVELL, E. R., & GREEN, F. L., & KORFMACHER, J. E. (1990). Do young children think of television images as pictures or real objects? *Journal of Broadcasting & Electronic Media, 34,* 339–419.

FLAVELL, J. H., FRIEDRICHS, A. G., & HOYT, J. D. (1970). Developmental changes in memorization processes. *Cognitive Psychology, 1,* 324–340.

FLAVELL, J. H., GREEN, F. L., & FLAVELL, E. R. (1986). Development of knowledge about the appearance-reality distinction. *Monographs of the Society for Research in Child Development, 51,* (1, Serial No. 212).

FLAVELL, J. H., GREEN, F. L., & FLAVELL, E. R (1990). Developmental changes in young children's knowledge about the mind. *Cognitive Development, 5,* 1–27.

FLAVELL, J. H., GREEN, F. L., WAHL, K. R., & FLAVELL, E. R. (1987). The effects of question clarification and memory aids on young children's performance on appearance-reality tasks. *Cognitive Development, 2,* 127–144.

FODOR, J. (1983). *The modularity of mind.* Cambridge, MA: MIT Press.

FOGELSON, R. D. (1982). Person, self, and identity: Some anthropological retrospects, circumspects, and prospects. In B. Lee (Ed.), *Psychosocial theories of the self.* New York: Plenum Press.

FOORMAN, B. R., & SIEGEL, A. W. (Eds.). (1986). *Acquisition of reading skills: Cultural constraints and cognitive universals.* Hillsdale, NJ: Erlbaum.

FORD, C. S., & BEACH, F. A. (1951). *Patterns of sexual behavior.* New York: Harper & Row.

FORDHAM, S., & OGBU, J. U. (1986). Black students school success: Coping with the "burden of 'acting white.'" *Urban Review, 18*(3), 176–206.

FORGAYS, D. G., & FORGAYS, J. W. (1952). The nature of the effect of free-environmental experience in the rat. *Journal of Comparative and Physiological Psychology, 45,* 322–328.

FORMAN, E. (1989). The role of peer interaction in the social construction of mathematical knowledge. *International Journal of Educational Research, 13,* 55–70.

FORTES, M. (1950). Kinship and marriage among the Ashanti. In A. R. Radcliffe-Brown & D. Forde (Eds.), *African systems of kinship and marriage*. London: Oxford University Press.

FOX, N. (1977). Attachment of Kibbutz infants to mother and metapelet. *Child Development, 48,* 1228–1239.

FOX, N., & BELL, M. A. (1990). Electrophysiological indices of frontal lobe development. *Annals of the New York Academy of Sciences, 608,* 677–704.

FOX, N., KAGAN, J., & WESIKOPF, S. (1979). The growth of memory during infancy. *Genetic Psychology Monographs, 99,* 91–130.

FOX, N. A., KIMMERLY, N. L., & SCHAFER, W. D. (1991). Attachment to mother/ Attachment to father: A meta-analysis. *Child Development, 62,* 210–225.

FOX, V. C. (1977). Is adolescence a phenomenon of modern times? *Journal of Psychohistory, 5,* 271–295.

FRAIBERG, S. H. (1959). *The magic years: Understanding and handling the problems of early childhood*. New York: Scribner.

FRAIBERG, S. H. (1974). Blind infants and their mothers: An examination of the sign system. In M. Lewis & L. Rosenblum (Eds.), *The effect of the infant on its caregiver*. New York: Wiley.

FRAIBERG, S. H. (1977). *Every child's birthright: In defense of mothering*. New York: Basic Books.

FRANCIS, P. L., SELF, P. A., & HOROWITZ, F. D. (1987). The behavioral assessment of the neonate: An overview. In J. D. Osofsky (Ed.), *Handbook of infant development* (2nd ed.). New York: Wiley.

FRANCO, F., & BUTTERWORTH, G. (1991, April). Infant pointing: Prelinguistic reference and co-reference. Paper presented at Society for Research in Child Development Biennial Meeting, Seattle, WA.

FRANK, A. (1975). *The diary of a young girl*. New York: Pocket Books.

FRANKEL, K., & BATES, J. (1990). Mother-toddler problem solving: Antecedents in attachment, home behavior, and temperament. *Child Development, 61,* 810–819.

FRANKENBURG, W. K., & DODDS, J. B. (1967). The Denver developmental screening test. *The Journal of Pediatrics, 71,* 181–191.

FREED, K. (1983, March 14). Cubatao—a paradise lost to pollution. *Los Angeles Times,* pp. 1, 12, 13.

FREEDMAN, D. (1974). *Human infancy: An evolutionary perspective*. Hillsdale, NJ: Erlbaum.

FREEMAN, D. (1983). *Margaret Mead and Samoa*. Cambridge, MA: Harvard University Press.

FREMGEN, A., & FAY, D. (1980). Overextensions in production and comprehension: A methodological clarification. *Journal of Child Language, 7,* 201–211.

FRENKEL-BRUNSWIK, E. (1963). Adjustments and reorientation in the course of the life-span. In R. E. Kuhlen & G. G. Thompson (Eds.), *Psychological studies of human development*. New York: Appleton-Century-Crofts.

FREUD, A. (1946). *Ego and the mechanisms of defense*. New York: International Universities Press.

FREUD, S. (1920/1924). The psychogenesis of a case of homosexuality in a woman. (B. Low & R. Gabler, Trans.). *Collected Papers* (Vol. 2). London: Hogarth Press.

FREUD, S. (1930). Civilization and its discontents. In J. Strachey (Ed. & Trans.), *The standard edition of the complete psychological works of Sigmund Freud* (Vol. 21). London: Hogarth Press.

FREUD, S. (1921/1949). Group psychology—The analysis of the Ego. In J. Strachey (Ed. & Trans.), *The standard edition of the complete psychological works of Sigmund Freud* (Vol. 18). London: Hogarth Press.

FREUD, S. (1937/1953). Analysis terminable and interminable. In J. Strachey (Ed.), *The standard edition of the complete psychological works of Sigmund Freud.* (Vol. 5). London: Hogarth Press.

FREUD, S. (1905/1953a). Three essays on the theory of sexuality. In J. Strachey (Ed. and Trans.), *The standard edition of the complete psychological works of Sigmund Freud* (Vol. 7).London: Hogarth Press.

FREUD, S. (1905/1953b). The transformation of puberty. In J. Strachey (Ed. & Trans.), *The standard edition of the complete psychological works of Sigmund Freud* (Vol. 7). London: Hogarth Press.

FREUD, S. (1920/1955). Beyond the pleasure principle. In J. Strachey (Ed. and Trans.), *The standard edition of the complete psychological works of Sigmund Freud* (Vol. 18). London: Hogarth Press.

FREUD, S. (1925/1961). Some psychical consequences of the anatomical distinctions between the sexes. In J. Strachey (Ed. & Trans.), *The standard edition of the complete psychological works of Sigmund Freud* (Vol. 19). London: Hogarth Press.

FREUD, S. (1933/1964). *New introductory lectures in psychoanalysis.* (J. Strachey, Ed. & Trans.). New York: W. W. Norton.

FREUD, S. (1940/1964). An outline of psychoanalysis. In J. Strachey (Ed. and Trans.), *The standard edition of the complete psychological works of Sigmund Freud* (Vol. 23). London: Hogarth Press.

FRIEDLANDER, B. Z., WHETSTONE, S., & SCOTT, L. (1974). Suburban preschool children's comprehension of an age-appropriate information television program. *Child Development, 45,* 561–565.

FRIEDMAN, S. L., & SIGMAN, M. (Eds.). (1980). *Preterm birth and psychological development.* New York: Academic Press.

FRIEDRICH, L. K., & STEIN, A. H. (1973). Aggressive and prosocial television programs and the natural behavior of preschool children. *Monographs of the Society for Research in Child Development, 38,* (4, Serial No. 151).

FRIES, J. F. & CRAPO, L. M. (1981). *Vitality and Aging: Implications of the rectangular curve.* San Francisco: W. H. Freeman.

FRISCH, R. E. (1978). Menarche and fatness. *Science, 200,* 1509–1513.

FRITH, C. D., & FRITH, U. (1978). Feature selection and classification: A developmental study. *Journal of Experimental Child Psychology, 25,* 413–428.

FRITH, U. (1989). *Autism.* Oxford: Oxford University Press.

FRODI, A. (1985). When empathy fails: Aversive infant crying and children abuse. In B. M. Lester & C. F. Z. Boukydis (Eds.), *Infant crying: Theoretical and research prospectives.* New York: Plenum Press.

FRODI, A. M., LAMB. M. E., LEAVITT, L. A., & DONOVAN, W. L. (1978). Fathers' and mothers' responses to the faces and cries of normal premature infants. *Developmental Psychology, 14,* 490–498.

FROST, R. (1916/1969). The road not taken. In E. C. Lathem (Ed.), *The poetry of Robert Frost.* New York: Holt, Rinehart and Winston.

FRY, C. I. (1988). Theories of age and culture. In J. Berren & V. Bingtson (Eds.), *Emergent theories of aging.* New York: Springer-Verlag.

FRY, D. P. (1988). Intercommunity differences in aggression among Zapotec children. *Child Development, 59,* 1008–1018.

FRYE, D., & MOORE, C. (Eds.) (1991). *Children's theories of mind: Mental states and social understanding.* Hillsdale, NJ: Erlbaum.

FUKUSHIMA, O., & KATO, M. (1976). The effects of vicarious experiences on children's altruistic behavior. *Bulletin of Tokyo Gakuge University, 27* (Series 1), 90–94.

FULLARD, W., & REILING, A. M. (1976). An investigation of Lorenz's babyness. *Child Development, 47,* 1191–1193.

FURMAN, W., RAHE, D. F., & HARTUP, W. W. (1979). Rehabilitation of socially withdrawn preschool children through mixed-age and same-age socialization. *Child Development, 50*(4), 915–922.

FURSTENBERG, F. F., JR., & CHERLIN, A. J. (1991). *Divided families: What happens to children when parents part.* Cambridge, MA: Harvard University Press.

FURSTENBERG, F. F., JR., BROOKS-GUNN, J., & CHASE-LANSDALE, L. (1989). Teenage pregnancy and childbearing. *American Psychologist, 44,* 313–320.

FURTH, H. G. (1980). *The world of grownups: Children's conceptions of society.* New York: Elsevier.

FUSTER, J. M. (1990). Prefrontal cortex and the bridging of temporal gaps in the perception-action cycle. *Annals of the New York Academy of Sciences, 68,* 318–336.

FUTUYMA, D. J. (1990). *Evolutionary biology* (2nd ed.). Sunderland, MA: Sinauer Associates.

GADDIS, A., & BROOKS-GUNN, J. (1985). The male experience of pubertal change. *Journal of Youth and Adolescence, 14*(1), 61–69.

GAGNON, J. H., & SIMON, W. (1973). *Sexual conduct: The social sources of human sexuality.* Chicago: Aldine.

GALLER, J. R., RAMSEY, F., & SOLIMANO, G. (1985). A follow-up study of the effects of early malnutrition on subsequent development. II. Fine motor skills. *Pediatric Research, 19,* 524–527.

GALLUP. G. G., JR. (1970). Chimpanzees: Self-recognition. *Science, 167,* 86–87.

GAMBLE, T., & ZIGLER. E. (1986). Effects of infant day care: Another look at the evidence. *American Journal of Orthopsychiatry, 56,* 26–42.

GARDNER, H. (1980). *Artful scribbles: The significance of children's drawings.* New York: Basic Books.

GARDNER, H. (1983). *Frames of mind: The theory of multiple intelligences.* New York: Basic Books.

GARDNER, H. (1991). *The unschooled mind: How children think and how schools should teach.* New York: Basic Books.

GARDNER, J., & GARDNER, H. (1970). A note on selective imitation by a six-week-old infant. *Child Development, 41,* 1209–1213.

GARDNER, R. A., & GARDNER, B. T. (1969). Teaching sign language to a chimpanzee. *Science, 165,* 664–672.

GARDNER, W., & ROGOFF, B. (1990). Children's deliberateness of planning according to task circumstances. *Developmental Psychology, 26,* 480–487.

GARMEZY, N. & RUTTER, M. (Eds.) (1988). *Stress, coping, and development in children.* Baltimore: Johns Hopkins Press.

GARVEY, C. (1977). *Play.* Cambridge, MA: Harvard University Press.

GARVEY, C. (1990). *Play* (enlarged ed.). Cambridge, MA: Harvard University Press.

GARVEY, C., & BERNDT, R. (1977). Organization of pretend play. Paper presented at the meetings of the American Psychological Association, Chicago, IL.

GASKINS, S. (1990). *Exploratory play and development in Maya infants.* Unpublished doctoral dissertation, University of Chicago.

GASKINS, S., & GÖNCÜ, A. (1992). Cultural variation in play: A challenge to Piaget and Vygotsky. *Quarterly Newsletter of the Laboratory of Comparative Human Cognition, 14*(3), 31–35.

GAY, J., & COLE, M. (1967). *The new mathematics and an old culture.* New York: Holt, Rinehart & Winston.

GEARHART, M., & NEWMAN, D. (1980). Learning to draw a picture: The social context of individual activity. *Discourse Processes, 3,* 169–184.

GEERTZ, C. (1973). *The interpretation of cultures.* New York: Basic Books.

GEERTZ, C. (1984). From the native's point of view: On the nature of anthropological understanding. In R. Shweder & R. Levine (Eds.), *Culture theory.* Cambridge: Cambridge University Press.

GELLES, R. J. (1973). Child abuse as psychopathology: A sociological critique and reformulation. *American Journal of Orthopsychiatry, 43,* 611–621.

GELMAN, R., & BAILLARGEON, R. (1983). A review of some Piagetian concepts. In P. Mussen (Ed.), *Handbook of child development:* Vol. 3. *Cognitive development.* New York: Wiley.

GELMAN, R., MECK, E., & MERKIN, S. (1986). Young children's mathematical competence. *Cognitive Development, 1,* 1–29.

GELMAN, S. A., & BYRNES, J. P. (1991). *Perspectives on language and thought: Interrelations in development.* New York: Cambridge University Press.

GENOVESE, E. D. (1976). *Role, Jordan, Roll.* New York: Random House.

GERBNER, G., GROSS, L., SIGNORELLI, N., & MORGAN, M. (1986). *Television's mean world: Violence profile no. 14–16.* Philadelphia: Annenberg School of Communication.

GESELL, A. (1929). *Infancy and human growth.* New York: Macmillan.

GESELL, A. (1940). *The first five years of life* (9th ed.). New York: Harper & Row.

GESELL, A. (1945). *The embryology of behavior.* New York: Harper & Row.

GESELL, A., & AMATRUDA, C. S. (1947). *Developmental diagnosis: Normal and abnormal child development* (3rd ed.). Hagerstown, MD: Harper & Row.

GESELL, A., & ILG, F. L. (1943). *Infant and child in the culture of today.* New York: Harper & Row.

GIBBS, G. T., & HUANG, L. N. (Eds.) (1989). *Children of color.* San Francisco: Jossey-Bass.

GIBSON, E. J. (1988). Exploratory behavior in the development of perceiving, acting, and the acquiring of knowledge. *Annual Review of Psychology, 39,* 1–41.

GIL, D. (1970). *Violence against children: Physical child abuse in the United States.* Cambridge, MA: Harvard University Press.

GILLIGAN, C. (1977). In a different voice: Women's conceptions of the self and of morality. *Harvard Educational Review, 47,* 481–517.

GILLIGAN, C. (1982). *In a different voice: Psychological theory and women's development.* Cambridge, MA: Harvard University Press.

GILLIGAN, C., & BELENKY, M. (1980). A naturalistic study of abortion practices. In R. Selman & R. Yondo (Eds.), *Clinical developmental psychology* (*New directions for child development,* No. 7). San Francisco: Jossey-Bass.

GILLIGAN, C., & MURPHY, J. M. (1979). Development from adolescence to adulthood: The philosopher and the "dilemma of the fact." In D. Kuhn (Ed.), *Intellectual development beyond childhood* (*New directions for child development*, No. 5). San Francisco: Jossey-Bass.

GILLIS, J. R. (1974). *Youth and history: Tradition and change in European age relations 1770–present.* New York: Academic Press.

GINSBURG, H. (1977). *Children's arithmetic.* New York: Van Nostrand.

GJERDE, P. F. (1986). The interpersonal structure of family interaction settings: Parent-adolescent relations in dyads and triads. *Developmental Psychology, 22,* 297–304.

GLADWIN, E. T. (1970). *East is a big bird.* Cambridge, MA: Harvard University Press.

GLEITMAN, H. (1963). *Psychology.* New York: W. W. Norton.

GLEITMAN, L., NEWPORT, E., & GLEITMAN, H. (1984). The current status of the motherese hypothesis. *Journal of Child Language, 11,* 43–80.

GLYNN, T. J. (1981). From family to peer: A review of transitions of influence among drug using youth. *Journal of youth and adolescence, 10,* 363–383.

GOELMAN, H. (1988). The relationship between structure and process variables in home and day care settings on children's language development. In A. R. Pence (Ed.), *Ecological research with children and families.* New York: Teachers College Press.

GOLBUS, M. S. (1980). Teratology for the obstetrician: Current status. *Journal of the American College of Obstetricians and Gynecologists, 55,* 269–276.

GOLDBERG, S., & DIVITTO, B. A. (1983). *Born too soon: Premature birth and early development.* New York: W. H. Freeman.

GOLDING, W. (1954). *The lord of the flies.* New York: Putnam.

GOLDIN-MEADOW, S. (1982). The resilience of recursion: A study of a communication system developed without a conventional language model. In E. Wanner & L. R. Gleitman (Eds.), *Language acquisition: The state of the art.* New York: W. W. Norton.

GOLDIN-MEADOW, S. (1985). Language development under atypical learning conditions. In K. E. Nelson (Ed.), *Children's language* (Vol. 5). Hillsdale, NJ: Erlbaum.

GOLDIN-MEADOW, S., & MYLANDER, C. (1990). The role of parental input in the development of a morphological system. *Journal of Child Language, 17,* 527–563.

GOLDMAN-RAKIC, P. S. (1987). Development of cortical circuitry and cognitive function. *Child Development, 58,* 601–622.

GOLDSMITH, H. H. (1987). Roundtable: What is temperament? Four Approaches. *Child Development, 58,* 505–529.

GOLDSMITH, H. H., & CAMPOS, J. J. (1982). Toward a theory of infant temperament. In R. N. Emde & R. Harmon (Eds.), *The development of attachment and affiliative systems.* New York: Plenum Press.

GOLDSMITH, H. H., & GOTTESMAN, I. I. (1981). Origins of variation in behavior style: A longitudinal study of young twins. *Child Development, 52,* 91–103.

GOLOMB, C. (1974). *Young children's sculpture and drawing.* Cambridge, MA: Harvard University Press.

GOMES-SCHWARTZ, B., HOROWITZ, J. M., & CARDARELLI, A. P. (1990). *Child sexual abuse: Initial effects.* Newbury Park, CA: Sage Publications.

GÖNCÜ, A., & KESSEL, F. S. (1988). Preschoolers' collaborative construction in planning and maintaining imaginative play. *International Journal of Behavioral Development, 11,* 327–344.

GONSIOREK, J.C., & WEINRICH, J. D. (Eds.) (1991). *Homosexuality: Research implications for public policy.* Newbury Park, CA: Sage Publications.

GOOD, T. L., SIKES, J., & BROPHY, J. (1973). Effects of teacher sex and student sex on classroom interaction. *Journal of Educational Psychology, 65,* 74–87.

GOODALL, J. (1986). *The chimpanzees of Gombe: Patterns of behavior.* Cambridge, MA: Harvard University Press.

GOODENOUGH, F. L. (1931/1975). *Anger in young children.* Minneapolis: University of Minnesota Press.

GOODENOUGH, W. H. (1953). Native astronomy in the Central Carolines. *Museum Monographs.* Philadelphia: University Museum, University of Pennsylvania.

GOODMAN, G. (1984). Children's testimony in historical perspective. *Journal of Social Issues, 40,* 9–31.

GOODMAN, G. S., AMAN, C., HIRSCHMAN, J. (1987). Child's sexual and physical abuse: Children's testimony. In S. J. Ceci, M. P. Toglia, & D. Ross (Eds.), *Children's eyewitness memory.* New York: Springer-Verlag.

GOODMAN, G. S., LEVINE, M., MELTON, G. B., & OGDEN, D. W. (1991). Child witnesses and the confrontation clause. *Law and Human Behavior, 15,* 13–29.

GOODMAN, G. S., RUDY, L., BOTTOMS, B. L., & AMAN, C. (1990). Children's concerns and memory: Issues of ecological validity in the study of children's eyewitness testimony. In R. Fivush & J. A. Hudson (Eds.), *Knowing and remembering in young children.* New York: Cambridge University Press.

GOODMAN, K. S., SMITH, E. B., MERIDETH, R., & GOODMAN, Y. E. (1987). *Language and thinking in school.* New York: Owen.

GOODMAN, Y. E., & GOODMAN, K. S. (1990). Vygotsky and the whole-language perspective. In L.C. Moll (Ed.), *Vygotsky and education: Instructional implications and applications of sociohistorical psychology.* New York: Cambridge University Press.

GOODNOW, J. (1984). Parents' ideas about parenting and development. In A. L. Brown & B. Rogoff (Eds.), *Advances in developmental psychology* (Vol. 3). Hillsdale, NJ: Erlbaum.

GOODNOW, J. (1990). The socialization of cognition: What's involved? In J. W. Stigler, R. A. Shweder, & G. Herdt (Eds.), *Cultural psychology: Essays on comparative human development.* New York: Cambridge University Press.

GOODNOW, J., & BURNS, A. (1985). *Home and school: A child's-eye view.* Sydney: Allen & Unwin.

GOODNOW, J. J. (1977). *Children drawing.* Cambridge, MA: Harvard University Press.

GOODNOW, J. J., CASHMORE, J., COTTON, S., & KNIGHT, R. (1984). Mothers' developmental timetables in two cultural groups. *International Journal of Psychology, 19,* 193–205.

GOODY, E. N. (Ed.) (1978). *Questions and politeness: Strategies in social interaction.* Cambridge: Cambridge University Press.

GOODY, E. N. (1989). Learning, apprenticeship, and the division of labor. In M. Coy (Ed.), *Apprenticeship: From theory to method and back again.* Albany, NY: SUNY Press.

GOODY, J. (1977). *Domestication of the savage mind.* Cambridge: Cambridge University Press.

GOOSSENS, F. A., & VAN IJZENDOORN, M. H. (1990). Quality of infants' attachments to professional caregivers: Relation to infant-parent attachment and day-care characteristics. *Child Development, 61,* 832–837.

GOPNIK, A. (1982). Words and plans: early language and the development of intelligent action. *Journal of Child Language, 9,* 301–318.

GOPNIK, A., & MELTZOFF, A. N. (1986). Words, plans, things, and locations: Interactions between semantic and cognitive development at the one-word stage. In S. R. Kuczaj & M. D. Barrett (Eds.), *The development of word meaning.* New York: Springer-Verlag.

GOPNIK, A., & MELTZOFF, A. N. (1987). Language and thought in the child: Early semantic developments and their relations to object permanence, means-ends understanding, and categorization. In K. Nelson & Van Kleeck (Eds.), *Children's language* (Vol. 6). Hillsdale, NJ: Erlbaum.

GORDON, J. S., & HAIRE, D. (1981). Alternatives in childbirth. In P. Ahmed (Ed.), *Pregnancy, childbirth, and parenthood.* New York: Elsevier.

GOREN, C. C., SARTY, J., & WU, P. Y. (1975). Visual following and pattern discrimination of face-like stimuli by newborn infants. *Pediatrics, 56,* 544–549.

GORN, G. J., GOLDEBERG, M. E., & KANANGO, R. N. (1976). The role of educational television in changing intergroup attitudes of children. *Child Development, 47,* 277–280.

GOTTESMAN, I. I. (1991). *Schizophrenia genesis: The origins of madness.* New York: W. H. Freeman.

GOTTFRIED, A. E., GOTTFRIED, A. W., & BATHHURST, K. (1988). Maternal employment, family environment and children's development: Infancy through the school years. In A. E. Gottfried & A. W. Gottfried (Eds.), *Maternal employment and children's development: Longitudinal research.* New York: Plenum Press.

GOTTLIEB, G. (1983). The psychobiological approach to developmental issues. In P. H. Mussen (Ed.), *Handbook of child psychology*: Vol. 2. *Infancy and developmental psychobiology.* New York: Wiley.

GOTTMAN, J. M. (1983). How children become friends. *Monographs of the Society for Research in Child Development, 48*(3).

GOULD, S. J. (1977a). *Ever since Darwin.* New York: W. W. Norton.

GOULD, S. J. (1977b). *Ontogeny and phylogeny.* Cambridge, MA: Harvard University Press.

GOULD, S. J. (1981). *The mismeasure of man.* New York: W. W. Norton.

GRAHAM, F. K., MATARAZZO, R. G., & CALDWELL, B. M. (1956). Behavioral differences between normal and traumatized newborns: II. Standardization, reliability, and validity. *Psychological Monographs, 70* (21, Serial No. 428).

GRAHAM, P., RUTTER, M., & GEORGE, S. (1973). Temperamental characteristics as predictors of behavior disorders in children. *American Journal of Orthopsychiatry, 43,* 328–339.

GRAVES, Z., & GLICK, J. A. (1978). The effect of context on mother-child interaction: A progress report. *Quarterly Newsletter of the Laboratory of Comparative Human Cognition, 2,* 41–46.

GREEN, G. (1984). On the appropriateness of adaptations in primary-level basal readers: Reactions to remarks by Bertran Bruce. In R. C. Anderson, J. Osborn & R. J. Tierney (Eds.), *Learning to read in American schools.* Hillsdale, NJ: Erlbaum.

GREENBERG, M. T., & CRNIC, K. A. (1988). Longitudinal predictors of developmental status and social interaction in premature and full-term infants at age two. *Child Development, 59,* 554–570.

GREENBERGER, E., & STEINBERG, L. (1981). The workplace as a context for the socialization of youth. *Journal of Youth and Adolescence, 10,* 185–210.

GREENBERGER, E., & STEINBERG, L. (1986). *When teenagers work: The psychological and social costs of adolescent employment.* New York: Basic Books.

GREENBERGER, E., STEINBERG, L., & RUGGIERO, M. (1982). A job is a job is a job . . . or is it? Behavioral observations in the adolescent work place. *Work and Occupations, 9,* 79–96.

GREENFIELD, P. M. (1966). On culture and conservation. In J. S. Bruner, R. R. Olver, & P. M. Greenfield (Eds.), *Studies in cognitive growth.* New York: Wiley.

GREENFIELD, P. M. (1976). Cross-cultural Piagetian research: Paradox and progress. In K. F. Riegel & J. A. Meacham (Eds.), *The developing individual in a changing world: Historical and cultural issues* (Vol. 1). Chicago: Aldine.

GREENFIELD, P. M. (1984). *Mind and media: The effects of television, video, games and computers.* Cambridge, MA: Harvard University Press.

GREENFIELD, P. M. (1991). Language, tools and brain: The ontogeny and phylogeny of hierarchically organized sequential behavior. *Behavioral and Brain Sciences, 14,* 531–594.

GREENFIELD, P. M., BRAZELTON, T. B., & CHILDS, C. P. (1989). From birth to maturity in Zinacantan: Ontogenesis in cultural context. In V. Bricker & G. Gossen (Eds.), *Ethnographic encounters in southern Mesoamerica: Celebratory essays in honor of Evon Z. Vogt.* Albany, NY: Institute of Mesoamerican Studies, State University of New York.

GREENFIELD, P. M., & LAVE, J. (1982). Cognitive aspects of informal education. In D. A. Wagner & H. E. Stevenson (Eds.), *Cultural perspectives on child development.* New York: W. H. Freeman.

GREENFIELD, P. M., & SAVAGE-RUMBAUGH, E. S. (1990). Grammatical combination in *Pan paniscus:* Processes of learning and invention in the evolution and development of language. In S. T. Parker & K. R. Gibson (Eds.), *Language and intelligence in monkeys and apes.* Cambridge: Cambridge University Press.

GREENFIELD, P. M., & SMITH, J. H. (1976). *The structure of communication in early language development.* New York: Academic Press.

GREENOUGH, W. T. (1991). Experience as a component of normal development: Evolutionary considerations. *Developmental Psychology, 27,* 14–17.

GREGG, N. M. (1941). Cogenital cataracts following German measles in mothers. *Transcripts of the Ophthalmological Society of Australia, 3,* 35.

GREGOR, J. A., & MCPHERSON, D. A. (1966). Racial preference and ego identity among White and Bantu children in the Republic of South Africa. *Genetic Psychology Monographs, 73,* 218–253.

GRIBBIN, J. R., & CHERFAS, J. (1982). *The monkey puzzle: Reshaping the evolutionary tree.* New York: Pantheon Books.

GRICE, H. P. (1975). Logic and conversation. In P. Cole & J. L. Morgan (Eds.), *Syntax and semantics:* Vol. 3. *Speech acts.* New York: Academic Press.

GRIFFIN, P. (1983). Personal communication.

GRIMWADE, J. C., WALKER, D. W., BARTLETT, M., GORDON, S., & WOOD, C. (1970). Human fetal heartrate change and movement-response to sound and vibration. *American Journal of Obstetrics and Gynecology, 109,* 86–90.

GRISWOLD DEL CASTILLO, R. (1984). *La familia: Chicano families in the urban southwest, 1848 to the present.* Notre Dame, IN: University of Notre Dame Press.

GRONLUND, N. E. (1959). *Sociometry in the classroom.* New York: Harper Brothers.

GROSSMANN, K. FREMMER-BOMBIK, E., RUDOLPH, J., & GROSSMANN, K. (1987, January). Maternal attachment in relation to patterns of infant-mother attachment and maternal care during the first year. Paper presented at Conference of Intrafamilial Relationships, Cambridge, England.

GROSSMANN, K., GROSSMANN, K. E., SPANGLER, S., SUESS, G., & UNZNER, L. (1985). Maternal sensitivity and newborn orientation responses as related to quality of attachment in Northern Germany. *Monographs of the Society for Research in Child Development, 50* (1–2 Serial No. 209).

GROSSMAN, K. E., & GROSSMAN, K. (1990). The wider concept of attachment in cross-cultural research. *Human Development, 33*, 31–47.

GROTBERG, E. (1969). *Review of Head Start research, 1965–1969*. Washington, DC: OEO Pamphlet 1608:13 ED02308).

GROTEVANT, H. (1986). Assessment of identity development: Current issues and future directions. *Journal of Adolescent Research, 1*, 175–181.

GROTEVANT, H., & COOPER, C. (1985). Patterns of interaction in family relationships and the development of identity exploration in adolescence. *Developmental Psychology, 56*, 415–428.

GROTEVANT, H. D., THORBECKE, W., & MEYER, M. L. (1982). An extension of Marcia's identity status interview in the interpersonal domain. *Journal of Youth and Adolescence, 11*, 33–47.

GUERRA, N. G., & SLABY, R. G. (1990). Cognitive mediators of aggression in adolescent offenders: 2. Intervention. *Developmental Psychology, 26*, 269–277.

GUIDUBALDI, J., PERRY, J. D., CLEMINSHAW, H. K. & MCLOUGHLIN, C. S. (1983). The impact of parental divorce on children: Report of the nationwide NASP study. *School Psychology Review, 12*(3), 300–323.

GUILFORD, J. P. (1967). *The nature of human intelligence*. New York: McGraw-Hill.

GUSTAFSON, G. E., & HARRIS, K. L. (1990). Women's responses to young infants' cries. *Developmental Psychology, 26*, 144–152.

HAAF, R. A., SMITH, P. H., & SMITELY, S. (1983). Infant response to facelike patterns under fixed-trial and infant control procedures. *Child Development, 54*, 172–177.

HAAN, N., LANGER, J., & KOHLBERG, L. (1976). Family patterns of moral reasoning. *Child Development, 47*, 1204–1206.

HAAN, N., SMITH, B., & BLOCK, J. (1968). The moral reasoning of young adults. *Journal of Personality and Social Psychology, 10*, 183–201.

HAAN, N., WEISS, R., & JOHNSON, V. (1982). The role of logic in moral reasoning and development. *Developmental Psychology, 18*, 245–256.

HAGEN, J. W., MEACHAM, J. A., & MESIBOV, G. (1970). Verbal labeling, rehearsal, and short-term memory. *Cognitive Psychology, 1*, 47–58.

HAITH, M. M. (1980). *Rules that babies look by: The organization of newborn visual activity*. Hillsdale, NJ: Erlbaum.

HAITH, M. M. (1990). Progress in the understanding of sensory and perceptual processes in early infancy. *Merrill Palmer Quarterly, 36*, 1–26.

HAITH, M. M., BERMAN, T., & MOORE, M. J. (1977). Eye contact and face scanning in early infancy. *Science, 198*, 853–855.

HALL, G. S. (1904). *Adolescence: Its psychology and its relations to psychology, anthropology, sociology, sex, crime, religion, and education*. New York: Appleton-Century-Crofts.

HALL, G. S. (1921). The dangerous age. *Pedagogical Seminary, 28*, 275–294.

HALL, G. S. (1922). *Senescence: The last half of life*. New York: Appleton-Century-Crofts.

HALL, W. S. (1989). Reading comprehension. *American Psychologist, 44*, 157–161.

HALLOWELL, A. I. (1955). The self and its behavioral environment. In A. I. Hallowell (Ed.), *Culture and experience*. Philadelphia: University of Pennsylvania Press.

HALLPIKE, C. R. (1979). *The foundations of primitive thought*. Oxford: Clarendon Press.

HALPERN, D. F. (1986). *Sex differences in cognitive abilities*. Hillsdale, NJ: Erlbaum.

HALPERN, R. (1990). Poverty and early childhood parenting: Toward a framework for intervention. *American Journal of Orthopsychiatry, 60*(1), 6–18.

HAMBURGER, V. (1957). The concept of "development" in biology. In D. B. Harris (Ed.), *The concept of development*. Minneapolis: University of Minnesota Press.

HAMBURGER, V. (1975). Cell death in the development of the lateral motor column of the chick embryo. *Journal of Comparative Neurology, 160*, 1121–1125.

HAMOND, N. R., & FIVUSH, R. (1991). Memories of Mickey Mouse: Young children recount their trip to Disneyworld. *Cognitive Development, 6,* 483–448.

HANSON, J. W., STREISSGUTH, A. P., & SMITH, D. W. (1978). The effects of moderate alcohol consumption during pregnancy on fetal growth and morphogenesis. *Journal of Pediatrics, 92,* 457–460.

HAREVEN, T. K. (1978). The last stage: Historical adulthood and old age. In E. H. Erikson (Ed.), *Adulthood.* New York: W. W. Norton.

HAREVEN, T. K., & ADAMS, K. (Eds.). (1982). *Aging and life course transitions: An interdisciplinary perspective.* New York: Guildford.

HARKNESS, S. (1990). A cultural model for the acquisition of language: Implications for the innateness debate. *Developmental Psychobiology, 23,* 727–740.

HARKNESS, S., EDWARDS, C. P., & SUPER, C. M. (1981). Social roles and moral reasoning: A case study in a rural African community. *Developmental Psychology, 17,* 595–603.

HARKNESS, S., & SUPER, C. M. (1983). The cultural construction of child development: A framework for the socialization of emotion. *Ethos, 11,* 221–231.

HARKNESS, S., & SUPER, C. M. (1985). The cultural context of gender segregation in children's peer groups. *Child Development, 56,* 219–224.

HARLEY, G. W. (1941). Notes on the Poro in Liberia. In B. B. Sommer (Ed.), *Puberty and adolescence.* New York: Oxford University Press.

HARLOW, H. (1959). Love in infant monkeys. *Scientific American, 200*(6), 68–74.

HARLOW, H. (1971). *Learning to love.* San Francisco: Albion.

HARLOW, H. F., & HARLOW, M. K. (1962). Social deprivation in monkeys. *Scientific American, 207,* 136–146.

HARLOW, H. F., & HARLOW, M. K. (1969). Effects of various mother-infant relationships on rhesus monkey behaviors. In B. M. Foss (Ed.), *Determinants of infant behavior* (Vol. 4). London: Methuen.

HARLOW, H. F., & NOVAK, M. A. (1973). Psychopathological perspectives. *Perspectives in Biology and Medicine,* Spring, 461–478.

HARLOW, H. F., & ZIMMERMAN, R. (1959). Affectional responses in the infant monkey. *Science, 130,* 421–432.

HARRINGTON, M. (1963). *The other America: Poverty in the United States.* New York: Macmillan.

HARRIS, B. (1979). Whatever happened to little Albert? *American Psychologist, 34,* 151–160.

HARRIS, P. L. (1983). Infant cognition. In P. H. Mussen (Ed.), *Handbook of child psychology:* Vol. 2. *Infancy and developmental psychobiology.* New York: Wiley.

HARRIS, P. L. (1989). *Children and emotion.* Oxford: Blackwell.

HARRIS, P. L., DONNELLY, K., GUZ, G. R., & PITT-WATSON, R. (1986). Children's understanding of the distinction between real and apparent emotion. *Child Development, 57,* 895–909.

HARRIS, P. L., & GROSS, D. (1988). Children's understanding of real and apparent motion. In J. W. Astington, P. L. Harris, & D. R. Olson (Eds.), *Developing theories of mind.* New York: Cambridge University Press.

HARRIS, R. (1986). *The origin of writing.* La Salle, IL: Open Court.

HARRISON, A. O., WILSON, M. N., PINE, C. J., CHAN, S. Q., & BURIEL, R. (1990). Family ecologies of ethnic minority children. *Child Development, 61,* 347–362.

HART, C. H., LADD, G. W., & BURLESON, B. R. (1990). Children's expectations of the outcomes of social strategies: Relations with sociometric status and maternal disciplinary styles. *Child Development, 61,* 127–137.

HARTER, S. (1982). The perceived competence scale for children. *Child Development, 53,* 87–97.

HARTER, S. (1983). Development perspectives on the self-system. In P. M. Mussen (Ed.), *Handbook of Child Psychology:* Vol. 4. *Socialization, personality, and social development.* New York: Wiley.

HARTER, S. (1986). Cognitive-developmental processes in integration of concepts about emotion and the self. *Social Cognition, 4,* 119–151.

HARTER, S. (1987). The determinants and mediational role of global self-worth in children. In N. Eisenberg (Ed.), *Contemporary topics in developmental psychology.* New York: Wiley.

HARTER, S. (1990). Issues in the development of the self-concept of children and adolescents. In A. LaGreca (Ed.), *Through the eyes of a child.* Boston: Allyn and Bacon.

HARTER, S. (1990). Self and identity development. In S. S. Feldman and G. R. Elliott (Eds.), *At the threshold: The developing adolescent.* Cambridge, MA: Harvard University Press.

HARTER, S., & MONSOUR, A. (1992). Developmental analysis of conflict caused by opposing attributes in the adolescent self-portrait. *Developmental Psychology, 28,* 251–260.

HARTER, S., & PIKE, R. (1984). The pictorial scale of perceived competence and social acceptance for young children. *Child Development, 55,* 1969–1982.

HARTUP, W. W. (1974). Aggression in childhood. Developmental perspectives. *American Psychologist, 29,* 336–341.

HARTUP, W. W. (1978). Children and their friends. In H. McGurk (Ed.), *Issues in childhood social development.* London: Methuen.

HARTUP, W. W. (1984). The peer context in middle childhood. In A. Collins (Ed.), *Development during middle childhood: The years from six to twelve.* Washington, DC: National Academy Press.

HARTUP, W. W. (1992). Friendships and their developmental significance. In H. McGurk, (Ed.), *Childhood social development: Contemporary perspectives.* London: Erlbaum.

HASHER, L., & CLIFTON, D. (1974). A developmental study of attribute encoding in free recall. *Journal of Experimental Child Psychology, 1,* 332–346.

HASKINS, R. (1985). Public school aggression among children with varying day-care experience. *Child Development, 56,* 687–703.

HASKINS, R. (1989). Beyond metaphor: The efficacy of early childhood education. *American Psychologist, 44,* 274–282.

HATANO, G. (1987). How do Japanese children learn to read?: Orthographic and eco-cultural variables. In B. R. Foorman & A. W. Siegel (Eds.), *Acquisition of reading skills: Cultural constraints and cognitive universals.* Hillsdale, NJ: Erlbaum.

HAUGAARD, J. J., & REPPUCCI, N. D. (1988). *The sexual abuse of children.* San Francisco: Jossey-Bass.

HAVIGHURST, R. J. (1967). *Developmental tasks and education.* New York: David McKay.

HAYES, C. D., & KAMERMAN, S. B. (Eds.). (1983). *Children of working parents: Experiences and outcomes.* Washington, DC: National Academy Press.

HAYES, K., & HAYES, C. (1951). The intellectual development of a home-raised chimpanzee. *Proceedings of the American Philosophical Society, 95,* 105–109.

HAYFLICK, L. (1980). The cell biology of human aging. *Scientific American, 242,* 58–65.

HAYNE, H., ROVEE-COLLIER, C., & PERRIS, E. E. (1987). Categorization and memory retrieval by three-month-olds. *Child Development, 58,* 750–767.

HAZEN, N. L., & BLACK, B. (1989). Preschool peer communication skills: A longitudinal study. *Child Development, 60,* 867–876.

HEARNSHAW, L. S. (1979). *Cyril Burt, psychologist.* Ithaca, NY: Cornell University Press.

HEATH, S. B. (1982). What no bedtime story means: Narrative skills at home and school. *Language in Society, 11,* 49–77.

HEATH, S. B. (1984). *Ways with words: Language, life, and work in communities and classrooms.* Cambridge: Cambridge University Press.

HECOX, K., & DEEGAN, D. M. (1985). Methodological issues in the study of auditory development. In G. Gottlieb & N. A. Krasnegor (Eds.), *Measurement of audition and vision in the first year of postnatal life: A methodological overview.* Norwood, NJ: Ablex Publishing Corp.

HELD, R., & HEIN, A. (1963). Movement-produced stimulation and the development of visually guided behaviors. *Journal of Comparative and Physiological Psychology, 56,* 872–876.

HENDERSON, H., & HENDERSON, R. (1982). Traditional Onitsha Ibo maternity beliefs and practices. In M. A. Kay (Ed.), *Anthropology of human birth.* Philadelphia: F. A. Davis.

HENDERSON, L. (1982). *Orthography and word recognition in reading.* New York: Academic Press.

HENMON, V. A. C. (1921). Intelligence and its measurement: A symposium. *Journal of Educational Psychology, 12,* 195–198.

HERDT, G. (Ed.). (1989). *Gay and lesbian youth.* New York: Harrington Park Press.

HERSKOVITZ, M. J. (1948). *Man and his works: The science of cultural anthropology.* New York: Knopf.

HESS, R. D., KASHIWAGI, K., AZUMA, H., PRICE, G., & DICKSON, W. P. (1980). Maternal expectations for mastery of developmental tasks in Japan and the United States. *International Journal of Psychology, 15,* 259–271.

HETHERINGTON, E. M. (1988). Parents, children, and siblings: Six years after divorce. In R. A. Hinde & J.

Stevenson-Hinde (Eds.), *Relationships within families: Mutual influences*. Oxford: Oxford University Press.

HETHERINGTON, E. M. (1989). Coping with family transitions: Winners, losers, and survivors. *Child Development, 60*, 1–14.

HETHERINGTON, E. M., & CLINGEMPEEL, W. G. (1992). Coping with marital transitions. *Monographs of the Society for Research in Child Development, 57*, (2–3, Serial No. 227).

HETHERINGTON, E. M., COX, M., & COX, R. (1982) Long-term effects of divorce and remarriage on the adjustment of children. *Journal of the American Academy of Child Psychiatry, 24*, 518–530.

HETHERINGTON, E. M., LERNER, R. M., & PERLMUTTER, M. (Eds.) (1988). *Child development in life-span perspective*. Hillsdale, NJ: Erlbaum.

HETHERINGTON, E. M., STANLEY-HAGEN, M., & ANDERSON, E. R. (1989). Marital transitions. A child's perspective. *American Psychologist, 41*, 303–312.

HICKS, L. E., LANGHAM, R. A., & TAKENAKA, J. (1982). Cognitive and health measures following early nutritional supplementation: A sibling study. *American Journal of Public Health, 72*, 1110–1118.

HILL, J. P. (1988). Adapting to menache: Familial control and conflict. In M. R. Gunner, & W. A. Collins (Eds.), *Development during the transition to adolescence. Minnesota Symposia on Child Psychology* (Vol. 21). Hillsdale, NJ: Erlbaum.

HILL, R. C., & STAFFORD, F. P. (1980). Parental care of children: Time diary estimates of quantity, predictability, and variety. *Journal of Human Research, 15*, 219–239.

HINDE, R. A. (1982). Attachment: Some conceptual and biological issues. In C. Parkes & J. Stevenson-Hinde (Eds.), *The place of attachment in human behavior*. New York: Basic Books.

HINDE, R. A. (1987). *Relationships and culture: Links between ethology and the social sciences*. Cambridge: Cambridge University Press.

HINER, N. R., & HAWES, J. M. (Eds.). (1985). *Growing up in America: Children in historical perspective*. Champaign, IL: University of Illinois Press.

HIRSCH, H. V. B., & SPINELLI, D. N. (1971). Modification of the distribution of receptive field orientation in cats by selective visual exposure during development. *Experimental Brain Research, 13*, 509–527.

HIRSH-PASEK, K., TREIMAN, R., & SCHNEIDERMAN, M. (1984). Brown and Hanlon revisited: Mothers' sensitivity to ungrammatical forms. *Journal of Child Language, 11*, 81–88.

HODGES, J., & TIZARD, B. (1989a). IQ and behavioral adjustments of ex-institutional adolescents. *Journal of Child Psychology and Psychiatry, 30*, 53–75.

HODGES, J., & TIZARD, B. (1989b). Social and family relationships of ex-institutional adolescents. *Journal of Child Psychology and Psychiatry, 30*, 77–97.

HOFER, M. A. (1981). *The roots of human behavior: An introduction to the psychobiology of early development*. New York: W. H. Freeman.

HOFFMAN, L. W. (1980). The effects of maternal employment on the academic attitudes and performance of school age children. *School Psychology Reveiw, 9*, 319–335.

HOFFMAN, L. W. (1984). Maternal employment and the young child. In M. Perlmutter (Ed.), *Parent-child interactions and parent-child relations in child development. Minnesota Symposia on Child Psychology* (Vol. 17). Hillsdale, NJ: Erlbaum.

HOFFMAN, L. W. (1989). Effects of maternal employment in the two-parent family. *American Psychologist, 44*, 283–292.

HOFFMAN, L. W. (1991). The influence of the family environment on personality: Accounting for sibling differences. *Psychological Bulletin, 110*, 187–203.

HOFFMAN, M. L. (1970). Moral development. In P. H. Mussen (Ed.), *Carmichael's manual of child psychology: Vol. 2, Part 4. Socialization* (3rd ed.). New York: Wiley.

HOFFMAN, M. L. (1975). Altruistic behavior and the parent-child relationship. *Journal of Personality and Social Psychology, 31*, 937–943.

HOFFMAN, M. L. (1980). Moral development in adolescence. In J. Adelson (Ed.), *Handbook of adolescent psychology*. New York: Wiley.

HOFFMAN, M. L. (1981). The development of empathy. In P. Rushton & R. M. Sorrentino (Eds.), *Altruism and helping behavior: Social, personality, and developmental perspectives*. Hillsdale, NJ: Erlbaum.

HOFFMAN, M. L. (1983). Affective and cognitive processes in moral internalization. In E. T. Higgins, D. N. Ruble, & W. W. Hartup (Eds.), *Social cognition and social behavior: Developmental perspectives*. Cambridge: Cambridge University Press.

HOFSTADER, D. (1979). *Godel, Escher, Bach: An eternal golden braid.* New York: Basic Books.

HOGGE, A. W. (1990). Teratology. In I. R. Merkatz & J. E. Thompson (Eds.), *New perspectives on prenatal care.* New York: Elsevier.

HOLLINGSHEAD, A. B. (1975). *Elmtown's youth and Elmtown revisited.* New York: Wiley.

HOLLOS, M. (1975). Logical operations and role-taking abilities in two cultures: Norway and Hungary. *Child Development, 46,* 638–649.

HOLLOS, M., & COWAN, P. A. (1973). Social isolation and cognitive development: Logical operations and role-taking abilities in three Norwegian social settings. *Child Development, 44,* 630–641.

HOLMES, L. D. (1983). *Other cultures, elder years: An introduction to cultural gerontology.* Minneapolis: Burgess Publishing Company.

HOLMES, S. T., & HOLMES, T. H. (1969). Short-term intrusions into the lifestyle routine. *Journal of Psychosomatic Research, 14,* 1–7.

HOLSTEIN, C. (1976). Development of moral judgment: A longitudinal study of males and females. *Child Development, 47,* 51–61.

HOLT, J. (1964). *How children fail.* New York: Dell.

HOOK, E. B. (1982). Epidemiology of Down Syndrome. In S. M. Pueschel & J. E. Rynders (Eds.), *Advances in biomedicine and behavioral sciences.* Cambridge, MA: Ware Press.

HOOKER, D. (1952). *The prenatal origins of behavior.* New York: Hafner.

HOORWEG, J., & STANFIELD, J. P. (1976). The effects of protein energy malnutrition in early childhood on intellectual and motor abilities in later childhood and adolescence. *Developmental Medicine and Child Neurology, 18,* 330–350.

HOPKINS, B., & WESTEN, T. (1988). Maternal handling and motor development: An intracultural study. *Genetic Psychology Monographs, 14,* 377–420.

HORN, J. L., & DONALDSON, G. (1980). Cognitive development in adulthood. In O. G. Brim & J. Kagan (Eds.), *Constancy and change in human development.* Cambridge, MA: Harvard University Press.

HOWES, C. (1987). Peer interaction of young children. *Monographs of the Society for Research in Child Development, 53*(1, Serial No. 217).

HOWES, C. (1990). Can the age of entry into child care and the quality of child care predict adjustment in kindergarten? *Developmental Psychology, 26,* 292–303.

HOWES, C., & OLENICK, M. (1986). Family and childcare influences on toddlers' compliance. *Child Development, 57,* 202–216.

HOWES, C., & RUBENSTEIN, J. (1985). Determinants of toddlers' experience in day care: Age of entry and quality of entry and quality of setting. *Child Care Quarterly, 14,* 140–151.

HSIA, D. Y., DRISCOLL, K. W., TROLL, W., & KNOX, W. E. (1956). Detection of phenylalanine tolerance tests heterozygous carriers of phenylketonuria. *Nature, 176,* 1239–1240.

HUBA, G. J., & BENTLER, P. M. (1980). The role of peer and adult models for drug taking at different stages of adolescence. *Journal of Youth and Adolescence, 9,* 449–468.

HUBEL, D. H., & WIESEL, T. N. (1979). Brain mechanisms of vision. *Scientific American, 241,* 130–139.

HUGHES, M. (1986). *Children and number: Difficulties in learning mathematics.* New York: Blackwell.

HUTCHINS, E. (1980). *Culture and inference.* Cambridge, MA: Harvard University Press.

HUTCHINS, E. (1983). Understanding Micronesian navigation. In D. Gentner & A. Stevens (Eds.), *Mental models.* Hillsdale, NJ: Erlbaum.

HUTTENLOCHER, P. R. (1990). Morphometric study of human cerebral cortex development. Neuropsychologia, 28, 517–527.

HYDE, J. S. (1981). How large are cognitive gender differences? A meta-analysis using W and D. *American Psychologist, 36,* 892–901.

HYMEL, S., WAGNER, E., & BUTLER, L. J. (1990). Reputational bias: View from the peer group. In S. R. Asher & J. D. Coie (Eds.), *Peer rejection in childhood.* Cambridge: Cambridge University Press.

INHELDER, B., & PIAGET, J. (1958). *The growth of logical thinking from childhood to adolescence.* New York: Basic Books.

INHELDER, B., & PIAGET, J. (1964). *The early growth of logic in the child.* New York: Harper & Row.

IRVINE, S. H., & BERRY, J. W. (1987). *Human abilities in cultural context.* New York: Cambridge University Press.

ISAACS, S. (1966). *Intellectual growth in young children.* New York: Schocken.

ISABELLA, R. A., & BELSKY, J. (1991). Interactional synchrony and the origins of infant-mother attachment: A replication study. *Child Development, 60,* 373–384.

ISHIYAMA, F. I., & CHABASSOL, D. J. (1985). Adolescents' fear of social consequences of academic success as a function of age and sex. *Adolescence, 14,* 37–46.

ITARD, J. M. G. (1801/1982). *The wild boy of Aveyron* (G. Humphrey & M. Humphrey, Trans.). New York: Appleton-Century-Crofts.

IZARD, C. (1977). *Human emotions.* New York: Plenum Press.

IZARD, C. E., HUEBNER, R. R., RISSER, D., MCGINNES, G. C., & DOUGHERTY, L. M. (1980). The young infant's ability to produce discrete emotion expressions. *Developmental Psychology, 16,* 132–140.

JACKLIN, C. N., & MACCOBY, E. E. (1978). Social behavior at 33 months in same-sex and mixed-sex dyads. *Child Development, 49,* 557–569.

JACOB, F. (1982). *The possible and the actual.* New York: Pantheon Books.

JACOBS, J. (1975). *Older persons and retirement communities.* Springfield, IL: Charles C. Thomas.

JAHODA, M. (1958). *Current concepts of positive mental health.* New York: Basic Books.

JAHODA, G. (1980). Theoretical and systematic approaches in mass-cultural psychology. In H. C. Triandis & W. W. Lambert (Eds.), *Handbook of cross-cultural psychology* (Vol. 1). Boston: Allyn and Bacon.

JAHODA, G. (1983). European "lag" in the development of an economic concept: A study in Zimbabwe. *British Journal of Developmental Psychology, 1,* 113–120.

JAMES, W. T. (1890). *The principles of psychology.* New York: Holt, Rinehart and Winston.

JAMES, W. T. (1951). Social organization among dogs of different temperaments: Terriers and beagles, reared together. *Journal of Comparative and Physiological Psychology, 44,* 71–77.

JAMESON, S. (1986, July 11). South Korean parents tip birth ratio. *Los Angeles Times,* p. 1, 18.

JANES, M. D. (1975). Physical and psychological growth and development. *Environmental Child Health, 121,* 26–30.

JEANS, P. C., SMITH, M. B., & STEARNS, G. (1955). Incidence of prematurity in relation to maternal nutrition. *Journal of the American Dietary Association, 31,* 576–581.

JENCKS, C. (1972). *Inequality: A reassessment of the effect of family and schooling in America.* New York: Basic Books.

JENKINS, J. B. (1979). *Genetics* (2nd ed.). Boston: Houghton Mifflin.

JENKINS, J. M., SMITH, M. A., & GRAHAM, P. J. (1989). Coping with parental quarrels. *Journal of the American Academy of Child and Adolescent Psychiatry, 28,* 182–189.

JENSEN, A. R. (1969). How much can we boost I.Q. and scholastic achievement? *Harvard Educational Review, 29,* 1–123.

JENSEN, A. R. (1980). *Bias in mental testing.* New York: Free Press.

JERRISON, H. J. (1982). The evolution of biological intelligence. In R. J. Sternberg (Ed.), *Handbook of human intelligence.* Cambridge: Cambridge University Press.

JESSOR, R., & JESSOR, S. L. (1977). *Problem behavior and psychosocial development: A longitudinal study of youth.* New York: Academic Press.

JOFFE, C. (1977). *Friendly intruders: Child care professionals and family life.* Berkeley: University of California Press.

JOHNSON, F. E., BORDEN, M., & MACVEAN, R. B. (1973). Height, weight, and their growth velocities in Guatemalan private school children of high socioeconomic class. *Human Biology, 45,* 627–641.

JONES, C. L., & LOPEZ, R. E. (1990). Drug abuse and pregnancy. In I. R. Merkatz & J. E. Thompson (Eds.), *New perspectives on prenatal care.* New York: Elsevier.

JONES, M. C. (1965). Psychological correlates of somatic development. *Child Development, 36,* 899–911.

JONES, M. C., & BAYLEY, N. (1950). Physical maturing among boys as related to behavior. *Journal of Educational Psychology, 41,* 129–184.

JORDAN, C. (1981). The selection of culturally compatible teaching practices. *Educational Perspectives, 20,* 16–19.

KAGAN, J. (1972). A conception of early adolescence. In J. Kagan & R. Coles (Eds.), *Twelve to sixteen: Early adolescence.* New York: W. W. Norton.

KAGAN, J. (1981). *The second year*. Cambridge, MA: Harvard University Press.

KAGAN, J. (1982). *Psychological research on the human infant: An evaluative summary*. New York: William T. Grant Foundation.

KAGAN, J. (1984). *The nature of the child*. New York: Basic Books.

KAGAN, J. (1989). *Unstable ideas*. Cambridge, MA: Harvard University Press.

KAGAN, J., & HAMBURG, M. (1981). The enhancement of memory in the first year. *Journal of Genetic Psychology, 138,* 3–14.

KAGAN, J., KEARSLEY, R. B., & ZELAZO, P. (1978). *Infancy: Its place in human development*. Cambridge, MA: Harvard University Press.

KAGAN, J., KLEIN, R. E., FINLEY, G. E., ROGOFF, B., & NOLAN, E. (1979). A cross-cultural study of cognitive development. *Monographs of the Society for Research in Child Development, 44*(5, Serial No. 180).

KAGAN, J., & LAMB, S. (1987). *The emergence of morality in young children*. Chicago: University of Chicago Press.

KAGAN, J., & MOSS, H. A. (1962). *Birth to maturity*. New York: Wiley.

KAGAN, J., & SNIDMAN, N. (1991a). Infant predictors of inhibited and uninhibited profiles. *Psychological Science, 2,* 40–44.

KAGAN, J., & SNIDMAN, N. (1991b). Temperamental factors in human development. *American Psychologist, 46*(8), 856–862.

KAGAN, S., & MADSEN, M. C. (1971). Cooperation and competition of Mexican, Mexican-American, and Anglo-American children of two ages under four instructional sets. *Developmental Psychology, 5,* 32–39.

KAIL, R. (1986). Sources of age differences in speed of processing. *Child Development, 57,* 969–987.

KAIL, R. (1990). *The development of memory in children* (3rd. ed.). New York: W. H. Freeman.

KAIL, R. (1991). Processing time declines exponentially during childhood and adolescence. *Developmental Psychology, 27,* 259–266.

KAITZ, M., MESCHULACH-SARFATY, O., AUERBACH, J., & EIDELMAN, A. (1988). A Reexamination of newborns' ability to imitate facial expressions. *Developmental Psychology, 24,* 3–7.

KAMARA, A. I., & EASLEY, J. A., JR. (1977). Is the rate of cognitive development uniform across cultures? A methodological critique with new evidence from Themne children. In P. R. Dasen (Ed.), *Piagetian psychology: Cross-cultural contributions*. New York: Gardner.

KAMINSKY, H. (1984). Moral development in historical perspective. In W. M. Kurtines & J. L. Gewirtz (Eds.), *Morality, moral behavior, and moral development*. New York: Wiley.

KANDEL, D. B. (1986). Processes of peer influences in adolescence. In R. K. Silbereisen, K. Eyferth, & G. Rudinger (Eds.), *Development as action in context: Problem behavior and normal youth development*. Berlin: Springer-Verlag.

KANDEL, D. B., & LESSER, G. S. (1972). *Youth in two worlds: United States and Denmark*. San Francisco: Jossey-Bass.

KAPLAN, H., & DOVE, H. (1987) Infant development among the Ache of Eastern Paraguay. *Developmental Psychology, 23,* 190–198.

KARMILOFF-SMITH, A. (1986). On the structure-dependent nature of stages of development. In L. Levin (Ed.), *Stage and structure: Reopening the debate*. Norwood, NJ: Ablex Publishing Corp.

KARMILOFF-SMITH, A. (1991). Beyond modularity: Innate constraints and developmental change. In S. Carey & R. Gelman (Eds.), *The epigenesis of mind: Essays on biology and cognition*. Hillsdale, NJ: Erlbaum.

KARNIOL, R. (1989). The role of manual manipulative stages in the infant's acquisition of perceived control over object. *Developmental Review, 9,* 205–233.

KATCHADOURIAN, H. A. (1977). *The biology of adolescence*. New York: W. H. Freeman.

KATCHADOURIAN, H. A. (1987). *Fifty: Midlife in perspective*. New York: W. H. Freeman.

KATCHADOURIAN, H. A. (1990). Sexuality. In S. S. Feldman & G. R. Elliott (Eds.), *At the threshold: The developing adolescent*. Cambridge, MA: Harvard University Press.

KATCHADOURIAN, H. A., & LUNDE, D. T. (1975). *Fundamentals of human sexuality* (2nd ed.). New York: Holt, Rinehart and Winston.

KAUFMAN, J., & ZIGLER, E. (1989). The intergenerational transmission of child abuse. In D. Cicchetti & V. Carlson (Eds.), *Child maltreatment: Theory and research on the causes and consequences of child abuse and neglect*. Cambridge: Cambridge University Press.

KAYE, K. (1982). *The mental and social life of babies.* Chicago: University of Chicago Press.

KEATING, D. (1980). Thinking processes in adolescence. In J. Adelson (Ed.), *Handbook of adolescent psychology.* New York: Wiley.

KEATING, D. (1990). Adolescent thinking. In S. S. Feldman & G. R. Elliott (Eds.), *At the threshold: The developing adolescent.* Cambridge, MA: Harvard University Press.

KEENEY, T. J., CANNIZZO, S. D., & FLAVELL, J. H. (1967). Spontaneous and induced verbal rehearsal in a recall task. *Child Development, 38,* 935–966.

KEGAN, R. (1982). *The emerging self: Problem and process in human development.* Cambridge, MA: Harvard University Press.

KELLER, A., FORD, L. H., & MEACHAM, J. A. (1978). Dimensions of self concept in preschool children. *Developmental Psychology, 14,* 483–489.

KELLEY, R. K. (1972). The premarital sexual revolution: Comments on research. *Family Coordinator, 21,* 334–336.

KELLOGG, R. (1969). *Analyzing children's art.* Palo Alto, CA: National Press Books.

KELLOGG, W. N., & KELLOGG, L. A. (1933). *The ape and the child: A study of environmental influences upon early behavior.* New York: Whittlesey House.

KEMPE, R., & KEMPE, C. H. (1978). *Child Abuse.* Cambridge, MA: Harvard University Press.

KEMPE, C., SILVERMAN, E., STEELE, B., DROEGEMUELLER, W., & SILVER, H. (1962). The battered child syndrome. *Journal of the American Medical Association, 181,* 17–24.

KENNELL, J. H., JERAULD, R., WOLFE, H., CHESTER, D., KREGER, N., MCALPINE, W., STEFFA, M., & KLAUS, M. H. (1974). Maternal behavior one year after early and extended post-partum contact. *Developmental Medicine and Child Neurology, 16,* 172–179.

KENNELL, J. H., VOOS, D. K., & KLAUS, M. H. (1979). Parent-infant bonding. In J. D. Osofsky (Ed.), *Handbook of infant development.* New York: Wiley.

KENISTON, K. (1970). Youth: As a stage of life. *American Scholar, 39,* 631–654.

KENYATTA, J. (1938). *Facing Mt. Kenya: The tribal life of the Kikuyu.* London: Secker & Warburg.

KESSEN, W. (1965). *The child.* New York: Wiley.

KETT, J. F. (1977). *Rites of passage: Adolescence in America 1790 to the present.* New York: Basic Books.

KIELL, N. (1964). *The universal experience of adolescence.* New York: International Universities Press.

KING, M. A., & YUILLE, J. C. (1987). Suggestibility and the child witness. In S. J. Ceci, M. P. Toglia, & D. F. Ross (Eds.), *Children's eyewitness memory.* New York: Springer-Verlag.

KINSBOURNE, M., & HISCOCK, M. (1983). Development of lateralization of the brain. In P. Mussen (Ed.), *Handbook of child development:* Vol. 2. *Infancy and developmental psychobiology.* New York: Wiley.

KINSEY, A. C., POMEROY, W. B., & MARTIN, C. E. (1948). *Sexual behavior in the human male.* Philadelphia: Saunders.

KINSEY, A. C., POMEROY, W. B., MARTIN, C. E., & GEBHARD, P. H. (1953). *Sexual behavior in the human female.* Philadelphia: Saunders.

KITCHER, P. (1985). *Vaulting ambition: Sociobiology and the quest for human nature.* Cambridge, MA: MIT Press.

KITZINGER, S. (1971). *Giving birth: The parents' emotions at birth.* New York: Taplinger.

KLAHR, D. (1982). Nonmonotone assessment of monotone development: An information processing analysis. In S. Strauss (Ed.), *U-shaped behavioral-growth.* New York: Academic Press.

KLAHR, D., & WALLACE, J. G. (1976). *Cognitive development: An information-processing view.* Hillsdale, NJ: Erlbaum.

KLAPPER, Z. S., & BIRCH, H. G. (1969). Perceptual and action equivalence of objects and photographs in children. *Perceptual and Motor Skills, 29,* 763–771.

KLAUS, M. H., & KENNELL, J. H. (1976). *Maternal-infant bonding: The impact of early separation or loss on family development.* St. Louis, MO: Mosby.

KLAUS, M. H., KENNELL, J. H., PLUMB, N., & ZUEHLKE, S. (1970). Human maternal behavior at the first contact with her young. *Pediatrics, 46,* 187.

KLEIN, A., & STARKEY, P. (1987). The origins and development of numerical cognition. In J. A. Sloboda & D. Rogers (Eds.), *Cognitive processes in mathematics.* Oxford: Clarendon Press.

KLEIN, M. & STERN, L. (1971). Low birthweight and the battered child syndrome. *American Journal of the Disabled Child, 122,* 15–18.

KLEITMAN, N. (1963). *Sleep and wakefulness.* Chicago: University of Chicago Press.

KLIEGL, R., & BALTES, P. (1987). Theory-guided analysis of mechanisms of development and aging through test-the-limits and research on expertise. In C. Schooler & K. W. Schaie (Eds.), *Cognitive functioning and social structure over the life course.* Norwood, NJ: Ablex Publishing Corp.

KLINEBERG, O. (1935). *Race differences.* New York: Harper & Row.

KLINEBERG, O. (1980). Historical perspectives: Cross-cultural psychology before 1960. In H. Triandis & W. Lambert (Eds.), *Handbook of cross-cultural psychology* (Vol 1). Boston: Allyn and Bacon.

KLOPFER, P. H., ADAMS, D. K., & KLOPFER, M. S. (1964). Maternal imprinting in goats. *Proceedings of the National Academy of Sciences, 52,* 911–914.

KLUCKHOHN, C., & KELLY, W. H. (1945). The concept of culture. In R. Linton (Ed.), *The science of man in the world crisis.* New York: Columbia University Press.

KLUCKHOHN, C., MURRAY, H. A., & SCHNEIDER, D. M. (1953). *Personality in nature, society, and culture.* New York: Knopf.

KOCHANSKA, G., KUCZYNSKI, L., & RADKE-YARROW, M. (1989). Correspondence between mothers' self-reported and observed child-rearing practices. *Child Development, 60,* 56–63.

KOHLBERG, L. (1966). A cognitive-developmental analysis of childrens' sex role concepts and attitudes. In E. E. Maccoby (Ed.), *The development of sex differences.* Stanford, CA: Stanford University Press.

KOHLBERG, L. (1969). Stage and sequence: The cognitive-developmental approach to socialization. In D. A. Goslin (Ed.), *Handbook of socialization theory and research.* Chicago: Rand McNally.

KOHLBERG, L. (1976). Moral stages and moralization: The cognitive-developmental approach. In J. Lickona (Ed.), *Moral development behavior: Theory, research and social issues.* New York: Holt, Rinehart and Winston.

KOHLBERG, L. (1984). *The psychology of moral development: The nature and validity of moral stages* (Vol. 2). New York: Harper & Row.

KOHLBERG, L., HICKEY, J., & SCHARF, P. (1972). The justice structure of the prison: A theory and intervention. *Prison Journal, 51,* 3–14.

KOHLBERG, L., & KRAMER, R. (1969). Continuities and discontinuities in childhood and adult moral development. *Human Development, 12,* 93–120.

KOHLBERG, L., & RYNCARZ, R. (1990). Beyond justice reasoning: Moral development and considerations of a seventh stage. In C. Alexander & E. Langer (Eds.), *Higher stages of human development: Perspectives on adult growth.* New York: Oxford University Press.

KOHLBERG, L., YAEGER, J., & HJERTHOLM, E. (1968). Private speech: Four studies and a review of theories. *Child Development, 39,* 691–736.

KOHN, M. L. (1977). *Class and conformity* (2nd ed.). Chicago: University of Chicago Press.

KOHNSTAMM, G. A., BATES, J. E., & ROTHBART, M. K. (1989). *Temperament in childhood.* New York: Wiley.

KOLATA, G. (1987, Sept. 22). Flaws reported in new prenatal test. *New York Times,* Section 1, p. 12.

KOLB, B., & WHISHAW, I. Q. (1985). *Fundamentals of human neuropsychology* (2nd ed.). New York: W. H. Freeman.

KOLUCHOVA, J. (1972). Severe deprivation in twins: A case study. *Journal of Child Psychology and Psychiatry, 13,* 107–114.

KOLUCHOVA, J. (1976). A report on the further development of twins after severe and prolonged deprivation. In A. M. Clarke & A. D. B. Clarke (Eds.), *Early experience: Myth and evidence.* London: Open Books.

KONNER, M. (1977). Evolution in human behavior development. In P. H. Leiderman, S. Tulkin, & A. Rosenfeld (Eds.), *Culture and infancy: Variations in human experience.* New York: Academic Press.

KOPP, C. B. (1983). Risk factors in development. In P. H. Mussen (Ed.), *Handbook of child development:* Vol. 2. *Infancy and developmental psychobiology.* New York: Wiley.

KOPP, C. B. (1987). The growth of self-regulation: Caregivers and children. In N. Eisenberg (Ed.), *Contemporary trends in developmental psychology.* New York: Wiley.

KOPP, C. B., & KALER, S. R. (1989). Risk in infancy: Origins and implications. *American Psychologist, 44,* 224–230

KOPP, C. B., & KRAKOW, J. B. (1983). The developmentalist and the study of biological risk: A view of the past with an eye toward the future. *Child Development, 54,* 1086–1108.

KOPP, C. B., & MCCALL, R. B. (1982). Predicting later mental performance for normal, at-risk, and handicapped infants. In P. B. Baltes & O. G. Brim (Eds.), *Life span development and behavior* (Vol. 4). New York: Academic Press.

KOPP, C. B., & PARMELEE, A. H. (1979). Prenatal and perinatal influences on behavior. In J. D. Osofsky (Ed.), *Handbook of infant development*. New York: Wiley.

KORNER, A. F. (1987). Preventive intervention with high-risk newborns: Theoretical conceptual and methodological perspectives. In J. D. Osofsky (Ed.), *Handbook of infant development* (2nd ed.). New York: Wiley.

KORNER, A. F., & GROBSTEIN, R. (1966). Visual alertness as related to soothing in neonates. *Child Development, 37,* 867–876.

KORNER, A. F., & THOMAN, E. (1970). Visual alertness in neonates as evoked by maternal care. *Journal of Experimental Child Psychology, 10,* 67–78.

KOTELCHUCK, M. (1976). The infant's relationship to the father: Experimental evidence. In M. E. Lamb (Ed.), *The role of the father in child development*. New York: Wiley.

KOTELCHUCK, M., SCHWARTZ, J. B., ANDERKA, M. T., & FINISON, K. S. (1984). WIC participation and pregnancy outcomes: Massachusetts statewide evaluation project. *American Journal of Public Health, 74,* 1086–1091.

KOZOL, J. (1985). *Illiterate America*. Garden City, NY: Doubleday.

KRASNOGORSKI, N. I. (1907/1967). The formation of artificial conditioned reflexes in young children. In Y. Brackbill & G. G. Thompson (Eds.), *Behavior in infancy and early childhood: A book of readings*. New York: Free Press.

KRAUSS, R. M., & GLUCKSBERG, S. (1969). The development of communication: Competence as a function of age. *Child Development, 42,* 255–266.

KRETSCHMANN, H. J., KAMMRADT, I., KRAUTHAUSEN, I., SAUER, B., WINGERT, F. (1986). Growth of the hippocampal formation in man. *Bibliotheca Anatomica, 28,* 27–52.

KREUTZER, M. A., LEONARD, S. C., & FLAVELL, J. H. (1975). An interview study of children's knowledge about memory. *Monographs of the Society for Research in Child Development, 40*(1, Serial No. 159).

KROGER, J. (1989). *Identity in adolescence: The balance between self and other*. London: Routledge.

KUHL, P. K., & MILLER, J. D. (1978). Speech perception by the chinchilla: Identification functions for synthetic VOT stimuli. *Journal of the Acoustical Society of America, 63,* 905–917.

KUHL, P. K., WILLIAMS, K. A., LACERDA, F., STEVENS, K. N., & LINDBLOM, B. (1992). Linguistic experiences alters phonetic perception in infants by 6 months of age. *Science, 255,* 606–608.

KUHN, D. (1976). Short-term longitudinal evidence for the sequentiality of Kohlberg's early stages of moral judgment. *Developmental Psychology, 12,* 162–166.

KUNDERA, M. (1988). *The art of the novel*. New York: Grove Press.

KUPERSMIDT, J. B., COIE, J. D., & DODGE, K. A. (1990). The role of poor peer relationships in the development of disorder. In S. R. Asher & J. D. Coie (Eds.), *Peer rejection in childhood*. New York: Cambridge University Press.

KURTINES, W. M., & GEWIRTZ, J. L. (Eds.). (1991). *Handbook of moral behavior and development:* Vol. 1. *Theory*. Hillsdale, NJ: Erlbaum.

KURTINES, W. M., & GRIEF, E. B. (1974). The development of moral thought: Review and evaluation of Kohlberg's approach. *Psychological Bulletin, 81,* 453–470.

LABORATORY OF COMPARATIVE HUMAN COGNITION. (1983). Culture and cognitive development. In P. Mussen (Ed.), *Handbook of child psychology:* Vol. 1. *History, theory, and methods*. New York: Wiley.

LABOUVIE-VIEF, G. (1982). Individual time, social time, intellectual aging. In T. Hareven & K. Adams (Eds.), *Aging and life course transitions: An interdisciplinary perspective*. New York: Guilford Press.

LABOUVIE-VIEF, G. (1990). Wisdom as integrated thought: Historical and developmental perspectives. In J. Sternberg (Ed.), *Wisdom: Its nature, origins, and development*. New York: Cambridge University Press.

LABOUVIE-VIEF, G., HAKIM-LARSON, J., DE VOE, M., & SCHOEBERLEIN, S. (1989). Emotions and self-regulation: A life span view. *Human Development, 32*(5), 279–289.

LABOV, W., & ROBBINS, C. (1969). A note on the relation of reading failure to peer-group status in urban ghettos. *Florida Language Reporter, 167,* 54–57.

LADYGINA-KOTS, N. N. (1935). *Infant, ape, and human child*. Moscow: Darwin Museum.

LAGERCRANTZ, H., & SLOTKIN, T. A. (1986). The "stress" of being born. *Scientific American, 254,* 100–107.

LAMB, M. E. (1976). Interactions between eight-month-old children and their fathers and mothers. In M. E. Lamb (Ed.), *The Role of the Father in Child Development.* New York: Wiley.

LAMB, M. E. (1977a). The development of mother-infant and father-infant attachments in the second year of life. *Developmental Psychology, 13,* 637–648.

LAMB, M. E. (1977b). Father-infant and mother-infant interaction in the first year of life. *Child Development, 48,* 167–181.

LAMB, M. E. (1982). What can "research experts" tell parents about effective socialization? In E. Zigler, M. E. Lamb, & I. L. Child (Eds.), *Socialization and personality development.* Oxford: Oxford University Press.

LAMB, M. E. (Ed.). (1987). *The Father's Role: Cross-Cultural Perspectives.* Hillsdale, NJ: Erlbaum.

LAMB, M. E., & BORNSTEIN, M. H. (1992). *Development in infancy: An introduction* (3rd ed.). New York: Random House.

LAMB, M. E., & HWANG, C. P. (1982). Maternal attachment and mother-neonate bonding: A critical review. In M. E. Lamb & A. L. Brown (Eds.), *Advances for developmental psychology* (Vol. 2). Hillsdale, NJ: Erlbaum.

LAMB, M. E., PLECK, J. H., CHARNOV, E. L., & LEVINE, J. A. (1987). A biosocial perspective on paternal behavior and involvement. In J. B. Lancaster, J. Altmann, A. Rossi, & L. R. Sherrod (Eds.), *Parenting across the lifespan: Biosocial perspectives.* Hawthorne, NY: Aldine de Gruyter.

LANDSBAUM, J., & WILLIS, R. (1971). Conformity in early and late adolescence. *Developmental Psychology, 4,* 334–337.

LANE, H. (1976). *The wild boy of Aveyron.* Cambridge, MA: Harvard University Press.

LANGE, G. (1978). Organization-related processes in children's recall. In P. A. Ornstein (Ed.), *Memory development in children.* Hillsdale, NJ: Erlbaum.

LANGER, E. J., & RODIN, J. (1976). The effects of choice and enhanced personal responsibilities for the aged: A field experiment in an institutional setting. *Journal of Personality and Social Psychology, 34,* 191–198.

LANGER, E. J., RODIN, J., BECK, P., WEINMAN, C., & SPITZER, L. (1979). Environmental determinants of memory improvement in late adulthood. *Journal of Personality and Social Psychology, 37,* 2003–2013.

LANGLOIS, J. (1986). From the eye of the beholder to behavioral reality: Development of social behaviors and social relations as a function of physical attractiveness. In C. P. Herman, M. P. Zanna, & E. T. Higgins (Eds.), *Physical appearance, stigma, and social behavior: The Ontario Symposium* (Vol. 3). Hillsdale, NJ: Erlbaum.

LARSEN, M. T. (1986). Writing on clay: From pictograph to alphabet. *Quarterly Newsletter of the Laboratory of Comparative Human Cognition, 8,* 3–9.

LATOUR, B. (1987). *Science in action.* Cambridge, MA: Harvard University Press.

LAU v. NICHOLS (1974). 414 U.S. 563.

LAVE, J. (1977). Tailor-made experiments and evaluating the intellectual consequences of apprenticeship training. *Quarterly News Letter of the Institute of Comparative Human Development, 1,* 1–3.

LAVE, J. (1988). *Cognition in practice: Mind, mathematics, and culture in everyday life.* Cambridge: Cambridge University Press.

LAVE, J. (1991). Situating learning in communities of practice. In L. B. Resnick, J. M. Levine, & S. D. Teasley (Eds.), *Perspectives on socially shared cognition.* Washington, DC: American Psychological Association.

LAVE, J., & WENGER, E. (1991). *Situated learning: Legitimate peripheral practice.* New York: Cambridge University Press.

LAVIGNE, M. (1982). Rubella's disabled children: Research and rehabilitation. *Columbia, 7,* 10–17.

LAVIK, N. J. (1977). Urban-rural differences in rates of disorder: A comparative psychiatric population study of Norwegian adolescents. In P. T. Graham (Ed.), *Epidemiological approaches in child psychiatry.* London: Academic Press.

LAWTON, M. P. (1977). The impact of the environment on aging and behavior. In J. E. Birren & K. W. Schaie (Eds.), *Handbook of the psychology of aging.* New York: Van Nostrand Reinhold.

LECOURS, A. R. (1975). Mylogenetic correlates of the development of speech and language. In E. H. Lenneberg & E. Lenneberg (Eds.), *Foundations of language development* (Vol. 1). New York: Academic Press.

LECOURS, A. R. (1982). Correlates of developmental behavior in brain maturation. In T. Bever (Ed.), *Regressions in mental development.* Hillsdale, NJ: Erlbaum.

LEE, L. (1965). *Cider with Rosie.* London: Hogarth Press.

LEE, R. B., & DEVORE, I. (Eds.). (1976). *Kalahari hunter-gatherers*. Cambridge, MA: Harvard University Press.

LEGAULT, F., & STRAYER, F. F. (1990). The emergence of sex-segregation in preschool peer groups. In F. F. Strayer (Ed.), *Social interaction and behavioral development during early childhood*. Montreal: La Maison D'Ethologie de Montreal.

LEGG, C., SHERICK, I., & WADLAND, W. (1974). Reaction of preschool children to the birth of a sibling. *Child Psychiatry and Human Development, 5,* 3–39.

LEINBACH, M. D., & HORT, B. (1989, April). Bears are for boys: "Metaphorical" associations in the young child's gender schema. Paper presented at the biennial meeting of the Society for Research in Child Development, Kansas City, MO.

LE MARE, L. J., & RUBIN, K. H. (1987). Perspective taking and peer interaction: Structural and developmental analyses. *Child Development, 58,* 306–315.

LEMISH, D., & RICE, M. L. (1986). Television as a talking picture book: A prop for language acquisition. *Journal of Child Language, 13,* 251–274.

LENNEBERG, E. H. (1967). *The biological foundations of language*. New York: Wiley.

LENNEBERG, E. H., REBELSKY, F. G., & NICHOLS, I. A. (1965). The vocalizations of infants born to hearing and deaf parents. *Human Development, 8,* 23–27.

LEONARD, L. B., CHAPMAN, K., ROWAN, L. E., & WEISS, A. L. (1983). Three hypotheses concerning young children's imitations of lexical items. *Developmental Psychology, 19,* 591–601.

LEONI, L. (1964). *Tico and the golden wings*. New York: Pantheon.

LEONTIEV, A. N. (1981). *Problems of the development of the mind*. Moscow: Progress Publishers.

LEOPOLD, W. F. (1949). *Speech development of a bilingual child: A linguist's record*. Vol. 2. *Diary from age two*. Evanston, IL: Northwestern University Press.

LEPPER, M. R., & GREENE, D. (Eds.). (1978). *The hidden costs of reward*. Hillsdale, NJ: Erlbaum.

LERNER, M. I., & LIBBY, W. J. (1976). *Heredity, evolution, and society*. New York: W. H. Freeman.

LERNER, R. M. (1988). Personality development: A life-span perspective. In E. M. Hetherington, R. M. Lerner, & M. Perlmutter (Eds.), *Child development in life-span perspective*. Hillsdale, NJ: Erlbaum.

LERNER, R. M. (1991). Changing organism-context relations as the basic process of development: A developmental contextual perspective. *Developmental Psychology, 27,* 27–32.

LERNER, R. M., & FOCH, T. T. (Eds.) (1987). *Biological-psychosocial interactions in early adolescence*. Hillsdale, NJ: Erlbaum.

LESLIE, A. M. (1986). Getting development off the ground: Modularity and the infant's perception of causality. In P. Van Geert (Ed.), *Theory building and development*. Amsterdam: Elsevier.

LESLIE, A. M., & KEEBLE, S. (1987). Do six month old infants perceive causality? *Cognition, 25,* 265–288.

LESSER, G. S. (1974). *Children and television*. New York: Random House.

LESTER, B. M. (1984). A biosocial model of infant crying. In L. P. Lipsitt (Ed.), *Advances in infancy research*. New York: Academic Press.

LESTER, B. M., ALS, H., & BRAZELTON, T. B. (1982). Regional obstetric anesthesia and newborn behavior: A reanalysis towards synergistic effects. *Child Development, 53,* 687–692.

LESTER, B. M., & ZESKIND, P. S. (1982). A biobehavioral perspective on crying in early infancy. In H. Fitzgerald, B. Lester, & M. Yogman (Eds.), *Theory and research in behavioral pediatrics* (Vol. 1). New York: Plenum Press.

LEVER, J. (1978). Sex differences in the complexity of children's play and games. *American Sociological Review, 43,* 471–483.

LEVINE, R. A. (1974). Parental goals: A cross cultural view. In H. J. Leichter (Ed.), *The family as educator*. New York: Teachers College Press.

LEVINSON, P. J., & CARPENTER, R. L. (1974). An analysis of analogical reasoning in children. *Child Development, 45,* 857–861.

LEWIS, M., & BROOKS-GUNN, J. (1979). *Social cognition and the acquisition of self*. New York: Plenum Press.

LEWIS, M., & FEIRING, C. (1989). Infant, mother, and mother-infant interaction behavior and subsequent attachment. *Child Development, 60,* 831–837.

LEWIS, M., & ROSENBLUM, L. A. (Eds.) (1974). *The effect of the infant on its caretaker*. New York: Wiley.

LEWIS, M., & SAARNI, C. (1985). *The socialization of emotions*. New York: Plenum Press.

LEWIS, M., & STARR, M. (1979). Developmental continuity. In J. Osofsky (Ed.), *Handbook of infant development*. New York: Wiley.

LEWIS, M., SULLIVAN, M. W., STANGER, C., & WEISS, M. (1989). Self development and self-conscious emotions. *Child Development, 23,* 690–697.

LEWONTIN, R. (1982). *Human diversity.* New York: Scientific American Books.

LEWONTIN, R., ROSE, R., & KAMIN, L. (1984). *Not in our genes.* New York: Pantheon.

LEWONTIN, R. C. (1976). Race and intelligence. In N. J. Block & G. Dworkin (Eds.), *The IQ controversy.* New York: Pantheon.

LICKONA, T. (Ed.) (1976). *Moral development and behavior: Theory, research and social issues.* New York: Holt, Rinehart, & Winston.

LIEBERMAN, P. (1984). *The biology and evolution of language.* Cambridge, MA: Harvard University Press.

LIEBERMAN, P. (1991). *Uniquely human: The evolution of speech, thought, and selfless behavior.* Cambridge, MA: Harvard University Press.

LIEBERT, R. M. (1984). What develops in moral development? In W. K. Kurtines & J. L. Gewirtz (Eds.), *Morality, moral behavior, and moral development.* New York: Wiley.

LIEBERT, R. M., & SPRAVKIN, J. N. (1988). *The early window: Effects of television on children and youth* (3rd ed.). New York: Pergamon Press.

LIFTER, K., & BLOOM, L. (1989). Object knowledge and the emergence of language. *Infant Behavior and Development, 12,* 395–424.

LINAZA, J. (1984). Piaget's marbles: The study of children's games and their knowledge of rules. *Oxford Review of Education, 10,* 271–274.

LINN, M. C. (1983). Content, context, and process in reasoning. *Journal of Early Adolescence, 3,* 63–82.

LINN, M. C., DE BENEDICTUS, T., & DELUCCHI, K. (1982). Adolescent reasoning about advertisements: Preliminary investigations. *Child Development, 53,* 1599–1613.

LINN, M. C., & PULOS, S. (1983). Male-female differences in predicting displaced volume: Strategy usage, aptitude relationships, and experience influences. *Journal of Educational Psychology, 75,* 86–96.

LINN, M. C., & SWEENEY, S. F., JR. (1981). Individual differences in formal thought: Role of expectations and attitudes. *Journal of Educational Psychology, 73,* 274–286.

LIPSITT, L. P. (1977). Taste in human neonates: Its effects on sucking and heart rate. In J. M. Weiffenbach (Ed.), *Taste and development: The genesis of sweet preference.* Washington, DC: U.S. Government Printing Office.

LIPSITT, L. P. (1990). Learning and memory in infants. *Merrill Palmer Quarterly, 36,* 53–66.

LIPSITT, L. P., & LEVY, N. (1959). Electrotactual threshold in the neonate. *Child Development, 30,* 547–554.

LOCK, A. (1980). *The guided reinvention of language.* New York: Academic Press.

LOCKE, J. (1938). *Some thoughts concerning education.* London: Churchill. (Original work published 1699).

LOEB, R. C., HORST, L., & HORTON, P. J. (1980). Family interaction patterns associated with self-esteem in preadolescent boys and girls. *Merrill-Palmer Quarterly, 26,* 203–217.

LOFTUS, E. F. (1979). *Eyewitness testimony.* Cambridge, MA: Harvard University Press.

LOFTUS, E. F., & DAVIES, G. M. (1984). Distortions in the memory of children. *Journal of Social Issues, 40,* 51–67.

LOGAN, R. K. (1986). *The alphabet effect.* New York: Morrow.

LOMAX, E. M., KAGAN, J., & ROSENKRANTZ, B. G. (1978). *Science and patterns of child care.* New York: W. H. Freeman.

LORENZ, K. (1943). Die Angebornen Formen mogicher Erfahrung. *Zeitschrift für Tierpsychologie, 5,* 233–409.

LORENZ, K. (1966). *On aggression.* New York: Harcourt, Brace & World.

LUCARIELLO, J., & RIFKIN, A. (1986). Event representations as the basis of categorical knowledge. In K. Nelson (Ed.), *Event knowledge: Structure and function in development.* Hillsdale, NJ: Erlbaum.

LUNZER, E. A. (1965). Problems of formal reasoning in test situations. In P. H. Mussen (Ed.), *Handbook of child psychology: Vol. 3. Cognitive development.* New York: Wiley.

LURIA, A. R. (1961). *The role of speech in the regulation of normal and abnormal behavior.* New York: Pergamon Press.

LURIA, A. R. (1973). *The working brain.* New York: Basic Books.

LURIA, A. R. (1976). *Cognitive development*. Cambridge, MA: Harvard University Press.

LURIA, A. R. (1981). *Language and cognition*. New York: Wiley.

LUTZ, C. (1987). Goals, events, and understanding Ifaluk emotion theory. In D. Holland & N. Quinn (Eds.), *Cultural models in language and thought*. Cambridge: Cambridge University Press.

LYNN, R. (1982). IQ in Japan and the United States shows a growing disparity. *Nature, 297,* 222–223.

MAAS, H. (1963). The young adult adjustment of twenty wartime residential nursery children. *Child Welfare, 42,* 57–72.

MACCOBY, E. E. (1980). *Social development: Psychological growth and the parent-child relationship*. New York: Harcourt Brace Jovanovich.

MACCOBY, E. E. (1984). Middle childhood in the context of the family. In W. A. Collins (Ed.), *Development during middle childhood: The years from six to twelve*. Washington, DC: National Academy Press.

MACCOBY, E. E., & MARTIN, J. A. (1983). Socialization in the context of the family: Parent-child interaction. In P. H. Mussen (Ed.), *Handbook of child psychology: Vol. 4. Socialization, personality, and social behavior*. New York: Wiley.

MACDONALD, K. (1988). *Social and personality development: An evolutionary synthesis*. New York: Plenum Press.

MACDONALD, K., & PARKE, R. (1984). Bridging the gap: Parent-child play interaction and peer interactive competence. *Child Development, 55,* 1265–1277.

MACFARLANE, A. (1975). Olfaction in the development of social preferences in the human neonate. *Parent-infant interaction (CIBA Foundation symposium 33)*. New York: Elsevier.

MACFARLANE, A. (1977). *The psychology of childbirth*. Cambridge, MA: Harvard University Press.

MACKENZIE, B. (1984). Explaining race differences in I.Q. *American Psychologist, 39,* 1214–1233.

MACLUSKY, N. J., & NAFTOLIN, F. (1981). Sexual differentiation in the central nervous system. *Science, 211,* 1294–1303.

MADSEN, M. C., & SHAPIRA, A. (1970). Cooperative and competitive behavior of urban Afro-American, Anglo-American, Mexican-American, and Mexican village children. *Developmental Psychology, 3,* 16–20.

MAIN, M. (1973). *Play, exploration, and competence as related to child-adult attachment*. Unpublished doctoral dissertation, Johns Hopkins University.

MAIN, M., & WESTON, D. (1981). The quality of the toddler's relationship to mother and father: Related to conflict behavior and the readiness to establish new relationships. *Child Development, 52,* 932–940.

MALINA, R. M. (1975). *Growth and development: The first twenty years in man*. Minneapolis: Burgess.

MALLICK, S. K., & MCCANDLESS, B. R. (1966). A study of catharsis of aggression. *Journal of Personality and Social Psychology, 4,* 590–596.

MANDLER, J. (1983). Representation. In P. H. Mussen (Ed.), *Handbook of child psychology: Vol 3. Cognitive development*. New York: Wiley.

MANDLER, J. (1990). Recall of events by preverbal children. *Annals of the New York Academy of Sciences, 608,* 485–516.

MANDLER, J. M., & BAUER., P. J. (1988). The cradle of categorization: Is the basic level basic? *Cognitive Development, 3,* 247–264.

MANDLER, J., SCRIBNER, S., COLE, M., & DE FOREST, M. (1980). Cross-cultural invariance in story recall. *Child Development, 51,* 19–26.

MARATSOS, M. (1973). Nonegocentric communication abilities in preschool children. *Child Development, 44,* 697–700.

MARATSOS, M. (1983). Some issues in the study of the acquisition of grammar. In P. Mussen (Ed.), *Handbook of child psychology: Vol 3. Cognitive development*. New York: Wiley.

MARCIA, J. E. (1966). Development and validation of ego identity status. *Journal of Personality and Social Psychology, 3,* 551–558.

MARCIA, J. E. (1980). Identity in adolescence. In J. Adelson (Ed.), *Handbook of Adolescent Psychology*. New York: Wiley.

MARCIA, J. E. (1987). The identity status approach to the study of ego identity. In T. Honess & K. Yardley (Eds.), *Self and identity: Perspectives across the lifespan*. London: Routledge & Kegan Paul.

MARKMAN, E. M. (1987). *Categorization and Naming In Children*. Cambridge, MA: M.I.T. Press.

MARKOVA, A. K. (1979). *The teaching and mastery of language*. White Plains, NY: M. E. Sharpe.

MARKSTROM, C. A. (1987). A comparison of psychosocial maturity between four ethnic groups during middle adolescence. Paper presented at the biennial meetings of the Society for Research in Child Development, Baltimore, MD.

MARKUS, H. R., & KITAYAMA, S. (1991). Culture and the self: Implications for cognition, emotion, and motivation. *Psychological Review, 98*, 224–253.

MARQUIS, D. (1931). Can conditioned reflexes be established in the newborn infant? *Journal of Genetic Psychology, 39*, 479–492.

MARSHALL, W. A., & TANNER, J. M. (1974). Puberty. In J. A. Davis & J. Dobbing (Eds.), *Scientific foundations of pediatrics*. Philadelphia: Saunders.

MARTIN, G. B., & CLARK, R. D. (1987). Distress crying in neonates: Species and peer specificity. *Developmental Psychology, 18*, 3–9.

MATAS, L., AREND, R., & SROUFE, L. A. (1978). Continuity of adaptation in the second year. The relationship between quality of attachment and later competence. *Child Development, 49*, 547–556.

MATHEW, A. & COOK, M. (1990). The control of reaching movements by young infants. *Child development, 61*, 1238–1257.

MATTHEWS, K. A., BATESON, C. D., HORN, J., & ROSENMAN, R. H. (1981). Principles in his nature which interest him in the fortune of others. . . . The heritability of empathic concern for others. *Journal of Personality, 49*, 237–247.

MCADOO, H. P. (1985). Racial attitude and self-concept of young black children over time. In H. P. McAdoo & J. L. McAdoo (Eds.), *Black children: Social, educational, and parental environments*. Beverly Hills: Sage.

MCADOO, H. P., & MCADOO, J. L. (1985). *Black children: Social, educational, and parental environments*. Beverly Hills: Sage.

MCCALL, R. B. (1981). Nature, nurture and the two realms of development: A proposed integration with respect to mental development. *Child Development, 52*, 1–12.

MCCALL, R. B., EICHORN, D. H., & HOGARTY, P. S. (1977). Transitions in early mental development. *Monographs of Society for Research Child Development, 42*(3, Serial No. 171).

MCCALL, R. B., MEYERS, E. D., JR., HARTMAN, J., & ROCHE, A. F. (1983). Developmental changes in head-circumference and mental-performance growth rates: A test of Epstein's phrenoblysis hypothesis. *Developmental Psychobiology, 16*, 457–458.

MCCARTHY, J., & HODGE, D. (1982). Analysis of age effects in longitudinal studies of adolescent self-esteem. *Developmental Psychology, 18*, 372–379.

MCCARTNEY, K. (1984). The effect of quality of day care environment upon children's language development. *Developmental Psychology, 20*, 244–260.

MCCARTNEY, K., SCARR, S., PHILLIPS, D., & GRAJEK, S. (1985). Day care as intervention: Comparisons of varying quality programs. *Journal of Applied Developmental Psychology, 6*, 247–260.

MCCONNELL, T. M. (1934/1958). Discover or be told! In C. W. Hunnicutt & W. J. Iverson (Eds.), *Research in the three R's*. New York: Harper & Row.

MCCORD, J. (1990). Problem Behaviors. In S. S. Feldman & G. R. Elliott (Eds.), *At the threshold: The developing adolescent*. Cambridge, MA: Harvard University Press.

MCCUNE-NICOLICH, L., & BRUSKIN, C. (1982). Combinatorial competency in symbolic play and language. In D. J. Pepler & K. H. Rubin (Eds.), *The play of children: Current theory and research*. Basal: S. Krieger.

MCDONALD, K. B. (1988). *Social and personality development: An evolutionary synthesis*. New York: Plenum.

MCDONOUGH, L., & MANDLER, J. M. (1989). Immediate and deferred imitation with 11-month-olds: A comparison between novel and familiar actions. Poster presented at the biennial meeting of the Society for Research in Child Development, Kansas City, MO.

MCGRAW, M. B. (1975). *Growth: A study of Johnny and Jimmy*. New York: Arno Press. (Original work published 1935).

MCGROARTY, M. (1992). The societal context of bilingual education. *Educational Researcher, 21*, 7–9.

MCKNIGHT, C. C., CROSSWHITE, F. J., DOSSEY, J. A., KIFER, E., SWAFFORD, J. O., TRAVERS, K. J., & COONEY, T. J. (1987). *The underachieving curriculum: Assessing U.S. school mathematics from an international perspective*. Champaign, IL: Stipes.

MCKUSICK, V. A. (1986). *Mendelian inheritance in man: Catalog of autosomal dominant, autosomal recessive, and x-linked phenotypes* (8th ed.). Baltimore: Johns Hopkins University Press.

MCLANE, J. B., & MCNAMEE, G. D. (1990). *Early literacy*. Cambridge, MA: Harvard University Press.

MCLOYD, V. (1990). The impact of economic hardship on black families and children: Psychological distress, parenting, and socioemotional development. *Child Development, 61*, 311–346.

MCMILLEN, M. M. (1979). Differential mortality by sex in fetal and neonatal deaths. *Science, 204*, 89–91.

MCNEILL, D. (1966). Developmental psycholinguistics. In S. Smith & G. A. Miller (Eds.), *The genesis of language: A psycholinguistic approach.* Cambridge, MA: MIT Press.

MCNEILL, D. (1970). *The acquisition of language: The study of developmental psycholinguistics.* New York: Harper & Row.

MEAD, M. (1935). *Sex and temperament.* New York: William Morrow.

MEAD, M. (1928/1973). *Coming of age in Samoa: A psychological study of primitive youth.* New York: American Museum of Natural History.

MEAD, M., & MACGREGOR, F. C. (1951). *Growth and culture.* New York: Putnam.

MEAD, M., & NEWTON, N. (1967). Cultural patterning of perinatal behavior. In S. Richardson & A. Guttmacher (Eds.), *Childbearing: Its social and psychological aspects.* Baltimore: Williams & Wilkins.

MEDICUS, G. (1992). The inapplicability of the biogenetic rule to behavioral development. *Human Development, 35*, 1–7.

MEDRICH, E. A., ROIZEN, J., RUBIN, V., & BUCKLEY, S. (1982). *The serious business of growing up.* Berkeley: University of California Press.

MEEHAN, A. M. (1984). A meta-analysis of sex differences in formal operational thought. *Child Development, 55*, 1110–1124.

MEHAN, H. (1979). What time is it, Denise? Asking known information questions in classroom discourse. *Theory into Practice, 18*, 285–294.

MEHLER, J., LAMBERTZ, G., JUSCZYK, P., & AMIEL-TISON, C. (1986). Discrimination de la langue maternelle par le nouveau-né. *Comptes rendus de l'Academie de Science, 303*(3), 637–640.

MELTZOFF, A. N. (1988a). Imitation of televised models by infants. *Child Development, 59*, 1221–1229.

MELTZOFF, A. N. (1988b). Infant imitation and memory: Nine-month-olds in immediate and deferred tests. *Child Development, 59*, 217–225.

MELTZOFF, A. N. (1990). Towards a developmental cognitive science: The implications of cross-modal matching and imitation for the development of representation and memory in infancy. *Annals of the New York Academy of Sciences, 608*, 1–37.

MELTZOFF, A. N., & BORTON, R. W. (1979). Intermodal matching by human neonates. *Nature, 282*, 403–404.

MELTZOFF, A. N., & GOPNIK, A. (1989). On linking nonverbal imitation, representation, and language learning in the first two years of life. In G. E. Speidel & K. E. Nelson (Eds.), *The many faces of imitation in language learning.* New York: Springer Verlag.

MELTZOFF, A. N., & MOORE, M. K. (1977). Imitation of facial and manual gestures by human neonates. *Science, 198*, 75–78.

MELTZOFF, A. N., & MOORE, M. K. (1983). The origins of imitation in infancy: Paradigm, phenomena, and theories. In L. Lipsitt & C. Rovee-Collier (Eds.), *Advances in infancy research* (Vol 2). Norwood, NJ: Ablex.

MELTZOFF, A. N. & MOORE, M. K. (1989). Imitation in newborn infants: Exploring the range of gestures imitated and the underlying mechanisms. *Developmental Psychology, 25*, 954–962.

MERKATZ, I. R., & THOMPSON, J. E. (Eds.). (1990). *New perspectives on prenatal care.* New York: Elsevier.

MESSER, S. B. (1976). Reflection-impulsivity: A review. *Psychological Bulletin, 83*, 1026–1052.

MICHALSON, L., & LEWIS, M. (1985). What do children know about emotions and when do they know it? In M. Lewis & C. Saarni (Eds.), *The socialization of emotions.* New York: Plenum Press.

MICHEL, G. F. (1981). Right handedness: A consequence of infant supine head orientation preference. *Science, 212*, 385–387.

MIDDLETON, D., BUCHANAN, K., & SUURMOND, J. (1991, June). Communities of Memory: Issues of 'Re-membering' and belonging in reminiscence work with the elderly. Paper presented at the British Psychological Society's Special Interest Group in the Elderly, Annual Conference *Thriving into the Nineties,* Durham, NC.

MILES, H. L. (1990). The cognitive foundations for reference in a signing orangutan. In S. T. Parker & K. R. Gibson (Eds.), *Language and intelligence in monkeys and apes.* Cambridge: Cambridge University Press.

MILLER, G. A. (1981). *Language and speech.* New York: W. H. Freeman.

MILLER, G. A. (1988). The challenge of universal literacy. *Science, 241*, 1293–1298.

MILLER, G. A. (1991). *The science of words.* New York: Scientific American Library.

MILLER, N. E., & DOLLARD, J. (1941). *Social learning and imitation.* New Haven: Yale University Press.

MILLER, P. (1982). *Amy, Wendy and Beth: Learning language in south Baltimore.* Austin: University of Texas Press.

MILLER, P. H. (1989). *Theories of developmental psychology* (2nd ed.). New York: W. H. Freeman.

MILLER, S. A. (1987). *Developmental research methods.* Englewood Cliffs, NJ: Prentice-Hall.

MILLER, S. A., SHELTON, J., & FLAVELL, J. H. (1970). A test of Luria's hypothesis concerning the development of verbal self-regulation. *Child Development, 41,* 651–665.

MINTON, H. L. & SCHNEIDER, F. W. (1980). *Differential psychology.* Monterey, CA: Brooks/Cole.

MINUCHIN, P. P., & SHAPIRO, E. K. (1983). The school as a context of social development. In P. H. Mussen (Ed.), *Handbook of child psychology: Vol. 4. Socialization, personality, and social development.* New York: Wiley.

MISCHEL, W. (1966). A social learning view of sex differences in behavior. In E. M. Maccoby (Ed.), *The development of sex differences.* Stanford: Stanford University Press.

MISCHEL, W. (1968). *Personality and assessment.* New York: Wiley.

MIYAKI, K., CAMPOS, J., BRADSHAW, D. L., & KAGAN, J. (1986). Issues in socioemotional development. In H. Stevenson, H. Azuma, & K. Hakuta (Eds.), *Child development and education in Japan.* New York: W. H. Freeman.

MIYAKE, K., CHEN, S. & CAMPOS, J. J. (1985). Infant temperament, mother's mode of interaction, and attachment in Japan. An interim report. *Monographs of the Society for Research in Child Development, 50*(1–2, Serial No. 209).

MIZUKAMI, K., KOBAYASHI, N., ISHII, T., & IWATA, H. (1990). First selective attachment begins in early infancy: A study using telethermography. *Infant Behavior and Development, 13,* 257–273.

MODELL, J., & GOODMAN, M. (1990). Historical Perspectives. In S. S. Feldman & G. R. Elliott (Eds.), *At the threshold: The developing adolescent.* Cambridge, MA: Harvard University Press.

MODGIL, S., & MODGIL, C. (1986). *Lawrence Kohlberg, consensus and controversy.* Philadelphia: Falmer.

MOLL, L. C. (1992). Bilingual classroom studies and community analysis. *Educational Researcher, 21,* 20–24.

MOLL, L. C., & GREENBERG, J. B. (1990). Creating zones of possibilities: Combining social contexts for instruction. In L. C. Moll (Ed.), *Vygotsky and education: Instructional implications and applications of sociohistorical psychology.* New York: Cambridge University Press.

MONEY, J. & EHRHARDT, A. A. (1972). *Man and woman, boy and girl.* Baltimore: Johns Hopkins University Press.

MONTEMAYOR, R. (1982). The relationship between parent-adolescent conflict and the amount of time adolescents spend alone and with their parents and peers. *Child Development, 53,* 1512–1519.

MONTEMAYOR, R. (1990). Continuity and change in the behavior of nonhuman primates during the transition to adolescence. In R. Montemayor, G. Adams, & T. Gullota (Eds.), *From childhood to adolescence.* Newbury Park, CA: Sage.

MONTESSORI, M. (1912/1964). *The Montessori method.* New York: Schocken Books.

MOON, C., & FIFER, W. P. (1990). Syllables as signals for 2-day-old infants. *Infant Behavior and Development, 13,* 377–390.

MOORE, K. L. (1982). *The developing human: Clinically oriented embryology* (3rd ed.). Philadelphia: Saunders.

MOORE, T. R., ORIGEL, W., KEY, T. C., & RESNIK, R. (1986). The perinatal and economic impact of prenatal care in a low socioeconomic population. *American Journal of Obstetrics and Gynecology, 154,* 29–33.

MORRISON, F. J. (1988). Development of phonemic awareness: A natural experiment. Paper presented at the Annual Meeting of the Psychonomic Society, Chicago.

MORTON, J., & JOHNSON, M. H. (1991). CONSPEC and CONLEARN: A two-process theory of infant face recognition. *Psychological Review, 98,* 164–181.

MOWBRAY, C. T., LANIR, S., & HULCE, M. (1982). Stress, mental health, and motherhood. *Birth Psychology Bulletin, 3,* 10–33.

MOWRER, O. H. (1950). *Learning theory and personality.* New York: Ronald Press.

MUNN, P., & DUNN, J. (1988). Temperament and the developing relationship between siblings. *International Journal of Behavioral Development, 12,* 433–451.

MURDOCK, G. P. (1949). *Social structure.* New York: Macmillan.

NAEYE, R. L. (1978). Effects of maternal cigarette smoking on the fetus and placenta. *Journal of Obstetrics and Gynecology of the British Commonwealth, 85,* 732–735.

NAGATA, D. (1989). Japanese-American children and adolescents. In G. T. Gibbs & L. N. Huang (Eds.), *Children of color.* San Francisco: Jossey-Bass.

NASH, M. (1967). *Machine age Maya.* Chicago: University of Chicago Press.

NATIONAL ACADEMY OF EDUCATION. COMMISSION ON READING (1985). *Becoming a nation of readers: The report of the Commission on reading.* Washington, DC: U.S. Department of Education.

NATIONAL ACADEMY OF SCIENCES. COMMITTEE ON DIETARY ALLOWANCES, FOOD, AND NUTRITION BOARD, NATIONAL RESEARCH COUNCIL. (1989). *Recommended dietary allowances.* Washington, DC: National Academy of Sciences.

NATIONAL CENTERS FOR DISEASE CONTROL. (January, 1992). Sexual Behavior Among High School Students—United States, 1990. *Morbidity and Mortality Weekly Report, 40,* (Nos. 51 & 52, 885–887). Washington, DC: U.S. Government Printing Office.

NATIONAL COMMISSION ON YOUTH. (1980). *The transition of youth to adulthood: A bridge too long.* Boulder, CO: Westview Press.

NATIONAL PANEL ON HIGH SCHOOL AND ADOLESCENT EDUCATION. (1976). *The education of adolescents.* HEW Publication (OE) 76–00004. Washington, DC: U.S. Government Printing Office.

NATIONAL RESEARCH COUNCIL (U. S.). PANEL ON ADOLESCENT PREGNANCY AND CHILDBEARING. (1987). C. Hayes (Ed.), *Risking the future: Adolescent sexuality, pregnancy and childbearing.* Washington, DC: National Academy Press.

NEEDHAM, J. (1968). *Order and life.* Cambridge, MA: MIT Press.

NEIMARK, E. D. (1975). Longitudinal development of formal operational thought. *Genetic Psychology Monographs, 91,* 171–225.

NEISSER, U. (1976). *General, academic, and artificial intelligence.* Hillsdale, NJ: Erlbaum.

NELSON, K. (1973). Structure and strategy in learning to talk. *Monographs of the Society for Research in Child Development, 38*(2, Serial No. 149).

NELSON, K. (1976). Some attributes of adjectives used by young children. *Cognition, 4,* 13–30.

NELSON, K. (1977). The syntagmatic-paradigmatic shift revisited: A review of research and theory. *Psychological Bulletin, 84,* 93–116.

NELSON, K. (1978). Semantic development and the development of semantic memory. In K. E. Nelson (Ed.), *Children's language* (Vol. 1). New York: Gardner Press.

NELSON, K. (1979). Exploration in the development of a functional system. In W. Collins (Ed.), *Children's language and communication. The Minnesota Symposia on Child Psychology, 12.* Hillsdale, NJ: Erlbaum.

NELSON, K. (1981). Social cognition in a script framework. In J. H. Flavell & L. Ross (Eds.), *Social cognitive development.* Cambridge: Cambridge University Press.

NELSON, K. (1986). *Event knowledge: Structure and function in development.* Hillsdale, NJ: Erlbaum.

NELSON, K. (1988). Constraints on word learning? *Cognitive Development, 3,* 221–246.

NELSON, K. E. (1976). Facilitating syntax acquisition. *Developmental Psychology, 13,* 101–107.

NERLOVE, S. B., ROBERTS, J. M., KLEIN, R. E., YARBROUGH, C., & HABICHT, J. P. (1974). Natural indicators of cognitive ability. *Ethos, 2,* 265–295.

NETTER, F. H. (1965). *The CIBA collection of medical illustrations.* Summit, NJ: Ciba Pharmaceutical Products.

NEUGARTEN, B. L. (Ed.). (1968). *Middle age and aging.* Chicago: University of Chicago Press.

NEUGARTEN, B. L., & HAGISTAD, G. O. (1976). Age and the life course. In R. H. Binstock & E. Shanas (Eds.), *Handbook of aging and the social sciences.* New York: Van Nostrand Reinhold.

NEUGARTEN, B. L., WOOD, V., KRAMAS, R. J., & LOOMIS, B. (1963). Women's attitudes toward menopause. *Vita Humana, 6,* 140–151.

NEWPORT, E. (1991). Contrasting concepts of the critical period for language. In S. Carey & R. Gelman (Eds.), *The epigenesis of mind: Essays on biology and cognition.* Hillsdale, NJ: Erlbaum.

NEWSON, J., & NEWSON, E. (1976). *Seven years old in the home environment.* New York: Wiley.

NEWTON, N., & NEWTON, M. (1972). Lactation: Its psychological component. In J. G. Howells (Ed.), *Modern perspectives in psycho-obstetrics*. New York: Brunner/Mazel.

NIGHTINGALE, E. O., & MEISTER, S. B. (1987). *Prenatal screening, policies and values: The example of neural tube defects*. Cambridge, MA: Harvard University Press.

NILSSON, L. (1981). *A child is born: The drama of life before birth*. (With text by A. Ingelman-Sundberg & C. Wirsen). New York: Dell.

NINIO, A., & BRUNER, J. (1978). The achievement of antecedents of labelling. *Journal of Child Language, 5*, 1–5.

NISWANDER, K. R. (1981). *Obstetrics: Essentials of clinical practice* (2nd ed.). Boston: Little Brown.

NUCCI, L. P. (1981). The development of personal concepts: A domain distinct from moral or societal concepts. *Child Development, 52*, 114–121.

NUCCI, L., TURIEL, E., & ENCARNACION-GAWRYCH, G. E. (1983). Children's social interactions and social concepts: Analyses of morality and convention in the Virgin Islands. *Journal of Cross-cultural Psychology, 14*, 469–487.

NUCCI, L. P., & TURIEL, E. (1978). Social interactions and the development of social concepts in preschool children: Methods, issues, and illustrations. *Child Development, 49*, 400–407.

NUNNER-WINKLER, G. (1984). Two moralities: A critical discussion of an ethic of care and responsibility versus an ethic of rights and justice. In W. M. Kurtines & J. L. Gewirtz (Eds.), *Morality, moral behavior, and moral development*. New York: Wiley.

NYITI, R. M. (1976). The development of conservation in the Meru children of Tanzania. *Child Development, 47*, 1122–1129.

NYITI, R. M. (1982). The validity of "cultural differences explanations" for cross-cultural variation in the rate of Piagetian cognitive development. In D. Wagner & H. Stevenson (Eds.), *Cultural perspectives on child development*. New York: W. H. Freeman.

O'BRYAN, K. G. & BOERSMA, F. T. (1971). Eye movement, perceptual activity, and conservation development. *Journal of Experimental Child Psychology, 12*, 157–169.

OCHS, E. (1982). Talking to children in Western Samoa. *Language in Society, 11*, 77–104.

OCHS, E., & SCHIEFFELIN, B. (1984). Language acquisition and socialization. Three developmental stories and their implications. In R. Shweder & R. LeVine (Eds.), *Culture theory*. Cambridge: Cambridge University Press.

OCHS, E., TAYLOR, C., RUDOLPH, D., & SMITH, R. (1991). Storytelling as a theory-building activity. *Discourse Processes, 15*(1), 37–72.

OFFER, D., OSTROV, E., HOWARD, K. I., ATKINSON, R. (1988). *The teenage world: Adolescents' self-image in ten countries*. New York: Plenum Press

OLDS, D. L., & HENDERSON, C. R., JR. (1989). The prevention of maltreatment. In D. Cicchetti & V. Carlson (Eds.), *Child Maltreatment: Theory and research on the causes and consequences of child abuse and neglect*. New York: Cambridge University Press.

OLINER, S. B., & OLINER, P. (1988). *The altruistic personality: Rescuers of Jews in Nazi Germany*. New York: Macmillan.

OLLER, D. K. (1978). The emergence of the sounds of speech in infancy. In G. H. Yeni-Komshian, J. F. Kavanaugh, & C. A. Ferguson (Eds.), *Child Phonology: Perception and production*. New York: Academic Press.

OLLER, D. K., & EILERS, R. E. (1988). The Role of audition in infant babbling. *Child Development, 59*, 441–449.

OLSON, D. R. (1978). The language of instruction. In S. Spiro (Ed.), *Schooling and the acquisition of knowledge*. Hillsdale, NJ: Erlbaum.

OMMEN, G. S. (1978). Prenatal diagnosis of genetic disorders. *Science, 200*, 952–958.

OPPEL, W. C., HARPER, P. A., & REDER, R. V. (1968). The age of attaining bladder control. *Pediatrics, 42*(4), 614–626.

OPPENHEIM, R. W. (1981). Ontogenetic adaptation and retrogressive processes in the development of the nervous system and behavior: A neuroembryological perspective. In K. J. Connolly & H. F. R. Prechtl (Eds.), *Maturation and development: Biological and psychological perspectives*. Philadelphia: Lippincott.

OSTREA, E. M., & CHAVEZ, C. J. (1979). Perinatal problems (excluding neonatal withdrawal) in maternal drug addiction: A study of 830 cases. *Journal of Pediatrics, 94*, 292–295.

OVERMEIR, J. B., & SELIGMAN, M. E. P. (1967). Effects of inescapable shock upon subsequent escape and avoidance learning. *Journal of Comparative and Physiological Psychology, 63*, 23–33.

OWEN, M. T., & COX, J. J. (1988). Maternal employment and the transition to parenthood. In A. E. Gottfried & A. W. Gottfried (Eds.), *Maternal employment and children's development*. New York: Plenum Press.

PADDEN, C., & HUMPHRIES, T. (1989). *Deaf in America: Voices from a culture*. Cambridge, MA: Harvard University Press.

PALEY, V. G. (1981). *Wally's stories*. Cambridge, MA: Harvard University Press.

PALEY, V. G. (1984). *Boys and girls*. Chicago: University of Chicago Press.

PALEY, V. G. (1986). *Mollie is three: Growing up in school*. Chicago: University of Chicago Press.

PALEY, V. G. (1990). *The boy who would be a helicopter*. Cambridge, MA: Harvard University Press.

PALINCSAR, A. S., & BROWN, A. L. (1984). Reciprocal teaching of comprehension fostering and monitoring activities. *Cognition and Instruction, 1*, 117–175.

PALMER, C. E. (1989). The discriminating nature of infants' exploratory actions. *Developmental Psychology, 25*, 885–893.

PARIS, S. G., NEWMAN, R. S., & JACOBS, J. E. (1985). Social contexts and functions of children's remembering. In M. Pressley & C. Brainard (Eds.), *Cognitive learning and memory in children: Progress in cognitive development research*. Berlin: Springer-Verlag.

PARKE, R. D. (1981). *Fathers*. Cambridge, MA: Harvard University Press.

PARKE, R. & COLLMER, C. (1975). Child abuse: An interdisciplinary review. In E. M. Hetherington (Ed.), *Review of child developent research* Vol 5. Chicago: University of Chicago Press.

PARKE, R. D., & SLABY, R. G. (1983). The development of aggression. In P. H. Mussen (Ed.), *Handbook of child psychology: Vol. 4. Socialization, personality, and social behavior*. New York: Wiley.

PARKE, R. D., & SAWIN, D. B. (1975). Infant characteristics and behavior as initiators of maternal and paternal responsivity. Paper presented at the Biennial Meeting of the Society for Research in Child Development, Denver, CO.

PARKE, R. D., & TINSLEY, B. R. (1981). The father's role in infancy: Determinants of involvement in caregiving and play. In M. E. Lamb (Ed.), *The role of the father in child development* (2nd ed.). New York: Wiley.

PARKER, J. G., & ASHER, S. R. (1987). Peer relations and later personal adjustment: Are low-accepted children "at risk"? *Psychological Bulletin, 102*, 357–389.

PARKER, J. G., & GOTTMAN, J. M. (1989). Social and emotional development in a relational context: friendship interactions from early childhood to adolescence. In T. J. Berndt & G. W. Ladd (Eds.), *Peer relationships in child development*. New York: Wiley.

PARKER, S. T., & GIBSON, K. R. (Eds.). (1990). *"Language" and intelligence in monkey and apes: Comparative developmental perspectives*. Cambridge: Cambridge University Press.

PARSONSON, B. S., & NAUGHTON, K. A. (1988). Training generalized conservation in 5-year-old children. *Journal of Experimental Child Psychology, 46*, 372–390.

PASCUAL-LEONE, J. (1988). Organismic processes for neo-Piagetian theories: A dialetical causal account of cognitive development. In A. Demetriou (Ed.), *The neo-Piagetian theories of cognitive development: Toward an integration*. Amsterdam: Elsevier.

PATTEN, B. M. (1968). *Human embryology* (3rd ed.). New York: McGraw-Hill.

PATTERSON, G. R. (1976). The aggressive child: Victim and architect of a coercive system. In E. J. Marsh, L. A. Hamerlynk, & L. C. Handy (Eds.), *Behavior modification and families: Vol. 1. Theory and research*. New York: Brunner/Mazel.

PATTERSON, G. R. (1979). A performance theory of coercive family interaction. In R. Cairns (Ed.), *Social Interaction: Methods*. Hillsdale, NJ: Erlbaum.

PATTERSON, G. R. (1982). *Coercive family processes*. Eugene, OR: Castalia Press.

PATTERSON, G. R., DEBARYSHE, B. D., & RAMSEY, E. (1989). A developmental perspective on anti-social behavior. *American Psychologist, 44*, 329–335.

PATTERSON, G. R., LITTMAN, R. A., & BRICKER, W. (1967). Assertive behavior in young children: A step toward a theory of aggression. *Monographs of the Society for Research for Child Development, 32*(Serial No. 113).

PAVLOV, I. P. (1927). *Conditioned reflexes*. Oxford: Oxford University Press.

PEEVERS, B. H., & SECORD, P. F. (1973). Developmental changes in attribution of descriptive concepts to persons. *Journal of Personality and Social Psychology, 27*, 120–128.

PEIPER, A. (1963). *Cerebral function in infancy and childhood*. New York: Consultants Bureau.

PENCE, A. R. (Ed.) (1988). *Ecological research with children and families: From concepts to methodology*. New York: Teachers College Press.

PEPPER, S. C. (1942). *World hypotheses, a study in evidence*. Berkeley: University of California Press.

PERCY, W. (1975). *The message in the bottle*. New York: Farrar, Straus & Giroux.

PERLMUTTER, M. (1986). A life-span view of memory. In P. B. Baltes & D. Featherman (Eds.). *Life-span development and behavior*: Vol. 7. San Diego: Academic Press.

PERLMUTTER, M., KAPLAN, M., & NYQUIST, L. (1990). Development of adaptive competence in adulthood. *Human Development, 33,* 185–197.

PERNOLL, M. L., BENDA, G. I., & BABSON, S. G. (1986). *Diagnosis and management of the fetus and neonate at risk: A guide for team care* (5th ed.). St. Louis: Mosby.

PERRET-CLERMONT, A. N., PERRET, J. F., & BELL, N. (1991). The social construction of meaning and cognitive activity in elementary school children. In L. B. Resnick, J. M. Levine, & S. D. Teaseley (Eds.), *Perspectives on socially shared cognition*. Washington, DC: American Psychological Association.

PERRY, D. G., & BUSSEY, K. (1984). *Social development*. Englewood Cliffs, NJ: Prentice-Hall.

PERSAUD, T. V. N. (1977). *Problems of birth defects: From Hippocrates to thalidomide and after*. Baltimore: University Park Press.

PESKIN, H. (1967). Pubertal onset and ego functioning. *Journal of Abnormal Psychology, 72,* 1–15.

PESKIN, J. (1980). Female performance and Inhelder's and Piaget's tests of formal operations. *Genetic Psychology Monographs, 101,* 245–256.

PETERSEN, A. C., & CROCKER, L. (1985). Pubertal timing and grade effects on adjustment. *Journal of Youth and Adolescence, 14,* 191–206.

PETTITO, L. A. & MARENTETTE, P. F. (1991). Babbling in the manual mode: Evidence for the ontogeny of language. *Science, 251,* 1493–1496.

PFEIFFER, J. (1977). *The emergence of society: A prehistory of the establishment*. New York: McGraw-Hill.

PHILLIPS, D., MCCARTNEY, K., SCARR, S., & HOWES, C. (1987). Selective review of infant day care research: A cause for concern! *Zero to Three, 1*(3), 18–21.

PIAGET, J. (1926). *The language and thought of the child*. New York: Meridian Books.

PIAGET, J. (1928). *Judgment and reasoning in the child*. London: Routledge & Kegan Paul.

PIAGET, J. (1930). *The child's conception of physical causality*. New York: Harcourt Brace.

PIAGET, J. (1952a). *The child's conception of number*. New York: W. W. Norton.

PIAGET, J. (1952b). *The origins of intelligence in children*. New York: International Universities Press.

PIAGET, J. (1954). *The construction of reality in the child*. New York: Basic Books.

PIAGET, J. (1962). *Play, dreams and imitation*. New York: W. W. Norton.

PIAGET, J. (1965). *The moral judgment of the child*. New York: Free Press. (Original work published 1932).

PIAGET, J. (1967). *Six psychological studies*. New York: Random House.

PIAGET, J. (1972). Intellectual evolution from adolescence to adulthood. *Human Development, 15,* 1–12.

PIAGET, J. (1973). *The psychology of intelligence*. Totowa, NJ: Littlefield & Adams.

PIAGET, J. (1966/1974). Nécessité et signification des recherches comparatives en psychologie génétique. [Need and significance of cross-cultural studies in genetic psychology.] In. J. W. Berry & P. R. Dasen (Eds.), *Culture and Cognition*. London: Methuen.

PIAGET, J. (1977). *The development of thought: Equilibration of cognitive structure*. New York: Viking.

PIAGET, J. (1929/1979). *The child's conception of the world*. New York: Harcourt Brace.

PIAGET, J. (1980). Schemes of action and language learning. In M. Piattelli-Palmarini (Ed.), *Language and Learning: The debate between Jean Piaget and Noam Chomsky*. Cambridge, MA: Harvard University Press.

PIAGET, J. (1983). Piaget's theory. In P. H. Mussen (Ed.), *Handbook of child psychology*: Vol 1. *History, theory and methods*. New York: Wiley.

PIAGET, J., & INHELDER, B. (1956). *The child's conception of space*. London: Routledge & Kegan Paul.

PIAGET, J., & INHELDER, B. (1969). *The psychology of the child*. New York: Basic Books.

PIAGET, J., & INHELDER, B. (1973). *Memory and intelligence.* New York: Basic Books.

PIANTA, R., EGELAND, B., & ERICKSON, M. F., (1989). Results of the mother-child interaction research project. In D. Cicchetti & V. Carlson (Eds.), *Child Maltreatment: Theory and research on the causes and consequences of child abuse and neglect.* Cambridge: Cambridge University Press.

PIATTELLI-PALMARINI, M. (1980). *Language and learning.* Cambridge, MA: Harvard University Press.

PINKER, S. (1989). *Learnability and cognition.* Cambridge, MA: MIT Press.

PLATO. (1945). *The republic.* (F. M. Cornford, Trans.). London: Oxford University Press.

PLOMIN, R. (1986). *Developmental genetics and psychology.* Hillsdale, NJ: Erlbaum.

PLOMIN, R. (1990). *Nature and nurture: An introduction to human behavioral genetics.* Pacific Grove, CA: Brooks/Cole.

PLOMIN, R., & BERGEMAN, C. S. (1991). The nature of nuture: Genetic influence on "environmental" measures. *Behavioral and Brain Sciences, 14*(3), 373–427.

PLOMIN, R., & DEFRIES, J. C. (1983). The Colorado adoption project. *Child Development, 54,* 276–289.

PLOMIN, R., & DE FRIES, J. C. (1985). *Origins of individual differences in infancy.* New York: Academic Press.

PLOMIN, R., DE FRIES, J. C., & MCCLEARN, G. (1990). *Behavioral genetics: A primer* (2nd ed.). New York: W. H. Freeman.

PLONIM, R., & DANIELS, D. (1987). Why are children in the same family so different from each other? *The Behavioral and Brain Sciences, 10,* 1–16.

PLOMIN, R. & DUNN, J. (1986). *The study of temperament: Changes, continuities and challenges.* Hillsdale, NJ: Erlbaum.

POTTS, R., HUSTON, A., & WRIGHT, J. (1986). The effects of television form and violent content on boys' attention and social behavior. *Journal of Experimental Child Psychology, 41,* 1–17.

POWER, C. HIGGINS, A., & KOHLBERG, L. (1989). *Lawrence Kohlberg's approach to moral education.* New York: Columbia University Press.

PRATT, H. (1954). The neonate. In L. Carmichael (Ed.), *Manual of child psychology* (2nd ed.). New York: Wiley.

PRECHTL, H. (1977). *The neurological examination of the full-term newborn infant* (2nd ed.). Philadelphia: Lippincott.

PREISSER, D. A., HODSON, B. W., & PADEN, E. P. (1988). Developmental phonology: 18–29 months. *Journal of Speech and Hearing Disorders, 53,* 125–130.

PREMACK, D., & PREMACK, A. J. (1983). *The mind of an ape.* New York: W. W. Norton.

PRESCOTT, E., & JONES, E. (1971). Day care of children—assets and liabilities. *Children, 18,* 54–58.

PRESIDENT'S SCIENCE ADVISORY COMMITTEE (1974). *Youth: Transition to adulthood.* Chicago: University of Chicago Press.

PROVINE, R. R. (1986). Behavioral neuro-embryology: Motor perspectives. In W. J. Greenough & J. Juraska (Eds.), *Developmental neuropsychology.* New York: Academic Press.

PRICE-WILLIAMS, D., GORDON, W., & RAMIREZ, M. (1969). Skill and conservation: A study of pottery-making children. *Developmental Psychology, 1,* 769.

PRITCHARD, J. A., & MACDONALD, P. C. (1980). *Williams' Obstetrics* (16th ed.). New York: Appleton-Century-Crofts.

PURVES, D., & LICHTMAN, J. W. (1985). *Principles of neural development.* Sunderland, MA: Sinauer Associates.

PUTALLAZ, M. (1983). Predicting children's sociometric status from their behavior. *Child Development, 54,* 1417–1426.

PUTALLAZ, M. (1987). Maternal behavior and children's sociometric status. *Child Development, 58,* 324–340.

PUTALLAZ, M., & GOTTMAN, J. M. (1981). Social skills and group acceptance. In S. R. Asher & J. M. Gottman (Eds.), *The development of children's friendships.* Cambridge: Cambridge University Press.

PUTALLAZ, M. & HEFLIN, A. H. (1990). Parent-child interaction. In S. R. Asher & J. D. Coie (Eds.), *Peer rejection in childhood.* New York: Cambridge University Press.

QUANTY, M. B. (1976). Aggression catharsis: Experimental investigations and implications. In R. G. Green & E. C. O'Neal (Eds.), *Perspectives on aggression.* New York: Academic Press.

QUINTON, D., & RUTTER, M. (1976). Early hospital admissions and later disturbances of behavior: An attempted replication of Douglas' findings. *Developmental Medicine and Child Neurology, 18,* 447–459.

QUINTON, D., & RUTTER, M. (1985). Parenting behavior of mothers raised "in care." In A. R. Nicol (Ed.), *Longitudinal studies in child psychology and psychiatry: Practical lessons from research experience.* New York: Wiley.

RABIN, A. J. (1965). *Growing up in the kibbutz.* New York: Springer-Verlag.

RABINOWICZ, T. (1979). The differentiate maturation of the human cerebral cortex. In F. Falkner & J. M. Tanner (Eds.), *Human growth:* Vol. 3. *Neurobiology and nutrition.* New York: Plenum Press.

RADER, N., BAUSANO, M., & RICHARDS, J. (1980). On the nature of the visual-cliff avoidance response in human infants. *Child Development, 51,* 61–68.

RADKE-YARROW, M., ZAHN-WAXLER, C., & CHAPMAN, M. (1983). Children's prosocial dispositions and behavior. In P. H. Mussen (Ed.), *Handbook of child psychology:* Vol. 4. *Socialization, personality, and social behavior.* New York: Wiley.

RANK, O. (1929). *The trauma of birth.* New York: Harcourt Brace.

RASMUSSEN, L., HIGHTOWER, R., & RASMUSSEN, P. (1964). *Mathematics for the primary school teacher.* Chicago: Learning Materials.

RAUM, O. F. (1940/1967). *Chaga childhood.* Oxford: Oxford University Press.

RAUSCH, W. A., BARRY, R. K., HERTEL, R. K., & SWAIN, M. A. (1974). *Communication, conflict, and marriage.* San Francisco: Jossey-Bass.

RAVEN, J. C. (1962). *Coloured progressive matrices.* London: H. K. Lewis & Co., Ltd.

RAWLS, J. (1971). *A theory of justice.* Cambridge, MA: Harvard University Press.

READ, M. (1960/1968). *Children of their fathers: Growing up among the Ngoni of Malawi.* New York: Holt, Rinehart & Winston.

REICHEL-DOMATOFF, G., & REICHEL-DOLMATOFF, A. (1961). *The people of Aritama.* London: Routledge & Kegan Paul.

REISS, I. L. (1972). Premarital sexuality: Past, present and future. In I. L. Reiss (Ed.), *Readings on the family system.* New York: Holt, Rinehart & Winston.

REISSLAND, N. (1988). Neonatal imitation in the first hour of life: Observations in rural Nepal. *Developmental Psychology, 24,* 464–469.

RESNICK, D. P., & RESNICK, L. B. (1977). The nature of literacy: A historical exploration. *Harvard Educational Review, 47,* 370–385.

RESNICK, L. B., & FORD, W. W. (1981). *The psychology of mathematics instruction.* Hillsdale, NJ: Erlbaum.

REST, J. R. (1979). *Development in judging moral issues.* Minneapolis: University of Minnesota Press.

REST, J. R. (1983). Morality. In P. H. Mussen (Ed.), *Handbook of child psychology:* Vol. 3. *Cognitive development.* New York: Wiley.

REYNOLDS, P. (1989). *Childhood in crossroads: Cognition and society in South Africa.* Grand Rapids, MI: Eerdmans Publishing.

RHEINGOLD, H. L. (1982). Little children's participation in the work of adults, a nascent prosocial behavior. *Child Development, 53,* 114–125.

RICE, M. L. (1990). Preschooler's QUIL: Quick incidental learning of words. In G. Conti Ramsden & C. E. Snow (Eds.), *Children's Language:* Vol. 7. Hillsdale, NJ: Erlbaum.

RICE, M. L., & WOODSMALL, L. (1988). Lessons from television: Children's word learning when viewing. *Child Development, 59,* 420–429.

RICHARDS, J., & RADER, N. (1981). Crawlingonset age predicts visual cliff avoidance in infants. *Journal of Experimental Psychology: Human Perception and Performance, 7,* 382–387.

RICHARDSON, G. A., DAY, N. L., & TAYLOR, P. M. (1989). The effects of prenatal alcohol, marijuana, and tobacco exposure. *Infant Behavior and Development, 12,* 199–210.

RIESEN, A. H. (1950). Arrested vision. *Scientific American, 183,* 16–19.

RIMLAND, B. (1964). *Infantile autism: The syndrome and its implications for a neural theory of behavior.* New York: Appleton-Century-Crofts.

RITTER, K. (1978). The development of an external retrieval cue strategy. *Child Development, 49,* 1227–1230.

ROBBINS, L. C. (1963). The accuracy of parental remembering of aspects of child development and of child rearing practices. *Journal of Abnormal and Social Psychology, 66,* 261–270.

ROBBINS, L. N., & RUTTER, M. (1990). *Straight and devious paths from childhood to adulthood.* New York: Cambridge University Press.

ROBINSON, J. P. (1989). Caring for kids. *American Demographics, 11,* 52.

ROBSON, K. S., & MOSS, H. A. (1970). Patterns and determinants of maternal attachment. *Journal of Pediatrics, 77,* 976–985.

ROCHAT, P. (1989). Object manipulation and exploration in 2- to 5-month-old infants. *Developmental Psychology, 25,* 871–886.

RODIN, J. (1986). Aging and health: Effects of the sense of control. *Science, 233,* 1271–1275.

RODIN, J., & LANGER, E. J. (1977). Long-term effects of a control-relevant intervention with the institutionalized aged. *Journal of Personality and Social Psychology, 35,* 897–902.

ROGOFF, B. (1978). Spot observation: An introduction and examination. *Quarterly Newsletter of the Laboratory of Comparative Human Cognition, 2,* 21–26.

ROGOFF, B. (1981). Schooling and the development of cognitive skills. In H. C. Triandis & A. Heron (Eds.), *Handbook of cross-cultural psychology* (Vol. 4). Boston: Allyn & Bacon.

ROGOFF, B. (1982). Integrating context and cognitive development. In M. E. Lamb & A. L. Brown (Eds.), *Advances in developmental psychology* (Vol. 2). Hillsdale, NJ: Erlbaum.

ROGOFF, B. (1990). *Apprenticeship in thinking: Cognitive development in social context.* Oxford: Oxford University Press.

ROGOFF, B., & LAVE, J. (1984). *Everyday cognition.* Cambridge, MA: Harvard University Press.

ROGOFF, B., & MISTRY, J. (1990). The social and functional context of children's remembering. In R. Fivush & J. A. Hudson (Eds.), *Knowing and remembering in young children.* New York: Cambridge University Press.

ROGOFF, B., NEWCOMBE, N., FOX, N., & ELLIS, S. (1980). Transitions in children's roles and capabilities. *International Journal of Psychology, 15,* 181–200.

ROGOFF, B., SELLERS, M. J., PIRROTTA, S., FOX, N., & WHITE, S. H. (1975). Age of assignment of roles and responsibilities to children: A cross-cultural survey. *Human Development, 18,* 353–369.

ROGOFF, B., & WADDELL, K. J. (1982). Memory for information organized in a scene by children from two cultures. *Child Development, 53,* 1224–1228.

ROSALDO, M. Z. (1984). Toward an ethnography of self and feeling. In R. Shweder & R. A. LeVine (Eds.), *Culture theory: Essays on mind, self, and emotion.* Cambridge: Cambridge University Press.

ROSALDO, M. Z., & LAMPHERE, L. (Eds.). (1974). *Women, culture, and society.* Stanford: Stanford University Press.

ROSE, S. A., FELDMAN, J. F., WALLACE, I. F., & MCCARTON, C. (1991). Information processing at 1 year: Relation to birth status and developmental outcome during the first 5 years. *Developmental Psychology, 27,* 723–737.

ROSENBLITH, J. F., & SIMS-KNIGHT, J. E. (1985). *In the beginning: development in the first two years of life.* Monterey, CA: Brooks/Cole.

ROSENSTEIN, D., & OSTER, H. (1988). Differential facial responses to four basic tastes in newborns. *Child Development, 59,* 1555–1568.

ROSENTHAL, R. (1987). Pygmalian effects: Existence, magnitude, and social importance. *Educational Researcher, 16(9),* 37–41.

ROSENTHAL, R., BARATZ, S. S., & HALL, C. M. (1974). Teacher behavior, teacher expectations, and gains in pupils' rated creativity. *Journal of Genetic Psychology, 124,* 115–121.

ROSENTHAL, R., & JACOBSEN, L. (1968). *Pygmalion in the classroom: Teacher expectation and pupils' intellectual development.* New York: Holt, Rinehart & Winston.

ROSENTHAL, R., & RUBIN, D. B. (1978). Interpersonal expectancy effects: The first 345 studies. *Behavioral and Brain Sciences, 3,* 377–415.

ROSENZWEIG, M. R. (1984). Experience, memory, and the brain. *American Psychologist, 39,* 365–376.

ROSENZWEIG, M. R., BENNETT, E. L., & DIAMOND, M. C. (1972). Brain changes in response to experience. *The nature and nurture of behavior: Development psychobiology.* New York: W. H. Freeman.

ROSIER, P. (1977). *A comparative study of two approaches of introducing initial reading to Navajo children: The direct method and the native language method.* Ph.D. dissertation, Northern Arizona University.

ROSSO, P. (1990). *Nutrition and metabolism in pregnancy.* Oxford: Oxford University Press.

ROUSSEAU, J. J. (1762/1911). *Emile; or On education.* London: Dent.

ROVEE-COLLIER, C. K. (1984). The ontogeny of learning in infancy. In R. V. Kail, Jr. & N. E. Spear (Eds.), *Comparative perspectives on the development of memory.* Hillsdale, NJ: Erlbaum.

ROVEE-COLLIER, C. K. (1987). Learning and memory. In J. D. Osofsky (Ed.), *Handbook of infant development* (2nd ed.). New York: Wiley.

ROVEE-COLLIER, C. K. (1990). The "memory system" of prelinguistic infants. *Annals of the New York Academy of Sciences, 608,* 517–542.

ROVEE-COLLIER, C. K., SULLIVAN, M. W., ENRIGHT, M., LUCAS, D., & FAGAN, J. W. (1980). Reactivation of infant memory. *Science, 208,* 1159–1161.

ROVET, J., & NETLEY, C. (1982). Processing deficits in Turner's syndrome. *Developmental Psychology, 18,* 77–94.

RUBIN, J. Z., PROVEZANO, F. J., & LURIA, Z. (1974). The eye of the beholder: Parents' view on sex of newborns. *American Journal of Orthopsychiatry, 44,* 512–519.

RUBIN, K. H. (1973). Egocentrism in childhood: A unitary construct? *Child Development, 44,* 102–110.

RUBIN, K. H., FEIN, G. G., & VANDENBERG, B. (1983). Play. In P. H. Mussen (Ed.), *Handbook of child psychology: Vol. 4. Socialization, personality, and social behavior.* New York: Wiley.

RUBIN, Z. (1980). *Children's friendships.* Cambridge, MA: Harvard University Press.

RUBLE, D. N., BOGGIANO, A. K., FELDMAN, N. S., & LOEBL, J. H. (1980). Developmental analysis of the role of social comparison in self-evaluation. *Developmental Psychology, 16,* 105–115.

RUBLE, D. N., & BROOKS-GUNN, J. (1982). The experience of menarche. *Child Development, 53,* 1557–1666.

RUBLE, D. N., & FREY, K. S. (1991). Changing patterns of comparative behavior as skills are acquired: A functional model of self-evaluation. In J. Suls & T. H. Wells (Eds.), *Social comparison: Contemporary theory and research.* Hillsdale, NJ: Erlbaum.

RUFF, H. (1978). Infant recognition of the invariant form of objects. *Child Development, 49,* 293–306.

RUOPP, R., TRAVERS, J., GLANTZ, F., & COELEN, C. (1979). *Children at the center. Final report of the national day care study.* Cambridge: Abt Books.

RUTTER, M. (1976). Maternal deprivation 1972–1978: New findings, new concepts, new approaches. *Child Development, 50,* 283–305.

RUTTER, M. (1985). Psychopathology and development: Links between childhood and adult life. In M. Rutter & L. Hersov (Eds.), *Child and adolescent psychiatry: Modern approaches* (2nd ed.). Oxford: Oxford University Press.

RUTTER, M. (1989). Pathways from childhood to adult life. *Journal of Child Psychology and Psychiatry, 30,* 23–51.

RUTTER, M., & GARMEZY, N. (1983). Developmental psychopathology. In P. H. Mussen (Ed.), *Handbook of child psychology: Vol. 4. Socialization, personality, and social development.* New York: Wiley.

RUTTER, M., & HERSOV, L. (1985). *Child and adolescent psychiatry: Modern approaches* (2nd. ed.). Oxford: Oxford University Press.

RUTTER, M., MAUGHAN, B., MORTIMORE, P., & OUSTON, J. (1979). *Fifteen thousand hours: Secondary schools and their effects on children.* Cambridge, MA: Harvard University Press.

RUTTER, M. QUINTON, D., & HILL, J. (1990). Adult outcome of insitution-reared children. In L. Robins & M. Rutter (Eds.), *Straight and devious pathways from childhood to adulthood.* Cambridge: Cambridge University Press.

RUTTER, M., YULE, B., QUINTON, D., ROWLAND, O., YULE, W., & BERGER, M. (1975). Attainment and adjustment in two geographical areas: III. Some factors accounting for area differences. *British Journal of Psychiatry, 126,* 520–533.

SACHS, J., BARD, B., & JOHNSON, M. (1981). Language learning with restricted input; Case studies of two hearing children of deaf parents. *Applied Psycholinguistics, 2,* 33–54.

SACHS, J., & DEVIN, J. (1973). Young children's knowledge of age-appropriate speech styles. Paper presented to Linguistic Society of America.

SAGI, A., LAMB, M. E., LEWKOWICZ, K. S., SHOHAM, R., DVIR, R., & ESTES, D. (1985). Security of infant-mother, -father, and metapelet attachments among kibbutz reared Israeli children. *Monographs of the Society for Research in Child Development, 50*(1–2, Serial No. 209).

SALAPATEK, P. (1975). Pattern perception in early infancy. In L. B. Cohen & P. Salapatek (Eds.), *Basic visual processes:* Vol. 1. *Infant perception: From sensation to cognition.* New York: Academic Press.

SALE, R. (1978). *Fairy tales and after.* Cambridge, MA: Harvard University Press.

SALK, L. (1973). The role of the heartbeat in the relationship between mother and infant. *Scientific American, 228*(3), 24–29.

SALKIND, N. J., & NELSON, C. F. (1980). A note on the developmental nature of reflection-impulsivity. *Developmental Psychology, 16*, 237–238.

SALOMON, G. L. (1984). Television is "easy" and print is "tough': The differential investment of mental effort in learning as a function of perceptions and attributions. *Journal of Educational Psychology, 76*, 647–658.

SALZINGER, S. (1990). Social networks in child rearing and child development. In S. M. Pfafflin, J. A. Sechzer, J. M. Fish, & R. L. Thompson (Eds.), *Psychology: Perspectives and practice.* New York: New York Academy of Science.

SAMELSON, R. (1980). J. B. Watson's little Albert, Cyril Burt's twins, and the need for a critical science. *American Psychologist, 35*, 619-625.

SAMEROFF, A. (1978). Organization and stability of newborn behavior: A commentary on the Brazelton Neonatal Behavior Assessment Scale. *Monographs of Society for Research in Child Development, 43*(5–6, Serial No. 177).

SAMEROFF, A. J. (1983). Developmental systems: Contexts and evolutions. In P. H. Mussen (Ed.), *Handbook of child psychology:* Vol. 1. *History, theory and methods.* New York: Wiley.

SAMEROFF, A. J. (1989). Models of developmental regulation: The environtype. In D. Cicchetti (Ed.). *The emergence of a discipline: Rochester Symposium on Developmental Psychopathology* Vol. 1. Hillsdale, NJ: Erlbaum.

SAMEROFF, A. J., & CAVANAUGH, P. J. (1979). Learning in infancy: A developmental perspective. In J. D. Osofsky (Ed.), *Handbook of infant development.* New York: Wiley.

SAMEROFF, A. J., & CHANDLER, M. J. (1975). Reproductive risk and the continuum of caretaking casualty. In F. D. Horowitz (Ed.), *Review of child development research*, Vol. 4. Chicago: University of Chicago Press.

SAMEROFF, A. J., SEIFER, R., BAROCAS, R., ZAX, M., & GREENSPAN, S. (1987). Intelligence quotient scores of 4-year-old children: Social environmental risk factors. *Pediatrics, 79*, 343–350.

SANDVEN, K. & RESNICK, M. (1990). Informal adoption among black adolescent mothers. *American Journal of Orthopsychiatry, 60*, 210–224.

SAVAGE-RUMBAUGH, S. (1990). Language as a cause-effect communication system. *Philosophical Psychology, 3*, 55–76.

SAVAGE-RUMBAUGH, S., MCDONALD, K., SEVCIK, R. A., HOPKINS, W. D., & RUBERT, E. (1986). Spontaneous symbol acquisition and communication use by pygmy chimpanzees. *Journal of Experimental Psychology: General, 115*, 211–235.

SAVIN-WILLIAMS, R. C. (1987). *Adolescence: An ethological perspective.* New York: Springer-Verlag.

SAVIN-WILLIAMS, R. C. (1990). *Gay and Lesbian Youth: Expressions of identity.* New York: Hemisphere Publishing Corporation.

SAVIN-WILLIAMS, R. C. & BERNDT, T. J. (1990). Friendships and peer relations. In S. S. Feldman & G. R. Elliott (Eds.), *At the threshhold: The developing adolescent.* Cambridge, MA: Harvard University Press.

SAXE, G. B. (1981). Body parts as numerals: A developmental analysis of numeration among the Oksapmin in Papua, New Guinea. *Child Development, 52*, 306–316.

SAXE, G. B. (1991). *Culture and cognitive development: Studies in mathematical understanding.* Hillsdale, NJ: Erlbaum.

SCANZONI, L., & SCANZONI, J. (1976). *Men, women and change: A sociology of marriage and family.* New York: McGraw-Hill.

SCARR, S. (1981). *Race, social class and individual differences in I.Q.* Hillsdale, NJ: Erlbaum.

SCARR. S. (1992). Developmental theories for the 1990's: Development and individual differences. *Child Development, 63*, 1–19.

SCARR, S., & MCCARTNEY, K. (1983). How people make their own environments: A theory of genotype-environment effects. *Child Development, 54*, 424–435.

SCARR, S., PHILLIPS, D., & MCCARTNEY, K. (1990). Facts, fantasies, and the future of child care in the United States. *Psychological Science, 1*, 26–35.

SCARR, S., & WEINBERG, R. A. (1976). IQ performance of black children adopted by white families. *American Psychologist, 31*, 726–739.

SCARR, S., & WEINBERG, R. (1977). Intellectual similarities within families of both adopted and biological children. *Intelligence, 2,* 170–191.

SCARR, S. & WEINBERG. R. A. (1983). The Minnesota adoption studies: Genetic differences and malleability. *Child Development, 54,* 260–267.

SCHAEFER, E. S. (1959). A circumplex model for maternal behavior. *Journal of Abnormal and Social Psychology, 59,* 226–235.

SCHAFFER, H. R. (1974). Cognitive components of the infant's response to strangeness. In M. Lewis & L. Rosenblum (Eds.), *The origins of fear.* New York: Wiley.

SCHAIE, K. W. (1990). Developmental design revisited. In H. W. Reese & S. H. Cohen (Eds.), *Life-span developmental psychology: Methodological issues.* Hillsdale, NJ: Erlbaum.

SCHAIE, K. W., & HERTZOG, C. (1985). Measurement in the psychology of aging. In J. E. Birren & K. W. Schaie (Eds.), *Handbook of the psychology of aging* (2nd ed.). New York: Van Nostrand Reinhold.

SCHAIE, K. W., & LABOUVIE-VIEF, G. (1974). Generational versus ontogenetic components of change in adult cognitive behavior. *Developmental Psychology, 10,* 305–320.

SCHAIE, K. W., & WILLS, S. L. (1991). *Adult development and aging.* (3rd ed.). New York: Harper & Row.

SCHALLER, S. (1991). *A man without words.* New York: Summit.

SCHEINFELD, A. (1972). *Heredity in humans.* Philadelphia: Lippincott.

SCHEPER-HUGHES, N. (1992). *Death without weeping: The violence of everyday life in Brazil.* Berkeley: University of California Press.

SCHINDLER, P. J., MOELY, B., & FRANK, A. L. (1987). Time in day care and social participation of young children. *Developmental Psychology, 23,* 255–261.

SCHLEGEL, A., & BARRY, H. (1991). *Adolescence: An anthropological inquiry.* New York: Free Press.

SCHMANDT-BESSERAT, D. (1978). The earliest precursor of writing. *Scientific American, 283,* 50–59.

SCHNEIDER, B. H., ATTILI, G., NADEL, J., & WEISSBERG, R. P. (Eds.). (1989). *Social competence in developmental perspective: Proceedings of the NATO advanced study institute on social competence in developmental perspective, Les Arcs, France, July 8–18.* Dordecht, The Netherlands: Kluwer Academic Publishers.

SCHNEIDER-ROSEN, K., BRAUNWALD, K., CARLSON, V., & CICCHETTI, D. (1985). Current perspectives in attachment theory: Illustration from the study of maltreated infants. *Monographs of the Society for Research in Child Development, 50*(1–2, Serial No. 209).

SCHNOLL, S. H. (1986). Drug use in pregnancy: Mother and child. In I. J. Chasnoff (Ed.), *Pharmacologic basis of perinatal addiction.* Lancaster, England: MTP Press.

SCHOGGEN, P. (1989). *Behavior settings: a revision and extension of Roger G. Barker's Ecological Psychology.* Stanford, CA: Stanford University Press.

SCHRAMM, W., BARNES, D., & BLACK-WELL, J. (1987). Neonatal mortality in Missouri home births. *American Journal of Public Health, 77,* 930–935.

SCHOOLER, C., & SCHAIE, K. W. (Eds.). (1987). *Cognitive functioning and social structure over the life course.* Norwood, NJ: Ablex.

SCHWARTZMAN, H. B. (1980). *Play and culture.* West Point, NY: Leisure Press.

SCRIBNER, S., & COLE, M. (1973). Cognitive consequences of formal and informal education. *Science, 182,* 553–559.

SEARLE, J. (1969). *Speech acts.* Cambridge: Cambridge University Press.

SEARS, R., MACCOBY, E., & LEVIN, H. (1957). *Patterns of childrearing.* Evanston, IL: Row, Peterson.

SEBALD, H. (1981). Adolescent's concept of popularity and unpopularity: Comparing 1960 with 1976. *Adolescence, 16,* 187–193.

SECORD, P., & PEEVERS, B. H. (1974). The development and attribution of person concepts. In T. Mischel (Ed.), *Understanding other persons.* Totowa, NJ: Rowman and Littlefield.

SEGALL, M. H., DASEN, P. R., BERRY, J. W., & POORTINGA, Y. H. (1990). *Human behavior in global perspective: An introduction to cross-cultural psychology.* New York: Pergamon Press.

SELFE, L. (1977). *Nadia: A case of extraordinary drawing ability in an autistic child.* New York: Academic Press.

SELFE, L. (1983). *Normal and anomalous representational drawing ability in children.* New York: Academic Press.

SELIGMAN, M. (1975). *Helplessness: On depression, development, and death.* New York: W. H. Freeman.

SELMAN, R. L. (1976). Social cognitive understanding. In T. Lickona (Ed.), *Moral development and behavior: Theory, research, and social issues.* New York: Holt, Rinehart & Winston.

SELMAN, R. L. (1980). *The growth of interpersonal understanding: Developmental and clinical analysis.* New York: Academic Press.

SELMAN, R. L. (1981). The child as a friendship philosopher. In S. R. Asher & J. M. Gottman (Eds.), *The development of children's friendships.* Cambridge: Cambridge University Press.

SELMAN, R. L., & SCHULTZ, L. H. (1990). *Making a friend in youth: Developmental theory and pair therapy.* Chicago: University of Chicago Press.

SEPKOWSKI. C. (1985). Maternal obstetric medication and newborn behavior. In J. W. Scanlon (Ed.), *Prenatal anesthesia.* London: Blackwell.

SERBIN, L. A., O'LEARY, K. D., KENT, R. N., & TONICK, I. J. (1973). A comparison of teacher response to the preacademic and problem behavior of boys and girls. *Child Development, 44,* 796–804.

SEVERNE, L. (1982). Psychosocial aspects of the menopause. In A. M. Voda, M. Dinnerstein, & S. O'Donnell (Eds.), *Changing perspectives on menopause.* Austin: University of Texas Press.

SEXTON, P. C. (1961). *Education and income.* New York: Viking Press.

SHAPIRA, A., & MADSEN, M. C. (1969). Cooperative and competitive behavior of kibbutz and urban children in Israel. *Child Development, 4,* 609–617.

SHARP, D. W., COLE, M., & LAVE, C. (1979). Education and cognitive development: The evidence from experimental research. *Monographs of the Society for Research in Child Development, 4,* (1–2, Serial No. 178).

SHATZ, M. (1974). The comprehension of indirect directives: Can you shut the door? Paper presented at Linguistics Society of America, Amherst, MA.

SHATZ, M. (1978). Children's comprehension of question-directives. *Journal of Child Language, 5,* 39–46.

SHATZ, M. (1983). Communication. In P. H. Mussen (Ed.), *Handbook of child psychology:* Vol. 3. *Cognitive development.* New York: Wiley.

SHATZ, M., & GELMAN, R. (1973). The development of communication skills: Modification in the speech of young children as a function of listener. *Monographs of the Society for Research in Child Development, 38*(5, Serial No. 152).

SHAW, G. B. (1963). *George Bernard Shaw on language.* A. Tauben (Ed.). London: Peter Owen.

SHERIF, M., & SHERIF, C. W. (1953). *Groups in harmony and tension.* New York: Harper & Row.

SHERIF, M., & SHERIF, C. W. (1956). *An outline of social psychology.* New York: Harper & Row.

SHERROD, K. B., O'CONNOR, S., VIETZE, P. M., & ALTEMEIER, W. A., III. (1984). Child health and maltreatment. *Child development, 55,* 1174–1183.

SHERROD, L. R. (1979). Social cognition in infants: Attention to the human face. *Infant Behavior and Development, 2,* 279–294.

SHOCK, N. (1960, December). Aging—some social and biological aspects. Symposia presented at the meeting of the American Association for the Advancement of Science, Chicago, IL.

SHOCK, N. (1977). Systems integration. In L. Hayflick & C. E. Finch (Eds.), *Handbook of the biology of aging.* New York: Van Nostrand Reinhold.

SHOPEN, T. (1980). How Pablo says "love" and "store." In T. Shopen & J. M. Williams (Eds.), *Standards and dialects in English.* Cambridge: Winthrop.

SHOSTAK, M. (1981). *Nissa: The life and words of a !Kung Woman.* Cambridge, MA: Harvard University Press.

SHUY, R., & GRIFFIN, P. (Eds.) (1986). The study of children's functional language and education in the early years. *Final report to the Carnegie Corporation of New York.* Arlington, VA: Center for Applied Linguistics.

SHWEDER, R. A. (1982). Liberalism as destiny. *Contemporary Psychology, 27,* 421–424.

SHWEDER, R. A., & BOURNE, E. J. (1984). Does the concept of person vary cross-culturally? In R. A. Shweder & R. A. LeVine (Eds.) *Culture theory: Essays on mind, self, and emotion.* Cambridge: Cambridge University Press.

SHWEDER, R. A., MAHAPATPA, M., & MILLER, J. G. (1987). Culture and moral development. In J. Kagan & S. Lamb (Eds.), *The emergence of morality in young children.* Chicago: University of Chicago Press.

SIEGAL, M. (1991). *Knowing children: Experiments in conversation and cognition.* Hillsdale, NJ: Erlbaum.

SIEGLER, R. S. (1976). Three aspects of cognitive development. *Cognitive Psychology, 8,* 481–520.

SIEGLER, R. S. (1983). Information processing approaches to development. In P. H. Mussen (Ed.), *Handbook of child psychology: Vol. 1. History, theory and methods*. New York: Wiley.

SIEGLER, R. S. (1991). *Children's thinking* (2nd ed.). Englewood Cliffs, NJ: Prentice-Hall.

SIEGLER, R. S., & CROWLEY, K. (1991). The microgenetic method. *American Psychologist, 46, 606–620.*

SIEGLER, R. S., & LIEBERT, R. M. (1975). Acquisition of formal scientific reasoning by 10-and 13-year-olds: Designing a factorial experiment. *Developmental Psychology, 11, 401–402.*

SIEGLER, R. S., & SHRAGER, J. (1984). Strategy choices in addition and subtraction: How do children know what to do? In C. Sophian (Ed.), *Origins of cognitive skills*. Hillsdale, NJ: Erlbaum.

SIGEL, I. E. (Ed.) (1985). *Parental belief systems*. Hillsdale, NJ: Erlbaum.

SIGMAN, M., & PARMELEE, A. H. (1979). Longitudinal evaluation of the preterm infant. In T. M. Field, A. M. Sostek, S. Goldberg, & H. H. Shuman (Eds.), *Infants born at risk: Behavior and development*. Jamaica, NY: Spectrum.

SILVERSTEIN, B. & KRATE, R. (1975). *Children of the dark ghetto: A developmental psychology*. New York: Praeger.

SIMMONS, R. G., & BLYTH, D. A. (1987). *Moving into adolescence: The impact of pubertal change in school context*. New York: A. de Gruyter.

SIMMONS, R. G., BURGESON, R., CARLTON-FORD & BLYTH, D., (1987). The impact of cumulative change in early adolescence. *Child Development, 58, 1220–1234.*

SIMPSON. E. L. (1974). Moral development research: A case of scientific cultural bias. *Human Development, 17, 81–106.*

SINCLAIR DE ZWART, H. (1967). *Acquisition du langage et developpement de la pensée*. Paris: Dunod.

SINCLAIR, J., & COULTHARD, R. M. (1975). *Towards an analysis of discourse: The English used by teachers and pupils*. Oxford: Oxford University Press.

SINGER, D. G., SINGER, J. L., & ZUCKERMAN, D. M. (1980). *Getting the most out of TV*. Santa Monica, CA: Goodyear.

SINGER, J. L. (1980). The powers and limitations of television. In P. Tannenbaum (Ed.), *The entertainment functions of television*. Hillsdale, NJ: Erlbaum.

SINGER, J. L., & SINGER, D. G. (1980). Television viewing, family style and aggressive behavior in preschool children. In M. Green (Ed.), *Violence and the family: Psychiatric, sociological and historical implications*. Boulder, CO: Westview Press.

SINGER, D. G., & SINGER, J. L. (1990). *The house of makebelieve*. Cambridge, MA: Harvard University Press.

SIQUELAND, E. R. (1968). Reinforcement patterns and extinction in human newborns. *Journal of Experimental Child Psychology, 6, 431–432.*

SKINNER. B. F. (1938). *The behavior of organisms*. New York: Appleton-Century-Crofts.

SKINNER, B. F. (1953). *Science and human behavior*. New York: Appleton-Century-Crofts.

SKINNER, B. F. (1957). *Verbal behavior*. New York: Appleton-Century-Crofts.

SKINNER, B. F. & VAUGHN, B. E. (1988). *Enjoying old age*. New York: W. W. Norton.

SKUSE, D. (1984a). Extreme deprivation in early childhood-I. Diverse outcomes for three siblings from an extraordinary family. *Journal of Child Psychology and Psychiatry, 25, 523–541.*

SKUSE, D. (1984b). Extreme deprivation in early childhood -II. Theoretical issues and a comparative review. *Journal of Child Psychology and Psychiatry, 25, 543–572.*

SMELSER, N. J. (1980). Issues in the study of work and love in adulthood. In N. J. Smelser & E. H. Erikson (Eds.), *Themes of work and love in adulthood*. Cambridge, MA: Harvard University Press.

SMETANA, J. G. (1989). Adolescents' and parents' reasoning about actual family conflict. *Child Development, 60, 1052–1067.*

SMITH, E., & UDRY, J. (1985). Coital and non-coital sexual behaviors of white and black adolescents. *American Journal of Public Health, 75, 1200–1203.*

SMITH, L. K. (1989). The influence of education on memory development. Paper presented at the annual meeting of the American Educational Research Association, San Francisco.

SMITH, M. E. (1926). An investigation of the development of the sentence and the extent of vocabulary in young children. *University of Iowa Studies in Child Welfare, 3* (No. 5), 1–92

SMITH, N. V. (1971, Oct. 2). How children learn to speak. *The Listener.*

SMITH, P. K. (1982). Does play matter: Functional and evolutionary aspects of animal and human play. *Behavioral and Brain Sciences, 5,* 139–184.

SMITH, P. K. (1988). Children's play and its role in early development: A re-evaluation of the "play ethos." In A. D. Pellegrini (Ed.), *Psychological bases for early education.* New York: Wiley.

SMITH, P. K. (1990). Rough-and-tumble play, aggression and dominance: Perception and behavior in children's encounters. *Human Development, 33,* 271–282.

SMITH, P. K., & DAGLISH, L. (1977). Sex differences in parent and infant behavior in the home. *Child Development, 48,* 1250–1254.

SMITH, R., ANDERSON, D. R., & FISCHER, C. (1985). Young children's comprehension of montage. *Child Development, 56,* 962–971.

SMITH, R. P. (1958). *Where did you go? OUT. What did you do? Nothing.* New York: W. W. Norton.

SMUTS, H. B. & HAGEN, J. W. (Eds.). (1985). History and research in child development. *Monographs of the Society for Research in Child Development, 50*(4–5, Serial No. 211).

SMYTHE, D. W. (1954). Reality as presented by television. *Public Opinion Quarterly, 18,* 143–156.

SNAREY, J. R. (1985). Cross-cultural universality of social moral development: A critical review of Kohlbergian research. *Psychological Bulletin, 97,* 202–232.

SNOW, C. E. (1972). Mother's speech to children learning language. *Child Development, 43,* 549–565.

SNOW, C. E., ARLMAN-RUPP, A., MASSING, Y., JOBSE, J., JOOSKEN, J., & VORSTER, J. (1976). Mother's speech in three social classes. *Journal of Psycholinguistic Research, 5,* 1–20.

SNOW, C. E., & FERGUSON, C. A. (Eds.). (1977). *Talking to children.* Cambridge: Cambridge University Press.

SNOW, R. E., & YALOW, E. (1982). Education and intelligence. In R. J. Sternberg (Ed.), *Handbook of human intelligence.* Cambridge: Cambridge University Press.

SNYDER, J. J., & PATTERSON, G. R. (1986). The effects of consequences on patterns of social interaction: A quasi-experimental approach to reinforcement in natural interaction. *Child Development, 57,* 1257–1268.

SONG, M., SMETANA, J. G., & KIM, S. Y. (1987). Korean children's conceptions of moral and conventional transgressions. *Developmental Psychology, 23,* 577–582.

SONTAG. L. W. (1941). The significance of fetal environmental differences. *American Journal of Obstetrics and Gynecology, 42,* 996–1003.

SORENSON, R. C. (1973). *Adolescent sexuality in contemporary America.* New York: World.

SOYINKA, W. (1981). *Aké, the years of childhood.* New York: Random House.

SPEARMAN, C. (1927). *The abilities of man.* New York: Macmillan.

SPEIDEL, G. E., & NELSON, K. E. (1989). A fresh look at imitation in language learning. In G. E. Speidel & K. E. Nelson (Eds.), *The many faces of imitation in language learning.* New York: Springer-Verlag.

SPELKE, E. S. (1976). Infants' intermodal perception of events. *Cognitive Psychology, 8,* 553–560.

SPELKE, E. S. (1984). The development of intermodal perception. In L. B. Cohen & P. Salapatek (Eds.), *Handbook of infant perception.* New York: Academic Press.

SPELKE, E. S. (1990). Principles of object perception. *Cognitive Science, 14,* 29–56.

SPELKE, E. S. (1991). Physical knowledge in infancy: Reflections on Piaget's theory. In S. Carey & R. Gelman (Eds.), *The epigenesis of mind.* Hillsdale, NJ: Erlbaum.

SPENCER, M. B. (1988). Self concept development. In D. T. Slaughter (Ed.), *Perspectives on black child development: New directions for child development.* San Francisco: Jossey-Bass.

SPENCER, M. B., & HOROWITZ, F. D. (1973). Effects of systematic social and token reinforcement on the modification of racial and color concept attitudes in black and white preschool children. *Developmental Psychology, 9,* 246–254.

SPENCER, M. B., & MARKSTROM-ADAMS, C. (1990). Identity processes among racial and ethnic minority children in America. *Child Development, 61,* 290–310.

SPIRO, M. E. (1965). *Children of the kibbutz.* New York: Schocken.

SPOCK, B. (1968). *Baby and child care* (rev. ed.). New York: Pocket Books.

SPRUNGER, L., BOYCE, W. T., & GAINS, J. A. (1985). Family-infant congruence: Routines and rhythmicity in family adaptations to a young infant. *Child Development, 56,* 564–572.

SROUFE. L. A. (1979). Socioemotional development. In J. Osofsky (Ed.), *Handbook of infant development.* New York: Wiley.

SROUFE, L. A. (1988). An organizational prespective on the self. In D. Cicchetti & M. Beeghly (Eds.), *Transitions from infancy to childhood: The self.* Chicago: University of Chicago Press.

SROUFE. L. A., & FLEESON, J. (1986). Attachment and the construction of relationships. In W. W. Hartup & Z. Rubin (Eds.), *Relationships and development.* Hillsdale, NJ: Erlbaum.

STAATS, A. W. (1968). *Learning, language, and cognition.* New York: Holt, Rinehart & Winston.

STAHL, S. A., & MILLER, P. A. (1989). Whole language and language experience approaches for beginning readers: A quantitative research synthesis. *Review of Educational Research, 59,* 87–116.

STARKEY, D. (1981). The origins of concept formation: Object sorting and object preference in early infancy. *Child Development, 52,* 489–497.

STATTIN, H., & MAGNUSSON, D. (1990). *Pubertal maturation in female development.* Hillsdale, NJ: Erlbaum

STEIN, Z., SUSSER, M., SAENGER, G., & MAROLLA, F. (1975). *Famine and development: The Dutch hunger winter of 1944–1945.* Oxford: Oxford University Press.

STEINBERG, L. (1989). Pubertal maturation and parent-adolescent distance: An evolutionary perspective. In G. Adams, R. Montemayor, & T. Gullota (Eds.), *Advances in adolescent development* (Vol. 1). Beverly Hills, CA: Sage Publications.

STEINBERG, L. & DORNBUSCH, S. M. (1991). Negative correlates of part-time employment during adolescence: Replication and elaboration. *Developmental Psychology, 27*(2), 304–313.

STEINBERG, L., ELMAN, J. D., & MOUNTS, S. (1989). Authoritative parenting, psychosocial maturity, and academic success among adolescents. *Child Development, 60,* 1424–1436.

STEINER, J. E. (1977). Facial expressions of the neonate infant indicating the hedonics of food related chemical stimuli. In J. N. Weiffenbach (Ed.), *Taste and development: The genesis of sweet preference.* Washington, DC: U.S. Government Printing Office.

STEINER, J. E. (1979). Human facial expressions in response to taste and smell stimulation. In H. W. Reese & L. P. Lipsitt (Eds.), *Advances in child development and behavior* (Vol. 13). New York: Academic Press.

STEPHAN, C. W., & LANGLOIS, J. H. (1984). Baby beautiful: Adult attributions of infant competence as a function of infant attractiveness. *Child Development, 55,* 576–585.

STEPHENS, W. N. (1963). *The family in cross-cultural perspective.* New York: Holt, Rinehart & Winston.

STERN, D. (1977). *The first relationship.* Cambridge, MA: Harvard University Press.

STERN, D. (1985). *The interpersonal world of the infant: A view from psychoanalysis and developmental psychology.* New York: Basic Books.

STERN, D. N., SPIEKER, S., BARNETT, R. K., & MACKAIN, K. (1983). The prosody of maternal speech: Infant age and context related changes. *Journal of Child Language, 10,* 1–15.

STERN, W. (1910). Abstracts of lectures on the psychology of testimony and on the study of individuality. *American Journal of Psychology, 21,* 273–282.

STERN, W. (1912). *Psychologische methoden der intelligenz-prufung.* Leipzig: Barth.

STERNBERG, R. J. (1983). *Handbook of intelligence.* New York: Cambridge University Press.

STERNBERG, R. J. (1985). *Beyond IQ: A triarchic theory of human intelligence.* New York: Cambridge University Press.

STERNBERG, R. J. (1988). What theorists of intellectual development among children can learn from their counterparts studying adults. In E. M. Hetherington, R. Lerner, & M. Perlmutter (Eds.), *Child development in life-span perspective.* Hillsdale, NJ: Erlbaum.

STERNBERG, R. J., & NIGRO, G. (1980). Developmental patterns in the solution of verbal analogies. *Child Development, 51,* 27–38.

STERNBERG, R. J., & POWELL, J. S. (1983). The development of intelligence. In P. H. Mussen (Ed.), *Handbook of child psychology:* Vol. 3. *Cognitive development.* New York: Wiley.

STEVENS, J. (1984). Black grandmothers' and black adolescent mothers' knowledge about parenting. *Developmental Psychology, 20,* 1017–1025.

STEVENSON, H. W., LEE, S., & STIGLER, J. W. (1986). Mathematics achievement of Chinese, Japanese, and American children. *Science, 231,* 693–699.

STEVENSON, H. W., & STIGLER, J. W. (1992). *The learning gap: Why our schools are failing and what we can learn from Japanese and Chinese education.* New York: Summit Books.

STEVENSON, H. W., STIGLER, J. W., LEE, S., LUCKER, G. W., KITAMURA, S., &

HSU, C. (1985). Cognitive performance and academic achievement of Japanese, Chinese, and American children. *Child Development, 56,* 718–734.

STEVENSON, R. (1977). *The fetus and newly born infant: Influence of the prenatal environment* (2nd ed.). St. Louis: Mosby.

STEWART, R. B., & MARVIN, R. S. (1984). Sibling relations: The role of conceptual perspective taking in the ontogeny of sibling caregiving. *Child Development, 55,* 1322–1332.

STIFTER, C. A. & FOX, N. A. (1990). Infant reactivity: Physiological correlates of newborn and 5-month temperament. *Developmental Psychology, 26,* 582–588.

STIGLER, J. W., & PERRY, M. (1990). Mathematics learning in Japanese, Chinese, and American classrooms. In J. W. Stigler, R. A. Shweder & G. Herdt (Eds.), *Cultural psychology: Essays on comparative human development.* New York: Cambridge University Press.

STIPEK, D. J. (1981). Children's perceptions of their own and their classmates' ability. *Journal of Educational Psychology, 73,* 404–410.

STOCKER, C., DUNN, J., & PLOMIN, R. (1989). Sibling relationships: Links with child temperament, maternal behavior, and family structure. *Child Development, 60,* 715–727.

STOLLER, R. J. (1980). A different view of the Oedipal conflict. In S. I. Greenspan & G. H. Pollock (Eds.), *The course of life,* Vol. 1. *Infancy and early childhood.* Adelphi, MD: Mental Health Study Center.

STONE, C. A., & DAY, M. C. (1980). Competence and performance models and the characterization of formal operational skills. *Human Development, 23,* 323–353.

STONE, J. L., & CHURCH, J. (1957). *Childhood and adolescence: A psychology of the growing person.* New York: Random House.

STRAUSS, S. (Ed.) (1988). *Ontongeny, phylogeny and historical development.* Norwood, NJ: Ablex.

STRAYER, F. F. (1980). Social ecology of the preschool peer group. In W. A. Collins (Ed.), *Development of cognition, affect, and social relations: Minnesota Symposia in Child Development* (Vol. 13). Hillsdale, NJ: Erlbaum.

STRAYER, F. F. (1991). The development of agonistic and affiliative structures in preschool play groups. In J. Silverberg & P. Gray (Eds.), *To fight or not to fight: Violence and peacefulness in humans and other primates.* Oxford: Oxford University Press.

STRERI, A., & SPELKE, E. S. (1988). Haptic perception of objects in infancy. *Cognitive Psychology, 20,* 1–23.

STROMMEN, E. A. (1973). Verbal self-regulation in a children's game: Impulsive errors on "Simon Says." *Child Development, 44,* 849–853.

SUBBOTSKI, E. V. (1991). A life span approach to object permanence. *Human Development, 34,* 125–137.

SUGARMAN, S. (1983). *Children's early thought.* Cambridge: Cambridge University Press.

SULLIVAN, H. S. (1953). *The interpersonal theory of psychiatry.* New York: W. W. Norton.

SULLIVAN, M. W., ROVEE-COLLIER, C. K., & TYNES, D. M. (1979). A conditioning analysis of infant long-term memory. *Child Development, 50,* 152–162.

SULLOWAY, F. J. (1979). *Freud, biologist of the mind: Beyond the psychoanalytic legend.* New York: Basic Books.

SUOMI, S. J., & HARLOW, H. F. (1972). Social rehabilitation of isolate-reared monkeys. *Developmental Psychology, 6,* 487–496.

SUOMI, S. J., HARLOW, H. F., & MCKINNY, W. T., JR. (1972). Monkey psychiatrists. *American Journal of Psychiatry, 128,* 927–932.

SUPER, C. M. (1976). Environmental effects on motor development: A case of African infant precocity. *Developmental Medicine and Child Neurology, 18,* 561–567.

SUPER, C. M. (1981). Behavioral development in infancy. In R. H. Munroe, R. L. Munroe, & B. B. Whiting (Eds.), *Handbook of cross-cultural human development.* New York: Garland.

SUPER, C. M., & HARKNESS, S. (1972). The infant's niche in rural Kenya and metropolitan America. In L. Adler (Ed.), *Issues in cross-cultural research.* New York: Academic Press.

SUPER, C., & HARKNESS, S. (1986). The developmental niche: A conceptualization at the interface of society and the individual. *International Journal of Behavioral Development, 9,* 545–570.

SUPER, C. M., HERRERA, M. G., & MORA, J. O. (1990). Long-term effects of food supplementation and psychosocial intervention on the physical growth of Colombian infants at risk of malnutrition. *Child Development, 61,* 29–49.

SUSSMAN, E. J., NOTTLEMANN, E. D., INHOFF-GERMAIN, G. E., DORN, L. D.,

CUTLER, G. B., JR., LORIAUX, D. L., & CHROUSOS, G. P. (1985). The relation of development and social-emotional behavior in young adolescents. *Journal of Youth and Adolescence, 14,* 245–264.

SUTTON-SMITH, B. (1979). *Play and learning.* New York: Gardner.

SWENSON, E. J. (1922/1958). How to teach for memory and application. In C. W. Hunnicutt & W. J. Iverson (Eds.), *Research in the three R's.* New York: Harper & Row.

SWIFT, J. (1726/1970). *Gulliver's travels.* New York: W. W. Norton.

TAGGART, R. (1980). Youth knowledge development report 2:12. *Youth employment policies and programs for the 1980's: Background analysis for the Department of Labor Employment and Training Components of the Youth Act of 1980.* Washington DC: U.S. Department of Labor.

TAKAHASHI, K. (1990a). Affective relationships and their lifelong development. In P. B. Baltes, D. L. Featherman, & R. M. Lerner (Eds.), *Life-span development and behavior.* Hillsdale, NJ: Erlbaum.

TAKAHASHI, K. (1990b). Are the key assumptions of the "strange situation" procedure universal? *Human Development, 33,* 23–30.

TANNER, J. M. (1978). *Fetus into man: Physical growth from conception to maturity.* Cambridge, MA: Harvard University Press.

TANNER, N. M. (1981). *On becoming human.* Cambridge: Cambridge University Press.

TANYZER, H., & KARL, J. (1972). *Reading, children's books, and our pluralistic society.* Newark, DE: International Reading Association.

TAVRIS, C., & OFFIR, C. (1977). *The longest war. Sex differences in perspective.* San Diego: Harcourt Brace Jovanovich.

TAYLOR, M., & HORT, B. C. (1990). Can children be trained to make the appearance reality distinction? *Cognitive Development, 5,* 89–99.

TEALE, W. H., & SULZBY, E. (Eds.) (1986). *Emergent literacy: Writing and reading.* Norwood, NJ: Ablex.

TELLER, D. Y., & BORNSTEIN, M. H. (1987). Infant color vision and color perception. In P. Salapatek & L. B. Cohen (Eds), *Handbook of infant perception.* New York: Academic Press.

TELZROW, R. W., CAMPOS, J. J., SHEPHERD, A., BERTENTHAL, B. I., & ATWATER, S. (1987). Spatial understanding in infants with motor handicaps. In K. Jaffe (Ed.), *Childhood powered mobility: Developmental, technical and clinical perspectives.*

TEMPLIN, M. C. (1957). *Certain language skills in children.* Minneapolis: University of Minnesota Press.

TERMAN, L. M. (1925). *Genetic studies of genius.* Stanford: Stanford University Press.

TERRACE, H. (1984). Apes who "talk": Language or projection of language by their teachers? In J. De Luce & H. T. Wilder (Eds.), *Language in primates.* New York: Springer-Verlag.

THATCHER, R. W. (1991) Maturation of the human frontal lobes: Physiological evidence for staging. *Developmental Neuropsychology, 7*(3), 397–419.

THELEN, E. (1984). Learning to walk: Ecological demands and phylogenetic constraints. In L. P. Lipsitt & C. Rovee-Collier (Eds), *Advances in infancy research* (Vol. 3). Norwood, NJ: Ablex.

THELEN, E. (1986). Treadmill-elicited stepping in seven month old infants. *Child Development, 57,* 1498–1506.

THELEN, E, & ULRICH, B. D. (1991). Hidden skills. *Monographs of the Society for Research in Child Development, 56*(1, Serial No. 223).

THELEN, E., ULRICH, B. D., & JENSEN, J. L. (1989). The developmental origins of locomotion. In M. Woollacott & A. Shumway-Cook (Eds.), *The development of posture and gait across the lifespan.* Columbia, SC: University of South Carolina Press.

THOMAN, E. B. & WHITNEY, M. P. (1989). Sleep states of infants monitored in the home: Individual differences, develpmental trends, and origins of cyclicity. *Infant Behavior and Development, 12,* 59–75.

THOMAS, A., & CHESS, S. (1977). *Temperament and development.* New York: Brunner/Mazel.

THOMAS, A., & CHESS, S. (1984). Genesis and evaluation of behavioral disorders: From infancy to early adult life. *American Journal of Psychiatry, 141,* 1–9.

THOMAS, A., & CHESS, S. (1989). Temperament and personality. In G. A. Kohnstamm, J. E. Bates, & M. K. Rothbart (Eds.), *Temperament in childhood.* New York: Wiley.

THOMAS, A., CHESS, S., BIRCH, H. G., HERTZIG, M. E., & KORN, S. (1963). *Behavioral individuality in early childhood.* New York: New York University Press.

THOMPSON, J. E. (1990). Maternal stress, anxiety, and social support during pregnancy: Possible directions for prenatal intervention. In I. R. Merkatz & J. E. Thompson (Eds.), *New perspectives on prenatal care.* New York: Elsevier.

THOMPSON, L. A., FAGAN, J. F., & WALKER, D. W. (1991). Longitudinal prediction of specific cognitive abilities from infant novelty preference. *Child Development, 62,* 530–538.

THORBECKE, W., & GROTEVANT, H. D. (1982). Gender differences in adolescent interpersonal identity formation. *Journal of Youth and Adolescence, 11,* 479–492.

THORKILDSEN, T. A. (1989). Pluralism in children's moral reasoning about social justice. *Child Development, 60,* 965–972.

THORNDIKE, E. L. (1911). *Animal intelligence: Experimental studies.* New York: Macmillan.

THORNDIKE, E. L. (1922). *The psychology of arithmetic.* New York: Macmillan.

THURSTONE, L. L. (1938). Primary mental abilities. *Psychometric Monographs, 1,* (1).

TIETJEN, A. M. (1989). The ecology of children's social support networks. In D. Belle (Ed.), *Children's social networks and social supports.* New York: Wiley.

TIETJEN, A. M., & WALKER, L. J. (1985). Moral reasoning and leadership among men in a Papua New Guinea society. *Child Development, 21,* 982–992.

TIKHOMIROV, O. K. (1978). The formation of voluntary movements in children of preschool age. In M. Cole (Ed.), *The selected writings of A. R. Luria.* White Plains, NY: Merle Sharp.

TISAK, M. S., & TURIEL, E. (1988). Variation in seriousness of transgression and children's moral and conventional concepts. *Developmental Psychology, 24,* 352–357.

TIZARD, B., & HODGES, J. (1978). The effect of early institutional rearing on the development of eight-year-old children. *Journal of Child Psychology and Psychiatry, 19,* 99–118.

TIZARD, B., & REES, J. (1975). The effect of early institutional rearing on the behavioral problems and affectional relationship of four-year-old children. *Journal of Child Psychology and Psychiatry, 16,* 61–73.

TOBIN, J. J., WU, D. Y. H., & DAVISON, D. H. (1989). *Preschool in three cultures: Japan, China, and the United States.* New Haven: Yale University Press.

TOMASELLO, M., (1988). The role of joint attention in early language development. *Language Sciences, 11,* 69–88.

TOMASSELO, M. (1990). Cultural transmission in the tool use and communicatory signalling of chimpanzees? In S. Parker & E. Gibson (Eds.), *"Language" and intelligence in animals: Developmental perspectives.* Cambridge: Cambridge University Press.

TOMASELLO, M. (1992). The social bases of language acquisition. *Social Development, 1,* 67–87.

TOMASELLO, M., & FARRAR, J. (1986). Joint attention and early language. *Child Development, 57,* 1454–1463.

TOMASELLO, M., & MANLE, S. (1985). Pragmatics of sibling speech to one-year-olds. *Child Development, 56,* 911–917.

TORAN-ALLERAND, C. D. (1984). On the genesis of sexual differentiation of the central nervous system: Morphogenetic consequences of steroidal exposure and possible role of *a*-Fetoprotein. In G. J. De Vries, J. P. C. Bruin, H. B. M. Uylings, & M. A. Corner (Eds.), *Progress in Brain Research, 61,* 63–98.

TORNEY-PURTA, J. (1990). Youth in relation to social institutions. In S. S. Feldman & G. R. Elliott (Eds.), *At the threshold: The developing adolescent.* Cambridge, MA: Harvard University Press.

TRAVERS, J., & RUOPP, R. (1978). *National day care study: Preliminary findings and their implications.* Cambridge: Abt.

TREVARTHEN, C. (1980). The foundations of intersubjectivity: Development of interpersonal and cooperative understanding in infants. In D. Olson (Ed.), *The social foundations of language and thought.* New York: W. W. Norton.

TROIDEN, R. R. (1988). *Gay and lesbian identity: A sociological analysis.* Dix Hills, NY: General Hall, Inc.

TRONICK, E. Z., WINN, S., & MORELLI, G. A. (1985) Multiple caretaking in the context of human evolution: Why don't the Efe know the western prescription for child care? In M. Reite & T. Field (Eds.), *The Psychobiology of attachment and separation.* Orlando, FL: Academic Press.

TSCHIRGI, J. E. (1980). Sensible reasoning: A hypothesis about hypotheses. *Child Development, 51,* 1–10.

TUCHMANN-DUPLESSIS, H. (1975). *Drug effects on the fetus.* Acton, MA: Publishing Science Group Inc.

TULVISTE, P. (1991). *The cultural-historical development of verbal thinking.* Commack, NY: Nova.

TURIEL, E. (1978). Social regulation and domains of social concepts. In W. Damon (Ed.), *Social cognition (New directions for child development, No. 1)*. San Francisco: Jossey-Bass.

TURIEL, E. (1983). *The development of social knowledge: Morality and convention*. Cambridge: Cambridge University Press.

TURIEL, E., & DAVIDSON, P. (1986). Heterogeneity, inconsistency, and asynchrony in the development of cognitive structures. In I. Levin (Ed.), *Stage and structure: Reopening the debate*. Norwood, NJ: Ablex.

TURIEL, E., KILLEN, M., & HELWIG, C. C. (1987). Morality: Its structure, functions, and vagaries. In J. Kagan & S. Lamb (Eds.), *The emergence of morality*. Chicago: Chicago University Press.

TYSON, P., & TYSON, R. L. (1990). *Psychoanalytic theories of development: An integration*. New Haven: Yale University Press.

UHLENBERG, P. (1980). Death and the family. *Journal of Family History, 5*, 313–320.

U.S. BUREAU OF THE CENSUS (1990). *Statistical Abstract of the United States: 1990* (110th ed.). Washington, DC: U.S. Government Printing Office.

U.S. BUREAU OF THE CENSUS (1991). *Statistical Abstract of the United States: 1991* (111th ed.). Washington, DC: U.S. Government Printing Office.

U.S. BUREAU OF THE CENSUS, CURRENT POPULATION REPORTS (1990, March). *Marital Status and Living Arrangements*. (Series P-20, No. 450). Washington, DC: U.S. Government Printing Office.

U.S. BUREAU OF THE CENSUS, POPULATION DIVISION. (1988, March). Marital status and living arrangements: March 1987. *Current Reports,* Series P-20, No. 423. Washington, DC: U.S. Government Printing Office.

U.S. BUREAU OF THE CENSUS (1991). Daily disruption and economic hardship; the shortrun picture for children. *Current Population Report,* Series P-70, No. 3.

U.S. CONGRESS, SENATE COMMITTEE ON HUMAN RESOURCES (1978). *Obstetrical practices in U.S.* Hearings before the subcommittee on Health and scientific research of the Committee on Human Resources. Washington, DC: U.S. Government Printing Office.

U.S. DEPARTMENT OF EDUCATION. NATIONAL COMMISSION ON EXCELLENCE IN EDUCATION (1983). *A nation at risk: The imperative for educational reform.* Washington, DC: U.S. Government Printing Office.

U.S. DEPARTMENT OF EDUCATION, OFFICE OF EDUCATIONAL RESEARCH AND IMPROVEMENT (1991). *Youth indicators 1991: Trends in the well-being of American youth.* Washington, DC: U.S. Government Printing Office.

U.S. DEPARTMENT OF HEALTH AND HUMAN SERVICES, NATIONAL CENTER FOR HEALTH STATISTICS (Jan. 13, 1992). *Monthly Vital Statistics Report, 40(9),* 1.

U.S. DEPARTMENT OF HEALTH AND HUMAN SERVICES (1988). *Study of national incidence and prevalence of child abuse and neglect.* Washington, DC: U.S. Government Printing Office.

U.S. DEPARTMENT OF LABOR (1985). *Handbook of Labor Statistics, Bureau of Labor Statistics Bulletin, 2217.* Washington, DC: U.S. Government Printing Office.

U.S. DEPARTMENT OF LABOR, BUREAU OF LABOR STATISTICS (1991, March). *Current population survey.* Washington, DC: U.S. Government Printing Office.

U.S. NATIONAL CENTER FOR HEALTH STATISTICS (annual). *Vital Statistics of the U.S.* Washington, DC: U.S. Government Printing Office.

U.S. SELECT PANEL FOR THE PROMOTION OF CHILD HEALTH (1981). *Better health for our children: A national strategy: Report of the Select Panel for the Promotion of Child Health to the U.S. Congress.* Washington, DC: U.S. Government Printing Office.

UNITED NATIONS CHILDREN'S FUND (UNICEF) (1987). *The state of the world's children 1987.* Oxford: Oxford University Press.

UNITED NATIONS CHILDREN'S FUND (UNICEF) (1988). *The state of the world's children 1988.* Oxford: Oxford University Press.

UZGIRIS, I. C., & HUNT, J. (1975). *Assessment in infancy: Ordinal scales of psychological development.* Champaign: University of Illinois Press.

VALENZUELA, M. (1990). Attachment in chronically underweight young children. *Child Development, 61,* 1984–1996.

VALSINER, J. (1988). *Child development within culturally structured environments,* Vol. 2: *Social co-construction and environmental guidance in development.* Norwood, NJ: Ablex.

VALSINER, J. (1989). *Constructing the subject.* Lexington, MA: Lexington Books.

VANDELL, D. L., & RAMANAN, J. (1991). Children of the National Longitudinal Survey of Youth: Choices in after-school care and child development. *Developmental Psychology, 27,* 636–643.

VANDER LINDE, E., MORRONGIELLO, B. A., & ROVEE-COLLIER, C. K. (1985). Determinants of retention in 8-week-olds. *Developmental Psychology, 21,* 601–613.

VAUGHN, B., EGELAND, B., SROUFE, L. A., & WATERS, E. (1979). Individual differences in infant-mother attachment at twelve and eighteen months: Stability and change in families under stress. *Child Development, 50,* 971–975.

VAUGHN, B. E., & LANGLOIS, J. H. (1983). Physical attractiveness as a correlate of peer status and social competence in preschool children. *Developmental Psychology, 19,* 550–560.

VAUGHN, B. E., LEFEVER, G. B., SEIFER, R., & BARGLOW, P. (1989). Attachment behavior, attachment security, and temperament during infancy. *Child Development, 60,* 728–737.

VERNY, T., & KELLY, J. (1981). *The secret life of the unborn child.* New York: Summit Books.

VINTER, A. (1986). The role of movement in eliciting early imitation. *Child Development, 57,* 66–71.

VON HOFSTEN, C. (1984). Developmental changes in the organization of prereaching movements. *Developmental Psychology, 20,* 369–382.

VON HOFSTEN, C., & RONNQVIST, L. (1988). Preparations for grasping an object: A developmental study. *Journal of Experimental Psychology, 14,* 610–621.

VORHEES, C. V., & MOLLNOW, E. (1987). Behavior teratogenesis: Long-term influences on behavior. In J. D. Osofsky (Ed.), *Handbook of infant development* (2nd ed.). New York: Wiley.

VURPILLOT, E. (1968). The development of scanning strategies and their relation to visual differentiation. *Journal of Experimental Child Psychology, 6,* 632–650.

VYGOTSKY, L. S. (1978). *Mind in society.* Cambridge, MA: Harvard University Press.

VYGOTSKY, L. S. (1934/1987). Thinking and speech. In *The collected works of L. S.* Vol 1. *Problems of general psychology.* (N. Minick, Trans.). New York: Plenum Press.

WADDINGTON, C. H. (1947). *Organizers and genes.* Cambridge: Cambridge University Press.

WADDINGTON. C. H. (1966). *Principles of development and differentiation.* New York: Macmillian.

WAGNER, D. A. (1974). The development of short-term and incidental memory: A cross cultural study. *Child Development, 48,* 389–396.

WAGNER, D. A. (1978). Memories of Morocco: The influence of age, schooling, and environment on memory. *Cognitive Psychology, 10,* 1–28.

WAGNER, R. K., & STERNBERG, R. J. (1985). Practical intelligence in real-world pursuits: The role of tacit knowledge. *Journal of Personality and Social Psychology, 49,* 436–458.

WALCZYK, J. J. (1990). The relation between error detection, sentence verification, and low-level reading skills in fourth graders. *Journal of Educational Psychology, 82(3),* 491–497.

WALDEN, T. A. & BAXTER, A. (1989). The effect of context and age on social referencing. *Child Development, 60,* 1511–1518.

WALDROP, M. F., & HALVERSON, C. F., Jr. (1975). Intensive and extensive peer behavior. *Child Development, 46,* 19–26.

WALKER, L. J. (1980). Sex differences in moral reasoning. In W. M. Kurtines & J. L. Gerwirtz (Eds.), *Handbook of moral behavior and development,* Vol. 2. Hillsdale, NJ: Erlbaum.

WALKER, L. J. (1984). Sex differences in the development of moral reasoning: A critical review. *Child Development, 55,* 677–691.

WALKER, L. J. (1986). Sex differences in the development of moral reasoning: A rejoinder to Baumrind. *Child Development, 57,* 522–526.

WALKER, L. J. (1988). The development of moral reasoning. *Annals of Child Development, 5,* 33–78.

WALKER, L. J., & DE VRIES, B., (1985). Moral stages/moral orientations: Do the sexes really differ? In C. Black (Ed.), *Gender differences in research in moral development.* Symposium conducted at the meetings of the American Psychological Association, Los Angeles.

WALKER, L. J., DE VRIES, B., & TREVETHAN, S. D. (1987). Moral stages and moral orientations in real-life and hypothetical dilemmas. *Child Development, 58,* 842–858.

WALLERSTEIN, J. S. (1983). Children of divorce: Stress and developmental tasks. In N. Garmezy & M. Rutter (Eds.), *Stress, coping and development in children.* New York: McGraw Hill.

WALLERSTEIN, J. S. (1984). Parent-child relations following divorce. In J. Anthony & C. Chiland (Eds.), *Clinical parenthood* Vol. 8. *The yearbook of the International Association of Child and Adolescent Psychiatry. New York: Wiley.*

WALLERSTEIN, J. S. (1987). Children of divorce: Report of a ten-year follow-up of early latency-age children. *American Journal of Orthopsychiatry, 57*(2), 199–211.

WALTERS, W. A. W., & SINGER, P. (1982). *Test-tube babies.* New York: Oxford Univesity Press.

WARTON, P. M., & GOODNOW, J. J. (1991). The nature of responsibility: Children's understanding of "Your Job." *Child Development, 62,* 156–165.

WASIK, B. H., RAMEY, C. T., BRYANT, D. M., & SPARLING, J. J. (1990). A longitudinal study of two early intervention strategies: Project CARE. *Child Development, 61,* 1682–1696.

WASZ-HOCKERT, O., LIND, J., VUOREN-KOSKI, V., PARTANEN, T., & VALANNE, E. (1968). *The infant cry: A spectographic and auditory analysis.* Clinics in developmental medicine, No. 29. Lavenham, Suffolk: Spastics International Medical Publications and William Heinemann Medical Books, Ltd.

WATERMAN, A. S. (1985). Identity in the context of adolescent psychology. In A. S. Waterman (Ed.), *Identity in adolescence: Progress and contents: (New directions for child development,* No. 30). San Francisco: Jossey-Bass.

WATERMAN, A. S., & ARCHER, S. L. (1990). A life-span perspective on identity formation: Developments in form, function, & process. In P. B. Baltes, D. L. Featherman, & R. M. Lerner (Eds.), *Life-span development and behavior.* Hillsdale, NJ: Erlbaum.

WATERMAN, A. S., & WATERMAN, C. K. (1971). A longitudinal study of changes in ego identity status during the freshman year at college. *Developmental Psychology, 5,* 167–173.

WATERS, E. (1978). The reliability and stability of individual differences in infant-mother attachment. *Child Development, 49,* 483–494.

WATSON, J. B. (1930). *Behaviorism.* Chicago: Chicago University Press.

WATSON, J. B., & RAYNER, R. (1920). Conditioned emotional reactions. *Journal of Experimental Psychology, 3,* 1–14.

WATSON, J. S. (1971). Cognitive-perceptual development in infancy: Setting for the seventies. *Merrill-Palmer Quarterly, 17,* 139–152.

WATSON, J. S. (1972). Smiling, cooing and "the game." *Merrill-Palmer Quarterly, 18,* 323–340.

WATSON, J. S. (1984). Memory in learning: Analysis of the momentary reactions of infants. In R. Kail & N. E. Spear (Eds.), *Comparative perspectives on the development of memory.* Hillsdale, NJ: Erlbaum.

WATSON, M. W., & FISCHER, K. W. (1977). A developmental sequence of agent use in late infancy. *Child Development, 48,* 828–835.

WATSON, M. W., & FISCHER, K. W. (1980). Development of social roles in elicited spontaneous behavior during the preschool years. *Developmental Psychology, 16,* 483–494.

WAXMAN, S. R., & GELMAN, R. (1986). Preschoolers use of superordinate relations in classification. *Cognitive Development, 1,* 139–156.

WEBER, D. J., REDFIELD, R. R., & LEMON, S. M. (1986). Acquired immunodeficiency syndrome: Epidemiology and significance for the obstetrician and gynecologist. *American Journal of Obstetrics and Gynecology, 155*(2), 235–239.

WECHSLER, D. (1939). *The measurement of adult intelligence.* Baltimore: Williams & Wilkins.

WECHSLER, D. (1974). *Manual for the Wechsler intelligence scale for children.* New York: Psychology Corporation.

WEILL, B. C. (1930). Are you training your child to be happy? *Lesson material in child management.* Washington, DC: U.S. Government Printing Office.

WEINBRAUB, M., JAEGER, E., & HOFFMAN, L. W. (1988). Predicting infant outcomes in families of employed and non-employed mothers. *Early Childhood Research Quarterly, 3,* 361–378.

WEISNER, T. S. (1984). Ecocultural niches of middle childhood. In W. A. Collins (Ed.), *Development during middle childhood: The years from six to twelve.* Washington, DC: National Academy Press.

WEISNER, T. S., GALLIMORE, R., & JORDAN, C. (1988). Unpackaging cultural effects on classroom learning: Hawaiian peer assistance and child-generated activity. *Anthropology and Education Quarterly, 19,* 327–353.

WEISNER, T. S., & WILSON-MITCHELL, J. (1990). Nonconventional family lifestyles and sex typing in six-year-olds. *Child Development, 62,* 1915–1933.

WEISS, M. J., ZELAZO, P. R., & SWAIN, I. U. (1988). Newborn response to auditory stimulus discrepancy. *Child Development, 59,* 1530–1541.

WEISSBERG, J. A., & PARIS, S. G. (1986). Young children's remembering in different contexts: A reinterpretation of Istomina's study. *Child Development, 57,* 1123–1129.

WELLMAN, H. M., CROSS, D., & BARTSCH, K. (1987). Infant search and object permanence: A meta-analysis of the A-not-B error. *Monographs of the Society for Research in Child Development, 51*(Serial No. 214).

WELLMAN, H. M. & GELMAN, S. A. (1992). Cognitive development: Foundational theories and core domains. *Annual Review of Psychology, 43,* 337–376.

WELLMAN, H., & LEMPERS, J. D. (1977). The naturalistic communication abilities of two-year-olds. *Child Development, 48,* 1052–1057.

WELLS, G. (Ed.). (1981). *Learning through interaction.* Cambridge: Cambridge University Press.

WERNER, E., & SMITH, R. S. (1982). *Vulnerable but invincible: A longitudinal study of resilient children and youth.* New York: McGraw-Hill.

WERNER, H. (1948). *Comparative psychology of mental development.* New York: International Universities Press.

WERNER, H., & KAPLAN, B. (1952). The acquisition of word meanings: A developmental study. *Monographs of the Society for Research in Child Development, 15*(1, Serial No. 51).

WERNER, J. S., & LIPSITT, L. P. (1981). The infancy of human sensory systems. In E. S. Gollin (Ed.), *Developmental plasticity: Behavioral and biological aspects of variations in development.* New York: Academic Press.

WERNER, J. S., & WOOTEN, B. R. (1979). Human infant color vision and color perception. *Infant Behavior and Development, 2,* 241–273.

WERNER, L. A., & GILLENWATER, J. M. (1990). Pure tone sensitivity of 2-to 5-week-old infants. *Infant Behavior and Development, 13,* 355–374.

WERTSCH, J. (1985). *Vygotsky and the social formation of mind.* Cambridge, MA: Harvard University Press.

WESTINGHOUSE LEARNING CORPORATION. (1969). *The impact of Head Start: An evaluation of the effects of Head Start on children's cognitive and affectional development.* Executive summary, Ohio University report to the Office of Economic Opportunity. Washington, DC: Learning House for Federal Scientific and Technical Informations.

WEXLER, K. (1990). Innateness and maturation in linguistic development. *Developmental Psychobiology, 23,* 645–660.

WHITE, B. L. (1975). *The first three years of life.* Englewood Cliffs, NJ: Prentice-Hall.

WHITE, B. L., & WATTS, J. C. (1973). *Experience and environment: Major influences on the development of the young child.* Englewood Cliffs, NJ: Prentice-Hall.

WHITE, L. A. (1949). *The science of culture.* New York: Grove Press.

WHITE, L. A. (1959). The concept of culture. *American Anthropologist, 61,* 227–251.

WHITE, M. (1987). *The Japanese education challenge: A commitment to children.* New York: Free Press.

WHITE, M. L. (1976). *Children's literature: Criticism and response.* Columbus, OH: Charles E. Merrill.

WHITE, R. W. (1959). Motivation re-considered: The concept of competence. *Psychological Review, 66,* 279–333.

WHITE, S. H., & PILLEMER, D. B. (1979). Childhood amnesia and the development of a socially accessible memory system. In J. F. Kihlstrom & F. J. Evans (Eds.), *Functional disorders of memory.* Hillsdale, NJ: Erlbaum.

WHITELY, R. J., & GOLDENBERG, R. L. (1990). Infectious disease in the prenatal period and recommendations for screening. In I. R. Merkatz & J. E. Thompson (Eds.), *New perspectives on prenatal care.* New York: Elsevier.

WHITING, B. (1980). Culture and social behavior: A model for the development of social behavior. *Ethos, 8,* 95–116.

WHITING, B. B. (1986). The effect of experience on peer relationships. In E. C. Mueller, & C. R. Cooper (Eds.), *Process and outcome in peer relationships.* Orlando, FL: Academic Press.

WHITING, B. B., & EDWARDS, C. P. (1988). *Children of different worlds: The formation of social behavior.* Cambridge, MA: Harvard University Press.

WHITING, B. B., & WHITING, J. W. M. (1975). *Children of six cultures: A psycho-cultural analysis.* Cambridge, MA: Harvard University Press.

WHITING, J. W. M., BURBANK, V. K., & RATNER, M. S. (1986). The duration of maidenhood. In J. B. Lancaster & B. A. Hamburg, (Eds.), *School age pregnancy and parenthood.* Hawthorne, NY: Aldine de Gruyter.

WILCOX, A. J., WEINBERG, C. R., O'CONNER, J. F., BAIRD, D. D., SCHLATTERER, J. P., CANFIELD, R. E., ARMSTRONG, E. G., & NISULA, B. C. (1988). Incidence of early loss in pregnancy. *New England Journal of Medicine, 319*(4), 189–194.

WILLIAMS, J. M., & WHITE, K. A. (1983). Adolescent status system for males and females at three age levels. *Adolescence, 18,* 381–390.

WILLATS, J. (1987). Marr and pictures: An information processing account of children's drawings. *Archives de Psychologie, 55,* 105–125.

WILSON, E. O. (1975). *Sociobiology: The new synthesis.* Cambridge, MA: Harvard University Press.

WILSON, J. D., GEORGE, F. W., & GRIFFIN, J. E. (1981). The hormonal control of sexual development. *Science, 211,* 1278–1284.

WILSON, J. G. (1977). Current status of teratology. In J. G. Wilson & F. C. Fraser (Eds.), *Handbook of teratology* (Vol. 1). New York: Plenum Press.

WILSON, M. N. (1986). The black extended family: An analytical consideration. *Developmental Psychology, 22,* 246–258.

WILSON, M. N. (1989). Child development in the context of the black extended family. *American Psychologist, 44,* 380–383.

WILSON, W. J. (1987). *The truly disadvantaged: The inner city, the underclass, and public policy.* Chicago: University of Chicago Press.

WINCHESTER, A. M. (1972). *Genetics.* Boston: Houghton Mifflin.

WINEBERG, S. S. (1987). The self-fulfillment of the self-fulfilling prophecy. *Educational Researcher, 16,* 28–36.

WINNER, E. (1988). *The Point of Words.* Cambridge, MA: Harvard University Press.

WINNER, E., MCCARTHY, M., KLEINMAN, S., & GARDNER, H. (1979). First metaphors. In D. Wolfe (Ed.), *Early symbolization (New directions for child development,* No. 3). San Francisco: Jossey-Bass.

WOLFENSTEIN, M. (1953). Trends in infant care. *American Journal of Orthopsychiatry, 33,* 120–130.

WOLFF, P. H. (1966). The causes, controls, and organization of behavior in the neonate. *Psychological Issues, 5,* 1–105.

WOLFF, P. H. (1969). The natural history of crying and other vocalizations in infancy. In B. M. Foss (Ed.), *Determinants of infant behavior* (Vol. 4). London: Methuen.

WOLKIND, S., & RUTTER, M. (1985). Separation, loss and family relationships. In M. Rutter & L. Hersov (Eds.), *Child and adolescent psychiatry.* Oxford: Blackwell.

WONG-FILLMORE, L. (1985). Second language learning in children: A proposed model. In R. Eshch, & J. Provinzano (Eds.), *Issues in English language development.* Rosslyn, VA.: National Clearing House for Bilingual Education.

WOODRUFF-PAK, D. S., LOGAN, C. G., & THOMPSON, R. F. (1990). Neurobiological substrates of classical conditioning across the life-span. *Annals of the New York Academy of Sciences, 608,* 150–178.

WORTHINGTON-ROBERTS, B. S. & KLERMAN, L. V. (1990). Maternal nutrition. In I. R. Merkatz & J. E. Thompson (Eds.), *New perspectives on prenatal care.* New York: Elsevier.

WORTHMAN, C. M., & WHITING, J. W. M. (1987). Social change in adolescent sexual behavior, mate selection, and premarital pregnancy rates in a Kikuyu community. *Ethos, 15,* 145–165.

WRIGHT, H. F. (1956). Psychological development in Midwest. *Child Development, 27,* 265–286.

WRIGHT, J. D., HUSTON, A. C., ROSS, R. P., CLAVERT, S. L., ROLANDELLI, D., WEEKS, L. A., RAEISSI, P., & POTTS, R. (1984). Pace and continuity of television programs: Effects on children's attention and comprehension. *Developmental Psychology, 20,* 653–666.

YAKOVLEV, P. I., & LECOURS, A. P. (1967). The myclogenetic cycles of regional maturation of the brain. In A. Menkowski (Ed.), *Regional development of the brain in early life.* Oxford: Blackwell.

YARROW, M. R., SCOTT, P. M., & WAXLER, C. Z. (1973). Learning concern for others. *Developmental Psychology, 8,* 240–260.

YERKES, R. M. (Ed.). (1921). Psychological examining in the United States Army. *Memoirs of the National Academy of Sciences, 15.*

YOUNG, K. T. (1990). American conceptions of infant development from 1955 to 1984: What the experts are telling parents. *Child Development, 61,* 17–28.

YOUNG, W. W., GOY, R., & PHOENIX, C. (1964). Hormones and sexual behavior. *Science, 143,* 212–218.

YOUNGER, B., & COHEN, L. B. (1986). Developmental change in infants' perception of correlation among attributes. *Child Development, 57,* 803–813.

YOUNISS, J. (1980). *Parents and peers in social development.* Chicago: University of Chicago Press.

YOUNISS, J. (1983). Social construction of adolescence by adolescents and their parents. In H. D. Grotevant & C. R. Cooper (Eds.), *Adolescent development in the family (New directions for child development,* No. 22). San Francisco: Jossey-Bass.

YOUNISS, J., & SMOLLAR, J. (1985). *Adolescent relations with mothers, fathers, and friends.* Chicago: University of Chicago Press.

YOUNISS, J., & VOLPE, J. (1978). A relational analysis of friendship. In W. Damon (Ed.), *Social cognition (New directions for child development,* No. 1). San Francisco: Jossey-Bass.

ZAHAVI, S., & ASHER, S. R. (1978). The effects of verbal instruction on preschool children's aggressive behavior. *Journal of School Psychology, 16,* 146–153.

ZAHN-WAXLER, C., & RADKE-YARROW, M. (1982). The development of altruism: Alternative research strategies. In N. Eisenberg (Ed.), *The development of prosocial behavior.* New York: Academic Press.

ZAHN-WAXLER, C., RADKE-YARROW, M., & KING, R. (1979). Child rearing and children's prosocial initiations toward victims of distress. *Child Development, 50,* 319–330.

ZASLAVSKY, C. (1973). *Africa counts.* Boston: Prindle, Weber, and Schmidt.

ZEGIOB, L. E., ARNOLD, S., & FOREHAND, R. (1975). An examination of observer effects in parent child interaction. *Child Development, 46,* 509–512.

ZELAZO, P. R. (1983). The development of walking: New findings and old assumptions. *Journal of Motor Behavior, 15,* 99–137.

ZELAZO, P. R., ZELAZO, N. A., & KOLB, S. (1972). Walking in the newborn. *Science, 179,* 314–315.

ZELNIK, M., & KANTNER, J. F. (1980). Sexual activity, contraceptive use, and pregnancy among metropolitan area teens, 1971–1979. *Family Planning Perspectives, 12*(2), 69–76.

ZELNIK, M., & SHAH, F. K. (1983). First intercourse among Americans. *Family Planning Perspectives, 15,* 64–72.

ZESKIND, P. S. (1983). Cross-cultural differences in maternal perceptions of cries of low- and high-risk infants. *Child Development, 54,* 1119–1128.

ZESKIND, P. S., & RAMEY, C. T. (1978). Fetal malnutrition: An experimental study of its consequences in two caregiving environments. *Child Development, 49,* 1155–1162.

ZESKIND, P. S., & RAMEY, C. T. (1981). Preventing intellectual and interactional sequelae of fetal malnutrition: A longitudinal, transactional and synergistic approach to development. *Child Development, 52,* 213–218.

ZESKIND, P. S., SALE, J., MAIO, M. C., HUNTINGTON, L., & WEISEMAN, J. R. (1985). Adult perceptions of pain and hunger cries: A synchrony of arousal. *Child Development, 56,* 549–554.

ZIGLER, E. (1980). Controlling child abuse: do we have the knowledge and/or the will? In G. Gerbner, C. J. Ross, & E. Zigler (Eds.), *Child abuse: An agenda for action.* New York: Oxford University Press.

ZIGLER, E., & HALL, N. W. (1989). Physical child abuse in America: Past, present, and future. In D. Cicchetti & V. Carlson (Eds.), *Child maltreatment: Theory and research on the causes and consequences of child abuse and neglect.* New York: Cambridge University Press.

ZIGLER, E., & VALENTINE, J. (Eds.). (1979). *Project Head Start: A legacy of the war on poverty.* New York: Free Press.

ZINCHENKO, V. P., CHZHI-TSIN, V., & TARAKANOV, V. V. (1963). The formation and development of perceptual activity. *Soviet Psychology, 2,* 3–12.

ZUKOW, P. G. (1989). *Sibling interaction across cultures.* New York: Springer-Verlag.

SOURCES OF PHOTOGRAPHS

CHAPTER 1

Opener: Lennart Nilsson, *A Child Is Born,* 1990 ed., Dell Publishing Company; p. 2: Jean-Loup Charmet, Paris; p. 5: Lewis W. Hine Collection, NYPL; p. 8: Kari Rene Hall, *Los Angeles Times;* p. 11: Thomas McAvoy, *LIFE* Magazine, 1955, Time, Inc.; p. 15: Herbert Gehr, *LIFE* Magazine, Time, Inc.; p. 16: G. L. Engel, F. Reichman, V. T. Harway, D. W. Hess. Monica: Infant-feeding behavior of a mother gastric fistula-fed as an infant: A 30-year longitudinal study of enduring effects, pp. 29–90, in E. J. Anthony and G. H. Pollock (Eds.). *Parental Influences in Health and Disease.* Boston: Little, Brown & Co., 1985; p. 17: Yves de Braines/Black Star; p. 18: (*top*) David Burnett/Woodfin Camp and Associates; (*bottom*) Hiroyuki Matsumoto/Black Star; p. 19: (*top*) Macduff Everton; (*bottom*) V. Chiasson/Gamma Liaison; p. 23: Down House and the Royal College of Surgeons of England; p. 25: Doonesbury copyright 1992 G. B. Trudeau. Reprinted with permission of UNIVERSAL PRESS SYNDICATE. All rights reserved; pp. 28, 29: Joseph Campos, University of Illinois; p. 30: Benjamin Harris; p. 33: James Wilson/Woodfin Camp & Associates.

CHAPTER 2

Opener: Jim Brandenberg/Minden Pictures; p. 50: Dr. Robert Langridge, Computer Graphics Laboratory, UCSF, copyright Regents, University of California; p. 52: Kathryn Abbe and Frances McLaughlin-Gill; p. 53: Barbara Rogoff; p. 54: (*bottom*) David Ward, Yale School of Medicine; p. 56: Moravian Museum, Brno; p. 62: (*top*) Frank Siteman/Stock Boston, (*middle*) Joan Lifton, UNICEF, (*bottom*) Eastphoto; p. 64: Gary Mortimore/Tony Stone Worldwide; p. 67: Patricia N. Farnsworth; p. 68: Bruce Roberts/Photo Researchers.

CHAPTER 3

Opener: Copyright Lennart Nilsson, *A Child Is Born,* 1990 ed., Dell Publishing Company; p. 80: Copyright Lennart Nilsson, *A Child Is Born,* 1990 ed., Dell Publishing Company; p. 82: Copyright Lennart Nilsson, *Behold Man,* Little, Brown & Co.; p. 86: Copyright Lennart Nilsson, *A Child Is Born,* 1976 ed., Dell Publishing Company; p. 90: Anthony De Casper, photo Walter Salinger; p. 91: Copyright Lennart Nilsson, *A Child Is Born,* 1990 ed., Dell Publishing Com-

pany; p. 93: Lawrence Migdale; p. 97: Marie Dorigny/REA; p. 98: from Ann Pytkowicz Streissguth et al. (18 July 1980). Teratogenic effects of alcohol in humans and laboratory animals, *Science 209,* 353–361, figs. 2, 3, 4. Copyright 1980 by the American Association for the Advancement of Science. Photographs courtesy University of Washington, School of Medicine; p. 101: Aileen & W. Eugene Smith/Black Star; p. 102: Vincent Leloup/Gamma Liaison; p. 106: 1992 New African Visions Inc., D. Michael Cheers, from *Songs of My People;* p. 112: John Ficara/Woodfin Camp & Associates.

CHAPTER 4

Opener: Stuart Cohen/Comstock; p. 130: James Kilkelly, *Scientific American, 252,* 46–52; p. 132: David Linton, *Scientific American, 204,* 66–72; p. 135: Courtesy Jacob E. Steiner, The Hebrew University–Hadassah School of Dental Medicine, Jerusalem; p. 138: Carroll Izard; p. 146: Stephen Trimble; p. 152: E. Gamper (1926), *Zeitschrift fur der gesamte Neurologie und Psychiatrie, 104,* 65, fig. 14; p. 153: (*top, bottom*) Heather Angel/Biofotos; p. 157: courtesy Einar R. Siqueland, Brown University; pp. 158–159: Tiffany M. Field et al., Discrimination and imitation of facial expressions by neonates, *Science, 218,* 179–182. Copyright 1980 by the American Association for the Advancement of Science; p. 163: Laura Dwight; p. 166: Bernard Wolff, UNICEF; p. 168: (*left*) Comstock, (*right*) Frans Lanting/Minden Pictures, (*bottom*) David Turnley/Black Star; p. 170: Beryl Goldberg; p. 171: D. G. Freedman, *Human Infancy: An Evolutionary Perspective,* Erlbaum, 1974; p. 172: Elizabeth Crews.

CHAPTER 5

p. 176: Michael Newman/Photo Edit; p. 179: Sam McVicker/Comstock; p. 182: (*top*) Lew Merrim/Monkmeyer, (*bottom*) Joel Gordon; p. 184: Library of Congress; p. 185: Martha Cooper; p. 186: Randy Taylor/Sygma; p. 189: D. Goodman/Monkmeyer; p. 191: Adele Diamond; p. 192: Elizabeth Crews; p. 196: Carolyn Rovee Collier, Rutgers University; p. 198: A. N. Meltzoff (1988), *Child Development, 59,* 1221–1229. Photo A. N. Meltzoff; p. 199: Charles Gatewood/The Image Works; p. 202: Laura Dwight; p. 203: UNICEF.

CHAPTER 6

p. 208: Tony Freeman/Photo Edit; p. 211: Laura Dwight; p. 213: Erika Stone; p. 216: Laura Dwight; p. 219: George S. Zimbel/Monkmeyer; p. 224: Lawrence Manning/Click; pp. 227–228: Harlow Primate Laboratory, University of Wisconsin; p. 229: Sheila Cole; pp. 230–231: Mary D. Ainsworth; p. 233: Catherine Karnow/Woodfin Camp and Associates; p. 234: Elizabeth Crews; p. 235: David M. Grossman; p. 238: Susan Lapides/Design Conceptions; p. 239: Erika Stone.

CHAPTER 7

Opener: Peter Turnley/Black Star; p. 247: Ellan Young/Photo Researchers; p. 248: John Chiasson/Gamma Liaison; p. 250: Christopher Morris/Black Star; p. 251: Anthony Suau/Black Star; p. 253: Ed Malitsky/Gamma Liaison; p. 255: Murrae Haynes; pp. 262–263: Harlow Primate Laboratory, University of Wisconsin; p. 264: April Saul/*The Philadelphia Inquirer.*

CHAPTER 8

Opener: Catherine Karnow/Woodfin Camp & Assoc.; p. 281: Phiz Mezey/Taurus; p. 282: Beryl Goldberg; p. 288: Erika Stone; p. 293: Myrleen Ferguson/Photo Edit; p. 295: Novosti from Sovfoto; p. 300: Teresa Zabala/Monkmeyer; p. 302: H. Terrace; p. 304: Ursula Bellugi, The Salk Institute for Biological Studies; p. 307: Erika Stone.

CHAPTER 9

Opener: Laura Dwight; p. 317: Bonnie Kamin; p. 321: The Exploratorium, San Francisco; p. 322: Rheta De Vries; p. 323: (*left*) Mimi Forsyth/Monkmeyer, (*right*) Joel Gordon; p. 326: Helene Borke; p. 331: Al Seib, *Los Angeles Times*; p. 339: Catherine Karnow/Woodfin Camp and Associates; p. 341: (*top*) Bernard Wolff/Omni-Photo Communications, (*bottom*) Karen R. Preuss/Taurus; p. 343: Eastfoto; p. 346: Carrie Hogan; p. 348: Lorna Selfe, *Nadia: A Case of Extraordinary Drawing Ability in an Autistic Child.* © 1977 Academic Press, plates 20 and 27; p. 349: U.S. Committee for UNICEF; p. 350: Lawrence Migdale.

CHAPTER 10

Opener: Cotton Coulson/Woodfin Camp and Associates; p. 358: Michelle Bogre; p. 359: Lynn Johnson/Black Star; p. 360: Austrian Press and Information Service; p. 365: Joseph Rodriquez/Black Star; p. 367: Marlene Wallace/Photo Edit; p. 372: Photo by Jill Krementz, courtesy of Erik Erikson; p. 376: Herlinde Koelbl/Betty Dornheim Picture Service; p. 379: Albert Bandura, Stanford University; p. 380: Film Study Center, Harvard; p. 382: UPI/Bettmann Newsphotos; p. 385: Janet Kelly/*Eagle-Times*, Reading, Pennsylvania; p. 386: David M. Grossman.

CHAPTER 11

Opener: Erika Stone; p. 397: Arthur Pollack, *Boston Herald;* p. 399: Eastcott/Momatiuk/Woodfin Camp and Associates; p. 400: Stephanie Maze/Woodfin Camp and Associates; p. 405: Tony Freeman/Photo Edit; p. 407: April Saul/*The Philadelphia Inquirer;* p. 408: Peter Turnley/Black Star; p. 413: Check Keeler/Tony Stone Worldwide; p. 415: 1992 Watterson/Universal Press Syndicate; p. 416: Joseph Rodriquez/Black Star; p. 418: Barbara Rios/Photo Researchers; p. 422: Eastfoto; p. 424: Elizabeth Crews/Stock Boston; p. 425: Erika Stone; p. 429: Paul Conklin/Photo Edit.

CHAPTER 12

Opener: Frans Lanting/Minden Pictures; p. 441: Roger Werth/Woodfin Camp and Associates; p. 442: Lawrence Migdale; p. 443: NIH; p. 445: (*top*) Joe Traver/Gamma Liaison, (*bottom*) Martha Cooper; p. 447: Martha Cooper; p. 452: "Love is Hell" © 1985 by Matt Groening. All Rights Reserved. Reprinted by permission of Pantheon Books, a division of Random House, NY; p. 455: Beryl Goldberg; p. 463: Macduff Everton.

CHAPTER 13

Opener: Tony Freeman/Photo Edit; p. 472: Macduff Everton; p. 473: From Schmandt-Besserat, 1978; p. 475: Bonnie Kamin; p. 477: Lawrence Migdale; p. 480: Ulrike Welsch/Photo Researchers; p. 484: Elizabeth Crews; p. 485: Anthony Hewett, UNICEF; p. 491: Michael Cole; p. 510: Lawrence Migdale.

CHAPTER 14

Opener: Lawrence Migdale; p. 517: Shirley Zeiberg/Taurus; p. 518: Frans Lanting/Minden Pictures; p. 521: Don Spiro/Tony Stone Worldwide; p. 522: © 1992 New African Visions Inc., C. W. Griffin, from *Songs of My People;* p. 537: Joseph Rodriquez/Black Star; p. 539: Lawrence Migdale; p. 556: Shirley Zeiberg/Taurus.

CHAPTER 15

Opener: Peter D'Angelo/Comstock; p. 579: Joseph Rodriquez/Black Star; p. 581: Stephen Trimble; p. 584: Skip Barron/Comstock; p. 586: Joel Gordon; p. 590: Gary S. Chapman and Mark Sadan; p. 594: Alon Reininger/Woodfin Camp and Associates; p. 596: Sven Martson/Comstock; p. 597: (*left*) UPI/Bettmann Newsphotos, (*right*) Phil McCarten/Photo Edit; p. 601: Ron Levine/Black Star.

CHAPTER 16

Opener: Arthur Tilley/Tony Stone Worldwide; p. 611: Air Products and Chemicals Inc.; p. 621: Stephen D. Thomas,

NAME INDEX

SUBJECT INDEX